USA TODAY BASEBALL WEEKLY

ALMANAC

1992

EDITED BY:
Editor / *Baseball Weekly*, Paul White
Managing Editor / Sports, *USA TODAY*, Gene Policinski
Assistant to Managing Editor / Sports, *USA TODAY*, Robert Barbrow

With contributions from the staffs of *Baseball Weekly*
and *USA TODAY* Sports

Managing Editor, Liz Barrett

A Balliett & Fitzgerald Book

HYPERION

ISBN # 1-56282-978-5

FIRST EDITION
10 9 8 7 6 5 4 3 2 1

Acknowledgments
We are grateful, first of all, for the vision, support, skill and good humor of Susan Bokern and Silvia Molina at Gannett New Business, without whom this book would not have been possible; also many thanks to Stephanie Hart, and the support staff at USA TODAY. We send kudos to everyone at Hyperion, especially publisher Bob Miller, who wanted it, and Leslie Wells, who let us know just how much. We could never have completed this book without our own hard-working and talented production staff. We truly appreciate the efforts of designer Michael Harvey, page artists Keith Halper, Jim Kirchman and Jeanette Christopher; and assistant editor Elizabeth Mitchell.
And finally many thanks to our friends and families who suffered through our hectic schedules.

Contents

Leading off

By Paul White

Well, we survived the year of the ex-manager, at least all of us did except the dozen or so guys who were major league managers in 1991 but aren't in 1992.

The way managers come and go—and the way free agency and trades keep players on the move—there's never been a more appropriate time for the old phrase: "You can't tell the players without a scorecard."

And since *Baseball Weekly* is a scorecard of sorts all year long—keeping fans up to date on every game, every stat, every player move and just about anything else that's going on in baseball—it seemed logical to give you a handy way to look back at last season and ahead to the 1992 season.

The *Baseball Weekly Almanac* has all of the basic elements to do just that: 1991 season reviews and 1992 previews of the majors and minors, coverage of the hottest issues facing our favorite pastime, and plenty of stats and facts. But because we know so many of you are comfortable with what you've become used to in *Baseball Weekly*, we also included all of our regular elements.

We have information on collectibles and fantasy leagues. We've gone back and brought up to date some of the best memories of 1991, *Baseball Weekly's* rookie year.

And what a rookie year it was. Every time we thought we would be overwhelmed by the mayhem that comes with putting out a newspaper every week, we just took a look at what was going on in baseball. Just like putting out our weekly chronicle, watching the year on the field and in the stands was exciting, unpredictable and, in the end, rewarding.

As good as we feel getting the paper to you every week, that feeling couldn't come close to the excitement of the '91 World Series—seven games of drama to cap a year of, well, everything:

▶Fans getting a chance to meet players up close and personal, with Jose Canseco and Albert Belle paying personal visits and Rob Dibble sending his message via fastball.

▶Fans starting the season by saying hello to the new Comiskey Park and ending the year by saying goodbye to Baltimore's Memorial Stadium.

▶And even a couple of fans managing to see every major and minor league ballpark in one summer. That's the ultimate road trip.

How will we ever top that in 1992?

Well, the Houston Astros will be on the road long enough during one unconventional trip this summer that they could probably throw in the Japanese leagues too.

We get a new stadium in Baltimore on opening day. And enough other cities are on the way toward new stadiums that we're having the first great ballpark boom since the runaway cookie-cutters went wild in the '60s and '70s. (Oh, and how that big cookie in Montreal is crumbling.)

At least this time they're letting real grass grow in the new places and making it fun for the fans. Baltimore this year; Atlanta, Cleveland and Texas on the horizon; probably Milwaukee and Detroit. . . . this could be fun.

Speaking of fun, let's just get this season going. I'm ready for another year of Hector (as in Villanueva) homers, winning some minor league lucky number drawings and seeing as many doubleheaders as I can find.

Ranking the free agents

Free agents are divided into five categories:

▶**Starting pitchers**

▶**Relief pitchers**

▶**Catchers**

▶**Middle infielders/third basemen**

▶**First basemen/outfielders/designated hitters.**

Players are ranked within each category according to their performance—compared to other players at the same position:

▶**Type A: Top 30%**

▶**Type B: 31% to 50%**

▶**Type C: 51% to 60%**

Rankings are based on statistics from the past two seasons, and include players on the rosters as of August 31. Here's how they figure the rankings:

▶**First they arrive at an average.** For example, each first baseman is ranked against other first basemen in terms of plate appearances, batting average, on-base average, home runs, and runs batted in. He is given a rank in each of those categories. Those ranks are used to figure an average ranking value.

▶**Then they put them in order.** That average ranking value is subtracted from the total number of players at the position, then divided by the total number, and multiplied by 100—to get a whole number. At the end of 1991, for example, Rafael Palmiero was No.1 among American League first basemen, Cecil Fielder was No. 2, and so on.

▶**Then they rate them as Type A, B or C.** Since 26 first basemen were considered in the league, those who were ranked 1 through 9 were Type A players, 10 through 13 were Type B players, and No. 14 (Todd Benzinger) was a Type C player. Below that, no compensation is offered.

Nobody likes the system

Until the 1981 strike, teams who lost free agents could draft a player from a pool of minor leaguers; the pool was made up of the 27th-best players of each team that signed up to negotiate with free agents. Teams that signed free agents didn't really lose anything but money. And that, owners realized, allowed the balance of power to swing too much.

So the compensation system was introduced as part of the collective bargaining agreement that settled the infamous strike. But nobody likes it.

▶The Major League Baseball Players Association believes the system is unnecessary. They think players should be allowed to work for any team they choose, at a salary that is determined in the free market.

▶Owners believe that everybody gets hurt—even if they don't sign or lose free agents—because the "sandwich" picks take top prospects out of the draft.

So why is the system still in place? "That's a rational and reasonable thought," said Mark Belanger of the MLBPA. "And nothing is rational and reasonable in collective bargaining."

—Rick Lawes

Free Agent Compensation: How does it work?

Each year major league clubs anxiously await free agent rankings to see what kind of compensation they will gain or lose in free agent signings. In the 14 years that the system has been in place, clubs have often sacrificed potential future stars for a quick fix.

The system provides compensation to the clubs that lose free agents, based upon the player's ranking:

▶Clubs that sign Type A free agents lose their first-round draft pick in the next June draft, unless they finish the season among the 13th worst teams. (In that case, they lose a second-round

Free Agent Compensation: How does it work? (cont.)

pick.)

▶Clubs that lose Type A free agents get that first-round draft pick the signing team lost, plus a "sandwich" pick—a supplemental selection between the first and second rounds of the draft.

▶Clubs that lose Type B free agents get the signing team's highest available regular pick (the first 13 picks are exempt).

▶Clubs that lose Type C free agents get a pick between the second and third rounds.

1992 Free Agents

Bobby Bonilla made the headlines when he signed a $29 million deal with the New York Mets, leaving a gaping hole in the Pirates' lineup and making Mets' fans very happy customers.

But Bonilla certainly wasn't the only player up for grabs. Listed below are all of the players who filed for free agency by the Nov. 11 deadline.

Players with six or more seasons of major league service whose contracts had expired and were not bound by repeater-rights restrictions were eligible to file.

The letter in parentheses after the player's name (A, B, or C) indicates his free-agent compensation rating; where no letter exists, he is a non-compensation player. (See "Free agent compensation: How does it work?" for an explanation of what the rating means to the team losing the player.)

▶Atlanta: Jim Clancy, rhp; Otis Nixon (B), of; Alejandro Pena (A), rhp; Doug Sisk, rhp.

▶Baltimore: Glenn Davis (B), 1b; Dwight Evans, of.

▶Boston: Joe Hesketh (B), lhp; Dennis Lamp, rhp; Steve Lyons, 2b; Dan Petry, rhp.

▶California: Bert Blyleven, rhp; Donnie Hill (C), inf; Wally Joyner (A), 1b; Kirk McCaskill (C), rhp; Jeff Robinson, rhp; Dick Schofield (B), ss; Max Venable, of;

Dave Winfield (A), of.

▶Chicago Cubs: Rick Sutcliffe, rhp.

▶Chicago White Sox: Carlton Fisk (A), c; Scott Fletcher (C), 2b; Dan Pasqua (A), of.

▶Cincinnati: Mariano Duncan (B), 2b; Carmelo Martinez, of; Ted Power (B), rhp; Herm Winningham, of.

▶Cleveland: None.

▶Detroit: Dave Bergman (B), 1b; John Cerutti, lhp; Jerry Don Gleaton (A), lhp; Pete Incaviglia (C), of; Lloyd Moseby (C), of; Mark Salas, c.

▶Houston: Jim Deshaies, lhp; Rafael Ramirez, ss.

▶Kansas City: Steve Crawford (C), rhp; Jim Eisenreich (B), of; Kurt Stillwell (A), ss; Danny Tartabull (A), of.

▶Los Angeles: Alfredo Griffin, ss; Orel Hershiser (C), rhp; Jay Howell (A), rhp; Mike Morgan (A), rhp; Eddie Murray (A), 1b; Juan Samuel (A), 2b; Mitch Webster, of.

▶Milwaukee: Jim Gantner (B), 2b; Willie Randolph (B), 2b.

▶Minnesota: Steve Bedrosian (B), rhp; Dan Gladden (C), of; Brian Harper (A), c; Terry Leach (B), rhp; Jack Morris (A), rhp; Al Newman, inf; Junior Ortiz (B), c; Mike Pagliarulo (B), 3b.

▶Montreal: Mike Fitzgerald (A), c; Ron Hassey, c.

▶New York Mets: Daryl Boston (B), of; Garry Templeton (C), ss; Frank Viola (A), lhp.

▶New York Yankees: None.

▶Oakland: Ron Darling, rhp; Mike Gallego (B), 2b; Brook Jacoby (A), 3b; Carney Lansford (C), 3b; Ernest Riles, 3b; Curt Young, lhp.

▶Philadelphia: Danny Cox, rhp; Steve Lake, c; Steve Ontiveros, rhp; Randy Ready (C), 2b; Rick Schu, inf; Dickie Thon (B), ss; Mitch Williams (A), lhp.

▶Pittsburgh: Bobby Bonilla (A), of; Steve Buechele (A), 3b; Bob Kipper (C), lhp; Mike LaValliere (A), c; Bob Walk (B), rhp; Curtis Wilkerson, ss.

▶St.Louis: Pedro Guerrero (A), 1b.

▶San Diego: Atlee Hammaker, lhp; Jack Howell (B), 3b; Dennis Rasmussen (B), lhp; Tim Teufel, 2b.

▶San Francisco: Dave Anderson (C), ss; Terry Kennedy, c; Don Robinson (C), rhp.

▶Seattle: Alvin Davis (C), 1b; Bill Krueger (B), lhp; Tracy Jones, of.

▶Texas: Dennis "Oil Can" Boyd (B), rhp; Brian Downing (C), of; Rich Gossage, rhp; Geno Petralli (B), c; John Russell, c.

▶Toronto: Jim Acker (C), rhp; Tom Candiotti (A), rhp; Dave Parker (B), of;

The Survivors: 1992 team managers

After the dust settled on a rash of firings that made major league baseball look like a temporary employment agency, the following managers were set for 1992:

▶National League East

Chicago Cubs: Jim Lefebvre
Montreal Expos: Tom Runnels
New York Mets: Jeff Torborg
Philadelphia Phillies: Jim Fregosi
Pittsburgh Pirates: Jim Leyland
St. Louis Cardinals: Joe Torre

▶National League West

Atlanta Braves: Bobby Cox
Cincinnati Reds: Lou Piniella
Houston Astros: Art Howe
Los Angeles Dodgers: Tom Lasorda
San Diego Padres: Greg Riddoch
San Francisco Giants: Roger Craig

▶American League East

Baltimore Orioles: John Oates
Boston Red Sox: Butch Hobson
Cleveland Indians: Mike Hargrove
Detroit Tigers: Sparky Anderson
Milwaukee Brewers: Phil Garner
New York Yankees: Buck Showalter
Toronto Blue Jays: Cito Gaston

▶American League West

California Angels: Buck Rodgers
Chicago White Sox: Gene Lamont
Kansas City Royals: Hal McRae
Minnesota Twins: Tom Kelly
Oakland Athletics: Tony La Russa
Seattle Mariners: Bill Plummer
Texas Rangers: Bobby Valentine

Winter meetings: Winners and losers

By Paul White

As advertised, Whitey Herzog rode Gene Autry's wallet into the winter meetings, immediately got things started with a trade–and promptly was upstaged.

Herzog made no secret that he was bound and determined to rebuild, refurbish and otherwise resurrect the California Angels. Getting Von Hayes from Philadelphia was a nice start but Dave Gallagher for Hubie Brooks and a three-pitcher (nobody the world could get excited about) swap with Milwaukee was hardly the way to keep attention.

In fact, Whitey got more attention for berating agent Dennis Gilbert in a hotel coffee shop than for anything else he did during the week in Miami.

Ahhh, Gilbert, the man who helped steer Bobby Bonilla out from under Herzog and into a megabucks shocker with the Mets.

Ahhh, Gilbert, who represents the other big-name bopper that could fill Herzog's offensive needs: Danny Tartabull.,

So as Whitey simmered on the back burner, he quietly signed left-handed ace Chuck Finley to head off a half dozen or so rumored deals.

Meanwhile, back in the lobby, a few awards:

▶Most head-scratching: To the Giants for sending Kevin Mitchell to the Mariners for three pitchers, none of whom were likely to solidify the Giants' always-sore rotation. (Honorable mention goes to the Mariners for announcing the same deal, the biggest in franchise history, before 6 a.m. Seattle time.)

▶Biggest block busted: Easily the Mets for breaking up what could have been the first defensive lineup with all eight guys playing out of position. Sure, getting Bret Saberhagen was interesting, but with Bill Pecota, they have a guy who can play just about anywhere and not be caught out of position.

▶Flying fastest into the face of conventional wisdom: "We need pitching, but then, everybody needs pitching" is the most common general managers' quote. So, just what are the Reds and Royals doing anyway? Here's Kansas City sending away Saberhagen and Storm Davis, not getting any starting pitchers in return and still having more candidates for the rotation than they know what to do with.

And the Reds put together the best rotation in baseball before they get to the meetings, deal away Randy Myers and John Wetteland and still leave Miami with 21 pitchers on their 40-man roster (14 of them with major league experience).

▶Son of stockpiling: It wasn't enough for Reds' GM Bob Quinn to have all that pitching. He deals Eric Davis and heads home with seven outfielders who have been in the majors.

▶Focus award: The Astros were determined to get Craig Biggio out from behind the plate. A young catching prospect would do the trick. Eddie Taubensee from Cleveland seemed like a good name. So what if it cost them impact center fielder of the future Kenny Lofton.

▶Good sense award (this one's not given annually): The Dodgers and Royals make the perfect deal. Each team gets something it dearly needs and gives up something it will never miss. Todd Benzinger went to L.A., giving the Dodgers a hedge against young Eric Karros at first base and someone to spell Eric Davis in left. Benzinger was out of a job in K.C. with George Brett at DH and Wally Joyner at first base. Chris Gwynn, who had no job in L.A., ended up with a team that had a hole in the outfield.

A

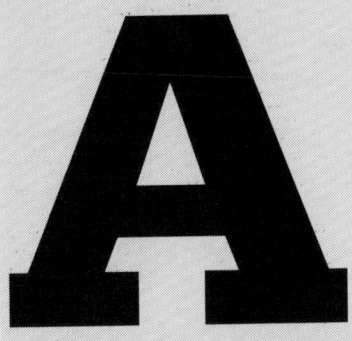

round the
League

USA SNAPSHOTS®

A look at statistics that shape the sports world

Equal opportunity in baseball

The same

More opportunities

35%

48%

17%

Fewer

How members of the USA TODAY Sports Team view management opportunities for minorities in Major League Baseball vs. the business community:

Source: Call-in survey of USA TODAY Sports Team members, all of whom volunteered to serve for one month

By Bob Laird, USA TODAY

Rickey Henderson: Man of Steal

Rickey's 939th: For the record

The stolen base that broke Brock's record came May 1, 1991, against Henderson's old team, the Yankees.

▶Time: 1:53 p.m. PDT
▶Score: 3-2, Oakland
▶Inning: Fourth
▶Base: Third
▶Battery: Tim Leary pitching; Matt Nokes catching
▶Count: 1-0
▶How Henderson reached base: On an error by Alvaro Espinoza. Went to second on a Dave Henderson infield single, then stole third where he stayed after a Jose Canseco flyout.
▶His previous at-bats: In the first inning he walked, but was thrown out (by Nokes) trying to steal second. Struck out (looking) in the second.

By Tim Wendel

It took 21 games to do it, but Rickey Henderson stole his third base of the season—939th of his career—on May 1, 1991, surpassing Lou Brock's mark to become the greatest base thief of all time.

Though some people see him as brash and cocky, it is Henderson's discipline at the plate and fearlessness on the basepaths that impressed his mentor, Tom Trebelhorn.

"Rickey was never afraid of the consequences of running," says Trebelhorn, who managed Henderson in 1976 and 1977 in the A's farm system.

Before night games in rookie ball, Henderson and Trebelhorn met at the ballpark for special instruction. Henderson would go to first base, Trebelhorn to the mound. The manager would go through the moves pitchers use to hold runners on. After several hours, Henderson would move to second, and the process would start all over again.

"People who think I have all this ability should have seen me then," Henderson says.

Other players are known as base-stealers, but none has come close to Henderson's record pace. He has singlehandedly kept the running game alive in the American League, insists Trebelhorn.

Once he takes his lead off first, Henderson has been clocked at less than 3.3 seconds in reaching second. He stole the base that broke Brock's record in a bat of an eyelash.

Oakland's Rickey Henderson became the all-time greatest base thief in 1992.

Nolan Ryan added to his legend with his seventh no-hitter.

Nolan Ryan: Deep in the heart of Texas

By Tim Wendel

Nolan Ryan has been in the majors longer than some of his Texas teammates have been alive. He ranks among the all-time top 10 in strikeouts, shutouts and games started, and the top 20 in innings pitched, earned run average and victories.

He's often the only active player on such roll calls, surrounded by such names as Cy Young, Walter Johnson, Tom Seaver and Warren Spahn.

But he still gets ready for upcoming seasons by throwing to his neighbor, former major-leaguer Harry Spilman, in his backyard or out in a pasture where he has a modest pitching mound.

After Ryan pitched his seventh career no-hitter—upstaging Rickey Henderson's stolen base record of the same day—he gave his neighbor credit for getting him in shape.

Nolan Ryan is an old-fashioned cowboy with a Hall-of-Fame fastball. At age 44, he pitched 173 innings, made 27 starts, and held opposing hitters to just .172 against him—far and away the best in the American League.

He's a living legend. They like 'em that way in Texas.

Boxscore of 7th no-hitter

TEXAS	3
TORONTO	0

Toronto.....000 000 000 0
Texas.........003 000 00x 3

TORONTO	ab	r	h	bi	lo	bb	so	avg
White, cf	4	0	0	0	0	0	3	.316
Alomar, 2b	4	0	0	0	0	0	3	.244
Gruber, 3b	2	0	0	0	0	1	1	.250
Carter, lf	2	0	0	0	1	1	1	.329
Olerud, 1b	2	0	0	0	1	0	1	.250
Whiten, rf	3	0	0	0	0	0	1	.293
Hill, dh	3	0	0	0	0	0	3	.333
Myers, c	3	0	0	0	0	0	2	.231
Lee, ss	3	0	0	0	0	0	1	.250
Totals	27	0	0	0	2	2	16	

▶BASERUNNING - Team LOB: 2.
▶FIELDING - E: Gruber (2, ground ball); Myers (1, throw); Lee (5, throw).

TEXAS	ab	r	h	bi	lo	bb	so	avg
Pettis, cf	4	1	1	0	1	0	2	.286
Daugherty, lf	4	0	1	0	2	0	1	.143
Palmiero, 1b	4	1	2	0	0	0	0	.329
Sierra, rf	4	1	1	2	2	0	1	.271
Franco, 2b	4	0	0	0	0	0	1	.225
Gonzales, dh	3	0	1	0	0	0	0	.412
Stanley, c	3	0	1	0	1	1	0	.235
Buechele, 3b	4	0	1	0	4	0	1	.255
Huson, ss	2	0	0	0	3	0	1	.233
TOTALS	32	3	8	2	13	1	7	

▶BATTING - 2B: Gonzales (3, off Key); Stanley (1, off Fraser). HR: Sierra (5, 3rd inning, off Key, 1 on, 1 out). RBI, scoring position, less than 2 outs: Pettis 0-1, Sierra 1-1, Buechele 0-2; S: Huson.
▶BASERUNNING - SB: Pettis (8, 3rd base off Key/Myers). CS: Gonzales (1, HP by Fraser/Myers). Team LOB: 8.
▶FIELDING - E: Palmiero (1, dropped throw).

PITCHING	ip	h	r	er	bb	so	era
TORONTO							
Key L,4-1	6	5	3	3	1	5	2.31
MacDonald	1	2	0	0	0	2	0.00
Fraser	1	1	0	0	0	0	1.35
TEXAS							
Ryan W,3-2	9	0	0	0	2	16	3.03

HBP: Gonzales by Fraser. Pitches-strikes: Ryan 122-83; Key 99-64; MacDonald 16-12; Fraser 12-7. Ground balls-fly balls: Ryan 3-7; Key 10-6; MacDonald 2-0; Fraser 1-1.

▶GAME DATA - T: 2:25. A: 33,439.
▶UMPIRES - HP: Tschida. 1B: Coble. 2B: Shulock. 3B: Johnson.

MONTREAL 2
LOS ANGELES 0

Montreal...... 000 000 200 - 2
Los Angeles... 000 000 000 - 0

MONTREAL	ab	r	h	bi	lo	bb	so	avg
DeShields, 2b	3	0	1	0	0	1	0	.254
Grissom, cf	4	0	0	0	4	0	1	.264
Da.Martinez, rf	4	1	0	0	2	0	1	.268
Calderon, lf	3	0	0	0	0	0	1	.306
Wallach, 3b	4	0	0	0	1	0	1	.238
Walker, 1b	4	1	1	1	0	0	0	.243
Hassey, c	3	0	1	0	0	0	1	.245
Owen, ss	3	0	0	0	1	0	0	.223
De.Martinez, p	3	0	1	0	0	0	1	.130
Totals	**31**	**2**	**4**	**1**	**8**	**1**	**5**	

▶BATTING - 3B: Walker (2, off Morgan). 2-out RBI: Walker. RBI, scoring position, less than 2 outs: Grissom 0-2, Wallach 0-1. S: Calderon.

▶BASERUNNING - CS: Hassey (1, 2nd base by Morgan/Scioscia). Team LOB: 4.

LOS ANGELES	ab	r	h	bi	lo	bb	so	avg.
Butler, cf	3	0	0	0	0	0	1	.296
Samuel, 2b	3	0	0	0	0	0	0	.297
Murray, 1b	3	0	0	0	0	0	0	.251
Strawberry, rf	3	0	0	0	0	0	0	.242
Daniels, lf	3	0	0	0	0	0	2	.265
Harris, 3b	3	0	0	0	0	0	1	.289
Scioscia, c	3	0	0	0	0	0	0	.272
Griffin, ss	2	0	0	0	0	0	0	.253
Javier, ph	1	0	0	0	0	0	1	.201
Morgan, p	2	0	0	0	0	0	0	.064
Gwynn, ph	1	0	0	0	0	0	0	.242
Totals	**27**	**0**	**0**	**0**	**0**	**0**	**5**	

▶FIELDING - E: Griffin 2 (20, ground ball; ground ball).

PITCHING	ip	h	r	er	bb	so	era
MONTREAL							
De.Martinez	9	0	0	0	0	5	2.05
LOS ANGELES							
Morgan L,9-6	9	4	2	0	1	5	2.53

WP: Morgan. Pitches-strikes: Morgan 108-69; De.Martinez 95-65. Ground balls-fly balls: Morgan 15-9; De.Martinez 16-5.

▶GAME DATA - T: 2:14. A: 45,560.
▶UMPIRES - HP: Poncino. 1B: Froemming. 2B: DeMuth. 3B: Bonin

Dennis Martinez pitched a perfect game and led the NL in ERA, complete games, and shutouts.

Dennis Martinez: El perfecto

By Rob Rains

"Dennis Martinez was already the most popular person in the country before he pitched the perfect game," said Tito Rondon, sports editor of Nicaragua's afternoon newspaper, *La Prensa*.

Martinez, the first of five players born in Nicaragua to play in the major leagues and the only one still active, became the first Latin pitcher to pitch a perfect game when the Montreal Expos' right-hander stopped the Dodgers 2-0 on July 28.

"I saw the list of all the pitchers who have thrown perfect games, like Cy Young and Sandy Koufax. I never thought I would be participating with them in something special, especially being from Nicaragua."

As it does for all of Martinez's starts, the state radio network in Nicaragua kept listeners abreast of his perfect game by calling Dodger Stadium every three innings. Said Rene Cardenas, one of the Dodgers' Spanish network broadcasters who is from Nicaragua. "The whole country stopped still."

Canseco and Fielder: In their own league

By Tim Wendel

Not since 1967 — when Carl Yastrzemski tied Harmon Killebrew for home runs on his way to the Triple Crown—have fans been treated to the type of long-ball *mano a mano* that Jose Canseco and Cecil Fielder slugged out in the American League last season.

The two AL hitters vied neck-and-neck all season long, with Fielder's final homer (No. 44) tying Canseco's mark in time to share the 1991 home run crown with him. But making history—the potential to put up Ruthian numbers—is about the only common ground these two appear to share. They have become the slugging version of the odd couple.

While Canseco's physique borders on Hulk Hogan's, Fielder inspires the couch potato in all of us—visible proof that you can have your cake and eat it too.

Canseco makes no bones about his chances to be remembered as one of the all-time home-run hitters. After his 200th career home run on Aug. 19, he characteristically said, "If I stay healthy, I could hit 600 or 700. If I average 35 a year, it could happen."

Such boasting, along with the speeding tickets and the late-night rendezvous with Madonna, hasn't endeared the 27-year-old Canseco to many fans. From the shoulder shrugs after a strikeout, to the hands clasped over his head after another home run, he's often seen as too big and too bad for public consumption.

But beneath all this bravado dwells a ballplayer with a refreshing sense of humor. A guy who's ready to be guest host on *Saturday Night Live*.

After the A's lost a stretch-drive heartbreaker to the Twins, the players filed out of the closed clubhouse with stern faces. Canseco slammed the door behind him and momentarily glared at reporters. Then his face broke into a big schoolboy grin.

"Just kidding," he said, sauntering off.

Sluggers Jose Conseco (above) and Cecil Fielder (below) vied neck-and-neck all season long for the American League home run crown.

In their own league
(continued)

A's manager Tony La Russa adds, "Jose's a big target, mainly because of his talent, his appearance."

Canseco followed Fielder's home run prowess nightly on ESPN, and even though Fielder didn't acknowledge it, the habit was probably mutual.

"He's one of the best," Fielder says of Canseco.

There was laughter in the Tigers' camp when the ballclub was caught up in the divisional race, but for several seasons the joke was on Fielder.

Vada Pinson recalls sitting in the Detroit dugout when Fielder was trying to win a job with the Toronto Blue Jays: "You'd hear them (players) saying things like, 'His thighs are rubbing together.' People were laughing and not realizing what the person could do.

"Look at Babe Ruth—he had a gut on him. With Cecil, I tried to block out his appearance and just see what he did."

After a year in Japan, Fielder signed with Detroit as a free agent and in 1990 became the first player since the Reds' George Foster to hit more than 50 home runs in a season. In 1991, Fielder picked up where he left off and the racial mix of the crowds at Tiger Stadium began to slowly transform.

For many years, the only black fans Pinson saw on a consistent basis were a family in the reserved seats and a smattering in the bleachers—less than a dozen.

"Now there's a lot more pepper coming in with salt," Pinson says. "They're coming in because the team is winning and because of Cecil Fielder."

Tony Phillips, formerly Canseco's teammate and now Fielder's, says it's difficult to choose between the two.

"They're both in the same category," he says. "As far as home runs, they'll be pushing each other a lot of years.

"They're both big, they can hit with power, they're both in their prime. They do things I can't even dream about. They're in a league by themselves."

Great home run races are rare

To find a race that was as heated as 1991's Canseco-Fielder duel, one has to go back at least a half-century.

▶**1929**: The Phillies' Chuck Klein and the Giants' Mel Ott were tied with 42 homers apiece going into the last day. Philadelphia and New York locked up in a season-ending doubleheader, and in the first game Klein hit his 43rd off the Giants' Carl Hubbell. In the second game, the Phillies intentionally walked Ott five straight times to make sure one of their own was homer king.

▶**1927**: Lou Gehrig led Yankee teammate Babe Ruth in home runs on July 4 and was only one dinger behind on Aug. 30. But Ruth homered the next day, and then blasted 17 more in September.

▶**1931**: Gehrig and Ruth ended the season tied with 46 homers. Yet one Gehrig homer, back on April 26 in Washington, was disallowed when Lyn Lary of the Yankees, who was on base with Gehrig at the plate, thought a long drive by Gehrig had been caught and left the basepaths. Actually the blast had carried into the stands and dropped onto the field. Lary touched third base and ran into the New York dugout. Still circling the bases, Gehrig touched home plate but was awarded only a triple.

—Tim Wendel

TV contracts can make or break teams

By Tim Wendel

George Steinbrenner might be officially gone from baseball, but a landmark television deal he made for the New York Yankees is threatening to divide baseball into a few big-city "haves"and a growing number of "have nots."

Thanks to Steinbrenner, the Yankees are locked into a 12-year, $500 million local television package with the Madison Square Garden Network—an agreement that netted the New York club more than $41 million in 1991 alone.

Small-city teams such as Seattle, Milwaukee and Pittsburgh cannot come close to such a lucrative local TV contract. As a result, it's becoming increasingly difficult for such teams to outbid franchises in larger cities for free-agent talent.

The 26 major-league teams evenly split the $1.5 billion CBS-ESPN national television deal—about $14 million to each ballclub last season. Yet there is no sharing of a team's own media coverage. Local television, cable and radio generated more than $200 million for the 26 major-league clubs last season, ranging from the Yankees' windfall to a low of $4 million in smaller markets such as Seattle.

The Yankees, Mets, Phillies and Dodgers net more than 35% of total rights fees—an indication of how far apart some teams are financially.

Comparing bottom lines for individual teams isn't an exact science. The books for most ballclubs are closed, little more than tax write-offs for corporations like Turner Broadcasting (Braves) and Domino's Pizza (Tigers).

The Pittsburgh Pirates, however, are publicly held by a coalition of local corporations, universities and individuals who combined in October 1985 to keep the team from leaving the Steel City. The Pirates' local broadcasting revenue in 1989 was $5.8 million. That's $2.4 million less than the average major-league club, and far short of the Mets' $29 million and the Cubs' $22 million.

It's no coincidence, then, that the Pirates lost Sid Bream, Wally Backman, Rafael Belliard and Ted Power to free agency and went to arbitration with 1990 Cy Young winner Doug Drabek, 1990 MVP Barry Bonds and 1990 MVP runner-up Bobby Bonilla before the 1991 season even began. Meanwhile, the Cubs, backed by the Tribune Co. ($525.3 million in revenues last year), signed George Bell, Dave Smith and Danny Jackson.

Pittsburgh's player payroll ($23 million) is slightly above average for the National League. It's no surprise that four of the five teams with larger payrolls—Los Angeles ($33.3 million), New York ($32.9

In 1959 when Ted Williams batted .254—his only sub-.300 season in the major leagues—he earned $125,000. With no discussion at all, Boston Red Sox owner Tom Yawkey sent Williams a contract for 1960 at the same amount. Ted looked at the numbers, didn't like what he saw, marched into Yawkey's office and tore up the contract.

"I looked him straight in the eyes and said, 'I'm taking a $35,000 cut,'" Williams recalled. A self-imposed salary cut?

"I signed for $90,000," Williams said. "It was the only fair thing to do . . . I couldn't function right. I didn't think it was fair to take $125,000."

Salaries today? Williams says some players make more for one game than he did for a whole season.

"I don't resent it one bit," he said. "It's not the players' fault they're able to demand that kind of money. Television has created a situation where the clubs get a lot more revenue; the players have a tremendous advantage. They can go to any team they want or not go to some they don't want to go to. It was never that way in the past. Conditions favor the player, and I must admit, I'm all for the player. The game can't be played without them."

million), San Francisco ($30.8 million) and Chicago ($26.8 million)—are in larger television markets.

"The system we have just doesn't work, especially for small-market teams," says Pirates' president Carl Barger. "We can't continue the way it is."

In the American League, Mariners' owner Jeff Smulyan jokes that when Ken Griffey Jr.'s contract expires, he and the budding superstar will simply switch places—Smulyan will go to work for Griffey. To hang on to Griffey, Smulyan says he might commit up to "90 percent" of his team's payroll.

Ballpark prices: Fans pay for 'bells and whistles'

Don't bet that baseball's TV money will keep going up—or that player salaries will slow down. But you can take this to the bank: Ballpark prices will continue to inch up as long as fans let them.

Clubs don't always give fans more for their money—at least on the field—so they're looking to improve things in the stands.

"We've moved from a baseball business to an entertainment," says Andy Dolich, vice-president of business operations for the Oakland Athletics. "More clubs are thinking of training their employees to be customer-service representatives."

And ballparks themselves are changing. Oakland has added automatic teller machines, smoking bans and a family rest area with TV monitors for parents to keep abreast of game action—and small food portions and toy blocks for the kids. For business people during day games, Oakland offers cellular phones in the stands and hopes, eventually, to add secretarial services and fax machines.

In the works: offering services such as dry-cleaning and film development and interactive computers to let fans settle arguments about baseball trivia.

Fans at the All-Star Game in Toronto this summer got a taste of the elaborate bells-and-whistles in baseball's future. In an All-Star "FanFest," according to event sponsor Coca-Cola, the Metro Toronto Convention Centre became a "ballpark-theme park." Among the attractions, for fans paying $12: a "Field of Dreams" county fair, a bullpen where fans can pitch, and the world's largest baseball.

Sometimes clubs work simply to improve more mundane matters. San Diego Padres' vice president Andy Strasberg says the club paid about $50,000 to a consultant to analyze traffic patterns to make it easier to exit Jack Murphy Stadium.

"We're always looking," he says, "to improve the ambiance of the ballpark." —*Michael Hiestand*

Grass vs. turf: The great debate

By Rick Lawes

In the list of hallmark dates defining baseball history, one that may have changed the game forever came on July 19, 1966, when the Philadelphia Phillies played the Houston Astros in the Astrodome—the first major-league baseball game played on a field completely covered with artificial turf.

Since then, the ersatz grass has changed the way all sports are played. It has led to the proliferation of domed ballparks, brought an entirely new lexicon to the game, and even affected the way general managers look at building their clubs.

But, with the possible exception of those domes, is it still necessary to cover the playing fields with what has been less than affectionately called "fuzzy concrete?" After all, as any purist will tell you, baseball was meant to be played on green grass under sunny skies.

And, while there is no chance of tearing out the lights in the stadiums, advances in the quality of natural grass are chipping away at many of the arguments for the plastic stuff.

The multi-use argument

The primary reason for the move toward artificial turf was the proliferation of multi-purpose stadiums. The new stadiums were housing baseball and football teams, and it was said that real grass couldn't stand up over the long haul.

But George Toma of the Kansas City Royals, considered one of the game's best groundskeepers, disputes that: "People expect too much from natural grass and give it too little in return. The owners have a lot of money invested in their ballplayers, in getting better coaches and managers. . . but when it comes to the playing field, that's where the money stops."

The rain-out argument

While the multi-use argument doesn't work for the Royals—their carpeted stadium is strictly a baseball park—the selling point that a game still can be played on AstroTurf shortly after it rains certainly applies. Royals' GM Herk Robinson noted that the team has had "a minimum number of rainouts here."

Yet advances in natural grass—specifically the draining systems under the fields—now give teams a sense of security against rain.

"I can think of maybe a half-dozen games that would have been rained out in the six years I've been here," said Terry Savarese, Chicago White Sox vice president for stadium operations. "We can play 20 minutes after it rains with Roger's system."

Roger is Comiskey's head groundskeeper Roger Bossard, who installed a new drainage system under its natural grass. AstroTurf claims it can drain 20 inches of rain per hour. But, as Savarese says, if it rained 20 inches in an hour no one would be able to get to the ballpark. He says the Comiskey system can handle as heavy a rain as three or four inches an hour.

The White Sox's system has drawn interest from other clubs. While Houston, Seattle, Toronto and Minnesota are doomed to life on turf—they all play in domes—success in Chicago could mean some AstroTurf fields could be converted back to natural grass.

The hardness argument

AstroTurf proponents say that some of the natural grass drainage systems compound a major concern leveled at artificial turf: hardness.

"A sand-filled system is harder than an artificial system or a good grass system," says Ed Milner, former president of AstroTurf Industries. "Remember, wet-packed sand is what they used to race cars on at Daytona."

But Chicago Cubs outfielder Andre Dawson says "there's really no comparison. On grass you can dig into it, you can tear it up, you can slide on it and it gives. It doesn't provide the shock to the joints. It's very easy to get stiffness and

Turf debut got mixed reviews

Opinions of AstroTurf really haven't changed in 25 years. After they laid the carpet down in the outfield to complete the first full artificially-covered field, Phillies' manager Gene Mauch took the opportunity to run in the outfield.

"It's got to be better. I got out there and ran around on it myself before the game and it's not nearly as hard as the old (grass)," Mauch told The Houston Post on July 19, 1966. "On top of that," he added, "it's a hell of a lot prettier."

"I was a little concerned at first," said Phillies' right fielder Johnny Callison, "but you get used to it in a hurry."

Cookie Rojas, who would get very used to the turf as a Kansas City Royals second baseman, played center field for the Phils that night.

The starting third baseman for the Phillies that night was Dick Allen, who didn't even want to try to get used to it. Allen was later quoted as saying: "If cows don't eat it, I ain't playing on it."

—Rick Lawes

Grass vs. turf (continued)

soreness if you play on turf for any length of time."

Yet the Royals' Toma says artificial turf can be a forgiving surface; it just depends upon the base, he says. AstroTurf generally must be replaced about every eight years. The foam padding underneath compacts and hardens over time and under usage.

The St. Louis Cardinals have made their living on the turf. They always have been known as a speed team, using the turf and Busch's spacious alleys. But general manager Dal Maxvill says that argument has been overplayed.

"Guys that can run, can run on grass or dirt or turf. It really doesn't matter," he says, though he concedes that turf helps offense. "I think most AstroTurf fields probably raise offense. Ground balls sneak through that might not sneak through on grass."

Cardinal Ozzie Smith disagrees. "It's like the DH rule," he says. "They say it's supposed to generate more offense, but they've got statistics that say it doesn't."

—*Contributing: Rob Rains and Tim Wendel.*

Turftalk

Artificial turf has changed the way we talk about the game. Some turf-terms:

▶**True hop:** Ground balls take a "true hop" on fake turf. On grass infields, bad-hop base hits are a fact of life.

▶**Turf bounce:** The turf hop wasn't always perfect —especially in the outfield. "Turf bounce" describes the high hops that carom wildly all around the outfield. Outfielders learned right away to play deeper and to forget diving for shallow fly balls.

▶**Concepcion play:** Possibly the greatest shortstop artisan on the ersatz grass was the Reds' Davey Concepcion. He quickly discovered that a sharply hit ball didn't slow down through the infield. So he started playing much deeper—almost in shallow left field—to get greater range. His throws had to be longer, but he made them lower, so they would one-hop into the first baseman's glove.

▶**Turf toe:** Artificial turf grabs at shoes better than natural grass, but when the torque of a moving human body is applied, something has to give. The injurious result is "turf toe." The sole of the shoe remains virtually glued to the turf, while the big toe is jammed into the front of the shoe. Yes, it does hurt—and yes, it can end careers.

▶**Speed:** Despite the claims of some general managers that base-stealers can steal anywhere, turf gives the runner an extra step over 90 feet. Plus, ground balls dart through the infield and go through gaps in the outfield, also making the turf game faster.

Expansion: Your questions answered

Q: When will Miami and Denver begin play?
A: In April 1993.
Q: Where will the two teams play?
A: Denver will play its first two seasons in Mile High Stadium. Voters have OK'd construction of an open-air, grass stadium. Miami will play in Joe Robbie Stadium, located between Miami and Fort Lauderdale. It will be renovated for baseball—it's home to the NFL Dolphins—and has a grass surface.
Q: Will the two divisions be realigned?
A: Not likely—at least not right away.
Q: How will the new teams get players?
A: An expansion draft is scheduled for November 1992. Each of the 26 major league teams will contribute three players to stock the two new organizations with 39 players each. The new teams will probably participate in next summer's amateur free agent draft, but likely will not be allowed to sign free agents from other teams until after their first season.
Q: What will be the biggest problem playing in Denver?
A: Denver could become the home run capital of the majors. Studies have shown that at Denver's altitude of 5,280 feet, a batted ball travels 40 feet farther than a ball hit at sea level.
Q: What will be the biggest problem in Miami?
A: The weather. Even though most people say the summer rain usually comes in the afternoon and clears by evening, the minor-league Miami Miracle had nine rainouts in 68 home games last year. Projected over an 81-game home schedule, that would translate into 10 rainouts. The average major league total last year was 1.9 rainouts per team, not counting the five teams that play in domed stadiums.
Q: What happens to the other cities (Buffalo, Orlando, Tampa-St. Petersburg and Washington, D.C.) not selected?
A: They might talk to some of the existing clubs that are for sale, but it isn't likely the major leagues will allow more than one team to move. The most-often mentioned candidates are the Expos, Mariners, Astros and Giants.
Q: What can the fans in Denver and Miami expect?
A: Probably several years of bad baseball. The average record for a first-year team in the four previous expansions was 59-102. But this time, expansion clubs will select players out of both leagues, so there should be more talent—and hopefully more wins—available.   —*Rob Rains*

The new ballparks

Here's a look at the dimensions of the National League's new ballparks. Miami will play at Joe Robbie Stadium. Denver will spend its first two seasons at Mile High Stadium while Coors Stadium is constructed.

Stadium	LF	CF	RF
Joe Robbie	335	410	345
Mile High	335	423	370
Coors	335	420	345

Tropical baseball

1. PUERTO RICO
First player: Hiram Bithorn (1942); Current stars: Ruben Sierra, Ivan Calderon, Danny Tartabull, Roberto Alomar, Sandy Alomar Jr., Juan Gonzalez; Current major leaguers born in Puerto Rico: 30

2. DOMINICAN REPUBLIC
First player: Ozzie Virgil (1956); Current stars: George Bell, Julio Franco, Jose Rijo, Ramon Martinez, Juan Samuel, Felix Jose, Pedro Guerrero, Luis Polonia, Tony Pena; Current major leaguers born in Dominican Republic: 34

3. CUBA
First player: Esteban Bellan (1871); Current stars: Jose Canseco, Rafael Palmeiro; Current major leaguers born in Cuba: 3

4. MEXICO
First player: Melo Almeda (1933); Current stars: Teddy Higuera, Vicente Palacios; Fernando Valenzuela; Current major leaguers born in Mexico: ?

5. BELIZE
First player: Chito Martinez (1991); Current star: Chito Martinez; Current major leaguers born in Belize: 1

6. HONDURAS
First player: Gerald Young (1987); Current star: Gerald Young; Current major leaguers born in Honduras: 1

7. NICARAGUA
First player: Dennis Martinez (1976); Current star: Dennis Martinez; Current major leaguers born in Nicaragua: 1

8. PANAMA
First player: Hector Lopez and Humberto Robinson (1955); Current stars: Roberto Kelly, Juan Berenguer; Current major leaguers born in Panama: 3

9. COLOMBIA
First player: Luis Castro (1906); Current star: No active Colombian players

10. VENEZUELA
First player: Alejandro Carrasquel (1939); Current stars: Ozzie Guillen, Andres Galarraga, Carlos Quintana; Current major leaguers born in Venezuela: 11

By Rob Ruck

Since Rico Carty went to the USA to play ball in the 1960s, the town of San Pedro De Macoris, Dominican Republic, has sent Alfredo Griffin, Joaquin Andujar, Sammy Sosa, Pedro Guerrero, Juan Samuel, Tony Fernandez, Julio Franco, George Bell, Manny Lee, Jose Offerman, Mariano Duncan, and Rafael Ramirez on to the big leagues.

Hundreds of others played in the minors; thousands more train daily for a baseball career. This town of 80,000 may be the only one in the world that could form a major-league franchise solely on local talent.

Although it was Rico Carty who helped put this town on the sports map, it is his mother, Oliva, once the town's midwife, for whom a street is named. Carty Street stretches from Santa Ana Church—once home of a fabled baseball team—to a giant sugar mill, which runs the town's baseball program and dominates daily life.

Carty opened eyes at the 1959 Pan American Games in Chicago. Nine U.S. clubs made him offers to play professionally. Carty accepted them all: "I just go ahead and sign 'cause all I want to do is play baseball. I get baseball in my blood and I keep on signing." He also signed with all four Dominican winter clubs—only the intervention of the president of the minor leagues saved him from permanent exile from the game. He played his first game in the majors in 1963 for Milwaukee.

After Carty's .366 average led the majors in 1970, a flood of Dominican ballplayers signed pro contracts. Among them were boys from the local amateur team, which sent five shortstops in a row to the majors.

Of the hundred-plus Dominicans to have played in the majors by 1988, more than a third came via San Pedro. And while the best Dominicans, like Juan Marichal and Tony Pena, initially came from elsewhere in the nation, since the '70s, San Pedro has provided the most bountiful harvests.

There is no comparable alternative to a baseball career in San Pedro—at least not a legal one—and the local boys know it.

But there is baseball—almost around the clock. Both the government and the sugar mills sponsor extensive amateur ball, while camps are run by major-league teams throughout the year.

While only the best and luckiest players will make it, almost all of them will return to San Pedro each winter. Every boy who returns a major-leaguer raises the town's fever for the game another notch.

Bad boys

Extreme prejudice: Crashes at the plate

By Rod Beaton

Most baseball fans like nothing better than a good, old-fashioned, bone-rattling, home-plate collision—and they had plenty to savor last season. In one week alone: Eric Yelding, skinny Houston shortstop, ran into and over Cincinnati catcher Jeff Reed; Barry Larkin, Cincinnati shortstop, from a family of football players, belted Atlanta catcher Mike Heath and knocked Heath out of action; Joe Carter, all 225 pounds of him, crunched Royals' catcher Mike Macfarlane, who suffered torn knee ligaments and was sidelined for 6-8 weeks.

Nothing out of the ordinary. Runners and catchers are meeting at the plate—with extreme prejudice—more than ever before.

"It sure seems that way," said Cleveland catcher Sandy Alomar, Jr. Granted, Alomar has a rather limited perspective; it's his second full season. But his theory is widely shared. Explanations that have been proffered:

▶**Macho, macho men**: Players like contact. Players want to prove they're playing all out. Players are just ornery.

"I've seen a lot of players on TV, when the guy's not blocking the plate and he gets hit anyway," said Alomar. "Some guys just enjoy doing that. They think they're playing football."

Benito Santiago, San Diego's All-Star catcher, agreed: "Some people play clean baseball, a lot of them don't. Baseball is a dirty game now."

▶**Your cheatin' heart:** Mike Scioscia of Los Angeles is the No. 1 practitioner of the block-the-plate-before-you-have-the-ball routine. It's effective. It's dangerous. It's illegal.

"(Scioscia) drops in front of the plate. All the time," said Reds' catcher Reed. "That's why Norm (Charlton) took him on (in 1990) and took him out."

▶**Give, so you don't receive:** A catch-er can put a serious hurt on an unwary runner. Shin guards are hard. Chest protectors are heavy. The man wearing both is heavier. Hit him, the theory goes, on your terms, before he buries you.

The best way, said Reds' third baseman Chris Sabo, is the sneak attack.

"The only way to hit a catcher is if he's not looking," Sabo said. "I'm not a big guy. If he's waiting for me, I've got no chance."

The slamdance is not likely to abate any time soon.

Catchers' gear: The 'tools of ignorance'

Ever wonder why so many catchers become managers, coaches and broadcasters? All those collisions knock some sense into them.

Baltimore skipper John Oates knows. Dave Parker got him on Opening Day 1976, when Parker was as fast as he is big. And Oates, catching for the Phillies, was as crushed as you can get.

"I got it pretty good," said Oates, "but I was doing my job. I'd do it again."

That's the attitude catchers have brought to the plate since they first strapped on masks. Perhaps that is also why they call their gear "the tools of ignorance."

Pete Rose took on Ray Fosse in the 1970 All-Star Game in Cincinnati. Fosse's career was taking off. Rose drove into his shoulder. Fosse was never the same, and neither was his promising career.

Hall of Fame Reds' catcher Johnny Bench "got run over by Gary Matthews in 1975." Rick Dempsey met Bo Jackson at the plate, and found out that Bo knows KOs. Houston catcher Craig Biggio "got run over by a freight train" in the form of Philadephia's Danny Cox. Sandy Alomar, Jr., was hit by Bob Boone and Mackey Sasser in the same year.

The list goes on and on. But before you start feeling too sorry for the catchers, remember: sometimes the runners don't come out so well, either. You might remember Dave Parker breaking his face on a catcher and wearing a football faceguard afterwards.

—Rod Beaton

Baylor: Brushback pitch a dying art

Don Baylor was never one to shy away from the brushback pitch. He was hit a major-league record 267 times to prove it.

"Most of them were not intentional," Baylor said. "I just stood on the plate. That was my style of hitting more than anything else."

Baylor's style was also a dare, and many pitchers he faced couldn't take it.

"A lot of times, I knew they couldn't pitch inside," he said. "If they made a mistake inside, I took advantage of it." Baylor clubbed 338 home runs with 1,276 RBI and a .260 batting average in his 19-year playing career with Baltimore, Oakland, California, the New York Yankees, Boston and Minnesota.

During two seasons as the Milwaukee Brewers' hitting coach, he's seen a change in players' attitudes about being pitched inside.

"A lot of them are .200 hitters and they feel like somebody's throwing at them," Baylor said. "You don't throw at guys hitting .200, but they don't understand the situation."

Baylor, 42, calls the brushback "one of those lost and dying arts. Now, when guys pitch inside, they're tossed out of the ballgame."

The rash of mound-charging by hitters these days, Baylor said, is "about money." If players are put on the disabled list, Baylor explained, "they will lose time of service and won't have their numbers to go to arbitration and free agency." *—Chuck Johnson*

Feller: No sympathy for today's hitters

Hall of Fame pitcher Bob Feller has no empathy for today's hitters who think the brushback pitch is a threat to their livelihood.

"All they want is for the pitcher to throw the ball right over the plate so they can hit it out of the ballpark and

make $4 million a year," Feller said. "If I was pitching today, I'd throw it in high and tight and snap the bat right out of their hands."

King turns shutout into punchout

The Cleveland Indians added to their reputation as the new American League "bad boys" when pitcher Eric King celebrated a 2-hit shutout of the Texas Rangers (early August) by allegedly punching a fan in the eye after the game.

Ronald Johnston of Keller, Texas said King socked him in the right eye after he followed King and other players back to their rooms. Johnston said he was trying to retrieve his cowboy hat, which the players took from him while they were in the hotel bar.

At the time of the incident, three of King's teammates—Albert Belle, Carlos Martinez and Mark Whiten—had already been suspended, topping any team in the league.

Reds' Charlton adds insult to injury

The Dodgers weren't happy when Reds' pitcher Norm Charlton said he hit catcher Mike Scioscia on purpose (Sept.9), and they certainly weren't pleased when he appealed his suspension and was eligible to play against the Dodgers.

When Charlton finally was to serve his suspension, it coincided with a series against Atlanta, the team battling the Dodgers for the NL West lead. League president Bill White delayed the suspension until after the Braves' series.

Charlton admits he made a mistake in speaking out after hitting Scioscia, whom he alleged had been stealing his signs. And he knows it could present him with more trouble in the future.

"Every time I come in (with a pitch) now, it's going to be a thought in people's minds and maybe the umpires' minds that maybe I'm throwing at people," Charlton said. "I'll probably be more apt to get warned."

Stargell: Hitting well is the best revenge

Hall of Fame slugger Willie Stargell says the batter has to protect himself against brushback pitches, but should use discretion.

"If you get a pitcher coming in and he misses, that's a difference," Stargell said. "But if somebody with a history of good control is throwing at you or behind you, he's not concerned about your welfare."

Stargell believes there's a better remedy for a brushed-back hitter than charging the mound.

"Personally, the way I feel you should get back at him is to get a good pitch and turn on it," he said.

Sabo on fan abuse:"There is no story"

Cincinnati Reds' third baseman Chris Sabo pushed an autograph-seeker into a Busch Stadium window after a late-July loss to the St. Louis Cardinals, a witness said.

"He was totally, completely, out of hand," said Alex Neuman, who said more than 20 fans witnessed the incident. "I've never seen a jerk like Chris Sabo in my life. Nothing at all provoked him to do this."

Neuman said the fan asked Sabo to sign an autograph. After Sabo refused, the fan asked why not and a brief scuffle ensued. In the scuffle, the fan was thrown into the ground-floor window, shattering it, Neuman said.

The fan, who was not identified, did not appear to be injured and decided not to press charges, authorities said.

Sabo, reached at the team's hotel across the street from Busch Stadium, declined to comment on the incident.

"There is no story," Sabo said before hanging up the phone. Reds' manager Lou Piniella said Sabo would not face disciplinary action.

"It wasn't a window, just a little plate glass," Piniella said. "A fan was bothering him for autographs and it was just a little bit of a scuffle. Everything has been handled."

USA SNAPSHOTS®

A look at statistics that shape the sports world

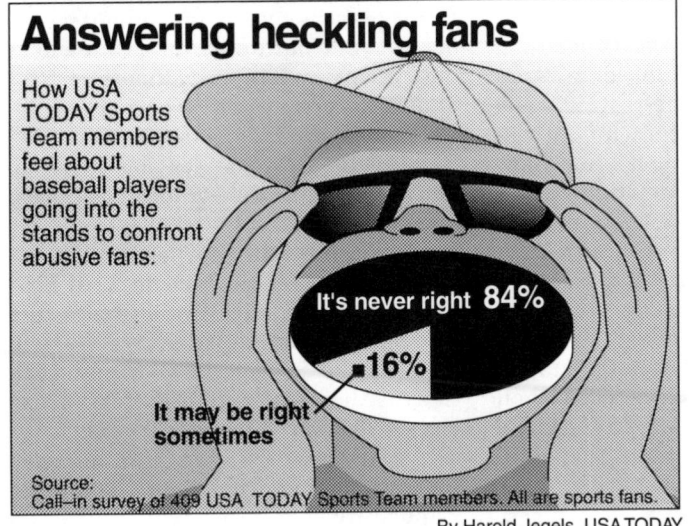

Answering heckling fans

How USA TODAY Sports Team members feel about baseball players going into the stands to confront abusive fans:

It's never right **84%**

16%

It may be right sometimes

Source: Call-in survey of 409 USA TODAY Sports Team members. All are sports fans.

By Harold Jegels, USA TODAY

Commentary

Rob Dibble: Armed and dangerous

By Tom Weir

Cincinnati pitcher Rob Dibble has brought new meaning to the term "scatter-armed"—the world seems to be his strike zone. First, he threw a pitch behind Houston's Eric Yelding last April, an offense for which he served a three-day suspension. In May, he finished off a Cincinnati victory by firing a ball into the centerfield seats—winging a female fan.

Then, after being badly beaten to first on a squeeze-bunt play by Chicago's Doug Dascenzo, Dibble fired the ball at Dascenzo's backside and hit him in the lower leg.

Dibble's initial defense was that the ball that struck Dascenzo merely slipped. It also no doubt slipped in Class AAA ball (1987), when Dibble reacted to giving up a home run by throwing the next ball he touched out of Herschel Greer Stadium.

And there must have been an entire batch of slippery ones the night Dibble was called in and threw his first four warmups into his own team's dugout.

Or what about that 1989 exhibition where giving up the game-costing home run resulted in Dibble launching furniture into a pond? That just must have been some sort of failed aviation experiment. And the bat he sent sailing up the screen behind home plate? Surely he was just aiming for the bat rack—he only missed by 40 yards.

It has been 71 years since Carl Mays made Ray Chapman the only major-leaguer killed by a pitch, and baseball better wake up to the fact that Dibble is demonstrating a frightening capability to challenge that exclusivity.

Is that too harsh, Rob? Sorry. It just slipped.

According to the Cinncinnati Reds, Dibble has entered a counseling program and has met the team's requirements.

Save the doubleheader

By Paul White

The Tigers and Brewers tried to revive a baseball tradition last Memorial Day: the holiday doubleheader.They played just one game, but it did last five hours, 37 minutes—enough innings to get a reprise of The Beer Barrel Polka. (I wonder how many folks were able to handle a second seventh-inning stretch on an 82-degree day in a stadium that doesn't cut off beer sales before game's end.)

Of course, you knew right away when I mentioned a holiday doubleheader that they weren't scheduled to play two. Nobody is these days. In fact, four American League teams weren't scheduled to play any games at all on Memorial Day.

Not only aren't there any holiday doubleheaders, there aren't any Sunday doubleheaders. C'mon fans, give me one good reason why we shouldn't have twinbills, double-dips, two for the price of one, a lidlifter followed by the afterpiece. The only redeeming value I can find is that it's refreshing to find something players and management agree on: Players hate playing two; owners hate giving up a precious home date.

Look closely at last year's schedule. There was one doubleheader not caused by a rainout. Only one. It's time to rise up and speak out for an endangered species.

Forget the whales, the elephants and the manatee for one night. Save the doubleheader!

We found a regularly scheduled doubleheader in 1992: Cleveland's Saturday opener (April 12) vs. Boston. Let's make it baseball's Woodstock (maybe they'll play Jimi Hendrix's version of *The Star-Spangled Banner*).

No matter where it is, let's all pack up and go. Even if it's in Cleveland. Especially if it's in Cleveland. Let's pack the place. Let's show the major leagues that we still want doubleheaders.

Maybe next year they'll schedule two.

F.Y.I.

Let's hear it for the good guys

While a handful of players were racking up points toward the "bad boy" title for 1991, many of baseball's true champions were quietly spending their time helping others. Twenty-two of these players were nominated for the annual Roberto Clemente Award, presented at 1991's All-Star Game to Seattle second baseman Harold Reynolds.

Reynolds—recognized as a "Daily Point of Light" by President Bush—says there are many more athletes who work diligently for humanitarian causes, and most of them don't seek publicity for their good deeds.

"I've done a lot of big things that draw a lot of attention," Reynolds said. "But there are little things guys do on a daily basis. I'd say about 90 percent of the guys are involved in the community in some way or another."

The award is named after the Hall of Fame outfielder who died during a mercy mission in Nicaragua on New Year's Eve in 1972.

Past Roberto Clemente winners

1971 Willie Mays
1972 Brooks Robinson
1973 Al Kaline
1974 Willie Stargell
1975 Lou Brock
1976 Pete Rose
1977 Rod Carew
1978 Greg Luzinski
1979 Andre Thornton
1980 Phil Niekro
1981 Steve Garvey
1982 Ken Singleton
1983 Cecil Cooper
1984 Ron Guidry
1985 Don Baylor
1986 Garry Maddox
1987 Rick Sutcliffe
1988 Dale Murphy
1989 Gary Carter
1990 Dave Stewart

Field of deans: Players with a past

Players 36 and older lead some teams—and sit on others. Here's a list of regulars and role players in 1991, and their ages when they started the season.

▶**Stars**
Nolan Ryan, P, Rangers, 44
Carlton Fisk, C, White Sox, 43
Charlie Hough, P, White Sox, 43
Rick Reuschel, P, Giants, 41
Brian Downing, DH, Rangers, 40
Bert Blyleven, P, Angels, 40
Dave Winfield, OF, Angels, 39
Dwight Evans, DH-OF, Orioles, 39
Dave Parker, DH, Angels, 39
George Brett, 1B, Royals, 37
Jim Gantner, 2B, Brewers, 37
John Candelaria, P, Dodgers, 37
Frank Tanana, P, Tigers, 37
Dennis Eckersley, P, A's, 36
Andre Dawson, OF, Cubs, 36
Willie Randolph, 2B, Brewers, 36
Ozzie Smith, SS, Cardinals, 36
Dave Smith, P, Cubs, 36

▶**Role players**
Rick Dempsey, C, Brewers, 41
Ken Griffey Sr., OF, Mariners, 40
Mike Flanagan, P, Orioles, 39
Ron Hassey, C, Expos, 38
Ernie Whitt, C, Orioles, 38
Dave Bergman, 1B, Tigers, 37
Gary Carter, C, Dodgers, 37
Keith Hernandez, 1B, Indians, 37
Terry Leach, P, Twins, 37
Rick Mahler, P, Expos, 37
Rick Honeycutt, P, A's, 36
Jamie Quirk, C, A's, 36
Rick Cerone, C, Mets, 36
Mike Heath, C, Braves, 36
Denny Walling, 1B-DH, Rangers, 36
Dan Schatzeder, P, Royals, 36
Ted Power, P, Reds, 36
Juan Berenguer, P, Braves, 36

How waivers work

The waiver system is required for most transactions during the season and virtually all after Aug. 1. Waivers are used to:

▶**Trade a player after July 31.** These are major-league waivers. Any team can put in a claim for the player. If there are no claims, he can be traded. If he is claimed by and awarded to a team, he can be traded to that team, allowed to go for the waiver price of $20,000, or the waivers can be revoked (he stays with his original team, but if waived again that season, those waivers are irrevocable).

▶**Outright a player to the minors.** A player may be sent to the minors on an optional or outright assignment. If optioned, no waivers are needed. The player is still "under control" (on the 40-man roster).

▶**Release a player.** If a player is waived to give him an unconditional release, the team cannot recall him. If claimed, he has five days to report to his new team or opt for free agency, voiding his contract (and walking away from a guaranteed full year's pay).

When a team places a player on waivers:

▶**The major league office must be notified by computer by 2 p.m. EDT.** A list of all the day's waivers is sent to all teams, by computer. Teams can place a maximum of seven players on the waiver wire per day.

▶**Teams have three business days to put in a claim.**

▶**Teams within the same league have first shot;** the worst-record team has priority. If no one in the league claims him, teams in the other league get a chance.

—David Steele and Rick Lawes

MLB to players: Snuff it!

By Deron Snyder

Quick, what are two types of baseball spitters? Answer: Illegal pitches and tobacco chewers. Both are part of baseball's lore, but only one was illegal—until now.

Attempts are under way—from the college level to the major leagues—to snuff out the love affair between baseball and smokeless tobacco.

Players in last year's College World Series were banned from using smokeless tobacco on the field or in the dugout. The ban was passed by the NCAA executive committee in December and covers all NCAA championships. Frank Uryasz, NCAA director of sports sciences, says other athletes are affected, but none more than baseball players.

"We get letters reminding us that college athletes are role models, and it doesn't help our tobacco education programs to have role models on the field chewing tobacco," Uryasz says.

Major League Baseball has embarked on its own arduous task of disassociating itself from jaws of chaws. Players in the lowest levels of professional baseball—short-season Class A and rookie leagues—are now prohibited from using tobacco products.

"Basically the commissioner requested it," says MLB spokesman Jim Small. "We wanted to start at a low level. The players at that level are 18, 19 years old. We wanted to catch them while they're young."

Small says the ban is "the dramatic part" of an overall effort to reduce the presence of tobacco in baseball. MLB has commissioned a study outlining the dangers of smokeless tobacco, and has produced a video for each team.

In addition, MLB and the National Cancer Institute worked together to produce a 16-page guide—"Beat the Smokeless Habit"—published last season and made available to players. The guide includes stars such as Nolan Ryan, John Franco, Andy Van Slyke and Tim Wallach—all of whom have kicked the habit.

Reader Survey: You made the call

If you are a true fan, you don't just eat, sleep and watch baseball, you argue about it. More than 3,000 fans responded to our survey last May, which included questions about player salaries, artificial turf, expansion, and many other hotly debated issues in baseball. Here's how they answered:

Which two cities deserve to have the new National League teams?

Denver 62%
Tampa/St. Petersburg 37%
Buffalo 33%
Washington, D.C. 26%
Miami 25%
Orlando 12%

Which cities ought to lose their major league teams?

National League

Montreal 21%
Houston 17%
Pittsburgh 12%
Atlanta 9%
San Francisco 7%
New York 2%
Philadelphia 2%
San Diego 2%
Chicago 1%
Cincinnati 1%
Los Angeles 1%
St. Louis 1%

American League

Cleveland 21%
Seattle 11%
Toronto 6%
Milwaukee 4%
Minnesota 4%
California 3%
Texas 2%
Baltimore 2%
Detroit 2%
New York 2%
Kansas City 1%
Oakland 1%
Chicago 1%
Boston 0%

Would you rather:

Hit 50 HRS 44%
Manage the team 29%
Win 20 games 23%
Steal 100 bases 4%

Your son is considered a major league prospect—would you rather have him:

Go to college, get an education and then try for majors. 78%

Go straight to the minor leagues. 21%

Go to college, get an education and do something more worthwhile than playing baseball. 1%

Your daughter is considered a major league prospect—would you rather she:

Make a serious effort to be the first woman in the big leagues. 48%

Bag the idea—no woman will ever play in the big leagues. 33%

Bag the idea—maybe some women will play, but why should my little darling go through all the discrimination the first woman will face? 12%

Bag the idea—no daughter of mine is going to play professional baseball if I can help it. 6%

You're an owner.

What's the most you'll pay a player?
(Only 13% of those under 30 set the cap at less than $1 million, compared with 38% of those 50 and older)
$1 million-$3 million a year 52%
Less than $1 million a year 19%
More than $5 million a year 15%
$4 million-$5 million a year 13%

You have a top player the caliber of Rickey Henderson, and he asks to renegotiate his new contract before spring training starts. Do you:

Tell him "see you on the field or in the courtroom." Nobody's that important. 60%

Reader Survey (cont.)

Delay saying anything, and hope critics and disappointed fans will force the player to back down. 29%

Give him a new deal and cut down the hassle factor. He's that important. 11%

(17% of those 30 and under are willing to give him a new deal, only 4% of those 50 and older. 69% of the 50 and older crowd say "see you in court" vs. only 49% of the under 30 crew)

You're the commissioner.

Do you allow the use of aluminum bats?

Yes   8%   No   92%

Do you ban artificial turf in stadiums?

Yes   65%   No   35%

Do you have most games on cable TV?

Yes   50%   No   50%

Do you keep the designated hitter in the American League?

Yes   48%   No   52%

Do you ban the sale of beer at all ballparks after the 7th inning?

Yes   81%   No   19%

You're the player.

Who would you most want as your manager?

Harrelson 30%	Leyland 6%
Lasorda 16%	Piniella 4%
La Russa 15%	Craig 3%
Anderson 12%	Other 14%

A fan asks you who is the greatest baseball player ever. You say:

Mays 15%	Cobb 3%
Ted Williams 8%	Rose 3%
DiMaggio 7%	Aaron 3%
Mantle 6%	Other 25%
Gehrig 4%	

(Ruth is tops with every age group; after him, over-50 types lean heavily toward Williams and DiMaggio, 40s like Mays, Aaron and Rose don't get much support from any age group.)

Jim Palmer's comeback try didn't work last spring. Would you tell guys like Palmer to stay retired?

No, everybody loves a comeback try; it's good for the game. 74%

Yes, they're an embarrassment; it's bad for the game. 26%

Which kind of career would you rather have:

One like Willie Randolph—solid, respected, but unspectacular for more than 15 years. 75%

One like Kirk Gibson—playing all-out for a few moments of ultimate glory, but a lot of time on the disabled list. 12%

One like Bo Jackson—doing some things so spectacularly no one else can do them, but not considered a great all-around ballplayer. 12%

When fans ask you for autographs, you:

Sign them for everyone, free of charge, whenever you're asked. 53%

Sign them free at the ballpark for everyone, and charge everyone a reasonable fee at card shows and other commercial events. 30%

Sign them free at ballparks for kids only, and charge everyone a reasonable fee at card shows and other commercial events. 18%

Avoid the situation at the ballpark, and charge everyone a reasonable fee at card shows and other commercial events. 8%

Should Bo Jackson have played football?

Yes   58%

No   43%

(69% of those under 30 said yes, as did 56% of the 30-somethings, 44% of the 40-somethings and 46% of the 50-and-over crew)

N L/AL Beat

USA SNAPSHOTS®

A look at statistics that shape the sports world

Feeling pitcher's loss

USA TODAY Sports Team members are nearly united about the designated hitter's worst impact on the game:

Batting order
1B
2B
CF
Pitcher

Removes pitcher from strategy	**75%**
Makes games too long, high scoring	**18%**
Makes manager's job too easy	**7%**

Source: Call-in survey of 380 USA TODAY Sports Team members. All are sports fans.

By Julie Stacey, USA TODAY

NL East: Don't forget the Pirates

By Rob Rains

Though it was overshadowed by the Braves' worst-to-first climb, the Pirates became the first team in 13 years to repeat as the champion of either division of the National League. No NL team had been able to pull off the trick since the Phillies and Dodgers both repeated in 1978.

No one thought the Pirates could do it, especially after a celebrated blowup in spring training between manager Jim Leyland and star outfielder Barry Bonds. There were too many distractions, everybody said, and marked the Pirates down for third or fourth place.

Wrong. Not only did the Pirates repeat, they moved into first place before April was over, and eventually won the division by 14 games over the second-place Cardinals.

NL East Standings May 24, 1991

Team	W	L	Pct	GB
Pittsburgh	24	15	.615	-
New York	22	17	.584	2
St. Louis	22	18	.550	2 1/2
Chicago	21	20	.512	4
Philadelphia	20	21	.488	5
Montreal	19	22	.463	6

The Pirates proved the skeptics wrong with big seasons from Bonds and free-agent-to-be Bobby Bonilla, both of whom topped 100 RBI for the second straight year. They also got 20 victories from left-hander John Smiley, a career offensive year from shortstop Jay Bell, and 51 saves from a bullpen without a No. 1 closer.

Joe Torre's Cardinals were almost as much of a surprise in the division as the Pirates. Picked by almost everybody to finish last, they managed to come in second, six games over .500. And they did it without top starter Joe Magrane, who missed the entire season after undergoing elbow surgery in spring training.

No teams were bigger busts than the Cubs and Mets, expected to finish ahead of the Pirates. The Cubs spent $33 million on free agents Danny Jackson, Dave Smith and George Bell and got virtually nothing to show for

their investment. Jackson was on the disabled list twice and won just one game. Smith saved 17 games, but pitched a total of only 33 innings. Bell had a decent season, 25 homers and 86 RBI, but he faded out down the stretch.

NL East Standings (All-Star Break)

Team	W	L	Pct	GB
Pittsburgh	48	31	.608	-
New York	46	34	.575	2 1/2
St. Louis	44	37	.543	5
Chicago	38	44	.463	11 1/2
Montreal	35	47	.427	14 1/2
Philadelphia	33	49	.402	16 1/2

The Mets' Howard Johnson led the NL in home runs (38) and RBI (117) but the supporting cast wasn't able to keep up with his pace. Dwight Gooden won only 13 games—the second-lowest total of his career—and ended the year with shoulder surgery. Frank Viola couldn't win a game the last two months.

The Phillies and Expos were not expected to contend, and they didn't. Any hopes Philadelphia had of being a factor ended when Lenny Dykstra crashed his car into a tree, and the Expos had too many young players to be a threat. It also didn't help Montreal to be forced to play the final 26 games of the season on the road because of concerns about the safety of Olympic Stadium.

Mirroring the rest of 1991 baseball, it was the year of mass manager switches—for every NL East team but the Pirates and Cardinals. The Cubs fired two managers—Don Zimmer and Jim Essian—the Phillies dismissed Nick Leyva, the Expos fired Buck Rodgers, and the Mets said goodbye to Bud Harrelson.

NL East Final Standings

Team	W	L	Pct	GB
Pittsburgh	98	64	.605	-
St. Louis	84	78	.519	14
Philadelphia	78	84	.481	20
Chicago	77	83	.481	20
New York	77	84	.475	20 1/2
Montreal	71	90	.441	26 1/2

NL West: Braves' new world

By Rob Rains

Not even the most rabid Braves' fan could have predicted the 1991 season, rising from what seemed like a perennial hold on last place to beat the Los Angeles Dodgers in a sizzling pennant race and win their first division title since 1982.

The pitching materialized: Tom Glavine won 20 games—and the Cy Young award. Steve Avery, 21, was right behind with 18 wins. And John Smoltz, after a trip to the psychologist over the All-Star break, was almost unbeatable the second half, finishing with 14 wins.

With the addition of Charlie Leibrandt's 15 wins, the Braves became the first National League team since the 1917 New York Giants to have three lefthanders win 15 or more games.

The Braves' rally caps in action.

The Dodgers—after signing free agents Darryl Strawberry and Brett Butler—were expected to be the team to beat. They had a five-game lead at the All-Star break with a 49-31 record—the best in the majors.

NL West Standings (All-Star Break)

Team	W	L	Pct	GB
Los Angeles	49	31	.613	-
Cincinnati	44	36	.550	5
Atlanta	39	40	.494	9 1/2
San Diego	40	43	.482	10 1/2
San Francisco	35	46	.432	14 1/2
Houston	34	47	.420	15 1/2

The offense wasn't bad either. Terry Pendleton won the NL batting title (.319), and racked up a career-high 22 homers and 86 RBI. Ronnie Gant became only the third player in history to repeat a 30-30 season (32 homers, 34 stolen bases). He had 105 RBI.

The Braves survived the loss of David Justice and Sid Bream for almost two months because of injuries, thanks to Otis Nixon, who was hitting .297 and leading the league with 72 stolen bases before he was suspended Sept. 16 for violating his drug treatment program.

Relief pitcher Juan Berenguer saved 17 games before a season-ending arm injury in August, but general manager John Schuerholz traded for reliever Alejandro Pena (Mets), who was almost perfect in September. Pena's two wins and 11 saves allowed the Braves to hold off the Dodgers. They clinched the pennant on the next-to-the-last day of the season.

NL West Standings July 20, 1991

Team	W	L	Pct	GB
Los Angeles	51	39	.567	-
Atlanta	46	42	.523	4
Cincinnati	45	44	.506	5 1/2
San Diego	43	49	.467	9
San Francisco	39	51	.433	12
Houston	37	53	.411	14

But troubles on the road hurt them in July and August, and the Braves climbed back into the race from a nine-game deficit. Strawberry finished with 28 homers and 99 RBI, and Butler hit .296 and scored 112 runs, but it wasn't enough to hold off Atlanta.

No other team was ever in the race. San Diego hung on to finish third, while the Giants and Reds were major disappointments, finishing in the second division.

Houston, in a rebuilding program, finished last—as expected—but was a better team than many predicted. They uncovered some future stars, including NL Rookie of the Year Jeff Bagwell, who hit .294 with 15 home runs and 82 RBI.

NL West Final Standings

Team	W	L	Pct	GB
Atlanta	94	68	.580	-
Los Angeles	93	69	.574	1
San Diego	84	78	.519	10
San Francisco	75	87	.463	19
Cincinnati	74	88	.457	20
Houston	65	97	.401	29

AL East: Jinx vs. curse

By Tim Wendel

It was the jinx versus the curse in the American League East last year. Two of the most star-crossed franchises in sports—the Toronto Blue Jays and Boston Red Sox—did their best to keep each other in contention as this race went into late September.

The Blue Jays experimented with team chemistry during the offseason, bringing in Joe Carter, Devon White and Roberto Alomar to take the place of George Bell, Tony Fernandez and Fred McGriff. The moves barely paid off as the Blue Jays' pitchers eventually carried the team to its second divisional crown in three years.

Toronto dealt outfielders Mark Whiten and Glenallen Hill to the Cleveland Indians for Tom Candiotti, while rookie Juan Guzman took over for an injured Dave Stieb. Mike Timlin, another rookie, filled in admirably in the bullpen.

AL East Standings (All-Star Break)

Team	W	L	Pct	GB
Toronto	49	34	.590	-
Boston	42	38	.525	5 1/2
Detroit	41	40	.506	7
New York	38	40	.487	8 1/2
Milwaukee	36	44	.450	11 1/2
Baltimore	33	47	.413	14 1/2
Cleveland	26	53	.329	21

Rookie Phil Plantier helped spark the Red Sox's second-half surge. Eleven games out on Aug. 8, Boston closed to within a half-game of Toronto by Sept. 21.

Joe Hesketh unexpectedly became the team's No. 2 starter behind Roger Clemens, while Jack Clark and Wade Boggs had great second halfs.

But a comment by Boston closer Jeff Reardon on national television caught the Blue Jays' interest and may have been the Red Sox's undoing. Reardon hinted that his club had the momentum while Toronto stumbled along the West Coast.

AL East Standings August 9, 1991

Team	W	L	Pct	GB
Toronto	62	48	.564	-
Detroit	56	52	.519	5
Boston	51	57	.472	10
New York	48	57	.457	11 1/2
Milwaukee	48	61	.440	13 1/2
Baltimore	43	65	.398	18
Cleveland	35	72	.327	25 1/2

"You learn to keep quiet," the Blue Jays' Carter said weeks later, after his team had wrapped up the division.

Into late August, the Detroit Tigers—not the Red Sox—were the team chasing the Blue Jays. Despite an overwhelming number of strikeouts, the Tigers hit home runs by the truckload. Tony Phillips and Travis Fryman proved to be adaptable, holding down every position except pitcher and catcher between them, while Cecil Fielder had an encore MVP-caliber season.

Their leader was manager Sparky Anderson, who adhered to the "Don't Worry, Be Happy" school of baseball philosophy. Unfortunately for Anderson and the Tigers, the season grabbed them by the tail when closer Mike Henneman missed more than a month with a sore shoulder.

The Milwaukee Brewers rallied from eight games below .500 to four games above and a near second-place finish by the end of the season. But that didn't save manager Tom Trebelhorn's job.

The Baltimore Orioles were considered a dark-horse contender when the season opened. Their season went downhill fast, though, when Glenn Davis went out of the lineup with a neck injury, leaving MVP candidate Cal Ripken to carry on, mostly on his own. John Oates took over as manager when Frank Robinson was fired.

The Cleveland Indians also ended the season with a new manager: Mike Hargrove taking over for John McNamara. Despite the change in command, the bullpen and starting staffs were in need of a transfusion by the end of the season. One-time closer Doug Jones found himself in the rotation and, surprisingly, won four games.

AL East Final Standings

Team	W	L	Pct	GB
Toronto	91	71	.562	-
Boston	84	78	.519	7
Detroit	84	78	.519	7
Milwaukee	83	79	.512	8
New York	71	91	.438	20
Baltimore	67	95	.414	24
Cleveland	57	105	.352	34

AL West: The year of the streak

By Tim Wendel

In '91, the American League West was the division of streaks. First, the Seattle Mariners won eight in a row. Then there were the Texas Rangers' 14 straight. Finally, divisional honors—and ultimately the World Series—went to the Minnesota Twins, whose 15 consecutive victories put them in first place.

In a division where every team finished the season with a .500 record or better, streaks were important—both winning and losing.

"This race will go to the most consistent team," said Rangers' manager Bobby Valentine in midseason. His team proved him right by riding a rollercoaster out of contention. After their 14-win streak, the Rangers immediately lost 11 of 12 and were never heard from again.

AL West Standings May 31, 1991

Team	W	L	Pct	GB
Texas	26	17	.605	-
Oakland	28	19	.596	-
California	26	21	.553	2
Seattle	25	23	.521	3 1/2
Minnesota	23	25	.479	5 1/2
Chicago	21	23	.477	5 1/2
Kansas City	21	25	.457	6 1/2

Strangely, neither were the defending AL champion Oakland A's—after the All-Star break. Despite injuries to their bullpen and starting rotation, Carney Lansford's career-threatening knee injury and Rickey Henderson's reluctant start to the season, the A's were tied for fourth place, only two games out at the All-Star break.

For some reason, though, the healthier the A's got, the worse they played.

"Some people have pointed to our pitching, others to our offense," said Oakland manager Tony La Russa. "The simple fact is that it's been all of that. We didn't do the job this season."

AL West Standings (All-Star Break)

Team	W	L	Pct	GB
Texas	44	33	.571	—
Minnesota	47	36	.566	—
California	44	37	.543	2
Chicago	43	37	.538	2 1/2
Oakland	44	38	.537	2 1/2
Seattle	40	42	.488	6 1/2
Kansas City	36	44	.450	9 1/2

The Kansas City Royals enjoyed the kind of second half that A's fans expected from their team. Eight games below .500 at the break, the Royals, under new manager Hal McRae, came on to finish two games above the break-even mark.

But that didn't count for much in the AL West. The Royals were nine games out at the All-Star break and 13 games behind by the end of the regular season.

Jim Lefebvre managed the Mariners to the promised land of .500 baseball. But that wasn't enough for him to hang on to his job.

The Angels were picked by many to win, or at least contend, for the division. The team's offense was so lousy, though, it couldn't win despite having starters Jim Abbott, Mark Langston and Chuck Finley, as well as the league's premier closer in '91, Bryan Harvey.

The White Sox stayed in contention until late September. Frank Thomas, Robin Ventura and this generation's "Six Million Dollar Man" Bo Jackson (we have the technology, we can rebuild him) give this franchise a bright future. Too bad former manager Jeff Torborg, who opted for the bright lights of New York, won't be around to enjoy it.

In the end, the division—and the season itself—belonged to the Twins. For the second time in four seasons, they captured the World Series while proving once again they couldn't win a game on the road in the fall classic without Walter Johnson pitching. But their formidable blend of youth and experience, speed and defense, was enough to win it all in '91.

AL West Final Standings

Team	W	L	Pct	GB
Minnesota	95	67	.586	-
Chicago	87	75	.537	8
Texas	85	77	.525	10
Oakland	84	78	.519	11
Seattle	83	79	.512	12
Kansas City	82	80	.506	13
California	81	81	.500	14

Baseball Weekly's 1991 All-Stars

Fans' choice: Top vote-getters

▶**NATIONAL LEAGUE**

CATCHER: 1. Benito Santiago, San Diego, 1,751,399; 2. Craig Biggio, Houston, 910,659; 3. Mike Scioscia, Los Angeles, 850,396.

FIRST BASE: 1. Will Clark, San Francisco, 1,534,203; 2. Fred McGriff, San Diego, 1,474,502; 3. Mark Grace, Chicago, 541,465.

SECOND BASE: 1. Ryne Sandberg, Chicago, 2,526,747; 2. Delino DeShields, Montreal, 637,022; 3. Juan Samuel, Los Angeles, 522,468.

THIRD BASE: 1. Chris Sabo, Cincinnati, 1,325,774; 2. Matt Williams, San Francisco, 782,392; 3. Tim Wallach, Montreal, 715,502.

SHORTSTOP: 1. Ozzie Smith, St. Louis, 1,280,495; 2, Tony Fernandez, San Diego, 1,083,010; 3. Barry Larkin, Cincinnati, 875,591.

OUTFIELD: 1. Darryl Strawberry, Los Angeles, 1,393,009; 2. Tony Gwynn, San Diego, 1,381,602; 3. Andre Dawson, Chicago, 1,108,585; 4. Bobby Bonilla, Pittsburgh, 1,085,233; 5. Kevin Mitchell, San Francisco, 1,001,357; 6. David Justice, Atlanta, 986,238; 7. George Bell, Chicago, 871,299; 8. Barry Bonds, Pittsburgh, 870,457; 9. Eric Davis, Cincinnati, 751,005.

▶**AMERICAN LEAGUE**

CATCHER: 1. Sandy Alomar, Cleveland, 1,367,734; 2. Carlton Fisk, Chicago, 998,340; 3. Terry Steinbach, Oakland, 648,087.

FIRST BASE: 1. Mark McGwire, Oakland, 912,052; 2. Cecil Fielder, Detroit, 861,426.

SECOND BASE: 1. Roberto Alomar, Toronto, 1,661,039; 2. Julio Franco, Texas, 709,981; 3. Steve Sax, New York, 683,563.

THIRD BASE: 1. Wade Boggs, Boston, 1,651,716 2. Kelly Gruber, Toronto, 1,023,763; 3. Edgar Martinez, Seattle, 562,914.

SHORTSTOP: 1. Cal Ripken, Baltimore, 2,060,109; 2. Ozzie Guillen, Chicago, 623,152; 3. Manuel Lee, Toronto, 610,279.

OUTFIELD: 1. Ken Griffey Jr., Seattle, 2,224,396; 2. D. Henderson, Oakland, 1,570,507; 3. R. Henderson, Oakland, 1,477,838; 4. Kirby Puckett, Minnesota, 1,159,981; 5. Jose Canseco, Oakland, 1,134,654; 6. Joe Carter, Toronto, 1,047,886; 7. Ruben Sierra, Texas, 741,159; 8. Devon White, Toronto, 630,899.

There are two basic rules when it comes to picking an All-Star team: Choose the best players and make sure every team is represented. Here were our choices at the All-Star break (no hindsight has been added):

NATIONAL LEAGUE

MIKE SCIOSCIA, C, Dodgers: Nobody at the position was having a terrific season at the time, but Scioscia was our choice over runner-up Craig Biggio (Houston Astros).

WILL CLARK, 1B, Giants: Clark came on strong after the Giants' slow start and earned the nod from us, edging out the Padres' Fred McGriff.

JUAN SAMUEL, 2B, Dodgers: There was no greater comeback in the league than Samuel's. At the All-Star break, he hadn't gone two consecutive games without a hit. Backup: Ryne Sandberg (Chicago Cubs).

OZZIE SMITH, SS, Cardinals: Smith had fewer homers than our backup choice, Barry Larkin (Cincinnati Reds), but was as good or better in every other offensive and defensive category.

TERRY PENDLETON, 3B, Braves: Pendleton was a big reason why the Braves played so well in 1991. He does it all. Backup: Todd Zeile (St. Louis Cardinals).

TONY GWYNN, OF, Padres: Why Gwynn hasn't earned the respect of the fans for four batting titles is a mystery. Maybe if he hits .400, the recognition will come.

DAVID JUSTICE, OF, Braves: He was the second-best player in the league—behind Gwynn—the first half of the season. At age 25, he could be a regular All-Star selection through the 1990s. (His bad back didn't allow him to play in 1991.)

BOBBY BONILLA, OF, Pirates: His offensive numbers were solid, and he was an especially important cog in the Pittsburgh machine when Barry Bonds was struggling early in the year. Backups: Paul O'Neill (Cincinnati), Ivan Calderon (Montreal Expos) and Willie McGee (San Francisco).

HOWARD JOHNSON, DH, Mets: Johnson was on the ballot as a shortstop and was playing third, but his best All-Star position was DH. No comments are needed about his power at the plate. Backup: George Bell (Chicago).

TOM GLAVINE, SP, Braves: This honor usually goes to the pitcher with the most rest coming into the game, but Glavine deserved the assignment. He was the league's best pitcher in the first half of the season.

ROB DIBBLE, RP, Reds: Dibble was one of the league's most controversial players last season, but he was also the top reliever in the first half. Backup: Lee Smith (St. Louis).

AMERICAN LEAGUE

TERRY STEINBACH, C, A's: He kept his sanity while helping inexperienced A's pitchers to their first major-league victories. He also showed courage coming back after being beaned by Bobby Thigpen. Backups: Carlton Fisk (Chicago White Sox) and Brian Harper (Minnesota Twins).

CECIL FIELDER, 1B, Tigers: The big man's bid to become the first AL player since Jimmie Foxx (1932-33) to lead the majors in RBI two consecutive years edged out Mark McGwire (Oakland), Frank Thomas (Chicago), and Wally Joyner (California).

JULIO FRANCO, 2B, Rangers: Our backup choice, Roberto Alomar (Toronto Blue Jays), may have better range and steal more bases, but what other second baseman bats cleanup?

CAL RIPKEN, SS, Orioles: With Glenn Davis injured, Ripken showed everybody he could do it alone. Backup: Ozzie Guillen (Chicago).

WADE BOGGS, 3B, Red Sox: Boggs was one of the few consistent players in a Boston attack that was supposed to be much better. Backup: Edgar Martinez (Seattle Mariners).

DAVE HENDERSON, OF, A's: Oakland wouldn't have survived the first half without him. He was among the leaders in average, home runs, runs and RBI. And you have to love that smile.

JOE CARTER, OF, Blue Jays: His midseason home-run heroics distanced him from such outfield competition as Mike Greenwell, Luis Polonia, Tim Raines and Rickey Henderson.

RUBEN SIERRA, OF, Rangers: He proved that last year's offensive show was no fluke. His defense improved, too. Backups: Dave Winfield (California), Kirby Puckett (Minnesota), and Jose Canseco (Oakland).

HAROLD BAINES, DH, A's: He hit nearly .400 after a subpar April. He keeps his mouth shut and his mind on the game—Baines lets his bat do his talking. Backup: Chili Davis (Minnesota).

SCOTT ERICKSON, SP, Twins: The Twins' ace was on the DL instead of the mound for the AL squad, but he deserved to start. Backups: Mark Langston and Chuck Finley (California), Roger Clemens (Boston) and Jack McDowell (Chicago).

DENNIS ECKERSLEY, RP, A's: "Eck" did the job in 1991 despite the extended absences of teammates Rick Honeycutt, Gene Nelson and Todd Burns. Backups: Jeff Reardon (Boston), Rick Aguilera (Minnesota) and Bryan Harvey (California).

All-Star game box score

AMERICAN 4
NATIONAL 2

```
National......100 100 000 —2
American......003 000 10x —4
```

NATIONAL	AB	R	H	RBI	PO	A	E
Gwynn, cf	4	1	2	0	6	0	0
Butler, pr-cf	1	0	0	0	0	0	0
Sandberg, 2b	3	0	1	0	2	1	0
Samuel, 2b	1	0	0	0	2	1	0
Clark, 1b	2	0	1	0	2	0	0
Murray, 1b	1	0	0	0	3	0	0
Bonilla, dh	4	0	2	0	0	0	0
Dawson, rf	2	1	1	1	0	0	0
Jose, rf	2	0	1	0	1	0	0
Calderon, lf	2	0	1	0	1	0	0
O'Neill, lf	2	0	0	0	0	0	0
Sabo, 3b	2	0	0	0	1	0	0
Johnson, 3b	2	0	0	0	0	0	0
Santiago, c	3	0	0	0	4	0	0
Biggio, c	1	0	0	0	2	0	1
O. Smith, ss	1	0	0	0	0	1	0
Larkin, ss	1	0	0	0	0	2	0
Bell, ph	1	0	0	0	0	0	0
Glavine, p	-	-	-	-	0	0	0
D. Mrtinz, p	-	-	-	-	0	0	0
Viola, p	-	-	-	-	0	0	0
Harnisch, p	-	-	-	-	0	0	0
Smiley, p	-	-	-	-	0	0	0
Dibble, p	-	-	-	-	0	1	0
Morgan, p	-	-	-	-	0	1	0
Totals	**35**	**2**	**10**	**2**	**24**	**7**	**1**

AMERICAN	AB	R	H	RBI	PO	A	E
R. Hendrsn, lf	2	1	1	0	0	0	0
Carter, lf	1	1	1	0	1	0	0
Boggs, 3b	2	1	1	0	1	2	0
Molitor, 3b	0	0	0	0	0	0	0
Ripken, ss	3	1	2	3	1	1	0
Guillen, ss	0	0	0	0	1	0	0
Fielder, 1b	3	0	0	0	6	2	0
Pimeiro, 1b	0	0	0	0	2	0	0
Tartabull, dh	2	0	0	0	0	0	0
Baines, dh	1	0	0	1	0	0	0
D. Hendrsn, rf	2	0	0	0	2	0	0
Sierra, rf	2	0	0	0	2	0	0
Griffey Jr. cf	3	0	2	0	2	0	0
Puckett, cf	1	0	0	0	2	0	0
S. Alomar, c	2	0	0	0	2	0	0
Fisk, c	2	0	1	0	5	0	0
R. Alomar, c	2	0	0	0	2	0	0
Morris, p	-	-	-	-	0	1	0
Key, p	-	-	-	-	1	0	0
Clemens, p	-	-	-	-	0	0	0
McDowell, p	-	-	-	-	0	0	0
Reardon, p	-	-	-	-	0	0	0
Aguilera, p	-	-	-	-	0	0	0
Eckrsly, p	-	-	-	-	0	1	
Totals	**30**	**4**	**8**	**4**	**27**	**12**	**0**

(continued on next page)

All-Star report card

All-Star game box score (continued)

NL Pitching	IP	H	R	ER	BB	K
Glavine	2	1	0	0	1	3
D. Martinez,L	2	4	3	3	0	0
Viola	1	0	0	0	1	0
Harnisch	1	2	0	0	0	1
Smiley	0	1	1	1	0	0
Dibble	1	0	0	0	1	1
Morgan	1	0	0	0	0	1
Totals	8	8	4	4	3	6

AL Pitching	IP	H	R	ER	BB	K
Morris	2	4	1	1	0	1
Key, W	1	1	0	0	0	1
Clemens	1	1	1	1	0	0
McDowell	2	1	0	0	2	0
Reardon	.2	1	0	0	0	0
Aguilera	1.1	2	0	0	0	3
Eckersley, Save	1	0	0	0	0	1
Totals	9	10	2	2	2	5

NL BATTING - 2B: Sandberg (1, off Key). HR: Dawson (1, 4th inning off Clemens, 0 on, 0 out). RBI, scoring position, less than 2 outs: Clark 0-1, Bonilla 1-1, Dawson 0-1, Jose 0-1, O'Neill 0-1, Santiago 0-1. BB: O. Smith, Clark. Struck out: Santiago, Bonilla, Murray, O'Neill, Johnson, Bell. GDP: Dawson, Gwynn.
AL BATTING - HR: Ripken (1, 3rd inning off D. Martinez, 2 on, 1 out). S. Guillen. SF: Baines. RBI, scoring position, less than 2 outs: Ripken 2-2, Fielder 0-1, Baines 1-2. BB: Boggs, Carter. IBB: Palmeiro off Dibble. Struck out: Fielder, Tartabull, D. Henderson, Sierra 2, Fisk.
NL BASERUNNING - SB: Calderon (1, 3rd base off Morris/Alomar Jr). TEAM LOB: 8.
AL BASERUNNING - TEAM LOB: 8.
NL FIELDING - E: Biggio (1, interference).
AL FIELDING - DP: 2.
IBB: Palmeiro by Dibble.
GAME DATA - T: 3:04. A: 52,383. Temp: 75. Wind: 9 mph, in from left.
UMPIRES - HP: Joe Brinkman (AL), 1B: John McSherry (NL), 2B: Ken Kaiser (AL), 3B: Jim Quick (NL), LF: Larry Young (AL), RF: Greg Bonin (NL).

Rod Beaton grades the 1991 teams

▶**Pitching**

NATIONAL LEAGUE: **C**. Montreal's Dennis Martinez delivered a room-service, hanging curve to Ripken. He served quite a few line drives.

AMERICAN LEAGUE: **B**. Starter Jack Morris had shaky start, giving up first-inning run. Everyone was most effective with men on. One-run lead was held for five innings.

▶**Hitting**

NATIONAL LEAGUE: **C-**. Ryne Sandberg's third-inning double was the National League's first extra-base hit since 1987. But too many runners were stranded.

AMERICAN LEAGUE: **B-**. Cal Ripken buried his homer, just like he did in the home-run derby. Harold Baines had critical SF in 7th. Not much more.

▶**Fielding**

NATIONAL LEAGUE: **C**. Clark, Sandberg, Tony Gwynn made strong plays. Clark mishandled throw before Ripken's HR, 2B Samuel made bad turn on DP try.

AMERICAN LEAGUE: **A+**. They turned two excellent double plays. Credit 3B Wade Boggs and 2B Robby Alomar. 1B Cecil Fielder threw out Will Clark at the plate.

▶**Managers**

NATIONAL LEAGUE: **C**. Lou Piniella pinch hit twice for favorable matchups in a futile sixth-inning threat. He used an intentional walk (to Palmeiro), an All-Star rarity.

AMERICAN LEAGUE: **A**. All of LaRussa's moves worked. He had his closers lined up to nurse lead over last three innings, including saving his own Dennis Eckersley for end.

SkyFacts

Since opening June 5, 1989, Toronto's SkyDome has been one of the most visited venues in sports history. Last year, the Blue Jays broke their own major league attendance record with over 4 million fans.

▶**First game:** June 5, 1989 (Milwaukee 5, Toronto 3).

▶**1991 total attendance:** 4,001,526

▶**Average attendance:** 49,402

▶**1991 sellouts:** 66 out of 81 home dates; only one home game after May 15 was not a sellout.

▶**1991 sellout percentage:** 98% of all seats were sold for the season; only 74,000 seats were unsold over 81 dates.

▶**Roof:** The retractable roof can open or close in 20 minutes. When closed, it covers eight acres and rises to an inside height equivalent to a 31-story building—almost twice as high as the Metrodome in Minneapolis.

▶**Scoreboard:** The world's largest video display board was built by Sony and uses 420,000 light bulbs.

▶**Entertainment:** A Hard Rock Cafe built into the third deck in right field; a 35,000-square-foot Fitness Club; and Sightlines, a 420-seat open-air bar. Seventy rooms at the SkyDome Hotel provide views of the field at $150-$750 a night.

Obituaries

NL champions honor lost friends

Both teams in the National League Championship Series carried reminders of members of their organizations who passed away during the 1991 season.

▶**Braves' JWM:** The Atlanta Braves wore "JWM" on their left uniform sleeves to honor vice president John W. Mullen, who passed away during spring training. Mullen served as special assistant to general manager John Schuerholz. He was with the Braves franchise for 32 years, and was the only member left in the organization who has been with the club in Boston, Milwaukee and Atlanta.

▶**Pirates' H:** The Pittsburgh Pirates wore a gold "H" in a black circle in memory of long-time equipment manager John Hallahan, who died Sept. 11. Hallahan, 64, was in the middle of his 50th season with the club. The Pirates had planned to name the home clubhouse after him following the season, which they did.

Negro Leagues' quick 'Cool Papa' Bell dies

James "Cool Papa" Bell, a Hall of Famer once considered the fastest player in the Negro Leagues, died March 7 in St. Louis University Hospital after a brief illness. He was 89. Bell played 29 summer seasons and 21 winter seasons, batting .407 in 1946, his final season. Inducted into the Baseball Hall of Fame in 1974, his plaque reads: "Combined speed, daring and batting skill to rank among best players in Negro Leagues." Contemporaries rated him fastest man on base paths.

Burgess, NL All-Star, is dead

Forrest Harrill "Smoky" Burgess, one of baseball's greatest hitters in a pinch, died Sept. 15. He was 64.

Burgess died at Rutherford Hospital in Asheville, N.C. The cause of death was undisclosed. Burgess was a five-time member of the NL All-Star team and hit .333 in the 1960 World Series for the champion Pirates. He ended his career with a .295 batting average and 126 lifetime home runs.

Negro league star Renfroe dies

Othello "Chico" Renfroe, a former Negro league shortstop and sports broadcaster, died of a heart attack Sept. 3. He was 68.

Renfroe, who teamed with Jackie Robinson and Satchel Paige on the Kansas City Monarchs, was a sports broadcaster for WIGO in Atlanta and sports editor of *The Atlanta Daily World.*

Bespectacled umpire dies at 73

Frank Umont, the American League umpire who became famous for wearing eyeglasses, died Thursday. He was 73.

Umont worked in the AL from 1954 until retiring after the 1973 season (four World Series, four All-Star games, and an AL Championship Series). In 1969, Umont ejected Baltimore manager Earl Weaver for smoking a cigarette in the dugout before the game. The next day, Weaver brought the Orioles' lineup card to home plate with a candy cigarette between his lips. Before becoming an umpire, Umont was a 220-pound tackle for the NFL's New York Giants.

William Shea dies in New York

William Shea, the man most responsible for bringing National League baseball back to New York, died Oct. 3 in his apartment in Manhattan. He was 84.

Obituaries (continued)

After the Brooklyn Dodgers and New York Giants left for California following the 1957 season, Shea tried to persuade existing franchises (Pittsburgh, Cincinnati, Philadelphia) to move. Then he tried to pressure the NL into expansion. When both efforts were unsuccessful, Shea teamed with Branch Rickey to bring baseball back to New York via the Continental League, a proposed third major league.

The planned league was to begin play in 1961 in eight cities, including New York, Houston and Minneapolis. To head off a possible risk to the exemption from federal antitrust laws that baseball enjoyed, Major League Baseball agreed to expand—the Mets and the Astros were born.

Leo Durocher gave Willie Mays his break.

Leo 'The Lip' dies at 86

Leo Durocher, who died Oct. 7 in Palm Springs, Calif. at age 86, had just one passion. That was victory. It didn't matter if he was with the Dodgers, the Giants or a Little League team in his native West Springfield, Mass.

He was loud, profane, colorful and combative. But above all else, he wanted to win.

"Nice guys finish last," he said, in reference to the beloved Mel Ott, his predecessor as manager of the Giants.

He also supposedly said he would trip his grandmother rounding third base if it meant a victory.

Durocher is credited with helping young Willie Mays break into the majors in 1951. After coming up from Minneapolis, Mays got off to an 0-for-12 start. He sat at his locker crying and asked Durocher to ship him back to the minors. Durocher put his arm around Mays and assured him he would be the Giants' center fielder the rest of the season. In his next game, Mays homered against Warren Spahn and was on his way to Cooperstown.

Seventeen of his former players went on to manage in the majors. The list includes Al Dark, Gene Mauch, Bill Rigney, Gil Hodges and Doug Rader.

As manager of the Dodgers, Durocher had constant run-ins with president and general manager Branch Rickey. They argued about everything from salaries to personnel. Finally, on July 16, 1948, he left Brooklyn and was hired by the archrival Giants.

Commissioner A.B. "Happy" Chandler suspended Durocher in 1947 for "conduct detrimental to baseball." It was assumed Durocher was sent to the sideline for his alleged association with gamblers, but that was never proven.

The suspension is the primary reason Durocher is not in the Hall of Fame. He is one of just six managers with 2,000 or more victories; the other five have been inducted.

Although Durocher had later stints with the Chicago Cubs (close call in 1969!) and Houston Astros, he always will be known for his accomplishments in New York.

He was a Dodger. A Giant. And a giant.

—Bill Koenig

NATIONAL LEAGUE LEADERS
(Final 1991 Stats)

Batting

BATTING AVERAGE

	G	AB	R	H	AVG
Pendleton, Atl	153	586	94	187	.319
Morris, Cin	136	478	72	152	.318
Gwynn, SD	134	530	69	168	.317
McGee, SF	131	497	67	155	.312
Jose, StL	154	568	69	173	.305
Larkin, Cin	123	464	88	140	.302
Bonilla, Pitt	157	577	102	174	.302
Clark, SF	148	565	84	170	.301
Sabo, Cin	153	582	91	175	.301
Calderon, Mtl	134	470	69	141	.300

HOME RUNS

Johnson, NY	38
Williams, SF	34
Gant, Atl	32
Dawson, Chi	31
McGriff, SD	31
Clark, SF	29
O'Neill, Cin	28
Strawberry, LA	28
Mitchell, SF	27
2 tied	26

RUNS SCORED

Butler, LA	112
Johnson, NY	108
Sandberg, Chi	104
Bonilla, Pitt	102
Gant, Atl	101
Bell, Pitt	96
O. Smith, StL	96
Bonds, Pitt	95
Pendleton, Atl	94
Sabo, Cin	91

RUNS BATTED IN

Johnson, NY	117
Bonds, Pitt	116
Clark, SF	116
McGriff, SD	106
Gant, Atl	105
Dawson, Chi	104
Bonilla, Pitt	100
Sandberg, Chi	100
Strawberry, LA	99
Williams, SF	98

HITS

Pendleton, Atl	187
Butler, LA	182
Sabo, Cin	175
Bonilla, Pitt	174
Jose, StL	173
Clark, SF	170
Finley, Hou	170
Sandberg, Chi	170
Grace, Chi	169
Gwynn, SD	168

STOLEN BASES

Grissom, Mtl	76
Nixon, Atl	72
DeShields, Mtl	56
Lankford, StL	44
Bonds, Pitt	43
Butler, LA	38
Coleman, NY	37
O. Smith, StL	35
Finley, Hou	34
Gant, Atl	34

BASES ON BALLS

Butler, LA	108
Bonds, Pitt	107
McGriff, SD	105
DeShields, Mtl	95
Bonilla, Pitt	90
Sandberg, Chi	87
Magadan, NY	83
O. Smith, StL	83
Johnson, NY	78
2 tied	75

SLUGGING PERCENTAGE

Clark, SF	.536
Johnson, NY	.535
Pendleton, Atl	.517
Bonds, Pitt	.514
Larkin, Cin	.506
Sabo, Cin	.505
Williams, SF	.499
Gant, Atl	.496
McGriff, SD	.494
Bonilla, Pitt	.492

DOUBLES

Bonilla, Pitt	44
Jose, StL	40
O'Neill, Cin	36
Zeile, StL	36
Gant, Atl	35
Sabo, Cin	35
Johnson, NY	34
Pendleton, Atl	34
Morris, Cin	33
Murphy, Phil	33

TRIPLES

Lankford, StL	15
Gwynn, SD	11
Finley, Hou	10
Gonzalez, Hou	9
Grissom, Mtl	9
Bell, Pitt	8
Owen, Mtl	8
Pendleton, Atl	8
4 tied	7

ON-BASE PERCENTAGE

Bonds, Pitt	.410
Butler, LA	.401
McGriff, SD	.396
Bonilla, Pitt	.391
Bagwell, Hou	.387
O. Smith, StL	.380
Sandberg, Chi	.379
Magadan, NY	.378
Larkin, Cin	.378
Morris, Cin	.374

TOTAL BASES

Clark, SF	303
Pendleton, Atl	303
Johnson, NY	302
Sabo, Cin	294
Williams, SF	294
Bonilla, Pitt	284
Sandberg, Chi	284
Gant, Atl	278
Dawson, Chi	275
Bonds, Pitt	262

Pitching

EARNED RUN AVERAGE

De. Martinez, Mtl	2.39
Rijo, Cin	2.51
Glavine, Atl	2.55
Belcher, LA	2.62
Harnisch, Hou	2.70
DeLeon, StL	2.71
Morgan, LA	2.78
Tomlin, Pitt	2.98
Benes, SD	3.03
Drabek, Pitt	3.07

WON-LOST

Smiley, Pitt	20	8
Glavine, Atl	20	11
Avery, Atl	18	8
Martinez, LA	17	13
Smith, Pitt	16	10
Mulholland, Phil	16	13
6 tied	15	

GAMES PITCHED

Jones, Mtl	77
Assenmacher, Chi	75
Stanton, Atl	74
Agosto, StL	72
Burke, Mtl -NY	72
McDowell, Phil-LA	71
McElroy, Chi	71
Osuna, Hou	71
Innis, NY	69
Williams, Phil	69

SAVES

L. Smith, StL	47
Dibble, Cin	31
Franco, NY	30
Williams, Phil	30
Righetti, SF	24
Lefferts, SD	23
Berenguer, Atl	17
Landrum, Pitt	17
Da. Smith, Chi	17
2 tied	16

INNINGS PITCHED

Maddux, Chi	263.0
Glavine, Atl	246.2
Morgan, LA	236.1
Drabek, Pitt	234.2
Cone, NY	232.2
Mulholland, Phil	232.0
Viola, NY	231.1
Browning, Cin	230.1
Leibrandt, Atl	229.2
Smoltz, Atl	229.2

STRIKEOUTS

Cone, NY	241
Maddux, Chi	198
Glavine, Atl	192
Harnisch, Hou	172
Rijo, Cin	172
Benes, SD	167
Belcher, LA	156
Greene, Phil	154
Gooden, NY	150
Martinez, LA	150

COMPLETE GAMES

Glavine, Atl	9
De. Martinez, Mtl	9
Mulholland, Phil	8
Maddux, Chi	7
Martinez, LA	6
Smith, Pitt	6
Cone, NY	5
Drabek, Pitt	5
Morgan, LA	5
Smoltz, Atl	5

SHUTOUTS

De. Martinez, Mtl	5
Martinez, LA	4
Black, SF	3
Mulholland, Phil	3
Smith, Pitt	3
7 tied	2

AMERICAN LEAGUE LEADERS
(Final 1991 Stats)

Batting

BATTING AVERAGE

	G	AB	R	H	AVG
Franco, Tex	146	589	108	201	.341
Boggs, Bos	144	546	93	181	.332
Randolph, Mil	124	431	60	141	.327
Griffey Jr., Sea	154	548	76	179	.327
Molitor, Mil	158	665	133	216	.325
C. Ripken, Balt	162	650	99	210	.323
Palmeiro, Tex	159	631	115	203	.322
Puckett, Minn	152	611	92	195	.319
Thomas, Chi	158	559	104	178	.318
Tartabull, KC	132	484	78	153	.316

HOME RUNS

Canseco, Oak	44
Fielder, Det	44
C. Ripken, Balt	34
Carter, Tor	33
Thomas, Chi	32
Tartabull, KC	31
Tettleton, Det	31
Davis, Minn	29
3 tied	28

RUNS BATTED IN

Fielder, Det	133
Canseco, Oak	122
Sierra, Tex	116
C. Ripken, Balt	114
Thomas, Chi	109
Carter, Tor	108
Gonzalez, Tex	102
Griffey Jr., Sea	100
Tartabull, KC	100
Ventura, Chi	100

STOLEN BASES

R. Henderson, Oak	58
Alomar, Tor	53
Raines, Chi	51
Polonia, Cal	48
Cuyler, Det	41
Franco, Tex	36
White, Tor	33
R. Kelly, NY	32
Sax, NY	31
Pettis, Tex	29

SLUGGING PERCENTAGE

Tartabull, KC	.593
C. Ripken, Balt	.566
Canseco, Oak	.556
Thomas, Chi	.553
Palmeiro, Tex	.532
Griffey Jr., Sea	.527
Fielder, Det	.513
Davis, Minn	.507
Carter, Tor	.503
Sierra, Tex	.502

TRIPLES

Johnson, Chi	13
Molitor, Mil	13
Alomar, Tor	11
Devereaux, Balt	10
White, Tor	10
Gladden, Minn	9
McRae, KC	9
Mack, Minn	8
Polonia, Cal	8

RUNS SCORED

Molitor, Mil	133
Canseco, Oak	115
Palmeiro, Tex	115
Sierra, Tex	110
White, Tor	110
Franco, Tex	108
R. Henderson, Oak	105
Thomas, Chi	104
Fielder, Det	102
Raines, Chi	102

HITS

Molitor, Mil	216
C. Ripken, Balt	210
Palmeiro, Tex	203
Sierra, Tex	203
Franco, Tex	201
Sax, NY	198
Puckett, Minn	195
Alomar, Tor	188
Boggs, Bos	181
White, Tor	181

BASES ON BALLS

Thomas, Chi	138
Tettleton, Det	101
R. Henderson, Oak	98
Clark, Bos	96
Davis, Minn	95
McGwire, Oak	93
Whitaker, Det	90
Boggs, Bos	89
Deer, Det	89
2 tied	84

DOUBLES

Palmeiro, Tex	49
C. Ripken, Balt	46
Sierra, Tex	44
Boggs, Bos	42
Carter, Tor	42
Griffey Jr., Sea	42
Reed, Bos	42
Alomar, Tor	41
Brett, KC	40
White, Tor	40

TOTAL BASES

C. Ripken, Balt	368
Palmeiro, Tex	336
Sierra, Tex	332
Molitor, Mil	325
Carter, Tor	321
Fielder, Det	320
Canseco, Oak	318
Thomas, Chi	309
White, Tor	292
Griffey Jr., Sea	289

ON-BASE PERCENTAGE

Thomas, Chi	.453
Randolph, Mil	.424
Boggs, Bos	.421
Franco, Tex	.408
E. Martinez, Sea	.405
R. Henderson, Oak	.400
Molitor, Mil	.399
Griffey Jr., Sea	.399
Tartabull, KC	.397
Whitaker, Det	.391

Pitching

EARNED RUN AVERAGE

Clemens, Bos	2.62
Candiotti, Clev-Tor	2.65
Wegman, Mil	2.84
J. Abbott, Cal	2.89
Ryan, Tex	2.91
Moore, Oak	2.96
Tapani, Minn	2.99
Langston, Cal	3.00
Key, Tor	3.05
Saberhagen, KC	3.07

WON-LOST

Erickson, Minn	20	8
Gullickson, Det	20	9
Langston, Cal	19	8
Finley, Cal	18	9
Clemens, Bos	18	10
J. Abbott, Cal	18	11
Morris, Minn	18	12
Moore, Oak	17	8
McDowell, Chi	17	10
3 tied	16	

GAMES PITCHED

D. Ward, Tor	81
Jackson, Sea	72
Olson, Balt	72
Swift, Sea	71
Eichhorn, Cal	70
Jeffcoat, Tex	70
Cadaret, NY	68
Gibson, Det	68
Je. Russell, Tex	68
5 tied	67

SAVES

Harvey, Cal	46
Eckersley, Oak	43
Aguilera, Minn	42
Reardon, Bos	40
Montgomery, KC	33
Henke, Tor	32
Olson, Balt	31
Je. Russell, Tex	30
Thigpen, Chi	30
2 tied	23

INNINGS PITCHED

Clemens, Bos	271.1
McDowell, Chi	253.2
Morris, Minn	246.2
Langston, Cal	246.1
Tapani, Minn	244.0
J. Abbott, Cal	243.0
Candiotti, Clev-Tor	238.0
Swindell, Clev	238.0
Navarro, Mil	234.0
Finley, Cal	227.1

STRIKEOUTS

Clemens, Bos	241
Johnson, Sea	228
Ryan, Tex	203
McDowell, Chi	191
Langston, Cal	183
Finley, Cal	171
Swindell, Clev	169
Candiotti, Clev-Tor	167
Gordon, KC	167
Morris, Minn	163

COMPLETE GAMES

McDowell, Chi	15
Clemens, Bos	13
Morris, Minn	10
Navarro, Mil	10
Terrell, Det	8
Langston, Cal	7
Saberhagen, KC	7
Swindell, Clev	7
Wegman, Mil	7
Welch, Oak	7

SHUTOUTS

Clemens, Bos	4
Appier, KC	3
Erickson, Minn	3
Holman, Sea	3
McDowell, Chi	3
10 tied	2

Postseason

USA SNAPSHOTS®

A look at statistics that shape the sports world

Double-digit victories

Nolan Ryan is the second pitcher to have at least 10 victories in each of 20 seasons. Number of seasons top pitchers have reached double figures in games won:

Seasons

Don Sutton	21
Cy Young	19
Phil Niekro	19
Walter Johnson	18
Steve Carlton	18

Source: American League of Professional Baseball Clubs

By Marty Baumann, USA TODAY

ALCS Playoffs

MINNESOTA 5, TORONTO 4

Great play: Roberto Alomar made the defensive play of the game when he fielded Kent Hrbek's sharply hit grounder in the seventh, tagged Kirby Puckett, who was trying to advance to second, and then threw on to first to get Hrbek.

The Flydome: Trying to flag down flyballs in the Metrodome proved to be difficult for both teams. Blue Jays' right fielder Joe Carter misjudged Shane Mack's third-inning line drive into an RBI double; the Twins' Dan Gladden barely held on to Candy Maldonado's drive in the sixth; rookie Chuck Knoblauch helped set up Toronto's three-run sixth by losing Roberto Alomar's towering popup against the background of the roof: "A simple popup can be an adventure here," Knoblauch said.

Ump record: Larry Barnett, who was behind the plate for Game One, was umpiring in his sixth LCS, the most ever in the AL.

Good news, bad news: The Jays' Kelly Gruber had a good day offensively, going 2-for-4 with two RBI and a stolen base. But he made two of Toronto's three errors.

TORONTO 5, MINNESOTA 2

No freebies for Jays: When Blue Jays' designated hitter Rance Mulliniks walked to open the fourth inning, it was the first postseason free pass for Toronto since Game 4 of the 1989 ALCS—a span of 22 innings.

Rookie report: Twins' rookie Chuck Knoblauch went 2-for-3 and scored 2 runs in Game 2.

Homerless hankies: Neither team homered in the first two games of the series, hankies or no hankies.

Bullpen goose eggs: The Blue Jays' bullpen pitched 8 scoreless innings in the first two games.

It had to end sometime: The Game 2 loss to Toronto was the Twins' first postseason loss ever in the Metrodome. After losing to Baltimore in Game 2 of the 1970 ALCS at Metropolitan Stadium, they had won seven straight postseason contests at home. That streak fell one shy of the postseason record, set by the New York Yankees over four World Series from 1927-36.

Gladden stopped his own streak: The Twins' Dan Gladden went 0-for-3 to end his postseason game hit streak at nine games.

MINNESOTA 3, TORONTO 2

Pitching notes: Mike Pagliarulo's home run off Mike Timlin was the first the Blue Jays' rookie allowed since Aug. 17 at Detroit. Joe Carter's first-inning home run was the ALCS's first long ball since Boston's Wade Boggs took Oakland's Dave Stewart deep in the fourth inning of Game 1 in 1990. That five-game homerless streak was the longest in postseason play in 43 years. Rick Aguilera pitched one scoreless inning to pick up his second save in as many opportunities in this ALCS.

Maldonado broke his slump: Candy Maldonado snapped an 0-for-15 slump in league championship play with a first-inning double that drove in Toronto's second run of the game. His last LCS hit, a single, had come four years before—Oct. 11, 1987 (NLCS Game Five, for San Francisco).

Gruber went on hitting: Kelly Gruber singled in the first inning to extend his postseason hitting streak to five games.

Hrbek went south: Kent Hrbek, usually the Twins' cleanup hitter, was dropped to sixth in the club's batting order. He went 0-for-3 in Game Three, falling to 0-for-11 in the series.

Wild West: The two wild pitches thrown by the Twins' David West in the fifth inning tied an LCS mark for most in an inning. It has happened three times, most recently by the Astros' Jeff Calhoun in the '86 NLCS.

MINNESOTA 9, TORONTO 3

Pag's twin talents—glove and bat: Mike Pagliarulo's pinch-hit home run won Game Three; his diving grab of Roberto Alomar's line drive in the fifth inning was

(continued on page 44)

ALCS COMPOSITE BOX (Through 5 games)

TORONTO BLUE JAYS BATTING

	G	AB	R	H	2B	3B	HR	RBI	SO	BB	Avg.	PO	A	E	Pct.
Alomar 2b	5	19	3	9	0	0	0	4	3	2	.474	14	8	0	1.000
White cf	5	22	5	8	1	0	0	0	3	2	.364	17	0	0	1.000
Borders c	5	19	0	5	1	0	0	2	0	0	.263	38	5	2	.956
Carter rf-dh	5	19	3	5	2	0	1	4	5	1	.263	4	1	0	1.000
Wilson pr-dh-lf	3	8	1	2	0	0	0	0	3	1	.250	3	0	0	1.000
Gruber 3b	5	21	1	5	0	0	0	4	4	0	.238	3	7	3	.769
Olerud 1b	5	19	1	4	1	0	0	3	1	3	.211	39	3	0	1.000
Lee ss	5	16	3	2	0	0	0	0	5	1	.125	8	16	1	.960
Mulliniks dh-ph	5	8	1	1	0	0	0	0	0	3	.125	0	0	0	.—
Maldonado lf-rf	5	20	1	2	1	0	0	1	6	1	.100	5	0	0	1.000
Ducey pr-rf	1	1	0	0	0	0	0	0	0	0	.000	0	0	0	.—
Tabler ph	1	1	0	0	0	0	0	0	0	1	.000	0	0	0	.—
Gonzals pr-1b-ss	2	0	0	0	0	0	0	0	0	0	.—	2	0	0	1.000
Acker p	0	0	0	0	0	0	0	0	0	0	.—	0	0	0	.—
Candiotti p	2	0	0	0	0	0	0	0	0	0	.—	0	2	0	1.000
Guzman p	1	0	0	0	0	0	0	0	0	0	.—	0	0	0	.—
Henke p	1	0	0	0	0	0	0	0	0	0	.—	0	2	0	1.000
Key p	1	0	0	0	0	0	0	0	0	0	.—	0	3	0	1.000
MacDonald p	0	0	0	0	0	0	0	0	0	0	.—	0	0	0	.—
Stottlemyre p	1	0	0	0	0	0	0	0	0	0	.—	1	0	0	1.000
Timlin p	4	0	0	0	0	0	0	0	0	0	.—	0	2	1	.667
Ward p	2	0	0	0	0	0	0	0	0	0	.—	0	0	0	.—
Wells p	4	0	0	0	0	0	0	0	0	0	.—	1	1	0	1.000
Totals	5	173	19	43	6	0	1	18	30	15	.249	135	50	7	.964

MINNESOTA TWINS BATTING

	G	AB	R	H	2B	3B	HR	RBI	SO	BB	Avg.	PO	A	E	Pct.
Puckett cf	5	21	4	9	1	0	2	6	4	1	.429	13	1	0	1.000
Knoblauch 2b	5	20	5	7	2	0	0	3	3	3	.350	8	14	0	1.000
Mack rf	5	18	4	6	1	1	0	3	4	2	.333	3	0	1	.750
Pagliarulo 3b-ph	5	15	3	5	1	0	1	3	2	0	.333	5	10	0	1.000
Davis dh	5	17	3	5	2	0	0	2	8	5	.294	0	0	0	.—
Harper c	5	18	1	5	2	0	0	1	2	0	.278	25	1	1	.963
Gladden lf	5	23	4	6	0	0	0	3	3	1	.261	20	0	0	1.000
Gagne ss	5	17	2	4	0	0	0	1	5	1	.235	9	9	2	.900
Hrbek 1b	5	21	0	3	0	0	0	3	3	1	.143	41	8	0	1.000
Sorrento ph	1	1	0	0	0	0	0	0	0	0	.000	0	0	0	.—
Larkin ph	3	3	0	0	0	0	0	0	1	0	.000	0	0	0	.—
Ortiz c	3	3	0	0	0	0	0	0	0	0	.000	7	0	0	1.000
Leius ph-3b	3	4	0	0	0	0	0	0	1	1	.000	0	4	0	1.000
Newman 3b-ss	2	0	0	0	0	0	0	0	0	0	.—	0	0	0	.—
Brown pr	1	0	1	0	0	0	0	0	0	0	.—	0	0	0	.—
Aguilera p	3	0	0	0	0	0	0	0	0	0	.—	0	0	0	.—
Bedrosian p	2	0	0	0	0	0	0	0	0	0	.—	0	0	0	.—
Erickson p	1	0	0	0	0	0	0	0	0	0	.—	1	1	0	1.000
Guthrie p	2	0	0	0	0	0	0	0	0	0	.—	0	1	0	1.000
Morris p	2	0	0	0	0	0	0	0	0	0	.—	3	2	0	1.000
Tapani p	2	0	0	0	0	0	0	0	0	0	.—	3	0	0	1.000
West p	2	0	0	0	0	0	0	0	0	1	.—	0	0	0	.—
Willis p	3	0	0	0	0	0	0	0	0	0	.—	0	0	0	.—
Totals	5	181	27	50	9	1	3	25	37	15	.276	138	51	4	.979

TORONTO BLUE JAYS PITCHING

	G	CG	IP	H	R	BB	SO	HB	WP	W	L	Sv	Pct.	ER	ERA
Acker	1	0	.2	1	0	0	0	0	0	0	0	0	.—	0	0.00
Henke	2	0	2.2	0	0	1	5	0	0	0	0	0	.—	0	0.00
Wells	4	0	7.2	6	2	2	9	0	0	0	0	0	.—	2	2.35
Key	1	0	6	5	2	1	6	0	0	0	0	0	.—	2	3.00
Guzman	1	0	5.2	4	2	4	2	0	0	1	1	0	1.000	2	3.18
Timlin	4	0	5.2	5	4	2	5	0	0	0	1	0	.000	2	3.18
Ward	2	0	4.1	4	3	1	6	0	0	0	1	1	.000	3	6.23
Candiotti	2	0	7.2	17	9	2	5	0	0	1	1	0	.000	7	8.22
MacDonald	1	0	1	1	1	1	0	0	0	0	0	0	.—	1	9.00
Stottlemyre	1	0	3.2	7	4	1	3	1	0	0	1	0	.000	4	9.81
Totals	5	0	45	50	27	15	37	1	0	2	1	4	1	.200	23	4.60

MINNESOTA TWINS PITCHING

	G	CG	IP	H	R	BB	SO	HB	WP	W	L	Sv	Pct.	ER	ERA
West	2	0	5.2	1	0	4	4	0	0	2	1	0	1.000	0	0.00
Willis	3	0	5.1	2	0	0	3	0	0	0	0	0	.—	0	0.00
Aguilera	3	0	3.1	1	0	0	3	0	0	0	0	3	.—	0	0.00
Guthrie	2	0	2.2	0	0	0	0	0	0	0	1	0	1.000	0	0.00
Bedrosian	2	0	1.1	3	2	2	2	0	0	0	0	0	.—	0	0.00
Morris	2	0	13.1	17	6	1	7	0	0	1	2	0	1.000	6	4.05
Erickson	1	0	4	3	2	5	2	0	0	0	0	0	.—	2	4.50
Tapani	2	0	10.1	16	9	3	9	0	0	0	1	0	.000	9	7.84
Totals	5	0	46	43	19	15	30	0	0	3	4	1	3	.800	17	3.33

Miscellaneous

SCORE BY INNINGS

Toronto	315	304	201	0—19
Minnesota	332	417	141	1—27

DP: Toronto 5, Minnesota 3. **LOB:** Toronto 35, Minnesota 38. **SB:** Knoblauch 2, Gruber, Davis, Mack 2, White 3, Gladden 3, Alomar 2, Wilson. **CS:** Knoblauch, Mack, Carter, Gagne 2. **S:** Alomar 2, Borders, Pagliarulo. **SF:** Carter, Puckett, Mack. Erickson pitched to 2 batters in the 5th (Game 3); Candiotti pitched to 2 batters in the 6th (Game 5). **HBP:** by Stottlemyre (Gagne). **PB:** Borders 2. Umpires: Barnett; Johnson; Roe; Welke; Reilly; McKean. **Official scorers:** Games 1-5: Joe Sawchuk (Ontario Hydro); Games 1,2,4 and 5: Tom Mee (Minnesota Twins). **Time:** Game 1 at Minnesota, 3:17. Game 2 at Minnesota, 3:02. Game 3 at Toronto, 3:36. Game 4 at Toronto, 3:15. Game 5 at Toronto, 3:29. **Attendance:** Game 1 at Minnesota, 54,766. Game 2 at Minnesota, 54,816. Game 3 at Toronto, 51,454. Game 4 at Toronto, 51,526. Game 5 at Toronto, 51,425.

ALCS Scores

Minnesota Twins win playoffs 4-1
Oct. 8: Minnesota 5, Toronto 4
Oct. 9: Toronto 5, Minnesota 2
Oct. 11: Minn. 3, Toronto 2 (10 inn.)
Oct. 12: Minnesota 9, Toronto 3
Oct. 13: Minnesota 8, Toronto 5

ALCS: Where they played

Hubert H. Humphrey Metrodome (Minnesota Twins)

Capacity: 55,883
Surface: Artificial turf
Left-field line: 343 feet
Center field: 400 feet
Right-field line: 327 feet
Power alleys: 385 feet
Walls: LF 13 feet; CF 7 feet; RF 23 feet

Skydome (Toronto Blue Jays)

Capacity: 50,516
Surface: Artificial turf
Left-field line: 328 feet
Center field: 400 feet
Right-field line: 400 feet
Power alleys: 375 feet
Walls: 10 feet high

ALCS Playoffs (cont.)

one of the biggest plays in Game 4.

Take two: The double steal by Toronto in the third inning was the first in ALCS play since Game 3 of the 1990 ALCS when Jose Canseco and Harold Baines did it.

The call of the wild: The four wild pitches by Minnesota through Game 4 set an ALCS record. It tied the overall league championship series record set by Los Angeles against Philadelphia in the '83 NLCS.

The third's the charm: Kelly Gruber committed his third error of the series in the seventh inning, tying the LCS record for most errors by a third baseman in post-season play. It has been done twice previously, both times in the ALCS play, by George Brett in 1976 and Doug DeCinces in 1982.

ALCS: Game Five

MINNESOTA 8, TORONTO 5

Puckett named MVP: The Twins' Kirby Puckett was named ALCS MVP. Puckett went 3-for-4 in Game 5 with the game-winning hit in the eighth inning, and batted .429 with two home runs and 6 RBI in the five-game series. He was 6-for-9 with four RBI in the last two games and became the 10th player in ALCS history to homer in consecutive games.

The F-word did it: Toronto manager Cito Gaston said his ejection from Game 5 had nothing to do with trying to motivate his team. Home plate umpire Mike Reilly explained why he ejected the Blue Jays' manager between the second and third inning: "He called me over and said, 'Hey, Mike, you got to give us a good game.' I said, 'You are getting a good game.' He said, '(expletive) you.' That was it."

They hit, they ran, they won: The 17 runs scored by the Twins in Games 4 and 5 are the most by one team in consecutive ALCS games since Boston beat California 10-4 and 8-1 in 1986. Everybody in the Twins' lineup hit in Game 5, and their 14 team hits were the most by one club in an ALCS game since Minnesota had 15 in Game 5 of the '87 ALCS against Detroit.

—Tim Wendel

NLCS Playoffs

NLCS: Game One

PITTSBURGH 5, ATLANTA 1

Game hero: Andy Van Slyke homered and drove in two runs.

Braves' manager wanted the Jays: Atlanta manager Bobby Cox made no secret of the fact that he wanted to see Toronto win the American League playoffs. "Nothing against Minnesota, but all my ties are with the Blue Jays," he said. Cox was fired by the Braves in 1981 and hired by the Jays four days later. He left the Jays after 1985—when he led them to within one game of the World Series—and came back to the Braves.

Braves' coach also an ex-Jay: Atlanta's third-base coach Jimmy Williams also used to manage the Toronto Blue Jays. He took over after Cox left, but was fired 36 games into the 1989 season and replaced by Cito Gaston.

Where were the other 1,382 Bucs fans? While fans in other cities scrambled for tickets, they could've walked up to the ticket window in Pittsburgh and bought one the night of the game. Game 1 was not a sellout, but the crowd of 57,347 was the largest ever to see a baseball game in Pittsburgh.

NLCS: Game Two

ATLANTA 1, PITTSBURGH 0

Young guns: Steve Avery was the youngest pitcher to start a playoff game since Kansas City's Bret Saberhagen in 1984. He is the youngest to start a National League playoff game since Fernando Valenzuela in 1980. Dwight Gooden was six months older than Avery when he started for the Mets in 1986. Unlike Avery, none of those pitchers won their starts.

Look Ma, I'm in the playoffs: Braves' reliever Marvin Freeman traveled with his team despite being unable to pitch while recovering from back surgery. His locker is next to Avery's, and he wanted Avery to stand there for post-game interviews. "Get a shot of it so my mother will know where I am," Freeman said.

Braves' broadcaster shut out Pirates: The last time the Pirates had been shut out in a playoff game was Game 1 in 1974, 3-0 by Dodgers' pitcher Don Sutton—now a broadcaster for the Braves.

Tied up: This was the first NL playoff game to be tied 0-0 after five innings since Game 3 of the 1980 series between the Phillies and Astros.

A gang of thieves: Ron Gant's three stolen bases tied an NLCS record. Joe Morgan and Ken Griffey Sr. did it for the Reds in 1975, and Steve Sax did it for the Dodgers in a 12-inning game in 1988.

One was all it took: The Braves tied an NLCS record by making just one out-field putout. That had been done three times previously.

NLCS: Game Three

ATLANTA 10, PITTSBURGH 3

The stars came out: It was a star-studded crowd that witnessed the Braves' first postseason win in Atlanta since the franchise moved there in 1966. Seated in the front row, doing the Tomahawk Chop with the rest of the crowd, were Braves' owner Ted Turner, actress Jane Fonda and former President Jimmy Carter with his wife Rosalynn. In the broadcast booth, and later in the Braves' clubhouse, was rap star M.C. Hammer.

No mercy from Merced: John Smoltz had not allowed a homer in 96 innings—since Barry Bonds connected July 31—when Orlando Merced hit the first pitch of the game over the right-center field wall. Merced became the fourth player in history to lead off a playoff game with a homer, and the first to do it since Bob Dernier of the Cubs in 1984.

First pitcher to steal: When Smoltz stole second base in the sixth inning, it was the first time in the 22-year history of the National League playoffs that a pitcher had stolen a base.

Proud papa: Pirates' manager Jim Leyland arrived in Atlanta about five hours before the game after spending the off-day in Pittsburgh, where his wife Katie gave birth to the couple's first son, Patrick James.

NLCS: Game Four

PITTSBURGH 3, ATLANTA 2

Bonilla liked Atlanta fans: Bobby Bonilla and the rest of the Pirates were excited by the festive atmosphere of the Tomahawk chopping-crowd in Atlanta. "It's nice to see the city excited like that," Bonilla said. "We've all gotten a kick out of it. (The fans) are having a great time, and that's what it's all about."

Killer Bs, the sequel—Bell and Buechele: The Pirates' best hitters through Game Four were shortstop Jay Bell and third baseman Steve Buechele, each of whom tied a playoff record. Bell tied the record of six hits in two consecutive games, last accomplished by the Giants' Will Clark in 1989. Buechele tied a record of five consecutive hits over two games, also last accomplished by Clark. Bell had a .471 average through four games, Buechele .462.

Where's the bat? The league's best hitter in the regular season, Atlanta's Terry Pendleton, struggled through the first four games, going 3-for-17 (.176). Pendleton was only the fourth batting champion to play in a playoff series and the first since the Cardinals' Willie McGee in 1985.

Working overtime: Game 4 was the first extra-inning game in the NLCS since 1988's Game Four went 12 innings.

Don't blame Justice: Pitcher Charlie Leibrandt accepted the responsibility for David Justice's throwing error on the Pirates' tying run in the fifth inning, blaming himself for not properly backing up third base.

NLCS: Game Five

PITTSBURGH 1, ATLANTA 0

No regrets: Pittsburgh's Zane Smith was once one of the Braves' young pitchers, but he was traded to Montreal in 1989 and moved on to Pittsburgh in 1990. He thinks the moves have been good for him: "I think if you talk to any player who has been on one team for a long time there comes a time when they need a change of scenery," Smith said. "The Braves helped me out by trading me."

Failed suicide squeeze a 'miracle': The Braves' tried a suicide squeeze bunt with two strikes on pitcher Tom Glavine in the second inning. The bases were loaded with one out. Glavine missed the sign, and tried to bunt only after he saw baserunner Brian Hunter breaking from third. He missed, and Hunter was caught in a rundown and tagged out for a rally-ending double play. The play perhaps failed because Smith failed to throw a strike, a pitch Glavine likely would have been able to bunt. "We had no idea it was coming," said Pittsburgh manager Jim Leyland. "We caught a break . . . It was basically a miracle."

Pendleton on ice: Braves' third baseman Terry Pendleton was unable to take infield practice and had to have his knee iced after every game. "I don't think it's any secret I'm going to have to get it taken care of," said Pendleton, who said his sore knee was not the reason for his paltry .238 average in the series.

NLCS: Game Six
ATLANTA 1, PITTSBURGH 0

Drabek was great: Even though he gave up the only run of the game in the ninth inning, Doug Drabek lowered his ERA for the series to 0.60, one earned run in 15 innings. His career ERA of 1.15 in four playoff games is the third best all-time of pitchers who have worked 20 or more innings.

But Avery was better: As good as Drabek was, however, the Braves' Steve Avery was even better. His eight scoreless innings gave him an NLCS record of 16 1/3 consecutive scoreless innings. The previous mark was set by Mike Scott of Houston with 16 consecutive scoreless innings against the Mets in the 1986 series.

Gant stole record: The Braves' Ron Gant stole his sixth base of the series in the ninth inning, setting up the run. It broke the record for most steals in a series, 5, set by Dave Lopes of Los Angeles in 1981 and tied by Steve Sax of the Dodgers in 1988.

Off the bench—finally: Atlanta replaced second baseman Mark Lemke with Jeff Treadway, who had been bothered by a bone spur in his right hand. He said it was a relief to be off the bench.

On the bench—still: Nick Esasky sat on the bench all year, as he continued his battle against vertigo. He was in uniform, though, at the request of Braves' general manager John Schuerholz. ". . . I guess I'm kind of like a cheerleader," Esasky said, " . . . but that's OK. I'll take whatever piece of this I can get."

NLCS: Game Seven
ATLANTA 4, PITTSBURGH 0

Avery credited his teammates: On the strength of his masterful pitching performance, Steve Avery was named MVP for the NLCS, but he refused to accept the award for his individual performance. "It's a team trophy," he said.

Hero of Game Seven: Brian Hunter, Braves. He hit a two-run homer in the first inning and added an RBI single in the fifth.

Goat of Game Seven: John Smiley, Pittsburgh. The Pirates' starter allowed three Atlanta runs and didn't last the first inning.

000 000 000 000 000 000 000 000 000: That's what the Pirates' scorecard looked like for the final 27 innings at Three Rivers Stadium.

Empty seats and empty coffers: There were more than 11,000 unsold seats for the seventh game of the NLCS, adding to the team's mounting financial problems. If the Pirates had won the game and gone to the World Series, team officials estimated their annual loss for 1991 in the neighborhood of $3 million. By missing out on the opportunities provided by the Series, the loss would jump to about $6 million.

Braves' bonus: The Braves got more than a financial bonus by winning the NLCS. One added benefit from playing in the World Series would be realized in 1992. The commissioner's office said that post-season days counted toward suspension time for outfielder Otis Nixon. The extra weeks in the Series meant that Nixon could be allowed to return to the lineup before the end of April.

NLCS COMPOSITE BOX (Through 7 games)

ATLANTA BRAVES BATTING

	G	AB	R	H	2B	3B	HR	RBI	SO	BB	Avg.	PO	A	E	Pct.
Olson c	7	24	3	8	1	0	1	4	3	4	.333	62	1	0	1.000
Smoltz p	2	5	0	1	0	0	0	0	4	1	.200	3	0	0	1.000
Treadway 2b	1	3	0	1	0	0	0	0	0	0	.333	2	2	0	1.000
Bream 1b-ph	4	10	1	3	0	0	1	3	1	0	.300	20	3	0	1.000
Hunter 1b	5	18	2	6	2	0	1	4	2	0	.333	30	4	0	1.000
L.Smith lf	7	24	3	6	3	0	0	5	4	4	.250	10	2	0	1.000
Gant cf	7	27	4	7	1	0	1	3	4	2	.259	15	2	0	1.000
Glavine p	2	4	0	1	0	0	0	0	2	0	.250	1	3	0	1.000
Gregg ph	4	4	0	1	0	0	0	0	2	0	.250	0	0	0	—
Lemke 2b	7	20	1	4	1	0	0	1	0	4	.200	12	10	1	.957
Justice rf	7	25	4	5	1	0	1	2	7	3	.200	17	0	1	.944
Belliard ss	7	19	4	4	0	0	0	1	3	3	.211	8	14	1	.957
Pendleton 3b	7	30	1	5	1	1	0	1	3	1	.167	5	11	0	1.000
Avery p	2	7	0	1	0	0	0	0	4	0	.143	1	2	0	1.000
Leibrandt p	1	1	0	0	0	0	0	0	0	0	.000	0	1	0	1.000
Blauser ss-ph	2	2	0	0	0	0	0	0	0	0	.000	0	1	1	.500
Willard ph	2	2	0	0	0	0	0	0	1	0	.000	0	0	0	—
Mitchell pr-lf-ph	5	4	0	0	0	0	0	1	0	0	.000	2	0	0	1.000
Clancy p	1	0	0	0	0	0	0	0	0	0	—	0	0	0	—
Mercker p	1	0	0	0	0	0	0	0	0	0	—	0	0	0	—
Pena p	4	0	0	0	0	0	0	0	0	0	—	1	2	0	1.000
Stanton p	3	0	0	0	0	0	0	0	0	0	—	0	2	0	1.000
Wohlers p	3	0	0	0	0	0	0	0	0	0	—	0	1	0	1.000
Totals	**7**	**229**	**19**	**53**	**10**	**1**	**5**	**19**	**42**	**22**	**.231**	**189**	**61**	**4**	**.984**

PITTSBURGH PIRATES BATTING

	G	AB	R	H	2B	3B	HR	RBI	SO	BB	Avg.	PO	A	E	Pct.
Varsho ph	2	2	0	1	0	0	0	1	0	0	.500	0	0	0	—
Bell ss	7	29	2	12	2	0	1	1	10	0	.414	13	19	1	.970
Buechele 3b	7	23	2	7	2	0	0	0	6	4	.304	8	14	0	1.000
LaValliere c-ph	3	6	0	2	0	0	0	1	0	2	.333	14	3	0	1.000
Bonilla rf	7	23	2	7	2	0	0	1	2	6	.304	12	1	0	1.000
Slaught c-ph	6	17	0	4	0	0	0	1	4	1	.235	30	5	0	1.000
Drabek p	2	5	0	1	1	0	0	1	2	0	.200	3	0	0	1.000
Merced 1b-ph	3	9	1	2	0	0	1	1	1	0	.222	13	0	1	.929
Lind 2b	7	25	0	4	0	0	0	3	6	0	.160	12	24	1	.973
Van Slyke cf	7	25	3	4	2	0	1	2	5	5	.160	18	1	0	1.000
Redus 1b	5	19	1	3	0	0	0	4	1	1	.158	51	0	2	.962
Bonds lf	7	27	1	4	1	0	0	4	4	2	.148	14	1	1	.938
Espy ph	2	2	0	0	0	0	0	0	2	0	.000	0	0	0	—
Mason p	3	1	0	0	0	0	0	0	1	0	.000	0	0	0	—
Walk p	3	2	0	0	0	0	0	0	2	0	.000	0	0	0	—
McClendn ph-1b	3	2	0	0	0	0	0	0	0	1	.000	0	0	0	—
Tomlin p	1	2	0	0	0	0	0	0	0	0	.000	1	0	0	1.000
Wilkerson ph	4	4	0	0	0	0	0	0	3	0	.000	0	0	0	—
Z.Smith p	2	5	0	0	0	0	0	0	4	0	.000	0	3	0	1.000
Belinda p	3	0	0	0	0	0	0	0	0	0	—	0	1	0	1.000
Kipper p	1	0	0	0	0	0	0	0	0	0	—	0	1	0	1.000
Landrum p	1	0	0	0	0	0	0	0	0	0	—	0	0	0	—
Patterson p	1	0	0	0	0	0	0	0	0	0	—	0	0	0	—
Rodriguez p	1	0	0	0	0	0	0	0	0	0	—	0	0	0	—
Smiley p	2	0	0	0	0	0	0	0	0	0	—	0	0	0	—
Totals	**7**	**228**	**12**	**51**	**10**	**0**	**3**	**1157**		**22**	**.224**	**18973**		**6**	**.978**

ATLANTA BRAVES PITCHING

	G	CG	IP	H	R	BB	SO	HB	WP	W	L	Sv	Pct.	ER	ERA
Avery	2	0	16.1	9	0	4	17	0	0	2	0	0	1.000	0	0.00
Pena	4	0	4.1	1	0	4	0	1	0	0	0	3	—	0	0.00
Wohlers	3	0	1.2	3	0	1	1	0	0	0	0	0	—	0	0.00
Clancy	1	0	0.1	0	0	0	0	0	0	0	0	0	—	0	0.00
Leibrandt	1	0	6.2	8	2	3	6	0	0	0	1	0	—	1	1.35
Stanton	3	0	3.2	4	1	3	3	0	1	0	0	0	—	1	2.45
Glavine	2	0	14	12	5	6	11	0	0	0	2	0	.000	5	3.21
Smoltz	2	1	15.1	14	3	3	15	0	0	2	0	0	1.000	3	1.76
Mercker	1	0	.2	0	1	2	0	0	0	0	1	0	.000	1	13.50
Totals	**7**	**1**	**63**	**51**	**12**	**22**	**57**	**0**	**2**	**4**	**3**	**3**	**.571**	**11**	**1.57**

PITTSBURGH PIRATES PITCHING

	G	CG	IP	H	R	BB	SO	HB	WP	W	L	Sv	Pct.	ER	ERA
Belinda	3	0	5	0	0	3	4	0	0	1	0	0	1.000	0	0.00
Mason	3	0	4.1	3	0	1	2	0	0	0	0	1	—	0	0.00
Patterson	1	0	2	1	0	3	0	0	0	0	0	0	—	0	0.00
Drabek	2	0	15	10	1	5	10	0	0	1	1	0	.500	1	0.60
Z.Smith	2	0	14	15	1	3	10	1	0	1	1	0	.500	1	0.61
Walk	3	0	9.1	5	2	3	5	0	0	0	1	1	—	2	1.93
Tomlin	1	0	6	6	2	2	1	0	0	0	0	0	—	2	3.00
Kipper	1	0	2	2	1	0	1	0	0	0	0	0	—	1	4.50
Landrum	1	0	1	2	1	2	2	0	0	0	0	0	—	1	9.00
Smiley	2	0	2.2	8	8	1	3	1	0	0	2	0	.000	7	23.63
Rodriguez	1	0	1	1	3	2	1	0	0	0	0	0	—	3	27.00
Totals	**7**	**1**	**63**	**53**	**19**	**22**	**42**	**2**	**0**	**3**	**4**	**2**	**.429**	**18**	**2.57**

Miscellaneous

SCORE BY INNINGS

Atlanta	911	011	132	0—19
Pittsburgh	212	121	110	1—12

DP: Atlanta 6, Pittsburgh 3. **LOB:** Atlanta 51, Pittsburgh 54. **SB:** Redus 2, Bonds 3, Gant 7, L. Smith 2, Olson, Smoltz, Van Slyke. **CS:** Justice, Bonilla, Hunter, L. Smith. **S:** Bell, Belliard 2, Leibrandt, Buechele, Slaught, Treadway, Merced , Smoltz. **SF:** Lind, Gant. **HBP:** by Z. Smith (Gant), by Smiley (L. Smith). **Balk:** Walk. **Umpires:** Harvey; Pulli; DeMuth; Gregg; Davidson; Froemming. **Official scorers:** Games 1, 2, 6 and 7: Tony Krizmanich (Pittsburgh), Nick Peters (San Francisco Chronicle); Games 3, 4 and 5: Paul Newberry (Atlanta), Peters. **Time:** Game 1 at Pittsburgh, 2:51. Game 2 at Pittsburgh, 2:46. Game 3 at Atlanta, 3:21. Game 4 at Atlanta, 3:43. Game 5 at Atlanta, 2:51. Game 6 at Pittsburgh, 3:09. Game 7 at Pittsburgh, 3:04. **Attendance:** Game 1 at Pittsburgh, 57,347. Game 2 at Pittsburgh, 57,533. Game 3 at Atlanta, 50,905. Game 4 at Atlanta, 51,109. Game 5 at Atlanta, 51,109. Game 6 at Pittsburgh, 54,508. Game 7 at Pittsburgh, 46,932.

NLCS Scores

Oct. 9: Pittsburgh 5, Atlanta 1
Oct. 10: Atlanta 1, Pittsburgh 0
Oct. 12.: Atlanta 10, Pittsburgh 3
Oct. 13: Pitt. 3, Atlanta 2 (10 inn.)
Oct. 14: Pittsburgh 1, Atlanta 0
Oct. 16: Atlanta 1, Pittsburgh 0
Oct. 17: Atlanta 4, Pittsburgh 0

NLCS: Where they played

Atlanta-Fulton County Stadium
(Atlanta Braves)
Capacity: 52,007
Surface: Grass
Left-field line: 330 feet
Center-field: 402 feet
Right-field line: 330 feet
Power alleys: 385 feet
Walls: 10 feet high

Three Rivers Stadium
(Pittsburgh Pirates)
Capacity: 58,729
Surface: Artificial turf
Left-field line: 335 feet
Center field: 400 feet
Right-field line: 335 feet
Power alleys: 375 feet
Walls: 10 feet high

World Series 1991

World Series: Game One

MINNESOTA 5, ATLANTA 2

Hero: Twins' shortstop Greg Gagne put the game out of Atlanta's reach with a three-run homer in the fifth.

Great play: Twins' second baseman Chuck Knoblauch went to his knees to start a two-on, eighth-inning double play. The Braves followed with a walk and RBI single, so the play was crucial to blunting their comeback bid.

Pivotal pitch: Atlanta starter Charlie Leibrandt tried to run a fastball in onto Gagne's fists. It worked for him in the past. This time, the pitch stayed over the plate until Gagne swatted it just over the left-field fence.

Baserunning mistake: Minnesota's Dan Gladden did not hold third base on Kirby Puckett's one-out liner to left. He ran back to the bag when the ball was caught and was easily thrown out at home.

World Series: Game Two

MINNESOTA 3, ATLANTA 2

Perfect pen: Twins' closer Rick Aguilera became the first pitcher to save Games 1 and 2 of the World Series since the Yankees' Goose Gossage did it in 1981 against the Dodgers.

Hero: Twins' rookie Scott Leius, whose solo homer in the eighth inning won the game.

Goat: The Braves will long claim it was first base umpire Drew Coble who ruled that Ron Gant was out at first in a collision with the Twins' Kent Hrbek.

Safe at last: Terry Pendleton finally broke an 0-for-18 streak against right-handers in postseason play with a sixth-inning single.

...but injured again: Pendleton reinjured his left knee when he slid into first base in beating out an infield hit in the eighth inning.

Good odds for Minnesota: Teams that have taken a 2-0 lead in the World Series have gone on to win 31 of 41—including the '87 Twins, '88 Dodgers, '89 A's and '90 Reds. (Make that 32—add the '91 Twins).

Game 1 box score
Twins 5, Braves 2

```
Atlanta     000 001 010  2
Minnesota   001 031 00x  5
```

ATLANTA	ab	r	h	bi	lo	bb	so	avg
L.Smith, dh	3	1	0	0	0	1	0	.000
Treadway, 2b	3	1	1	0	1	1	2	.333
Pendleton, 3b	4	0	0	0	3	0	0	.000
Justice, rf	2	0	1	0	0	2	0	.500
Gant, cf	4	0	3	2	1	0	0	.750
Bream, 1b	4	0	0	0	6	0	1	.000
Hunter, lf	4	0	0	0	1	0	0	.000
Olson, c	3	0	1	0	0	1	0	.333
Belliard, ss	1	0	0	0	1	0	0	.000
Blauser, ph-ss	2	0	0	0	0	0	0	.000
Totals	30	2	6	2	13	5	3	

▶BATTING — Two-out RBI: Gant 2. RBI, scoring position, less than two outs: L.Smith 0-1, Pendleton 0-1. S:Belliard. GDP:Pendleton, Belliard.
▶BASERUNNING — Team LOB:7.
▶FIELDING — E: Treadway (1, ground ball). Outfield assist:Justice (Knoblauch at 2B); Hunter (Gladden at HP). DP:2.

MINNESOTA	ab	r	h	bi	lo	bb	so	avg
Gladden, lf	2	1	0	0	2	0	0	.000
Knoblauch, 2b	3	0	3	1	0	1	0	1.000
Puckett, cf	4	0	0	0	2	0	2	.000
Davis, dh	3	0	0	0	2	1	1	.000
Harper, c	4	0	2	0	3	0	0	.500
Mack, rf	4	0	0	0	2	0	1	.000
Hrbek, 1b	4	2	2	1	0	0	1	.500
Leius, 3b	2	1	1	0	0	0	0	.500
Pagliarulo, ph-3b	1	0	0	0	0	0	0	.000
Gagne, ss	3	1	1	3	0	0	1	.333
Totals	30	5	9	5	9	4	6	

▶BATTING — 2B: Harper(1, off Leibrandt); Hrbek (1, off Leibrandt). HR:Hrbek (1, 6th inning off Clancy, 0 on, 1 out); Gagne (1, 5th inning off Leibrandt, 2 on, 0 out). Two-out RBI:Knoblauch. RBI, scoring position, less than two outs: Puckett 0-1, Harper 0-2, Mack 0-1, Gagne 2-2.
▶BASERUNNING — SB: Gladden(1, 2nd base off Leibrandt/Olson); Knoblauch 2(2, 2nd base off Leibrandt/Olson; 2nd base off Clancy/Olson). CS:Gladden (1, 2nd base by Wohlers/Olson). Team LOB:5.
▶FIELDING — E:Gladden (1, mishandled base hit). DP:2.

▶PITCHING	ip	h	r	er	bb	so	era
ATLANTA							
Leibrandt L, 0-1	4	7	4	4	1	3	9.00
Clancy	2	1	1	1	2	0	4.50
Wohlers	1	1	0	0	1	1	0.00
Stanton	1	0	0	0	0	2	0.00
MINNESOTA							
Morris W, 1-0	7	5	2	2	4	3	2.57
Guthrie H,1	.2	0	0	0	1	0	0.00
Aguilera S,1	1.1	1	0	0	0	0	0.00

Leibrandt pitched to 3 batters in 5th; Morris pitched to 2 batters in 8th.
▶IBB:Davis by Clancy. Inherited runners/scored:Guthrie 2/0; Aguilera 2/1. Pitches-strikes:Morris 100-60; Guthrie 7-3; Aguilera 18-13; Leibrandt 79-50; Clancy 32-17; Wohlers 18-9; Stanton 11-7. Ground balls-fly balls:Morris 8-8; Guthrie 1-0; Aguilera 1-2; Leibrandt 3-3; Clancy 4-3; Wohlers 2-0; Stanton 1-0.
▶GAME DATA — T:3:00. A:55,108. Indoors.
▶UMPIRES — HP:Denkinger. 1B:Wendelstedt. 2B:Coble. 3B:Tata. LF: Reed. RF: Montague.

Game 2 box score
Twins 3, Braves 2

```
Atlanta     010 010 000  2
Minnesota   200 000 01x  3
```

ATLANTA	ab	r	h	bi	lo	bb	so	avg
L.Smith, dh	3	0	0	0	0	0	0	.000
Pendleton, 3b	4	0	2	0	1	0	1	.250
Gant, cf	4	0	1	0	3	0	0	.500
Justice, rf	4	1	1	0	3	0	0	.333
Bream, 1b	4	0	1	0	1	0	1	.125
Hunter, lf	3	0	1	1	0	0	1	.143
Olson, c	4	1	1	0	2	0	1	.286
Lemke, 2b	3	0	0	0	1	0	1	.000
Gregg, ph	1	0	0	0	1	0	1	.000
Belliard, ss	2	0	1	1	0	0	0	.333
Totals	32	2	8	2	12	0	6	

▶BATTING — 2B: Bream (1, off Tapani); Olson (1, off Tapani). RBI, scoring position, less than 2 outs: Gant 0-1, Hunter 1-2, Olson 0-1, Lemke 0-1, Belliard 1-1. S: L.Smith. SF: Belliard, Hunter.
▶BASERUNNING — Team LOB: 6.
▶FIELDING — E: Justice (1, 2-base fly). DP: 2.

MINNESOTA	ab	r	h	bi	lo	bb	so	avg
Gladden, lf	4	0	0	0	1	0	1	.000
Knoblauch, 2b	3	1	0	0	0	1	0	.500
Puckett, cf	4	0	0	0	3	0	1	.000
Davis, dh	3	1	1	2	0	0	0	.167
Harper, c	2	0	1	0	0	1	0	.500
Mack, rf	3	0	0	0	2	0	2	.000
Hrbek, 1b	2	0	0	0	1	1	1	.333
Leius, 3b	3	1	1	1	0	0	0	.400
Gagne, ss	3	0	1	0	0	0	1	.333
Totals	27	3	4	3	8	3	6	

▶BATTING — HR: Davis (1, 1st inning off Glavine, 1 on, 2 out); Leius (1, 8th inning off Glavine, 0 on, 0 out). 2-out RBI: Davis 2. RBI, scoring position, less than 2 outs: Knoblauch 0-1, Puckett 0-1. GDP: Leius, Puckett.
▶BASERUNNING — Team LOB: 3.
▶FIELDING — E: Leius (1, ground ball). Outfield assist: Gladden (Gant at 1B).

▶PITCHING	ip	h	r	er	bb	so	era
ATLANTA							
Glavine L,0-1	8	4	3	3	3	6	3.38
MINNESOTA							
Tapani W,1-0	8	7	2	2	0	3	2.25
Aguilera S,2	1	1	0	0	0	3	0.00

Balks: Glavine. Pitches-strikes: Tapani 105-69; Aguilera 19-13; Glavine 108-66. Ground balls-fly balls: Tapani 11-11; Glavine 14-5.
▶GAME DATA — T: 2:37. A: 55,145. Indoors.
▶UMPIRES — HP: Wendelstedt. 1B: Coble. 2B: Tata. 3B: Reed. LF: Montague. RF: Denkinger.

World Series: Game Three

ATLANTA 5, MINNESOTA 4 (12 innings)

Hero: Atlanta second baseman Mark Lemke. He nearly cost the Braves the game with an error in the top of the 12th, then he won it with a single in the bottom half.

Goat: Braves' relief pitcher Alejandro Pena, who surrendered a two-run homer to the Twins' Chili Davis in the eighth inning to wipe out a 4-2 Atlanta lead.

Great play: Braves' right fielder David Justice slid home just ahead of catcher Brian Harper's tag to score the winning run. He beat the throw from Twins' left fielder Dan Gladden.

Big blooper: Atlanta's Justice and center fielder Ron Gant converged on a lead-

Game 3 box score
Braves 5 Twins 4

```
Minnesota   100 000 120 000  4
Atlanta     101 200 000 001  5
```

MINNESOTA	ab	r	h	bi	lo	bb	so	avg
Gladden lf	6	1	3	0	0	0	1	.250
Knoblauch 2b	5	0	1	1	2	0	0	.364
Hrbek,1b	6	0	1	0	5	0	2	.250
Puckett cf	4	1	1	1	2	2	2	.083
Mack rf	4	0	0	0	2	0	2	.000
Willis p	0	0	0	0	0	0	0	-
Sorrento ph	1	0	0	0	2	0	1	.000
Guthrie p	0	0	0	0	0	0	0	-
Aguilera ph-p	1	0	0	0	3	0	0	.000
Leius 3b	3	0	0	0	0	0	1	.250
Pagliarulo ph-3b	1	0	0	0	0	0	1	.000
Newman ph-3b	1	0	0	0	0	0	0	.000
Gagne ss	5	0	0	0	0	0	1	.182
Ortiz c	2	0	1	0	0	0	0	.500
Harper ph-c	3	1	1	0	0	0	0	.444
Erickson p	1	0	0	0	0	0	1	.000
West p	0	0	0	0	0	0	0	-
Leach p	0	0	0	0	0	0	0	-
Larkin ph	1	0	1	0	0	0	0	1.000
Bedrosian p	0	0	0	0	0	0	0	-
Davis ph	1	1	1	2	0	0	0	.286
Brown rf	0	0	0	0	0	0	0	-
Bush ph-rf	2	0	0	0	1	0	1	.000
Totals	47	4	10	4	17	2	13	

▶BATTING — 3B: Gladden (1 off Avery). HR: Puckett (1 7th inning off Avery 0 on 0 out); Davis (2 8th inning off Pena 1 on 0 out).
▶BASERUNNING — SB: Knoblauch (3 2nd base off Mercker/Olson). Team LOB: 10.
▶FIELDING — E: Knoblauch (1 ground ball).

ATLANTA	ab	r	h	bi	lo	bb	so	avg
L.Smith lf	4	1	1	1	0	0	1	.100
Mitchell lf	2	0	0	0	1	0	1	.000
Pendleton 3b	4	1	0	0	2	0	0	.167
Gant cf	6	0	0	0	3	0	0	.286
Justice rf	6	2	2	1	0	0	1	.333
Bream 1b	3	0	1	0	0	1	0	.182
Hunter ph-1b	2	0	0	0	1	0	0	.111
Olson c	3	1	1	1	1	3	0	.300
Lemke 2b	5	0	2	1	3	1	1	.250
Belliard ss	3	0	1	1	1	1	0	.333
Blauser ph-ss	1	0	0	0	2	0	0	.000
Avery p	3	0	0	0	2	0	2	.000
Pena p	0	0	0	0	0	0	0	-
Treadway ph	0	0	0	0	0	0	0	.333
Stanton p	0	0	0	0	0	0	0	-
Cabrera ph	1	0	0	0	0	0	0	.000
Wohlers p	0	0	0	0	0	0	0	-
Mercker p	0	0	0	0	0	0	0	-
Clancy p	0	0	0	0	0	0	0	-
Totals	43	5	8	5	14	8	6	

▶BATTING — 2B: Bream (2 off Erickson); Olson (2 off Guthrie). HR: L.Smith (1 5th inning off Erickson 0 on 1 out); Justice (1 4th inning off Erickson 0 on 0 out).
▶BASERUNNING — SB: Justice (1 2nd base off Aguilera/Harper). Team LOB: 12.
▶FIELDING — E: Pendleton (1 ground ball); Lemke (1 mishandled base hit).

▶PITCHING	ip	h	r	er	bb	so	era
MINNESOTA							
Erickson	4.2	5	4	3	2	3	5.79
West	0	0	0	0	2	0	-
Leach	.1	0	0	0	0	1	0.00
Bedrosian	2	0	0	0	0	1	0.00
Willis	2	0	0	0	2	0	0.00
Guthrie	2	1	0	0	1	1	0.00
Aguilera L,0-1	.2	2	1	1	1	0	3.00
ATLANTA							
Avery	7	4	3	2	0	5	2.57
Pena BS,1	2	4	1	1	0	4	4.50
Stanton	2	1	0	0	1	3	0.00
Wohlers	.1	0	0	0	0	0	0.00
Mercker	.1	0	0	0	0	1	0.00
Clancy W,1-0	.1	0	0	0	0	0	3.86

West pitched to 2 batters in 5th; Avery pitched to 1 batter in 8th.
IBB: Pendleton by Willis; Puckett 2 by Stanton; by Clancy. WP: Pena Erickson.
▶GAME DATA — T: 4:04. A: 50,878.
▶UMPIRES — HP: Coble. 1B: Tata. 2B: Reed. 3B: Montague. LF: Denkinger RF: Wendlestadt.

off drive by Gladden that fell between them for a triple. Either could have—should have—made the play. The misplay brought an end to Steve Avery's streak of 16 scoreless postseason innings.

Exciting confrontation: Atlanta's Kent Mercker struck out Kent Hrbek with the go-ahead run on third with one out in the Twins' 12th. It delighted Twins' fans, who had been chanting "Cheater!" at Hrbek after he made a hard tag and appeared to lift Braves' Gant off the bag in Game 2.

Youth on the mound: The starting matchup of Steve Avery and Scott Erickson was the youngest for a World Series game since Dave Righetti of the Yankees faced Fernando Valenzuela of the Dodgers in 1981.

Pinch-hit parade: The Twins set a record by using eight pinch-hitters; the combined total of 11 for both teams was also a record. Twins' closer Rick Aguilera became the first pitcher to be used as a pinch-hitter since the Dodgers' Don Drysdale in the 1965 series against the Twins.

World Series: Game Four

ATLANTA 3, MINNESOTA 2

Hero: Braves' Jerry Willard, a journeyman minor leaguer placed on the roster 10 minutes before the plane left for the first NLCS game in Pittsburgh. He drove in the winning run on a sacrifice fly in the bottom of the ninth.

Lemke again: Willard hit the sacrifice fly, but Mark Lemke gets credit for avoiding Brian Harper's tag at home to score the winning run. Lemke had tripled to left with one out to get into scoring position.

Goat: Twins' Carl Willis, who allowed Lonnie Smith's game-tying solo homer in the seventh inning.

Rookie record: Minnesota's Chuck Knoblauch doubled in the first inning for his 12th hit of the postseason—a record among rookies.

Game 4 box score
Braves 3 Twins 2

Minnesota	010 000 100 2
Atlanta	001 000 101 3

MINNESOTA	ab	r	h	bi	lo	bb	so	avg
Gladden lf	4	0	0	0	0	0	0	.188
Knoblauch 2b	3	0	1	0	0	1	1	.357
Puckett cf	4	0	1	0	2	0	0	.125
Hrbek 1b	4	0	0	0	3	0	1	.188
Harper c	4	1	2	0	0	0	0	.462
Mack rf	4	0	0	0	2	0	2	.000
Pagliarulo 3b	3	1	3	2	0	0	0	.600
Leius ph-3b	1	0	0	0	0	0	0	.222
Bedrosian p	0	0	0	0	0	0	0	-
Gagne ss	3	0	0	0	2	0	3	.143
Morris p	2	0	0	0	1	0	1	.000
Larkin ph	1	0	0	0	0	0	0	.500
Willis p	0	0	0	0	0	0	0	-
Guthrie p	0	0	0	0	0	0	0	-
Newman 3b	0	0	0	0	0	0	0	.000
Totals	33	2	7	2	10	1	8	

▶**BATTING** — 2B: Knoblauch (1 off Smoltz); Harper (2 off Smoltz). HR: Pagliarulo (1 7th inning off Smoltz 0 on 1 out). RBI scoring position less than 2 outs: Puckett 0-1 Mack 0-1 Pagliarulo 1-1 Gagne 0-1.
▶**BASERUNNING** — SB: Knoblauch (4 2nd base off Stanton/Olson). CS: Mack (1 HP by Smoltz/Olson). Team LOB: 5.
▶**FIELDING** — Outfield assist: Puckett (L.Smith at HP).

ATLANTA	ab	r	h	bi	lo	bb	so	avg
L.Smith lf	4	1	2	1	0	0	1	.214
Pendleton 3b	4	1	2	1	0	0	0	.250
Gant cf	3	0	1	0	0	1	0	.294
Justice rf	3	0	0	0	1	1	1	.267
Bream 1b	3	0	0	0	2	0	1	.143
Hunter ph-1b	1	0	0	0	0	0	0	.100
Olson c	3	0	0	0	0	1	1	.231
Lemke 2b	4	1	3	0	0	0	0	.417
Belliard ss	2	0	0	1	3	0	0	.250
Treadway ph	1	0	0	0	0	0	0	.250
Blauser ss	0	0	0	0	0	1	0	.000
Smoltz p	2	0	0	0	1	0	1	.000
Gregg ph	1	0	0	0	0	0	1	.000
Wohlers p	0	0	0	0	0	0	0	-
Stanton p	0	0	0	0	0	0	0	-
Cabrera ph	0	0	0	0	0	0	0	.000
Willard ph	0	0	0	1	0	0	0	-
Totals	31	3	8	3	7	4	6	

▶**BATTING** — 2B: Pendleton (1 off Morris); Lemke (1 off Morris). 3B: Lemke (1 off Guthrie). HR: L.Smith (2 7th inning off Willis 0 on 2 out); Pendleton (1 3rd inning off Morris 0 on 2 out). 2-out RBI: L.Smith Pendleton. RBI scoring position less than 2 outs: Belliard 0-1 Willard 1-1. SF: Willard.
▶**BASERUNNING** — SB: L.Smith (1 2nd base off Morris/Harper); Gant (1 2nd base off Morris/Harper). Team LOB: 7.

▶PITCHING	ip	h	r	er	bb	so	era
MINNESOTA							
Morris	6	6	1	1	3	4	2.08
Willis,BS,1	1.1	1	1	1	0	1	2.70
Guthrie,L,0-1	1	1	1	1	1	1	2.45
Bedrosian	.1	0	0	0	0	0	0.00
ATLANTA							
Smoltz	7	7	2	2	0	7	2.57
Wohlers	.1	0	0	0	1	0	1-0
Stanton W,1-0	1.2	0	0	0	0	1	0.00

IBB: Blauser by Guthrie. **WP:** Morris. Inherited runners/scored: Stanton 1/0; Bedrosian 2/1. Pitches-strikes: Smoltz 96-66; Wohlers 10-6; Stanton 26-17; Morris 94-50; Willis 17-12; Guthrie 14-8; Bedrosian 4-3. Ground balls-fly balls: Smoltz 9-7; Wohlers 1-0; Stanton 0-3; Morris 5-8; Willis 1-3; Guthrie 1-2; Bedrosian 0-1.
▶**GAME DATA** — T: 2:57. A: 50,878. Temp: 72. Wind: 6 mph right to left.
▶**UMPIRES** — HP: Tata. 1B: Reed. 2B: Montague. 3B: Denkinger. LF: Wendelstedt RF: Coble.

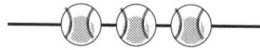

World Series: Game Five

ATLANTA 14, MINNESOTA 5

Hero: David Justice. His two-run homer started the offensive explosion, and he finished with 5 RBI.

Goat: Twins' reliever David West, who failed to retire any of the six batters he faced in his two appearances—including four batters in Game 5.

Back-to-back-to-back homers: Lonnie Smith joined an elite group when he homered in his third consecutive game. He is the first in the National League to accomplish the feat, and the fifth overall. All four of the others did it while playing for the Yankees: Lou Gehrig, 1928; Johnny Mize, 1953; Hank Bauer, 1958; Reggie Jackson, 1977.

Red hot Chili: Chili Davis said he started Game 5 in the outfield because Twins' manager Tom Kelly "got kind of tired of seeing me on the bench."

Fans got to Hrbek: Did the threatening phone calls and constant chanting by the Braves' fans affect Twin Kent Hrbek's play in Atlanta? Manager Kelly said Hrbek was quieter than usual and that he wished umpire Drew Coble "had called (Gant) safe so we wouldn't have to listen to all this crap." Hrbek himself went so far as to confront a Braves fan in an Atlanta restaurant after hearing the man refer to him as a cheater. "I asked him how he was doing," Hrbek told the *St. Paul Pioneer Press*. Nothing came of the incident.

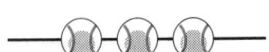

Game 5 box score
Braves 14, Twins 5

```
MINNESOTA    000 003 011  5
ATLANTA      000 410 63x  14
```

TWINS	ab	r	h	bi	lo	bb	so	avg
Gladden, lf	5	1	1	0	1	0	1	.190
Knoblauch, 2b	3	1	1	0	0	1	1	.353
Bedrosian, p	0	0	0	0	0	0	0	-
Ortiz, c	1	0	0	1	0	0	0	.333
Puckett, cf	2	1	1	0	0	0	0	.167
Brown, ph-cf	2	0	0	0	0	0	0	.000
Davis, rf	3	2	1	0	0	1	0	.300
Willis, p	0	0	0	0	0	0	0	-
Harper, c	2	0	1	1	1	1	1	.400
Bush, ph-rf	1	0	0	0	0	0	0	.000
Leius, 3b	2	0	1	1	0	1	1	.273
West, p	0	0	0	0	0	0	0	-
Newman, 2b	1	0	1	1	0	0	0	.500
Hrbek, 1b	3	0	0	1	0	0	0	.158
Sorrento, ph-1b	0	0	0	0	0	1	0	.000
Gagne, ss	4	0	1	0	4	0	0	.167
Tapani, p	1	0	0	0	0	0	0	.000
Larkin, ph	1	0	0	0	1	0	0	.333
Leach, p	0	0	0	0	0	0	0	-
Pagliarulo, ph-3b	2	0	0	0	0	0	0	.429
TOTALS	**33**	**5**	**7**	**5**	**7**	**5**	**4**	

▶BATTING — 2B: Gagne (1, off Glavine). 3B: Gladden (2, off St. Claire); Newman (1, off Clancy). 2-out RBI: Newman.
▶RBI, scoring position, less than 2 outs: Ortiz 0-1, Davis 0-1, Harper 1-1, Leius 1-1, Hrbek 1-2, Tapani 0-1. S: Puckett.
▶BASERUNNING—CS: Leius (1, 2nd base by Glavine). Team LOB: 7.
▶FIELDING — E: Harper (1, throw). DP: 1.

ATLANTA	ab	r	h	bi	lo	bb	so	avg
L.Smith, lf	5	1	1	1	2	0	1	.211
Mitchell, lf	0	0	0	0	0	0	0	.000
Pendleton, 3b	4	3	2	0	0	1	0	.300
Gant, cf	4	3	3	1	0	1	1	.381
Justice, rf	5	2	2	5	0	0	1	.300
Bream, 1b	2	0	0	0	1	1	1	.125
Hunter, ph-1b	2	2	2	2	0	0	0	.250
Olson, c	5	1	3	0	4	0	0	.333
St. Claire, p	0	0	0	0	0	0	0	-
Lemke, 2b	4	2	2	3	1	1	1	.438
Belliard, ss	4	0	2	2	2	0	0	.333
Glavine, p	2	0	0	0	0	0	0	.000
Mercker, p	0	0	0	0	0	0	0	-
Gregg, ph	1	0	0	0	0	0	0	.000
Clancy, p	1	0	0	0	1	0	1	.000
Cabrera, c	0	0	0	0	0	0	0	.000
TOTALS	**39**	**14**	**17**	**14**	**11**	**4**	**6**	

▶BATTING — 2B: Pendleton (2, off Willis); Belliard (1, off Tapani). 3B: Gant (1, off Willis); Lemke 2 (3, off Tapani; off Bedrosian). HR: L.Smith (3, 7th inning off West, 0 on, 0 out); Justice (2, 4th inning off Tapani, 1 on, 0 out); Hunter (1, 8th inning off Willis, 0 on, 1 out). RBI, scoring position, less than 2 outs: Gant 1-1, Justice 4-4, Bream 0-1, Hunter 1-1, Olson 0-1, Lemke 3-3, Belliard 2-2, Glavine 0-1. GDP: Lemke.
▶BASERUNNING — SB: Justice (2, 2nd base off Leach/Harper); Olson (1, 2nd base off Tapani/Harper). Team LOB: 5.
▶FIELDING — E: Pendleton (2, ground ball).

▶PITCHING	IP	H	R	ER	BB	SO	ERA
MINNESOTA							
Tapani L,1-1	4	6	4	4	2	4	4.50
Leach	2	2	1	1	0	1	3.86
West	0	2	4	4	2	0	-
Bedrosian	1	3	2	2	0	1	5.40
Willis	1	4	3	3	0	0	8.31
ATLANTA							
Glavine W,1-1	5.1	4	3	3	4	2	4.05
Mercker H,1	.2	0	0	0	0	0	0.00
Clancy H,1	2	2	1	1	1	2	4.15
St. Claire	1	1	1	1	0	0	9.00

▶WP: Bedrosian. Inherited runners/scored: Mercker 3/1; Bedrosian 2/2. Pitches-strikes: Glavine 85-43; Mercker 5-3; Clancy 37-23; St. Claire 6-5; Tapani 54-33; Leach 30-19; West 14-4; Bedrosian 25-18; Willis 16-11. Ground balls-fly balls: Glavine 10-5; Mercker 2-0; Clancy 4-0; St. Claire 1-2; Tapani 6-2; Leach 3-3; West 1-1; Bedrosian 2-2; Willis 2-1.
▶GAME DATA — T: 2:59. A: 50,878. Temp: 72. Wind: 9 mph, right to left.
▶UMPIRES — HP: Reed. 1B: Montague. 2B: Denkinger. 3B: Wendelstedt.

MINNESOTA 4, ATLANTA 3
(11 innings)

Best post-game quote: "I'm just glad this is over with. I feel like I just went 15 rounds with Evander Holyfield." —Kirby Puckett.

Hero: Puckett, who hit a solo homer in the bottom of the 11th inning, making sure the series went to seven games. That was after he hit an RBI triple down the third base line in the first inning and made a leaping catch of a sure double by Ron Gant in the third inning. He also hit an RBI fly, singled, and stole a base for good measure.

Goat: Braves' Charlie Liebrandt, who saw his fourth pitch of the night disappear into the centerfield seats, above the Harmon Killebrew sign.

Defense saved Erickson: Twins' starter Scott Erickson survived six-plus innings on offspeed stuff and a little help from his friends. Outfielder Dan Gladden made a running grab of Sid Bream's opposite-field line drive in the first inning with two men on base, third baseman Scott Leius leapt to snare Brian Hunter's line drive and, of course, Puckett tracked down Gant's long fly to center field in the third inning.

Just one more great play: With the game tied in the top of the 10th inning and Braves' Terry Pendleton on first, Gant smashed a hit-and-run liner, but Twins' shortstop Greg Gagne moved to the bag and gloved it. Instead of men on first and third with no outs, it was a double play. The Twins won it an inning later.

Missed opportunities: The Twins were 2 for their last 35 at-bats with runners in scoring position.

Tape-measure foul: Atlanta slugger David Justice ripped a Scott Erickson pitch into the upper deck in right field. It was foul by the width of one seat.

Broken bat, broken slump: Minnesota's Shane Mack, who was benched for Game 5 in Atlanta, broke out of an 0-for-15 slump with a broken-bat RBI single in the first inning. He went 2-for-4 in the game.

Game 6 box score
Twins 4, Braves 3

Atlanta	000 020 100 00	3				
Minnesota	200 010 000 01	4				

ATLANTA	ab	r	h	bi	lo	bb	so	avg
L.Smith, dh	3	1	0	0	2	1	0	.182
Pendleton, 3b	5	1	4	2	1	0	0	.400
Gant, cf	5	0	0	1	2	0	0	.308
Justice, rf	4	0	0	0	3	1	1	.250
Bream, 1b	4	0	1	0	2	1	0	.150
Mitchell, pr-lf	0	0	0	0	0	0	0	.000
Hunter, lf-1b	5	0	0	0	1	0	0	.176
Olson, c	5	0	0	0	1	0	1	.261
Lemke, 2b	4	1	2	0	1	0	0	.450
Belliard, ss	2	0	1	0	1	0	1	.357
Gregg, ph	0	0	0	0	0	0	0	.000
Blauser, ph-ss	2	0	1	0	1	0	1	.200
Totals	39	3	9	3	15	3	4	

▶BATTING — HR: Pendleton (2, 5th inning off Erickson, 1 on, 1 out).
RBI, scoring position, less than 2 outs: Pendleton 1-1, Gant 1-2. GDP:
L.Smith.
▶BASERUNNING — CS: Mitchell (1, 2nd base by Aguilera/Harper).
Team LOB:
▶FIELDING — E: Hunter (1, 2-base fly). DP: 2.

MINNESOTA	ab	r	h	bi	lo	bb	so	avg
Gladden, lf	4	1	0	0	1	1	0	.160
Knoblauch, 2b	5	1	1	0	0	0	0	.318
Puckett, cf	4	2	3	3	0	0	1	.273
Davis, dh	4	0	0	0	2	0	1	.214
Mack, rf	4	0	2	1	1	0	0	.105
Leius, 3b	3	0	2	0	1	0	0	.357
Pagliarulo, ph-3b	1	0	0	0	0	0	1	.375
Hrbek, 1b	4	0	0	0	3	0	1	.130
Ortiz, c	2	0	0	0	2	0	1	.200
Harper, ph-c	2	0	0	0	0	0	1	.353
Gagne, ss	4	0	1	0	2	0	0	.182
Totals	37	4	9	4	12	1	6	

▶BATTING — 2B: Mack (1, off Avery). 3B: Puckett (1, off Avery). HR:
Puckett (2, 11th inning off Leibrandt, 0 on, 0 out). 2-out RBI: Mack.
RBI, scoring position, less than 2 outs: Knoblauch 0-1, Puckett 2-2,
Davis 0-1, Leius 0-1, Ortiz 0-2. SF: Puckett. GDP: Gladden, Hrbek.
▶BASERUNNING — SB: Gladden (2, 2nd base off Avery/Olson); Puckett (1, 2nd base off Stanton/Olson). Team LOB: 5.
▶FIELDING — DP: 2.

▶PITCHING ATLANTA	ip	h	r	er	bb	so	era
Avery	6	6	3	3	1	3	3.46
Stanton	2	2	0	0	0	1	0.00
Pena	2	0	0	0	0	2	2.25
Leibrandt L,0-2	0	1	1	1	0	0	11.25
MINNESOTA							
Erickson	6	5	3	3	2	2	5.06
Guthrie H,2	.1	1	0	0	1	1	2.25
Willis B S,2	2.2	1	0	0	0	1	5.14
Aguilera W,1-1	2	2	0	0	0	0	1.80

Erickson pitched to 1 batter in 7th; Leibrandt pitched to 1 batter
in 11th. HBP: L.Smith by Erickson. WP: Guthrie. Inherited run-
ners/scored: Guthrie 1/0; Willis 3/1. Pitches-strikes: Erickson 102-58;
Guthrie 13-8; Willis 33-21; Aguilera 15-11; Avery 83-55; Stanton 36-
24; Pena 24-16; Leibrandt 4-2. Ground balls-fly balls: Erickson 11-6;
Guthrie 1-0; Willis 4-3; Aguilera 1-3; Avery 10-7; Stanton 2-3; Pena
3-1; Leibrandt 0-1.
▶GAME DATA — T: 3:46. A: 55,155. Indoors.
▶UMPIRES — HP: Montague. 1B: Denkinger. 2B: Wendelstedt. 3B:
Coble. LF: Tata RF: Reed

MINNESOTA 1, ATLANTA 0
(10 innings)

When nine full innings of Game 7 had been played and neither team had won the Series—or even scored a run—most fans were satisfied that the 1991 World Series was, in fact, a draw.

Even the players saw it that way. Atlanta batting champion Terry Pendleton said Twins' catcher Brian Harper "told me in the 10th inning, the way both teams had played, why didn't we just quit and call it a tie."

But there are no ties in baseball—at least not officially—and eventually Dan Gladden scored the lone run that would give the Twins a hard-earned victory. Both teams accepted the outcome graciously, but no one could deny that it was heartbreaking to see either team lose this one.

It was left to 21-year-old Steve Avery—the youngest member of the Atlanta Braves—to display the emotion that the whole team must have felt. Sitting on a chair pulled deep into his locker, Avery buried his head into a towel and cried.

Some of the game's highlights:

MVP: Jack Morris, a not-so-old man at 36, threw a 10-inning shutout, escaping tough innings and getting stronger in his last two innings. He stretched his scoreless streak to 13 innings.

Hero: Gene Larkin, whose RBI single in the bottom of the 10th inning gave the Twins the world championship.

Goat: Lonnie Smith, who went for a fake throw from second baseman Chuck Knoblauch to shortstop Greg Gagne on a double by Terry Pendleton in the eighth inning, hesitated, and cost the Braves a run—and probably the championship game.

Great play: Rookie Chuck Knoblauch got down a 10th-inning sacrifice to move Dan Gladden to third with one out.

Worst inning: The eighth. The Braves and Twins took turns loading 'em up with one out and then hitting into a double play to waste the opportunity.

Home field advantage: Both teams won every home game, but the Twins were favored by the schedule—they played four at home and won the series.

Game 7 box score
Twins 1 Braves 0

Atlanta	000 000 000 0 - 0
Minnesota	000 000 000 1 - 1

ATLANTA	ab	r	h	bi	lo	bb	so	avg
L.Smith dh	4	0	2	0	0	1	1	.231
Pendleton 3b	5	0	1	0	4	0	0	.367
Gant cf	4	0	0	0	6	0	2	.267
Justice rf	3	0	1	0	0	1	1	.259
Bream 1b	4	0	0	0	3	0	0	.125
Hunter lf	4	0	1	0	1	0	1	.190
Olson c	4	0	0	0	2	0	1	.222
Lemke 2b	4	0	1	0	0	0	1	.417
Belliard ss	2	0	1	0	0	0	1	.375
Blauser ph-ss	1	0	0	0	0	0	0	.167
Totals	35	0	7	0	16	2	8	

▸BATTING — 2B: Pendleton (3 off Morris); Hunter (1 off Morris). RBI scoring position less than 2 outs: Pendleton 0-2 Gant 0-2 Bream 0-2 Hunter 0-1. S: Belliard. GDP: Bream.
▸BASERUNNING — Team LOB: 8.
▸FIELDING — DP: 3.

MINNESOTA	ab	r	h	bi	lo	bb	so	avg
Gladden lf	5	1	3	0	1	0	1	.233
Knoblauch 2b	4	0	1	0	1	0	0	.308
Puckett cf	2	0	0	0	1	3	1	.250
Hrbek 1b	3	0	0	0	4	1	0	.115
Davis dh	4	0	1	0	2	0	1	.222
Brown pr-dh	0	0	0	0	0	0	0	.000
Larkin ph	1	0	1	1	0	0	0	.500
Harper c	4	0	2	0	1	0	0	.381
Mack rf	4	0	1	0	3	0	0	.130
Pagliarulo 3b	3	0	0	0	2	1	0	.273
Gagne ss	2	0	0	0	0	0	1	.167
Bush ph	1	0	1	0	0	0	0	.250
Newman pr-ss	0	0	0	0	0	0	0	.500
Sorrento ph	1	0	0	0	2	0	1	.000
Leius ss	0	0	0	0	0	0	0	.357
Totals	34	1	10	1	17	5	5	

▸BATTING — 2B: Gladden 2 (2 off Smoltz; off Pena). RBI scoring position less than 2 outs: Knoblauch 0-1 Hrbek 0-2 Larkin 1-1 Mack 0-1. S: Knoblauch. GDP: Mack Davis.
▸BASERUNNING — Team LOB: 12.
▸FIELDING — PB: Harper. DP: 1.

▸PITCHING	ip	h	r	er	bb	so	era
ATLANTA							
Smoltz	7.1	6	0	0	1	4	1.26
Stanton	.2	2	0	0	1	0	0.00
Pena L,0-1	1.1	2	1	1	3	1	3.38
MINNESOTA							
Morris W,2-0	10	7	0	0	2	8	1.17

Stanton pitched to 2 batters in 9th.
▸IBB: Puckett 2 by Stanton; by Pena; Hrbek by Pena; Pagliarulo by Pena; Justice by Morris. HBP: Hrbek by Smoltz. Inherited runners/scored: Stanton 2/0; Pena 2/0. Pitches-strikes: Morris 122-79; Smoltz 104-68; Stanton 16-11; Pena 12-11. Ground balls-fly balls: Morris 12-9; Smoltz 9-10; Stanton 0-1; Pena 1-2.
▸GAME DATA — T: 3:23. A: 55,118. Indoors.
▸UMPIRES — HP: Denkinger. 1B: Wendelstedt. 2B: Coble. 3B: Tata. LF: Reed. RF: Montague.

53

The World Series

Series had marks of excellence, error

A look at the 1991 World Series participants who pitched, batted or fielded their way into the record book:

CHUCK KNOBLAUCH—Most postseason hits by a rookie (15): The favorite for AL Rookie of the Year hustled his way into the record book past Fred Lynn (Boston, 1975) and Jimmy Sebring (Pittsburgh, 1903), who each had 11 hits.

LONNIE SMITH—Most clubs, total series, playing one or more games (4): Smith is hitting .290 in World Series after championships with Phillies (1980), Cardinals (1982) and Royals (1985).

RON GANT—Most at-bats, extra-inning game, no hits (6): There have been only 47 extra-inning World Series games (more in 1991 alone than in all of the 1980s) and only one game longer than 12 innings. Gant tied several players with his 0-for-6 in Game Three.

MARK LEMKE—Most triples, game (2): In Atlanta's 14-5 Game Five rout, had two triples (off Kevin Tapani and Steve Bedrosian) and three RBI. He was the sixth player to triple twice and the first since Tommy Davis in 1963 for the Dodgers.

MARK LEMKE—Most triples, seven-game series (3): In Game Four, Lemke tripled and scored on Jerry Willard's sacrifice fly in the bottom of the ninth.

JACK MORRIS—Most games started, seven-game series (3): tied record held by many, many pitchers, the last one being Frank Viola of the Mets in 1987.

JACK MORRIS—Most wild pitches, game (2): the first double-wild pitch World Series game since the earthquake. Again, a popular record, done 12 times previously. Oakland's Mike Moore, the last pitcher to accomplish the feat, threw two pitches away in Game Two of the 1989 Series.

CHARLIE LEIBRANDT—Most games lost, seven-game series (2): Some questioned his start in Game One, where he gave up four runs and seven hits in four innings. Then he served up Kirby Puckett's game-winner in a relief role in 11th inning of Game Six. The last pitcher to tie this record was Danny Cox of the St. Louis Cardinals, who also had Twin losses in 1987.

TOM GLAVINE—Most bases-on-balls, inning (4): After cruising through the first five innings of Game Five allowing three hits and no walks, Glavine suddenly couldn't throw a strike, walking in two runs.

TOM GLAVINE—Most consecutive bases-on-balls (3): Chili Davis, Brian Harper and Scott Leius were the beneficiaries, with Harper and Leius picking up cheap RBI. Of course, the Braves still won the game by nine runs.   — *John Hunt*

The Players' Share

The spoils of victory—and defeat.

The Twins' World Series victory brought them a record payday and brought four young players more than they earned during the regular season.

A full winning share was $119,593, which was almost $20,000 more than the major league minimum paid to Minnesota series stalwarts Scott Leius and Chuck Knoblauch during the rest of the year.

The full losers' share for the Atlanta Braves was $73,331. Players vote on share distribution before the season ends, and Otis Nixon, who missed the postseason because of his suspension, was voted a full share.

One for the books

Even critics who argued that the two teams may not have been the best in baseball, agreed that they were certainly the most closely matched. It was the first time in 67 years that Game 7 went into extra innings. Here are some other down-to-the-wire facts about the 1991 classic:

Four games decided in the last at-bat.

Four games decided in the last inning.

Five games decided by one run.

Three games went into extra innings.

All games won by the home team.

Game 7 was the first extra-inning finale since 1924, when the Washington Senators beat the N.Y. Giants 4-3 in 12 innings.

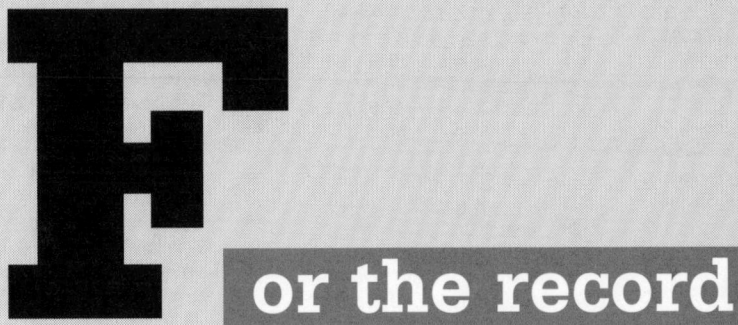

For the record

USA SNAPSHOTS®

A look at statistics that shape the sports world

Counting division titles

Major league baseball teams finishing first the most and least times in 23 years of divisional play:

Most — Oakland **9** American League — Least — Cleveland, Seattle[1], Texas[2] **0**

Pittsburgh **8** National League — Montreal, San Diego **1**

1—Began play in 1977   2—Moved from Washington in 1972

Source: USA TODAY research   By Keith Carter, USA TODAY

Active player records

Games played: Most, career, active players

2606	Dwight Evans, 1972-1991
2579	Robin Yount, 1974-1991
2551	Dave Winfield, 1973-1991
2466	Dave Parker, 1973-1991
2412	Carlton Fisk, 1969-1991
2410	George Brett, 1973-1991
2288	Eddie Murray, 1977-1991
2237	Brian Downing, 1973-1991
2201	Gary Carter, 1974-1991
2167	Andre Dawson, 1976-1991

At-bats: Most, career, active players

9997	Robin Yount, 1974-1991
9464	Dave Winfield, 1973-1991
9358	Dave Parker, 1973-1991
9197	George Brett, 1973-1991
8996	Dwight Evans, 1972-1991
8573	Eddie Murray, 1977-1991
8515	Carlton Fisk, 1969-1991
8348	Andre Dawson, 1976-1991
7856	Dale Murphy, 1976-1991
7732	Willie Randolph, 1975-1991

Runs: Most, career, active players

1499	Robin Yount, 1974-1991
1470	Dwight Evans, 1972-1991
1459	George Brett, 1973-1991
1459	Dave Winfield, 1973-1991
1395	Rickey Henderson, 1979-1991
1279	Eddie Murray, 1977-1991
1272	Dave Parker, 1973-1991
1262	Carlton Fisk, 1969-1991
1210	Willie Randolph, 1975-1991
1199	Andre Dawson, 1976-1991

Hits: Most, career, active players

2878	Robin Yount, 1974-1991
2836	George Brett, 1973-1991
2712	Dave Parker, 1973-1991
2697	Dave Winfield, 1973-1991
2502	Eddie Murray, 1977-1991
2446	Dwight Evans, 1972-1991
2354	Andre Dawson, 1976-1991
2303	Carlton Fisk, 1969-1991
2143	Ken Griffey Sr, 1973-1991
2138	Willie Randolph, 1975-1991

Total bases: Most, career, active players

4566	George Brett, 1973-1991
4535	Dave Winfield, 1973-1991
4405	Dave Parker, 1973-1991
4341	Robin Yount, 1974-1991
4230	Dwight Evans, 1972-1991
4181	Eddie Murray, 1977-1991
4086	Andre Dawson, 1976-1991
3928	Carlton Fisk, 1969-1991
3709	Dale Murphy, 1976-1991
3400	Gary Carter, 1974-1991

2B: Most, career, active players

599	George Brett, 1973-1991
526	Dave Parker, 1973-1991
518	Robin Yount, 1974-1991
483	Dwight Evans, 1972-1991
460	Dave Winfield, 1973-1991
425	Eddie Murray, 1977-1991
417	Andre Dawson, 1976-1991
417	Carlton Fisk, 1969-1991
400	Wade Boggs, 1982-1991
369	Paul Molitor, 1978-1991

3B: Most, career, active players

137	Willie Wilson, 1976-1991
129	George Brett, 1973-1991
120	Robin Yount, 1974-1991
106	Garry Templeton, 1976-1991
92	Andre Dawson, 1976-1991
88	Brett Butler, 1981-1991
87	Tim Raines, 1979-1991
81	Willie McGee, 1982-1991
81	Juan Samuel, 1983-1991
80	Dave Winfield, 1973-1991

HR: Most, career, active players

406	Dave Winfield, 1973-1991
398	Eddie Murray, 1977-1991
396	Dale Murphy, 1976-1991
385	Dwight Evans, 1972-1991
377	Andre Dawson, 1976-1991
372	Carlton Fisk, 1969-1991
339	Dave Parker, 1973-1991
335	Jack Clark, 1975-1991
319	Gary Carter, 1974-1991
304	Lance Parrish, 1977-1991

RBI: Most, career, active players

1602	Dave Winfield, 1973-1991
1493	Dave Parker, 1973-1991
1469	Eddie Murray, 1977-1991
1459	George Brett, 1973-1991
1384	Dwight Evans, 1972-1991
1335	Andre Dawson, 1976-1991
1305	Carlton Fisk, 1969-1991
1278	Robin Yount, 1974-1991
1252	Dale Murphy, 1976-1991
1196	Gary Carter, 1974-1991

SB: Most, career, active players

994	Rickey Henderson, 1979-1991
685	Tim Raines, 1979-1991
632	Willie Wilson, 1976-1991
586	Vince Coleman, 1985-1991
499	Ozzie Smith, 1978-1991
407	Steve Sax, 1981-1991
396	Brett Butler, 1981-1991
381	Paul Molitor, 1978-1991
356	Lonnie Smith, 1978-1991
341	Juan Samuel, 1983-1991

BB: Most, career, active players

1391	Dwight Evans, 1972-1991
1206	Jack Clark, 1975-1991
1203	Willie Randolph, 1975-1991
1191	Rickey Henderson, 1979-1991
1135	Brian Downing, 1973-1991
1081	Eddie Murray, 1977-1991
1044	Dave Winfield, 1973-1991
1022	George Brett, 1973-1991
980	Dale Murphy, 1976-1991
966	Lou Whitaker, 1977-1991

HBP: Most, career, active players

141	Carlton Fisk, 1969-1991
121	Brian Downing, 1973-1991
83	Lonnie Smith, 1978-1991
81	Andre Dawson, 1976-1991
66	Gary Carter, 1974-1991
58	Lloyd Moseby, 1980-1991
58	Juan Samuel, 1983-1991
58	Willie Wilson, 1976-1991
57	Carney Lansford, 1978-1991
56	Dave Parker, 1973-1991
56	Tim Wallach, 1980-1991

GIDP: Most, career, active players

282	Dave Winfield, 1973-1991
227	Dwight Evans, 1972-1991
215	Eddie Murray, 1977-1991
213	Willie Randolph, 1975-1991
209	Dave Parker, 1973-1991
202	Carlton Fisk, 1969-1991
201	Dale Murphy, 1976-1991
200	George Brett, 1973-1991
196	Robin Yount, 1974-1991
193	Cal Ripken, 1981-1991

BA: Highest, career, active players

.345	Wade Boggs, 1982-1991
.328	Tony Gwynn, 1982-1991
.320	Kirby Puckett, 1984-1991
.314	Don Mattingly, 1982-1991
.311	Mike Greenwell, 1985-1991
.308	George Brett, 1973-1991
.302	Rafael Palmeiro, 1986-1991
.302	Julio Franco, 1982-1991
.302	Pedro Guerrero, 1978-1991
.302	Luis Polonia, 1987-1991

Slug avg: Highest, career, active players

.527	Cecil Fielder, 1985-1991
.522	Fred McGriff, 1986-1991
.518	Jose Canseco, 1985-1991
.517	Kevin Mitchell, 1984-1991
.516	Darryl Strawberry, 1983-1991
.514	Danny Tartabull, 1984-1991
.512	Will Clark, 1986-1991
.509	Eric Davis, 1984-1991
.496	George Brett, 1973-1991
.491	Don Mattingly, 1982-1991

Extra-base hits: Most, career, active players

1019	George Brett, 1973-1991
946	Dave Winfield, 1973-1991
941	Dwight Evans, 1972-1991
940	Dave Parker, 1973-1991
886	Andre Dawson, 1976-1991
873	Robin Yount, 1974-1991
853	Eddie Murray, 1977-1991

835 Carlton Fisk, 1969-1991
783 Dale Murphy, 1976-1991
702 Gary Carter, 1974-1991

Pitchers

Games: Most, career, active players

897 Rich Gossage, 1972-1991
776 Charlie Hough, 1970-1991
767 Nolan Ryan, 1966-1991
751 Jeff Reardon, 1979-1991
717 Lee Smith, 1980-1991
671 Dennis Eckersley, 1975-1991
667 Bert Blyleven, 1970-1991
618 Dennis Lamp, 1977-1991
613 Bob McClure, 1975-1991
608 Steve Bedrosian, 1981-1991

Complete games: Most, career, active players

241 Bert Blyleven, 1970-1991
220 Nolan Ryan, 1966-1991
164 Jack Morris, 1977-1991
140 Frank Tanana, 1973-1991
107 Fern. Valenzuela, 1980-1991
102 Charlie Hough, 1970-1991
102 Dennis Martinez, 1976-1991
102 Rick Reuschel, 1972-1991
102 Dave Stieb, 1979-1991
101 Mike Flanagan, 1975-1991

Shutouts: Most, career, active players

61 Nolan Ryan, 1966-1991
60 Bert Blyleven, 1970-1991
34 Frank Tanana, 1973-1991
30 Dave Stieb, 1979-1991
29 Roger Clemens, 1984-1991
29 Fern. Valenzuela, 1980-1991
28 Bob Welch, 1978-1991
26 Jack Morris, 1977-1991
26 Rick Reuschel, 1972-1991
23 Orel Hershiser, 1983-1991
23 Dennis Martinez, 1976-1991

Wins: Most, career, active players

314 Nolan Ryan, 1966-1991
279 Bert Blyleven, 1970-1991
220 Frank Tanana, 1973-1991
216 Jack Morris, 1977-1991
214 Rick Reuschel, 1972-1991
195 Charlie Hough, 1970-1991
188 Bob Welch, 1978-1991
177 Dennis Martinez, 1976-1991
175 John Candelaria, 1975-1991
174 Dennis Eckersley, 1975-1991

Losses: Most, career, active players

278 Nolan Ryan, 1966-1991
238 Bert Blyleven, 1970-1991
208 Frank Tanana, 1973-1991
191 Rick Reuschel, 1972-1991
179 Charlie Hough, 1970-1991
167 Jim Clancy, 1977-1991
162 Jack Morris, 1977-1991
145 Dennis Martinez, 1976-1991

144 Dennis Eckersley, 1975-1991
143 Mike Flanagan, 1975-1991

HR allowed: Most, career, active players

413 Bert Blyleven, 1970-1991
398 Frank Tanana, 1973-1991
339 Jack Morris, 1977-1991
327 Charlie Hough, 1970-1991
307 Nolan Ryan, 1966-1991
302 Dennis Eckersley, 1975-1991
288 Floyd Bannister, 1977-1991
274 Dennis Martinez, 1976-1991
258 Frank Viola, 1982-1991
248 Mike Flanagan, 1975-1991

BB: Most career, active players

2686 Nolan Ryan, 1966-1991
1476 Charlie Hough, 1970-1991
1293 Bert Blyleven, 1970-1991
1178 Jack Morris, 1977-1991
1110 Frank Tanana, 1973-1991
960 Dave Stieb, 1979-1991
947 Jim Clancy, 1977-1991
935 Rick Reuschel, 1972-1991
918 Fern. Valenzuela, 1980-1991
901 Rick Sutcliffe, 1976-1991

K: Most, career, active players

5511 Nolan Ryan, 1966-1991
3631 Bert Blyleven, 1970-1991
2566 Frank Tanana, 1973-1991
2143 Jack Morris, 1977-1991
2095 Charlie Hough, 1970-1991
2025 Dennis Eckersley, 1975-1991
2015 Rick Reuschel, 1972-1991
1815 Bob Welch, 1978-1991
1764 Fern. Valenzuela, 1980-1991
1693 Floyd Bannister, 1977-1991

Wild pitches: Most, career, active players

265 Nolan Ryan, 1966-1991
170 Jack Morris, 1977-1991
149 Charlie Hough, 1970-1991
111 Bert Blyleven, 1970-1990
101 Jim Clancy, 1977-1991
101 Frank Tanana, 1973-1991
98 Dave Stewart, 1978-1991
95 Fern. Valenzuela, 1980-1991
89 Rick Reuschel, 1972-1991
88 Rick Sutcliffe, 1976-1991

Win pct: Highest, career, active players

.714 Dwight Gooden, 1984-1991
.687 Roger Clemens, 1984-1991
.622 Teddy Higuera, 1985-1991
.620 David Cone, 1986-1991
.613 Orel Hershiser, 1983-1991
.606 Bob Welch, 1978-1991
.606 John Candelaria, 1975-1991
.602 Jimmy Key, 1984-1991
.588 John Smiley, 1986-1991
.588 Tom Browning, 1984-1991

ERA: Lowest, career, active players

2.67 Dave Smith, 1980-1991
2.77 Orel Hershiser, 1983-1991
2.82 Jesse Orosco, 1979-1991
2.84 Lee Smith, 1980-1991
2.85 Roger Clemens, 1984-1991
2.90 Alejandro Pena, 1981-1991
2.91 Dwight Gooden, 1984-1991
2.94 Rich Gossage, 1972-1991
2.99 Tim Belcher, 1987-1991
3.03 Craig Lefferts, 1983-1991

Innings: Most, career, active players

5162.1 Nolan Ryan, 1966-1991
4837.0 Bert Blyleven, 1970-1991
3799.0 Frank Tanana, 1973-1991
3548.1 Rick Reuschel, 1972-1991
3307.0 Charlie Hough, 1970-1991
3289.1 Jack Morris, 1977-1991
2933.0 Dennis Martinez, 1976-1991
2891.1 Dennis Eckersley, 1975-1991
2735.1 Mike Flanagan, 1975-1991
2733.0 Bob Welch, 1978-1991

American League single-season records

(active players in caps)

At-bats: Most, season, AL

705 WILLIE WILSON, KC-1980
692 Bobby Richardson, NY-1962
691 KIRBY PUCKETT, Min-1985
689 Sandy Alomar, Cal-1971
687 TONY FERNANDEZ, Tor-1986
686 Horace Clarke, NY-1970
680 KIRBY PUCKETT, Min-1986
679 Harvey Kuenn, Det-1953
679 Bobby Richardson, NY-1964
677 DON MATTINGLY, NY-1986
677 Jim Rice, Bos-1978

Runs: Most, season, AL

177 Babe Ruth, NY-1921
167 Lou Gehrig, NY-1936
163 Lou Gehrig, NY-1931
163 Babe Ruth, NY-1928
158 Babe Ruth, NY-1920
158 Babe Ruth, NY-1927
152 Al Simmons, Phi-1930
151 Joe DiMaggio, NY-1937
151 Jimmie Foxx, Phi-1932
151 Babe Ruth, NY-1923

Hits: Most, season, AL

257 George Sisler, StL-1920
253 Al Simmons, Phi-1925
248 Ty Cobb, Det-1911
246 George Sisler, StL-1922
241 Heinie Manush, StL-1928
240 WADE BOGGS, Bos-1985
239 Rod Carew, Min-1977
238 DON MATTINGLY, NY-1986
237 Harry Heilmann, Det-1921
236 Jack Tobin, StL-1921

Total bases: Most, season, AL

457	Babe Ruth, NY-1921
447	Lou Gehrig, NY-1927
438	Jimmie Foxx, Phi-1932
419	Lou Gehrig, NY-1930
418	Joe DiMaggio, NY-1937
417	Babe Ruth, NY-1927
410	Lou Gehrig, NY-1931
409	Lou Gehrig, NY-1934
406	Jim Rice, Bos-1978
405	Hal Trosky, Cle-1936

2B: Most, season, AL

67	Earl Webb, Bos-1931
64	George Burns, Cle-1926
63	Hank Greenberg, Det-1934
60	Charlie Gehringer, Det-1936
59	Tris Speaker, Cle-1923
56	George Kell, Det-1950
55	Gee Walker, Det-1936
54	Hal McRae, KC-1977
53	DON MATTINGLY, NY-1986
53	Al Simmons, Phi-1926
53	Tris Speaker, Bos-1912

3B: Most, season, AL

26	Sam Crawford, Det-1914
26	Joe Jackson, Cle-1912
25	Sam Crawford, Det-1903
24	Ty Cobb, Det-1911
24	Ty Cobb, Det-1917
23	Ty Cobb, Det-1912
23	Earle Combs, NY-1927
23	Sam Crawford, Det-1913
23	Dale Mitchell, Cle-1949
22	Bill Bradley, Cle-1903
22	Earle Combs, NY-1930
22	Birdie Cree, NY-1911
22	Elmer Flick, Cle-1906
22	Tris Speaker, Bos-1913
22	Snuffy Stirnweiss, NY-1945

HR: Most, season, AL

61	Roger Maris, NY-1961
60	Babe Ruth, NY-1927
59	Babe Ruth, NY-1921
58	Jimmie Foxx, Phi-1932
58	Hank Greenberg, Det-1938
54	Mickey Mantle, NY-1961
54	Babe Ruth, NY-1920
54	Babe Ruth, NY-1928
52	Mickey Mantle, NY-1956
51	CECIL FIELDER, Det-1990

RBI: Most, season, AL

184	Lou Gehrig, NY-1931
183	Hank Greenberg, Det-1937
175	Jimmie Foxx, Bos-1938
175	Lou Gehrig, NY-1927
174	Lou Gehrig, NY-1930
171	Babe Ruth, NY-1921
170	Hank Greenberg, Det-1935
169	Jimmie Foxx, Phi-1932
167	Joe DiMaggio, NY-1937
165	Lou Gehrig, NY-1934
165	Al Simmons, Phi-1930

SB: Most, season, AL

130	RICKEY HENDERSON, Oak-1982
108	RICKEY HENDERSON, Oak-1983
100	RICKEY HENDERSON, Oak-1980
96	Ty Cobb, Det-1915
93	RICKEY HENDERSON, NY-1988
88	Clyde Milan, Was-1912
87	RICKEY HENDERSON, NY-1986
83	Ty Cobb, Det-1911
83	WILLIE WILSON, KC-1979
81	Eddie Collins, Phi-1910

BB: Most, season, AL

170	Babe Ruth, NY-1923
162	Ted Williams, Bos-1947
162	Ted Williams, Bos-1949
156	Ted Williams, Bos-1946
151	Eddie Yost, Was-1956
149	Eddie Joost, Phi-1949
148	Babe Ruth, NY-1920
146	Mickey Mantle, NY-1957
145	Harmon Killebrew, Min-1969
145	Ted Williams, Bos-1941
145	Ted Williams, Bos-1942

K: Most, season, AL

186	ROB DEER, Mil-1987
185	PETE INCAVIGLIA, Tex-1986
182	CECIL FIELDER, Det-1990
179	ROB DEER, Mil-1986
175	JOSE CANSECO, Oak-1986
175	ROB DEER, Det-1991
175	Dave Nicholson, Chi-1963
175	Gorman Thomas, Mil-1979
172	BO JACKSON, KC-1989
172	JIM PRESLEY, Sea-1986

GIDP: Most, season, AL

36	Jim Rice, Bos-1984
35	Jim Rice, Bos-1985
32	Jackie Jensen, Bos-1954
32	CAL RIPKEN, Bal-1985
31	Tony Armas, Bos-1983
31	Bobby Doerr, Bos-1949
31	Jim Rice, Bos-1983
30	Billy Hitchcock, Phi-1950
30	DAVE WINFIELD, NY-1983
30	Carl Yastrzemski, Bos-1964

BA: Highest, season, AL

.426	Nap Lajoie, Phi-1901
.420	George Sisler, StL-1922
.420	Ty Cobb, Det-1911
.410	Ty Cobb, Det-1912
.408	Joe Jackson, Cle-1911
.407	George Sisler, StL-1920
.406	Ted Williams, Bos-1941
.403	Harry Heilmann, Det-1923
.401	Ty Cobb, Det-1922
.398	Harry Heilmann, Det-1927

Slug avg: Highest, season, AL

.847	Babe Ruth, NY-1920
.846	Babe Ruth, NY-1921
.772	Babe Ruth, NY-1927
.765	Lou Gehrig, NY-1927
.764	Babe Ruth, NY-1923
.749	Jimmie Foxx, Phi-1932
.739	Babe Ruth, NY-1924
.737	Babe Ruth, NY-1926
.735	Ted Williams, Bos-1941
.732	Babe Ruth, NY-1930

Extra-base hits: Most, season, AL

119	Babe Ruth, NY-1921
117	Lou Gehrig, NY-1927
103	Hank Greenberg, Det-1937
100	Jimmie Foxx, Phi-1932
100	Lou Gehrig, NY-1930
99	Hank Greenberg, Det-1940
99	Babe Ruth, NY-1920
99	Babe Ruth, NY-1923
98	Hank Greenberg, Det-1935
97	Babe Ruth, NY-1927

Pitchers

Games: Most, season, AL

90	Mike Marshall, Min-1979
89	MARK EICHHORN, Tor-1987
88	Wilbur Wood, Chi-1968
85	MITCH WILLIAMS, Tex-1987
84	Dan Quisenberry, KC-1985
83	Ken Sanders, Mil-1971
82	Eddie Fisher, Chi-1965
81	DUANE WARD, Tor-1991
81	John Wyatt, KC-1964
80	Willie Hernandez, Det-1984
80	MITCH WILLIAMS, Tex-1986

Complete games: Most, season, AL

48	Jack Chesbro, NY-1904
42	George Mullin, Det-1904
42	Ed Walsh, Chi-1908
41	Cy Young, Bos-1902
40	Cy Young, Bos-1904
39	Bill Dinneen, Bos-1902
39	Joe McGinnity, Bal-1901
39	Rube Waddell, Phi-1904
38	Walter Johnson, Was-1910
38	Jack Powell, NY-1904
38	Cy Young, Bos-1901

Saves: Most, season, AL

57	BOBBY THIGPEN, Chi-1990
48	DENNIS ECKERSLEY, Oak-1990
46	BRYAN HARVEY, Cal-1991
46	DAVE RIGHETTI, NY-1986
45	DENNIS ECKERSLEY, Oak-1988
45	Dan Quisenberry, KC-1983
44	Dan Quisenberry, KC-1984
43	DENNIS ECKERSLEY, Oak-1991
43	DOUG JONES, Cle-1990
42	RICK AGUILERA, Min-1991
42	JEFF REARDON, Min-1988

Shutouts: Most, season, AL

13	Jack Coombs, Phi-1910
11	Dean Chance, LA-1964
11	Walter Johnson, Was-1913
11	Ed Walsh, Chi-1908
10	Bob Feller, Cle-1946

10	Bob Lemon, Cle-1948
10	Jim Palmer, Bal-1975
10	Ed Walsh, Chi-1906
10	Joe Wood, Bos-1912
10	Cy Young, Bos-1904

Wins: Most, season, AL

41	Jack Chesbro, NY-1904
40	Ed Walsh, Chi-1908
36	Walter Johnson, Was-1913
34	Joe Wood, Bos-1912
33	Walter Johnson, Was-1912
33	Cy Young, Bos-1901
32	Cy Young, Bos-1902
31	Jim Bagby, Cle-1920
31	Jack Coombs, Phi-1910
31	Lefty Grove, Phi-1931
31	Denny McLain, Det-1968

Losses: Most, season, AL

26	Pete Dowling, Mil-Cle-1901
26	Bob Groom, Was-1909
26	Happy Townsend, Was-1904
25	Patsy Flaherty, Chi-1903
25	Fred Glade, StL-1905
25	Walter Johnson, Was-1909
25	Scott Perry, Phi-1920
25	Red Ruffing, Bos-1928
24	Joe Bush, Phi-1916
24	Pat Caraway, Chi-1931
24	Sam Gray, StL-1931
24	Tom Hughes, NY-Was-1904

HR allowed: Most, season, AL

50	Bert Blyleven, Min-1986
46	Bert Blyleven, Min-1987
43	Pedro Ramos, Was-1957
42	Denny McLain, Det-1966
40	Fergie Jenkins, Tex-1979
40	JACK MORRIS, Det-1986
40	Orlando Pena, KC-1964
40	Ralph Terry, NY-1962
39	Catfish Hunter, Oak-1973
39	JACK MORRIS, Det-1987
39	Jim Perry, Min-1971
39	Pedro Ramos, Min-1961

BB: Most season, AL

208	Bob Feller, Cle-1938
204	NOLAN RYAN, Cal-1977
202	NOLAN RYAN, Cal-1974
194	Bob Feller, Cle-1941
192	Bobo Newsom, StL-1938
183	NOLAN RYAN, Cal-1976
181	Bob Turley, Bal-1954
179	Tommy Byrne, NY-1949
177	Bob Turley, NY-1955
171	Bump Hadley, Chi-StL-1932

K: Most, season, AL

383	NOLAN RYAN, Cal-1973
367	NOLAN RYAN, Cal-1974
349	Rube Waddell, Phi-1904
348	Bob Feller, Cle-1946
341	NOLAN RYAN, Cal-1977

329	NOLAN RYAN, Cal-1972
327	NOLAN RYAN, Cal-1976
325	Sam McDowell, Cle-1965
313	Walter Johnson, Was-1910
308	Mickey Lolich, Det-1971

Win pct: Highest, season, AL

.938	Johnny Allen, Cle-1937
.893	Ron Guidry, NY-1978
.886	Lefty Grove, Phi-1931
.872	Joe Wood, Bos-1912
.862	Whitey Ford, NY-1961
.862	Bill Donovan, Det-1907
.857	ROGER CLEMENS, Bos-1986
.850	Chief Bender, Phi-1914
.849	Lefty Grove, Phi-1930
.842	Ralph Terry, NY-1961
.842	Schoolboy Rowe, Det-1940
.842	Sandy Consuegra, Chi-1954

ERA: Lowest, season, AL

0.96	Dutch Leonard, Bos-1914
1.14	Walter Johnson, Was-1913
1.16	Addie Joss, Cle-1908
1.26	Cy Young, Bos-1908
1.27	Ed Walsh, Chi-1910
1.27	Walter Johnson, Was-1918
1.30	Jack Coombs, Phi-1910
1.35	Walter Johnson, Was-1910
1.39	Walter Johnson, Was-1912
1.39	Harry Krause, Phi-1909

Innings: Most, season, AL

464.0	Ed Walsh, Chi-1908
454.2	Jack Chesbro, NY-1904
422.1	Ed Walsh, Chi-1907
393.0	Ed Walsh, Chi-1912
390.1	Jack Powell, NY-1904
384.2	Cy Young, Bos-1902
383.0	Rube Waddell, Phi-1904
382.1	George Mullin, Det-1904
382.0	Joe McGinnity, Bal-1901
380.0	Cy Young, Bos-1904

American League club records

Highest Batting Average season, AL

.316	Detroit, 1921
.313	St.Louis, 1922
.309	New York, 1930
.308	St.Louis, 1920
.308	Cleveland, 1921

Lowest Batting Average season, AL

.211	Chicago, 1910
.214	New York, 1968
.217	Texas, 1972
.218	St.Louis, 1910
.221	Chicago, 1909

Highest Slugging Percentage season, AL

.489	New York, 1927
.488	New York, 1930
.483	New York, 1936
.465	Boston, 1977
.464	New York, 1921

Most Runs season, AL

1067	New York, 1931
1065	New York, 1936
1062	New York, 1930
1027	Boston, 1950
1002	New York, 1932

Most Homers season, AL

240	New York, 1961
225	Minnesota, 1963
225	Detroit, 1987
221	Minnesota, 1964
216	Milwaukee, 1982

Most Stolen Bases season, AL

341	Oakland, 1976
288	New York, 1910
287	Washington, 1913
280	Chicago, 1901
280	Detroit, 1909

Most Grounded into Double Plays season, AL

174	Boston, 1990
171	Boston, 1982
171	Boston, 1983
170	Philadelphia, 1950
169	Boston, 1949
169	Boston, 1951
169	Boston, 1989

Fielding Average season, AL

.986	Toronto, 1990
.986	Baltimore, 1989
.986	Minnesota, 1988
.986	Oakland, 1990
.985	Baltimore, 1991

Most Errors season, AL

410	Detroit, 1901
401	Baltimore, 1901
393	Milwaukee, 1901
385	St.Louis, 1910
382	New York, 1912

Fewest Errors season, AL

84	Minnesota, 1988
86	Toronto, 1990
87	Oakland, 1990
87	Baltimore, 1989
91	Baltimore, 1991

Most Double Plays season, AL

217	Philadelphia, 1949
214	New York, 1956
208	Philadelphia, 1950
207	Boston, 1949

206	Boston, 1980
206	Toronto, 1980

Lowest Earned Run Average season, AL

1.78	Philadelphia, 1910
1.93	Philadelphia, 1909
1.99	Chicago, 1905
2.02	Cleveland, 1908
2.03	Chicago, 1910

Most Shutouts season, AL

32	Chicago, 1906
28	Los Angeles, 1964
27	Cleveland, 1906
27	Philadelphia, 1907
27	Philadelphia, 1909

Most Homers Allowed season, AL

226	Baltimore, 1987
220	Kansas City, 1964
219	Cleveland, 1987
212	California, 1987
210	Minnesota, 1987

Fewest Homers Allowed season, AL

6	Boston, 1913
7	St.Louis, 1908
8	Philadelphia, 1910
8	Chicago, 1909
8	Detroit, 1907
8	Cleveland, 1907

Most Walks Allowed season, AL

827	Philadelphia, 1915
812	New York, 1949
801	St.Louis, 1951
779	Washington, 1949
770	Cleveland, 1971

National League single-season records

(active players in caps)

At-bats: Most, season, NL

701	JUAN SAMUEL, Phi-1984
699	Dave Cash, Phi-1975
698	Matty Alou, Pit-1969
696	Woody Jensen, Pit-1936
695	Omar Moreno, Pit-1979
695	Maury Wills, LA-1962
689	Lou Brock, StL-1967
687	Dave Cash, Phi-1974
681	Jo-jo Moore, NY-1935
681	Lloyd Waner, Pit-1931

Runs: Most, season, NL

192	Billy Hamilton, Phi-1894
166	Billy Hamilton, Phi-1895
165	Willie Keeler, Bal-1894
165	Joe Kelley, Bal-1894
162	Willie Keeler, Bal-1895
160	Jesse Burkett, Cle-1896

160	Hugh Duffy, Bos-1894
159	Hughie Jennings, Bal-1895
158	Chuck Klein, Phi-1930
158	Bobby Lowe, Bos-1894

Hits: Most, season, NL

254	Lefty O'Doul, Phi-1929
254	Bill Terry, NY-1930
250	Rogers Hornsby, StL-1922
250	Chuck Klein, Phi-1930
241	Babe Herman, Bro-1930
240	Jesse Burkett, Cle-1896
239	Willie Keeler, Bal-1897
238	Ed Delahanty, Phi-1899
237	Hugh Duffy, Bos-1894
237	Joe Medwick, StL-1937
237	Paul Waner, Pit-1927

Total bases: Most, season, NL

450	Rogers Hornsby, StL-1922
445	Chuck Klein, Phi-1930
429	Stan Musial, StL-1948
423	Hack Wilson, Chi-1930
420	Chuck Klein, Phi-1932
416	Babe Herman, Bro-1930
409	Rogers Hornsby, Chi-1929
406	Joe Medwick, StL-1937
405	Chuck Klein, Phi-1929
400	Hank Aaron, Mil-1959

2B: Most, season, NL

64	Joe Medwick, StL-1936
62	Paul Waner, Pit-1932
59	Chuck Klein, Phi-1930
57	Billy Herman, Chi-1935
57	Billy Herman, Chi-1936
56	Joe Medwick, StL-1937
55	Ed Delahanty, Phi-1899
53	Stan Musial, StL-1953
53	Paul Waner, Pit-1936
52	Johnny Frederick, Bro-1929
52	Enos Slaughter, StL-1939

3B: Most, season, NL

36	Chief Wilson, Pit-1912
31	Heinie Reitz, Bal-1894
29	Perry Werden, StL-1893
28	Harry Davis, Pit-1897
27	George Davis, NY-1893
27	Jimmy Williams, Pit-1899
26	Kiki Cuyler, Pit-1925
26	John Reilly, Cin-1890
26	George Treadway, Bro-1894
25	Roger Connor, NY-StL-1894
25	Larry Doyle, NY-1911
25	Buck Freeman, Was-1899
25	Tom Long, StL-1915

HR: Most, season, NL

56	Hack Wilson, Chi-1930
54	Ralph Kiner, Pit-1949
52	George Foster, Cin-1977
52	Willie Mays, SF-1965
51	Ralph Kiner, Pit-1947
51	Willie Mays, NY-1955
51	Johnny Mize, NY-1947

49	ANDRE DAWSON, Chi-1987
49	Ted Kluszewski, Cin-1954
49	Willie Mays, SF-1962

RBI: Most, season, NL

190	Hack Wilson, Chi-1930
170	Chuck Klein, Phi-1930
166	Sam Thompson, Det-1887
165	Sam Thompson, Phi-1895
159	Hack Wilson, Chi-1929
154	Joe Medwick, StL-1937
153	Tommy Davis, LA-1962
152	Rogers Hornsby, StL-1922
151	Mel Ott, NY-1929
149	George Foster, Cin-1977
149	Rogers Hornsby, Chi-1929

SB: Most, season, NL

118	Lou Brock, StL-1974
111	Billy Hamilton, Phi-1891
111	Monte Ward, NY-1887
110	VINCE COLEMAN, StL-1985
109	VINCE COLEMAN, StL-1987
107	VINCE COLEMAN, StL-1986
104	Maury Wills, LA-1962
102	Jim Fogarty, Phi-1887
102	Billy Hamilton, Phi-1890
99	Jim Fogarty, Phi-1889

BB: Most, season, NL

148	Eddie Stanky, Bro-1945
148	Jim Wynn, Hou-1969
147	Jimmy Sheckard, Chi-1911
144	Eddie Stanky, NY-1950
137	Ralph Kiner, Pit-1951
137	Willie McCovey, SF-1970
137	Eddie Stanky, Bro-1946
136	Jack Clark, StL-1987
136	Jack Crooks, StL-1892
132	Jack Clark, SD-1989
132	Joe Morgan, Cin-1975

K: Most, season, NL

189	Bobby Bonds, SF-1970
187	Bobby Bonds, SF-1969
180	Mike Schmidt, Phi-1975
169	ANDRES GALARRAGA, Mon-1990
168	JUAN SAMUEL, Phi-1984
163	Donn Clendenon, Pit-1968
162	JUAN SAMUEL, Phi-1987
161	Dick Allen, Phi-1968
158	ANDRES GALARRAGA, Mon-1989
156	Tommie Agee, NY-1970
156	Dave Kingman, NY-1982

GIDP: Most, season, NL

30	Ernie Lombardi, Cin-1938
29	Ted Simmons, StL-1973
28	Sid Gordon, Bos-1951
27	John Bateman, Mon-1971
27	Carl Furillo, Bro-1956
27	Ron Santo, Chi-1973
27	Ken Singleton, Mon-1973
26	Sid Gordon, NY-1943

26	Cleon Jones, NY-1970	
26	Billy Jurges, NY-1939	
26	Ernie Lombardi, Cin-1933	
26	Willie Montanez, Phi-SF-1975	
26	Willie Montanez, SF-Atl-1976	
26	DAVE PARKER, Cin-1985	
26	Joe Torre, Mil-1964	

BA: Highest, season, NL

.440	Hugh Duffy, Bos-1894
.424	Willie Keeler, Bal-1897
.424	Rogers Hornsby, StL-1924
.410	Ed Delahanty, Phi-1899
.410	Jesse Burkett, Cle-1896
.409	Jesse Burkett, Cle-1895
.407	Ed Delahanty, Phi-1894
.404	Billy Hamilton, Phi-1894
.404	Ed Delahanty, Phi-1895
.403	Rogers Hornsby, StL-1925

Slug avg: Highest, season, NL

.756	Rogers Hornsby, StL-1925
.723	Hack Wilson, Chi-1930
.722	Rogers Hornsby, StL-1922
.702	Stan Musial, StL-1948
.696	Rogers Hornsby, StL-1924
.694	Hugh Duffy, Bos-1894
.687	Chuck Klein, Phi-1930
.679	Rogers Hornsby, Chi-1929
.678	Babe Herman, Bro-1930
.669	Hank Aaron, Atl-1971

Extra-base hits: Most, season, NL

107	Chuck Klein, Phi-1930
103	Chuck Klein, Phi-1932
103	Stan Musial, StL-1948
102	Rogers Hornsby, StL-1922
97	Joe Medwick, StL-1937
97	Hack Wilson, Chi-1930
95	Joe Medwick, StL-1936
94	Babe Herman, Bro-1930
94	Rogers Hornsby, Chi-1929
94	Chuck Klein, Phi-1929

Pitchers

Games: Most, season, NL

94	Kent Tekulve, Pit-1979
92	Mike Marshall, Mon-1973
91	Kent Tekulve, Pit-1978
90	Wayne Granger, Cin-1969
90	Kent Tekulve, Phi-1987
87	ROB MURPHY, Cin-1987
85	Kent Tekulve, Pit-1982
85	Frank Williams, Cin-1987
84	Ted Abernathy, Chi-1965
84	Enrique Romo, Pit-1979
84	Dick Tidrow, Chi-1980

Complete games: Most, season, NL

75	Will White, Cin-1879
73	Charley Radbourn, Pro-1884
72	Jim Galvin, Buf-1883
72	Jim McCormick, Cle-1880
71	Jim Galvin, Buf-1884
68	John Clarkson, Chi-1885

68	John Clarkson, Bos-1889
67	Bill Hutchinson, Chi-1892
66	Jim Devlin, Lou-1876
66	Charley Radbourn, Pro-1883

Saves: Most, season, NL

47	LEE SMITH, StL-1991
45	Bruce Sutter, StL-1984
44	MARK DAVIS, SD-1989
41	Jeff Reardon, Mon-1985
40	Steve Bedrosian, Phi-1987
39	JOHN FRANCO, Cin-1988
37	Clay Carroll, Cin-1972
37	Rollie Fingers, SD-1978
37	Bruce Sutter, Chi-1979
36	LEE SMITH, Chi-1987
36	Bruce Sutter, StL-1982
36	MITCH WILLIAMS, Chi-1989
36	Todd Worrell, StL-1986

Shutouts: Most, season, NL

16	Pete Alexander, Phi-1916
16	George Bradley, StL-1876
13	Bob Gibson, StL-1968
12	Pete Alexander, Phi-1915
12	Jim Galvin, Buf-1884
11	Tommy Bond, Bos-1879
11	Sandy Koufax, LA-1963
11	Christy Mathewson, NY-1908
11	Charley Radbourn, Pro-1884
10	John Clarkson, Chi-1885
10	Mort Cooper, StL-1942
10	Carl Hubbell, NY-1933
10	Juan Marichal, SF-1965
10	John Tudor, StL-1985

Wins: Most, season, NL

59	Charley Radbourn, Pro-1884
53	John Clarkson, Chi-1885
49	John Clarkson, Bos-1889
48	Charlie Buffinton, Bos-1884
48	Charley Radbourn, Pro-1883
47	Al Spalding, Chi-1876
47	Monte Ward, Pro-1879
46	Jim Galvin, Buf-1883
46	Jim Galvin, Buf-1884
45	George Bradley, StL-1876
45	Jim McCormick, Cle-1880

Losses: Most, season, NL

48	John Coleman, Phi-1883
42	Will White, Cin-1880
40	George Bradley, Tro-1879
40	Jim McCormick, Cle-1879
37	George Cobb, Bal-1892
36	Bill Hutchinson, Chi-1892
36	Stump Weidman, KC-1886
35	Jim Devlin, Lou-1876
35	Red Donahue, StL-1897
35	Jim Galvin, Buf-1880

HR allowed: Most, season, NL

46	Robin Roberts, Phi-1956
41	Phil Niekro, Atl-1979
41	Robin Roberts, Phi-1955
40	Phil Niekro, Atl-1970

40	Robin Roberts, Phi-1957
39	Murry Dickson, StL-1948
38	Lew Burdette, Mil-1959
38	Warren Hacker, Chi-1955
38	Don Sutton, LA-1970
36	TOM BROWNING, Cin-1988
36	Larry Jansen, NY-1949
36	Art Mahaffey, Phi-1962
36	ED WHITSON, SD-1987

BB: Most season, NL

289	Amos Rusie, NY-1890
267	Amos Rusie, NY-1892
262	Amos Rusie, NY-1891
227	Mark Baldwin, Pit-1891
218	Amos Rusie, NY-1893
213	Cy Seymour, NY-1898
203	John Clarkson, Bos-1889
200	Amos Rusie, NY-1894
199	Bill Hutchinson, Chi-1890
194	Mark Baldwin, Pit-1892

K: Most, season, NL

441	Charley Radbourn, Pro-1884
417	Charlie Buffinton, Bos-1884
382	Sandy Koufax, LA-1965
369	Jim Galvin, Buf-1884
345	Mickey Welch, NY-1884
345	Jim Whitney, Bos-1883
341	Amos Rusie, NY-1890
337	Amos Rusie, NY-1891
333	Tim Keefe, NY-1888
323	Lady Baldwin, Det-1886

Win pct: Highest, season, NL

.880	Preacher Roe, Bro-1951
.875	Fred Goldsmith, Chi-1880
.870	DAVID CONE, NY-1988
.864	OREL HERSHISER, LA-1985
.857	DWIGHT GOODEN, NY-1985
.842	Emil Yde, Pit-1924
.842	Tom Hughes, Bos-1916
.838	Bill Hoffer, Bal-1895
.833	King Cole, Chi-1910
.833	Sandy Koufax, LA-1963
.833	Hoyt Wilhelm, NY-1952

ERA: Lowest, season, NL

1.04	Mordecai Brown, Chi-1906
1.12	Bob Gibson, StL-1968
1.14	Christy Mathewson, NY-1909
1.15	Jack Pfiester, Chi-1907
1.17	Carl Lundgren, Chi-1907
1.22	Pete Alexander, Phi-1915
1.23	George Bradley, StL-1876
1.27	Christy Mathewson, NY-1905
1.31	Mordecai Brown, Chi-1909
1.33	Jack Taylor, Chi-1902

Innings: Most, season, NL

680.0	Will White, Cin-1879
678.2	Charley Radbourn, Pro-1884
657.2	Jim McCormick, Cle-1880
656.1	Jim Galvin, Buf-1883
636.1	Jim Galvin, Buf-1884
632.1	Charley Radbourn, Pro-1883

627.0 Bill Hutchinson, Chi-1892
623.0 John Clarkson, Chi-1885
622.0 Jim Devlin, Lou-1876
620.0 John Clarkson, Bos-1889

National League club records

Highest Batting Average season, NL

.349   Philadelphia, 1894
.343   Baltimore, 1894
.337   Chicago, 1876
.331   Boston, 1894
.330   Philadelphia, 1895

Lowest Batting Average season, NL

.208   Washington, 1888
.208   Detroit, 1884
.210   Washington, 1886
.213   Brooklyn, 1908
.219   New York, 1963

Highest Slugging Percentage season, NL

.484   Boston, 1894
.483   Baltimore, 1894
.481   Chicago, 1930
.476   Philadelphia, 1894
.474   Brooklyn, 1953

Most Runs season, NL

1220   Boston, 1894
1171   Baltimore, 1894
1143   Philadelphia, 1894
1068   Philadelphia, 1895
1041   Chicago, 1894

Most Homers season, NL

221   New York, 1947
221   Cincinnati, 1956
209   Chicago, 1987
208   Brooklyn, 1953
207   Atlanta, 1966

Most Stolen Bases season, NL

441   Baltimore, 1896
415   New York, 1887
409   Brooklyn, 1892
401   Baltimore, 1897
382   Chicago, 1887

Most Grounded into Double Plays season, NL

166   St.Louis, 1958
157   Chicago, 1938
154   Atlanta, 1985
153   New York, 1939
151   Brooklyn, 1952

Highest Fielding Average season, NL

.984   Cincinnati, 1977
.984   Cincinnati, 1975

.984   Cincinnati, 1971
.984   Cincinnati, 1976
.983   Cincinnati, 1990

Most Errors season, NL

639   Philadelphia, 1883
607   Pittsburgh, 1890
595   Chicago, 1884
584   Baltimore, 1892
565   New York, 1892

Fewest Errors season, NL

95   Cincinnati, 1977
100   Cincinnati, 1958
102   Cincinnati, 1990
102   Cincinnati, 1976
102   Cincinnati, 1975

Most Double Plays season, NL

215   Pittsburgh, 1966
198   Los Angeles, 1958
197   Atlanta, 1985
195   Pittsburgh, 1963
195   Pittsburgh, 1970

Lowest Earned Run Average season, NL

1.22   St.Louis, 1876
1.61   Providence, 1884
1.64   Providence, 1880
1.67   Hartford, 1876
1.69   Louisville, 1876

Most Shutouts season, NL

32   Chicago, 1907
32   Chicago, 1909
30   Chicago, 1906
30   St.Louis, 1968
29   Chicago, 1908

Most Homers Allowed season, NL

192   New York, 1962
185   St. Louis, 1955
185   Atlanta, 1970
184   Chicago, 1966
179   Cincinnati, 1953
179   Cincinnati, 1957

Fewest Homers Allowed season, NL

5   Cincinnati, 1909
6   Chicago, 1909
8   Philadelphia, 1908
11   Chicago, 1907
12   Pittsburgh, 1909
12   Pittsburgh, 1907
12   Chicago, 1906
12   Pittsburgh, 1905

Most Walks Allowed season, NL

716   Monteal, 1970
715   San Diego, 1974
702   Monteal, 1969
701   St.Louis, 1911
701   Atlanta, 1977

Fewest Walks Allowed season, NL

257   Cincinnati, 1933
276   Cincinnati, 1932
280   Pittsburgh, 1920
288   New York, 1908
293   Cincinnati, 1924

Career records

Games played: Most, career, all-time

3562   Pete Rose, 1963-1986
3308   Carl Yastrzemski, 1961-1983
3298   Hank Aaron, 1954-1976
3035   Ty Cobb, 1905-1928
3026   Stan Musial, 1941-1963
2992   Willie Mays, 1951-1973
2951   Rusty Staub, 1963-1985
2896   Brooks Robinson, 1955-1977
2834   Al Kaline, 1953-1974
2826   Eddie Collins, 1906-1930
2820   Reggie Jackson, 1967-1987
2808   Frank Robinson, 1956-1976
2792   Honus Wagner, 1897-1917
2789   Tris Speaker, 1907-1928
2777   Tony Perez, 1964-1986
2730   Mel Ott, 1926-1947
2700   Graig Nettles, 1967-1988
2687   Darrell Evans, 1969-1989
2670   Rabbit Maranville, 1912-1935
2649   Joe Morgan, 1963-1984

At-bats: Most, career, all-time

14053   Pete Rose, 1963-1986
12364   Hank Aaron, 1954-1976
11988   Carl Yastrzemski, 1961-1983
11434   Ty Cobb, 1905-1928
10972   Stan Musial, 1941-1963
10881   Willie Mays, 1951-1973
10654   Brooks Robinson, 1955-1977
10430   Honus Wagner, 1897-1917
10332   Lou Brock, 1961-1979
10272   Cap Anson, 1871-1897
10230   Luis Aparicio, 1956-1973
10195   Tris Speaker, 1907-1928
10116   Al Kaline, 1953-1974
10078   Rabbit Maranville, 1912-1935
10006   Frank Robinson, 1956-1976
9997   ROBIN YOUNT, 1974-1991
9948   Eddie Collins, 1906-1930
9864   Reggie Jackson, 1967-1987
9778   Tony Perez, 1964-1986
9720   Rusty Staub, 1963-1985

Runs: Most, career, all-time

2245   Ty Cobb, 1905-1928
2174   Hank Aaron, 1954-1976
2174   Babe Ruth, 1914-1935
2165   Pete Rose, 1963-1986
2062   Willie Mays, 1951-1973
1996   Cap Anson, 1871-1897
1949   Stan Musial, 1941-1963
1888   Lou Gehrig, 1923-1939
1882   Tris Speaker, 1907-1928
1859   Mel Ott, 1926-1947
1829   Frank Robinson, 1956-1976

1819 Eddie Collins, 1906-1930
1816 Carl Yastrzemski, 1961-1983
1798 Ted Williams, 1939-1960
1774 Charlie Gehringer, 1924-1942
1751 Jimmie Foxx, 1925-1945
1736 Honus Wagner, 1897-1917
1733 Jim O'Rourke, 1872-1904
1720 Jesse Burkett, 1890-1905
1719 Willie Keeler, 1892-1910

Hits: Most, career, all-time

4256 Pete Rose, 1963-1986
4190 Ty Cobb, 1905-1928
3771 Hank Aaron, 1954-1976
3630 Stan Musial, 1941-1963
3514 Tris Speaker, 1907-1928
3419 Carl Yastrzemski, 1961-1983
3415 Honus Wagner, 1897-1917
3413 Cap Anson, 1871-1897
3310 Eddie Collins, 1906-1930
3283 Willie Mays, 1951-1973
3242 Nap Lajoie, 1896-1916
3152 Paul Waner, 1926-1945
3053 Rod Carew, 1967-1985
3023 Lou Brock, 1961-1979
3007 Al Kaline, 1953-1974
3000 Roberto Clemente, 1955-1972
2987 Sam Rice, 1915-1934
2961 Sam Crawford, 1899-1917
2943 Frank Robinson, 1956-1976
2932 Willie Keeler, 1892-1910

Total bases: Most, career, all-time

6856 Hank Aaron, 1954-1976
6134 Stan Musial, 1941-1963
6066 Willie Mays, 1951-1973
5855 Ty Cobb, 1905-1928
5793 Babe Ruth, 1914-1935
5752 Pete Rose, 1963-1986
5539 Carl Yastrzemski, 1961-1983
5373 Frank Robinson, 1956-1976
5101 Tris Speaker, 1907-1928
5060 Lou Gehrig, 1923-1939
5041 Mel Ott, 1926-1947
4956 Jimmie Foxx, 1925-1945
4884 Ted Williams, 1939-1960
4862 Honus Wagner, 1897-1917
4852 Al Kaline, 1953-1974
4834 Reggie Jackson, 1967-1987
4712 Rogers Hornsby, 1915-1937
4706 Ernie Banks, 1953-1971
4685 Al Simmons, 1924-1944
4599 Billy Williams, 1959-1976

2B: Most, career, all-time

792 Tris Speaker, 1907-1928
746 Pete Rose, 1963-1986
725 Stan Musial, 1941-1963
724 Ty Cobb, 1905-1928
657 Nap Lajoie, 1896-1916
646 Carl Yastrzemski, 1961-1983
640 Honus Wagner, 1897-1917
624 Hank Aaron, 1954-1976
605 Paul Waner, 1926-1945
599 GEORGE BRETT, 1973-1991
582 Cap Anson, 1871-1897

---

574 Charlie Gehringer, 1924-1942
542 Harry Heilmann, 1914-1932
541 Rogers Hornsby, 1915-1937
540 Joe Medwick, 1932-1948
539 Al Simmons, 1924-1944
534 Lou Gehrig, 1923-1939
529 Al Oliver, 1968-1985
528 Frank Robinson, 1956-1976
526 DAVE PARKER, 1973-1991

3B: Most, career, all-time

309 Sam Crawford, 1899-1917
295 Ty Cobb, 1905-1928
252 Honus Wagner, 1897-1917
243 Jake Beckley, 1888-1907
233 Roger Connor, 1880-1897
222 Tris Speaker, 1907-1928
220 Fred Clarke, 1894-1915
205 Dan Brouthers, 1879-1904
194 Joe Kelley, 1891-1908
191 Paul Waner, 1926-1945
188 Bid McPhee, 1882-1899
186 Eddie Collins, 1906-1930
185 Ed Delahanty, 1888-1903
184 Sam Rice, 1915-1934
182 Jesse Burkett, 1890-1905
182 Edd Roush, 1913-1931
181 Ed Konetchy, 1907-1921
178 Buck Ewing, 1880-1897
177 Rabbit Maranville, 1912-1935
177 Stan Musial, 1941-1963

HR: Most, career, all-time

755 Hank Aaron, 1954-1976
714 Babe Ruth, 1914-1935
660 Willie Mays, 1951-1973
586 Frank Robinson, 1956-1976
573 Harmon Killebrew, 1954-1975
563 Reggie Jackson, 1967-1987
548 Mike Schmidt, 1972-1989
536 Mickey Mantle, 1951-1968
534 Jimmie Foxx, 1925-1945
521 Willie McCovey, 1959-1980
521 Ted Williams, 1939-1960
512 Ernie Banks, 1953-1971
512 Eddie Mathews, 1952-1968
511 Mel Ott, 1926-1947
493 Lou Gehrig, 1923-1939
475 Stan Musial, 1941-1963
475 Willie Stargell, 1962-1982
452 Carl Yastrzemski, 1961-1983
442 Dave Kingman, 1971-1986
426 Billy Williams, 1959-1976

RBI: Most, career, all-time

2297 Hank Aaron, 1954-1976
2213 Babe Ruth, 1914-1935
1995 Lou Gehrig, 1923-1939
1951 Stan Musial, 1941-1963
1937 Ty Cobb, 1905-1928
1922 Jimmie Foxx, 1925-1945
1903 Willie Mays, 1951-1973
1895 Cap Anson, 1871-1897
1860 Mel Ott, 1926-1947
1844 Carl Yastrzemski, 1961-1983
1839 Ted Williams, 1939-1960

1827 Al Simmons, 1924-1944
1812 Frank Robinson, 1956-1976
1732 Honus Wagner, 1897-1917
1702 Reggie Jackson, 1967-1987
1652 Tony Perez, 1964-1986
1636 Ernie Banks, 1953-1971
1609 Goose Goslin, 1921-1938
1602 DAVE WINFIELD, 1973-1991
1599 Nap Lajoie, 1896-1916

SB: Most, career, all-time

994 RICKEY HENDERSON, 1979-1991
938 Lou Brock, 1961-1979
912 Billy Hamilton, 1888-1901
891 Ty Cobb, 1905-1928
744 Eddie Collins, 1906-1930
739 Arlie Latham, 1880-1909
738 Max Carey, 1910-1929
722 Honus Wagner, 1897-1917
689 Joe Morgan, 1963-1984
685 TIM RAINES, 1979-1991
657 Tom Brown, 1882-1898
649 Bert Campaneris, 1964-1983
632 WILLIE WILSON, 1976-1991
616 George Davis, 1890-1909
594 Dummy Hoy, 1888-1902
586 Maury Wills, 1959-1972
583 George Vanhaltren, 1887-1903
574 Hugh Duffy, 1888-1906
568 Bid McPhee, 1882-1899
557 Davey Lopes, 1972-1987

BB: Most, career, all-time

2056 Babe Ruth, 1914-1935
2019 Ted Williams, 1939-1960
1865 Joe Morgan, 1963-1984
1845 Carl Yastrzemski, 1961-1983
1733 Mickey Mantle, 1951-1968
1708 Mel Ott, 1926-1947
1614 Eddie Yost, 1944-1962
1605 Darrell Evans, 1969-1989
1599 Stan Musial, 1941-1963
1566 Pete Rose, 1963-1986
1559 Harmon Killebrew, 1954-1975
1508 Lou Gehrig, 1923-1939
1507 Mike Schmidt, 1972-1989
1499 Eddie Collins, 1906-1930
1464 Willie Mays, 1951-1973
1452 Jimmie Foxx, 1925-1945
1444 Eddie Mathews, 1952-1968
1420 Frank Robinson, 1956-1976
1402 Hank Aaron, 1954-1976
1391 DWIGHT EVANS, 1972-1991

HBP: Most, career, all-time

273 Hughie Jennings, 1891-1918
272 Tommy Tucker, 1887-1899
267 Don Baylor, 1970-1988
243 Ron Hunt, 1963-1974
198 Frank Robinson, 1956-1976
192 Minnie Minoso, 1949-1980
171 Curt Welch, 1884-1893
164 Jake Beckley, 1888-1907
151 Chet Lemon, 1975-1990
146 Dan McGann, 1896-1908
142 Nellie Fox, 1947-1965

141 CARLTON FISK, 1969-1991
141 Art Fletcher, 1909-1922
132 Steve Brodie, 1890-1902
129 John McGraw, 1891-1906
126 Fred Clarke, 1894-1915
126 Dummy Hoy, 1888-1902
121 BRIAN DOWNING, 1973-1991
115 Jimmy Dykes, 1918-1939
115 Sherm Lollar, 1946-1963

K: Most, career, all-time

2597 Reggie Jackson, 1967-1987
1936 Willie Stargell, 1962-1982
1883 Mike Schmidt, 1972-1989
1867 Tony Perez, 1964-1986
1816 Dave Kingman, 1971-1986
1757 Bobby Bonds, 1968-1981
1730 Lou Brock, 1961-1979
1720 DALE MURPHY, 1976-1991
1710 Mickey Mantle, 1951-1968
1699 Harmon Killebrew, 1954-1975
1697 DWIGHT EVANS, 1972-1991
1570 Lee May, 1965-1982
1556 Dick Allen, 1963-1977
1550 Willie McCovey, 1959-1980
1537 DAVE PARKER, 1973-1991
1532 Frank Robinson, 1956-1976
1526 Willie Mays, 1951-1973
1513 Rick Monday, 1966-1984
1495 Greg Luzinski, 1970-1984
1487 Eddie Mathews, 1952-1968

GIDP: Most, career, all-time

328 Hank Aaron, 1954-1976
323 Carl Yastrzemski, 1961-1983
315 Jim Rice, 1974-1989
297 Brooks Robinson, 1955-1977
297 Rusty Staub, 1963-1985
287 Ted Simmons, 1968-1988
284 Joe Torre, 1960-1977
282 DAVE WINFIELD, 1973-1991
277 George Scott, 1966-1979
275 Roberto Clemente, 1955-1972
271 Al Kaline, 1953-1974
270 Frank Robinson, 1956-1976
268 Tony Perez, 1964-1986
266 Dave Concepcion, 1970-1988
261 Ernie Lombardi, 1931-1947
256 Ron Santo, 1960-1974
255 Buddy Bell, 1972-1989
254 Al Oliver, 1968-1985
251 Steve Garvey, 1969-1987
251 Willie Mays, 1951-1973

BA: Highest, career, all-time

.366 Ty Cobb, 1905-1928
.359 Rogers Hornsby, 1915-1937
.356 Joe Jackson, 1908-1920
.346 Ed Delahanty, 1888-1903
.345 WADE BOGGS, 1982-1991
.345 Tris Speaker, 1907-1928
.344 Ted Williams, 1939-1960
.344 Billy Hamilton, 1888-1901
.342 Dan Brouthers, 1879-1904
.342 Babe Ruth, 1914-1935
.342 Harry Heilmann, 1914-1932

.342 Pete Browning, 1882-1894
.341 Willie Keeler, 1892-1910
.341 Bill Terry, 1923-1936
.340 George Sisler, 1915-1930
.340 Lou Gehrig, 1923-1939
.338 Jesse Burkett, 1890-1905
.338 Nap Lajoie, 1896-1916
.336 Riggs Stephenson, 1921-1934
.334 Al Simmons, 1924-1944

Slug avg: Highest, career, all-time

.690 Babe Ruth, 1914-1935
.634 Ted Williams, 1939-1960
.632 Lou Gehrig, 1923-1939
.609 Jimmie Foxx, 1925-1945
.605 Hank Greenberg, 1930-1947
.579 Joe DiMaggio, 1936-1951
.577 Rogers Hornsby, 1915-1937
.562 Johnny Mize, 1936-1953
.559 Stan Musial, 1941-1963
.558 Willie Mays, 1951-1973
.557 Mickey Mantle, 1951-1968
.554 Hank Aaron, 1954-1976
.548 Ralph Kiner, 1946-1955
.545 Hack Wilson, 1923-1934
.543 Chuck Klein, 1928-1944
.540 Duke Snider, 1947-1964
.537 Frank Robinson, 1956-1976
.535 Al Simmons, 1924-1944
.534 Dick Allen, 1963-1977
.534 Earl Averill, 1929-1941

Extra-base hits: Most, career, all-time

1477 Hank Aaron, 1954-1976
1377 Stan Musial, 1941-1963
1356 Babe Ruth, 1914-1935
1323 Willie Mays, 1951-1973
1190 Lou Gehrig, 1923-1939
1186 Frank Robinson, 1956-1976
1157 Carl Yastrzemski, 1961-1983
1136 Ty Cobb, 1905-1928
1131 Tris Speaker, 1907-1928
1117 Jimmie Foxx, 1925-1945
1117 Ted Williams, 1939-1960
1075 Reggie Jackson, 1967-1987
1071 Mel Ott, 1926-1947
1041 Pete Rose, 1963-1986
1019 GEORGE BRETT, 1973-1991
1015 Mike Schmidt, 1972-1989
1011 Rogers Hornsby, 1915-1937
1009 Ernie Banks, 1953-1971
995 Al Simmons, 1924-1944
993 Honus Wagner, 1897-1917

Pitchers

Games: Most, career, all-time

1070 Hoyt Wilhelm, 1952-1972
1050 Kent Tekulve, 1974-1989
987 Lindy McDaniel, 1955-1975
944 Rollie Fingers, 1968-1985
931 Gene Garber, 1969-1988
906 Cy Young, 1890-1911
899 Sparky Lyle, 1967-1982
898 Jim Kaat, 1959-1983

897 RICH GOSSAGE, 1972-1991
874 Don McMahon, 1957-1974
864 Phil Niekro, 1964-1987
848 Roy Face, 1953-1969
824 Tug McGraw, 1965-1984
802 Walter Johnson, 1907-1927
777 Gaylord Perry, 1962-1983
776 CHARLIE HOUGH, 1970-1991
774 Don Sutton, 1966-1988
767 NOLAN RYAN, 1966-1991
765 Darold Knowles, 1965-1980
760 Tommy John, 1963-1989

Complete games: Most, career, all-time

749 Cy Young, 1890-1911
646 Jim Galvin, 1875-1892
554 Tim Keefe, 1880-1893
531 Walter Johnson, 1907-1927
531 Kid Nichols, 1890-1906
525 Bobby Mathews, 1871-1887
525 Mickey Welch, 1880-1892
489 Charley Radbourn, 1880-1891
485 John Clarkson, 1882-1894
468 Tony Mullane, 1881-1894
466 Jim McCormick, 1878-1887
448 Gus Weyhing, 1887-1901
438 Pete Alexander, 1911-1930
434 Christy Mathewson, 1900-1916
422 Jack Powell, 1897-1912
410 Eddie Plank, 1901-1917
394 Will White, 1877-1886
392 Amos Rusie, 1889-1901
388 Vic Willis, 1898-1910
386 Tommy Bond, 1874-1884

Saves: Most, career, all-time

341 Rollie Fingers, 1968-1985
327 JEFF REARDON, 1979-1991
312 LEE SMITH, 1980-1991
308 RICH GOSSAGE, 1972-1991
300 Bruce Sutter, 1976-1988
248 DAVE RIGHETTI, 1979-1991
244 Dan Quisenberry, 1979-1990
238 Sparky Lyle, 1967-1982
227 Hoyt Wilhelm, 1952-1972
218 Gene Garber, 1969-1988
216 DAVE SMITH, 1980-1991
211 JOHN FRANCO, 1984-1991
193 Roy Face, 1953-1969
188 DENNIS ECKERSLEY, 1975-1991
188 Mike Marshall, 1967-1981
186 TOM HENKE, 1982-1991
184 STEVE BEDROSIAN, 1981-1991
184 Kent Tekulve, 1974-1989
180 Tug McGraw, 1965-1984
179 Ron Perranoski, 1961-1973
178 BOBBY THIGPEN, 1986-1991
172 Lindy McDaniel, 1955-1975
154 Stu Miller, 1952-1968
153 Don McMahon, 1957-1974
150 Greg Minton, 1975-1990

Shutouts: Most, career, all-time

110 Walter Johnson, 1907-1927
90 Pete Alexander, 1911-1930

79	Christy Mathewson, 1900-1916	482	Phil Niekro, 1964-1987	187	Tommy John, 1963-1989
76	Cy Young, 1890-1911	472	Don Sutton, 1966-1988	183	Steve Carlton, 1965-1988
69	Eddie Plank, 1901-1917	434	Warren Spahn, 1942-1965	172	Joe Niekro, 1967-1988
63	Warren Spahn, 1942-1965	414	Steve Carlton, 1965-1988	170	JACK MORRIS, 1977-1991
61	NOLAN RYAN, 1966-1991	413	BERT BLYLEVEN, 1970-1990	160	Gaylord Perry, 1962-1983
61	Tom Seaver, 1967-1986	399	Gaylord Perry, 1962-1983	156	Red Ames, 1903-1919
60	BERT BLYLEVEN, 1970-1990	398	FRANK TANANA, 1973-1991	155	Walter Johnson, 1907-1927
58	Don Sutton, 1966-1988	395	Jim Kaat, 1959-1983	149	CHARLIE HOUGH, 1970-1991
57	Jim Galvin, 1875-1892	380	Tom Seaver, 1967-1986	140	Sam McDowell, 1961-1975
57	Ed Walsh, 1904-1917	374	Catfish Hunter, 1965-1979	128	Jim Kaat, 1959-1983
56	Bob Gibson, 1959-1975	372	Jim Bunning, 1955-1971	126	Tom Seaver, 1967-1986
55	Mordecai Brown, 1903-1916	347	Mickey Lolich, 1963-1979	126	Will White, 1877-1886
55	Steve Carlton, 1965-1988	346	Luis Tiant, 1964-1982	124	Mickey Lolich, 1963-1979
53	Jim Palmer, 1965-1984	339	JACK MORRIS, 1977-1991	124	Jim Maloney, 1960-1971
53	Gaylord Perry, 1962-1983	338	Early Wynn, 1939-1963	123	George Bradley, 1875-1888
52	Juan Marichal, 1960-1975	327	CHARLIE HOUGH, 1970-1991	119	Larry Cheney, 1911-1919
50	Rube Waddell, 1897-1910	324	Doyle Alexander, 1971-1989	119	Tony Cloninger, 1961-1972
50	Vic Willis, 1898-1910	320	Juan Marichal, 1960-1975	118	Joe Coleman, 1965-1979

Wins: Most, career, all-time

		BB: Most career, all-time		Win pct: Highest, career, all-time	
511	Cy Young, 1890-1911	2686	NOLAN RYAN, 1966-1991	.796	Al Spalding, 1871-1878
417	Walter Johnson, 1907-1927	1833	Steve Carlton, 1965-1988	.717	Spud Chandler, 1937-1947
373	Pete Alexander, 1911-1930	1809	Phil Niekro, 1964-1987	.714	DWIGHT GOODEN, 1984-1991
373	Christy Mathewson, 1900-1916	1775	Early Wynn, 1939-1963	.690	Dave Foutz, 1884-1896
364	Jim Galvin, 1875-1892	1764	Bob Feller, 1936-1956	.690	Whitey Ford, 1950-1967
363	Warren Spahn, 1942-1965	1732	Bobo Newsom, 1929-1953	.688	Bob Caruthers, 1884-1893
361	Kid Nichols, 1890-1906	1704	Amos Rusie, 1889-1901	.687	ROGER CLEMENS, 1984-1991
342	Tim Keefe, 1880-1893	1566	Gus Weyhing, 1887-1901	.686	Don Gullett, 1970-1978
329	Steve Carlton, 1965-1988	1541	Red Ruffing, 1924-1947	.680	Lefty Grove, 1925-1941
328	John Clarkson, 1882-1894	1476	CHARLIE HOUGH, 1970-1991	.671	Joe Wood, 1908-1922
326	Eddie Plank, 1901-1917	1442	Bump Hadley, 1926-1941	.667	Vic Raschi, 1946-1955
324	Don Sutton, 1966-1988	1434	Warren Spahn, 1942-1965	.665	Larry Corcoran, 1880-1887
318	Phil Niekro, 1964-1987	1431	Earl Whitehill, 1923-1939	.665	Christy Mathewson, 1900-1916
314	Gaylord Perry, 1962-1983	1408	Tony Mullane, 1881-1894	.660	Sam Leever, 1898-1910
314	NOLAN RYAN, 1966-1991	1396	Sam Jones, 1914-1935	.657	Sal Maglie, 1945-1958
311	Tom Seaver, 1967-1986	1390	Tom Seaver, 1967-1986	.656	Dick McBride, 1871-1876
309	Charley Radbourn, 1880-1891	1379	Gaylord Perry, 1962-1983	.655	Sandy Koufax, 1955-1966
307	Mickey Welch, 1880-1892	1371	Mike Torrez, 1967-1984	.654	Johnny Allen, 1932-1944
300	Lefty Grove, 1925-1941	1362	Walter Johnson, 1907-1927	.651	Ron Guidry, 1975-1988
300	Early Wynn, 1939-1963	1343	Don Sutton, 1966-1988	.650	Lefty Gomez, 1930-1943

Losses: Most, career, all-time

		K: Most, career, all-time		ERA: Lowest, career, all-time	
316	Cy Young, 1890-1911	5511	NOLAN RYAN, 1966-1991	1.82	Ed Walsh, 1904-1917
310	Jim Galvin, 1875-1892	4136	Steve Carlton, 1965-1988	1.89	Addie Joss, 1902-1910
279	Walter Johnson, 1907-1927	3640	Tom Seaver, 1967-1986	2.06	Mordecai Brown, 1903-1916
278	NOLAN RYAN, 1966-1991	3631	BERT BLYLEVEN, 1970-1990	2.10	Monte Ward, 1878-1894
274	Phil Niekro, 1964-1987	3574	Don Sutton, 1966-1988	2.13	Christy Mathewson, 1900-1916
265	Gaylord Perry, 1962-1983	3534	Gaylord Perry, 1962-1983	2.16	Rube Waddell, 1897-1910
256	Don Sutton, 1966-1988	3509	Walter Johnson, 1907-1927	2.17	Walter Johnson, 1907-1927
254	Jack Powell, 1897-1912	3342	Phil Niekro, 1964-1987	2.22	Al Spalding, 1871-1878
251	Eppa Rixey, 1912-1933	3192	Fergie Jenkins, 1965-1983	2.23	Orval Overall, 1905-1913
248	Bobby Mathews, 1871-1887	3117	Bob Gibson, 1959-1975	2.28	Will White, 1877-1886
245	Robin Roberts, 1948-1966	2855	Jim Bunning, 1955-1971	2.28	Ed Reulbach, 1905-1917
245	Warren Spahn, 1942-1965	2832	Mickey Lolich, 1963-1979	2.30	Jim Scott, 1909-1917
244	Steve Carlton, 1965-1988	2800	Cy Young, 1890-1911	2.31	Tommy Bond, 1874-1884
244	Early Wynn, 1939-1963	2583	Warren Spahn, 1942-1965	2.35	Eddie Plank, 1901-1917
238	BERT BLYLEVEN, 1970-1990	2581	Bob Feller, 1936-1956	2.35	Larry Corcoran, 1880-1887
237	Jim Kaat, 1959-1983	2566	FRANK TANANA, 1973-1991	2.38	George McQuillan, 1907-1918
232	Gus Weyhing, 1887-1901	2556	Jerry Koosman, 1967-1985	2.38	Eddie Cicotte, 1905-1920
231	Tommy John, 1963-1989	2527	Tim Keefe, 1880-1893	2.38	Ed Killian, 1903-1910
230	Bob Friend, 1951-1966	2502	Christy Mathewson, 1900-1916	2.39	Doc White, 1901-1913
230	Ted Lyons, 1923-1946	2486	Don Drysdale, 1956-1969	2.42	George Bradley, 1875-1888

HR allowed: Most, career, all-time

		Wild pitches: Most, career, all-time		Innings: Most, career, all-time	
505	Robin Roberts, 1948-1966	265	NOLAN RYAN, 1966-1991	7355.1	Cy Young, 1890-1911
484	Fergie Jenkins, 1965-1983	226	Phil Niekro, 1964-1987	6003.1	Jim Galvin, 1875-1892

5923.2 Walter Johnson, 1907-1927
5404.1 Phil Niekro, 1964-1987
5350.1 Gaylord Perry, 1962-1983
5282.1 Don Sutton, 1966-1988
5243.2 Warren Spahn, 1942-1965
5217.1 Steve Carlton, 1965-1988
5189.1 Pete Alexander, 1911-1930
5162.1 NOLAN RYAN, 1966-1991
5061.1 Tim Keefe, 1880-1893
5057.1 Kid Nichols, 1890-1906
4956.0 Bobby Mathews, 1871-1887
4837.0 BERT BLYLEVEN, 1970-1990
4802.0 Mickey Welch, 1880-1892
4782.2 Tom Seaver, 1967-1986
4781.0 Christy Mathewson, 1900-1916
4710.1 Tommy John, 1963-1989

General club records

Highest percentage for league champion

.832 St. Louis, UA-1884
.798 Chicago, NL-1880
.788 Chicago, NL-1876
.777 Chicago, NL-1885
.763 Chicago, NL-1906

Lowest percentage for league champion

.509 New York, NL-1973
.525 Minnesota, AL-1987
.551 New York, AL-1981
.556 Philadelphia, NL-1983
.556 Oakland, AL-1974

Most Wins

116 Chicago, NL-1906
111 Cleveland, AL-1954
110 Pittsburgh, NL-1909
110 New York, AL-1927
109 New York, AL-1961
109 Baltimore, AL-1969

Fewest Wins

36 Philadelphia, AL-1916
38 Washington, AL-1904
38 Boston, NL-1935
40 New York, NL-1962
42 Washington, AL-1909
42 Philadelphia, NL-1942
42 Pittsburgh, NL-1952

Most league championships

33 New York, AL
21 Brooklyn-Los Angeles, NL
19 New York-San Francisco, NL
16 Chicago, NL
15 St. Louis, NL
15 Philadelphia-Oakland, AL

Individual fielding records

Most Gold Gloves, Pitcher

16 Jim Kaat
9   Bob Gibson
8   Bobby Shantz
5   Phil Niekro
5   Ron Guidry
4   Jim Palmer
3   Harvey Haddix
2   Andy Messersmith
2   Mike Norris
2   RICK REUSCHEL
2   MARK LANGSTON

Most Gold Gloves, Catcher

10 Johnny Bench
7   Bob Boone
6   Jim Sundberg
5   Bill Freehan
4   Del Crandall
3   Sherm Lollar
3   Earl Battey
3   Thurman Munson
3   GARY CARTER
3   LANCE PARRISH
3   TONY PENA
3   BENITO SANTIAGO

Most Gold Gloves, First base

11 Keith Hernandez
8   George Scott
7   Vic Power
7   Bill White
6   Wes Parker
5   DON MATTINGLY
4   Steve Garvey
3   Gil Hodges
3   Joe Pepitone
3   EDDIE MURRAY

Most Gold Gloves, Second base

8   Bill Mazeroski
8   Frank White
8   RYNE SANDBERG
5   Bobby Richardson
5   Joe Morgan
4   Bobby Grich
3   Nellie Fox
3   Bobby Knoop
3   Davey Johnson
3   Manny Trillo
3   LOU WHITAKER
3   HAROLD REYNOLDS

Most Gold Gloves, Third base

16 Brooks Robinson
10 Mike Schmidt
6   Buddy Bell
5   Ken Boyer
5   Ron Santo
5   Doug Rader
4   GARY GAETTI
3   Frank Malzone

3   TIM WALLACH
2   Graig Nettles
2   TERRY PENDLETON

Most Gold Gloves, Shortstop

11 OZZIE SMITH
9   Luis Aparicio
8   Mark Belanger
5   Dave Concepcion
4   ALAN TRAMMELL
4   TONY FERNANDEZ
3   Roy McMillan
2   Maury Wills
2   Zoilo Versalles
2   Gene Alley
2   Don Kessinger
2   Larry Bowa

Most Gold Gloves, Outfield

12 Roberto Clemente
12 Willie Mays
10 Al Kaline
8   Paul Blair
8   Garry Maddox
8   ANDRE DAWSON
8   DWIGHT EVANS
7   Curt Flood
7   Carl Yastrzemski
7   DAVE WINFIELD

Fielding Average, Pitcher (92 chances accepted)

1.000 Kid Nichols, Bos/N-1896
1.000 Frank Owen, Chi/A-1904
1.000 Mordecai Brown, Chi/N-1908
1.000 Pete Alexander, Phi/N-1913
1.000 Walter Johnson, Was/A-1913
1.000 Eppa Rixey, Phi/N-1917
1.000 Walter Johnson, Was/A-1917
1.000 Hal Schumacher, NY/N-1935
1.000 Larry Jackson, Chi/N-1964
1.000 Randy Jones, SD/N-1976
1.000 GREG MADDUX, Chi/N-1990

Fielding Average, Catcher

1.000 Spud Davis, Phi/N-1939
1.000 Buddy Rosar, Phi/A-1946
1.000 Lou Berberet, Was/A-1957
1.000 Pete Daley, Bos/A-1957
1.000 Yogi Berra, NY/A-1958
1.000 RICK CERONE, Bos/A-1988
.999   Joe Azcue, Cle/A-1967
.999   Wes Westrum, NY/N-1950
.998   Thurman Munson, NY/A-1971
.998   MIKE LaVALLIERE, Pit/N-1991

Fielding Average, First Base

1.000 Steve Garvey, SD/N-1984
.999   Stuffy McInnis, Bos/A-1921
.999   Frank McCormick, Phi/N-1946
.999   Steve Garvey, LA/N-1981
.999   Jim Spencer, Cal-Tex/A-1973
.999   Wes Parker, LA/N-1968
.999   EDDIE MURRAY, Bal/A-1981
.998   Jim Spencer, Chi/A-1976
.998   Jim Spencer, NY-Oak/A-1981

.998 Joe Judge, Was/A-1930

Fielding Average, Second Base

.997 Bobby Grich, Cal/A-1985
.996 JOSE OQUENDO, StL/N-1990
.995 RYNE SANDBERG, Chi/N-1991
.995 Rob Wilfong, Min/A-1980
.995 Bobby Grich, Bal/A-1973
.994 Frank White, KC/A-1988
.994 JOSE OQUENDO, StL/N-1989
.994 Jerry Adair, Bal/A-1964
.994 RYNE SANDBERG, Chi/N-1986
.994 Tim Cullen, Was/A-1970

Fielding Average, Shortstop

.996 CAL RIPKEN, Bal/A-1990
.992 TONY FERNANDEZ, Tor/A-1989
.991 Larry Bowa, Phi/N-1979
.990 Ed Brinkman, Det/A-1972
.990 CAL RIPKEN, Bal/A-1989
.989 SPIKE OWEN, Mon/N-1990
.989 TONY FERNANDEZ, Tor/A-1990
.987 OZZIE SMITH, StL/N-1991
.987 Larry Bowa, Phi/N-1972
.987 OZZIE SMITH, StL/N-1987

Fielding Average, Third Base

.991 STEVE BUECHELE, Tex/A-1991
*(counting Pit/N, Buechele's
average was .983)*
.989 Don Money, Mil/A-1974
.988 Hank Majeski, Phi/A-1947
.987 Aurelio Rodriguez, Det/A-1978
.984 Willie Kamm, Cle/A-1933
.983 George Kell, Phi-Det/A-1946
.983 Heinie Groh, NY/N-1924
.983 CARNEY LANSFORD, Cal/A-1979
.982 George Kell, Det/A-1950
.982 Pinky Whitney, Phi/N-1937

Fielding Average, Outfield

1.000 Danny Litwhiler, Phi/N-1942
1.000 Willard Marshall, Bos/N-1951
1.000 Tony Gonzalez, Phi/N-1962
1.000 Don Demeter, Phi/N-1963
1.000 Rocky Colavito, Cle/A-1965
1.000 Curt Flood, StL/N-1966
1.000 Johnny Callison, Phi/N-1968
1.000 Mickey Stanley, Det/A-1968
1.000 Ken Harrelson, Bos/A-1968
1.000 Ken Berry, Chi/A-1969
1.000 Mickey Stanley, Det/A-1970
1.000 Roy White, NY/A-1971
1.000 Al Kaline, Det/A-1971
1.000 Ken Berry, Cal/A-1972
1.000 Carl Yastrzemski, Bos/A-1977
1.000 TERRY PUHL, Hou/N-1979
1.000 Gary Roenicke, Bal/A-1980
1.000 Ken Landreaux, LA/N-1981
1.000 TERRY PUHL, Hou/N-1981
1.000 Ken Singleton, Bal/A-1981
1.000 BRIAN DOWNING, Cal/A-1982
1.000 John Lowenstein, Bal-A/1982
1.000 BRIAN DOWNING, Cal-A/1984
1.000 BRETT BUTLER, LA-A/1991

Fielding Average, Pitcher, active players (63 Chances accepted)

1.000 Greg Maddux, Chi/N-1990
1.000 Dan Petry, Det-A-1982
1.000 Bert Blyleven, Min-Tex/A-1976
1.000 Rick Reuschel, Pit/N-1985
1.000 Fern. Valenzuela, LA/N-1985
1.000 Bob Welch, LA/N-1987

Fielding Average, Catcher, active players

1.000 Rick Cerone, Bos/A-1988
.998 Mike LaValliere, Pit/N-1991
.998 Rick Cerone, NY/A-1987
.998 Chris Hoiles, Bal/A-1991
.998 Rick Dempsey, Bal/A-1981

Fielding Average, First Base, active players

.999 Eddie Murray, Bal/A-1981
.998 Dave Magadan, NY/N-1990
.997 Wally Joyner, Cal/A-1989
.997 Kent Hrbek, Min/A-1990
.997 Pete O'Brien, Sea/A-1991
.997 Will Clark, SF/N-1991
.997 Eddie Murray, Bal/A-1982
.997 Mark McGwire, Oak/A-1991

Fielding Average, Second Base, active players

.996 Jose Oquendo, StL/N-1990
.995 Ryne Sandberg, Chi/N-1991
.994 Jose Oquendo, StL/N-1989
.994 Ryne Sandberg, Chi/N-1986
.994 Lou Whitaker, Det/A-1991

Fielding Average, Third Base, active players

.991 Steve Buechele, Tex/A-1991
*(counting Pit/N, Buechele's
average was .983)*
.983 Carney Lansford, Cal/A-1979
.980 Carney Lansford, Oak/A-1987
.979 Carney Lansford, Oak/A-1988
.979 Ken Oberkfell, Atl/N-1987

Fielding Average, Shortstop, active players

.996 Cal Ripken, Bal/A-1990
.992 Tony Fernandez, Tor/A-1989
.990 Cal Ripken, Bal/A-1989
.989 Spike Owen, Mon/N-1990
.989 Tony Fernandez, Tor/A-1990

Fielding Average, Outfield, active players

1.000 Terry Puhl, Hou/N-1979
1.000 Terry Puhl, Hou/N-1981
1.000 Brian Downing, Cal/A-1982
1.000 Brian Downing, Cal/A-1984
1.000 Brett Butler, LA/N-1991

Assists, Pitcher

227 Ed Walsh, Chi/A-1907
223 Will White, Cin/N-1882

190 Ed Walsh, Chi/A-1908
178 Harry Howell, StL/A-1905
177 Tony Mullane, Lou/A-1882
174 John Clarkson, Chi/N-1885
172 John Clarkson, Bos/N-1889
166 Jack Chesbro, NY/A-1904
163 George Mullin, Det/A-1904
160 Ed Walsh, Chi/A-1911

Assists, Catcher

238 Bill Rariden, New/F-1915
215 Bill Rariden, Ind/F-1914
214 Pat Moran, Bos/N-1903
212 Oscar Stanage, Det/A-1911
212 Art Wilson, Chi/F-1914
210 Gabby Street, Was/A-1909
204 Frank Snyder, StL/N-1915
203 George Gibson, Pit/N-1910
202 Bill Bergen, Bro/N-1909
202 Claude Berry, Pit/F-1914

Assists, First Base

184 Bill Buckner, Bos/A-1985
180 MARK GRACE, Chi/N-1990
167 MARK GRACE, Chi/N-1991
166 SID BREAM, Pit/N-1986
161 Bill Buckner, Chi/N-1983
159 Bill Buckner, Chi/N-1982
157 Bill Buckner, Bos/A-1986
155 Mickey Vernon, Cle/A-1949
152 Fred Tenney, Bos/N-1905
152 EDDIE MURRAY, Bal/A-1985

Assists, Second Base

641 Frankie Frisch, StL/N-1927
588 Hughie Critz, Cin/N-1926
582 Rogers Hornsby, NY/N-1927
572 Ski Melillo, StL/A-1930
571 RYNE SANDBERG, Chi/N-1983
568 Rabbit Maranville, Pit/N-1924
562 Frank Parkinson, Phi/N-1922
559 Tony Cuccinello, Bos/N-1936
557 Johnny Hodapp, Cle/A-1930
555 Lou Bierbauer, Pit/N-1892

Assists, Shortstop

621 OZZIE SMITH, SD/N-1980
601 Glenn Wright, Pit/N-1924
598 Dave Bancroft, Phi-NY/N-1920
597 Tommy Thevenow, StL/N-1926
595 Ivan DeJesus, Chi/N-1977
583 CAL RIPKEN, Bal/A-1984
581 W. Wietelmann, Bos/N-1943
579 Dave Bancroft, NY/N-1922
574 Rabbit Maranville, Bos/N-1914
573 Don Kessinger, Chi/N-1968

Assists, Third Base

412 Graig Nettles, Cle/A-1971
410 Graig Nettles, NY/A-1973
410 Brooks Robinson, Bal/A-1974
405 Harlond Clift, StL/A-1937
405 Brooks Robinson, Bal/A-1967
404 Mike Schmidt, Phi/N-1974
399 Doug DeCinces, Cal/A-1982
396 Clete Boyer, NY/A-1962

396   Mike Schmidt, Phi/N-1977
396   Buddy Bell, Tex/A-1982

Assists, Outfield

50   Orator Shaffer, Chi/N-1879
48   Hugh Nicol, StL/A-1884
45   Hardy Richardson, Buf/N-1881
44   Tommy McCarthy, StL/A-1888
44   Chuck Klein, Phi/N-1930
43   Charlie Duffee, StL/A-1889
43   Jimmy Bannon, Bos/N-1894
42   Jim Fogarty, Phi/N-1889
41   Orator Shaffer, Buf/N-1883
41   Jim Lillie, Buf/N-1884

Assists, Pitcher, active players

64   Fern. Valenzuela, LA/N-1982
60   Orel Hershiser, LA/N-1988
59   Dennis Martinez, Bal/A-1979
58   Dave Stieb, Tor/A-1980
56   Rick Reuschel, Chi/N-1980
56   Dwight Gooden, NY/N-1988

Assists, Catcher, active players

108   Gary Carter, Mon/N-1980
107   Gary Carter, Mon/N-1983
104   Gary Carter, Mon/N-1982
101   Gary Carter, Mon/N-1977
100   Tony Pena, Pit/N-1985
100   Benito Santiago, SD/N-1991

Assists, First Base, active players

180   Mark Grace, Chi/N-1990
167   Mark Grace, Chi/N-1991
166   Sid Bream, Pit/N-1986
152   Eddie Murray, Bal/A-1985
146   Pete O'Brien, Tex/A-1987

Assists, Second Base, active players

571   Ryne Sandberg, Chi/N-1983
550   Ryne Sandberg, Chi/N-1984
522   Ryne Sandberg, Chi/N-1988
515   Ryne Sandberg, Chi/N-1991
512   Jim Gantner, Mil/A-1983

Assists, Third Base, active players

392   Terry Pendleton, StL/N-1989
383   Tim Wallach, Mon/N-1985
373   George Brett, KC/A-1979
371   Terry Pendleton, StL/N-1986
369   Terry Pendleton, StL/N-1987

Assists, Shortstop, active players

621   Ozzie Smith, SD/N-1980
583   Cal Ripken, Bal/A-1984
570   Ozzie Guillen, Chi/A-1988
555   Ozzie Smith, SD/N-1979
549   Ozzie Smith, StL/N-1985

Assists, Outfield, active players

26   Dave Parker, Pit/N-1977
24   Warren Cromartie, Mon/N-1978
22   Jesse Barfield, Tor/A-1985
22   Joe Orsulak, Bal/A-1991
21   Tim Raines, Mon/N-1983

Individual records

Most consecutive games played, lifetime

2130   Lou Gehrig, 1925-1939
1573   Cal Ripken, 1982-1991
1307   Everett Scott, 1916-1925
1207   Steve Garvey, 1975-1983
1117   Billy Williams, 1963-1970
1103   Joe Sewell, 1922-1930
895   Stan Musial, 1951-1957
829   Eddie Yost, 1949-1955
822   Gus Suhr, 1931-1937
798   Nellie Fox, 1955-1960

Most consecutive games played, lifetime, active players

1573   Cal Ripken, 1982-1991
503   Joe Carter, 1988-1991
214   Cecil Fielder, 1990-1991
173   Mark Grace, 1990-1991

Most consecutive games batted safely, season

56   Joe DiMaggio, NY/AL-1941
44   Willie Keeler, Bal/NL-1897
44   Pete Rose, Cin/NL-1978
42   Bill Dahlen, Chi/NL-1894
41   George Sisler, StL/AL-1922
40   Ty Cobb, Det/AL-1911
39   Paul Molitor, Mil/AL-1987
37   Tommy Holmes, Bos/NL-1945
36   Billy Hamilton, Phi/NL-1894
35   Fred Clarke, Lou/NL-1895
35   Ty Cobb, Det/AL-1917
34   George Sisler, StL/AL-1925
34   George McQuinn, StL/AL-1938
34   Dom DiMaggio, Bos/AL-1949
34   Benito Santiago, SD/NL-1987
33   George Davis, NY/NL-1893
33   Rogers Hornsby, StL/NL-1922
33   Heinie Manush, Was/AL-1933
31   Ed Delahanty, Phi/NL-1899
31   Sam Rice, Was/AL-1924
31   Willie Davis, LA/NL-1969
31   Rico Carty, Atl/NL-1970
31   Ken Landreaux, Min/AL-1980
30   Elmer Smith, Cin/NL-1898
30   Tris Speaker, Bos/AL-1912
30   Goose Goslin, Det/AL-1934
30   Stan Musial, StL/NL-1950
30   Ron LeFlore, Det/AL-1976
30   George Brett, KC/AL-1980
30   Jerome Walton, Chi/NL-1989

Most consecutive games batted safely, season, active players

39   Paul Molitor, Mil/AL-1987
34   Benito Santiago, SD/NL-1987
30   George Brett, KC/AL-1980
30   Jerome Walton, Chi/NL-1989
28   Wade Boggs, Bos/AL-1985
26   Jack Clark, SF/AL-1978
25   Tony Gwynn, SD/NL-1983

25   Steve Sax, LA/NL-1986
25   Wade Boggs, Bos/AL-1987
25   Brian Harper, Min/AL-1990

Most pinch hits, lifetime

150   Manny Mota, 1962-1982
145   Smoky Burgess, 1949-1967
143   Greg Gross, 1973-1989
123   Jose Morales, 1973-1984
116   Jerry Lynch, 1954-1966
114   Red Lucas, 1923-1938
113   Steve Braun, 1971-1985
108   Terry Crowley, 1969-1983
107   Gates Brown, 1963-1975
107   DENNY WALLING, 1975-1991
103   Mike Lum, 1967-1981
102   Jim Dwyer, 1973-1990
100   Rusty Staub, 1963-1985
95   Larry Biittner, 1970-1983
95   Vic Davalillo, 1963-1980
94   Jerry Hairston, 1973-1989
93   Dave Philley, 1941-1962
93   Joel Youngblood, 1976-1989
92   Jay Johnstone, 1966-1985
90   Ed Kranepool, 1962-1979
90   Elmer Valo, 1940-1961

Most pinch hits, lifetime, active players

107   Denny Walling, 1975-1991
71   Ken Griffey Sr., 1973-1991
65   Dave Bergman, 1975-1991
62   Danny Heep, 1979-1991
61   Randy Bush, 1982-1991
61   Terry Puhl, 1977-1991
57   Max Venable, 1979-1991
44   Herm Winningham, 1984-1991
43   Candy Maldonado, 1981-1991
42   Kevin Bass, 1982-1991

Most pinch hit home runs, lifetime

20   Cliff Johnson, 1972-1986
18   Jerry Lynch, 1954-1966
16   Gates Brown, 1963-1975
16   Smoky Burgess, 1949-1967
16   Willie McCovey, 1959-1980
14   George Crowe, 1952-1961
12   Joe Adcock, 1950-1966
12   Bob Cerv, 1951-1962
12   Jose Morales, 1973-1984
12   Graig Nettles, 1967-1988
11   Jeff Burroughs, 1970-1985
11   Jay Johnstone, 1966-1985
11   Fred Whitfield, 1962-1970
11   Cy Williams, 1912-1930
10   Jim Dwyer, 1973-1990
10   Mike Lum, 1967-1981
10   Ken McMullen, 1962-1977
10   Don Mincher, 1960-1972
10   Wally Post, 1949-1964
10   Champ Summers, 1974-1984
10   Jerry Turner, 1974-1983
10   Gus Zernial, 1949-1959

Most pinch hit home runs, lifetime, active players

9   Candy Maldonado, 1981-1991
8   Mark Carreon, 1987-1991
6   Jesse Barfield, 1981-1991
6   Randy Bush, 1982-1991
6   Tommy Gregg, 1987-1991
6   Ron Kittle, 1982-1991
6   Lloyd McClendon, 1987-1991
6   Tim Teufel, 1983-1991
6   Denny Walling, 1975-1991
5   Danny Heep, 1979-1991
5   Sam Horn, 1987-1991
5   Ernie Riles, 1985-1991

Most consecutive scoreless innings, season

59 OREL HERSHISER, LA/NL - August 30 to September 28, 1988
58 Don Drysdale, LA/NL - May 14 to June 8, 1968
55 Walter Johnson, Was/AL - April 10 to May 14, 1913
47 Bob Gibson, StL/NL - June 2 to 26, 1968
45 Cy Young, Bos/AL - April 25 to May 17, 1904
45 Doc White, Chi/AL - September 12 to 30, 1904
45 Carl Hubbell, NY/NL - July 13 to August 1, 1933
45 Sal Maglie, NY/NL - August 16 to September 14, 1950
44 Ed Reulbach, Chi/NL - September 17 to October 3, 1908 (end of season) *added 6 more innings on April 17, 1909 for a total of 50*
41 Grover Cleveland Alexander, Phi/NL - September 7 to 24, 1911
41 Luis Tiant, Cle/AL - April 28 to May 17, 1968
39 Mordecai Brown, Chi/NL - June 8 to July 8, 1908
39 Billy Pierce, Chi/AL - August 3 to 19, 1953
39 Gaylord Perry, SF/NL - September 1 to 23, 1970
38 Bill Lee, Chi/NL - September 5 to 26, 1938
38 Mike Torrez, Oak/AL - August 29 to September 15, 1976
37 Joel Horlen, Chi/AL - May 11 to 29, 1968
36 Ed Morris, Pit/NL - September 5 to 17, 1888
36 Ed Walsh, Chi/AL - August 4 to 14, 1910
36 Hal Brown, Bal/AL - July 7 to August 8, 1961
36 Jim McGlothlin, Cal/AL - May 22 to June 11, 1967
36 CHARLIE HOUGH, Tex/AL - August 23 to September 14, 1983 *(GREGG OLSON, Ball/AL had a streak of 41 consecutive scoreless*

innings over two seasons from August 4, 1989 to May 4, 1990, 26 in 1989 and 15 in 1990)

Most strikeouts, game

21 Tom Cheney, Was/AL - September 12, 1962 (16 innings)
20 Roger Clemens, Bos/AL- April 29, 1986
19 Charlie Sweeney, Pro/NL- June 7, 1884
19 Hugh (One Arm) Daily, Chi/UA - July 7, 1884
19 Luis Tiant, Cle/AL - July 3, 1968 (10 innings)
19 Steve Carlton, StL/NL - September 15, 1969
19 Tom Seaver, NY/NL - April 22, 1970
19 Nolan Ryan, Cal/AL - June 14, 1974 (12 innings)
19 Nolan Ryan, Cal/AL - August 12, 1974
19 Nolan Ryan, Cal/AL - August 20, 1974 (11 innings)
19 Nolan Ryan, Cal/AL - June 8, 1977 (10 innings)
19 David Cone, NY/NL - October 6, 1991
18 Jim Whitney, Bos/NL - June 14, 1884 (15 innings)
18 Dupee Shaw, Bos/UA - July 19, 1884
18 Henry Porter, Mil/UA - October 3, 1884
18 Jack Coombs, Phi/AL - September 1, 1906 (24 innings)
18 Bob Feller, Cle/AL - October 2, 1938 (1st g)
18 Warren Spahn, Bos/NL - June 14, 1952 (15 innings)
18 Sandy Koufax, LA/NL - August 31, 1959
18 Sandy Koufax, LA/NL - April 24, 1962
18 Jim Maloney, Cin/NL - June 14, 1965 (11 innings)
18 Chris Short, Phi/NL - October 2, 1965 (15 innings in an 18 inning game)
18 Don Wilson, Hou/NL - July 14, 1968
18 Nolan Ryan, Cal/AL - September 10, 1976
18 Ron Guidry, NY/AL - June 17, 1978
18 Bill Gullickson, Mon/NL - September 10, 1980
18 Ramon Martinez, LA/NL - June 4, 1990

Most bases on balls, game

16 Bill George, NY/NL - May 30, 1887 (1st game)
16 George Van Haltren, Chi/NL - June 27, 1887
16 Henry Gruber, Cle/PL - April 19, 1890

16 Bruno Haas, Phi/AL - June 23, 1915
16 Tommy Byrne, NY/AL - August 22, 1951 (13 innings)
15 Carroll Brown, Phi/AL - July 12, 1913
14 Ed Crane, Was/NL - September 1, 1886
14 Charlie Hickman, Bos/NL - August 16, 1899 (2nd game)
14 Henry Mathewson, NY/NL - October 5, 1906
14 Skipper Friday, Was/AL - June 17, 1923
13 Bill George, NY/NL - May 17, 1887
13 John Kirby, Ind/NL - June 9, 1887
13 Cy Seymour, NY/NL - May 24, 1899 (10 innings)
13 Mal Eason, Bos/NL - September 3, 1902
13 Pete Schneider, Cin/NL - July 6, 1918
13 George Turbeville, Phi/AL - August 24, 1935 (15 innings)
13 Tommy Byrne, NY/AL - June 8, 1949
13 Dick Weik, Was/AL - September 1, 1949
13 Bud Podbielan, Cin/NL - May 18, 1953 (11 innings)

No-hit games, nine or more innings (number to left is career total if greater than 1)

Joe Borden, Phi vs Chi NA, 4-0; July 28, 1875.
George Bradley, StL vs Har NL, 2-0; July 15, 1876.
Lee Richmond, Wor vs Cle NL, 1-0; June 12, 1880 (perfect game).
Monte Ward, Pro vs Buf NL, 5-0; June 17, 1880 (perfect game).
Larry Corcoran, Chi vs Bos NL, 6-0; August 19, 1880.
Jim Galvin, Buf at Wor NL, 1-0; August 20, 1880.
Tony Mullane, Lou at Cin AA, 2-0; September 11, 1882.
Guy Hecker, Lou at Pit AA, 3-1; September 19, 1882.
2 Larry Corcoran, Chi vs Wor NL, 5-0; September 20, 1882.
Charley Radbourn, Pro at Cle NL, 8-0; July 25, 1883.
Hugh (One Arm) Daily, Cle at Phi NL; 1-0; September 13, 1883.
Al Atkisson, Phi vs Pit AA, 10-1; May 24, 1884.
Ed Morris, Col at Pit AA, 5-0; May 29, 1884.
Frank Mountain, Col at Was AA, 12-0; June 5, 1884.
3 Larry Corcoran, Chi vs Pro NL, 6-0; June 27, 1884.
2 Jim Galvin, Buf at Det NL, 18-0;

August 4, 1884.

Dick Burns, Cin at KC UA, 3-1; August 26, 1884.

Ed Cushman, Mil vs Was UA, 5-0; September 28, 1884.

Sam Kimber, Bro vs Tol AA, 0-0; October 4, 1884 (ten innings, darkness).

John Clarkson, Chi at Pro NL, 4-0; July 27, 1885.

Charlie Ferguson, Phi vs Pro NL, 1-0; August 29, 1885.

2 Al Atkisson, Phi vs NY AA, 3-2; May 1, 1886.

Adonis Terry, Bro vs StL AA, 1-0; July 24, 1886.

Matt Kilroy, Bal at Pit AA, 6-0; October 6, 1886.

2 Adonis Terry, Bro vs Lou AA, 4-0; May 27, 1888.

Henry Porter, KC at Bal AA, 4-0; June 6, 1888.

Ed Seward, Phi vs Cin AA, 12-2; July 26, 1888.

Gus Weyhing, Phi vs KC AA, 4-0; July 31, 1888.

Silver King, Chi vs Bro PL, 0-1; June 21, 1890 (8 innings,lost the game; bottom of 9th not played).

Cannonball Titcomb, Roch vs Syr AA, 7-0; September 15, 1890.

Tom Lovett, Bro vs NY NL, 4-0; June 22, 1891.

Amos Rusie, NY vs Bro NL, 6-0; July 31, 1891.

Ted Breitenstein, StL vs Lou AA, 8-0; October 4, 1891 (1st game,first start in the major leagues).

Jack Stivetts, Bos vs Bro NL, 11-0; August 6, 1892.

Ben Sanders, Lou vs Bal NL, 6-2; August 22, 1892.

Bumpus Jones, Cin vs Pit NL, 7-1; October 15, 1892 (first game in the major leagues).

Bill Hawke, Bal vs Was NL, 5-0; August 16, 1893.

Cy Young, Cle vs Cin NL, 6-0; September 18, 1897 (1st game).

2 Ted Breitenstein, Cin vs Pit NL, 11-0; April 22, 1898.

Jim Hughes, Bal vs Bos NL, 8-0; April 22, 1898.

Red Donahue, Phi vs Bos NL, 5-0; July 8, 1898.

Walter Thornton, Chi vs Bro NL, 2-0; August 21, 1898 (2nd game).

Deacon Phillippe, Lou vs NY NL, 7-0; May 25, 1899.

Noodles Hahn, Cin vs Phi NL, 4-0; July 12, 1900.

Earl Moore, Cle vs Chi AL, 2-4; May 9, 1901 (lost on two hits in the tenth).

Christy Mathewson, NY vs StL NL, 5-

0; July 15, 1901.

Nixey Callahan, Chi vs Det AL, 3-0; September 20, 1902 (1st game).

Chick Fraser, Phi at Chi NL; 10-0; September 18, 1903 (2nd game).

2 Cy Young, Bos vs Phi AL, 3-0; May 5, 1904 (perfect game).

Bob Wicker, Chi at NY NL, 1-0; June 11, 1904 (won in 12 innings after allowing one hit in the tenth).

Jesse Tannehill, Bos at Chi AL, 6-0; August 17, 1904.

2 Christy Mathewson, NY at Chi NL, 1-0; June 13, 1905.

Weldon Henley, Phi at StL AL, 6-0; July 22, 1905 (1st game).

Frank Smith, Chi at Det AL, 15-0; September 6, 1905 (2nd game).

Bill Dinneen, Bos vs Chi AL, 2-0; September 27, 1905 (1st game).

Johnny Lush, Phi at Bro NL, 6-0; May 1, 1906.

Mal Eason, Bro at StL NL, 2-0; July 20, 1906.

Harry McIntyre, Bro vs Pit NL, 0-1; August 1, 1906 (lost on 4 hits in 13 innings after allowing the first hit in the 11th).

Frank (Jeff) Pfeffer, Bos vs Cin NL, 6-0; May 8, 1907.

Nick Maddox, Pit vs Bro NL, 2-1; September 20, 1907.

3 Cy Young, Bos at NY AL, 8-0; June 30, 1908.

Hooks Wiltse, NY vs Phi NL, 1-0; July 4, 1908 (1st game, ten innings).

Nap Rucker, Bro vs Bos NL, 6-0; September 5, 1908 (2nd game).

Dusty Rhoades, Cle vs Bos AL, 2-1; September 18, 1908.

2 Frank Smith, Chi vs Phi AL, 1-0; September 20, 1908.

Addie Joss, Cle vs Chi AL, 1-0; October 2, 1908 (perfect game).

Red Ames, NY vs Bro NL. 0-3; April 15, 1909 (lost on 7 hits in 13 innings after allowing the first hit in the tenth).

2 Addie Joss, Cle vs Chi AL, 1-0; April 20, 1910.

Chief Bender, Phi vs Cle AL, 4-0; May 12, 1910.

Tom L. Hughes, NY vs Cle AL, 0-5; August 30, 1910 (2nd game) (lost on 7 hits in 11 innings after allowing the first hit in the tenth)

Joe Wood, Bos vs StL AL, 5-0; July 29, 1911 (1st game).

Ed Walsh, Chi vs Bos AL, 5-0; August 27, 1911.

George Mullin, Det vs StL AL, 7-0; July 4, 1912 (2nd game).

Earl Hamilton, StL at Det AL, 5-1; August 30, 1912.

Jeff Tesreau, NY at Phi NL, 3-0;

September 6, 1912 (1st game).

Jim Scott, Chi at Was AL, 0-1; May 14, 1914 (lost on 2 hits in the tenth).

Joe Benz, Chi vs Cle AL, 6-1; May 31, 1914.

George Davis, Bos vs Phi NL, 7-0; September 9, 1914 (2nd game).

Ed Lafitte, Bro vs KC FL, 6-2; September 19, 1914.

Rube Marquard, NY vs Bro NL, 2-0; April 15, 1915.

Frank Allen, Pit vs StL FL, 2-0; April 24, 1915.

Claude Hendrix, Chi vs Pit FL, 10-0; May 15, 1915.

Alex Main, KC vs Buf FL, 5-0; August 16, 1915.

Jimmy Lavender, Chi at NY NL, 2-0; August 31, 1915 (1st game).

Dave Davenport, StL vs Chi FL, 3-0; September 7, 1915.

2 Tom L. Hughes, Bos vs Pit NL, 2-0; June 16, 1916.

Rube Foster, Bos vs NY AL, 2-0; June 21, 1916.

Joe Bush, Phi vs Cle AL, 5-0; August 26, 1916.

Hubert (Dutch) Leonard, Bos vs StL AL, 4-0; August 30, 1916.

Eddie Cicotte, Chi at StL AL, 11-0; April 14, 1917.

George Mogridge, NY at Bos AL, 2-1; April 24, 1917.

Fred Toney, Cin at Chi NL, 1-0; May 2, 1917 (ten innings).

Hippo Vaughn, Chi vs Cin NL, 0-1; May 2, 1917 (lost on two hits in the 10th, Toney pitched a no-hitter in this game).

Ernie Koob, StL vs Chi AL, 1-0; May 5, 1917.

Bob Groom, StL vs Chi AL, 3-0; May 6, 1917 (2nd game).

Ernie Shore, Bos vs Was AL, 4-0; June 23, 1917 (1st game, perfect game. Shore relieved Babe Ruth in the first inning after Ruth had been thrown out of the game for protesting a walk to the first batter. The runner was caught stealing and Shore retired the remaining 26 batters in order).

2 Hubert (Dutch) Leonard, Bos at Det AL, 5-0; June 3, 1918.

Hod Eller, Cin vs StL NL, 6-0; May 11, 1919.

Ray Caldwell, Cle at NY AL, 3-0; September 10, 1919 (1st game).

Walter Johnson, Was at Bos AL, 1-0; July 1, 1920.

Charlie Robertson, Chi at Det AL, 2-0; April 30, 1922 (perfect game).

Jesse Barnes, NY vs Phi NL, 6-0; May 7, 1922.

Sam Jones, NY at Phi AL, 2-0;

September 4, 1923.

Howard Ehmke, Bos at Phi AL, 4-0; September 7, 1923.

Jesse Haines, StL vs Bos NL, 5-0; July 17, 1924.

Dazzy Vance, Bro vs Phi NL, 10-1; September 13, 1925 (1st game).

Ted Lyons, Chi at Bos AL, 6-0; August 21, 1926.

Carl Hubbell, NY vs Pit NL, 11-0; May 8, 1929.

Wes Ferrell, Cle vs StL AL, 9-0; April 29, 1931.

Bobby Burke, Was vs Bos AL, 5-0; August 8, 1931.

Bobo Newsom, StL vs Bos AL, 1-2; September 18, 1934 (lost on 1 hit in the tenth).

Paul Dean, StL at Bro NL, 3-0; September 21, 1934 (2nd game).

Vern Kennedy, Chi vs Cle AL, 5-0; August 31, 1935.

Bill Dietrich, Chi vs StL AL, 8-0; June 1, 1937.

Johnny Vander Meer, Cin vs Bos NL, 3-0; June 11, 1938

2 Johnny Vander Meer, Cin at Bro NL, 6-0; June 15, 1938 (next start after June 11)

Monte Pearson, NY vs Cle AL, 13-0; August 27, 1938 (2nd game).

Bob Feller, Cle at Chi AL, 1-0; April 16, 1940 (opening day).

Tex Carleton, Bro at Cin NL, 3-0; April 30, 1940.

Lon Warneke, StL at Cin NL, 2-0; August 30, 1941.

Jim Tobin, Bos vs Bro NL, 2-0; April 27, 1944.

Clyde Shoun, Cin vs Bos NL, 1-0; May 15, 1944.

Dick Fowler, Phi vs StL AL, 1-0; September 9, 1945 (2nd game).

Ed Head, Bro vs Bos NL, 5-0; April 23, 1946.

2 Bob Feller, Cle at NY AL, 1-0; April 30, 1946.

Ewell Blackwell, Cin vs Bos NL, 6-0; June 18, 1947.

Don Black, Cle vs Phi AL, 3-0; July 10, 1947 (1st game).

Bill McCahan, Phi vs Was AL, 3-0; September 3, 1947.

Bob Lemon, Cle at Det AL, 2-0; June 30, 1948.

Rex Barney, Bro vs NY NL, 2-0; September 9, 1948.

Vern Bickford, Bos vs Bro NL, 7-0; August 11, 1950.

Cliff Chambers, Pit at Bos NL, 3-0; May 6, 1951 (2nd game).

3 Bob Feller, Cle vs Det AL, 2-1; July 1, 1951 (1st game).

Allie Reynolds, NY at Cle AL, 1-0; July 12, 1951.

2 Allie Reynolds, NY vs Bos AL, 8-0;

September 28, 1951 (1st game).

Virgil Trucks, Det vs Was AL, 1-0; May 15, 1952.

Carl Erskine, Bro vs Chi NL, 5-0; June 19, 1952.

2 Virgil Trucks, Det at NY AL, 1-0; August 25, 1952.

Bobo Holloman, StL vs Phi AL, 6-0; May 6, 1953 (first start in the major leagues).

Jim Wilson, Mil vs Phi NL, 2-0; June 12, 1954.

Sam Jones, Chi vs Pit NL, 4-0; May 12, 1955.

2 Carl Erskine, Bro vs NY NL, 3-0; May 12, 1956.

Johnny Klippstein (7 innings), Hershell Freeman (1 inning) and Joe Black (3 innings), Cin at Mil NL, 1-2; May 26, 1956 (lost on 3 hits in 11 innings after allowing the first hit in the tenth).

Mel Parnell, Bos vs Chi AL, 4-0; July 14, 1956.

Sal Maglie, Bro vs Phi NL, 5-0; September 25, 1956.

Don Larsen, NY AL vs Bro NL, 2-0; October 8, 1956 (World Series, perfect game).

Bob Keegan, Chi vs Was AL, 6-0; August 20, 1957 (2nd game).

Jim Bunning, Det at Bos AL, 3-0; July 20, 1958 (1st game).

Hoyt Wilhelm, Bal vs NY AL, 1-0; September 20, 1958

Harvey Haddix, Pit at Mil NL, 0-1; May 26, 1959 (lost on 1 hit in 13 innings after pitching 12 perfect innings).

Don Cardwell, Chi vs StL NL, 4-0; May 15, 1960 (2nd game).

Lew Burdette, Mil vs Phi NL, 1-0; August 18, 1960.

Warren Spahn, Mil vs Phi NL, 4-0; September 16, 1960.

2 Warren Spahn, Mil vs SF NL, 1-0; April 28, 1961.

Bo Belinsky, LA vs Bal AL, 2-0; May 5, 1962.

Earl Wilson, Bos vs LA AL, 2-0; June 26, 1962.

Sandy Koufax, LA vs NY NL, 5-0; June 30, 1962.

Bill Monbouquette, Bos vs Chi AL, 1-0; August 1, 1962.

Jack Kralick, Min vs KC AL, 1-0; August 26, 1962.

2 Sandy Koufax, LA vs SF NL, 8-0; May 11, 1963.

Don Nottebart, Hou vs Phi NL, 4-1; May 17, 1963.

Juan Marichal, SF vs Hou NL, 1-0; June 15, 1963.

Ken T. Johnson, Hou vs Cin NL, 0-1; April 23, 1964 (lost the game).

3 Sandy Koufax, LA at Phi NL, 3-0;

June 4, 1964.

2 Jim Bunning, Phi at NY NL, 6-0; June 21, 1964 (1st game, perfect game).

Jim Maloney, Cin vs NY NL, 0-1; June 14, 1965 (lost on 2 hits in 11 innings after pitching 10 hitless innings).

2 Jim Maloney, Cin at Chi NL, 1-0; August 19, 1965 (1st game, 10 innings).

4 Sandy Koufax, LA vs Chi NL, 1-0; September 9, 1965 (perfect game).

Dave Morehead, Bos vs Cle AL, 2-0; September 16, 1965.

Sonny Siebert, Cle vs Was AL, 2-0; June 10, 1966.

Steve D. Barber (8 2/3 innings) and Stu Miller (1/3 inning) Bal vs Det AL, 1-2; April 30, 1967 (1st game, lost the game)

Don Wilson, Hou vs Atl NL, 2-0; June 18, 1967.

Dean Chance, Min at Cle AL, 2-1; August 25, 1967 (2nd game).

Joe Horlen, Chi vs Det AL, 6-0; September 10, 1967 (1st game).

Tom Phoebus, Bal vs Bos AL, 6-0; April 27, 1968.

Catfish Hunter, Oak vs Min AL, 4-0; May 8, 1968 (perfect game).

George Culver, Cin at Phi NL, 6-1; July 29, 1968 (2nd game).

Gaylord Perry, SF vs StL NL, 1-0; September 17, 1968.

Ray Washburn, StL at SF NL, 2-0; September 18, 1968.

Bill Stoneman, Mon at Phi NL, 7-0; April 17, 1969.

3 Jim Maloney, Cin vs Hou NL, 10-0; April 30, 1969.

2 Don Wilson, Hou at Cin NL, 4-0; May 1, 1969.

Jim Palmer, Bal vs Oak AL, 8-0; August 13, 1969.

Ken Holtzman, Chi vs Atl NL, 3-0; August 19, 1969.

Bob Moose, Pit at NY NL, 4-0; September 20, 1969.

Dock Ellis, Pit at SD NL, 2-0; June 12, 1970 (1st game).

Clyde Wright, Cal vs Oak AL, 4-0; July 3, 1970.

Bill Singer, LA vs Phi NL, 5-0; July 20, 1970.

Vida Blue, Oak vs Min AL, 6-0; September 21, 1970.

2 Ken Holtzman, Chi at Cin NL, 1-0; June 3, 1971.

Rick Wise, Phi at Cin NL, 4-0; June 23, 1971.

Bob Gibson, StL at Pit NL, 11-0; August 14, 1971.

Burt Hooton, Chi vs Phi NL, 4-0; April 16, 1972.

Milt Pappas, Chi vs SD NL, 8-0; September 2, 1972.

2 Bill Stoneman, Mon vs NY NL, 7-0; October 2, 1972 (1st game).

Steve Busby, KC at Det AL, 3-0; April 16, 1973.

Nolan Ryan, Cal at KC AL, 3-0; May 15, 1973.

2 Nolan Ryan, Cal at Det AL, 6-0; July 15, 1973.

Jim Bibby, Tex at Oak AL, 6-0; July 20, 1973.

Phil Niekro, Atl vs SD NL, 9-0; August 5, 1973.

2 Steve Busby, KC at Mil AL, 2-0; June 19, 1974.

Dick Bosman, Cle vs Oak AL, 4-0; July 19, 1974.

3 Nolan Ryan, Cal vs Min AL, 4-0; September 28, 1974.

4 Nolan Ryan, Cal vs Bal AL, 1-0; June 1, 1975.

Ed Halicki, SF vs NY NL, 6-0; August 24, 1975 (2nd game).

Vida Blue (5 innings), Glenn Abbott (1 inning), Paul Lindblad (1 inning) and Rollie Fingers (2 innings), Oak vs Cal AL, 5-0; September 28, 1975.

Larry Dierker, Hou vs Mon NL, 6-0; July 9, 1976.

Blue Moon Odom (5 innings) and Francisco Barrios (4 innings),Chi at Oak AL, 2-1; July 28, 1976.

John Candelaria, Pit vs LA NL, 2-0; August 9, 1976.

John Montefusco, SF at Atl NL, 9-0; September 29, 1976.

Jim Colborn, KC vs Tex AL, 6-0; May 14, 1977.

Dennis Eckersley, Cle vs Cal AL, 1-0; May 30, 1977.

Bert Blyleven, Tex at Cal AL, 6-0; September 22, 1977.

Bob Forsch, StL vs Phi NL, 5-0; April 16, 1978.

Tom Seaver, Cin vs StL NL, 4-0; June 16, 1978.

Ken Forsch, Hou vs Atl NL, 6-0; April 7, 1979.

Jerry Reuss, LA at SF NL, 8-0; June 27, 1980.

Charlie Lea, Mon vs SF NL, 4-0; May 10, 1981 (2nd game).

Len Barker, Cle vs Tor AL, 3-0; May 15, 1981 (perfect game).

5 Nolan Ryan, Hou vs LA NL, 5-0; September 26, 1981.

Dave Righetti, NY vs Bos AL, 4-0; July 4, 1983.

2 Bob Forsch, StL vs Mon NL, 3-0; September 26, 1983.

Mike Warren, Oak vs Chi AL, 3-0; September 29, 1983.

Jack Morris, Det at Chi AL, 4-0; April 7, 1984.

Mike Witt, Cal at Tex AL, 1-0; September 30, 1984 (perfect game).

Joe Cowley, Chi at Cal AL, 7-1; September 19, 1986.

Mike Scott, Hou vs SF NL, 2-0; September 25, 1986.

Juan Nieves, Mil at Bal AL, 7-0; April 15, 1987.

Tom Browning, Cin vs LA NL, 1-0; September 16, 1988 (perfect game).

Mark Langston (7 innings) and Mike Witt (2 innings), Cal vs Sea AL, 1-0; April 11, 1990.

Randy Johnson, Sea vs Det AL, 2-0; June 2, 1990.

6 Nolan Ryan, Tex at Oak AL, 5-0; June 11, 1990.

Dave Stewart, Oak at Tor AL, 5-0; June 29, 1990.

Fern. Valenzuela, LA vs StL NL, 6-0; June 29, 1990.

Andy Hawkins, NY at Chi AL, 0-4; July 1, 1990 (8 innings, lost the game; bottom of 9th not played).

Terry Mulholland, Phi vs SF NL, 6-0; August 15, 1990.

Dave Stieb, Tor at Det AL, 3-0; September 2, 1990.

7 Nolan Ryan, Tex vs Tor AL, 3-0; May 1, 1991.

Tommy Greene, Phi at Mon NL, 2-0; May 23, 1991.

Bob Milacki (6 innings), Mike Flanagan (1 inning), Mark Williamson (1 inning) and Gregg Olson (1 inning), Bal at Oak AL, 2-0; July 13, 1991.

Mark Gardner, Mon at LA NL, 0-1; July 26, 1991 (9 innings,lost on 2 hits in 10th, relieved by Jeff Fassero, who allowed 1 more hit).

Dennis Martinez, Mon at LA NL, 2-0; July 28, 1991 (perfect game).

Wilson Alvarez, Chi at Bal AL, 7-0; August 11, 1991.

Bret Saberhagen, KC vs Chi AL, 7-0; August 26, 1991.

Kent Mercker (6 innings), Mark Wohlers (2 innings) and Alejandro Pena (1 inning), Atl at SD NL, 1-0; September 11, 1991.

No hit games, less than 9 innings

Larry McKeon, six innings, rain, Ind at Cin AA, 0-0; May 6, 1884.

Charlie Gagus, eight innings, darkness, Was vs Wil UA, 12-1; August 21, 1884.

Charlie Getzien, six innings, rain, Det vs Phi NL, 1-0; October 1, 1884.

Charlie Sweeney (2 innings) and

Henry Boyle (3 innings), five innings, rain, StL vs StP UA, 0-1; October 5,1884.

Dupee Shaw, five innings, agreement, Pro at Buf NL, 4-0; October 7, 1885 (1st game).

George Van Haltren, six innings, rain, Chi vs Pit NL, 1-0, June 21,1888.

Ed Crane, seven innings, darkness, NY vs Was NL, 3-0; September 27, 1888.

Matt Kilroy, seven innings, darkness, Bal vs StL AA, 0-0; July 29, 1889 (2nd game).

George Nicol, seven innings, darkness, StL vs Phi AA, 21-2; September 23, 1890.

Hank Gastright, eight innings, darkness assumed, Col vs Tol AA, 6-0; October 12, 1890.

Jack Stivetts, five innings, called so Boston could catch train to Cleveland for Temple Club playoffs, Bos at Was NL, 6-0; October 15, 1892 (2nd game).

Elton Chamberlain, seven innings, darkness, Cin vs Bos NL, 6-0; September 23, 1893 (2nd game).

Ed Stein, six innings, rain, Bro vs Chi NL, 6-0; June 2, 1894.

Red Ames, five innings, darkness, NY at StL NL, 5-0; September 14, 1903 (2nd game, first game in the major leagues).

Rube Waddell, five innings, rain, Phi vs StL AL, 2-0; August 15, 1905.

Jake Weimer, seven innings, agreement, Cin vs Bro NL, 1-0; August 24, 1906 (2nd game).

Jimmy Dygert (3 innings) and Rube Waddell (2 innings), five innings, rain, Phi vs Chi AL, 4-3; August 29, 1906. (Waddell allowed hit and two runs in 6th, but rain caused game to revert to 5 innings).

Stoney McGlynn, seven innings, agreement, StL at Bro NL, 1-1; September 24, 1906 (2nd game).

Lefty Leifield, six innings, darkness, Pit at Phi NL, 8-0; September 26, 1906 (2nd game).

Ed Walsh, five innings, rain, Chi vs NY AL, 8-1; May 26, 1907.

Ed Karger, seven perfect innings, agreement, StL vs Bos NL, 4-0; August 11, 1907 (2nd game).

Howie Camnitz, five innings, agreement, Pit at NY NL, 1-0; August 23, 1907 (2nd game).

Rube Vickers, five perfect innings, darkness, Phi at Was AL, 4-0; October 5, 1907 (2nd game).

Johnny Lush, six innings, rain, StL at Bro NL, 2-0; August 6, 1908.

King Cole, seven innings, called so

Chicago could catch train, Chi at StL NL, 4-0; July 31, 1910 (2nd game).

Jay Cashion, six innings, called so Cleveland could catch train, Was vs Cle AL, 2-0; August 20, 1912 (2nd game).

Walter Johnson, seven innings, rain, Was vs StL AL, 2-0; August 25, 1924.

Fred Frankhouse, seven and two-thirds innings, rain, Bro vs Cin NL, 5-0; August 27, 1937.

John Whitehead, six innings, rain, StL vs Det AL, 4-0; August 5, 1940 (2nd game).

Jim Tobin, five innings, darkness, Bos vs Phi NL, 7-0; June 22, 1944 (2nd game).

Mike McCormick, five innings, rain, SF at Phi NL, 3-0; June 12, 1959 (allowed hit in 6th, but rain caused game to revert to 5 innings).

Sam Jones, seven innings, rain, SF at StL NL, 4-0; September 26, 1959.

Dean Chance, five perfect innings, rain, Min vs Bos AL, 2-0; August 6, 1967.

David Palmer, five perfect innings, rain, Mon at StL NL, 4-0; April 21, 1984 (2nd game).

Pascual Perez, five innings, rain, Mon at Phi NL, 1-0; September 24, 1988.

Melido Perez, six innings, rain, Chi at NY AL, 8-0; July 12, 1990.

Fan Daniel Richard risked it all for a souvenir of the 1960 World Series at Forbes Field.

Lee Richmond, Wor vs Cle NL, 1-0; June 12, 1880

CLEVELAND	ab	r	h	po	a	e
Dunlap,2b	3	0	0	4	2	2
Hankinson,3b	3	0	0	0	0	0
Kennedy,c	3	0	0	9	1	0
Phillips,lb	3	0	0	7	0	0
Shaffer,rf	3	0	0	2	0	0
McCormick,p	3	0	0	0	10	0
Gilligan,cf	3	0	0	1	0	0
Glasscock,ss	3	0	0	0	2	0
Hanlon,lf	3	0	0	1	0	0
Team	27	0	0	24	15	2

WORCESTER	ab	r	h	po	a	e
Wood,lf	4	0	0	0	0	0
Richmond,p	3	0	1	0	6	0
Knight,rf	3	0	0	1	1	0
Irwin,ss	3	0	2	2	3	0
Bennett,c	2	0	0	8	0	0
Whitney,3b	3	0	0	1	2	0
Sullivan,lb	3	0	0	14	0	0
Corey,cf	3	0	0	1	0	0
Creamer,2b	3	0	0	0	4	0
Team	27	1	3	27	16	0

Cleveland	000	000	000	–0
Worcester	000	010	00x	–1

Runs batted in - none
Double play - Glasscock, Dunlap and Phillips

	ip	h	r	er	bb	so
McCormick (L)	8	3	1	0	1	7
Richmond (W)	9	0	0	0	0	5

Time - 1:27
Umpire - Bradley
Attendance - 700

John Montgomery Ward, Pro vs Buf NL, 5-0; June 17, 1880 (A.M.)

PROVIDENCE	ab	r	h	po	a	e
Hines,cf	5	0	2	2	0	0
Start,lb	5	1	1	14	0	0
Dorgan,rf	5	0	2	0	0	0
Gross,c	5	0	0	5	1	0
Farrell,2b	4	3	3	0	2	0
Ward,p	4	0	1	2	6	0
Peters,ss	4	0	1	0	6	0
York,lf	4	0	2	3	0	0
Bradley,3b	4	1	1	1	4	0
Team	40	5	13	27	19	0

BUFFALO	ab	r	h	po	a	e
Crowley,rf-c	3	0	0	4	0	2
Richardson,3b	3	0	0	0	1	0
Rowe,c-rf	3	0	0	3	1	0
Walker,lf	3	0	0	3	0	1
Hornung,2b	3	0	0	2	3	0
Mack,ss	3	0	0	3	3	1
Esterbrook,lb	3	0	0	10	0	0
Poorman,cf	3	0	0	2	0	1
Galvin,p	3	0	0	0	5	0
Team	27	0	0	27	13	5

Providence	010	100	111	–5
Buffalo	000	000	000	–0

Double - Farrell

Triples - Start, York, Bradley
Runs batted in - Ward, Hines, Dorgan
Passed ball - Crowley

	ip	h	r	er	bb	so
Ward (W)	9	0	0	0	0	6
Galvin (L)	9	13	5	3	0	2

Wild pitches - Galvin 2
Time - 1:40
Umpire - Daniels
Attendance - 2000

Cy Young, Bos vs Phi AL, 3-0; May 5, 1904

PHILADELPHIA	ab	r	h	po	a	e
Hartsel,lf	1	0	0	0	0	0
Hoffman,lf	2	0	0	2	1	0
Pickering,cf	3	0	0	1	0	0
Davis,lb	3	0	0	5	0	1
L.Cross,3b	3	0	0	4	1	0
Seybold,rf	3	0	0	2	0	0
Murphy,2b	3	0	0	1	2	0
M.Cross,ss	3	0	0	2	3	0
Schreck,c	3	0	0	7	0	0
Waddell,p	3	0	0	0	1	0
Team	27	0	0	24	8	1

BOSTON	ab	r	h	po	a	e
Dougherty,lf	4	0	1	1	0	0
Collins,3b	4	0	2	2	0	0
Stahl,cf	4	1	1	3	0	0
Freeman,rf	4	0	1	2	0	0
Parent,ss	4	0	2	1	4	0
LaChance,lb	3	0	1	9	0	0
Ferris,2b	3	1	1	0	3	0
Criger,c	3	1	1	9	0	0
Young,p	3	0	0	0	2	0
Team	32	3	10	27	9	0

Philadelphia	000	000	000	–0
Boston	000	001	20x	–3

Doubles - Collins, Criger
Triples - Stahl, Freeman, Ferris
Runs batted in - Freeman, Criger
Sacrifice - LaChance
Double plays - Hoffman and Schreck; L.Cross and Davis

	ip	h	r	er	bb	so
Waddell (L)	8	10	3	2	0	6
Young (W)	9	0	0	0	0	8

Time - 1:30
Umpire - Dwyer
Attendance - 10,267

Addie Joss, Cle vs Chi AL, 1-0; October 2, 1908

CHICAGO	ab	r	h	po	a	e
Hahn,rf	3	0	0	1	0	0
Jones,cf	3	0	0	0	0	0
Isbell,lb	3	0	0	6	1	1
Dougherty,lf	3	0	0	0	0	0
Davis,2b	3	0	0	1	0	0
Parent,ss	3	0	0	0	3	0
Schreck,c	2	0	0	13	1	0
Shaw,c	0	0	0	2	0	0
White,ph	1	0	0	0	0	0

	ab	r	h	po	a	e
Tannehill,3b	2	0	0	0	0	0
Donohue,ph	1	0	0	0	0	0
Walsh,p	2	0	0	1	3	0
Anderson,ph	1	0	0	0	0	0
Team	27	0	0	24	8	1

CLEVELAND	ab	r	h	po	a	e
Good,rf	4	0	0	1	0	0
Bradley,3b	4	0	0	0	1	0
Hinchman,lf	3	0	0	3	0	0
Lajoie,2b	3	0	1	2	8	0
Stovall,1b	3	0	0	16	0	0
Clarke,c	3	0	0	4	1	0
Birmingham,cf	4	1	2	0	0	0
Perring,ss	2	0	1	1	1	0
Joss,p	3	0	0	0	5	0
Team	29	1	4	27	16	0
Chicago	000	000	000	–0		
Cleveland	001	000	00x	–1		

Runs batted in - none
Stolen bases - Birmingham 2

	ip	h	r	er	bb	so
Walsh (L)	8	4	1	0	1	15
Joss (W)	9	0	0	0	0	3

Wild pitch - Walsh
Time - 1:40
Umpires - Connolly and O'Loughlin
Attendance - 10,598

Ernie Shore, Bos vs Was AL, 4-0; June 23, 1917 (1st game)

WASHINGTON	ab	r	h	po	a	e
Morgan,2b	2	0	0	4	2	0
Foster,3b	3	0	0	1	3	2
Leonard,3b	0	0	0	0	1	0
Milan,cf	3	0	0	1	0	0
Rice,rf	3	0	0	3	0	1
Gharrity,1b	0	0	0	0	0	0
Judge,1b	3	0	0	11	1	0
Jamieson,lf	3	0	0	0	0	0
Shanks,ss	3	0	0	1	2	0
Henry,c	3	0	0	1	0	0
Ayers,p	2	0	0	2	8	0
Menosky,ph	1	0	0	0	0	0
Team	26	0	0	24	17	3

BOSTON	ab	r	h	po	a	e
Hooper,rf	4	0	1	0	0	0
Barry,2b	4	0	0	2	1	0
Hoblitzel,1b	4	0	0	12	2	0
Gardner,3b	4	1	1	2	1	0
Lewis,lf	4	0	3	2	0	0
Walker,cf	3	1	1	4	0	0
Scott,ss	3	0	0	1	5	0
Thomas,c	0	0	0	0	0	0
Agnew,c	3	1	3	2	1	0
Ruth,p	0	0	0	0	0	0
Shore,p	2	1	0	2	6	0
Team	31	4	9	27	16	0
Washington	000	000	000	–0		
Boston	010	000	30x	–4		

Doubles - Walker, Agnew
Runs batted in - Agnew 2, Hooper 2
Sacrifices - Walker, Shore, Scott
Caught stealing - Morgan
Double plays - Ayers, Foster and Judge; Ayers and Judge

	ip	h	r	er	bb	so
Ayers (L)	8	9	4	2	0	0
Ruth	0	0	0	0	1	0
Shore (W)	9	0	0	0	0	2

Time 1:40
Umpires - Owens, McCormick and Dinneen
Attendance - 16,158

Charlie Robertson, Chi at Det AL, 2-0; April 30, 1922

CHICAGO	ab	r	h	po	a	e
Mulligan,ss	4	0	1	0	0	0
McClellan,3b	3	0	1	1	3	0
Collins,2b	3	0	1	4	3	0
Hooper,rf	3	1	0	3	0	0
Mostil,lf	4	1	1	3	0	0
Strunk,cf	3	0	0	0	0	0
Sheely,1b	4	0	2	9	0	0
Schalk,c	4	0	1	7	1	0
Robertson,p	4	0	0	0	1	0
Team	32	2	7	27	8	0

DETROIT	ab	r	h	po	a	e
Blue,1b	3	0	0	11	3	1
Cutshaw,2b	3	0	0	2	3	0
Cobb,cf	3	0	0	1	0	0
Veach,lf	3	0	0	2	0	0
Heilmann,rf	3	0	0	1	0	0
Jones,3b	3	0	0	1	5	0
Rigney,ss	2	0	0	2	1	0
Clark,ph	1	0	0	0	0	0
Manion,c	3	0	0	7	1	0
Pillette,p	2	0	0	0	3	0
Bassler,ph	1	0	0	0	0	0
Team	27	0	0	27	16	1
Chicago	020	000	000	–2		
Detroit	000	000	000	–0		

Doubles - Mulligan, Sheely
Runs batted in - Sheely 2
Sacrifices - McClellan, Collins, Strunk

	ip	h	r	er	bb	so
Robertson (W)	9	0	0	0	0	6
Pillette (L)	9	7	2	2	2	5

Time - 1:55
Umpires - Nallin and Evans
Attendance - 25,000

Don Larsen, NY AL vs Bro NL, 2-0; October 8, 1956 (World Series)

BROOKLYN	ab	r	h	po	a	e
Gilliam,2b	3	0	0	2	0	0
Reese,ss	3	0	0	4	2	0
Snider,cf	3	0	0	1	0	0
Robinson,2b	3	0	0	2	4	0
Hodges,1b	3	0	0	5	1	0
Amoros,lf	3	0	0	3	0	0
Furillo,rf	3	0	0	0	0	0
Campanella,c	3	0	0	7	2	0
Maglie,p	2	0	0	0	1	0
Mitchell,ph	1	0	0	0	0	0
Team	27	0	0	24	10	0

NEW YORK	ab	r	h	po	a	e
Bauer,rf	4	0	1	4	0	0
Collins,1b	4	0	1	7	0	0
Mantle,cf	3	1	1	4	0	0

Berra,c	3	0	0	7	0	0
Slaughter,lf	2	0	0	1	0	0
Martin,2b	3	0	1	3	4	0
McDougald,ss	2	0	0	0	2	0
Carey,3b	3	1	1	1	1	0
Larsen,p	2	0	0	0	1	0
Team	26	2	5	27	8	0
Brooklyn	000	000	000	−0		
New York	000	101	00x	−2		

Home run - Mantle

Runs batted in - Mantle, Bauer

Sacrifice - Larsen

Double plays - Reese and Hodges; Hodges, Campanella, Robinson, Campanella and Robinson

	ip	h	r	er	bb	so
Maglie (L)	8	5	2	2	2	5
Larsen (W)	9	0	0	0	0	7

Time - 2:06

Umpires - Pinelli, Soar, Boggess, Napp, Gorman, Runge

Attendance - 64,519

Harvey Haddix, Pit at Mil NL, 0-1; May 26, 1959 (12 perfect innings, lost on one-hit in the 13th inning)

PITTSBURGH	ab	r	h	po	a	e
Schofield,ss	6	0	3	2	4	0
Virdon,cf	6	0	1	8	0	0
Burgess,c	5	0	0	8	0	0
Nelson,1b	5	0	2	14	0	0
Skinner,lf	5	0	1	4	0	0
Mazeroski,2b	5	0	1	1	1	0
Hoak,3b	5	0	2	0	6	1
Mejias,rf	3	0	1	1	0	0
Stuart,ph	1	0	0	0	0	0
Christopher,rf	1	0	0	0	0	0
Haddix,p	5	0	1	0	2	0
Team	47	0	12	38	13	1

MILWAUKEE	ab	r	h	po	a	e
O'Brien,2b	3	0	0	2	5	0
Rice,ph	1	0	0	0	0	0
Mantilla,2b	1	1	0	1	2	0
Mathews,3b	4	0	0	2	3	0
Aaron,rf	4	0	0	1	0	0
Adcock,1b	5	0	1	17	3	0
Covington,lf	4	0	0	4	0	0
Crandall,c	4	0	0	3	5	0
Pafko,cf	4	0	0	6	0	0
Logan,ss	4	0	0	3	5	0
Burdette,p	4	0	0	1	3	0
Team	38	1	1	39	22	0
Pittsburgh	000	000	000	000	0–0	
Milwaukee	000	000	000	000	1–1	

Double - Adcock

Run batted in - Adcock

Sacrifice - Mathews

Double plays - Adcock, Logan and Adcock; Mathews, O'Brien and Adcock; Adcock and Logan

	ip	h	r	er	bb	so
Haddix (L)	12 2/3	1	1	0	1	8
Burdette (W)	13	12	0	0	0	2

Time - 2:54

Umpires - Smith, Dascoli, Secory and Dixon

Attendance - 19,194

Jim Bunning, Phi at NY NL, 6-0; June 21, 1964

PHILADELPHIA	ab	r	h	po	a	e
Briggs,cf	4	1	0	2	0	0
Herrnstein,1b	4	0	0	7	0	0
Callison,rf	4	1	2	1	0	0
Allen,3b	3	0	1	0	2	0
Covington,lf	2	0	0	1	0	0
Wine,pr-ss	1	1	0	2	1	0
T.Taylor,2b	3	2	1	0	3	0
Rojas,ss-lf	3	0	1	3	0	0
Triandos,c	4	1	2	11	1	0
Bunning,p	4	0	1	0	0	0
Team	32	6	8	27	7	0

NEW YORK	ab	r	h	po	a	e
Hickman,cf	3	0	0	2	0	0
Hunt,2b	3	0	0	3	2	0
Kranepool,1b	3	0	0	8	1	0
Christopher,rf	3	0	0	4	0	0
Gonder,c	3	0	0	6	2	0
R.Taylor,lf	3	0	0	1	0	0
C.Smith,ss	3	0	0	2	1	0
Samuel,3b	2	0	0	0	1	0
Altman,ph	1	0	0	0	0	0
Stallard,p	1	0	0	0	2	0
Wakefield,p	0	0	0	0	0	0
Kanehl,ph	1	0	0	0	0	0
Sturdivant,p	0	0	0	1	0	0
Stephenson,ph	1	0	0	0	0	0
Team	27	0	0	27	9	0
Philadelphia	110	004	000	−6		
New York	000	000	000	−0		

Doubles - Triandos, Bunning

Home run - Callison

Runs batted in - Callison, Allen, Triandos 2, Bunning 2

Sacrifices - Hernstein, Rojas

	ip	h	r	er	bb	so
Bunning (W)	9	0	0	0	0	10
Stallard (L)	5 2/3	7	6	6	4	3
Wakefield	1/3	0	0	0	0	0
Sturdivant	3	1	0	0	0	3

Wild pitch - Stallard

Time - 2:19

Umpires - Sudol, Pryor, Secory and Burkhart

Attendance - 32,026

Sandy Koufax, LA vs Chi NL, 1-0; September 9, 1965

CHICAGO	ab	r	h	po	a	e
Young,cf	3	0	0	5	0	0
Beckert,2b	3	0	0	1	1	0
Williams,rf	3	0	0	0	0	0
Santo,3b	3	0	0	1	2	0
Banks,1b	3	0	0	13	0	0
Browne,lf	3	0	0	1	0	0
Krug,c	3	0	0	3	0	1
Kessinger,ss	2	0	0	0	2	0
Amalfitano,ph	1	0	0	0	0	0
Hendley,p	2	0	0	0	5	0
Kuenn,ph	1	0	0	0	0	0
Team	27	0	0	24	10	1

LOS ANGELES	ab	r	h	po	a	e
Wills,ss	3	0	0	0	2	0
Gilliam,3b	3	0	0	0	1	0
W.Davis,cf	3	0	0	2	0	0
Johnson,lf	2	1	1	2	0	0
Fairly,rf	2	0	0	3	0	0
Lefebvre,2b	3	0	0	1	0	0
Tracewski,2b	0	0	0	0	0	0
Parker,lb	3	0	0	4	0	0
Torborg,c	3	0	0	15	0	0
Koufax,p	2	0	0	0	0	0
Team	24	1	1	27	3	0
Chicago	000	000	000	−0		
Los Angeles	000	010	00x	−1		

Double - Johnson
Runs batted in - none
Sacrifice - Fairly
Stolen base - Johnson

	ip	h	r	er	bb	so
Hendley (L)	8	1	1	0	1	3
Koufax (W)	9	0	0	0	0	14

Time - 1:43
Umpires - Vargo, Pelekoudas, Jackowski and Pryor
Attendance - 29,139

Jim "Catfish" Hunter, Oak vs Min AL, 4-0; May 8, 1968

MINNESOTA	ab	r	h	po	a	e
Tovar,3b	3	0	0	1	2	0
Carew,2b	3	0	0	4	1	0
Killebrew,lb	3	0	0	5	0	0
Oliva,rf	3	0	0	3	0	0
Uhlaender,cf	3	0	0	2	0	0
Allison,lf	3	0	0	0	0	0
Hernandez,ss	2	0	0	2	4	0
Roseboro,ph	1	0	0	0	0	0
Look,c	3	0	0	7	2	0
Boswell,p	2	0	0	0	1	1
Perranoski,p	0	0	0	0	0	0
Reese,ph	1	0	0	0	0	0
Team	27	0	0	24	10	1

OAKLAND	ab	r	h	po	a	e
Campaneris,ss	4	0	2	1	3	0
Jackson,rf	4	0	0	3	0	0
Bando,3b	3	0	1	0	2	0
Webster,lb	4	1	2	7	0	0
Donaldson,2b	3	0	0	1	2	0
Pagliaroni,c	3	1	0	11	0	0
Monday,cf	3	2	2	2	0	0
Rudi,lf	3	0	0	2	0	0
Robinson,ph	0	0	0	0	0	0
Cater,ph	0	0	0	0	0	0
Hershberger,lf	0	0	0	0	0	0
Hunter,p	4	0	3	0	0	0
Team	31	4	10	27	7	0
Minnesota	000	000	000 - 0			
Oakland	000	000	13x - 4			

Doubles - Hunter, Monday
Runs batted in - Hunter 3, Cater
Stolen base - Campaneris
Double plays - Boswell, Hernandez and Killebrew;
  Hernandez, Carew and Killebrew

	ip	h	r	er	bb	so
Boswell (L)	7 2/3	9	4	4	4	6
Perranoski	1/3	1	0	0	1	0

Hunter (W)	9	0	0	0	0	11

Hit by pitch - by Boswell (Donaldson)
Wild pitches - Boswell 2
Time - 2:28
Umpires - Napp, Salerno, Haller and Neudecker
Attendance - 6,298

Len Barker, Cle vs Tor AL, 3-0; May 15, 1981

TORONTO	ab	r	h	po	a	e
Griffin,ss	3	0	0	1	1	1
Moseby,rf	3	0	0	4	0	0
Bell,lf	3	0	0	2	0	0
Mayberry,lb	3	0	0	4	1	1
Upshaw,dh	3	0	0	0	0	0
Garcia,2b	3	0	0	3	2	1
Bosetti,cf	3	0	0	3	0	0
Ainge,3b	2	0	0	1	0	0
Woods,ph	1	0	0	0	0	0
B.Martinez,c	2	0	0	5	1	0
Whitt,ph	1	0	0	0	0	0
Leal,p	0	0	0	1	1	0
Team	27	0	0	24	6	3

CLEVELAND	ab	r	h	po	a	e
Manning,cf	4	1	1	4	0	0
Orta,rf	4	1	3	0	0	0
Hargrove,lb	4	1	1	9	0	0
Thornton,dh	3	0	0	0	0	0
Hassey,c	4	0	1	11	0	0
Harrah,3b	4	0	1	2	0	0
Charbonneau,lf	3	0	0	1	0	0
Kuiper,2b	3	0	0	0	4	0
Veryzer,ss	3	0	0	0	3	0
Barker,p	0	0	0	0	0	0
Team	32	3	7	27	7	0
Toronto	000	000	000 - 0			
Cleveland	200	000	01x - 3			

Home run - Orta
Runs batted in - Thornton, Hassey, Orta
Sacrifice - Thornton

	ip	h	r	er	bb	so
Leal (L)	8	7	3	1	0	5
Barker (W)	9	0	0	0	0	11

Time - 2:09
Umpires - Garcia, Kosc, Denkinger and McKean
Attendance - 7,290

Mike Witt, Cal at Tex AL, 1-0; September 30, 1984
(last game of the season)

CALIFORNIA	ab	r	h	po	a	e
Wilfong,2b	4	0	0	0	8	0
Sconiers,lb	3	0	0	10	1	0
Grich,lb	0	0	0	2	0	0
Lynn,cf-rf	4	0	2	1	0	0
DeCinces,3b	4	1	2	0	1	0
Downing,lf	4	0	1	1	0	0
Thomas,lf	0	0	0	0	0	0
Re.Jackson,dh	4	0	0	0	0	0
M.Brown,rf	3	0	3	2	0	0
Pettis,cf	0	0	0	0	0	0
Boone,c	3	0	0	10	0	0
Schofield,ss	2	0	0	0	3	0
Witt,p	0	0	0	1	0	0
Team	31	1	7	27	13	0

TEXAS	ab	r	h	po	a	e
Rivers,dh	3	0	0	0	0	0
Tolleson,2b	3	0	0	4	5	0
Ward,lf	3	0	0	0	0	0
Parrish,3b	3	0	0	0	3	0
O'Brien,1b	3	0	0	13	0	0
G.Wright,cf	3	0	0	3	0	0
Dunbar,rf	3	0	0	1	0	0
Scott,c	2	0	0	4	3	0
B.Jones,ph	1	0	0	0	0	0
Wilkerson,ss	2	0	0	2	4	0
Foley,ph	1	0	0	0	0	0
Hough,p	0	0	0	0	2	0
Team	27	0	0	27	17	0

California	000	000	100 - 1
Texas	000	000	000 - 0

Double - Brown

Triple - Brown

Run batted in - Jackson

Double plays - Parrish, Tolleson and O'Brien; Tolleson, Wilkerson and O'Brien

Passed ball - Scott

	ip	h	r	er	bb	so
Witt (W)	9	0	0	0	0	10
Hough (L)	9	7	1	0	3	3

Wild pitch - Hough

Time - 1:49

Umpires - Kosc, Hendry, Coble and Evans

Attendance - 8,375

Tom Browning, Cin vs LA NL, 1-0; September 16, 1988

LOS ANGELES	ab	r	h	po	a	e
Griffin,ss	3	0	0	0	4	0
Hatcher,1b	3	0	0	10	0	0
Gibson,lf	3	0	0	1	0	0
Gonzalez,lf	0	0	0	0	0	0
Marshall,rf	3	0	0	2	0	0
Shelby,cf	3	0	0	2	0	0
Hamilton,3b	3	0	0	0	1	1
Dempsey,c	3	0	0	7	0	0
Sax,2b	3	0	0	2	2	0
Belcher,p	2	0	0	0	2	0
Woodson,ph	1	0	0	0	0	0
Team	27	0	0	24	9	0

CINCINNATI	ab	r	h	po	a	e
Larkin,ss	3	1	1	0	4	0
Sabo,3b	3	0	1	0	3	0
Daniels,lf	3	0	0	3	0	0
Davis,cf	2	0	0	1	0	0
O'Neill,rf	3	0	0	4	0	0
Esasky,1b	3	0	0	10	1	0
Reed,c	3	0	0	7	0	0
Oester,2b	3	0	1	1	1	0
Browning,p	3	0	1	1	0	0
Team	26	1	3	27	9	0

Los Angeles	000	000	000 - 0
Cincinnati	000	001	00x - 1

Double - Larkin

Run batted in - none

	ip	h	r	er	bb	so
Belcher (L)	8	3	1	0	1	7
Browning (W)	9	0	0	0	0	7

Time - 1:51

Umpires - Quick, Hirschbeck, Kibler and Gregg

Attendance - 16,591

Dennis Martinez, Mon at LA NL, 2-0; July 28, 1991

MONTREAL	ab	r	h	po	a	e
DeShields,2b	3	0	1	0	9	0
Grissom,cf	4	0	0	2	0	0
Da.Martinez,rf	4	1	0	0	0	0
Calderon,lf	3	0	0	2	0	0
Wallach,3b	4	0	0	1	1	0
Walker,1b	4	1	1	17	0	0
Hassey,c	3	0	1	5	0	0
Owen,ss	3	0	0	0	2	0
De.Martinez,p	3	0	1	0	2	0
Team	31	2	4	27	14	0

LOS ANGELES	ab	r	h	po	a	e
Butler,cf	3	0	0	1	0	0
Samuel,2b	3	0	0	1	3	0
Murray,1b	3	0	0	8	2	0
Strawberry,rf	3	0	0	4	0	0
Daniels,lf	3	0	0	3	0	0
Harris,3b	3	0	0	0	0	0
Scioscia,c	3	0	0	5	1	0
Griffin,ss	2	0	0	4	4	2
Javier,ph	1	0	0	0	0	0
Morgan,p	2	0	0	1	2	0
Gwynn,ph	1	0	0	0	0	0
Team	27	0	0	26	12	2

Montreal	000	000	200 - 2
Los Angeles	000	000	000 - 0

Triple - Walker

Run batted in - Walker

Caught stealing - Hassey

	ip	h	r	er	bb	so
De.Martinez (W)	9	0	0	0	0	5
Morgan (L)	9	4	2	0	1	5

Wild pitch - Morgan

Time - 2:14

Umpires - Poncino, Froemming, DeMuth and Bonin

Attendance - 45,560

M ajor

L eague

R eport

Pittsburgh Pirates

80

Pittsburgh ace John Smiley won 20 games in 1991.

'Killer Bs' lead Bucs to repeat

Before this season began, most observers gave the Pittsburgh Pirates little chance to repeat as champions of the National League East. They saw distractions and contract problems and put the Pirates down for a third or fourth-place finish.

Perhaps fueled by their skeptics, the Pirates got to first place by the end of April and stayed there for the rest of the season.

By the end of the year, they had won 98 games and the division by 14 games. They became the first National League team to repeat a division title since the 1978 Dodgers and Phillies.The players, led by outfielder Barry Bonds and Bobby Bonilla, used the fact that nobody expected to repeat as motivation.

"All this team needs is a challenge," said Bonds, who didn't quite repeat his MVP numbers of 1990 but came close with a .292 average, 25 homers and 116 RBI.

Bonilla, perhaps playing his final year with the Pirates before free agency, hit .302 with 18 homers and 100 RBI. They became the first two Pirates in history to repeat 100-RBI seasons.

Shortstop Jay Bell had the best season of his career, hitting 16 homers with 67 RBI, and outfielder Andy Van Slyke hit 17 homers and drove in 83 runs.

"I don't think we've gotten the respect we deserve," Van Slyke said.

The pitching staff was led by John Smiley, who became the first Pirate lefthander since John Candelaria to win 20 games in a season. Zane Smith won 16 and Doug Drabek 15.

"People didn't realize we'd get better," Bell said. "We're more mature, more confident. I see guys that supposedly had career years last year turn around and do it again."

The biggest holes the Pirates had before the season were at first base and in the leadoff spot. Rookie Orlando Merced, platooning with Gary Redus, filled both of them, hitting .275 with 10 homers and 50 RBI.

When Jeff King and rookie John Wehner went down with back injuries, general manager Larry Doughty filled that potential hole by trading for Steve Buechele from the Texas Rangers. That trade helped convince the players and manager Jim Leyland that 1991 was going to be a good season.

"In the last two years I don't think I've ever seen as many smiles in the clubhouse as after we acquired Buechele and last year after we picked up Zane Smith," Leyland said. "I think making trades like that sends a message to your players. It really shows the players that top management wants to win."

—Rob Rains

Pirates 1992 preview

The Pirates won their second consecutive NL East division title last season, but again failed to advance to the World Series. It will be harder to defend the title this season, with Bobby Bonilla gone to the Mets.

Such a gaping hole in the lineup is impossible to fill, but the Pirates again rely on good starting pitching and strong defense to keep them in games.

John Smiley, Zane Smith and Doug Drabek anchor the staff. Shortstop Jay Bell contributed at the plate last year (.267, 16 HR, 67 RBI, 98 runs)—and should continue to be a steady defensive player and team leader.

Two problem areas: no bona fide closer, and third base—especially if Steve Buechele leaves and Jeff King and John Wehner continue to suffer from back injuries.

But despite the shortcomings, this club has a better chance of winning any game with Jim Leyland as manager.

82

1992 prophecy: Pirates

▸The Pirates will sign flashy slugger Barry Bonds to a new lucrative lifetime agreement with the stipulation that he not play in any postseason games.

▸A sportswiter will be fired for criticizing the play of Pittsburgh quote machine Andy Van Slyke.

—John Hunt

Bucs' team name has dubious history

By Norman Macht

When the Pittsburgh Pirates won their second straight NL East title, they flew the flag of the oldest continuously-used team name in professional sports.

It was 100 years ago that the Smokey City Club was branded the Pirates for hijacking a player from another team. Here is the way it happened:

When the players revolted in 1890 and formed their own league, second baseman Lou Bierbauer was among more than 100 who deserted the two major leagues of the time, the National and the American Association. Bierbauer had been with the Philadelphia Athletics of the AA for four years, and was on their reserve list at the time he jumped.

The Players' League folded after one season, and the terms of the peace treaty provided for all players to be returned to their original teams. But the Philadelphia owners had neglected to write Bierbauer's name on their reserve list, and the NL's Pittsburgh Alleghenys signed him. Despite the Athletics' clerical oversight, the AA and the public considered this an unethical act and a violation of the spirit of the agreement.

Nasty words flew between the Pennsylvania cities; the one that stuck was "pirates," and the Jolly Roger has flown the Pittsburgh masthead ever since.

Bierbauer played for the Bucs for six

years, batted .267 for his 13-year career and led second basemen in assists five times.

Note: Cincinnati carried the name Reds since 1890, but in 1952—during the McCarthy era—they changed their name to the Redlegs. In 1959 they went back to the Reds.

—Norman Macht is a member of the Society for American Baseball Research.

How the '91 champs became Pirates

Name	Pos	How obtained
J. Bell	SS	March 1989, trade with Cleveland for IF Felix Fermin
B.Bonds	LF	1st round draft pick 1985; major league debut 1986
B.Bonilla	RF	July 1986 trade with Chicago White Sox for P Jose DeLeon
D.Drabek	RHP	Nov. 1986 trade with New York Yankees, along with Ps Logan Easley and Brian Fisher Pat Clements, Cecilio Guante and Rick Rhoden
J.King	3B	1st round draft pick 1986; major league debut 1989
B.Landrum	RHP	Signed as free agent Jan. 1989
M.LaValliere	C	Apr. 1987 trade with St. Louis, along with Andy Van Slyke and P Mike Dunne for C Tony Pena
J. Lind	2B	Signed as non-drafted free agent Dec. 1982; major league debut 1987
O.Merced	1B	Signed as non-drafted free agent Feb. 1985; major league debut 1991

Name	Pos	How obtained
G.Redus	1B/OF	Aug. 1988 trade with Chicago White Sox for OF/1B Mike Diaz
D.Slaught	C	Dec 1989 trade with New York Yankees for Ps Jeff Robinson and Willie Smith
J.Smiley	LHP	12th-round draft pick 1983; major league debut 1986
Z.Smith	LHP	Aug. 1990 trade with Montreal for P Scott Ruskin, SS Willie Greene and OF Moises Alou (named later)
R.Tomlin	LHP	18th-round draft pick 1988; major league debut 1990
A.Van Slyke	CF	April 1987 trade with St. Louis, along with Mike LaValliere and P Mike Dunne for C Tony Pena

SOURCE: Pittsburgh Pirates

Bucs went to play-offs, Heaton went home

When the rest of his team went to battle the Atlanta Braves for the National League pennant, pitcher Neal Heaton went home to East Patchogue, N.J. He was upset about being left off of the Pirates' postseason roster, along with fellow pitcher Vicente Palacios and catcher Tom Prince.

"I really don't want to talk about it," Heaton said. "You understand."

Manager Jim Leyland understood, but said that he had to take the 11 pitchers he thought were the best. Heaton was on the All-Star team in 1990, but suffered shoulder inflammation that limited him to a 2-5 record after the break. He was relegated to the bullpen in 1991, and had a 3-3 record with no saves and a 4.33 ERA in 42 games.

"He took it real tough," Leyland said.

"Believe me, it was tough to tell him. It's a tough thing for these guys. They've worked hard, all of them."

Leyland asked the three players to stay with the team during the postseason, but said he would understand if they chose to go home. Heaton and Palacios went home; Prince said he would stay.

Palacios was 6-3 in 1991, but all of his losses were to the Braves.

Team directory

▶Owner: Pittsburgh Baseball Associates

▶General Manager: Larry Doughty

▶Ballpark:
Three Rivers Stadium
600 Stadium Circle, Pittsburgh, Pennsylvania
800-BUY-BUCS
Capacity 58,729
Pay parking lot; $4
Public transportation available
Family and wheelchair sections, ramps, guest relations

▶Team publications:
Yearbook, Scorecard, Official Record and Info Guide

▶TV, radio broadcast stations:
KDKA 1020 AM, KDKA Channel 2, TCI Cable

▶Camps and/or clinics:
TBA, 412-323-5000

▶Spring Training:
McKechnie Field
Bradenton, Florida
Capacity 5,000
813-748-4610

PITTSBURGH PIRATES 1991 Final Stats

Batting	AVG	SLG	OB	G	AB	R	H	TB	2B	3B	HR	RBI	BB	SO	SB	CS	E
Banister	1.000	1.000	1.000	1	1	0	1	1	0	0	0	0	0	0	0	0	0
Wehner	.340	.406	.381	37	106	15	36	43	7	0	0	7	7	17	3	0	6
Bonilla	.302	.492	.391	157	577	102	174	284	44	6	18	100	90	67	2	4	15
Slaught	.295	.395	.363	77	220	19	65	87	17	1	1	29	21	32	1	0	5
Bonds	.292	.514	.410	153	510	95	149	262	28	5	25	116	107	73	43	13	3
LaValliere	.289	.360	.351	108	336	25	97	121	11	2	3	41	33	27	2	1	1
McClendon	.288	.460	.366	85	163	24	47	75	7	0	7	24	18	23	2	1	3
Merced	.275	.399	.373	120	411	83	113	164	17	2	10	50	64	81	8	4	12
Varsho	.273	.417	.344	99	187	23	51	78	11	2	4	23	19	34	9	2	1
Bell	.270	.428	.330	157	608	96	164	260	32	8	16	67	52	99	10	6	24
Lind	.265	.339	.306	150	502	53	133	170	16	6	3	54	30	56	7	4	9
Van Slyke	.265	.446	.355	138	491	87	130	219	24	7	17	83	71	85	10	3	1
Prince	.265	.441	.405	26	34	4	9	15	3	0	1	2	7	3	0	0	1
Garcia	.250	.417	.280	12	24	2	6	10	0	2	0	1	1	8	0	0	1
Richardson	.250	.250	.250	6	4	0	1	1	0	0	0	0	0	3	0	0	0
Redus	.246	.393	.324	98	252	45	62	99	12	2	7	24	28	39	17	3	6
Buechele	.246	.412	.315	31	114	16	28	47	5	1	4	19	10	28	0	1	4
Espy	.244	.329	.281	43	82	7	20	27	4	0	1	11	5	17	4	0	2
King	.239	.376	.328	33	109	16	26	41	1	1	4	18	14	15	3	1	2
Wilkerson	.188	.277	.243	85	191	20	36	53	9	1	2	18	15	40	2	1	2
Redfield	.111	.111	.273	11	18	1	2	2	0	0	0	0	4	1	0	1	1
Gonzalez	.042	.104	.078	58	48	5	2	5	0	0	1	3	2	15	0	0	0
Bullett	.000	.000	.200	11	4	2	0	0	0	0	0	0	0	3	1	1	0
Schulz	.000	.000	.000	3	3	0	0	0	0	0	0	0	0	2	0	0	0

Pitching	W-L	ERA	G	GS	CG	GF	Sho	SV	IP	H	R	ER	HR	BB	SO
Tomlin	8-7	2.98	31	27	4	0	2	0	175	170	75	58	9	54	104
Mason	3-2	3.03	24	0	0	6	0	3	29.2	21	11	10	2	6	21
Drabek	15-14	3.07	35	35	5	0	2	0	234.2	245	92	80	16	62	142
Smiley	20-8	3.08	33	32	2	0	1	0	207.2	194	78	71	17	44	129
Landrum	4-4	3.18	61	0	0	43	0	17	76.1	76	32	27	4	19	45
Smith	16-10	3.20	35	35	6	0	3	0	228	234	95	81	15	29	120
Belinda	7-5	3.45	60	0	0	37	0	16	78.1	50	30	30	10	35	71
Walk	9-2	3.60	25	20	0	0	0	0	115	104	53	46	10	35	67
Palacios	6-3	3.75	36	7	1	8	1	3	81.2	69	34	34	12	38	64
Rodriguez	1-1	4.11	18	0	0	8	0	6	15.1	14	7	7	1	8	10
Patterson	4-3	4.11	54	1	0	19	0	2	65.2	67	32	30	7	15	57
Heaton	3-3	4.33	42	1	0	5	0	0	68.2	72	37	33	6	21	34
Kipper	2-2	4.65	52	0	0	18	0	4	60	66	34	31	7	22	38
Miller	0-0	5.40	1	1	0	0	0	0	5	4	3	3	0	3	2
Huismann	0-0	7.20	5	0	0	0	0	0	5	7	6	4	0	2	5
Fajardo	0-0	9.95	2	2	0	0	0	0	6.1	10	7	7	0	7	8
Reed	0-0	10.38	1	1	0	0	0	0	4.1	8	6	5	1	1	2

1992 Preliminary Roster

Pitchers (18)

Joe Ausanio
Miguel Batista
Stan Belinda
Victor Cole
Doug Drabek
Neal Heaton
Bill Landrum
Roger Mason
Paul Miller
Blas Minor
Vicente Palacios
Bob Patterson
Rick Reed
Rosario Rodriguez
Mike Roesler
John Smiley
Zane Smith
Randy Tomlin

Catchers (3)

Tom Prince
Mandy Romero
Don Slaught

Infielders (10)

Mike LaValliere
Jay Bell
Carlos Garcia
Jeff King
Jose Lind

Orlando Merced
Gary Redus
Jeff Richardson
Ben Shelton
John Wehner

Outfielders (9)

Barry Bonds
Scott Bullett
Cecil Espy
Albert Martin
Lloyd McClendon
Terry McDaniel
Daryl Ratliff
Andy Van Slyke
Gary Varsho

Games played by position

	G	C	1B	2B	3B	SS	OF
Banister,J	1	0	0	0	0	0	0
Bell,Ja	157	0	0	0	0	156	0
Bonds,B	153	0	0	0	0	0	150
Bonilla,B	157	0	4	0	67	0	104
Buechele,S	31	0	0	0	31	0	0
Bullett,J	11	0	0	0	0	0	3
Espy,C	43	0	0	0	0	0	35
Garcia,C	12	0	0	1	2	9	0
Gonzalez,Jo	58	0	0	0	0	0	41
King,J	33	0	0	0	33	0	0
LaValliere,M	108	105	0	0	0	0	0
Lind,J	150	0	0	149	0	0	0
McClendon,L	85	2	22	0	0	0	32
Merced,O	120	0	105	0	0	0	7
Prince,T	26	19	1	0	0	0	0
Redfield,J	11	0	0	0	9	0	0
Redus,G	98	0	47	0	0	0	33
Richardson,Je	6	0	0	0	3	2	0
Schulz,J	3	0	0	0	0	0	0
Slaught,D	77	69	0	0	1	0	0
Van Slyke,A	138	0	0	0	0	0	135
Varsho,G	99	0	3	0	0	0	54
Wehner,J	37	0	0	0	36	0	0
Wilkerson,C	85	0	0	30	14	15	0

Sick call: 1991 DL report

Player	Days on the DL
Bob Walk	65*
Jeff King	31*
Don Slaught	22
Vincente Palacios	24
Tom Prince	19
John Wehner	39

On DL twice (not counting administrative transfers from one DL to another).

Minor League Report

Class AAA-Buffalo finished 81-62, first in the American Association East. It was Buffalo's first division title since 1959. The Bisons lost to Denver in the playoffs. Buffalo set a minor-league attendance record with 1,205,335 fans, breaking its own 1988 record. RHP Rick Reed (14-4, 2.15) led the league in wins and ERA and was named Most Valuable Pitcher. RHP Steve Fireovid was 9-8 and second in league with a 2.90 ERA. OF Cecil Espy hit .312 with 22 SBs. Utility man Keith Miller hit .261 with 9 HRs and 68 RBIs. OF Greg Tubbs (.273) had 34 SBs, a 17-game hitting streak and led league with 11 triples... Class AA-- Carolina finished 67-75, third in the first half and fifth in the second half in the Southern league Eastern Division. The Mudcats drew a franchise-record 217,054 fans, including 143,545 after moving into their new stadium in Zebulon, N.C. 3B Kevin Young hit .342. 2B Terry Crowley Jr. hit .264 with 7 HRs, 45 RBI, OF Darwin Pennye (.257) had 20 doubles and 7 triples. RHP Tim Wakefield (15-8, 2.90) had 8 CGs.... Class A--Salem finished 63-77, third in both halves in the Carolina League Northern Division. OF Kevin Young (.318, 10, 46) was second in the league batting race. OF Alberto de los Santos hit .279 with 17 doubles, 9 HRs, 56 RBI and 24 SBs. RHP Paul Wagner (11-6, 3.12) had 113 strikeouts. RHP Dave Tellers (6-4, 1.39) had 10 saves.... Augusta finished 68-74, third in the first ha;lf and seventh in the second half in the South Atlantic League Southern Division. 2B Joe Sondrini hit .306 with 45 RBI. OF Scott Bullett hit .284 with 48 SBs before his promotion to Salem. The Pirates had a league-high 16 -game winning streak May 26-June 10. RHP Kurt Miller was 6-7 with a 2.50 ERA and 103 SOs. Augusta pitchers set a league record by hitting 83 batters.... Welland finished 30-47, sixth in the NY-P League Stedler Division. 1B-3B Jeff Leatherman (.271) was named team MVP. OF Antonio Mitchell hit .270 with a team-record 10HRs and 38 RBI. INF Tony Womack hit .277 with 26 SBs in 54 games. RHP Marc Pisciotta (1-1) had an 0.26 ERA in 24 relief appearances.

Tops in the Organization

BATTING LEADERS	Club	Avg.	G	AB	R	H	HR	RBI
Kevin Young	Buf	.328	135	473	75	155	9	63
Cecil Espy	Buf	.312	102	398	69	124	2	43
Paul List	Sal	.308	113	389	68	119	11	58
Joe Sondrini	Aug	.306	106	376	66	115	1	45
Jeff Schulz	Buf	.300	122	437	55	131	2	54

HOME RUNS			WINS		
Ben Shelton	Car	15	Tim Wakefield	Car	15
G. Campusano	Aug	13	Rick Reed	Buf	14
Paul List	Sal	12	Paul Miller	Buf	12
Several players tied		9	Paul Wagner	Sal	11
RBI			Dave Bird	Sal	10
Ben Shelton	Car	75	SAVES		
Eddie Zambrano	Buf	74	Mike Roesler	Buf	14
Keith Miller	Buf	68	Victor Cole	Car	12
Kevin Young	Buf	63	David Tellers	Sal	11
Carlos Garcia	Buf	60	Brian Shouse	Sal	11
STOLEN BASES			Mike Zimmerman	Sal	9
Scott Bullett	Sal	63	STRIKE OUTS		
Daryl Ratliff	Car	42	Hector Fajardo	Buf	151
Ramon Martinez	Aug	35	Tim Wakefield	Car	124
Greg Tubbs	Buf	34	Paul Wagner	Sal	113
Carlos Garcia	Buf	30	Steve Buckholz	Car	113
			Dave Bird	Sal	111

PITCHING LEADERS	Club	W-L	ERA	IP	H	BB	SO
Paul Miller	Buf	12-4	2.01	156	110	64	99
Rick Reed	Buf	14-4	2.15	168	151	26	102
Kurt Miller	Aug	6-7	2.50	115	89	57	103
Stephen Cooke	Car	9-7	2.79	129	103	56	103
Steve Fireovid	Buf	9-8	2.90	130	127	43	72

Pittsburgh (1887-1991)

Runs: Most, career, all-time

1521	Honus Wagner, 1900-1917
1493	Paul Waner, 1926-1940
1416	Roberto Clemente, 1955-1972
1414	Max Carey, 1910-1926
1195	Willie Stargell, 1962-1982

Hits: Most, career, all-time

3000	Roberto Clemente, 1955-1972
2967	Honus Wagner, 1900-1917
2868	Paul Waner, 1926-1940
2416	Max Carey, 1910-1926
2416	Pie Traynor, 1920-1937

2B: Most, career, all-time

558	Paul Waner, 1926-1940
551	Honus Wagner, 1900-1917
440	Roberto Clemente, 1955-1972
423	Willie Stargell, 1962-1982
375	Max Carey, 1910-1926

3B: Most, career, all-time

232	Honus Wagner, 1900-1917
187	Paul Waner, 1926-1940
166	Roberto Clemente, 1955-1972
164	Pie Traynor, 1920-1937
156	Fred Clarke, 1900-1915

HR: Most, career, all-time

475	Willie Stargell, 1962-1982
301	Ralph Kiner, 1946-1953
240	Roberto Clemente, 1955-1972
166	DAVE PARKER, 1973-1983
163	Frank Thomas, 1951-1958

RBI: Most, career, all-time

1540	Willie Stargell, 1962-1982
1475	Honus Wagner, 1900-1917
1305	Roberto Clemente, 1955-1972
1273	Pie Traynor, 1920-1937
1177	Paul Waner, 1926-1940

SB: Most, career, all-time

688	Max Carey, 1910-1926
639	Honus Wagner, 1900-1917
412	Omar Moreno, 1975-1982
312	Patsy Donovan, 1892-1899
271	Tommy Leach, 1900-1918

BB: Most, career, all-time

937	Willie Stargell, 1962-1982
918	Max Carey, 1910-1926
909	Paul Waner, 1926-1940

877	Honus Wagner, 1900-1917
795	Ralph Kiner, 1946-1953

BA: Highest, career, all-time

.340	Paul Waner, 1926-1940
.336	Kiki Cuyler, 1921-1927
.328	Honus Wagner, 1900-1917
.327	Matty Alou, 1966-1970
.324	Arky Vaughan, 1932-1941
.324	Elmer Smith, 1892-1901

Slug avg: Highest, career, all-time

.567	Ralph Kiner, 1946-1953
.529	Willie Stargell, 1962-1982
.512	Dick Stuart, 1958-1962
.512	Kiki Cuyler, 1921-1927
.494	DAVE PARKER, 1973-1983

Games started: Most, career, all-time

477	Bob Friend, 1951-1965
371	Wilbur Cooper, 1912-1924
364	Vern Law, 1950-1967
354	Babe Adams, 1907-1926
299	Sam Leever, 1898-1910
271	JOHN CANDELARIA, 1975-1985 (6)

Saves: Most, career, all-time

188	Roy Face, 1953-1968
158	Kent Tekulve, 1974-1985
133	Dave Giusti, 1970-1976
59	Al McBean, 1961-1970
56	BILL LANDRUM, 1989-1991

Shutouts: Most, career, all-time

44	Babe Adams, 1907-1926
39	Sam Leever, 1898-1910
35	Bob Friend, 1951-1965
33	Wilbur Cooper, 1912-1924
29	Lefty Leifield, 1905-1912
20	Bob Veale, 1962-1972 (9)

Wins: Most, career, all-time

202	Wilbur Cooper, 1912-1924
194	Babe Adams, 1907-1926
194	Sam Leever, 1898-1910
191	Bob Friend, 1951-1965
168	Deacon Phillippe, 1900-1911
124	JOHN CANDELARIA, 1975-1985 (9)

K: Most, career, all-time

1682	Bob Friend, 1951-1965

1652	Bob Veale, 1962-1972
1191	Wilbur Cooper, 1912-1924
1142	JOHN CANDELARIA, 1975-1985
1092	Vern Law, 1950-1967

Win pct: Highest, career, all-time

.683	Nick Maddox, 1907-1910
.667	Jesse Tannehill, 1897-1902
.660	Sam Leever, 1898-1910
.659	Vic Willis, 1906-1909
.656	Emil Yde, 1924-1927
.627	Dave Giusti, 1970-1976 (10)

ERA: Lowest, career, all-time

2.08	Vic Willis, 1906-1909
2.38	Lefty Leifield, 1905-1912
2.47	Sam Leever, 1898-1910
2.50	Deacon Phillippe, 1900-1911
2.60	Bob Harmon, 1914-1918
2.68	Kent Tekulve, 1974-1985 (7)

Runs: Most, season

148	Jake Stenzel, 1894
145	Patsy Donovan, 1894
144	Kiki Cuyler, 1925
142	Paul Waner, 1928
140	Max Carey, 1922
112	Bobby Bonilla, 1990 (*)

Hits: Most, season

237	Paul Waner, 1927
234	Lloyd Waner, 1929
231	Matty Alou, 1969
223	Lloyd Waner, 1927
223	Paul Waner, 1928

2B: Most, season

62	Paul Waner, 1932
53	Paul Waner, 1936
50	Paul Waner, 1928
47	Adam Comorosky, 1930
45	DAVE PARKER, 1979
45	Honus Wagner, 1900

3B: Most, season

36	Chief Wilson, 1912
28	Harry Davis, 1897
27	Jimmy Williams, 1899
26	Kiki Cuyler, 1925
23	Adam Comorosky, 1930

23	Elmer Smith, 1893
15	Andy Van Slyke, 1988 (*)

HR: Most, season

54	Ralph Kiner, 1949
51	Ralph Kiner, 1947
48	Willie Stargell, 1971
47	Ralph Kiner, 1950
44	Willie Stargell, 1973

RBI: Most, season

131	Paul Waner, 1927
127	Ralph Kiner, 1947
127	Ralph Kiner, 1949
126	Honus Wagner, 1901
125	Willie Stargell, 1971

SB: Most, season

96	Omar Moreno, 1980
77	Omar Moreno, 1979
71	Omar Moreno, 1978
71	Billy Sunday, 1888
70	Frank Taveras, 1977

BB: Most, season

137	Ralph Kiner, 1951
122	Ralph Kiner, 1950
119	Elbie Fletcher, 1940
118	Elbie Fletcher, 1941
118	Arky Vaughan, 1936
107	BARRY BONDS, 1991 (10)

BA: Highest, season

.385	Arky Vaughan, 1935
.381	Honus Wagner, 1900
.380	Paul Waner, 1927
.374	Jake Stenzel, 1895
.373	Paul Waner, 1936
.357	Roberto Clemente, 1967 (13)

Slug avg: Highest, season

.658	Ralph Kiner, 1949
.646	Willie Stargell, 1973
.639	Ralph Kiner, 1947
.628	Willie Stargell, 1971
.627	Ralph Kiner, 1951

Games started: Most, season

55	Ed Morris, 1888
53	Mark Baldwin, 1892
50	Mark Baldwin, 1891
50	Jim Galvin, 1888
50	Pink Hawley, 1895
50	Frank Killen, 1896
39	Ron Kline, 1956 (15)

Saves: Most, season

34	JIM GOTT, 1988
31	Kent Tekulve, 1978
31	Kent Tekulve, 1979
30	Dave Giusti, 1971
28	Roy Face, 1962

Shutouts: Most, season

8	Babe Adams, 1920
8	Jack Chesbro, 1902
8	Lefty Leifield, 1906
8	Al Mamaux, 1915
7	Steve Blass, 1968
7	Wilbur Cooper, 1917
7	Sam Leever, 1903
7	Bob Veale, 1965
7	Vic Willis, 1908

Wins: Most, season

36	Frank Killen, 1893
31	Pink Hawley, 1895
30	Frank Killen, 1896
29	Ed Morris, 1888
28	Jack Chesbro, 1902
28	Jim Galvin, 1887
22	Doug Drabek, 1990 (*)

K: Most, season

276	Bob Veale, 1965
250	Bob Veale, 1964
229	Bob Veale, 1966
213	Bob Veale, 1969
199	Larry McWilliams, 1983

Win pct: Highest, season

.842	Emil Yde, 1924
.824	Jack Chesbro, 1902
.806	Howie Camnitz, 1909
.800	JOHN CANDELARIA, 1977
.800	Ed Doheny, 1902
.800	Sam Leever, 1905

ERA: Lowest, season

1.56	Howie Camnitz, 1908
1.62	Howie Camnitz, 1909
1.66	Sam Leever, 1907
1.73	Vic Willis, 1906
1.87	Lefty Leifield, 1906
2.05	Bob Veale, 1968 (12)

Most pinch-hit homers, season

3	Ham Hyatt, 1913
3	Al Rubeling, 1944
3	Bob Skinner, 1956
3	Dick Stuart, 1959
3	Gene Freese, 1964

3	Jose Pagan, 1969
3	Willie Stargell, 1982

Most pinch-hit, homers, career

7	Willie Stargell

Most consecutive games, batting safely

27	Jimmy Williams, 1899
26	Danny O'Connell, 1953

Most consecutive scoreless innings

36	Ed Morris, 1888

No hit games

Nick Maddox, Pit vs Bro NL, 2-1; September 20, 1907.

Cliff Chambers, Pit at Bos NL, 3-0; May 6, 1951 (2nd game).

Harvey Haddix, Pit at Mil NL, 0-1; May 26, 1959 (lost on 1 hit in 13 innings after pitching 12 perfect innings).

Bob Moose, Pit at NY NL, 4-0; September 20, 1969.

Dock Ellis, Pit at SD NL, 2-0; June 12, 1970 (1st game).

John Candelaria, Pit vs LA NL, 2-0; August 9, 1976.

Lefty Leifield, six innings, darkness, Pit at Phi NL, 8-0; September 26, 1906 (2nd game).

Howie Camnitz, five innings, agreement, Pit at NY NL, 1-0; August 23, 1907 (2nd game).

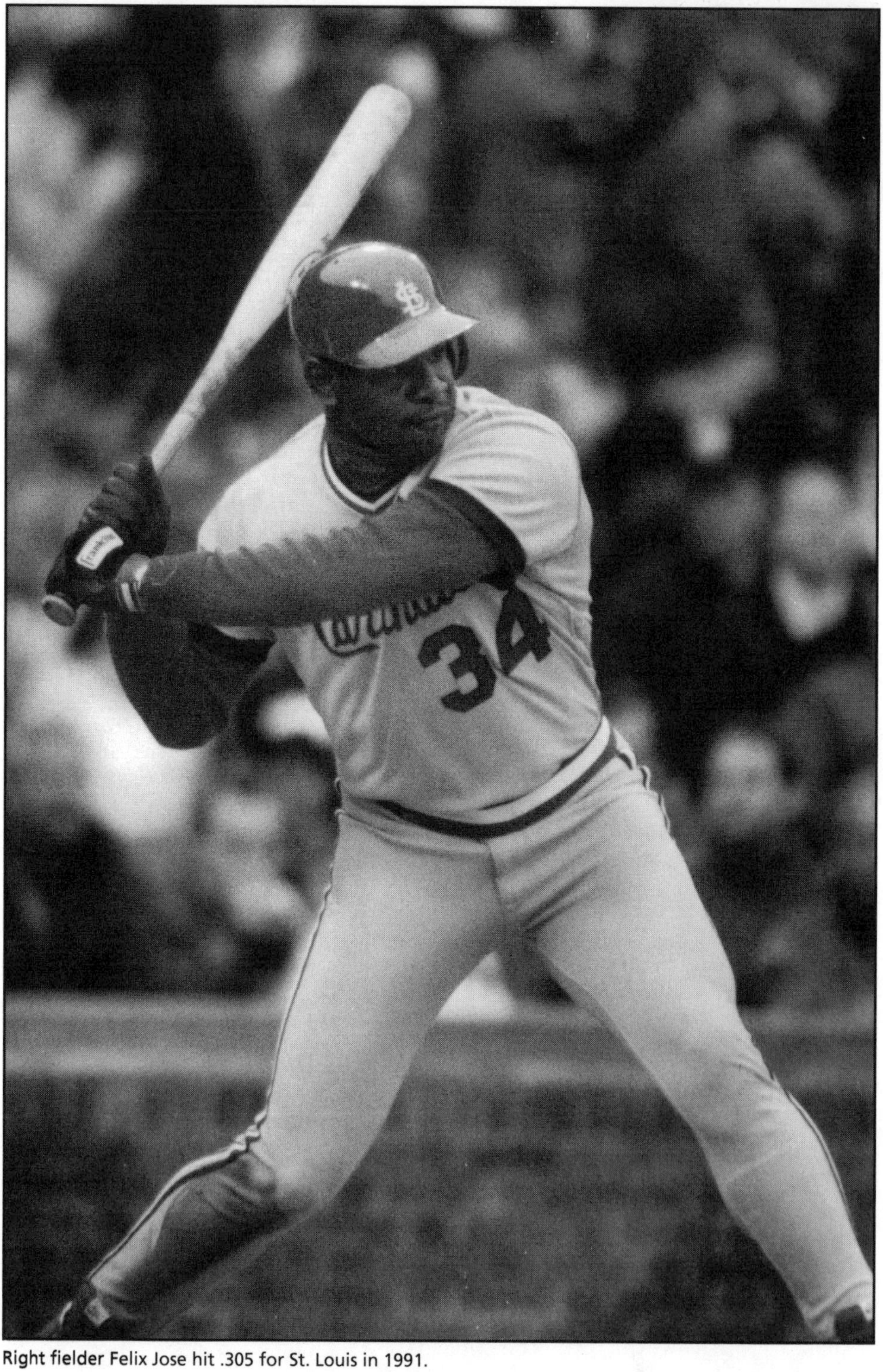

Right fielder Felix Jose hit .305 for St. Louis in 1991.

They got more than they expected

Neither general manager Dal Maxvill or manager Joe Torre really knew what to expect from the Cardinals in 1991. In 1990, the team had finished last for the first time since 1918. Many changes had been made in personnel and the Cardinals were relying on those young players. Most observers picked them to again finish last or at best fifth.

"Most of the time you put guys on the field, you pretty much know what to expect," Torre said. "Not this year."

What Maxvill, Torre and the Cardinals got was probably better than even they could have hoped for. Virtually all of the new players lived up to—or exceeded—their expectations. The result was 84 victories and a second-place finish behind the Pirates.

Specifically, the Cardinals found they had a good rookie centerfielder in Ray Lankford, a good rightfielder in Felix Jose, a good third baseman in Todd Zeile and a good catcher in Tom Pagnozzi, none of whom had performed for a full year on the major-league level before.

They also found out Ozzie Smith still was one of the best shortstops in the game, as he set a career record by making only eight errors. They also found out Lee Smith was as good as advertised, setting a league-record by saving 47 games.

The Cardinals padded their rapidly improving roster with two rookie pitchers—righthander Omar Olivares and lefthander Rheal Cormier. With the expected return of lefthander Joe Magrane after a year off for elbow surgery, and the continued improvement of righthander Ken Hill, starting pitching could be a strength for the Cardinals in 1992.

The Cardinals never really contended with the Pirates, although they did get within four games with a 5-1 victory on Aug. 9 in the opener of a four-game series at Pittsburgh. Pirate wins the next two days, however, brought the Bucs' lead to six games, and just when it looked as if the Cardinals might cut it back to five, Barry Bonds hit a two-run homer off Lee Smith in the 11th inning, stretching the margin to seven games.

The Cardinals proved to be an entertaining team to watch, winning 21 games in their final at-bat and leading the league with 37 one-run victories. But they were shut out 14 times, and Torre thought that was too many.

Overall, however, for a team that had so many question marks at the start of the season, 1991 was a very successful year for the Cardinals.

"We wanted to show people we had some players," Pagnozzi said. "We wanted to show management they made the right choice in who they kept. I think they kept the right players."

—Rob Rains

Cardinals 1992 preview

The Cardinals unveiled a group of young players that might take them places in the '90s. Ray Lankford (.251 with 69 RBI and 44 steals) and Felix Jose (.305, 40 doubles and 77 RBI) provide a solid nucleus in the outfield.

Todd Zeile made the transition from catcher to full-time third baseman and thrived at the plate, batting .280 with 81 RBI. Catcher Tom Pagnozzi and pitcher Omar Oliveras round out the Cardinals' young guns.

Nonetheless, the same problem that has plagued the Cards for the last few seasons—lack of run production— threatens to resurface again this year. New comer Andres Galarraga must replace Pedro Guerrero, who had 70 RBI last season. After being touted as a top rookie, outfielder Bernard Gilkey batted just .216. He needs to restore his confidence.

But there's no lack of confidence in the bullpen; closer Lee Smith broke Bruce Sutter's NL record with 47 saves.

▶The entire Cardinals outfield will go on the disabled list after they fail to realize the fences had been moved in at Busch Stadium.

▶Felix Jose will wake up one day, look at himself in the mirror and say, "Hey, I should be hitting home runs."

—*John Hunt*

Smith: 300th just 'another save'

Lee Smith was low-key about his 300th career save—a milestone reached by only four other pitchers.

"It's another save," Smith said after the Aug. 25 game. "I don't worry too much about those things now. After the season, I might look at the statistics. Right now, I don't look at it."

The league's save leader also saved the Cardinals' win against the Giants the following night to tie his career high of 36 saves set for the Cubs in 1987. (Smith finished the season with a 6-3 record, 2.34 ERA, and 47 saves.)

It took 702 total appearances for Smith to hit the 300 mark, second only to Bruce Sutter (300 saves in his 661st game).

Don't fence them in

Two members of the Cardinals think the decision to move in and lower walls at Busch Stadium next season will hurt the team.

Catcher Tom Pagnozzi and pitcher Lee Smith said they thought the move would benefit the Cardinals' opponents.

"I think it's stupid," Pagnozzi said. "I think you do it when you have a power pitching staff. From a hitter's standpoint it's good, but I don't have enough power to begin with."

Said Smith, "It still isn't going to be as small as Wrigley Field or Fenway Park, but I don't think it's going to do us a whole lot of good. It's going to do a lot

for Kevin Mitchell or Will Clark."

The Cardinals said they were moving in the fences for the first time since 1976. The distance will stay at 330 feet down the foul lines, but will be shortened from 383 feet to 375 in right and left center and from 414 to 402 in center field. The height of the fence also will be lowered from 10 feet, 6 inches to 8 feet.

Cardinals winter league news

▶Instructional League: St. Petersburg, Fla. The Cardinals' Instructional League team finished 24-14. St. Louis sent 73 players to St. Petersburg and divided them up between three teams. The "A" team played against other Instructional teams, while the remaining players played against each other. . . . IF Geronimo Pena, who spent the entire season in St. Louis, came to camp for four days to work on playing the outfield. "We brought him down for the sake of adding another position to his game," said St. Louis director of player development Ted Simmons. "With Jose Oquendo and Ozzie Smith up the middle, he has to be flexible." . . . St. Louis officials were very impressed with the play of first-round picks Dmitri Young and P Brian Barber . . . SS Aaron Holbert, the Cardinals' No. 1 pick in the 1990 draft, was in camp to get extra instruction on offense and defense. Holbert has played two minor league seasons, but won't turn 19 until January.

▶Winter leagues: The Cardinals sent players to all four Latin American winter leagues. . . . OF Bernard Gilkey, who missed five weeks during the season with a broken thumb, made up the time with the Mayaguez Indians in Puerto Rico. "We're convinced he's a major league player," Simmons said. "We've been pleased with the way he's played." . . . 1B Rod Brewer, who missed four weeks with a shoulder separation, also tried to make up lost time in Puerto Rico. "He's as fine a defensive first baseman as there is anywhere,"

Simmons said. . . . SS Bien Figueroa and IF Geronimo Pena played at home in the Dominican Republic. . . . OF Lonnie Maclin, who played winter ball for the Mayaguez Indians last year, played in Venezuela this winter. . . . IF Luis Alicea played at home in Puerto Rico.

▸Winter leagues roster: Luis Alicea, IF, San Juan Metros, Puerto Rico; Rod Brewer, 1B, Mayaguez Indians, Puerto Rico; Greg Carmona, SS, Tigres (Tigers) de Licey, D.R.; John Ericks, RHP, Ponce Lions, Puerto Rico; Fidel Compres, RHP, Leones (Lions) Escogido, Dominican Republic; Joey Fernandez, 1B, Culiacan Tomateros (Tomato growers), Mexico; Bien Figueroa, SS, Leones (Lions) Escogido, Dominican Republic; Bernard Gilkey, OF, Mayaguez Indians, Puerto Rico; Lonnie Maclin, OF, Venezuela; Mauricio Nunez, IF, Estrellas Orientales, (Eastern Stars), Stars Oriente), D.R.; Gabriel Ozuna, RHP, Tigres de Licey, D.R.; Geronimo Pena, IF, Tigres (Tigers) de Licey, D.R.; Stan Royer, 3B, Ponce Lions, Puerto Rico.

Team directory

▸Owner: August A. Busch III

▸General Manager: Dal Maxvill

▸Ballpark:
Busch Stadium
250 Stadium Plaza, St. Louis, Missouri
314-421-3060
Capacity 56,227
Parking for over 7,000 cars; $4
Public transportation
Wheelchair section, ramps

▸Team publications:
Yearbook, Media Guide, a magazine in 1992
314-421-3060

▸TV, radio broadcast stations:
KMOX 1120 AM, KPLR Channel 11

▸Spring Training:
Al Lang Stadium
Petersburg, Florida
Capacity 7,600
314-421-2799

St. LOUIS CARDINALS 1991 Final Stats

Batting	AVG	SLG	OB	G	AB	R	H	TB	2B	3B	HR	RBI	BB	SO	SB	CS	E
Thompson	.307	.442	.368	115	326	55	100	144	16	5	6	34	32	53	16	9	2
Jose	.305	.438	.360	154	568	69	173	249	40	6	8	77	50	113	20	12	3
Royer	.286	.333	.318	9	21	1	6	7	1	0	0	1	1	2	0	0	0
Stephens	.286	.286	.375	6	7	0	2	2	0	0	0	0	0	1	3	0	0	0
O. Smith	.285	.367	.380	150	550	96	157	202	30	3	3	50	83	36	35	9	8
Zeile	.280	.412	.353	155	565	76	158	233	36	3	11	81	62	94	17	11	25
Guerrero	.272	.361	.326	115	427	41	116	154	12	1	8	70	37	46	4	2	16
Pagnozzi	.264	.351	.319	140	459	38	121	161	24	5	2	57	36	63	9	13	7
Lankford	.251	.392	.301	151	566	83	142	222	23	15	9	69	41	114	44	20	6
Pena	.243	.400	.322	104	185	38	45	74	8	3	5	17	18	45	15	5	6
Oquendo	.240	.301	.357	127	366	37	88	110	11	4	1	26	67	48	1	2	9
Perry	.240	.300		109	242	29	58	92	8	4	6	36	22	34	15	8	5
Hudler	.227	.309	.260	101	207	21	47	64	10	2	1	15	10	29	12	8	2
Gilkey	.216	.313	.316	81	268	28	58	84	7	2	5	20	39	33	14	8	1
Alicea	.191	.235	.276	56	68	5	13	16	3	0	0	0	8	19	0	1	0
Wilson	.171	.195	.222	60	82	5	14	16	2	0	0	13	6	10	0	0	2
Jones	.167	.250	.222	16	24	1	4	6	2	0	0	2	2	6	0	1	0
Gedman	.106	.213	.140	46	94	7	10	20	1	0	3	8	4	15	0	1	5
Brewer	.077	.077	.077	19	13	0	1	1	0	0	0	1	0	5	0	0	1

Pitching	W-L	ERA	G	GS	CG	GF	Sho	SV	IP	H	R	ER	HR	BB	SO
Grater	0-0	0.00	3	0	0	2	0	0	3	5	0	0	0	2	0
L. Smith	6-3	2.34	67	0	0	61	0	47	73	70	19	19	5	13	67
DeLeon	5-9	2.71	28	28	1	0	0	0	162.2	144	57	49	15	61	118
Terry	4-4	2.80	65	0	0	13	0	1	80.1	76	31	25	1	32	52
McClure	1-1	3.13	32	0	0	9	0	0	23	24	8	8	1	8	15
Tewksbury	11-12	3.25	30	30	3	0	0	0	191	206	86	69	13	38	75
Hill	11-10	3.57	30	30	0	0	0	0	181.1	147	76	72	15	67	121
Olivares	11-7	3.71	28	24	0	2	0	1	167.1	148	72	69	13	61	91
B. Smith	12-9	3.85	31	31	3	0	0	0	198.2	188	95	85	16	45	94
Clark	1-1	4.03	7	2	0	1	0	0	22.1	17	10	10	3	11	13
Cormier	4-5	4.12	11	10	2	1	0	0	67.2	74	35	31	5	8	38
Carpenter	10-4	4.23	59	0	0	19	0	0	66	53	31	31	6	20	47
Agosto	5-3	4.81	72	0	0	22	0	2	86	92	52	46	4	39	34
Fraser	3-3	4.93	35	0	0	16	0	0	49.1	44	28	27	9	21	25
Moyer	0-5	5.74	8	7	0	1	0	0	31.1	38	21	20	5	16	20
Perez	0-2	5.82	14	0	0	2	0	0	17	19	11	11	1	7	7
Sherrill	0-0	8.16	10	0	0	3	0	0	14.1	20	13	13	2	3	4
Oquendo	0-0	27.00	1	0	0	1	0	0	1	2	3	3	0	2	1

1992 Preliminary Roster

Pitchers (18)

Juan Agosto
Cris Carpenter
Mark Clark
Fidel Compres
Rheal Cormier
Jose DeLeon
Frank DiPino
John Ericks
Willie Fraser
Joe Magrane
Bob McClure
Mike Milchin
Omar Olivares
Bryn Smith
Lee Smith
Scott Terry
Bob Tewksbury
Todd Worrell

Catchers (3)

Jose Fernandez
Rich Gedman
Tom Pagnozzi

Infielders (13)

Luis Alicea
Rod Brewer
Greg Carmona
Andres Galarraga
Rex Hudler
Tim Jones
Jose Oquendo
Geronimo Pena
Gerald Perry
Stan Royer
Ozzie Smith
Craig Wilson
Todd Zeile

Outfielders (6)

Bernard Gilkey
Brian Jordan
Felix Jose
Ray Lankford
Lonnie Maclin
Milt Thompson

Games played by position

	G	C	1B	2B	3B	SS	OF
Alicea,L	56	0	0	11	2	1	0
Brewer,R	19	0	15	0	0	0	3
Gedman,R	46	43	0	0	0	0	0
Gilkey,B	81	0	0	0	0	0	74
Guerrero,P	115	0	112	0	0	0	0
Hudler,R	101	0	12	5	0	0	58
Jones,Ti	16	0	0	4	0	14	0
Jose,F	154	0	0	0	0	0	153
Lankford,R	151	0	0	0	0	0	149
Oquendo,J	127	0	3	118	0	22	0
Pagnozzi,T	140	139	3	0	0	0	0
Pena,G	104	0	0	83	0	0	4
Perry,G	109	0	61	0	0	0	5
Royer,S	9	0	0	0	5	0	0
Smith,O	150	0	0	0	0	150	0
Stephens,R	6	6	0	0	0	0	0
Thompson,M	115	0	0	0	0	0	91
Wilson,C	60	0	4	3	12	0	5
Zeile,T	155	0	0	0	154	0	0

Sick call: 1991 DL report

Player	Days on the DL
Frank DiPino	182
Todd Worrell	182
Joe Magrane	182
Bernard Gilkey	27
Pedro Guerrero	39
Ken Hill	21

Minor League Report

Class AAA — Louisville finished 51-92, fourth in the American Association East. That was the worst record in club history. The 92 losses were most in modern league history. Manager Mark DeJohn resigned after the season, citing personal reasons. Despite record, Redbirds drew 565,716 fans, second-highest total in minors this season. 3B Stan Royer (.254-14-74) was team MVP. He hit for the cycle against Denver July 19. After being called up to St. Louis Sept. 1, Royer singled in his first major league at-bat. OF Lonnie Maclin hit .287. LHP Rheal Cormier (7-9, 4.23) led league with 3 shutouts and had won three games with the St. Louis Cardinals since he was called up. . . . **Class AA** — Arkansas finished 49-87, tied for third in the first half and fourth in the second half in the Texas League Eastern Division. Despite the record, the Travelers drew 265,268 fans in just 57 dates. 1B John Sellick hit .245 with 18 doubles, 18 HRs and 63 RBI. OF Cliff Brannon hit .281 with 26 doubles. Former first-round draft picks RHP John Ericks and LHP Donovan Osborne were 5-14 and 8-12, respectively. . . . **Class A** — St. Petersburg finished 47-84, fifth in both halves in the Florida State League Western Division. That was worst record in club history. However, the Cardinals did lead league in fielding (.975). OF Skeets Thomas hit .298 with 10 triples and 46 RBI. 2B Brad Beanblossom hit .254 with 28 doubles. C Paul Ellis hit with 6 HRs and 42 RBI. Top pitchers were LHP Tom Urbani (8-7, 2.35) and RHP Rick Shackle (8-9, 2.65). . . . Springfield finished 58-79, tied for sixth in the first half and fifth in the second half in the Midwest League Southern Division. C Andy Beasley hit .284 with 12 HRs and 60 RBI. 2B Mateo Ozuna led league with 78 SBs. RHP Clyde Keller was 5-0 with 0.75 ERA and 32 saves. . . . Savannah finished 61-77, seventh in the first half and third in the second half in the South Atlantic League Southern Division. OF Terry Bradshaw hit .237 with 42 RBI, 64 SBs and 99 walks. RHP John Kelly (6-5, 1.38) had 30 saves. RHP Roy Bailey (8-2, 2.49) and LHP Bryan Eversgerd (1-5, 3.47) ranked 1-2 in the minor leagues with 73 and 72 appearances, respectively. . . . Hamilton finished 35-42, tied for fourth in the NY-P League Stedler Division. 1B John O'Brien (.308-10-44 with league-leading 23 doubles) was team MVP. OF John Mabry (.310) led league with 10 assists. RHP Duff Brumley (2-6, 3.64) was top pitcher. . . . Johnson City finished 40-26, second in the Appalachian League Southern Division. Darrel Deak hit .302 with 23 doubles, 9 HRs and 34 RBI. RHP Gerrald Santos (2-0, 2.23, 13 saves) had just 5 walks and 55 strikeouts in 32 innings.

Tops in the Organization

BATTING LEADERS	Club	Avg.	G	AB	R	H	HR	RBI
John Thomas	Stp	.298	115	429	51	128	3	46
Andy Beasley	Spr	.284	100	338	40	96	12	60
Cliff Brannon	Ark	.281	119	399	46	112	4	44
Jose Trujillo	Sav	.268	99	339	45	91	3	46
Mike Fiore	Ark	.263	123	453	60	119	8	50

HOME RUNS			WINS		
John Sellick	Ark	18	Tom Urbani	Stp	11
Stan Royer	Lou	14	Kevin Nielsen	Stp	10
Joey Hamilton	Lou	13	Luis Faccio	Ark	10
Jose Fernandez	Ark	12	Paul Anderson	Spr	9
Andy Beasley	Spr	12	Several players tied		8

RBI			SAVES		
Stan Royer	Lou	74	Clyde Keller	Spr	32
Rod Eldridge	Sav	64	John Kelly	Sav	30
John Sellick	Ark	63	Gab Ozuna	Ark	15
Andy Beasley	Spr	60	Troy Salvior	Stp	13
Rod Brewer	Lou	52	Mark Grater	Lou	12

STOLEN BASES			STRIKEOUT		
Mateo Ozuna	Spr	78	Kevin Nielsen	Stp	146
Terry Bradshaw	Sav	64	Donovan Osbourne	Ark	130
Tremayne Donald	Spr	38	Luis Faccio	Ark	114
Juan Andujar	Sav	34	Paul Anderson	Spr	109
Tracey Ealy	Sav	31	Tom Urbani	Stp	106

PITCHING LEADERS	Club	W-L	ERA	IP	H	BB	SO
Tom Urbani	Stp	11-9	2.28	166	154	31	106
Rick Shackle	Stp	8-9	2.65	129	125	36	94
Kevin Nielsen	Stp	10-10	3.17	176	159	49	146
Frank Cimorelli	Spr	8-14	3.43	192	203	51	98
Jeremy McGarity	Sav	7-12	3.44	175	144	75	100

St. Louis (1892-1991)

Runs: Most, career, all-time

1949	Stan Musial, 1941-1963
1427	Lou Brock, 1964-1979
1089	Rogers Hornsby, 1915-1933
1071	Enos Slaughter, 1938-1953
1025	Red Schoendienst, 1945-1963

Hits: Most, career, all-time

3630	Stan Musial, 1941-1963
2713	Lou Brock, 1964-1979
2110	Rogers Hornsby, 1915-1933
2064	Enos Slaughter, 1938-1953
1980	Red Schoendienst, 1945-1963

2B: Most, career, all-time

725	Stan Musial, 1941-1963
434	Lou Brock, 1964-1979
377	Joe Medwick, 1932-1948
367	Rogers Hornsby, 1915-1933
366	Enos Slaughter, 1938-1953

3B: Most, career, all-time

177	Stan Musial, 1941-1963
143	Rogers Hornsby, 1915-1933
135	Enos Slaughter, 1938-1953
121	Lou Brock, 1964-1979
119	Jim Bottomley, 1922-1932

HR: Most, career, all-time

475	Stan Musial, 1941-1963
255	Ken Boyer, 1955-1965
193	Rogers Hornsby, 1915-1933
181	Jim Bottomley, 1922-1932
172	Ted Simmons, 1968-1980

RBI: Most, career, all-time

1951	Stan Musial, 1941-1963
1148	Enos Slaughter, 1938-1953
1105	Jim Bottomley, 1922-1932
1072	Rogers Hornsby, 1915-1933
1001	Ken Boyer, 1955-1965

SB: Most, career, all-time

888	Lou Brock, 1964-1979
549	VINCE COLEMAN, 1985-1990
352	OZZIE SMITH, 1982-1991
274	WILLIE McGEE, 1982-1990
203	Jack Smith, 1915-1926

BB: Most, career, all-time

1599	Stan Musial, 1941-1963
838	Enos Slaughter, 1938-1953
694	OZZIE SMITH, 1982-1991

681	Lou Brock, 1964-1979
660	Rogers Hornsby, 1915-1933

BA: Highest, career, all-time

.359	Rogers Hornsby, 1915-1933
.336	Johnny Mize, 1936-1941
.335	Joe Medwick, 1932-1948
.331	Stan Musial, 1941-1963
.326	Chick Hafey, 1924-1931
.308	Joe Torre, 1969-1974 (9)

Slug avg: Highest, career, all-time

.600	Johnny Mize, 1936-1941
.568	Rogers Hornsby, 1915-1933
.568	Chick Hafey, 1924-1931
.559	Stan Musial, 1941-1963
.545	Joe Medwick, 1932-1948
.475	Ken Boyer, 1955-1965 (8)

Games started: Most, career, all-time

482	Bob Gibson, 1959-1975
401	Bob Forsch, 1974-1988
388	Jesse Haines, 1920-1937
319	Bill Doak, 1913-1929
243	Bill Sherdel, 1918-1932

Saves: Most, career, all-time

127	Bruce Sutter, 1981-1984
126	Todd Worrell, 1985-1989
74	LEE SMITH, 1990-1991
64	Lindy McDaniel, 1955-1962
60	Al Brazle, 1943-1954
60	Joe Hoerner, 1966-1969

Shutouts: Most, career, all-time

56	Bob Gibson, 1959-1975
30	Bill Doak, 1913-1929
28	Mort Cooper, 1938-1945
25	Harry Brecheen, 1940-1952
24	Jesse Haines, 1920-1937

Wins: Most, career, all-time

251	Bob Gibson, 1959-1975
210	Jesse Haines, 1920-1937
163	Bob Forsch, 1974-1988
153	Bill Sherdel, 1918-1932
144	Bill Doak, 1913-1929

K: Most, career, all-time

3117	Bob Gibson, 1959-1975
1095	Dizzy Dean, 1930-1937
1079	Bob Forsch, 1974-1988

979	Jesse Haines, 1920-1937
951	Steve Carlton, 1965-1971

Win pct: Highest, career, all-time

.718	Ted Wilks, 1944-1951
.705	John Tudor, 1985-1990
.677	Mort Cooper, 1938-1945
.667	Al Hrabosky, 1970-1977
.641	Dizzy Dean, 1930-1937

ERA: Lowest, career, all-time

2.52	John Tudor, 1985-1990
2.67	Slim Sallee, 1908-1916
2.67	Jack Taylor, 1904-1906
2.74	Johnny Lush, 1907-1910
2.74	Red Ames, 1915-1919

Runs: Most, season

142	Jesse Burkett, 1901
141	Rogers Hornsby, 1922
135	Stan Musial, 1948
133	Rogers Hornsby, 1925
132	Joe Medwick, 1935
126	Lou Brock, 1971 (10)

Hits: Most, season

250	Rogers Hornsby, 1922
237	Joe Medwick, 1937
235	Rogers Hornsby, 1921
230	Stan Musial, 1948
230	Joe Torre, 1971

2B: Most, season

64	Joe Medwick, 1936
56	Joe Medwick, 1937
53	Stan Musial, 1953
52	Enos Slaughter, 1939
51	Stan Musial, 1944
48	Keith Hernandez, 1979 (7)

3B: Most, season

29	Perry Werden, 1893
25	Tom Long, 1915
20	Jim Bottomley, 1928
20	Duff Cooley, 1895
20	Rogers Hornsby, 1920
20	Stan Musial, 1943
20	Stan Musial, 1946
19	GARRY TEMPLETON, 1979 (8)

HR: Most, season

43	Johnny Mize, 1940

42	Rogers Hornsby, 1922
39	Rogers Hornsby, 1925
39	Stan Musial, 1948
36	Stan Musial, 1949
35	JACK CLARK, 1987 (6)

RBI: Most, season

154	Joe Medwick, 1937
152	Rogers Hornsby, 1922
143	Rogers Hornsby, 1925
138	Joe Medwick, 1936
137	Jim Bottomley, 1929
137	Johnny Mize, 1940
137	Joe Torre, 1971

SB: Most, season

118	Lou Brock, 1974
110	VINCE COLEMAN, 1985
109	VINCE COLEMAN, 1987
107	VINCE COLEMAN, 1986
81	VINCE COLEMAN, 1988

BB: Most, season

136	JACK CLARK, 1987
136	Jack Crooks, 1892
121	Jack Crooks, 1893
116	Miller Huggins, 1910
107	Stan Musial, 1949

BA: Highest, season

.424	Rogers Hornsby, 1924
.403	Rogers Hornsby, 1925
.401	Rogers Hornsby, 1922
.397	Rogers Hornsby, 1921
.396	Jesse Burkett, 1899
.363	Joe Torre, 1971 (16)

Slug avg: Highest, season

.756	Rogers Hornsby, 1925
.722	Rogers Hornsby, 1922
.702	Stan Musial, 1948
.696	Rogers Hornsby, 1924
.652	Chick Hafey, 1930
.597	JACK CLARK, 1987 (21)

Games started: Most, season

50	Ted Breitenstein, 1894
50	Ted Breitenstein, 1895
47	Jack Taylor, 1898
45	Kid Gleason, 1892
45	Kid Gleason, 1893
38	Joaquin Andujar, 1985 (16)

Saves: Most, season

47	LEE SMITH, 1991

45	Bruce Sutter, 1984
36	Bruce Sutter, 1982
36	Todd Worrell, 1986
33	Todd Worrell, 1987

Shutouts: Most, season

13	Bob Gibson, 1968
10	Mort Cooper, 1942
10	John Tudor, 1985
7	Harry Brecheen, 1948
7	Mort Cooper, 1944
7	Dizzy Dean, 1934
7	Bill Doak, 1914

Wins: Most, season

30	Dizzy Dean, 1934
28	Dizzy Dean, 1935
27	Ted Breitenstein, 1894
26	Cy Young, 1899
24	Dizzy Dean, 1936
24	Jesse Haines, 1927
23	Bob Gibson, 1970 (7)

K: Most, season

274	Bob Gibson, 1970
270	Bob Gibson, 1965
269	Bob Gibson, 1969
268	Bob Gibson, 1968
245	Bob Gibson, 1964

Win pct: Highest, season

.811	Dizzy Dean, 1934
.810	Ted Wilks, 1944
.789	Harry Brecheen, 1945
.778	Johnny Beazley, 1942
.767	Bob Gibson, 1970

ERA: Lowest, season

1.12	Bob Gibson, 1968
1.72	Bill Doak, 1914
1.78	Mort Cooper, 1942
1.90	Max Lanier, 1943
1.93	John Tudor, 1985

Most pinch-hit homers, season

4	George Crowe, 1959
4	George Crowe, 1960
4	Carl Sawatski, 1961

Most pinch-hit, homers, career

8	George Crowe, 1959-1961

Most consecutive games, batting safely

33	Rogers Hornsby, 1922

Most consecutive scoreless innings

47	Bob Gibson, 1968

No hit games

George Bradley, StL vs Har NL, 2-0; July 15, 1876.

Jesse Haines, StL vs Bos NL, 5-0; July 17, 1924.

Paul Dean, StL at Bro NL, 3-0; September 21, 1934 (2nd game).

Lon Warneke, StL at Cin NL, 2-0; August 30, 1941.

Ray Washburn, StL at SF NL, 2-0; September 18, 1968.

Bob Gibson, StL at Pit NL, 11-0; August 14, 1971.

Bob Forsch, StL vs Phi NL, 5-0; April 16, 1978.

Bob Forsch, StL vs Mon NL, 3-0; September 26, 1983.

Stoney McGlynn, seven innings, agreement, StL at Bro NL, 1-1; September 24, 1906 (2nd game).

Ed Karger, seven perfect innings, agreement, StL vs Bos NL, 4-0; August 11, 1907 (2nd game).

Johnny Lush, six innings, rain, StL at Bro NL, 2-0; August 6, 1908.

Lenny Dykstra's car crash hurt the whole team in 1991.

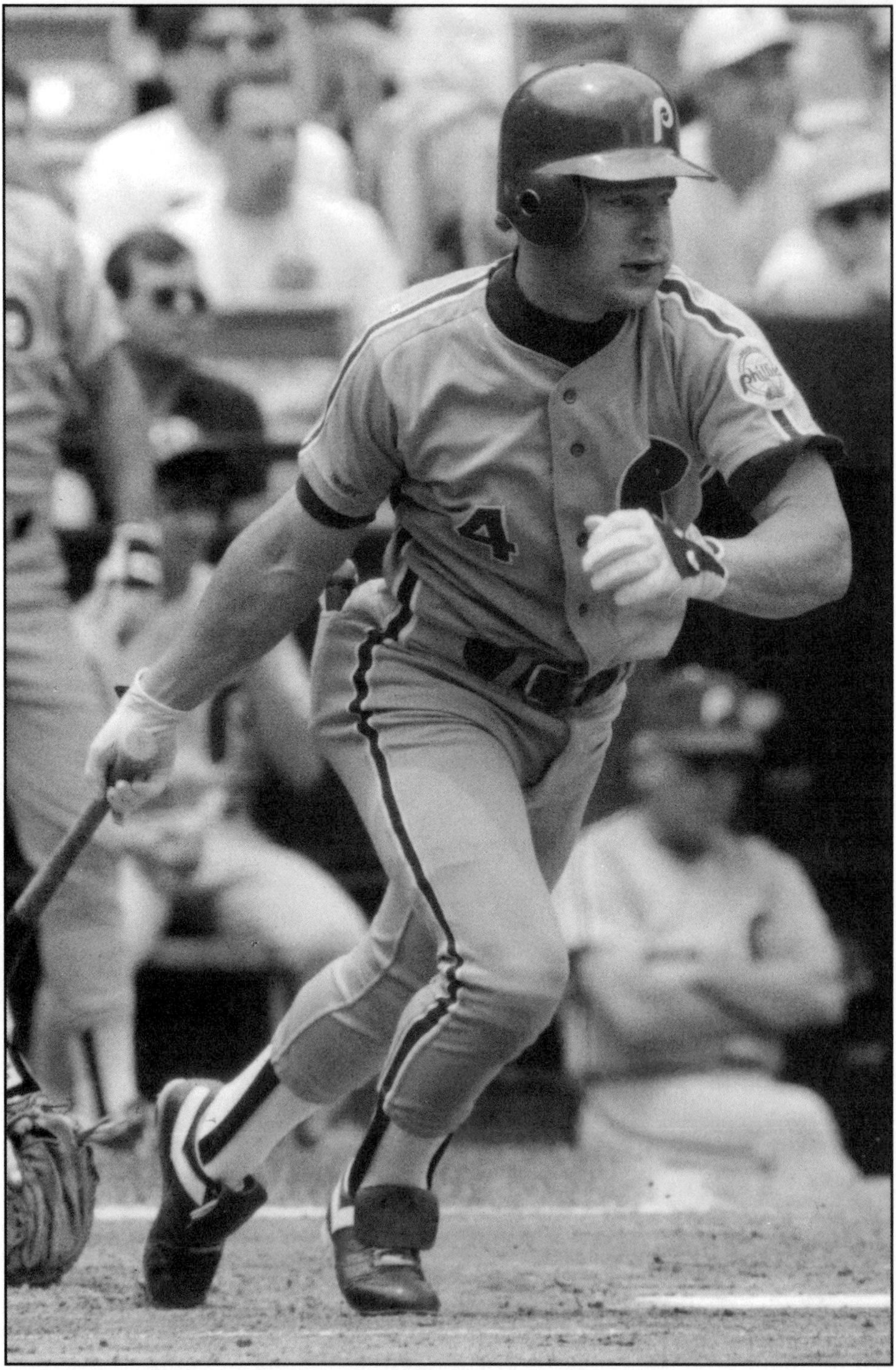

Dykstra crashed Phillies' hopes

Any hopes the Philadelphia Phillies may have harbored of contending for the National League East crown were effectively lost when Len Dykstra crashed his Mercedes in an alcohol-related accident with catcher Darren Daulton as a passenger May 6.

Dykstra, the scrappy center fielder and catalyst of the Phillies' offense (.325 with 33 stolen bases in 1990), was lost for two months with a broken collarbone. He returned in August only to be lost for the season when he aggravated the injury in an outfield collision at Riverfront Stadium Aug. 26 that caused Cincinnati officials to pledge to pad the outfield wall.

Daulton, who signed a lucrative contract after a career year in 1990, hit .196 in only 89 games.

The Phillies spent much of the first half in last place, and Nick Leyva became the first managerial casualty of the season when he was fired April 23. New manager Jim Fregosi guided the team to a 25-13 mark from July 15 to Aug. 26 and the Phillies rode a 13-game August winning streak to finish 78-84 and in a third-place tie in the NL East.

Although injuries and ineffectiveness made pitching a major concern entering the season, the Phillies closed the campaign with a staff solidly anchored by three youngsters. Tommy Greene, acquired as a throw-in from Atlanta in 1990 with Dale Murphy, went 13-7 and no-hit Montreal May 23. Jose DeJesus, continued to have control problems, but finished 10-9 while lefthander Terry Mulholland went 16-13.

First baseman John Kruk (.294, 21 HRs and 92 RBI) enjoyed his best season since 1987 and was rewarded with a multi-year contract. His play made a reserve out of Ricky Jordan, who along with third baseman Charlie Hayes and injured outfielder Von Hayes were frequently mentioned in trade talks.

Von Hayes' trade value plummeted when he was lost for the season June

14 after he broke his left wrist on a pitch by Cincinnati's Tom Browning. Hayes' injury, along with Dykstra's extended absence, opened the way for rookie Wes Chamberlain, who provided 13 HRs and 50 RBI in 383 at-bats.

Philadelphia officials made it a priority to resign Kruk during the season, but postponed talks with free agent-to-be Mitch Williams, who went 12-5 with 30 saves. His early-season acquisition from Chicago made Roger McDowell expendable—McDowell was shipped to Los Angeles for pitcher Mike Hartley and minor league outfielder Braulio Castillo.

Murphy hit 18 home runs, breaking a 13-year streak of 20-plus home run seasons while rookie infielders Mickey Morandini and Dave Hollins showed promise for 1992.

—Pete Williams

Phillies 1992 preview

The "X" factor for the Phillies entering last season—starting pitching—is now a plus sign. Terry Mulholland (16-13, 3.61), Tommy Greene (13-7, 3.38) and Jose DeJesus (10-9, 3.42) form the nucleus of what became a steady rotation in 1991. Top draft choice Tyler Green and rookie Kyle Abbott may fit into the equation.

First baseman John Kruk bore the brunt of the offense (.294, 21 HR, 92 RBI) and is expected to do so again. Some help is needed, though, and a likely place to look is the hot corner, where Dave Hollins appears to be the third baseman of the future.

Dale Murphy's best years may be behind him, but he still provides some pop in the lineup (18 homers, 81 RBI). The main concerns are settling on the middle of the infield and a legitimate cleanup hitter.

The bullpen is set, but if ace closer Mitch Williams hasn't re-signed, look for a bullpen by committee.

1992 prophecy: Phillies

▸Dale Murphy and Lenny Dykstra will room together on road trips in an effort to keep the centerfielder in line.
▸Mariano Duncan will play every position except pitcher and catcher.

—John Hunt

Players are up against the wall

Several members of the Phillies were quick to criticize the Reds' unpadded walls at Riverfront Stadium when Lenny Dykstra was injured in late August. But Cincinnati was not the only errant team in the National League.

At the start of this season, half of the National League clubs—Cincinnati, Los Angeles, Philadelphia, Atlanta, San Francisco and Chicago—did not have padded walls. The Phillies added the pads in April, the Dodgers in May after Darryl Strawberry injured his shoulder crashing into the wall.

After the flap about Dykstra's injury, the Reds also added pads.

With key players being injured on unpadded walls, it's difficult to understand why some clubs have been hesitant to protect baseball's most expensive investment—the players. The cost is not prohibitive—about $40,000 for the average major-league stadium.

Bob Smith, the Dodgers' vice president of stadium operations, said the cost of their pads was only about $25,000, but Ken John, president of the company that performed the work (Promats of Denver, Colo.), cautioned that Dodger Stadium was a relatively easy ballpark, keeping the cost low.

John said his company has installed the pads at 50 major league, minor league and spring training stadiums. He has had discussions with all of the teams that don't have pads. Most teams recognize the need to protect their players, John said. They also find that adding pads can add an extra defensive edge in a game.

"In the facilities that we have done over the years," John continued, "not only are there less injuries to the players but we've found players become more aggressive in trying to field balls."

So why haven't more teams padded their outfield walls?

"I can't believe economics is the reason," John said. "You tell me why they wouldn't do it."

Wild Thing not wild about wins

By Ray Finocchiaro

Toward the end of last August, some of the Phillies thought that closer Mitch "Wild Thing" Williams might become baseball's first pitcher to join the 20-20 club.

"They're making such a big deal of Jose Canseco's 40-40 homer-steal thing that Mitch's going for 20-20: 20 saves and 20 wins," joked manager Jim Fregosi after Charlie Hayes' ninth-inning homer gave Philadelphia a 6-5 victory over the hot Atlanta Braves on Aug. 24. "No pitcher's ever done that."

Informed that Williams was 8-1 with four saves and an 0.95 earned run average that month, Fregosi feigned dismay.

"Only 8-1 this month?" he asked? "I'm not using him enough. How many days do I have left?"

But Wild Thing wasn't in a joking mood. Relievers don't like to win—or lose—games; closers are expected to save victories for starters.

"I won because I blew the save for Danny Cox," said Williams, who pitched out of a bases-loaded jam in the eighth after the Braves had tied the score. "That's three blown saves for me. I stunk."

Williams won four more games before the season ended, finishing 12-5 (2.34 ERA). He fell short of his 20 wins, but he was fourth in the league with 30 saves.

Ray Finocchiaro writes for the Wilmington (Del.) News Journal

Phils' better half came after the break

The Phillies were limping along at 33-49 at the All-Star break, when team president Bill Giles made them a deal: If they could post the best record in the NL East for the second half, he would give each player a trophy.

They turned their record around—logging 45 wins and 35 losses—but it wasn't enough to beat out the Pirates 50-33 second half. It was enough, though, for third place in their division, the team's best finish since 1986.

They won just one more game than in 1990, but they did it without catcher Darren Daulton and outfielders Von Hayes and Lenny Dykstra for long stretches. (Hayes, who hit 43 home runs 1989-90, hit none at all in '91.)

Even though they didn't win the trophies, the players' second-half performance pleased Giles.

"I'll remember the way we came back in the late innings to win so many games," he said. "It reminds me of the late '70s and early '80s, when we had really good teams."

Phillies winter league news

▶Winter leagues: With a number of pitchers competing for spots on the Philadelphia staff, three went to the winter leagues hoping to gain an edge on their competition. "We have some good young arms," said Philadelphia director of player development Del Unser. "Spring training should be very competitive. We have some question marks in guys coming off injuries like (Ken) Howell and (Pat) Combs. It might mean that our Class AAA staff will have some good pitchers." RHP Jason Grimsley was trying to rediscover the effective changeup he had several years ago. . . . RHP Cliff Brantley and veteran minor league RHP Jay Baller also got more work in Puerto Rico. . . . OF Bruce Dostal, who missed five weeks last season with a leg injury, worked out in Mexico. OF Nikco Riesgo, who hit 14 home runs and drove in 66 RBI at Class AA Reading, played for Hermosillo, Mexico.

▶Winter roster: Jay Baller, RHP, Bayamon Cowboys, Puerto Rico; Cliff Brantley, RHP, Bayamon Cowboys, Puerto Rico; Sil Campusano, OF, Tigres (Tigers) de Licey, D.R.; Braulio Castillo, OF, Tigres de (Tigers) Licey, D.R.; Bruce Dostal, OF, Hermosillo Naranjeros (Orange growers), Mexico; Jason Grimsley, RHP, Bayamon Cowboys, Puerto Rico; Julio Peguero, OF, Aguilas Cibaena (Eagles), D.R.; Nikco Riesgo, OF, Navojoa, Mexico.

Team directory

▶Owner: Bill Giles

▶General Manager: Lee Thomas

▶Ballpark:
Veterans Stadium
Broad St. & Pattison Ave.,
Philadelphia, Pennsylvania
215-463-1000
Capacity 62,382
Parking for 10,000 cars; $4
Public transportation available
Wheelchair section and ramps, telephone service for the hearing impaired
(215-463-2998)

▶Team publications:
Media Guide, Yearbook, Scorecard
Program

▶TV, radio broadcast stations:
WOGL 1210 AM, WTXF-TV Channel 29

▶Spring Training:
Jack Russell Memorial Stadium
Clearwater, Florida
Capacity 7,350
813-442-8496

PHILADELPHIA PHILLIES 1991 Final Stats

Batting	AVG	SLG	OB	G	AB	R	H	TB	2B	3B	HR	RBI	BB	SO	SB	CS	E
Lindeman	.337	.389	.413	65	95	13	32	37	5	0	0	12	13	14	0	1	0
Hollins	.298	.510	.378	56	151	18	45	77	10	2	6	21	17	26	1	1	8
Dykstra	.297	.427	.391	63	246	48	73	105	13	5	3	12	37	20	24	4	4
Kruk	.294	.483	.367	152	538	84	158	260	27	6	21	92	67	100	7	0	3
Jordan	.272	.452	.304	101	301	38	82	136	21	3	9	49	14	49	0	2	9
Thon	.252	.351	.283	146	539	44	136	189	18	4	9	44	25	84	11	5	21
Murphy	.252	.415	.309	153	544	66	137	226	33	1	18	81	48	93	1	0	5
Morandini	.249	.317	.313	98	325	38	81	103	11	4	1	20	29	45	13	2	6
Ready	.249	.322	.385	76	205	32	51	66	10	1	1	20	47	25	2	1	3
Backman	.243	.308	.344	94	185	20	45	57	12	0	0	15	30	30	3	2	4
Chamberlain	.240	.399	.300	101	383	51	92	153	16	3	13	50	31	73	9	4	3
C. Hayes	.230	.363	.257	142	460	34	106	167	23	1	12	53	16	75	3	3	15
Fletcher	.228	.309	.255	46	136	5	31	42	8	0	1	12	5	15	0	1	2
Lake	.228	.285	.238	58	158	12	36	45	4	1	1	11	2	26	0	0	2
Booker	.226	.245	.236	28	53	3	12	13	1	0	0	7	1	7	0	0	0
V. Hayes	.225	.285	.303	77	284	43	64	81	15	1	0	21	31	42	9	2	2
Batiste	.222	.222	.250	10	27	2	6	6	0	0	0	1	1	8	0	1	1
Morris	.220	.276	.293	85	127	15	28	35	2	1	1	6	12	25	2	0	2
Daulton	.196	.365	.297	89	285	36	56	104	12	0	12	42	41	66	5	0	8
Castillo	.173	.231	.189	28	52	3	9	12	3	0	0	2	1	15	1	1	1
Jones	.154	.231	.214	28	26	0	4	6	2	0	0	3	2	9	0	0	0
Campusano	.114	.200	.139	15	35	2	4	7	0	0	1	2	1	10	0	0	0
Schu	.091	.091	.125	17	22	1	2	2	0	0	0	2	1	7	0	0	1
Lindsey	.000	.000	.000	1	3	0	0	0	0	0	0	0	0	3	0	0	0

Pitching	W-L	ERA	G	GS	CG	GF	Sho	SV	IP	H	R	ER	HR	BB	SO
:Williams	12-5	2.34	69	0	0	60	0	30	88.1	56	24	23	4	62	84
Ritchie	1-2	2.50	39	0	0	13	0	0	50.1	44	17	14	4	17	26
Greene	13-7	3.38	36	27	3	3	2	0	207.2	177	85	78	19	66	154
Brantley	2-2	3.41	6	5	0	0	0	0	31.2	26	12	12	0	19	25
DeJesus	10-9	3.42	31	29	3	1	0	1	181.2	147	74	69	7	128	118
Mulholland	16-13	3.61	34	34	8	0	3	0	232	231	100	93	15	49	142
Ruffin	4-7	3.78	31	15	1	2	1	0	119	125	52	50	6	38	85
Boever	3-5	3.84	68	0	0	27	0	0	98.1	90	45	42	10	54	89
Searcy	2-1	4.15	18	0	0	4	0	0	30.1	29	16	14	2	14	21
Hartley	4-1	4.21	58	0	0	16	0	2	83.1	74	40	39	11	47	63
Cox	4-6	4.57	23	17	0	2	0	0	102.1	98	57	52	14	39	46
Grimsley	1-7	4.87	12	12	0	0	0	0	61	60	34	33	4	41	42
Combs	2-6	4.90	14	13	1	0	0	0	64.1	64	41	35	7	43	41
Akerfelds	2-1	5.26	30	0	0	11	0	0	49.2	49	30	29	5	27	31
Ashby	1-5	6.00	8	8	0	0	0	0	42	41	28	28	5	19	26
Mauser	0-0	7.59	3	0	0	1	0	0	10.2	18	10	9	3	3	6
Carreno	0-0	16.20	3	0	0	1	0	0	3.1	5	6	6	1	3	2
LaPoint	0-1	16.20	2	2	0	0	0	0	5	10	10	9	0	6	3

1992 Preliminary Roster

Pitchers (15)

Kyle Abbott
Andy Ashby
Bob Ayrault
Joe Boever
Toby Borland
Cliff Brantley
Pat Combs
Jose DeJesus
Tommy Greene
Jason Grimsley
Mike Hartley
Ken Howell
Terry Mulholland
Wally Ritchie
Steve Searcy

Catchers (3)

Darren Daulton
Doug Lindsey
Todd Prott

Infielders (9)

Wally Backman
Kim Batiste
Mariano Duncan
Charlie Hayes
David Hollins
Ricky Jordan
John Kruk
Mickey Morandini

Dale Sveum

Outfielders (11)

Ruben Amaro
Braulio Castillo
Wes Chamberlain
Bruce Dostal
Lenny Dykstra
Von Hayes
Jim Lindeman
Anthony Longmire
Dale Murphy
Julio Peguero
Cary Williams

Games played by position

	G	C	1B	2B	3B	SS	OF
Backman,W	94	0	0	36	20	0	0
Batiste,K	10	0	0	0	0	7	0
Booker,R	28	0	0	0	3	20	0
Campusano,S	15	0	0	0	0	0	15
Castillo,B	28	0	0	0	0	0	26
Chamberlain,W	101	0	0	0	0	0	98
Daulton,D	89	88	0	0	0	0	0
Dykstra,L	63	0	0	0	0	0	63
Fletcher,D	46	45	0	0	0	0	0
Hayes,C	142	0	0	0	138	2	0
Hayes,V	77	0	0	0	0	0	72
Hollins,D	56	0	6	0	36	0	0
Jones,R	28	0	0	0	0	0	0
Jordan,R	101	0	72	0	0	0	0
Kruk,J	152	0	102	0	0	0	52
Lake,S	58	58	0	0	0	0	0
Lindeman,J	65	0	1	0	0	0	30
Lindsey,D	1	1	0	0	0	0	0
Morandini,M	98	0	0	97	0	0	0
Morris,Jo	85	0	0	0	0	0	57
Murphy,D	153	0	0	0	0	0	147
Ready,R	76	0	0	66	0	0	0
Schu,R	17	0	1	0	3	0	0
Thon,D	146	0	0	0	0	146	0

Sick call: 1991 DL report

Player	Days on the DL
Ron Jones	56
Steve Ontiveros	182
Sil Campusano	18
Darren Daulton	66**
Lenny Dykstra	111*
Danny Cox	29
Ken Howell	182
Wally Ritchie	22
Jason Grimsley	77
Randy Ready	34
Von Hayes	83
Pat Combs	102
Roger McDowell	17
Dave Hollins	21

On DL twice (not counting administrative transfers from one DL to another).
**On DL three times (not counting administrative transfers from one DL to another).*

Minor League Report

Class AAA — Scranton/Wilkes-Barre finished 65-78, fourth in the International League East. SS Kim Batiste (.292 with 25 doubles) won the Paul Owens Award as the top Phillies minor-league player. He committed 29 errors his first 60 games; 9 errors his final 62 games. 3B Rick Schu topped the farm system with a .321 average and had 14 HRs and 57 RBI. 1B Gary Alexander had 17 HRs and 48 RBI in 79 games. RHPs Bob Ayrault (68) and Jay Baller (61) ranked 1-2 in the IL in appearances. RHP Andy Ashby was 11-5. . . . Class AA — Reading finished 72-68, fifth in the Eastern League. Reading drew a club-record 250,610 fans, the fifth-highest total in league history. OF Bruce Dostal (.313 with 38 SBs) was team MVP and a league All-Star. OF Nikco Riesgo hit .258 with 14 HRs and 66 RBI. OF Tony Longmire hit .288 with 56 RBI. 2B Pat Austin hit .289. RHP Andy Carter was 11-5. Reliever Toby Borland (8-3, 2.70) had club-record 24 saves and was named Phillies Minor League Pitcher of the Year. . . . Class A — Clearwater finished 81-49, winning both halves of the Florida State League Western Division. The Phillies beat St. Lucie and lost to West Palm Beach in the playoffs. SS Troy Paulsen hit .288. OF Tom Nuneviller hit .283. 1B Ron Lockett hit .268 with 10 HRs and 71 RBI. OF Sam Taylor hit .259 with 73 RBI. RHP Donnie Elliott (8-5, 2.78) allowed 78 hits in 107 innings with 103 strikeouts. . . . Spartanburg finished 70-70, fifth in the first half and second in the second half in the South Atlantic League Northern Division. OF Mike Farmer hit .238 with 12 HRs, 77 RBI and 31 SBs. C Mike Lieberthal hit .305 in 72 games. LHP J.J. Munoz was 8-6 with a 3.58 ERA. RHP Eric Hill (7-10, 3.15) had 143 strikeouts in 143 innings. . . . Batavia finished 38-40, third in the NY-P League McNamara West Division. David Tokheim hit .326. Craig Billeci (.267) had 11 HRs and 45 RBI. RHP Craig Holman was 6-2 with a 1.93 ERA. . . . Martinsville finished 27-41, third in the Appalachian League Northern Division. Lamar Cherry hit .275 with 10 HRs and 32 RBI. RHP Dominick DeSantis was 6-6 with a 2.19 ERA. RHP Dan Brown (3-0, 1.72) had 10 saves.

Tops of the Organization

BATTING LEADERS	Club	Avg.	G	AB	R	H	HR	RBI
Rick Schu	Swb	.321	106	355	69	114	14	57
Bruce Dostal	Rea	.313	96	364	68	114	5	34
Kim Batiste	Swb	.292	122	462	54	135	1	41
Greg Legg	Swb	.290	111	352	58	102	3	41
Troy Paulsen	Clw	.288	122	441	62	127	1	47

HOME RUNS			WINS		
Gary Alexander	Swb	17	Mike Williams	Rea	14
Nikco Riesgo	Rea	14	Donnie Elliott	Clw	11
Rick Schu	Swb	14	Andy Carter	Rea	11
Casey Waller	Rea	12	Andy Ashby	Swb	11
Mike Farmer	Spt	12	Several players tied		10

RBI			SAVES		
Mike Farmer	Spt	77	Toby Borland	Rea	24
Sam Taylor	Clw	73	Matt Stevens	Rea	19
Ron Lockett	Clw	71	Jay Baller	Swb	17
Sean Ryan	Rea	70	Ray Domecq	Spt	13
Nikco Riesgo	Rea	66	Mike Sullivan	Clw	11

STOLEN BASES			STRIKE OUTS		
Bruce Dostal	Rea	38	Donnie Elliott	Clw	184
Leroy Ventress	Clw	35	Eric Hill	Spt	143
Mike Farmer	Spt	33	Mike Williams	Rea	127
R.A. Neitzel	Clw	32	Elliott Gray	Rea	117
Jeff Jackson	Spt	29	Paul Fletcher	Rea	117

PITCHING LEADERS	Club	W-L	ERA	IP	H	BB	SO
Cliff Brantley	Swb	6-7	2.69	117	94	50	79
Mike Williams	Rea	14-8	2.76	196	158	50	127
Elliott Gray	Rea	10-6	3.00	147	133	64	117
Paul Fletcher	Rea	7-10	3.06	150	133	64	117
Eric Hill	Spt	7-10	3.15	143	126	48	143

Philadelphia (1883-1991)

Runs: Most, career, all-time

1506	Mike Schmidt, 1972-1989
1367	Ed Delahanty, 1888-1901
1114	Richie Ashburn, 1948-1959
963	Chuck Klein, 1928-1944
924	Sam Thompson, 1889-1898

Hits: Most, career, all-time

2234	Mike Schmidt, 1972-1989
2217	Richie Ashburn, 1948-1959
2213	Ed Delahanty, 1888-1901
1812	Del Ennis, 1946-1956
1798	Larry Bowa, 1970-1981

2B: Most, career, all-time

442	Ed Delahanty, 1888-1901
408	Mike Schmidt, 1972-1989
337	Sherry Magee, 1904-1914
336	Chuck Klein, 1928-1944
310	Del Ennis, 1946-1956

3B: Most, career, all-time

157	Ed Delahanty, 1888-1901
127	Sherry Magee, 1904-1914
106	Sam Thompson, 1889-1898
97	Richie Ashburn, 1948-1959
84	Johnny Callison, 1960-1969

HR: Most, career, all-time

548	Mike Schmidt, 1972-1989
259	Del Ennis, 1946-1956
243	Chuck Klein, 1928-1944
223	Greg Luzinski, 1970-1980
217	Cy Williams, 1918-1930

RBI: Most, career, all-time

1595	Mike Schmidt, 1972-1989
1286	Ed Delahanty, 1888-1901
1124	Del Ennis, 1946-1956
983	Chuck Klein, 1928-1944
957	Sam Thompson, 1889-1898

SB: Most, career, all-time

508	Billy Hamilton, 1890-1895
411	Ed Delahanty, 1888-1901
387	Sherry Magee, 1904-1914
289	Jim Fogarty, 1884-1889
288	Larry Bowa, 1970-1981

BB: Most, career, all-time

1507	Mike Schmidt, 1972-1989
946	Richie Ashburn, 1948-1959
946	Roy Thomas, 1899-1911

693	Willie Jones, 1947-1959
643	Ed Delahanty, 1888-1901

BA: Highest, career, all-time

.361	Billy Hamilton, 1890-1895
.348	Ed Delahanty, 1888-1901
.338	Elmer Flick, 1898-1901
.333	Sam Thompson, 1889-1898
.326	Chuck Klein, 1928-1944
.295	Tony Gonzalez, 1960-1968
	(16)

Slug avg: Highest, career, all-time

.553	Chuck Klein, 1928-1944
.530	Dick Allen, 1963-1976
.527	Mike Schmidt, 1972-1989
.510	Dolph Camilli, 1934-1937
.508	Ed Delahanty, 1888-1901

Games started: Most, career, all-time

499	Steve Carlton, 1972-1986
472	Robin Roberts, 1948-1961
301	Chris Short, 1959-1972
279	Pete Alexander, 1911-1930
262	Curt Simmons, 1947-1960

Saves: Most, career, all-time

103	STEVE BEDROSIAN, 1986-1989
94	Tug McGraw, 1975-1984
90	Ron Reed, 1976-1983
65	Turk Farrell, 1956-1969
59	Jack Baldschun, 1961-1965

Shutouts: Most, career, all-time

61	Pete Alexander, 1911-1930
39	Steve Carlton, 1972-1986
35	Robin Roberts, 1948-1961
24	Chris Short, 1959-1972
23	Jim Bunning, 1964-1971

Wins: Most, career, all-time

241	Steve Carlton, 1972-1986
234	Robin Roberts, 1948-1961
190	Pete Alexander, 1911-1930
132	Chris Short, 1959-1972
115	Curt Simmons, 1947-1960

K: Most, career, all-time

3031	Steve Carlton, 1972-1986
1871	Robin Roberts, 1948-1961
1585	Chris Short, 1959-1972
1409	Pete Alexander, 1911-1930
1197	Jim Bunning, 1964-1971

Win pct: Highest, career, all-time

.676	Pete Alexander, 1911-1930
.642	Tom Seaton, 1912-1913
.607	Charlie Ferguson, 1884-1887
.606	Charlie Buffinton, 1887-1889
.603	Red Donahue, 1898-1901
.600	Ron Reed, 1976-1983 (6)

ERA: Lowest, career, all-time

1.79	George McQuillan, 1907-1916
2.18	Pete Alexander, 1911-1930
2.47	Tully Sparks, 1897-1910
2.61	Frank Corridon, 1904-1909
2.63	Earl Moore, 1908-1913
2.93	Jim Bunning, 1964-1971 (12)

Runs: Most, season

192	Billy Hamilton, 1894
166	Billy Hamilton, 1895
158	Chuck Klein, 1930
152	Chuck Klein, 1932
152	Lefty O'Doul, 1929
125	Dick Allen, 1964 (19)

Hits: Most, season

254	Lefty O'Doul, 1929
250	Chuck Klein, 1930
238	Ed Delahanty, 1899
226	Chuck Klein, 1932
223	Chuck Klein, 1933
213	Dave Cash, 1975 (12)

2B: Most, season

59	Chuck Klein, 1930
55	Ed Delahanty, 1899
50	Chuck Klein, 1932
49	Ed Delahanty, 1895
48	Dick Bartell, 1932
46	VON HAYES, 1986 (6)

3B: Most, season

23	Nap Lajoie, 1897
21	Ed Delahanty, 1892
21	Sam Thompson, 1895
19	JUAN SAMUEL, 1984
19	George Wood, 1887

HR: Most, season

48	Mike Schmidt, 1980

45	Mike Schmidt, 1979
43	Chuck Klein, 1929
41	Cy Williams, 1923
40	Dick Allen, 1966
40	Chuck Klein, 1930
40	Mike Schmidt, 1983

RBI: Most, season

170	Chuck Klein, 1930
165	Sam Thompson, 1895
146	Ed Delahanty, 1893
145	Chuck Klein, 1929
143	Don Hurst, 1932
130	Greg Luzinski, 1977 (9)

SB: Most, season

111	Billy Hamilton, 1891
102	Jim Fogarty, 1887
102	Billy Hamilton, 1890
99	Jim Fogarty, 1889
98	Billy Hamilton, 1894
72	JUAN SAMUEL, 1984 (7)

BB: Most, season

128	Mike Schmidt, 1983
126	Billy Hamilton, 1894
125	Richie Ashburn, 1954
121	VON HAYES, 1987
120	Mike Schmidt, 1979

BA: Highest, season

.410	Ed Delahanty, 1899
.407	Ed Delahanty, 1894
.404	Billy Hamilton, 1894
.404	Ed Delahanty, 1895
.398	Lefty O'Doul, 1929
.339	Tony Gonzalez, 1967 (*)

Slug avg: Highest, season

.687	Chuck Klein, 1930
.657	Chuck Klein, 1929
.654	Sam Thompson, 1895
.646	Chuck Klein, 1932
.644	Mike Schmidt, 1981

Games started: Most, season

61	John Coleman, 1883
55	Kid Gleason, 1890
50	Ed Daily, 1885
49	Gus Weyhing, 1892
47	Charlie Ferguson, 1884
41	Jim Bunning, 1966 (18)
41	Steve Carlton, 1972 (18)

Saves: Most, season

| 40 | STEVE BEDROSIAN, 1987 |

30	MITCH WILLIAMS, 1991
29	STEVE BEDROSIAN, 1986
29	Al Holland, 1984
28	STEVE BEDROSIAN, 1988

Shutouts: Most, season

16	Pete Alexander, 1916
12	Pete Alexander, 1915
9	Pete Alexander, 1913
8	Pete Alexander, 1917
8	Steve Carlton, 1972
8	Ben Sanders, 1888

Wins: Most, season

38	Kid Gleason, 1890
33	Pete Alexander, 1916
32	Gus Weyhing, 1892
31	Pete Alexander, 1915
30	Pete Alexander, 1917
30	Charlie Ferguson, 1886
27	Steve Carlton, 1972 (12)

K: Most, season

310	Steve Carlton, 1972
286	Steve Carlton, 1980
286	Steve Carlton, 1982
275	Steve Carlton, 1983
268	Jim Bunning, 1965

Win pct: Highest, season

.800	Robin Roberts, 1952
.769	Charlie Ferguson, 1886
.760	Larry Christenson, 1977
.760	John Denny, 1983
.756	Pete Alexander, 1915

ERA: Lowest, season

1.22	Pete Alexander, 1915
1.53	George McQuillan, 1908
1.55	Pete Alexander, 1916
1.83	Lew Richie, 1908
1.83	Pete Alexander, 1917
1.97	Steve Carlton, 1972 (9)

Most pinch-hit homers, season

5	Gene Freese, 1959
4	Rip Repulski, 1958
4	Del Unser, 1979

Most pinch-hit, homers, career

| 9 | Cy Williams, 1918-1930 |

Most consecutive games, batting safely

| 36 | Billy Hamilton, 1894 |
| 26 | Chuck Klein, 1930 (2 streaks) |

Most consecutive scoreless innings

| 41 | Grover Cleveland Alexander, 1911 |

No hit games

Charlie Ferguson, Phi vs Pro NL, 1-0; August 29, 1885.
Red Donahue, Phi vs Bos NL, 5-0; July 8, 1898.
Chick Fraser, Phi at Chi NL; 10-0; September 18, 1903 (2nd game).
Johnny Lush, Phi at Bro NL, 6-0; May 1, 1906.
Jim Bunning, Phi at NY NL, 6-0; June 21, 1964 (1st game, perfect game).
Rick Wise, Phi at Cin NL, 4-0; June 23, 1971.
Terry Mulholland, Phi vs SF NL, 6-0; August 15, 1990.
Tommy Greene, Phi at Mon NL, 2-0; May 23, 1991.

Chicago Cubs

Chicago needs a repeat performance from Andre Dawson in 1992.

Big money deals didn't pay off

One-for-three gets it done in the batter's box.

Not in the game of big-money free agents.

During the offseason the Chicago Cubs opened the corporate vault of the Tribune Co., and signed right fielder George Bell and pitchers Dave Smith and Danny Jackson to multi-million dollar extended deals.

Bell rang true.

Smith and Jackson were flops.

Bell hit .285 with 25 HRs and 86 RBI after signing for $2.1 million a year. Smith, who earns $1.9 million annually, battled injuries throughout the season and pitched in just 35 games. He had 17 saves before he went out for the season and finished with a 0-6 record and a 6.00 ERA.

Jackson had a similar fate. He pulled a groin muscle early in the season and never found his stride. He struggled to a 1-5 record with a 6.75 ERA and made just 14 starts.

(The injuries did not stop with just high-priced free agents. Starters Les Lancaster, Mike Harkey and Shawn Boskie all suffered arm injuries during the season.)

Meanwhile, Don Zimmer was not around to see most of the season. He was dismissed May 21 after the Cubs struggled to an 18-19 start, and was replaced by Jim Essian who—after leading the Cubs to a disappointing 77-83 mark—twisted in the wind awaiting announcement of his fate. In the fashion of the season, he, too, was fired.

Ryne Sandberg was an all-star again, but could become a free agent after the 1992 season and was awaiting negotiations on a new contract. Sandberg hit .291 with 26 HR and 100 RBI.

Shawon Dunston will return next year after signing a four-year deal worth $12 million, but the team was unable to find a third baseman after prospect Gary Scott failed.

After briefly considering retirement during an ineffective rehab stint in the minors, Rick Sutcliffe got it back together, pitched well during the final two months of the season, then became a free agent.

The Cubs also landed lauded pitching prospect Turk Wendell from the Atlanta Braves in a late-season trade that cost them pitcher Mike Bielecki and catcher Damon Berryhill.

—*A. Reid*

Cubs 1992 preview

The Cubs will need repeat performances from Ryne Sandberg and Andre Dawson this season. If Sandberg comes close to a third consecutive 100-run, 100-RBI season, and Dawson can defy Father Time with more numbers like 31 homers and 104 RBI, there will be two fewer areas of concern.

One pressing need is a speedy center fielder who can also bat leadoff. Jerome Walton, 1989 NL Rookie of the Year, needs to reverse his downward spiral at the plate, where his average has dropped from .293 to .219. Dawson and George Bell solidify the other outfield positions.

The two biggest infield problems: Hector Villanueva has yet to prove he's an everyday backstop, and no one has stamped his name on the hot corner.

Pitching is a thin spot, although injury-free seasons by Danny Jackson, Mike Harkey and Dave Smith may help alleviate lack of depth. Free-agent Mike Morgan provides additional help on the mound for Greg Maddux.

1992 prophecy: Cubs

▸In a desperate move to reverse its team's historical losing trend, Cubs management will shock baseball traditionalists by installing artificial turf at Wrigley Field. Andre Dawson will then quit.

▸Feeling sorry for first baseman Mark Grace's throbbing right hand, shortstop Shawon Dunston will throw 85 mph sliders to first.

—*John Hunt*

'Escobar' gave game character

By Tom Weir

When Jim Essian was promoted to manager of the Chicago Cubs, I had a flashback about the first time I really noticed the bent-nosed guy they call "Escobar." It was in an airport waiting area, after he had just been traded for the second of an eventual six times. With the Oakland A's flight delayed, players began doing what baseball most prepares them for—killing time.

For Essian, this meant disappearing into a corner, assuming the lotus position and commencing a venture into the world of transcendental meditation. A's manager Bobby Winkles walked by and gave Essian that "Wheaties" look— the one managers reserve for the flakiest of flakes. Ask Essian about this now and he cops a plea, blaming his first team, the Philadelphia Phillies, who at the time were apparently studying California's granola circuit for new training ideas.

Essian eventually wound through five managing stops and two championships in the minor leagues. The term "players' manager" is an overused one, but it sticks to Essian like pine tar on a bat.

During a stint in the American Association, Essian was in the third-base coaching box when an Oklahoma City pitcher threw at one of Essian's players. The 40-year-old rushed the mound and attacked the pitcher. (It cost him a three-day suspension.)

"It's a little different in the minors," Essian explained. Among the parade of managers Essian played for was Billy Martin, from whom he learned the question-dodging skills every manager must acquire. As the A's catcher when "six or seven of the pitchers were using a foreign substance," Essian mastered the blank look baseball people must wear when the topic of greasy fastballs arises.

That a free spirit like Essian was hired at a time when baseball is marching more and more to the beat of the corporate drum seemed to say that there's still a little room for the characters, the guys who think of baseball as a game rather than a business. Baseball lost one of those characters when the Cubs dumped Don Zimmer, and another when they dumped Essian in the managerial musical chairs game that reached an all-time peak in 1991.

Smith celebrated 100th win

Bryn Smith knows his 100th career victory might not have the same significance as other pitchers' milestones.

"This is like 300 for me," Smith said. "I know I'll never win 200. I never like to go out on a limb and say I deserve this, but I think I deserve this. It's come from a lot of hard work."

Smith didn't make the majors until he was 26. He got win No. 100 Aug. 9, two days before his 36th birthday, against the Pirates—after two previous attempts.

He celebrated with a bottle of champagne that pitcher Scott Terry had bought before Smith's first attempt.

"I'd been carrying it around for two weeks," Smith said.

Teammate Bob Tewksbury, an accomplished artist, drew a caricature of Smith, and a fan from St. Louis sent roses.

Dunston stays with Cubs

Shawon Dunston signed a four-year contract worth $12 million, believed to make him the highest-paid shortstop in the game at the time.

The deal includes a clause stipulating that Dunston cannot be traded to several specific teams—Cleveland, Toronto and Montreal reportedly among them.

Dunston, who made $2.1 million in 1991, was relieved to re-sign with the Cubs before the free agency deadline. Unlike many players in today's high-stakes market, Dunston's priority was staying with his team.

"People might say I could make more elsewhere," Dunston said. "I don't want to make more. I want to stay here."

When he signed, the deal moved Dunston into third place on the Cubs' payroll behind Andre Dawson and George Bell.

To be safe, the Cubs had acquired Jose Vizcaino and had groomed Rey Sanchez as possible replacements for Dunston. The rumor mill had Dunston possibly signing with the Dodgers.

Cubs' winter league news

▶Winter leagues: Chicago sent the largest group of players to winter ball, assigning a number of players from its major league roster. OF George Bell was to play in his native Dominican Republic for the first time in seven years. Licey, which has owned the rights to Bell since the outfielder led the Tigers to the league title seven years ago, acquired Bell from Azucareros Este for SS Jose Offerman and RHP Pedro J. Martinez. Bell was slated to make his debut for Azucareros in January . . . RHP Heathcliff Slocumb (2-1, 3.45 in 52 relief appearances with the Cubs) and RHP Bob Scanlan (7-8, 3.89) played winter ball to get additional work. 3B Luis Salazar (.258-14-38) was one of many native players competing in Venezuela . . . Third baseman Gary Scott went to Venezuela to reha-

bilitate a broken wrist suffered late last season and to try to find the batting stroke that looked so promising in spring training last year. . . . C Hector Villanueva played at home in Puerto Rico for the San Juan Metros. He will compete with C Rick Wilkins and C Joe Girardi for the Cubs' starting job next season. Wilkins also played for San Juan. . . . RHP Turk Wendell (11-3, 2.56 at Class AA Greenville), acquired in the late-season trade that sent C Damon Berryhill and RHP Mike Bielecki to Atlanta, played in Puerto Rico for the Santurce Crabbers. LHP Yorkis Perez (12-3, 3.79 at Class AAA Richmond), acquired in the same trade, played at home in the Dominican Republic for Licey. . . . LHP Lance Dickson (4-4, 3.11) continued to rehabilitate from a stress fracture of his right foot after missing two months at Iowa. . . . IF Jose Vizcaino played at home in the Dominican Republic. . . . OF Phil Dauphin played in Australia for the Sydney team.

Team directory

▶Owner: Tribune Company

▶General Manager: James G. Frey

▶Ballpark: Wrigley Field
Clark and Addison Streets, Chicago, Illinois
312-404-2827
Capacity 38,710
Parking for 900; $10 (private lots available)
Public transportation available
Family and wheelchair sections, ramps

▶Team publications:
Yearbook, Vineline, game date program 800-248-WINS

▶TV, radio broadcast stations:
WGN 720 AM, WGN Channel 9

▶Spring Training:
HoHoKam Park
Mesa, Arizona
Capacity 8,963
800-638-4253 or 602-678-2222

CHICAGO CUBS 1991 Final Stats

Batting	AVG	SLG	OB	G	AB	R	H	TB	2B	3B	HR	RBI	BB	SO	SB	CS	E
Strange	.444	.556	.455	3	9	0	4	5	1	0	0	1	0	1	1	0	1
Sandberg	.291	.485	.379	158	585	104	170	284	32	2	26	100	87	89	22	8	4
Bell	.285	.468	.323	149	558	63	159	261	27	0	25	86	32	62	2	6	10
Villanueva	.276	.542	.346	71	192	23	53	104	10	1	13	32	21	30	0	0	6
Grace	.273	.373	.346	160	619	87	169	231	28	5	8	58	70	53	3	4	8
Dawson	.272	.488	.302	149	563	69	153	275	21	4	31	104	22	80	4	5	3
Vizcaino	.262	.297	.283	93	145	7	38	43	5	0	0	10	5	18	2	1	7
Sanchez	.261	.261	.370	13	23	1	6	6	0	0	0	2	4	3	0	0	0
Dunston	.260	.407	.292	142	492	59	128	200	22	7	12	50	23	64	21	6	21
Salazar	.258	.432	.292	103	333	34	86	144	14	1	14	38	15	45	0	3	10
Walker	.257	.337	.315	124	374	51	96	126	10	1	6	34	33	57	13	5	8
Dascenzo	.255	.314	.327	118	239	40	61	75	11	0	1	18	24	26	14	7	2
Landrum	.233	.279	.313	56	86	28	20	24	2	1	0	6	10	18	27	5	2
Dw. Smith	.228	.347	.279	90	167	16	38	58	7	2	3	21	11	32	2	3	3
D. May	.227	.455	.280	15	22	4	5	10	2	0	1	3	2	1	0	0	0
Wilkins	.222	.355	.307	86	203	21	45	72	9	0	6	22	19	56	3	3	3
Walton	.219	.330	.275	123	270	42	59	89	13	1	5	17	19	55	7	3	3
Girardi	.191	.234	.283	21	47	3	9	11	2	0	0	6	6	6	0	0	3
Pappas	.176	.176	.222	7	17	1	3	3	0	0	0	2	1	5	0	0	0
Scott	.165	.241	.305	31	79	8	13	19	3	0	1	5	13	14	0	1	2

Pitching	W-L	ERA	G	GS	CG	GF	Sho	SV	IP	H	R	ER	HR	BB	SO
Dascenzo	0-0	0.00	3	0	0	3	0	0	4	2	0	0	0	2	2
McElroy	6-2	1.95	71	0	0	12	0	3	101.1	73	33	22	7	57	92
Perez	1-0	2.08	3	0	0	0	0	0	4.1	2	1	1	0	2	3
Assenmacher	7-8	3.24	75	0	0	31	0	15	102.2	85	41	37	10	31	117
Maddux	15-11	3.35	37	37	7	0	2	0	263	232	113	98	18	66	198
Slocumb	2-1	3.45	52	0	0	21	0	1	62.2	53	29	24	3	30	34
Lancaster	9-7	3.52	64	11	1	21	0	3	156	150	68	61	13	49	102
Scanlan	7-8	3.89	40	13	0	16	0	1	111	114	60	48	5	40	44
Sutcliffe	6-5	4.10	19	18	0	0	0	0	96.2	96	52	44	4	45	52
Castillo	6-7	4.35	18	18	4	0	0	0	111.2	107	56	54	5	33	73
Boskie	4-9	5.23	28	20	0	2	0	0	129	150	78	75	14	52	62
Harkey	0-2	5.30	4	4	0	0	0	0	18.2	21	11	11	3	6	15
Da. Smith	0-6	6.00	35	0	0	28	0	17	33	39	22	22	6	19	16
Jackson	1-5	6.75	17	14	0	0	0	0	70.2	89	59	53	8	48	31
Renfroe	0-1	13.50	4	0	0	2	0	0	4.2	11	7	7	1	2	4
S. May	0-0	18.00	2	0	0	1	0	0	2	6	4	4	0	1	1
Pavlas	0-0	18.00	1	0	0	1	0	0	1	3	2	2	1	0	0

1992 Preliminary Roster

Pitchers (16)

Paul Assenmacher
Shawn Boskie
Jim Bullinger
Frank Castillo
Lance Dickson
Mike Harkey
Jeff Hartsock
Danny Jackson
Les Lancaster
Greg Maddux
Chuck McElroy
Mike Morgan
Bob Scanlan
Heathcliff Slocumb
Dave Smith
Turk Wendell

Catchers (4)

Joe Girardi
George Pedre
Hector Villanueva
Rick Wilkins

Infielders (11)

Alex Arias
Pedro Castellano
Shawon Dunston
Mark Grace
Elvin Paulino
Luis Salazar
Rey Sanchez
Ryne Sandberg
Gary Scott
Doug Strange
Jose Vizcaino

Outfielders (10)

George Bell
Steve Carter
Doug Dascenzo
Andre Dawson
Ced Landrum
Derrick May
Kevin Roberson
Dwight Smith
Chico Walker

Games Played by position

Head:	G	C	1B	2B	3B	SS	OF
Bell,G	149	0	0	0	0	0	146
Dascenzo,D	118	0	0	0	0	0	86
Dawson,A	149	0	0	0	0	0	137
Dunston,S	142	0	0	0	0	142	0
Girardi,J	21	21	0	0	0	0	0
Grace,M	160	0	160	0	0	0	0
Landrum,C	56	0	0	0	0	0	44
May,D	15	0	0	0	0	0	7
Pappas,E	7	6	0	0	0	0	0
Salazar,L	103	0	7	0	86	0	1
Sanchez,R	13	0	0	2	0	10	0
Sandberg,R	158	0	0	157	0	0	0
Scott,G	31	0	0	0	31	0	0
Smith,Dw	90	0	0	0	0	0	42
Strange,D	3	0	0	0	3	0	0
Villanueva,H	71	55	6	0	0	0	0
Vizcaino,J	93	0	0	9	57	33	0
Walker,C	124	0	0	6	57	0	53
Walton,J	123	0	0	0	0	0	101
Wilkins,R	86	82	0	0	0	0	0

Sick call: 1991 DL report

Player	Days on the DL
Hector Villanueva	20
Rick Sutcliffe	74 *
Joe Girardi	111
Danny Jackson	94 *
Mike Harkey	63
Dave Smith	40
Frank Castillo	16

On DL twice (not counting admininstrative transfers from one DL to another.

Minor League Report

Class AAA — Iowa finished 78-66, second in the American Association West. The Cubs led the division for all but 8 days, but lost 9 of their final 11 games and were overtaken by Denver at the end. Hitting leaders were 3B Doug Strange (.293-8-56 with 35 doubles), SS Rey Sanchez (.290) and OF Steve Carter (.287-8-67 with league-leading 11 triples). RHP Laddie Renfroe (8-5, 4.21) led league with club-record 18 saves. . . . **Class AA** — Charlotte finished 74-70, fourth in the first half and third in the second half in the Southern League Eastern Division. The Knights drew a club-record 313,351 fans, best in Double-A. 1B Elvin Paulino (.257) became first Charlotte player to lead SL in HRs (24) and RBI (81) during the same season. OF Fernando Ramsey hit .276 with 37 SBs. SS Alex Arias hit .275 with 26 doubles. OF Kevin Roberson hit 19 HRs. Top pitchers included RHP John Salles (10-7, 3.00); RHP Tim Parker (11-9, 3.73) and RHP John Gardner (7-8, 3.51, 122 hits in 154 innings). . . . **Class A** — Winston-Salem finished 83-57, second in the first half and second in the second half in the Carolina League Southern Division. 3B Pete Castellano (.304-11-88) was league MVP. OF John Jensen (.256) was second in league to Castellano with 81 RBI. RHP Ryan Hawblitzel (15-2) tied for the league lead in wins, while RHP Travis Willis had 26 saves. . . . Peoria finished 62-76, tied for sixth in the first half and fourth in the second half in the Midwest League Southern Division. OF Phil Dauphin hit .296 with 11 HRs and 49 RBI. OF Earl Cunningham (.239-19-70) set a team record with 7 RBI against Appleton July 21. 3B Jose Viera (.265-6-55) set a club mark with 37 doubles. OF Mike Little hit .274 with 10 HRs. RHP Jason Doss was 11-11 with a 3.34 ERA. . . . Geneva finished 35-43, fourth in the NY-P League McNamara West Division. The Cubs drew a club-record 35,577 fans. OF Ozzie Timmons hit .221 with 12 HRs and 47 RBI. OF Doug Glanville hit .303 with 17 SBs. RHP Pedro Perez (4-4, 3.06) had 95 strikeouts in 100 innings. . . . Huntington finished 25-42, fifth in the Appalachian League Northern Division. Top hitters were OF Pedro Valdez (.287), SS Ken Arnold (.275-6-43) and 3B Mitch Root (.268). RHP Hector Trinidad was 6-3 with a 2.87 ERA.

Tops in the Organization

BATTING LEADERS	Avg.	G	AB	R	H	HR	RBI
Pedro Castellano	Chr	.308	136	478	61	147	10	90
Phil Dauphin	Peo	.296	120	426	74	126	11	49
Doug Strange	Iwa	.293	131	509	76	149	8	56
Rey Sanchez	Iwa	.290	126	417	60	121	2	46
Steve Carter	Iwa	.287	136	519	79	149	8	67

HOME RUNS			WINS		
Elvin Paulino	Chr	24	Ryan Hawblitzel	Chr	16
Earl Cunningham	Peo	19	Jose Nunez	Iwa	12
Kevin Roberson	Chr	19	Jim Bullinger	Iwa	12
Paul Torres	Peo	15	Jason Doss	Peo	11
Russ McGinnis	Iwa	15	Tim Parker	Chr	11

RBI			SAVES		
Pedro Castellano	Chr	90	Travis Willis	Wns	26
Elvin Paulino	Chr	81	Laddie Renfroe	Iwa	18
John Jensen	Wns	78	Tim Watkins	Chr	13
Mike Grace	Chr	71	Scott May	Iwa	10
Several players tied		70	Julio Strauss	Chr	9

STOLEN BASES			STRIKEOUTS		
Fernando Ramsey	Chr	37	Jim Bullinger	Iwa	158
Ty Griffin	Wns	28	Jason Doss	Peo	154
Victor Cancel	Peo	22	Ryan Hawblitzel	Chr	128
Alex Arias	Chr	22	Jose Nunez	Iwa	118
Jerrone Williams	Wns	22	John Gardner	Chr	116

PITCHING LEADERS	Club	W-L	ERA	IP	H	BB	SO
Dave Swartzbaugh	Chr	10-10	2.17	133	98	60	109
Ryan Hawblitzel	Chr	16-4	2.47	168	141	59	128
Troy Bradford	Wns	9-5	2.59	118	103	48	72
John Salles	Chr	10-7	3.00	150	141	37	74
Jason Doss	Peo	11-11	3.34	143	136	68	154

Chicago (1876-1991)

Runs: Most, career, all-time

1719	Cap Anson, 1876-1897	
1409	Jimmy Ryan, 1885-1900	
1306	Billy Williams, 1959-1974	
1305	Ernie Banks, 1953-1971	
1239	Stan Hack, 1932-1947	

Hits: Most, career, all-time

2995	Cap Anson, 1876-1897
2583	Ernie Banks, 1953-1971
2510	Billy Williams, 1959-1974
2193	Stan Hack, 1932-1947
2171	Ron Santo, 1960-1973

2B: Most, career, all-time

528	Cap Anson, 1876-1897
407	Ernie Banks, 1953-1971
402	Billy Williams, 1959-1974
391	Gabby Hartnett, 1922-1940
363	Stan Hack, 1932-1947

3B: Most, career, all-time

142	Jimmy Ryan, 1885-1900
124	Cap Anson, 1876-1897
117	Frank Schulte, 1904-1916
106	Bill Dahlen, 1891-1898
99	Phil Cavarretta, 1934-1953
90	Ernie Banks, 1953-1971 (7)

HR: Most, career, all-time

512	Ernie Banks, 1953-1971
392	Billy Williams, 1959-1974
337	Ron Santo, 1960-1973
231	Gabby Hartnett, 1922-1940
205	Bill Nicholson, 1939-1948
205	RYNE SANDBERG, 1982-1991

RBI: Most, career, all-time

1879	Cap Anson, 1876-1897
1636	Ernie Banks, 1953-1971
1353	Billy Williams, 1959-1974
1290	Ron Santo, 1960-1973
1153	Gabby Hartnett, 1922-1940

SB: Most, career, all-time

400	Frank Chance, 1898-1912
399	Bill Lange, 1893-1899
369	Jimmy Ryan, 1885-1900
304	Joe Tinker, 1902-1916
297	RYNE SANDBERG, 1982-1991

BB: Most, career, all-time

1092	Stan Hack, 1932-1947
1071	Ron Santo, 1960-1973
952	Cap Anson, 1876-1897
911	Billy Williams, 1959-1974
794	Phil Cavarretta, 1934-1953

BA: Highest, career, all-time

.336	Riggs Stephenson, 1926-1934
.330	Bill Lange, 1893-1899
.329	Cap Anson, 1876-1897
.325	Kiki Cuyler, 1928-1935
.323	Bill Everett, 1895-1900
.300	Bill Buckner, 1977-1984 (15)

Slug avg: Highest, career, all-time

.590	Hack Wilson, 1926-1931
.517	ANDRE DAWSON, 1987-1991
.512	Hank Sauer, 1949-1955
.503	Billy Williams, 1959-1974
.500	Ernie Banks, 1953-1971

Games started: Most, career, all-time

347	Fergie Jenkins, 1966-1983
343	RICK REUSCHEL, 1972-1984
340	Bill Hutchinson, 1889-1895
339	Charlie Root, 1926-1941
296	Bill Lee, 1934-1947

Saves: Most, career, all-time

180	LEE SMITH, 1980-1987
133	Bruce Sutter, 1976-1980
63	Don Elston, 1953-1964
60	Phil Regan, 1968-1972
52	MITCH WILLIAMS, 1989-1990

Shutouts: Most, career, all-time

48	Mordecai Brown, 1904-1916
35	Hippo Vaughn, 1913-1921
31	Ed Reulbach, 1905-1913
29	Fergie Jenkins, 1966-1983
28	Orval Overall, 1906-1913

Wins: Most, career, all-time

201	Charlie Root, 1926-1941
188	Mordecai Brown, 1904-1916
182	Bill Hutchinson, 1889-1895
175	Larry Corcoran, 1880-1885
167	Fergie Jenkins, 1966-1983

K: Most, career, all-time

2038	Fergie Jenkins, 1966-1983

1432	Charlie Root, 1926-1941
1367	RICK REUSCHEL, 1972-1984
1226	Bill Hutchinson, 1889-1895
1138	Hippo Vaughn, 1913-1921

Win pct: Highest, career, all-time

.800	Al Spalding, 1876-1878
.773	Jim McCormick, 1885-1886
.706	John Clarkson, 1884-1887
.686	Mordecai Brown, 1904-1916
.677	Ed Reulbach, 1905-1913
.569	MIKE BIELECKI, 1988-1991
(23)	

ERA: Lowest, career, all-time

1.80	Mordecai Brown, 1904-1916
1.85	Jack Pfiester, 1906-1911
1.91	Orval Overall, 1906-1913
2.15	Jake Weimer, 1903-1905
2.24	Ed Reulbach, 1905-1913
3.18	Bill Hands, 1966-1972 (20)

Runs: Most, season

156	Rogers Hornsby, 1929
155	Kiki Cuyler, 1930
155	King Kelly, 1886
152	Woody English, 1930
150	George Gore, 1886
137	Billy Williams, 1970 (10)

Hits: Most, season

229	Rogers Hornsby, 1929
228	Kiki Cuyler, 1930
227	Billy Herman, 1935
214	Woody English, 1930
212	Frank Demaree, 1936
205	Billy Williams, 1970 (11)

2B: Most, season

57	Billy Herman, 1935
57	Billy Herman, 1936
50	Kiki Cuyler, 1930
49	Riggs Stephenson, 1932
47	Rogers Hornsby, 1929
41	Bill Buckner, 1980 (12)
41	RAFAEL PALMEIRO, 1988 (12)

3B: Most, season

21	Vic Saier, 1913
21	Frank Schulte, 1911
19	Bill Dahlen, 1892
19	Bill Dahlen, 1896
19	RYNE SANDBERG, 1984

HR: Most, season

56	Hack Wilson, 1930	
49	ANDRE DAWSON, 1987	
48	Dave Kingman, 1979	
47	Ernie Banks, 1958	
45	Ernie Banks, 1959	

RBI: Most, season

190	Hack Wilson, 1930	
159	Hack Wilson, 1929	
149	Rogers Hornsby, 1929	
147	Cap Anson, 1886	
143	Ernie Banks, 1959	

SB: Most, season

84	Bill Lange, 1896	
76	Walt Wilmot, 1890	
74	Walt Wilmot, 1894	
73	Bill Lange, 1897	
67	Frank Chance, 1903	
67	Bill Lange, 1895	
54	RYNE SANDBERG, 1985 (14)	

BB: Most, season

147	Jimmy Sheckard, 1911	
122	Jimmy Sheckard, 1912	
116	Richie Ashburn, 1960	
113	Cap Anson, 1890	
108	Johnny Evers, 1910	
103	Gary Matthews, 1984 (7)	

BA: Highest, season

.389	Bill Lange, 1895	
.388	King Kelly, 1886	
.380	Rogers Hornsby, 1929	
.372	Heinie Zimmerman, 1912	
.371	Cap Anson, 1886	
.354	Bill Madlock, 1975 (14)	

Slug avg: Highest, season

.723	Hack Wilson, 1930	
.679	Rogers Hornsby, 1929	
.630	Gabby Hartnett, 1930	
.618	Hack Wilson, 1929	
.614	Ernie Banks, 1958	

Games started: Most, season

71	Bill Hutchinson, 1892	
70	John Clarkson, 1885	
66	Bill Hutchinson, 1890	
60	Larry Corcoran, 1880	
60	Al Spalding, 1876	
42	Fergie Jenkins, 1969 (18)	

Saves: Most, season

37	Bruce Sutter, 1979	
36	LEE SMITH, 1987	
36	MITCH WILLIAMS, 1989	
33	LEE SMITH, 1984	
33	LEE SMITH, 1985	

Shutouts: Most, season

10	John Clarkson, 1885	
9	Pete Alexander, 1919	
9	Mordecai Brown, 1906	
9	Mordecai Brown, 1908	
9	Bill Lee, 1938	
9	Orval Overall, 1909	
7	Fergie Jenkins, 1969 (11)	

Wins: Most, season

53	John Clarkson, 1885	
47	Al Spalding, 1876	
44	Bill Hutchinson, 1891	
43	Larry Corcoran, 1880	
42	Bill Hutchinson, 1890	
24	Fergie Jenkins, 1971 (*)	

K: Most, season

316	Bill Hutchinson, 1892	
313	John Clarkson, 1886	
308	John Clarkson, 1885	
289	Bill Hutchinson, 1890	
274	Fergie Jenkins, 1970	

Win pct: Highest, season

.875	Fred Goldsmith, 1880	
.833	King Cole, 1910	
.833	Jim McCormick, 1885	
.826	Ed Reulbach, 1906	
.813	Mordecai Brown, 1906	
.720	MIKE BIELECKI, 1989 (25)	

ERA: Lowest, season

1.04	Mordecai Brown, 1906	
1.15	Jack Pfiester, 1907	
1.17	Carl Lundgren, 1907	
1.31	Mordecai Brown, 1909	
1.33	Jack Taylor, 1902	
2.11	Dick Ellsworth, 1963 (*)	

Most pinch-hit homers, season

3	Willie Smith, 1969	
3	Thad Bosley, 1985	

Most pinch-hit, homers, career

6	Thad Bosley, 1983-1986	

Most consecutive games, batting safely

42	Bill Dahlen, 1894	
30	Jerome Walton, 1989	

Most consecutive scoreless innings

50	Ed Reulbach, 1908-09	

No hit games

Larry Corcoran, Chi vs Bos NL, 6-0; August 19, 1880.
Larry Corcoran, Chi vs Wor NL, 5-0; September 20, 1882.
Larry Corcoran, Chi vs Pro NL, 6-0; June 27, 1884.
John Clarkson, Chi at Pro NL, 4-0; July 27, 1885.
Walter Thornton, Chi vs Bro NL, 2-0; August 21, 1898 (2nd game).
Bob Wicker, Chi at NY NL, 1-0; June 11, 1904 (won in 12 innings after allowing one hit in the tenth).
Jimmy Lavender, Chi at NY NL, 2-0; August 31, 1915 (1st game).
Hippo Vaughn, Chi vs Cin NL, 0-1; May 2, 1917. (lost on two hits in the 10th, Toney pitched a no-hitter in this game).
Sam Jones, Chi vs Pit NL, 4-0; May 12, 1955.
Don Cardwell, Chi vs StL NL, 4-0; May 15, 1960 (2nd game).
Ken Holtzman, Chi vs Atl NL, 3-0; August 19, 1969.
Ken Holtzman, Chi at Cin NL, 1-0; June 3, 1971.
Burt Hooton, Chi vs Phi NL, 4-0; April 16, 1972.
Milt Pappas, Chi vs SD NL, 8-0; September 2, 1972.
George Van Haltren, six innings, rain, Chi vs Pit NL, 1-0, June 21, 1888.
King Cole, seven innings, called so Chicago could catch train, Chi at StL NL, 4-0; July 31, 1910 (2nd game).

New York's Howard Johnson led the league with 38 home runs in 1991.

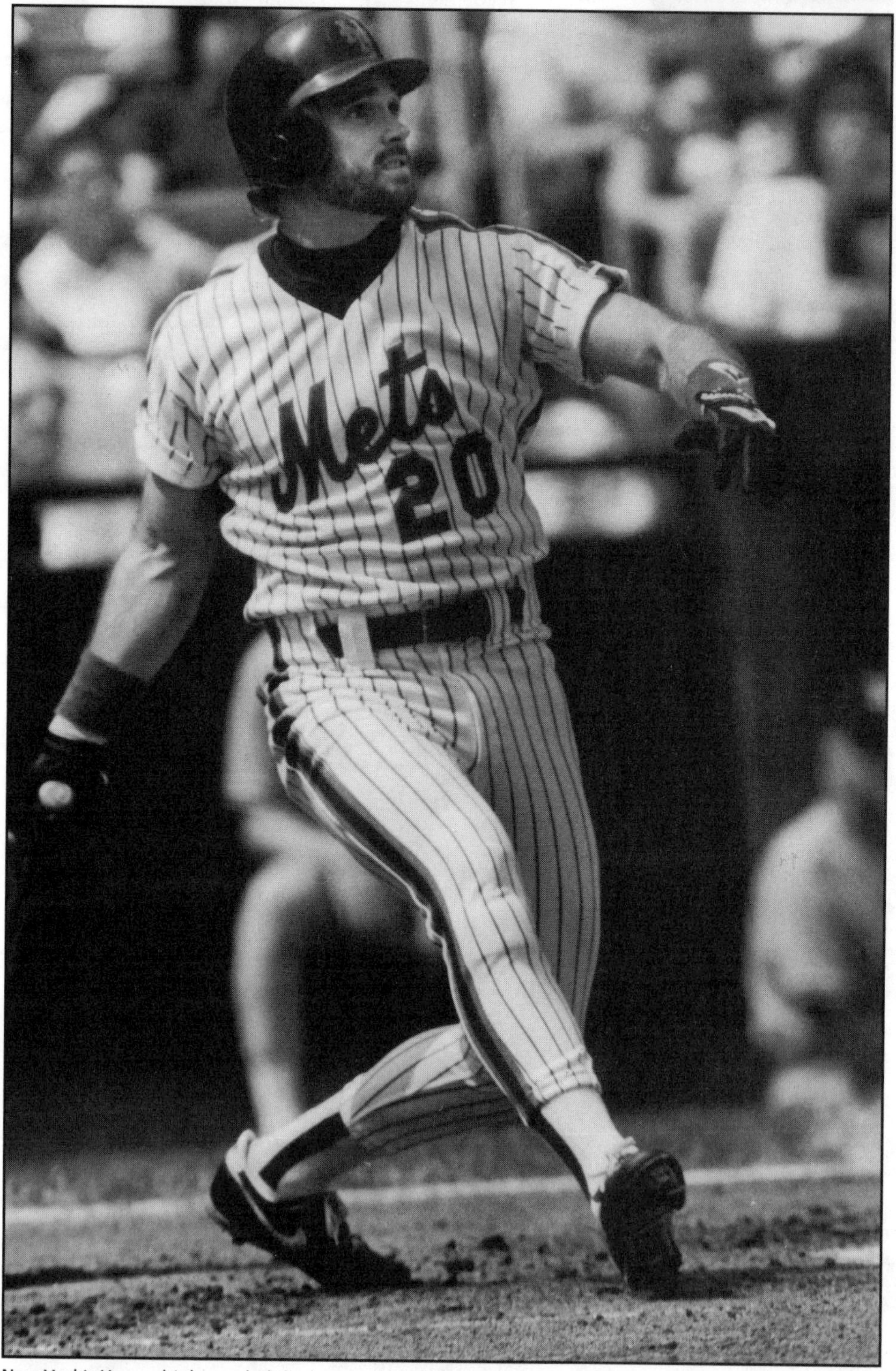

Weak bats + bad gloves = fifth place

The New York Mets found themselves in an unfamiliar position last season. They finished lower than second place in the National League East for the first time since 1983.

Prognosticators already had pegged the Mets as a middle-of-the-pack team, primarily due to a porous defense. But no one expected a fifth-place finish.

In the long run, the starting rotation of Dwight Gooden, David Cone, Frank Viola, Sid Fernandez and Ron Darling—the Mets' strong suit—could not overcome poor fielding and a weak offense. (Darling was traded to Montreal, where he stayed briefly before going to the American League to join Oakland's struggling pitching staff.) New York committed the second-most errors in the league and was eighth in runs scored.

The pitching staff was disrupted when Fernandez suffered a broken arm in spring training, making him unavailable until July.

But the Mets stayed competitive with a 10-game winning streak in July, pulling within two games of first-place at the All-Star break.

By August they were done. The Mets lost seven of nine games in California after the break. Sure signs of crumbling arose when the Cubs swept a four-game series at Shea Stadium.

The bottom fell out during an 0-10 road trip that ended Aug. 18, following visits to Chicago, St. Louis and Pittsburgh.

The anemic defense was no surprise, with Gregg Jefferies, Howard Johnson and others playing musical chairs in the infield. But the hitting was another matter:

▶Dave Magadan competed for the batting title in 1990 and finished third (.328), but he fell to .258 last season.

▶Hubie Brooks, acquired from Los Angeles to ease the loss of Darryl Strawberry, had 16 homers and 50 RBI: roughly half Strawberry's average output.

▶Vince Coleman was signed to help transform the Mets into a speed-based team, but injuries limited him to 72 games and his average dropped from .295 to .255.

▶Usually reliable Kevin McReynolds had his worst power numbers since 1985—16 homers and 74 RBI.

Johnson was the lone bright spot offensively, with a league-leading 38 homers and 117 RBI.

Cone tied Roger Clemens for the major-league lead in strikeouts (241), and tied an NL record on the season's final day by striking out 19 batters. But manager Bud Harrelson wasn't there to witness the feat.

Harrelson was fired the week before. Jeff Torborg was named manager after the season ended, and one of his first tasks will be easing the the tense clubhouse atmpsphere.

—Deron Snyder

Mets 1992 preview

New manager Jeff Torborg takes over with Howard Johnson coming off a career year. Bobby Bonilla, Eddie Murray and Bret Saberhagen return a star quality to the Mets' lineup..

Despite Saberhagen and David Cone, who threw 19 strikeouts on the final day of last season, Dwight Gooden and Sid Fernandez are coming off surgery.

The infield remains a question mark with only Eddie Murray set at first base. Johnson concluded last season in the outfield and may return there. Bill Pecota will play somewhere and Kevin Elster gets another shot at shortstop.

If Vince Coleman can bounce back from an off-year, the outfield could be the best in the league.

Young Randy Hundley could finally solve the Mets' catching problems.

1992 prophecy: Mets

▶Mackey Sasser will be cured of his mysterious throwing ailment when the Mets sign 6-foot-10 pitcher Randy Johnson.

▶David Cone will be everyone's preseason choice for Cy Young, but he will continue to confound hitters by giving up runs and losing games.

—*John Hunt*

Record day closed poor year

It wasn't a good year for the New York Mets, but pitcher David Cone and outfielder Howard Johnson made history the final day of the season Oct. 6 in Philadelphia.

Cone struck out 19 Phillies in a 7-0 victory, tying Steve Carlton and Tom Seaver for the NL record for strikeouts in a nine-inning game. Appropriately, it was Fan Appreciation Day.

"I wouldn't compare myself to those guys (Carlton, Seaver) as a pitcher," Cone said, "but it's great to tie a record that they held."

Boston's Cy Young winner, Roger Clemens, holds the major-league record of 20. Cone wound up with Clemens for the major-league lead with 241 strikeouts.

Johnson finished with a league-leading 117 RBI. Johnson is the first Mets player and first switch-hitter to lead the NL in RBI. (Mickey Mantle, Eddie Murray and Ruben Sierra have led the AL).

Is Schourek for real?

The Mets hope the real Pete Schourek is the one who tossed a one-hitter against the Montreal Expos in September—not the one who had a tumultuous rookie season.

"The one hit was a breaking ball I hung a little," Schourek said. "Sure, I knew it was the first hit, but I'm not superstitious and I didn't let it bother me. In fact, after the hit, I just relaxed."

It was Schourek's first win since May. In the start prior to his one-hitter, the left-hander gave up four runs, four hits and three walks in 1 2/3 innings.

His one-hitter was the first by a Met since David Cone one-hit the San Francisco Giants Aug. 29, 1988, and the first by a Met rookie since Dwight Gooden dominated the Chicago Cubs Sept. 7, 1984.

Hojo got there early

When Howard Johnson drove in three runs against Chicago Sept. 12, it gave him 101 RBI and marked the earliest point that a Mets player has reached the 100-RBI plateau.

Johnson—who got No. 100 in the 140th game—broke Darryl Strawberry's record, set in 1990, of 100 RBI in 143 games.

Johnson finished the season leading the league in home runs (38) and RBI (117), and was second in slugging percentage (.535)—one point behind San Francisco's Will Clark (.536).

Murray, Bonilla beef up Mets chances

Bobby Bonilla said he thought the Mets "felt like they were one player away from winning" after they signed Eddie Murray. Bonilla was that one player—and he cost them at least $29 million dollars, a figure that could balloon considerably if he earns the $3.35 million the Mets have agreed to pay him in bonuses for finishing third or better in MVP voting during his five-year contract.

The deal made Bonilla the highest-paid player in baseball history, but it wasn't just the money that swayed him to sign with the Mets.

"New York City was in my heart," said Bonilla, a native of the South Bronx who grew up rooting for the Yankees.

"It's a special place."

Bonilla had similar offers from the Philadelphia Phillies and the California Angels, but in the end he chose his hometown.

"I kept thinking what it would be like to play at Shea Stadium," he said. "I had the opportunity to get out of the South Bronx, and to be given an opportunity to play there at this level just breaks me up, so to speak."

It broke up the Pittsburgh Pirates, too. The loss of Bonilla is a serious blow to their lineup. Yet Bonilla indicated that he would have signed with the Pirates for less than the $29 million he got from the Mets, even as late as September.

"It was a frustrating process with the Pirates," he said. "But I leave with no hard feelings."

It's up to you New York, New York.

Let's make a deal

Those little town blues are certainly melting away for Bobby Bonilla, whose free-agent negotiations netted him a cool $29 million to move back to his native New York.

The five-year paycheck
▶Signing bonus: $1.5 million
▶1992 salary: $5.5 million
▶1993 salary: $5.6 million
▶1994 salary: $5.7 million
▶1995 salary: $4.7 million
▶1996 salary: $4.5 million

Endorsements
▶The Mets agreed to guarantee $1.5 million in endorsement income during the contract and to pay the difference if Bonilla doesn't sign endorsement agreements totaling $1.5 million.

Bonuses
▶$200,000 if traded.
▶$100,000 for winning MVP or finishing second or third.
▶$250,000 for winning two MVPs or finishing second or third.
▶$1 million for winning three MVPs or finishing second or third.
▶$2 million for winnning four MVPs or finishing second or third.

—USA TODAY

Mets winter league news

▶Winter leagues: Eight players from the Mets' organization played for the Arecibo Wolves in Puerto Rico. RHP Brad Moore 8-5, 3.33 at Class AAA Tidewater) left the Wolves to join the Navegantes del Magallanes team in Venezuela. Moore has struggled with this consistency in the past, and is working on avoiding getting behind in the count. . . Arecibo's general manager is Felix Millan, a former Mets' infielder. His son Bernie Millan, a designated hitter in the Mets' minor leagues, played for the Wolves this winter. . . . 2B Alberto Diaz, RHP Julian Vasquez and RHP Jose Martinez played at home in the Dominican Republic for Aguilas Cibae-na.

Team directory

▶Owner: Fred Wilpon

▶General Manager: Frank Cashen

▶Ballpark:
William A. Shea Municipal Stadium
126th Street and Roosevelt Avenue, Flushing, New York
718-507-TIXX
Capacity 55,601
Parking for 6,000 cars; $4.50
Public transportation available
Family and wheelchair sections, ramps

▶Team publications:
Inside Pitch
919-688-0218

▶TV, radio broadcast stations:
WFAN 660 AM, WWOR Channel 9, Sportschannel America

▶Camps and/or clinics:
Ulti-Met Week, 407-788-2222

▶Spring Training:
St. Lucie County Stadium
Port St. Lucie, Florida
Capacity 7,000
407-871-2115

NEW YORK METS 1991 Final Stats

Batting	AVG	SLG	OB	G	AB	R	H	TB	2B	3B	HR	RBI	BB	SO	SB	CS	E
Miller	.280	.411	.345	98	275	41	77	113	22	1	4	23	23	44	14	4	10
Boston	.275	.416	.350	137	255	40	70	106	16	4	4	21	30	42	15	8	3
Cerone	.273	.357	.360	90	227	18	62	81	13	0	2	16	30	24	1	1	6
Sasser	.272	.417	.298	96	228	18	62	95	14	2	5	35	9	19	0	2	3
Jefferies	.272	.374	.336	136	486	59	132	182	19	2	9	62	47	38	26	5	17
Carreon	.260	.331	.297	106	254	18	66	84	6	0	4	21	12	26	2	1	3
Johnson	.259	.535	.342	156	564	108	146	302	34	4	38	117	78	120	30	16	31
McReynolds	.259	.416	.322	143	522	65	135	217	32	1	16	74	49	46	6	6	2
Magadan	.258	.342	.378	124	418	58	108	143	23	0	4	51	83	50	1	1	5
Coleman	.255	.327	.347	72	278	45	71	91	7	5	1	17	39	47	37	14	3
Elster	.241	.351	.318	115	348	33	84	122	16	2	6	36	40	53	2	3	14
Brooks	.238	.409	.324	103	357	48	85	146	11	1	16	50	44	62	3	1	5
Donnels	.225	.247	.330	37	89	7	20	22	2	0	0	5	14	19	1	1	2
Templeton	.221	.304	.246	112	276	25	61	84	10	2	3	26	10	38	3	2	8
McDaniel	.207	.241	.233	23	29	3	6	7	1	0	0	2	1	11	2	0	0
O'Brien	.185	.256	.272	69	168	16	31	43	6	0	2	14	17	25	0	2	4
Carr	.182	.182	.182	12	11	1	2	2	0	0	0	1	0	2	1	0	0
Gardner	.162	.162	.238	13	37	3	6	6	0	0	0	0	1	4	6	0	6
Hundley	.133	.217	.221	21	60	5	8	13	0	1	1	7	6	14	0	0	0
Torve	.000	.000	.000	10	8	0	0	0	0	0	0	0	0	1	0	0	0

Pitching	W-L	ERA	G	GS	CG	GF	Sho	SV	IP	H	R	ER	HR	BB	SO
Valera	0-0	0.00	2	0	0	1	0	0	2	1	0	0	0	4	3
Bross	0-0	1.80	8	0	0	4	0	0	10	7	2	2	1	3	5
Innis	0-2	2.66	69	0	0	29	0	0	84.2	66	30	25	2	23	47
Beatty	0-0	2.79	5	0	0	1	0	0	9.2	9	3	3	0	4	7
Fernandez	1-3	2.86	8	8	0	0	0	0	44	36	18	14	4	9	31
Franco	5-9	2.93	52	0	0	48	0	30	55.1	61	27	18	2	18	45
Young	2-5	3.10	10	8	0	2	0	0	49.1	48	20	17	4	12	20
Cone	14-14	3.29	34	34	5	0	2	0	232.2	204	95	85	13	73	241
Castillo	2-1	3.34	17	3	0	6	0	0	32.1	40	16	12	4	11	18
Burke	6-7	3.36	72	0	0	31	0	6	101.2	96	46	38	8	26	59
Gooden	13-7	3.60	27	27	3	0	1	0	190	185	80	76	12	56	150
Viola	13-15	3.97	35	35	3	0	0	0	231.1	259	112	102	25	54	132
Whitehurst	7-12	4.19	36	20	0	6	0	1	133.1	142	67	62	12	25	87
Schourek	5-4	4.27	35	8	1	7	1	2	86.1	82	49	41	7	43	67
Simons	2-3	5.19	42	1	0	11	0	1	60.2	55	40	35	5	19	38
Sauveur	0-0	10.80	6	0	0	0	0	0	3.1	7	4	4	1	2	4

1992 Preliminary Roster

Pitchers (19)

Terry Bross
Tim Burke
Tony Castillo
David Cone
Sid Fernandez
John Franco
Dwight Gooden
Eric Hillman
Jeff Innis
John Johnstone
Steve Rosenberg
Bret Saberhagen
Pete Schourek
Doug Simons
Julio Valera
Julian Vasquez
Joe Vitko
Wally Whitehurst
Anthony Young

Catchers (4)

Brook Fordyce
Todd Hundley
Charlie O'Brien
Mackey Sasser

Infielders (9)

Kevin Baez
Chris Donnels
Kevin Elster
Terrel Hansen
Dave Magadan
Eddie Murray
Tito Navarro
Junior Noboa
Bill Pecota

Outfielders (6)

Bobby Bonilla
Mark Carreon
Vince Coleman
Dave Gallagher
Pat Howell
Howard Johnson

Games played by position

	G	C	1B	2B	3B	SS	OF
Boston,D	137	0	0	0	0	0	115
Brooks,H	103	0	0	0	0	0	100
Carr,C	12	0	0	0	0	0	9
Carreon,M	106	0	0	0	0	0	77
Cerone,R	90	81	0	0	0	0	0
Coleman,V	72	0	0	0	0	0	70
Donnels,C	37	0	15	0	11	0	0
Elster,K	115	0	0	0	0	107	0
Gardner,J	13	0	0	3	0	8	0
Hundley,T	21	20	0	0	0	0	0
Jefferies,G	136	0	0	77	51	0	0
Johnson,H	156	0	0	0	104	28	30
Magadan,D	124	0	122	0	0	0	0
McDaniel,T	23	0	0	0	0	0	14
McReynolds,K	143	0	0	0	0	0	141
Miller,K	98	0	0	60	2	2	28
O'Brien,C	69	67	0	0	0	0	0
Sasser,M	96	43	10	0	0	0	21
Templeton,G	112	0	25	0	17	41	2
Torve,K	10	0	1	0	0	0	0

Sick call: 1991 DL report

Player	Days on the DL
Gregg Jefferies	16
Kevin Elster	15
Keith Miller	20
Vince Coleman	84*
Sid Fernandez	101
Wally Whitehurst	15
Hubie Brooks	49
Chuck Carr	15
Dwight Gooden	44

On DL twice (not counting administrative transfers from one DL to another).

Minor League Report

Class AAA — Tidewater finished 77-65, second in the International League West. C Todd Hundley hit .273 with 24 doubles, 14 HRs and 66 RBI. 3B Chris Donnels hit .303 with 18 doubles and 56 RBI. OF Chuck Carr had 27 SBs. Top pitchers were LHP Blaine Beatty (12-9, 4.11), RHP Mark Dewey (12-3, 3.34) and LHP Rich Sauveur (2-2, 2.38). RHP Brad Moore had 13 saves. . . . **Class AA** — Williamsport finished 60-79, seventh in the Eastern League. OF Jeromy Burnitz hit .225 and led the league with 31 HRs and 85 RBI. He also had 31 SBs, 10 triples and 104 walks. SS Tito Navarro hit .288 with 42 SBs. OF D.J. Dozier hit .278 with 8 HRs and 30 RBI in 74 games, then hit .269 in 43 games at Tidewater. 1B Paul Williams hit .259 with 29 doubles and 72 RBI. RHP Dave Telgheder (13-11, 3.60) led the league in wins. RHP Doug Kline was 2-5 with a 2.47 ERA. RHP Bryan Rogers had 15 saves. . . . **Class A** — St. Lucie finished 69-58, fifth in the first half and first in the second half in the Florida State League Eastern Division. The Mets beat Sarasota and lost to Clearwater in the playoffs. OF Curtis Pride hit .260 with 21 doubles, 9 HRs, 37 RBI and 24 SBs. C Brook Fordyce hit .239 with 55 RBI. OF Pat Howell had 37 SBs at St. Lucie and 27 more at Williamsport. RHP Joe Vitko was 11-8 with a 2.24 ERA and 5 CGs. RH reliever Julian Vasquez (3-2, 0.28, 25 saves) gave up just 35 hits and 2 ERs in 64 innings. . . . Columbia finished 86-54, first in the first half and second in the second half in the South Atlantic League Southern Division. The Mets beat Macon and Charleston (W. Va.) to win the playoffs and league championship. RHP Jose Martinez (20-4) became only the second 20-game winner in league history. 3B Butch Huskey hit .287 with league-leading 26 HRs and 99 RBI. OF Tim McClinton hit .249 with 14 HRs and 91 RBI. OF Jay Davis hit .297 with 29 doubles. . . . Pittsfield finished 51-26, first in the NY-P League McNamara East Division. The Mets beat Elmira and lost to Jamestown in the playoffs. OF Randy Curtis hit .288 with 25 SBs. 1B Frank Jacobs hit .233 with 9 HRs and 50 RBI. LHP Chris Shanahan was 10-2 with a 2.92 ERA, while LHP Ottis Smith was 7-2 with a 2.61 ERA. . . . Kingsport finished 36-31, fourth in the Appalachian League Southern Division. OF Ricky Otero hit .345 to win the league batting title. He also had 16 doubles, 7 HRs and 52 RBI. 2B Quilvio Veras hit .336, second in the league, with 38 SBs. RHP Hector Ramirez was 8-2 with a 2.54 ERA. LHP Joe Crawford had 11 saves and a 1.11 ERA.

Tops of the Organization

BATTING LEADERS	Club	Avg.	G	AB	R	H	HR	RBI
Jay Davis	Clb	.297	132	511	79	152	0	63
Jeff Gardner	Tdw	.292	136	504	73	147	1	56
Tito Navarro	WPt	.288	128	482	69	139	2	42
Butch Huskey	Clb	.287	134	492	88	141	26	99
Ed Fully	Clb	.277	122	448	69	124	5	56

HOME RUNS:			WINS		
Jeromy Burnitz	WPt	31	Jose Martinez	Clb	20
Butch Huskey	Clb	26	Dave Telgheder	WPt	13
Tim McClinton	Clb	14	Mark Dewey	Tdw	12
Todd Hundley	Tdw	14	Juan Castillo	Clb	12
Terrel Hansen	Tdw	12	Blaine Beatty	Tdw	12

RBI			SAVES		
Butch Huskey	Clb	99	Julian Vasquez	Slu	25
Tim McClinton	Clb	91	Bryan Rogers	WPt	15
Jeromy Burnitz	WPt	85	Brad Moore	Tdw	13
Paul Williams	WPt	72	Andy Reich	Slu	10
Todd Hundley	Tdw	66	Mark Dewey	Tdw	9

STOLEN BASES			STRIKE OUTS		
Pat Howell	WPt	64	Jose Martinez	Clb	158
Tito Navarro	WPt	42	Juan Castillo	Clb	144
Fernando Vina	Clb	42	Tom Wegmann	Slu	138
D.J. Dozier	Tdw	33	Todd Douma	WPt	126
Jeromy Burnitz	WPt	31	Several players tied		117

PITCHING LEADERS	Club	W-L	ERA	IP	H	BB	SO
Jose Martinez	Clb	20-4	1.49	193	162	30	158
Joe Vitko	Slu	11-8	2.24	140	102	39	105
Greg Langbehn	Slu	10-12	2.52	175	149	44	106
Todd Douma	WPt	10-7	3.05	159	161	33	126
Rob Rees	Clb	6-8	3.08	114	108	44	95

New York (1962-1991)

Runs: Most, career, all-time

662	DARRYL STRAWBERRY, 1983-1990
592	MOOKIE WILSON, 1980-1989
563	Cleon Jones, 1963-1975
547	HOWARD JOHNSON, 1985-1991
536	Ed Kranepool, 1962-1979

Hits: Most, career, all-time

1418	Ed Kranepool, 1962-1979
1188	Cleon Jones, 1963-1975
1112	MOOKIE WILSON, 1980-1989
1029	Bud Harrelson, 1965-1977
1025	DARRYL STRAWBERRY, 1983-1990

2B: Most, career, all-time

225	Ed Kranepool, 1962-1979
187	HOWARD JOHNSON, 1985-1991
187	DARRYL STRAWBERRY, 1983-1990
182	Cleon Jones, 1963-1975
170	MOOKIE WILSON, 1980-1989

3B: Most, career, all-time

62	MOOKIE WILSON, 1980-1989
45	Bud Harrelson, 1965-1977
33	Cleon Jones, 1963-1975
31	Steve Henderson, 1977-1980
30	DARRYL STRAWBERRY, 1983-1990

HR: Most, career, all-time

252	DARRYL STRAWBERRY, 1983-1990
178	HOWARD JOHNSON, 1985-1991
154	Dave Kingman, 1975-1983
118	Ed Kranepool, 1962-1979
118	KEVIN McREYNOLDS, 1987-1991

RBI: Most, career, all-time

733	DARRYL STRAWBERRY, 1983-1990
614	Ed Kranepool, 1962-1979
560	HOWARD JOHNSON, 1985-1991
521	Cleon Jones, 1963-1975
468	Keith Hernandez, 1983-1989

SB: Most, career, all-time

281	MOOKIE WILSON, 1980-1989
191	DARRYL STRAWBERRY, 1983-1990
174	HOWARD JOHNSON, 1985-1991
152	Lee Mazzilli, 1976-1989
116	LENNY DYKSTRA, 1985-1989

BB: Most, career, all-time

580	DARRYL STRAWBERRY, 1983-1990
573	Bud Harrelson, 1965-1977
482	Wayne Garrett, 1969-1976
471	Keith Hernandez, 1983-1989
458	HOWARD JOHNSON, 1985-1991

BA: Highest, career, all-time

.297	Keith Hernandez, 1983-1989
.294	DAVE MAGADAN, 1986-1991
.283	WALLY BACKMAN, 1980-1988
.281	Cleon Jones, 1963-1975
.278	LENNY DYKSTRA, 1985-1989

Slug avg: Highest, career, all-time

.520	DARRYL STRAWBERRY, 1983-1990
.478	HOWARD JOHNSON, 1985-1991
.463	KEVIN McREYNOLDS, 1987-1991
.453	Dave Kingman, 1975-1983
.429	Keith Hernandez, 1983-1989

Games started: Most, career, all-time

395	Tom Seaver, 1967-1983
346	Jerry Koosman, 1967-1978
241	RON DARLING, 1983-1991
236	DWIGHT GOODEN, 1984-1991
200	SID FERNANDEZ, 1984-1991

Saves: Most, career, all-time

107	JESSE OROSCO, 1979-1987
86	Tug McGraw, 1965-1974
84	ROGER McDOWELL, 1985-1989
69	Neil Allen, 1979-1983
65	Skip Lockwood, 1975-1979

Shutouts: Most, career, all-time

44	Tom Seaver, 1967-1983
26	Jerry Koosman, 1967-1978
26	Jon Matlack, 1971-1977
21	DWIGHT GOODEN, 1984-1991
10	DAVID CONE, 1987-1991
10	RON DARLING, 1983-1991
10	Al Jackson, 1962-1969

Wins: Most, career, all-time

198	Tom Seaver, 1967-1983
140	Jerry Koosman, 1967-1978
132	DWIGHT GOODEN, 1984-1991
99	RON DARLING, 1983-1991
82	Jon Matlack, 1971-1977

K: Most, career, all-time

2541	Tom Seaver, 1967-1983
1799	Jerry Koosman, 1967-1978
1541	DWIGHT GOODEN, 1984-1991
1175	SID FERNANDEZ, 1984-1991
1148	RON DARLING, 1983-1991

Win pct: Highest, career, all-time

.714	DWIGHT GOODEN, 1984-1991
.620	DAVID CONE, 1987-1991
.615	Tom Seaver, 1967-1983
.586	RON DARLING, 1983-1991
.564	SID FERNANDEZ, 1984-1991

ERA: Lowest, career, all-time

2.57	Tom Seaver, 1967-1983
2.91	DWIGHT GOODEN, 1984-1991
3.03	Jon Matlack, 1971-1977
3.09	Jerry Koosman, 1967-1978
3.12	BOB OJEDA, 1986-1990
3.12	DAVID CONE, 1987-1991

Runs: Most, season

108	HOWARD JOHNSON, 1991
108	DARRYL STRAWBERRY, 1987
107	Tommie Agee, 1970
104	HOWARD JOHNSON, 1989
101	DARRYL STRAWBERRY, 1988

Hits: Most, season

191	Felix Millan, 1975	
185	Felix Millan, 1973	
183	Keith Hernandez, 1985	
182	Tommie Agee, 1970	
181	Lee Mazzilli, 1979	

2B: Most, season

41	HOWARD JOHNSON, 1989
40	GREGG JEFFERIES, 1990
37	LENNY DYKSTRA, 1987
37	HOWARD JOHNSON, 1990
37	Felix Millan, 1975
37	Joel Youngblood, 1979

3B: Most, season

10	MOOKIE WILSON, 1984
9	Steve Henderson, 1978
9	Charlie Neal, 1962
9	Frank Taveras, 1979
9	MOOKIE WILSON, 1982

HR: Most, season

39	DARRYL STRAWBERRY, 1987
39	DARRYL STRAWBERRY, 1988
38	HOWARD JOHNSON, 1991
37	Dave Kingman, 1976
37	Dave Kingman, 1982
37	DARRYL STRAWBERRY, 1990

RBI: Most, season

117	HOWARD JOHNSON, 1991
108	DARRYL STRAWBERRY, 1990
105	GARY CARTER, 1986
105	Rusty Staub, 1975
104	DARRYL STRAWBERRY, 1987

SB: Most, season

58	MOOKIE WILSON, 1982
54	MOOKIE WILSON, 1983
46	MOOKIE WILSON, 1984
42	Frank Taveras, 1979
41	HOWARD JOHNSON, 1989
41	Lee Mazzilli, 1980

BB: Most, season

97	Keith Hernandez, 1984
97	DARRYL STRAWBERRY, 1987
95	Bud Harrelson, 1970
94	Keith Hernandez, 1986
93	Lee Mazzilli, 1979

BA: Highest, season

.340	Cleon Jones, 1969
.328	DAVE MAGADAN, 1990
.319	Cleon Jones, 1971
.311	Keith Hernandez, 1984
.310	Keith Hernandez, 1986

Slug avg: Highest, season

.583	DARRYL STRAWBERRY, 1987
.559	HOWARD JOHNSON, 1989
.545	DARRYL STRAWBERRY, 1988
.535	HOWARD JOHNSON, 1991
.518	DARRYL STRAWBERRY, 1990

Games started: Most, season

36	Jack Fisher, 1965
36	Tom Seaver, 1970
36	Tom Seaver, 1973
36	Tom Seaver, 1975
35	RON DARLING, 1985
35	Gary Gentry, 1969
35	DWIGHT GOODEN, 1985
35	Jerry Koosman, 1973
35	Jerry Koosman, 1974
35	Jon Matlack, 1976
35	Tom Seaver, 1968
35	Tom Seaver, 1969
35	Tom Seaver, 1971
35	Tom Seaver, 1972
35	Craig Swan, 1979
35	FRANK VIOLA, 1990
35	FRANK VIOLA, 1991

Saves: Most, season

33	JOHN FRANCO, 1990
31	JESSE OROSCO, 1984
30	JOHN FRANCO, 1991
27	Tug McGraw, 1972
26	RANDY MYERS, 1988

Shutouts: Most, season

8	DWIGHT GOODEN, 1985
7	Jerry Koosman, 1968
7	Jon Matlack, 1974
6	Jerry Koosman, 1969
6	Jon Matlack, 1976

Wins: Most, season

25	Tom Seaver, 1969
24	DWIGHT GOODEN, 1985
22	Tom Seaver, 1975
21	Jerry Koosman, 1976
21	Tom Seaver, 1972

K: Most, season

289	Tom Seaver, 1971
283	Tom Seaver, 1970
276	DWIGHT GOODEN, 1984
268	DWIGHT GOODEN, 1985
251	Tom Seaver, 1973

Win pct: Highest, season

.870	DAVID CONE, 1988
.857	DWIGHT GOODEN, 1985
.783	BOB OJEDA, 1986
.781	Tom Seaver, 1969
.739	DWIGHT GOODEN, 1986

ERA: Lowest, season

1.53	DWIGHT GOODEN, 1985
1.76	Tom Seaver, 1971
2.08	Tom Seaver, 1973
2.08	Jerry Koosman, 1968
2.20	Tom Seaver, 1968

Most pinch-hit homers, season

4	Danny Heep, 1983
4	Mark Carreon, 1989

Most pinch-hit, homers, career

8	Mark Carreon, 1987-1991

Most consecutive games, batting safely

24	Hubie Brooks, 1984

Most consecutive scoreless innings

31	Jerry Koosman, 1973

No hit games

N/A

Delino DeShields stole 56 bases for Montreal in 1991.

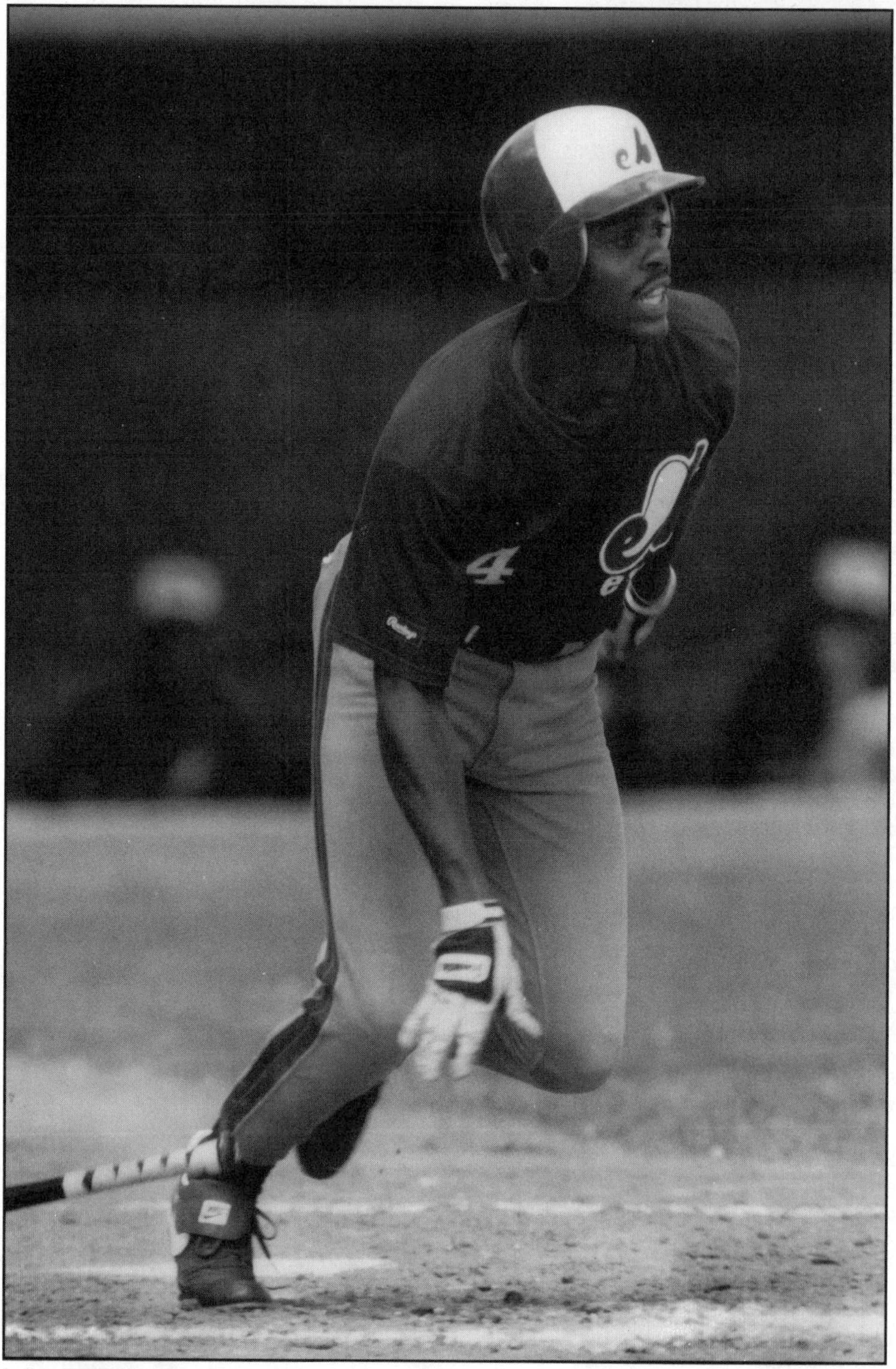

Expos: Wrap Up

By Bill Koenig

It would be fair to say the roof almost caved in on the Montreal Expos last season.

The Expos were forced to play their final 26 games on the road after a cement beam at Olympic Stadium collapsed Sept. 13.

In truth, things fell apart long before that.

The Expos finished last in the National League East with a 71-90 record, their worst since 1976.

Fans stayed away in droves. The Expos were the only major-league team to fail to draw 1 million spectators. Their season attendance of 978,045 was the lowest since the team left Jarry Park in 1977.

Even the front office bailed out after the season. General Manager Dave Dombrowski left for a similar job with the new Florida Marlins, and took scouting director Gary Hughes and his assistant Frank Wren with him.

New GM Dan Duquette, 33, has one tough rebuilding job on his hands–and he must operate under the most difficult financial constraints in the league because of Canadian tax laws and the exchange of currency.

The Expos were last in the league with 579 runs and hit just .245 as a team. They lost 39 one-run games.

First baseman Andres Galarraga (.219, 33 RBI) and third baseman Tim Wallach (.225), the team's mainstays, had horrible years.

However, the cupboard isn't completely bare, and the 1991 season wasn't without any highlights.

Right-hander Dennis Martinez (14-11, 2.39) was the league ERA champion and pitched the Expos' first perfect game in history July 28 against the Los Angeles Dodgers.

Two nights earlier, Mark Gardner (9-11) carried a no-hitter into the 10th inning before losing to the Dodgers.

Outfielder Marquis Grissom hit .267 and led the league with 76 stolen bases.

Outfielder Ivan Calderon came over from the Chicago White Sox, hit .300 with 19 home runs and 75 RBI and made the NL All-Star team.

Outfielder Larry Walker (.290-16-64) gave the Expos' their long-sought left-handed bat.

Dave Martinez hit .295.

Perhaps most encouraging is the fact the Expos' farm system is one of the best in the business. It ranked fourth in 1991 with a .552 winning percentage.

Prospects such as outfielder John Vanderwal, shortstop Wilfredo Cordero and second baseman and outfielder Rondell White will be heard from soon.

The Expos still need a bullpen closer and a lot more offensive punch, but it's doubtful things can bottom out any more than they did in 1991.

Expos 1992 preview

Ivan Calderon should be even better in his second National League season. The team will look to him for leadership on the field and in the dugout.

Montreal also needs more offense from third baseman Tim Wallach—who batted 40 points lower than his .267 career average—and catcher, where four players combined for just seven homers and 69 RBI.

Larry Walker (.290, 16 HR, 64 RBI) and Marquis Grissom (major league-leading 76 stolen bases) provide a solid offensive base with Calderon.

Dennis Martinez and Mark Gardner anchor the young pitching staff, which needs an improved defense to back it up—only three NL teams committed more errors than the Expos (133).

▸The Expos will move out of crumbling Olympic Stadium and refurbish old Jarry Park.
▸By May, Gary Carter will want to know why he isn't starting every day.
—John Hunt

Buck saw it coming

By Rod Beaton

The Montreal Expos weren't winning. They weren't drawing. And manager Buck Rodgers knew what came next.

"I knew this would be my last year in Montreal," Rodgers said. "I figured I'd go hard as I could as long as I could, like I tell my pitchers."

He was right. The Expos fired him after six seasons and 49 games. The team was 20-29, dead last in the NL East. General manager David Dombrowski had his sights set on a new man, his man—coach Tom Runnells.

"I knew and the players knew that Tommy Runnells was Dave Dombrowski's man," said Rodgers. "I wasn't from the start." Rodgers said he clashed with Dombrowski over the care and feeding of young players. In Montreal, where free agents flee when the opportunity arises, young players are always the flavor of the month. Under those circumstances, Rodgers' 520-499 record was commendable— good enough, in fact, to net him the manager's job with the California Angels after Doug Rader was fired over there.

Rodgers' record with the Expos:

Year	Record	Pct.	Pos.
1985	84-77	.522	3rd
1986	78-83	.484	4th
1987	91-71	.562	3rd
1988	81-81	.500	3rd
1989	81-81	.500	4th
1990	85-77	.525	3rd
1991	20-29	.408	6th
Total	520-499	.510	-

▸Winningest manager in Expos' history.
▸Named NL manager of the year in 1987.

Grissom is king of stolen bases

Marquis Grissom sprained his ankle during an October game against St. Louis, when he made an awkward hookslide into third base in the second inning. The injury ended his season early, but he already had collected 76 stolen bases, enough to lead the National League.

Grissom battled Atlanta's Otis Nixon for the stolen base crown for much of the season, but took over the lead in September after Nixon was suspended for failing a drug test.

Grissom's 76 is the fourth-highest, single-year stolen base total in Expos history. Ahead of him in the team record book are Ron LeFlore (97 in 1980) and Tim Raines (90 in 1983 and 78 in 1982).

Doctors feared that the ankle was broken after initial X-rays showed a crack in the bone, but the crack proved to be a line in the film. Grissom was congratulated by teammates after the game.

"It's funny to be congratulating a guy when he's on crutches, but I am pretty happy with my year," Grissom said. "My goal was to get 500 at-bats. I did that and I played pretty good defense, stole a lot of bases.

"All it would have taken to have made it a great year for me would have been if I had shown a little more discipline at the plate. But that will come."

Martinez no-no made Gardner nervous

Mark Gardner was trying to forget about the nine-inning no-hitter he pitched, and lost, for the Expos against the Dodgers when he sat down in the dugout to watch Dennis Martinez go to work on July 28.

What he didn't know was that he was going to be on the edge of his seat watching Martinez go for a perfect game, less than 48 hours after his own attempt.

"I was more nervous watching Dennis than when I was out there pitching," Gardner said. "My hands were all clammy. I didn't sit there and think how nice it would have been to get some runs in my game. All I thought about was, 'Wow, I'm actually watching a perfect game.' There aren't too many people who can say that."

Martinez also addressed the fact that Gardner suffered a cruel fate when he failed to win his no-hit effort only because the Expos failed to score any runs.

"Sometimes this is an unfair game," Martinez said. "If Mark had gotten some runs he might have had his no-hitter, and he deserved it."

Expos winter league news

▸Winter leagues: The Expos sent one of the larger contingents to Mexico, splitting their players between Navojoa and Hermosillo. . . . OF Moises Alou, acquired from Pittsburgh in the 1990 deal for LHP Zane Smith, played at home in the Dominican Republic for Aguilas Cibae-na. Alou's father, former major leaguer Felipe Alou, is the manager of the Leones (Lions) Escogido, a rival league team. . . 1B Andres Galarraga (.219-9-33 in 375 at-bats) the top name playing winter ball in 1991-92, competed in his hometown of Caracas, Venezuela. Galarraga, sidelined part of the year due to injury, had his worst year as a major leaguer and used winter ball to regain his batting stroke. While he was there, he learned he had been traded to St. Louis. But perhaps the biggest reason for Galarraga's presence in winter ball was a concentrated effort on Venezuela's part to lure its big league natives back home. . . . RHP Doug Piatt (6-4, 3.45 at

Class AAA Indianapolis), RHP Matt Maysey (3-6, 5.14 at Indianapolis), LHP Phil Harrison (7-1, 2.40 at Class AA Harrisburg) went to Mexico to get extra innings. . . . The entire 1991 Harrisburg infield of 1B Archi Cianfrocco (.316-9-77), 2B Matt Stairs (.333-13-78), 2B F.P. Santangelo (.245-5-42), SS Chris Martin (.224 in 294 at-bats) and 3B Bryn Kosco (.241-10-58) were reunited in Mexico, with everyone but Kosco playing for Navojoa. . . . C Bob Natal (.256-13-53 at Harrisburg) played in Venezuela. . . . RHP Bill Brennan (3-2, 3.12 at Harrisburg) signed with the Santurce Crabbers in Puerto Rico shortly after the season began.

Team directory

▸Owner: Montreal Baseball Club Limited

▸General Manager: Dan Duquette

▸Ballpark:
Olympic Stadium
4549 Avenue Pierre-de-Coubertin, Montreal, Canada
514-253-3434
Capacity 43,739
Parking for 4,000 cars; $5
Public transportation available
Wheelchair sections, ramps, extensive food concessions

▸Team publications:
Yearbook
P.O. Box 500, Station M, Montreal QC, H1V 3P2

▸TV, radio broadcast stations:
CFCF 600 AM, CTV, TSN (English), CKAC 730 AM, CBFT-TV, RDS (French)

▸Spring Training:
Municipal Stadium
West Palm Beach, Florida
Capacity 7,500
407-684-6801

MONTREAL EXPOS 1991 Final Stats

Batting	AVG	SLG	OB	G	AB	R	H	TB	2B	3B	HR	RBI	BB	SO	SB	CS	E
Barberie	.353	.515	.435	57	136	16	48	70	12	2	2	18	20	22	0	0	5
Calderon	.300	.481	.368	134	470	69	141	226	22	3	19	75	53	64	31	16	7
Da. Martinez	.295	.419	.332	124	396	47	117	166	18	5	7	42	20	54	16	7	4
Walker	.290	.458	.349	137	487	59	141	223	30	2	16	64	42	102	14	9	6
Williams	.271	.400	.311	34	70	11	19	28	5	2	0	1	3	22	2	1	2
Grissom	.267	.373	.310	148	558	73	149	208	23	9	6	39	34	89	76	17	6
Owen	.255	.366	.321	139	424	39	108	155	22	8	3	26	42	61	2	6	8
Santovenia	.250	.365	.255	41	96	7	24	35	5	0	2	14	2	18	0	0	3
Noboa	.242	.305	.250	67	95	5	23	29	3	0	1	2	1	8	2	3	1
DeShields	.238	.332	.347	151	563	83	134	187	15	4	10	51	95	151	56	23	27
Hassey	.227	.319	.301	52	119	5	27	38	8	0	1	14	13	16	1	1	2
Wallach	.225	.334	.292	151	577	60	130	193	22	1	13	73	50	100	2	4	14
Bullock	.222	.319	.305	73	72	6	16	23	4	0	1	6	9	13	6	1	1
Galarraga	.219	.336	.268	107	375	34	82	126	13	2	9	33	23	86	5	6	9
Reyes	.217	.261	.285	83	207	11	45	54	9	0	0	13	19	51	2	4	11
Vanderwal	.213	.361	.222	21	61	4	13	22	4	1	1	8	1	18	0	0	0
Foley	.208	.286	.269	86	168	12	35	48	11	1	0	15	14	30	2	0	6
Fitzgerald	.202	.308	.278	71	198	17	40	61	5	2	4	28	22	35	4	2	2
Riesgo	.143	.143	.400	4	7	1	1	1	0	0	0	0	3	1	0	0	1

Pitching	W-L	ERA	G	GS	CG	GF	Sho	SV	IP	H	R	ER	HR	BB	SO
De. Martinez	14-11	2.39	31	31	9	0	5	0	222	187	70	59	9	62	123
Fassero	2-5	2.44	51	0	0	30	0	8	55.1	39	17	15	1	17	42
Piatt	0-0	2.60	21	0	0	3	0	0	34.2	29	11	10	3	17	29
Jones	4-9	3.35	77	0	0	46	0	13	88.2	76	35	33	8	33	46
Boyd	6-8	3.52	19	19	1	0	1	0	120.1	115	49	47	9	40	82
Nabholz	8-7	3.63	24	24	1	0	0	0	153.2	134	66	62	5	57	99
Rojas	3-3	3.75	37	0	0	13	0	6	48	42	21	20	4	13	37
Gardner	9-11	3.85	27	27	0	0	0	0	168.1	139	78	72	17	75	107
Sampen	9-5	4.00	43	8	0	8	0	0	92.1	96	49	41	13	46	52
Haney	3-7	4.04	16	16	0	0	0	0	84.2	94	49	38	6	43	51
Barnes	5-8	4.22	28	27	1	0	0	0	160	135	82	75	16	84	117
Ruskin	4-4	4.24	64	0	0	24	0	6	63.2	57	31	30	4	30	46
Darling	5-8	4.37	20	20	0	0	0	0	119.1	121	66	58	15	33	69
Frey	0-1	4.99	31	0	0	5	0	1	39.2	43	31	22	3	23	21
Wainhouse	0-1	6.75	2	0	0	1	0	0	2.2	2	2	2	0	4	1
Schmidt	0-1	10.38	4	0	0	1	0	0	4.1	9	5	5	2	2	3
Long	0-0	10.80	3	0	0	1	0	0	1.2	4	2	2	0	4	0

1992 Preliminary Roster

Pitchers (19)

Brian Barnes
Kent Bottenfield
Howard Farmer
Jeff Fassero
Steve Frey
Mark Gardner
Chris Haney
Ken Hill
Jonathan Hurst
Matt Karchner
Dennis Martinez
Chris Nabholz
Doug Piatt
Bill Risley
Mel Rojas
Bill Sampen
David Wainhouse
John Wetteland
Pete Young

Catchers (6)

Gary Carter
Greg Colbrunn
Jimmy Kremers
Tim Laker
Robert Natal
Gilberto Reyes

Infielders (8)

Bret Barberie
George Canale
Wilfredo Cordero
Delino DeShields
Tom Foley
Spike Owen
Matt Stairs
Tim Wallach

Outfielders (6)

Moises Alou
Ivan Calderon
Marquis Grissom
Darren Reed
John Vanderwal
Larry Walker

Games Played by position

	G	C	1B	2B	3B	SS	OF
Barberie,B	57	0	1	10	10	19	0
Bullock,E	73	0	3	0	0	0	9
Calderon,I	134	0	4	0	0	0	122
DeShields,D	151	0	0	148	0	0	0
Fitzgerald,M	71	54	3	0	0	0	3
Foley,T	86	0	31	2	6	43	0
Galarraga,A	107	0	105	0	0	0	0
Grissom,M	148	0	0	0	0	0	138
Hassey,R	52	34	0	0	0	0	0
Martinez,D	124	0	0	0	0	0	112
Noboa,J	67	0	1	6	2	2	7
Owen,S	139	0	0	0	0	133	0
Reyes,G	83	80	0	0	0	0	0
Riesgo,N	4	0	0	0	0	0	2
Santovenia,N	41	30	7	0	0	0	0
Vanderwal,J	21	0	0	0	0	0	17
Walker,L	137	0	39	0	0	0	102
Wallach,T	151	0	0	0	149	0	0
Williams,K	34	0	0	0	0	0	24

Sick call: 1991 DL report

Player	Days on the DL
Mark Gardner	36
Greg McCarthy	182
Nikco Riesgo	10
Howard Farmer	44
Darren Reed	182
Brian Barnes	27
Andres Galarraga	39
Mike Fitzgerald	49
Moises Alou	182
Kenny Williams	15
Chris Nabholz	48
Larry Walker	15

Minor League Report

Class AAA — Indianapolis finished 75-68, second in the American Association East. OF John Vanderwal (.293-15-71 with 36 doubles and 8 triples) was team MVP. 2B Todd Haney hit .312 with 32 doubles. SS Wil Cordero hit .261 with 11 HRs in 98 games before breaking his wrist. INF Bret Barberie hit .312 with 10 HRs in 71 games. RHP Eddie Dixon was 6-7 with a 2.91 ERA. . . . **Class AA** — Harrisburg finished 87-53, first in the Eastern League. The Senators beat Canton-Akron and lost to Albany-Colonie in the playoffs. 2B Matt Stairs (.333-13-78 with 30 doubles) led the league in batting and was named MVP. 1B Archi Cianfrocco hit .316, second in the league, with 77 RBI. OF Rob Katzaroff hit .290 with 33 SBs. Senators led EL with a 2.97 ERA. LHP Chris Pollack was 11-8 with a 2.75 ERA. . . . **Class A** — West Palm Beach finished 70-57, tied for third in the first half and second in the second half in the Florida State League Eastern Division. The Expos beat Vero Beach, Lakeland and Clearwater to win the playoffs and league championship. Expos had second-best ERA (2.70) in league, but second-lowest batting average (.218). OF Troy Ricker hit .221 in regular season, but .370 in playoffs. 3B Willie Greene hit .217 with 12 HRs and 43 RBI. 3B-DH Chad McDonald hit .253 with 7 HRs and 48 RBI. RHP Doug Bochtler (12-9, 2.92) tied for the league lead in victories. . . . Rockford finished 76-61, second in both halves in the Midwest League Northern Division. Top hitters were OF Shaun Murphy (.299-3-47), OF Mike Weimerskirch (.269-4-58) and OF Glen Murray (.236-5-60). RHP Mike Mathile was 9-3 with a 2.47 ERA. RHP Corey Powell was 12-8 with a 3.16 ERA. . . . Sumter finished 64-75, sixth in the first half and fourth in the second half in the South Atlantic League Northern Division. OF Rondell White hit .260 with 13 HRs, 68 RBI and 51 SBs. OF Todd Samples (.259) had a league-record 29 assists from RF. RHP Tavo Alvarez (12-10, 3.24) was third in league with 158 strikeouts. RHP Kevin Foster (10-4, 2.74) had 114 strikeouts in 102 innings. . . . Jamestown finished 51-27, first in the NY-P League Stedler Division. The Expos beat Erie and Pittsfield to win the playoffs and league championship. C Mike Daniel (.253) led league with 62 RBI. Expos had league's 3-4-5 hitters in 1B Derrick White (.328), OF Jim Austin (.326) and 3B-OF Scott Campbell (.324). LHP Brian Looney (7-1) led league with a 1.16 ERA. RHP Heath Haynes was 10-1 with 11 saves and 2.08 ERA.

Tops of the Organization

BATTING LEADERS	Club	Avg.	G	AB	R	H	HR	RBI
Matt Stairs	HRb	.333	129	505	87	168	13	78
Archi Cianfrocco	HRb	.316	124	456	71	144	9	77
Todd Haney	Ind	.312	132	510	68	159	2	39
Shaun Murphy	Rkf	.299	117	401	54	120	3	47
John Vanderwal	Ind	.293	133	478	84	140	15	71

HOME RUNS:			WINS	
John Vanderwal	Ind	15	Tavo Alvarez	Sum 12
Chris Cassels	HRb	13	Corey Powell	Rkf 12
Bob Natal	HRb	13	Doug Bochtler	WPb 12
Cesar Hernandez	HRb	13	Several players tied	11
Matt Stairs	HRb	13		

RBI			SAVES	
Matt Stairs	HRb	78	Mike Thomas	Sum 20
Archi Cianfrocco	HRb	77	Bob Baxter	WPb 19
John Vanderwal	Ind	71	Steve Long	Sum 17
Rondell White	Sum	67	Pete Young	HRb 13
Todd Samples	Sum	63	Doug Piatt	Ind 13

STOLEN BASES			STRIKE OUTS	
Rondell White	Sum	51	Tavo Alvarez	Sum 158
Cesar Hernandez	HRb	34	Gabe White	Sum 140
Rob Katzaroff	HRb	33	Matt Maysey	Ind 131
Mike Weimerskirch	Rkf	32	Corey Powell	Rkf 120
Wayne Johnson	Rkf	27	Kevin Foster	Sum 111

PITCHING LEADERS	Club	W-L	ERA	IP	H	BB	SO
Reid Cornelius	HRb	10-4	2.46	128	94	50	93
Mike Mathile	Rkf	9-3	2.47	117	100	19	66
Chris Pollack	HRb	11-8	2.75	157	147	68	83
Eddie Dixon	Ind	6-7	2.91	118	120	30	63
Doug Bochtler	WPb	12-9	2.92	160	148	54	109

Runs: Most, career, all-time

934	TIM RAINES, 1979-1990
828	ANDRE DAWSON, 1976-1986
684	TIM WALLACH, 1980-1991
683	GARY CARTER, 1974-1984
446	WARREN CROMARTIE, 1974-1983

Hits: Most, career, all-time

1598	TIM RAINES, 1979-1990
1575	ANDRE DAWSON, 1976-1986
1574	TIM WALLACH, 1980-1991
1365	GARY CARTER, 1974-1984
1063	WARREN CROMARTIE, 1974-1983

2B: Most, career, all-time

331	TIM WALLACH, 1980-1991
295	ANDRE DAWSON, 1976-1986
273	TIM RAINES, 1979-1990
256	GARY CARTER, 1974-1984
222	WARREN CROMARTIE, 1974-1983

3B: Most, career, all-time

81	TIM RAINES, 1979-1990
67	ANDRE DAWSON, 1976-1986
30	WARREN CROMARTIE, 1974-1983
30	TIM WALLACH, 1980-1991
25	MITCH WEBSTER, 1985-1988

HR: Most, career, all-time

225	ANDRE DAWSON, 1976-1986
215	GARY CARTER, 1974-1984
195	TIM WALLACH, 1980-1991
118	Bob Bailey, 1969-1975
106	ANDRES GALARRAGA, 1985-1991

RBI: Most, career, all-time

846	TIM WALLACH, 1980-1991
838	ANDRE DAWSON, 1976-1986
794	GARY CARTER, 1974-1984
552	TIM RAINES, 1979-1990
466	Bob Bailey, 1969-1975

SB: Most, career, all-time

634	TIM RAINES, 1979-1990

253	ANDRE DAWSON, 1976-1986
139	Rodney Scott, 1976-1982
133	OTIS NIXON, 1988-1990
96	MITCH WEBSTER, 1985-1988

BB: Most, career, all-time

775	TIM RAINES, 1979-1990
549	GARY CARTER, 1974-1984
502	Bob Bailey, 1969-1975
464	TIM WALLACH, 1980-1991
370	Ron Fairly, 1969-1974

BA: Highest, career, all-time

.301	TIM RAINES, 1979-1990
.294	Rusty Staub, 1969-1979
.288	Ellis Valentine, 1975-1981
.280	WARREN CROMARTIE, 1974-1983
.280	ANDRE DAWSON, 1976-1986

Slug avg: Highest, career, all-time

.497	Rusty Staub, 1969-1979
.476	ANDRE DAWSON, 1976-1986
.476	Ellis Valentine, 1975-1981
.461	GARY CARTER, 1974-1984
.441	HUBIE BROOKS, 1985-1989

Games started: Most, career, all-time

393	Steve Rogers, 1973-1985
193	BRYN SMITH, 1981-1989
192	Steve Renko, 1969-1976
170	BILL GULLICKSON, 1979-1985
167	DENNIS MARTINEZ, 1986-1991

Saves: Most, career, all-time

152	JEFF REARDON, 1981-1986
101	TIM BURKE, 1985-1991
75	Mike Marshall, 1970-1973
52	Woodie Fryman, 1975-1983
33	Dale Murray, 1974-1980

Shutouts: Most, career, all-time

37	Steve Rogers, 1973-1985
15	Bill Stoneman, 1969-1973
13	DENNIS MARTINEZ, 1986-1991
8	Woodie Fryman, 1975-1983
8	Charlie Lea, 1980-1987
8	SCOTT SANDERSON, 1978-1983
8	BRYN SMITH, 1981-1989

Wins: Most, career, all-time

158	Steve Rogers, 1973-1985
81	BRYN SMITH, 1981-1989
72	BILL GULLICKSON, 1979-1985
69	DENNIS MARTINEZ, 1986-1991
68	Steve Renko, 1969-1976

K: Most, career, all-time

1621	Steve Rogers, 1973-1985
838	BRYN SMITH, 1981-1989
831	Bill Stoneman, 1969-1973
810	Steve Renko, 1969-1976
688	DENNIS MARTINEZ, 1986-1991

Win pct: Highest, career, all-time

.623	TIM BURKE, 1985-1991
.573	Charlie Lea, 1980-1987
.570	DENNIS MARTINEZ, 1986-1991
.556	Mike Torrez, 1971-1974
.544	SCOTT SANDERSON, 1978-1983

ERA: Lowest, career, all-time

3.02	DENNIS MARTINEZ, 1986-1991
3.17	Steve Rogers, 1973-1985
3.28	BRYN SMITH, 1981-1989
3.32	Charlie Lea, 1980-1987
3.33	SCOTT SANDERSON, 1978-1983

Runs: Most, season

133	TIM RAINES, 1983
123	TIM RAINES, 1987
115	TIM RAINES, 1985
107	ANDRE DAWSON, 1982
106	TIM RAINES, 1984

Hits: Most, season

204	Al Oliver, 1982
194	TIM RAINES, 1986
192	TIM RAINES, 1984
189	ANDRE DAWSON, 1983
188	Dave Cash, 1977

2B: Most, season

46	WARREN CROMARTIE, 1979
43	Al Oliver, 1982
42	Dave Cash, 1977

42	ANDRES GALARRAGA, 1988
42	TIM WALLACH, 1987
42	TIM WALLACH, 1989

3B: Most, season

13	TIM RAINES, 1985
13	Rodney Scott, 1980
13	MITCH WEBSTER, 1986
12	ANDRE DAWSON, 1979
11	Ron LeFlore, 1980

HR: Most, season

32	ANDRE DAWSON, 1983
31	GARY CARTER, 1977
30	Larry Parrish, 1979
30	Rusty Staub, 1970
29	GARY CARTER, 1980
29	GARY CARTER, 1982
29	ANDRES GALARRAGA, 1988
29	Rusty Staub, 1969

RBI: Most, season

123	TIM WALLACH, 1987
113	ANDRE DAWSON, 1983
109	Al Oliver, 1982
106	GARY CARTER, 1984
103	Ken Singleton, 1973

SB: Most, season

97	Ron LeFlore, 1980
90	TIM RAINES, 1983
78	TIM RAINES, 1982
76	MARQUIS GRISSOM, 1991
75	TIM RAINES, 1984

BB: Most, season

123	Ken Singleton, 1973
112	Rusty Staub, 1970
110	Rusty Staub, 1969
100	Bob Bailey, 1974
97	Bob Bailey, 1971
97	TIM RAINES, 1983

BA: Highest, season

.334	TIM RAINES, 1986
.331	Al Oliver, 1982
.330	TIM RAINES, 1987
.320	TIM RAINES, 1985
.311	Rusty Staub, 1971

Slug avg: Highest, season

.553	ANDRE DAWSON, 1981
.551	Larry Parrish, 1979
.540	ANDRES GALARRAGA, 1988
.539	ANDRE DAWSON, 1983
.526	Rusty Staub, 1969

| .526 | TIM RAINES, 1987 |

Games started: Most, season

40	Steve Rogers, 1977
39	Bill Stoneman, 1971
38	Steve Rogers, 1974
37	Carl Morton, 1970
37	Steve Renko, 1971
37	Steve Rogers, 1979
37	Steve Rogers, 1980

Saves: Most, season

41	JEFF REARDON, 1985
35	JEFF REARDON, 1986
31	Mike Marshall, 1973
28	TIM BURKE, 1989
26	JEFF REARDON, 1982

Shutouts: Most, season

5	DENNIS MARTINEZ, 1991
5	Steve Rogers, 1979
5	Steve Rogers, 1983
5	Bill Stoneman, 1969
4	MARK LANGSTON, 1989
4	Charlie Lea, 1983
4	Carl Morton, 1970
4	Steve Rogers, 1976
4	Steve Rogers, 1977
4	Steve Rogers, 1980
4	Steve Rogers, 1982
4	Bill Stoneman, 1972

Wins: Most, season

20	Ross Grimsley, 1978
19	Steve Rogers, 1982
18	Carl Morton, 1970
18	BRYN SMITH, 1985
17	BILL GULLICKSON, 1983
17	Steve Rogers, 1977
17	Steve Rogers, 1983
17	Bill Stoneman, 1971

K: Most, season

251	Bill Stoneman, 1971
206	Steve Rogers, 1977
202	Floyd Youmans, 1986
185	Bill Stoneman, 1969
179	Steve Rogers, 1982

Win pct: Highest, season

.783	BRYN SMITH, 1985
.704	Steve Rogers, 1982
.696	DENNIS MARTINEZ, 1989
.652	Mike Torrez, 1974
.645	Ross Grimsley, 1978

ERA: Lowest, season

2.39	DENNIS MARTINEZ, 1991
2.39	MARK LANGSTON, 1989
2.40	Steve Rogers, 1982
2.44	PASCUAL PEREZ, 1988
2.47	Steve Rogers, 1978

Most pinch-hit homers, season

| 4 | Hal Breeden, 1973 |

Most pinch-hit, homers, career

| 5 | Jose Morales. 1973-1977 |

Most consecutive games, batting safely

| 19 | Warren Cromartie, 1979 |
| 19 | Andre Dawson, 1980 |

Most consecutive scoreless innings

| 32 | Woodie Fryman, 1975 |

No hit games

Bill Stoneman, Mon at Phi NL, 7-0; April 17, 1969.

Bill Stoneman, Mon vs NY NL, 7-0; October 2, 1972 (1st game).

Charlie Lea, Mon vs SF NL, 4-0; May 10, 1981 (2nd game).

Mark Gardner, Mon at LA NL, 0-1; July 26, 1991 (9 innings, lost on 2 hits in 10th, relieved by Jeff Fassero, who allowed 1 more hit).

Dennis Martinez, Mon at LA NL, 2-0; July 28, 1991 (perfect game).

David Palmer, five perfect innings, rain, Mon at StL NL, 4-0; April 21, 1984 (2nd game).

Pascual Perez, five innings, rain, Mon at Phi NL, 1-0; September 24, 1988.

Atlanta Braves

Atlanta's Tom Glavine won the NL Cy Young award in 1991.

Pendleton said, 'Why not?'

It was in spring training, before anyone was predicting anything more than a .500 season, that new Atlanta Braves' third baseman Terry Pendleton offered his analysis of what the club might do in 1991.

"I'm not saying we will win the division, but I don't see why that can't happen," Pendleton said. "It should be our goal, no matter what has happened here before. And remember, it's baseball ... anything can happen."

Anything certainly did. Riding a career year by Pendleton that included winning the batting championship—and a pitching performance that netted Tom Glavine the Cy Young award—the Braves became the first NL team in history to finish last one season and first the next.

For years, scouts and other observers raved about the pitching prospects in the Braves' farm system. The predictions of stardom for Tom Glavine, Steve Avery and John Smoltz started to come true in 1991, with Glavine winning 20 games, Avery 18 and Smoltz going 12-2 after the All-Star break following a terrible first half.

The Braves also won a franchise-record 94 games behind the play of Pendleton, who was one of three key free agents signed in the off-season by new general manager John Schuerholz.

Pendleton hit 22 homers, drove in 86 runs and hit .319 in the best year of his career, also providing much of the intangible quality of leadership that the woebegone Braves had been missing for so many years. He also was particularly valuable during a two-month stretch in the middle of the season when David Justice and Sid Bream were out with injuries.

Schuerholz also signed Bream and reliever Juan Berenguer, who was almost perfect, converting 17 of 18 save opportunities and allowing only one inherited runner to score, before he was injured Aug. 12 and missed the rest of the season. To replace Berenguer, Schuerholz traded for Alejandro Pena, who converted 11 straight save opportunities during September.

Schuerholz had also engineered a spring training trade for outfielder Otis Nixon, who proved to be a catalyst, leading the league with 72 stolen bases, until he was suspended Sept. 16 for failing a drug test.

That the Braves were able to win despite the long absences of several key players was due in large part to the performance of Pendleton and center-fielder Ron Gant (32 home runs, 105 runs batted in, 34 stolen bases).

The Braves made up a 9 1/2 game deficit to Los Angeles in the second half of the season to sprint past the Dodgers the second-to-last day of the season. The divison title was theirs.

The biggest blow of the year was a two-run homer by Justice on Oct. 1, off the Reds' Rob Dibble, which capped a comeback from a 6-0 deficit against Jose Rijo, at the time leading the league in ERA. It was one of eight straight wins for the Braves in their drive to the pennant.

Asked about the odds of coming back to win that game, Justice said he thought they would have been about a billion to one, only slightly greater than the odds most people would have given the Braves on winning before the season began.

—*Rob Rains*

Braves 1992 preview

The Braves are in good shape to attempt an encore of last season's NL championship. Even if Terry Pendleton doesn't post numbers similar to last season (.319, 22 HR, 86 RBI) the Braves offense shouldn't suffer too much—as long as David Justice remains healthy.

Second baseman Mark Lemke demonstrated in the postseason that he can be a force offensively, and center fielder Ron Gant had his second consecutive

30-30 season.

The pitching staff boasts three left-handed starters, and a solid bullpen in Juan Berenguer and Alejandro Pena, if he re-signs.

A lack of production from catcher and shortstop may be bothersome; Damon Berryhill will get a shot at the backstop job, while shortstop apparently remains a platoon of Rafael Belliard and Jeff Blauser.

Otis Nixon should provide a spark with his offense and base-stealing once his suspension ends.

Braves 1992 prophecy

▶Jane Fonda will overthrow Ted Turner as owner of the Braves and begin attending Atlanta home games with her faithful dog "Fondzie."

▶The Braves will become the first team in baseball history to go from worst to first to worst, and Braves' fans will replace the "tomahawk chop" with the "nodding off drop."

—John Hunt

130

Pendleton won batting crown

Terry Pendleton won his first batting title the same way the Braves won the NL West—with a big finish.

Pendleton charged ahead of Tony Gwynn and Hal Morris by hitting .353 in his final 28 games, getting at least one hit in 26 of them. That raised his overall average to .319 and allowed him to finish one point ahead of Morris and two points ahead of Gwynn.

"I never thought I would win it with guys like Tony Gwynn and Willie McGee in the league," Pendleton said.

Pendleton had a career low .230 in 1990 with the Cardinals, and said the reason for his big turnaround in 1991 was that he was more relaxed and patient at the plate.

Pendleton led Morris the season's last day and sat out the final game.

He wasn't asked by manager Bobby

Cox if he wanted to play, but he said he would have declined anyway.

Morris needed four hits to beat Pendleton on the final day. He got three.

"I felt like I had done all I could do," Pendleton said after the final game. "If I'd gone out and gone 4-for-4, or 0-for-4, I'd still have done all I could do. If (Morris) had come out and gone 4-for-4, I'd have tipped my hat to him.

"I haven't had a day off since June 14," he continued. "That was 104 games ago. The idea is to get me ready for the play-offs."

Pendleton—who also hit a career-high 22 homers and drove in 86 runs—had already been mentioned as an MVP candidate, but he said winning the batting title was more meaningful to him.

"To win the batting title, you have to beat out everybody," he said. "The MVP is a vote and the writers decide it."

It came down to the last inning

The Braves said the NL West race would go to the final weekend. They were right.

The Giants wanted to spoil it for the Dodgers. They did.

"Unless something goes wrong here, I fully expect it to go down to the last day," said Giants' first baseman Will Clark. "I remember (in 1989) Tom Lasorda saying he didn't want us to celebrate in front of him. There's the same feeling in this clubhouse."

San Francisco manager Roger Craig also thought it would be a nail-biter.

"I think it's going to go down to the last inning, last pitch just like it did (in LA's 3-2 win on Sept. 29)," Craig said.

It went to the next-to-last game, but it was often the Braves who were pressed to the final pitch of the final inning.

▶Sept.27: Atlanta scored four runs in the eighth inning, including a pair of two-out RBI singles from Greg Olson and Jeff Blauser, to beat the Astros 4-2.

▶Sept. 28: Atlanta scored two runs in the seventh, one in the eighth, and one in the ninth to overcome a 3-1 Houston lead for a 5-4 win.

▶Sept. 29: Atlanta blew a 5-0 lead, but held on and came back to win 6-5 in 13 innings.

▶Oct. 1: Down 6-0 after one inning (with Jose Rijo pitching for Cincinnati), David Justice put the Braves chances at "about a billion to one." But the Braves rallied to 6-5 entering the ninth, then Justice slammed a two-run homer to complete an unbelievable comeback for a 7-6 win.

"Every pitch, every swing, that's the way it is with this club," said manager Bobby Cox. "It's been that way for a long time. We have a very highly competitive ball-club. There is a lot of spirit and desire."

There was enough, in fact, to take the Braves through the last inning of the seven-game League Championship Series and then to extra innings in the seventh game of the World Series, where they were defeated by one run.

Piniella said they'd fold; Lasorda knew otherwise

By Rob Rains

The first salvo was fired by the Dodgers' Darryl Strawberry, who said: "I've never been concerned about Atlanta. They've been chasing us and they've been playing extremely well. But we've always played extremely well against them. If the Giants and Padres were that close, it would be a different story."

"He'd better start rethinking what he said," said catcher Greg Olson. "The Dodgers have real good starting pitching and we have real good starting pitching.

"Our bullpen is better than their bullpen. They're not hitting, and we are knocking it around. We'll see who's talking in October."

Dodgers manager Tom Lasorda didn't share Strawberry's belief, but the Dodger outfielder did find some support in Cincinnati manager Lou Piniella, who also said he didn't believe

the Braves could stay in the race.

"I think Atlanta is going to fold up and collapse," Piniella said.

Said Lasorda, "I've been saying all along that Atlanta was for real and they would be a part of it. Check all my interviews. I don't expect them to fall out."

Team Directory

▶Owner: Ted Turner

▶General Manager: John Schuerholz

▶Ballpark:
Atlanta-Fulton County Stadium
521 Capitol Avenue, SW, Atlanta, Georgia
404-614-1309
Capacity 52,007
Parking for 6,500 cars; $4
Public transportation available
Family and wheelchair sections, non-alcohol section

▶Team publications:
Fan Magazine
404-688-1537
Homestands Magazine (Gwinett Daily News)
404-963-0311

▶TV, radio broadcast stations:
WSB 750-AM, WTBS Channel 17

▶Camps and/or clinics:
Braves Fantasy Camp (ages 30+), February, 800-8-BRAVES

▶Spring Training:
Municipal Stadium
West Palm Beach, Florida
Capacity 7,200
407-683-6100

ATLANTA BRAVES 1991 Final Stats

Batting	AVG	SLG	OB	G	AB	R	H	TB	2B	3B	HR	RBI	BB	SO	SB	CS	E
Heep	.417	.500	.462	14	12	4	5	6	1	0	0	3	1	4	0	1	0
Treadway	.320	.418	.368	106	306	41	98	128	17	2	3	32	23	19	2	2	15
Pendleton	.319	.517	.363	153	586	94	187	303	34	8	22	86	43	70	10	2	24
Mitchell	.318	.409	.392	48	66	11	21	27	0	0	2	5	8	12	3	1	1
Nixon	.297	.327	.371	124	401	81	119	131	10	1	0	26	47	40	72	21	3
Justice	.275	.503	.377	109	396	67	109	199	25	1	21	87	65	81	8	8	7
L. Smith	.275	.394	.377	122	353	58	97	139	19	1	7	44	50	64	9	5	5
Blauser	.259	.409	.358	129	352	49	91	144	14	3	11	54	54	59	5	6	17
Bream	.253	.423	.313	91	265	32	67	112	12	0	11	45	25	31	0	3	3
Gant	.251	.496	.338	154	561	101	141	278	35	3	32	105	71	104	34	15	6
Hunter	.251	.450	.296	97	271	32	68	122	16	1	12	50	17	48	0	2	8
Belliard	.249	.286	.296	149	353	36	88	101	9	2	0	27	22	63	3	1	18
Cabrera	.242	.432	.284	44	95	7	23	41	6	0	4	23	6	20	1	1	3
Olson	.241	.345	.316	133	411	46	99	142	25	0	6	44	44	48	1	1	4
Lemke	.234	.312	.305	136	269	36	63	84	11	2	2	23	29	27	1	2	10
Willard	.214	.429	.313	17	14	1	3	6	0	0	1	4	2	5	0	0	0
Heath	.209	.266	.250	49	139	4	29	37	3	1	1	12	7	26	0	0	2
Castilla	.200	.200	.200	12	5	1	1	1	0	0	0	0	0	2	0	0	0
Sanders	.191	.345	.270	54	110	16	21	38	1	2	4	13	12	23	11	3	3
Berryhill	.188	.325	.243	63	160	13	30	52	7	0	5	14	11	42	1	2	8
Gregg	.187	.308	.275	72	107	13	20	33	8	1	1	4	12	24	2	2	0
Bell	.133	.233	.188	17	30	4	4	7	0	0	1	1	2	7	1	0	2
Rossy	.000	.000	.000	5	1	0	0	0	0	0	0	0	0	1	0	0	0

Pitching	W-L	ERA	G	GS	CG	GF	Sho	SV	IP	H	R	ER	HR	BB	SO
Berenguer	0-3	2.24	49	0	0	35	0	17	64.1	43	18	16	5	20	53
Pena	8-1	2.40	59	0	0	36	0	15	82.1	74	23	22	6	22	62
Glavine	20-11	2.55	34	34	9	0	1	0	246.2	201	83	70	17	69	192
Mercker	5-3	2.58	50	4	0	28	0	6	73.1	56	23	21	5	35	62
Stanton	5-5	2.88	74	0	0	20	0	7	78	62	27	25	6	21	54
Freeman	1-0	3.00	34	0	0	6	0	1	48	37	19	16	2	13	34
Wohlers	3-1	3.20	17	0	0	4	0	2	19.2	17	7	7	1	13	13
Avery	18-8	3.38	35	35	3	0	1	0	210.1	189	89	79	21	65	137
Leibrandt	15-13	3.49	36	36	1	0	1	0	229.2	212	105	89	18	56	128
Smoltz	14-13	3.80	36	36	5	0	0	0	229.2	206	101	97	16	77	148
Clancy	3-5	3.91	54	0	0	22	0	8	89.2	73	42	39	8	34	50
St. Claire	0-0	4.08	19	0	0	5	0	0	28.2	31	17	13	4	9	30
Bielecki	13-11	4.46	41	25	0	9	0	0	173.2	171	91	86	18	56	75
Mahler	2-4	4.50	23	8	0	2	0	0	66	70	37	33	4	28	27
Sisk	2-1	5.02	14	0	0	2	0	0	14.1	21	14	8	1	8	5
P. Smith	1-3	5.06	14	10	0	2	0	0	48	48	33	27	5	22	29
Petry	0-0	5.55	10	0	0	4	0	0	24.1	29	17	15	2	14	9
Reynoso	2-1	6.17	6	5	0	1	0	0	23.1	26	18	16	4	10	10
Parrett	1-2	6.33	18	0	0	9	0	1	21.1	31	18	15	2	12	14

1992 Preliminary Roster

Pitchers (18)

Steve Avery
Juan Berenguer
Mike Bielecki
Dennis Burlingame
Marvin Freeman
Tom Glavine
Pat Gomez
Mark Grant
Charlie Leibrandt
Kent Mercker
Matt Murray
David Nied
Armando Reynoso
Bienvenido Rivera
Pete Smith
John Smoltz
Mike Stanton
Mark Wohlers

Catchers (6)

Damon Berryhill
Francisco Cabrera
Mike Heath
Javier Lopez
Greg Olson
Jerry Willard

Infielders (9)

Rafael Belliard
Jeff Blauser
Sid Bream
Ramon Caraballo
Vinny Castilla
Brian Hunter
Mark Lemke
Terry Pendleton
Jeff Treadway

Outfielders (7)

Ron Gant
Tommy Gregg
David Justice
Keith Mitchell
Mel Nieves
Deion Sanders
Lonnie Smith

Games played by position

	G	C	1B	2B	3B	SS	OF
Bell,M	17	0	14	0	0	0	0
Belliard,R	149	0	0	0	0	145	0
Berryhill,D	63	49	0	0	0	0	0
Blauser,J	129	0	0	32	18	85	0
Bream,S	91	0	85	0	0	0	0
Cabrera,F	44	17	14	0	0	0	0
Castilla,V	12	0	0	0	0	12	0
Gant,R	154	0	0	0	0	0	148
Gregg,T	72	0	13	0	0	0	14
Heath,M	49	45	0	0	0	0	0
Heep,D	14	0	1	0	0	0	1
Hunter,B	97	0	85	0	0	0	6
Justice,D	109	0	0	0	0	0	106
Lemke,M	136	0	0	110	15	0	0
Mitchell,Ke	48	0	0	0	0	0	34
Nixon,O	124	0	0	0	0	0	115
Olson,Gr	133	127	0	0	0	0	0
Pendleton,T	153	0	0	0	148	0	0
Rossy,R	5	0	0	0	0	1	0
Sanders,D	54	0	0	0	0	0	44
Smith,L	122	0	0	0	0	0	99
Treadway,J	106	0	0	93	0	0	0
Willard,J	17	1	0	0	0	0	0

Sick call: 1991 DL report

Player	Days on the DL
Mark Grant	175*
Pete Smith	45
Tommy Gregg	42
Lonnie Smith	20
Doug Sisk	136
Nick Esasky	182
Sid Bream	61*
Dave Justice	54
Mike Heath	86
Kent Mercker	15
Juan Berenguer	19
Marvin Freeman	50

* On DL twice (not counting administrative transfers from one DL to another).

Minor League Report

Class AAA — Richmond finished 65-79, fourth in the International League West. C Jerry Willard hit .300 with 8 HRs and 39 RBI. 3B Tracy Woodson hit .277 with 6 HRs and 56 RBI. 2B Rico Rossy (.257) had 25 doubles and 48 RBI. RHP Armando Reynoso (10-6, 2.61) led the IL in ERA. RHP Randy St. Claire (6-2, 1.19) gave up 39 hits in 68 innings. . . . **Class AA** — Greenville finished 88-56, first in the first half and second in the second half in the Southern League Eastern Division. The 88 victories were a franchise record. The Braves lost to Orlando in the playoffs. 1B Ryan Klesko (.291-14-67) was named MVP. RHP Mark Wohlers (21 saves, 0.57 ERA before mid-season promotion) was named Most Outstanding Pitcher. RHP Nap Robinson (16-6) led the SL in wins. That was a team record, as was RHP Bill Taylor's 22 saves. Chris Chambliss was Manager of the Year. . . . **Class A** — Durham finished 79-58, third in the first half and second in the second half in the Carolina League Southern Division. Top hitters included INF Tim Gillis (.246 with 26 doubles), C Javy Lopez (.245-11-51) and OF Melvin Nieves (.264). and OF Tony Tarasco (.250-12-38).RHP Dennis Burlingame (11-7, 3.01) gave up 143 hits in 161.1 innings. RHP Scott Taylor (10-3, 2.18) gave up 94 hits in 111.1 innings. . . . Macon finished 83-58, second in the first half and first in the second half in the South Atlantic League Southern Division. The Braves lost to Columbia in the playoffs. SS Chipper Jones hit .323 with 11 triples, 15 HRs and 98 RBI. He was second in the league with 153 hits and tied for first with 104 runs. OF Troy Hughes (.300) had 33 doubles. OF Lee Heath (.236) tied for second with 60 SBs.Macon led the league with 257 SBs and set league record with 22 shutouts. RHP Joe Roa was 13-3 with a 2.11 ERA. . . . Pulaski finished 45-23, first in the Appalachian League Southern Division. The Braves beat Burlington to win the playoffs and league championship. OF Don Robinson hit .286, SS Manny Jimenez hit .282 and 1B Lance Marks hit .281 with 12 HRs and 42 RBI. RHP Kevin Lomon was 6-0 with an 0.61 ERA. RHP John Wilder was 8-2 with a 2.51 ERA. . . . Idaho Falls finished 39-30, second in the Pioneer League Southern Division. The Braves hit .303 as a team and scored 477 runs in 69 games. Top hitters were 2B Dario Paulino (.371), SS Tony Graffagnino (.347) and C Brad Rippelmeyer (.342). RHP Brad Woodall had 11 saves.

Tops in the Organization

BATTING LEADERS

	Club	Avg.	G	AB	R	H	HR	RBI
Chipper Jones	Mac	.326	136	473	104	154	15	98
Troy Hughes	Mac	.300	112	404	69	121	9	80
Ryan Klesko	Grv	.291	126	419	64	122	14	67
Sean Ross	Grv	.282	113	429	52	121	8	40
Boi Rodriguez	Rmd	.281	134	484	64	136	9	63

HOME RUNS

Chipper Jones	Mac	15
Vinny Castilla	Rmd	14
Ryan Klesko	Grv	14
Several players tied		12

RBI

Chipper Jones	Mac	98
Vinny Castilla	Rmd	80
Troy Hughes	Mac	80
Rick Karcher	Mac	79
Ryan Klesko	Grv	67

STOLEN BASES

Lee Heath	Mac	61
Ramon Caraballo	Dur	53
Jose Olmeda	Grv	43
Chipper Jones	Mac	39
Ed Alicea	Grv	34

WINS

Napoleon Robinson	Grv	16
Henry Werland	Dur	15
David Nied	Grv	15
Scott Taylor	Grv	13
Joe Roa	Mac	13

SAVES

Mark Wohlers	Rmd	32
Bill Taylor	Grv	22
Don Strange	Grv	20
Mark Ross	Rmd	9
Ray Mack	Mac	9

STRIKEOUTS

David Nied	Grv	178
Turk Wendell	Rmd	140
Nate Minchey	Dur	138
Ben Rivera	Grv	116
Pat Gomez	Rmd	112

PITCHING LEADERS

	Club	W-L	ERA	IP	H	BB	SO
David Nied	Grv	15-6	2.01	170	125	43	178
Joe Roa	Mac	13-3	2.11	141	106	33	96
Napoleon Robinson	Grv	16-6	2.27	175	172	48	107
Nate Minchey	Dur	11-9	2.34	184	153	60	138
Pedro Borbon	Grv	4-4	2.41	120	108	45	101

Runs: Most, career, all-time

2107	Hank Aaron, 1954-1974
1452	Eddie Mathews, 1952-1966
1291	Herman Long, 1890-1902
1134	Fred Tenney, 1894-1911
1103	DALE MURPHY, 1976-1990

Hits: Most, career, all-time

3600	Hank Aaron, 1954-1974
2201	Eddie Mathews, 1952-1966
1994	Fred Tenney, 1894-1911
1901	DALE MURPHY, 1976-1990
1900	Herman Long, 1890-1902

2B: Most, career, all-time

600	Hank Aaron, 1954-1974
338	Eddie Mathews, 1952-1966
306	DALE MURPHY, 1976-1990
295	Herman Long, 1890-1902
291	Tommy Holmes, 1942-1951

3B: Most, career, all-time

103	Rabbit Maranville, 1912-1935
96	Hank Aaron, 1954-1974
90	Herman Long, 1890-1902
80	John Morrill, 1876-1888
79	Bill Bruton, 1953-1960

HR: Most, career, all-time

733	Hank Aaron, 1954-1974
493	Eddie Mathews, 1952-1966
371	DALE MURPHY, 1976-1990
239	Joe Adcock, 1953-1962
215	Bob Horner, 1978-1986

RBI: Most, career, all-time

2202	Hank Aaron, 1954-1974
1388	Eddie Mathews, 1952-1966
1143	DALE MURPHY, 1976-1990
964	Herman Long, 1890-1902
927	Hugh Duffy, 1892-1900

SB: Most, career, all-time

431	Herman Long, 1890-1902
331	Hugh Duffy, 1892-1900
274	Billy Hamilton, 1896-1901
260	Bobby Lowe, 1890-1901
260	Fred Tenney, 1894-1911
240	Hank Aaron, 1954-1974 (6)

BB: Most, career, all-time

1376	Eddie Mathews, 1952-1966
1297	Hank Aaron, 1954-1974
912	DALE MURPHY, 1976-1990
750	Fred Tenney, 1894-1911
598	Billy Nash, 1885-1895

BA: Highest, career, all-time

.338	Billy Hamilton, 1896-1901
.332	Hugh Duffy, 1892-1900
.327	Chick Stahl, 1897-1900
.317	Rico Carty, 1963-1972
.317	Ralph Garr, 1968-1975

Slug avg: Highest, career, all-time

.567	Hank Aaron, 1954-1974
.533	Wally Berger, 1930-1937
.517	Eddie Mathews, 1952-1966
.511	Joe Adcock, 1953-1962
.508	Bob Horner, 1978-1986

Games started: Most, career, all-time

635	Warren Spahn, 1942-1964
595	Phil Niekro, 1964-1987
501	Kid Nichols, 1890-1901
330	Lew Burdette, 1951-1963
302	Vic Willis, 1898-1905

Saves: Most, career, all-time

141	Gene Garber, 1978-1987
78	Cecil Upshaw, 1966-1973
57	Rick Camp, 1976-1985
50	Don McMahon, 1957-1962
41	STEVE BEDROSIAN, 1981-1985

Shutouts: Most, career, all-time

63	Warren Spahn, 1942-1964
44	Kid Nichols, 1890-1901
43	Phil Niekro, 1964-1987
30	Lew Burdette, 1951-1963
29	Tommy Bond, 1877-1881

Wins: Most, career, all-time

356	Warren Spahn, 1942-1964
329	Kid Nichols, 1890-1901
268	Phil Niekro, 1964-1987
179	Lew Burdette, 1951-1963
151	Vic Willis, 1898-1905

K: Most, career, all-time

2912	Phil Niekro, 1964-1987
2493	Warren Spahn, 1942-1964
1667	Kid Nichols, 1890-1901
1161	Vic Willis, 1898-1905
1157	Jim Whitney, 1881-1885 (12)

Win pct: Highest, career, all-time

.679	Fred Klobedanz, 1896-1902
.655	Harry Staley, 1891-1894
.645	John Clarkson, 1888-1892
.643	Kid Nichols, 1890-1901
.631	Tommy Bond, 1877-1881
.581	Tony Cloninger, 1961-1968

ERA: Lowest, career, all-time

2.21	Tommy Bond, 1877-1881
2.49	Jim Whitney, 1881-1885
2.52	Art Nehf, 1915-1919
2.62	Dick Rudolph, 1913-1927
2.74	Pat Ragan, 1915-1919
3.20	Phil Niekro, 1964-1987 (16)

Runs: Most, season

160	Hugh Duffy, 1894
158	Bobby Lowe, 1894
152	Billy Hamilton, 1896
152	Billy Hamilton, 1897
149	Herman Long, 1893
131	DALE MURPHY, 1983 (9)

Hits: Most, season

237	Hugh Duffy, 1894
224	Tommy Holmes, 1945
223	Hank Aaron, 1959
219	Ralph Garr, 1971
218	Felipe Alou, 1966

2B: Most, season

51	Hugh Duffy, 1894
47	Tommy Holmes, 1945
46	Hank Aaron, 1959
44	Wally Berger, 1931
44	Lee Maye, 1964

3B: Most, season

20	Dick Johnston, 1887
20	Harry Stovey, 1891
19	Chick Stahl, 1899

18	Dick Johnston, 1888
18	Ray Powell, 1921
17	Ralph Garr, 1974 (6)

HR: Most, season

47	Hank Aaron, 1971
47	Eddie Mathews, 1953
46	Eddie Mathews, 1959
45	Hank Aaron, 1962
44	Hank Aaron, 1957
44	Hank Aaron, 1963
44	Hank Aaron, 1966
44	Hank Aaron, 1969
44	DALE MURPHY, 1987

RBI: Most, season

145	Hugh Duffy, 1894
135	Eddie Mathews, 1953
132	Hank Aaron, 1957
132	Jimmy Collins, 1897
130	Hank Aaron, 1963
130	Wally Berger, 1935

SB: Most, season

84	King Kelly, 1887
83	Billy Hamilton, 1896
72	OTIS NIXON, 1991
68	King Kelly, 1889
66	Billy Hamilton, 1897

BB: Most, season

131	Bob Elliott, 1948
127	Jim Wynn, 1976
126	Darrell Evans, 1974
124	Darrell Evans, 1973
124	Eddie Mathews, 1963

BA: Highest, season

.440	Hugh Duffy, 1894
.387	Rogers Hornsby, 1928
.373	Dan Brouthers, 1889
.369	Billy Hamilton, 1898
.366	Rico Carty, 1970

Slug avg: Highest, season

.694	Hugh Duffy, 1894
.669	Hank Aaron, 1971
.636	Hank Aaron, 1959
.632	Rogers Hornsby, 1928
.627	Eddie Mathews, 1953

Games started: Most, season

72	John Clarkson, 1889
67	Charlie Buffinton, 1884
64	Tommy Bond, 1879
63	Jim Whitney, 1881

59	Tommy Bond, 1878
44	Phil Niekro, 1979 (22)

Saves: Most, season

30	Gene Garber, 1982
27	Cecil Upshaw, 1969
25	Gene Garber, 1979
24	Gene Garber, 1986
23	Bruce Sutter, 1985

Shutouts: Most, season

11	Tommy Bond, 1879
9	Tommy Bond, 1878
8	Charlie Buffinton, 1884
8	John Clarkson, 1889
7	Kid Nichols, 1890
7	Togie Pittinger, 1902
7	Warren Spahn, 1947
7	Warren Spahn, 1951
7	Warren Spahn, 1963
7	Irv Young, 1905
6	Phil Niekro, 1974 (11)

Wins: Most, season

49	John Clarkson, 1889
48	Charlie Buffinton, 1884
43	Tommy Bond, 1879
40	Tommy Bond, 1877
40	Tommy Bond, 1878
24	Tony Cloninger, 1965 (*)

K: Most, season

417	Charlie Buffinton, 1884
345	Jim Whitney, 1883
284	John Clarkson, 1889
270	Jim Whitney, 1884
262	Phil Niekro, 1977

Win pct: Highest, season

.842	Tom Hughes, 1916
.810	Phil Niekro, 1982
.788	Fred Klobedanz, 1897
.788	Bill James, 1914
.783	Jack Manning, 1876

ERA: Lowest, season

1.87	Phil Niekro, 1967
1.90	Bill James, 1914
1.96	Tommy Bond, 1879
2.02	Lefty Tyler, 1916
2.06	Tommy Bond, 1878

Most pinch-hit homers, season

5	Butch Nieman, Bos-1945
4	Tommy Gregg, 1990

Most pinch-hit, homers, career

7	Joe Adcock, Mil-1953-1962
6	Tommy Gregg, 1988-1991

Most consecutive games, batting safely

37	Tommy Holmes, Bos-1945
31	Rico Carty, 1970

Most consecutive scoreless innings

N/A

No hit games

Jack Stivetts, Bos vs Bro NL, 11-0; August 6, 1892.
Frank (Jeff) Pfeffer, Bos vs Cin NL, 6-0; May 8, 1907.
George Davis, Bos vs Phi NL, 7-0; September 9, 1914 (2nd game).
Tom L. Hughes, Bos vs Pit NL, 2-0; June 16, 1916.
Jim Tobin, Bos vs Bro NL, 2-0; April 27, 1944.
Vern Bickford, Bos vs Bro NL, 7-0; August 11, 1950.
Jim Wilson, Mil vs Phi NL, 2-0; June 12, 1954.
Lew Burdette, Mil vs Phi NL, 1-0; August 18, 1960.
Warren Spahn, Mil vs Phi NL, 4-0; September 16, 1960.
Warren Spahn, Mil vs SF NL, 1-0; April 28, 1961.
Phil Niekro, Atl vs SD NL, 9-0; August 5, 1973.
Kent Mercker (6 innings), Mark Wohlers (2 innings) and Alejandro Pena (1 inning), Atl at SD NL, 1-0; September 11, 1991.
Jack Stivetts, five innings, called so Boston could catch train to Cleveland for Temple Club playoffs, Bos at Was NL, 6-0; October 15, 1892 (2nd game).
Jim Tobin, five innings, darkness, Bos vs Phi NL, 7-0; June 22, 1944 (2nd game).

Los Angeles Dodgers

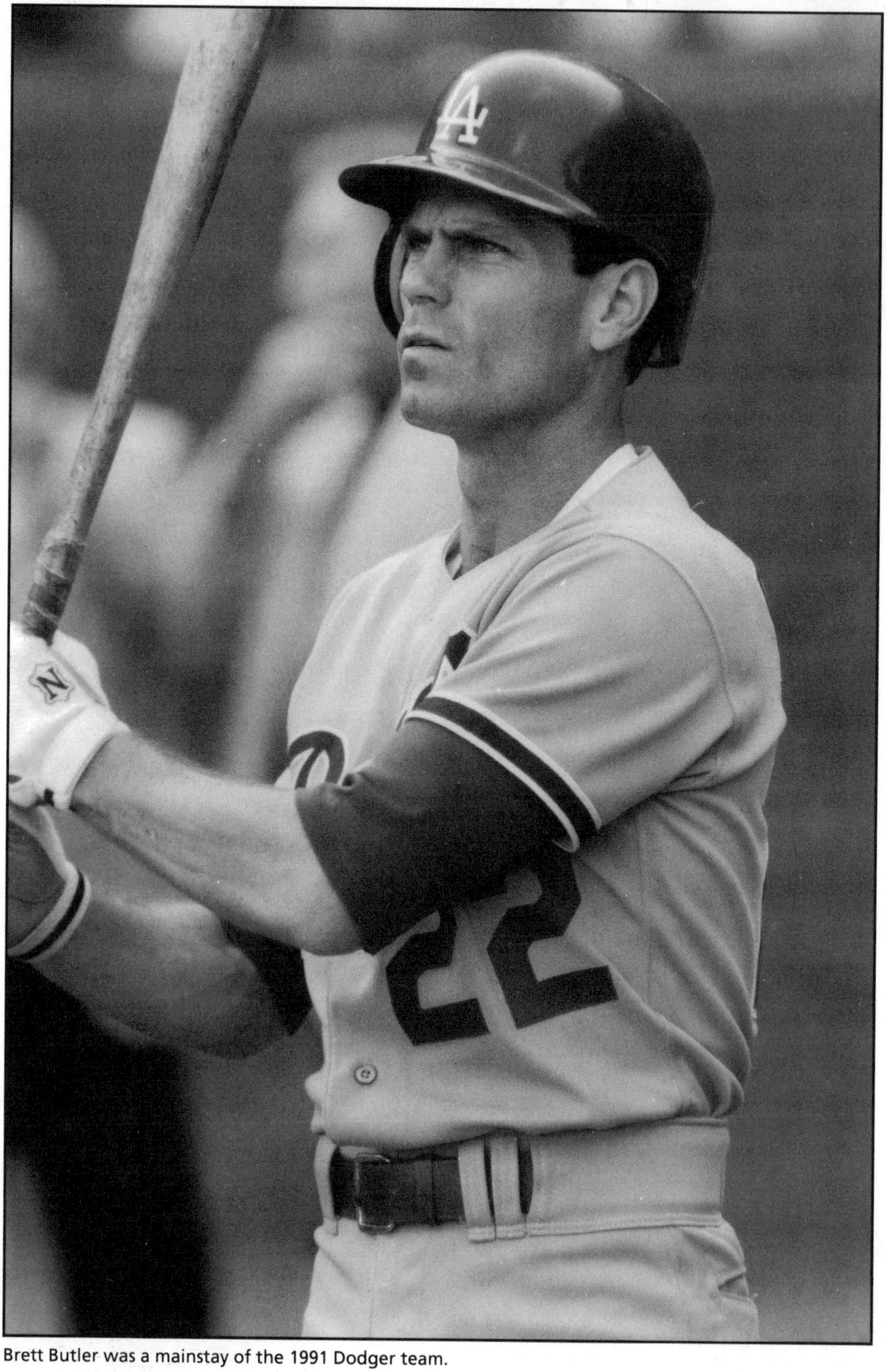

Brett Butler was a mainstay of the 1991 Dodger team.

Los Angeles Dodgers: Wrap Up

The Los Angeles Dodgers spent mightily in the offseason to sign free agents Darryl Strawberry, Brett Butler and Kevin Gross, making them the favorites to win the NL West.

They came close, falling just one game behind the Atlanta Braves despite having the fourth best record in the major leagues.

The reason they didn't win, at least according to Butler and Strawberry, was because of a factor money couldn't buy — heart.

"We didn't have enough of this right here," said Strawberry, putting his hand over the upper left side of his chest. "Just didn't have enough."

Said Butler, "We were a team, but we were not a family ... and the Braves were both. We came to the park, we worked, and then we went our separate ways. We were too many individuals and not enough of a group."

The Dodgers led the division for 134 days, falling into a tie with Atlanta with three games remaining. But while the Braves were winning two straight games over Houston, Los Angeles lost two in a row in San Francisco and the race was over.

The biggest stretch of the season likely was the two-week period following the All-Star break, and that was the point many players felt was when the season got away.

They started the second half going 2-9 on an East Coast road trip, wiping out much of a 9 1/2 game lead over the Braves they enjoyed at the break, when they had the best record in baseball.

"There was not enough guys with enough fire," Strawberry said.

Strawberry, adjusting to Los Angeles as well as to his new Christian beliefs, took the first half of the season to become comfortable, but then had a big second half and finished the year with 28 homers and 99 RBI.

Butler also played well as a catalyst, and the Dodgers saw the return of Orel Hershiser after his recovery from shoulder surgery. Mike Morgan had the best season of his career and Ramon Martinez won 17 games, but it wasn't enough to catch the Braves.

The loss of shortstop Alfredo Griffin to injuries at three separate points in the season hurt the Dodger, as did a second-half slump by All-Star Juan Samuel and the sore knees of Kal Daniels, which kept him out of 25 games.

The bullpen suffered from the loss of reliever Jay Howell, who led the team with 16 saves. General Manager Fred Claire tried to fill the void by trading for Roger McDowell, who pitched well, but wasn't the deciding factor either.

When the Dodgers played a late-season series in Pittsburgh, most of the players found themselves thinking they would be back in October for the playoffs, but it was the Braves who were there instead.

Dodgers 1992 preview

You can bet the Los Angeles Dodgers will be bearing down right after the All-Star break this year. Most observers feel that's when the NL West title got away last year.

It's also fair to assume that the esprit de corps will be a little better, too. Outfielders Darryl Strawberry and Brett Butler suggested team camaraderie wasn't all it should have been last season, but now Strawberry's pal Eric Davis is on board to provide a little more right-handed offensive punch.

On paper, there is no reason the Dodgers can't battle Atlanta down to the wire again. The pitching is solid with Ramon Martinez, Tom Candiotti, Bob Ojeda, Kevin Gross and Orel Hershiser—if he's healthy.

1992 prophecy: Dodgers

▶Ramon's younger brother Pedro Martinez will join the staff, and the Dodgers will trade for Montreal's Dennis Martinez—the staff will be known as the "Three Martinez Bunch."

▶The Dodgers will be 10 games behind San Francisco in September, and Darryl Strawberry will be quoted as saying, "We're not afraid of the Giants."

—John Hunt

Second fiddles

The Los Angeles Dodgers like finishing second—it means that the next season they are championship bound.

▶1976-77: When they finished second to Cincinnati in 1976, they went on to win the pennant in '77—Tom Lasorda's first season.

▶1980-81: When they tied Houston in 1980, but lost a special playoff, they turned around and won the World Series in '81.

▶1982-83: When they finished second to Atlanta in 1982, they won the NL West title in '83.

▶The spoiler—1990-91: Up until the last two days of 1991, it looked like history would continue to repeat itself. The Dodgers had finished second to the Reds in 1990, and were leading the NL West in '91. But the Braves refused to lose, and it was the Dodgers' archrival team—the San Francisco Giants—who put an ironic end to LA's two-one punch.

Lasorda: a Dodger blue-blood

By Rob Rains

On Sept. 22, Dodgers manager Tom Lasorda celebrated his 64th birthday. Although he's the senior manager in the league in age and experience, 1991 wasn't an easy year for him—on or off the field.

On more than one occasion last sea-son, Lasorda said that if he survived the year, he would live to be 105.

Losing a down-to-the-wire pennant race to the Atlanta Braves wasn't Lasorda's biggest hurt. Earlier in the year he had to cope with the death of his 33-year-old son, Tom Jr., after a long illness. He has been able to handle that tragedy better because of his job, Lasorda said.

"No matter how tired or dejected or depressed I might be, when I walk through that clubhouse door I've got to put on a new face," Lasorda said. "I've got to put on a winning face of self-con-fidence. If I walk in here and I'm dejected and depressed and hanging my head, what is going to be the attitude and atmosphere of this clubhouse?"

Lasorda has sometimes been criticized for his positive, rah-rah approach to life and baseball; he's often been called a cheerleader.

He agrees that he tries to be a positive person, and he doesn't apologize.

"Vin Scully was interviewing me the day I got the job as manager of the Dodgers and asked me how I felt about replacing a guy like Walter Alston, who had managed the team for 23 years, a future Hall of Famer, one of the great-est managers who ever lived. He said, 'Don't you think there's going to be a lot of pressure on you?' I said, 'I'm not wor-ried about that. I'm worried about the guy who's going to have to replace me.' "

While other, younger managers think about getting out of the game because of the toll that stress and pressure takes on them, Lasorda thrives.

"I'm sorry to see it happen, but it isn't going to happen to me," Lasorda said of the problems other managers face.

Since he became manager of the Dodgers in 1977, he has won six divi-sion titles, four pennants and two World Series. He has gone to the last day of the season with a chance to win the division on two occasions, and lost on the second-to-last day once (1991).

"I don't get heart attacks, I give them," Lasorda proudly announced. "I don't get ulcers, I give them. There's no way I'm taking off this uniform. I'm not quitting. They're going to have to cut it off me."

Dodgers loved Atlanta fans

Outfielder Brett Butler wished the Los Angeles fans would watch their counterparts in Atlanta during the final weeks of the pennant race.

"I love our fans," Butler said. "They are the best in baseball, but it's just a fact that they are different. they are more spoiled. It's like they've won so much, it's not that big of a deal. They get to the park in the second inning, they leave in the seventh . . . They don't act like the fans in Atlanta.

"The fans in Atlanta, because they have never seen anything like this before, are unbelievable," Butler continued. "They are awesome. They really charge everything up. This may give the Braves a little more of an edge than we get at home."

Pitcher Bob Ojeda agreed with Butler.

"We have great fans, but playing in Atlanta really made me realize what kind of excitement you can have. I loved it. You can just feel the energy (there). It's a lot different than in Los Angeles."

Butler wasn't quite so happy with the Atlanta fans when he got to his home in suburban Duluth, Ga., however, and found a police car sitting in his driveway. Some overzealous fans had thrown eggs and toilet paper at his house and in his trees.

▶Owner: Peter O'Malley

▶General Manager: Fred Claire

▶Ballpark:
Dodger Stadium
1000 Elysian Park Avenue, Los Angeles, California
213-224-1400
Capacity 56,000
Parking for 16,000 cars; $4
Wheelchair section and ramps

▶Team publications:
Dodger Magazine, Media Guide, 30th Anniversary of Dodger Stadium Commemorative Yearbook
800-762-1770

▶TV, radio broadcast stations:
KABC 790 AM, KWKW 1330 AM (Spanish), KTTV Channel 11

▶Camps and/or clinics:
Twenty clinics per year, 213-224-1435

▶Spring Training:
Holman Stadium
Dodgertown
Vero Beach, Florida
Capacity 6,500
407-569-4900

LOS ANGELES DODGERS 1991 Final Stats

Batting	AVG	SLG	OB	G	AB	R	H	TB	2B	3B	HR	RBI	BB	SO	SB	CS	E
Butler	.296	.343	.401	161	615	112	182	211	13	5	2	38	108	79	38	28	0
Harris	.287	.350	.349	145	429	59	123	150	16	1	3	38	37	32	12	3	20
Sharperson	.278	.375	.355	105	216	24	60	81	11	2	2	20	25	24	1	3	4
Samuel	.271	.389	.328	153	594	74	161	231	22	6	12	58	49	133	23	8	17
Hansen	.268	.393	.293	53	56	3	15	22	4	0	1	5	2	12	1	0	0
Strawberry	.265	.491	.361	139	505	86	134	248	22	4	28	99	75	125	10	8	5
Scioscia	.264	.391	.353	119	345	39	91	135	16	2	8	40	47	32	4	3	7
Murray	.260	.403	.321	153	576	69	150	232	23	1	19	96	55	74	10	3	7
Gwynn	.252	.410	.301	94	139	18	35	57	5	1	5	22	10	23	1	0	0
Daniels	.249	.397	.337	137	461	54	115	183	15	1	17	73	63	116	6	1	5
Carter	.246	.375	.323	101	248	22	61	93	14	0	6	26	22	26	2	2	5
Griffin	.243	.271	.286	109	350	27	85	95	6	2	0	27	22	49	5	4	22
Hamilton	.223	.298	.255	41	94	4	21	28	4	0	1	14	4	21	0	0	5
Webster	.222	.363	.296	94	171	21	38	62	8	5	2	19	18	52	0	1	2
Hernandez	.214	.286	.250	15	14	1	3	4	1	0	0	1	0	5	1	0	1
Javier	.205	.284	.268	121	176	21	36	50	5	3	1	11	16	36	7	1	3
Offerman	.195	.212	.345	52	113	10	22	24	2	0	0	3	25	32	3	2	10
Goodwin	.143	.143	.143	16	7	3	1	1	0	0	0	0	0	0	1	1	0
Karros	.071	.143	.133	14	14	0	1	2	1	0	0	1	1	6	0	0	0
Davis	.000	.000	.000	1	1	0	0	0	0	0	0	0	0	0	0	0	0
Lyons	.000	.000	.000	9	9	0	0	0	0	0	0	0	0	2	0	0	0
Smith	.000	.000	.000	5	3	1	0	0	0	0	0	0	0	2	0	0	0

Pitching	W-L	ERA	G	GS	CG	GF	Sho	SV	IP	H	R	ER	HR	BB	SO
Christopher	0-0	0.00	3	0	0	2	0	0	4	2	0	0	0	3	2
Wetteland	1-0	0.00	6	0	0	3	0	0	9	5	2	0	0	3	9
Cook	1-0	0.51	20	1	0	5	0	0	17.2	12	3	1	0	7	8
Wilson	0-0	2.61	19	0	0	5	0	2	20.2	14	7	6	1	9	14
Belcher	10-9	2.62	33	33	2	0	1	0	209.1	189	76	61	10	75	156
Morgan	14-10	2.78	34	33	5	1	1	1	236.1	197	85	73	12	61	140
McDowell	9-9	2.93	71	0	0	34	0	10	101.1	100	40	33	4	48	50
Gott	4-3	2.96	55	0	0	26	0	5	76	63	28	25	5	32	73
Howell	6-5	3.18	44	0	0	35	0	16	51	39	19	18	3	11	40
Ojeda	12-9	3.18	31	31	2	0	1	0	189.1	181	78	67	15	70	120
Martinez	17-13	3.27	33	33	6	0	4	0	220.1	190	89	80	18	69	150
Crews	2-3	3.43	60	0	0	17	0	6	76	75	30	29	7	19	53
Hershiser	7-2	3.46	21	21	0	0	0	0	112	112	43	43	3	32	73
Gross	10-11	3.58	46	10	0	16	0	3	115.2	123	55	46	10	50	95
Candelaria	1-1	3.74	59	0	0	10	0	2	33.2	31	16	14	3	11	38

1992 Preliminary Roster

Pitchers (17)

Pedro Astacio
John Candelaria
Tom Candiotti
Tim Crews
Jim Gott
Kevin Gross
Kip Gross
Orel Hershiser
Mike James
Pedro Martinez
Ramon Martinez
Jamie McAndrew
Roger McDowell
Bob Ojeda
Rudy Seanez
Zak Shinall
Steve Wilson

Catchers (4)

Bryan Baar
Carlos Hernandez
Mike Piazza
Mike Scioscia

Infielders (9)

Todd Benzinger
Jeff Hamilton
Dave Hansen
Lenny Harris
Eric Karros
Jose Offerman
Mike Sharperson
Greg Smith
Eric Young

Outfielders (9)

Billy Ashley
Brett Butler
Kal Daniels
Eric Davis
Tom Goodwin
Stan Javier
Raul Mondesi
Henry Rodriguez
Darryl Strawberry

Games played by position

	G	C	1B	2B	3B	SS	OF
Butler,B	161	0	0	0	0	0	161
Carter,G	101	68	10	0	0	0	0
Daniels,K	137	0	0	0	0	0	132
Davis,B	1	0	0	0	0	0	0
Goodwin,T	16	0	0	0	0	0	5
Griffin,A	109	0	0	0	0	109	0
Gwynn,C	94	0	0	0	0	0	41
Hamilton,J	41	0	0	0	33	1	0
Hansen,D	53	0	0	0	21	1	0
Harris,L	145	0	0	27	113	20	1
Hernandez,C	15	13	0	0	1	0	0
Javier,S	121	0	2	0	0	0	69
Karros,E	14	0	10	0	0	0	0
Lyons,B	9	6	0	0	0	0	0
Murray,E	153	0	149	0	1	0	0
Offerman,J	52	0	0	0	0	50	0
Samuel,J	153	0	0	152	0	0	0
Scioscia,M	119	115	0	0	0	0	0
Sharperson,M	105	0	10	5	68	16	0
Smith,G	5	0	0	1	0	0	0
Strawberry,D	139	0	0	0	0	0	136
Webster,M	94	0	1	0	0	0	65

Sick call: 1991 DL report

Player	Days on the DL
Alfredo Griffin	41*
Mike Sharperson	22
Orel Hershiser	51
Darryl Strawberry	15
Jeff Hamilton	78
Jay Howell	33
Mike Scioscia	5

On DL twice (not counting administrative transfers from one DL to another).

Minor League Report

Class AAA — Albuquerque finished 80-58, third in the first half and second in the second half in the PCL Southern Division. The Dukes had the best overall record in the league, the best home record (43-25) and the best road record (37-33) but failed to make the playoffs. Manager Kevin Kennedy resigned after the season. C Carlos Hernandez hit .345, but was 6 plate appearances shy of qualifying for league leaders. 1B Eric Karros hit .316 with 33 doubles, 8 triples, 22 HRs and 101 RBI (second in the PCL). 2B Jose Munoz hit .326. OF Tom Goodwin hit .273 with 48 SBs. RHP Jeff Hartsock (12-6, 3.80) led the league with 123 strikeouts. RHPs John Wetteland and Mike Christopher combined for 36 saves. The Dukes set a franchise record with a .976 fielding percentage. . . . **Class AA** — San Antonio finished 61-75, third in the first half and fourth in the second half in the Texas League Western Division. Top hitters were 2B Eric Young (.280 with 71 SBs), OF Brett Magnusson (.265-11-66) and 1B Brian Traxler (.256-7-61). RHP Dennis Springer (10-10, 4.43) led the league with 138 strikeouts. RHP Pedro Martinez was 7-5 with a 1.76 ERA. . . . **Class A** — Bakersfield finished 85-51, first in the first half and second in the second half in the California League Southern Division. The Dodgers lost to High Desert in the playoffs. C Mike Piazza hit .277 with 29 HRs and 80 RBI. 2B Domingo Mota hit .275 with 37 SBs. OF Garey OK Ingram hit .297 with 61 RBI and 30 SBs. Top pitchers were RHP Greg Hansell (14-5, 2.87), LHP Mark Mimbs (12-6, 2.22, 164 strikeouts) and RHP Terry McFarlin (14-6, 2.66). . . . Vero Beach finished 79-52, first in the first half and third in the second half in the Florida State League Eastern Division. 1B John Deutsch hit .300 with 24 doubles, 12 HRs and 66 RBI. 2B Matt Howard hit .262 with 50 SBs. OF Marc Griffin hit .239 with 42 SBs. LHP Michael Mimbs (12-4, 2.67) had 132 strikeouts. RHP Sean Snedeker was 7-3 with a 2.52 ERA and a perfect game against St. Lucie Aug. 28. . . . Yakima finished 44-32, first in the Northwest League Northern Division. The Bears lost to Boise in the playoffs. 1B Murph Proctor hit .309 with 25 doubles and 61 RBI. OF Vernon Spearman hit .290 with 56 SBs. RHP David Baumann was 8-3 with a 5.23 ERA. . . . Great Falls finished 46-24, first in the Pioneer League Northern Division. The Dodgers lost to Salt Lake in the playoffs. Top hitters were OF Javier Puchales (.360 in 40 games), INF Willis Otanez (.288-6-39) and C Jay Kirkpatrick (.321). and INF Randall Graves (.303). RHP Chris Sinacori was 6-1 with a 1.57 ERA and 7 saves.

Tops in the Organization

BATTING LEADERS	Club	Avg.	G	AB	R	H	HR	RBI
Carlos Hernandez	Abq	.345	95	345	60	119	8	44
Jose Munoz	Abq	.324	132	512	74	166	0	78
Chris Morrow	San	.318	109	362	42	115	5	37
Eric Karros	Abq	.316	132	488	88	154	22	101
John Deutsch	Vrb	.300	123	433	59	130	12	66

HOME RUNS		
Mike Piazza	Bak	29
Eric Karros	Abq	22
Jerry Brooks	Abq	13
Brock McMurray	Vrb	12
John Deutsch	Vrb	12

RBI		
Eric Karros	Abq	101
Jerry Brooks	Abq	82
Mike Piazza	Bak	80
Jose Munoz	Abq	78
Several players tied		69

STOLEN BASES		
Eric Young	Abq	71
Matt Howard	Vrb	50
Tom Goodwin	Abq	48
Marc Griffin	Vrb	42
Domingo Mota	Bak	37

WINS		
Pedro Martinez	Abq	18
Greg Hansell	Bak	14
Terric McFarlin	Bak	14
Several players tied		12

SAVES		
John Wetteland	Abq	20
Mike Christopher	Abq	16
Gordon Tipton	Bak	14
Ray Calhoun	San	13
Brian Piotrowicz	Bak	11

STRIKEOUTS		
Pedro Martinez	Abq	192
Mark Mimbs	Bak	164
Dennis Springer	San	138
Michael Mimbs	Vrb	132
Greg Hansell	Bak	132

PITCHING LEADERS	Club	W-L	ERA	IP	H	BB	SO
William Wengert	Vrb	7-6	2.06	127	100	42	114
Mark Mimbs	Bak	12-6	2.22	170	134	59	164
Pedro Martinez	Abq	18-8	2.29	177	126	66	192
Terric McFarlin	Bak	14-6	2.66	152	139	56	128
Michael Mimbs	Vrb	12-4	2.67	142	124	70	132

Los Angeles (1958-1991), incl. Brooklyn (1890-1957)

Runs: Most, career, all-time

1338	Pee Wee Reese, 1940-1958
1255	Zack Wheat, 1909-1926
1199	Duke Snider, 1947-1962
1163	Jim Gilliam, 1953-1966
1088	Gil Hodges, 1943-1961
1004	Willie Davis, 1960-1973 (6)

Hits: Most, career, all-time

2804	Zack Wheat, 1909-1926
2170	Pee Wee Reese, 1940-1958
2091	Willie Davis, 1960-1973
1995	Duke Snider, 1947-1962
1968	Steve Garvey, 1969-1982

2B: Most, career, all-time

464	Zack Wheat, 1909-1926
343	Duke Snider, 1947-1962
333	Steve Garvey, 1969-1982
330	Pee Wee Reese, 1940-1958
324	Carl Furillo, 1946-1960

3B: Most, career, all-time

171	Zack Wheat, 1909-1926
110	Willie Davis, 1960-1973
97	Hy Myers, 1909-1922
87	Jake Daubert, 1910-1918
82	John Hummel, 1905-1915
82	Duke Snider, 1947-1962

HR: Most, career, all-time

389	Duke Snider, 1947-1962
361	Gil Hodges, 1943-1961
242	Roy Campanella, 1948-1957
228	Ron Cey, 1971-1982
211	Steve Garvey, 1969-1982

RBI: Most, career, all-time

1271	Duke Snider, 1947-1962
1254	Gil Hodges, 1943-1961
1210	Zack Wheat, 1909-1926
1058	Carl Furillo, 1946-1960
992	Steve Garvey, 1969-1982

SB: Most, career, all-time

490	Maury Wills, 1959-1972
418	Davey Lopes, 1972-1981
335	Willie Davis, 1960-1973
298	Tom Daly, 1890-1901
290	STEVE SAX, 1981-1988

BB: Most, career, all-time

1210	Pee Wee Reese, 1940-1958
1036	Jim Gilliam, 1953-1966
925	Gil Hodges, 1943-1961
893	Duke Snider, 1947-1962

765	Ron Cey, 1971-1982

BA: Highest, career, all-time

.352	Willie Keeler, 1893-1902
.339	Babe Herman, 1926-1945
.337	Jack Fournier, 1923-1926
.317	Zack Wheat, 1909-1926
.315	Babe Phelps, 1935-1941
.315	Manny Mota, 1969-1982 (6)

Slug avg: Highest, career, all-time

.557	Babe Herman, 1926-1945
.553	Duke Snider, 1947-1962
.552	Jack Fournier, 1923-1926
.528	Reggie Smith, 1976-1981
.512	PEDRO GUERRERO, 1978-1988

Games started: Most, career, all-time

533	Don Sutton, 1966-1988
465	Don Drysdale, 1956-1969
335	Claude Osteen, 1965-1973
332	Brickyard Kennedy, 1892-1901
326	Dazzy Vance, 1922-1935

Saves: Most, career, all-time

125	Jim Brewer, 1964-1975
101	Ron Perranoski, 1961-1972
83	Clem Labine, 1950-1960
81	JAY HOWELL, 1988-1991
64	Tom Niedenfuer, 1981-1987

Shutouts: Most, career, all-time

52	Don Sutton, 1966-1988
49	Don Drysdale, 1956-1969
40	Sandy Koufax, 1955-1966
38	Nap Rucker, 1907-1916
34	Claude Osteen, 1965-1973

Wins: Most, career, all-time

233	Don Sutton, 1966-1988
209	Don Drysdale, 1956-1969
190	Dazzy Vance, 1922-1935
177	Brickyard Kennedy, 1892-1901
165	Sandy Koufax, 1955-1966

K: Most, career, all-time

2696	Don Sutton, 1966-1988
2486	Don Drysdale, 1956-1969
2396	Sandy Koufax, 1955-1966
1918	Dazzy Vance, 1922-1935
1759	FERNANDO VALENZUELA, 1980-1990

Win pct: Highest, career, all-time

.715	Preacher Roe, 1948-1954
.674	Tommy John, 1972-1978
.674	Jim Hughes, 1899-1902
.658	Billy Loes, 1950-1956
.655	Sandy Koufax, 1955-1966

ERA: Lowest, career, all-time

2.31	Jeff Pfeffer, 1913-1921
2.42	Nap Rucker, 1907-1916
2.56	Ron Perranoski, 1961-1972
2.58	Rube Marquard, 1915-1920
2.62	Jim Brewer, 1964-1975

Runs: Most, season

148	Hub Collins, 1890
143	Babe Herman, 1930
140	Mike Griffin, 1895
140	Willie Keeler, 1899
136	Mike Griffin, 1897
130	Maury Wills, 1962 (10)

Hits: Most, season

241	Babe Herman, 1930
230	Tommy Davis, 1962
221	Zack Wheat, 1925
219	Lefty O'Doul, 1932
217	Babe Herman, 1929

2B: Most, season

52	Johnny Frederick, 1929
48	Babe Herman, 1930
47	Wes Parker, 1970
44	Johnny Frederick, 1930
43	Augie Galan, 1944
43	Babe Herman, 1931
43	STEVE SAX, 1986

3B: Most, season

26	George Treadway, 1894
22	Hy Myers, 1920
20	Dan Brouthers, 1892
20	Tommy Corcoran, 1894
19	Jimmy Sheckard, 1901
16	Willie Davis, 1970 (12)

HR: Most, season

43	Duke Snider, 1956
42	Gil Hodges, 1954
42	Duke Snider, 1953
42	Duke Snider, 1955
41	Roy Campanella, 1953
33	Steve Garvey, 1977 (11)
33	PEDRO GUERRERO, 1985 (11)

RBI: Most, season

153	Tommy Davis, 1962
142	Roy Campanella, 1953

136	Duke Snider, 1955
130	Jack Fournier, 1925
130	Babe Herman, 1930
130	Gil Hodges, 1954
130	Duke Snider, 1954

SB: Most, season

104	Maury Wills, 1962
94	Maury Wills, 1965
88	Monte Ward, 1892
85	Hub Collins, 1890
77	Davey Lopes, 1975

BB: Most, season

148	Eddie Stanky, 1945
137	Eddie Stanky, 1946
119	Dolph Camilli, 1938
116	Pee Wee Reese, 1949
114	Augie Galan, 1945
110	Jim Wynn, 1975

BA: Highest, season

.393	Babe Herman, 1930
.381	Babe Herman, 1929
.379	Willie Keeler, 1899
.375	Zack Wheat, 1924
.368	Lefty O'Doul, 1932
.346	Tommy Davis, 1962

Slug avg: Highest, season

.678	Babe Herman, 1930
.647	Duke Snider, 1954
.628	Duke Snider, 1955
.627	Duke Snider, 1953
.612	Babe Herman, 1929
.577	PEDRO GUERRERO, 1985

Games started: Most, season

44	George Haddock, 1892
44	Brickyard Kennedy, 1893
44	Adonis Terry, 1890
43	Tom Lovett, 1891
42	Don Drysdale, 1963
42	Don Drysdale, 1965
42	Ed Stein, 1892

Saves: Most, season

28	JAY HOWELL, 1989
24	Jim Brewer, 1970
24	Jim Hughes, 1954
22	Jim Brewer, 1971
22	CHARLIE HOUGH, 1977

Shutouts: Most, season

11	Sandy Koufax, 1963
9	Don Sutton, 1972
8	TIM BELCHER, 1989
8	Don Drysdale, 1968
8	OREL HERSHISER, 1988
8	Sandy Koufax, 1965
8	FERNANDO VALENZUELA, 1981

Wins: Most, season

30	Tom Lovett, 1890
29	George Haddock, 1892
28	Jim Hughes, 1899
28	Joe McGinnity, 1900
28	Dazzy Vance, 1924
25	Don Drysdale, 1962

K: Most, season

382	Sandy Koufax, 1965
317	Sandy Koufax, 1966
306	Sandy Koufax, 1963
269	Sandy Koufax, 1961
262	Dazzy Vance, 1924
251	Don Drysdale, 1963

Win pct: Highest, season

.880	Preacher Roe, 1951
.864	OREL HERSHISER, 1985
.833	Sandy Koufax, 1963
.824	Jim Hughes, 1899
.824	Dazzy Vance, 1924

ERA: Lowest, season

1.58	Rube Marquard, 1916
1.68	Ned Garvin, 1904
1.73	Sandy Koufax, 1966
1.74	Sandy Koufax, 1964
1.87	Kaiser Wilhelm, 1908
2.03	OREL HERSHISER, 1985

Most pinch-hit homers, season

6	Johnny Frederick, 1932
5	Lee Lacy, 1978

Most pinch-hit, homers, career

8	Johnny Frederick, 1929-1934
8	Lee Lacy, 1972-78

Most consecutive games, batting safely

31	Willie Davis, 1969

Most consecutive scoreless innings

59	Orel Hershiser, 1988

No hit games

Tom Lovett, Bro vs NY NL, 4-0; June 22, 1891.

Mal Eason, Bro at StL NL, 2-0; July 20, 1906.

Harry McIntyre, Bro vs Pit NL, 0-1; August 1, 1906 (lost on 4 hits in 13 innings after allowing the first hit in the 11th).

Nap Rucker, Bro vs Bos NL, 6-0; September 5, 1908 (2nd game).

Dazzy Vance, Bro vs Phi NL, 10-1; September 13, 1925 (1st game).

Tex Carleton, Bro at Cin NL, 3-0; April 30, 1940.

Ed Head, Bro vs Bos NL, 5-0; April 23, 1946.

Rex Barney, Bro at NY NL, 2-0; September 9, 1948.

Carl Erskine, Bro vs Chi NL, 5-0; June 19, 1952.

Carl Erskine, Bro vs NY NL, 3-0; May 12, 1956.

Sal Maglie, Bro vs Phi NL, 5-0; September 25, 1956.

Sandy Koufax, LA vs NY NL, 5-0; June 30, 1962.

Sandy Koufax, LA vs SF NL, 8-0; May 11, 1963.

Sandy Koufax, LA at Phi NL, 3-0; June 4, 1964.

Sandy Koufax, LA vs Chi NL, 1-0; September 9, 1965 (perfect game).

Bill Singer, LA vs Phi NL, 5-0; July 20, 1970.

Jerry Reuss, LA at SF NL, 8-0; June 27, 1980.

Fernando Valenzuela, LA vs StL NL, 6-0; June 29, 1990.

Ed Stein, six innings, rain, Bro vs Chi NL, 6-0; June 2, 1894.

Fred Frankhouse, seven and two-thirds innings, rain, Bro vs Cin NL, 5-0; August 27, 1937.

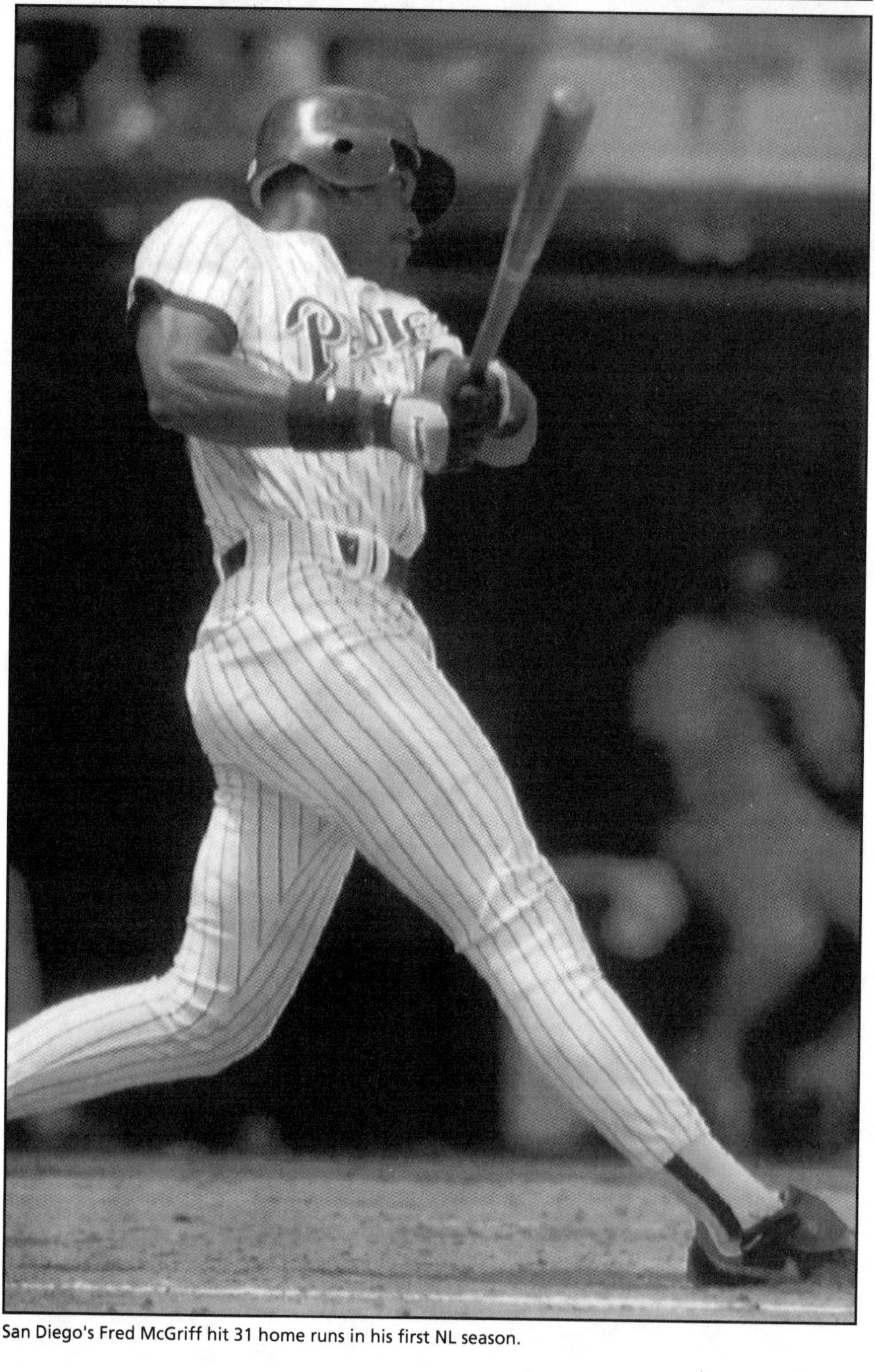

San Diego's Fred McGriff hit 31 home runs in his first NL season.

Who's on third?

You couldn't tell the 1991 San Diego Padres without a scorecard—and maybe not even with one. The Padres used a club-record 48 players last year, including 18 who started the season at Class AAA Las Vegas.

There were 22 different pitchers, seven third basemen and six second basemen.

Somehow, manager Greg Riddoch juggled all the combinations into a winning season. The Padres were 84-78, their third-best record ever.

The Padres got great mileage out of their blockbuster trade with Toronto. First baseman Fred McGriff hit .278 with 31 home runs and 106 RBI, and should be even better this season after a year around the league. The Padres had no other slugger to protect him in the lineup last year—he walked 105 times.

Shortstop Tony Fernandez hit .272 with 27 doubles and 23 stolen bases. He had surgery to correct ligament damage in his right thumb after the season.

Bip Roberts divided his time between second base and outfield and hit .281 as a leadoff hitter.

Center fielder Darrin Jackson came alive, hitting .262 with 21 HRs. Only Atlanta's Ron Gant hit more among National League center fielders.

And, of course, right fielder Tony Gwynn had another typical year, free of the sniping and backbiting that plagued him in 1990. He hit .317 in 134 games and led the league much of the year. However, he hurt his knee and missed the final 21 games, then underwent arthroscopic surgery.

There were disappointments as well. Outfielder Shawn Abner, the first player taken in the 1984 draft by the New York Mets, hit .165 and was traded to the California Angels for Jack Howell. Howell didn't do much better, hitting .206 in 58 games.

Outfielder Jerald Clark hit just .228 with 10 HRs. Catcher Benito Santiago hit .267 with 17 HRs and a career-high 87 RBI, but demanded a trade and was booed by San Diego fans.

On the mound, left-hander Bruce Hurst quietly put together a solid year (15-8, 3.29). The pitching staff has a solid nucleus for the future with Andy Benes (15-11, 3.03), Greg Harris (9-5, 2.23) and Hurst.

Craig Lefferts led the bullpen with 23 saves, but the search for a top-gun closer was the No. 1 priority after the season. The Padres also had holes at second and third base.

—Bill Koenig

Padres 1992 preview

If the San Diego Padres can find a third baseman . . . If they can find a second baseman . . . If they can find a slugger to hit behind Fred McGriff . . .

Those are the points to ponder for the Padres, who are coming off their third-best record ever (84-78). Of course, they'll need a catcher, too, if Santiago is traded.

The trade that brought first baseman McGriff (.278-31-106) and shortstop Tony Fernandez (.272) to San Diego from Toronto was beneficial to both teams. However, McGriff walked 105 times and Fernandez is coming off thumb surgery.

Outfielder Tony Gwynn, who missed 21 games after knee surgery last year, always will hit. And the Padres are hoping center fielder Darrin Jackson follows up on his solid year.

The starting rotation is solid with Bruce Hurst, Andy Benes and Greg Harris, and Randy Myers provides help in the bullpen.

1992 prophecy: Padres

▶The Padres will struggle early, become mathematically eliminated, then become the hottest team in baseball in the second half of September.

▶Fred McGriff will hit .000 with an on-base percentage of 1.000 after drawing a walk in every at-bat.

—*John Hunt*

Larry Andersen: Comic relief

By Rob Rains

There is nothing outwardly funny about Larry Andersen's career. But Andersen is one of the funniest men in baseball.

The San Diego Padres' reliever, who has been pitching professionally since 1971 but never has become a star, has developed a reputation of taking ordinary events and turning them into one-liners.

Andersen said there is so much idle time in baseball, particularly for a reliever, that he sits in the bullpen and thinks about clever sayings. He said if he didn't use humor as his release, "I'd be a basket case by the seventh inning.

"And I'm close enough to that without it," Andersen said.

Andersen thinks his long tenure in the minor leagues—from 1971 through 1981 with the exception of 22 games in Cleveland scattered over three seasons—helped shape his personality.

He knew during those seasons that if he couldn't enjoy the game and the people, he was in the wrong business.

"In the Houston bullpen one time, Juan Agosto was struggling and he said he just couldn't put three and two together," Andersen said. "That made me think, why does it always have to be two and two that makes things work? What's wrong with it being three and two?

"I'm more concerned with who decided this thing. Why couldn't three and

three do it?

"Why does it always have to rain cats and dogs? How about yaks and wilde-beests? We got into a big discussion last year in Philadelphia about how and why flies land on the ceiling. Do they fly upside down or do they flip over just before they land?"

Andersen also would like an explanation on why the plate is shaped the way it is. "Why isn't it just a square?" he asked.

"The bottom line is having fun. I'm a firm believer in having fun. If I can say something stupid or do something stupid and a couple of people laugh, then that's good.

"I don't know how my mind works. I don't know if it does work."

Andersen does have a philosophy on life, however: "All I want is less to do, more time to do it in and to get paid more for not getting it done . . . which is pretty much the way this season started."

Larry asks:

▶How do you know when you run out of invisible ink?

▶Why does sour cream have an expiration date?

▶Why is it when you send something by ship it's cargo and when you send it by car it's shipment?

▶Why do you drive on the parkway and park on the driveway?

Guess who's back?

Surprise! Manager Greg Riddoch was rehired by the Padres after being under the gun all last year.

"How many times was I fired (last) year?" he asked rhetorically. "I wasn't going to make it to the All-Star break. But someone was thoughtful enough to give me some fuel. The way I am, if someone says I can't do something, that fuels the tank to make me say I can do it."

Riddoch must have felt he had a tiger in his tank, with all of the sniping the past couple of seasons. In 1990, shortstop Garry Templeton said Riddoch was the worst guy he met in 15 years in the business. First baseman Jack Clark merely called him "a snake."

But "other people's expectations of you are unimportant," Riddoch said. "It's what I expect of myself that counts. That (criticism) was a pretty nice challenge. I used to say to myself, 'Let's see who's standing when the smoke clears.'"

The Padres were standing, all right. Only the Braves had a better record in the NL West the second half. Riddoch said he was happy with San Diego's third-place finish, but "never satisfied."

The front office was satisfied enough to give the skipper a one-year contract for an estimated $220,000.

Padres winter league news

▶Winter leagues: San Diego sent four players to the Mayaguez Indians of the Puerto Rican league to fine-tune their skills for the 1992 season. LHP Derrick Lilliquist (4-6, 5.38 ERA at Class AAA Las Vegas) is trying to work his way back to the majors. Lilliquist started 60 games between Atlanta and San Diego in 1989-90. . . . RHP Jim Lewis (6-3, 3.38 at Las Vegas) and RHP Brian Wood (3-8, 5.48 at Las Vegas) also competed in Puerto Rico to make a run at San Diego's roster in spring training. . . . IF Paul Faries, who hit .177 in 57 games with San Diego this season, worked on his hitting. . . . OF Will Taylor, who stole 62 bases at Las Vegas, joined Faries, Lewis and Lilliquist at Mayaguez. . . . OF Vince Harris (48 steals at Class AA Wichita) played for Culiacan in the Mexican winter league. . . . 1B Guillermo Velasquez (.295-21-100 at Wichita) played in his hometown of Mexicali. . . . RHP Pedro A. Martinez (11-10, 5.23 ERA at Wichita) played at home in the Dominican Republic for Tigres (Tigers) de Licey, the same team that has RHP Pedro J. Martinez, the brother of Los Angeles RHP Ramon Martinez.
▶Winter leagues roster: Roberto Arredondo, 1B, Aguilas Cibaeƒna (Eagles), D.R.; Paul Faries, IF,

Mayaguez Indians, Puerto Rico; Juan Guerrero, 3B, Tigres (Tigers) de Licey, D.R.; Vince Harris, OF, Culiacan Tomateros (Tomato growers), Mexico; Jim Lewis, RHP, Mayaguez Indians, Puerto Rico; Derrick Lilliquist, LHP, Mayaguez Indians, Puerto Rico; Pedro A. Martinez, LHP, Tigres (Tigers) de Licey, D.R.; Will Taylor, OF, Mayaguez Indians, Puerto Rico; Guillermo Velasquez, 1B, Mexicali Aguila (Eagle), Mexico; Brian Wood, RHP, Arecibo Wolves, Puerto Rico.

Team directory

▶Owner: San Diego Padres Baseball Partnership

▶General Manager: Joe McIlvaine

▶Ballpark:
San Diego Jack Murphy Stadium
9449 Friars Road, San Diego, California
619-283-4494
Capacity 59,254
Parking for 18,751 cars; $4
Public transportation available
Wheelchair sections, ramps, AAA in parking lot, pre-registration for telephone paging, ATM machines

▶Team publications:
Padre Magazine, Fanfare (for season ticket holders)
619-283-4494

▶TV, radio broadcast stations:
KFMB 760 AM, XEXX AM, KUSI Channel 51, Cox Cable

▶Spring Training:
Desert Sun Stadium
Yuma, Arizona
Capacity 7,000
602-726-6040

SAN DIEGO PADRES 1991 Final Stats

Batting	AVG	SLG	OB	G	AB	R	H	TB	2B	3B	HR	RBI	BB	SO	SB	CS	E
Gwynn	.317	.432	.355	134	530	69	168	229	27	11	4	62	34	19	8	8	3
Stephenson	.286	.286	.444	11	7	0	2	2	0	0	0	0	2	3	0	0	0
Roberts	.281	.347	.342	117	424	66	119	147	13	3	3	32	37	71	26	11	10
McGriff	.278	.494	.396	153	528	84	147	261	19	1	31	106	105	135	4	1	14
Shipley	.275	.341	.298	37	91	6	25	31	3	0	1	6	2	14	0	1	7
Fernandez	.272	.360	.337	145	558	81	152	201	27	5	4	38	55	74	23	9	20
Bilardello	.269	.423	.345	15	26	4	7	11	2	1	0	5	3	4	0	0	0
Santiago	.267	.403	.296	152	580	60	155	234	22	3	17	87	23	114	8	10	14
Jackson	.262	.476	.315	122	359	51	94	171	12	1	21	49	27	66	5	3	2
Howard	.249	.356	.309	106	281	30	70	100	12	3	4	22	24	57	10	7	1
Azocar	.246	.281	.267	38	57	5	14	16	2	0	0	9	1	9	2	0	2
Ward	.243	.402	.308	44	107	13	26	43	7	2	2	8	9	27	1	4	1
Clark	.228	.352	.295	118	369	26	84	130	16	0	10	47	31	90	2	1	2
Mota	.222	.222	.282	17	36	4	8	8	0	0	0	2	2	7	0	0	3
Teufel	.217	.370	.319	117	341	41	74	126	16	0	12	44	51	77	9	3	9
Coolbaugh	.217	.306	.294	60	180	12	39	55	8	1	2	15	19	45	0	3	1
Howell	.206	.350	.287	58	160	24	33	56	3	1	6	16	18	33	0	0	2
Vatcher	.200	.200	.333	17	20	3	4	4	0	0	0	2	4	6	1	0	1
Lampkin	.190	.276	.230	38	58	4	11	16	3	1	0	3	3	9	0	0	0
Barrett	.188	.438	.235	12	16	1	3	7	1	0	1	3	0	3	0	0	0
Faries	.177	.215	.262	57	130	13	23	28	3	1	0	7	14	21	3	1	2
Abner	.165	.243	.218	53	115	15	19	28	4	1	1	5	7	25	0	0	0
Presley	.136	.186	.200	20	59	3	8	11	0	0	1	5	4	16	0	1	3
Dorsett	.083	.083	.083	11	12	0	1	1	0	0	0	1	0	3	0	0	0
Aldrete	.000	.000	.167	12	15	2	0	0	0	0	0	1	3	4	0	1	0

Pitching	W-L	ERA	G	GS	CG	GF	Sho	SV	IP	H	R	ER	HR	BB	SO
Hernandez	0-0	0.00	9	0	0	7	0	2	14.1	8	1	0	0	5	9
Harris	9-5	2.23	20	20	3	0	2	0	133	116	42	33	16	27	95
Andersen	3-4	2.30	38	0	0	24	0	13	47	39	13	12	0	13	40
Maddux	7-2	2.46	64	1	0	27	0	5	98.2	78	30	27	4	27	57
Benes	15-11	3.03	33	33	4	0	1	0	223	194	76	75	23	59	167
Costello	1-0	3.09	27	0	0	6	0	0	35	37	15	12	2	17	24
Rodriguez	3-1	3.26	64	1	0	19	0	0	80	66	31	29	8	44	40
Melendez	8-5	3.27	31	9	0	10	0	3	93.2	77	35	34	11	24	60
Hurst	15-8	3.29	31	31	4	0	0	0	221.2	201	89	81	17	59	141
Rasmussen	6-13	3.74	24	24	1	0	1	0	146.2	155	74	61	12	49	75
Clements	1-0	3.77	12	0	0	4	0	0	14.1	13	8	6	0	9	8
Lefferts	1-6	3.91	54	0	0	40	0	23	69	74	35	30	5	14	48
Lewis	0-0	4.15	12	0	0	2	0	0	13	14	7	6	2	11	10
Peterson	3-4	4.45	13	11	0	0	0	0	54.2	50	33	27	10	28	37
Bones	4-6	4.83	11	11	0	0	0	0	54	57	33	29	3	18	31
Whitson	4-6	5.03	13	12	2	0	0	0	78.2	93	47	44	13	17	40
Hammaker	0-1	5.79	1	1	0	0	0	0	4.2	8	7	3	0	3	1
Rosenberg	1-1	6.94	10	0	0	5	0	0	11.2	11	9	9	3	5	6
Gardner	0-1	7.08	14	0	0	2	0	1	20.1	27	16	16	1	12	9
Lilliquist	0-2	8.79	6	2	0	1	0	0	14.1	25	14	14	3	4	7
Jackson	0-0	9.00	1	0	0	1	0	0	2	3	2	2	0	2	0
Scott	0-0	9.00	2	0	0	1	0	0	1	2	1	1	0	0	1
Nolte	3-2	11.05	6	6	0	0	0	0	22	37	27	27	6	10	15

1992 Preliminary Roster

Pitchers (18)
Larry Andersen
Andy Benes
Ricky Bones
Doug Brocail
Greg Harris
Jeremy Hernandez
Bruce Hurst
Craig Lefferts
Jim Lewis
Mike Linskey
Mike Maddux
Jose Melendez
Randy Myers
Adam Peterson

Rich Rodriguez
Frank Seminara
Rafael Valdez
Ed Whitson
Catchers (3)
Dann Bilardello
Tom Lampkin
Benito Santiago
Infielders (12)
Paul Faries
Tony Fernandez
Jeff Gardner
Ray Holbert
Luis Lopez

Fred McGriff
Tom Redington
Craig Shipley
Dave Staton
Phil Stephenson
Jose Valentin
Guillermo Velasquez
Outfielders (7)
Oscar Azocar
Jerald Clark
Tony Gwynn
Thomas Howard
Darrin Jackson
Will Taylor
Jim Vatcher

Games Played by position

	G	C	1B	2B	3B	SS	OF
Abner,S	53	0	0	0	0	0	39
Aldrete,M	12	0	0	0	0	0	5
Azocar,O	38	0	1	0	0	0	13
Barrett,M	12	0	0	2	2	0	0
Bilardello,D	15	13	0	0	0	0	0
Clark,Je	118	0	16	0	0	0	96
Coolbaugh,S	60	0	0	0	54	0	0
Dorsett,B	11	0	2	0	0	0	0
Faries,P	57	0	0	36	12	8	0
Fernandez,T	145	0	0	0	0	145	0
Gwynn,T	134	0	0	0	0	0	134
Howard,T	106	0	0	0	0	0	86
Howell,J	58	0	0	0	54	0	0
Jackson,Dj	122	0	0	0	0	0	98
Lampkin,T	38	11	0	0	0	0	0
McGriff,F	153	0	153	0	0	0	0
Mota,A	17	0	0	13	0	3	0
Presley,J	20	0	0	0	16	0	0
Roberts,B	117	0	0	68	0	0	46
Santiago,B	152	151	0	0	0	0	1
Shipley,C	37	0	0	14	0	19	0
Stephenson,P	11	0	0	0	0	0	0
Teufel,T	117	0	6	66	53	0	0
Vatcher,J	17	0	0	0	0	0	11

Sick call: 1991 DL report

Player	Days on the DL
Atlee Hammaker	143*
Dennis Rasmussen	47
Phil Stephenson	153*
G.W. Harris	72
Pat Clements	131
Larry Andersen	41*
Jerald Clark	19
Marty Barrett	33
Paul Faries	25
Ed Whitson	115*
Bip Roberts	30

* On DL twice (not counting administrative transfers from one DL to another).

Minor League Report

Class AAA — Las Vegas finished 65-75, fourth in the first half and fifth in the second half in the PCL Southern Division. C Dan Walters hit .317 in 96 games. OF Jim Vatcher hit .266 with 17 HRs and 67 RBI. OF Will Taylor hit .257 with 62 SBs. INFs Jose Mota and Kevin Higgins each hit .289. RHP A.J. Sager was 7-5 with a 4.71 ERA. . . . **Class AA** — Wichita finished 71-64, second in the first half and third in the second half in the Texas League Western Division. 1B Guillermo Velasquez (.295-21-100) set a Wichita Double-A record for RBI. He had a 15-game streak with at least one RBI. RHP Frank Seminara (15-10, 3.38) led the league in victories. RHP Kerry Knox had the league's only no-hitter, May 17 against Tulsa. RHP Doug Brocail (10-7, 3.87) had three consecutive shutouts. The Wranglers were hurt by a 10-22 record against El Paso. . . . **Class A** — High Desert finished 73-63, third in the first half and first in the second half in the California League Southern Division. The Mavericks beat Bakersfield and Stockton to win the playoffs and league championship. OF Matt Mieske (.341-15-119) won the batting title and was named league MVP. 1B Jay Gainer led the league with 32 HRs and 120 RBI. OF J.D. Noland had a league-high 81 SBs. RHP Ed Zinter had 18 saves. High Desert drew a California League record 204,638 fans during the regular season. . . . Waterloo finished 75-63, fifth in the first half and second in the second half in the Midwest League Southern Division. OF Darius Gash hit .307 with 27 doubles, 60 RBI and 31 SBs. He led the league with 154 hits. Other top hitters were 1B Roberto Arredondo (.313), OF Tookie Spann (.312) and SS Brent Bish (.294). LHP Lance Painter (14-8, 2.30) was second in the league in ERA and strikeouts (201). RHP Linty Ingram was 8-4 and third with a 2.41 ERA. The Diamonds had 17 shutouts. . . . Charleston (S.C.) finished 68-73, fifth in the first half and fourth in the second half in the South Atlantic League Southern Division. 2B Billy Hall hit .301 in 72 games. OF Ray McDavid (.247) had 60 SBs. OF Brian Beck (.202) had 14 HRs and 56 RBI. LHP Jeff Brown (13-8, 2.45) had 45 walks and 152 strikeouts. Former first-round pick LHP Robbie Beckett (2-14, 8.23) had 117 walks and 96 strikeouts in 109 innings. RHP Bill Johnson led the league with 26 WPs. . . . Spokane finished 24-52, fourth in the Northwest League Northern Division. OF David Lebak

just missed hitting .300 (he finished .2994) after batting .356 the final month.OF Shawn Robertson hit .284 with 38 RBI. LHP Chris Benhardt was 3-3 with a 3.73 ERA.

Tops in the Organization

BATTING LEADERS

	Club	Avg.	G	AB	R	H	HR	RBI
Matt Mieske	Hds	.341	133	492	108	168	15	119
Darius Gash	Wlo	.307	130	501	84	154	5	60
Brent Bish	Wlo	.297	119	394	65	117	2	44
Oscar Azocar	Lvg	.296	107	361	51	107	7	50
Guillermo Velasquez	Wch	.295	130	501	72	148	21	100

HOME RUNS

Jay Gainer	Hds	32
Dave Staton	Lvg	24
Guillermo Velasquez	Wch	21
Jose Valentin	Wch	17
Jim Vatcher	Lvg	17

WINS

Frank Seminara	Wch	15
Lance Painter	Wlo	14
Tim Worrell	Hds	13
Linty Ingram	Wlo	13
Jeff Brown	CSc	13

RBI

Jay Gainer	Hds	120
Matt Mieske	Hds	119
Guillermo Velasquez	Wch	100
Dave Staton	Lvg	74
Several players tied		68

SAVES

Mark Ettles	Wlo	20
Ed Zinter	Hds	18
Rick Davis	Wch	13
Jeremy Hernandez	Lvg	13
Scott Fredrickson	Hds	13

STOLEN BASES

J.D. Noland	Hds	81
Will Taylor	Lvg	62
Ray McDavid	CSc	60
Vince Harris	Wch	48
Darrell Sherman	Wch	43

STRIKEOUTS

Lance Painter	Wlo	201
Tim Worrell	Hds	153
Jeff Brown	CSc	152
Joe Waldron	CSc	141
Linty Ingram	Wlo	136

PITCHING LEADERS

	Club	W-L	ERA	IP	H	BB	SO
Lance Painter	Wlo	14-8	2.30	200	162	57	201
Jeff Brown	CSc	13-8	2.45	165	134	45	152
Linty Ingram	Wlo	13-10	2.78	184	170	38	136
Scott Sanders	Hds	12-6	3.17	159	131	78	111
Frank Seminara	Wch	15-10	3.38	176	173	68	107

Runs: Most, career, all-time

765	TONY GWYNN, 1982-1991	
599	DAVE WINFIELD, 1973-1980	
484	Gene Richards, 1977-1983	
442	Nate Colbert, 1969-1974	
430	GARRY TEMPLETON, 1982-1991	

Hits: Most, career, all-time

1699	TONY GWYNN, 1982-1991
1135	GARRY TEMPLETON, 1982-1991
1134	DAVE WINFIELD, 1973-1980
994	Gene Richards, 1977-1983
817	TERRY KENNEDY, 1981-1986

2B: Most, career, all-time

248	TONY GWYNN, 1982-1991
195	GARRY TEMPLETON, 1982-1991
179	DAVE WINFIELD, 1973-1980
158	TERRY KENNEDY, 1981-1986
130	Nate Colbert, 1969-1974

3B: Most, career, all-time

72	TONY GWYNN, 1982-1991
63	Gene Richards, 1977-1983
39	DAVE WINFIELD, 1973-1980
36	GARRY TEMPLETON, 1982-1991
29	Cito Gaston, 1969-1974

HR: Most, career, all-time

163	Nate Colbert, 1969-1974
154	DAVE WINFIELD, 1973-1980
82	CARMELO MARTINEZ, 1984-1989
77	Cito Gaston, 1969-1974
76	TERRY KENNEDY, 1981-1986

RBI: Most, career, all-time

626	DAVE WINFIELD, 1973-1980
550	TONY GWYNN, 1982-1991
481	Nate Colbert, 1969-1974
427	GARRY TEMPLETON, 1982-1991
424	TERRY KENNEDY, 1981-1986

SB: Most, career, all-time

246	TONY GWYNN, 1982-1991
242	Gene Richards, 1977-1983
171	Alan Wiggins, 1981-1985
147	OZZIE SMITH, 1978-1981
133	DAVE WINFIELD, 1973-1980

BB: Most, career, all-time

463	DAVE WINFIELD, 1973-1980
460	TONY GWYNN, 1982-1991
423	Gene Tenace, 1977-1980
350	Nate Colbert, 1969-1974
338	Gene Richards, 1977-1983

BA: Highest, career, all-time

.328	TONY GWYNN, 1982-1991
.291	Gene Richards, 1977-1983
.286	Johnny Grubb, 1972-1976
.284	DAVE WINFIELD, 1973-1980
.275	Steve Garvey, 1983-1987

Slug avg: Highest, career, all-time

.468	Nate Colbert, 1969-1974
.464	DAVE WINFIELD, 1973-1980
.434	TONY GWYNN, 1982-1991
.422	Gene Tenace, 1977-1980
.410	BENITO SANTIAGO, 1986-1991

Games started: Most, career, all-time

253	Randy Jones, 1973-1980
230	ERIC SHOW, 1981-1990
208	ED WHITSON, 1983-1991
172	ANDY HAWKINS, 1982-1988
170	Clay Kirby, 1969-1973

Saves: Most, career, all-time

108	Rollie Fingers, 1977-1980
83	RICH GOSSAGE, 1984-1987
74	MARK DAVIS, 1987-1989
64	CRAIG LEFFERTS, 1984-1991
49	Gary Lucas, 1980-1983

Shutouts: Most, career, all-time

18	Randy Jones, 1973-1980
11	Steve Arlin, 1969-1974
11	ERIC SHOW, 1981-1990
7	ANDY HAWKINS, 1982-1988
7	Clay Kirby, 1969-1973

Wins: Most, career, all-time

100	ERIC SHOW, 1981-1990
92	Randy Jones, 1973-1980
77	ED WHITSON, 1983-1991
60	ANDY HAWKINS, 1982-1988
53	Dave Dravecky, 1982-1987

K: Most, career, all-time

951	ERIC SHOW, 1981-1990
802	Clay Kirby, 1969-1973
767	ED WHITSON, 1983-1991
677	Randy Jones, 1973-1980
489	ANDY HAWKINS, 1982-1988

Win pct: Highest, career, all-time

.594	BRUCE HURST, 1989-1991
.535	ERIC SHOW, 1981-1990
.517	ED WHITSON, 1983-1991
.515	Dave Dravecky, 1982-1987
.508	ANDY HAWKINS, 1982-1988

ERA: Lowest, career, all-time

3.12	Dave Dravecky, 1982-1987
3.30	Randy Jones, 1973-1980
3.59	ERIC SHOW, 1981-1990
3.69	ED WHITSON, 1983-1991
3.73	Clay Kirby, 1969-1973

Runs: Most, season

119	TONY GWYNN, 1987
107	TONY GWYNN, 1986
106	Alan Wiggins, 1984
104	BIP ROBERTS, 1990
104	DAVE WINFIELD, 1977

Hits: Most, season

218	TONY GWYNN, 1987
213	TONY GWYNN, 1984
211	TONY GWYNN, 1986
203	TONY GWYNN, 1989
197	TONY GWYNN, 1985

2B: Most, season

42	TERRY KENNEDY, 1982
36	Johnny Grubb, 1975
36	TONY GWYNN, 1987
36	BIP ROBERTS, 1990
34	Ollie Brown, 1970
34	Steve Garvey, 1985
34	Ruppert Jones, 1981

3B: Most, season

13	TONY GWYNN, 1987
12	Gene Richards, 1978
12	Gene Richards, 1981
11	Bill Almon, 1977
11	TONY GWYNN, 1991

11   Gene Richards, 1977

HR: Most, season

38	Nate Colbert, 1970
38	Nate Colbert, 1972
34	DAVE WINFIELD, 1979
31	FRED McGRIFF, 1991
29	Cito Gaston, 1970

RBI: Most, season

118	DAVE WINFIELD, 1979
115	JOE CARTER, 1990
111	Nate Colbert, 1972
106	FRED McGRIFF, 1991
98	TERRY KENNEDY, 1983

SB: Most, season

70	Alan Wiggins, 1984
66	Alan Wiggins, 1983
61	Gene Richards, 1980
57	OZZIE SMITH, 1980
56	TONY GWYNN, 1987
56	Gene Richards, 1977

BB: Most, season

132	JACK CLARK, 1989
125	Gene Tenace, 1977
105	FRED McGRIFF, 1991
105	Gene Tenace, 1979
104	JACK CLARK, 1990

BA: Highest, season

.370	TONY GWYNN, 1987
.352	TONY GWYNN, 1984
.336	TONY GWYNN, 1989
.329	TONY GWYNN, 1986
.319	Cito Gaston, 1970

Slug avg: Highest, season

.558	DAVE WINFIELD, 1979
.543	Cito Gaston, 1970
.511	TONY GWYNN, 1987
.509	Nate Colbert, 1970
.508	Nate Colbert, 1972

Games started: Most, season

40	Randy Jones, 1976
39	Randy Jones, 1979
37	Steve Arlin, 1972
37	Gaylord Perry, 1978
36	Randy Jones, 1975
36	Randy Jones, 1978
36	Clay Kirby, 1971

Saves: Most, season

44	MARK DAVIS, 1989

37	Rollie Fingers, 1978
35	Rollie Fingers, 1977
28	MARK DAVIS, 1988
26	RICH GOSSAGE, 1985

Shutouts: Most, season

6	Randy Jones, 1975
6	Fred Norman, 1972
5	Randy Jones, 1976
4	Steve Arlin, 1971
4	BRUCE HURST, 1990

Wins: Most, season

22	Randy Jones, 1976
21	Gaylord Perry, 1978
20	Randy Jones, 1975
18	ANDY HAWKINS, 1985
16	La Marr Hoyt, 1985
16	Tim Lollar, 1982
16	ERIC SHOW, 1988
16	ED WHITSON, 1989

K: Most, season

231	Clay Kirby, 1971
185	Pat Dobson, 1970
179	BRUCE HURST, 1989
175	Clay Kirby, 1972
167	ANDY BENES, 1991
167	Fred Norman, 1972

Win pct: Highest, season

.778	Gaylord Perry, 1978
.692	ANDY HAWKINS, 1985
.667	La Marr Hoyt, 1985
.652	BRUCE HURST, 1991
.640	Tim Lollar, 1982

ERA: Lowest, season

2.10	Dave Roberts, 1971
2.24	Randy Jones, 1975
2.60	ED WHITSON, 1990
2.66	ED WHITSON, 1989
2.69	BRUCE HURST, 1989

Most pinch-hit homers, season

5	Jerry Turner, 1978

Most pinch-hit, homers, career

9	Jerry Turner, 1974-1983

Most consecutive games, batting safely

34	Benito Santiago, 1987

Most consecutive scoreless innings

30	Randy Jones, 1980

No hit games

N / A

San Francisco Giants

Gold Glove winner Will Clark also hit .301 with 29 homers and 116 RBI.

They spoiled it for the Dodgers

They may not have celebrated the 40th anniversary of Bobby Thomson's shot heard 'round the world with their own pennant in '91, but at least they spoiled it for their archrival Dodgers.

With a newly acquired pitcher and a highly touted rookie catcher, the San Francisco Giants hoped the electrifying combination of Black and Decker would provide the spark to an already deep roster.

That was not to be. Bud Black, who was 83-82 in nine seasons with three teams, won 12 games for the Giants but led the league in losses with 16. Steve Decker hit .206 in 79 games and spent the bulk of his season at Triple-A Phoenix.

The pair set the tone for the Giants, who had been picked by many prognosticators to capture the National League West title but spent April 27 to June 4 in last place.

Veteran pitchers Mike LaCoss and Rick Reuschel were released by the All-Star break, and Kevin Mitchell missed three weeks in June after arthroscopic surgery on his left knee.

The Giants were 12-29 on May 24, but went 43-26 from that day until Aug. 11 and were within six games of the NL West lead in mid-August. First baseman Will Clark was in contention for the triple crown as late as Labor Day, but finished the year eighth in the batting race (.301) with 29 home runs (sixth) and 116 RBI (tied for second).

Outfielder Willie McGee finished fourth in the league in batting (.312) while third baseman Matt Williams, who battled teammates Clark and Mitchell for the home run title for much of the season, finished with 34, second to New York's Howard Johnson.

Mike Felder, who was claimed on waivers from Milwaukee at the end of spring training, stole 21 bases. Kelly Downs, a former starter, found a home in the bullpen.

But the Giants' surge came too late, and a September slump brought them to 75-87 and a fourth place finish, 19 games behind the Atlanta Braves.

But the Giants weren't locked out of pennant fever: San Francisco brought an old-time flavor to the NL West race, pledging to bring down the Los Angeles Dodgers during the teams' season-ending showdown in Candlestick Park Oct. 4-6. The Giants made good on their promise, defeating the Dodgers in the first two games of the set to help the Braves clinch their first division title since 1982.

—Pete Williams

Giants 1992 preview

The San Francisco Giants' mission is simple: get some quality starts from their pitching staff and get out of the gate faster than last season. A year ago, it was an uphill battle out of the cellar from June 4 on; the Giants pulled within six games of the top in mid-August before running out of gas.

San Francisco has decent starters in John Burkett and Trevor Wilson. Lefty Bud Black has to improve on his 12-16 mark.

The Giants also are hoping their catching and shortstop situations are improved. Highly touted catcher Steve Decker hit just .206 in 79 games last year. Shortstop Royce Clayton may get a shot to show why he's one of the game's top-rated prospects. Outfielders Darren Lewis and Ted Wood also should get a long look.

1992 prophecy: Giants

▶The Royals will not be the only team drawing militant protests of their nickname. Led by a 7-foot-4 wrestler named Andre, thousands of freakishly large people will picket outside Candlestick Park, scaring away fans and raising public awareness.

—John Hunt

Fielder's choice: glove over bat

San Francisco first baseman Will Clark finished the 1991 season with a .301 average (eighth in the National League), 29 home runs (sixth), 116 runs batted in (second), and led the league in total bases (303) and slugging percentage (.536).

For the better part of the season, he was a serious contender for the triple crown. Yet it was not his accomplishments at the plate that he wanted to talk about.

Clark is proudest of his Gold Glove. He called it the most consistent facet of his game last year, and said that the fact he had committed only four errors all year was his proudest achievement.

"I can hit," Clark said. "I know I'm going to hit. But I'm very pleased with my defense. It hasn't come natural to me at all. It's something that I've spent more time with over the years than my offense.

"It was always hard for me to go out and take ground balls. But now I've reached a comfortable point in the field, where you want the ball to hit you."

Clark deserves to be proud of his glove. His fielding percentage for 1991 was .997, the best among full-time first basemen.

Count out of the money

Former San Francisco pitcher John "The Count" Montefusco won his first game in the major leagues and hit a home run in his first at-bat.

But he struck out at the race track in his professional harness racing debut at Freehold (N.C.) Raceway on Oct. 2.

Montefusco finished eighth and sixth in a pair of eight-horse fields. In the first race, driving Blue's Express, he was dead last, 15 lengths behind the winner. In the second race, with Rudder Tree, he finished 5 3/4 lengths behind the leader.

"It was like when I was pitching," Montefusco said. "Some days I had it, some days I didn't."

Black's record makes him blue

Bud Black, who signed a four-year, $13-million contract with the Giants, realizes he might not have lived up to his end of the bargain.

At the time of the signing, general manager Al Rosen said the veteran would win more games than any other free agent pitcher. He finished the season 12-16, and his 25 homers allowed was third in the National League.

"I try not to look at my record, but it's reality," Black said.

"I like to think I've pitched better than my record shows, but maybe I haven't. That's what's frustrating."

Still, he insists that he's had a relatively successful year.

"In '85 (when he was 10-15 for Kansas City) we won the World Series and I pitched not as well as I have this year, but I won key games down the stretch and that kind of bolstered things a little."

Brace yourself: Robinson got a save

They gave him the call, and he thought they were kidding. It was the ninth inning, and Dave Righetti was on the mound for the Giants.

Don Robinson hadn't earned a save in more than three years when he got the nod on Sept. 28. Why would they want him?

"I didn't even have my knee brace on," Robinson said. "I was leaning against the bullpen fence watching the game. When they told me to get up, I said 'you gotta be kidding.' "

But they weren't joking. And neither was Robinson. He reported for duty, got the job done, and got the save.

Robinson finished the season with 5 wins, 9 losses—and 1 save.

Giants winter league news

▶Instructional League: none.
▶Winter leagues: First baseman Jim Wilson (.300-21-78 at Class AAA Phoenix) headlined a small contingent of players from the San Francisco organization in the winter leagues, although as a six-year free agent Wilson was eligible to sign elsewhere. . . RHP Johnny Ard (12-8 between Phoenix and Class AA Shreveport) worked on his delivery and tried to develop another pitch to add to his repertoire in Puerto Rico. . . . RHP Rod Beck (4-3, 2.02 at Phoenix) concentrated on improving his forkball. . . . LHP Kevin Rogers (4-6, 3.36 at Shreveport) got additional innings in Mexico. . . . RHP Vlad Perez (1-1, 3.35 at Shreveport), 2B Andres Santana (45 steals at Phoenix) and RHP Jose Segura (5-5, 3.43 at Phoenix) played at home in the Dominican Republic.
▶Winter leagues roster: Johnny Ard, RHP, Arecibo Wolves, Puerto Rico; Rod Beck, RHP, Tigres (Tigers) de Licey, D.R.; Vlad Perez , RHP, Tigres (Tigers) de Licey, D.R.; Kevin Rogers, LHP, Guasave Algodoneros (Cotton growers), Mexico; Andres Santana 2B, Estrellas Orientales (Eastern Stars), D.R.; Jose Segura, RHP, Tigres (Tigers) de Licey, D.R.; Salomon Torres, RHP, Tigres (Tigers) de Licey, D.R.; Jim Wilson, 1B, Hermosillo Naranjeros, (Orange growers), Mexico.

Team directory

▶Owner: Bob Lurie

▶General Manager: Al Rosen

▶Ballpark:
Candlestick Park
Jamestown Ave. & Harney Way, San Francisco, California
415-467-8000
Capacity 62,000
Parking for 30,400 cars; $4-$5
Public transportation
Family and wheelchair sections, ramps, battery charger plug-ins for wheelchairs, designated handicapped pick-up and drop-off sights

▶Team publications:
Giants Magazine
415-468-3700 X478

▶TV, radio broadcast stations:
KNBR 680 AM, KTVU Channel 2

▶Camps and/or clinics:
Rob Andrews Baseball, June and July, 510-935-3505

▶Spring Training:
Scottsdale Stadium
Scottsdale, Arizona
Capacity 7,500-10,000
800-944-SFGIANTS

SAN FRANCISCO GIANTS 1991 Final Stats

Batting	AVG	SLG	OB	G	AB	R	H	TB	2B	3B	HR	RBI	BB	SO	SB	CS	E
McGee	.312	.408	.357	131	497	67	155	203	30	3	4	43	34	74	17	9	6
Clark	.301	.536	.359	148	565	84	170	303	32	7	29	116	51	91	4	2	4
Williams	.268	.499	.310	157	589	72	158	294	24	5	34	98	33	128	5	5	16
Felder	.264	.328	.325	132	348	51	92	114	10	6	0	18	30	31	21	6	4
Thompson	.262	.447	.352	144	492	74	129	220	24	5	19	48	63	95	14	7	11
Mitchell	.256	.515	.338	113	371	52	95	191	13	1	27	69	43	57	2	3	6
Anderson	.248	.314	.286	100	226	24	56	71	5	2	2	13	12	35	2	4	11
Lewis	.248	.311	.358	72	222	41	55	69	5	3	1	15	36	30	13	7	0
Leonard	.240	.357	.306	63	129	14	31	46	7	1	2	14	12	25	0	1	0
Kennedy	.234	.339	.283	69	171	12	40	58	7	1	3	13	11	31	0	0	6
Bass	.233	.366	.307	124	361	43	84	132	10	4	10	40	36	56	7	4	4
Perezchica	.229	.354	.260	23	48	2	11	17	4	1	0	3	2	12	0	1	2
Manwaring	.225	.275	.271	67	178	16	40	49	9	0	0	19	9	22	1	1	4
Uribe	.221	.303	.283	90	231	23	51	70	8	4	1	12	20	33	3	4	11
Coles	.214	.214	.214	11	14	1	3	3	0	0	0	0	0	2	0	0	0
Herr	.209	.270	.344	102	215	23	45	58	8	1	1	21	45	28	9	2	0
Decker	.206	.309	.262	79	233	11	48	72	7	1	5	24	16	44	0	1	7
Kingery	.182	.236	.280	91	110	13	20	26	2	2	0	8	15	21	1	0	1
Litton	.181	.276	.250	59	127	13	23	35	7	1	1	15	11	25	0	2	2
Benjamin	.123	.208	.188	54	106	12	13	22	3	0	2	8	7	26	3	0	3
Wood	.120	.120	.185	10	25	0	3	3	0	0	0	1	2	11	0	0	1
Clayton	.115	.154	.148	9	26	0	3	4	1	0	0	2	1	6	0	0	3
Parker	.071	.071	.133	13	14	0	1	1	0	0	0	0	1	5	0	0	0

Pitching	W-L	ERA	G	GS	CG	GF	Sho	SV	IP	H	R	ER	HR	BB	SO
Brantley	5-2	2.45	67	0	0	39	0	15	95.1	78	27	26	8	52	81
Righetti	2-7	3.39	61	0	0	49	0	24	71.2	64	29	27	4	28	51
Wilson	13-11	3.56	44	29	2	6	1	0	202	173	87	80	13	77	139
Hickerson	2-2	3.60	17	6	0	4	0	0	50	53	20	20	3	17	43
Beck	1-1	3.78	31	0	0	10	0	1	52.1	53	22	22	4	13	38
Heredia	0-2	3.82	7	4	0	1	0	0	33	27	14	14	4	7	13
Oliveras	6-6	3.86	55	1	0	17	0	3	79.1	69	36	34	12	22	48
Black	12-16	3.99	34	34	3	0	3	0	214.1	201	104	95	25	71	104
Burkett	12-11	4.18	36	34	3	0	1	0	206.2	223	103	96	19	60	131
Downs	10-4	4.19	45	11	0	4	0	0	111.2	99	59	52	12	53	62
Reuschel	0-2	4.22	4	1	0	1	0	0	10.2	17	5	5	0	7	4
Remlinger	2-1	4.37	8	6	1	1	1	0	35	36	17	17	5	20	19
Robinson	5-9	4.38	34	16	0	7	0	1	121.1	123	64	59	12	50	78
Segura	0-1	4.41	11	0	0	2	0	0	16.1	20	11	8	1	5	10
McClellan	3-6	4.56	13	12	1	1	0	0	71	68	41	36	12	25	44
Gunderson	0-0	5.40	2	0	0	1	0	1	3.1	6	4	2	0	1	2
Garrelts	1-1	6.41	8	3	0	2	0	0	19.2	25	14	14	5	9	8
Lacoss	1-5	7.23	18	5	0	6	0	0	47.1	61	39	38	4	24	30
Litton	0-0	9.00	1	0	0	1	0	0	1	1	1	1	0	3	0

1992 Preliminary Roster

Pitchers (21)

Johnny Ard
Rod Beck
Bud Black
Jeff Brantley
Dave Burba
John Burkett
Kelly Downs
Scott Garrelts
Eric Gunderson
Chris Hancock
Gil Heredia
Bryan Hickerson
MIke Jackson
Dave Masters
Paul McClellan
Jim Myers
Francisco Oliveras
Dave Righetti
Kevin Rogers
Bill Swift
Trevor Wilson

Catchers (2)

Steve Decker
Kirk Manwaring

Infielders (9)

Mike Benjamin
Will Clark
Royce Clayton
Greg Litton
John Patterson
Andres Santana
Robby Thompson
Jose Uribe
Matt Williams

Outfielders (7)

Kevin Bass
Mike Felder
Steve Hosey
Mark Leonard
Darren Lewis
Willie McGee
Ted Wood

156

Games played by position

	G	C	1B	2B	3B	SS	OF
Anderson,D	100	0	16	6	11	63	0
Bass,K	124	0	0	0	0	0	101
Benjamin,M	54	0	0	0	1	51	0
Clark,W	148	0	144	0	0	0	0
Clayton,R	9	0	0	0	0	8	0
Coles,D	11	0	1	0	0	0	3
Decker,S	79	78	0	0	0	0	0
Felder,M	132	0	0	1	3	0	107
Herr,T	102	0	0	72	3	0	1
Kennedy,T	69	58	2	0	0	0	0
Kingery,M	91	0	6	0	0	0	38
Leonard,M	63	0	0	0	0	0	34
Lewis,D	72	0	0	0	0	0	68
Litton,G	59	1	15	15	11	9	6
Manwaring,K	67	67	0	0	0	0	0
McGee,W	131	0	0	0	0	0	128
Mitchell,K	113	0	1	0	0	0	100
Parker,R	13	0	0	0	0	0	4
Perezchica,T	23	0	0	6	0	13	0
Thompson,Ro	144	0	0	144	0	0	0
Uribe,J	90	0	0	0	0	87	0
Williams,Ma	157	0	0	0	154	4	0
Wood,T	10	0	0	0	0	0	8

Sick call: 1991 DL report

Player	Days on the DL
Kelly Downs	9
Jose Uribe	46*
Scott Garrelts	141*
Rick Reuschel	56
Rick Parker	38
Kirt Manwaring	41
Mike Felder	15
Kevin Mitchell	22
Kevin Bass	34
Willie McGee	19
Don Robinson	16
Greg Litton	17

On DL twice (not counting administrative transfers from one DL to another).

Minor League Report

Class AAA — Phoenix finished 68-70, second in the first half and fourth in the second half in the PCL Southern Division. It was Phoenix's fourth consecutive year under .500, the longest streak in club history. OF Ted Wood hit .311 with 38 doubles, 11 HRs and league-leading 109 RBI (also a club record). He had 159 hits. 2B Andres Santana hit .316 with 45 SBs. OF Darren Lewis hit .340 with 52 RBI and 32 SBs in 81 games. RHP Gil Heredia (9-11, 2.82, 5 CGs) became the first Phoenix pitcher to lead the PCL in ERA. Veteran RHP Craig McMurtry was 10-6 with a 4.38 ERA. The team went through 95 player transactions. . . . **Class AA** — Shreveport finished 86-50, winning both halves in the Texas League Eastern Division. The Captains beat El Paso to win the playoffs and their second consecutive league championship. Shreveport led the league with a 3.48 ERA. Top hurlers were RHP Larry Carter (9-8, 2.95), RHP Johnny Ard (9-3, 2.74), RHP Pat Rapp (6-2, 2.69) and RHP Dan Rambo (12-6, 3.67). Carter won the league ERA championship (Ard and Rapp didn't qualify). 3B Juan Guerrero (.334-19-94) was team MVP. OF Steve Hosey hit .293 with 17 HRs and 74 RBI. 1B Dan Lewis hit .291 with 13 HRs and 90 RBI. . . . **Class A** — San Jose finished 92-44 (the best record in baseball), winning both halves in the California League Northern Division. The Giants lost to Stockton in the playoffs. RHP Rick Huisman (16-4, 1.83, 216 strikeouts in 182.1 innings) was Cal League Pitcher of the Year. RHP Gary Sharko had league-record 31 saves. Ron Wotus was Manager of the Year. . . . Clinton finished 81-58, third in the first half and first in the second half in the Midwest League Southern Division. The Giants beat Burlington and Madison to win the playoffs and league championship. RHP Salomon Torres (16-5, 1.41) led the league in ERA and strikeouts (214) and was named league MVP. RHP Rod Huffman had 36 saves. 3B Ricky Ward hit .278 with 11 HRs and 64 RBI. . . . Everett finished 37-39, tied for second in the Northwest League Northern Division. OF Matt Brewer (.347) was second in the league, C Frank Charles (.318) was fifth and OF Dax OK Jones (.306) was ninth. The Giants' .261 team average was highest in club history. RHP Lenny Ayres (8-5, 2.85) and RHP Bill VanLandingham (8-4, 4.09) tied for league lead in wins. RHP Doug VanderWeele (6-4) was second with 1.97 ERA.

Tops in the Organization

BATTING LEADERS	Club	Avg.	G	AB	R	H	HR	RBI
Juan Guerrero	Shr	.334	128	479	78	160	19	94
Dave Patterson	Phx	.332	115	346	58	115	4	51
Andres Santana	Phx	.316	113	456	84	144	1	35
Ted Wood	Phx	.311	137	512	90	159	11	109
Jim Wilson	Phx	.300	116	433	62	130	21	78

HOME RUNS			WINS		
Jim Wilson	Phx	21	Dan Carlson	Cln	16
Juan Guerrero	Shr	19	Richard Huisman	Sjo	16
Steve Hosey	Shr	17	Salomon Torres	Cln	16
Adell Davenport	Shr	13	Several players tied		13
Dan Lewis	Shr	13			

RBI			SAVES		
Ted Wood	Phx	109	Rod Huffman	Cln	35
Juan Guerrero	Shr	94	Gary Sharko	Sjo	31
Dan Lewis	Shr	90	Jim Myers	Shr	24
Jim Wilson	Phx	78	Steve Reed	Phx	13
Joey James	Sjo	75	Several players tied		6

STOLEN BASES			STRIKEOUTS		
Jason McFarlin	Sjo	46	Richard Huisman	Sjo	216
Andres Santana	Phx	45	Salomon Torres	Cln	214
John Patterson	Shr	40	Kevin McGehee	Sjo	171
Reuben Smiley	Shr	37	Dan Carlson	Cln	164
Several players tied		36	Dan Henrikson	Cln	150

PITCHING LEADERS	Club	W-L	ERA	IP	H	BB	SO
Salomon Torres	Cln	16-5	1.41	211	148	47	214
Richard Huisman	Sjo	16-4	1.83	182	126	73	216
Kevin McGehee	Sjo	13-6	2.33	174	129	87	171
Dan Henrikson	Cln	12-8	2.56	162	141	68	150
Pat Rapp	Shr	13-7	2.57	150	140	59	119

Runs: Most, career, all-time

2011	Willie Mays, 1951-1972
1859	Mel Ott, 1926-1947
1313	Mike Tiernan, 1887-1899
1120	Bill Terry, 1923-1936
1113	Willie McCovey, 1959-1980

Hits: Most, career, all-time

3187	Willie Mays, 1951-1972
2876	Mel Ott, 1926-1947
2193	Bill Terry, 1923-1936
1974	Willie McCovey, 1959-1980
1834	Mike Tiernan, 1887-1899

2B: Most, career, all-time

504	Willie Mays, 1951-1972
488	Mel Ott, 1926-1947
373	Bill Terry, 1923-1936
308	Willie McCovey, 1959-1980
291	Travis Jackson, 1922-1936

3B: Most, career, all-time

162	Mike Tiernan, 1887-1899
139	Willie Mays, 1951-1972
131	Roger Connor, 1883-1894
117	Larry Doyle, 1907-1920
112	Bill Terry, 1923-1936

HR: Most, career, all-time

646	Willie Mays, 1951-1972
511	Mel Ott, 1926-1947
469	Willie McCovey, 1959-1980
226	Orlando Cepeda, 1958-1966
189	Bobby Thomson, 1946-1957

RBI: Most, career, all-time

1860	Mel Ott, 1926-1947
1859	Willie Mays, 1951-1972
1388	Willie McCovey, 1959-1980
1078	Bill Terry, 1923-1936
929	Travis Jackson, 1922-1936

SB: Most, career, all-time

428	Mike Tiernan, 1887-1899
354	George Davis, 1893-1903
336	Willie Mays, 1951-1972
334	George Burns, 1911-1921
332	Monte Ward, 1883-1894

BB: Most, career, all-time

1708	Mel Ott, 1926-1947
1394	Willie Mays, 1951-1972
1168	Willie McCovey, 1959-1980

747	Mike Tiernan, 1887-1899
631	George Burns, 1911-1921

BA: Highest, career, all-time

.341	Bill Terry, 1923-1936
.332	George Davis, 1893-1903
.322	Ross Youngs, 1917-1926
.322	Frankie Frisch, 1919-1926
.321	George Vanhaltren, 1894-1903
.308	Orlando Cepeda, 1958-1966 (12)

Slug avg: Highest, career, all-time

.564	Willie Mays, 1951-1972
.549	Johnny Mize, 1942-1949
.536	KEVIN MITCHELL, 1987-1991
.535	Orlando Cepeda, 1958-1966
.533	Mel Ott, 1926-1947

Games started: Most, career, all-time

550	Christy Mathewson, 1900-1916
446	Juan Marichal, 1960-1973
431	Carl Hubbell, 1928-1943
412	Mickey Welch, 1883-1892
403	Amos Rusie, 1890-1898

Saves: Most, career, all-time

127	Gary Lavelle, 1974-1984
125	Greg Minton, 1975-1987
83	Randy Moffitt, 1972-1981
78	Frank Linzy, 1963-1970
58	Marv Grissom, 1946-1958

Shutouts: Most, career, all-time

79	Christy Mathewson, 1900-1916
52	Juan Marichal, 1960-1973
36	Carl Hubbell, 1928-1943
29	Amos Rusie, 1890-1898
28	Mickey Welch, 1883-1892

Wins: Most, career, all-time

372	Christy Mathewson, 1900-1916
253	Carl Hubbell, 1928-1943
238	Juan Marichal, 1960-1973
238	Mickey Welch, 1883-1892
233	Amos Rusie, 1890-1898

K: Most, career, all-time

2499	Christy Mathewson, 1900-1916
2281	Juan Marichal, 1960-1973
1819	Amos Rusie, 1890-1898
1677	Carl Hubbell, 1928-1943
1606	Gaylord Perry, 1962-1971

Win pct: Highest, career, all-time

.693	Sal Maglie, 1945-1955
.680	Tim Keefe, 1885-1891
.664	Christy Mathewson, 1900-1916
.656	Jesse Barnes, 1918-1923
.651	Doc Crandall, 1908-1913
.630	Juan Marichal, 1960-1973 (11)

ERA: Lowest, career, all-time

2.12	Christy Mathewson, 1900-1916
2.38	Joe McGinnity, 1902-1908
2.43	Jeff Tesreau, 1912-1918
2.45	Red Ames, 1903-1913
2.48	Hooks Wiltse, 1904-1914
2.82	Gary Lavelle, 1974-1984 (12)

Runs: Most, season

147	Mike Tiernan, 1889
139	Bill Terry, 1930
138	Mel Ott, 1929
137	Johnny Mize, 1947
136	George Vanhaltren, 1896
134	Bobby Bonds, 1970 (6)

Hits: Most, season

254	Bill Terry, 1930
231	Freddy Lindstrom, 1928
231	Freddy Lindstrom, 1930
226	Bill Terry, 1929
225	Bill Terry, 1932
208	Willie Mays, 1958 (13)

2B: Most, season

46	JACK CLARK, 1978
43	Willie Mays, 1959
43	Bill Terry, 1931
42	George Kelly, 1921
42	Bill Terry, 1932

3B: Most, season

27	George Davis, 1893

25	Larry Doyle, 1911
22	Roger Connor, 1887
21	Mike Tiernan, 1890
21	Mike Tiernan, 1895
21	George Vanhaltren, 1896
20	Willie Mays, 1957 (7)

HR: Most, season

52	Willie Mays, 1965
51	Willie Mays, 1955
51	Johnny Mize, 1947
49	Willie Mays, 1962
47	Willie Mays, 1964
47	KEVIN MITCHELL, 1989

RBI: Most, season

151	Mel Ott, 1929
142	Orlando Cepeda, 1961
141	Willie Mays, 1962
138	Johnny Mize, 1947
136	George Davis, 1897
136	George Kelly, 1924

SB: Most, season

111	Monte Ward, 1887
65	George Davis, 1897
62	George Burns, 1914
62	Monte Ward, 1889
61	Josh Devore, 1911
58	Billy North, 1979 (7)

BB: Most, season

144	Eddie Stanky, 1950
137	Willie McCovey, 1970
127	Eddie Stanky, 1951
121	Willie McCovey, 1969
118	Mel Ott, 1938

BA: Highest, season

.401	Bill Terry, 1930
.379	Freddy Lindstrom, 1930
.372	Bill Terry, 1929
.371	Roger Connor, 1885
.369	Mike Tiernan, 1896
.347	Willie Mays, 1958 (22)

Slug avg: Highest, season

.667	Willie Mays, 1954
.659	Willie Mays, 1955
.656	Willie McCovey, 1969
.645	Willie Mays, 1965
.635	KEVIN MITCHELL, 1989

Games started: Most, season

| 65 | Mickey Welch, 1884 |

64	Tim Keefe, 1886
63	Amos Rusie, 1890
61	Amos Rusie, 1892
59	Mickey Welch, 1886
41	Gaylord Perry, 1970 (*)

Saves: Most, season

30	Greg Minton, 1982
24	DAVE RIGHETTI, 1991
22	Greg Minton, 1983
21	Frank Linzy, 1965
21	Greg Minton, 1981

Shutouts: Most, season

11	Christy Mathewson, 1908
10	Carl Hubbell, 1933
10	Juan Marichal, 1965
9	Joe McGinnity, 1904
8	Tim Keefe, 1888
8	Juan Marichal, 1969
8	Christy Mathewson, 1902
8	Christy Mathewson, 1905
8	Christy Mathewson, 1907
8	Christy Mathewson, 1909
8	Jeff Tesreau, 1914
8	Jeff Tesreau, 1915

Wins: Most, season

44	Mickey Welch, 1885
42	Tim Keefe, 1886
39	Mickey Welch, 1884
37	Christy Mathewson, 1908
36	Amos Rusie, 1894
26	Juan Marichal, 1968 (25)

K: Most, season

345	Mickey Welch, 1884
341	Amos Rusie, 1890
337	Amos Rusie, 1891
333	Tim Keefe, 1888
291	Tim Keefe, 1886
248	Juan Marichal, 1963 (11)

Win pct: Highest, season

.833	Hoyt Wilhelm, 1952
.818	Sal Maglie, 1950
.814	Joe McGinnity, 1904
.813	Carl Hubbell, 1936
.810	Doc Crandall, 1910

ERA: Lowest, season

1.14	Christy Mathewson, 1909
1.27	Christy Mathewson, 1905
1.43	Christy Mathewson, 1908
1.44	Fred Anderson, 1917
1.58	Tim Keefe, 1885

| 1.99 | Bobby Bolin, 1968 (16) |

Most pinch-hit homers, season

4	Ernie Lombardi, NY-1946
4	Bill Taylor, NY-1955
4	Mike Ivie, 1978
4	Candy Maldonado, 1986
4	Ernie Riles, 1990

Most pinch-hit, homers, career

| 13 | Willie McCovey, 1959-1980 |

Most consecutive games, batting safely

| 33 | George Davis, NY-1893 |
| 26 | Jack Clark, 1978 |

Most consecutive scoreless innings

45	Carl Hubbell, NY-1933
45	Sal Maglie, NY-1950
39	Gaylord Perry, 1970

No hit games

Amos Rusie, NY vs Bro NL, 6-0; July 31, 1891.

Christy Mathewson, NY at StL NL, 5-0; July 15, 1901.

Christy Mathewson, NY at Chi NL, 1-0; June 13, 1905.

Hooks Wiltse, NY vs Phi NL, 1-0; July 4, 1908 (1st game, ten innings).

Red Ames, NY vs Bro NL. 0-3; April 15, 1909 (lost on 7 hits in 13 innings after allowing the first hit in the tenth).

Jeff Tesreau, NY at Phi NL, 3-0; September 6, 1912 (1st game).

Rube Marquard, NY vs Bro NL, 2-0; April 15, 1915.

Jesse Barnes, NY vs Phi NL, 6-0; May 7, 1922.

Carl Hubbell, NY vs Pit NL, 11-0; May 8, 1929.

Juan Marichal, SF vs Hou NL, 1-0; June 15, 1963.

Gaylord Perry, SF vs StL NL, 1-0; September 17, 1968.

Ed Halicki, SF vs NY NL, 6-0; August 24, 1975 (2nd game).

John Montefusco, SF at Atl NL, 9-0; September 29, 1976.

Ed Crane, seven innings, darkness, NY vs Was NL, 3-0; September 27, 1888.

Red Ames, five innings, darkness, NY at StL NL, 5-0; September 14, 1903(2nd game, first game in the major leagues).

Mike McCormick, five innings, rain, SF at Phi NL, 3-0; June 12, 1959. (allowed hit in 6th, but rain caused game to revert to 5 innings)

Sam Jones, seven innings, rain, SF at StL NL, 4-0; September 26, 1959.

Cincinnati Reds

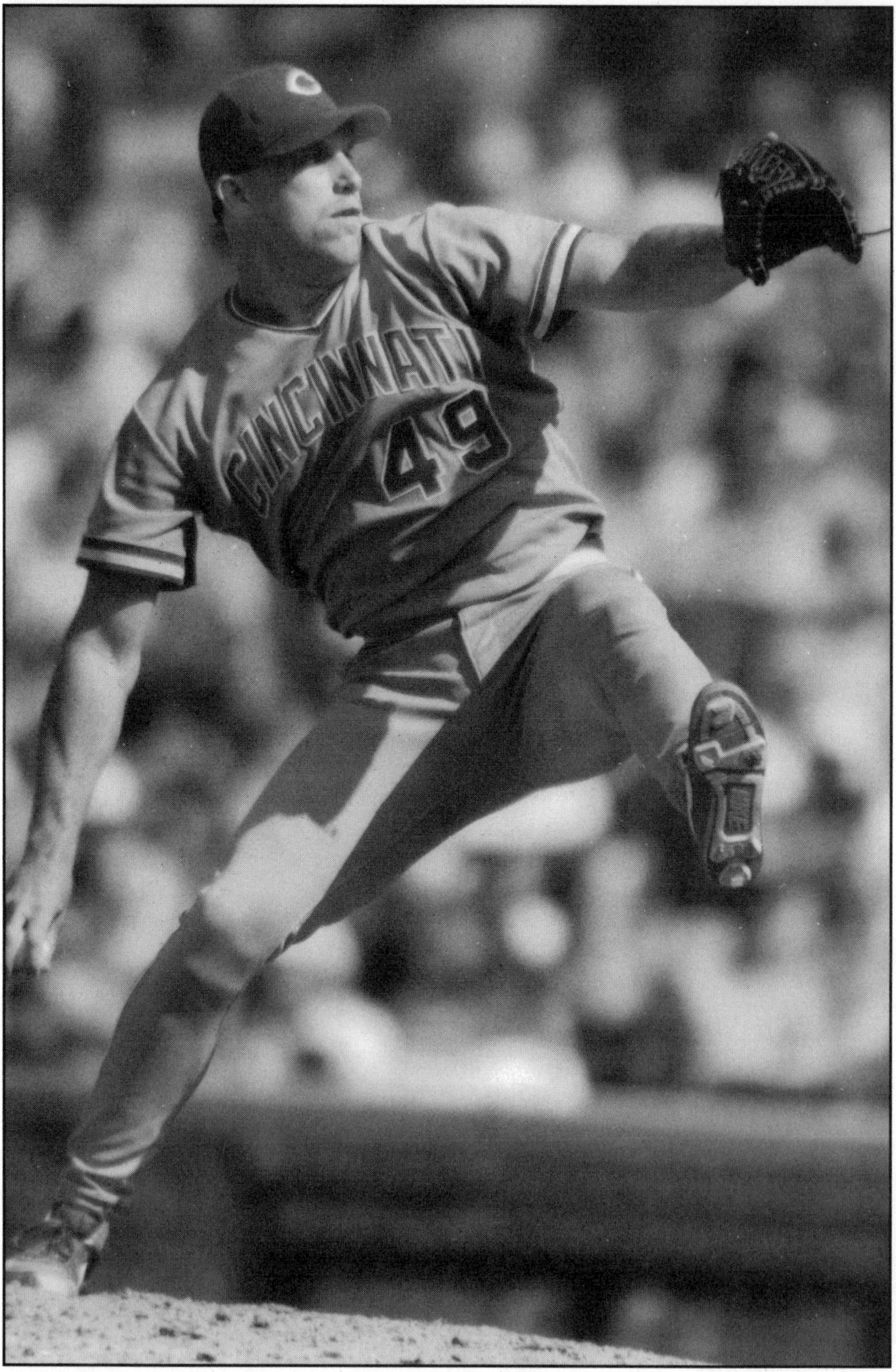

Cinncinati's Rob Dibble explodes with his fastball—and his temper.

Blame it on the pitching

The Cincinnati Reds' 1991 season can be summed up in one pitch.

October 1, Riverfront Stadium. Reds vs. Braves. Reds up 6-5 in the ninth, with ace reliever Rob Dibble on the mound. With one on and one out, Braves right fielder Dave Justice jumps on a Dibble fastball, and drives it high and deep over the right-field wall for a two-run homer.

For the Reds, who blew a 6-0 lead that night, the 7-6 loss represented how far the Reds had fallen since going wire-to-wire and winning a World Championship in 1990.

A year after finishing 91-71 and 26 games ahead of the last-place Braves, the fifth-place Reds finished 74-88 and 20 games behind Atlanta.

The starting pitching that anchored the World Championship team was beset by injuries and inconsistencies. Jose Rijo, 1990 World Series MVP, was the only starter to come close to replicating his season—15-6, 2.51 ERA—despite missing a month with a broken ankle.

Tom Browning gave the Reds plenty of innings (14-14, 36 starts), but his ERA was abnormally high.

After that, the Reds had no one they could depend on. Jack Armstrong, 1990 All-Star starter, had such a miserable season that he was sent to the minors at one point to straighten himself out. Scott Scudder, Kip Gross and Chris Hammond all showed flashes of brilliance and baffling inconsistency.

"We need pitching," admitted Reds' manager Lou Piniella. "We need to fine-tune some places, but the major focus is pitching."

So Armstrong, Scudder and Gross were traded for the more proven Greg Swindel and Tim Belcher.

The Nasty Boys in the bullpen were broken up and subject to breaking down. Ace reliever Rob Dibble was 23-for-23 in saves with a 1.30 ERA before the All-Star Game. The he went 3-5, was just 8-for-13 in saves and had a 4.87 ERA. He also got two suspensions and a fine for ball-throwing episodes.

Norm Charlton moved into the rotation at the start of the season, but had tendinitis in his left shoulder and missed a month. Randy Myers came out of the bullpen to take his spot and pitched effectively, but was victimized by a lack of run support.

The Reds fell to eighth in the league in ERA in 1991 (3.83) after finishing second (3.39) in 1990. The offense was there—Cincinnati led the league in homers (164) and was second in batting average (.258)—but it wasn't enough to overcome the hurting hurlers.

Reds 1992 preview

The Cincinnati Reds' primary goal is to improve their mound staff. Aside from Jose Rijo (15-6, 2.51), no one did the job last year. The acquisition of Greg Swindell and Tim Belcher adds stability, but Tom Browning must be more than mediocre and youngsters such as Chris Hammond must be more consistent.

Reliever Rob Dibble fell apart after the All-Star break and fell in and out of trouble for his antics, such as hitting a fan with a baseball.

Offensively, there's no need to panic. The Reds led the NL in home runs (164) last year and ranked second in batting (.258), even though the traded Eric Davis—who played hurt—hit just .235 with 33 RBI.

There is reason for optimism with Hal Morris (.318) at first base and Chris Sabo (.301, 26 HR, 88 RBI) at third. Barry Larkin and Bill Doran complete a solid infield.

▶Eric Davis will spontaneously combust.
▶"Honest, it slipped," Rob Dibble will say after his errant fastball nails team owner Marge Schott in the left ear, prompting a one-game suspension.
▶Still grieving over the loss of her beloved companion Schottzie, Cincinnati's owner will adopt third baseman Chris Sabo as her new pet.

—John Hunt

Rijo fell just short of bonus

Most critics say the Reds' pitching fell apart in 1991, with the exception of one bright spot: Jose Rijo. Ironically, Rijo missed qualifiying for a $62,500 incentive bonus by two outs. He said he deserves the money just the same.

"I hope they give it to me," he said. "I've been pitching hurt for the club."

Rijo would have earned the money automatically by pitching 205 innings this season. He went eight innings in his final start Oct. 6 in San Diego, but didn't pitch the bottom of the ninth since the Reds won 3-1.

Rijo said if the Reds don't pay up, they'll be dealing "with one (ticked) off Dominican."

Rijo, the 1990 World Series MVP, finished 15-6 and was second in the league with a 2.51 ERA.

Dibble: On the air

By Rory Glynn

Rob Dibble called a Cincinnati radio sports talk show in July and got a few things off his chest. In a 15-minute conversation with hosts Cris Collinsworth and Andy Furman, Dibble stirred up controversy when he called some of his Reds teammates dogs, denied trying to hit Chicago's Doug Dascenzo, admitted intentionally throwing at a player two years ago when told to do so, and criticized teammates for not supporting him.

"I get tired of listening to hitters say, 'The pitchers don't protect us,' " Dibble said. "I've taken suspensions because guys have asked me to hit people, and I've done it. I've knocked guys down for these guys, and when I need a little bit of backing, what do they do? They go and run and start popping off."

Dibble said any Red would say he's "a great guy," but that he isn't trying to win popularity contests.

"There's a lot of guys who don't like my style of play, and I don't like the way they play," he said. "I think we've got some dogs on our team. But I don't say that (stuff), because it causes dissension.

"What's worse, me taking three days off (for a suspension), or a guy taking two weeks off?" Dibble asked. "I've seen guys go down with unbelievable injuries. That's the sickness here ... a lot of guys aren't even hurt."

Dibble said he tries to channel his anger by throwing bats and tantrums.

"I can be the kind of guy who'll throw a 100 mph fastball in your face, and stand out there while you're bleeding on the ground," Dibble said. "I did it one time, and I didn't like it. I don't have a taste for that.

"I hit Tim Teufel (in 1989, with New York) and I shouldn't have done that because I was told to do that," Dibble said. "But other than that, I've never intentionally hit a guy. And when I start doing that (stuff), I need to get out of the game."

Suspension ruling upset Charlton

Norm Charlton didn't like the way his suspension for hitting Dodgers' catcher Mike Scioscia was handled.

Charlton agreed to drop his appeal and begin serving the seven-game suspension Sept. 29 to end his season early. But three of the Reds' final games were against the Braves, who were contending for the NL West title.

So National League president Bill White reinstated Charlton and ordered him onto the roster for that series.

White said, "It is imperative that all teams play with their full complement of players in order to guarantee that competition is fair and balanced."

Charlton, who had been eligible for three games against the Dodgers after appealing his suspension, said he didn't understand White's reasoning.

"There was the thing called integrity of the game that Pete Rose got kicked out for," Charlton said. "Yet Bill White suspends me against Los Angeles, I drop my appeal against Atlanta and he makes me play."

Charlton apparently was reinstated after the Dodgers protested his missing the three games against Atlanta, and serves the rest of the suspension at the start of the 1992 season.

Manager Lou Piniella said he understood White's decision: "There was a pennant race and Charlton pitched the full complement of games against the Dodgers."

Said Charlton, "My first responsibility is not to Los Angeles."

Braves manager Bobby Cox said the incident showed the problems with the suspension and appeal process.

"There has got to be a system . . . where this doesn't happen. Give them a 24-hour appeal and get on with it."

Team directory

▶Owner: Marge Schott and a limited partnership

▶General Manager: Bob Quinn

▶Ballpark:
Riverfront Stadium
Pete Rose Way, Cincinnati, Ohio
513-421-7337 or 800-829-5353
Capacity 52,952
Parking for 5,022 cars; $3.50-$5
Wheelchair locations, ramps

▶Team publications:
Media Guide, Yearbook program
513-651-7200

▶TV, radio broadcast stations:
WLW 700 AM, WLWT Channel 5

▶Spring Training:
Plant City Stadium
Plant City, Florida
Capacity 6,700
813-752-1878

CINCINNATI REDS 1991 Final Stats

Batting	AVG	SLG	OB	G	AB	R	H	TB	2B	3B	HR	RBI	BB	SO	SB	CS	E
Morris	.318	.479	.374	136	478	72	152	229	33	1	14	59	46	61	10	4	9
Larkin	.302	.506	.378	123	464	88	140	235	27	4	20	69	55	64	24	6	15
Sabo	.301	.505	.354	153	582	91	175	294	35	3	26	88	44	79	19	6	12
Jones	.292	.416	.304	52	89	14	26	37	1	2	2	6	2	31	2	1	0
Benavides	.286	.302	.303	24	63	11	18	19	1	0	0	3	1	15	1	0	2
Doran	.280	.374	.359	111	361	51	101	135	12	2	6	35	46	39	5	4	7
Reed	.267	.370	.321	91	270	20	72	100	15	2	3	31	23	38	0	1	5
Hatcher	.262	.360	.312	138	442	45	116	159	25	3	4	41	26	55	11	9	5
Braggs	.260	.432	.323	85	250	36	65	108	10	0	11	39	23	46	11	3	5
Duncan	.258	.411	.288	100	333	46	86	137	7	4	12	40	12	57	5	4	9
O'Neill	.256	.481	.346	152	532	71	136	256	36	0	28	91	73	107	12	7	2
Davis	.235	.386	.353	89	285	39	67	110	10	0	11	33	48	92	14	2	3
Martinez	.234	.383	.301	64	154	13	36	59	5	0	6	19	16	39	0	0	6
Winningham	.225	.290	.272	98	169	17	38	49	6	1	1	4	11	40	4	4	5
Quinones	.222	.325	.297	97	212	15	47	69	4	3	4	20	21	31	1	2	7
Oliver	.216	.379	.265	94	269	21	58	102	11	0	11	41	18	53	0	0	11
Sanders	.200	.275	.200	9	40	6	8	11	0	0	1	3	0	9	1	1	0
Benzinger	.187	.268	.244	51	123	7	23	33	3	2	1	11	10	20	2	0	2
Scott	.158	.158	.158	10	19	0	3	3	0	0	0	0	0	2	0	0	0
R. Jefferson	.143	.571	.250	5	7	1	1	4	0	0	1	1	1	2	0	0	0
Sutko	.100	.100	.250	10	10	0	1	1	0	0	0	1	2	6		0	3
S. Jefferson	.053	.053	.100	13	19	2	1	1	0	0	0	0	1	3	2	0	0
Lee	.000	.000	.000	3	6	0	0	0	0	0	0	0	0	2	0	0	0

Pitching	W-L	ERA	G	GS	CG	GF	Sho	SV	IP	H	R	ER	HR	BB	SO
Foster	0-0	1.93	11	0	0	5	0	0	14	7	5	3	1	4	11
Brown	0-0	2.25	11	0	0	3	0	0	12	15	4	3	0	6	4
Rijo	15-6	2.51	30	30	3	0	1	0	204.1	165	69	57	8	55	172
Charlton	3-5	2.91	39	11	0	10	0	1	108.1	92	37	35	6	34	77
Dibble	3-5	3.17	67	0	0	57	0	31	82.1	67	32	29	5	25	124
Gross	6-4	3.47	29	9	1	6	0	0	85.2	93	43	33	8	40	40
Myers	6-13	3.55	58	12	1	18	0	6	132	116	61	52	8	80	108
Power	5-3	3.62	68	0	0	22	0	3	87	87	37	35	6	31	51
Hill	1-1	3.78	22	0	0	8	0	0	33.1	36	14	14	1	8	20
Sanford	1-2	3.86	5	5	0	0	0	0	28	19	14	12	3	15	31
Hammond	7-7	4.06	20	18	0	0	0	0	99.2	92	51	45	4	48	50
Browning	14-14	4.18	36	36	1	0	0	0	230.1	241	124	107	32	56	115
Scudder	6-9	4.35	27	14	0	4	0	1	101.1	91	52	49	6	56	51
Carman	0-2	5.25	28	0	0	10	0	1	36	40	23	21	8	19	15
Armstrong	7-13	5.48	27	24	1	1	0	0	139.2	158	90	85	25	54	93
Minutelli	0-2	6.04	16	3	0	2	0	0	25.1	30	17	17	5	18	21
Layana	0-2	6.97	22	0	0	9	0	0	20.2	23	18	16	1	11	14

1992 Preliminary Roster

Pitchers (20)

Bobby Ayala
Tim Belcher
Tom Browning
Norm Charlton
Rob Dibble
Steve Foster
Victor Garcia
Chris Hammond
Dwayne Henry
Milton Hill
Trevor Hoffman
Tim Layana
Gino Minutelli
Ross Powell
Tim Pugh
Jose Rijo
Scott Ruskin
Mo Sanford
Jason Satre
Greg Swindell

Catchers (4)

Bob Geren
Joe Oliver
Jeff Reed
Glenn Sutko

Infielders (7)

Freddie Benavides
Jeff Branson
Bill Doran
Brian Lane
Barry Larkin
Hal Morris
Chris Sabo

Outfielders (9)

Glenn Braggs
Jacob Brumfield
Cesar Hernandaz
Billy Hatcher
Chris Jones
Dave Martinez
Paul O'Neill
Bip Roberts
Reggie Sanders

Games Played by position

	G	C	1B	2B	3B	SS	OF
Benavides,F	24	0	0	3	0	20	0
Benzinger,T	51	0	21	0	0	0	15
Braggs,G	85	0	0	0	0	0	74
Davis,E	89	0	0	0	0	0	81
Doran,B	111	0	4	88	0	0	6
Duncan,M	100	0	0	62	0	32	7
Hatcher,B	138	0	0	0	0	0	121
Jefferson,R	5	0	2	0	0	0	0
Jefferson,S	13	0	0	0	0	0	5
Jones,Ji	52	0	0	0	0	0	26
Larkin,B	123	0	0	0	0	119	0
Lee,T	3	0	2	0	0	0	0
Martinez,Cs	64	0	33	0	0	0	16
Morris,H	136	0	128	0	0	0	1
Oliver,J	94	90	0	0	0	0	0
O'Neill,P	152	0	0	0	0	0	150
Quinones,L	97	0	0	33	19	5	0
Reed,Js	91	89	0	0	0	0	0
Sabo,C	153	0	0	0	151	0	0
Sanders,R	9	0	0	0	0	0	9
Scott,D	10	8	0	0	0	0	0
Sutko,G	10	9	0	0	0	0	0
Winningham,H	98	0	0	0	0	0	66

Sick call: 1991 DL report

Player	Days on the DL
Brian Lane	182
Bill Doran	22
Barry Larkin	17
Norm Charlton	48*
Scott Scudder	68*
Eric Davis	41*
Jose Rijo	34
Gino Minutelli	15
Jeff Reed	18
Chris Hammond	36
Mariano Duncan	15
Reggie Sanders	27
Glenn Braggs	42

On DL twice (not counting administrative transfers from one DL to another).

Minor League Report

Class AAA — Nashville finished 65-78, third in the American Association East. The Sounds were in third place from May 1 to the end of the season. 1B Terry Lee hit .304 with 15 HRs and 67 RBI. OF Todd Trafton hit .285 with 9 HRs and 41 RBI in 75 games. OF Adam Casillas hit .275. RHP Keith Brown (2-5, 3.48) had 16 saves. LHP Ross Powell was 8-8 with a 4.37 ERA. Frank Funk was named pitching coach for 1992. . . . **Class AA** — Chattanooga finished 73-71, second in the first half and third in the second half in the Southern League Western Division. OF Benny Covard (.280-17-68 with 23 doubles and 8 triples) was named team MVP. OF Reggie Sanders hit .315 with 8 HRs and 49 RBI. RHP Mike Anderson was 10-9 with a 4.40 ERA. RHP Trevor Hoffman had 8 saves and a 1.93 ERA. The Lookouts drew 186,029 fans, their most in 39 years. Utility man Frank Kremblas played all 9 positions against Carolina Sept. 3. . . . **Class A** — Charleston (W.Va.) finished 92-50, winning both halves in the South Atlantic League Northern Division. The Wheelers lost to Columbia in the playoff finals. Top hitters were OF Steve Gibralter (.267 with 36 doubles and 71 RBI); OF Keith Gordon (.268 with 10 triples and 25 SBs) and 1B Tom Raffo (.277-13-68). and 3B Bobby Perna (.248-9-57). RHP John Roper (14-9, 2.31) led the league with 189 strikeouts. RHP Johnny Ray was 16-9 with a 3.36 ERA. RHP Sean Doty and LHP Scott Duff combined for 34 saves. . . . Cedar Rapids finished 66-74, fourth in the first half and sixth in the second half in the Midwest League Southern Division. Jamie Dismuke hit .254 with 35 doubles, 8 HRs and 72 RBI. Kevin Riggs hit .268 with 21 doubles and 23 SBs. Top pitchers were RHP Larry Luebbers (8-10, 3.12) and RHP Scott Robinson (8-9, 3.77). and RHP Mark Borcherding (9-8, 4.40). . . . Billings finished 25-44, third in the Pioneer League Northern Division. Top hitters were Gene Taylor (.289), Mike Mitchell (.275), Bob Jesperson (.273) and Joe DeBerry (.263-10-47). RHP Charles McClain (5-7, 3.38) gave up 63 hits in 80 innings. . . . Princeton finished 24-40, fourth in the Appalachian League Northern Division. C Toby Rumfield (.274-3-30) was team MVP. SS Calvin Reese, the Reds' top 1991 draft pick, hit .238 with 27 RBI. RHP John Hrusovsky was 4-4 with a 1.83 ERA. RHP Kevin Jarvis was 5-6 with a 2.42 ERA.

Tops in the Organization

BATTING LEADERS	Club	Avg.	G	AB	R	H	HR	RBI
Terry Lee	Nvl	.304	126	437	70	133	15	67
Dan Wilson	Cng	.280	133	489	57	137	5	67
Benny Colvard	Cng	.280	125	468	62	131	17	68
Tom Raffo	Cwv	.277	133	473	63	131	13	68
Adam Casillas	Nvl	.275	128	422	44	116	5	52

HOME RUNS			WINS		
Benny Colvard	Cng	17	John Ray	Cwv	16
Todd Trafton	Nvl	15	John Roper	Cwv	14
Terry Lee	Nvl	15	Tim Pugh	Nvl	10
Tom Raffo	Cwv	13	Mike Anderson	Cng	10
Several players tied		10	Mo Sanford	Nvl	10

RBI			SAVES		
Todd Trafton	Nvl	75	Steve Foster	Nvl	22
James Dismuke	Cdr	72	Trevor Hoffman	Cng	20
Steve Gibralter	Cwv	71	Sean Doty	Cwv	20
Tom Raffo	Cwv	68	Keith Brown	Nvl	16
Benny Colvard	Cng	68	Scott Duff	Cwv	15

STOLEN BASES			STRIKEOUTS		
Motorboat Jones	Cdr	26	John Roper	Cwv	189
Keith Gordon	Cwv	25	Jason Satre	Cng	174
Kevin Riggs	Cwv	23	Mo Sanford	Nvl	162
Brian Koelling	Cdr	22	Carl Stewart	Cwv	135
Several players tied		20	John Ray	Cwv	120

PITCHING LEADERS	Club	W-L	ERA	IP	H	BB	SO
John Roper	Cwv	14-9	2.31	187	134	67	189
Mo Sanford	Nvl	10-4	2.44	129	88	77	162
Larry Luebbers	Cdr	8-10	3.12	185	177	64	98
Tim Cecil	Cwv	8-4	3.18	130	129	49	70
Jason Satre	Cng	9-13	3.21	177	138	93	174

Cincinnati (1890-1991)

Runs: Most, career, all-time

1741	Pete Rose, 1963-1986
1091	Johnny Bench, 1967-1983
1043	Frank Robinson, 1956-1965
993	Dave Concepcion, 1970-1988
978	Vada Pinson, 1958-1968

Hits: Most, career, all-time

3358	Pete Rose, 1963-1986
2326	Dave Concepcion, 1970-1988
2048	Johnny Bench, 1967-1983
1934	Tony Perez, 1964-1986
1881	Vada Pinson, 1958-1968

2B: Most, career, all-time

601	Pete Rose, 1963-1986
389	Dave Concepcion, 1970-1988
381	Johnny Bench, 1967-1983
342	Vada Pinson, 1958-1968
339	Tony Perez, 1964-1986

3B: Most, career, all-time

152	Edd Roush, 1916-1931
115	Pete Rose, 1963-1986
112	Bid McPhee, 1890-1899
96	Vada Pinson, 1958-1968
94	Curt Walker, 1924-1930

HR: Most, career, all-time

389	Johnny Bench, 1967-1983
324	Frank Robinson, 1956-1965
287	Tony Perez, 1964-1986
251	Ted Kluszewski, 1947-1957
244	George Foster, 1971-1981

RBI: Most, career, all-time

1376	Johnny Bench, 1967-1983
1192	Tony Perez, 1964-1986
1036	Pete Rose, 1963-1986
1009	Frank Robinson, 1956-1965
950	Dave Concepcion, 1970-1988

SB: Most, career, all-time

406	Joe Morgan, 1972-1979
337	Arlie Latham, 1890-1895
321	Dave Concepcion, 1970-1988
319	Bob Bescher, 1908-1913
316	Bid McPhee, 1890-1899

BB: Most, career, all-time

1210	Pete Rose, 1963-1986
891	Johnny Bench, 1967-1983
881	Joe Morgan, 1972-1979
736	Dave Concepcion, 1970-1988
698	Frank Robinson, 1956-1965

BA: Highest, career, all-time

.332	Cy Seymour, 1902-1906
.331	Edd Roush, 1916-1931
.325	Jake Beckley, 1897-1903
.314	Bubbles Hargrave, 1921-1928
.311	Rube Bressler, 1917-1927
.307	Pete Rose, 1963-1986 (9)

Slug avg: Highest, career, all-time

.554	Frank Robinson, 1956-1965
.514	George Foster, 1971-1981
.512	Ted Kluszewski, 1947-1957
.509	ERIC DAVIS, 1984-1991
.498	Wally Post, 1949-1963

Games started: Most, career, all-time

356	Eppa Rixey, 1921-1933
322	Paul Derringer, 1933-1942
319	Dolf Luque, 1918-1929
296	Bucky Walters, 1938-1948
278	Johnny Vander Meer, 1937-1949
258	Jim Maloney, 1960-1970 (7)

Saves: Most, career, all-time

148	JOHN FRANCO, 1984-1989
119	Clay Carroll, 1968-1975
88	Tom Hume, 1977-1987
76	Pedro Borbon, 1970-1979
73	Wayne Granger, 1969-1971

Shutouts: Most, career, all-time

32	Bucky Walters, 1938-1948
30	Jim Maloney, 1960-1970
29	Johnny Vander Meer, 1937-1949
25	Ken Raffensberger, 1947-1954
24	Paul Derringer, 1933-1942
24	Noodles Hahn, 1899-1905
24	Dolf Luque, 1918-1929

Wins: Most, career, all-time

179	Eppa Rixey, 1921-1933
161	Paul Derringer, 1933-1942
160	Bucky Walters, 1938-1948
154	Dolf Luque, 1918-1929
134	Jim Maloney, 1960-1970

K: Most, career, all-time

1592	Jim Maloney, 1960-1970
1449	Mario Soto, 1977-1988
1289	Joe Nuxhall, 1944-1966
1251	Johnny Vander Meer, 1937-1949
1062	Paul Derringer, 1933-1942

Win pct: Highest, career, all-time

.674	Don Gullett, 1970-1976
.653	Pedro Borbon, 1970-1979
.636	JOSE RIJO, 1988-1991
.623	Jim Maloney, 1960-1970
.623	Clay Carroll, 1968-1975

ERA: Lowest, career, all-time

2.18	Fred Toney, 1915-1918
2.37	Bob Ewing, 1902-1909
2.52	Noodles Hahn, 1899-1905
2.62	Hod Eller, 1917-1921
2.65	Pete Schneider, 1914-1918
2.73	Clay Carroll, 1968-1975 (7)

Runs: Most, season

134	Frank Robinson, 1962
131	Vada Pinson, 1959
130	Pete Rose, 1976
129	Arlie Latham, 1894
126	Tommy Harper, 1965

Hits: Most, season

230	Pete Rose, 1973
219	Cy Seymour, 1905
218	Pete Rose, 1969
215	Pete Rose, 1976
210	Pete Rose, 1968
210	Pete Rose, 1975

2B: Most, season

51	Frank Robinson, 1962
51	Pete Rose, 1978
47	Vada Pinson, 1959
47	Pete Rose, 1975
45	George Kelly, 1929
45	Pete Rose, 1974

3B: Most, season

26	John Reilly, 1890
22	Sam Crawford, 1902
22	Jake Daubert, 1922
22	Bid McPhee, 1890
22	Mike Mitchell, 1911
14	Vada Pinson, 1963 (*)

HR: Most, season

52	George Foster, 1977
49	Ted Kluszewski, 1954
47	Ted Kluszewski, 1955
45	Johnny Bench, 1970
40	Johnny Bench, 1972
40	George Foster, 1978
40	Ted Kluszewski, 1953
40	Tony Perez, 1970
40	Wally Post, 1955

RBI: Most, season

149	George Foster, 1977
148	Johnny Bench, 1970
141	Ted Kluszewski, 1954
136	Frank Robinson, 1962
130	Deron Johnson, 1965

SB: Most, season

87	Arlie Latham, 1891
80	Bob Bescher, 1911
80	ERIC DAVIS, 1986
79	Dave Collins, 1980
76	Dusty Miller, 1896

BB: Most, season

132	Joe Morgan, 1975
120	Joe Morgan, 1974
117	Joe Morgan, 1977
115	Joe Morgan, 1972
114	Joe Morgan, 1976

BA: Highest, season

.377	Cy Seymour, 1905
.372	Bug Holliday, 1894
.351	Edd Roush, 1923
.351	Mike Donlin, 1903
.348	Edd Roush, 1924
.348	Pete Rose, 1969 (6)

Slug avg: Highest, season

.642	Ted Kluszewski, 1954
.631	George Foster, 1977
.624	Frank Robinson, 1962
.611	Frank Robinson, 1961
.595	Frank Robinson, 1960

Games started: Most, season

49	Elton Chamberlain, 1892
47	Tony Mullane, 1891
45	Billy Rhines, 1890
43	Billy Rhines, 1891
42	Noodles Hahn, 1901
42	Pete Schneider, 1917
42	Fred Toney, 1917
40	Jack Billingham, 1973 (8)

Saves: Most, season

39	JOHN FRANCO, 1988
37	Clay Carroll, 1972
35	Wayne Granger, 1970
32	JOHN FRANCO, 1987
32	JOHN FRANCO, 1989

Shutouts: Most, season

7	Jack Billingham, 1973
7	Hod Eller, 1919
7	Fred Toney, 1917
6	Ewell Blackwell, 1947
6	Noodles Hahn, 1902
6	Jack Harper, 1904
6	DANNY JACKSON, 1988
6	Dolf Luque, 1923
6	Jim Maloney, 1963
6	Ken Raffensberger, 1952
6	Billy Rhines, 1890
6	Fred Toney, 1915
6	Johnny Vander Meer, 1941
6	Bucky Walters, 1944
6	Jake Weimer, 1906

Wins: Most, season

28	Billy Rhines, 1890
27	Pink Hawley, 1898
27	Dolf Luque, 1923
27	Bucky Walters, 1939
25	Paul Derringer, 1939
25	Eppa Rixey, 1922
23	DANNY JACKSON, 1988 (9)
23	Jim Maloney, 1963 (9)

K: Most, season

274	Mario Soto, 1982
265	Jim Maloney, 1963
244	Jim Maloney, 1965
242	Mario Soto, 1983
239	Noodles Hahn, 1901

Win pct: Highest, season

.826	Elmer Riddle, 1941
.821	Bob Purkey, 1962
.783	TOM BROWNING, 1988
.781	Paul Derringer, 1939
.771	Dolf Luque, 1923

ERA: Lowest, season

1.58	Fred Toney, 1915
1.73	Bob Ewing, 1907
1.77	Noodles Hahn, 1902
1.82	Dutch Ruether, 1919
1.86	Andy Coakley, 1908
1.99	Gary Nolan, 1972 (9)

Most pinch-hit homers, season

5	Jerry Lynch, 1961
4	Bob Thurman, 1957

Most pinch-hit, homers, career

13	Jerry Lynch, 1957-1963

Most consecutive games, batting safely

44	Pete Rose, 1978

Most consecutive scoreless innings

N/A

No hit games

Bumpus Jones, Cin vs Pit NL, 7-1; October 15, 1892 (first game in the major leagues).
Ted Breitenstein, Cin vs Pit NL, 11-0; April 22, 1898.
Noodles Hahn, Cin vs Phi NL, 4-0; July 12, 1900.
Fred Toney, Cin at Chi NL, 1-0; May 2, 1917 (ten innings).
Hod Eller, Cin vs StL NL, 6-0; May 11, 1919.
Johnny Vander Meer, Cin vs Bos NL, 3-0; June 11, 1938
Johnny Vander Meer, Cin at Bro NL, 6-0; June 15, 1938 (next start after June 11)

Clyde Shoun, Cin vs Bos NL, 1-0; May 15, 1944.
Ewell Blackwell, Cin vs Bos NL, 6-0; June 18, 1947.
Johnny Klippstein (7 innings), Hershell Freeman (1 inning) and Joe Black (3 innings), Cin at Mil NL, 1-2; May 26, 1956 (lost on 3 hits in 11 innings after allowing the first hit in the tenth)
Jim Maloney, Cin vs NY NL, 0-1; June 14, 1965 (lost on 2 hits in 11 innings after pitching 10 hitless innings).
Jim Maloney, Cin at Chi NL, 1-0; August 19, 1965 (1st game, 10 innings).
George Culver, Cin at Phi NL, 6-1; July 29, 1968 (2nd game).
Jim Maloney, Cin vs Hou NL, 10-0; April 30, 1969.
Tom Seaver, Cin vs StL NL, 4-0; June 16, 1978.
Tom Browning, Cin vs LA NL, 1-0; September 16, 1988 (perfect game).
Elton Chamberlain, seven innings, darkness, Cin vs Bos NL, 6-0; September 23, 1893 (2nd game).
Jake Weimer, seven innings, agreement, Cin vs Bro NL, 1-0; August 24, 1906 (2nd game).

Houston Astros

Steve Finley hit a solid .285, stole 34 bases, and anchored center field.

Well, the future looks brighter

The Houston Astros like to think they saw their future as they watched the Atlanta Braves jump from last place to first in the National League West.

"We were able to see how quickly a team can turn around," manager Art Howe said. "We hope we're on the same track as they are."

There are some similarities. The Astros tied a club record with 97 losses in 1991. That's exactly how many the Braves lost in 1990. And like Atlanta, the Houston strategy is to build from within, with young players.

The Astros said good-bye to veterans Glenn Davis, Terry Puhl and Glenn Wilson, and welcomed newcomers such as Jeff Bagwell, Steve Finley, Luis Gonzalez and Pete Harnisch.

Bagwell was playing third base for the Class AA New Britain (Conn.) Red Sox two years ago. He was obtained in a trade for pitcher Larry Andersen, switched to first base and responded with a great rookie season. He hit .294 and led the team with 15 home runs and 82 runs batted in. Only catcher Craig Biggio (.295) hit higher.

Finley and Harnisch came from Baltimore with pitcher Curt Schilling in the Davis trade. Finley, a former International League batting champion, hit a solid .285, stole 34 bases and anchored center field. Harnisch was 12-9 despite frequent lapses in support, and posted a 2.70 earned run average (2.41 in the Astrodome).

Gonzalez, who hit 24 homers at Class AA Columbus, Ga., in 1990, made the jump to the majors and hit .254 with 28 doubles, 13 HRs and 69 RBI. He was moved from first base to left field in spring training. Third baseman Ken Caminiti hit .253 and drove in 80 runs.

The problem was pitching depth. Ace Mike Scott made just two starts, pitching a total of seven innings, before he was sidelined for the year with recurring shoulder problems. Jim Deshaies, once thought to be on the verge of stardom, was just 5-12 with a 4.98 ERA.

The bullpen could have applied for disaster relief. With a record of 20-34, the relief corps had as many losses as saves. Left-hander Al Osuna led the staff with 12 saves, but the bullpen blew a whopping 19 save opportunities.

In addition, the Astros led the major leagues with 161 errors.

Still, the general mood at the end of the season was upbeat. Nobody expected the team to win big after trimming its payroll from $20 million to $12 million. This was a rebuilding year, and the team found plenty of reasons for optimism.

After watching Atlanta clinch the division at his team's expense Oct. 5, Howe motioned to his team and said, "These guys got to see what waits for them—hopefully."

—Bill Koenig

Astros 1992 preview

Don't look for the Houston Astros to join the worst-to-first fad this season—that would be too much of a miracle.

But do look for significant improvement from a club that definitely is headed in the right direction. The Astros are young, eager and getting better.

NL Rookie of the Year first baseman Jeff Bagwell (.294, 15 HR, 82 RBI) heads a crop of first- or second-year players that also includes outfielders Steve Finley and Luis Gonzalez, infielder Andujar Cedeno and pitcher Pete Harnisch.

The middle of the lineup could use a solid run producer.

The pitching staff has potential with starters such as Ryan Bowen, Darryl Kile, Jeff Juden and Harnisch.

The bullpen (led by Rob Mallicoat, Curt Schilling, Al Osuna and Dean Wilkins) has to improve after blowing 19 save opportunities last year.

▸Pete Harnisch will become the first pitcher in major-league history to go an entire season without giving up an earned run. Harnisch will finish the season with a 9-10 record.

▸After the AstroDome hosts the Republican National Convention, Dan Quayle will embark on a new career as Astros batboy.

Astro-youth: Such a deal

By Gary Gillette

After Houston's fire sale on veteran players, the Astros wound up with the most inexperienced—and least expensive—roster in the National League last year: $12 million total.

This thrifty payroll was kept down by filling the roster with lots of players who are not yet eligible for arbitration. Houston had more players in this class than any other National League team, and fewer with three or more years of service. In fact, only 37% (10 of 27) of the Astros had any negotiating leverage going into the 1991 season, compared to the 59% average for all other teams in the league.

Major league service is measured in years and days.

Players with less than two years of service and most players with more than two but less than three years service are not eligible for salary arbitration. Those with more than three but less than six years of service are automatically eligible for salary arbitration. Players with six or more years of service are eligible for free agency.

Attempt to switch has hitch

Houston's third baseman Ken Caminiti said he would decide at the end of the season whether to continue switch-hitting.

Caminiti has struggled batting left-handed for the past two seasons. When he made the remark in September, he was hitting over .300 right-handed, but less than .200 from the left side of the plate. He finished the season .310 from the right and .213 from the left.

"Sometimes I'd rather just be a right-handed hitter," Caminiti said. "But I'm not. I know I could put up some big numbers just hitting right, but I don't know where I'd be now.

"My natural way is right-handed," Caminiti explained. "It comes easy for me. If I get into a slump I can get myself out. But left-handed, the swing is not mine. When I get in a slump, I have no idea what I'm doing wrong. I can't get myself out of it without some help, some supervision."

Caminiti said the most frustrating part of his decision is that he has had some success batting left-handed in the past. He became a switch-hitter in college, nine years ago.

Braves gave Astros hope

The Astros were more than innocent bystanders at the Atlanta Braves' NL West victory celebration on Oct. 5. Observing from the third-base dugout at Atlanta-Fulton County Stadium after their loss gave the Braves the title, the Astros saw just how quickly a team's fortunes can change.

A year earlier, the Braves lost 97 games. In 1991, they won the pennant. Last year the Astros lost 97 games. Next year?

"As far as our season, it couldn't have ended in a better spot," said manager Art Howe. "We were able to see how quickly a team can turn around. We hope we're on the same track as they are. These guys got to see what waits for them—hopefully."

Catcher Craig Biggio is another wishful thinker.

"I was just wondering what it would

be like to be on the receiving end of something like this," he said after watching the Braves and their fans whoop it up.

"I mean, we lost 97 games and it has been a long, long season. These guys were in the same spot last year. Now here they are, with 45,000 people singing and chanting the last weekend of the season. Incredible.

"The only time I had anything like this happen to me was in Class A ball (Asheville, N.C.). There were 6,000 people there and I thought that was a heck of a deal."

The Astros didn't play favorites. Between Sept. 11 and Oct. 5, they were 0-5 against Atlanta and 0-4 against the Los Angeles Dodgers.

Their 97 losses in 1991 tied a club record set in 1965 and 1975.

Astros winter league news

▶Winter leagues: Houston sent one of the larger contingents of players to the winter leagues. OF Eric Anthony, whose career has stalled after back-to-back minor league seasons of 28 or more home runs in 1988 and 1989, looked to find enough consistency at the plate to make the permanent jump to the majors from Class AAA Tucson, where he hit .336 in 318 at-bats in 1991. . . .Between Anthony, Javier Ortiz and Karl Rhodes, who all played in Venezuela, the Astros hope to find their right fielder of the future. . . . OF Gerald Young was to have played with the Mayaguez Indians in Puerto Rico but returned home with a broken arm. . . . RHP Shane Reynolds (8-9, 4.47 at Class AA Jackson) worked on control and velocity in Venezuela.
▶Partial winter leagues roster: Harold Allen, P, Los Mochis Caneros (Sugar cane growers), Mexico; Eric Anthony, OF, Navegantes del Magallanes, Venezuela; Andujar Cedeno, SS, Azucareros Este, (Sugarmen), D.R.; Carlo Columbino, 3B, Los Mochis Caneros, Mexico; Tony Eusebio, C, Azucareros Este, (Sugar East), D.R.; Dean Hartgraves, LHP, Bayamon Cowboys, P. R..

Team directory

▶Owner: Dr. John J. McMullen

▶General Manager: Bill Wood

▶Ballpark:
Houston Astrodome
8400 Kirby Drive, Houston, Texas
713-799-9555
Capacity 54,816
Parking for 26,000 cars; $4
Public transportation by bus
Wheelchair section and ramps

▶Team publications:
Astros Magazine, Astros Media Guide, Liftoff
713-799-9500

▶TV, radio broadcast stations:
KPRC 950 AM, KTXH Channel 20, Home Sports Entertainment Cable

▶Camps and/or clinics:
Astros Youth Clinics during the season, 713-799-9500

▶Spring Training:
Osceola County Stadium
Kissimmee, Florida
Capacity 5,100
407-933-2520

HOUSTON ASTROS 1991 Final Stats

Batting	AVG	SLG	OB	G	AB	R	H	TB	2B	3B	HR	RBI	BB	SO	SB	CS	E
Biggio	.295	.374	.358	149	546	79	161	204	23	4	4	46	53	71	19	6	11
Bagwell	.294	.437	.387	156	554	79	163	242	26	4	15	82	75	116	7	4	12
Finley	.285	.406	.331	159	596	84	170	242	28	10	8	54	42	65	34	18	5
Ortiz	.277	.386	.381	47	83	7	23	32	4	1	1	5	14	14	0	0	0
Candaele	.262	.362	.319	151	461	44	121	167	20	7	4	50	40	49	9	3	10
Tolentino	.259	.389	.305	44	54	6	14	21	4	0	1	6	4	9	0	0	1
Gonzalez	.254	.433	.320	137	473	51	120	205	28	9	13	69	40	101	10	7	5
Caminiti	.253	.383	.312	152	574	65	145	220	30	3	13	80	46	85	4	5	23
Cooper	.250	.313	.368	9	16	1	4	5	1	0	0	2	3	6	0	0	1
Cedeno	.243	.418	.270	67	251	27	61	105	13	2	9	36	9	74	4	3	18
Yelding	.243	.301	.276	78	276	19	67	83	11	1	1	20	13	46	11	9	20
Ramirez	.236	.292	.274	101	233	17	55	68	10	0	1	20	13	40	3	3	8
Oberkfell	.229	.286	.357	53	70	7	16	20	4	0	0	14	14	8	0	0	2
Young	.218	.275	.327	108	142	26	31	39	3	1	1	11	24	17	16	5	0
Rhodes	.213	.272	.289	44	136	7	29	37	3	1	1	12	14	26	2	2	4
Simms	.203	.317	.301	49	123	18	25	39	5	0	3	16	18	38	1	0	6
Lofton	.203	.216	.253	20	74	9	15	16	1	0	0	0	5	19	2	1	1
Nichols	.196	.255	.268	20	51	3	10	13	3	0	0	1	5	17	0	0	3
Davidson	.190	.275	.263	85	142	10	27	39	6	0	2	15	12	28	0	0	0
Mota	.189	.244	.198	27	90	4	17	22	2	0	1	6	1	17	2	0	3
Servais	.162	.243	.244	16	37	0	6	9	3	0	0	6	4	8	0	0	1
Anthony	.153	.229	.227	39	118	11	18	27	6	0	1	7	12	41	1	0	1
McLemore	.148	.164	.221	21	61	6	9	10	1	0	0	2	6	13	0	1	2
Rohde	.122	.122	.217	29	41	3	5	5	0	0	0	0	5	8	0	0	0
Eusebio	.105	.158	.320	10	19	4	2	3	1	0	0	0	0	8	0	0	1

Pitching	W-L	ERA	G	GS	CG	GF	Sho	SV	IP	H	R	ER	HR	BB	SO
Harnisch	12-9	2.70	33	33	4	0	2	0	216.2	169	71	65	14	83	172
Capel	1-3	3.03	25	0	0	13	0	3	32.2	33	14	11	3	15	23
Henry	3-2	3.19	52	0	0	25	0	2	67.2	51	25	24	7	39	51
Osuna	7-6	3.42	71	0	0	32	0	12	81.2	59	39	31	5	46	68
Kile	7-11	3.69	37	22	0	5	0	0	153.2	144	81	63	16	84	100
Corsi	0-5	3.71	47	0	0	15	0	0	77.2	76	37	32	6	23	53
Williams	0-1	3.75	2	2	0	0	0	0	12	11	5	5	2	4	4
Schilling	3-5	3.81	56	0	0	34	0	8	75.2	79	35	32	2	39	71
Mallicoat	0-2	3.86	24	0	0	4	0	1	23.1	22	10	10	2	13	18
Gardner	1-2	4.01	5	4	0	0	0	0	24.2	19	12	11	5	14	12
Jones	6-8	4.39	26	22	1	0	1	0	135.1	143	73	66	9	51	88
Portugal	10-12	4.49	32	27	1	3	0	1	168.1	163	91	84	19	59	120
Hernandez	2-7	4.71	32	6	0	8	0	3	63	66	34	33	6	32	55
Deshaies	5-12	4.98	28	28	1	0	0	0	161	156	90	89	19	72	98
Bowen	6-4	5.15	14	13	0	0	0	0	71.2	73	43	41	4	36	49
Juden	0-2	6.00	4	3	0	0	0	0	18	19	14	12	3	7	11
Wilkins	2-1	11.25	7	0	0	3	0	1	8	16	14	10	0	10	4
Scott	0-2	12.86	2	2	0	0	0	0	7	11	10	10	2	4	3

1992 Preliminary Roster

Pitchers (20)

Willie Blair
Ryan Bowen
Mike Capel
Chris Gardner
Brian Griffiths
Pete Harnisch
Butch Henry
Xavier Hernandez
Jimmy Jones
Todd Jones
Jeff Juden
Darryl Kile
Rob Mallicoat
Al Osuna
Mark Portugal
Shane Reynolds
Curt Schilling
Richie Simon
Matt Turner
Brian Williams

Catchers (5)

Craig Biggio
Tony Eusebio
Scott Servais
Ed Taubensee
Eddie Tucker

Infielders (9)

Jeff Bagwell
Ken Caminiti
Casey Candaele
Andujar Cedeno
Gary Cooper
Juan Guerrero
Orlando Miller
Andy Mota
Eric Yelding

Outfielders (6)

Eric Anthony
Steve Finley
Luis Gonzalez
Karl Rhodes
Mike Simms
Gerald Young

Games Played by position

	G	C	1B	2B	3B	SS	OF
Anthony,E	39	0	0	0	0	0	37
Bagwell,J	156	0	155	0	0	0	0
Biggio,C	149	139	0	3	0	0	2
Caminiti,K	152	0	0	0	152	0	0
Candaele,C	151	0	0	109	11	0	26
Cedeno,A	67	0	0	0	0	66	0
Cooper,G	9	0	0	0	4	0	0
Davidson,M	85	0	0	0	0	0	63
Eusebio,T	10	9	0	0	0	0	0
Finley,S	159	0	0	0	0	0	153
Gonzalez,L	137	0	0	0	0	0	133
Lofton,K	20	0	0	0	0	0	20
McLemore,M	21	0	0	19	0	0	0
Mota,An	27	0	0	27	0	0	0
Nichols,C	20	17	0	0	0	0	0
Oberkfell,K	53	0	13	0	4	0	0
Ortiz,Jo	47	0	0	0	0	0	24
Ramirez,R	101	0	0	27	2	45	0
Rhodes,K	44	0	0	0	0	0	44

Sick call: 1991 DL report

Player	Days on the DL
Mike Scott	76
Mark McLemore	47
Xavier Hernandez	23
Mark Portugal	26
Scott Servais	34
Jimmy Jones	47
Luis Gonzalez	5

Minor League Report

Class AAA — Tucson finished 79-61, first in the first half and third in the second half in the PCL Southern Division. The Toros beat Colorado Springs and Calgary to win the playoffs and league championship. Top hitters were INF Dave Rohde (.372), 3B Gary Cooper (.305-14-75), OF Eric Anthony (.336-9-63) and OF Kenny Lofton (.308 with 17 triples, 50 RBI and 40 SBs). 1B Rob Nelson (.278 with 25 RBI in 25 games after being traded from Vancouver). RHP Terry Clark (14-7, 4.66) tied for the league lead in victories. RHP Dean Wilkins had 20 saves. . . . **Class AA** — Jackson finished 70-66, second both halves in the Texas League Eastern Division. 1B Howard Prager hit .305 with 11 HRs and 65 RBI. OF Joe Mikulik hit .293 with 15 HRs and 94 RBI. 2B Trent Hubbard hit .297 with 39 SBs. Three others had 20 or more SBs (OF Bert Hunter 31, OF Bernie Jenkins 21, Mikulik 20). The pitching staff set a franchise record with 947 strikeouts. RHP Chris Gardner was 13-5 with a 3.15 ERA. RHP Richie Simon (4-2, 2.18) had 20 saves. Five Generals earned promotions to Houston. . . . **Class A** — Osceola finished 64-63, second in the first half and third in the second half in the Florida State League Central Division. SS Orlando Miller hit .298, 3B Jeff Ball hit .245 with 51 RBI and OF Brian Williams hit in 20 of his last 21 games to raise his average to .240. OF Brian Hunter had 32 SBs. C Ed Beuerlein hit 7 HRs in 63 games. RHP Ed Ponte (6-6, 1.78, 11 saves) was team MVP. . . . Burlington finished 67-70, first in the first half and seventh in the second half in the Midwest League Southern Division. The Astros lost to Clinton in the playoffs. Top hitters were OF Ruben Cruz (.278-8-59), OF Chris Hatcher (.235-15-65) C Tony Gilmore (.272) and 2B Fletcher Thompson (.271 with 34 SBs). LHP Wally Trice (4-2, 0.99, 18 saves) had 9 walks and 53 strikeouts in 46 innings. LHP Anthony Gutierrez (7-4, 2.69) had 126 strikeouts in 107 innings. RHP Donnie Wall (7-5, 2.03) had 21 walks and 102 strikeouts in 107 innings. . . . Asheville finished 55-83, seventh in the first half and tied for fifth in the second half in the South Atlantic League Northern Division. SS Tom Nevers hit .252 with 16 HRs and 71 RBI. C Lance Smith hit .280 with 20 doubles and 41 RBI. . . . Auburn finished 38-39, second in the NY-P League McNamara West Division. Eric Martinez hit .320 with 9 HRs and 58 RBI. James Mouton hit .264 with 10 triples and 60 SBs. LHP Mark Loughlin (8-2, 2.01) gave up 73 hits in 94 innings.

Tops in the Organization

BATTING LEADERS	Club	Avg.	G	AB	R	H	HR	RBI
Kenny Lofton	Tcn	.308	130	545	93	168	2	50
Gary Cooper	Tcn	.305	120	406	86	124	14	75
Andujar Cedeno	Tcn	.303	93	347	49	105	7	55
Howard Prager	Jck	.303	123	400	63	121	11	72
Andy Mota	Tcn	.299	123	462	65	138	2	46

HOME RUNS			WINS		
Rob Nelson	Tcn	16	Terry Clark	Tcn	14
Tom Nevers	Ash	16	Donnie Wall	Osc	13
Joe Mikulik	Tcn	15	Chris Gardner	Jck	13
Mike Simms	Tcn	15	Doug Ketchen	Ash	10
Gary Cooper	Tcn	14	Butch Henry	Tcn	10

RBI			SAVES		
Joe Mikulik	Tcn	94	Jim Dougherty	Ash	27
Gary Cooper	Tcn	75	Rich Simon	Jck	20
Howard Prager	Jck	72	Dean Wilkins	Tcn	20
Tom Nevers	Ash	71	Wally Trice	Jck	19
Chris Hatcher	Bur	65	Montie Phillips	Osc	11

STOLEN BASES			STRIKEOUTS		
Kenny Lofton	Tcn	40	Donnie Wall	Osc	164
Trent Hubbard	Tcn	39	Troy Dovey	Bur	130
Fletcher Thompson	Bur	34	Anthony Gutierrez	Bur	126
Several players tied		32	Jeff Juden	Tcn	126
			Shane Reynolds	Jck	116

PITCHING LEADERS	Club	W-L	ERA	IP	H	BB	SO
Donnie Wall	Osc	13-8	2.05	184	128	32	164
Dean Hartgraves	Tcn	9-5	2.83	118	107	45	62
Troy Dovey	Bur	7-6	3.02	116	88	74	130
Jeff Juden	Tcn	9-5	3.14	152	140	69	126
Chris Gardner	Jck	13-5	3.15	131	116	75	72

Houston (1962-1991)

Runs: Most, career, all-time

890	Cesar Cedeno, 1970-1981	
871	Jose Cruz, 1975-1987	
829	Jim Wynn, 1963-1973	
676	TERRY PUHL, 1977-1990	
640	Bob Watson, 1966-1979	

Hits: Most, career, all-time

1937	Jose Cruz, 1975-1987
1659	Cesar Cedeno, 1970-1981
1448	Bob Watson, 1966-1979
1357	TERRY PUHL, 1977-1990
1291	Jim Wynn, 1963-1973

2B: Most, career, all-time

343	Cesar Cedeno, 1970-1981
335	Jose Cruz, 1975-1987
241	Bob Watson, 1966-1979
228	Jim Wynn, 1963-1973
226	TERRY PUHL, 1977-1990

3B: Most, career, all-time

80	Jose Cruz, 1975-1987
63	Joe Morgan, 1963-1980
62	Roger Metzger, 1971-1978
56	TERRY PUHL, 1977-1990
55	Cesar Cedeno, 1970-1981
55	Craig Reynolds, 1979-1989

HR: Most, career, all-time

223	Jim Wynn, 1963-1973
166	GLENN DAVIS, 1984-1990
163	Cesar Cedeno, 1970-1981
139	Bob Watson, 1966-1979
138	Jose Cruz, 1975-1987

RBI: Most, career, all-time

942	Jose Cruz, 1975-1987
782	Bob Watson, 1966-1979
778	Cesar Cedeno, 1970-1981
719	Jim Wynn, 1963-1973
600	Doug Rader, 1967-1975

SB: Most, career, all-time

487	Cesar Cedeno, 1970-1981
288	Jose Cruz, 1975-1987
219	Joe Morgan, 1963-1980
217	TERRY PUHL, 1977-1990
191	Enos Cabell, 1975-1985
191	BILL DORAN, 1982-1990

BB: Most, career, all-time

847	Jim Wynn, 1963-1973
730	Jose Cruz, 1975-1987
678	Joe Morgan, 1963-1980
585	BILL DORAN, 1982-1990
534	Cesar Cedeno, 1970-1981

BA: Highest, career, all-time

.297	Bob Watson, 1966-1979
.292	Jose Cruz, 1975-1987
.289	Cesar Cedeno, 1970-1981
.282	Jesus Alou, 1969-1979
.281	Enos Cabell, 1975-1985

Slug avg: Highest, career, all-time

.483	GLENN DAVIS, 1984-1990
.454	Cesar Cedeno, 1970-1981
.445	Jim Wynn, 1963-1973
.444	Bob Watson, 1966-1979
.429	Jose Cruz, 1975-1987

Games started: Most, career, all-time

320	Larry Dierker, 1964-1976
301	Joe Niekro, 1975-1985
282	NOLAN RYAN, 1980-1988
267	Bob Knepper, 1981-1989
259	MIKE SCOTT, 1983-1991

Saves: Most, career, all-time

199	DAVE SMITH, 1980-1990
76	Fred Gladding, 1968-1973
72	Joe Sambito, 1976-1984
50	Ken Forsch, 1970-1980
43	Frank DiPino, 1982-1986

Shutouts: Most, career, all-time

25	Larry Dierker, 1964-1976
21	Joe Niekro, 1975-1985
21	MIKE SCOTT, 1983-1991
20	Don Wilson, 1966-1974
19	J.R. Richard, 1971-1980

Wins: Most, career, all-time

144	Joe Niekro, 1975-1985
137	Larry Dierker, 1964-1976
110	MIKE SCOTT, 1983-1991
107	J.R.Richard, 1971-1980
106	NOLAN RYAN, 1980-1988

K: Most, career, all-time

1866	NOLAN RYAN, 1980-1988
1493	J.R. Richard, 1971-1980
1487	Larry Dierker, 1964-1976
1318	MIKE SCOTT, 1983-1991
1283	Don Wilson, 1966-1974

Win pct: Highest, career, all-time

.609	Jim Ray, 1965-1973
.601	J.R. Richard, 1971-1980
.576	MIKE SCOTT, 1983-1991
.571	DANNY DARWIN, 1986-1990
.554	Joe Niekro, 1975-1985

ERA: Lowest, career, all-time

2.53	DAVE SMITH, 1980-1990
3.13	NOLAN RYAN, 1980-1988
3.15	Don Wilson, 1966-1974
3.15	J.R. Richard, 1971-1980
3.18	Ken Forsch, 1970-1980

Runs: Most, season

117	Jim Wynn, 1972
113	Jim Wynn, 1969
103	Cesar Cedeno, 1972
102	Joe Morgan, 1970
102	Jim Wynn, 1967

Hits: Most, season

195	Enos Cabell, 1978
189	Jose Cruz, 1983
187	Jose Cruz, 1984
185	Jose Cruz, 1980
185	Greg Gross, 1974

2B: Most, season

44	Rusty Staub, 1967
40	Cesar Cedeno, 1971
39	Cesar Cedeno, 1972
38	Bob Watson, 1977
37	Rusty Staub, 1968

3B: Most, season

14	Roger Metzger, 1973
13	Jose Cruz, 1984
12	Joe Morgan, 1965
11	BILL DORAN, 1984
11	Roger Metzger, 1971
11	Joe Morgan, 1967
11	Joe Morgan, 1971
11	Craig Reynolds, 1984

HR: Most, season

37	Jim Wynn, 1967
34	GLENN DAVIS, 1989
33	Jim Wynn, 1969
31	GLENN DAVIS, 1986
30	GLENN DAVIS, 1988

RBI: Most, season

110	Bob Watson, 1977
107	Jim Wynn, 1967
105	Lee May, 1973
102	Cesar Cedeno, 1974
102	Bob Watson, 1976

SB: Most, season

65	GERALD YOUNG, 1988
64	ERIC YELDING, 1990
61	Cesar Cedeno, 1977
58	Cesar Cedeno, 1976
57	Cesar Cedeno, 1974

BB: Most, season

148	Jim Wynn, 1969
110	Joe Morgan, 1969
106	Jim Wynn, 1970
103	Jim Wynn, 1972
102	Joe Morgan, 1970

BA: Highest, season

.333	Rusty Staub, 1967
.324	Bob Watson, 1975
.320	Cesar Cedeno, 1972
.320	Cesar Cedeno, 1973
.318	Jose Cruz, 1983

Slug avg: Highest, season

.537	Cesar Cedeno, 1973
.537	Cesar Cedeno, 1972
.507	Jim Wynn, 1969
.498	Bob Watson, 1977
.495	Jim Wynn, 1967

Games started: Most, season

40	Jerry Reuss, 1973
39	J.R. Richard, 1976
38	Bob Knepper, 1986
38	Joe Niekro, 1979
38	Joe Niekro, 1983
38	Joe Niekro, 1984
38	J.R. Richard, 1979

Saves: Most, season

33	DAVE SMITH, 1986
29	Fred Gladding, 1969
27	DAVE SMITH, 1985
27	DAVE SMITH, 1988
25	DAVE SMITH, 1989

Shutouts: Most, season

6	Dave Roberts, 1973
5	Larry Dierker, 1972
5	Bob Knepper, 1981
5	Bob Knepper, 1986
5	Joe Niekro, 1979
5	Joe Niekro, 1982
5	MIKE SCOTT, 1986
5	MIKE SCOTT, 1988

Wins: Most, season

21	Joe Niekro, 1979
20	Larry Dierker, 1969
20	Joe Niekro, 1980
20	J.R. Richard, 1976
20	MIKE SCOTT, 1989

K: Most, season

313	J.R. Richard, 1979
306	MIKE SCOTT, 1986
303	J.R. Richard, 1978
270	NOLAN RYAN, 1987
245	NOLAN RYAN, 1982

Win pct: Highest, season

.692	MIKE SCOTT, 1985
.667	MIKE SCOTT, 1989
.656	Joe Niekro, 1979
.652	Larry Dierker, 1972
.643	MIKE SCOTT, 1986

ERA: Lowest, season

2.18	Bob Knepper, 1981
2.21	DANNY DARWIN, 1990
2.22	Mike Cuellar, 1966
2.22	MIKE SCOTT, 1986
2.33	Larry Dierker, 1969

Most pinch-hit homers, season

5	Cliff Johnson, 1974

Most pinch-hit, homers, career

8	Cliff Johnson, 1972-1977

Most consecutive games, batting safely

23	Art Howe, 1981

Most consecutive scoreless innings

31	J. R. Richard, 1980

No hit games

Don Nottebart, Hou vs Phi NL, 4-1; May 17, 1963.

Ken T. Johnson, Hou vs Cin NL, 0-1; April 23, 1964 (lost the game).

Don Wilson, Hou vs Atl NL, 2-0; June 18, 1967.

Don Wilson, Hou at Cin NL, 4-0; May 1, 1969.

Larry Dierker, Hou vs Mon NL, 6-0; July 9, 1976.

Ken Forsch, Hou vs Atl NL, 6-0; April 7, 1979.

Nolan Ryan, Hou vs LA NL, 5-0; September 26, 1981.

Mike Scott, Hou vs SF NL, 2-0; September 25, 1986.

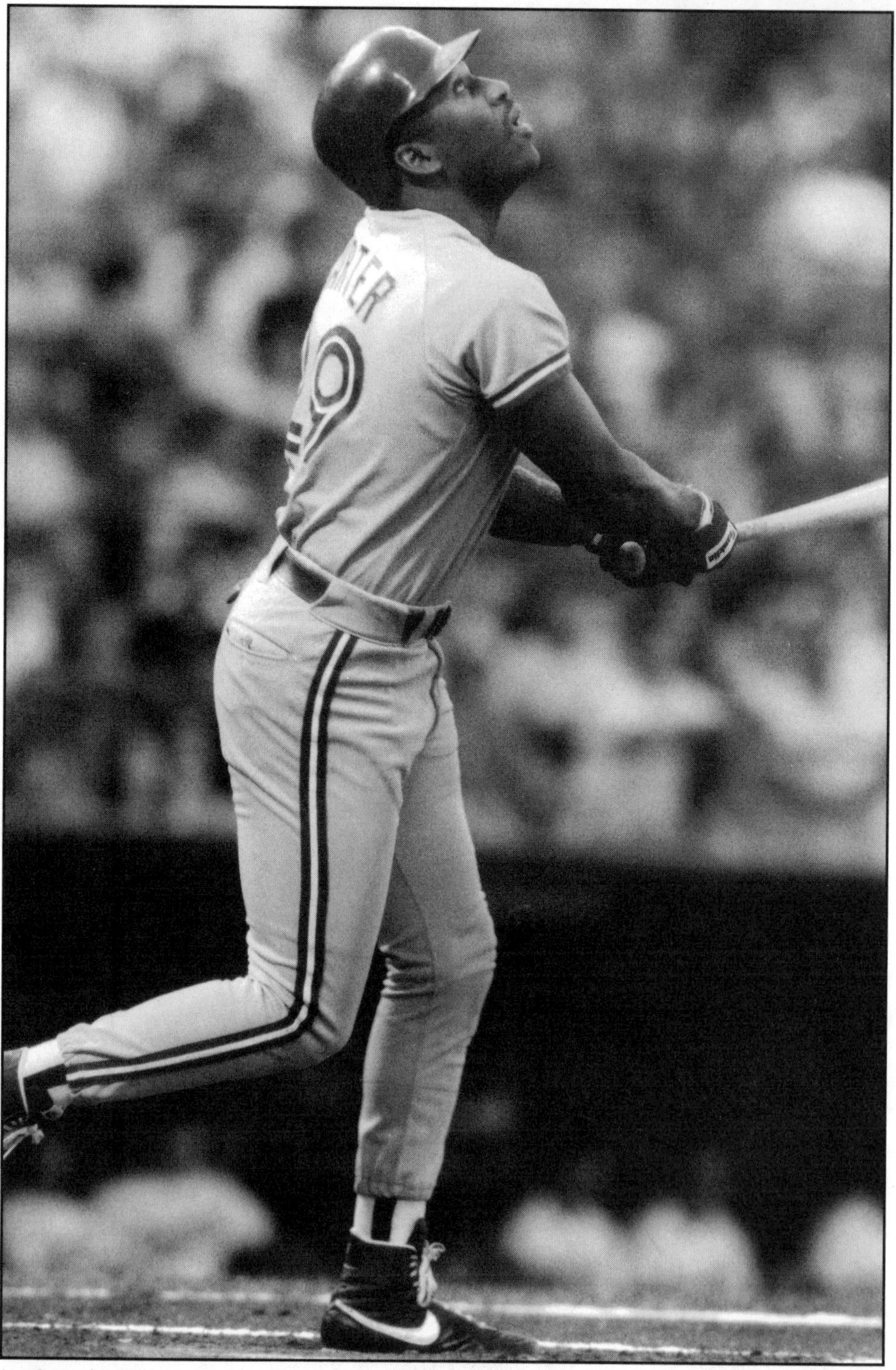

Joe Carter hit 33 home runs for Toronto, but was hurt for the ALCS.

The chemistry experiment worked

General manager Pat Gillick proved he knew something about team chemistry before the '91 season when he dealt Fred McGriff and Tony Fernandez to San Diego for Joe Carter and Roberto Alomar.

Teamed with Devon White, another newcomer, the new trio held down the top three spots in Toronto's batting order and paced the Blue Jays to the American League East title, accounting for nearly half of the team's offense.

"The deal actually had two parts," Gillick later explained. "McGriff for Carter, Fernandez for Alomar. I wouldn't have made the deal with only one part."

White, who finished '90 in the minors, quickly served notice that he could still hit major league pitching, going 3-for-5 in his second game with the Jays.

When the Toronto pitching staff was asked anonymously who was the team's MVP, all but two of them named White because of his stellar defense in center field. White's 33 stolen bases were second only to Alomar's 53 on the Jays and seventh-best in the AL.

"I can't believe the Angels let him get away," said the Twins' Chili Davis, who also fled Anaheim before the '91 season. "Devon's one of those players who doesn't come along every day. He's got great speed and he can hit."

Staff ace Dave Stieb went down first with shoulder problems and then a back injury, making just nine starts. In his place, rookie Juan Guzman steppped in, winning 10 straight games down the stretch as Toronto held off first Detroit and then Boston.

"He's got the best stuff in the league," said Jays' All-Star pitcher Jimmy Key of Guzman. "He's come a long way."

White adds, "He says he's a rookie, but I don't believe him."

Knuckleballer Tom Candiotti, who arrived in a trade from Cleveland, was runner-up to the Red Sox's Roger Clemens in the ERA race. "Who knows how many I would have won if I'd been here all year," said Candiotti, 14-13, who went to Los Angeles as a free agent in December.

Manager Cito Gaston missed 33 games with a herniated disk, an injury similar to Stieb's. Batting coach Gene Tenace, whose only previous managerial experience was on an interim basis with Prince William of the Carolina League, took over the club. He was handed a two-game lead in the AL East, and even though that was shaved to just a half-game in late September, Toronto was still two ahead when Gaston returned.

"I'm proud of the job I did," said Tenace, who was being touted for a number of mangerial openings as the Jays went to the American League playoffs. "We didn't lose any ground."

—Tim Wendel

Blue Jays 1992 preview

The Toronto Blue Jays and Boston Red Sox have been alternating AL East titles every year since 1988. Even though 1992 is Boston's turn, there is no good reason why the Blue Jays can't repeat.

They have the proper chemistry and a good nucleus in outfielders Joe Carter (33 HR, 108 RBI) and Devon White, and second baseman Roberto Alomar. Alomar and White shored up the defense and combined to steal 86 bases.

International League MVP Derek Bell was enjoying a career-year at Syracuse and should step in this season. Solid contributions from Bell and a healthy Kelly Gruber at third base should give Toronto enough offense.

With Candiotti gone, much hinges on the status of pitcher Dave Stieb, who made just nine starts last year because of shoulder and back injuries. Juan Guzman stepped up and won 10 consecutive games, joining a good rotation with Jimmy Key, Todd Stottlemyre and David Wells.

1992 prophecy: Blue Jays

▶The Blue Jays will have the most talented team in the American League, but they will not make it to the World Series. What a surprise.

▶A group of neighborhood kids will ask catcher Pat Borders to join them in a friendly game of "tag." Borders will respectfully decline.

—John Hunt

How do you spell relief? T-e-n-a-c-e.

With 35 games left and the Blue Jays only one game up on Detroit, skipper Cito Gaston had to be replaced indefinitely. Gaston, who has managed the Blue Jays since 1989, had a herniated disk (the same injury that ended Dave Stieb's season and sidelined former Orioles manager Frank Robinson for several weeks during the 1988 season), and was also suffering from numbness in his leg caused by an inflamed sciatic nerve.

The team turned to batting coach Gene Tenace, but a question lingered. How important is a manager's experience to a ballclub?

Tenace enjoyed a 17-year playing career, but his only managing experience came in 1988 when he was the interim manager for Class A Prince William of the Carolina League. He wasn't even playing professional baseball when the Tigers' Sparky Anderson began managing in 1964.

When he took over Aug. 21, Tenace told Gaston he wanted to talk with him on the phone daily. But Gaston told his relief manager that he was running the club now and didn't need to be checking in so frequently.

Tenace talked over pitching moves with coach Galen Cisco, but he said, "I make the final decision. Being an ex-catcher helps."

Except for moving Candy Maldonado up in the lineup, Tenace kept the Jays' regular batting order intact. He said he'd like to see the Blue Jays bunt and hit-and-run more, but observers say neither happened.

"I'm trying to keep things basic," Tenace said. "Get six or seven innings out of my starters and then go to my bullpen—just trying to follow common sense, really.

"I feel when all's said and done, it'll be our pitching. That's the key. Pitching and defense—that's what will win it for us."

And it certainly did.

Down the stretch: Did experience count?

Coming down the stretch—with Cito Gaston's 11 years of coaching experience sidelined—Toronto's coaching staff had 48 fewer years of experience than Detroit's. Listed is each staff's experience, as coaches and managers, and as managers only:

DETROIT	Position	Yrs	Yrs
Sparky Anderson	Manager	27	27
Billy Consolo	Dugout	13	0
Jim Davenport	Infield	18	4
Alex Grammas	Third base	26	3
Billy Muffett	Pitching	18	0
Vada Pinson	Hitting	15	0
Dick Tracewski	First base	20	1
Total		137	35

TORONTO	Position	Yrs	Yrs
Cito Gaston	(sidelined)	0	0
Gene Tenace	Batting/Mgr	7	1
Galen Cisco	Pitching	22	0
Rich Hacker	Third base	10	4
Mike Squiares	First base	7	0
John Sullivan	Bullpen	20	6
Hector Torres	Instructor	7	2
Total		73	13

Pitching tandem posted key effort

Jimmy Key downplayed a memorable milestone in Baltimore Aug. 26. After two unsuccessful attempts, Key won his 100th career game, with Tom Henke coming on to save the contest (his 30th of the season).

"It wasn't something I was thinking about. It was going to come," Key said, noting that the Blue Jays were in a pennant race and needed to concentrate on reaching that goal. "That was the first and foremost thing on my mind."

But Henke, who pitched the ninth inning to nail down the win, admitted that the game would have significance for both of them down the road.

"A few years from now I can see us sitting in a fishing boat, after we've retired," the Jays' closer said, "and I'll be able to say to him, 'Remember that night in Baltimore? You owe me a six-pack for that.'"

Alomar brothers fulfill dream of playing together

By Mike Terry

This brother act is the hottest in town. And the surname isn't Marx, Smothers or Grimm.

It's Alomar and Alomar. Roberto, 23, and Sandy, 25. Both are rising stars and both were American League starters in the 1991 All-Star Game.

It was the third time in All-Star history that blood brothers started for the same team. The Coopers (catcher Walker and pitcher Mort) represented St. Louis for the National League in 1942, and the DiMaggios—Joe (Yankees) and Dom (Red Sox)—were on the American League roster in 1949.

Overall, the Alomars are the seventh brother combination to appear in the same game.

For Sandy and Roberto, it represents the coming true of a dream that started back in their Little League days.

"It's probably the dream of every boy to be in the big leagues," said Sandy, "and for us the dream was to play together. But I never thought it could be like this; in my first two years I play against my brother and now with him."

"We know about the DiMaggios," said Roberto, commenting on the last pair of brothers to play on the same All-Star team. "They were great players. That's why this is such a thrill to be with my brother. We know this is something that doesn't happen that often."

There are those who think the Alomars were destined to be together in the big leagues. Their father, Sandy Sr., played 15 years in the majors and is currently a minor league instructor for the Cubs.

Team directory

▶Owner: Labatt's Breweries and the Canadian Imperial Bank of Commerce

▶General Manager: Pat Gillick

▶Ballpark:
Skydome
Toronto, Ontario
416-341-1000
Capacity 51,000
Public transportation available
Family and wheelchair sections, non-alcohol sections, ramps, Playland

▶Team publications:
Scorebook Magazine
416-341-2800

▶TV, radio broadcast stations:
CTV Telecasts, CJCL 1430 Toronto

▶Spring Training:
Dunedin Stadium
at Grant Field
311 Douglas Avenue
Dunedin, Florida
Capacity 6,218
813-733-0429

TORONTO BLUE JAYS 1991 Final Stats

Batting	AVG	SLG	OB	G	AB	R	H	TB	2B	3B	HR	RBI	BB	SO	SB	CS	E
Alomar	.295	.436	.354	161	637	88	188	278	41	11	9	69	57	86	53	11	15
White	.282	.455	.342	156	642	110	181	292	40	10	17	60	55	135	33	10	1
Sprague	.275	.394	.361	61	160	17	44	63	7	0	4	20	19	43	0	3	14
Carter	.273	.503	.330	162	638	89	174	321	42	3	33	108	49	112	20	9	8
Myers	.262	.411	.306	107	309	25	81	127	22	0	8	36	21	45	0	0	11
Olerud	.256	.438	.353	139	454	64	116	199	30	1	17	68	68	84	0	2	5
Gruber	.252	.443	.308	113	429	58	108	190	18	2	20	65	31	70	12	7	13
Maldonado	.250	.427	.342	86	288	37	72	123	15	0	12	48	36	76	4	0	2
Mulliniks	.250	.333	.364	97	240	27	60	80	12	1	2	24	44	44	0	0	0
Borders	.244	.354	.271	105	291	22	71	103	17	0	5	36	11	45	0	0	4
Wilson	.241	.349	.277	86	241	26	58	84	12	4	2	28	8	35	11	3	2
Parker	.239	.365	.288	132	502	47	120	183	26	2	11	59	33	98	3	3	0
T. Ward	.239	.301	.306	48	113	12	27	34	7	0	0	7	11	18	0	0	0
Ducey	.235	.368	.297	39	68	8	16	25	2	2	1	4	6	26	2	0	4
Lee	.234	.288	.274	138	445	41	104	128	18	3	0	29	24	107	7	2	19
Tabler	.216	.270	.318	82	185	20	40	50	5	1	1	21	29	21	0	0	3
Williams	.207	.379	.314	13	29	5	6	11	2	0	1	3	4	5	1	0	0
Gonzales	.195	.246	.289	71	118	16	23	29	3	0	1	6	12	22	0	0	7
Snyder	.175	.265	.216	71	166	14	29	44	4	1	3	17	9	60	0	0	3
Giannelli	.167	.208	.310	9	24	2	4	5	1	0	0	0	5	9	1	0	1
Zosky	.148	.259	.148	18	27	2	4	7	1	1	0	2	0	8	0	0	0
Bell	.143	.143	.314	18	28	5	4	4	0	0	0	1	6	5	3	2	2
Knorr	.000	.000	.500	3	1	0	0	0	0	0	0	0	1	1	0	0	0

Pitching	W-L	ERA	G	GS	CG	GF	Sho	SV	IP	H	R	ER	HR	BB	SO
Horsman	0-0	0.00	4	0	0	2	0	0	4	2	0	0	0	3	2
Weston	0-0	0.00	2	0	0	2	0	0	2	1	0	0	0	1	1
Henke	0-2	2.32	49	0	0	43	0	32	50.1	33	13	13	4	11	53
Hentgen	0-0	2.45	3	1	0	1	0	0	7.1	5	2	2	1	3	3
Candiotti	13-13	2.65	34	34	6	0	0	0	238	202	82	70	12	73	167
D. Ward	7-6	2.77	81	0	0	46	0	23	107.1	80	36	33	3	33	132
MacDonald	3-3	2.85	45	0	0	10	0	0	53.2	51	19	17	5	25	24
Guzman	10-3	2.99	23	23	1	0	0	0	138.2	98	53	46	6	66	123
Key	16-12	3.05	33	33	2	0	2	0	209.1	207	84	71	12	44	125
Timlin	11-6	3.16	63	3	0	17	0	3	108.1	94	43	38	6	50	85
Stieb	4-3	3.17	9	9	1	0	0	0	59.2	52	22	21	4	23	29
Wells	15-10	3.72	40	28	2	3	0	1	198.1	188	88	82	24	49	106
Stottlemyre	15-8	3.78	34	34	1	0	0	0	219	194	97	92	21	75	116
Weathers	1-0	4.91	15	0	0	4	0	0	14.2	15	9	8	1	17	13
Acker	3-5	5.20	54	4	0	11	0	1	88.1	77	53	51	16	36	44
Fraser	0-2	6.15	13	1	0	6	0	0	26.1	33	20	18	4	11	12
Dayley	0-0	6.23	8	0	0	3	0	0	4.1	7	3	3	0	5	3
Wills	0-1	16.62	4	0	0	3	0	0	4.1	8	8	8	2	5	2
Leiter	0-0	27.00	3	0	0	1	0	0	1.2	3	5	5	0	5	1

1992 Preliminary Roster

Pitchers (15)

Ken Dayley
Juan Guzman
Tom Henke
Pat Hentgen
Vince Horsman
Jimmy Key
Al Leiter
Bob MacDonald
Dave Stieb
Todd Stottlemyre
Mike Timlin
Rick Trlicek
Duane Ward
Dave Weathers
David Wells

Catchers (3)

Pat Borders
Randy Knorr
Greg Myers

Infielders (11)

Roberto Alomar
Kelly Gruber
Jeff Kent
Manuel Lee
Domingo Martinez
Rance Mulliniks
John Olerud
Tom Quinlan
Ed Sprague
Pat Tabler
Eddie Zosky

Outfielders(9)

Derek Bell
Joe Carter
Rob Ducey
Candy Maldonado
Robert Perez
Ryan Thompson
Turner Ward
Devon White
Nigel Wilson

Games Played by position

	G	C	1B	2B	3B	SS	OF	DH
Alomar,R	161	0	0	160	0	0	0	0
Bell,D	18	0	0	0	0	0	13	0
Borders,P	105	102	0	0	0	0	0	0
Carter,J	162	0	0	0	0	0	151	11
Ducey,R	39	0	0	0	0	0	24	2
Giannelli,R	9	0	0	0	9	0	0	0
Gonzales,R	71	0	2	11	26	36	0	0
Gruber,K	113	0	0	0	111	0	0	2
Knorr,R	3	3	0	0	0	0	0	0
Lee,M	138	0	0	0	0	138	0	0
Maldonado,C	86	0	0	0	0	0	76	9
Mulliniks,R	97	0	0	0	5	0	0	81
Myers,G	107	104	0	0	0	0	0	0
Olerud,J	139	0	135	0	0	0	0	1
Parker,D	132	0	0	0	0	0	0	130
Snyder,C	71	0	22	0	3	0	43	3
Sprague,E	61	2	22	0	35	0	0	2
Tabler,P	82	0	20	0	0	0	1	57
Ward,T	48	0	0	0	0	0	44	0
White,D	156	0	0	0	0	0	156	0
Williams,K	13	0	0	0	0	0	9	2
Wilson,M	86	0	0	0	0	0	41	34
Zosky,E	18	0	0	0	0	18	0	0

Sick call: 1991 DL report

Player	Days on the DL
Ken Dayley	163*
Tom Henke	35
Al Leiter	168
Rance Mulliniks	31
Kelly Gruber	41
Dave Steib	137
Mike Timlin	15

* On DL twice (not counting administrative transfers from one DL to another).

Minor League Report

Class AAA — Syracuse finished 73-71, third in the International League East. OF Derek Bell (.346-13-93) was league MVP and led the IL in batting and RBI. He also had 12 triples and 27 SBs. RHP Mickey Weston was 12-6 with a 3.74 ERA. RHP Steve Wapnick (6-3, 2.76) led the league with 20 saves, and RHP Pat Hentgen (8-9, 4.47) led the league with 155 strikeouts. . . . **Class AA** — Knoxville finished 67-77, fourth in the first half and first in the second half in the Southern League Western Division. The Blue Jays lost to Birmingham in the play-offs. 2B Jeff Kent (.256-12-61) was team MVP. RHP Jesse Cross was 10-9 with a 2.83 ERA and 128 strikeouts. RHP Rick Trlicek had 16 saves, despite missing the final month. . . . **Class A** — Dunedin finished 59-72, fourth in the first half and third in the second half in the Florida State League Western Division. OF Robert Perez won the league batting title with a .302 average, one point ahead of teammate Nigel Wilson. Perez went 1-for-4 and Wilson 0-for-4 against Sarasota the final day of the season. Perez also led the league with 145 hits. However, Wilson had 12 HRs, 55 RBI, 26 SBs and a club-record 13 triples and was named team MVP. RHP Paul Menhart was 10-6 with a 2.66 ERA. LHP Graeme Lloyd (2-5, 2.24) had a club-record 24 saves. Dunedin set a team attendance record with 67,040. . . . Myrtle Beach finished 59-80, sixth in both halves in the South Atlantic League Southern Division. 3B Howard Battle hit .283 with 20 HRs and 86 RBI. LHP Ricardo Jordan (9-8, 2.74) gave up 100 hits in 145 innings with 152 strikeouts. . . . St. Catharines finished 35-42, tied for fourth in the NY-P League Stedler Division. OF Rob Butler hit .338 and tied for the league batting title. RHP Giovanni Carrara (5-2, 1.61) gave up 66 hits in 89 innings. . . . Medicine Hat finished 24-45, fourth in the Pioneer League Northern Division. 2B Felipe Crespo (.304-4-31) was team MVP. LHP Michael Taylor was 6-4 with a 3.10 ERA.

Tops in the Organization

BATTING LEADERS	Club	Avg.	G	AB	R	H	HR	RBI
Derek Bell	Syr	.346	119	457	89	158	13	93
Domingo Martinez	Syr	.313	126	467	61	146	17	83
Nigel Wilson	Dun	.301	119	455	64	137	12	55
Robert Perez	Syr	.298	131	500	52	149	4	51
Carlos Delgado	Syr	.284	133	444	72	126	18	70

HOME RUNS		
Howard Battle	Myr	20
Carlos Delgado	Syr	18
Domingo Martinez	Syr	17
Julian Yan	Knx	16
Derek Bell	Syr	13

RBI		
Derek Bell	Syr	93
Howard Battle	Myr	87
Domingo Martinez	Syr	83
Carlos Delgado	Syr	70
Several players tied		61

STOLEN BASES		
Ernesto Rodriguez	Myr	42
Lonell Roberts	Myr	35
Brent Bowers	Myr	35
Ron Reams	Myr	30
Several players tied		27

WINS		
Rick Steed	Myr	12
John Shea	Syr	12
Mickey Weston	Syr	12
Several players tied		10

SAVES		
Graeme Lloyd	Knx	24
Steve Wapnick	Syr	20
Rick Trlicek	Knx	16
Huck Flener	Myr	13
Woody Williams	Syr	9

STRIKEOUTS		
Pat Hentgen	Syr	155
Ricardo Jordan	Myr	152
Joe Ganote	Dun	140
Thomas Singer	Myr	131
Jesse Cross	Knx	128

PITCHING LEADERS	Club	W-L	ERA	IP	H	BB	SO
Dave Weathers	Knx	10-7	2.45	139	121	49	114
Tim Brown	Dun	8-3	2.49	123	113	37	87
Paul Menhart	Dun	10-6	2.66	128	114	34	114
Aaron Small	Dun	8-7	2.73	148	129	42	92
Ricardo Jordan	Myr	9-8	2.74	145	100	79	152

Toronto (1977-1991)

182

Runs: Most, career, all-time
768 LLOYD MOSEBY, 1980-1989
641 GEORGE BELL, 1981-1990
538 Willie Upshaw, 1978-1987
530 JESSE BARFIELD, 1981-1989
510 TONY FERNANDEZ, 1983-1990

Hits: Most, career, all-time
1319 LLOYD MOSEBY, 1980-1989
1294 GEORGE BELL, 1981-1990
1142 TONY FERNANDEZ, 1983-1990
1028 Damaso Garcia, 1980-1986
982 Willie Upshaw, 1978-1987

2B: Most, career, all-time
242 LLOYD MOSEBY, 1980-1989
237 GEORGE BELL, 1981-1990
204 RANCE MULLINIKS, 1982-1991
192 TONY FERNANDEZ, 1983-1990
177 Willie Upshaw, 1978-1987

3B: Most, career, all-time
61 TONY FERNANDEZ, 1983-1990
60 LLOYD MOSEBY, 1980-1989
50 ALFREDO GRIFFIN, 1979-1984
42 Willie Upshaw, 1978-1987
32 GEORGE BELL, 1981-1990

HR: Most, career, all-time
202 GEORGE BELL, 1981-1990
179 JESSE BARFIELD, 1981-1989
149 LLOYD MOSEBY, 1980-1989
131 ERNIE WHITT, 1977-1989
125 FRED McGRIFF, 1986-1990

RBI: Most, career, all-time
740 GEORGE BELL, 1981-1990
651 LLOYD MOSEBY, 1980-1989
527 JESSE BARFIELD, 1981-1989
518 ERNIE WHITT, 1977-1989
478 Willie Upshaw, 1978-1987

SB: Most, career, all-time
255 LLOYD MOSEBY, 1980-1989
194 Damaso Garcia, 1980-1986
138 TONY FERNANDEZ, 1983-1990
76 ALFREDO GRIFFIN, 1979-1984
76 Willie Upshaw, 1978-1987

BB: Most, career, all-time
547 LLOYD MOSEBY, 1980-1989
415 RANCE MULLINIKS, 1982-1991
403 ERNIE WHITT, 1977-1989
390 Willie Upshaw, 1978-1987
352 FRED McGRIFF, 1986-1990

BA: Highest, career, all-time
.289 TONY FERNANDEZ, 1983-1990
.288 Damaso Garcia, 1980-1986
.286 GEORGE BELL, 1981-1990
.280 RANCE MULLINIKS, 1982-1991
.278 FRED McGRIFF, 1986-1990

Slug avg: Highest, career, all-time
.530 FRED McGRIFF, 1986-1990
.486 GEORGE BELL, 1981-1990
.483 JESSE BARFIELD, 1981-1989
.461 Otto Velez, 1977-1982
.450 John Mayberry, 1978-1982

Games started: Most, career, all-time
391 DAVE STIEB, 1979-1991
345 JIM CLANCY, 1977-1988
217 JIMMY KEY, 1984-1991
151 Luis Leal, 1980-1985
108 JOHN CERUTTI, 1985-1990

Saves: Most, career, all-time
183 TOM HENKE, 1985-1991
64 DUANE WARD, 1986-1991
31 Joey McLaughlin, 1980-1984
30 Roy Lee Jackson, 1981-1984
16 Bill Caudill, 1985-1986

Shutouts: Most, career, all-time
30 DAVE STIEB, 1979-1991
11 JIM CLANCY, 1977-1988
8 JIMMY KEY, 1984-1991
4 Jesse Jefferson, 1977-1980
3 Doyle Alexander, 1983-1986
3 Luis Leal, 1980-1985
3 Dave Lemanczyk, 1977-1980

Wins: Most, career, all-time
170 DAVE STIEB, 1979-1991
128 JIM CLANCY, 1977-1988
103 JIMMY KEY, 1984-1991
51 Luis Leal, 1980-1985
46 Doyle Alexander, 1983-1986
46 JOHN CERUTTI, 1985-1990

K: Most, career, all-time
1586 DAVE STIEB, 1979-1991
1237 JIM CLANCY, 1977-1988
827 JIMMY KEY, 1984-1991
598 TOM HENKE, 1985-1991
491 Luis Leal, 1980-1985

Win pct: Highest, career, all-time
.639 Doyle Alexander, 1983-1986
.602 JIMMY KEY, 1984-1991
.588 DAVID WELLS, 1987-1991
.574 DAVE STIEB, 1979-1991
.554 JOHN CERUTTI, 1985-1990

ERA: Lowest, career, all-time
3.33 DAVE STIEB, 1979-1991
3.41 JIMMY KEY, 1984-1991
3.56 Doyle Alexander, 1983-1986
3.87 JOHN CERUTTI, 1985-1990
4.10 JIM CLANCY, 1977-1988

Runs: Most, season
111 GEORGE BELL, 1987
110 DEVON WHITE, 1991
107 JESSE BARFIELD, 1986
106 LLOYD MOSEBY, 1987
104 LLOYD MOSEBY, 1983

Hits: Most, season
213 TONY FERNANDEZ, 1986
198 GEORGE BELL, 1986
188 ROBERTO ALOMAR, 1991
188 GEORGE BELL, 1987
186 TONY FERNANDEZ, 1987
186 TONY FERNANDEZ, 1988

2B: Most, season
42 JOE CARTER, 1991
41 ROBERTO ALOMAR, 1991
41 GEORGE BELL, 1989
41 TONY FERNANDEZ, 1988
40 DEVON WHITE, 1991

3B: Most, season
17 TONY FERNANDEZ, 1990
15 Dave Collins, 1984
15 ALFREDO GRIFFIN, 1980

15   LLOYD MOSEBY, 1984
11   ROBERTO ALOMAR, 1991

HR: Most, season

47	GEORGE BELL, 1987
40	JESSE BARFIELD, 1986
36	FRED McGRIFF, 1989
35	FRED McGRIFF, 1990
34	FRED McGRIFF, 1988

RBI: Most, season

134	GEORGE BELL, 1987
118	KELLY GRUBER, 1990
108	JESSE BARFIELD, 1986
108	GEORGE BELL, 1986
108	JOE CARTER, 1991

SB: Most, season

60	Dave Collins, 1984
54	Damaso Garcia, 1982
53	ROBERTO ALOMAR, 1991
46	Damaso Garcia, 1984
39	LLOYD MOSEBY, 1984
39	LLOYD MOSEBY, 1987

BB: Most, season

119	FRED McGRIFF, 1989
94	FRED McGRIFF, 1990
79	FRED McGRIFF, 1988
78	LLOYD MOSEBY, 1984
78	Willie Upshaw, 1986

BA: Highest, season

.322	TONY FERNANDEZ, 1987
.315	LLOYD MOSEBY, 1983
.311	Bob Bailor, 1977
.310	TONY FERNANDEZ, 1986
.310	Damaso Garcia, 1982

Slug avg: Highest, season

.605	GEORGE BELL, 1987
.559	JESSE BARFIELD, 1986
.552	FRED McGRIFF, 1988
.536	JESSE BARFIELD, 1985
.532	GEORGE BELL, 1986

Games started: Most, season

40	JIM CLANCY, 1982
38	Luis Leal, 1982
38	DAVE STIEB, 1982
37	JIM CLANCY, 1987
36	Doyle Alexander, 1985
36	JIM CLANCY, 1984
36	JIMMY KEY, 1987
36	DAVE STIEB, 1983
36	DAVE STIEB, 1985

Saves: Most, season

34	TOM HENKE, 1987
32	TOM HENKE, 1990
27	TOM HENKE, 1986
25	TOM HENKE, 1988
23	DUANE WARD, 1991

Shutouts: Most, season

5	DAVE STIEB, 1982
4	DAVE STIEB, 1980
4	DAVE STIEB, 1983
4	DAVE STIEB, 1988
3	JIM CLANCY, 1982
3	JIM CLANCY, 1986

Wins: Most, season

18	DAVE STIEB, 1990
17	Doyle Alexander, 1984
17	Doyle Alexander, 1985
17	JIMMY KEY, 1987
17	DAVE STIEB, 1982
17	DAVE STIEB, 1983
17	DAVE STIEB, 1989

K: Most, season

198	DAVE STIEB, 1984
187	DAVE STIEB, 1983
180	JIM CLANCY, 1987
167	DAVE STIEB, 1985
166	MARK EICHHORN, 1986

Win pct: Highest, season

.750	DAVE STIEB, 1990
.739	Doyle Alexander, 1984
.680	JIMMY KEY, 1987
.680	DAVE STIEB, 1989
.667	DAVE STIEB, 1984
.667	DAVE STIEB, 1988

ERA: Lowest, season

2.48	DAVE STIEB, 1985
2.76	JIMMY KEY, 1987
2.83	DAVE STIEB, 1984
2.93	DAVE STIEB, 1990
3.00	JIMMY KEY, 1985

Most pinch-hit homers, season

2	Al Woods, 1977
2	Otto Velez, 1979
2	Rico Carty, 1979
2	Ernie Whitt, 1982
2	Jeff Burroughs, 1985

Most pinch-hit, homers, career

| 4 | Ernie Whitt, 1977-1989 |
| 4 | Jesse Barfield, 1981-1989 |

Most consecutive games, batting safely

| 22 | George Bell, 1989 |

Most consecutive scoreless innings

| 31 | Dave Stieb, 1988 |

No hit games

Dave Stieb, Tor at Det AL, 3-0;
September 2, 1990.

Boston Red Sox

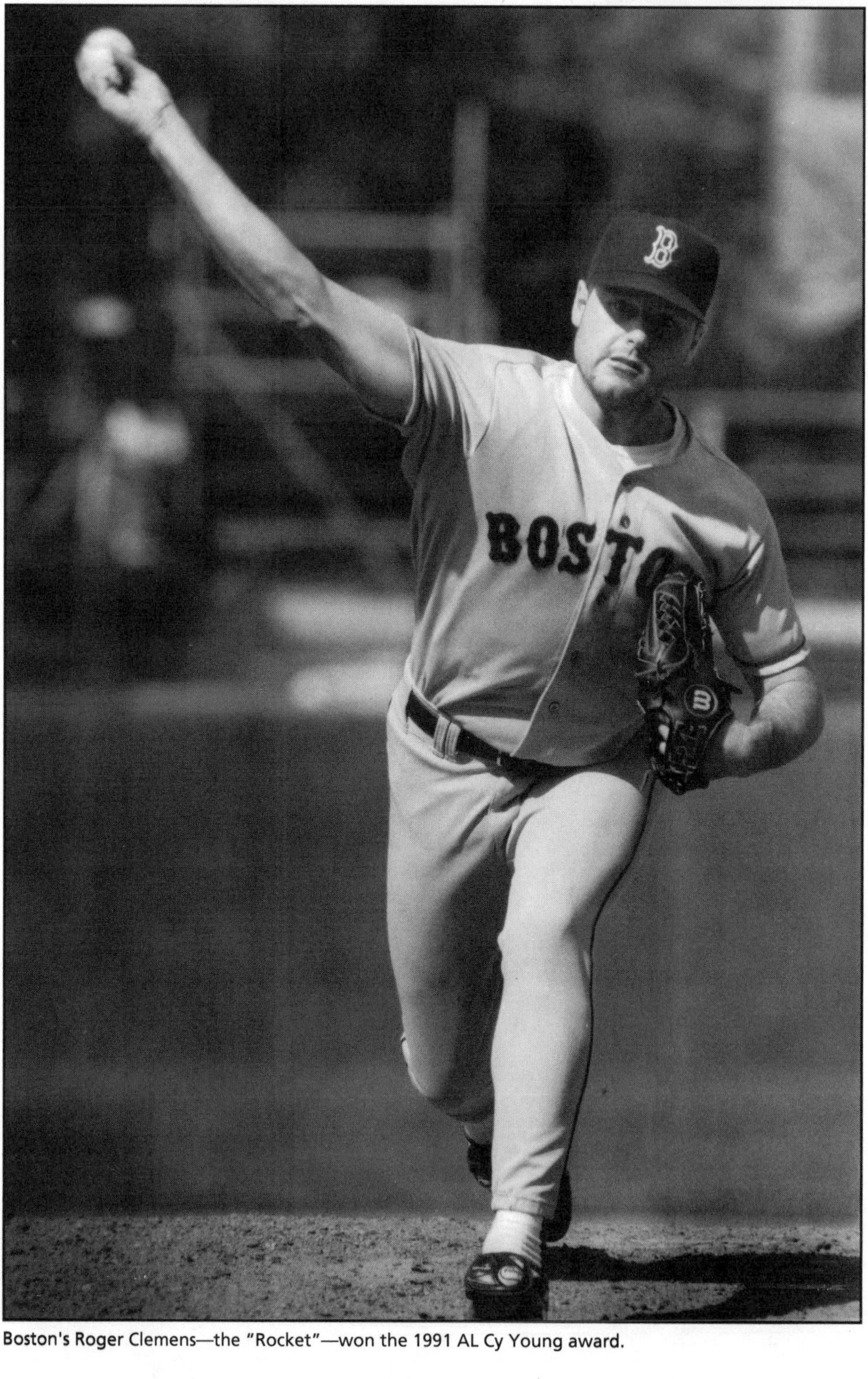

Boston's Roger Clemens—the "Rocket"—won the 1991 AL Cy Young award.

Riding on one horse

There may be no greater heartache than being a Red Sox fan. Once again in 1991, the Olde Towne Team brought their fans to the brink of delirium—only to fall just short.

While in the past there have been true collapses, it was a heroic effort by the '91 Red Sox to even pull into contention, though in the end, they just could not overcame a rash of injuries to key players.

On Aug. 7, the Sox were 11 games behind the division-leading Toronto Blue Jays. Even diehard Sox fans had given up: a mock funeral procession was held on Yawkey Way.

But Boston stormed back, winning 31 of their next 41 games. A four-game sweep of Toronto started the streak, which led to the Sox coming within a half-game of the Jays on Sept. 21. But Boston closer Jeff Reardon gave up a two-out, two-strike, ninth-inning home run to the Yankees' Roberto Kelly the next day, and the Red Sox lost in 10 innings to fall one game back.

They would get no closer. After 11 losses in their final 14 games—including six losses in seven games against Milwaukee down the stretch—Boston ended up in a second-place tie with Detroit.

The Red Sox had come close with just one horse—Cy Young winner Roger Clemens—dragging the rest of a makeshift pitching staff by himself. Clemens again finished with top numbers: 18-10, AL-leading 2.62 ERA and tied for the major league strikeout lead with the Mets' David Cone at 241.

Danny Darwin and Matt Young, both high-priced offseason acquisitions, were injured much of the season. Stepping in to carry the load down the stretch were rookie Mike Gardiner (9-10, 4.85 in 22 starts) and Joe Hesketh (12-4, 3.29).

Offensively, Ellis Burks, Wade Boggs, Tom Brunansky, Mike Greenwell and Jeff Gray all missed significant parts of the season—including key games in the stretch run.

Boggs still had a Boggsian-season, batting .332 with 42 doubles. Jody Reed chipped in with a .283 average and 42 doubles, and Jack Clark (.245, 27 homers, 85 RBI) and Mike Greenwell (.300, 83 RBI) did what was expected.

But in the end, even the great comeback over the final two months couldn't save manager Joe Morgan. He was fired Oct. 8, replaced by Butch Hobson.

Nevertheless, the season provided some considerable hope for the future. Though Mike Marshall's lack of production meant rookies Mo Vaughn and Phil Plantier were called up before the Red Sox' brass wanted, their ability left fans wondering what would have been if Marshall had been dumped earlier.

Plantier, who hit .331 with 11 homers and 35 RBI in 53 games, played well enough to put Carlos Quintana and Greenwell on the trading block. Vaughn hit .260 with four homers in 74 games, and will start at first next season if Quintana is dealt.

But Boston fans, who haven't seen a World Championship since 1918, continue to live and die with their Sox: a record 2,562,435 fans came to Fenway in 1991. Again in 1992, they'll dream that the curse of the Bambino may finally be broken.

—*Rick Lawes*

Red Sox 1992 preview

Boston's new manager, Butch Hobson, will inherit three familiar problems in his first season at Fenway Park: No pitching depth, no team speed and the Curse of the Bambino.

Cy Young winner Roger Clemens did his best to pull up the Sox last year, and it wouldn't be a surprise if he repeated similar numbers. But in order for the Sox to contend, Joe Hesketh will have to duplicate his career-year (12-4), youngsters Mike Gardiner and Kevin Morton will have to pick it up a notch and Danny Darwin, Matt Young and Jeff Gray must bounce back from injuries and illness.

Offensively, Wade Boggs, Jody Reed and Jack Clark are coming off fine years, and youngsters Mo Vaughn and Phil Plantier give Boston even more punch.

However, outfielders Ellis Burks and Tom Brunansky must regain their old form.

1992 prophecy: Red Sox

▶Jack Clark will hit for a high average and endear himself to his teammates and the media with his wit and charm . . . not!

▶Wade Boggs will bounce back from a dismal .332 season in 1991 to flirt with .400.

▶Mo Vaughn, after an offseason conditioning program, will make Boston fans forget about Sam Horn.

—John Hunt

Red Sox to Greenwell: Pull over, put it in park

By Mel Antonen and Hal Bodley

Boston outfielder Mike Greenwell, who owns a stock car in Florida, took a ride in one during the season and the Red Sox said he violated his contract. Red Sox general manager Lou Gorman said, "The contract doesn't allow him to be involved in any way, shape or form in competitive racing, either in the car as a driver or a passenger. Even being around the pits is a question. There are conflicting stories as to what he did."

Cindy DeLicio of East Providence, R.I., owner of the 1991 Chevrolet Lumina, said Greenwell didn't race at Seekonk (Mass.) Speedway.

"He drove around the track five times," she said.

"There were two other cars on the track and one did a 360." Greenwell took the lower part of the track to avoid the spinning car. DeLicio estimated his speed at 40 mph.

"We haven't got a racing motor in the car. It's not prepared for racing," she said.

Gorman said, " . . . if it happens again, we'll take action against him."

Greenwell insisted, however, that the joy ride was "nothing but a parade to promote racing."

Would he do it again? "I think I would talk to Lou," Greenwell said. "Maybe I would invite him to come and watch."

The curse of the Bambino

By Rick Lawes

In 1918, the last time the Red Sox won the World Series, Ruth led the league with 11 homers (in 317 at-bats) while winning 13 of 19 starts on the mound. He extended his World Series record to 29 1/3 scoreless innings pitched. The next year, Babe's last in Boston, he hit an unheard-of 29 homers in 432 at-bats.

As Ruth's popularity increased with that of the homer, Boston owner Harry Frazee knew he had a marketable commodity.

Frazee was an owner for whom the bright lights of Broadway held more attraction than the crack of the bat. Since he purchased the Red Sox in 1917, he found the value of his ballplayers to be more than enough to finance his new shows.

During the 1919-20 offseason, Frazee came up short in his financing for his new musical *No, No, Nanette*. Having already found a market with the Yankees for Red Sox talent, Frazee knew where to find his big payoff.

Thus, for $125,000, Babe became a pinstriper.

The curse didn't take long to take hold: Shortly after Red Sox fans were driven to drink by the sale of the Bambino, prohibition was enacted.

On the field, the Bostonians fell to fifth place in 1920. They didn't rise out of the second division until 1934 and then, only reaching fourth.

But the curse has not shown any signs of giving way. The Red Sox have been in four World Series since their last victory in 1918—and have lost all four in seven games.

The misery stretches from Enos Slaughter's scoring from first—on what was essentially a single—with the winning run in 1946, to Mookie Wilson's grounder dribbling through Bill Buckner's legs 40 years later. Oh, that didn't end the series, but there was no doubt about what would happen in Game Seven.

For Frazee, he showed he knew more about the future on Broadway than on the diamond—while the curse of Bambino was to become the rueful future of the Red Sox, Frazee's *No, No, Nanette* was his most popular production of a 20-plus-year career.

Fenway fans are tough customers

By Dave Albee

When the Olde Towne Team is winning here, there is no better place to watch a baseball game. Of course, when they're not winning—or not winning enough, as is always the case with the Boston Red Sox—there is no place to hide.

Fans at Fenway Park are rough on their players. You can be a legend and still get bounced around.

"You're always going to get a few people that are going to get on you hard. I don't care who you are or what you've done," said Oakland A's third baseman Carney Lansford, who played for the Red Sox in 1981-82.

It is both a magical and maniacal kingdom for baseball.

Ted Williams used to shoot pigeons in right field. Reggie Smith wore a batting helmet in center field because his own fans were throwing junk at him. Ed Jurak once fielded a large rodent with his first baseman's mitt.

One night in 1975, a fan dressed as a witch doctor to remove a curse put on Luis Tiant by another witch doctor from Baltimore.

"It seems like more interesting things can happen in this ballpark than any other park in baseball," said A's hitting coach Rick Burleson, who played shortstop for the BoSox from 1974-80.

Inside Fenway Park is a tour of lore. There's the Green Monster—the infamous 37-foot high wall in left field—and the Jagged Edge that juts out from the visiting dugout to the left field foul line.

Then there's the curse of the Bambino, which Boston has found to be its karma for trading Babe Ruth.

But many of the players find that it is not the fans who make it a challenge to play at Fenway.

"The only negative I found in the seven years I was playing here was that the press was tough," Burleson said.

Team directory

▶Owner: JRY Corporation

▶General Manager: James (Lou) Gorman

▶Ballpark:
Fenway Park
4 Yawkey Way, Boston, Massachusetts
617-267-8661
Capacity 34,142
Public transportation available
Family, wheelchair, and vision-impaired sections, sound amplification for hearing impaired, ramps, TDD Ticket Info

▶Team publications:
Media Guide; Game Scorebook
617-267-9440

▶TV, radio broadcast stations:
WRKO-AM, WSBK Channel 38, New England Sports Network Cable TV

▶Spring Training:
Chain O'Lakes Park
Winter Haven, Florida
Capacity 4,545
813-293-3900

BOSTON RED SOX 1991 Final Stats

Batting	AVG	SLG	OB	G	AB	R	H	TB	2B	3B	HR	RBI	BB	SO	SB	CS	E
Wedge	1.00	1.00	1.00	1	1	0	1	1	0	0	0	0	0	0	0	0	0
Cooper	.457	.686	.486	14	35	6	16	24	4	2	0	7	2	2	0	0	2
Boggs	.332	.460	.421	144	546	93	181	251	42	2	8	51	89	32	1	2	12
Plantier	.331	.615	.420	53	148	27	49	91	7	1	11	35	23	38	1	0	2
Greenwell	.300	.419	.350	147	544	76	163	228	26	6	9	83	43	35	15	5	3
Quintana	.295	.412	.375	149	478	69	141	197	21	1	11	71	61	66	1	0	9
Reed	.283	.382	.349	153	618	87	175	236	42	2	5	60	60	53	6	5	14
Marzano	.263	.333	.271	49	114	10	30	38	8	0	0	9	1	16	0	0	3
Vaughn	.260	.370	.339	74	219	21	57	81	12	0	4	32	26	43	2	1	6
Rivera	.258	.384	.318	129	414	64	107	159	22	3	8	40	35	86	4	4	24
Burks	.251	.422	.314	130	474	56	119	200	33	3	14	56	39	81	6	11	2
Housie	.250	.375	.333	11	8	2	2	3	1	0	0	0	1	3	1	0	0
Clark	.249	.466	.374	140	481	75	120	224	18	1	28	87	96	133	0	2	0
Lyons	.241	.354	.277	87	212	15	51	75	10	1	4	17	11	35	10	3	3
Pena	.231	.321	.291	141	464	45	107	149	23	2	5	48	37	53	8	3	5
Brunansky	.229	.390	.303	142	459	54	105	179	24	1	16	70	49	72	1	2	3
Brumley	.212	.254	.273	63	118	16	25	30	5	0	0	5	10	22	2	0	7
Romine	.164	.255	.207	44	55	7	9	14	2	0	1	7	3	10	1	1	1
Zupcic	.160	.280	.192	18	25	3	4	7	0	0	1	3	1	6	0	0	2
Naehring	.109	.127	.197	20	55	1	6	7	1	0	0	3	6	15	0	0	3

Pitching	W-L	ERA	G	GS	CG	GF	Sho	SV	IP	H	R	ER	HR	BB	SO
Lyons	0-0	0.00	1	0	0	1	0	0	1	2	0	0	0	0	1
Plympton	0-0	0.00	4	0	0	3	0	0	5.1	5	0	0	0	4	2
Gray	2-3	2.34	50	0	0	20	0	1	61.2	39	17	16	7	10	41
Clemens	18-10	2.62	35	35	13	0	4	0	271.1	219	93	79	15	65	241
Reardon	1-4	3.03	57	0	0	51	0	40	59.1	54	21	20	9	16	44
Hesketh	12-4	3.29	39	17	0	5	0	0	153.1	142	59	56	19	53	104
Fossas	3-2	3.47	64	0	0	18	0	1	57	49	27	22	3	28	29
Harris	11-12	3.85	53	21	1	15	0	2	173	157	79	74	13	69	127
Morton	6-5	4.59	16	15	1	0	0	0	86.1	93	49	44	9	40	45
Lamp	6-3	4.70	51	0	0	12	0	0	92	100	54	48	8	31	57
Petry	2-3	4.79	30	6	0	8	0	1	77	87	52	41	12	31	30
Gardiner	9-10	4.85	22	22	0	0	0	0	130	140	79	70	18	47	91
Darwin	3-6	5.16	12	12	0	0	0	0	68	71	39	39	15	15	42
Young	3-7	5.18	19	16	0	1	0	0	88.2	92	55	51	4	53	69
Bolton	8-9	5.24	25	19	0	4	0	0	110	136	72	64	16	51	64
Irvine	0-0	6.00	9	0	0	5	0	0	18	25	13	12	2	9	8
Kiecker	2-3	7.36	18	5	0	3	0	0	40.1	56	34	33	6	23	21
Dopson	0-0	18.00	1	0	0	1	0	0	1	2	2	2	0	1	0
Manzanillo	0-0	18.00	1	0	0	1	0	0	1	2	2	2	0	3	1

1992 Preliminary Roster

Pitchers (20)

Tom Bolton
Roger Clemens
Danny Darwin
John Dopson
Tom Fischer
Tony Fossas
Mike Gardiner
Jeff Gray
Greg Harris
Peter Hoy
Daryl Irvine
Dana Kiecker
Derek Livernois
Josias Manzanillo
Kevin Morton
Jeff Plympton
Paul Quantrill
Jeff Reardon
Scott Taylor
Matt Young

Catchers (3)

John Marzano
Tony Pena
Eric Wedge

Infielders (10)

Wade Boggs
Mike Brumley
Jack Clark
Scott Cooper
Tim Naehring
Carlos Quintana
Jody Reed
Luis Rivera
John Valentin
Mo Vaughn

Outfielders (7)

Tom Brunansky
Ellis Burks
Mike Greenwell
Wayne Housie
Jeff McNeely
Phil Plantier
Bob Zupcic

188

Games played by position

	G	C	1B	2B	3B	SS	OF	DH
Boggs,W	144	0	0	0	140	0	0	0
Brumley,M	63	0	0	7	17	31	4	2
Brunansky,T	142	0	0	0	0	0	137	1
Burks,E	130	0	0	0	0	0	126	2
Clark,Ja	140	0	0	0	0	0	0	135
Cooper,S	14	0	0	0	13	0	0	0
Greenwell,M	147	0	0	0	0	0	143	1
Housie,W	11	0	0	0	0	0	4	2
Lyons,S	87	0	2	16	12	1	45	2
Marzano,J	49	48	0	0	0	0	0	0
Naehring,T	20	0	0	1	2	17	0	0
Pena,T	141	140	0	0	0	0	0	0
Plantier,P	53	0	0	0	0	0	40	5
Quintana,C	149	0	138	0	0	0	13	1
Reed,Jo	153	0	0	152	0	6	0	0
Rivera,L	129	0	0	0	0	129	0	0
Romine,K	44	0	0	0	0	0	23	14
Vaughn,M	74	0	49	0	0	0	0	16
Wedge,E	1	0	0	0	0	0	0	1
Zupcic,B	18	0	0	0	0	0	16	0

Sick call: 1991 DL report

Player	Days on the DL
John Dopson	148
David Owen	116
Mike Miller	182
Danny Darwin	123*
Tim Naehring	142
Dana Kiecker	55
Mike Marshall	16
Matt Young	57
Mike Gardiner	98
Tom Bolton	22
Jeff Gray	70
Daryl Irvine	67

* On DL twice (not counting administrative transfers from one DL to another).

Minor League Report

Class AAA — Pawtucket finished 79-64, first in the International League East. That was an 18.1-game improvement over 1990 (62-84). The PawSox lost to Columbus in the Governors' Cup playoffs. Pawtucket drew a club-record 362,342 fans — the first time over 300,000 — and sold out 20 of its final 27 games. OF Phil Plantier hit .305 with 16 HRs and 61 RBI in 84 games. 3B Scott Cooper (.277-15-72) was team MVP. Butch Hobson was IL Manager of the Year. . . . Class AA — New Britain finished 47-93, eighth in the Eastern League. That was the worst record in the team's 9-year history, but the Red Sox set an attendance record with 146,632 fans. OF Wayne Housie hit .277 with 43 SBs. RHP Al Sanders (4-15, 4.95) set a team mark with 15 losses. . . . Class A — Lynchburg finished 67-72, second in the first half and first in the second half in the Carolina League Northern Division. The Red Sox beat Prince William and lost to Kinston in the playoffs. OF Jeff McNeely led the league with a .322 average and ranked fourth with 38 SBs. RHP Tim Smith (12-9) had 8 complete games and led the league with a 2.16 ERA. . . . Winter Haven finished 43-85, fourth in the Florida State League Central Division. Top hitters were C Scott Hatteberg (.277) and OF Bryan Brown (.276). RHP Tom Niles had a 3.78 ERA despite a 3-14 record. RHP Aaron Sele, Boston's top 1991 draft pick, was 3-6 with a 4.96 ERA. . . . Elmira finished 47-30, first in the NY-P League McNamara West Division. SS Frank Rodriguez hit .271 with 6 HRs and 31 RBI. RHP Chris Davis was 9-3 with a 2.19 ERA.:

Tops in the Organization

BATTING LEADERS	Club	Avg.	G	AB	R	H	HR	RBI
Jeff McNeely	Lyn	.322	106	382	58	123	4	38
Willie Tatum	Lyn	.287	126	421	54	121	8	54
Wayne Housie	Paw	.285	134	523	72	149	8	34
Jeff Stone	Paw	.281	104	352	63	99	8	44
Scott Cooper	Paw	.277	137	483	55	134	15	72

HOME RUNS:			WINS		
Rick Lancellotti	Paw	21	Paul Quantrill	Paw	12
Bob Zupcic	Paw	18	Tim Smith	Lyn	12
Phil Plantier	Paw	16	Erik Plantenberg	Lyn	11
Scott Cooper	Paw	15	Eric Hetzel	Paw	9
Several players tied		14	Andy Rush	Lyn	9

RBI			SAVES		
Bruce Chick	Lyn	73	Peter Hoy	Paw	20
Scott Cooper	Paw	72	Daryl Irvine	Paw	17
Bob Zupcic	Paw	70	Dave Walters	Paw	12
Boo Moore	Lyn	69	Kevin Uhrhan	Lyn	12
Rick Lancellotti	Paw	64	Paul Brown	Nbr	10

STOLEN BASES			STRIKE OUTS		
Wayne Housie	Paw	45	Andy Rush	Lyn	144
Jeff McNeely	Lyn	38	Ed Riley	Lyn	122
Jim Morrison	Whv	29	Gar Finnvold	Nbr	121
Jim Byrd	Nbr	23	Gary Painter	Nbr	105
Garrett Jenkins	Whv	21	Tim Smith	Lyn	103

PITCHING LEADERS	Club	W-L	ERA	IP	H	BB	SO
Tim Smith	Lyn	12-9	2.16	175	149	34	103
Jim Dennison	Lyn	3-8	3.38	133	134	32	68
Ed Riley	Lyn	8-10	3.53	163	169	56	122
Eric Hetzel	Paw	9-5	3.57	116	110	58	83
Thomas Niles	Whv	3-14	3.78	136	119	85	91

Runs: Most, career, all-time

1816	Carl Yastrzemski, 1961-1983
1798	Ted Williams, 1939-1960
1435	DWIGHT EVANS, 1972-1990
1249	Jim Rice, 1974-1989
1094	Bobby Doerr, 1937-1951

Hits: Most, career, all-time

3419	Carl Yastrzemski, 1961-1983
2654	Ted Williams, 1939-1960
2452	Jim Rice, 1974-1989
2373	DWIGHT EVANS, 1972-1990
2042	Bobby Doerr, 1937-1951

2B: Most, career, all-time

646	Carl Yastrzemski, 1961-1983
525	Ted Williams, 1939-1960
474	DWIGHT EVANS, 1972-1990
400	WADE BOGGS, 1982-1991
381	Bobby Doerr, 1937-1951

3B: Most, career, all-time

130	Harry Hooper, 1909-1920
106	Tris Speaker, 1907-1915
90	Buck Freeman, 1901-1907
89	Bobby Doerr, 1937-1951
87	Larry Gardner, 1908-1917
79	Jim Rice, 1974-1989 (6)

HR: Most, career, all-time

521	Ted Williams, 1939-1960
452	Carl Yastrzemski, 1961-1983
382	Jim Rice, 1974-1989
379	DWIGHT EVANS, 1972-1990
223	Bobby Doerr, 1937-1951

RBI: Most, career, all-time

1844	Carl Yastrzemski, 1961-1983
1839	Ted Williams, 1939-1960
1451	Jim Rice, 1974-1989
1346	DWIGHT EVANS, 1972-1990
1247	Bobby Doerr, 1937-1951

SB: Most, career, all-time

300	Harry Hooper, 1909-1920
267	Tris Speaker, 1907-1915
168	Carl Yastrzemski, 1961-1983
141	Heinie Wagner, 1906-1918
134	Larry Gardner, 1908-1917

BB: Most, career, all-time

2019	Ted Williams, 1939-1960
1845	Carl Yastrzemski, 1961-1983
1337	DWIGHT EVANS, 1972-1990
930	WADE BOGGS, 1982-1991
826	Harry Hooper, 1909-1920

BA: Highest, career, all-time

.345	WADE BOGGS, 1982-1991
.344	Ted Williams, 1939-1960
.337	Tris Speaker, 1907-1915
.320	Pete Runnels, 1958-1962
.320	Jimmie Foxx, 1936-1942

Slug avg: Highest, career, all-time

.634	Ted Williams, 1939-1960
.605	Jimmie Foxx, 1936-1942
.520	Fred Lynn, 1974-1980
.502	Jim Rice, 1974-1989
.492	Vern Stephens, 1948-1952

Games started: Most, career, all-time

297	Cy Young, 1901-1908
240	ROGER CLEMENS, 1984-1991
238	Luis Tiant, 1971-1978
232	Mel Parnell, 1947-1956
228	Bill Monbouquette, 1958-1965

Saves: Most, career, all-time

132	Bob Stanley, 1977-1989
104	Dick Radatz, 1962-1966
91	Ellis Kinder, 1948-1955
69	Sparky Lyle, 1967-1971
61	JEFF REARDON, 1990-1991

Shutouts: Most, career, all-time

38	Cy Young, 1901-1908
29	ROGER CLEMENS, 1984-1991
28	Joe Wood, 1908-1915
26	Luis Tiant, 1971-1978
25	Dutch Leonard, 1913-1918

Wins: Most, career, all-time

192	Cy Young, 1901-1908
134	ROGER CLEMENS, 1984-1991
123	Mel Parnell, 1947-1956
122	Luis Tiant, 1971-1978
116	Joe Wood, 1908-1915

K: Most, career, all-time

1665	ROGER CLEMENS, 1984-1991
1341	Cy Young, 1901-1908
1075	Luis Tiant, 1971-1978
1043	BRUCE HURST, 1980-1988
986	Joe Wood, 1908-1915

Win pct: Highest, career, all-time

.695	Roger Moret, 1970-1975
.687	ROGER CLEMENS, 1984-1991
.684	Dave Ferriss, 1945-1950
.674	Joe Wood, 1908-1915
.659	Babe Ruth, 1914-1919

ERA: Lowest, career, all-time

1.99	Joe Wood, 1908-1915
2.00	Cy Young, 1901-1908
2.12	Ernie Shore, 1914-1917
2.13	Dutch Leonard, 1913-1918
2.19	Babe Ruth, 1914-1919
2.85	ROGER CLEMENS, 1984-1991 (12)

Runs: Most, season

150	Ted Williams, 1949
142	Ted Williams, 1946
141	Ted Williams, 1942
139	Jimmie Foxx, 1938
136	Tris Speaker, 1912
128	WADE BOGGS, 1988 (13)

Hits: Most, season

240	WADE BOGGS, 1985
222	Tris Speaker, 1912
214	WADE BOGGS, 1988
213	Jim Rice, 1978
210	WADE BOGGS, 1983

2B: Most, season

67	Earl Webb, 1931
53	Tris Speaker, 1912
51	WADE BOGGS, 1989
51	Joe Cronin, 1938
47	WADE BOGGS, 1986
47	George Burns, 1923
47	Fred Lynn, 1975

3B: Most, season

22	Tris Speaker, 1913
20	Buck Freeman, 1903
19	Buck Freeman, 1902

19	Buck Freeman, 1904
19	Larry Gardner, 1914
19	Chick Stahl, 1904
15	Jim Rice, 1977 (17)
15	Jim Rice, 1978 (17)

HR: Most, season

50	Jimmie Foxx, 1938
46	Jim Rice, 1978
44	Carl Yastrzemski, 1967
43	Tony Armas, 1984
43	Ted Williams, 1949

RBI: Most, season

175	Jimmie Foxx, 1938
159	Vern Stephens, 1949
159	Ted Williams, 1949
145	Ted Williams, 1939
144	Walt Dropo, 1950
144	Vern Stephens, 1950
139	Jim Rice, 1978 (8)

SB: Most, season

54	Tommy Harper, 1973
52	Tris Speaker, 1912
46	Tris Speaker, 1913
42	Tris Speaker, 1914
40	Harry Hooper, 1910
40	Billy Werber, 1934

BB: Most, season

162	Ted Williams, 1947
162	Ted Williams, 1949
156	Ted Williams, 1946
145	Ted Williams, 1941
145	Ted Williams, 1942
128	Carl Yastrzemski, 1970 (8)

BA: Highest, season

.406	Ted Williams, 1941
.388	Ted Williams, 1957
.383	Tris Speaker, 1912
.369	Ted Williams, 1948
.368	WADE BOGGS, 1985

Slug avg: Highest, season

.735	Ted Williams, 1941
.731	Ted Williams, 1957
.704	Jimmie Foxx, 1938
.694	Jimmie Foxx, 1939
.667	Ted Williams, 1946
.637	Fred Lynn, 1979 (9)

Games started: Most, season

43	Cy Young, 1902
42	Bill Dinneen, 1902
41	Babe Ruth, 1916
41	Cy Young, 1901
41	Cy Young, 1904
39	Jim Lonborg, 1967 (6)

Saves: Most, season

40	JEFF REARDON, 1991
33	Bob Stanley, 1983
31	Bill Campbell, 1977
29	Dick Radatz, 1964
29	LEE SMITH, 1988

Shutouts: Most, season

10	Joe Wood, 1912
10	Cy Young, 1904
9	Babe Ruth, 1916
8	ROGER CLEMENS, 1988
8	Carl Mays, 1918

Wins: Most, season

34	Joe Wood, 1912
33	Cy Young, 1901
32	Cy Young, 1902
28	Cy Young, 1903
26	Cy Young, 1904
24	ROGER CLEMENS, 1986 (9)

K: Most, season

291	ROGER CLEMENS, 1988
258	Joe Wood, 1912
256	ROGER CLEMENS, 1987
246	Jim Lonborg, 1967
241	ROGER CLEMENS, 1991

Win pct: Highest, season

.872	Joe Wood, 1912
.857	ROGER CLEMENS, 1986
.806	Dave Ferriss, 1946
.793	Ellis Kinder, 1949
.792	Dutch Leonard, 1914

ERA: Lowest, season

0.96	Dutch Leonard, 1914
1.26	Cy Young, 1908
1.49	Joe Wood, 1915
1.62	Ray Collins, 1910
1.62	Cy Young, 1901
1.91	Luis Tiant, 1972 (14)

Most pinch-hit homers, season

5	Joe Cronin, 1943
4	Del Wilber, 1953

Most pinch-hit, homers, career

7	Ted Williams, 1939-1960

Most consecutive games, batting safely

34	Dom DiMaggio, 1949

Most consecutive scoreless innings

45	Cy Young, 1904

No hit games

Cy Young, Bos vs Phi AL, 3-0; May 5, 1904 (perfect game).

Jesse Tannehill, Bos at Chi AL, 6-0; August 17, 1904.

Bill Dinneen, Bos vs Chi AL, 2-0; September 27, 1905 (1st game).

Cy Young, Bos at NY AL, 8-0; June 30, 1908.

Joe Wood, Bos vs StL AL, 5-0; July 29, 1911 (1st game).

Rube Foster, Bos vs NY AL, 2-0; June 21, 1916.

Hubert (Dutch) Leonard, Bos vs StL AL, 4-0; August 30, 1916.

Ernie Shore, Bos vs Was AL, 4-0; June 23, 1917 (1st game, perfect game). (Shore relieved Babe Ruth in the first inning after Ruth had been thrown out of the game for protesting a walk to the first batter. The runner was caught stealing and Shore retired the remaining 26 batters in order).

Hubert (Dutch) Leonard, Bos at Det AL, 5-0; June 3, 1918.

Howard Ehmke, Bos at Phi AL, 4-0; September 7, 1923.

Mel Parnell, Bos vs Chi AL, 4-0; July 14, 1956.

Earl Wilson, Bos vs LA AL, 2-0; June 26, 1962.

Bill Monbouquette, Bos at Chi AL, 1-0; August 1, 1962.

Dave Morehead, Bos vs Cle AL, 2-0; September 16, 1965.

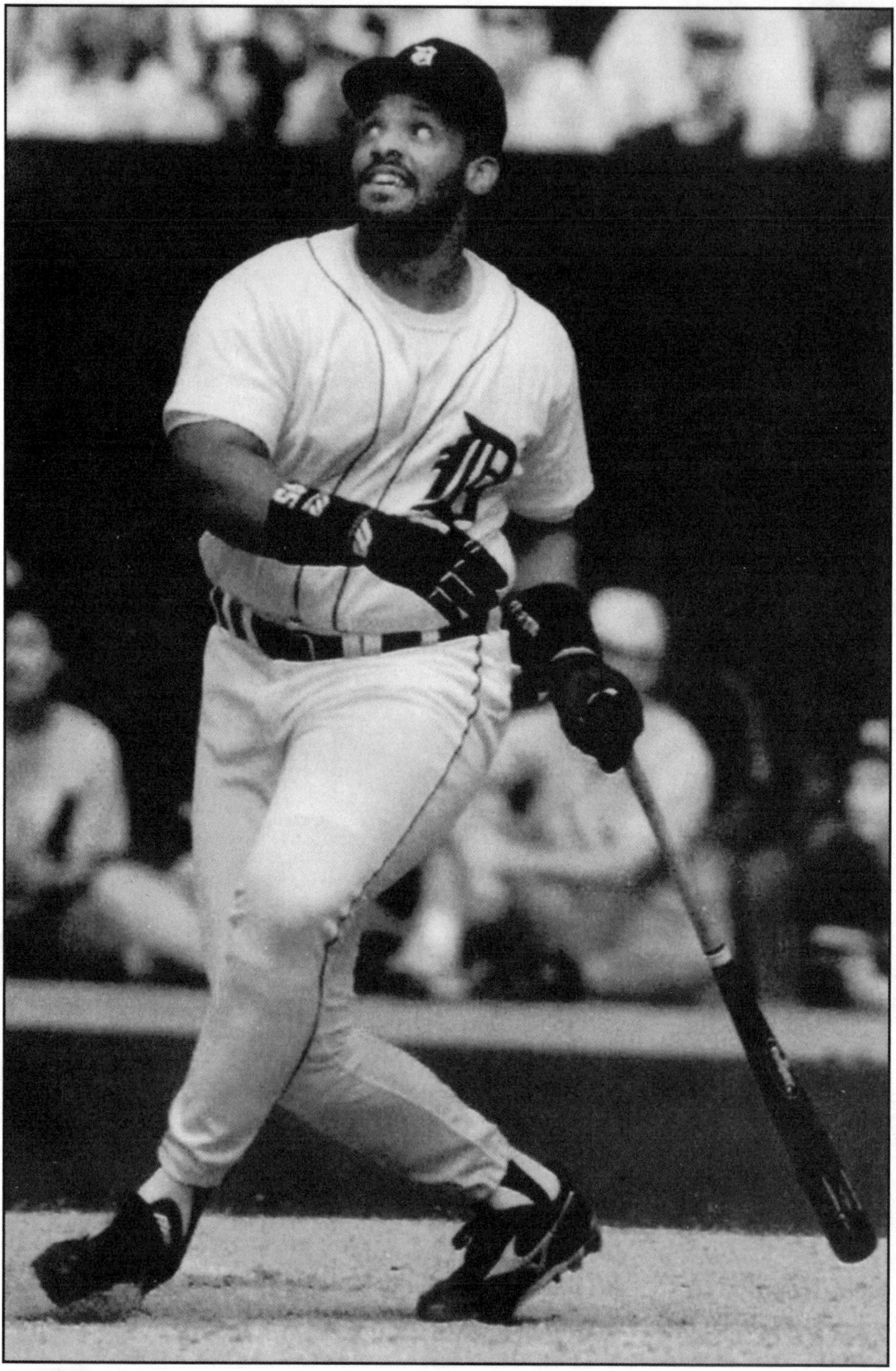

Cecil Fielder hit 44 home runs but finished second in the MVP vote.

Fielder led the hit parade

Picked to finish near the bottom of the American League East, the Detroit Tigers combined bashers and journeyman pitchers into a team that contended well into September.

Manager Sparky Anderson, who has already won World Series titles in both leagues, fashioned a squad heavy on hitting and light on pitching. But the mix proved highly successful for the Tigers, who became the most unlikely of powerhouses.

Warhorses Bill Gullickson (20-9), Frank Tanana (13-12), and Walt Terrell (12-14) anchored a staff whose fourth and fifth starters were often "Undecided,"—a phenomenon so common that Anderson, when queried on his future starters, frequently replied: "I don't know, (triple-A) Toledo's only an hour away."

Gullickson won more than 17 games for the first time in his career and allowed only 31 unintentional walks. But opposing hitters batted .288 against him.

That often didn't matter for the Tigers, whose explosive offense included six players with 17 or more home runs. Hefty slugger Cecil Fielder hit 44 home runs, and with 133 RBI, became the first player since George Foster in 1976-77 to lead the major leagues in RBI in back-to-back seasons.

Second baseman Lou Whitaker provided 23 home runs and 78 RBI, while Tony Phillips—who played five field positions and designated hitter—added 17 HRs and 72 RBI.

Catcher Mickey Tettleton hit 31 home runs and drove in 89 runs, while Rob Deer had almost as many strikeouts (175) as points in his batting average (.179). Deer had 25 homers–the sixth consecutive year he's had 20-plus–but his 64 RBI were the lowest for a full season in his career.

Center fielder Milt Cuyler emerged as a Rookie of the Year candidate, bolstering the Tigers' defense while stealing 41 bases. Second-year third baseman Travis Fryman was second in the club with 91 RBI and led the Tigers with 36 doubles, batting .259.

The Tigers fought Toronto and Boston for the AL East flag, a title that at times no team seemed to want, but in the end could not match the superior pitching staffs of the Blue Jays and Red Sox.

But Detroit proved that a team does not have to follow conventional formulas to win, a fact not lost on Tettleton, who, after watching Pete Incaviglia become the first player to hit the light standard above Fenway Park's "Green Monster" with a homer, said, "We've done a lot of things this year that haven't been done before."

—Pete Williams

Tigers 1992 preview

The Detroit Tigers probably will rely on the Big Bang Theory again this season. A year ago, they hit 209 home runs but struck out 1,185 times and became one of the most entertaining teams to watch. Feast or famine.

First baseman Cecil Fielder and catcher Mickey Tettleton will lead an explosive offense in cozy Tiger Stadium. Rob Deer may even make occasional contact.

The future looks bright with center fielder Milt Cuyler and third baseman Travis Fryman.

The pitching is another story. Bill Gullickson will be hard-pressed to repeat his 20-win season. Even if he comes close, he'll need solid support from Frank Tanana, Walt Terrell, Mark Leiter, Scott Aldred and rookie Greg Gohr.

The Tigers also need a bridge to get from their starters to closer Mike Henneman.

1992 prophecy: Tigers

▶The Tigers, in need of more home runs and strikeouts, will bring Dave Kingman out of retirement and try him at third base. Manager Sparky Anderson will proclaim him the very best third baseman he's ever seen.

▶But Travis Fryman will regain his third base job after an injury to Kingman, and Anderson will proclaim Fryman the very best third baseman he's ever seen.

▶Cecil Fielder will hit 62 home runs and drive in 200 runs but lose in MVP voting to Sandy Alomar.

—John Hunt

Rob Deer: Not your average slugger

By Rick Lawes

Rob Deer carved out a dubious distinction for himself in 1991: He set a major league record for most RBI while batting under .200.

Deer is in stellar company: Mike Schmidt, Reggie Jackson and Harmon Killebrew all had seasons in which they had averages below .200 and 40-plus RBI.

Deer almost set another improbable record in 1991: With a season batting average of .179 and 175 strikeouts, Deer just missed becoming the first player in major league history to record more strikeouts than points in his batting average.

The only other batter who came close was Reggie Jackson, who struck out 146 times while compiling a .194 average for California in 1983.

Player	Avg	RBI	Team, year
Rob Deer	.179	64	Detroit,1991
Tim Laudner	.191	43	Minnesota, 1987
Reggie Jackson	.194	49	California, 1983
Harmon Killebrew	.199	44	Kansas City, 1975
Pedro Garcia	.199	54	Milwaukee, 1974
Mike Schmidt	.196	52	Phila., 1973
Bob Robertson	.193	41	Pittsburgh, 1972

Player	Avg	RBI	Team, year
Roger Repoz	.199	42	California, 1971
Coco Laboy	.199	53	Montreal, 1970
Tom Tresh	.195	52	Yankees, 1968
Ed Kirkpatrick	.192	44	California, 1966
Jack Dittmer	.193	41	Bos. Braves, 1952
Eddie Ainsmith	.191	42	Senators, 1917
Jimmy Esmond	.195	40	Cincinnati, 1912
John Gouchnaur	.185	48	Cleveland, 1903
Monte Cross	.197	44	Phila., 1901

Source: Fluffy Saccucci, SABR

Phillips a virtuoso in art of baseball

When Tony Phillips left Oakland to sign with Detroit at the end of the '89 season, A's manager Tony La Russa said he would miss him as much as departing slugger Dave Parker.

The most versatile fielder in the American League, Phillips not only flourished defensively, he helped keep the Tigers in contention with his bat.

While Cecil Fielder is undoubtedly the main man in Detroit, Phillips deserves some votes as Tigers' MVP. He has had great stretches at the plate—notably his last season in Oakland, where he hit .345 in September—but it's with the glove that he's made his mark.

In 1991 Phillips played more than 30 games at second base, third base and in the outfield, as well as regular duty at shortstop.

"If it wasn't for my glove, I wouldn't be in the majors," he says. "Some guys play different positions for something to do. I do it to survive."

In the clubhouse, Phillips' high-pitched laughter is infectious, and his well-timed barbs find everybody, even manager Sparky Anderson.

"Any team of the 26 (major league ballclubs) that has Tony Phillips will be better for it," says Anderson. "I don't care if it's the world champions. They would have to be better with Tony."

Cecil Fielder: Nobody does it better

Cecil Fielder is, without a doubt, one of the most admired players in the game today. Not only did he tie Jose Canseco for the major league lead in home runs (44) and knock in more runs than anybody in the majors (133), he played in every single game of the year in 1991.

He stepped up to the plate 624 times, got on base more than one-third of those at-bats (163 hits, 78 walks), maintained a slugging average of .513 (25 doubles, 44HR) and scored 102 runs.

Fielder was the first Tiger to play in every game since Rusty Staub did it in 1978. But Staub was Detroit's designated hitter that year, while Fielder played defense along with being baseball's most powerful hitter.

Being one of the season's iron men was quite a feat for Fielder, who spoke admiringly of Baltimore's 1,500-game iron man Cal Ripken.

"I don't know how Rip does it," Fielder said. "You have to give yourself a rest. Not that I don't want to play every game, but I can feel it."

Tigers winter league news

▶Winter leagues: The Tigers have a partial working agreement with Aguilas del Zulia in Venezuela, and sent eight players there this winter, including RHP Steve Cummings (5-5, 4.68 at Class AAA Toledo), RHP Greg Gohr (10-8, 4.61 at Toledo), RHP John Kiely (4-2, 2.13 at Toledo), OF Eric Mangham (.241-4-35), 2B Johnny Paredes (.284, 36 steals at Toledo). . . . IF Victor Rosario (.300 at Toledo), OF Domingo Michel (.269 at Class AA London), OF Basilio Cabrera, and 1B Luis Del los Santos (.284 at Toledo) played winter ball at home in the Dominican Republic.
▶Winter leagues roster: Andy Allanson, C, Obregon Yaqui (Yaqui Indians), Mexico; Basillo abrera, OF, Azucareros del Este (Sugarmen), D.R.; Steve Cummings, RHP, Aguilas del Zulia, Venezuela; Luis De los Santos, 1B, Leones (Lions) Escogido, D.R.; Greg Gohr, RHP, Aquilas del Zulia, Venezuela; Adrian Jordan, OF, Aguilas del Zulia, Venezuela; Manny Jose, OF, Azucareros Este, (Sugar East), D.R.; John Kiely, RHP, Aguilas del Zulia, Venezuela; Dan Lewis, OF, Aguilas del Zulia, Venezuela; Eric Mangham, OF, Aguilas del Zulia, Venezuela; Randy Marshall, LHP, Culiacan Tomateros (Tomato growers), Mexico; Domingo Michel, OF, Azucareros Este, (Sugar East), D.R.; Johnny Paredes, 2B, Aguilas del Zulia, Venezuela; Victor Rosario, IF, Azucareros Este, (Sugar East), D.R.; Leo Torres, RHP, Azucaeros Este, (Sugar East), D.R.; Rob Wassenaar, RHP, Aguilas del Zulia, Venezuela.

Team directory

▶Owner: Thomas S. Monaghan

▶General Manager: Glenn E. "Bo" Schembechler

▶Ballpark:Tiger Stadium
2121 Trumbull Avenue, Detroit, Michigan
313-962-4000
Capacity 52,416
Pay parking lot
Public transportation available
Wheelchair section, ramps, Group Sales department

▶Team publications:
Tiger Yearbook, Scorebook/Program

▶TV, radio broadcast stations:
WJR 760AM, WDIV Channel 4

▶Camps and/or clinics:
Jim Price's Sports Fantasy, 313-353-5643

▶Spring Training:
Marchant Stadium
Lakeland, Florida
Capacity 7,027
813-682-1401

DETROIT TIGERS 1991 Final Stats

Batting	AVG	SLG	OB	G	AB	R	H	TB	2B	3B	HR	RBI	BB	SO	SB	CS	E
Paredes	.333	.333	.333	16	18	4	6	6	0	0	0	0	0	1	1	1	1
Livingstone	.291	.378	.341	44	127	19	37	48	5	0	2	11	10	25	2	1	2
Barnes	.289	.491	.325	75	159	28	46	78	13	2	5	17	9	24	10	7	2
Phillips	.284	.438	.371	146	564	87	160	247	28	4	17	72	79	95	10	5	8
Whitaker	.279	.489	.391	138	470	94	131	230	26	2	23	78	90	45	4	2	4
Tettleton	.263	.491	.387	154	501	85	132	246	17	2	31	89	101	131	3	3	6
Moseby	.262	.396	.321	74	260	37	68	103	15	1	6	35	21	43	8	1	6
Fielder	.261	.513	.347	162	624	102	163	320	25	0	44	133	78	151	0	0	8
Fryman	.259	.447	.309	149	557	65	144	249	36	3	21	91	40	149	12	5	23
Cuyler	.257	.337	.335	154	475	77	122	160	15	7	3	33	52	92	41	10	6
Rowland	.250	.250	.333	4	4	0	1	1	0	0	0	1	1	2	0	0	0
Trammell	.248	.373	.320	101	375	57	93	140	20	0	9	55	37	39	11	2	9
Bergman	.237	.407	.351	86	194	23	46	79	10	1	7	29	35	40	1	1	1
Allanson	.232	.318	.266	60	151	10	35	48	10	0	1	16	7	31	0	1	5
Incaviglia	.214	.353	.290	97	337	38	72	119	12	1	11	38	36	92	1	3	3
Deer	.179	.386	.314	134	448	64	80	173	14	2	25	64	89	175	1	3	7
Bernazard	.167	.167	.167	6	12	0	2	2	0	0	0	0	0	4	0	0	1
delos Sants	.167	.233	.219	16	30	1	5	7	2	0	0	2	4	4	0	0	1
Shelby	.154	.287	.204	53	143	19	22	41	8	1	3	8	8	23	0	2	2
Salas	.088	.158	.117	33	57	2	5	9	1	0	1	7	0	10	0	0	0
Hare	.053	.105	.143	9	19	0	1	2	1	0	0	0	2	1	0	0	0
Moses	.048	.095	.130	13	21	5	1	2	1	0	0	1	2	7	4	0	0

Pitching	W-L	ERA	G	GS	CG	GF	Sho	SV	IP	H	R	ER	HR	BB	SO
Henneman	10-2	2.88	60	0	0	50	0	21	84.1	81	29	27	2	34	61
Dalton	0-0	3.38	4	0	0	1	0	0	8	3	3	2	2	4	4
Tanana	13-12	3.77	33	33	3	0	2	0	217.1	217	98	91	26	78	107
Gullickson	20-9	3.90	35	35	4	0	0	0	226.1	256	109	98	22	44	91
Gleaton	3-2	4.06	47	0	0	16	0	2	75.1	74	37	34	7	39	47
Leiter	9-7	4.21	38	15	1	7	0	1	134.2	125	66	63	16	50	103
Terrell	12-14	4.24	35	33	8	1	2	0	218.2	257	115	103	16	79	80
Cerutti	3-6	4.57	38	8	1	10	0	2	88.2	94	49	45	9	37	29
Gibson	5-7	4.59	68	0	0	28	0	8	96	112	51	49	10	48	52
Aldred	2-4	5.18	11	11	1	0	0	0	57.1	58	37	33	9	30	35
Meacham	2-1	5.20	10	4	0	1	0	0	27.2	35	17	16	4	11	14
Gakeler	1-4	5.74	31	7	0	11	0	2	73.2	73	52	47	5	39	43
Haas	1-0	6.75	11	0	0	0	0	0	10.2	8	8	8	1	12	6
Searcy	1-2	8.41	16	5	0	4	0	0	40.2	52	40	38	8	30	32
Kaiser	0-1	9.00	10	0	0	4	0	2	5	6	5	5	1	5	4
Munoz	0-0	9.64	6	0	0	4	0	0	9.1	14	10	10	0	5	3
Ritz	0-3	11.74	11	5	0	3	0	0	15.1	17	22	20	1	22	9
Kiely	0-1	14.85	7	0	0	3	0	0	6.2	13	11	11	0	9	1

196

1992 Preliminary Roster

Pitchers (19)

Scott Aldred
Steve Cummings
John DeSilva
John Doherty
Dan Gakeler
Paul Gibson
Greg Gohr
Buddy Groom
Bill Gullickson
David Haas
Mike Henneman
Jeff Kaiser
John Kiely
Kurt Knudsen
Mark Leiter
Mike Munoz
Kevin Ritz
Frank Tanana
Walt Terrell

Catchers (3)

Andy Allanson
Rich Rowland
Mickey Tettleton

Infielders (10)

Dave Bergman
Rico Brogna
Cecil Fielder
Travis Fryman
Scott Livingstone
Johnny Paredes
Tony Phillips
Victor Rosario
Alan Trammell
Lou Whitaker

Outfielders (8)

Skeeter Barnes
Milt Cuyler
Rob Deer
Shawn Hare
Jody Hurst
Riccardo Ingram
Steve Pegues
Rudy Pemberton

Games played by position

	G	C	1B	2B	3B	SS	OF	DH
Allanson,A	60	56	2	0	0	0	0	1
Barnes,Br	75	0	9	7	17	0	33	3
Bergman,D	86	0	49	0	0	0	4	13
Bernazard,T	6	0	0	2	0	0	0	2
Cuyler,M	154	0	0	0	0	0	151	0
Deer,R	134	0	0	0	0	0	132	2
Delossantos,L	16	0	2	0	2	0	3	9
Fielder,C	162	0	122	0	0	0	0	42
Fryman,T	149	0	0	0	85	71	0	0
Hare,S	9	0	0	0	0	0	6	2
Incaviglia,P	97	0	0	0	0	0	54	41
Livingstone,S	44	0	0	0	43	0	0	0
Moseby,L	74	0	0	0	0	0	64	7
Moses,J	13	0	0	0	0	0	12	0
Paredes,J	16	0	0	7	1	1	0	2
Phillips,T	146	0	0	36	46	13	56	18
Rowland,R	4	2	0	0	0	0	0	1
Salas,M	33	11	5	0	0	0	0	8
Shelby,J	53	0	0	0	0	0	47	4
Tettleton,M	154	125	1	0	0	0	3	24
Trammell,A	101	0	0	0	1	91	0	6
Whitaker,L	138	0	0	135	0	0	0	3

Sick call: 1991 DL report

Player	Days on the DL
Lloyd Moseby	48**
Mark Leiter	18
Pete Incaviglia	45*
Jerry Don Gleaton	38
Alan Trammell	27
Mike Henneman	16

On DL twice (not counting administrative transfers from one DL to another).
**On DL three times (not counting administrative transfers from one DL to another).*

Minor League Report

Class AAA — Toledo finished 74-70, third in the International League West. The Mud Hens were 44-28 at home, their best record in Toledo since 1968. The club set a season attendance record with 229,419 fans, breaking its 1980 record of 210,685. C Rich Rowland (.271-13-66) threw out 51.1% of baserunners attempting to steal (46 of 90). . . . **Class AA** — London finished 61-78, sixth in the Eastern League. Top hitters were OF Riccardo Ingram (.271-18-64) and 1B Rico Brogna (.273-13-51 in 77 games). LHP Buddy Groom was 7-1 with a 3.48 ERA and LHP Randy Marshall was 8-10 with a 4.47 ERA. . . . **Class A** — Lakeland finished 72-56, winning both halves in the Florida State League Central Division. The Tigers lost to West Palm Beach in the playoffs. OF Basilio Cabrera hit .286 in 74 games. LHP Frank Gonzales was 11-5 with a 3.39 ERA. Reliever Jeff Braley (4-4, 2.63) had 24 saves. . . . Fayetteville finished 59-78, third in the first half and seventh in the second half in the South Atlantic League Northern Division. OF Jeff Goodale hit .326, C Joe Perona hit .272 and 1B Danny Rogers hit .230 with 11 HRs and 67 RBI. Top pitchers included RHP Phil Stidham (0-1, 1.60, 8 saves); RHP Bob Undorf (4-1, 1.60) and LHP Mike Guilfoyle (1-4, 2.47, 8 saves). . . . Niagara Falls finished 36-42, third in the NY-P League Stedler Division. 3B Rob Grable hit .303 with 7 HRs and 46 RBI. LHP Jimmy Henry was 8-4 with a 2.22 ERA. . . . Bristol finished 22-44, fifth in the Appalachian League Southern Division. The Tigers hit .208 as a team, but Tom Mezzanotte hit .304 with 10 doubles and 25 RBI. LHP Matt Bauer was 5-3 with a 3.19 ERA.

Tops in the Organization

BATTING LEADERS	Club	Avg.	G	AB	R	H	HR	RBI
Scott Livingstone	Tol	.302	92	331	48	100	3	62
Victor Rosario	Tol	.300	116	423	59	127	1	48
Shawn Hare	Tol	.297	111	377	64	112	13	70
Johnny Paredes	Tol	.284	135	514	82	146	1	53
Dean Decillis	Tol	.283	98	368	45	104	3	50

HOME RUNS:			WINS		
Mitch Lyden	Tol	18	Steve Wolf	Lon	11
Riccardo Ingram	Lon	18	Brian Warren	Lak	11
Rico Brogna	Tol	15	Frank Gonzales	Lak	11
Shawn Hare	Tol	13	Greg Coppeta	Fay	11
Rich Rowland	Tol	13	Several players tied		10

RBI			SAVES		
Shawn Hare	Tol	70	Jeff Braley	Lak	24
Rich Rowland	Tol	68	John Doherty	Lon	15
Danny Rogers	Fay	67	Mike Munoz	Tol	8
Rico Brogna	Tol	64	Phil Stidham	Fay	8
Riccardo Ingram	Lon	64	Mike Guilfoyle	Fay	8

STOLEN BASES			STRIKE OUTS		
Lou Frazier	Lon	42	John Desilva	Tol	136
Johnny Paredes	Tol	36	David Haas	Tol	133
Eric Mangham	Lon	29	Steve Wolf	Lon	126
Skeeter Barnes	Tol	27	Ed Rodriguez	Fay	119
Rudy Pemberton	Lak	25	Mike Garcia	Lak	109

PITCHING LEADERS	Club	W-L	ERA	IP	H	BB	SO
Brian Warren	Lak	11-3	2.44	129	104	20	103
Tom Drell	Lak	6-10	2.91	130	115	43	56
Rusty Meacham	Tol	9-7	3.09	125	117	40	70
Mike Garcia	Lak	6-8	3.13	144	130	41	109
Kevin Ritz	Tol	8-7	3.28	126	116	60	105

Detroit (1901-1991)

Runs: Most, career, all-time

2087	Ty Cobb, 1905-1926
1774	Charlie Gehringer, 1924-1942
1622	Al Kaline, 1953-1974
1242	Donie Bush, 1908-1921
1209	Harry Heilmann, 1914-1929

Hits: Most, career, all-time

3901	Ty Cobb, 1905-1926
3007	Al Kaline, 1953-1974
2839	Charlie Gehringer, 1924-1942
2499	Harry Heilmann, 1914-1929
2466	Sam Crawford, 1903-1917

2B: Most, career, all-time

665	Ty Cobb, 1905-1926
574	Charlie Gehringer, 1924-1942
498	Al Kaline, 1953-1974
497	Harry Heilmann, 1914-1929
402	Sam Crawford, 1903-1917

3B: Most, career, all-time

284	Ty Cobb, 1905-1926
249	Sam Crawford, 1903-1917
146	Charlie Gehringer, 1924-1942
145	Harry Heilmann, 1914-1929
136	Bobby Veach, 1912-1923
75	Al Kaline, 1953-1974 (6)

HR: Most, career, all-time

399	Al Kaline, 1953-1974
373	Norm Cash, 1960-1974
306	Hank Greenberg, 1930-1946
262	Willie Horton, 1963-1977
239	Rudy York, 1934-1945

RBI: Most, career, all-time

1804	Ty Cobb, 1905-1926
1583	Al Kaline, 1953-1974
1442	Harry Heilmann, 1914-1929
1427	Charlie Gehringer, 1924-1942
1264	Sam Crawford, 1903-1917

SB: Most, career, all-time

864	Ty Cobb, 1905-1926
400	Donie Bush, 1908-1921
317	Sam Crawford, 1903-1917
294	Ron LeFlore, 1974-1979
210	ALAN TRAMMELL, 1977-1991

BB: Most, career, all-time

1277	Al Kaline, 1953-1974
1186	Charlie Gehringer, 1924-1942
1148	Ty Cobb, 1905-1926
1125	Donie Bush, 1908-1921
1025	Norm Cash, 1960-1974

BA: Highest, career, all-time

.368	Ty Cobb, 1905-1926
.342	Harry Heilmann, 1914-1929
.337	Bob Fothergill, 1922-1930
.325	George Kell, 1946-1952
.321	Heinie Manush, 1923-1927
.297	Al Kaline, 1953-1974 (17)

Slug avg: Highest, career, all-time

.616	Hank Greenberg, 1930-1946
.518	Harry Heilmann, 1914-1929
.516	Ty Cobb, 1905-1926
.503	Rudy York, 1934-1945
.501	Rocky Colavito, 1960-1963
.490	Norm Cash, 1960-1974 (6)

Games started: Most, career, all-time

459	Mickey Lolich, 1963-1975
408	JACK MORRIS, 1977-1990
395	George Mullin, 1902-1913
388	Hooks Dauss, 1912-1926
373	Hal Newhouser, 1939-1953

Saves: Most, career, all-time

125	John Hiller, 1965-1980
120	Willie Hernandez, 1984-1989
85	Aurelio Lopez, 1979-1985
80	MIKE HENNEMAN, 1987-1991
55	Terry Fox, 1961-1966

Shutouts: Most, career, all-time

39	Mickey Lolich, 1963-1975
34	George Mullin, 1902-1913
33	Tommy Bridges, 1930-1946
33	Hal Newhouser, 1939-1953
29	Bill Donovan, 1903-1918

Wins: Most, career, all-time

222	Hooks Dauss, 1912-1926
209	George Mullin, 1902-1913
207	Mickey Lolich, 1963-1975
200	Hal Newhouser, 1939-1953
198	JACK MORRIS, 1977-1990

K: Most, career, all-time

2679	Mickey Lolich, 1963-1975
1980	JACK MORRIS, 1977-1990
1770	Hal Newhouser, 1939-1953
1674	Tommy Bridges, 1930-1946
1406	Jim Bunning, 1955-1963

Win pct: Highest, career, all-time

.700	MIKE HENNEMAN, 1987-1991
.654	Denny McLain, 1963-1970
.639	Aurelio Lopez, 1979-1985
.629	Schoolboy Rowe, 1933-1942
.616	Harry Coveleski, 1914-1918

ERA: Lowest, career, all-time

2.34	Harry Coveleski, 1914-1918
2.38	Ed Killian, 1904-1910
2.42	Ed Summers, 1908-1912
2.49	Bill Donovan, 1903-1918
2.61	Ed Siever, 1901-1908
2.83	John Hiller, 1965-1980 (7)

Runs: Most, season

147	Ty Cobb, 1911
144	Ty Cobb, 1915
144	Charlie Gehringer, 1930
144	Charlie Gehringer, 1936
144	Hank Greenberg, 1938
126	Ron LeFlore, 1978 (15)

Hits: Most, season

248	Ty Cobb, 1911
237	Harry Heilmann, 1921
227	Ty Cobb, 1912
227	Charlie Gehringer, 1936
225	Ty Cobb, 1917
225	Harry Heilmann, 1925
212	Ron LeFlore, 1977 (14)

2B: Most, season

63	Hank Greenberg, 1934
60	Charlie Gehringer, 1936
56	George Kell, 1950
55	Gee Walker, 1936
50	Charlie Gehringer, 1934
50	Hank Greenberg, 1940
50	Harry Heilmann, 1927
42	Lance Parrish, 1983

3B: Most, season

26	Sam Crawford, 1914
25	Sam Crawford, 1903
24	Ty Cobb, 1911
24	Ty Cobb, 1917
23	Ty Cobb, 1912
23	Sam Crawford, 1913
13	Larry Herndon, 1982)

41   George Mullin, 1905

HR: Most, season

58	Hank Greenberg, 1938
51	CECIL FIELDER, 1990
45	Rocky Colavito, 1961
44	CECIL FIELDER, 1991
44	Hank Greenberg, 1946

RBI: Most, season

183	Hank Greenberg, 1937
170	Hank Greenberg, 1935
150	Hank Greenberg, 1940
146	Hank Greenberg, 1938
140	Rocky Colavito, 1961
133	CECIL FIELDER, 1991 (12)

SB: Most, season

96	Ty Cobb, 1915
83	Ty Cobb, 1911
78	Ron LeFlore, 1979
76	Ty Cobb, 1909
68	Ty Cobb, 1916
68	Ron LeFlore, 1978

BB: Most, season

137	Roy Cullenbine, 1947
135	Eddie Yost, 1959
125	Eddie Yost, 1960
124	Norm Cash, 1961
120	Eddie Lake, 1947

BA: Highest, season

.420	Ty Cobb, 1911
.410	Ty Cobb, 1912
.403	Harry Heilmann, 1923
.401	Ty Cobb, 1922
.398	Harry Heilmann, 1927
.361	Norm Cash, 1961 (23)

Slug avg: Highest, season

.683	Hank Greenberg, 1938
.670	Hank Greenberg, 1940
.668	Hank Greenberg, 1937
.662	Norm Cash, 1961
.632	Harry Heilmann, 1923

Games started: Most, season

45	Mickey Lolich, 1971
44	George Mullin, 1904
42	Mickey Lolich, 1973
42	George Mullin, 1907
41	Joe Coleman, 1974
41	Mickey Lolich, 1972
41	Mickey Lolich, 1974
41	Denny McLain, 1968
41	Denny McLain, 1969

Saves: Most, season

38	John Hiller, 1973
32	Willie Hernandez, 1984
31	Willie Hernandez, 1985
27	Tom Timmermann, 1970
24	Willie Hernandez, 1986

Shutouts: Most, season

9	Denny McLain, 1969
8	Ed Killian, 1905
8	Hal Newhouser, 1945
7	Billy Hoeft, 1955
7	George Mullin, 1904
7	Dizzy Trout, 1944

Wins: Most, season

31	Denny McLain, 1968
29	George Mullin, 1909
29	Hal Newhouser, 1944
27	Dizzy Trout, 1944
26	Hal Newhouser, 1946

K: Most, season

308	Mickey Lolich, 1971
280	Denny McLain, 1968
275	Hal Newhouser, 1946
271	Mickey Lolich, 1969
250	Mickey Lolich, 1972

Win pct: Highest, season

.862	Bill Donovan, 1907
.842	Schoolboy Rowe, 1940
.838	Denny McLain, 1968
.808	Bobo Newsom, 1940
.784	George Mullin, 1909

ERA: Lowest, season

1.64	Ed Summers, 1908
1.71	Ed Killian, 1909
1.78	Ed Killian, 1907
1.81	Hal Newhouser, 1945
1.91	Ed Siever, 1902
1.96	Denny McLain, 1968 (7)

Most pinch-hit homers, season

3	Gus Zernial, 1958
3	Norm Cash, 1960
3	Vic Wertz, 1962
3	Gates Brown, 1968
3	Ben Oglivie, 1976
3	John Grubb, 1984
3	Larry Herndon, 1986

Most pinch-hit, homers, career

16	Gates Brown, 1963-1975

Most consecutive games, batting safely

40	Ty Cobb, 1911

Most consecutive scoreless innings

N/A

No hit games

George Mullin, Det vs StL AL, 7-0;
July 4, 1912 (2nd game).
Virgil Trucks, Det vs Was AL, 1-0;
May 15, 1952.
Virgil Trucks, Det at NY AL, 1-0;
August 25, 1952.
Jim Bunning, Det at Bos AL, 3-0; July
20, 1958 (1st game).
Jack Morris, Det at Chi AL, 4-0; April
7, 1984.

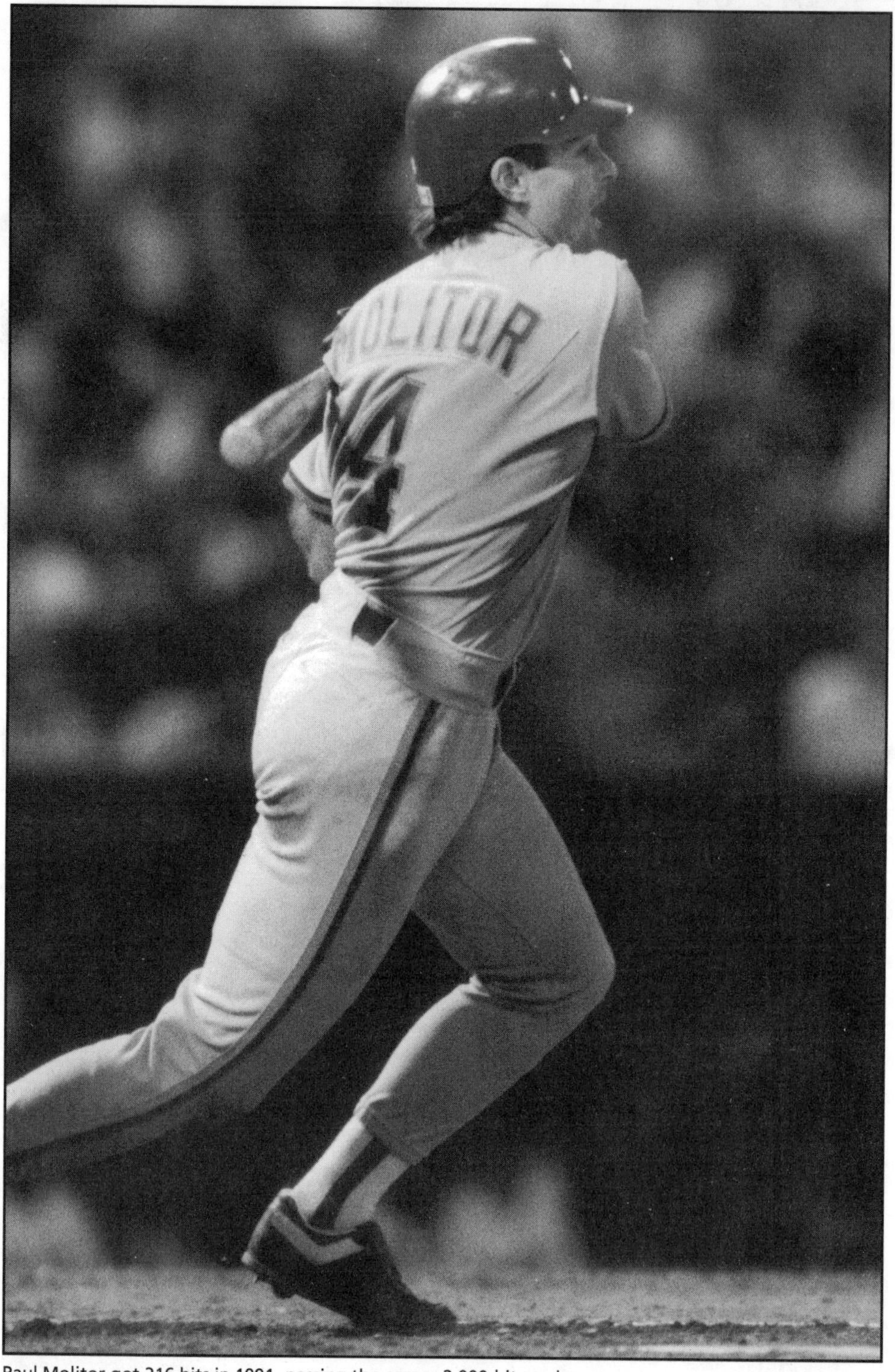

Paul Molitor got 216 hits in 1991, passing the career 2,000-hit mark.

A 'halfway decent season'

A banner at County Stadium the final day of the season summed up the season for the Milwaukee Brewers: "Thanks for a halfway decent season."

If the season had started on Aug. 1, the Brewers would have been in great shape. They won 40 of their last 59 games, but the damage already had been done. They finished 83-79, fourth in the American League East.

If nothing else, the Brewers played "spoilers" against Boston, beating the Red Sox six out of seven games during the last two weekends of the season. That knocked the Bosox into a second-place tie with Detroit, just one game ahead of Milwaukee.

The season was followed immediately by the Big Purge: General Manager Harry Dalton was named senior vice president for special projects, former third baseman Sal Bando was hired as GM and Tom Trebelhorn was replaced by Phil Garner as manager. In addition, farm director Bruce Manno was promoted to vice president of baseball operations.

Dalton was on the hot seat for signing pitcher Teddy Higuera and first baseman Franklin Stubbs to big contracts.

Higuera signed for $13.4 million over four years, but pitched just seven times because of a torn rotator cuff.

Stubbs was paid $2.1 million last season and hit .213 with 11 home runs and 38 runs batted in.

Other big contracts went to starter Ron Robinson, who made just one appearance because of elbow surgery, and reliever Edwin Nunez, who made 23 appearances and required back surgery.

Outfielder Candy Maldonado, who was solid in spring training, broke his foot the second game of the season, and eventually was traded to Toronto.

In addition, infielder Gary Sheffield's season ended in July with a shoulder injury and a final .194 batting average. Ironically, that injury made veteran Willie Randolph a regular, and he responded with his finest year ever. He hit a career-high .327, third in the batting race. His .424 on-base percentage was second in the league to Chicago's Frank Thomas.

Veteran Paul Molitor enjoyed another solid season, hitting .325 with 17 HRs and 75 RBI. Molitor led the league with 216 hits and 133 runs.

Robin Yount missed a month with a kidney stone and wound up batting .260 with 77 RBI.

The Brewers uncovered a couple of good, young players in outfielders Greg Vaughn (.244-27-98) and Darryl Hamilton (.311-1-57).

The brightest spot on the mound was Bill Wegman, who won 9 of his last 12 starts to finish 15-7. Jaime Navarro was 15-12; Chris Bosio 14-10.

—Bill Koenig

Brewers 1992 preview

The Milwaukee Brewers closed last season with a rush, winning 40 of their last 59 games—but it wasn't enough to save Tom Trebelhorn's job. New manager Phil Garner is hoping the final two months were no fluke.

The Brewers have the makings of a decent rotation with Chris Bosio, Bill Wegman, Jaime Navarro, Dan Plesac and rookie Cal Eldred. If Ted Higuera can bounce back from a torn rotator cuff, it will be icing on the cake.

Look for solid years from veterans Robin Yount and Paul Molitor, and hope young outfielders Greg Vaughn and Darryl Hamilton continue to mature.

The Brewers simply have to get more production from first baseman Franklin Stubbs, their $2 million man. On the other hand, infielder Gary Sheffield, whose season was cut short by a shoulder injury, probably won't hit .194 again.

1992 prophecy: Brewers

▸Paul "Iron Horse" Molitor will once again play in 158 games.

▸The Brewers will shy away from free agents, remembering Franklin Stubbs' .213 season of 1991 where he was paid $52,631.58 for each of his measly 38 RBI.

▸Todd Worrell will sign with Milwaukee and have the healthiest shoulder on the staff.

—*John Hunt*

Molitor stayed healthy and slugged it out

Paul Molitor surpassed the 2,000 career hit mark at the end of last July, getting No. 1,999 and No. 2,000 off of Kansas City's Bret Saberhagen, who has had considerable success against the veteran slugger.

Molitor, who has been injury-plagued throughout his career, would probably have had several hundred more hits if he had been as healthy in earlier years as he was in '91.

"You think about that sometimes," he said, "but there's really nothing you can do about it."

Earlier in the season, Molitor had talked about retiring after 1992, but conceded that he'd stick around if he was wanted.

"I think about that," he said, "but I could also decide to play for three or four more years if they want me."

After finishing 1991 with a league-leading 216 hits in 665 at-bats, fifth in batting (.325), first in runs scored (133), fourth in total bases (325) and second in triples (13), there's no question that they want him.

They've got the bug

The Brewers have been bitten by the injury bug since Rollie Fingers had to have elbow surgery in 1982. During the past four years (1988-91), the team has lost almost 2,400 player days—the equivalent of 15 individual seasons—to injuries.

Trainer John Adam can't explain the curse.

"I don't know what the answer is," he said, ". . . we just seem to have lousy luck."

The team hired strength and conditioning coach Toby Oldham to supervise a year-round program that will try to keep the players healthy. Oldham, who has worked with the Toronto Blue Jays and the Florida State baseball team, planned to visit players around the country during the offseason.

Team officials had complained that many of the players don't stick to their conditioning programs once the season is over. But even those who do have had problems.

"Nobody works harder than Paul Molitor during the offseason," Adam said, "but he's a Murphy's Law waiting for an injury to happen."

Ironically, Molitor had a healthy 1991 and wound up among the league leaders in five offensive categories. If the rest of the team could follow suit, there's no telling what the "Bruise Crew" might do.

"Someday we'll come out of this," Adam said. "But I wonder if I'll be here to see it."

Broadcaster joined Brewers' DL

Nobody in Milwaukee is immune to the injury curse—not even the broadcasters. Bob Uecker, the Brewers' radio voice since 1971, underwent surgery last July on two aneurysms in his abdominal aorta.

But before he took himself out of the lineup, Uecker called the game as scheduled—even though he knew he was to have the life-threatening surgery three days later.

In a press conference after the successful surgery, the announcer joked that he had called the July game because he had an "aneurysm clause" in his contract.

"You work with an aneurysm, you get a bonus," he teased.

Brewers winter league news

▸Instructional League: none.
▸Winter leagues: OF Matias Carrillo, who hit .276 with 8 HRs and 56 RBI at Class AAA Denver, played for the Mexicali Aguila in Mexico with SS Jim Tatum (.320-18-128 at Class AA El Paso). . . . OF Shon Ashley (.308-24-100 at El Paso), LHP Tim Fortugno (5-1, 1.99 at El Paso) and SS Pat Listach (44 RBI between El Paso and Denver) got additional experience playing for the Mazatlan Venados. . . . OF Jim Olander (.325-9-78 at Denver) was Milwaukee's only player in Puerto Rico.
▸Winter leagues roster: Shon Ashley, OF, Mazatlan Venados (Deer), Mexico; Matias Carrillo, OF, Mexicali Aguila (Eagle), Mexico; Tim Fortugno, LHP, Mazatlan Venados, (Deer), Mexico; Pat Listach, 2B, Mazatlan Venados, (Deer), Mexico; Julio Machado, P, Aguilas del Zulia, Venezuela; Jim Olander, OF, San Juan Metros, Puerto Rico; Ramon Sambo, OF, Azucareros Este (Sugarmen), D.R.; William Suero, 2B, Leones (Lions) Escogido, D.R.; Jim Tatum, SS, Mil, Mexicali Aguila (Eagle) Mexico.

Team directory

▸Owner: Allan H. (Bud) Selig

▸General Manager: Sal Bando

▸Ballpark:
 Milwaukee County Stadium
 201 South 46th Street, Milwaukee, Wisconsin
 414-933-1818
 Capacity 53,192
 Pay parking lot; $4
 Public transportation available
 Family and wheelchair sections, ramps, Designated Driver Program including free taxi transportation for single ticket holders participating in the DDP

▸Team publications:
 What's Brewing, game program, Yearbook
 414-933-4114

▸TV, radio broadcast stations:
 WTMJ 620 AM, WCGV-TV 24

▸Camps and/or clinics:
 Gatorade Youth Camp, during the season, 414-933-4114
 Fantasy Camp, January, 414-933-4114

▸Spring Training:
 Compadre Stadium
 Chandler, Arizona
 Capacity 5,000
 602-895-1200

MILWAUKEE BREWERS 1991 Final Stats

Batting	AVG	SLG	OB	G	AB	R	H	TB	2B	3B	HR	RBI	BB	SO	SB	CS	E
Mcintosh	.364	.727	.364	7	11	2	4	8	1	0	1	1	0	4	0	0	0
Randolph	.327	.374	.424	124	431	60	141	161	14	3	0	54	75	38	4	2	20
Molitor	.325	.489	.399	158	665	133	216	325	32	13	17	75	77	62	19	8	6
Hamilton	.311	.385	.361	122	405	64	126	156	15	6	1	57	33	38	16	6	1
Surhoff	.289	.372	.319	143	505	57	146	188	19	4	5	68	26	33	5	8	4
Brock	.283	.400	.419	31	60	9	17	24	4	0	1	6	14	9	1	1	0
Gantner	.283	.361	.320	140	526	63	149	190	27	4	2	47	27	34	4	6	12
Spiers	.283	.401	.337	133	414	71	117	166	13	6	8	54	34	55	14	8	17
Yount	.260	.376	.332	130	503	66	131	189	20	4	10	77	54	79	6	4	2
Vaughn	.244	.456	.319	145	542	81	132	247	24	5	27	98	62	125	2	2	2
Sveum	.241	.365	.320	90	266	33	64	97	19	1	4	43	32	78	2	4	10
Bichette	.238	.393	.272	134	445	53	106	175	18	3	15	59	22	107	14	8	7
Dempsey	.231	.347	.329	61	147	15	34	51	5	0	4	21	23	20	0	2	2
Stubbs	.213	.359	.282	103	362	48	77	130	16	2	11	38	35	71	13	4	9
Sheffield	.194	.320	.277	50	175	25	34	56	12	2	2	22	19	15	5	5	8
Canale	.176	.500	.318	21	34	6	6	17	2	0	3	10	8	6	0	0	2
Olander	.000	.000	.182	12	9	2	0	0	0	0	0	0	2	5	0	0	0
Carrillo	—	—	—	3	0	0	0	0	0	0	0	0	0	0	0	0	0

Pitching	W-L	ERA	G	GS	CG	GF	Sho	SV	IP	H	R	ER	HR	BB	SO
Henry	2-1	1.00	32	0	0	25	0	15	36	16	4	4	1	14	28
Wegman	15-7	2.84	28	28	7	0	2	0	193.1	176	76	61	16	40	89
George	0-0	3.00	2	1	0	1	0	0	6	8	2	2	0	0	2
Bosio	14-10	3.25	32	32	5	0	1	0	204.2	187	80	74	15	58	117
Machado	3-3	3.45	54	0	0	13	0	3	88.2	65	36	34	12	55	98
Lee	2-5	3.86	62	0	0	9	0	1	67.2	72	33	29	10	31	43
Navarro	15-12	3.92	34	34	10	0	2	0	234	237	117	102	18	73	114
Plesac	2-7	4.29	45	10	0	25	0	8	92.1	92	49	44	12	39	61
Higuera	3-2	4.46	7	6	0	1	0	0	36.1	37	18	18	2	10	33
Dempsey	0-0	4.50	2	0	0	2	0	0	2	3	1	1	0	1	0
Eldred	2-0	4.50	3	3	0	0	0	0	16	20	9	8	2	6	10
Crim	8-5	4.63	66	0	0	29	0	3	91.1	115	52	47	9	25	39
Holmes	1-4	4.72	40	0	0	9	0	3	76.1	90	43	40	6	27	59
August	9-8	5.47	28	23	1	3	1	0	138.1	166	87	84	18	47	62
Brown	2-4	5.51	15	10	0	0	0	0	63.2	66	39	39	6	34	30
Ignasiak	2-1	5.68	4	1	0	0	0	0	12.2	7	8	8	2	8	10
Nunez	2-1	6.04	23	0	0	18	0	8	25.1	28	20	17	6	13	24
Robinson	0-1	6.23	1	1	0	0	0	0	4.1	6	3	3	0	3	0
Hunter	0-5	7.26	8	6	0	0	0	0	31	45	26	25	3	17	14
Knudson	1-3	7.97	12	7	0	3	0	0	35	54	33	31	8	15	23
Austin	0-0	8.31	5	0	0	1	0	0	8.2	8	8	8	1	11	3

1992 Preliminary Roster

Pitchers (23)

James Austin
Chris Bosio
Kevin Brown
Cal Eldred
Narciso Elvira
Mike Fetters
Chris George
Otis Green
Doug Henry
Ted Higuera
Darren Holmes
Mike Ignasiak
Mark Kiefer
Mark Lee
Julio Machado
Angel Miranda
Jamie Navarro
Edwin Nunez
Jesse Orosco
Dan Plesac
Ron Robinson
Bruce Ruffin
Bill Wegman

Catchers (3)

Joe Kmak
Dave Nilsson
B.J. Surhoff

Infielders (9)

John Jaha
Pat Listach
Tim McIntosh
Paul Molitor
Gary Sheffield
Bill Spiers
Franklin Stubbs
William Suero
Jim Tatum

Outfielders (6)

Dante Bichette
Mickey Brantley
Darryl Hamilton
Jim Olander
Greg Vaughn
Robin Yount

Games played by position

	G	C	1B	2B	3B	SS	OF	DH
Bichette,D	134	0	0	0	1	0	127	0
Brock,G	31	0	25	0	0	0	0	0
Canale,G	21	0	19	0	0	0	0	0
Carrillo,M	3	0	0	0	0	0	3	0
Dempsey,R	61	56	1	0	0	0	0	0
Gantner,J	140	0	0	59	90	0	0	0
Hamilton,D	122	0	0	0	0	0	117	0
McIntosh,T	7	0	1	0	0	0	4	2
Molitor,P	158	0	46	0	0	0	0	112
Olander,J	12	0	0	0	0	0	9	3
Randolph,W	124	0	0	121	0	0	0	2
Sheffield,G	50	0	0	0	43	0	0	5
Spiers,B	133	0	0	0	0	128	1	2
Stubbs,F	103	0	92	0	0	0	4	4
Surhoff,B	143	127	0	1	5	0	2	6
Sveum,D	90	0	0	2	38	51	0	3
Vaughn,G	145	0	0	0	0	0	135	10
Yount,R	130	0	0	0	0	0	117	13

Sick call: 1991 DL report

Player	Days on the DL
Bill Wegman	25
Candy Maldonado	75
Ron Robinson	178
Mark Knudson	36
Ed Nunez	86
Darryl Hamilton	24
Ted Higuera	144*
Gary Sheffield	95*
Chris Bosio	15
Darren Holmes	15
Robin Yount	24
Jim Austin	41
Mike Ignasiak	28

On DL twice (not counting administrative transfers from one DL to another).

Minor League Report

Class AAA — Denver finished 79-65, first in American Association West. The Zephyrs beat Buffalo to win the league title, then advanced to Triple-A Classic against Columbus. Denver had a top-flight OF in Jim Olander (.325-9-78 with 32 doubles and 10 triples), Carmen Castillo (.302-14-72) and Mickey Brantley (.301-15-78). RHP Cal Eldred was 13-9 with a 3.75 ERA, while RHP Mark Kiefer was 9-5 with a 4.62 ERA. The Zephyrs drew 554,297 fans. . . . **Class AA** — El Paso finished 81-55, winning the first half and finishing second the second half in the Texas League Western Division. The Diablos beat Midland and lost to Shreveport in the playoffs. Hitting leaders were 1B John Jaha (.344-30-134) and SS Jim Tatum (.320-18-128). RHP Jeff Schwarz was 11-8 with a 4.89 ERA. The Diablos drew a club-record 274,055 fans. . . . **Class A** — Stockton finished 71-65, second in the first half and fourth in the second half in the California League Northern Division. The Ports shocked San Jose in the playoffs before losing to High Desert. Tim Clark hit .274 with 19 doubles and 56 RBI. LHP Otis Green was 9-1 with a 1.92 ERA; RHP Tim Dell was 10-9 with a 2.69 ERA. . . . Beloit finished 70-67, third in the first half and fifth in the second half in the Midwest League Northern Division. Beloit led the Midwest League with 299 SBs in 137 games, just 20 short of the league record. OF Tony Diggs hit .270 with 52 SBs. RHP Larry Carter was 14-3 with a 3.17 ERA. . . . Helena finished 44-26, second in the Pioneer League Northern Division. The Brewers had a .293 batting average, led by Andy Fairman (.373-8-62), Mike Basse (.367) and Jeff Cirillo (.350-10-51). RHP Brian Souza was 8-2 with a 3.14 ERA.

Tops in the Organization

BATTING LEADERS	Club	Avg.	G	AB	R	H	HR	RBI
Dave Nilsson	Den	.366	93	344	62	126	6	71
John Jaha	Elp	.344	130	486	121	167	30	134
Jim Olander	Den	.325	134	498	89	162	9	78
Jim Tatum	Elp	.320	130	493	99	158	18	128
Ruben Escalera	Elp	.316	114	443	101	140	6	67

HOME RUNS:			WINS		
John Jaha	Elp	30	Mark Kiefer	Den	16
Shon Ashley	Elp	24	Larry Carter	Blt	14
Tim McIntosh	Den	18	Cal Eldred	Den	13
Jim Tatum	Elp	18	Otis Green	Elp	12
Kenny Jackson	Elp	17	Jeff Schwarz	Elp	11

RBI			SAVES		
John Jaha	Elp	134	Doug Henry	Den	14
Jim Tatum	Elp	128	Angel Miranda	Den	13
Shon Ashley	Elp	100	Jim Czajkowski	Elp	11
Tim McIntosh	Den	91	James Smith	Blt	9
John Byington	Elp	89	Pat Miller	Blt	9

STOLEN BASES			STRIKE OUTS		
Tony Diggs	Blt	52	Cal Eldred	Den	168
Mike Carter	Blt	46	Otis Green	Elp	155
Duane Singleton	Blt	42	Steve Sparks	Stk	149
Pat Listach	Den	37	Mark Kiefer	Den	140
Several players tied		27	Jeff Schwarz	Elp	134

PITCHING LEADERS	Club	W-L	ERA	IP	H	BB	SO
Otis Green	Elp	12-4	2.43	126	76	58	155
Tim Dell	Stk	10-9	2.69	150	127	55	131
Larry Carter	Blt	14-3	3.30	134	147	46	97
Steve Monson	Elp	10-6	3.38	160	158	56	113
Linc Mikkelsen	Stk	5-5	3.42	121	116	42	103

Runs: Most, career, all-time

1499	ROBIN YOUNT, 1974-1991
1186	PAUL MOLITOR, 1978-1991
821	Cecil Cooper, 1977-1987
704	JIM GANTNER, 1976-1991
596	Don Money, 1973-1983

Hits: Most, career, all-time

2878	ROBIN YOUNT, 1974-1991
2086	PAUL MOLITOR, 1978-1991
1815	Cecil Cooper, 1977-1987
1633	JIM GANTNER, 1976-1991
1168	Don Money, 1973-1983

2B: Most, career, all-time

518	ROBIN YOUNT, 1974-1991
369	PAUL MOLITOR, 1978-1991
345	Cecil Cooper, 1977-1987
250	JIM GANTNER, 1976-1991
215	Don Money, 1973-1983

3B: Most, career, all-time

120	ROBIN YOUNT, 1974-1991
79	PAUL MOLITOR, 1978-1991
42	Charlie Moore, 1973-1986
37	JIM GANTNER, 1976-1991
33	Cecil Cooper, 1977-1987

HR: Most, career, all-time

235	ROBIN YOUNT, 1974-1991
208	Gorman Thomas, 1973-1986
201	Cecil Cooper, 1977-1987
176	Ben Oglivie, 1978-1986
148	PAUL MOLITOR, 1978-1991

RBI: Most, career, all-time

1278	ROBIN YOUNT, 1974-1991
944	Cecil Cooper, 1977-1987
701	PAUL MOLITOR, 1978-1991
685	Ben Oglivie, 1978-1986
605	Gorman Thomas, 1973-1986

SB: Most, career, all-time

381	PAUL MOLITOR, 1978-1991
247	ROBIN YOUNT, 1974-1991
136	Tommy Harper, 1969-1971
131	JIM GANTNER, 1976-1991
108	MIKE FELDER, 1985-1990

BB: Most, career, all-time

869	ROBIN YOUNT, 1974-1991
682	PAUL MOLITOR, 1978-1991
501	Gorman Thomas, 1973-1986

440	Don Money, 1973-1983
432	Ben Oglivie, 1978-1986

BA: Highest, career, all-time

.302	PAUL MOLITOR, 1978-1991
.302	Cecil Cooper, 1977-1987
.288	ROBIN YOUNT, 1974-1991
.283	George Scott, 1972-1976
.277	Ben Oglivie, 1978-1986

Slug avg: Highest, career, all-time

.470	Cecil Cooper, 1977-1987
.461	Gorman Thomas, 1973-1986
.461	Ben Oglivie, 1978-1986
.456	George Scott, 1972-1976
.452	Sixto Lezcano, 1974-1980

Games started: Most, career, all-time

268	Jim Slaton, 1971-1983
231	Moose Haas, 1976-1985
217	Mike Caldwell, 1977-1984
185	TEDDY HIGUERA, 1985-1991
157	Bill Travers, 1974-1980

Saves: Most, career, all-time

132	DAN PLESAC, 1986-1991
97	Rollie Fingers, 1981-1985
61	Ken Sanders, 1970-1972
44	Bill Castro, 1974-1980
42	CHUCK CRIM, 1987-1991

Shutouts: Most, career, all-time

19	Jim Slaton, 1971-1983
18	Mike Caldwell, 1977-1984
12	TEDDY HIGUERA, 1985-1991
10	Bill Travers, 1974-1980
8	Moose Haas, 1976-1985

Wins: Most, career, all-time

117	Jim Slaton, 1971-1983
102	Mike Caldwell, 1977-1984
92	TEDDY HIGUERA, 1985-1991
91	Moose Haas, 1976-1985
65	Bill Travers, 1974-1980

K: Most, career, all-time

1019	TEDDY HIGUERA, 1985-1991
929	Jim Slaton, 1971-1983
800	Moose Haas, 1976-1985
629	CHRIS BOSIO, 1986-1991
540	Mike Caldwell, 1977-1984

Win pct: Highest, career, all-time

.622	TEDDY HIGUERA, 1985-1991

.606	Pete Vuckovich, 1981-1986
.560	Mike Caldwell, 1977-1984
.535	Moose Haas, 1976-1985
.531	Lary Sorensen, 1977-1980

ERA: Lowest, career, all-time

3.37	TEDDY HIGUERA, 1985-1991
3.65	Jim Colborn, 1972-1976
3.72	Lary Sorensen, 1977-1980
3.74	Mike Caldwell, 1977-1984
3.79	CHRIS BOSIO, 1986-1991

Runs: Most, season

136	PAUL MOLITOR, 1982
133	PAUL MOLITOR, 1991
129	ROBIN YOUNT, 1982
121	ROBIN YOUNT, 1980
115	PAUL MOLITOR, 1988

Hits: Most, season

219	Cecil Cooper, 1980
216	PAUL MOLITOR, 1991
210	ROBIN YOUNT, 1982
205	Cecil Cooper, 1982
203	Cecil Cooper, 1983

2B: Most, season

49	ROBIN YOUNT, 1980
46	ROBIN YOUNT, 1982
44	Cecil Cooper, 1979
42	ROBIN YOUNT, 1983
41	PAUL MOLITOR, 1987

3B: Most, season

16	PAUL MOLITOR, 1979
13	PAUL MOLITOR, 1991
12	ROBIN YOUNT, 1982
11	ROBIN YOUNT, 1988
10	ROBIN YOUNT, 1980
10	ROBIN YOUNT, 1983

HR: Most, season

45	Gorman Thomas, 1979
41	Ben Oglivie, 1980
39	Gorman Thomas, 1982
38	Gorman Thomas, 1980
36	George Scott, 1975

RBI: Most, season

126	Cecil Cooper, 1983
123	Gorman Thomas, 1979
122	Cecil Cooper, 1980
121	Cecil Cooper, 1982
118	Ben Oglivie, 1980

SB: Most, season

73	Tommy Harper, 1969
45	PAUL MOLITOR, 1987
41	PAUL MOLITOR, 1982
41	PAUL MOLITOR, 1983
41	PAUL MOLITOR, 1988

BB: Most, season

98	Gorman Thomas, 1979
95	Tommy Harper, 1969
89	Darrell Porter, 1975
87	John Briggs, 1973
86	ROB DEER, 1987

BA: Highest, season

.353	PAUL MOLITOR, 1987
.352	Cecil Cooper, 1980
.331	ROBIN YOUNT, 1982
.327	WILLIE RANDOLPH, 1991
.325	PAUL MOLITOR, 1991

Slug avg: Highest, season

.578	ROBIN YOUNT, 1982
.573	Sixto Lezcano, 1979
.566	PAUL MOLITOR, 1987
.563	Ben Oglivie, 1980
.539	Cecil Cooper, 1980
.539	Gorman Thomas, 1979

Games started: Most, season

38	Jim Slaton, 1973
38	Jim Slaton, 1976
36	Jim Colborn, 1973
36	Marty Pattin, 1971
36	Lary Sorensen, 1978

Saves: Most, season

33	DAN PLESAC, 1989
31	Ken Sanders, 1971
30	DAN PLESAC, 1988
29	Rollie Fingers, 1982
24	DAN PLESAC, 1990

Shutouts: Most, season

6	Mike Caldwell, 1978
5	Marty Pattin, 1971
4	Mike Caldwell, 1979
4	Jim Colborn, 1973
4	TEDDY HIGUERA, 1986
4	Bill Parsons, 1971

Wins: Most, season

22	Mike Caldwell, 1978
20	Jim Colborn, 1973
20	TEDDY HIGUERA, 1986
18	TEDDY HIGUERA, 1987
18	Lary Sorensen, 1978
18	Pete Vuckovich, 1982

K: Most, season

240	TEDDY HIGUERA, 1987
207	TEDDY HIGUERA, 1986
192	TEDDY HIGUERA, 1988
173	CHRIS BOSIO, 1989
169	Marty Pattin, 1971

Win pct: Highest, season

.750	Pete Vuckovich, 1982
.727	Mike Caldwell, 1979
.710	Mike Caldwell, 1978
.682	BILL WEGMAN, 1991
.652	TEDDY HIGUERA, 1985

ERA: Lowest, season

2.36	Mike Caldwell, 1978
2.45	TEDDY HIGUERA, 1988
2.79	TEDDY HIGUERA, 1986
2.81	Bill Travers, 1976
2.83	Jim Lonborg, 1972

Most pinch-hit homers, season

2	Max Alvis, 1970
2	Andy Kosco, 1971
2	Bob Hansen, 1974
2	Bobby Darwin, 1975
2	Ken McMullen, 1977

Most pinch-hit, homers, career

2	Mike Hegan, Sea-1969, 1970-1977
2	Max Alvis, 1970
2	Andy Kosco, 1971
2	Bob Hansen, 1974-1976
2	Bobby Darwin, 1975-1976
2	Ken McMullen, 1977

Most consecutive games, batting safely

39	Paul Molitor, 1987

Most consecutive scoreless innings

32	Ted Higuera, 1987

No hit games

Juan Nieves, Mil at Bal AL, 7-0; April 15, 1987.

207

Gold Glove winner Don Mattingly made more news with his hair than his bat.

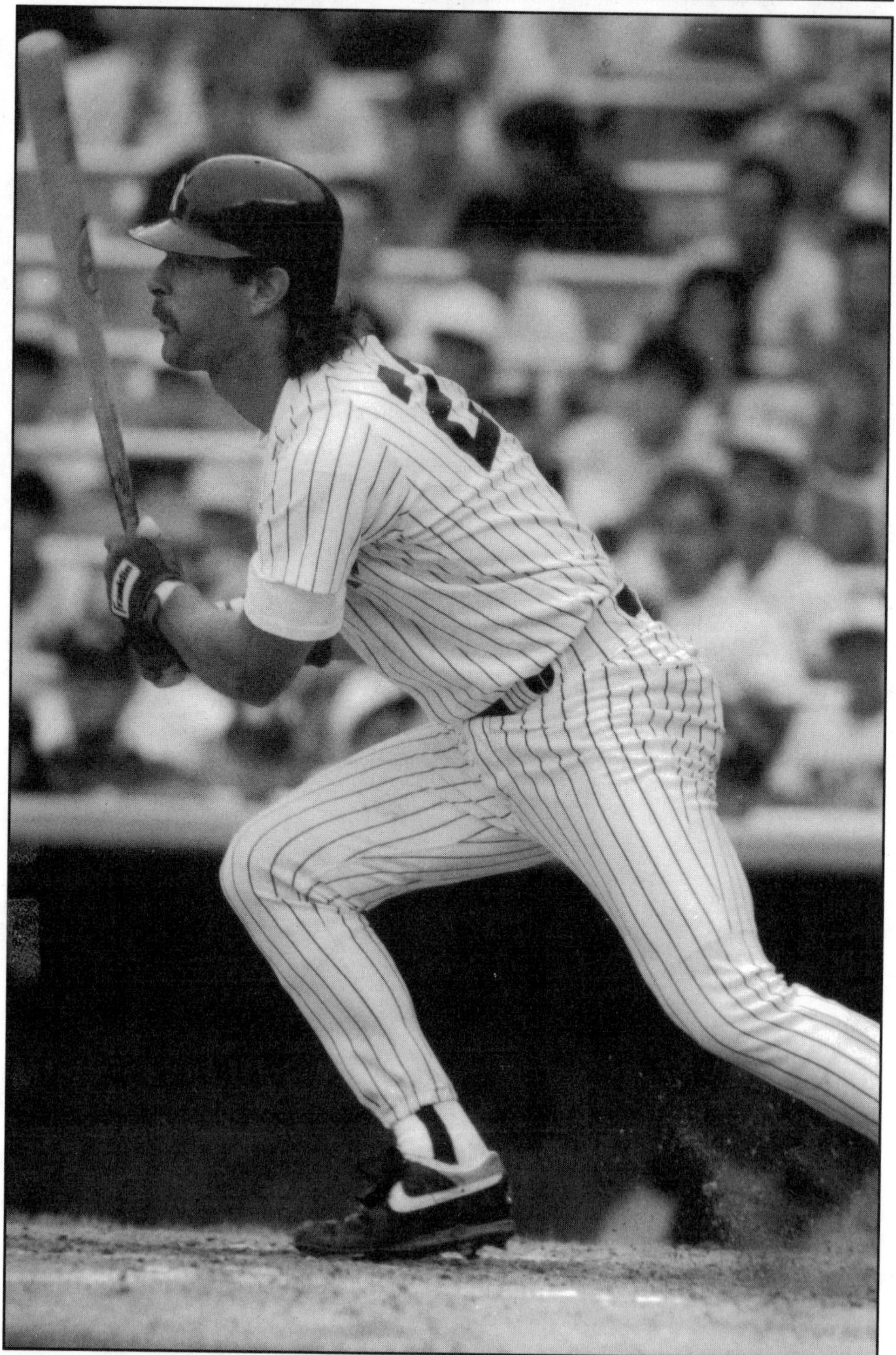

It wasn't all Stump's fault

For the first half of the 1991 season, it seemed the New York Yankees had taken over the heart of the Big Apple. As the Mets became more and more dull—and fell further and further back in the National League—the Yanks with their collection of youngsters were still in contention in the American League East.

But a 33-51 record after the All-Star break doomed the Yankees to a 71-91 record, their second straight 90-loss season—the first time that had happened since 1912-13.

And, ironically, on the day Leo Durocher died, a nice guy finished last: manager Stump Merrill, considered a "nice guy" by all but somewhat over-matched as Yankees' manager, was fired right after the season ended.

It wasn't all Merrill's fault.

The Yankees had crawled back from last year's disaster to one game over .500 on July 13. They had three rookies in the starting rotation, a rookie third baseman (Pat Kelly) playing great, and solid veteran leadership to count on.

But it all quickly unraveled:

▸Roberto Kelly went down with a sprained wrist July 5 and was out for six weeks.

▸Jesse Barfield suffered a stress fracture in his right ankle July 29, and was effectively done for the season.

▸Everything finally caught up with the rookies. Scott Kamieniecki, who ended the year 4-4, 3.90, was 4-1 until he suffered a bad back. Jeff Johnson's ERA was under 3.00 in July. He finished the season with a 5.95 ERA to go with his 6-11 record. Wade Taylor went 7-12 with a 6.27 ERA, while Pat Kelly committed 16 errors in 77 games at third.

▸Finally, the Yankees even messed with the only established marquee player in the lineup. On Aug. 15, Merrill—on orders from higher up—benched first baseman Don Mattingly when he refused to cut his hair. It became the most celebrated incident in Yankee Stadium since Billy Martin and Reggie Jackson sparred.

Mattingly ended the year hitting .288, with only nine homers and 68 RBI in 124 games. He still had problems with his back, but not of the same intensity that kept him out of 60 games in '90.

It wasn't all bad, either. Mel Hall had a fine season, taking over the starting left field job with a .285, 19-homer, 80-RBI season—and with a bad hand in the last month. Kevin Maas also had a tough year, batting just .220 and going from July 1 to Aug. 3 without a homer, but still hit 22.

With Gene Michael enjoying perhaps the most stability any Yankees general manager has enjoyed since the days of George Weiss, the Pinstripers seemed poised to again enter the free agent market with abandon.

The club was hoping to use 1991 as a true rebuilding year, and look for signs of progress. Though there was improvement—a scant four games—it wasn't quite to the level Michael was expecting, especially with the poor performance over the last half of the season.

But a couple of key free-agent additions coupled with consistent performance the rookies showed before July, and the Yankees may indeed steal the hearts of New Yorkers once again.

—*Rick Lawes*

Yankees 1992 preview

Will the real New York Yankees stand up this season? Are they the club that teased their fans the first half of last season, playing .500 ball as late as July 13? Or are they the team that sagged to 33-51 after the All-Star break, finished with 91 losses and cost manager Stump Merrill his job?

The Yankees have five good reasons for optimism: outfielder Bernie Williams, infielder Pat Kelly and 1990 rookie pitchers Wade Taylor, Jeff Johnson and Scott Kamieniecki. All showed promise last year.

In addition, outfielder Mel Hall had a fine season despite a bad back in September, and catcher Matt Nokes regained his rookie form from his Detroit days.

Outfielders Roberto Kelly and Jesse Barfield will have to bounce back from injuries and, hopefully, veteran Don Mattingly will have found a barber to the liking of GM Gene Michael. Heralded rookie Hensley Meulens, who didn't come anywhere near his potential, will have to contribute more.

1992 prophecy: Yankees

▶After firing manager "Stump" Merrill in favor of "Bucky" Showalter, the Yankees will hire Minnesota first base coach Wayne "Twig" Terwilliger. Showing typical pinstripe patience, the Yanks fire the Twig after two weeks and replace him with aging Houston Rockets center Wayne "Tree" Rollins. When the Yanks find themselves hopelessly out of the race by August, they will then hire the late Branch Rickey.

—*John Hunt*

The great Yankee hair crisis

By Glen Waggoner

They say baseball is a game of inches, and the Yankees proved them right.

It has been a pretty rough decade for the old National Pastime, what with the 1981 strike, the Pine Tar incident, the Rotisserie League thing, the Pete Rose unpleasantness, the lockout of 1989, and all. But the crisis in New York last season shook the very foundations of the game and threatened to rend it asunder. We're talking, of course, about the Great Yankee Hair Crisis.

Unless you spent the summer of '91 in a cave, you saw it on television, read it in the newspapers and heard it on the radio. The Yankees had a catastrophe on their hands. Their first baseman and team captain, veteran Don Mattingly,

was overdue for a haircut.

The crisis was of such proportions that the front office stepped in to remedy the situation:

▶General manager Gene "Stick" Michaels told the team's then-manager "Stump" Merrill to do something about it.

▶Stump, who got where he is today— fired—by following orders, told Mattingly to get a haircut or else.

▶Mattingly chose "else."

▶Stump scratched his best player from the lineup.

All hell broke loose in the Big Apple.

"Rules are rules," observed the ever-perceptive Stump the day the explosion rocked the House That Ruth Built. Benjamin Franklin couldn't have put it better.

It all makes perfect sense, if you look at the situation from Stick's perspective, which is that of the guy responsible for a fifth-place ballclub in the weakest division in the major leagues.

There's the Yankee tradition to uphold.

Not the Yankee tradition of barroom brawling—that was Billy Martin's bailiwick. Not the Yankee tradition of unbridled egoism, small-minded vindictiveness, hyper-machismo, lying, and hall-of-fame boorishness—that eternal fire is well-guarded by the Boss of bosses, George Steinbrenner.

No, what Don Mattingly had failed to buckle down and take seriously was the great Yankee tradition of short-haired first basemen.

Look at old pictures of Lou Gehrig. Do you see any long, sweaty, disgusting ringlets of hair hanging down from under his hat, as it does even in the cartoon rendering of Mattingly on the Yankees' 1991 media guide? Certainly not.

Bill Skowron? The Moose wore a crew cut.

Joe Pepitone? Also a crew cut, at least when he first came up. What's more, the Yankees' steep decline after 1964 corresponds exactly with the growing length of Pepitone's hair. (They traded him after the 1969 season, but by then it was too late.)

Chris Chambliss? Not enough hair for

a crew cut, but you can bet he'd have worn one if he'd been able to.

Fortunately, Mattingly took a long look in the mirror, took a second look at his bi-weekly pay stub, and decided to call in the Yankee clipper for assistance. Not Joe DiMaggio, but Carl Taylor, the Yankee bullpen catcher who also happens to be a professionally trained hair stylist.

The call of summer resumed: Play Bald!

Taylor's mom held out for 'Van Poppel-type money'

By Rick Lawes

The Todd Van Poppel case started innocently enough: Van Poppel, an 18-year-old pitcher from Arlington, Texas, simply said he wasn't going to turn pro. The Atlanta Braves were convinced, and opted for shortstop Chipper Jones.

The Oakland Athletics, on the other hand, decided to gamble on Van Poppel and six weeks later he signed for a record $1.2 million—including a $500,000 bonus.

When the '91 draft rolled around and the New York Yankees picked top prospect Brien Taylor, his mother Bettie announced what it would take to get her son in pinstripes: "Van Poppel-type money."

But as the negotiations dragged on, the name of Van Poppel's agent—Scott Boras—began to pop up. Boras was not allowed to enter into direct negotiations with the Yankees—nor was Taylor, or he would lose his college eligibility, his primary bargaining chip. But Boras was there every step of the way, letting Bettie Taylor know the true worth of her son.

"Brien Taylor is the best competitive high school player I've ever seen."

As the summer of '91 dragged on, the debate grew heated. At one point Bettie Taylor accused the Yankees of racism. She also refused to speak face-to-face with Yankee general manager Gene

Michael until he bettered the club's initial offer of $650,000.

Just five days before the young pitcher was to enroll at Louisburg (N.C.) College, Michael upped his bid. The $1.55 million deal they eventually agreed upon sent shock waves throughout the baseball community.

Team directory

▶Owner: George Steinbrenner

▶General Manager: Gene Michael

▶Ballpark:
Yankee Stadium
East 161st Street and River Avenue, Bronx, New York
212-293-4300
Capacity 57,545
Parking
Public transportation available
Family and wheelchair sections, ramps, Senior Citizen Discount ($1 tickets), Group Discounts, Holiday Gift Caravans for low-income neighborhoods, Silver Shield Benefit Game for families of police and firefighters killed in the line of duty, food drive, Holiday Party at the clubhouse for neighborhood children

▶Team publications:
Yankees Magazine
212-293-4300

▶TV, radio broadcast stations:
WABC 770 AM, WPIX Channel 11, MSG Network

▶Camps and/or clinics:
Project Achieve, during the season, 212-293-4300
Clinics in New York City Parks, during the season, 212-293-4300
Championship High School Games, June, 212-293-4300

▶Spring Training:
Fort Lauderdale Stadium
Fort Lauderdale, Florida
Capacity 8,340
305-776-1921

NEW YORK YANKEES 1991 Final Stats

Batting	AVG	SLG	OB	G	AB	R	H	TB	2B	3B	HR	RBI	BB	SO	SB	CS	E
Ramos	.308	.346	.310	10	26	4	8	9	1	0	0	3	1	3	0	0	0
Sax	.304	.414	.345	158	652	85	198	270	38	2	10	56	41	38	31	11	10
Mattingly	.288	.394	.339	152	587	64	169	231	35	0	9	68	46	42	2	0	5
Hall	.285	.455	.321	141	492	67	140	224	23	2	19	80	26	40	0	1	3
Nokes	.268	.469	.308	135	456	52	122	214	20	0	24	77	25	49	3	2	6
R. Kelly	.267	.444	.333	126	486	68	130	216	22	2	20	69	45	77	32	9	4
Espinoza	.256	.344	.282	148	480	51	123	165	23	2	5	33	16	57	4	1	21
Velarde	.245	.332	.322	80	184	19	45	61	11	1	1	15	18	43	3	1	15
P. Kelly	.242	.339	.288	96	298	35	72	101	12	4	3	23	15	52	12	1	18
Williams	.238	.350	.336	85	320	43	76	112	19	4	3	34	48	57	10	5	5
Barfield	.225	.447	.312	84	284	37	64	127	12	0	17	48	36	80	1	0	0
Meulens	.222	.319	.276	96	288	37	64	92	8	1	6	29	18	97	3	0	6
Maas	.220	.390	.333	148	500	69	110	195	14	1	23	63	83	128	5	1	6
Geren	.219	.289	.270	64	128	7	28	37	3	0	2	12	9	31	0	1	3
Sheridan	.204	.336	.286	62	113	13	23	38	3	0	4	7	13	30	1	1	0
Blowers	.200	.286	.282	15	35	3	7	10	0	0	1	1	4	3	0	0	3
Humphreys	.200	.200	.347	25	40	9	8	8	0	0	0	3	9	7	2	0	1
Rodriguez	.189	.189	.211	15	37	1	7	7	0	0	0	2	1	2	0	0	2
Leyritz	.182	.221	.300	32	77	8	14	17	3	0	0	4	13	15	0	1	3
Lovullo	.176	.216	.250	22	51	0	9	11	2	0	0	2	5	7	0	0	3
Lusader	.143	.143	.250	11	7	2	1	1	0	0	0	1	1	3	0	1	0

Pitching	W-L	ERA	G	GS	CG	GF	Sho	SV	IP	H	R	ER	HR	BB	SO
Espinoza	0-0	0.00	1	0	0	1	0	0	.2	0	0	0	0	0	0
Howe	3-1	1.68	37	0	0	10	0	3	48.1	39	12	9	1	7	34
Farr	5-5	2.19	60	0	0	48	0	23	70	57	19	17	4	20	60
Habyan	4-2	2.30	66	0	0	16	0	2	90	73	28	23	2	20	70
Perez	2-4	3.18	14	14	0	0	0	0	73.2	68	26	26	7	24	41
Cadaret	8-6	3.62	68	5	0	17	0	3	121.2	110	52	49	8	59	105
Monteleone	3-1	3.64	26	0	0	10	0	0	47	42	27	19	5	19	34
Guetterman	3-4	3.68	64	0	0	37	0	6	88	91	42	36	6	25	35
Sanderson	16-10	3.81	34	34	2	0	2	0	208	200	95	88	22	29	130
Kamieniecki	4-4	3.90	9	9	0	0	0	0	55.1	54	24	24	8	22	34
Mills	1-1	4.41	6	2	0	3	0	0	16.1	16	9	8	1	8	11
Plunk	2-5	4.76	43	8	0	6	0	0	111.2	128	69	59	18	62	103
Chapin	0-1	5.06	3	0	0	2	0	0	5.1	3	3	3	0	6	5
Eiland	2-5	5.33	18	13	0	4	0	0	72.2	87	51	43	10	23	18
Cary	1-6	5.91	10	9	0	0	0	0	53.1	61	35	35	6	32	34
Johnson	6-11	5.95	23	23	0	0	0	0	127	156	89	84	15	33	62
Taylor	7-12	6.27	23	22	0	0	0	0	116.1	144	85	81	13	53	72
Leary	4-10	6.49	28	18	1	4	0	0	120.2	150	89	87	20	57	83
Witt	0-1	10.13	2	2	0	0	0	0	5.1	8	7	6	1	1	0

1992 Preliminary Roster

Pitchers (21)

Greg Cadaret
Darrin Chapman
David Eiland
Steve Farr
Mike Gardella
Lee Guetterman
John Habyan
Steve Howe
Jeff Johnson
Scott Kamieniecki
Tim Leary
Ed Martel
Alan Mills
Rich Monteleone
Roberto Munoz
Pascual Perez
Scott Sanderson
Willie Smith
Russ Springer
Larry Stanford
Wade Taylor

Catchers (4)

Brad Ausmus
Jim Leyritz
Matt Nokes
John Ramos

Infielders (8)

Alvaro Espinoza
Pat Kelly
Kevin Maas
Don Mattingly
Steve Sax
Dave Silvestri
J.T. Snow
Randy Velarde

Outfielders (7)

Jesse Barfield
Mell Hall
Mike Humphreys
Roberto Kelly
Hensley Meulens
Bernie Williams
Gerald Williams

Games played by position

	G	C	1B	2B	3B	SS	OF	DH
Barfield,Je	84	0	0	0	0	0	81	0
Blowers,M	15	0	0	0	14	0	0	0
Espinoza,A	148	0	0	0	2	147	0	0
Geren,B	64	63	0	0	0	0	0	0
Hall,M	141	0	0	0	0	0	120	10
Humphreys,M	25	0	0	0	6	0	9	7
Kelly,P	96	0	0	19	80	0	0	0
Kelly,R	126	0	0	0	0	0	125	0
Leyritz,J	32	5	3	0	18	0	0	1
Lovullo,T	22	0	0	0	22	0	0	0
Lusader,S	11	0	0	0	0	0	4	1
Maas,K	148	0	36	0	0	0	0	109
Mattingly,D	152	0	127	0	0	0	0	22
Meulens,H	96	0	7	0	0	0	73	13
Nokes,M	135	130	0	0	0	0	0	3
Ramos,Jo	10	5	0	0	0	0	0	4
Rodriguez,C	15	0	0	3	0	11	0	0
Sax,S	158	0	0	149	5	0	0	4
Sheridan,P	62	0	0	0	0	0	34	2
Velarde,R	80	0	0	0	50	31	2	0
Williams,B	85	0	0	0	0	0	85	0

Sick call: 1991 DL report

Player	Days on the DL
Mike Witt	175*
Scott Lusader	47
Pascual Perez	112*
Dave Eiland	45
Roberto Kelly	38
Jesse Barfield	70
Scott Kamieniecki	65
Steve Howe	22

On DL twice (not counting administrative transfers from one DL to another).

Minor League Report

Class AAA — Columbus finished 85-59, first in the International League West. The Clippers swept Pawtucket to win the Governors' Cup, and advanced to the Triple-A Classic against Denver. C John Ramos hit .308 with 10 HRs and 63 RBI. OF Jim Walewander hit .225, but led the IL with 54 SBs. RHP Royal Clayton was 11-7 with a 3.84 ERA. RHP Darrin Chapin was 10-3 with a 1.95 ERA and 12 saves. . . . **Class AA** — Albany-Colonie finished 76-64, third in the Eastern League. However, the Yankees swept Hagerstown, then first-place Harrisburg to win the playoffs. Hitting leaders were SS Dave Silvestri (.262-19-83) and 1B J.T. Snow (.279-13-76). RHP Ed Martel (13-6, 2.81) gave up 129 hits in 163.1 innings. RHP Larry Stanford (2-3, 1.89) had 24 saves. . . . **Class A** — Prince William finished 71-68, winning the first half and finishing second the second half in the Carolina League Northern Division. The Cannons lost to Lynchburg in the playoffs, committing 12 errors in 2 games. OF Jason Robertson hit .264 with 54 RBI and 32 SBs. Top-flight pitching staff included RHP Sam Militello (12-2, 1.22) and RHP Trevor Hoffman (12-5, 2.87). Reliever Mark Ohlms had 26 saves. . . . Fort Lauderdale finished 60-68, third in the first half and fourth in the second half in the Florida State League Eastern Division. 3B Rey Noriega (.249-14-68) tied for the league lead in HRs. RHP Rich Batchelor tied for the league lead with 25 saves. . . . Greensboro finished 73-68, second in the first half and fifth in the second half in the South Atlantic League Northern Division. C Kiki Hernandez (.332-15-78) was named league MVP. LHP Rafael Quirico (12-8, 2.26) had 162 strikeouts in 155.1 innings. RHP Ron Frazier was 12-6 with a 2.40 ERA. The Hornets drew 186,434 fans to lead the league in attendance for the 13th consecutive year. . . . Oneonta finished 42-35, second in the NY-P League McNamara East Division. OF Lyle Mouton hit .309. Benjamin Short was second with 14 saves.

Tops in the Organization

BATTING LEADERS	Club	Avg.	G	AB	R	H	HR	RBI
Kiki Hernandez	Prw	.328	115	415	58	136	16	83
John Ramos	Col	.308	104	377	52	116	10	63
Billy Masse	Alb	.295	108	356	67	105	11	61
Bobby Dejardin	Alb	.295	129	482	74	142	2	53
Richard Barnwell	Alb	.290	91	317	54	92	5	37

HOME RUNS			WINS		
Dave Silvestri	Alb	19	Sam Militello	Alb	14
Kiki Hernandez	Prw	16	Ed Martel	Alb	13
Jay Knoblauh	Col	14	Ron Frazier	Gbo	12
Ray Noriega	Ftl	14	Jeff Hoffman	Prw	12
Several players tied		13	Rafael Quirico	Gbo	12

RBI			SAVES		
Vince Phillips	Alb	85	Mark Ohlms	Prw	26
Kiki Hernandez	Prw	83	Richard Batchelor	Alb	25
Dave Silvestri	Alb	83	Larry Stanford	Alb	24
Luis Gallardo	Gbo	77	Rich Monteleone	Col	17
J.T. Snow	Alb	76	Bo Siberz	Gbo	16

STOLEN BASES			STRIKE OUTS		
Jim Walewander	Col	54	Sam Militello	Alb	168
Lew Hill	Gbo	36	Rafael Quirico	Gbo	162
Mike Humphreys	Col	34	Russ Springer	Alb	155
Richard Barnwell	Alb	33	Darren Hodges	Prw	153
Jovino Carvajal	Ftl	33	Ed Martel	Alb	141

PITCHING LEADERS	Club	W-L	ERA	IP	H	BB	SO
Sam Militello	Alb	14-4	1.57	149	105	46	168
Rafael Quirico	Gbo	12-8	2.26	155	103	80	162
Ron Frazier	Gbo	12-6	2.40	169	140	42	127
Mark Hutton	Col	6-8	2.41	153	101	70	122
Kirt Ojala	Prw	8-7	2.53	157	120	61	112

Runs: Most, career, all-time

1959	Babe Ruth, 1920-1934
1888	Lou Gehrig, 1923-1939
1677	Mickey Mantle, 1951-1968
1390	Joe DiMaggio, 1936-1951
1186	Earle Combs, 1924-1935
1027	WILLIE RANDOLPH, 1976-1988 (7)

Hits: Most, career, all-time

2721	Lou Gehrig, 1923-1939
2518	Babe Ruth, 1920-1934
2415	Mickey Mantle, 1951-1968
2214	Joe DiMaggio, 1936-1951
2148	Yogi Berra, 1946-1963
1803	Roy White, 1965-1979 (8)

2B: Most, career, all-time

534	Lou Gehrig, 1923-1939
424	Babe Ruth, 1920-1934
389	Joe DiMaggio, 1936-1951
344	Mickey Mantle, 1951-1968
343	Bill Dickey, 1928-1946
323	DON MATTINGLY, 1982-1991 (8)

3B: Most, career, all-time

163	Lou Gehrig, 1923-1939
154	Earle Combs, 1924-1935
131	Joe DiMaggio, 1936-1951
121	Wally Pipp, 1915-1925
115	Tony Lazzeri, 1926-1937
58	WILLIE RANDOLPH, 1976-1988 (19)

HR: Most, career, all-time

659	Babe Ruth, 1920-1934
536	Mickey Mantle, 1951-1968
493	Lou Gehrig, 1923-1939
361	Joe DiMaggio, 1936-1951
358	Yogi Berra, 1946-1963
250	Graig Nettles, 1973-1983 (6)

RBI: Most, career, all-time

1995	Lou Gehrig, 1923-1939
1971	Babe Ruth, 1920-1934
1537	Joe DiMaggio, 1936-1951
1509	Mickey Mantle, 1951-1968
1430	Yogi Berra, 1946-1963
834	Graig Nettles, 1973-1983 (9)

SB: Most, career, all-time

326	RICKEY HENDERSON, 1985-1989
251	WILLIE RANDOLPH, 1976-1988
248	Hal Chase, 1905-1913
233	Roy White, 1965-1979
184	Ben Chapman, 1930-1936
184	Wid Conroy, 1903-1908

BB: Most, career, all-time

1847	Babe Ruth, 1920-1934
1733	Mickey Mantle, 1951-1968
1508	Lou Gehrig, 1923-1939
1005	WILLIE RANDOLPH, 1976-1988
934	Roy White, 1965-1979

BA: Highest, career, all-time

.349	Babe Ruth, 1920-1934
.340	Lou Gehrig, 1923-1939
.325	Earle Combs, 1924-1935
.325	Joe DiMaggio, 1936-1951
.314	DON MATTINGLY, 1982-1991

Slug avg: Highest, career, all-time

.711	Babe Ruth, 1920-1934
.632	Lou Gehrig, 1923-1939
.579	Joe DiMaggio, 1936-1951
.557	Mickey Mantle, 1951-1968
.526	Reggie Jackson, 1977-1981

Games started: Most, career, all-time

438	Whitey Ford, 1950-1967
391	Red Ruffing, 1930-1946
356	Mel Stottlemyre, 1964-1974
323	Ron Guidry, 1975-1988
319	Lefty Gomez, 1930-1942

Saves: Most, career, all-time

224	DAVE RIGHETTI, 1979-1990
151	RICH GOSSAGE, 1978-1989
141	Sparky Lyle, 1972-1978
104	Johnny Murphy, 1932-1946
76	Joe Page, 1944-1950

Shutouts: Most, career, all-time

45	Whitey Ford, 1950-1967
40	Red Ruffing, 1930-1946
40	Mel Stottlemyre, 1964-1974
28	Lefty Gomez, 1930-1942
27	Allie Reynolds, 1947-1954

Wins: Most, career, all-time

236	Whitey Ford, 1950-1967
231	Red Ruffing, 1930-1946
189	Lefty Gomez, 1930-1942
170	Ron Guidry, 1975-1988
168	Bob Shawkey, 1915-1927

K: Most, career, all-time

1956	Whitey Ford, 1950-1967
1778	Ron Guidry, 1975-1988
1526	Red Ruffing, 1930-1946
1468	Lefty Gomez, 1930-1942
1257	Mel Stottlemyre, 1964-1974

Win pct: Highest, career, all-time

.725	Johnny Allen, 1932-1935
.717	Spud Chandler, 1937-1947
.706	Vic Raschi, 1946-1953
.700	Monte Pearson, 1936-1940
.690	Whitey Ford, 1950-1967
.651	Ron Guidry, 1975-1988 (13)

ERA: Lowest, career, all-time

2.54	Russ Ford, 1909-1913
2.58	Jack Chesbro, 1903-1909
2.72	Al Orth, 1904-1909
2.73	Tiny Bonham, 1940-1946
2.73	George Mogridge, 1915-1920
2.97	Mel Stottlemyre, 1964-1974 (10)

Runs: Most, season

177	Babe Ruth, 1921
167	Lou Gehrig, 1936
163	Lou Gehrig, 1931
163	Babe Ruth, 1928
158	Babe Ruth, 1920
158	Babe Ruth, 1927
146	RICKEY HENDERSON, 1985 (12)

Hits: Most, season

238	DON MATTINGLY, 1986
231	Earle Combs, 1927
220	Lou Gehrig, 1930
218	Lou Gehrig, 1927
215	Joe DiMaggio, 1937

2B: Most, season

53	DON MATTINGLY, 1986
52	Lou Gehrig, 1927
48	DON MATTINGLY, 1985

47	Lou Gehrig, 1926
47	Lou Gehrig, 1928
47	Bob Meusel, 1927

3B: Most, season

23	Earle Combs, 1927
22	Earle Combs, 1930
22	Birdie Cree, 1911
22	Snuffy Stirnweiss, 1945
21	Earle Combs, 1928
13	Willie Randolph, 1979 (*)

HR: Most, season

61	Roger Maris, 1961
60	Babe Ruth, 1927
59	Babe Ruth, 1921
54	Mickey Mantle, 1961
54	Babe Ruth, 1920
54	Babe Ruth, 1928
41	Reggie Jackson, 1980 (19)

RBI: Most, season

184	Lou Gehrig, 1931
175	Lou Gehrig, 1927
174	Lou Gehrig, 1930
171	Babe Ruth, 1921
167	Joe DiMaggio, 1937
145	DON MATTINGLY, 1985 (16)

SB: Most, season

93	RICKEY HENDERSON, 1988
87	RICKEY HENDERSON, 1986
80	RICKEY HENDERSON, 1985
74	Fritz Maisel, 1914
61	Ben Chapman, 1931

BB: Most, season

170	Babe Ruth, 1923
148	Babe Ruth, 1920
146	Mickey Mantle, 1957
144	Babe Ruth, 1921
144	Babe Ruth, 1926
119	WILLIE RANDOLPH, 1980 (19)

BA: Highest, season

.393	Babe Ruth, 1923
.381	Joe DiMaggio, 1939
.379	Lou Gehrig, 1930
.378	Babe Ruth, 1924
.378	Babe Ruth, 1921
.352	DON MATTINGLY, 1986 (21)

Slug avg: Highest, season

.847	Babe Ruth, 1920

.846	Babe Ruth, 1921
.772	Babe Ruth, 1927
.765	Lou Gehrig, 1927
.764	Babe Ruth, 1923
.573	Don Mattingly, 1986 (*)

Games started: Most, season

51	Jack Chesbro, 1904
45	Jack Powell, 1904
42	Jack Chesbro, 1906
39	Pat Dobson, 1974
39	Whitey Ford, 1961
39	Catfish Hunter, 1975
39	Al Orth, 1906
39	Mel Stottlemyre, 1969
39	Ralph Terry, 1962

Saves: Most, season

46	DAVE RIGHETTI, 1986
36	DAVE RIGHETTI, 1990
35	Sparky Lyle, 1972
33	RICH GOSSAGE, 1980
31	DAVE RIGHETTI, 1984
31	DAVE RIGHETTI, 1987

Shutouts: Most, season

9	Ron Guidry, 1978
8	Whitey Ford, 1964
8	Russ Ford, 1910
7	Whitey Ford, 1958
7	Catfish Hunter, 1975
7	Allie Reynolds, 1951
7	Mel Stottlemyre, 1971
7	Mel Stottlemyre, 1972

Wins: Most, season

41	Jack Chesbro, 1904
27	Carl Mays, 1921
27	Al Orth, 1906
26	Joe Bush, 1922
26	Russ Ford, 1910
26	Lefty Gomez, 1934
26	Carl Mays, 1920
25	Ron Guidry, 1978 (8)

K: Most, season

248	Ron Guidry, 1978
239	Jack Chesbro, 1904
217	Al Downing, 1964
210	Bob Turley, 1955
209	Whitey Ford, 1961
209	Russ Ford, 1910

Win pct: Highest, season

.893	Ron Guidry, 1978

.862	Whitey Ford, 1961
.842	Ralph Terry, 1961
.839	Lefty Gomez, 1934
.833	Spud Chandler, 1943

ERA: Lowest, season

1.64	Spud Chandler, 1943
1.65	Russ Ford, 1910
1.74	Ron Guidry, 1978
1.82	Jack Chesbro, 1904
1.83	Hippo Vaughn, 1910

Most pinch-hit homers, season

4	Johnny Blanchard, 1961

Most pinch-hit, homers, career

9	Yogi Berra, 1946-1963

Most consecutive games, batting safely

56	Joe DiMaggio, 1941

Most consecutive scoreless innings

N/A

No hit games

Tom L. Hughes, NY vs Cle AL, 0-5; August 30, 1910 (2nd game) (lost on 7 hits in 11 innings after allowing the first hit in the tenth)

George Mogridge, NY at Bos AL, 2-1; April 24, 1917.

Sam Jones, NY at Phi AL, 2-0; September 4, 1923.

Monte Pearson, NY vs Cle AL, 13-0; August 27, 1938 (2nd game).

Allie Reynolds, NY at Cle AL, 1-0; July 12, 1951.

Allie Reynolds, NY vs Bos AL, 8-0; September 28, 1951 (1st game).

Don Larsen, NY vs Bro NL, 2-0; October 8, 1956 (World Series, perfect game).

Dave Righetti, NY vs Bos AL, 4-0; July 4, 1983.

Andy Hawkins, NY at Chi AL, 0-4; July 1, 1990 (8 innings, lost the game; bottom of 9th not played).

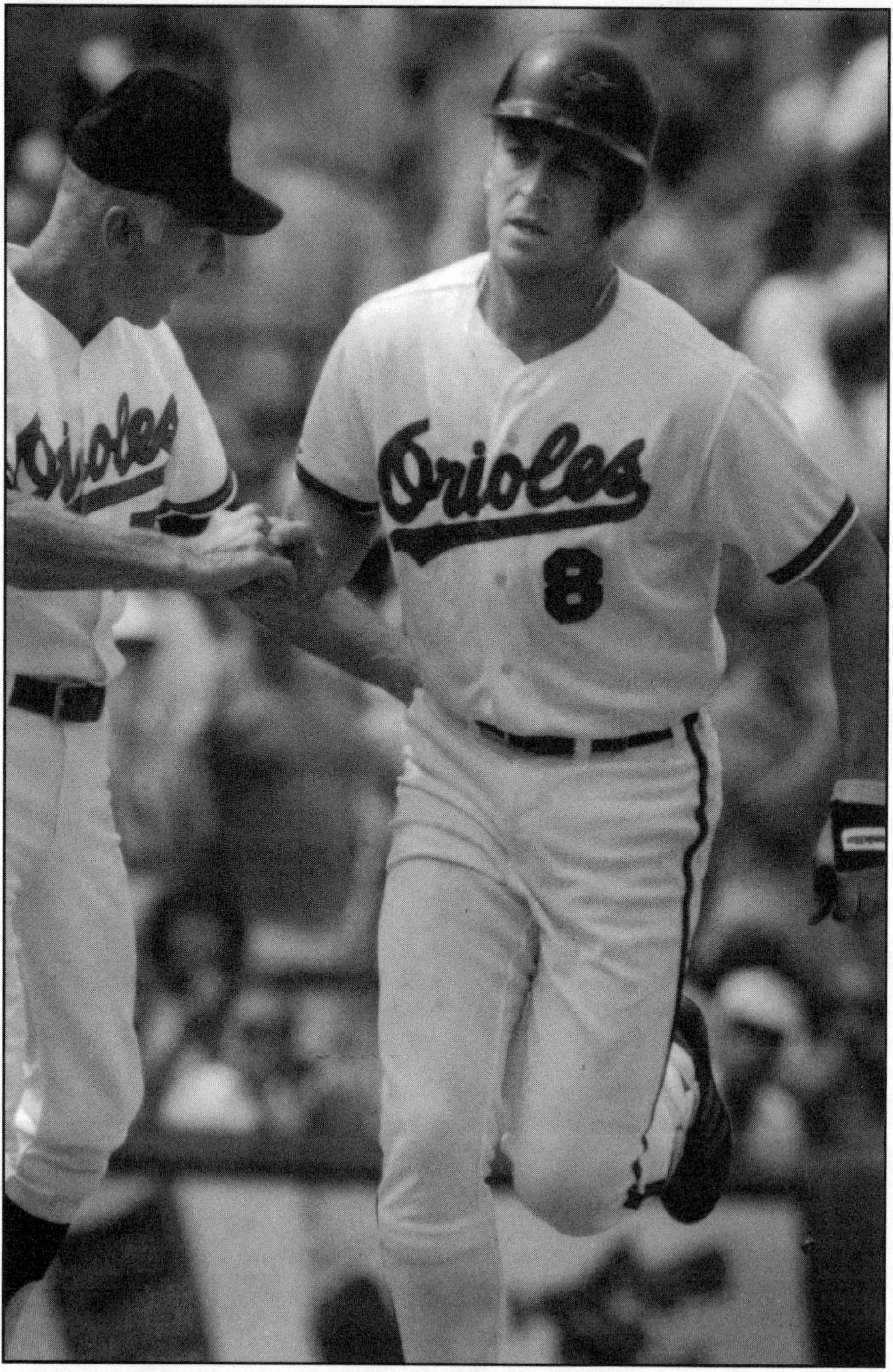

Cal Ripken Jr. (shown with his father) was the 1991 American League MVP

There's always Ripken

Before the Baltimore Orioles began their 38th and final season at Memorial Stadium, team officials dubbed the campaign "A Season to Remember." The Orioles, however, quickly realized it was a season they would just as soon forget.

Beset by injuries and ineffectiveness, the Baltimore pitching staff set the tone for the Orioles, who finished the year 67-95—24 games behind first-place Toronto. Frank Robinson was fired as manager May 23 and replaced by John Oates, who was given a contract extension at the end of the season.

Fireballer Ben McDonald, the No.1 pick in the 1989 draft, battled injuries for the second straight year and finished the season 6-8 with a 4.84 ERA. Bob Milacki—who along with Mike Flanagan, Mark Williamson and Gregg Olson threw a no-hitter against Oakland July 13—led the team Orioles with ten wins. For the second straight season, Baltimore did not have a pitcher work more than 190 innings.

Shortstop Cal Ripken had a most memorable season, reaching the 1,500 consecutive games played plateau and earning Most Valuable Player honors at the All-Star Game. Ripken batted .323 with 34 home runs and 114 RBI and heard prophetic chants of "M-V-P" during the Orioles final game at Memorial Stadium Oct.6.

Orioles' owner Eli Jacobs and Maryland Governor William Schaefer battled throughout the season about what to name Baltimore's new stadium being built on the former site of the Camden Yards railroad yard near Baltimore's Inner Harbor. Jacobs favored the Oriole Park while Schaefer preferred Camden Yards. The conflict ended with a lengthy compromise: Oriole Park at Camden Yards.

The Orioles completed their final year at Memorial Stadium in grand style Oct. 6. After the game—a 7-1 loss to Detroit—dozens of ex-Orioles, including hall of famers Jim Palmer, Brooks Robinson and Frank Robinson, took the field one last time as music from the movie Field of Dreams reverberated throughout the "House of Magic."

Veteran Detroit announcer Ernie Harwell, who broadcast the first game in Memorial Stadium in 1954, was on hand to call his final game for the Tigers. The Orioles' grounds crew arrived via police-escorted limousine in white and orange tuxedos to dig up home plate and escort it crosstown, where a half-hour later broadcaster Jim McKay—via the Memorial Stadium telescreen—conducted its replanting at Oriole Park at Camden Yards.

Longtime Orioles public address announcer Rex Barney was hospitalized before the final game, but appeared on the telescreen to utter the final words in Memorial Stadium—his trademark signoff: "Thank Yoouuuu."

—Pete Williams

Orioles 1992 preview

You could say the Baltimore Orioles are starting from the ground up. After losing 95 games last season, the Birds are moving into their new, state-of-the-art nest, Oriole Park at Camden Yards.

Manager John Oates is counting on another big year from shortstop Cal Ripken Jr., a nucleus of young players and improved health.

The youth movement will be most apparent on the mound. The rotation could include Mike Mussina, Ben McDonald, Arthur Rhodes and Bob Milacki. But McDonald must shake the injury bug which has plagued him his first two seasons.

The Orioles have a solid bullpen with Gregg Olson, Jim Poole and Todd Frohwirth.

Third baseman Leo Gomez led all major-league rookies with 16 home runs, while outfielder Chito Martinez added 13 HRs in just 67 games.

The Orioles will have to get more production from first baseman Glenn Davis, who was limited to 49 games by a neck injury and hit .227.

1992 prophecy: Orioles

▸To satisfy everyone, Baltimore's new ballpark will be renamed Babe Ruth's Memorial Oriole Park Stadium at Camden Yards Near Washington, D.C.
▸The Orioles organization will not sign any pitcher named Jose in 1992.
▸Jim Palmer will make another comeback but immediately retire upon noticing a gray chest hair.

—John Hunt

Palmer's 'horror' show

Baltimore Orioles Hall of Famer Jim Palmer, trying to turn back time to the 1970s, managed to evoke 1984 when he pitched against the Boston Red Sox during spring training last year. In two innings, Palmer, 45, gave up two runs and five hits; in '84, he walked 17 and struck out three in 17 innings. (The Orioles released him that May.)

Palmer's foiled comeback attempt—seven years later—was a nightmare. He got behind on almost every batter, had no control, no fastball, and no curve.

"The Red Sox are a horror highlight for a pitcher," Palmer said that day. "I have to pitch better than I did today." But Palmer's rematch was not to be. He pulled a hamstring warming up, and opted for the broadcast booth rather than the bullpen.

Oates gets new two-year contract

The day after leaving the Memorial Stadium field for the final time, the Orioles returned to give manager John Oates a two-year contract.

Oates replaced Frank Robinson on

May 23, and finished 54-71 with 35 one-run losses. The last time an American League team lost more one-run games was in 1968, when the White Sox set the AL record with 44.

Ripken bytes pitchers

Bored with card games and crossword puzzles, 1991 American League MVP Cal Ripken started taking a portable computer on the road. But what began as a way to entertain himself turned into a competitive edge at the plate.

Ripken used his computer manuals to put together a half-dozen personalized programs that plot how he fares against various pitchers.

"The books showed how to make up inventories and data bases," he said. "I put in what I know, which is baseball stats. There's a lot of information available, but it's difficult to make it useful to yourself.

"This started as a way to utilize time, learn a new skill. But I can see myself using it more and more."

Some of Ripken's programs are as basic as listing his statistics against pitchers, team by team. But others include comments and impressions of what a particular pitcher offered.

"It helps," he said. "(When) we were in Cleveland I couldn't remember what the pitcher threw me, so I punched it up on the computer."

Then he punched out another hit.

1991 AL MVP Quoting from the 'Book of Cal'

After Cal Ripken was voted 1991 American League MVP by the Baseball Writers Association of America, he told television reporters that he hoped his selection would silence those who criticized him during his 1,573-game hitting streak.

Earlier in the year, he answered questions about himself, his career with the Orioles, and the game itself.

▸On his 1,573-game streak: "The real reason I've played this long is not because I set out to do it; it's just I wanted to go and play, be in the lineup. It's symbolic of the way I approach the game. And I've been lucky enough to stay away from injuries."

▸On baseball: "The game has become a whole lot more specialized. Everyone's role seems to be scientifically defined. Before you just put nine people out there, and a starter was expected to pitch most of the game. I don't think it's taken anything away from the game; it's just been modified to get the best performance out of everyone. People now understand the importance of a bullpen, and they really understand the importance of a closer. When I first came up, there might have been a couple guys like Goose Gossage who were short men. Now every team is looking for that one guy."

▸On how long he'll play: "I guess when you just look at your career, I'd like to think I'm at the halfway point. That I could play another 10 years. Twenty years in the big leagues is probably a goal of everyone, to play as long as you can. And 20 years seems like a magic number."

Ripken's numbers

Cal Ripken Jr. won his second MVP award in 1991—the first was in 1983—by performing well above the level of his sixth-place team. En route to the honor, Ripken finished first in the league in total bases, extra-base hits and multi-hit games; second in slugging percentage, hits and doubles; third in home runs; fourth in runs batted in and sixth in hitting.

▸Batting average: .323
▸Home runs: 34
▸Runs batted in: 114
▸Hits: 210
▸Slugging percentage: .566
▸Doubles: 46

Team directory

▸Owner: Orioles Incorporated

▸General Manager: Roland Hemond

▸Ballpark:
Oriole Park at Camden Yards
Baltimore, Maryland
301-243-9800
Capacity over 47,000
Pay parking for 5,000 cars
Public transportation available
Family, hearing impaired and wheelchair sections, ramps, elevators, special menu selection board for the speaking impaired

▸Team publications:
The Thirty-third Street Gazette, The House of Magic, Daily Programs
301-243-9800

▸TV, radio broadcast stations:
WBAL 1090 AM, WMAR Channel 2, Home Team Sports Cable

▸Camps and/or clinics:
Fantasy Camp (ages 30+), February, 1-800-950-BIRD
Cal Ripken Senior Baseball Camp (ages 8-18), Mount St. Mary's, Emmitsburg, Md., late June and early July, 301-447-5296
L. Rod Hendricks Camp, McDonough School, McDonough, Md., July, 301-243-9800
Summer clinics, the Orioles region, during the season, 301-243-9800

▸Spring Training:
Al Lange Stadium
St. Petersburg, Florida
Capacity 7,600
301-243-9800

BALTIMORE ORIOLES 1991 Final Stats

Batting	AVG	SLG	OB	G	AB	R	H	TB	2B	3B	HR	RBI	BB	SO	SB	CS	E
C. Ripken	.323	.566	.374	162	650	99	210	368	46	5	34	114	53	46	6	1	11
Segui	.278	.340	.316	86	212	15	59	72	7	0	2	22	12	19	1	1	3
Orsulak	.278	.358	.321	143	486	57	135	174	22	1	5	43	28	45	6	2	1
Evans	.270	.378	.393	101	270	35	73	102	9	1	6	38	54	54	2	3	2
Martinez	.269	.514	.303	67	216	32	58	111	12	1	13	33	11	51	1	1	2
Milligan	.263	.406	.373	141	483	57	127	196	17	2	16	70	84	108	0	5	11
Devereaux	.260	.431	.313	149	608	82	158	262	27	10	19	59	47	115	16	9	3
Melvin	.250	.307	.279	79	228	11	57	70	10	0	1	23	11	46	0	0	1
Hoiles	.243	.384	.304	107	341	36	83	131	15	0	11	31	29	61	0	2	1
Whitt	.242	.274	.329	35	62	5	15	17	2	0	0	3	8	12	0	0	0
Horn	.233	.502	.326	121	317	45	74	159	16	0	23	61	41	99	0	0	0
Gomez	.233	.409	.302	118	391	40	91	160	17	2	16	45	40	82	1	1	7
Anderson	.230	.324	.338	113	256	40	59	83	12	3	2	27	38	44	12	5	3
Davis	.227	.460	.307	49	176	29	40	81	9	1	10	28	16	29	4	0	8
Worthington	.225	.373	.313	31	102	11	23	38	3	0	4	12	12	14	0	1	2
B. Ripken	.216	.261	.253	104	287	24	62	75	11	1	0	14	15	31	0	1	7
Hulett	.204	.350	.255	79	206	29	42	72	9	0	7	18	13	49	0	1	4
Mercedes	.204	.241	.259	19	54	10	11	13	2	0	0	2	4	9	0	0	0
Bell	.172	.249	.201	100	209	26	36	52	9	2	1	15	8	51	0	0	9
McKnight	.171	.195	.209	16	41	2	7	8	1	0	0	2	2	7	1	0	0
Tackett	.125	.125	.300	6	8	1	1	1	0	0	0	0	2	2	0	0	0
Turner	.000	.000	.000	4	1	0	0	0	0	0	0	0	0	0	0	0	0

Pitching	W-L	ERA	G	GS	CG	GF	Sho	SV	IP	H	R	ER	HR	BB	SO
Frohwirth	7-3	1.87	51	0	0	10	0	3	96.1	64	24	20	2	29	77
Poole	3-2	2.36	29	0	0	5	0	1	42	29	14	11	3	12	38
Flanagan	2-7	2.38	64	1	0	24	0	3	98.1	84	27	26	6	25	55
Mussina	4-5	2.87	12	12	2	0	0	0	87.2	77	31	28	7	21	52
Olson	4-6	3.18	72	0	0	62	0	31	73.2	74	28	26	1	29	72
Milacki	10-9	4.01	31	26	3	1	1	0	184	175	86	82	17	53	108
Telford	0-0	4.05	9	1	0	4	0	0	26.2	27	12	12	3	6	24
Jones	0-0	4.09	4	1	0	0	0	0	11	11	6	5	1	5	10
Williamson	5-5	4.48	65	0	0	21	0	4	80.1	87	42	40	9	35	53
de la Rosa	0-0	4.50	2	0	0	1	0	0	4	6	3	2	0	2	1
McDonald	6-8	4.84	21	21	1	0	0	0	126.1	126	71	68	16	43	85
Kilgus	0-2	5.08	38	0	0	14	0	1	62	60	38	35	8	24	32
Robinson	4-9	5.18	21	19	0	0	0	0	104.1	119	62	60	12	51	65
Smith	5-4	5.60	17	14	0	0	0	0	80.1	99	52	50	9	24	25
Ballard	6-12	5.60	26	22	0	1	0	0	123.2	153	91	77	16	28	37
Mesa	6-11	5.97	23	23	2	0	1	0	123.2	151	86	82	11	62	64
Johnson	4-8	7.07	22	14	0	4	0	0	84	127	68	66	18	24	38
Rhodes	0-3	8.00	8	8	0	0	0	0	36	47	35	32	4	23	23
Hickey	1-0	9.00	19	0	0	6	0	0	14	15	14	14	3	6	10
Bautista	0-1	16.88	5	0	0	3	0	0	5.1	13	10	10	1	5	3

1992 Preliminary Roster

Pitchers (17)

Storm Davis
Francisco de la Rosa
Mike Flanagan
Todd Frohwirth
Eric Hetzel
Richie Lewis
Ben McDonald
Jose Mesa
Bob Milacki
Mike Mussina
Gregg Olson
Mike Oquist
Brad Pennington
Jim Poole
Arthur Rhodes
Anthony Telford
Mark Williamson

Catchers (3)

Cesar Devares
Chris Hoiles
Jeff Tackett

Infielders (12)

Manny Alexander
Juan Bell
Glenn Davis
Leo Gomez
Ricky Gutierrez
Sam Horn
Tim Hulett
Randy Milligan
Bill Ripken
Cal Ripken
David Segui
Craig Worthington

Outfielders (7)

Brady Anderson
Mike Devereaux
Dwight Evans
Chito Martinez
Luis Mercedes
Joe Orsulak
Darrell Sherman

Games played by position

	G	C	1B	2B	3B	SS	OF	DH
Anderson,B	113	0	0	0	0	0	101	3
Bell,Ju	100	0	0	77	0	15	1	4
Davis,G	49	0	36	0	0	0	0	12
Devereaux,M	149	0	0	0	0	0	149	0
Evans,Dw	101	0	0	0	0	0	67	21
Gomez,L	118	0	3	0	105	0	0	10
Hoiles,C	107	89	2	0	0	0	0	13
Horn,S	121	0	0	0	0	0	0	102
Hulett,T	79	0	0	26	39	1	0	15
Martinez,C	67	0	1	0	0	0	54	4
McKnight,J	16	0	2	0	0	0	7	4
Melvin,B	79	72	0	0	0	0	0	4
Mercedes,L	19	0	0	0	0	0	15	1
Milligan,R	141	0	106	0	0	0	9	25
Orsulak,J	143	0	0	0	0	0	132	2
Ripken,C	162	0	0	0	0	162	0	0
Ripken,B	104	0	0	103	0	0	0	0
Segui,D	86	0	42	0	0	0	33	4
Tackett,J	6	6	0	0	0	0	0	0
Turner,S	4	0	0	1	0	0	0	1
Whitt,E	35	20	0	0	0	0	0	2
Worthington,C	31	0	0	0	30	0	0	0

Sick call: 1991 DL report

Player	Days on the DL
Ben McDonald	49*
Glenn Davis	116
Brian DuBois	182
Dave Johnson	68
Craig Worthington	29
Brady Anderson	17
Jeff McKnight	125
Dwight Evans	27
Billy Ripken	31
Mark Williamson	18
Jose Mesa	15

On DL twice (not counting administrative transfers from one DL to another).

Minor League Report

Class AAA — Rochester finished 76-68, second in the International League East. OF Luis Mercedes was second in the IL with a .334 average. RHP Mike Mussina (10-4, 2.87) was IL's Most Valuable Pitcher. . . . **Class AA** — Hagerstown finished 81-59, second in the Eastern League. The Suns were beaten three consecutive games by Albany in the playoffs. The Suns were 48-22 at home, but 33-37 on the road. 1B Ken Shamburg set Hagerstown Double-A records with 36 doubles and 82 RBI. 2B Rodney Lofton hit .284 with league-leading 56 SBs. RHP Mike Oquist (10-9, 4.06) had 136 strikeouts. . . . **Class A** — Frederick finished 58-82, fourth both halves in the Carolina League Northern Division. OF Sergio Cairo hit .314. SS Manny Alexander set club records with 134 games, 548 ABs and 143 hits. OF Damon Buford was hit by 10 pitches and had club-record 199 total bases. The Keys drew 318,354 fans, topping all Class A and Double-A clubs. . . . Kane County finished 68-67, seventh in the first half and first in the second half in the Midwest League Northern Division. The Cougars, who went 19-2 in the second half, lost to Madison in the playoffs. 1B Brent Miller (.286) had 9 HRs and 50 RBI, then added 10 more HRs and 31 RBI in 37 games at Frederick. The Cougars drew 240,290 fans, second in the Midwest League. . . . Bluefield finished 36-31, second in the Appalachian League Northern Division. Doug McConathy hit .402 with 10 doubles in 27 games. Clayton Byrne hit .321 with 25 RBI.

Tops in the Organization

BATTING LEADERS	Club	Avg.	G	AB	R	H	HR	RBI
Luis Mercedes	Roc	.334	102	374	68	125	2	36
Scott Meadows	Roc	.320	107	369	63	118	6	53
Tyrone Kingwood	Roc	.289	117	457	59	132	3	54
Tommy Shields	Roc	.289	116	412	69	119	6	52
Shane Turner	Roc	.282	110	404	49	114	1	57

HOME RUNS			WINS		
Chito Martinez	Roc	20	Matt Anderson	Knc	13
Brent Miller	Fre	19	Anthony Telford	Roc	12
Benny Distefano	Roc	18	Chuck Ricci	Fre	12
Melvin Wearing	Hag	14	Stacey Burdick	Hag	11
Tony Chance	Roc	14	Kip Yaughn	Fre	11

RBI			SAVES		
Ken Shamburg	Hag	85	Jeff Williams	Hag	23
Benny Distefano	Roc	83	Brad Pennington	Fre	17
Brent Miller	Fre	81	Todd Stephan	Hag	14
Melvin Wearing	Hag	77	Joe Borowski	Knc	13
Tim Holland	Hag	73	Several players tied		9

STOLEN BASES			STRIKE OUTS		
Rodney Lofton	Hag	56	Matt Anderson	Knc	166
Damon Buford	Fre	50	Kip Yaughn	Fre	155
Manny Alexander	Hag	47	Chuck Ricci	Fre	144
Tyrone Kingwood	Roc	38	Oswaldo Peraza	Hag	137
Tony Beasley	Fre	29	Mike Oquist	Hag	136

PITCHING LEADERS	Club	W-L	ERA	IP	H	BB	SO
Mike Mussina	Roc	10-4	2.87	122	108	31	107
John O'Donoghue	Fre	7-8	2.90	134	131	50	128
Pat Leinen	Hag	10-6	2.97	152	143	33	67
Stacey Burdick	Hag	11-4	2.99	136	99	100	102
Rob Blumberg	Fre	10-6	3.10	157	133	98	124

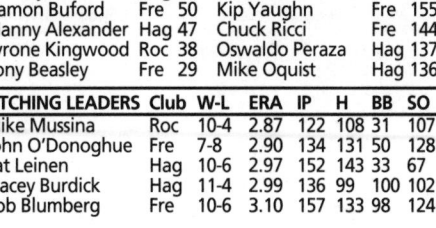

Baltimore (1954-1991), incl. St. Louis (1902-1953)

Runs: Most, career, all-time

1232	Brooks Robinson, 1955-1977
1091	George Sisler, 1915-1927
1048	EDDIE MURRAY, 1977-1988
1013	Harlond Clift, 1934-1943
970	CAL RIPKEN, 1981-1991

Hits: Most, career, all-time

2848	Brooks Robinson, 1955-1977
2295	George Sisler, 1915-1927
2021	EDDIE MURRAY, 1977-1988
1762	CAL RIPKEN, 1981-1991
1574	Boog Powell, 1961-1974

2B: Most, career, all-time

482	Brooks Robinson, 1955-1977
351	EDDIE MURRAY, 1977-1988
343	George Sisler, 1915-1927
340	CAL RIPKEN, 1981-1991
294	Harlond Clift, 1934-1943

3B: Most, career, all-time

145	George Sisler, 1915-1927
88	Baby Doll Jacobson, 1915-1926
72	Del Pratt, 1912-1917
72	Jack Tobin, 1916-1925
70	Ken Williams, 1918-1927
68	Brooks Robinson, 1955-1977 (6)

HR: Most, career, all-time

333	EDDIE MURRAY, 1977-1988
303	Boog Powell, 1961-1974
268	Brooks Robinson, 1955-1977
259	CAL RIPKEN, 1981-1991
185	Ken Williams, 1918-1927

RBI: Most, career, all-time

1357	Brooks Robinson, 1955-1977
1190	EDDIE MURRAY, 1977-1988
1063	Boog Powell, 1961-1974
959	George Sisler, 1915-1927
942	CAL RIPKEN, 1981-1991

SB: Most, career, all-time

351	George Sisler, 1915-1927
252	Al Bumbry, 1972-1984
247	Burt Shotton, 1909-1917
192	Jimmy Austin, 1911-1929
174	Del Pratt, 1912-1917

BB: Most, career, all-time

986	Harlond Clift, 1934-1943
889	Boog Powell, 1961-1974
886	Ken Singleton, 1975-1984
860	Brooks Robinson, 1955-1977
857	EDDIE MURRAY, 1977-1988

BA: Highest, career, all-time

.344	George Sisler, 1915-1927
.326	Ken Williams, 1918-1927
.318	Jack Tobin, 1916-1925
.317	Baby Doll Jacobson, 1915-1926
.309	Bob Dillinger, 1946-1949
.300	Frank Robinson, 1966-1971 (11)

Slug avg: Highest, career, all-time

.558	Ken Williams, 1918-1927
.543	Frank Robinson, 1966-1971
.512	Jim Gentile, 1960-1963
.500	EDDIE MURRAY, 1977-1988
.486	Bob Nieman, 1951-1959

Games started: Most, career, all-time

521	Jim Palmer, 1965-1984
384	Dave McNally, 1962-1974
328	MIKE FLANAGAN, 1975-1991
309	Scott McGregor, 1976-1988
283	Mike Cuellar, 1969-1976

Saves: Most, career, all-time

105	Tippy Martinez, 1976-1986
100	Stu Miller, 1963-1967
95	GREGG OLSON, 1988-1991
74	Eddie Watt, 1966-1973
58	Dick Hall, 1961-1971

Shutouts: Most, career, all-time

53	Jim Palmer, 1965-1984
33	Dave McNally, 1962-1974
30	Mike Cuellar, 1969-1976
27	Jack Powell, 1902-1912
26	Milt Pappas, 1957-1965

Wins: Most, career, all-time

268	Jim Palmer, 1965-1984
181	Dave McNally, 1962-1974
143	Mike Cuellar, 1969-1976
141	MIKE FLANAGAN, 1975-1991
138	Scott McGregor, 1976-1988

K: Most, career, all-time

2212	Jim Palmer, 1965-1984
1476	Dave McNally, 1962-1974
1280	MIKE FLANAGAN, 1975-1991
1011	Mike Cuellar, 1969-1976
944	Milt Pappas, 1957-1965

Win pct: Highest, career, all-time

.638	Jim Palmer, 1965-1984
.620	Wally Bunker, 1963-1968
.619	Dick Hall, 1961-1971
.619	Mike Cuellar, 1969-1976
.616	Dave McNally, 1962-1974

ERA: Lowest, career, all-time

2.06	Harry Howell, 1904-1910
2.52	Fred Glade, 1904-1907
2.62	Barney Pelty, 1903-1912
2.63	Jack Powell, 1902-1912
2.67	Carl Weilman, 1912-1920
2.86	Jim Palmer, 1965-1984 (6)

Runs: Most, season

145	Harlond Clift, 1936
137	George Sisler, 1920
134	George Sisler, 1922
132	Jack Tobin, 1921
128	Ken Williams, 1922
122	Frank Robinson, 1966 (7)

Hits: Most, season

257	George Sisler, 1920
246	George Sisler, 1922
241	Heinie Manush, 1928
236	Jack Tobin, 1921
224	George Sisler, 1925
211	CAL RIPKEN, 1983 (10)

2B: Most, season

51	Beau Bell, 1937
49	George Sisler, 1920
47	Heinie Manush, 1928
47	CAL RIPKEN, 1983
47	Joe Vosmik, 1937

3B: Most, season

20	Heinie Manush, 1928	
20	George Stone, 1906	
18	George Sisler, 1920	
18	George Sisler, 1921	
18	George Sisler, 1922	
18	Jack Tobin, 1921	
12	Paul Blair, 1967 (24)	

HR: Most, season

49	Frank Robinson, 1966
46	Jim Gentile, 1961
39	Boog Powell, 1964
39	Ken Williams, 1922
37	Boog Powell, 1969

RBI: Most, season

155	Ken Williams, 1922
141	Jim Gentile, 1961
134	Moose Solters, 1936
124	EDDIE MURRAY, 1985
123	Beau Bell, 1936

SB: Most, season

57	Luis Aparicio, 1964
51	George Sisler, 1922
46	Armando Marsans, 1916
45	George Sisler, 1918
44	Al Bumbry, 1980

BB: Most, season

126	Lu Blue, 1929
121	Roy Cullenbine, 1941
118	Harlond Clift, 1938
118	Burt Shotton, 1915
118	Ken Singleton, 1975

BA: Highest, season

.420	George Sisler, 1922
.407	George Sisler, 1920
.378	Heinie Manush, 1928
.371	George Sisler, 1921
.358	George Stone, 1906
.328	Ken Singleton, 1977 (*)

Slug avg: Highest, season

.646	Jim Gentile, 1961
.637	Frank Robinson, 1966
.632	George Sisler, 1920
.627	Ken Williams, 1922
.623	Ken Williams, 1923

Games started: Most, season

40	Mike Cuellar, 1970
40	MIKE FLANAGAN, 1978
40	Dave McNally, 1969
40	Dave McNally, 1970
40	Bobo Newsom, 1938
40	Jim Palmer, 1976

Saves: Most, season

37	GREGG OLSON, 1990
34	Don Aase, 1986
31	GREGG OLSON, 1991
27	Stu Miller, 1963
27	GREGG OLSON, 1989

Shutouts: Most, season

10	Jim Palmer, 1975
8	Steve Barber, 1961
7	Milt Pappas, 1964
6	Fred Glade, 1904
6	Harry Howell, 1906
6	Dave McNally, 1972
6	Jim Palmer, 1969
6	Jim Palmer, 1973
6	Jim Palmer, 1976
6	Jim Palmer, 1978

Wins: Most, season

27	Urban Shocker, 1921
25	Steve Stone, 1980
24	Mike Cuellar, 1970
24	Dave McNally, 1970
24	Urban Shocker, 1922

K: Most, season

232	Rube Waddell, 1908
226	Bobo Newsom, 1938
202	Dave McNally, 1968
199	Jim Palmer, 1970
198	Harry Howell, 1905

Win pct: Highest, season

.808	General Crowder, 1928
.808	Dave McNally, 1971
.800	Jim Palmer, 1969
.792	Wally Bunker, 1964
.781	Steve Stone, 1980

ERA: Lowest, season

1.59	Barney Pelty, 1906
1.77	Jack Powell, 1906
1.89	Harry Howell, 1908
1.89	Rube Waddell, 1908
1.93	Harry Howell, 1907
1.95	Dave McNally, 1968 (7)

Most pinch-hit homers, season

3	Whitey Herzog, 1962
3	Sam Bowens, 1967
3	Pat Kelly, 1979
3	Jim Dwyer, 1986
3	Sam Horn, 1991

Most pinch-hit, homers, career

9	Jim Dwyer, 1980-1988

Most consecutive games, batting safely

41	George Sisler, 1922
22	Eddie Murray, 1982
22	Doug DeCinces, 1978-1979

Most consecutive scoreless innings

41	Gregg Olson, 1989-1990

No hit games

Earl Hamilton, StL at Det AL, 5-1; August 30, 1912.

Ernie Koob, StL vs Chi AL, 1-0; May 5, 1917.

Bob Groom, StL vs Chi AL, 3-0; May 6, 1917 (2nd game).

Bobo Newsom, StL vs Bos AL, 1-2; September 18, 1934 (lost on 1 hit in the tenth).

Bobo Holloman, StL vs Phi AL, 6-0; May 6, 1953 (first start in the major leagues).

Hoyt Wilhelm, Bal vs NY AL, 1-0; September 20, 1958

Steve D. Barber (8 2/3 innings) and Stu Miller (1/3 inning), Bal vs Det AL, 1-2; April 30, 1967 (1st game, lost the game).

Tom Phoebus, Bal vs Bos AL, 6-0; April 27, 1968.

Jim Palmer, Bal vs Oak AL, 8-0; August 13, 1969.

Bob Milacki (6 innings), Mike Flanagan (1 inning), Mark Williamson, (1 inning) and Gregg Olson (1 inning), Bal at Oak AL, 2-0; July 13, 1991.

John Whitehead, six innings, rain, StL vs Det AL, 4-0; August 5, 1940 (2nd game).

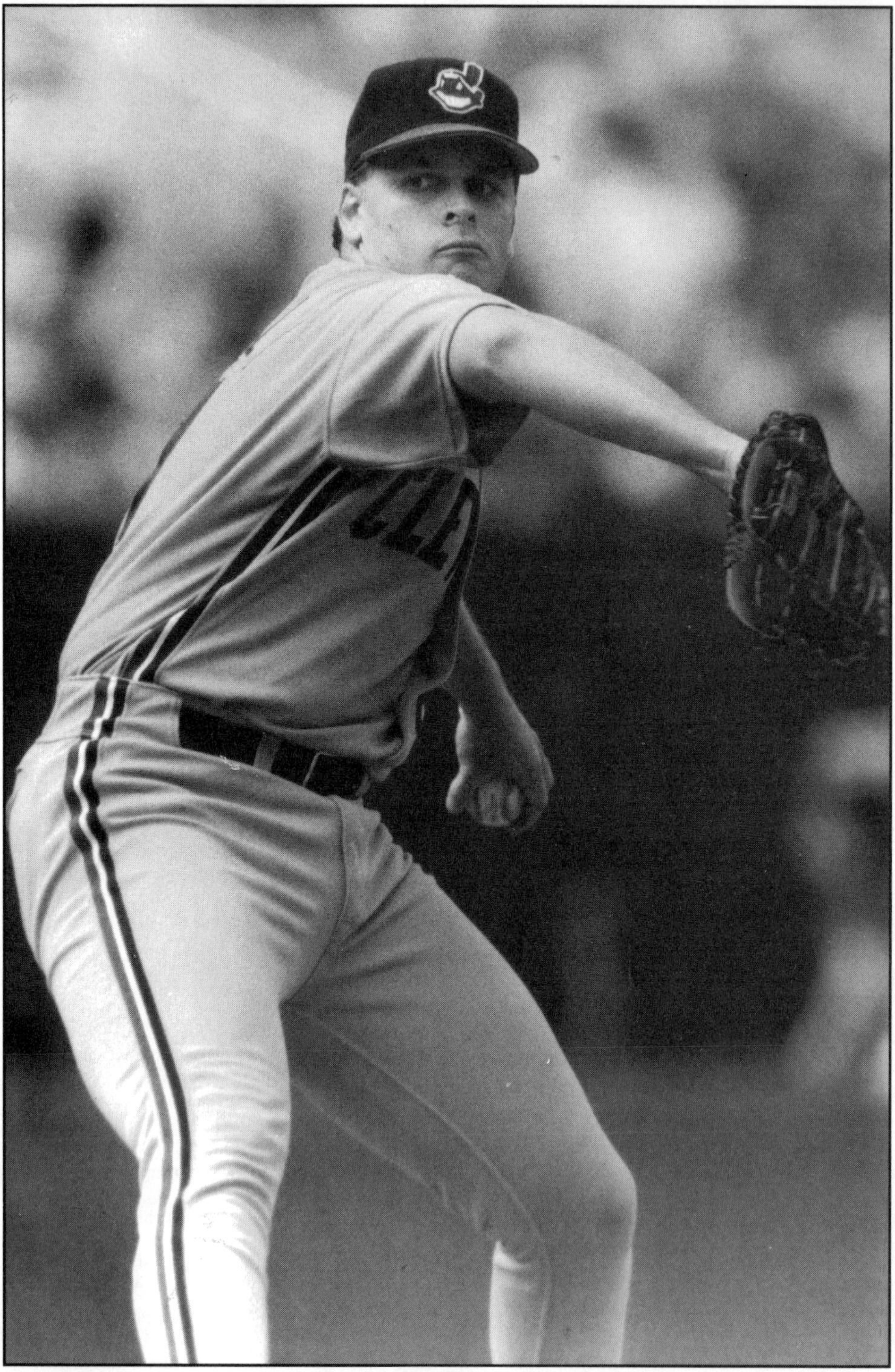

Cleveland traded ace Greg Swindell to Cincinnati.

Nowhere to go but up

If the Cleveland Indians win the American League pennant anytime in the next few years, they may look back on Oct. 2, 1991 as the day the franchise turned around their fortunes. On that day, the Tribe lost to Milwaukee 11-4 at Cleveland Stadium—a club-record 103rd loss.

But Cleveland won two of three games in the final weekend of the season in New York, winning both in their final at-bat.

"After what we went through in Cleveland when we lost our 103rd game, those games really showed me something about our talent," said manager Mike Hargrove. "We started on the road back in New York."

Hargrove himself became part of the long road back when he took the job as manager July 6, replacing the fired John McNamara. Just how long is the road?

▶The Indians committed 149 errors, most in the AL.

▶They were shutout 18 times, highest in the majors.

▶Their on-base percentage was worst in the league.

But the foundation is there for the Indians to build on. Despite his well-publicized difficulties, Albert Belle could be the key to the future. He hit .282 with 28 homers and 95 RBI in 123 games, although he was suspended for throwing a ball at a fan and sent down to the minors for not running out a grounder.

A couple of deals also brought some young talent to the organization. Taking advantage of a waiver snafu, the Indians picked up first baseman Reggie Jefferson from the Reds for former No. 1 pick, Tim Costo. In 26 games, Jefferson hit just .198, but is highly regarded.

The Tribe also dealt Tom Candiotti and outfielder Turner Ward to the Blue Jays for young outfielders Mark Whiten and Glenallen Hill and pitcher Denis Boucher. Hill batted .258 with eight homers and 25 RBI in 72 games, while Whiten hit .243 with nine homers and 45 RBI in 116 games.

Rookie second baseman Mark Lewis started off looking like a Rookie of the Year candidate, but was later sent down. He ended the year hitting .264. With Jefferson, Lewis, Carlos Baerga and third baseman Jim Thome, who hit over .300 in the minors, the Tribe could have an infield full of budding stars.

Although 1990 Rookie of the Year Sandy Alomar suffered through an injury-plagued year, he is also a potential superstar.

Cleveland's black hole is on the mound. After rejecting a three-year deal that would have made him the highest-paid player in the history of the team, lefthanded ace Greg Swindell (9-16, 3.48) was traded to the Cincinnati Reds in mid-November for three righthanders: Jack Armstrong (7-13, 5.48), Scott Scudder (6-9, 4.35) and minor-leaguer Joe Turek.

If youngsters Charles Nagy (10-15, 4.13), Eric King (6-11, 4.60), Rod Nichols (2-11, 3.54) and Dave Otto (2-8, 4.23) respond as Atlanta's young pitchers did, the Indians have the potential to be a force for a number of years.

—Rick Lawes

Indians 1992 preview

Things can't possibly get any worse in Cleveland, where the Indians lost a club-record 105 games last year. If the team's young players mature quickly, the Tribe could pick up quite a few more victories this season.

Even though he missed 30 games because of a suspension and demotion to the minors, Albert Belle hit 28 home runs and drove in 95 runs. That could be just scratching the surface of his potential.

Cleveland is looking for solid seasons from outfielders Mark Whiten and Glenallen Hill, and are hoping catcher Sandy Alomar bounces back from his dismal year.

The Indians could have their infield of the future in Jim Thome, Carlos Baerga, Mark Lewis and Reggie Jefferson.

Pitching is the Achilles heel. With Greg Swindell traded to Cincinnati, somebody will have to lead—by example—youngsters such as Charles Nagy, Eric King, Scott Scudder, Jack Armstrong, Derek Lilliquist and Rod Nichols. Perhaps former Oriole Eric Bell can help.

1992 prophecy: Indians

▸Sandy Alomar will have no home runs and three RBI at the break and be voted to his third All-Star game.
▸"Chest Protector Night" will draw 13,000 screaming fans to Municipal Stadium, all of whom will feel free to heckle Albert Belle.
▸The Indians will be the most improved team in baseball but finish 15 games under .500.

Buynak equipped for Hollywood

Cy Buynak, equipment manager for the Cleveland Indians, has never done anything close to working on stage, so it's easy to see why he was incredulous when a producer wanted him to come to Hollywood for a movie.

"I thought he was just horsing around," Buynak said. "Never in my life had I dreamed of something like this."

But Frank Pace, the producer of *Babe Ruth*, a made-for-TV movie about the Sultan of Swat, wasn't dreaming.

Buynak, 55, is 4'11" and weighs 165 pounds. When Pace saw Buynak in Tucson, Ariz., during spring training, he thought he looked like Eddie Bennett, the Yankees' batboy.

"I'm the roly-poly type," Buynak says.

Buynak grew up an Indians fan in Cleveland. After being laid off his first job, he was offered one as the assistant clubhouse man for Cleveland. He's now the equipment manager and has been

with the team for 26 seasons.

In the movie, Buynak was in six scenes. Two were in spring training, where he offered Ruth a hot dog. Another time, he gave Ruth ribs on the train. A couple of other scenes were in the clubhouse.

"Here's trivia for you," Buynak said. "What's Babe Ruth's other nickname? Everyone called him 'Sultan of Swat.' In one line, I say to him, 'Hey, Ginch.' I don't know where that came from."

When Buynak went to Hollywood for the film, he got the royal treatment—and his own dressing room.

"I didn't have to stand in line with the extras," Buynak said. "I didn't realize how lucky I was until I saw that."

McNamara knew it was coming

When John McNamara was fired as Indians' manager July 6 it did not surprise him.

"I saw it the last week or so," McNamara said. "No one would come around me."

McNamara, who at 59 has managed six major league clubs, a record shared with two other managers, said he hasn't ruled out managing again.

"I've learned never to say never," he said.

"Mac has a history of working well with young players," Indians' president Hank Peters said, "but he has never had to deal with this many young players at once."

Belle needs willpower

If only Albert Belle can maintain a little willpower, he'll have a lot more opportunity to use his estimable power at the plate to help his team. When he did play in 1991, the Indians' bad boy averaged an RBI every 5 or 6 at-bats, and a home run every 15 or so. That would've ranked him among the league leaders in both categories, but he didn't appear enough to even qualify.

Belle was suspended for six games when he winged a fan in the stands with a ball, and missed another 17 games when he was demoted to Triple-A Colorado Springs for failing to run out a ground ball.

"He could hit 30 to 35 home runs in a year," says Cleveland coaching assistant Billy Williams.

Belle commands such predictions even though he plays his home games in the cavernous Cleveland Stadium, where the fences were moved back before the season began to take advantage of the Indians' planned speed game. (The bunt-and-run attack never panned out, and Belle lost at least a dozen homers at home.)

Put him in a cozy ballpark and eliminate the temper tantrums, and Belle says, "I know I'd be among the home run and RBI leaders."

The fences in Cleveland will be moved in before the '92 season, so the stage will be set for the Indians' budding slugger. There's no doubt the talent is there. He simply has to prove that he can control himself.

Indians winter league news

▶Winter leagues: Cleveland sent RHP Gerald Dipoto (6-11, 3.81 at Class AA Canton-Akron), RHP Logan Easley (0-2, 3.60 at Canton-Akron), RHP Oscar Munoz (3-8, 5.72 at Canton-Akron) and RHP Bruce Egloff (1-2, 3.38 at Class AAA Colorado Springs) to gain additional experience in the Dominican Republic for Aguilas Cibaena (Eagles). . . . C Jesse Levis (.264-6-45 at Canton-Akron), OF Lee Tinsley (.295 at Canton-Akron), and OF Miguel Sabino (.219-5-26 at Canton-Akron) played for Aguilas Cibaena, D.R.

▶Winter leagues roster: Geronimo Berroa, OF, Leones (Lions) Escogido, D.R.; Gerald Dipoto, RHP, Aguilas Cibaena (Eagles), D.R.; Logan Easley, RHP, Aguilas Cibaena, (Eagle's Cibaena), D.R.; Bruce Egloff, RHP, Aguilas Cibaena, (Eagle's Cibaena),

D.R.; Apolinar Garcia, RHP, Aguilas Cibaena, (Eagle's Cibaena), D.R.; Jesse Levis, C, Aguilas Cibaena, (Eagle's Cibaena), D.R.; Oscar Munoz, RHP, Aguilas Cibaena, (Eagle's Cibaena), D.R.; Manny Ramirez, OF, Aguilas Cibaena, (Eagle's Cibaena), D.R.; Miguel Sabino, OF, Estrellas Orientales (Eastern Stars), D.R.; Paulino Tena, SS, Aguilas Cibaena, (Eagle's Cibaena), D.R.; Lee Tinsley, OF, Aguilas Cibaena, (Eagle's Cibaena), D.R.

Team directory

▶Owner: Henry J. Peters

▶General Manager: John Hart

▶Ballpark:
Cleveland Stadium
Boudreau Boulevard, Cleveland, Ohio
216-861-1200
Capacity 74,483
Parking for 4,000 vehicles; $4
Public transportation available
Family and wheelchair sections, ramps, Customer Service Center, and Designated Driver Program

▶Team publications:
Game Face Magazine
216-861-1200

▶TV, radio broadcast stations:
WWWE 1100AM, WUAB Channel 43, SportsChannel Ohio

▶Camps and/or clinics:
New York Life/Cleveland Indians Fantasy Camp, January, 800-666-1002

▶Spring Training:
Hi Corbett Field
Tucson, Arizona
Capacity 9,500
602-791-4266

CLEVELAND INDIANS 1991 Final Stats

Batting	AVG	SLG	OB	G	AB	R	H	TB	2B	3B	HR	RBI	BB	SO	SB	CS	E
Perezchica	.364	.455	.440	17	22	4	8	10	2	0	0	0	3	5	0	0	0
Cole	.295	.354	.386	122	387	58	114	137	17	3	0	21	58	47	27	17	8
Baerga	.288	.398	.346	158	593	80	171	236	28	2	11	69	48	74	3	2	27
Martinez	.284	.397	.310	72	257	22	73	102	14	0	5	30	10	43	3	2	8
Belle	.282	.540	.323	123	461	60	130	249	31	2	28	95	25	99	3	1	9
Lewis	.264	.318	.293	84	314	29	83	100	15	1	0	30	15	45	2	2	9
Aldrete	.262	.322	.380	85	183	22	48	59	6	1	1	19	36	37	1	2	2
Fermin	.262	.302	.307	129	424	30	111	128	13	2	0	31	26	27	5	4	12
Hill	.258	.421	.324	72	221	29	57	93	8	2	8	25	23	54	6	4	3
Thome	.255	.367	.298	27	98	7	25	36	4	2	1	9	5	16	1	1	8
Whiten	.243	.388	.297	116	407	46	99	158	18	7	9	45	30	85	4	3	7
Skinner	.243	.303	.279	99	284	23	69	86	14	0	1	24	14	67	0	2	5
Taubensee	.242	.303	.288	26	66	5	16	20	2	1	0	8	5	16	0	0	2
James	.238	.318	.273	115	437	31	104	139	16	2	5	41	18	61	3	4	0
Allred	.232	.328	.359	48	125	17	29	41	3	0	3	12	25	35	2	2	3
Browne	.228	.269	.292	107	290	28	66	78	5	2	1	29	27	29	2	4	14
Lopez	.220	.293	.261	35	82	7	18	24	4	1	0	7	4	7	0	0	2
Alomar	.217	.266	.264	51	184	10	40	49	9	0	0	7	8	24	0	4	4
Manto	.211	.313	.306	47	128	15	27	40	7	0	2	13	14	22	2	0	8
Kirby	.209	.256	.239	21	43	4	9	11	2	0	0	5	2	6	1	2	0
Escobar	.200	.200	.250	10	15	0	3	3	0	0	0	1	1	4	0	0	0
Jefferson	.198	.287	.219	26	101	10	20	29	3	0	2	12	3	22	0	0	2
Gonzalez	.159	.261	.284	33	69	10	11	18	2	1	1	4	11	27	8	0	1
Webster	.125	.125	.200	13	32	2	4	4	0	0	0	0	3	9	2	2	0
Medina	.063	.063	.118	5	16	0	1	1	0	0	0	0	1	7	0	0	0
Magallanes	.000	.000	.333	3	2	0	0	0	0	0	0	0	1	1	0	0	0

Pitching	W-L	ERA	G	GS	CG	GF	Sho	SV	IP	H	R	ER	HR	BB	SO
Bell	4-0	0.50	10	0	0	3	0	0	18	5	2	1	0	5	7
E. Valdez	0-0	1.50	7	0	0	0	0	0	6	5	1	1	0	3	1
Walker	0-1	2.08	5	0	0	3	0	0	4.1	6	1	1	0	2	2
Olin	3-6	3.36	48	0	0	32	0	17	56.1	61	26	21	2	23	38
Shaw	0-5	3.36	29	1	0	9	0	1	72.1	72	34	27	6	27	31
Swindell	9-16	3.48	33	33	7	0	0	0	238	241	112	92	21	31	169
Nichols	2-11	3.54	31	16	3	4	1	1	137.1	145	63	54	6	30	76
Orosco	2-0	3.74	47	0	0	20	0	0	45.2	52	20	19	4	15	36
Nagy	10-15	4.13	33	33	6	0	1	0	211.1	228	103	97	15	66	109
Otto	2-8	4.23	18	14	1	0	0	0	100	108	52	47	7	27	47
Hillegas	3-4	4.34	51	3	0	31	0	7	83	67	42	40	7	46	66
King	6-11	4.60	25	24	2	0	1	0	150.2	166	83	77	7	44	59
Egloff	0-0	4.76	6	0	0	2	0	0	5.2	8	3	3	0	4	8
S. Valdez	1-0	5.51	6	0	0	1	0	0	16.1	15	11	10	3	5	11
Jones	4-8	5.54	36	4	0	29	0	7	63.1	87	42	39	7	17	48
Boucher	1-7	6.05	12	12	0	0	0	0	58	74	41	39	12	24	29
Blair	2-3	6.75	11	5	0	1	0	0	36	58	27	27	7	10	13
York	1-4	6.75	14	4	0	3	0	0	34.2	45	29	26	2	19	19
Kiser	0-0	9.64	7	0	0	1	0	0	4.2	7	5	5	0	4	3
Mutis	0-3	11.68	3	3	0	0	0	0	12.1	23	16	16	1	7	6
Seanez	0-0	16.20	5	0	0	0	0	0	5	10	12	9	2	7	7
Kramer	0-0	17.36	4	0	0	1	0	0	4.2	10	9	9	1	6	4
Gozzo	0-0	19.29	2	2	0	0	0	0	4.2	9	10	10	0	7	3

1992 Preliminary Roster

Pitchers (19)

Jack Armstrong
Eric Bell
Denis Boucher
Mike Christopher
Dennis Cook
Gerry DiPoto
Bruce Egloff
Shawn Hillegas
Eric King
Tom Kramer
Derek Lilliquist
Jeff Mutis
Charles Nagy
Rod Nichols
Steve Olin
Dave Otto
Scott Scudder
Jeff Shaw
Kevin Wickander

Catchers (2)

Sandy Alomar
Joel Skinner

Infielders (9)

Carlos Baerga
Jerry Browne
Felix Fermin
Reggie Jefferson
Mark Lewis
Carlos Martinez
Tony Perezchica
Dave Rohde
Jim Thome

Outfielders (9)

Mike Aldrete
Albert Belle
Alex Cole
Glenallen Hill
Chris James
Kenny Lofton
Clyde Pough
Lee Tinsley
Mark Whiten

Games played by position

	G	C	1B	2B	3B	SS	OF	DH
Aldrete,M	85	0	47	0	0	0	16	7
Allred,B	48	0	0	0	0	0	42	1
Alomar,S	51	46	0	0	0	0	0	4
Baerga,C	158	0	0	75	89	2	0	0
Belle,J	123	0	0	0	0	0	89	32
Browne,J	107	0	0	47	15	0	17	7
Cole,A	122	0	0	0	0	0	107	6
Escobar,J	10	0	0	4	1	5	0	0
Fermin,F	129	0	0	0	0	129	0	0
Gonzalez,Jo	33	0	0	0	0	0	32	0
Hill,G	72	0	0	0	0	0	46	17
James,C	115	0	15	0	0	0	39	60
Jefferson,R	26	0	26	0	0	0	0	0
Kirby,W	21	0	0	0	0	0	21	0
Lewis,M	84	0	0	50	0	36	0	0
Lopez,L	35	12	10	0	1	0	1	6
Magallanes,E	3	0	0	0	0	2	0	0
Manto,J	47	5	14	0	32	0	1	0
Martinez,Ca	72	0	31	0	0	0	0	41
Medina,L	5	0	0	0	0	0	0	5
Perezchica,T	17	0	0	2	3	6	0	1
Skinner,J	99	99	0	0	0	0	0	0
Taubensee,E	26	25	0	0	0	0	0	0
Thome,X	27	0	0	0	27	0	0	0
Webster,M	13	0	0	0	0	0	10	0
Whiten,M	116	0	0	0	0	0	109	3

Sick call: 1991 DL report

Player	Days on the DL
John Farrell	182
Rudy Seanez	52*
Keith Hernandez	182
Felix Fermin	19
Brook Jacoby	17
Alex Cole	22
Sandy Alomar	103*
Eric King	45
Reggie Jefferson	15
Mike York	51
Glenallen Hill	28
Chris James	27

On DL twice (not counting administrative transfers from one DL to another)

Minor League Report

Class AAA — Colorado Springs finished 72-67, fifth in the first half and first in the second half in the PCL Southern Division. The SkySox lost to Tucson in the playoffs. Colorado Springs led the PCL with a .297 batting average. 1B-DH Luis Medina hit .324, tied for the PCL lead with 27 HRs and finished third with 98 RBI. RHP Mauro ``Goose'' Gozzo was 10-6 with a 5.25 ERA. . . . **Class AA** — Canton-Akron finished 75-65, fourth in the Eastern League. The Indians lost to Harrisburg in the playoffs. 3B Jim Thome hit .337 with 45 RBI in 84 games. LHP Jeff Mutis (11-5, 1.80, 7 complete games, 138 hits in 169 innings) was EL Most Valuable Pitcher. Reliever Rudy Seanez (4-2, 2.58) had 73 strikeouts in 38.1 innings. Canton set a team attendance record with 217,347 fans. . . . **Class A** — Kinston finished 89-49, first in the Carolina League. The Indians won both halves in the Southern Division, then swept Lynchburg to win the playoffs. OF Brian Giles hit .310 with 47 RBI. Reliever Mike Soper (3-2, 2.47) tied a minor-league record with 41 saves. . . . Columbus finished 74-68, fourth in the first half and fifth in the second half in the South Atlantic League Southern Division. OF Kyle Washington won the Sally League batting title with a .343 average. SS Jason Hardtke (.290-12-81) led the league with 155 hits and 104 runs, and also drew 75 walks. LHP Alan Embree was 10-8 with a 3.59 ERA. . . . Watertown finished 27-50, fourth in the NY-P League McNamara East Division. The team had a .228 batting average, but Mark Charbonnet hit .282 with 4 HRs and 19 RBI. RHP Sam Baker (3-8, 2.86) gave up 54 hits in 72.1 innings. . . . Burlington finished 40-27, first in the Appalachian League Northern Division. The Indians lost to Pulaski in the playoffs. OF Manny Ramirez hit .326 with 19 HRs and 63 games. Top pitchers were RHP Paul Gibbs (3-0, 1.22, 54 strikeouts in 37 innings) and LHP Chris Coulter (4-1, 2.30).

Tops in the Organization

BATTING LEADERS	Club	Avg.	G	AB	R	H	HR	RBI
Kyle Washington	Kin	.342	121	444	87	152	8	58
Luis Medina	CSp	.324	117	450	81	146	27	98
Geronimo Berroa	CSp	.322	125	478	81	154	18	91
Jim Thome	CSp	.319	125	445	67	142	7	73
Brian Giles	Kin	.310	125	394	70	122	4	47

HOME RUNS			WINS		
Luis Medina	CSp	27	Curtis Leskanic	Kin	15
Tracy Sanders	Kin	18	Shawn Bryant	Kin	11
Geronimo Berroa	CSp	18	Eric Bell	CSp	11
Marty Brown	CSp	15	Jeff Mutis	Can	11
Kelly Stinnett	Clm	14	Several players tied		10

RBI			SAVES		
Luis Medina	CSp	98	Michael Soper	Kin	41
Geronimo Berroa	CSp	91	Brian Cofer	Clm	12
Jason Hardtke	Clm	81	Mike Walker	Can	11
Raymond Harvey	Clm	80	Tom Kramer	CSp	10
Clyde Pough	CSp	75	Bill Wertz	Clm	9

STOLEN BASES			STRIKE OUTS		
John Cotton	Clm	56	Oscar Munoz	Can	182
Kyle Washington	Kin	51	Curtis Leskanic	Kin	163
Pat Bryant	Clm	30	Alan Embree	Clm	137
Wayne Kirby	CSp	29	Dave Mlicki	Clm	136
Miguel Flores	Kin	29	Andy Baker	Clm	118

PITCHING LEADERS	Club	W-L	ERA	IP	H	BB	SO
Jeff Mutis	Can	11-5	1.80	170	138	51	89
Chad Allen	Kin	9-8	2.48	153	146	51	82
Eric Bell	CSp	11-6	2.73	119	105	48	100
Curtis Leskanic	Kin	15-8	2.79	174	143	91	163
Oscar Munoz	Can	9-11	3.48	179	148	87	182

Cleveland (1901-1991)

Runs: Most, career, all-time

1154	Earl Averill, 1929-1939
1079	Tris Speaker, 1916-1926
942	Charlie Jamieson, 1919-1932
865	Nap Lajoie, 1902-1914
857	Joe Sewell, 1920-1930
650	Andy Thornton, 1977-1987
	(14)

Hits: Most, career, all-time

2046	Nap Lajoie, 1902-1914
1965	Tris Speaker, 1916-1926
1903	Earl Averill, 1929-1939
1800	Joe Sewell, 1920-1930
1753	Charlie Jamieson, 1919-1932
1102	BROOK JACOBY, 1984-1991
	(16)

2B: Most, career, all-time

486	Tris Speaker, 1916-1926
424	Nap Lajoie, 1902-1914
377	Earl Averill, 1929-1939
375	Joe Sewell, 1920-1930
367	Lou Boudreau, 1938-1950
193	Andy Thornton, 1977-1987
	(17)

3B: Most, career, all-time

121	Earl Averill, 1929-1939
108	Tris Speaker, 1916-1926
106	Elmer Flick, 1902-1910
89	Joe Jackson, 1910-1915
83	Jeff Heath, 1936-1945
45	BRETT BUTLER, 1984-1987
	(20)

HR: Most, career, all-time

226	Earl Averill, 1929-1939
216	Hal Trosky, 1933-1941
215	Larry Doby, 1947-1958
214	Andy Thornton, 1977-1987
192	Al Rosen, 1947-1956

RBI: Most, career, all-time

1084	Earl Averill, 1929-1939
919	Nap Lajoie, 1902-1914
911	Hal Trosky, 1933-1941
884	Tris Speaker, 1916-1926
869	Joe Sewell, 1920-1930
749	Andy Thornton, 1977-1987
	(8)

SB: Most, career, all-time

254	Terry Turner, 1904-1918

240	Nap Lajoie, 1902-1914
233	Ray Chapman, 1912-1920
207	Elmer Flick, 1902-1910
165	Harry Bay, 1902-1908
164	BRETT BUTLER, 1984-1987 (6)

BB: Most, career, all-time

857	Tris Speaker, 1916-1926
766	Lou Boudreau, 1938-1950
725	Earl Averill, 1929-1939
712	Jack Graney, 1908-1922
703	Larry Doby, 1947-1958
685	Andy Thornton, 1977-1987
	(6)

BA: Highest, career, all-time

.375	Joe Jackson, 1910-1915
.354	Tris Speaker, 1916-1926
.339	Nap Lajoie, 1902-1914
.327	George Burns, 1920-1928
.323	Ed Morgan, 1928-1933
.295	JULIO FRANCO, 1983-1988
	(20)

Slug avg: Highest, career, all-time

.551	Hal Trosky, 1933-1941
.542	Joe Jackson, 1910-1915
.542	Earl Averill, 1929-1939
.520	Tris Speaker, 1916-1926
.506	Jeff Heath, 1936-1945
.472	JOE CARTER, 1984-1989 (11)

Games started: Most, career, all-time

484	Bob Feller, 1936-1956
433	Mel Harder, 1928-1947
350	Bob Lemon, 1941-1958
320	Willis Hudlin, 1926-1940
305	Stan Coveleski, 1916-1924
295	Sam McDowell, 1961-1971 (7)

Saves: Most, career, all-time

128	DOUG JONES, 1986-1991
53	Ray Narleski, 1954-1958
46	Jim Kern, 1974-1986
46	Sid Monge, 1977-1981
45	Gary Bell, 1958-1967

Shutouts: Most, career, all-time

45	Addie Joss, 1902-1910
44	Bob Feller, 1936-1956
31	Stan Coveleski, 1916-1924
31	Bob Lemon, 1941-1958
27	Mike Garcia, 1948-1959
22	Sam McDowell, 1961-1971 (8)

Wins: Most, career, all-time

266	Bob Feller, 1936-1956
223	Mel Harder, 1928-1947
207	Bob Lemon, 1941-1958
172	Stan Coveleski, 1916-1924
164	Early Wynn, 1949-1963
122	Sam McDowell, 1961-1971
	(10)

K: Most, career, all-time

2581	Bob Feller, 1936-1956
2159	Sam McDowell, 1961-1971
1277	Bob Lemon, 1941-1958
1277	Early Wynn, 1949-1963
1160	Mel Harder, 1928-1947

Win pct: Highest, career, all-time

.667	Vean Gregg, 1911-1914
.663	Johnny Allen, 1936-1940
.630	Cal McLish, 1956-1959
.623	Addie Joss, 1902-1910
.622	Wes Ferrell, 1927-1933
.565	Bert Blyleven, 1981-1985
	(16)

ERA: Lowest, career, all-time

1.89	Addie Joss, 1902-1910
2.31	Vean Gregg, 1911-1914
2.39	Bob Rhoads, 1903-1909
2.45	Bill Bernhard, 1902-1907
2.50	Otto Hess, 1902-1908
2.71	Gaylord Perry, 1972-1975
	(8)

Runs: Most, season

140	Earl Averill, 1931
137	Tris Speaker, 1920
136	Earl Averill, 1936
133	Tris Speaker, 1923
130	Charlie Jamieson, 1923
108	Brett Butler, 1984
108	Joe Carter, 1986

Hits: Most, season

233	Joe Jackson, 1911
232	Earl Averill, 1936
227	Nap Lajoie, 1910
226	Joe Jackson, 1912
225	Johnny Hodapp, 1930
200	JOE CARTER, 1986
	(24)

2B: Most, season

64	George Burns, 1926

59	Tris Speaker, 1923
52	Tris Speaker, 1921
52	Tris Speaker, 1926
51	George Burns, 1927
51	Johnny Hodapp, 1930
51	Nap Lajoie, 1910

3B: Most, season

26	Joe Jackson, 1912
23	Dale Mitchell, 1949
22	Bill Bradley, 1903
22	Elmer Flick, 1906
20	Jeff Heath, 1941
20	Joe Vosmik, 1935
14	BRETT BUTLER, 1985 (21)
14	BRETT BUTLER, 1986 (21)

HR: Most, season

43	Al Rosen, 1953
42	Rocky Colavito, 1959
42	Hal Trosky, 1936
41	Rocky Colavito, 1958
37	Al Rosen, 1950
35	JOE CARTER, 1989 (6)

RBI: Most, season

162	Hal Trosky, 1936
145	Al Rosen, 1953
143	Earl Averill, 1931
142	Hal Trosky, 1934
136	Ed Morgan, 1930
121	JOE CARTER, 1986 (13)

SB: Most, season

61	Miguel Dilone, 1980
52	BRETT BUTLER, 1984
52	Ray Chapman, 1917
51	Braggo Roth, 1917
47	BRETT BUTLER, 1985

BB: Most, season

111	Mike Hargrove, 1980
109	Andy Thornton, 1982
106	Les Fleming, 1942
105	Jack Graney, 1919
102	Jack Graney, 1916

BA: Highest, season

.408	Joe Jackson, 1911
.395	Joe Jackson, 1912
.389	Tris Speaker, 1925
.388	Tris Speaker, 1920
.386	Tris Speaker, 1916
.341	Miguel Dilone, 1980

Slug avg: Highest, season

.644	Hal Trosky, 1936
.627	Earl Averill, 1936
.620	Rocky Colavito, 1958
.613	Al Rosen, 1953
.610	Tris Speaker, 1923
.524	Boog Powell, 1974

Games started: Most, season

44	George Uhle, 1923
42	Bob Feller, 1946
41	Gaylord Perry, 1973
40	Stan Coveleski, 1921
40	Bob Feller, 1941
40	Gaylord Perry, 1972
40	Dick Tidrow, 1973
40	George Uhle, 1922

Saves: Most, season

43	DOUG JONES, 1990
37	DOUG JONES, 1988
32	DOUG JONES, 1989
23	Ernie Camacho, 1984
21	Dave LaRoche, 1976
21	Dan Spillner, 1982

Shutouts: Most, season

10	Bob Feller, 1946
10	Bob Lemon, 1948
9	Stan Coveleski, 1917
9	Addie Joss, 1906
9	Addie Joss, 1908
9	Luis Tiant, 1968

Wins: Most, season

31	Jim Bagby, 1920
27	Bob Feller, 1940
27	Addie Joss, 1907
27	George Uhle, 1926
26	Bob Feller, 1946
26	George Uhle, 1923
24	Gaylord Perry, 1972 (9)

K: Most, season

348	Bob Feller, 1946
325	Sam McDowell, 1965
304	Sam McDowell, 1970
283	Sam McDowell, 1968
279	Sam McDowell, 1969

Win pct: Highest, season

.938	Johnny Allen, 1937
.773	Bill Bernhard, 1902
.767	Vean Gregg, 1911
.767	Bob Lemon, 1954
.741	Gene Bearden, 1948
.731	Bert Blyleven, 1984 (7)

ERA: Lowest, season

1.16	Addie Joss, 1908
1.59	Addie Joss, 1904
1.60	Luis Tiant, 1968
1.71	Addie Joss, 1909
1.72	Addie Joss, 1906

Most pinch-hit homers, season

3	Gene Green, 1962
3	Fred Whitfield, 1965
3	Ted Ulaender, 1970
3	Ron Kittle, 1987

Most pinch-hit, homers, career

8	Fred Whitfield, 1963-1967

Most consecutive games, batting safely

29	Bill Bradley, 1902

Most consecutive scoreless innings

41	Luis Tiant, 1968

No hit games

Earl Moore, Cle vs Chi AL, 2-4; May 9, 1901 (lost on two hits in the tenth).

Dusty Rhoades, Cle vs Bos AL, 2-1; September 18, 1908.

Addie Joss, Cle vs Chi AL, 1-0; October 2, 1908 (perfect game).

Addie Joss, Cle vs Chi AL, 1-0; April 20, 1910.

Ray Caldwell, Cle at NY AL, 3-0; September 10, 1919 (1st game).

Wes Ferrell, Cle vs StL AL, 9-0; April 29, 1931.

Bob Feller, Cle at Chi AL, 1-0; April 16, 1940 (opening day).

Bob Feller, Cle at NY AL, 1-0; April 30, 1946.

Don Black, Cle vs Phi AL, 3-0; July 10, 1947 (1st game).

Bob Lemon, Cle at Det AL, 2-0; June 30, 1948.

Bob Feller, Cle vs Det AL, 2-1; July 1, 1951 (1st game).

Sonny Siebert, Cle vs Was AL, 2-0; June 10, 1966.

Dick Bosman, Cle vs Oak AL, 4-0; July 19, 1974.

Dennis Eckersley, Cle vs Cal AL, 1-0; May 30, 1977.

Len Barker, Cle vs Tor AL, 3-0; May 15, 1981 (perfect game).

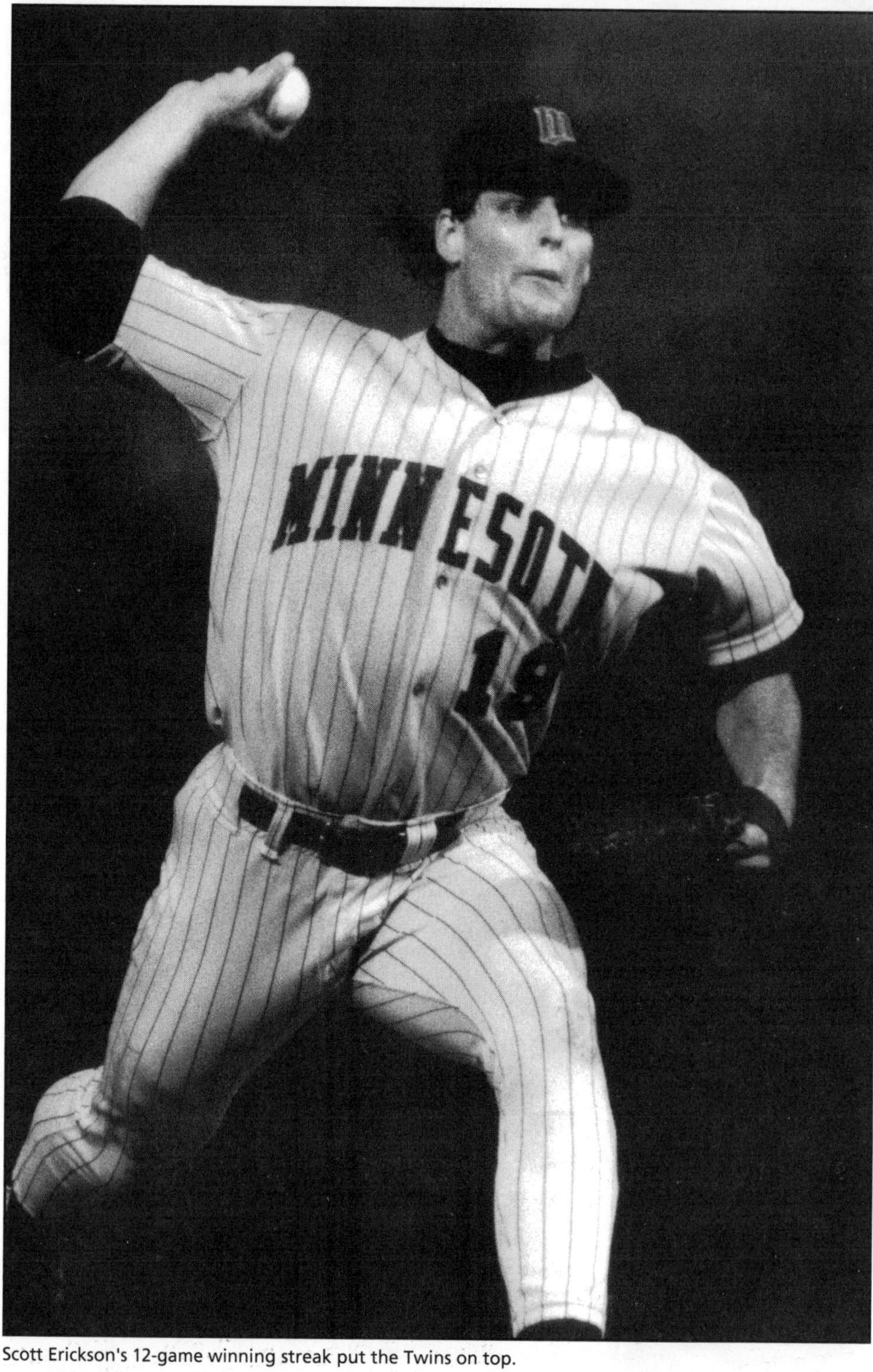

Scott Erickson's 12-game winning streak put the Twins on top.

They were never the 'worst'

Twins' manager Tom Kelly isn't proud about being labeled as the first team in the American League to go from worst to first in one year.

"We may have gone from last to first," he says, "but we weren't the worst team last year. We just decided to give our young pitchers a chance."

That move paid huge dividends for Minnesota as youngsters Scott Erickson and Kevin Tapani blossomed into Cy Young candidates in the American League, while veteran Jack Morris came home from Detroit to anchor the staff.

"As a kid, you dream about playing in championship games," Morris says, "and in those dreams I was always wearing a Twins uniform."

In the bullpen, Rick Aguilera, who arrived with Tapani as part of the Frank Viola trade with the Mets, took over as the team's closer.

"There's a feeling that if we can get the game to Aggie, we can wrap it up," says Kelly.

Switch-hitter Chili Davis, another newcomer, was signed as a free agent from California and balanced the Twins' batting order, which hit for the highest average in the league.

Kirby Puckett and Kent Hrbek, veterans from the Twins' '87 World Series triumph, showed little signs of letting up, while catcher Brian Harper, who contemplated retiring three years ago, hit .311 in '91.

"I didn't realize what a good hitting team they were until that first day in spring training," says hitting instructor Terry Crowley, who also was in his first year in Minnesota. "Top to bottom, we're as balanced as anybody in the league."

Rookie Chuck Knoblauch filled a big hole at second base and held down the No. 2 spot in the batting order, while adding speed with a team rookie record 25 steals.

Minnesota general manager Andy MacPhail says winning the AL West in 1991 was "more satisfying" than even capturing the World Series in 1987. "This is something that will stay with us in the front office for some time," he says. "To win your division in a year when no team in your division finished below .500. That's an accomplishment."

Morris adds that a major reason for the Twins' success has been Kelly's managing style. "There's nobody bad-mouthing him behind his back," says the veteran pitcher. "He uses everybody on this team."

Kelly says he's proud of the club because "we've always gone out there and played hard. We run out everything. There was no dogging it, no jaking, no half speed. I won't tolerate anything less."

—Tim Wendel

Twins 1992 preview

The Minnesota Twins are on top of the world after capping their worst-to-first season with a World Championship. Everybody in baseball's toughest division will be gunning for them, but barring key injuries, the Twins should be able to hold their own and contend again.

Kirby Puckett, Chili Davis and Kent Hrbek are genuine stars, and players such as Greg Gagne, Mike Pagliarulo and Brian Harper seem to complete the winning chemistry.

Rookie of the Year Chuck Knoblauch had a great postseason under pressure and doesn't seem likely to fall victim to the "sophomore jinx."

Outfielder Pedro Munoz should start and first baseman Paul Sorrento should contribute more off the bench this season.

On the mound, Scott Erickson took the world by storm the first half of last season, but fell off somewhat after the All-Star break. Kevin Tapani and Erickson should be solid again.

Rick Aguilera, Mark Guthrie and Carl Willis are a top-flight bullpen.

1992 prophecy: Twins

▶GM Andy MacPhail will acquire pitcher Bob Kipper, who will have a career year and win the Cy Young Award. MacPhail will then be elected mayor.

▶Kent Hrbek will quit baseball to pursue a professional wrestling career and will popularize a wrestling move called the "Atomic Gant Drop."

▶Brian Harper will undergo preseason surgery to remove Lonnie Smith's elbow from his chest.

—*John Hunt*

Erickson's 12-game winning streak

▶Complete games: 4
▶Shutouts: 3
▶Fewest hits: 2, May 1, 1-0 win vs. Boston; 2, June 25, 5-0 win vs. New York; 1, June 18 (6 inn.), 9-2 win vs. Baltimore.
▶Most hits: 10, May 23, vs. Texas(1).
▶Fewest innings: 6 vs. Baltimore, June 18.
▶Most earned runs: 4 vs. Texas, May 23.
▶Most strikeouts: 8 vs. Kansas City, June 2.
▶Most walks: 5 vs. Detroit, May 17; 5 vs. Baltimore, June 18.
▶No decision: 1

SOURCE: USA TODAY Research

Tapani happy he left New York

Kevin Tapani still follows his old team, the New York Mets. If he had stayed in New York, he figures he would have continued battling to win playing time on the perennially deep Mets pitching staff.

"Maybe I never would have gotten the chance in New York that I got here," said Tapani, who finished the year 16-9, with a 2.99 earned run average—and a World Series ring on his finger.

Tapani returned to his Midwest roots

in 1989 when he was dealt with pitchers Rick Aguilera, Tim Drummond, David West and Jack Savage for Frank Viola and outfielder Loy McBride.

"If I had my choice of any place in the league to play, this would be it," Tapani said. "It all worked out. Coming here, I got a chance to prove myself....I doubt if I could be saying the same thing if I was still in New York."

Twins dropped the name, kept the cap

By Ann Bauleke

All major league teams used to be named after their city—until the Minnesota Twins came along. Originally, they were to be the Twin City Twins, since Bloomington is between Minneapolis and St. Paul. "TC" went on the caps.

But owner Calvin Griffith became inspired at a Thanksgiving dinner after he got permission to move his Senators out of Washington 30 years ago: "Hell," he said, "as long as we're breaking with tradition, let's name the team after the whole state."

Everyone agreed. But "TC" remained on the cap for 23 years.

Ann Bauleke is a baseball writer for City Pages in Minneapolis.

How the Twins were built

Year	Free Agent or Draft (Round)	Trade
1978	Kent Hrbek(17)	
1979	Randy Bush(2)	
1980		
1981		
1982	Kirby Puckett(1)	Greg Gagne
1983		
1984	Gene Larkin(20)	
1985	Paul Abbott(3)	
	Lenny Webster(21)	
1986	Jarvis Brown(1)	
	Scott Leius (13)	

1987 Brian Harper
    Willie Banks(1)   Al Newman
    Mark Guthrie(7)   Dan Gladden
1988 Gary Wayne*   Paul Sorrento
1989 Chuck Knoblauch(1)Rick Aguilera
    Denny Neagle(3)   Kevin Tapani
    Scott Erickson(4) David West
1990 Shane Mack*   Steve Bedrosian
    Terry Leach   Junior Ortiz
    Carl Willis   Pedro Munoz
1991 Chili Davis
    Mike Pagliarulo
    Jack Morris

*Wayne (from Expos) and Mack (from Padres) were acquired via Major League Draft.

Trades

▶Shortstop Roy Smalley to New York Yankees for shortstop
Greg Gagne, pitcher Ron Davis and pitcher Paul Boris and cash.
▶Pitcher Mike Shade to Montreal for infielder Al Newman.
▶Pitcher Jose Dominguez and pitcher Ray Velasquez and a player to be named later (pitcher Bryan Hickerson) to San Francisco for outfielder Dan Gladden and pitcher David Blakley.
▶Pitcher Bert Blyleven and pitcher Kevin Trudeau to California for first baseman Paul Sorrento and pitcher Mike Cook and pitcher Rob Wassenaar.
▶Pitcher Frank Viola and outfielder Loy McBride to New York Mets for pitcher Rick Aguilera, pitcher Kevin Tapani, pitcher David West, pitcher Tim Drummond and a player to be named later (pitcher Jack Savage).
▶Pitcher Johnny Ard and a player to be named later (pitcher Jimmy Williams) to San Francisco for pitcher Steve Bedrosian.
▶Pitcher Mike Pomeranz to Pittsburgh for catcher Junior Ortiz and pitcher Orlando Lind.
▶Pitcher John Candelaria to Toronto for outfielder Pedro Munoz and second baseman Nelson Liriano.

Team directory

▶Owner: Carl R. Pohlad

▶General Manager: Andy MacPhail

▶Ballpark:
  Hubert H. Humphrey Metrodome
  501 Chicago Avenue South, Minneapolis, Minnesota
  612-375-7444
  Capacity 55,883
  Public transportation available
Family and wheelchair sections, elevators

▶Team publications:
  Twins Magazine, Twins Yearbook
  612-375-7481

▶TV, radio broadcast stations:
  WCCO 830 AM, WCCO-TV Channel 4

▶Camps and/or clinics:
  weekends throughout the summer,
  612-375-7481

▶Spring Training:
  Lee County Sports Complex
  Fort Myers, Florida
  Capacity 7,500
  612-375-7481

MINNESOTA TWINS 1991 Final Stats

Batting	AVG	SLG	OB	G	AB	R	H	TB	2B	3B	HR	RBI	BB	SO	SB	CS	E
Puckett	.319	.460	.352	152	611	92	195	281	29	6	15	89	31	78	11	5	6
Harper	.311	.447	.336	123	441	54	137	197	28	1	10	69	14	22	1	2	8
Mack	.310	.529	.363	143	442	79	137	234	27	8	18	74	34	79	13	9	7
Bush	.303	.485	.401	93	165	21	50	80	10	1	6	23	24	25	0	2	2
Webster	.294	.588	.390	18	34	7	10	20	1	0	3	8	6	10	0	0	1
Leius	.286	.417	.378	109	199	35	57	83	7	2	5	20	30	35	5	5	7
Larkin	.286	.373	.361	98	255	34	73	95	14	1	2	19	30	21	2	3	3
Hrbek	.284	.461	.373	132	462	72	131	213	20	1	20	89	67	48	4	4	8
Munoz	.283	.500	.327	51	138	15	39	69	7	1	7	26	9	31	3	0	1
Knoblauch	.281	.350	.351	151	565	78	159	198	24	6	1	50	59	40	25	5	18
Pagliarulo	.279	.384	.322	121	365	38	102	140	20	0	6	36	21	55	1	2	11
Davis	.277	.507	.385	153	534	84	148	271	34	1	29	93	95	117	5	6	0
Gagne	.265	.395	.310	139	408	52	108	161	23	3	8	42	26	72	11	9	9
Sorrento	.255	.553	.314	26	47	6	12	26	2	0	4	13	4	11	0	0	0
Gladden	.247	.356	.306	126	461	65	114	164	14	9	6	52	36	60	15	9	3
Brown	.216	.216	.256	48	37	10	8	8	0	0	0	0	2	8	7	1	1
Ortiz	.209	.261	.293	61	134	9	28	35	5	1	0	11	15	12	0	1	1
Newman	.191	.211	.260	118	246	25	47	52	5	0	0	19	23	21	4	5	4
Castillo	.167	.333	.231	9	12	0	2	4	0	1	0	0	0	2	0	0	0

Pitching	W-L	ERA	G	GS	CG	GF	Sho	SV	IP	H	R	ER	HR	BB	SO
Aguilera	4-5	2.35	63	0	0	60	0	42	69	44	20	18	3	30	61
Willis	8-3	2.63	40	0	0	9	0	2	89	76	31	26	4	19	53
Tapani	16-9	2.99	34	34	4	0	1	0	244	225	84	81	23	40	135
Erickson	20-8	3.18	32	32	5	0	3	0	204	189	80	72	13	71	108
Morris	18-12	3.43	35	35	10	0	2	0	246.2	226	107	94	18	92	163
Leach	1-2	3.61	50	0	0	22	0	0	67.1	82	28	27	3	14	32
Neagle	0-1	4.05	7	3	0	2	0	0	20	28	9	9	3	7	14
Edens	2-2	4.09	8	6	0	0	0	0	33	34	15	15	2	10	19
Guthrie	7-5	4.32	41	12	0	13	0	2	98	116	52	47	11	41	72
Bedrosian	5-3	4.42	56	0	0	22	0	6	77.1	70	42	38	11	35	44
West	4-4	4.54	15	12	0	0	0	0	71.1	66	37	36	13	28	52
Abbott	3-1	4.75	15	3	0	1	0	0	47.1	38	27	25	5	36	43
Anderson	5-11	4.96	29	22	2	4	0	0	134.1	148	82	74	24	42	51
Wayne	1-0	5.11	8	0	0	2	0	1	12.1	11	7	7	1	4	7
Banks	1-1	5.71	5	3	0	2	0	0	17.1	21	15	11	1	12	16
Casian	0-0	7.36	15	0	0	4	0	0	18.1	28	16	15	4	7	6

1992 Preliminary Roster

Pitchers (20)

Paul Abbott
Rick Aguilera
Allan Anderson
Willie Banks
Larry Casian
Jesse Cross
Tom Edens
Scott Erickson
Richard Garces
Mark Guthrie
Pat Mahomes
Denny Neagle
Al Newman
Kevin Tapani

Mike Trombley
George Tsamis
Rob Wassenaar
Gary Wayne
David West
Carl Willis

Catchers (2)

Derek Parks
Lenny Webster

Infielders (9)

Greg Gagne
Cheo Garcia
Shawn Gilbert
Kent Hrbek

Terry Jorgensen
Chuck Knoblauch
Gene Larkin
Scott Leius
Paul Sorrento

Outfielders (7)

Jarvis Brown
J.T. Bruett
Randy Bush
Chili Davis
Shane Mack
Pedro Munoz
Kirby Puckett

Games played by position

	G	C	1B	2B	3B	SS	OF	DH
Brown,J	38	0	0	0	0	0	32	4
Bush,R	93	0	12	0	0	0	38	10
Castillo,C	9	0	0	0	0	0	4	2
Davis,C	153	0	0	0	0	0	2	150
Gagne,G	139	0	0	0	0	137	0	1
Gladden,D	126	0	0	0	0	0	126	0
Harper,B	123	119	1	0	0	0	1	2
Hrbek,K	132	0	128	0	0	0	0	0
Knoblauch,C	151	0	0	148	0	2	0	0
Larkin,G	98	0	39	1	1	0	47	4
Leius,S	109	0	0	0	79	19	2	0
Mack,S	143	0	0	0	0	0	140	1
Munoz,P	51	0	0	0	0	0	44	2
Newman,A	118	0	1	35	35	55	1	3
Ortiz,J	61	60	0	0	0	0	0	0
Pagliarulo,M	121	0	0	1	118	0	0	0
Puckett,K	152	0	0	0	0	0	152	0
Sorrento,P	26	0	13	0	0	0	0	2
Webster,L	18	17	0	0	0	0	0	0

Sick call: 1991 DL report

Player	Days on the DL
David West	85
Junior Ortiz	15
Dan Gladden	25
Gene Larkin	15
Scott Erickson	15
Pedro Munoz	15
Denny Neagle	5

Minor League Report

Class AAA — Portland finished the season 70-68, winning the PCL's Northern Division in the first half of the season, and finishing third in the second half. RHP Tom Edens was voted to the PCL All-Star Team and finished second in the league in ERA with 3.01. RHP George Tsamis was third with 3.14. DH Bernardo Brito tied Colorado Springs' Luis Medina for the home run title with 27. Brito won the title outright last year. The Beavers' pitching staff led the league in ERA (3.81) and shutouts (13). , while the hitters struck out the fewest times in the league (644). . . . **Class AA** — Orlando won the Southern League Championship, defeating Birmingham 6-5 on Sept. 14 to win the best-of-five series three games to one. It finished the season with a 77-67 record, second in the Eastern Division of the Southern League in the first half, and first in the second half. CF Jay Kvasnicka hit a two-run homer, singled in the winning run and had a run-saving catch in the final game. He batted .417 in the playoffs. RHP Pat Mahomes and 3B Cheo Garcia were both named to the Southern League All-Star Team. , and utility player Shawn Gilbert was named Southern League Hustler of the Year. Mahomes led the League in ERA at 1.78, Gilbert led in stolen bases with 43 and RHP Mike Trombley led in strikeouts with 175. . . . **Class A** — Kenosha finished the season with a 63-74 record overall, fifth in the Northern Division for the first half of the season, and sixth in the second half. OF Midre Cummings won the Midwest League batting title, with a .322 average. . . . Visalia went 58-78 on the year, finishing fifth and last in the California League's Southern Division in the first half, and third in the second. A bright spot for the Oaks was INF Pat Meares, who came back from a slow start due to injury, and ended up batting .303 for the season. 3B Scott Stahoviak, the Twins' first round draft pick out of Creighton University, skipped the rookie level and hit .278 for the 43 games he played with Visalia. LH reliever Carlos Pulido (1-5, 2.01 ERA, 17 saves) led the team in ERA and was moved up to Triple-A Portland on Aug. 29.

Tops in the Organization

BATTING LEADERS

	Club	Avg.	G	AB	R	H	HR	RBI
Midre Cummings	Ken	.322	106	382	59	123	4	54
Paul Sorrento	Por	.308	113	409	59	126	13	79
Rex Delanuez	Vis	.308	111	406	78	125	11	65
Pat Meares	Vis	.303	89	360	53	109	6	44
Terry Jorgensen	Por	.298	126	456	74	136	11	59

HOME RUNS

Bernardo Brito	Por	27
Paul Russo	Ken	20
Chris Delarwelle	Vis	16
Several players tied		13

RBI

Paul Russo	Ken	100
Bernardo Brito	Por	83
Paul Sorrento	Por	79
Chris Delarwelle	Vis	77
Cheo Garcia	Orl	75

STOLEN BASES

David Rivera	Ken	52
Shawn Gilbert	Orl	43
Rex Delanuez	Vis	39
Mica Lewis	Vis	38
Midre Cummings	Ken	28

WINS

Mike Trombley	Orl	12
Pat Bangtson	Orl	12
Pat Mahomes	Por	11
Tim Persing	Ken	11
Alan Newman	Orl	11

SAVES

Greg Johnson	Orl	25
Carlos Pulido	Por	17
Dennis Hoppe	Vis	11
Fred White	Vis	10
Jason Klonoski	Vis	9

STRIKEOUTS

Pat Mahomes	Por	177
Mike Trombley	Orl	175
Alan Newman	Orl	132
Ed Gustafson	Vis	120
Several players tied		110

PITCHING LEADERS

	Club	W-L	ERA	IP	H	BB	SO
Pat Mahomes	Por	11-10	2.32	171	127	93	177
Mike Trombley	Orl	12-7	2.54	191	153	57	175
Tom Edens	Por	10-7	3.01	161	145	62	100
George Tsamis	Por	10-8	3.14	175	186	70	76
Alan Newman	Orl	11-9	3.16	159	139	79	132

238

Runs: Most, career, all-time

1466	Sam Rice, 1915-1933
1258	Harmon Killebrew, 1954-1974
1154	Joe Judge, 1915-1932
1037	Buddy Myer, 1925-1941
1004	Clyde Milan, 1907-1922

Hits: Most, career, all-time

2889	Sam Rice, 1915-1933
2291	Joe Judge, 1915-1932
2100	Clyde Milan, 1907-1922
2085	Rod Carew, 1967-1978
2024	Harmon Killebrew, 1954-1974

2B: Most, career, all-time

479	Sam Rice, 1915-1933
421	Joe Judge, 1915-1932
391	Mickey Vernon, 1939-1955
329	Tony Oliva, 1962-1976
305	Rod Carew, 1967-1978
305	Buddy Myer, 1925-1941

3B: Most, career, all-time

183	Sam Rice, 1915-1933
157	Joe Judge, 1915-1932
125	Goose Goslin, 1921-1938
113	Buddy Myer, 1925-1941
108	Mickey Vernon, 1939-1955
90	Rod Carew, 1967-1978 (8)

HR: Most, career, all-time

559	Harmon Killebrew, 1954-1974
256	Bob Allison, 1958-1970
243	KENT HRBEK, 1981-1991
220	Tony Oliva, 1962-1976
201	GARY GAETTI, 1981-1990

RBI: Most, career, all-time

1540	Harmon Killebrew, 1954-1974
1045	Sam Rice, 1915-1933
1026	Mickey Vernon, 1939-1955
1001	Joe Judge, 1915-1932
947	Tony Oliva, 1962-1976

SB: Most, career, all-time

495	Clyde Milan, 1907-1922
346	Sam Rice, 1915-1933
321	George Case, 1937-1947
271	Rod Carew, 1967-1978
210	Joe Judge, 1915-1932

BB: Most, career, all-time

1505	Harmon Killebrew, 1954-1974
1274	Eddie Yost, 1944-1958
943	Joe Judge, 1915-1932
864	Buddy Myer, 1925-1941
795	Bob Allison, 1958-1970

BA: Highest, career, all-time

.334	Rod Carew, 1967-1978
.328	Heinie Manush, 1930-1935
.323	Sam Rice, 1915-1933
.323	Goose Goslin, 1921-1938
.320	KIRBY PUCKETT, 1984-1991

Slug avg: Highest, career, all-time

.514	Harmon Killebrew, 1954-1974
.502	Goose Goslin, 1921-1938
.500	Roy Sievers, 1954-1959
.490	KENT HRBEK, 1981-1991
.481	Jimmie Hall, 1963-1966

Games started: Most, career, all-time

665	Walter Johnson, 1907-1927
433	Jim Kaat, 1959-1973
345	Bert Blyleven, 1970-1988
331	Camilo Pascual, 1954-1966
259	FRANK VIOLA, 1982-1989

Saves: Most, career, all-time

108	Ron Davis, 1982-1986
104	JEFF REARDON, 1987-1989
96	Firpo Marberry, 1923-1936
88	Al Worthington, 1964-1969
76	Ron Perranoski, 1968-1971

Shutouts: Most, career, all-time

110	Walter Johnson, 1907-1927
31	Camilo Pascual, 1954-1966
29	Bert Blyleven, 1970-1988
23	Jim Kaat, 1959-1973
23	Dutch Leonard, 1938-1946

Wins: Most, career, all-time

417	Walter Johnson, 1907-1927
190	Jim Kaat, 1959-1973
149	Bert Blyleven, 1970-1988
145	Camilo Pascual, 1954-1966
128	Jim Perry, 1963-1972

K: Most, career, all-time

3509	Walter Johnson, 1907-1927
2035	Bert Blyleven, 1970-1988
1885	Camilo Pascual, 1954-1966

1851	Jim Kaat, 1959-1973
1214	FRANK VIOLA, 1982-1989

Win pct: Highest, career, all-time

.622	Firpo Marberry, 1923-1936
.602	Sam Jones, 1928-1931
.599	Walter Johnson, 1907-1927
.598	Earl Whitehill, 1933-1936
.588	Mudcat Grant, 1964-1967

ERA: Lowest, career, all-time

2.17	Walter Johnson, 1907-1927
2.64	Doc Ayers, 1913-1919
2.75	Harry Harper, 1913-1919
2.76	Charlie Smith, 1906-1909
2.83	Bert Gallia, 1912-1917
3.15	Jim Perry, 1963-1972 (10)

Runs: Most, season

128	Rod Carew, 1977
127	Joe Cronin, 1930
126	Zoilo Versalles, 1965
122	Buddy Lewis, 1938
121	Heinie Manush, 1932
121	Sam Rice, 1930

Hits: Most, season

239	Rod Carew, 1977
234	KIRBY PUCKETT, 1988
227	Sam Rice, 1925
223	KIRBY PUCKETT, 1986
221	Heinie Manush, 1933

2B: Most, season

51	Mickey Vernon, 1946
50	Stan Spence, 1946
45	Joe Cronin, 1933
45	KIRBY PUCKETT, 1989
45	Zoilo Versalles, 1965

3B: Most, season

20	Goose Goslin, 1925
19	Joe Cassidy, 1904
19	Cecil Travis, 1941
18	Joe Cronin, 1932
18	Goose Goslin, 1923
18	Sam Rice, 1923
18	Howie Shanks, 1921
18	John Stone, 1935
16	Rod Carew, 1977 (11)

HR: Most, season

49	Harmon Killebrew, 1964

49	Harmon Killebrew, 1969
48	Harmon Killebrew, 1962
46	Harmon Killebrew, 1961
45	Harmon Killebrew, 1963

RBI: Most, season

140	Harmon Killebrew, 1969
129	Goose Goslin, 1924
126	Joe Cronin, 1930
126	Joe Cronin, 1931
126	Harmon Killebrew, 1962

SB: Most, season

88	Clyde Milan, 1912
75	Clyde Milan, 1913
63	Sam Rice, 1920
62	Danny Moeller, 1913
61	George Case, 1943
49	Rod Carew, 1976 (8)

BB: Most, season

151	Eddie Yost, 1956
145	Harmon Killebrew, 1969
141	Eddie Yost, 1950
131	Harmon Killebrew, 1967
131	Eddie Yost, 1954

BA: Highest, season

.388	Rod Carew, 1977
.379	Goose Goslin, 1928
.376	Ed Delahanty, 1902
.364	Rod Carew, 1974
.359	Rod Carew, 1975

Slug avg: Highest, season

.614	Goose Goslin, 1928
.606	Harmon Killebrew, 1961
.590	Ed Delahanty, 1902
.584	Harmon Killebrew, 1969
.579	Roy Sievers, 1957

Games started: Most, season

42	Walter Johnson, 1910
42	Jim Kaat, 1965
41	Jim Kaat, 1966
40	Bert Blyleven, 1973
40	Bob Groom, 1912
40	Walter Johnson, 1914
40	Jim Perry, 1970

Saves: Most, season

42	RICK AGUILERA, 1991
42	JEFF REARDON, 1988
34	Ron Perranoski, 1970
32	RICK AGUILERA, 1990
32	Mike Marshall, 1979

Shutouts: Most, season

11	Walter Johnson, 1913
9	Bert Blyleven, 1973
9	Walter Johnson, 1914
9	Bob Porterfield, 1953
8	Walter Johnson, 1910
8	Walter Johnson, 1917
8	Walter Johnson, 1918
8	Camilo Pascual, 1961

Wins: Most, season

36	Walter Johnson, 1913
33	Walter Johnson, 1912
28	Walter Johnson, 1914
27	Walter Johnson, 1915
26	General Crowder, 1932
25	Jim Kaat, 1966 (6)

K: Most, season

313	Walter Johnson, 1910
303	Walter Johnson, 1912
258	Bert Blyleven, 1973
249	Bert Blyleven, 1974
243	Walter Johnson, 1913

Win pct: Highest, season

.837	Walter Johnson, 1913
.800	Stan Coveleski, 1925
.800	Firpo Marberry, 1931
.774	FRANK VIOLA, 1988
.773	Bill Campbell, 1976

ERA: Lowest, season

1.14	Walter Johnson, 1913
1.27	Walter Johnson, 1918
1.35	Walter Johnson, 1910
1.39	Walter Johnson, 1912
1.49	Walter Johnson, 1919
2.50	Dave Goltz, 1978 (*)

Most pinch-hit homers, season

| 4 | Don Mincher, 1964 |

Most pinch-hit, homers, career

| 8 | Bob Allison, 1961-1970 (none with Was-1958-1960) |

Most consecutive games, batting safely

| 33 | Heine Manush, Was-1933 |
| 31 | Ken Landreaux, 1980 |

Most consecutive scoreless innings

| 55 | Walter Johnson, Was-1913 |

No hit games

Walter Johnson, Was at Bos AL, 1-0; July 1, 1920.
Bobby Burke, Was vs Bos AL, 5-0; August 8, 1931.
Jack Kralick, Min vs KC AL, 1-0; August 26, 1962.
Dean Chance, Min at Cle AL, 2-1; August 25, 1967 (2nd game).
Jay Cashion, six innings, called so Cleveland could catch train, Was vs Cle AL, 2-0; August 20, 1912 (2nd game).
Walter Johnson, seven innings, rain, Was vs StL AL, 2-0; August 25, 1924.
Dean Chance, five perfect innings, rain, Min vs Bos AL, 2-0; August 6, 1967.

Chicago White Sox

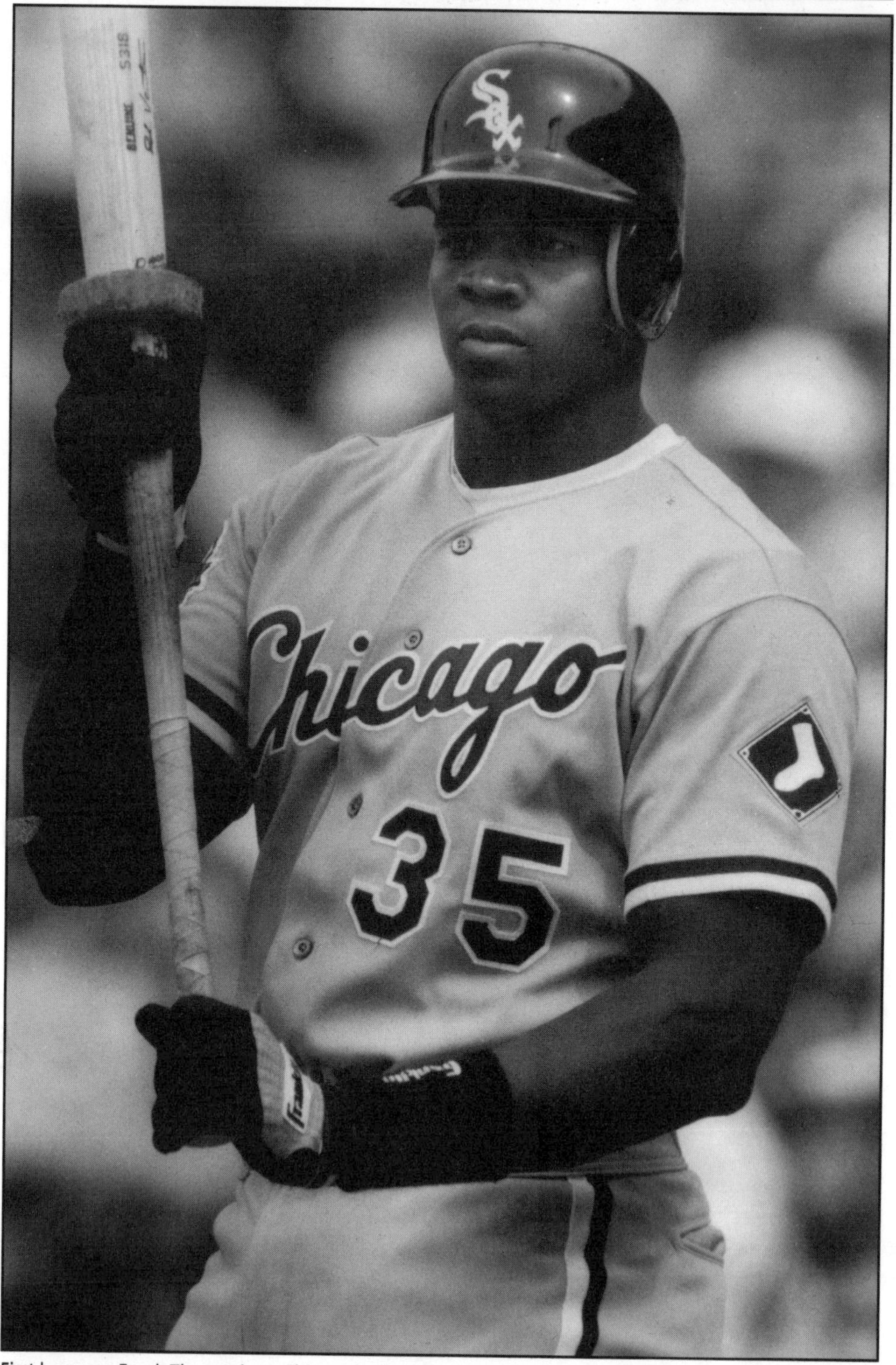

First baseman Frank Thomas kept Chicago in the race all season.

New park, new strategy, same old second place

The Chicago White Sox, who won 94 games in 1990 only to finish behind the Oakland Athletics, began 1991 confident that they could bring an American League western division crown to their new home at New Comiskey Park.

But they had trouble adjusting to their new $135 million stadium and spent much of the first half changing their attack from a hit-and-run offense to a lineup of bashers to take advantage of the new power-friendly ballpark.

New acquisitions Cory Snyder and Ron Kittle—who joined the White Sox for a third tour of duty—failed to bolster the lineup, and outfielder Sammy Sosa (15 HRs, 70 RBI in 1990) spent most of the season in the minors.

But first baseman Frank Thomas and third baseman Robin Ventura emerged as the league's top pair of cornerstones, keeping the Sox in the division race well into September. Outfielder Tim Raines, acquired in the offseason from Montreal for Ivan Calderon, provided a leadoff spark for Chicago, which won 20 of its 43 wins before the All-Star break in its last at-bat.

Thomas, who would have captured Rookie of the Year honors had he not lost his rookie status in a midseason callup in 1990, hit .318 with 32 home runs and 109 RBI while leading the league in walks (133) and on-base percentage (.457)—all while playing through a nagging shoulder injury that often limited him to designated hitting duty. Ventura racked up 23 home runs and 100 RBI.

Jack McDowell (17-10) emerged as the pitching ace White Sox management had hoped for, although his moonlighting as a rock singer continually annoyed general manager Ron Schueler. Veteran knuckleballer Charlie Hough provided 199 solid innings as the No. 2 starter, but the team often struggled with a patchwork group of rookies and youngsters rounding out its rotation.

Greg Hibbard (11-11) spent much of the year at Triple-A Vancouver. Melido Perez proved ineffective as a starter, but became one of the league's best middle relievers, while rookie Wilson Alvarez tossed a no-hitter in his first start since joining the team from Double-A Birmingham Aug. 11, but fizzled thereafter.

The White Sox tumbled as September approached, but were bolstered at the turnstiles by the unlikely return of Bo Jackson, who signed a $700,000 contract with the club after the Kansas City Royals released him following a career-threatening hip injury suffered while playing for the Los Angeles Raiders. Jackson, who underwent a much-publicized rehabilitation stint in the White Sox minor league system before returning to the majors Sept. 2, hit .225 in 23 games with the White Sox ,with three home runs and 14 RBI.

—Pete Williams

White Sox 1992 preview

Any team with a nucleus of Frank Thomas, Tim Raines, Robin Ventura and Jack McDowell should be in business. But the AL West is baseball's toughest dogfight and the Chicago White Sox will have their hands full.

One key will be outfielder Sammy Sosa. He hit just .203 last season, and his RBI production fell from 70 to 33. He wound up in the minors.

Another is outfielder Bo Jackson. Will he be able to come back from his hip injury? He hit .225 with 3 HRs in 23 games last September.

That leaves pitching. McDowell (17-10) took control as the staff leader, and veteran Charlie Hough may have enough flutter left in his knuckleball to contribute again. Beyond that, Greg Hibbard, Melido Perez, Alex Fernandez and Wilson

Alvarez will have to pick up the load.

Scott Radinsky and Bobby Thigpen lead a fine bullpen.

1992 prophecy: White Sox

▶The White Sox will call up Rodney McCray (the guy who ran through the wall) and threaten to trade him cross-town to the Cubs (the team with the brick wall) unless he hits .300.

▶A Chicago copy editor will be fired for writing five headlines in one week containing the phrase "Bo knows."

▶The Los Angeles Raiders, needing help at tight end, will sign Frank Thomas, who will give up baseball for football and TV commercials.

—John Hunt

Harrelson to Hrbek: 'Grab some bench'

There's nothing like a little bad blood to finish off the season between the Minnesota Twins and Chicago White Sox.

The Twins took exception to Ken Harrelson's pet phrase, "grab some bench." The White Sox announcer often makes that comment during telecasts when an opposing player strikes out.

Before one of the final 1991 games between the Twins and White Sox, several players, led by Kent Hrbek, yelled, "Grab some bench" in Hawk's direction. Hrbek called Harrelson's style "unprofessional."

Harrelson claimed he loved the attention. "I feel it shows we're doing our job," he said.

As for Hrbek, Harrelson added, "Kent Hrbek knows how I feel about him—he's over-weight and vastly overpaid. Talk about a lack of professionalism. He signs a big contract and comes into spring training at 280 pounds."

Hrbek wasn't the only Twin who could have lost a few pounds, but it didn't stop Minnesota from beating the White Sox in the AL West.

Bo knows cash flow

By Rick Lawes

Don't let that Bo Jackson limp fool you—he ran away with a truckload of cash he earned from football and baseball in 1991. His haul could exceed $4 million, not counting endorsements. Here's how:

Each game Bo played for the Chicago White Sox earns him $10,000 in incentive pay. (That's atop his $700,000 salary for '91).

Jackson didn't earn his projected $1.5 million to $4 million from football, due to a failed medical exam, but simply for reporting to the Los Angeles Raiders camp, Bo picked up a quick $100,000 and another $416,000 in deferred bonus money.

His attorneys are pursuing a $4 million payout on a disability insurance policy since his medical examination revealed that he will no longer be able to play football.

Way to go, Bo.

Urban designer mourns old Comiskey

By Tim Wendel

One of the nation's top advocates of traditional urban ballparks is not cheering the new Comiskey Park. Chicago architect Philip Bess claims the old Comiskey could have been saved as a park and the new stadium better built.

Bess, winner of a National Endowment for the Arts grant, had envisioned a new home for the White Sox on Armour Square Park, directly north of old Comiskey. Even though he did talk with the Illinois Sports Facility Authority, the merits of his concept, which was lauded by Inland Architect magazine, were never really discussed in Chicago.

"It's frustrating," said Bess. "The

whole procedure, the way it was done, the hype that's surrounding it—it's all very unfortunate. The feeling right now [in Chicago] is that it's all been worth it. . . . But I think we missed a chance."

Peter Bynoe, executive director of the Illinois Sports Facility Authority, said Bess' proposal came too late to be considered.

Bess contends that Chicago could have constructed a stadium more in tune with Wrigley Field and Boston's Fenway Park—including a section of old Comiskey stands as both a historic monument and a working grandstand. Old Comiskey would have been preserved for high school and American Legion teams, and a civic building (such as a branch library) would have been the centerpiece of a new commercial strip along 35th Street. Six thousand new parking spaces would have been hidden behind row houses.

McDowell had two good records

The White Sox's Jack McDowell completed a rare double play in 1991: He got rave reviews from his manager as well as Rolling Stone music critics.

The magazine said the debut album by his band V.I.E.W. "serves notice that these three jocks know how to rock."

Chicago reliever Wayne Edwards and former Stanford teammate Lee Plemel are the other band members. But McDowell is the lead singer, lyricist and the money man, having invested more than $100,000 in his rock 'n' roll hobby.

Winning over former White Sox manager Jeff Torborg proved as difficult as making a hit record.

Two years ago, unimpressed with McDowell's spirit, Torborg sent the right-hander down to the minors for the season. It was a move that Torborg later regretted.

"I just didn't know Jack at that time," Torborg said. "He's an aggressive personality. The way he's built and looks, he doesn't look that way. But he's as tough as there is."

CHICAGO WHITE SOX 1991 Final Stats

Batting	AVG	SLG	OB	G	AB	R	H	TB	2B	3B	HR	RBI	BB	SO	SB	CS	E
Thomas	.318	.553	.453	158	559	104	178	309	31	2	32	109	138	112	1	2	2
Newson	.295	.424	.419	71	132	20	39	56	5	0	4	25	28	34	2	2	2
McCray	.286	.286	.286	17	7	2	2	2	0	0	0	0	0	2	1	1	0
Ventura	.284	.442	.367	157	606	92	172	268	25	1	23	100	80	67	2	4	18
Grebeck	.281	.460	.386	107	224	37	63	103	16	3	6	31	38	40	1	3	10
Johnson	.274	.342	.304	159	588	72	161	201	14	13	0	49	26	58	26	11	2
Guillen	.273	.340	.284	154	524	52	143	178	20	3	3	49	11	38	21	15	21
Raines	.268	.345	.359	155	609	102	163	210	20	6	5	50	83	68	51	15	3
Pasqua	.259	.465	.358	134	417	71	108	194	22	5	18	66	62	86	0	2	6
Huff	.251	.346	.361	102	243	42	61	84	10	2	3	25	37	48	14	4	2
Karkovice	.246	.413	.310	75	167	25	41	69	13	0	5	22	15	42	0	0	4
Fisk	.241	.413	.299	134	460	42	111	190	25	0	18	74	32	86	1	2	6
Cora	.241	.276	.313	100	228	37	55	63	2	3	0	18	20	21	11	6	10
Merullo	.229	.343	.268	80	140	8	32	48	1	0	5	21	9	18	0	0	2
Wakamatsu	.226	.226	.250	18	31	2	7	7	0	0	0	0	1	6	0	0	0
Jackson	.225	.408	.333	23	71	8	16	29	4	0	3	14	12	25	0	1	0
Fletcher	.206	.266	.262	90	248	14	51	66	10	1	1	28	17	26	0	2	3
Sosa	.203	.335	.240	116	316	39	64	106	10	1	10	33	14	98	13	6	6
Kittle	.191	.319	.291	17	47	7	9	15	0	0	2	7	5	9	0	0	2
Beltre	.167	.167	.286	8	6	0	1	1	0	0	0	0	1	1	1	0	0

Pitching	W-L	ERA	G	GS	CG	GF	Sho	SV	IP	H	R	ER	HR	BB	SO
Wapnick	0-1	1.80	6	0	0	4	0	0	5	2	1	1	0	4	1
Radinsky	5-5	2.02	67	0	0	19	0	8	71.1	53	18	16	4	23	49
Pall	7-2	2.41	51	0	0	7	0	0	71	59	22	19	7	20	40
Patterson	3-0	2.83	43	0	0	13	0	1	63.2	48	22	20	5	35	32
Perez	8-7	3.12	49	8	0	16	0	1	135.2	111	49	47	15	52	128
Drahman	3-2	3.23	28	0	0	8	0	0	30.2	21	12	11	4	13	18
McDowell	17-10	3.41	35	35	15	0	3	0	253.2	212	97	96	19	82	191
Thigpen	7-5	3.49	67	0	0	58	0	30	69.2	63	32	27	10	38	47
Alvarez	3-2	3.51	10	9	2	0	1	0	56.1	47	26	22	9	29	32
Edwards	0-2	3.86	13	0	0	3	0	0	23.1	22	14	10	2	17	12
Hough	9-10	4.02	31	29	4	1	1	0	199.1	167	98	89	21	94	107
Hibbard	11-11	4.31	32	29	5	1	0	0	194	196	107	93	23	57	71
Fernandez	9-13	4.51	34	32	2	1	0	0	191.2	186	100	96	16	88	145
Carter	0-1	5.25	5	2	0	1	0	0	12	8	8	7	1	5	2
Garcia	4-4	5.40	16	15	0	0	0	0	78.1	79	50	47	13	31	40
Hernandez	1-0	7.80	9	3	0	1	0	0	15	18	15	13	1	7	6
Drees	0-0	12.27	4	0	0	1	0	0	7.1	10	10	10	4	6	2

1992 Preliminary Roster

Pitchers (20)

Wilson Alvarez
Jeff Carter
Brian Drahman
Wayne Edwards
Alex Fernandez
Ramon Garcia
Roberto Hernandez
Greg Hibbard
Charlie Hough
Chris Howard
Jack McDowell
Donn Pall
Ken Patterson
Melido Perez
Greg Perschke
Scott Radinsky
Johnny Ruffin
Rich Scheid
Bobby Thigpen
Steve Wapnick

Catchers (3)

Carlton Fisk
Ron Karkovice
Matt Merullo

Infielders (7)

Esteban Beltre
Joey Cora
Craig Grebeck
Ozzie Guillen
Norberto Martin
Frank Thomas
Robin Ventura

Outfielders (8)

Mike Huff
Bo Jackson
Lance Johnson
Derek Lee
Warren Newson
Dan Pasqua
Tim Raines
Sammy Sosa

Games played by position

	G	C	1B	2B	3B	SS	OF	DH
Beltre,E	8	0	0	0	0	8	0	0
Cora,J	100	0	0	80	0	5	0	2
Fisk,C	134	106	12	0	0	0	0	13
Fletcher,S	90	0	0	86	4	0	0	0
Grebeck,C	107	0	0	36	49	26	0	0
Guillen,O	154	0	0	0	0	149	0	0
Huff,M	102	0	0	4	0	0	96	2
Jackson,B	23	0	0	0	0	0	0	21
Johnson,L	159	0	0	0	0	0	157	0
Karkovice,R	75	69	0	0	0	0	1	0
Kittle,R	17	0	15	0	0	0	0	0
McCray,R	17	0	0	0	0	0	8	6
Merullo,M	80	27	16	0	0	0	0	6
Newson,W	71	0	0	0	0	0	50	3
Pasqua,D	134	0	83	0	0	0	59	8
Raines,T	155	0	0	0	0	0	133	19
Sosa,S	116	0	0	0	0	0	111	2
Thomas,F	158	0	56	0	0	0	0	101
Ventura,R	157	0	31	0	151	0	0	0
Wakamatsu,D	18	18	0	0	0	0	0	0

Sick call: 1991 DL report

Player	Days on the DL
Charlie Hough	5
Bo Jackson	147
Ron Karkovice	44
Brian Harrison	182
Joey Cora	18
Mike Huff	15

Minor League Report

Class AAA — Vancouver finished 49-86 in the Pacific Coast League's Northern Division, in last place during both halves of the season. 1B/DH Matt Stark led the team with 10 HRs. OF Derek Lee led the team with a .295 average. LHP Tom Drees was the team's top pitcher with an 8-8 record and a 3.52 ERA. . . . Class AA — Birmingham finished 77-66 in the Southern League's Western Division, first in the first half and last in the second half. The Barons defeated Knoxville three games to one in opening round playoff action, but lost the league championship to Orlando 3-1. 3B Ron Coomer, who had 13 HRs and a league runner-up 76 RBI, was named team MVP. The team pitcher of the year was LHP Wilson Alvarez, who was 10-6 with a 1.83 ERA before his promotion to Chicago, where he threw a no-hitter. The Barons' team ERA of 2.94 led the league. OF Scott Tedder was 12-for-23 in postseason play with eight runs scored and eight RBI. He reached base 20 times in his last 25 playoff plate appearances. . . . Class A — South Bend finished 69-70 in the Midwest League's Northern Division, third in the first half, third in the second half. SS Brandon Wilson set the all-time a South Bend record with a .313 average. OF Kevin Couglin played in a team-record 131 games. . . . Sarasota finished 75-56 in the Florida State League's Western Division, in second place during both halves of the season. . . . Utica completed its season 39-37 in third place in the McNamara (East) division of the New York-Penn League and set a record for attendance with 70,150. , beating the old record by 5,000.Mike Call (6-1, 1.26 ERA) was named the team's most valuable pitcher., and was also second in the league in ERA. P Larry Thomas (1-3, 1.47 ERA) was third.OF Harold Fleming (.275 BA, 3 HR, 30 RBI) was named the team's most valuable player.

Tops in the Organization

BATTING LEADERS	Club	Avg.	G	AB	R	H	HR	RBI
Brandon Wilson	Bir	.315	127	473	78	149	2	51
Scott Tedder	Bir	.307	137	486	59	149	0	49
Derek Lee	Van	.304	132	473	90	144	11	60
Kevin Coughlin	Sbn	.304	131	431	60	131	0	38
Scott Cepicky	Sar	.290	124	442	62	128	8	76

HOME RUNS			WINS		
Kevin Garner	Bir	14	Rodney Bolton	Bir	15
Ron Coomer	Bir	13	Bo Kennedy	Van	13
Derek Lee	Van	11	Domingo Jean	Sbn	12
Matt Stark	Van	10	Several players tied		11
Several players tied		9			

RBI			SAVES		
Scott Cepicky	Sar	76	Michael Mongiello	Sar	23
Ron Coomer	Bir	76	Rolando Caridad	Sbn	17
Kevin Garner	Bir	74	John Hudek	Bir	13
Matt Stark	Van	68	Brian Drahman	Van	12
Ron Plemmons	Sar	64	Keith Shepherd	Sar	12

STOLEN BASES			STRIKEOUTS		
Brandon Wilson	Bir	41	Wilson Alvarez	Bir	165
Kerry Valrie	Sbn	32	Jason Bere	Sbn	158
Kevin Castleberry	Bir	31	Domingo Jean	Sbn	141
Aubrey Waggoner	Bir	25	Rodney Bolton	Bir	134
Lindsay Foster	Bir	23	Danny Matznick	Sar	131

PITCHING LEADERS	Club	W-L	ERA	IP	H	BB	SO
Rodney Bolton	Bir	15-10	1.78	193	154	44	134
Wilson Alvarez	Bir	10-6	1.83	152	109	74	165
Brian Keyser	Bir	6-8	2.63	147	129	54	103
Scott Stevens	Sar	8-10	2.64	126	103	50	103
Kevin Tolar	Sbn	8-5	2.75	115	87	85	87

Chicago (1901-1991)

Runs: Most, career, all-time

1319	Luke Appling, 1930-1950
1187	Nellie Fox, 1950-1963
1063	Eddie Collins, 1915-1926
893	Minnie Minoso, 1951-1980
791	Luis Aparicio, 1956-1970

Hits: Most, career, all-time

2749	Luke Appling, 1930-1950
2470	Nellie Fox, 1950-1963
2005	Eddie Collins, 1915-1926
1576	Luis Aparicio, 1956-1970
1523	Minnie Minoso, 1951-1980

2B: Most, career, all-time

440	Luke Appling, 1930-1950
335	Nellie Fox, 1950-1963
267	HAROLD BAINES, 1980-1989
265	Eddie Collins, 1915-1926
260	Minnie Minoso, 1951-1980

3B: Most, career, all-time

104	Shano Collins, 1910-1920
104	Nellie Fox, 1950-1963
102	Luke Appling, 1930-1950
102	Eddie Collins, 1915-1926
82	Johnny Mostil, 1918-1929
79	Minnie Minoso, 1951-1980 (6)

HR: Most, career, all-time

210	CARLTON FISK, 1981-1991
186	HAROLD BAINES, 1980-1989
154	Bill Melton, 1968-1975
140	RON KITTLE, 1982-1991
135	Minnie Minoso, 1951-1980

RBI: Most, career, all-time

1116	Luke Appling, 1930-1950
819	HAROLD BAINES, 1980-1989
808	Minnie Minoso, 1951-1980
803	Eddie Collins, 1915-1926
740	Nellie Fox, 1950-1963

SB: Most, career, all-time

368	Eddie Collins, 1915-1926
318	Luis Aparicio, 1956-1970
250	Frank Isbell, 1901-1909
206	Fielder Jones, 1901-1908
192	Shano Collins, 1910-1920

BB: Most, career, all-time

1302	Luke Appling, 1930-1950
965	Eddie Collins, 1915-1926
658	Nellie Fox, 1950-1963
658	Minnie Minoso, 1951-1980
638	Ray Schalk, 1912-1928

BA: Highest, career, all-time

.340	Joe Jackson, 1915-1920
.331	Eddie Collins, 1915-1926
.317	Zeke Bonura, 1934-1937
.315	Bibb Falk, 1920-1928
.312	Taffy Wright, 1940-1948
.304	Minnie Minoso, 1951-1980 (9)

Slug avg: Highest, career, all-time

.518	Zeke Bonura, 1934-1937
.499	Joe Jackson, 1915-1920
.470	RON KITTLE, 1982-1991
.468	Minnie Minoso, 1951-1980
.464	HAROLD BAINES, 1980-1989

Games started: Most, career, all-time

484	Ted Lyons, 1923-1946
483	Red Faber, 1914-1933
390	Billy Pierce, 1949-1961
312	Ed Walsh, 1904-1916
301	Doc White, 1903-1913
286	Wilbur Wood, 1967-1978 (6)

Saves: Most, career, all-time

178	BOBBY THIGPEN, 1986-1991
98	Hoyt Wilhelm, 1963-1968
75	Terry Forster, 1971-1976
57	Wilbur Wood, 1967-1978
56	Bob James, 1985-1987

Shutouts: Most, career, all-time

57	Ed Walsh, 1904-1916
42	Doc White, 1903-1913
35	Billy Pierce, 1949-1961
29	Red Faber, 1914-1933
28	Eddie Cicotte, 1912-1920
24	Wilbur Wood, 1967-1978 (9)

Wins: Most, career, all-time

260	Ted Lyons, 1923-1946
254	Red Faber, 1914-1933
195	Ed Walsh, 1904-1916
186	Billy Pierce, 1949-1961
163	Wilbur Wood, 1967-1978

K: Most, career, all-time

1796	Billy Pierce, 1949-1961
1732	Ed Walsh, 1904-1916
1471	Red Faber, 1914-1933
1332	Wilbur Wood, 1967-1978
1098	Gary Peters, 1959-1969

Win pct: Highest, career, all-time

.648	Lefty Williams, 1916-1920
.644	Virgil Trucks, 1953-1955
.616	Jim Kaat, 1973-1975
.615	Juan Pizarro, 1961-1966
.609	Ed Walsh, 1904-1916

ERA: Lowest, career, all-time

1.81	Ed Walsh, 1904-1916
2.18	Frank Smith, 1904-1910
2.25	Eddie Cicotte, 1912-1920
2.30	Jim Scott, 1909-1917
2.30	Doc White, 1903-1913
2.92	Gary Peters, 1959-1969 (11)

Runs: Most, season

135	Johnny Mostil, 1925
120	Zeke Bonura, 1936
120	Fielder Jones, 1901
120	Johnny Mostil, 1926
120	Rip Radcliff, 1936
119	Minnie Minoso, 1954 (6)

Hits: Most, season

222	Eddie Collins, 1920
218	Joe Jackson, 1920
210	Buck Weaver, 1920
207	Rip Radcliff, 1936
204	Luke Appling, 1936
198	HAROLD BAINES, 1985 (10)

2B: Most, season

45	Floyd Robinson, 1962
44	IVAN CALDERON, 1990
44	Chet Lemon, 1979
43	Bibb Falk, 1926
43	Earl Sheely, 1925

3B: Most, season

21	Joe Jackson, 1916

20	Joe Jackson, 1920
18	Jack Fournier, 1915
18	Harry Lord, 1911
18	Minnie Minoso, 1954
18	Carl Reynolds, 1930

HR: Most, season

37	Dick Allen, 1972
37	CARLTON FISK, 1985
35	RON KITTLE, 1983
33	Bill Melton, 1970
33	Bill Melton, 1971

RBI: Most, season

138	Zeke Bonura, 1936
128	Luke Appling, 1936
121	Joe Jackson, 1920
119	Al Simmons, 1933
117	Eddie Robinson, 1951
116	Minnie Minoso, 1954 (6)

SB: Most, season

77	Rudy Law, 1983
56	Luis Aparicio, 1959
56	Wally Moses, 1943
53	Luis Aparicio, 1961
53	Eddie Collins, 1917

BB: Most, season

138	FRANK THOMAS, 1991
127	Lu Blue, 1931
122	Luke Appling, 1935
121	Luke Appling, 1949
119	Eddie Collins, 1915

BA: Highest, season

.388	Luke Appling, 1936
.382	Joe Jackson, 1920
.369	Eddie Collins, 1920
.360	Eddie Collins, 1923
.359	Carl Reynolds, 1930
.321	Harold Baines, 1989 (*)

Slug avg: Highest, season

.603	Dick Allen, 1972
.589	Joe Jackson, 1920
.584	Carl Reynolds, 1930
.573	Zeke Bonura, 1937
.563	Dick Allen, 1974

Games started: Most, season

49	Ed Walsh, 1908
49	Wilbur Wood, 1972
48	Wilbur Wood, 1973
46	Ed Walsh, 1907
43	Wilbur Wood, 1975

Saves: Most, season

57	BOBBY THIGPEN, 1990
34	BOBBY THIGPEN, 1988
34	BOBBY THIGPEN, 1989
32	Bob James, 1985
30	Ed Farmer, 1980
30	BOBBY THIGPEN, 1991

Shutouts: Most, season

11	Ed Walsh, 1908
10	Ed Walsh, 1906
8	Reb Russell, 1913
8	Ed Walsh, 1909
8	Wilbur Wood, 1972

Wins: Most, season

40	Ed Walsh, 1908
29	Eddie Cicotte, 1919
28	Eddie Cicotte, 1917
27	Ed Walsh, 1911
27	Ed Walsh, 1912
27	Doc White, 1907
24	La Marr Hoyt, 1983 (9)
24	Wilbur Wood, 1972 (9)
24	Wilbur Wood, 1973 (9)

K: Most, season

269	Ed Walsh, 1908
258	Ed Walsh, 1910
255	Ed Walsh, 1911
254	Ed Walsh, 1912
215	Gary Peters, 1967

Win pct: Highest, season

.842	Sandy Consuegra, 1954
.806	Eddie Cicotte, 1919
.774	Clark Griffith, 1901
.759	Richard Dotson, 1983
.750	Reb Russell, 1917
.750	Bob Shaw, 1959
.750	Monty Stratton, 1937
.750	Doc White, 1906

ERA: Lowest, season

1.27	Ed Walsh, 1910
1.41	Ed Walsh, 1909
1.42	Ed Walsh, 1908
1.52	Doc White, 1906
1.53	Eddie Cicotte, 1917
1.88	Joe Horlen, 1964 (15)

Most pinch-hit homers, season

3	Ron Northey, 1956
3	John Romano, 1959
3	Oscar Gamble, 1977

Most pinch-hit, homers, career

7	Jerry Hairston, 1973-1989

Most consecutive games, batting safely

27	Luke Appling, 1936

Most consecutive scoreless innings

45	Doc White, 1904

No hit games

Nixey Callahan, Chi vs Det AL, 3-0; September 20, 1902 (1st game).
Frank Smith, Chi at Det AL, 15-0; September 6, 1905 (2nd game).
Frank Smith, Chi vs Phi AL, 1-0; September 20, 1908.
Ed Walsh, Chi vs Bos AL, 5-0; August 27, 1911.
Jim Scott, Chi at Was AL, 0-1; May 14, 1914 (lost on 2 hits in the tenth).
Joe Benz, Chi vs Cle AL, 6-1; May 31, 1914.
Eddie Cicotte, Chi at StL AL, 11-0; April 14, 1917.
Charlie Robertson, Chi at Det AL, 2-0; April 30, 1922 (perfect game).
Ted Lyons, Chi at Bos AL, 6-0; August 21, 1926.
Vern Kennedy, Chi vs Cle AL, 5-0; August 31, 1935.
Bill Dietrich, Chi vs StL AL, 8-0; June 1, 1937.
Bob Keegan, Chi vs Was AL, 6-0; August 20, 1957 (2nd game).
Joe Horlen, Chi vs Det AL, 6-0; September 10, 1967 (1st game).
Blue Moon Odom (5 innings) and Francisco Barrios (4 innings), Chi at Oak AL, 2-1; July 28, 1976.
Joe Cowley, Chi at Cal AL, 7-1; September 19, 1986.
Wilson Alvarez, Chi at Bal AL, 7-0; August 11, 1991.
Ed Walsh, five innings, rain, Chi vs NY AL, 8-1; May 26, 1907.
Melido Perez, six innings, rain, Chi at NY AL, 8-0; July 12, 1990.

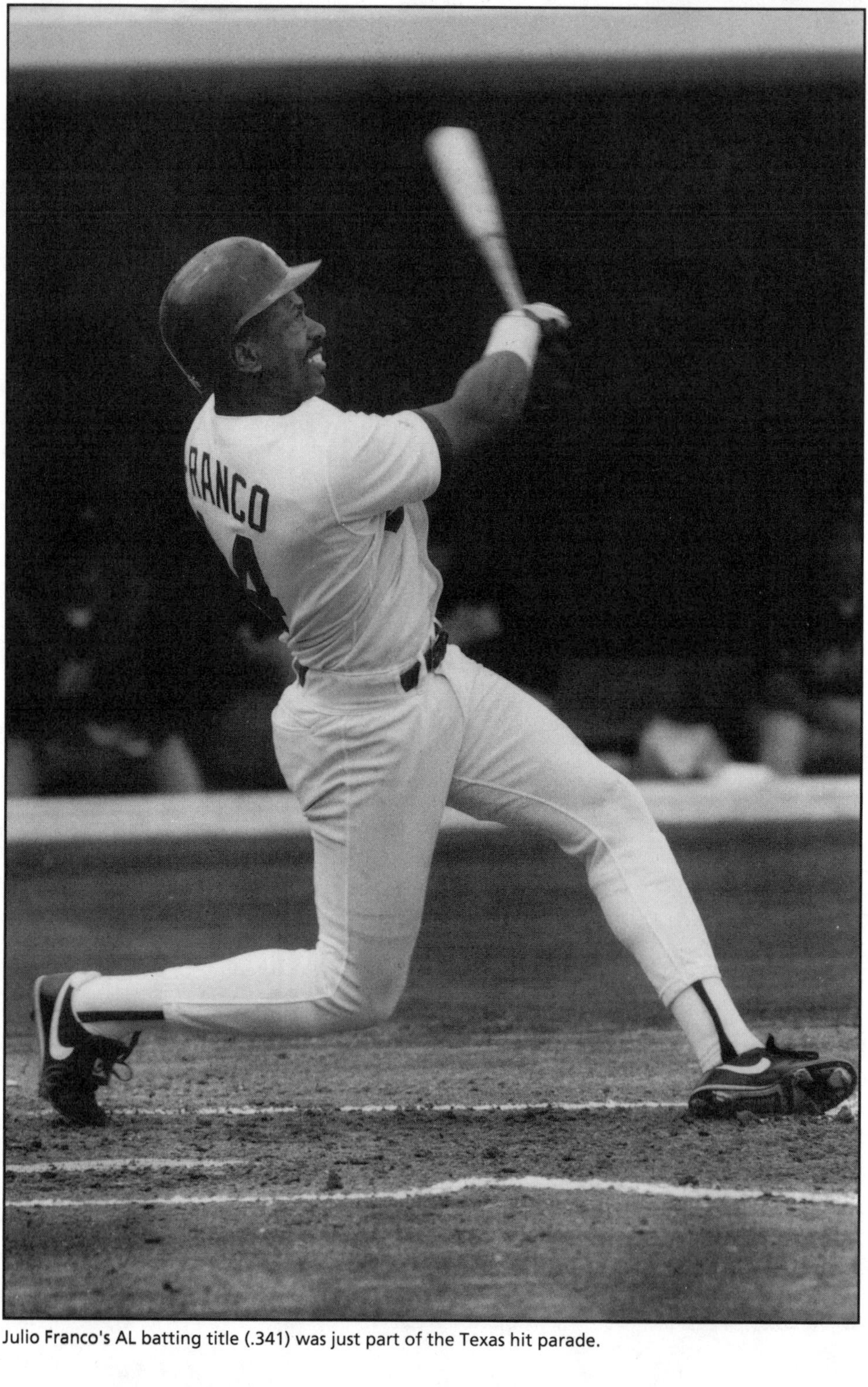

Julio Franco's AL batting title (.341) was just part of the Texas hit parade.

Hot bats weren't enough

For a while, the Rangers looked like 1991's Cinderella team—going on a 14-game winning streak from May 12-27, and sporting a 44-33 record in a first-place tie with Minnesota going into the All-Star break. But then, Minnesota took the glass slipper, and refused to give it back.

Texas, predicted by many to finish no higher than fourth or fifth, finished at 85-77—well above .500, but well behind Minnesota and first place. For a while, it seemed that the hot bats of eventual batting champion Julio Franco (.341), fellow contender Rafael Palmeiro (.322) and Ruben Sierra (.307), all of whom got 200 or more hits, could carry the team, but in the end, the pitching, or lack thereof, caught up.

Nolan Ryan proved he still has his stuff at age 44, going 12-6 with 203 strikeouts and pitching his record seventh no-hitter on May 1 against Toronto. However, he missed several weeks due to back soreness.

Logging even more DL time, however, were fellow hurlers Bobby Witt, who went on May 27 and missed most of the rest of the season due to a torn rotator cuff, and Scott Chiamparino, who went on on May 26, had reconstructive elbow surgery in July, and may be out until mid-1992. His injury was especially disappointing, as many figured on him to anchor the rotation along with Ryan.

The hero of the staff turned out to be Jose Guzman, who was waived in spring training, worked his way back on to the staff, and ultimately posted a 13-7 record with a 3.08 ERA, the most wins of any Ranger pitcher this year.

But Guzman couldn't carry a whole staff. While the offense led the majors in runs scored with 829, the pitching staff was 23rd in ERA at 4.47.

Next to Guzman, the other pleasant surprise for Texas had to be designated hitter Brian Downing, a castoff from the Angels who at age 40 was figured to be washed up. He proved his critics wrong, batting .278 with 17 homers, 49 RBI and 76 runs scored.

The Rangers may have solidfied their future in an August 30 trade, giving third baseman Steve Buechele to the Pirates in exchange for Kurt Miller and Hector Fajardo, two top pitching prospects. If either Miller or Fajardo is ready to move up to the majors, Guzman continues to come along, Witt is able to succesfully rehabilitate and Ryan continues rolling along, the Rangers would have a solid starting rotation.

Jeff Russell, coming off a solid season as the top closer (6-4, 30 saves, 3.29 ERA), must also perform well. With improved pitching and continued potent offense, the Rangers will definitely be a force to be reckoned with.

—Jeannie Chung

Rangers 1992 preview

The Texas Rangers have the American League batting champion, an ageless wonder and tons of potential. One of these years, they'll parlay all that into a division title.

If manager Bobby Valentine can get his pitching straightened out, the club has a chance.

Can Nolan Ryan do it again at age 45? He was 12-6 last year with 203 strikeouts and his seventh career no-hitter. That doesn't look like a man slowing down.

Can Jose Guzman come close to repeating his surprising 13-win season?

Will newcomers Kurt Miller and Hector Fajardo, obtained from Pittsburgh for Steve Buechele, be ready to contribute soon at the big-league level?

Offense is no problem. The Rangers led the majors with 829 runs last season. Second baseman Julio Franco (.341) won the batting title, first baseman Rafael Palmeiro (.322) and outfielder Ruben Sierra (.307) joined Franco in the 200-hit club, and rookies Juan

Gonzalez, Dean Palmer and Ivan Rodriguez flashed star potential last season.

1992 prophecy: Rangers

▸Julio Franco will actually play in the All-Star Game.
▸Nolan Ryan will take all the money from his bank in Alvin, Texas, and buy the Seattle Mariners and put Ken Griffey Jr. in centerfield.
▸The Rangers will laugh at an offer from Philadelphia of Mitch Williams for Rafael Palmeiro.
▸Texas will go to a one-man rotation of Ryan, since he's the only legitimate starter. He will set hundreds of new records, including most Advils taken in a season.

—*John Hunt*

Ryan trains during his 'days of rest'

By Mike Dodd

Nolan Ryan's ritual didn't change when he got his 300th victory in 1990 or pitched his seventh no-hitter in '91. And it won't change when he takes the mound in '92—or '93, or '94, or however long he stays in the game.

Win, lose or no-hitter, the Texas Rangers' living legend works out for 20 minutes on a stationary bike after every pitching outing. It's part of a regimen Ryan has followed for years to maintain strength in his legs.

The all-time strikeout leader and unparalleled no-hit king credits his overall conditioning as the reason he's throwing no-hitters at age 44. It takes more than skill to remain a viable force against hitters who weren't even born when Ryan started his pitching career—it takes stamina.

So Ryan maintains a competitive edge by making sure he is exceptionally fit. His training regimen is designed for overall conditioning and flexibility. Among other workouts, he lifts weights,

rides a stationary bike, runs in a pool, hikes up stairs and runs sideways drills.

How Ryan 'rests'

▸Day 1 (the day after he pitches): Running, aerobics, strength training. His heaviest workout is the day after he pitches. The strength training for his legs, as described in his book Nolan Ryan's Pitcher's Bible: Three sets—12 repetitions per set—of squats (which he says are a must for a pitcher), step-ups, lunges, leg extensions, leg curls and toe raises. Some are done with free weights, others on a weight-training machine.

One typical exercise: the lunge. With a weight bar across the back of his shoulders, Ryan lunges forward, bending his lead knee and lowering his back knee almost to the floor. He brings his legs back—feet together—then repeats, leading with the other leg.
▸Day 2: Running and aerobics. Ryan does outfield sprints and distance running (foul line to foul line along the outfield warning track). Aerobics augment his cardiovascular conditioning.
▸Day 3: Strength training (legs) and running or aerobics. Ryan does strength training for his legs two days later—the third day after he pitches.
▸Day 4: Stretching.
▸Day 5 (the day he pitches again): Pregame strength training. Ryan does a single set with very little weight. He runs sprints for five minutes before beginning his warm-ups in the bullpen.
▸In the offseason: Weight training and running/aerobics three times a week.

Texas hit list trio: Franco, Sierra, Palmeiro

The Rangers' big three—Julio Franco, Ruben Sierra and Rafael Palmeiro—put Texas among the top American League hitters in nine out of 12 offensive categories for 1991. The deeper you go, the more Rangers you see.

▶Batting: First, Franco (.341); seventh, Palmeiro (.322).
▶RBI: Third, Sierra (116); seventh, Gonzales (102).
▶Doubles: First, Palmeiro (49); third, Sierra (44).
▶Runs: Third, Palmeiro (115).
▶Hits: Third, Palmeiro (203) and Sierra (203); fourth, Franco (201).
▶Stolen bases: Sixth, Franco (36).
▶Total bases: Third, Palmeiro (336); fourth, Sierra (332).
▶On-base percentage: Fourth, Franco (.408).
▶Slugging percentage: Fifth, Palmeiro (.532).

Julio Franco's 1991 numbers

It was no big surprise that the Rangers' heavy lumber produced the American League batting champion. But Franco did a lot more than hit for average.

▶Games: 146
▶At-bats: 589
▶Batting average: .341
▶On-base percentage: .408
▶Slugging percentage: .474
▶Hits: 201
▶Runs scored: 108
▶Total bases: 279
▶Doubles: 27
▶Triples: 3
▶Home runs: 15
▶Runs batted in: 78
▶Walks: 65
▶Stolen bases: 36

Team directory

▶Owner: George W. Bush and Edward W. Rose

▶General Manager: Thomas A. Grieve

▶Ballpark:
Arlington Stadium
1700 Copeland Road, Arlington, Texas
817-273-5100
Capacity 43,521
Parking for 10,000 vehicles; $5
Public transportation available
Family and wheelchair sections, ramps

▶Team publications:
On Deck Newsletter, Yearbook, Program Magazine
817-273-5222

▶TV, radio broadcast stations:
WBAP-AM 820, KTVT-TV 11, Home Sports Entertainment

▶Camps and/or clinics:
Texas Ranger Coaches Clinic, June 5-7 and 19-21
817-273-5222

▶Spring Training:
Charlotte County Stadium
Port Charlotte, Florida
Capacity 6,026
817-625-9500

TEXAS RANGERS 1991 Final Stats

Batting	AVG	SLG	OB	G	AB	R	H	TB	2B	3B	HR	RBI	BB	SO	SB	CS	E
Harris	.375	.750	.444	18	8	4	3	6	0	0	1	2	1	3	1	0	0
Franco	.341	.474	.408	146	589	108	201	279	27	3	15	78	65	78	36	9	14
Palmeiro	.322	.532	.389	159	631	115	203	336	49	3	26	88	68	72	4	3	12
Sierra	.307	.502	.357	161	661	110	203	332	44	5	25	116	56	91	16	4	7
Downing	.278	.455	.377	123	407	76	113	185	17	2	17	49	58	70	1	1	0
Petralli	.271	.352	.339	87	199	21	54	70	8	1	2	20	21	25	2	1	11
Reimer	.269	.477	.332	136	394	46	106	188	22	0	20	69	33	93	0	3	6
Buechele	.267	.447	.335	121	416	58	111	186	17	2	18	66	39	69	0	4	3
Rodriguez	.264	.354	.276	88	280	24	74	99	16	0	3	27	5	42	0	1	10
Gonzalez	.264	.479	.321	142	545	78	144	261	34	1	27	102	42	118	4	4	6
Diaz	.264	.319	.318	96	182	24	48	58	7	0	1	22	15	18	0	1	7
Fariss	.258	.387	.395	19	31	6	8	12	1	0	1	6	7	11	0	0	0
Stanley	.249	.381	.372	95	181	25	45	69	13	1	3	25	34	44	0	0	6
Pettis	.216	.277	.341	137	282	37	61	78	7	5	0	19	54	91	29	13	6
Huson	.213	.287	.312	119	268	36	57	77	8	3	2	26	39	32	8	3	15
Daugherty	.194	.264	.270	58	144	8	28	38	3	2	1	11	16	23	1	0	1
Palmer	.187	.403	.281	81	268	38	50	108	9	2	15	37	32	98	0	2	9
Hernandez	.184	.224	.208	45	98	8	18	22	2	1	0	4	3	31	0	1	4
Green	.150	.200	.190	8	20	0	3	4	1	0	0	1	1	6	0	0	1
Jo. Russell	.111	.111	.138	22	27	3	3	3	0	0	0	1	1	7	0	0	0
Walling	.091	.114	.184	24	44	1	4	5	1	0	0	2	3	8	0	0	1
Maurer	.063	.125	.211	13	16	0	1	2	1	0	0	2	2	6	0	0	0
Kreuter	.000	.000	.000	3	4	0	0	0	0	0	0	0	0	1	0	0	0
Parent	.000	.000	.000	3	1	0	0	0	0	0	0	0	0	1	0	0	0
Scruggs	.000	.000	.000	5	6	1	0	0	0	0	0	0	0	1	0	0	0
Capra	–	–	1.000	2	0	1	0	0	0	0	0	0	1	0	0	0	0

Pitching	W-L	ERA	G	GS	CG	GF	Sho	SV	IP	H	R	ER	HR	BB	SO
Manuel	1-0	1.13	8	0	0	5	0	0	16	7	2	2	0	6	5
Ryan	12-6	2.91	27	27	2	0	2	0	173	102	58	56	12	72	203
Guzman	13-7	3.08	25	25	5	0	1	0	169.2	152	67	58	10	84	125
Je. Russell	6-4	3.29	68	0	0	56	0	30	79.1	71	36	29	11	26	52
Nolte	0-0	3.38	3	0	0	2	0	0	2.2	3	1	1	0	3	1
Gossage	4-2	3.57	44	0	0	16	0	1	40.1	33	16	16	4	16	28
Mathews	4-0	3.61	34	2	0	8	0	1	57.1	54	24	23	5	18	51
Chiamparino	1-0	4.03	5	5	0	0	0	0	22.1	26	11	10	1	12	8
Brown	9-12	4.40	33	33	0	0	0	0	210.2	233	116	103	17	90	96
Barfield	4-4	4.54	28	9	0	4	0	1	83.1	96	51	42	11	22	27
Jeffcoat	5-3	4.63	70	0	0	21	0	1	79.2	104	46	41	8	25	43
Bohanon	4-3	4.84	11	11	1	0	0	0	61.1	66	35	33	4	23	34
Alexander	5-3	5.24	30	9	0	4	0	0	89.1	93	56	52	11	48	50
Rosenthal	1-4	5.25	36	0	0	8	0	1	70.1	72	43	41	9	36	61
Rogers	10-10	5.42	63	9	0	20	0	5	109.2	121	80	66	14	61	73
Fajardo	0-2	5.68	4	3	0	1	0	0	19	25	13	12	2	4	15
Witt	3-7	6.09	17	16	1	0	1	0	88.2	84	66	60	4	74	82
Boyd	2-7	6.68	12	12	0	0	0	0	62	81	47	46	12	17	33
Bitker	1-0	6.75	9	0	0	2	0	0	14.2	17	11	11	4	8	16
Arnsberg	0-1	8.38	9	0	0	2	0	0	9.2	10	9	9	5	5	8
Schiraldi	0-1	11.57	3	0	0	1	0	0	4.2	5	6	6	3	5	1
Petkovsek	0-1	14.46	4	1	0	1	0	0	9.1	21	16	15	4	4	6

1992 Preliminary Roster

Pitchers (15)
Gerald Alexander
John Barfield
Brian Bohanon
Kevin Brown
Scott Chiamparino
Hector Fajardo
Jose Guzman
Barry Manuel
Terry Mathews
Robb Nen
Roger Pavlik
Kenny Rogers
Jeff Russell
Nolan Ryan
Bobby Witt

Catchers (3)
Bill Haselman
Geno Petralli
Ivan Rodriguez

Infielders (11)
Cris Colon
Monty Fariss
Julio Franco
Jeff Frye
Jose Hernandez
Jeff Huson
Jeff Kunkel
Rob Maurer
Jose Oliva
Rafael Palmeiro
Dean Palmer

Outfielders (8)
Jack Daugherty
Brian Downing
Juan Gonzalez
Donald Harris
Dan Peltier
Gary Pettis
Kevin Reimer
Ruben Sierra

Games played by position

	G	C	1B	2B	3B	SS	OF	DH
Buechele,S	121	0	0	13	111	4	0	0
Capra,N	2	0	0	0	0	0	2	0
Daugherty,J	58	0	11	0	0	0	37	1
Diaz,M	96	0	0	20	8	65	0	1
Downing,B	123	0	0	0	0	0	0	109
Fariss,M	19	0	0	4	0	0	8	4
Franco,Ju	146	0	0	146	0	0	0	0
Gonzalez,Ju	142	0	0	0	0	0	136	4
Green,G	8	0	0	0	0	8	0	0
Harris,D	18	0	0	0	0	0	12	3
Hernandez,J	45	0	0	0	1	44	0	0
Huson,J	119	0	0	2	1	116	0	0
Kreuter,C	3	1	0	0	0	0	0	0
Maurer,R	13	0	4	0	0	0	0	2
Palmeiro,R	159	0	157	0	0	0	0	2
Palmer,D	81	0	0	0	50	0	29	5
Parent,M	3	3	0	0	0	0	0	0
Petralli,G	87	66	0	0	7	0	0	5
Pettis,G	137	0	0	0	0	0	126	3
Reimer,K	136	0	0	0	0	0	66	56
Rodriguez,I	88	88	0	0	0	0	0	0
Russell,Jo	22	5	0	0	0	0	8	5
Scruggs,T	5	0	0	0	0	0	5	0
Sierra,R	161	0	0	0	0	0	161	0
Stanley,M	95	58	12	0	6	0	1	6
Walling,D	24	0	0	0	14	0	5	0

Sick call: 1991 DL report

Player	Days on the DL
Mark Parent	151
Jeff Kunkel	182
Brian Bohanon	84
Juan Gonzalez	18
Gary Green	39
Denny Walling	21
John Russell	70*
Brad Arnsberg	149*
Nolan Ryan	34*
Bobby Witt	66
Scott Chiamparino	134
Jack Daugherty	86*
Geno Petralli	40
Rich Gossage	51*
Mario Diaz	17
John Barfield	67
Jeff Huson	23
Gerald Alexander	28

On DL twice (not counting administrative transfers from one DL to another).

◆ 253

Minor League Report

Class AAA — Oklahoma City went 52-92 to finish last in the Western Division of the American Association. They did, however, post their second highest yearly attendance ever: 347,427. The highest yearly attendance was 1985, when the '89ers drew 364,247.3B Dean Palmer won the American Association home run title with 22, despite the fact that he was called up to the Texas Rangers on June 25 and remained there for the rest of the season. 1B Rob Maurer and DH/1B Steve Balboni each had 20 home runs.Palmer and 1B Rob Maurer were both voted to the American Association All-Star team, and Maurer, who had 20 HRs, was also American Association Rookie of the Year. An Oklahoma City player won the award for the second year in a row, Juan Gonzalez having won in 1990.SS Monty Fariss was voted to the Triple-A All-Star Team. A total of 26 players donned uniforms for both Oklahoma City and the Texas Rangers this year.... **Class AA** — Tulsa was 58-78 on the season, finishing tied for third in the Texas League's Eastern Division in both the first and second half. The team set an all-time attendance record for professional baseball in Tulsa — dating back to 1905 — of 260,864. They averaged 4,208 per game.C Ivan Rodriguez was named to the Texas League All-Star team. 2B Jeff Frye was ninth in the league in batting average, and led the team in that category, as well as in doubles (32), triples (11), walks (71) and stolen bases (15). He had 152 hits, one short of the franchise record.RH reliever Barry Manuel led the Texas League with 25 saves, also a franchise record. ... **Class A** — Gastonia finished with a record of 69-73, tied for third in the Northern Division of the South Atlantic League in the first half, and third again in the second half. 1B David Lowery led the team in both batting average (.294) and stolen bases (31). RF Marty Posey was the team's big slugger, with 11 home runs and 60 RBI. The top pitcher was LHP Terry Burrows (12 wins, 151 strikeouts), and the top reliever was RHP Matt Whiteside (29 saves). ... Port Charlotte was 62-70

on the season, third in the Western Division of the Florida State League for the first half of the season and fourth in the second half.

Tops in the Organization

BATTING LEADERS	Club	Avg.	G	AB	R	H	HR	RBI
Jeff Frye	Tul	.302	131	503	92	152	4	41
Rob Maurer	Okc	.301	132	459	76	138	20	77
Rusty Greer	Tul	.294	131	452	64	133	8	60
David Lowery	Gas	.294	133	507	55	149	9	49
Dan Rohrmeier	Tul	.292	121	418	67	122	5	62

HOME RUNS		
Dean Palmer	Okc	22
Steve Balboni	Okc	20
Rob Maurer	Okc	20
Jose Oliva	Chl	14
Monty Fariss	Okc	13

RBI		
Rob Maurer	Okc	77
Monty Fariss	Okc	73
Steve Balboni	Okc	63
Dan Rohrmeier	Tul	62
Several players tied		60

STOLEN BASES		
David Hulse	Chl	44
Timmie Morrow	Chl	33
David Lowery	Gas	31
Nick Capra	Okc	27
Ken Powell	Chl	19

WINS		
Christopher Gies	Tul	12
Terry Burrows	Gas	12
Jon Hurst	Tul	10
Several players tied		9

SAVES		
Matt Whiteside	Gas	29
Barry Manuel	Tul	25
Johnny Maldonado	Chl	14
Barry Goetz	Chl	12
Joe Bitker	Okc	7

STRIKEOUTS		
Terry Burrows	Gas	151
Christopher Gies	Tul	149
Nick Felix	Tul	135
Travis Buckley	Chl	131
Steve Dreyer	Gas	122

PITCHING LEADERS	Club	W-L	ERA	IP	H	BB	SO
Steve Dreyer	Gas	7-10	2.33	162	137	62	122
Jon Hurst	Tul	10-3	2.75	124	107	37	108
Christopher Gies	Tul	12-5	3.02	176	173	33	149
Mike Arner	Chl	8-8	3.17	145	112	44	96
Travis Buckley	Chl	8-9	3.23	128	115	67	131

Texas (1972-1991), incl. Washington (1961-1971)

Runs: Most, career, all-time

631	Toby Harrah, 1969-1986
544	Frank Howard, 1965-1972
505	RUBEN SIERRA, 1986-1991
482	Jim Sundberg, 1974-1989
471	Buddy Bell, 1979-1989

Hits: Most, career, all-time

1180	Jim Sundberg, 1974-1989
1174	Toby Harrah, 1969-1986
1141	Frank Howard, 1965-1972
1060	Buddy Bell, 1979-1989
993	RUBEN SIERRA, 1986-1991

2B: Most, career, all-time

200	Jim Sundberg, 1974-1989
197	Buddy Bell, 1979-1989
196	RUBEN SIERRA, 1986-1991
187	Toby Harrah, 1969-1986
161	PETE O'BRIEN, 1982-1988

3B: Most, career, all-time

37	RUBEN SIERRA, 1986-1991
30	Chuck Hinton, 1961-1964
27	Ed Brinkman, 1961-1975
27	Jim Sundberg, 1974-1989
24	Ed Stroud, 1967-1970

HR: Most, career, all-time

246	Frank Howard, 1965-1972
149	Larry Parrish, 1982-1988
139	RUBEN SIERRA, 1986-1991
124	Toby Harrah, 1969-1986
124	PETE INCAVIGLIA, 1986-1990

RBI: Most, career, all-time

701	Frank Howard, 1965-1972
586	RUBEN SIERRA, 1986-1991
568	Toby Harrah, 1969-1986
522	Larry Parrish, 1982-1988
499	Buddy Bell, 1979-1989

SB: Most, career, all-time

161	Bump Wills, 1977-1981
153	Toby Harrah, 1969-1986
144	Dave Nelson, 1970-1975
115	Oddibe McDowell, 1985-1988
92	Chuck Hinton, 1961-1964
92	Bill Sample, 1978-1984

BB: Most, career, all-time

708	Toby Harrah, 1969-1986
575	Frank Howard, 1965-1972
544	Jim Sundberg, 1974-1989
435	Mike Hargrove, 1974-1978
404	PETE O'BRIEN, 1982-1988

BA: Highest, career, all-time

.319	Al Oliver, 1978-1981
.303	Mickey Rivers, 1979-1984
.293	Mike Hargrove, 1974-1978
.293	Buddy Bell, 1979-1989
.280	RUBEN SIERRA, 1986-1991

Slug avg: Highest, career, all-time

.503	Frank Howard, 1965-1972
.474	RUBEN SIERRA, 1986-1991
.466	Al Oliver, 1978-1981
.459	PETE INCAVIGLIA, 1986-1990
.454	Larry Parrish, 1982-1988

Games started: Most, career, all-time

313	CHARLIE HOUGH, 1980-1990
190	Fergie Jenkins, 1974-1981
157	BOBBY WITT, 1986-1991
155	Dick Bosman, 1966-1973
123	Joe Coleman, 1965-1970

Saves: Most, career, all-time

83	Ron Kline, 1963-1966
83	JEFF RUSSELL, 1985-1991
64	Darold Knowles, 1967-1977
37	Jim Kern, 1979-1981
35	Steve Foucault, 1973-1976

Shutouts: Most, career, all-time

17	Fergie Jenkins, 1974-1981
12	Gaylord Perry, 1975-1980
11	CHARLIE HOUGH, 1980-1990
9	Dick Bosman, 1966-1973
8	Jim Bibby, 1973-1984

Wins: Most, career, all-time

139	CHARLIE HOUGH, 1980-1990
93	Fergie Jenkins, 1974-1981
59	Dick Bosman, 1966-1973
59	BOBBY WITT, 1986-1991
53	DANNY DARWIN, 1978-1984

K: Most, career, all-time

1452	CHARLIE HOUGH, 1980-1990
951	BOBBY WITT, 1986-1991
895	Fergie Jenkins, 1974-1981
736	NOLAN RYAN, 1989-1991
575	Gaylord Perry, 1975-1980

Win pct: Highest, career, all-time

.621	NOLAN RYAN, 1989-1991
.564	Fergie Jenkins, 1974-1981
.538	Doc Medich, 1978-1982
.531	CHARLIE HOUGH, 1980-1990
.527	Gaylord Perry, 1975-1980

ERA: Lowest, career, all-time

3.26	Gaylord Perry, 1975-1980
3.35	Dick Bosman, 1966-1973
3.41	Jon Matlack, 1978-1983
3.51	Joe Coleman, 1965-1970
3.56	Fergie Jenkins, 1974-1981

Runs: Most, season

115	RAFAEL PALMEIRO, 1991
111	Frank Howard, 1969
110	RUBEN SIERRA, 1991
108	JULIO FRANCO, 1991
105	Oddibe McDowell, 1986

Hits: Most, season

210	Mickey Rivers, 1980
209	Al Oliver, 1980
203	RAFAEL PALMEIRO, 1991
203	RUBEN SIERRA, 1991
201	JULIO FRANCO, 1991

2B: Most, season

49	RAFAEL PALMEIRO, 1991
44	RUBEN SIERRA, 1991
43	Al Oliver, 1980
42	Buddy Bell, 1979
42	Larry Parrish, 1984

3B: Most, season

14	RUBEN SIERRA, 1989
12	Chuck Hinton, 1963
10	RUBEN SIERRA, 1986
10	Ed Stroud, 1968
9	Ed Brinkman, 1966
9	Marty Keough, 1961

HR: Most, season

48	Frank Howard, 1969
44	Frank Howard, 1968
44	Frank Howard, 1970

254

36   Frank Howard, 1967
32   Larry Parrish, 1987

RBI: Most, season

126   Frank Howard, 1970
119   RUBEN SIERRA, 1989
118   Jeff Burroughs, 1974
117   Al Oliver, 1980
116   RUBEN SIERRA, 1991

SB: Most, season

52   Bump Wills, 1978
51   Dave Nelson, 1972
45   CECIL ESPY, 1989
44   Bill Sample, 1983
43   Dave Nelson, 1973

BB: Most, season

132   Frank Howard, 1970
113   Toby Harrah, 1985
109   Toby Harrah, 1977
107   Mike Hargrove, 1978
103   Mike Hargrove, 1977

BA: Highest, season

.341 JULIO FRANCO, 1991
.333 Mickey Rivers, 1980
.329 Buddy Bell, 1980
.324 Al Oliver, 1978
.323 Al Oliver, 1979

Slug avg: Highest, season

.574 Frank Howard, 1969
.552 Frank Howard, 1968
.546 Frank Howard, 1970
.543 RUBEN SIERRA, 1989
.533 RAFAEL PALMEIRO, 1991

Games started: Most, season

41   Jim Bibby, 1974
41   Fergie Jenkins, 1974
40   CHARLIE HOUGH, 1987
37   Fergie Jenkins, 1975
37   Fergie Jenkins, 1979

Saves: Most, season

38   JEFF RUSSELL, 1989
30   JEFF RUSSELL, 1991
29   Jim Kern, 1979
29   Ron Kline, 1965
27   Darold Knowles, 1970

Shutouts: Most, season

6   Bert Blyleven, 1976
6   Fergie Jenkins, 1974
5   Jim Bibby, 1974
5   Bert Blyleven, 1977
4   Joe Coleman, 1969

4   Fergie Jenkins, 1975
4   Fergie Jenkins, 1978
4   Camilo Pascual, 1968
4   Gaylord Perry, 1975
4   Gaylord Perry, 1977

Wins: Most, season

25   Fergie Jenkins, 1974
19   Jim Bibby, 1974
18   CHARLIE HOUGH, 1987
18   Fergie Jenkins, 1978
17   Doyle Alexander, 1977
17   Steve Comer, 1979
17   CHARLIE HOUGH, 1986
17   Fergie Jenkins, 1975
17   BOBBY WITT, 1990

K: Most, season

301   NOLAN RYAN, 1989
232   NOLAN RYAN, 1990
225   Fergie Jenkins, 1974
223   CHARLIE HOUGH, 1987
221   BOBBY WITT, 1990

Win pct: Highest, season

.692 Fergie Jenkins, 1978
.676 Fergie Jenkins, 1974
.630 CHARLIE HOUGH, 1986
.630 BOBBY WITT, 1990
.615 NOLAN RYAN, 1989

ERA: Lowest, season

2.19 Dick Bosman, 1969
2.27 Jon Matlack, 1978
2.40 Dick Donovan, 1961
2.42 RICK HONEYCUTT, 1983
2.60 Pete Richert, 1965

Most pinch-hit homers, season

3   Don Lock, Was-1966
3   Brant Alyea, Was-1969
3   Rick Reichardt, Was-1970
3   Tom McCraw, Was-1971
3   Darrell Porter, 1987

Most pinch-hit, homers, career

6   Brant Alyea, Was-1965-1969
5   Geno Petralli, 1985-1991

Most consecutive games, batting safely

24   Mickey Rivers, 1980

Most consecutive scoreless innings

36   Charlie Hough, 1983

No hit games

Jim Bibby, Tex at Oak AL, 6-0; July 20, 1973.
Bert Blyleven, Tex at Cal AL, 6-0; September 22, 1977.
Nolan Ryan, Tex at Oak AL, 5-0; June 11, 1990.
Nolan Ryan, Tex vs Tor AL, 3-0; May 1, 1991.

Even Jose Canseco's 44 home runs couldn't pull Oakland out of its slump.

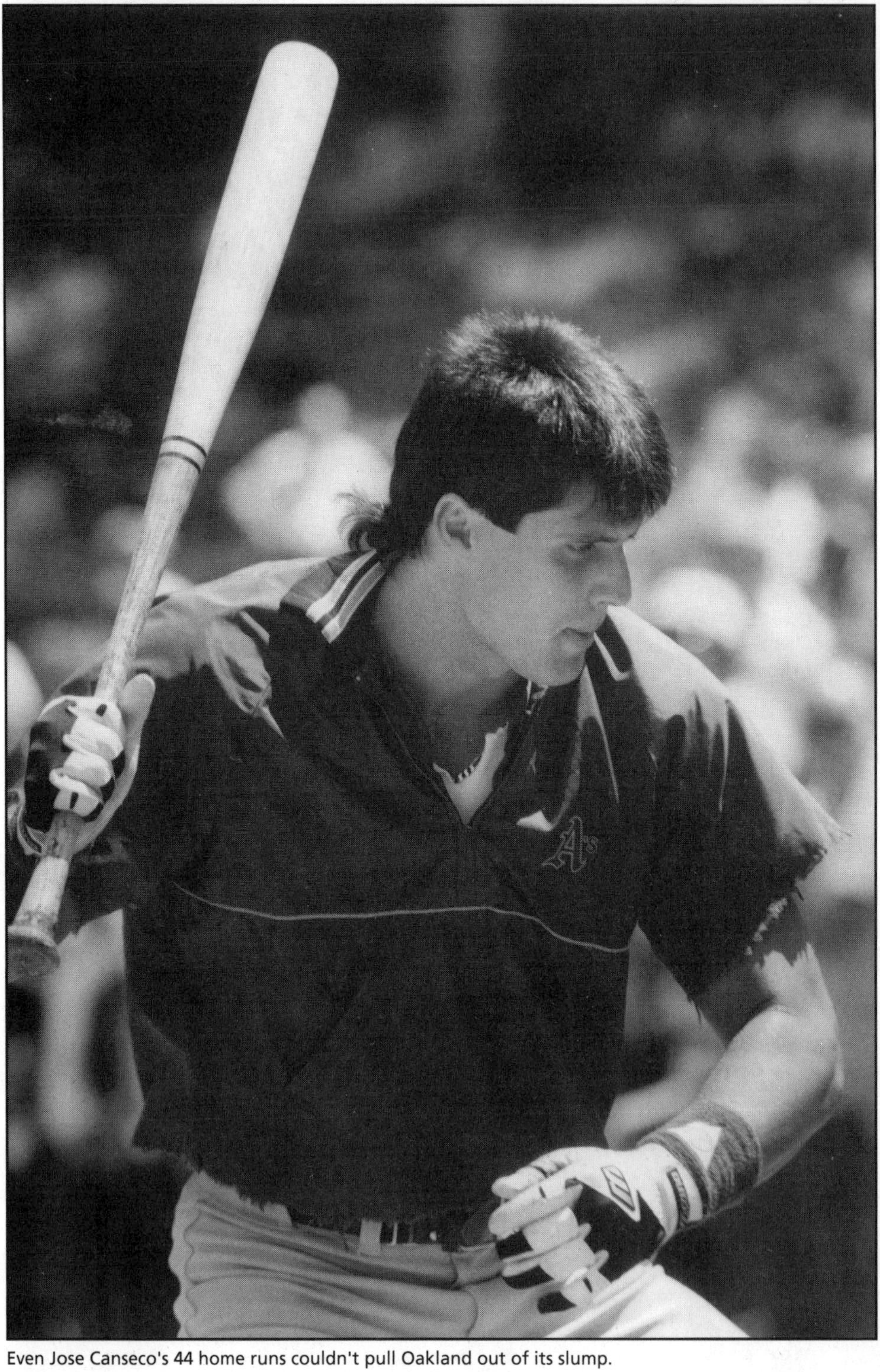

Pitching collapse deflates champs

Even with three consecutive American League championships, three of the last five Rookies of the Year and two of the last three Most Valuable Players, chinks were beginning to show in the Oakland Athletics' armor.

Before the '91 season got into full swing:

▶Carney Lansford, a valuable leader in the clubhouse, was out for the year after being injured in a freak offseason snowmobiling accident.

▶Former MVP Jose Canseco had a questionable back.

▶Former MVP Rickey Henderson was a disruptive force in spring training with his contract demands.

Still, the A's were expected to continue their domination and win their fourth consecutive pennant. But the preseason concerns—along with other unanticipated flaws—were too much for Oakland to overcome. The A's finished fourth, 11 games out of first.

One unexpected collapse was the pitching. The staff which led the league in ERA the previous season dropped to next-to-last. Only Mike Moore and Dennis Eckersley had ERAs below 4.00 among Oakland pitchers with more than 50 innings.

Dave Stewart's string of 20-win seasons was snapped at four. He was 11-11 and his ERA ballooned to 5.18. Bob Welch won 27 games and the Cy Young Award in 1990, but he finished at 12-13 in '91.

Mike Moore emerged as the A's most reliable pitcher, rebounding from a sub-.500 campaign in 1990 with a 17-8 record and 2.96 ERA. Ace reliever Dennis Eckersley again posted strong numbers (43 saves, 2.96), but was much more vulnerable than in 1990 .

Canseco was Oakland's only former Rookie of the Year who didn't have a disappointing season. Canseco tied Cecil Fielder with a major-league leading 44 homers, and added 122 RBI.

But fellow bash brother Mark McGwire had his worst offensive season, batting .201 with a career-low 22 homers. Shortstop Walt Weiss missed the final four months of the season with an ankle injury. His absence—along with Lansford's—made the infield unstable.

A familiar sight was Rickey Henderson leading the league in stolen bases, the 11th time in his 13-year career. Henderson became baseball's all-time leading thief May 1, when he surpassed Lou Brock's record of 938. Henderson ended the season with 58 swipes, for a career total of 994.

Another bright spot was the continued improvement of Mike Gallego, who established himself an everyday second baseman—.247 average and career-high 12 homers—before declaring himself as a free agent.

—Deron Snyder

Athletics 1992 preview

Can the A's rise from the ashes this year? Two big questions persist in Oakland, where the three-time American League champions' reign came to an abrupt end.

First, what will happen with Mark McGwire? The big first baseman's average has dropped steadily from .289 his Rookie of the Year season in 1987 to a meager .201 last year. The club kept him out of the lineup the final week so he wouldn't plummet below .200. He also hit less than 30 home runs for the first time in his major-league career.

Second, who plays third base? Carney Lansford may never be the same after his snowmobile ride two winters ago, and a committee of Vance Law, Ernest Riles and Brook Jacoby wasn't the answer last season.

Finally, what happened to pitchers Dave Stewart, Bob Welch and Dennis Eckersley? Was 1991 an aberration, or the first step on the backside of the hill?

Maybe the whole thing was a bad dream.

258

1992 prophecy: Athletics

▸The A's will lose six of eight games on a road trip in May and pack it in for the year.
▸Mark McGwire will go on the Tommy Lasorda diet and slim down to 180 pounds in an effort to hit his weight.

—John Hunt

Million-dollar debut

Although the Oakland A's claim that Todd Van Poppel's first major league start last September was merely a way to give struggling former Cy Young winner Bob Welch a day off, there is little doubt that the ballclub expects big things—and soon—from their million-dollar phenom.

Van Poppel must make the 25-man big league roster by opening day 1993, or the A's will have run out of options and Van Poppel would have to clear waivers or be sent to the minors.

The young right-hander had an auspicious start—striking out five of the first six batters he faced and carrying a no-hitter and a 1-0 lead into the fourth inning. But the Chicago White Sox caught up with him, batting around for five runs.

Thanks to Jose Canseco's 38th home run of a 44-homer season, Van Poppel wasn't tagged with a loss. He allowed five runs and seven hits, and struck out six before calling it a day.

La Russa can't wait to win again

By Tim Wendel

When his club was labeled a budding dynasty and he was nicknamed the "Mastermind" and popularized in a national best-seller, A's manager Tony La Russa never stepped forward to accept such accolades because he knew a season like 1991 was coming.

"The reason you never saw me jumping up and making any big claims about anything is that I know how humbling this game can be," said La Russa. "And I know how fragile that line of winning games can be. You can get on the wrong side of that line very easily."

The season of discontent gave La Russa greater satisfaction for what his team accomplished over the last three years.

"I'm really proud of '88, and even prouder of '89 and '90 . . . this year we just (weren't) good enough," said the skipper of the three-time American League champions.

La Russa believes that his "nucleus of the last five years" will still be there in 1992, more hungry than ever.

"Once you win, you can't wait to win again," he said at the end of the season. "I wish spring training was starting tomorrow."

Home run king loves Toronto's SkyDome

Many observers have agreed that if Jose Canseco can hit 44 home runs playing home games in the Coliseum, the sky would be the limit if he played in Toronto.

Canseco loves Toronto, and he believes the feeling is mutual.

"The fans love me (there)," Canseco said. "I don't want to disappoint them. Actually, the fans in Oakland are a lot more abusive towards me than they are in Toronto. . . It's always tougher to be booed at home."

Since the SkyDome opened, Canseco has hit over .360 there, with an armload of homers that include a 500-foot drive into the top deck in left field in the 1989 playoffs and a shot off a restaurant roof in center field.

"I love hitting (there)," Canseco said. "I love to take advantage of the good visibility and the fact that the ball carries well. The SkyDome is definitely my favorite place to hit."

After Canseco publicly praised the

Toronto fans and criticized his home fans, some of his Oakland faithful appeared at the Coliseum—long known as a "pitcher's park" because of the massive foul territory—with signs begging him to stay in town.

Will the American League home-run champ move to Toronto when his four-year contract with Oakland expires?

"Nope," said Canseco. "Too many taxes."

Jamie Quirk does it all

Jamie Quirk, the A's quintessential utilityman, has caught and played every infield and outfield position during his 17-year career.

Last season marked his second go-round with Oakland, after previous stops in Kansas City, Milwaukee, St. Louis, Chicago (White Sox), Cleveland, New York (Yankees) and Baltimore.

In 1991, 37-year-old Quirk played in 76 games—starting 49 behind the plate—and continued his overall improvement offensively. Quirk has said that he learned to catch after he was advised that a good catcher would never be out of a job. Without that skill, he remarked, he doubted if he would have been in the major leagues for 17 years.

A's winter league news

▶Winter leagues: OF Marco Armas, the younger brother of former Oakland and Boston OF Tony Armas, returned home to Venezuela to play for Caribes de Oriente. Armas hit .226 with 8 HRs and 53 RBI for Class AA Huntsville. . . C Troy Afenir, OF Eric Fox and IF Scott Hemond, who all played for Class AAA Tacoma in 1991, fine-tuned their games for the Santurce Crabbers (Puerto Rico) in hopes of making the jump to Oakland in spring training. Afenir hit .244 with 10 HRs and 38 RBI last season. Fox, who was a member of the 1983 and 1985 U.S. baseball teams that participated in the Pan American

games, hit .270 with 4 HRs and 52 RBI; Hemond hit .272 with 3 HRs and 31 RBI.

▶Winter leagues roster: Marco Armas, OF, Caribes de Oriente, Venezuela; Troy Afenir, C, Santurce Crabbers, Puerto Rico; Jorge Brito, C, Leones (Lions)Escogido, D.R.; Eric Fox, OF, Santurce Crabbers, Puerto Rico; Johnny Guzman, LHP, Aguilas Cibaeƒna (Eagles) D.R.; Scott Hemond, IF, Santurce Crabbers, Puerto Rico; Francisco Matos, SS, Aguilas Cibaeƒna, D.R.; Henry Mercedes, C, Azucareros Este (Sugarmen), D.R.; Wilfredo Tejada, C, Leones (Lions) Escogido, D.R.

Team directory

▶Owner: Walter A. Haas, Jr.

▶General Manager: Sandy Alderson

▶Ballpark:
Oakland Coliseum
Nimitz Freeway & Hegenberger Road, Oakland, California
510-568-5600
Capacity 47,313
Parking for 10,000 vehicles; $5
Public transportation available
Wheelchair section and ramps, picnic area

▶Team publications:
A's Magazine
510-638-4900, ext. 326

▶TV, radio broadcast stations:
KSFO 560 AM, KPIX Channel 5, KICU-TV Channel 36, SportsChannel

▶Camps and/or clinics:
Fantasy Camp and Youth Baseball Camp, 415-215-1000

▶Spring Training:
Phoenix Municipal Stadium
Phoenix, Arizona
Capacity 8,500
602-392-0074

OAKLAND ATHLETICS 1991 Final Stats

Batting	AVG	SLG	OB	G	AB	R	H	TB	2B	3B	HR	RBI	BB	SO	SB	CS	E
Baines	.295	.473	.383	141	488	76	144	231	25	1	20	90	72	67	0	1	1
D. Henderson	.276	.465	.346	150	572	86	158	266	33	0	25	85	58	113	6	6	1
Steinbach	.274	.386	.312	129	456	50	125	176	31	1	6	67	22	70	2	2	15
R. Henderson	.268	.423	.400	134	470	105	126	199	17	1	18	57	98	73	58	18	8
Canseco	.266	.556	.359	154	572	115	152	318	32	1	44	122	78	152	26	6	9
Quirk	.261	.296	.321	76	203	16	53	60	4	0	1	17	16	28	0	3	6
Blankenship	.249	.341	.336	90	185	33	46	63	8	0	3	21	23	42	12	3	3
Gallego	.247	.369	.343	159	482	67	119	178	15	4	12	49	67	84	6	9	12
Bordick	.238	.268	.289	90	235	21	56	63	5	1	0	21	14	37	3	4	11
Wilson	.238	.313	.290	113	294	38	70	92	14	4	0	28	18	43	20	5	3
Brosius	.235	.397	.268	36	68	9	16	27	5	0	2	4	3	11	3	1	0
Weiss	.226	.286	.286	40	133	15	30	38	6	1	0	13	12	14	6	0	5
Jacoby	.224	.308	.274	122	419	28	94	129	21	1	4	44	27	54	2	1	7
Hemond	.217	.217	.250	23	23	4	5	5	0	0	0	0	1	7	1	2	1
Riles	.214	.324	.290	108	281	30	60	91	8	4	5	32	31	42	3	2	11
Law	.209	.276	.303	74	134	11	28	37	7	1	0	9	18	27	0	0	5
McGwire	.201	.383	.330	154	483	62	97	185	22	0	22	75	93	116	2	1	4
Howitt	.167	.262	.182	21	42	5	7	11	1	0	1	3	1	12	0	0	0
Manrique	.143	.143	.217	9	21	2	3	3	0	0	0	0	2	1	0	0	1
Komminsk	.120	.160	.185	24	25	1	3	4	1	0	0	2	2	9	1	0	0
Jennings	.111	.111	.273	8	9	0	1	1	0	0	0	0	2	2	0	1	0
Afenir	.091	.091	.091	5	11	0	1	1	0	0	0	0	0	2	0	0	0
Lansford	.063	.063	.063	5	16	0	1	1	0	0	0	1	0	2	0	0	0
Witmeyer	.053	.053	.053	11	19	0	1	1	0	0	0	0	0	5	0	0	0

Pitching	W-L	ERA	G	GS	CG	GF	Sho	SV	IP	H	R	ER	HR	BB	SO
Law	0-0	0.00	1	0	0	1	0	0	.2	1	0	0	0	1	0
Campbell	1-0	2.74	14	0	0	2	0	0	23	13	7	7	4	14	16
Moore	17-8	2.96	33	33	3	0	1	0	210	176	75	69	11	105	153
Eckersley	5-4	2.96	67	0	0	59	0	43	76	60	26	25	11	9	87
Burns	1-0	3.38	9	0	0	5	0	0	13.1	10	5	5	2	8	3
Honeycutt	2-4	3.58	43	0	0	7	0	0	37.2	37	16	15	3	20	26
Darling	3-7	4.08	12	12	0	0	0	0	75	64	34	34	7	38	60
Chitren	1-4	4.33	56	0	0	20	0	4	60.1	59	31	29	8	32	47
Klink	10-3	4.35	62	0	0	10	0	2	62	60	30	30	4	21	34
Welch	12-13	4.58	35	35	7	0	1	0	220	220	124	112	25	91	101
Young	4-2	5.00	41	1	0	6	0	0	68.1	74	38	38	8	34	27
Stewart	11-11	5.18	35	35	2	0	1	0	226	245	135	130	24	105	144
Slusarski	5-7	5.27	20	19	1	0	0	0	109.1	121	69	64	14	52	60
Dressendorfer	3-3	5.45	7	7	0	0	0	0	34.2	33	28	21	5	21	17
Hawkins	4-6	5.52	19	17	1	2	0	0	89.2	91	56	55	10	42	45
Show	1-2	5.92	23	5	0	6	0	0	51.2	62	36	34	5	17	20
Walton	1-0	6.23	12	0	0	5	0	0	13	11	9	9	3	6	10
Nelson	1-5	6.84	44	0	0	11	0	0	48.2	60	38	37	12	23	23
Briscoe	0-0	7.07	11	0	0	9	0	0	14	12	11	11	3	10	9
Allison	1-1	7.36	11	0	0	4	0	0	11.0	16	9	9	0	5	4
Guzman	1-0	9.00	5	0	0	1	0	0	5.0	11	5	5	0	2	3
Van Poppel	0-0	9.64	1	1	0	0	0	0	4.2	7	5	5	1	2	6
Harris	0-0	12.00	2	0	0	1	0	0	3.0	5	4	4	0	3	2

260

1992 Preliminary Roster

Pitchers (19)

John Briscoe
Kevin Campbell
Steve Chitren
Kirk Dressendorfer
Dennis Eckersley
Scott Erwin
Johnny Guzman
Reggie Harris
Rick Honeycutt
Joe Klink
Mike Moore
Gene Nelson
Gavin Osteen
Eric Show
Joe Slusarski
Dave Stewart
Todd Van Poppel
Bruce Walton
Bob Welch

Catchers (3)

Henry Mercedes
Jamie Quirk
Terry Steinbach

Infielders (10)

Lance Blankenship
Mike Bordick
Scott Brosius
Scott Hemond
Dann Howitt
Carney Lansford
Mark McGwire
Craig Paquette
Walt Weiss
Ron Witmeyer

Outfielders (6)

Harold Baines
Jose Canseco
Dave Henderson
Rickey Henderson
Doug Jennings
Willie Wilson

Games played by position

	G	C	1B	2B	3B	SS	OF	DH
Afenir,M	5	4	0	0	0	0	0	1
Baines,H	141	0	0	0	0	0	13	125
Blankenship,L	90	0	0	45	14	0	28	6
Bordick,M	90	0	0	5	1	84	0	0
Brosius,S	36	0	0	18	7	0	13	1
Canseco,J	154	0	0	0	0	0	131	24
Gallego,M	159	0	0	135	0	55	0	0
Hemond,S	23	8	0	7	2	1	0	4
Henderson,D	150	0	0	1	0	0	140	7
Henderson,R	134	0	0	0	0	0	119	10
Howitt,D	21	0	1	0	0	0	20	0
Jacoby,B	122	0	58	0	67	0	0	0
Jennings,D	8	0	0	0	0	0	6	0
Komminsk,B	24	0	0	0	0	0	22	0
Lansford,C	5	0	0	0	4	0	0	1
Law,V	74	0	1	0	67	3	3	0
Manrique,F	9	0	0	2	0	7	0	0
McGwire,M	154	0	152	0	0	0	0	0
Quirk,J	76	54	8	0	1	0	0	1
Riles,E	108	0	5	7	69	20	0	0
Steinbach,T	129	117	9	0	0	0	0	2
Weiss,W	40	0	0	0	0	40	0	0
Wilson,W	113	0	0	0	0	0	87	9
Witmeyer,R	11	0	8	0	0	0	0	0

Sick call: 1991 DL report

Player	Days on the DL
Carney Lansford	176*
Rick Honeycutt	74
Eric Show	25
Gene Nelson	30
Rickey Henderson	15
Todd Burns	62
Vance Law	15
Dave Stewart	16
Kirk Dressendorfer	40
Curt Young	5
Joe Klink	35
Walt Weiss	137*
Mike Moore	17
Willie Wilson	17

On DL twice (not counting administrative transfers from one DL to another).

Minor League Report

Class AAA — Tacoma finished the season with a 63-73 record, third in the Pacific Coast League's Northern Division for the first half, and fourth for the second half. The Tigers' ``King of the Hill'' or most valuable pitcher award went to RH reliever Kevin Campbell (9-2, 1.80 ERA). Their MVP was also a RH reliever, Bruce Walton (1-1, 1.35 ERA), who led the PCL in saves with 20. The ``Big Stick'' or top offensive player award went to RF Dann Howitt (.267 BA, 14 HR, 73 RBI). All three were called up to Oakland.The fans' most popular player was CF Eric Fox, who also won the organization's Walter A. Haas Jr. Community LAchievement Award, given out by the Athletics at each level of their organization for the player most active in community service. . . . **Class AA** — Huntsville finished third in the Southern League's Northern Division in the first half and fourth in the second half, with a 61-83 record overall. RHP Todd Van Poppel won the Haas Jr. Community Achievement Award.Van Poppel made several visits to schools and youth groups during the season in Huntsville. Huntsville's team was devastated by the end of the season, losing OF Lee Tinsley and RHP Apolinar Garcia to a trade, RHP Dan Eskew to retirement and Van Poppel to the major league club. . . . **Class A** — Madison went 77-61 on the season, winning the first half of the season in the Northern Division of the Midwest League and finishing fourth in the second half. Their season attendance was 92,663, the best since 1985.OF Scott Lydy was voted Most Improved Player. OF Lee Sammons (.288 BA) was named Player of the Year. LHP Doug Johns was named Most Improved Pitcher, posting a record of 12-6, along with the only no-hitter ever in Madison history. RHP Tanyon Sturtze (10-5, 3.09 ERA) was named Pitcher of the Year. C Islay Molina received the Chelsea Baker Award for outstanding community service. . . . Modesto finished the season with a 68-68 record, third in the California League's Northern Division in the first half, and second in the second half. 3B Jim Waggoner was voted the team's most popular player. Enoch Simmons won the Walter A. Haas Jr. Award. , having spent much of the season speaking at schools in the Modesto area.CF Manny Martinez had the most impact offensively, batting .278 with 143 hits. RHP Chaon Garland led the pitchers with a 9-8 record. . . . Southern Oregon fin-

ished the season with a 40-36 record, third in the Northwest League's Southern Division. OF Mike Neill (.350 BA) was voted the team's MVP, as well as the Topps' Northwest League Player of the Month for August. SS Brent Gates was voted to the All-Northwest League Team.Southern Oregon set a team per-game attendance record, averaging 1,896 fans at each home game.

Tops in the Organization

BATTING LEADERS	Club	Avg.	G	AB	R	H	HR	RBI
Scott Henry	Mad	.289	105	322	49	93	1	51
Lee Sammons	Mad	.287	124	464	105	133	0	43
Eric Booker	Hvl	.279	104	384	71	107	2	61
Scott Hemond	Tac	.272	92	327	50	89	3	31
Troy Neel	Hvl	.272	128	423	71	115	23	75

HOME RUNS			WINS		
Troy Neel	Hvl	23	Mike Mohler	Hvl	13
Marcos Armas	Hvl	16	Gavin Osteen	Hvl	13
Ernie Young	Mad	15	Bronswell Patrick	Mod	12
Ron Witmeyer	Tac	15	Doug Johns	Mad	12
Dann Howitt	Tac	14	Tanyon Sturtze	Mad	10

RBI			SAVES		
Marcos Armas	Hvl	86	Tim Peek	Hvl	26
Ron Witmeyer	Tac	80	Bruce Walton	Tac	20
Troy Neel	Hvl	75	Ricky Strebeck	Mod	17
Dann Howitt	Tac	73	Todd Revenig	Hvl	13
Ernie Young	Mad	71	Several players tied		7

STOLEN BASES			STRIKEOUTS		
Lee Sammons	Mad	54	Mike Mohler	Hvl	125
Kevin Dattola	Hvl	44	Chaon Garland	Mod	117
Lee Tinsley	Hvl	36	Todd Van Poppel	Hvl	115
James Buccheri	Hvl	35	Gavin Osteen	Hvl	105
Francisco Matos	Mod	31	Several players tied		104

PITCHING LEADERS	Club	W-L	ERA	IP	H	BB	SO
Mike Mohler	Hvl	13-6	3.07	176	161	65	125
Tanyon Sturtze	Mad	10-5	3.09	163	136	58	88
Doug Johns	Mad	12-6	3.23	128	108	54	104
Bronswell Patrick	Mod	12-12	3.24	170	158	60	95
David Zancanaro	Hvl	5-10	3.38	165	151	92	104

Runs: Most, career, all-time

997	Bob Johnson, 1933-1942
983	Bert Campaneris, 1964-1976
975	Jimmie Foxx, 1925-1935
969	Al Simmons, 1924-1944
882	Max Bishop, 1924-1933
882	RICKEY HENDERSON, 1979-1991

Hits: Most, career, all-time

1882	Bert Campaneris, 1964-1976
1827	Al Simmons, 1924-1944
1705	Jimmy Dykes, 1918-1932
1617	Bob Johnson, 1933-1942
1500	Harry Davis, 1901-1917

2B: Most, career, all-time

365	Jimmy Dykes, 1918-1932
348	Al Simmons, 1924-1944
321	Harry Davis, 1901-1917
307	Bob Johnson, 1933-1942
292	Bing Miller, 1922-1934
270	Bert Campaneris, 1964-1976 (8)

3B: Most, career, all-time

102	Danny Murphy, 1902-1913
98	Al Simmons, 1924-1944
88	Frank Baker, 1908-1914
84	Eddie Collins, 1906-1930
82	Harry Davis, 1901-1917
70	Bert Campaneris, 1964-1976 (12)

HR: Most, career, all-time

302	Jimmie Foxx, 1925-1935
269	Reggie Jackson, 1967-1987
252	Bob Johnson, 1933-1942
209	JOSE CANSECO, 1985-1991
209	Al Simmons, 1924-1944

RBI: Most, career, all-time

1178	Al Simmons, 1924-1944
1075	Jimmie Foxx, 1925-1935
1040	Bob Johnson, 1933-1942
796	Sal Bando, 1966-1976
776	Reggie Jackson, 1967-1987

SB: Most, career, all-time

668	RICKEY HENDERSON, 1979-1991
566	Bert Campaneris, 1964-1976

376	Eddie Collins, 1906-1930
232	Billy North, 1973-1978
223	Harry Davis, 1901-1917

BB: Most, career, all-time

1043	Max Bishop, 1924-1933
853	Bob Johnson, 1933-1942
820	Elmer Valo, 1940-1956
792	Sal Bando, 1966-1976
785	RICKEY HENDERSON, 1979-1991

BA: Highest, career, all-time

.356	Al Simmons, 1924-1944
.339	Jimmie Foxx, 1925-1935
.336	Eddie Collins, 1906-1930
.321	Mickey Cochrane, 1925-1933
.321	Frank Baker, 1908-1914
.293	RICKEY HENDERSON, 1979-1991 (17)

Slug avg: Highest, career, all-time

.640	Jimmie Foxx, 1925-1935
.584	Al Simmons, 1924-1944
.520	Bob Johnson, 1933-1942
.518	JOSE CANSECO, 1985-1991
.496	Reggie Jackson, 1967-1987

Games started: Most, career, all-time

458	Eddie Plank, 1901-1914
340	Catfish Hunter, 1965-1974
288	Chief Bender, 1903-1914
267	Lefty Grove, 1925-1933
267	Rube Walberg, 1923-1933

Saves: Most, career, all-time

185	DENNIS ECKERSLEY, 1987-1991
136	Rollie Fingers, 1968-1976
73	John Wyatt, 1961-1969
61	JAY HOWELL, 1985-1987
58	Jack Aker, 1964-1968

Shutouts: Most, career, all-time

59	Eddie Plank, 1901-1914
37	Rube Waddell, 1902-1907
36	Chief Bender, 1903-1914
31	Catfish Hunter, 1965-1974
28	Vida Blue, 1969-1977
28	Jack Coombs, 1906-1914

Wins: Most, career, all-time

284	Eddie Plank, 1901-1914
195	Lefty Grove, 1925-1933
193	Chief Bender, 1903-1914
171	Eddie Rommel, 1920-1932
161	Catfish Hunter, 1965-1974

K: Most, career, all-time

1985	Eddie Plank, 1901-1914
1576	Rube Waddell, 1902-1907
1536	Chief Bender, 1903-1914
1523	Lefty Grove, 1925-1933
1520	Catfish Hunter, 1965-1974

Win pct: Highest, career, all-time

.712	Lefty Grove, 1925-1933
.670	BOB WELCH, 1988-1991
.654	Chief Bender, 1903-1914
.637	Eddie Plank, 1901-1914
.632	Jack Coombs, 1906-1914

ERA: Lowest, career, all-time

1.97	Rube Waddell, 1902-1907
2.15	Cy Morgan, 1909-1912
2.32	Chief Bender, 1903-1914
2.39	Eddie Plank, 1901-1914
2.60	Jack Coombs, 1906-1914
2.91	Rollie Fingers, 1968-1976 (8)

Runs: Most, season

152	Al Simmons, 1930
151	Jimmie Foxx, 1932
145	Nap Lajoie, 1901
144	Al Simmons, 1932
137	Eddie Collins, 1912
123	Reggie Jackson, 1969 (10)

Hits: Most, season

253	Al Simmons, 1925
232	Nap Lajoie, 1901
216	Al Simmons, 1932
214	Doc Cramer, 1935
213	Jimmie Foxx, 1932
187	Jose Canseco, 1988 (*)

2B: Most, season

53	Al Simmons, 1926
48	Nap Lajoie, 1901
48	Wally Moses, 1937

47	Harry Davis, 1905
47	Eric McNair, 1932
39	Reggie Jackson, 1975 (22)
39	Joe Rudi, 1974 (22)

3B: Most, season

21	Frank Baker, 1912
19	Frank Baker, 1909
18	Danny Murphy, 1910
17	Danny Murphy, 1904
16	Bing Miller, 1929
16	Al Simmons, 1930
16	Amos Strunk, 1915
12	Bert Campaneris, 1965 (*)
12	Phil Garner, 1976 (*)

HR: Most, season

58	Jimmie Foxx, 1932
49	MARK McGWIRE, 1987
48	Jimmie Foxx, 1933
47	Reggie Jackson, 1969
44	JOSE CANSECO, 1991
44	Jimmie Foxx, 1934

RBI: Most, season

169	Jimmie Foxx, 1932
165	Al Simmons, 1930
163	Jimmie Foxx, 1933
157	Al Simmons, 1929
156	Jimmie Foxx, 1930
124	JOSE CANSECO, 1988 (13)

SB: Most, season

130	RICKEY HENDERSON, 1982
108	RICKEY HENDERSON, 1983
100	RICKEY HENDERSON, 1980
81	Eddie Collins, 1910
75	Billy North, 1976

BB: Most, season

149	Eddie Joost, 1949
136	Ferris Fain, 1949
133	Ferris Fain, 1950
128	Max Bishop, 1929
128	Max Bishop, 1930
118	Sal Bando, 1970 (10)

BA: Highest, season

.426	Nap Lajoie, 1901
.390	Al Simmons, 1931
.387	Al Simmons, 1925
.381	Al Simmons, 1930
.365	Eddie Collins, 1911
.325	Rickey Henderson, 1990 (*)

Slug avg: Highest, season

.749	Jimmie Foxx, 1932
.708	Al Simmons, 1930
.703	Jimmie Foxx, 1933
.653	Jimmie Foxx, 1934
.643	Nap Lajoie, 1901
.618	MARK McGWIRE, 1987 (11)

Games started: Most, season

46	Rube Waddell, 1904
43	Eddie Plank, 1904
41	Catfish Hunter, 1974
41	Eddie Plank, 1905
40	Vida Blue, 1974
40	George Caster, 1938
40	Jack Coombs, 1911
40	Chuck Dobson, 1970
40	Ken Holtzman, 1973
40	Catfish Hunter, 1970
40	Eddie Plank, 1903
40	Eddie Plank, 1907

Saves: Most, season

48	DENNIS ECKERSLEY, 1990
45	DENNIS ECKERSLEY, 1988
43	DENNIS ECKERSLEY, 1991
36	Bill Caudill, 1984
33	DENNIS ECKERSLEY, 1989

Shutouts: Most, season

13	Jack Coombs, 1910
8	Vida Blue, 1971
8	Joe Bush, 1916
8	Eddie Plank, 1907
8	Rube Waddell, 1904
8	Rube Waddell, 1906

Wins: Most, season

31	Jack Coombs, 1910
31	Lefty Grove, 1931
28	Jack Coombs, 1911
28	Lefty Grove, 1930
27	Eddie Rommel, 1922
27	Rube Waddell, 1905
27	BOB WELCH, 1990

K: Most, season

349	Rube Waddell, 1904
302	Rube Waddell, 1903
301	Vida Blue, 1971
287	Rube Waddell, 1905
232	Rube Waddell, 1907

Win pct: Highest, season

| .886 | Lefty Grove, 1931 |
| .850 | Chief Bender, 1914 |

.849	Lefty Grove, 1930
.821	Chief Bender, 1910
.818	BOB WELCH, 1990

ERA: Lowest, season

1.30	Jack Coombs, 1910
1.39	Harry Krause, 1909
1.48	Rube Waddell, 1905
1.55	Cy Morgan, 1910
1.58	Chief Bender, 1910
1.82	Vida Blue, 1971 (10)

Most pinch-hit homers, season

| 4 | Jeff Burroughs, 1982 |

Most pinch-hit, homers, career

| 5 | Jeff Burroughs, 1982-1984 |

Most consecutive games, batting safely

| 29 | Billy Lamar, Phi-1925 |
| 24 | Carney Lansford, 1984 |

Most consecutive scoreless innings

| 38 | Mike Torrez, 1976 |

No hit games

Weldon Henley, Phi at StL AL, 6-0; July 22, 1905 (1st game).

Chief Bender, Phi vs Cle AL, 4-0; May 12, 1910.

Joe Bush, Phi vs Cle AL, 5-0; August 26, 1916.

Dick Fowler, Phi vs StL AL, 1-0; September 9, 1945 (2nd game).

Bill McCahan, Phi vs Was AL, 3-0; September 3, 1947.

Catfish Hunter, Oak vs Min AL, 4-0; May 8, 1968 (perfect game).

Vida Blue, Oak vs Min AL, 6-0; September 21, 1970.

Vida Blue (5 innings), Glenn Abbott (1 inning), Paul Lindblad (1 inning) and Rollie Fingers (2 innings), Oak vs Cal AL, 5-0; September 28, 1975.

Mike Warren, Oak vs Chi AL, 3-0; September 29, 1983.

Dave Stewart, Oak at Tor AL, 5-0; June 29, 1990.

Rube Waddell, five innings, rain, Phi vs StL AL, 2-0; August 15, 1905.

Jimmy Dygert (3 innings) and Rube Waddell (2 innings), five innings, rain, Phi vs Chi AL, 4-3; August 29, 1906. (Waddell allowed hit and two runs in 6th, but rain caused game to revert to 5 innings.)

Rube Vickers, five perfect innings, darkness, Phi at Was AL, 4-0; October 5, 1907 (2nd game).

Seattle Mariners

Seattle's Ken Griffey Jr. was a top vote-getter for the All-Star team.

Winning games, losing money

The 1991 season should have ended on a happy note for the Seattle Mariners, but instead there was only turmoil and confusion. The team won, the fans came, but the manager was fired and the owner wants to move.

The Mariners won six of their last eight games to finish 83-79. It was their first winning season in franchise history, something manager Jim Lefebvre called a milestone . . . a major step forward."

Yet four days after the final game, Lefebvre was fired by GM Woody Woodward. (Pitching coach Mike Paul also was let go.) Lefebvre was the Mariners' winningest manager, with a 233-252 record in three seasons. Under Lefebvre, the team finally appeared to be turning the corner and had a genuine superstar in Ken Griffey Jr., who set club records with his .327 average and 42 doubles.

The club also set a season attendance record of 2,147,905—the first time the M's broke the 2 million mark.

Despite that success on the field and at the box office, owner Jeff Smulyan said he was losing millions of dollars. Even though the team's lease at the Kingdome runs through 1996, there has been speculation that the club might move to the Suncoast Dome in St. Petersburg, Fla.

Smulyan also had until February to repay a $39.5 million loan from a local bank. That was interesting news for the 10 players heading to arbitration.

If that wasn't enough, popular Alvin Davis probably played his last game as a Mariner. Davis, a free agent, spent eight years with Seattle and holds most of the team's offensive records, including home runs and RBI. He hit just .221 last season and did not expect to be re-signed.

Davis, the 1984 AL Rookie of the Year, was given a pair of emotional standing ovations in what was probably his final game in the Kingdome.

In addition, pitcher Brian Holman (13-14, 3.69) had shoulder problems at the end of the season, and it was feared he might have a torn rotator cuff.

Lefebvre and the Mariners put together a winning season even though starters Randy Johnson (13-10), Erik Hanson (8-8) and Holman fell short of their potential. Johnson finished with 228 strikeouts, second in the league to Boston's Roger Clemens. He averaged 10.19 strikeouts per 9 innings.

But the season belonged to Griffey Jr., who hit 22 home runs and drove in 100 runs. He finished third in the batting race, and was named club MVP.

—Bill Koenig

Mariners 1992 preview

Where the Mariners play next season is anyone's guess. It could be Seattle, Vancouver, Portland—or all the above. And don't forget St. Petersburg, Fla.

How they will play this season is an even bigger mystery. 1991 was their first winning season in franchise history—but they fired the manager who got them there.

They still have a genuine superstar in center fielder Ken Griffey Jr. (.327, 42 doubles, 22 HR, 100 RBI). He'll give new manager Bill Plummer an instant reason to smile.

The most pressing need, a bona fide right-handed cleanup hitter, was solved with the acquisition of slugger Kevin Mitchell.

Starting pitchers Randy Johnson, Erik Hanson and Brian Holman form the nucleus of a solid staff, although none won more than 13 games and Holman had shoulder problems late in the season.

Ten players went through arbitration over the winter, something that won't help the team's bleak financial picture.

▶Ken Griffey Jr. will become the most recognizable face in St. Petersburg, Fla.
▶The Mariners will have their second winning season in franchise history but finish in fifth place, anyway—then fire their manager.

—John Hunt

Another Griffey may soon be in fold

The Mariners can't get enough Griffeys.

With Ken Griffey Jr. and Ken Griffey Sr. already in the fold, they selected Craig Griffey, Junior's little brother, in the 42nd round of the draft.

One catch: Craig, a sophomore at Ohio State, hasn't played baseball since he was 15. He's a defensive back for the Buckeye football team.

Although he was a catcher and short-stop in high school, the Mariners think his position may be in the outfield. His father says it may take a while for Craig to refine his skills.

Griffey Sr. was drafted 29th in 1969 and it took him four years to reach the majors. Griffey Jr., was the No. 1 pick in 1987. If signed, Craig is expected to be sent to the M's club in the Arizona Instructional League.

Griffey not kidding when game on line

By Mike Terry

As a star who shines brighter with each passing season, Ken Griffey Jr. still has to work at being himself. Life may be fun, but it's not easy being just 22 years old and already the Seattle Mariners' most identifiable personality.

"Oh, when I'm away from the ball-park, I'm still a big kid," said Griffey, eyes shining. "My girlfriend will tell you the same thing. I've got video games in the house, two dogs. My time is occupied with stuff I like to do."

His responsibilities, though, helped lead Seattle to a winning record for the first time in the club's 15-year history.

Some of his inspiration came from the season Seattle had. In the first half, when the Mariners were sloshing through the division's bottom half, Griffey was listless. He was hitting (for him) a soft .280 with 36 RBI, seven stolen bases and 46 strikeouts.

"I was down on myself more than I've ever been the first two years. I wanted to win so bad, and when we didn't it was like 'oh no, not again,' " he said.

But Junior was kicked into gear when local columnist Steve Kelly wrote a piece after the All-Star Game—of which Griffey was the AL's highest vote get-ter—asking him whether he wanted to fulfill the superstar destiny predicted for him or just slide by on talent and never grow.

"The article made me think about what I was doing," he said.

Mike Terry writes for the San Bernardino (Calif.) Sun.

Mariers winter league news

▶Winter leagues: First baseman Tino Martinez was to headline one of the largest contingents of players heading to the winter leagues. Martinez hit .326 with 18 home runs and 86 RBI at Class AAA Calgary, but hit only .205 in 36 games at Seattle in a late-season call-up. He opted to rest in the offseason rather than report to Puerto Rico. . . . Other top prospects who headed south for the winter include: 1B Jim Bowie (.310-10-67 at Class AA Jacksonville) and C Jim Campanis (.248-15-49 at Jacksonville), playing in Puerto Rico and Mexico, respectively. . . . OF Julio Fernandez, RHP Marcos Garcia, LHP Oscar Ortega and OF Jesus Tavarez played at home this winter in the Dominican Republic. Garcia played for Aguilas again, where he was 4-1 with an 0.39 ERA in eight starts last winter. Ortega played in one game for Escogido last winter. . . OF Alonzo Powell (.375-7-43 in 192 at-bats for Calgary) played for the Arecibo Wolves for the second consecutive winter. Powell hit .237 with 5 HRs and 34 RBI there last year. . . . RHP Kerry Woodson (4-6, 3.06 ERA at Jacksonville), LHP Dennis Powell (9-8, 4.15 ERA at Calgary) and Campanis played for three teams in the eight-team Mexican winter league.

▶Winter leagues rosters: Shawn Barton, LHP, Tiburones de La Guaira, Venezuela; Jim Bowie, 1B, Arecibo Wolves, Puerto Rico; Jim Campanis, C, Los Mochis Caneros (Sugarcane growers), Mexico; Dave Cochrane, C, Bayamon Cowboys, Puerto Rico; Julio Fernandez, OF, Aguilas Cibae–na (Eagles), D.R.; Marcos Garcia, RHP, Aguilas Cibae–na, D.R.; Gene Harris, RHP, Bayamon Cowboys, Puerto Rico; Calvin Jones, RHP, Bayamon Cowboys, Puerto Rico; Patrick Lennon, OF, Bayamon Cowboys, Puerto Rico; Edgar Martinez, OF, Aguilas Cibae–na (Eagle's Cibae–na), D.R.; Timber Mead, RHP, Mexicali Aguila (Eagle), Mexico; Jeff Nelson, RHP, Bayamon Cowboys, Puerto Rico; Oscar Ortega, LHP, Leones (Lions) Escogido, D.R.; Alonzo Powell, OF, Arecibo Wolves, Puerto Rico; Dennis Powell, LHP, Mazatlan Venados (Deer), Mexico; Jesus Tavarez, OF, Leones (Lions) Escogido, D.R.; Kerry Woodson, RHP, Hermosillo Naranjeros (Orange growers), Mexico.

Team directory

▶Owner: Jeff Smulyan

▶General Manager: Woody Woodward

▶Ballpark:
The Kingdome
201 South King Street, Seattle, Washington
206-628-3555
Capacity 57,748
Public transportation available
Parking for 2,500 vehicles; $5; $1 discount for car pools
Family and wheelchair sections, Fan Phone, Fantasy Play-by-Play, autograph booth, birthday package

▶Team publications:
Mariners Magazine
206-628-3555

▶TV, radio broadcast stations:
KIRO-AM 710, KSTW-TV Channel 11

▶Spring Training:
Tempe Stadium
2200 West Alameda
Tempe, Arizona
602-438-8900

SEATTLE MARINERS 1991 Final Stats

Batting	AVG	SLG	OB	G	AB	R	H	TB	2B	3B	HR	RBI	BB	SO	SB	CS	E
Griffey Jr	.327	.527	.399	154	548	76	179	289	42	1	22	100	71	82	18	6	4
E. Martinez	.307	.452	.405	150	544	98	167	246	35	1	14	52	84	72	0	3	15
Cotto	.305	.463	.347	66	177	35	54	82	6	2	6	23	10	27	16	3	2
Griffey Sr.	.282	.400	.380	30	85	10	24	34	7	0	1	9	13	13	0	0	0
Briley	.260	.336	.307	139	381	39	99	128	17	3	2	26	27	51	23	11	4
Reynolds	.254	.341	.332	161	631	95	160	215	34	6	3	57	72	63	28	8	18
T. Jones	.251	.360	.321	79	175	30	44	63	8	1	3	24	18	22	2	0	0
Schaefer	.250	.323	.272	84	164	19	41	53	7	1	1	11	5	25	3	1	6
Sinatro	.250	.250	.333	5	8	1	2	2	0	0	0	1	1	1	0	0	0
O'Brien	.248	.402	.300	152	560	58	139	225	29	3	17	88	44	61	0	1	5
Cochrane	.247	.354	.286	65	178	16	44	63	13	0	2	22	9	38	0	1	7
Buhner	.244	.498	.337	137	406	64	99	202	14	4	27	77	53	117	0	1	5
Vizquel	.230	.293	.302	142	426	42	98	125	16	4	1	41	45	37	7	2	13
Davis	.221	.335	.299	145	462	39	102	155	15	1	12	69	56	78	0	3	0
Powell	.216	.369	.288	57	111	16	24	41	6	1	3	12	11	24	0	2	2
T. Martinez	.205	.330	.272	36	112	11	23	37	2	0	4	9	11	24	0	0	2
Bradley	.203	.244	.280	83	172	10	35	42	7	0	0	11	19	19	0	0	4
Valle	.194	.299	.286	132	324	38	63	97	8	1	8	32	34	49	0	2	6
Howard	.167	.333	.286	9	6	1	1	2	1	0	0	0	1	2	0	0	0
Lennon	.125	.250	.364	9	8	2	1	2	1	0	0	1	3	1	0	0	0
Amaral	.063	.063	.167	14	16	2	1	1	0	0	0	0	1	5	0	2	2

Pitching	W-L	ERA	G	GS	CG	GF	Sho	SV	IP	H	R	ER	HR	BB	SO
Swift	1-2	1.99	71	0	0	30	0	17	90.1	74	22	20	3	26	48
C. Jones	2-2	2.53	27	0	0	6	0	2	46.1	33	14	13	0	29	42
Murphy	0-1	3.00	57	0	0	26	0	4	48	47	17	16	4	19	34
Rice	1-1	3.00	7	2	0	0	0	0	21	18	10	7	3	10	12
Jackson	7-7	3.25	72	0	0	35	0	14	88.2	64	35	32	5	34	74
Swan	6-2	3.43	63	0	0	11	0	2	78.2	81	35	30	8	28	33
Krueger	11-8	3.60	35	25	1	2	0	9	175	194	82	70	15	60	91
Schooler	3-3	3.67	34	0	0	23	0	7	34.1	25	14	14	2	10	31
Burba	2-2	3.68	22	2	0	11	0	1	36.2	34	16	15	6	14	16
Holman	13-14	3.69	30	30	5	0	3	0	195.1	199	86	80	16	77	108
Hanson	8-8	3.81	27	27	2	0	1	0	174.2	182	82	74	16	56	143
Johnson	13-10	3.98	33	33	2	0	1	0	201.1	151	96	89	15	152	228
Harris	0-0	4.05	8	0	0	3	0	1	13.1	15	8	6	1	10	6
Bankhead	3-6	4.90	17	9	0	2	0	0	60.2	73	35	33	8	21	28
DeLucia	12-13	5.09	32	31	0	0	0	0	182	176	107	103	31	78	98
Fleming	1-0	6.62	9	3	0	3	0	0	17.2	19	13	13	3	3	11
Comstock	0-0	54.00	1	0	0	0	0	0	.1	2	2	2	0	1	0

1992 Preliminary Roster

Pitchers (18)

Scott Bankhead
Rich DeLucia
Don Elliott
Dave Fleming
Erik Hanson
Gene Harris
Brian Holman
Randy Johnson
Calvin Jones
Brent Knackert
Rob Murphy
Jeff Nelson
Jim Newlin
Mike Remlinger
Mike Schooler
Russ Swan
Kerry Woodson
Clint Zavaras

Catchers (5)

Scott Bradley
Jim Campanis
Chris Howard
Greg Pirkl
Dave Valle

Infielders (8)

Rich Amaral
Dave Cochrane
Edgar Martinez
Tino Martinez
Pete O'Brien
Harold Reynolds
Jeff Schaefer
Omar Vizquel

Outfielders (7)

Greg Briley
Jay Buhner
Henry Cotto
Ken Griffey, Jr.
Patrick Lennon
Kevin Mitchell
Alonzo Powell

Games played by position

	G	C	1B	2B	3B	SS	OF	DH
Amaral,R	14	0	1	5	2	2	0	2
Bradley,S	83	65	1	0	4	0	0	2
Briley,G	139	0	0	1	1	0	125	2
Buhner,J	137	0	0	0	0	0	131	0
Cochrane,D	65	19	4	0	13	0	26	1
Cotto,H	66	0	0	0	0	0	56	6
Davis,A	145	0	14	0	0	0	0	126
Griffey,K	30	0	0	0	0	0	26	1
Griffey Jr,K	154	0	0	0	0	0	152	0
Howard,C	9	9	0	0	0	0	0	0
Jones,Tr	79	0	0	0	0	0	36	37
Lennon,P	9	0	0	0	0	0	1	5
Martinez,T	36	0	29	0	0	0	0	5
Martinez,E	150	0	0	144	0	0	0	2
O'Brien,P	152	0	132	0	0	0	13	18
Powell,A	57	0	7	0	0	0	40	7
Reynolds,H	161	0	0	159	0	0	0	1
Schaefer,J	84	0	0	11	30	46	0	1
Sinatro,M	5	5	0	0	0	0	0	0
Valle,D	132	129	2	0	0	0	0	0
Vizquel,O	142	0	0	1	0	138	0	0

Sick call: 1991 DL report

Player	Days on the DL
Ken Griffey Sr.	136*
Mike Schooler	91
Bill Swift	15
Scott Bankhead	101*
Erik Hanson	42*
Richie Amaral	49
Tracy Jones	30
Henry Cotto	65
Russ Swan	15
Keith Comstock	62

On DL twice (not counting administrative transfers from one DL to another).

Minor League Report

Class AAA — Calgary finished 72-64, its first season above .500 since 1987. It finished fourth in the Northern Division of the Pacific Coast League in the season's first half, and first in the second half. After sweeping Portland in the divisional playoffs, and winning two games from Southern Division champion Tucson, the Cannons lost the last three games of the best-of-five series. LHP Dennis Powell won game two of the series, and then started in game five, on two days rest, where he got a no-decision.INF Rich Amaral won the PCL batting title, with an average of .346 , the third Calgary player to do so. The first two were Edgar Martinez in 1988 and Bruce Field in 1989.1B Tino Martinez was the league's MVP, also the third Cannon to win the award. Danny Tartabull (1985) and Mike Campbell (1987) preceded him. . . . Class AA — Jacksonville posted a 74-69 record on the season, finishing second in the Eastern Division of the Southern League in the first half and fourth in the second half. 1B Jim Bowie, who finished the season at Triple-A Calgary, won the Southern League batting title with a .310 average. The Suns' batters led the league in home runs with 102, while their pitchers allowed the fewest number of walks (400). and were third in strikeouts with 965. . . . Class A — Peninsula finished last in the Southern Division of the Carolina League for the first and second half of the season. Their final record was 46-93. They won their final game of the season on Sept. 2 to snap a league record 22-game losing streak. . . . San Bernardino ended up 52-84, fourth in the first half and last in the second half in the California League's Southern Division. OF Marc Newfield (.300 BA, 22 2B, 11 HR, 68 RBI) and INF Ruben Santana (.302 BA, 3 HR 43 RBI, 34 SB) and CF Jesus Tavarez (.283 BA, 41 RBI, 69 SB) were bright spots offensively for the Spirit. They had only one winning pitcher, RHP Oscar Rivas (7-5, 4.17). RHPs Marcos Garcia (7-10, 3.46 ERA, 123 strikeouts), and Troy Kent (7-13, 3.25 ERA) led the team in ERA.

Tops in the Organization

BATTING LEADERS	Club	Avg.	G	AB	R	H	HR	RBI
Rich Amaral	CGy	.346	86	347	79	120	3	36
Pat Lennon	CGy	.329	112	416	75	137	15	74
Tino Martinez	CGy	.326	122	442	94	144	18	86
Jim Bowie	CGy	.313	137	498	60	156	11	74
Dave Brundage	CGy	.310	105	365	75	113	3	32

HOME RUNS			WINS		
Greg Pirkl	Sbr	20	Pat Rice	CGy	13
Bret Boone	Jax	19	Dave Fleming	CGy	12
Tino Martinez	CGy	18	Rick Balabon	Jax	11
Steve Springer	CGy	17	Marcos Garcia	Jax	10
Frank Bolick	Jax	16	Roger Salkeld	CGy	10

RBI			SAVES		
Greg Pirkl	Sbr	94	Jeff Nelson	CGy	19
Tino Martinez	CGy	86	Troy Kent	Sbr	15
Chuck Jackson	CGy	85	im Newlin	Jax	12
Alan Cockrell	CGy	81	Brad Holman	Pen	10
Bret Boone	Jax	75	Sal Urso	Pen	8

STOLEN BASES			STRIKEOUTS		
Tow Maynard	Jax	88	Roger Salkeld	CGy	180
Jesus Tavarez	Sbr	69	Marcos Garcia	Jax	165
Ruben Santana	Jax	34	Jim Converse	Pen	137
Ted Williams	Jax	34	Dave Fleming	CGy	125
Rich Amaral	CGy	30	John Cummings	Sbr	120

PITCHING LEADERS	Club	W-L	ERA	IP	H	BB	SO
Dave Fleming	CGy	12-6	2.54	156	140	28	125
Roger Salkeld	CGy	10-9	3.28	173	149	68	180
Johnny Wiggs	Jax	7-5	3.28	123	108	44	91
Marcos Garcia	Jax	10-12	3.68	171	138	78	165
John Cummings	Sbr	4-10	4.06	124	129	61	120

Seattle (1977-1991)

Runs: Most, career, all-time

563	ALVIN DAVIS, 1984-1991
488	HAROLD REYNOLDS, 1983-1991
402	Julio Cruz, 1977-1983
351	JIM PRESLEY, 1984-1989
346	Phil Bradley, 1983-1987

Hits: Most, career, all-time

1163	ALVIN DAVIS, 1984-1991
950	HAROLD REYNOLDS, 1983-1991
736	JIM PRESLEY, 1984-1989
697	Bruce Bochte, 1978-1982
649	Phil Bradley, 1983-1987
649	Julio Cruz, 1977-1983

2B: Most, career, all-time

212	ALVIN DAVIS, 1984-1991
177	HAROLD REYNOLDS, 1983-1991
147	JIM PRESLEY, 1984-1989
134	Bruce Bochte, 1978-1982
128	Al Cowens, 1982-1986

3B: Most, career, all-time

45	HAROLD REYNOLDS, 1983-1991
26	Phil Bradley, 1983-1987
23	SPIKE OWEN, 1983-1986
20	Ruppert Jones, 1977-1979
19	Dan Meyer, 1977-1981

HR: Most, career, all-time

160	ALVIN DAVIS, 1984-1991
115	JIM PRESLEY, 1984-1989
105	Ken Phelps, 1983-1988
79	DAVE HENDERSON, 1981-1986
64	Dan Meyer, 1977-1981

RBI: Most, career, all-time

667	ALVIN DAVIS, 1984-1991
418	JIM PRESLEY, 1984-1989
329	Bruce Bochte, 1978-1982
313	Dan Meyer, 1977-1981
271	DAVE HENDERSON, 1981-1986

SB: Most, career, all-time

290	Julio Cruz, 1977-1983
213	HAROLD REYNOLDS, 1983-1991
107	Phil Bradley, 1983-1987
74	HENRY COTTO, 1988-1991
70	JOHN MOSES, 1982-1987

BB: Most, career, all-time

672	ALVIN DAVIS, 1984-1991
346	HAROLD REYNOLDS, 1983-1991
330	Julio Cruz, 1977-1983
317	Ken Phelps, 1983-1988
313	Bruce Bochte, 1978-1982

BA: Highest, career, all-time

.301	Phil Bradley, 1983-1987
.290	Bruce Bochte, 1978-1982
.281	ALVIN DAVIS, 1984-1991
.265	Dan Meyer, 1977-1981
.262	HAROLD REYNOLDS, 1983-1991

Slug avg: Highest, career, all-time

.521	Ken Phelps, 1983-1988
.453	ALVIN DAVIS, 1984-1991
.449	Phil Bradley, 1983-1987
.433	DAVE HENDERSON, 1981-1986
.429	Bruce Bochte, 1978-1982

Games started: Most, career, all-time

217	MIKE MOORE, 1982-1988
173	MARK LANGSTON, 1984-1989
147	Jim Beattie, 1980-1986
146	Glenn Abbott, 1977-1983
127	MATT YOUNG, 1983-1990

Saves: Most, career, all-time

85	MIKE SCHOOLER, 1988-1991
52	Bill Caudill, 1982-1983
36	Shane Rawley, 1978-1981
35	EDWIN NUNEZ, 1982-1988
28	MIKE JACKSON, 1988-1991

Shutouts: Most, career, all-time

9	MARK LANGSTON, 1984-1989
9	MIKE MOORE, 1982-1988
7	FLOYD BANNISTER, 1979-1982
6	Jim Beattie, 1980-1986
5	BRIAN HOLMAN, 1989-1991
5	MATT YOUNG, 1983-1990

Wins: Most, career, all-time

74	MARK LANGSTON, 1984-1989
66	MIKE MOORE, 1982-1988
45	MATT YOUNG, 1983-1990
44	Glenn Abbott, 1977-1983
43	Jim Beattie, 1980-1986

K: Most, career, all-time

1078	MARK LANGSTON, 1984-1989
937	MIKE MOORE, 1982-1988
597	MATT YOUNG, 1983-1990
564	FLOYD BANNISTER, 1979-1982
563	Jim Beattie, 1980-1986

Win pct: Highest, career, all-time

.525	MARK LANGSTON, 1984-1989
.444	FLOYD BANNISTER, 1979-1982
.415	Glenn Abbott, 1977-1983
.407	MIKE MOORE, 1982-1988
.405	MATT YOUNG, 1983-1990

ERA: Lowest, career, all-time

3.75	FLOYD BANNISTER, 1979-1982
4.01	MARK LANGSTON, 1984-1989
4.04	BILL SWIFT, 1985-1991
4.13	MATT YOUNG, 1983-1990
4.14	Jim Beattie, 1980-1986

Runs: Most, season

109	Ruppert Jones, 1979
101	Phil Bradley, 1987
100	Phil Bradley, 1985
100	HAROLD REYNOLDS, 1990
98	EDGAR MARTINEZ, 1991

Hits: Most, season

192	Phil Bradley, 1985
184	HAROLD REYNOLDS, 1989
180	Willie Horton, 1979
180	Jack Perconte, 1984
179	Phil Bradley, 1987
179	KEN GRIFFEY JR, 1990
179	KEN GRIFFEY JR, 1991

2B: Most, season

42	KEN GRIFFEY JR, 1991
39	Al Cowens, 1982
38	Bruce Bochte, 1979
38	Phil Bradley, 1987
37	ALVIN DAVIS, 1987

3B: Most, season

11	HAROLD REYNOLDS, 1988
10	Phil Bradley, 1987
9	Ruppert Jones, 1979
9	HAROLD REYNOLDS, 1989
8	Phil Bradley, 1985
8	Al Cowens, 1982
8	Ruppert Jones, 1977
8	SPIKE OWEN, 1984
8	HAROLD REYNOLDS, 1987

HR: Most, season

32	Gorman Thomas, 1985
29	ALVIN DAVIS, 1987
29	Willie Horton, 1979
28	JIM PRESLEY, 1985
27	JAY BUHNER, 1991
27	ALVIN DAVIS, 1984
27	Ken Phelps, 1987
27	JIM PRESLEY, 1986
27	Leroy Stanton, 1977

RBI: Most, season

116	ALVIN DAVIS, 1984
107	JIM PRESLEY, 1986
106	Willie Horton, 1979
100	Bruce Bochte, 1979
100	ALVIN DAVIS, 1987
100	KEN GRIFFEY JR, 1991

SB: Most, season

60	HAROLD REYNOLDS, 1987
59	Julio Cruz, 1978
49	Julio Cruz, 1979
46	Julio Cruz, 1982
45	Julio Cruz, 1980

BB: Most, season

101	ALVIN DAVIS, 1989
97	ALVIN DAVIS, 1984
95	ALVIN DAVIS, 1988
90	ALVIN DAVIS, 1985
88	Ken Phelps, 1986

BA: Highest, season

.327	KEN GRIFFEY JR, 1991
.326	Tom Paciorek, 1981
.316	Bruce Bochte, 1979
.310	Phil Bradley, 1986
.307	EDGAR MARTINEZ, 1991

Slug avg: Highest, season

.527	KEN GRIFFEY JR, 1991
.516	ALVIN DAVIS, 1987
.515	Leon Roberts, 1978
.511	Leroy Stanton, 1977
.509	Tom Paciorek, 1981

Games started: Most, season

37	MIKE MOORE, 1986
36	MARK LANGSTON, 1986
35	FLOYD BANNISTER, 1982
35	MARK LANGSTON, 1987
35	MARK LANGSTON, 1988
35	MATT YOUNG, 1985

Saves: Most, season

33	MIKE SCHOOLER, 1989
26	Bill Caudill, 1982
26	Bill Caudill, 1983
17	BILL SWIFT, 1991
16	EDWIN NUNEZ, 1985
16	Enrique Romo, 1977

Shutouts: Most, season

3	FLOYD BANNISTER, 1982
3	BRIAN HOLMAN, 1991
3	MARK LANGSTON, 1987
3	MARK LANGSTON, 1988
3	MIKE MOORE, 1988

Wins: Most, season

19	MARK LANGSTON, 1987
18	ERIK HANSON, 1990
17	MARK LANGSTON, 1984
17	MIKE MOORE, 1985
15	MARK LANGSTON, 1988

K: Most, season

262	MARK LANGSTON, 1987
245	MARK LANGSTON, 1986
235	MARK LANGSTON, 1988
228	RANDY JOHNSON, 1991
211	ERIK HANSON, 1990

Win pct: Highest, season

.667	ERIK HANSON, 1990
.630	MARK LANGSTON, 1984
.630	MIKE MOORE, 1985
.594	MARK LANGSTON, 1987
.577	MARK LANGSTON, 1988

ERA: Lowest, season

3.24	ERIK HANSON, 1990
3.27	MATT YOUNG, 1983
3.34	SCOTT BANKHEAD, 1989
3.34	MARK LANGSTON, 1988
3.34	Jim Beattie, 1982

Most pinch-hit homers, season

2	Leon Roberts, 1978
2	Gary Gray, 1981
2	Ken Phelps, 1986

Most pinch-hit, homers, career

4	Ken Phelps, 1983-1988

Most consecutive games, batting safely

21	Dan Meyer, 1979
21	Richie Zisk, 1982

Most consecutive scoreless innings

34	Mark Langston, 1988

No hit games

Randy Johnson, Sea vs Det AL, 2-0; June 2, 1990.

Kansas City Royals

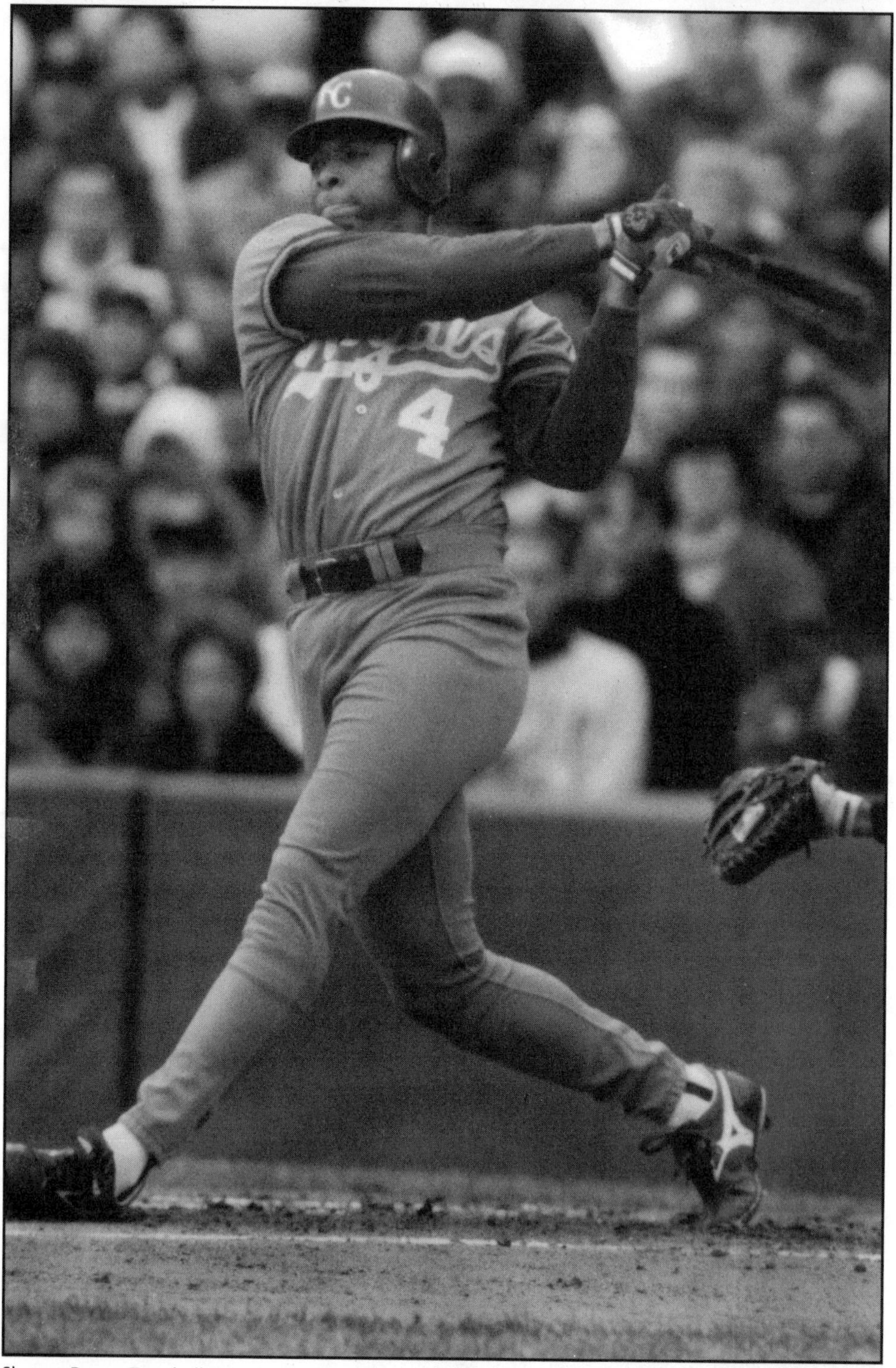

Slugger Danny Tartabull was among AL leaders in batting, home runs and RBI, then left for New York.

McRae brought slight improvement

The Kansas City Royals began the 1991 season much like the previous campaign, which had ended as the team's worst in its 22-year history. They ended the 1991 season with just a slightly better record, but with a new manager who was turning things around.

Hal McRae took over for John Wathan after the Royals started 16-23 (Kansas City had finished in last-place at 75-86 in 1990). McRae led the Royals to a 66-57 mark the rest of the season, as the team finished at 82-80 and avoided the cellar by one game.

One of McRae's first major decisions concerned the left side of his infield. Third baseman Kevin Seitzer and shortstop Kurt Stillwell were the better offensive players, but McRae opted for stronger defense, inserting Bill Pecota and David Howard. The move was a success on the field, but caused dissension as Seitzer and particularly Stillwell objected to their demotions.

The former starters both batted .265. Pecota made a case with his glove (4 errors) and his bat (.286). Stillwell was clearly a stronger force at the plate—eventually earning more playing time as Howard struggled—but Howard improved as a fulltime player. Batting just .093 at the All-Star break, Howard was .244 thereafter, for a .216 final average.

Next for McRae was the starting pitching, Kansas City's strongest point. Bret Saberhagen, who threw a no-hitter Aug. 26, and Kevin Appier led the staff with 13 wins apiece, and Mike Boddicker added a dozen.

McRae tinkered by moving Luis Aquino to the rotation and Storm Davis to the bullpen. Reliever Mark Davis excelled in a couple of late-season starts and will be tried as a starter in 1992.

Jeff Montgomery upped the career-high record of 24 saves he set the previous year. Montgomery notched 33 saves (fourth in the AL) and led the

team in appearances (67) for the second straight season.

Outfielder Danny Tartabull finished among the AL's top 10 in batting (.316), homers (31) and RBI (100). George Brett suffered a knee injury and missed a month of the season, which turned out to be a disappointment for the 1990 AL batting champ. Brett hit just .251 with 10 homers and 61 RBI.

Injury-plagued Kirk Gibson played in 132 games—the second-most he has appeared in since 1985—and had 16 home runs. Manager's son Brian McRae made his mark as the starting center fielder. He batted .261 with 64 RBI, and led the team in runs (86), hits (164) and stolen bases (20).

—*Deron Snyder*

Royals 1992 preview

George Brett's race to 3,000 hits could be the highlight of this season in Kansas City. The future Hall of Famer needs just 164 more to reach the milestone.

There might not be much else to excite the fans. The Royals avoided the cellar by a single game last season—they'll have to make some big strides this year. The Royals admitted they needed offense, especially when Danny Tartabull opted for free agency. So, they went anmd got some: Kevin McReynolds, Gregg Jefferies and Keith Miller from the Mets and Wally Joyner from the Angels.

Outfielder Brian McRae, son of manager Hal McRae, made his mark last year and should be an exciting player to watch. But he'll get no offensive help from the farm system.

The Royals do have solid pitching with starters Mike Boddicker, Kevin Appier and Mark Gubicza. Relievers Mark Davis and Tom Gordon could be tried as a starter. Jeff Montgomery is an excellent closer in the bullpen.

1992 prophecy: Royals

▶Hal McRae auditions his pitchers and comes up with an eight-man starting rotation.

▶Prince Charles and Lady Di will picket Royals Stadium, objecting to the team's socially insensitive nickname.

▶The Royals will announce the release of Kirk Gibson in a statement saying his play had "odoriferous emanations."

—John Hunt

Gibson will be platooned in '92

Kirk Gibson faces a platoon situation next season in left field.

After hitting just .197 against left-handed pitching, Gibson will share time with Gary Thurman. He learned of the plan after a meeting with manager Hal McRae before the final series of the year in California.

"I think it will help him to play just against righties. I don't know if he thinks it's the best but he struggled against left-handed pitching." said McRae. "He's disgusted he didn't do better. It's something he should not brood over, but it's hard not to when you're hitting .197. (But) he doesn't disagree with what I'm saying."

Gibson hit .236 with 16 homers and 55 RBI. He has one year left on his contract, including incentives for games played beginning at 120.

Brent Mayne: Shaking off stress

Royals' catcher Brent Mayne enjoyed one of the sweet moments in sports when he was on the receiving end of Bret Saberhagen's first career no-hitter on Aug. 26.

There was such synchronicity between pitcher and catcher that the veteran right-hander never shook off the rookie.

"He called a terrific game," says Saberhagen of Mayne. "I couldn't have asked for better."

The ability to relax in a stressful situation is a cornerstone of Mayne's training routine. For the last three seasons he's been a pupil of Ayurvedic medicine, a 6,000-year-old Sanskrit practice. A week before catching Saberhagen's no-hitter, Mayne traveled to the Maharishi Ayur-Veda Health Center for a mental tune-up.

Mayne doesn't meditate, but he says the physical training has helped his game. "I was looking for something to enhance my play and I stumbled upon it," he says. "It's helping me with dealing with stress."

Tartabull tried positive thinking

By Hal Bodley

Danny Tartabull said he'd never been happier. What? The sometimes moody, sometimes angry Kansas City Royals' outfielder? Get serious.

At the time, the Royals were bringing up the rear in the AL West, fighting off a six-game losing streak with a weekend in Oakland staring them in the face.

And he was happy? At that point you'd think the only thing that would have made Tartabull happy would be to get that nightmare of a season over with.

Instead, he said, he couldn't wait to get to the ballpark every day.

"I've never been this happy since I came to Kansas City (1987)," Tartabull said as he prepared to catch the team flight to Oakland. "Sure, we're in last place. Sure, we've lost six in a row, but believe me there's a new atmosphere here."

Tartabull was batting .305 with 12 home runs at the time. Was that the source of his newfound serenity?

"No, it started before that," Tartabull said. "When Herk Robinson took over as general manager last winter he called me. Said he would fly out (to Los Angeles) and visit. He kept his word.

He's backed up everything he promised. He's made us feel like a part of the family."

For Tartabull, another breath of fresh air was pumped into his career when Hal McRae took over as manager May 24.

"I'm in the best batting stroke of my career," said Tartabull, who finished the 1991 season among the league leaders in batting (.316), home runs (31) and RBI (100).

"Hal is the reason. He's got me hitting the ball to the middle of the field. I'm like a sponge around him. He helps me most with the approach to hitting. He doesn't mess with the mechanics that much. He keeps telling me to keep my head in the right place and take it from there."

In the past Tartabull's head has been one of his major problems.

It seemed like every time he picked up the paper he read that he was on the trading block. He hated for the phone to ring.

"It bothered me, was frustrating," he said. "Then, I got to thinking. If people are talking about getting me in a trade, then I'm needed—I'm wanted."

No kidding. When Tartabull declared himself a free agent after the season, he was on the most wanted list.

Royals winter league news

▶Winter leagues: RHP Scott Centala worked on his control in the Dominican Republic. "He'll have to have above average control to be effective in the major leagues because his velocity is less than what you would like," said Hegman. . . OF Kevin Koslofski, who has demonstrated exceptional speed but little proficiency in stealing bases, worked on base stealing technique. . . . LHP Dennis Moeller and RHP Steve Shifflett worked on their control. . . . RHP Mark Parnell tried to improve his consistency. . . . RHP Hipolito Pachardo played at home in the Dominican Republic.
▶Winter leagues roster: Scott Centala, RHP, Azucareros del Este (Sugarmen),

D.R.; Luis Encarnacion, RHP, Leones (Lions) Escogido, D.R.; Frank Laureano, IF, Estrellas Orientales (Eastern Stars), D.R.; Kevin Koslofski, OF, Azucareros Este (Sugar East), D.R.; Jim Lemasters, RHP, Azucareros Este, D.R.; Jeffrey Leonard, OF, released by KC, Culiacan, Mexico; Dennis Moeller, LHP, Azucareros Este, D.R.; Mark Parnell, RHP, Azucareros Este, D.R.; Hipolito Pachardo, RHP, Azucareros Este, D.R.;Jorge Pedre, C, Azucareros Este, D.R.; Steve Shifflett, RHP, Kansas City, Mazatlan Venados (Deer), Mexico.

Team directory

▶Owner: Ewing Kauffman

▶General Manager: Herk Robinson

▶Ballpark:
Royals Stadium
1 Royal Way, Kansas City, Missouri
816-921-8000
Capacity 40,625
Pay parking lot; $5
Public transportation available
Wheelchair section and ramps

▶Team publications:
Yearbook

▶TV, radio broadcast stations:
KMBZ 980 AM, WDAF-TV Channel 4

▶Camps and/or clinics:
Dream Week, Baseball City, Florida, February, 800-888-4376
Youth clinics, during the season, 816-921-8000

▶Spring Training:
Baseball City Stadium
Baseball City, Florida
Capacity 8,000
813-424-7211

KANSAS CITY ROYALS 1991 Final Stats

Batting	AVG	SLG	OB	G	AB	R	H	TB	2B	3B	HR	RBI	BB	SO	SB	CS	E
Liriano	.409	.409	.409	10	22	5	9	9	0	0	0	1	0	2	0	1	0
Moore	.357	.429	.400	18	14	3	5	6	1	0	0	0	1	2	3	2	0
Tartabull	.316	.593	.397	132	484	78	153	287	35	3	31	100	65	121	6	3	7
Cromartie	.313	.420	.381	69	131	13	41	55	7	2	1	20	15	18	1	3	1
Eisenreich	.301	.392	.333	135	375	47	113	147	22	3	2	47	20	35	5	3	5
Benzinger	.294	.386	.338	78	293	29	86	113	15	3	2	40	17	46	2	6	3
Pecota	.286	.399	.356	125	398	53	114	159	23	2	6	45	41	45	16	7	4
Thurman	.277	.359	.320	80	184	24	51	66	9	0	2	13	11	42	15	5	4
Macfarlane	.277	.506	.330	84	267	34	74	135	18	2	13	41	17	52	1	0	3
Pulliam	.273	.576	.333	18	33	4	9	19	1	0	3	4	3	9	0	0	2
Seitzer	.265	.350	.350	85	234	28	62	82	11	3	1	25	29	21	4	1	11
Stillwell	.265	.361	.322	122	385	44	102	139	17	1	6	51	33	56	3	4	18
Pedre	.263	.421	.364	10	19	2	5	8	1	1	0	3	3	5	0	0	1
Morman	.261	.261	.292	12	23	1	6	6	0	0	0	1	1	5	0	0	0
McRae	.261	.372	.288	152	629	86	164	234	28	9	8	64	24	99	20	11	3
Brett	.255	.402	.327	131	505	77	129	203	40	2	10	61	58	75	2	0	1
Mayne	.251	.325	.315	85	231	22	58	75	8	0	3	31	23	42	2	4	6
Gibson	.236	.403	.341	132	462	81	109	186	17	6	16	55	69	103	18	4	4
Puhl	.222	.222	.333	15	18	0	4	4	0	0	0	3	3	2	0	0	0
Shumpert	.217	.322	.283	144	369	45	80	119	16	4	5	34	30	75	17	11	16
Howard	.216	.258	.267	94	236	20	51	61	7	0	1	17	16	45	3	2	12
Martinez	.207	.355	.351	44	121	17	25	43	6	0	4	17	27	25	0	1	3
Clark	.200	.200	.273	11	10	1	2	2	0	0	0	1	1	1	0	0	0
Spehr	.189	.378	.282	37	74	7	14	28	5	0	3	14	9	18	1	0	3
Cole	.143	.143	.333	9	7	1	1	1	0	0	0	0	2	2	0	0	0
Berry	.133	.183	.212	31	60	5	8	11	3	0	0	1	5	23	0	0	2
Zuvella	–	–	–	2	0	0	0	0	0	0	0	0	0	0	0	0	0

Pitching	W-L	ERA	G	GS	CG	GF	Sho	SV	IP	H	R	ER	HR	BB	SO
Johnston	1-0	0.40	13	0	0	1	0	0	22.1	9	1	1	0	9	21
Gardner	0-0	1.59	3	0	0	2	0	0	5.2	5	4	1	0	2	3
Magnante	0-1	2.45	38	0	0	10	0	0	55	55	19	15	3	23	42
Montgomery	4-4	2.90	67	0	0	55	0	33	90	83	32	29	6	28	77
Saberhagen	13-8	3.07	28	28	7	0	2	0	196.1	165	76	67	12	45	136
Appier	13-10	3.42	34	31	6	1	3	0	207.2	205	97	79	13	61	158
Aquino	8-4	3.44	38	18	1	9	1	3	157	152	67	60	10	47	80
Corbin	0-0	3.86	2	0	0	2	0	0	2.1	3	1	1	0	2	1
Gordon	9-14	3.87	45	14	1	11	0	1	158	129	76	68	16	87	167
Boddicker	12-12	4.08	30	29	1	1	0	0	180.2	188	89	82	13	59	79
M. Davis	6-3	4.45	29	5	0	8	0	1	62.2	55	36	31	6	39	47
McGaffigan	0-0	4.50	4	0	0	1	0	0	8	14	5	4	0	2	3
Pecota	0-0	4.50	1	0	0	1	0	0	2	4	1	1	0	0	0
S. Davis	3-9	4.96	51	9	1	22	1	2	114.1	140	69	63	11	46	53
Gubicza	9-12	5.68	26	26	0	0	0	0	133	168	90	84	10	42	89
Crawford	3-2	5.98	33	0	0	17	0	1	46.2	60	31	31	3	18	38
Wagner	1-1	7.20	2	2	0	0	0	0	10	16	10	8	2	3	5
Maldonado	0-0	8.22	5	0	0	2	0	0	7.2	11	9	7	0	9	1
Schatzeder	0-0	9.45	8	0	0	2	0	0	6.2	11	9	7	0	7	4

1992 Preliminary Roster

Pitchers (17)

Kevin Appier
Luis Aquino
Mike Boddicker
Dera Clark
Archie Corbin
Mark Davis
Tom Gordon
Mark Gubicza
Joel Johnston
Mike Magnante
Carlos Maldonado
Rusty Meacham
Dennis Moeller
Jeff Montgomery
Hipolito Pichardo
Ed Pierce
Hector Wagner

Catchers (4)

Mike Macfarlane
Brent Mayne
Bob Melvin
Tim Spehr

Infielders (11)

Sean Berry
George Brett
Stu Cole
Jeff Conine
Bob Hamelin
Gregg Jefferies
Wally Joyner
Keith Miller
David Howard
Kevin Seitzer
Terry Shumpert

Outfielders (9)

David Clark
Kirk Gibson
Chris Gwynn
Kevin Koslofski
Brian McRae
Kevin McReynolds
Kerwin Moore
Harvey Pulliam
Gary Thurman

Games Played by position

	G	C	1B	2B	3B	SS	OF	DH
Benzinger,T	78	0	75	0	0	0	0	1
Berry,S	31	0	0	0	30	0	0	0
Brett,G	131	0	10	0	0	0	0	118
Clark,D	11	0	0	0	0	0	1	1
Cole,S	9	0	0	5	0	1	0	2
Cromartie,W	69	0	29	0	0	0	6	1
Eisenreich,J	135	0	15	0	0	0	105	1
Gibson,K	132	0	0	0	0	0	94	30
Howard,D	94	0	0	26	1	63	1	1
Liriano,N	10	0	0	10	0	0	0	0
Macfarlane,M	84	69	0	0	0	0	0	4
Martinez,Cs	44	0	43	0	0	0	0	1
Mayne,B	85	80	0	0	0	0	0	1
McRae,B	152	0	0	0	0	0	150	0
Moore,B	18	0	0	0	0	0	13	0
Morman,R	12	0	8	0	0	0	2	1
Pecota,B	125	0	8	34	102	9	1	2
Pedre,J	10	9	1	0	0	0	0	0
Puhl,T	15	0	0	0	0	0	1	2
Pulliam,H	18	0	0	0	0	0	15	0
Seitzer,K	85	0	0	0	68	0	0	3
Shumpert,T	144	0	0	144	0	0	0	0
Spehr,T	37	37	0	0	0	0	0	0
Stillwell,K	122	0	0	0	0	118	0	0
Tartabull,D	132	0	0	0	0	0	124	6
Thurman,G	80	0	0	0	0	0	72	0
Zuvella,P	2	0	0	0	2	0	0	0

Sick call: 1991 DL report

Player	Days on the DL
Mark Davis	63*
George Brett	31
Kevin Seitzer	34
Mike Boddicker	16
Mark Gubicza	36
Bret Saberhagen	30
Steve Crawford	73*
Mike Macfarlane	60
Kurt Stillwell	16
Gary Thurman	34

On DL twice (not counting administrative transfers from one DL to another).

Minor League Report

Class AAA — Omaha finished third in the Western Division of the American Association with a 73-71 record. It was the Royals' fourth consecutive winning season, a new club record. Omaha fell 864 fans shy of the record 341,129 attendance figure set in 1990. Royals LHP Bob Buchanan was named the league's top southpaw and C Tim Spehr joined Buchanan on the American Association postseason all-star team. OF Jacob Brumfield captured the league stolen base title with 36. OF David Clark finished sixth in the league in batting with a .301 average. Reliever Mark Huismann was second in the league in saves with 17. . . . **Class AA** — Memphis completed its season 61-83 in the Southern League's Western Division, in last place during the first half and in second place during the second half. OF Kevin Koslofski, who was promoted to Omaha in July with a .324 batting average, was named the Chicks' most valuable player. RHP Archie Corbin, who was 8-8, was named the team's top pitcher. RHP Steve Shifflett was the top reliever. The top defensive player award went to 2B Frank Laureano. OF Hugh Walker received the team hustle award. The team rookie of the year award went to utility player Darryl Robinson. . . . **Class A** — Baseball City finished 62-69 in the central division of the Florida State League, third in the first half and second in the second half. OF Kerwin Moore led the league with 61 stolen bases. and 130 games played and was second in the league with 77 walks. . . . Appleton completed its year 58-81 in the Northern Division of the Midwest League, third in the first half and last in the second half. . . . Eugene finished 42-34 and in second place in the Northwest League's Southern Division. 3B Joe Randa was named league MVP. Manager Tom Poquette was named manager of the year. OF Mark Johnson named to the league's postseason all-star team.

Tops in the Organization

BATTING LEADERS	Club	Avg.	G	AB	R	H	HR	RBI
Kevin Koslofski	Oma.	318	106	381	54	121	9	58
Dave Clark	Oma.	301	104	359	45	108	13	64
Frank Laureano	Mem.	291	105	378	60	110	4	39
Harry Guanchez	App	.280	109	375	40	105	2	50
Kevin Long	Mem.	275	106	407	60	112	3	35

HOME RUNS			WINS		
Dave Clark	Oma	13	Doug Harris	Bcy	12
Phil Hiatt	Mem	11	Dennis Moeller	Oma	11
Sean Berry	Oma	11	Steve Shifflett	Mem	11
Jorge Pedre	Oma	10	Bob Buchanan	Oma	11
Jeffrey Leonard	Oma	10	Brian Ahern	Bcy	9

RBI			SAVES		
Gary Caraballo	Bcy	68	Mark Huismann	Oma	17
Phil Hiatt	Mem	66	Skip Wiley	Bcy	17
Dave Clark	Oma	64	Mark Parnell	Mem	17
Jorge Pedre	Oma	63	David Hierholzer	App	14
Kevin Koslofski	Oma	58	Tony Long	Bcy	10

STOLEN BASES			STRIKEOUTS		
Kerwin Moore	Bcy	61	Archie Corbin	Mem	166
Darren Burton	App	37	Doug Harris	Bcy	123
Jacob Brumfield	Oma	36	Dera Clark	Oma	108
Bobby Moore	Oma	35	Dennis Moeller	Oma	105
Phil Hiatt	Mem	34	Shayne Rea	App	97

PITCHING LEADERS	Club	W-L	ERA	IP	H	BB	SO
Steve Shifflett	Mem	11-5	2.15	113	105	22	78
Doug Harris	Bcy	12-8	2.39	162	133	37	123
Kevin Shaw	Bcy	6-12	2.88	137	144	39	55
Dennis Moeller	Oma	11-8	2.95	131	122	61	105
Brian Ahern	Bcy	9-6	3.11	130	124	51	56

Kansas City (1969-1991)

Runs: Most, career, all-time

1459	GEORGE BRETT, 1973-1991
1074	Amos Otis, 1970-1983
1060	WILLIE WILSON, 1976-1990
912	Frank White, 1973-1990
873	Hal McRae, 1973-1987

Hits: Most, career, all-time

2836	GEORGE BRETT, 1973-1991
2006	Frank White, 1973-1990
1977	Amos Otis, 1970-1983
1968	WILLIE WILSON, 1976-1990
1924	Hal McRae, 1973-1987

2B: Most, career, all-time

599	GEORGE BRETT, 1973-1991
449	Hal McRae, 1973-1987
407	Frank White, 1973-1990
365	Amos Otis, 1970-1983
241	WILLIE WILSON, 1976-1990

3B: Most, career, all-time

133	WILLIE WILSON, 1976-1990
129	GEORGE BRETT, 1973-1991
65	Amos Otis, 1970-1983
63	Hal McRae, 1973-1987
58	Frank White, 1973-1990

HR: Most, career, all-time

291	GEORGE BRETT, 1973-1991
193	Amos Otis, 1970-1983
169	Hal McRae, 1973-1987
160	Frank White, 1973-1990
143	John Mayberry, 1972-1977

RBI: Most, career, all-time

1459	GEORGE BRETT, 1973-1991
1012	Hal McRae, 1973-1987
992	Amos Otis, 1970-1983
886	Frank White, 1973-1990
552	John Mayberry, 1972-1977

SB: Most, career, all-time

612	WILLIE WILSON, 1976-1990
340	Amos Otis, 1970-1983
336	Freddie Patek, 1971-1979
186	GEORGE BRETT, 1973-1991
178	Frank White, 1973-1990

BB: Most, career, all-time

1022	GEORGE BRETT, 1973-1991
739	Amos Otis, 1970-1983
616	Hal McRae, 1973-1987

561	John Mayberry, 1972-1977
413	Freddie Patek, 1971-1979

BA: Highest, career, all-time

.308	GEORGE BRETT, 1973-1991
.294	KEVIN SEITZER, 1986-1991
.293	Hal McRae, 1973-1987
.290	DANNY TARTABULL, 1987-1991
.289	WILLIE WILSON, 1976-1990

Slug avg: Highest, career, all-time

.518	DANNY TARTABULL, 1987-1991
.496	GEORGE BRETT, 1973-1991
.480	BO JACKSON, 1986-1990
.469	Willie Aikens, 1980-1983
.459	Steve Balboni, 1984-1988

Games started: Most, career, all-time

392	Paul Splittorff, 1970-1984
302	Dennis Leonard, 1974-1986
229	MARK GUBICZA, 1984-1991
226	BRET SABERHAGEN, 1984-1991
219	Larry Gura, 1976-1985

Saves: Most, career, all-time

238	Dan Quisenberry, 1979-1988
76	JEFF MONTGOMERY, 1988-1991
58	Doug Bird, 1973-1978
49	STEVE FARR, 1985-1990
40	Ted Abernathy, 1970-1972

Shutouts: Most, career, all-time

23	Dennis Leonard, 1974-1986
17	Paul Splittorff, 1970-1984
14	Larry Gura, 1976-1985
14	BRET SABERHAGEN, 1984-1991
12	MARK GUBICZA, 1984-1991

Wins: Most, career, all-time

166	Paul Splittorff, 1970-1984
144	Dennis Leonard, 1974-1986
111	Larry Gura, 1976-1985
110	BRET SABERHAGEN, 1984-1991
97	MARK GUBICZA, 1984-1991

K: Most, career, all-time

1323	Dennis Leonard, 1974-1986
1093	BRET SABERHAGEN, 1984-1991
1057	Paul Splittorff, 1970-1984
1010	MARK GUBICZA, 1984-1991
659	Steve Busby, 1972-1980

Win pct: Highest, career, all-time

.593	Al Fitzmorris, 1969-1976
.587	Larry Gura, 1976-1985
.585	BRET SABERHAGEN, 1984-1991
.576	Doug Bird, 1973-1978
.576	Dennis Leonard, 1974-1986

ERA: Lowest, career, all-time

2.55	Dan Quisenberry, 1979-1988
3.21	BRET SABERHAGEN, 1984-1991
3.46	Al Fitzmorris, 1969-1976
3.48	Marty Pattin, 1974-1980
3.52	Dick Drago, 1969-1973

Runs: Most, season

133	WILLIE WILSON, 1980
119	GEORGE BRETT, 1979
113	WILLIE WILSON, 1979
108	GEORGE BRETT, 1985
105	GEORGE BRETT, 1977
105	KEVIN SEITZER, 1987

Hits: Most, season

230	WILLIE WILSON, 1980
215	GEORGE BRETT, 1976
212	GEORGE BRETT, 1979
207	KEVIN SEITZER, 1987
195	GEORGE BRETT, 1975

2B: Most, season

54	Hal McRae, 1977
46	Hal McRae, 1982
45	GEORGE BRETT, 1978
45	GEORGE BRETT, 1990
45	Frank White, 1982

3B: Most, season

21	WILLIE WILSON, 1985
20	GEORGE BRETT, 1979
15	WILLIE WILSON, 1980

| 15 | WILLIE WILSON, 1982 |
| 15 | WILLIE WILSON, 1987 |

HR: Most, season

36	Steve Balboni, 1985
34	John Mayberry, 1975
34	DANNY TARTABULL, 1987
32	BO JACKSON, 1989
31	DANNY TARTABULL, 1991

RBI: Most, season

133	Hal McRae, 1982
118	GEORGE BRETT, 1980
112	GEORGE BRETT, 1985
112	Al Cowens, 1977
112	Darrell Porter, 1979

SB: Most, season

83	WILLIE WILSON, 1979
79	WILLIE WILSON, 1980
59	WILLIE WILSON, 1983
59	WILLIE WILSON, 1987
53	Freddie Patek, 1977

BB: Most, season

122	John Mayberry, 1973
121	Darrell Porter, 1979
119	John Mayberry, 1975
103	GEORGE BRETT, 1985
103	Paul Schaal, 1971

BA: Highest, season

.390	GEORGE BRETT, 1980
.335	GEORGE BRETT, 1985
.333	GEORGE BRETT, 1976
.332	Hal McRae, 1976
.332	WILLIE WILSON, 1982

Slug avg: Highest, season

.664	GEORGE BRETT, 1980
.593	DANNY TARTABULL, 1991
.585	GEORGE BRETT, 1985
.563	GEORGE BRETT, 1979
.563	GEORGE BRETT, 1983

Games started: Most, season

40	Dennis Leonard, 1978
38	Steve Busby, 1974
38	Dennis Leonard, 1980
38	Paul Splittorff, 1973
38	Paul Splittorff, 1978

Saves: Most, season

45	Dan Quisenberry, 1983
44	Dan Quisenberry, 1984
37	Dan Quisenberry, 1985
35	Dan Quisenberry, 1982
33	JEFF MONTGOMERY, 1991

| 33 | Dan Quisenberry, 1980 |

Shutouts: Most, season

6	Roger Nelson, 1972
5	Dennis Leonard, 1977
5	Dennis Leonard, 1979
4	Bill Butler, 1969
4	Dick Drago, 1971
4	Al Fitzmorris, 1974
4	MARK GUBICZA, 1988
4	Larry Gura, 1980
4	Dennis Leonard, 1978
4	BRET SABERHAGEN, 1987
4	BRET SABERHAGEN, 1989

Wins: Most, season

23	BRET SABERHAGEN, 1989
22	Steve Busby, 1974
21	Dennis Leonard, 1978
20	MARK GUBICZA, 1988
20	Dennis Leonard, 1977
20	Dennis Leonard, 1980
20	BRET SABERHAGEN, 1985
20	Paul Splittorff, 1973

K: Most, season

244	Dennis Leonard, 1977
206	Bob Johnson, 1970
198	Steve Busby, 1974
193	BRET SABERHAGEN, 1989
183	MARK GUBICZA, 1988
183	Dennis Leonard, 1978

Win pct: Highest, season

.800	Larry Gura, 1978
.793	BRET SABERHAGEN, 1989
.769	BRET SABERHAGEN, 1985
.727	Paul Splittorff, 1977
.714	MARK GUBICZA, 1988

ERA: Lowest, season

2.08	Roger Nelson, 1972
2.16	BRET SABERHAGEN, 1989
2.69	CHARLIE LEIBRANDT, 1985
2.70	MARK GUBICZA, 1988
2.71	Mike Hedlund, 1971

Most pinch-hit homers, season

| 2 | Hal McRae, 1986 |
| 2 | Carmelo Martinez, 1991 |

Most pinch-hit, homers, career

2	Chuck Harrison, 1969-1971
2	Bob Oliver, 1969-1972
2	Amos Otis, 1970-1983

2	Hal McRae, 1973-1987
2	Steve Balboni, 1984-1988
2	Jim Eisenreich, 1987-1991
2	Carmelo Martinez, 1991

Most consecutive games, batting safely

| 30 | George Brett, 1980 |

Most consecutive scoreless innings

| 31 | Bret Saberhagen, 1989 |

No hit games

Steve Busby, KC at Det AL, 3-0; April 16, 1973.

Steve Busby, KC at Mil AL, 2-0; June 19, 1974.

Jim Colborn, KC vs Tex AL, 6-0; May 14, 1977.

Bret Saberhagen, KC vs Chi AL, 7-0; August 26, 1991.

California Angels

California Angels

Jim Abbott was one of California's top pitchers in 1991.

Strong arms, weak bats, last place

The Minnesota Twins proved a team can go from last to first in one season. The California Angels proved a team can go from first to last in one month.

The Angels were leading the American League West on July 3, by .001. A month later, on Aug. 4, they were dead last in the division. And that's exactly where they finished the '91 campaign.

They also finished the season with a new manager and front office. General manager Mike Port was fired Apr. 30, replaced by Dan O'Brien. Doug Rader was swept out as skipper on Aug. 26, replaced by Buck Rodgers—who had been fired earlier in the season by the Montreal Expos. Finally, Whitey Herzog was named director of player personnel Sept. 6, and was given a great deal of latitude to make deals.

The Angels ended the year at .500 with an 81-81 record, the best ever for a last-place team. But how the Angels finished last with three starters who won at least 18 games apiece and the AL save leader seems a bit of a mystery.

Mark Langston (19-8), Chuck Finley (18-9) and Jim Abbott (18-11) gave the Angels the best starting trio in the league. Bryan Harvey became the dominant closer in the loop with 46 saves.

For both Langston and Abbott, the season was a vindication. In 1990, after signing a four-year, $15-million deal, Langston went 10-17. Abbott started the season with seven straight losses, and had critics screaming that the Angels had rushed him to the majors too quickly.

After the big three, though, there was little help on the Angels pitching staff. No. 4 starter Kirk McCaskill—a free agent at the end of the '91 season—struggled through a 10-19, 4.26 season, while the real black hole was the fifth starter spot. Through the end of August, pitchers such as Scott Lewis, Joe Grahe and Fernando Valenzuela had all been used—and had contributed a 1-16 record.

Where the Angels really fell short was offensively. The hitting simply disappeared during the team's fall from first. Overall, California finished 13th in runs, on-base percentage and slugging percentage. The .255 team batting average was tied for ninth.

Gary Gaetti—signed from the Twins just before the '91 season began—batted .246 and drove in just 66 runs, his lowest total since 1985. Lance Parrish—in the third year of a four-year deal—fell off to a .216 average with 19 homers, 51 RBI and 117 strikeouts.

But Wally Joyner had his best season in four years, batting .301 with 21 homers and 96 RBI—increasing his value in the free agent market.

The "Twin Creaks"—Dave Winfield and Dave Parker—did not have distinguished seasons. Winfield faded badly in the second half, ending with a .262 average, 28 homers and 86 RBI. Parker was released by the Angels—and picked up by the Blue Jays—after being relegated to part-time DH status.

Herzog has already promised the makeup of the Angels will be different. For years, it's been the "Old Folks Boogie" in Anaheim, as the club hired a bunch of aging stars to try to bring owner Gene Autry a World Championship. But both Herzog and Rodgers like the running game—meaning the team should have a younger look. If they can score runs to go with the outstanding pitching, the Angels could be the next team to go from last to first in a season.

—*Rick Lawes*

Angels 1992 preview

The Angels had the best last-place record in history last season (81-81). They are capable of much more. They had three of the league's top seven winners last year in starters Mark Langston (19-8), Chuck Finley (18-9)

and Jim Abbott (18-11); the top closer in Bryan Harvey (46 saves); and a great set-up man in Mark Eichhorn (1.98 ERA).

It wasn't enough to overcome a .255 team batting average (13th in runs and slugging).

New GM Whitey Herzog, hoping to work his magic that led to winners in Kansas City and St. Louis, wasted no time making changes.

The Angels released veterans Dave Winfield and Dave Parker as the team began its move toward younger, faster players. (Only outfielder Luis Polonia had more than 10 steals last year.)

Outfielder Junior Felix must overcome his injuries and veterans Von Hayes, Gary Gaetti and Lance Parrish have to bounce back from sub-par years.

1992 prophecy: Angels

▶General manager Whitey Herzog will acquire Don Mattingly from the Yankees and insist he adopt Herzog's hairstyle. Whitey will then trade the unhappy Mattingly to Oakland for Mark McGwire (after passing on Dennis Eckersley).

▶In a whirlwind of front office maneuvering, Herzog will also acquire Greg Swindell, Jimmy Key and Randy Johnson, so the Angels could be the only American League team with a quality left-handed starting pitcher.

—*John Hunt*

Winfield admitted to 400 club

By Mike Terry

Dave Winfield became the 23rd player in history to hit 400 or more home runs Aug. 14 in California's 7-4 win against Minnesota.

"What did I tell you guys out in Anaheim," Winfield, a native of nearby St. Paul, said. "Right here. Somehow you can dig down and do what you like to do in this game. You don't always do it when you want, but it was appropri-

ate here.

"To get off 399 . . . it sounds like something you purchase at a discount store. Four hundred sounds so much better."

Winfield cranked his historic hit off David West (3-3) in the fourth, with Dave Parker aboard, to give California a 3-2 lead. The home run put Winfield into 23rd place on the all-time list, ahead of Al Kaline; Winfield is No.1 among active home-run leaders.

Rader will miss people, not job

Former Angels manager Doug Rader—replaced by Buck Rodgers—said he didn't take his firing personally.

"The only thing that matters to me are the relationships I have with other people," Rodgers said. " . . . someday when I've got my grandchild on my knee I'm going to tell him about the time we beat Boston in the ninth. I'll say, 'I'd like to tell you a story about a right-handed pitcher named Kirk McCaskill.'

"I came here with a couple of friends and left with a whole bunch more. That's the hardest. The job itself is not the thing."

Rader knows he's the scapegoat for the Angels' last-place standing in its division—"that's part of the job description, isn't it?"

But he agrees the Angels didn't live up to expectations: "We just didn't hit, simple as that."

Abbott's big season eased Angels' pain

If the summer of 1991 holds any good memories for the California Angels, it will be the coming of age of Jim Abbott.

The images of the struggling young left-hander—as recent as last April when he opened the season 0-4—have faded in the face of the confident, hard-throwing 23-year-old who stepped to the mound every fifth day.

"He sure deserves (the success)," said ex-manager Doug Rader, who was primarily responsible for Abbott never having spent a day in the minors. "He's pitched well for very long and been in a terrific streak. But he's been consistent and competitive. He is special."

Catcher Lance Parrish has a simple formula for Abbott's streak, "One, he's getting ahead of the hitters; two, he's throwing the fastball on the outside corner to right-hand hitters on a consistent basis; and three, he's throwing his curves for strikes, so no one can just sit on the inside stuff," Parrish said.

Abbott himself had a word for it—control. "It has to do with experience and learning to throw the ball where I want to," said Abbott. "Everyone up here has control; it's who wants to trust it and throw over the plate."

Angels winter league news

▶Winter leagues: Several of California's top Latin American players went home to play winter ball, including OF Luis Polonia and OF Junior Felix in the Dominican Republic. . . .Most of the 1991 Edmonton pitching staff pitched in the winter leagues, including Abbott in Puerto Rico, LHP Sherm Corbett and RHP Tim Burcham in Mexico, and RHP Mike Erb, RHP Scott Lewis, RHP Fred Toliver and LHP Cliff Young in Venezuela. . . . The Angels have a partial working agreement with Tiburones de La Guaira of the Venezuelan league and sent six players there this winter. . 2B Luis Sojo, at home in Veneuzuela, played against his California teammates with the Cardenales de Lara squad. . . . OF Chad Curtis hit .490 with 14 RBI in his first 14 games in Venezuela. Aguilas Cibaena (Eagles), D.R.; Luis Sojo, 2B, Cardenales de Lara, Venezuela; Fred Toliver, RHP, Tiburones de La Guaira, Venezuela; Cliff Young, LHP, Tiburones de La Guaira, Venezuela.

Team directory

▶Owner: Gene Autry

▶General Manager: Buck Rodgers

▶Ballpark:
Anaheim Stadium
2000 Gene Autry Way, Anaheim, California
714-634-1300
Capacity 64,593
Parking for 15,000 vehicles; $4
Public transportation available
Family and wheelchair sections, escalators, ramps, picnic section

▶Team publications:
Halo Magazine

▶TV, radio broadcast stations:
KMPC 710AM, XPRS 1090 (Spanish), KTLA Channel 5, SportsChannel

▶Camps and/or clinics:
MCI/Angels Clinic, dates TBA, 714-937-6700
Angels Rookie League, dates TBA, 714-937-6700

▶Spring Training:
Gene Autry Park, Mesa, Arizona, 602-830-4137
Angels Stadium, Palm Springs, California, 619-323-3325

CALIFORNIA ANGELS 1991 Final Stats

Batting	AVG	SLG	OB	G	AB	R	H	TB	2B	3B	HR	RBI	BB	SO	SB	CS	E
Joyner	.301	.488	.360	143	551	79	166	269	34	3	21	96	52	66	2	0	8
Polonia	.296	.379	.352	150	604	92	179	229	28	8	2	50	52	74	48	23	5
Stevens	.293	.414	.354	18	58	8	17	24	7	0	0	9	6	12	1	2	1
Gallagher	.293	.367	.355	90	270	32	79	99	17	0	1	30	24	43	2	4	0
Felix	.283	.370	.321	66	230	32	65	85	10	2	2	26	11	55	7	5	3
Rose	.277	.431	.304	22	65	5	18	28	5	1	1	8	3	13	0	0	0
Winfield	.262	.472	.326	150	568	75	149	268	27	4	28	86	56	109	7	2	2
Marshall	.261	.362	.261	24	69	4	18	25	4	0	1	7	0	20	0	0	1
Sojo	.258	.327	.295	113	364	38	94	119	14	1	3	20	14	26	4	2	11
Venable	.246	.358	.292	82	187	24	46	67	8	2	3	21	11	30	2	1	3
Gaetti	.246	.379	.293	152	586	58	144	222	22	1	18	66	33	104	5	5	17
Hill	.239	.301	.335	77	209	36	50	63	8	1	1	20	30	21	1	0	8
Abner	.228	.366	.257	41	101	12	23	37	6	1	2	9	4	18	1	2	0
Schofield	.225	.260	.310	134	427	44	96	111	9	3	0	31	50	69	8	4	15
Amaro	.217	.261	.308	10	23	0	5	6	1	0	0	2	3	3	0	0	1
Parrish	.216	.388	.285	119	402	38	87	156	12	0	19	51	35	117	0	1	2
Disarcina	.211	.246	.274	18	57	5	12	14	2	0	0	3	3	4	0	0	4
Howell	.210	.309	.304	32	81	11	17	25	2	0	2	7	11	11	1	1	2
Orton	.203	.261	.313	29	69	7	14	18	4	0	0	3	10	17	0	1	1
Lyons	.200	.200	.200	2	5	0	1	1	0	0	0	0	0	0	0	0	0
Tingley	.200	.287	.258	45	115	11	23	33	7	0	1	13	8	34	1	1	3
Cron	.133	.133	.235	6	15	0	2	2	0	0	0	0	2	5	0	0	0
Flora	.125	.125	.222	3	8	1	1	1	0	0	0	0	1	5	1	0	2
Davis	.000	.000	.000	3	2	0	0	0	0	0	0	0	0	0	0	0	1

Pitching	W-L	ERA	G	GS	CG	GF	Sho	SV	IP	H	R	ER	HR	BB	SO
Harvey	2-4	1.60	67	0	0	63	0	46	78.2	51	20	14	6	17	101
Eichhorn	3-3	1.98	70	0	0	23	0	1	81.2	63	21	18	2	13	49
J. Abbott	18-11	2.89	34	34	5	0	1	0	243	222	85	78	14	73	158
Langston	19-8	3.00	34	34	7	0	0	0	246.1	190	89	82	30	96	183
Beasley	0-1	3.38	22	0	0	8	0	0	26.2	26	14	10	2	10	14
Finley	18-9	3.80	34	34	4	0	2	0	227.1	205	102	96	23	101	171
Bannister	0-0	3.96	16	0	0	2	0	0	25	25	12	11	5	10	16
Bailes	1-2	4.18	42	0	0	14	0	0	51.2	41	26	24	5	22	41
McCaskill	10-19	4.26	30	30	1	0	0	0	177.2	193	93	84	19	66	71
Young	1-0	4.26	11	0	0	6	0	0	12.2	12	6	6	3	3	6
K. Abbott	1-2	4.58	5	3	0	0	0	0	19.2	22	11	10	2	13	12
Grahe	3-7	4.81	18	10	1	2	0	0	73	84	43	39	2	33	40
Fetters	2-5	4.84	19	4	0	8	0	0	44.2	53	29	24	4	28	24
Robinson	0-3	5.37	39	0	0	16	0	3	57	56	34	34	9	29	57
Lewis	3-5	6.27	16	11	0	0	0	0	60.1	81	43	42	9	21	37
McClure	0-0	9.31	13	0	0	2	0	0	9.2	13	11	10	3	5	5
Valenzuela	0-2	12.15	2	2	0	0	0	0	6.2	14	10	9	3	3	5

1992 Preliminary Roster

Pitchers (16)
Jim Abbott
Scott Bailes
Chris Beasley
Michael Butcher
Mark Eichhorn
Michael Erb
Chuck Finley
Tim Fortugno
Joe Grahe
Bryan Harvey
Dave Holridge
Mark Langston
Scott Lewis

Paul Swingle
Cliff Young
Mark Zappelli

Catchers (3)
John Orton
Lance Parrish
Ron Tingley

Infielders (7)
Gary DiSarcina
Kevin Flora
Gary Gaetti
J.R. Phillips
Bobby Rose

Luis Sojo
Lee Stevens

Outfielders (9)
Shawn Abner
Hubie Brooks
Chad Curtis
Mark Davis
James Edmonds
Junior Felix
Von Hayes
Luis Polonia
Tim Salmon

Games played by position

	G	C	1B	2B	3B	SS	OF	DH
Abner,S	41	0	0	0	0	0	38	3
Amaro,R	10	0	0	4	0	0	5	1
Cron,C	6	0	5	0	0	0	0	1
Davis,M	3	0	0	0	0	0	3	0
Disarcina,G	18	0	0	7	2	10	0	0
Felix,J	66	0	0	0	0	0	65	0
Flora,K	3	0	0	3	0	0	0	0
Gaetti,G	152	0	0	0	152	0	0	0
Gallagher,D	90	0	0	0	0	0	87	2
Hill,D	77	0	3	39	0	29	0	0
Howell,J	32	0	3	12	8	0	5	1
Joyner,W	143	0	141	0	0	0	0	0
Lyons,B	2	0	2	0	0	0	0	0
Marshall,M	24	0	6	0	0	0	4	8
Orton,J	29	28	0	0	0	0	0	1
Parrish,L	119	111	3	0	0	0	0	5
Polonia,L	150	0	0	0	0	0	143	4
Rose,B	22	0	3	8	4	0	7	0
Schofield,D	134	0	0	0	0	133	0	0
Sojo,L	113	0	0	107	1	2	1	1
Stevens,L	18	0	11	0	0	0	9	0
Tingley,R	45	45	0	0	0	0	0	0
Venable,M	82	0	0	0	0	0	65	3
Winfield,D	150	0	0	0	0	0	115	34

Sick call: 1991 DL report

Player	Days on the DL
Bert Blyleven	182
Bob McClure	11
Jeff Richardson	182
Jack Howell	24
Floyd Bannister	31
Junior Felix	81*
Fernando Valenzuela	23
Lance Parrish	5
Scotty Bailes	15
Bobby Rose	44

On DL twice (not counting administrative transfers from one DL to another).

Minor League Report

Class AAA — Edmonton finished 70-66, second place in the Pacific Coast League's Northern Division during both halves of the season. SS Gary DiSarcina, who was named the Trappers' player of the year, led the PCL defensively with a .967 fielding percentage. and was 13th in the league with a batting .310 average.LHP Kyle Abbott and OF Ruben Amaro were named to the postseason PCL all-star team. Abbott tied for the league lead with 14 wins, tying a Trappers record and Abbott also finished second in the league with 120 strikeouts and was eighth in the league with a 3.99 ERA.led the league with 180.1 innings pitched. Amaro finished tied for third in the league with a .326 batting average and led the PCL with 95 runs and a team-record 42 doubles. He finished tied for third in the league with 154 hits.IF Chad Curtis finished with a .316 batting average and was third in the PCL with 46 stolen bases. 1B/OF Lee Stevens finished fourth in the league with 96 RBI. and was 11th in the league with a .314 average. . . . Class AA — Midland finished 67-68, fourth in the first half and first in the second half in the Texas League's Western Division. The Angels, who broke their all-time attendance record by drawing 180,616 fans, lost in the opening round, best-of-three playoffs to El Paso, two games to none. The previous attendance record was 168,742 set last year.3B/DH Mark Howie was voted MVP, and manager Don Long was voted Texas League manager of the year. He brought the Angels from a last-place finish in the first half to first place finish in the second half. 2B Kevin Flora (.285 avg.) led the Texas League with 15 triples. . . . Class A — Quad City finished 74-63, second in the first half and third in the second half in the Midwest League's southern division. DH Jeff Kipila (18 HRs, 77 RBI) was named to the Midwest League postseason All-Star team. RH reliever Daryl Scott led the minor leagues in opponents' batting average at .137. , and was second in strikeouts per nine innings with 14.7 INF Brian Grebeck was one of only three players in the Midwest League with 100 hits and 100 walks, and was also the league's top fielding shortstop.Quad City pitchers led the league with 1,131 strikeouts. . . . Palm Springs finished 65-71 in the California League's Southern Division, second in the first half and fourth in the second half. . . .

Boise captured the Northwest League's Southern Division title with a 50-26 record and defeated Northern Division winner Yakima two games to none in the best of three playoffs to win the Northwest League.

Tops in the Organization

BATTING LEADERS	Club	Avg.	G	AB	R	H	HR	RBI
Mark Howie	Mdl	.364	130	516	101	188	18	123
Ruben Amaro	Edm	.326	121	472	95	154	3	42
Don Barbara	Mdl	.324	129	450	72	146	15	88
Chad Curtis	Edm	.316	115	431	81	136	9	61
Lee Stevens	Edm	.314	123	481	75	151	19	96

HOME RUNS			WINS		
Tim Salmon	Mdl	23	Don Vidmar	Mdl	17
Chris Cron	Edm	22	Kyle Abbott	Edm	14
J.R. Phillips	Psp	20	Todd James	Mdl	12
Lee Stevens	Edm	19	Phillip Leftwich	Mdl	12
Several players tied		18	Several players tied		9

RBI			SAVES		
Mark Howie	Mdl	123	Darryl Scott	Qcy	19
Lee Stevens	Edm	96	Ken Edenfield	Qcy	15
Tim Salmon	Mdl	94	Mark Zappelli	Edm	11
Chris Cron	Edm	91	Paul Swingle	Psp	10
Don Barbara	Mdl	88	Several players tied		9

STOLEN BASES			STRIKEOUTS		
Clifton Garrett	Qcy	51	Phillip Leftwich	Mdl	166
Chad Curtis	Edm	46	Darryl Scott	Qcy	123
Kevin Flora	Mdl	40	Steve King	Psp	122
Ruben Amaro	Edm	36	Kyle Abbott	Edm	120
Marcus Lawton	Mdl	34	Justin Martin	Qcy	118

PITCHING LEADERS	Club	W-L	ERA	IP	H	BB	SO
Don Vidmar	Mdl	17-7	2.74	190	199	53	89
Phillip Leftwich	Mdl	12-9	3.27	179	163	64	166
Hilly Hathaway	Qcy	9-6	3.35	129	126	41	110
Steve Loubier	Psp	8-5	3.40	111	105	56	60
Dave Adams	Qcy	8-8	3.53	120	115	52	92

Runs: Most, career, all-time

889	BRIAN DOWNING, 1978-1990	
691	Jim Fregosi, 1961-1971	
601	Bobby Grich, 1977-1986	
481	Don Baylor, 1977-1982	
474	Rod Carew, 1979-1985	

Hits: Most, career, all-time

1588	BRIAN DOWNING, 1978-1990
1408	Jim Fregosi, 1961-1971
1103	Bobby Grich, 1977-1986
968	Rod Carew, 1979-1985
925	WALLY JOYNER, 1986-1991

2B: Most, career, all-time

282	BRIAN DOWNING, 1978-1990
219	Jim Fregosi, 1961-1971
183	Bobby Grich, 1977-1986
170	WALLY JOYNER, 1986-1991
149	Doug DeCinces, 1982-1987

3B: Most, career, all-time

70	Jim Fregosi, 1961-1971
32	Mickey Rivers, 1970-1975
27	DICK SCHOFIELD, 1983-1991
25	Bobby Knoop, 1964-1969
24	DEVON WHITE, 1985-1990

HR: Most, career, all-time

222	BRIAN DOWNING, 1978-1990
154	Bobby Grich, 1977-1986
141	Don Baylor, 1977-1982
130	Doug DeCinces, 1982-1987
123	Reggie Jackson, 1982-1986

RBI: Most, career, all-time

846	BRIAN DOWNING, 1978-1990
557	Bobby Grich, 1977-1986
546	Jim Fregosi, 1961-1971
523	Don Baylor, 1977-1982
518	WALLY JOYNER, 1986-1991

SB: Most, career, all-time

186	GARY PETTIS, 1982-1987
139	Sandy Alomar, 1969-1974
126	Mickey Rivers, 1970-1975
123	DEVON WHITE, 1985-1990
110	Jerry Remy, 1975-1977

BB: Most, career, all-time

866	BRIAN DOWNING, 1978-1990
630	Bobby Grich, 1977-1986
558	Jim Fregosi, 1961-1971
405	Rod Carew, 1979-1985
369	Albie Pearson, 1961-1966

BA: Highest, career, all-time

.314	Rod Carew, 1979-1985
.293	Juan Beniquez, 1981-1985
.288	WALLY JOYNER, 1986-1991
.275	Albie Pearson, 1961-1966
.271	BRIAN DOWNING, 1978-1990

Slug avg: Highest, career, all-time

.463	Doug DeCinces, 1982-1987
.455	WALLY JOYNER, 1986-1991
.448	Don Baylor, 1977-1982
.441	BRIAN DOWNING, 1978-1990
.440	Reggie Jackson, 1982-1986

Games started: Most, career, all-time

288	NOLAN RYAN, 1972-1979
272	MIKE WITT, 1981-1990
218	FRANK TANANA, 1973-1980
189	KIRK McCASKILL, 1985-1991
189	Clyde Wright, 1966-1973

Saves: Most, career, all-time

113	BRYAN HARVEY, 1987-1991
65	Dave LaRoche, 1970-1980
61	Donnie Moore, 1985-1988
58	Bob Lee, 1964-1966
43	Minnie Rojas, 1966-1968

Shutouts: Most, career, all-time

40	NOLAN RYAN, 1972-1979
24	FRANK TANANA, 1973-1980
21	Dean Chance, 1961-1966
14	George Brunet, 1964-1969
13	Geoff Zahn, 1981-1985

Wins: Most, career, all-time

138	NOLAN RYAN, 1972-1979
109	MIKE WITT, 1981-1990
102	FRANK TANANA, 1973-1980
87	Clyde Wright, 1966-1973
78	KIRK McCASKILL, 1985-1991

K: Most, career, all-time

2416	NOLAN RYAN, 1972-1979
1283	MIKE WITT, 1981-1990
1233	FRANK TANANA, 1973-1980
857	Dean Chance, 1961-1966
844	Rudy May, 1965-1974

Win pct: Highest, career, all-time

.569	CHUCK FINLEY, 1986-1991
.567	FRANK TANANA, 1973-1980
.557	Andy Messersmith, 1968-1972
.553	Geoff Zahn, 1981-1985
.533	NOLAN RYAN, 1972-1979

ERA: Lowest, career, all-time

2.78	Andy Messersmith, 1968-1972
2.83	Dean Chance, 1961-1966
3.07	NOLAN RYAN, 1972-1979
3.08	FRANK TANANA, 1973-1980
3.13	George Brunet, 1964-1969

Runs: Most, season

120	Don Baylor, 1979
115	Albie Pearson, 1962
114	CARNEY LANSFORD, 1979
110	BRIAN DOWNING, 1987
109	BRIAN DOWNING, 1982

Hits: Most, season

202	Alex Johnson, 1970
188	CARNEY LANSFORD, 1979
186	Don Baylor, 1979
186	Billy Moran, 1962
184	Johnny Ray, 1988

2B: Most, season

42	Doug DeCinces, 1982
42	Johnny Ray, 1988
38	Fred Lynn, 1982
37	BRIAN DOWNING, 1982
34	Rod Carew, 1980
34	WALLY JOYNER, 1991
34	Bob Rodgers, 1962

3B: Most, season

13	Jim Fregosi, 1968
13	Mickey Rivers, 1975
13	DEVON WHITE, 1989
12	Jim Fregosi, 1963
11	Bobby Knoop, 1966

11   Mickey Rivers, 1974

HR: Most, season

39	Reggie Jackson, 1982
37	Bobby Bonds, 1977
37	Leon Wagner, 1962
36	Don Baylor, 1979
34	Don Baylor, 1978
34	WALLY JOYNER, 1987

RBI: Most, season

139	Don Baylor, 1979
117	WALLY JOYNER, 1987
115	Bobby Bonds, 1977
107	Leon Wagner, 1962
104	Lee Thomas, 1962

SB: Most, season

70	Mickey Rivers, 1975
56	GARY PETTIS, 1985
50	GARY PETTIS, 1986
48	GARY PETTIS, 1984
48	LUIS POLONIA, 1991

BB: Most, season

106	BRIAN DOWNING, 1987
96	Albie Pearson, 1961
95	Albie Pearson, 1962
93	Jim Fregosi, 1969
92	Reggie Jackson, 1986
92	Albie Pearson, 1963

BA: Highest, season

.339	Rod Carew, 1983
.331	Rod Carew, 1980
.329	Alex Johnson, 1970
.326	BRIAN DOWNING, 1979
.319	Rod Carew, 1982

Slug avg: Highest, season

.548	Doug DeCinces, 1982
.543	Bobby Grich, 1981
.537	Bobby Grich, 1979
.532	Reggie Jackson, 1982
.530	Don Baylor, 1979

Games started: Most, season

41	NOLAN RYAN, 1974
40	Bill Singer, 1973
39	NOLAN RYAN, 1972
39	NOLAN RYAN, 1973
39	NOLAN RYAN, 1976
39	Clyde Wright, 1970

Saves: Most, season

46	BRYAN HARVEY, 1991
31	Donnie Moore, 1985
27	Minnie Rojas, 1967
25	BRYAN HARVEY, 1989
25	BRYAN HARVEY, 1990
25	Dave LaRoche, 1978

Shutouts: Most, season

11	Dean Chance, 1964
9	NOLAN RYAN, 1972
7	NOLAN RYAN, 1976
7	FRANK TANANA, 1977
6	Jim McGlothlin, 1967

Wins: Most, season

22	NOLAN RYAN, 1974
22	Clyde Wright, 1970
21	NOLAN RYAN, 1973
20	Dean Chance, 1964
20	Andy Messersmith, 1971
20	Bill Singer, 1973

K: Most, season

383	NOLAN RYAN, 1973
367	NOLAN RYAN, 1974
341	NOLAN RYAN, 1977
329	NOLAN RYAN, 1972
327	NOLAN RYAN, 1976

Win pct: Highest, season

.773	Bert Blyleven, 1989
.704	MARK LANGSTON, 1991
.692	Geoff Zahn, 1982
.690	Dean Chance, 1964
.667	CHUCK FINLEY, 1990
.667	CHUCK FINLEY, 1991

ERA: Lowest, season

1.65	Dean Chance, 1964
2.28	NOLAN RYAN, 1972
2.40	CHUCK FINLEY, 1990
2.43	FRANK TANANA, 1976
2.52	Andy Messersmith, 1969

Most pinch-hit homers, season

3	Joe Adcock, 1966
3	George Hendrick, 1987

Most pinch-hit, homers, career

4	Ruppert Jones, 1985-1987
4	George Hendrick, 1985-1988

Most consecutive games, batting safely

25   Rod Carew, 1982

Most consecutive scoreless innings

36   Jim McGlothlin, 1967

No hit games

Bo Belinsky, LA vs Bal AL, 2-0; May 5, 1962.
Clyde Wright, Cal vs Oak AL, 4-0; July 3, 1970.
Nolan Ryan, Cal at KC AL, 3-0; May 15, 1973.
Nolan Ryan, Cal at Det AL, 6-0; July 15, 1973.
Nolan Ryan, Cal vs Min AL, 4-0; September 28, 1974.
Nolan Ryan, Cal vs Bal AL, 1-0; June 1, 1975.
Mike Witt, Cal at Tex AL, 1-0; September 30, 1984 (perfect game).
Mark Langston (7 innings) and Mike Witt (2 innings), Cal vs Sea AL, 1-0; April 11, 1990.

1992: A peek into our editor's crystal ball

And now a word from the guy who picked the 1991 Cleveland Indians to win the American League East. . . . Hey, if I had picked the Braves and Twins to take it all you would have laughed, too. I just used logic and looked for my longshot in the worst division in baseball.

Now the chic prognosticating mode is to anticipate this year's surprise teams. So, I'll jump on the bandwagon—but again, I'll make the mistake of using logic.

I looked at teams that took long strides forward last year and figured that trend should continue. Obviously it's tough to look past Minnesota and Atlanta, especially considering how young the best of the Braves are. But, who else might sneak into the race?

You have to like the White Sox. Often teams that come from nowhere level off the next year, then either remain mediocre or resume their climb. The White Sox were the surprise of 1990, did OK in '91 and now have enough young players—Frank Thomas, Robin Ventura et al—to make their big move.

The Cardinals were a '91 surprise, again with a load of young talent. This could be that leveling off season, but without a dominant team in the NL East, watch out for St. Louis.

And then there are the teams that make a late-season rush from nowhere. Is it a tease? Do they sell a few extra season tickets then disappoint the new faithful? The Brewers and the Phillies are prime candidates in this category. But Milwaukee has a new, exciting management team, and Philadelphia can hope better health makes the difference.

Keep an eye on both of them.

Going in the other direction? Well maybe if I call Cleveland the dregs of the league, it will work in reverse.

—Paul White

USA SNAPSHOTS®

A look at statistics that shape the sports world

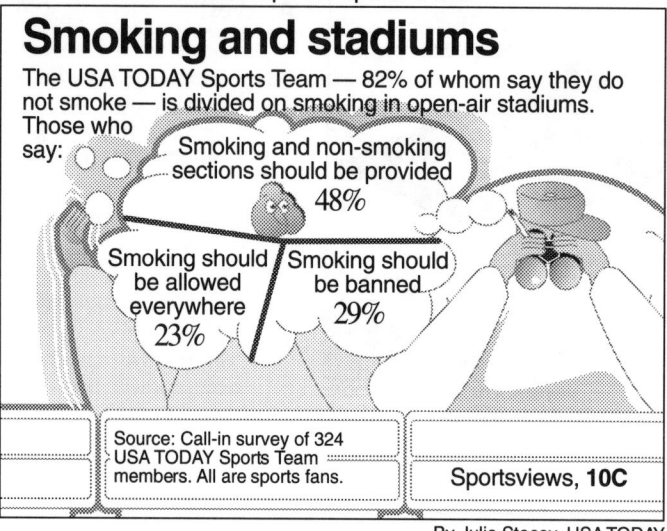

Smoking and stadiums

The USA TODAY Sports Team — 82% of whom say they do not smoke — is divided on smoking in open-air stadiums. Those who say:

Smoking and non-smoking sections should be provided 48%

Smoking should be allowed everywhere 23%

Smoking should be banned 29%

Source: Call-in survey of 324 USA TODAY Sports Team members. All are sports fans.

Sportsviews, **10C**

By Julie Stacey, USA TODAY

National League East: Can the Bucs do it again?

The walls are coming in in St. Louis. The roof may be caving in—literally—in Montreal. There are new managers in New York and Chicago. Free agents are fleeing from Pittsburgh.

So that should automatically leave the Phillies, that bastion of stability, as the favorite in the National League East in 1992, should it not?

Not.

The Phillies have their own share of question marks as they head into the 1992 season, leaving every team in the division in a state of uncertainty as the start of spring training approaches.

In New York, manager Jeff Torborg has to wait until March to see how all his injured players, including Dwight Gooden and Vince Coleman, are recovering.

The Cardinals, in addition to moving in and lowering the outfield walls, are counting on pitcher Joe Magrane to return after missing all of 1991 after elbow surgery. They also have to hope their young players can perform as well in their sophomore seasons as they did as rookies.

The Cubs are hoping their chances will improve with a change in managers and a return to form from injured pitchers Danny Jackson and Mike Harkey.

The Expos are awaiting clearance for Olympic Stadium—ordered closed last September because of safety concerns—to be ready for their season-opening game in April. They also have to hope Tim Wallach and Andres Galarraga can bounce back from sub-par performances in 1991.

The Phillies have to make sure Lenny Dykstra is troubled 1991 season and h. decide how they are going to hand. Dale Murphy/Von Hayes platoo. right field.

That leaves the two-time defendin. champion Pirates, and no team has more potential questions. How will they replace free agent defection Bobby Bonilla? Is either Jeff King or John Wehner healthy enough to play an entire season? Can they win again without a proven closer in the bullpen?

Manager Jim Leyland also likely will face more questions about Barry Bonds' future, and while that didn't hamper Bonilla's performance last year, the Bucs might not be so lucky in 1992.

At least Leyland and the Pirates will be used to the questions about the pressure of trying to repeat after weathering that storm last season. The question is: can they provide the same answers?

—*Rob Rains*

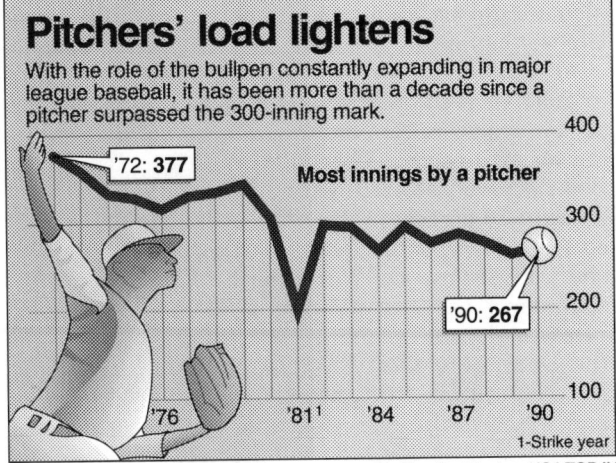

USA SNAPSHOTS®

A look at statistics that shape the sports world

Pitchers' load lightens

With the role of the bullpen constantly expanding in major league baseball, it has been more than a decade since a pitcher surpassed the 300-inning mark.

'72: 377

Most innings by a pitcher

'90: 267

'76 '81¹ '84 '87 '90

400
300
200
100

1-Strike year

Source: *The Baseball Encyclopedia*   By Ron Coddington, USA TODAY

National League West: Braves and Dodgers again

One thing is certain about the National League West 1992 pennant race—the Houston Astros will not make this worst-to-first thing a habit.

Nobody may have predicted the Braves' rise from sixth to the NL pennant in 1991, but even fewer people—not even Houston general manager Bill Wood—would even think of making such a claim for the Astros in 1992.

The Astros have a lot of good, young talent, including first baseman Jeff Bagwell, 1991 Rookie of the Year. In a couple of years, they will be a team to be reckoned with in this division, following the blueprint laid down by the Braves. But not this year.

This year, the two teams that fought it out for the 1991 title—the Braves and Dodgers—should do so again. The Reds, Giants and Padres all should be better than they were a year ago, but the question will be if that is good enough to close the gap on the Braves and Dodgers.

The Braves will have to see if they can deal with success, but with their young starting pitching all healthy, that shouldn't be a problem. If David Justice is healthy for a full year, he also should be able to produce more offense than he did a year ago.

Terry Pendleton won the batting title in 1991 with the best offensive season of his career, and he enters 1992 coming off arthroscopic knee surgery. Ron Gant will be shooting for his third straight 30-30 season, an unprecedented feat. The fact the Braves fell a run short of winning the World Series also should increase their desire in 1992.

Desire should not be a problem for the Dodgers, either. They fought the Braves until the 161st game of the season.

Darryl Strawberry, who said he needed time to adjust to life in Los Angeles and his new-found religious beliefs last season, won't be able to make that excuse this year. The biggest question for the team will be if their young players, especially Jose Offerman, are finally ready to occupy key roles for an extended period of time.

The Reds learned last season how difficult it is to repeat, especially when injuries wiped out most of their starting pitching and their best offensive player, Eric Davis. Manager Lou Piniella openly campaigned for changes in personnel, and how well and how quickly new players fit in could determine how serious a threat Cincinnati will be in 1992.

The Padres were never considered a threat last year, but never really went away either. Tony Gwynn is coming off arthroscopic knee surgery, which kept his production down the second half of 1991, and Fred McGriff has had a year to adjust to National League pitching, which should make him even more dangerous. Andy Benes was one of the two best starters in the league after the All-Star break, and San Diego hopes that streak can continue.

The Giants thought they had solved all of their problems last year by spending megabucks on free agents Bud Black, Dave Righetti and Willie McGee, but the team got off to a slow start and struggled all year. A similar performance early this year and manager Roger Craig might decide to ride off into the California sunset.

—*Rob Rains*

American League East:
Sox, Jays—and Indians?

LEAGUE FORECASTS

The American League East looks to be another close race between the Toronto Blue Jays and Boston Red Sox, with the Detroit Tigers and Milwaukee Brewers looking to jump on the pile.

The Blue Jays have the best pitching and defense, which was good enough to win the division last year. But questions remain about Dave Stieb's health, Juan Guzman's effectiveness during an entire season and the Blue Jays' void at designated hitter. Toronto DHs, excluding Joe Carter's cameos, combined for just eight home runs and 93 RBI between five players last year.

The Red Sox had plenty of pop, at least in the second half, and appear to have even more in '92, if Phil Plantier continues to develop and new manager Butch Hobson can straighten out Mo Vaughn. As always, Boston needs some pitching and speed.

The Tigers are excited about their collection of young arms. If Scott Aldred, Dan Gakeler, David Haas or Greg Gohr can take on more of the load, the Tigers won't fade away come September, no matter how many times they strike out.

The Brewers had a great second half, but new general manager Sal Bando wanted a tougher man at the helm, so he fired Tom Trebelhorn and hired Phil "Scrap Iron" Garner. Still, it won't matter if the Brewers are tough enough, if Robin Yount and Paul Molitor don't stay healthy.

In New York, Buck Showalter is the new man in charge. He's promised to cut

Don Mattingly's locks himself if it will help the Yankee superstar regain his power stroke.

The Yankees need to play hard the entire season, regardless of hair style. Even though there's plenty of talent on this team, last season they broke into two groups —the millionaires and the kids.

The Cleveland Indians are on the verge of a great young everyday lineup. They could begin the season with Sandy Alomar at catcher, Reggie Jefferson at first, Carlos Baerga at second, Mark Lewis at shortstop and Jim Thome at third. The outfield/DH jobs would be held down by Albert Belle, Glenallen Hill, Mark Whiten and Alex Cole.

This sounds even sweeter with the news that the fences at Cleveland Stadium will be moved back in for '92. Last year closer Doug Jones contended that his teammates needed beepers to play that home on the range. Unfortunately, the Indians still need somebody to pitch, since Greg Swindell was traded to Cincinnati.

293

USA SNAPSHOTS®

A look at statistics that shape the sports world

Home run derby

62   58

Thirty years ago, Roger Maris hit 61 home runs to break Babe Ruths' single-season record. After 153 games, the number of home runs hit by:

St. Louis Cardinals, 1991

Roger Maris, N.Y. Yankees, 1961

Source: Elias Sports Bureau

By Rod Little, USA TODAY

American League West: Any team could take it

Everybody's optimistic in the American League West, where all the teams finished .500 or better, even the last-place California Angels.

The reason everybody's smiling is that the Oakland A's, the three-time defending A.L. champs, failed to repeat in '91. In the Minnesota Twins' last-to-first place finish, a lot of teams—the Rangers, the Mariners, even the Royals —see themselves as this year's success stories.

The scary thing is they may all be right: Anybody can win this division in '92.

Every time has a hole or two, and the first team to patch and fill becomes the front-runner for next season.

The Angels have pitching and no hitting. The trio of Jim Abbott, Chuck Finley and Mark Langston, as well as closer Bryan Harvey, were among the best in '91. They may not all be in Angels uniforms come spring, though, as new general manager Whitey Herzog has said he'll talk to anybody about available power hitters.

The Rangers scored plenty of runs last season. What they're praying for in Texas is that Nolan Ryan has another good season left in his 45-year-old arm, and that somebody other than Jose Guzman knows how to record some outs. The best everyday hitting lineup in baseball is getting a little tired of swinging from the heels to keep themselves in games.

In Oakland, manager Tony La Russa believes that his nucleus—Henderson, Canseco, Stewart and Welch — has another banner campaign in them. But questions remain about who plays third and will Mark McGwire's batting average fall again for another season.

The Royals are hoping that manager Hal McRae's first full year as manager will lead them out of the woods. Yet things get a little dicey if free agent outfielder Danny Tartabull isn't re-signed.

The Mariners still boast some of the best young pitchers in the game. But they may have to unload one to secure that right-handed power hitter they sorely needed in '91.

The White Sox may finally rise above a third consecutive second-place finish, if a couple of their young pitchers make the quantum leap from prospect to regular starter.

The Twins are ready to repeat, and with Kirby Puckett, Chili Davis and pitchers Scott Erickson and Kevin Tapani already on board, their chances would appear good. Still, this is AL West, where everybody has a chance, even with the World Series champs in the same division.

USA SNAPSHOTS®

A look at statistics that shape the sports world

A history of no-hitters

Teams whose pitchers have thrown the most no-hitters and that have been no-hit most often[1]:

No-hitters
AL White Sox 17
NL Dodgers 16

Been no-hit
AL White Sox 14
NL Phillies 17

1— Since 1900

Source: USA TODAY research

By Marcia Staimer, USA TODAY

Final Player Stats

National League		American League	
Pitchers	307	Pitchers	296
Catchers	310	Catchers	299
First basemen	310	First basemen	300
Second basemen	311	Second basemen	300
Third basemen	312	Third basemen	301
Shortstops	312	Shortstops	302
Left fielders	313	Left fielders	303
Center fielders	314	Center fielders	304
Right fielders	315	Right fielders	304
		Designated hitters	305

Stats key for pitchers

T–Throws right or left; W–Wins; L–Losses; PCT–Percentage; ERA–Earned run average; G–Games; GS–Games started; CG – Complete games; SHO–Shutouts; SV–Saves; INN–Innings pitched; HR–Home runs allowed; BB–Bases on balls; SO–Strikeouts; WP–Wild pitches; SB–Stolen bases allowed; CS–Runners caught stealing; GAR–Ground out to air out ratio; BA–Batting average against; SLG–Slugging percentage against; OBP–On-base percentage against.

Stats key for batters

B–Bats; BA–Batting average; SLG–Slugging percentage; OBP–On-base percentage; G–Games; AB–At-bats; R–Runs; H–Hits; 2B–Doubles; 3B–Triples; HR–Home runs; RBI–Runs batted in; BB–Bases on balls; SO–Strikeouts; SB–Stolen bases; CS–Caught stealing; LHP–Batting vs. left-handed pitching; RHP–Batting vs. right-handed pitching; SP–Batting with runners in scoring position; SP2–Batting with runners in scoring position and two outs.

Statistics are provided by the Elias Sports Bureau. Minimum 15 innings played at that position

Players are listed alphabetically by position, within each league. Each player is listed at every position played (minimum 15 innings) during the season; all statistics are for the complete season.

American League Pitchers

Name	Team	T	W	L	PCT	ERA	G	GS	CG	SHO	SV	INN	HR	BB	SO	WP	SB	CS	GAR	BA	SLG	OBP
J. Abbott	Cal.	L	18	11	.621	2.89	34	34	5	1	0	243	14	73	158	1	12	14	1.83	.244	.336	.302
K. Abbott	Cal.	L	1	2	.333	4.58	5	3	0	0	0	19.2	2	13	12	1	1	2	1.50	.301	.438	.414
Abbott	Min.	R	3	1	.750	4.75	15	3	0	0	0	47.1	5	36	43	5	6	1	0.78	.232	.396	.365
Acker	Tor.	R	3	5	.375	5.20	54	4	0	0	1	88.1	16	36	44	7	10	3	1.31	.238	.424	.314
Aguilera	Min.	R	4	5	.444	2.35	63	0	0	0	42	69	3	30	61	3	7	0	0.63	.183	.275	.274
Aldred	Det.	L	2	4	.333	5.18	11	11	1	0	0	57.1	9	30	35	3	5	2	0.75	.266	.427	.352
Alexander	Tex.	R	5	3	.625	5.24	30	9	0	0	0	89.1	11	48	50	3	7	3	0.70	.272	.430	.364
Alvarez	ChiA	L	3	2	.600	3.51	10	9	2	1	0	56.1	9	29	32	2	0	4	1.12	.230	.407	.325
Anderson	Min.	L	5	11	.313	4.96	29	22	2	0	0	134.1	24	42	51	3	14	6	1.10	.281	.474	.336
Appier	K.C.	R	13	10	.565	3.42	34	31	6	3	0	207.2	13	61	158	7	10	8	1.01	.255	.357	.307
Aquino	K.C.	R	8	4	.667	3.44	38	18	1	1	3	157	10	47	80	1	10	6	0.95	.253	.374	.308
Arnsberg	Tex.	R	0	1	.000	8.38	9	0	0	0	0	9.2	5	5	8	1	0	0	1.44	.256	.641	.341
August	Mil.	R	9	8	.529	5.47	28	23	1	1	0	138.1	18	47	62	5	18	4	1.42	.301	.450	.358
Austin	Mil.	R	0	0	_	8.31	5	0	0	0	0	8.2	1	11	3	1	0	0	0.64	.276	.448	.500
Bailes	Cal.	L	1	2	.333	4.18	42	0	0	0	0	51.2	5	22	41	2	2	3	0.79	.218	.346	.310
Ballard	Bal.	L	6	12	.333	5.60	26	22	0	0	0	123.2	16	28	37	3	1	4	1.09	.302	.478	.340
Bankhead	Sea.	R	3	6	.333	4.90	17	9	0	0	0	60.2	8	21	28	0	8	0	0.71	.297	.467	.354
Banks	Min.	R	1	1	.500	5.71	5	3	0	0	0	17.1	1	12	16	3	2	0	1.92	.288	.356	.388
Barfield	Tex.	R	4	4	.500	4.54	28	9	0	0	1	83.1	11	22	27	0	1	3	1.28	.289	.464	.330
Beasley	Cal.	R	0	1	.000	3.38	22	0	0	0	0	26.2	2	10	14	2	0	1	1.50	.257	.366	.327
Bedrosian	Min.	R	5	3	.625	4.42	56	0	0	0	6	77.1	11	35	44	2	4	1	0.62	.243	.420	.327
Bell	Cle.	L	4	0	1.000	0.50	10	0	0	0	0	18	0	5	7	0	2	0	1.09	.091	.091	.180
Blair	Cle.	L	2	3	.400	6.75	11	5	0	0	0	36	7	10	13	1	1	1	1.11	.377	.565	.413
Boddicker	K.C.	R	12	12	.500	4.08	30	29	1	0	0	180.2	13	59	79	3	17	10	1.21	.272	.408	.340
Bohanon	Tex.	L	4	3	.571	4.84	11	11	1	0	0	61.1	4	23	34	3	5	0	0.82	.274	.378	.336
Bolton	Bos.	L	8	9	.471	5.24	25	19	0	0	0	110	16	51	64	3	5	2	1.91	.308	.485	.378
Bosio	Mil.	R	14	10	.583	3.25	32	32	5	1	0	204.2	15	58	117	5	9	4	1.29	.244	.350	.302
Boyd	Tex.	R	2	7	.222	6.68	12	12	0	0	0	62	12	17	33	0	3	3	0.94	.314	.519	.356
Brown	Tex.	R	9	12	.429	4.40	33	33	0	0	0	210.2	17	90	96	12	5	11	2.52	.264	.404	.362
Burba	Sea.	R	2	2	.500	3.68	22	2	0	0	1	36.2	6	14	16	1	1	1	0.96	.245	.453	.314
Cadaret	NY-A	L	8	6	.571	3.62	68	5	0	0	3	121.2	8	59	105	3	11	8	1.22	.246	.365	.335
Campbell	Oak.	R	1	0	1.000	2.74	14	0	0	0	0	23	4	14	16	0	1	0	1.17	.167	.359	.301
Candiotti	Tor.	R	13	13	.500	2.65	34	34	6	0	0	238	12	73	167	11	26	8	0.98	.228	.337	.288
Carter	ChiA	R	0	1	.000	5.25	5	2	0	0	0	12	1	5	2	0	1	0	1.40	.182	.318	.265
Cerutti	Det.	L	3	6	.333	4.57	38	8	1	0	2	88.2	9	37	29	4	5	2	1.21	.276	.412	.348
Chapin	NY-A	R	0	1	.000	5.06	3	0	0	0	0	5.1	0	6	5	2	1	0	1.20	.158	.263	.360
Chiamparino	Tex.	R	1	0	1.000	4.03	5	5	0	0	0	22.1	1	12	8	0	2	0	1.81	.295	.375	.380
Chitren	Oak.	R	1	4	.200	4.33	56	0	0	0	4	60.1	8	32	47	2	5	0	0.84	.258	.432	.356
Clemens	Bos.	R	18	10	.643	2.62	35	35	13	4	0	271.1	15	65	241	6	23	16	1.23	.221	.328	.270
Comstock	Sea.	L	0	0	_	54.00	1	0	0	0	0	0.1	0	1	0	0	0	0	0.00	.667	###	.750
Corbin	K.C.	R	0	0	_	3.86	2	0	0	0	0	2.2	0	2	1	0	0	0	2.00	.300	.300	.417
Crawford	K.C.	R	3	2	.600	5.98	33	0	0	0	1	46.2	3	18	38	5	9	2	0.79	.311	.440	.367
Crim	Mil.	R	8	5	.615	4.63	66	0	0	0	3	91.1	9	25	39	3	12	1	1.17	.305	.416	.351
Darling	Oak.	R	3	7	.300	4.08	12	12	0	0	0	75	9	38	60	3	7	1	0.93	.237	.374	.331
Darwin	Bos.	R	3	6	.333	5.16	12	12	0	0	0	68	15	15	42	2	5	1	0.41	.263	.500	.309
S. Davis	K.C.	R	3	9	.250	4.96	51	9	1	1	2	114.1	11	46	53	1	2	2	1.14	.306	.437	.367
M. Davis	K.C.	L	6	3	.667	4.45	29	5	0	0	1	62.2	6	39	47	1	4	3	0.97	.240	.376	.347
Dayley	Tor.	L	0	0	_	6.23	8	0	0	0	0	4.1	0	5	3	2	2	0	1.50	.368	.368	.500
de la Rosa	Bal.	R	0	0	_	4.50	2	0	0	0	0	4	0	2	1	0	0	0	1.75	.353	.471	.400
Delucia	Sea.	R	12	13	.480	5.09	32	31	0	0	0	182	31	78	98	10	4	9	0.61	.260	.457	.333
Dempsey	Mil.	R	0	0	_	4.50	2	0	0	0	0	2	0	1	0	0	0	0	2.00	.333	.444	.400
Dopson	Bos.	R	0	0	_	18.00	1	0	0	0	0	1	1	1	0	0	0	0	0.50	.500	.750	.500
Drahman	ChiA	R	3	2	.600	3.23	28	0	0	0	0	30.2	4	13	18	0	0	1	1.08	.193	.349	.276
Drees	ChiA	L	0	0	_	12.27	4	0	0	0	0	7.1	4	6	2	2	1	0	0.54	.345	.793	.444
Eckersley	Oak.	R	5	4	.556	2.96	67	0	0	0	43	76	11	9	87	1	8	1	0.58	.208	.365	.235
Edens	Min.	R	2	2	.500	4.09	8	6	0	0	0	33	2	10	19	1	2	1	1.61	.256	.391	.308
Eichhorn	Cal.	R	3	3	.500	1.98	70	0	0	0	1	81.2	2	13	49	0	3	3	2.05	.219	.309	.255
Eiland	NY-A	R	2	5	.286	5.33	18	13	0	0	0	72.2	10	23	18	0	6	1	1.44	.302	.510	.356
Eldred	Mil.	R	2	0	1.000	4.50	3	3	0	0	0	16	2	6	10	0	3	1	0.58	.299	.403	.356
Erickson	Min.	R	20	8	.714	3.18	32	32	5	3	0	204	13	71	108	4	4	10	2.12	.248	.364	.314
Espinoza	NY-A	R	0	0	_	0.00	1	0	0	0	0	0.2	0	0	0	0	0	0	1.00	.000	.000	.000
Fajardo	Tex.	R	0	2	.000	5.68	4	3	0	0	0	19	2	4	15	0	4	2	0.50	.329	.513	.357
Farr	NY-A	R	5	5	.500	2.19	60	0	0	0	23	70	4	20	60	2	2	2	1.25	.219	.312	.288
Fernandez	ChiA	R	9	13	.409	4.51	34	32	2	0	0	191.2	16	88	145	4	15	11	0.90	.259	.388	.337
Fetters	Cal.	R	2	5	.286	4.84	19	4	0	0	0	44.2	4	28	24	4	6	4	1.65	.305	.414	.410
Finley	Cal.	L	18	9	.667	3.80	34	34	4	2	0	227.1	23	101	171	6	15	14	1.00	.244	.385	.330
Flanagan	Bal.	L	2	7	.222	2.38	64	1	0	0	3	98.1	6	25	55	2	6	3	1.95	.236	.323	.289
Fleming	Sea.	L	1	0	1.000	6.62	9	3	0	0	0	17.2	3	3	11	1	1	1	2.33	.284	.537	.342
Fossas	Bos.	L	3	2	.600	3.47	64	0	0	0	1	57	3	28	29	2	5	2	1.82	.236	.327	.335
Frohwirth	Bal.	R	7	3	.700	1.87	51	0	0	0	3	96.1	2	29	77	0	10	4	2.82	.190	.267	.255

American League Pitchers

Name	Team	T	W	L	PCT	ERA	G	GS	CG	SHO	SV	INN	HR	BB	SO	WP	SB	CS	GAR	BA	SLG	OBP
Gakeler	Det.	R	1	4	.200	5.74	31	7	0	0	2	73.2	5	39	43	7	7	1	1.05	.256	.358	.345
Garcia	ChiA	R	4	4	.500	5.40	16	15	0	0	0	78.1	13	31	40	0	4	5	0.89	.269	.449	.340
Gardiner	Bos.	R	9	10	.474	4.85	22	22	0	0	0	130	18	47	91	1	11	5	1.14	.274	.438	.333
George	Mil.	R	0	0	—	3.00	2	1	0	0	0	6	0	2	0	1	0	1	1.29	.333	.458	.320
Gibson	Det.	R	5	7	.417	4.59	68	0	0	0	8	96	10	48	52	4	5	5	0.78	.297	.424	.379
Gleaton	Det.	L	3	2	.600	4.06	47	0	0	0	0	75.1	7	39	47	1	8	8	0.80	.269	.415	.355
Gordon	K.C.	R	9	14	.391	3.87	45	14	1	0	1	158	16	87	167	5	9	7	1.07	.221	.357	.324
Gossage	Tex.	R	4	2	.667	3.57	44	0	0	0	0	40.1	4	16	28	3	2	2	0.91	.228	.366	.317
Grahe	Cal.	R	3	7	.300	4.81	18	10	1	0	0	73	2	33	40	2	9	5	1.81	.288	.397	.365
Gray	Bos.	R	2	3	.400	2.34	50	0	0	0	0	61.2	7	10	41	2	5	3	0.91	.181	.338	.219
Gubicza	K.C.	R	9	12	.429	5.68	26	26	0	0	0	133	10	42	89	5	18	6	2.10	.308	.424	.361
Guetterman	NY-A	L	3	4	.429	3.68	64	0	0	0	6	88	6	25	35	4	4	3	2.15	.268	.388	.320
Gullickson	Det.	R	20	9	.690	3.90	35	35	4	0	0	226.1	22	44	91	4	15	8	1.02	.288	.435	.321
Guthrie	Min.	L	7	5	.583	4.32	41	12	0	0	2	98	11	41	72	7	9	5	1.08	.303	.465	.369
Guzman	Tex.	R	13	7	.650	3.08	25	25	5	1	0	169.2	10	84	125	8	12	13	1.26	.239	.341	.330
Guzman	Tor.	R	10	3	.769	2.99	23	23	1	0	0	138.2	6	66	123	10	11	6	0.93	.197	.268	.294
Haas	Det.	R	1	0	1.000	6.75	11	0	0	0	0	10.2	1	12	6	1	0	1	2.71	.242	.364	.438
Habyan	NY-A	R	4	2	.667	2.30	66	0	0	0	2	90	2	20	70	1	4	1	1.90	.225	.315	.274
Hanson	Sea.	R	8	8	.500	3.81	27	27	2	1	0	174.2	16	56	143	14	11	10	1.11	.269	.414	.323
Harris	Bos.	R	11	12	.478	3.85	53	21	1	0	2	173	13	69	127	6	1	6	1.39	.243	.363	.318
Harris	Sea.	R	0	0	—	4.05	8	0	0	0	1	13.1	1	10	6	1	0	0	1.40	.273	.400	.385
Harvey	Cal.	R	2	4	.333	1.60	67	0	0	0	46	78.2	6	17	101	2	12	0	1.73	.178	.266	.225
Henke	Tor.	R	0	2	.000	2.32	49	0	0	0	32	50.1	4	11	53	1	2	0	0.83	.184	.307	.232
Henneman	Det.	R	10	2	.833	2.88	60	0	0	0	21	84.1	2	34	61	5	3	2	1.40	.258	.344	.326
Henry	Mil.	R	2	1	.667	1.00	32	0	0	0	15	36	1	14	28	0	0	1	0.60	.133	.208	.221
Hentgen	Tor.	R	0	0	—	2.45	3	1	0	0	0	7.1	1	3	3	1	1	0	0.64	.208	.417	.345
Hernandez	ChiA	R	1	0	1.000	7.80	9	3	0	0	0	15	1	7	6	1	2	0	1.22	.290	.403	.362
Hesketh	Bos.	L	12	4	.750	3.29	39	17	0	0	0	153.1	19	53	104	8	7	8	1.47	.250	.424	.313
Hibbard	ChiA	L	11	11	.500	4.31	32	29	5	0	0	194	23	57	71	1	6	8	1.57	.266	.402	.320
Higuera	Mil.	L	3	2	.600	4.46	7	6	0	0	0	36.1	2	10	33	0	5	0	0.77	.262	.362	.314
Hillegas	Cle.	R	3	4	.429	4.34	51	3	0	0	7	83	7	46	66	5	6	3	0.74	.223	.340	.324
Holman	Sea.	R	13	14	.481	3.69	30	30	5	3	0	195.1	16	77	108	8	4	5	1.38	.268	.392	.343
Holmes	Mil.	R	1	4	.200	4.72	40	0	0	0	3	76.1	6	27	59	6	1	3	0.98	.295	.410	.351
Honeycutt	Oak.	L	2	4	.333	3.58	43	0	0	0	0	37.2	3	20	26	0	5	1	1.74	.261	.394	.358
Horsman	Tor.	L	0	0	—	0.00	4	0	0	0	0	4	0	3	2	0	0	0	0.50	.167	.167	.333
Hough	ChiA	R	9	10	.474	4.02	31	29	4	1	0	199.1	21	94	107	5	10	9	0.96	.229	.381	.320
Howe	NY-A	L	3	1	.750	1.68	37	0	0	0	3	48.1	1	7	34	2	1	0	1.26	.222	.284	.262
Ignasiak	Mil.	R	2	1	.667	5.68	4	1	0	0	0	12.2	2	8	10	0	2	0	0.59	.163	.349	.294
Irvine	Bos.	R	0	0	—	6.00	9	0	0	0	0	18	2	9	8	1	1	0	1.42	.321	.526	.404
Jackson	Sea.	R	7	7	.500	3.25	72	0	0	0	14	88.2	5	34	74	3	5	0	1.09	.201	.298	.290
Jeffcoat	Tex.	L	5	3	.625	4.63	70	0	0	0	0	79.2	8	25	43	3	5	2	1.10	.321	.466	.373
Johnson	Bal.	R	4	8	.333	7.07	22	14	0	0	0	84	18	24	38	0	3	3	0.78	.349	.563	.394
Johnson	Sea.	L	13	10	.565	3.98	33	33	2	1	0	201.1	15	152	228	12	18	9	1.10	.213	.325	.358
Johnson	NY-A	R	6	11	.353	5.95	23	23	0	0	0	127	15	33	62	5	18	4	1.74	.305	.453	.351
Johnston	K.C.	R	1	0	1.000	0.40	13	0	0	0	0	22.1	0	9	21	0	1	1	1.04	.120	.133	.214
C. Jones	Sea.	R	2	2	.500	2.53	27	0	0	0	2	46.1	0	29	42	6	5	1	1.07	.209	.247	.335
Jones	Cle.	R	4	8	.333	5.54	36	4	0	0	7	63.1	7	17	48	1	4	0	1.61	.320	.496	.357
Kaiser	Det.	L	0	1	.000	9.00	10	0	0	0	2	5	1	5	4	0	0	0	1.75	.286	.476	.423
Kamieniecki	NY-A	R	4	4	.500	3.90	9	9	0	0	0	55.1	8	22	34	1	4	2	1.22	.256	.455	.333
Key	Tor.	L	16	12	.571	3.05	33	33	2	2	0	209.1	12	44	125	1	6	2	0.99	.254	.347	.293
Kiecker	Bos.	R	2	3	.400	7.36	18	5	0	0	0	40.1	6	23	21	3	7	3	1.91	.344	.503	.429
King	Cle.	R	6	11	.353	4.60	25	24	2	1	0	150.2	7	44	59	2	8	3	1.11	.279	.384	.328
Kiser	Cle.	L	0	0	—	9.64	7	0	0	0	0	4.2	0	4	3	0	1	0	0.57	.368	.368	.500
Klink	Oak.	L	10	3	.769	4.35	62	0	0	0	2	62	4	21	34	4	4	2	1.25	.260	.364	.335
Kramer	Cle.	R	0	0	—	17.36	4	0	0	0	0	4.2	1	6	4	0	0	0	0.67	.476	.857	.533
Krueger	Sea.	L	11	8	.579	3.60	35	25	1	0	0	175	15	60	91	10	11	5	1.11	.289	.418	.346
Lamp	Bos.	R	6	3	.667	4.70	51	0	0	0	0	92	8	31	57	1	10	0	1.54	.275	.420	.335
Langston	Cal.	L	19	8	.704	3.00	34	34	7	0	0	246.1	30	96	183	6	10	15	0.73	.215	.360	.291
Law	Oak.	R	0	0	—	0.00	1	0	0	0	0	0.2	0	1	0	0	0	0	1.00	.333	.667	.500
Leach	Min.	R	1	2	.333	3.61	50	0	0	0	0	67.1	3	14	32	1	10	2	1.40	.299	.401	.332
Leary	NY-A	R	4	10	.286	6.49	28	18	1	0	0	120.2	20	57	83	10	10	5	1.13	.312	.511	.388
Lee	Mil.	L	2	5	.286	3.86	62	0	0	0	1	67.2	10	31	43	0	6	4	1.24	.283	.453	.362
Leiter	Tor.	L	0	0	—	27.00	3	0	0	0	0	1.2	0	5	1	0	0	0	0.33	.429	.714	.667
Leiter	Det.	R	9	7	.563	4.21	38	15	1	0	1	134.2	16	50	103	2	6	6	0.77	.245	.397	.316
Lewis	Cal.	R	3	5	.375	6.27	16	11	0	0	0	60.1	9	21	37	3	6	2	0.92	.316	.484	.373
Lyons	Bos.	R	0	0	—	0.00	1	0	0	0	0	1	0	0	0	0	0	0	0.00	.400	.600	.400
MacDonald	Tor.	L	3	3	.500	2.85	45	0	0	0	0	53.2	5	25	24	1	5	4	0.94	.252	.361	.332
Machado	Mil.	R	3	3	.500	3.45	54	0	0	0	3	88.2	12	55	98	5	5	0	0.70	.211	.364	.334
Magnante	K.C.	L	0	0	.000	2.45	38	0	0	0	0	55	3	23	42	1	1	2	1.16	.262	.386	.333
Manuel	Tex.	R	1	0	1.000	1.13	8	0	0	0	0	16	0	6	5	2	0	0	0.71	.143	.163	.224

Name	Team	T	W	L	PCT	ERA	G	GS	CG	SHO	SV	INN	HR	BB	SO	WP	SB	CS	GAR	BA	SLG	OBP
Manzanillo	Bos.	R	0	0	—	18.00	1	0	0	0	0	1	0	3	1	0	0	0	1.00	.400	.600	.625
Mathews	Tex.	R	4	0	1.000	3.61	34	2	0	0	1	57.1	5	18	51	5	8	3	0.84	.251	.419	.312
McCaskill	Cal.	R	10	19	.345	4.26	30	30	1	0	0	177.2	19	66	71	6	8	6	1.74	.283	.435	.347
McDonald	Bal.	R	6	8	.429	4.84	21	21	1	0	0	126.1	16	43	85	3	14	3	0.96	.261	.418	.321
McDowell	ChiA	R	17	10	.630	3.41	35	35	15	3	0	253.2	19	82	191	10	22	10	0.80	.228	.347	.292
Mesa	Bal.	R	6	11	.353	5.97	23	23	2	1	0	123.2	11	62	64	3	12	5	0.90	.307	.449	.385
Milacki	Bal.	R	10	9	.526	4.01	31	26	3	1	0	184	17	53	108	1	12	6	1.25	.253	.383	.305
Mills	NY-A	R	1	1	.500	4.41	6	2	0	0	0	16.1	1	8	11	2	3	0	1.00	.254	.333	.333
Monteleone	NY-A	R	3	1	.750	3.64	26	0	0	0	0	47	5	19	34	1	2	2	1.14	.236	.376	.307
Montgomery	K.C.	R	4	4	.500	2.90	67	0	0	0	33	90	6	28	77	6	4	0	1.54	.246	.355	.305
Moore	Oak.	R	17	8	.680	2.96	33	33	3	1	0	210	11	105	153	14	19	12	1.42	.229	.318	.324
Morris	Min.	R	18	12	.600	3.43	35	35	10	2	0	246.2	18	92	163	15	32	6	1.15	.245	.347	.315
Morton	Bos.	L	6	5	.545	4.59	16	15	1	0	0	86.1	9	40	45	1	4	2	1.03	.284	.448	.356
Murphy	Sea.	L	0	1	.000	3.00	57	0	0	0	4	48	4	19	34	4	5	0	0.67	.250	.410	.322
Mussina	Bal.	R	4	5	.444	2.87	12	12	2	0	0	87.2	7	21	52	3	4	4	0.78	.239	.354	.286
Nagy	Cle.	R	10	15	.400	4.13	33	33	6	1	0	211.1	15	66	109	6	23	7	1.47	.275	.403	.330
Navarro	Mil.	R	15	12	.556	3.92	34	34	10	2	0	234	18	73	114	10	23	7	1.33	.261	.370	.318
Neagle	Min.	L	0	1	.000	4.05	7	3	0	0	0	20.2	3	7	14	1	2	1	1.00	.329	.553	.380
Nelson	Oak.	R	1	5	.167	6.84	44	0	0	0	0	48.1	12	23	23	0	4	1	1.02	.306	.577	.381
Nichols	Cle.	R	2	11	.154	3.54	31	16	3	1	0	137.1	6	30	76	3	16	8	0.74	.273	.344	.316
Nunez	Mil.	R	2	1	.667	6.04	23	0	0	0	8	25.1	6	13	24	0	2	0	0.83	.277	.525	.353
Olin	Cle.	R	3	6	.333	3.36	48	0	0	0	17	56.1	2	23	38	0	3	2	2.44	.274	.354	.344
Olson	Bal.	R	4	6	.400	3.18	72	0	0	0	31	73.2	1	29	72	8	13	1	1.07	.262	.305	.332
Orosco	Cle.	L	2	0	1.000	3.74	47	0	0	0	0	45.2	4	15	36	1	5	0	0.61	.286	.396	.338
Otto	Cle.	L	2	8	.200	4.23	18	14	1	0	0	100	7	27	47	3	4	4	1.84	.283	.395	.333
Pall	ChiA	R	7	2	.778	2.41	51	0	0	0	0	71	7	20	40	2	4	5	1.58	.231	.337	.295
Patterson	ChiA	L	3	0	1.000	2.83	43	0	0	0	1	63.2	5	35	32	2	5	3	0.52	.214	.330	.321
Pecota	K.C.	R	0	0	—	4.50	1	0	0	0	0	2	0	0	0	0	0	0	1.00	.444	.778	.444
Perez	ChiA	R	8	7	.533	3.12	49	8	0	0	1	135.2	15	52	128	11	15	5	1.24	.224	.352	.299
Perez	NY-A	R	2	4	.333	3.18	14	14	0	0	0	73.2	7	24	41	3	4	1	1.53	.250	.371	.311
Petry	Bos.	R	2	3	.400	4.79	30	6	0	0	0	77	12	31	30	0	7	3	1.24	.286	.474	.353
Plesac	Mil.	L	2	7	.222	4.29	45	10	0	0	8	92.1	12	39	61	2	4	5	0.79	.263	.434	.336
Plunk	NY-A	R	2	5	.286	4.76	43	8	0	0	0	111.2	18	62	103	6	28	3	0.61	.286	.478	.371
Plympton	Bos.	R	0	0	—	0.00	4	0	0	0	0	5.1	0	4	2	1	0	0	0.56	.263	.316	.375
Poole	Bal.	L	3	2	.600	2.36	29	0	0	0	1	42	3	12	38	2	0	1	1.23	.196	.284	.252
Radinsky	ChiA	L	5	5	.500	2.02	67	0	0	0	8	71.1	4	23	49	0	1	0	0.99	.206	.288	.270
Reardon	Bos.	R	1	4	.200	3.03	57	0	0	0	40	59.1	9	16	44	0	3	1	0.61	.236	.419	.286
Rhodes	Bal.	L	0	3	.000	8.00	8	8	0	0	0	36	4	23	23	2	7	2	0.84	.320	.464	.405
Ritz	Det.	R	0	3	.000	11.74	11	5	0	0	0	15.1	1	22	9	0	3	0	0.90	.288	.390	.482
Robinson	Cal.	R	0	3	.000	5.37	39	0	0	0	3	57	9	29	57	10	4	0	1.43	.259	.444	.349
Robinson	Mil.	R	0	1	.000	6.23	1	1	0	0	0	4.1	0	3	0	0	1	0	1.00	.353	.588	.476
Rogers	Tex.	L	10	10	.500	5.42	63	9	0	0	5	109.2	14	61	73	3	1	3	1.14	.281	.444	.375
Rosenthal	Tex.	R	1	4	.200	5.25	36	0	0	0	1	70.1	9	36	61	8	6	1	0.79	.257	.425	.341
Je. Russell	Tex.	R	6	4	.600	3.29	68	0	0	0	30	79.1	11	26	52	6	1	0	1.44	.236	.365	.295
Ryan	Tex.	R	12	6	.667	2.91	27	27	2	2	0	173	12	72	203	8	24	8	0.61	.172	.285	.263
Saberhagen	K.C.	R	13	8	.619	3.07	28	28	7	2	0	196.1	12	45	136	8	9	9	1.04	.228	.327	.280
Sanderson	NY-A	R	16	10	.615	3.81	34	34	2	2	0	208	22	29	130	4	16	7	0.83	.252	.405	.293
Schooler	Sea.	R	3	3	.500	3.67	34	0	0	0	7	34.1	2	10	31	2	3	0	1.31	.198	.278	.255
Seanez	Cle.	R	0	0	—	16.20	5	0	0	0	0	5	2	7	7	2	0	0	2.00	.385	.692	.515
Shaw	Cle.	R	0	5	.000	3.36	29	1	0	0	1	72.1	6	27	31	6	1	3	1.32	.262	.371	.332
Show	Oak.	R	1	2	.333	5.92	23	5	0	0	0	51.2	5	17	20	2	4	1	0.93	.300	.464	.366
Slusarski	Oak.	R	5	7	.417	5.27	20	19	1	0	0	109.1	14	52	60	4	5	5	1.11	.283	.436	.364
Stewart	Oak.	R	11	11	.500	5.18	35	35	2	1	0	226	24	105	144	13	23	9	1.01	.278	.428	.356
Stieb	Tor.	R	4	3	.571	3.17	9	9	1	0	0	59.2	4	23	29	0	5	1	1.84	.243	.346	.321
Stottlemyre	Tor.	R	15	8	.652	3.78	34	34	1	0	0	219	21	75	116	4	24	3	0.93	.235	.356	.305
Swan	Sea.	L	6	2	.750	3.43	63	0	0	0	2	78.2	8	28	33	8	7	1	3.06	.269	.405	.330
Swift	Sea.	R	1	2	.333	1.99	71	0	0	0	17	90.1	3	26	48	2	1	1	4.73	.224	.276	.283
Swindell	Cle.	L	9	16	.360	3.48	33	33	7	0	0	238	21	31	169	3	9	11	0.75	.263	.393	.287
Tanana	Det.	L	13	12	.520	3.77	33	33	3	2	0	217.1	26	78	107	3	17	14	0.93	.265	.412	.327
Tapani	Min.	R	16	9	.640	2.99	34	34	4	1	0	244	23	40	135	3	18	3	1.16	.245	.382	.277
Taylor	NY-A	R	7	12	.368	6.27	23	22	0	0	0	116.1	13	53	72	3	12	6	1.34	.314	.477	.388
Telford	Bal.	R	0	0	—	4.05	9	1	0	0	0	26.2	3	6	24	1	1	0	1.20	.265	.402	.303
Terrell	Det.	R	12	14	.462	4.24	35	33	8	2	0	218.2	16	79	80	8	6	5	1.28	.301	.433	.358
Thigpen	ChiA	R	7	5	.583	3.49	67	0	0	0	30	69.2	10	38	47	2	8	5	1.15	.245	.409	.348
Timlin	Tor.	R	11	6	.647	3.16	63	3	0	0	3	108.1	6	50	85	5	11	5	2.51	.233	.297	.317
Van Poppel	Oak.	R	0	0	—	9.64	1	1	0	0	0	4.2	1	2	6	0	1	0	0.50	.368	.632	.429
Walton	Oak.	R	1	0	1.000	6.23	12	0	0	0	0	13	3	6	10	3	2	0	1.23	.229	.458	.321
Wapnick	ChiA	R	0	1	.000	1.80	6	0	0	0	0	5	0	4	1	0	0	0	0.36	.111	.167	.273
D. Ward	Tor.	R	7	6	.538	2.77	81	0	0	0	23	107.1	3	33	132	6	7	4	1.39	.207	.262	.271
Wayne	Min.	L	1	0	1.000	5.11	8	0	0	0	1	12.1	1	4	7	0	0	0	0.67	.244	.378	.314

American League Pitchers

Name	Team	T	W	L	PCT	ERA	G	GS	CG	SHO	SV	INN	HR	BB	SO	WP	SB	CS	GAR	BA	SLG	OBP
Weathers	Tor.	R	1	0	1.000	4.91	15	0	0	0	0	14.2	1	17	13	0	4	1	1.36	.263	.386	.442
Wegman	Mil.	R	15	7	.682	2.84	28	28	7	2	0	193.1	16	40	89	6	10	7	1.36	.242	.356	.286
Welch	Oak.	R	12	13	.480	4.58	35	35	7	1	0	220	25	91	101	3	12	16	0.91	.263	.404	.341
Wells	Tor.	L	15	10	.600	3.72	40	28	2	0	1	198.1	24	49	106	10	8	13	0.80	.252	.403	.297
West	Min.	L	4	4	.500	4.54	15	12	0	0	0	71.1	13	28	52	3	3	2	0.68	.244	.458	.314
Williamson	Bal.	R	5	5	.500	4.48	65	0	0	0	4	80.1	9	35	53	7	10	3	1.29	.275	.424	.343
Willis	Min.	R	8	3	.727	2.63	40	0	0	0	2	89	4	19	53	4	5	3	1.02	.232	.311	.273
Witt	NY-A	R	0	1	.000	10.13	2	2	0	0	0	5.1	1	1	0	1	1	0	2.40	.320	.520	.346
Witt	Tex.	R	3	7	.300	6.09	17	16	1	1	0	88.2	4	74	82	8	18	4	0.97	.254	.356	.388
York	Cle.	R	1	4	.200	6.75	14	4	0	0	0	34.2	2	19	19	2	4	2	1.28	.333	.489	.413
Young	Cal.	L	1	0	1.000	4.26	11	0	0	0	0	12.2	3	3	6	0	1	2	1.14	.261	.478	.306
Young	Oak.	L	4	2	.667	5.00	41	1	0	0	0	68.1	8	34	27	2	4	3	0.95	.278	.425	.363
Young	Bos.	L	3	7	.300	5.18	19	16	0	0	0	88.2	4	53	69	5	8	3	2.67	.266	.335	.365

American League Catchers

Name	Team	B	BA	SLG	OBP	G	AB	R	H	2B	3B	HR	RBI	BB	SO	SB	CS	LHP	RHP	SP	SP2
Allanson	Det.	R	.232	.318	.266	60	151	10	35	10	0	1	16	7	31	0	1	.217	.278	.310	.286
Alomar	Cle.	R	.217	.266	.264	51	184	10	40	9	0	0	7	8	24	0	4	.214	.218	.096	.100
Borders	Tor.	R	.244	.354	.271	105	291	22	71	17	0	5	36	11	45	0	0	.238	.250	.292	.194
Bradley	Sea.	L	.203	.244	.280	83	172	10	35	7	0	0	11	19	19	0	0	.182	.205	.229	.133
Cochrane	Sea.	R	.247	.354	.286	65	178	16	44	13	0	2	22	9	38	0	1	.245	.248	.438	.438
Dempsey	Mil.	R	.231	.347	.329	61	147	15	34	5	0	4	21	23	20	0	2	.237	.220	.289	.381
Fisk	ChiA	R	.241	.413	.299	134	460	42	111	25	0	18	74	32	86	1	2	.229	.248	.250	.218
Geren	NY-A	R	.219	.289	.270	64	128	7	28	3	0	2	12	9	31	0	1	.257	.043	.321	.333
Harper	Min.	R	.311	.447	.336	123	441	54	137	28	1	10	69	14	22	1	2	.316	.309	.313	.279
Hemond	Oak.	R	.217	.217	.250	23	23	4	5	0	0	0	0	1	7	1	2	.273	.167	.167	.000
Hoiles	Bal.	R	.243	.384	.304	107	341	36	83	15	0	11	31	29	61	0	2	.257	.237	.224	.176
Howard	Sea.	R	.167	.333	.286	9	6	1	1	1	0	0	0	1	2	0	0	.200	.000	.000	.000
Karkovice	ChiA	R	.246	.413	.310	75	167	25	41	13	0	5	22	15	42	0	0	.295	.217	.239	.241
Leyritz	NY-A	R	.182	.221	.300	32	77	8	14	3	0	0	4	13	15	0	1	.243	.125	.250	.143
Lopez	Cle.	R	.220	.293	.261	35	82	7	18	4	1	0	7	4	7	0	0	.234	.200	.150	.111
Macfarlane	K.C.	R	.277	.506	.330	84	267	34	74	18	2	13	41	17	52	1	0	.321	.245	.278	.216
Marzano	Bos.	R	.263	.333	.271	49	114	10	30	8	0	0	9	1	16	0	0	.300	.250	.280	.250
Mayne	K.C.	L	.251	.325	.315	85	231	22	58	8	0	3	31	23	42	2	4	.091	.268	.349	.259
Melvin	Bal.	R	.250	.307	.279	79	228	11	57	10	0	1	23	11	46	0	0	.269	.240	.305	.240
Merullo	ChiA	L	.229	.343	.268	80	140	8	32	1	0	5	21	9	18	0	0	.125	.235	.233	.130
Myers	Tor.	L	.262	.411	.306	107	309	25	81	22	0	8	36	21	45	0	0	.171	.274	.235	.143
Nokes	NY-A	L	.268	.469	.308	135	456	52	122	20	0	24	77	25	49	3	2	.261	.270	.256	.264
Ortiz	Min.	R	.209	.261	.293	61	134	9	28	5	1	0	11	15	12	0	1	.143	.239	.189	.294
Orton	Cal.	R	.203	.261	.313	29	69	7	14	4	0	0	3	10	17	0	1	.316	.160	.176	.111
Parrish	Cal.	R	.216	.388	.285	119	402	38	87	12	0	19	51	35	117	0	1	.219	.215	.250	.222
Pedre	K.C.	R	.263	.421	.364	10	19	2	5	1	1	0	3	3	5	0	0	.231	.333	.286	.333
Pena	Bos.	R	.231	.321	.291	141	464	45	107	23	2	5	48	37	53	8	3	.283	.215	.238	.254
Petralli	Tex.	L	.271	.352	.339	87	199	21	54	8	1	2	20	21	25	2	1	.111	.279	.265	.269
Quirk	Oak.	L	.261	.296	.321	76	203	16	53	4	0	1	17	16	28	0	3	.313	.257	.269	.250
Ramos	NY-A	R	.308	.346	.310	10	26	4	8	1	0	0	3	1	3	0	0	.333	.273	.000	–
Rodriguez	Tex.	R	.264	.354	.276	88	280	24	74	16	0	3	27	5	42	0	1	.239	.273	.333	.292
Jo. Russell	Tex.	R	.111	.111	.138	22	27	3	3	0	0	0	1	1	7	0	0	.133	.083	.000	.000
Salas	Det.	L	.088	.158	.117	33	57	2	5	1	0	1	7	0	10	0	0	.000	.093	.214	.000
Skinner	Cle.	R	.243	.303	.279	99	284	23	69	14	0	1	24	14	67	0	2	.307	.214	.176	.194
Spehr	K.C.	R	.189	.378	.282	37	74	7	14	5	0	3	14	9	18	1	0	.209	.161	.167	.083
Stanley	Tex.	R	.249	.381	.372	95	181	25	45	13	1	3	25	34	44	0	0	.277	.218	.250	.276
Steinbach	Oak.	R	.274	.386	.312	129	456	50	125	31	1	6	67	22	70	2	2	.266	.278	.285	.227
Surhoff	Mil.	L	.289	.372	.319	143	505	57	146	19	4	5	68	26	33	5	8	.255	.298	.313	.291
Tackett	Bal.	R	.125	.125	.300	6	8	1	1	0	0	0	0	2	2	0	0	.333	.000	.000	–
Taubensee	Cle.	L	.242	.303	.288	26	66	5	16	2	1	0	8	5	16	0	0	.400	.214	.333	.000
Tettleton	Det.	B	.263	.491	.387	154	501	85	132	17	2	31	89	101	131	3	3	.248	.268	.283	.231
Tingley	Cal.	R	.200	.287	.258	45	115	11	23	7	0	1	13	8	34	1	1	.212	.195	.184	.235
Valle	Sea.	R	.194	.299	.286	132	324	38	63	8	1	8	32	34	49	0	2	.232	.175	.163	.237
Wakamatsu	ChiA	R	.226	.226	.250	18	31	2	7	0	0	0	1	0	6	0	0	.313	.133	.000	.000
Webster	Min.	R	.294	.588	.390	18	34	7	10	1	0	3	8	6	10	0	0	.400	.250	.222	.400

American League First Basemen

Name	Team	B	BA	SLG	OBP	G	AB	R	H	2B	3B	HR	RBI	BB	SO	SB	CS	LHP	RHP	SP	SP2
Aldrete	Cle.	L	.262	.322	.380	85	183	22	48	6	1	1	19	36	37	1	2	.182	.267	.341	.273
Barnes	Det.	R	.289	.491	.325	75	159	28	46	13	2	5	17	9	24	10	7	.282	.297	.281	.313
Benzinger	K.C.	B	.294	.386	.338	78	293	29	86	15	3	2	40	17	46	2	6	.266	.307	.364	.283
Bergman	Det.	L	.237	.407	.351	86	194	23	46	10	1	7	29	35	40	1	1	.053	.257	.333	.353
Brett	K.C.	L	.255	.402	.327	131	505	77	129	40	2	10	61	58	75	2	0	.234	.266	.236	.200
Bush	Min.	L	.303	.485	.401	93	165	21	50	10	1	6	23	24	25	0	2	.000	.307	.262	.261
Canale	Mil.	L	.176	.500	.318	21	34	6	6	2	0	3	10	8	6	0	0	.000	.214	.222	.333
Cochrane	Sea.	B	.247	.354	.286	65	178	16	44	13	0	2	22	9	38	0	1	.245	.248	.438	.438
Cron	Cal.	R	.133	.133	.235	6	15	0	2	0	0	0	0	2	5	0	0	.250	.000	.000	.000
Daugherty	Tex.	L	.194	.264	.270	58	144	8	28	3	2	1	11	16	23	1	0	.233	.184	.128	.158
Davis	Sea.	L	.221	.335	.299	145	462	39	102	15	1	12	69	56	78	0	3	.238	.216	.259	.304
Davis	Bal.	R	.227	.460	.307	49	176	29	40	9	1	10	28	16	29	4	0	.255	.217	.190	.105
Eisenreich	K.C.	L	.301	.392	.333	135	375	47	113	22	3	2	47	20	35	5	3	.322	.295	.324	.255
Fielder	Det.	R	.261	.513	.347	162	624	102	163	25	0	44	133	78	151	0	0	.296	.249	.286	.224
Fisk	ChiA	R	.241	.413	.299	134	460	42	111	25	0	18	74	32	86	1	2	.229	.248	.250	.218
Hill	Cal.	B	.239	.301	.335	77	209	36	50	8	1	1	20	30	21	1	0	.257	.236	.327	.105
Hrbek	Min.	L	.284	.461	.373	132	462	72	131	20	1	20	89	67	48	4	4	.281	.284	.310	.371
Jacoby	Oak.	R	.224	.308	.274	122	419	28	94	21	1	4	44	27	54	2	1	.250	.215	.250	.283
James	Cle.	R	.238	.318	.273	115	437	31	104	16	2	5	41	18	61	3	1	.198	.255	.237	.300
Jefferson	Cle.	B	.198	.287	.219	26	101	10	20	3	0	2	12	3	22	0	0	.174	.205	.179	.214
Joyner	Cal.	L	.301	.488	.360	143	551	79	166	34	3	21	96	52	66	2	0	.275	.315	.329	.328
Larkin	Min.	L	.286	.373	.361	98	255	34	73	14	1	2	19	30	21	2	3	.273	.293	.190	.154
Lopez	Cle.	R	.220	.293	.261	35	82	7	18	4	1	0	7	4	7	0	0	.234	.200	.150	.111
Maas	NY-A	L	.220	.390	.333	148	500	69	110	14	1	23	63	83	128	5	1	.221	.219	.180	.155
Martinez	Cle.	R	.284	.397	.310	72	257	22	73	14	0	5	30	10	43	3	2	.338	.260	.360	.348
T. Martinez	Sea.	L	.205	.330	.272	36	112	11	23	2	0	4	9	11	24	0	0	.257	.182	.071	.083
Mattingly	NY-A	L	.288	.394	.339	152	587	64	169	35	0	9	68	46	42	2	0	.264	.303	.290	.288
McGwire	Oak.	R	.201	.383	.330	154	483	62	97	22	0	22	75	93	116	2	1	.200	.201	.238	.254
McKnight	Bal.	B	.171	.195	.209	16	41	2	7	1	0	0	2	2	7	1	0	.150	.190	.125	.125
Merullo	ChiA	L	.229	.343	.268	80	140	8	32	1	0	5	21	9	18	0	0	.125	.235	.233	.130
Meulens	NY-A	R	.222	.319	.276	96	288	37	64	8	1	6	29	18	97	3	0	.236	.200	.239	.250
Milligan	Bal.	R	.263	.406	.373	141	483	57	127	17	2	16	70	84	108	0	5	.229	.277	.305	.323
Molitor	Mil.	R	.325	.489	.399	158	665	133	216	32	13	17	75	77	62	19	8	.322	.326	.326	.338
O'Brien	Sea.	L	.248	.402	.300	152	560	58	139	29	3	17	88	44	61	0	1	.235	.255	.287	.273
Olerud	Tor.	L	.256	.438	.353	139	454	68	116	30	1	17	68	68	84	0	2	.217	.264	.233	.167
Palmeiro	Tex.	L	.322	.532	.389	159	631	115	203	49	3	26	88	68	72	4	3	.274	.342	.231	.211
Parrish	Cal.	R	.216	.388	.285	119	402	38	87	12	0	19	51	35	117	0	1	.219	.215	.250	.222
Pasqua	ChiA	L	.259	.465	.358	134	417	71	108	22	5	18	66	62	86	0	2	.265	.258	.243	.298
Pecota	K.C.	R	.286	.399	.356	125	398	53	114	23	2	6	45	41	45	16	7	.336	.263	.320	.279
Powell	Sea.	R	.216	.369	.288	57	111	16	24	6	1	3	12	11	24	0	2	.250	.163	.130	.111
Quintana	Bos.	R	.295	.412	.375	149	478	69	141	21	1	11	71	61	66	1	0	.340	.274	.277	.308
Quirk	Oak.	L	.261	.296	.321	76	203	16	53	4	0	1	17	16	28	0	3	.313	.257	.269	.250
Riles	Oak.	L	.214	.324	.290	108	281	30	60	8	4	5	32	31	42	3	2	.143	.219	.278	.333
Rose	Cal.	R	.277	.431	.304	22	65	5	18	5	1	1	8	3	13	0	0	.154	.154	.333	.286
Segui	Bal.	B	.278	.340	.316	86	212	15	59	7	0	2	22	12	19	1	1	.337	.228	.281	.226
Snyder	Tor.	R	.175	.265	.216	71	166	14	29	4	1	3	17	9	60	0	0	.164	.200	.163	.091
Sorrento	Min.	L	.255	.553	.314	26	47	6	12	2	0	4	13	4	11	0	0	.600	.214	.278	.000
Sprague	Tor.	R	.275	.394	.361	61	160	17	44	7	0	4	20	19	43	0	3	.267	.286	.289	.278
Stanley	Tex.	R	.249	.381	.372	95	181	25	45	13	1	3	25	34	44	0	0	.277	.218	.250	.276
Steinbach	Oak.	R	.274	.386	.312	129	456	50	125	31	1	6	67	22	70	2	2	.266	.278	.285	.227
Stevens	Cal.	L	.293	.414	.354	18	58	8	17	7	0	0	9	6	12	1	2	.294	.293	.214	.250
Stubbs	Mil.	L	.213	.359	.282	103	362	48	77	16	2	11	38	35	71	13	4	.250	.218	.211	.150	.160
Tabler	Tor.	R	.216	.270	.318	82	185	20	40	5	1	1	21	29	21	0	0	.190	.316	.234	.200
Thomas	ChiA	R	.318	.553	.453	158	559	104	178	31	2	32	109	138	112	1	2	.376	.293	.347	.345
Vaughn	Bos.	L	.260	.358	.339	74	219	21	57	12	0	4	32	26	43	2	1	.212	.269	.373	.323
Ventura	ChiA	L	.284	.442	.367	157	606	92	172	25	1	23	100	80	67	2	4	.260	.295	.331	.271
Witmeyer	Oak.	L	.053	.053	.053	11	19	0	1	0	0	0	0	0	5	0	0	.000	.056	.000	.000

American League Second Basemen

Name	Team	B	BA	SLG	OBP	G	AB	R	H	2B	3B	HR	RBI	BB	SO	SB	CS	LHP	RHP	SP	SP2
Alomar	Tor.	B	.295	.436	.354	161	637	88	188	41	11	9	69	57	86	53	11	.246	.316	.280	.203
Amaral	Sea.	R	.063	.063	.167	14	16	2	1	0	0	0	0	1	5	0	0	.143	.000	.000	.000
Amaro	Cal.	R	.217	.261	.308	10	23	0	5	1	0	0	2	3	3	0	0	.000	.263	.375	.600
Baerga	Cle.	B	.288	.398	.346	158	593	80	171	28	2	11	69	48	74	3	2	.329	.273	.280	.261
Barnes	Det.	R	.289	.491	.325	75	159	28	46	13	2	5	17	9	24	10	7	.282	.297	.281	.313
Bell	Bal.	B	.172	.249	.201	100	209	26	36	9	2	1	15	8	51	0	0	.104	.193	.106	.154
Blankenship	Oak.	R	.249	.341	.336	90	185	33	46	8	0	3	21	23	42	12	3	.222	.262	.241	.233
Bordick	Oak.	R	.238	.268	.289	90	235	21	56	5	1	0	21	14	37	3	4	.224	.243	.340	.375

American League Second Basemen

Name	Team	B	BA	SLG	OBP	G	AB	R	H	2B	3B	HR	RBI	BB	SO	SB	CS	LHP	RHP	SP	SP2
Brosius	Oak.	R	.235	.397	.268	36	68	9	16	5	0	2	4	3	11	3	1	.208	.250	.143	.143
Browne	Cle.	B	.228	.269	.292	107	290	28	66	5	2	1	29	27	29	2	4	.231	.226	.270	.289
Brumley	Bos.	B	.212	.254	.273	63	118	16	25	5	0	0	5	10	22	2	0	.308	.165	.172	.167
Cora	ChiA	B	.241	.276	.313	100	228	37	55	2	3	0	18	20	21	11	6	.298	.222	.196	.154
Diaz	Tex.	R	.264	.319	.318	96	182	24	48	7	0	1	22	15	18	0	1	.268	.260	.292	.370
Disarcina	Cal.	R	.211	.246	.274	18	57	5	12	2	0	0	3	3	4	0	0	.222	.205	.250	.000
Fariss	Tex.	R	.258	.387	.395	19	31	6	8	1	0	1	6	7	11	0	0	.261	.250	.286	.400
Fletcher	ChiA	R	.206	.266	.262	90	248	14	51	10	1	1	28	17	26	0	2	.188	.218	.254	.310
Flora	Cal.	R	.125	.125	.222	3	8	1	1	0	0	0	0	1	5	1	0	.000	.143	.000	.000
Franco	Tex.	R	.341	.474	.408	146	589	108	201	27	3	15	78	65	78	36	9	.368	.332	.322	.314
Gallego	Oak.	R	.247	.369	.343	159	482	67	119	15	4	12	49	67	84	6	9	.311	.225	.250	.196
Gantner	Mil.	L	.283	.361	.320	140	526	63	149	27	4	2	47	27	34	4	6	.266	.289	.236	.194
Gonzales	Tor.	R	.195	.246	.289	71	118	16	23	3	0	1	6	12	22	0	0	.212	.188	.097	.200
Grebeck	ChiA	R	.281	.460	.386	107	224	37	63	16	3	6	31	38	40	1	3	.304	.257	.276	.161
Hemond	Oak.	R	.217	.217	.250	23	23	4	5	0	0	0	0	1	7	1	2	.273	.167	.167	.000
Hill	Cal.	B	.239	.301	.335	77	209	36	50	8	1	1	20	30	21	1	0	.257	.236	.327	.105
Howard	K.C.	B	.216	.258	.267	94	236	20	51	7	0	1	17	16	45	3	2	.225	.212	.242	.243
Huff	ChiA	R	.251	.346	.361	102	243	42	61	10	2	3	25	37	48	14	4	.231	.270	.293	.294
Hulett	Bal.	R	.204	.350	.255	79	206	29	42	9	0	7	18	13	49	0	1	.139	.239	.137	.115
P. Kelly	NY-A	R	.242	.339	.288	96	298	35	72	12	4	3	23	15	52	12	1	.263	.231	.188	.229
Knoblauch	Min.	R	.281	.350	.351	151	565	78	159	24	6	1	50	59	40	25	5	.257	.290	.308	.288
Lewis	Cle.	R	.264	.318	.293	84	314	29	83	15	1	0	30	15	45	2	2	.276	.260	.324	.317
Lyons	Bos.	L	.241	.354	.277	87	212	15	51	10	1	4	17	11	35	10	3	.167	.245	.200	.182
Newman	Min.	B	.191	.211	.260	118	246	25	47	5	0	0	19	23	21	4	5	.242	.172	.189	.132
Paredes	Det.	R	.333	.333	.333	16	18	4	6	0	0	0	0	0	1	1	1	.357	.250	.333	.333
Pecota	K.C.	R	.286	.399	.356	125	398	53	114	23	2	6	45	41	45	16	7	.336	.263	.320	.279
Phillips	Det.	B	.284	.438	.371	146	564	87	160	28	4	17	72	79	95	10	5	.357	.256	.317	.296
Randolph	Mil.	R	.327	.374	.424	124	431	60	141	14	3	0	54	75	38	4	2	.358	.311	.373	.367
Reed	Bos.	R	.283	.382	.349	153	618	87	175	42	2	5	60	60	53	6	5	.267	.289	.304	.193
Reynolds	Sea.	B	.254	.341	.332	161	631	95	160	34	6	3	57	72	63	28	8	.264	.249	.322	.426
Riles	Oak.	L	.214	.324	.290	108	281	30	60	8	4	5	32	31	42	3	2	.143	.219	.278	.333
B. Ripken	Bal.	R	.216	.261	.253	104	287	24	62	11	1	0	14	15	31	0	1	.270	.187	.207	.286
Rose	Cal.	R	.277	.431	.304	22	65	5	18	5	1	1	8	3	13	0	0	.359	.154	.333	.286
Sax	NY-A	R	.304	.414	.345	158	652	85	198	38	2	10	56	41	38	31	11	.344	.284	.318	.246
Schaefer	Sea.	R	.250	.323	.272	84	164	19	41	7	1	1	11	5	25	3	1	.263	.232	.171	.143
Shumpert	K.C.	R	.217	.322	.283	144	369	45	80	16	4	5	34	30	75	17	11	.207	.222	.266	.333
Sojo	Cal.	R	.258	.327	.295	113	364	38	94	14	1	3	20	14	26	4	2	.298	.240	.225	.180
Whitaker	Det.	L	.279	.489	.391	138	470	94	131	26	2	23	78	90	45	4	2	.247	.287	.284	.220

American League Third Basemen

Name	Team	B	BA	SLG	OBP	G	AB	R	H	2B	3B	HR	RBI	BB	SO	SB	CS	LHP	RHP	SP	SP2
Baerga	Cle.	B	.288	.398	.346	158	593	80	171	28	2	11	69	48	74	3	2	.329	.273	.280	.261
Barnes	Det.	R	.289	.491	.325	75	159	28	46	13	2	5	17	9	24	10	7	.282	.297	.281	.313
Berry	K.C.	R	.133	.183	.212	31	60	5	8	3	0	0	1	5	23	0	0	.167	.100	.071	.000
Blankenship	Oak.	R	.249	.341	.336	90	185	33	46	8	0	3	21	23	42	12	3	.222	.262	.241	.233
Boggs	Bos.	L	.332	.460	.421	144	546	93	181	42	2	8	51	89	32	1	2	.265	.361	.310	.233
Bradley	Sea.	L	.203	.244	.280	83	172	10	35	7	0	0	11	19	19	0	0	.182	.205	.229	.133
Brosius	Oak.	R	.235	.397	.268	36	68	9	16	5	0	2	4	3	11	3	1	.208	.250	.143	.143
Browne	Cle.	B	.228	.269	.292	107	290	28	66	5	2	1	29	27	29	2	4	.231	.226	.270	.289
Brumley	Bos.	B	.212	.254	.273	63	118	16	25	5	0	0	5	10	22	2	0	.308	.165	.172	.167
Cochrane	Sea.	B	.247	.354	.286	65	178	16	44	13	0	2	22	9	38	0	1	.245	.248	.438	.438
Cooper	Bos.	L	.457	.686	.486	14	35	6	16	4	2	0	7	2	2	0	0	.667	.414	.667	.667
Diaz	Tex.	R	.264	.319	.318	96	182	24	48	7	0	1	22	15	18	0	1	.268	.260	.292	.370
Espinoza	NY-A	R	.256	.344	.282	148	480	51	123	23	2	5	33	16	57	4	1	.261	.254	.250	.170
Fryman	Det.	R	.259	.447	.309	149	557	65	144	36	3	21	91	40	149	12	5	.296	.244	.290	.260
Gaetti	Cal.	R	.246	.379	.293	152	586	58	144	22	1	18	66	33	104	5	5	.239	.248	.288	.254
Gantner	Mil.	L	.283	.361	.320	140	526	63	149	27	4	2	47	27	34	4	6	.266	.289	.236	.194
Gomez	Bal.	R	.233	.409	.302	118	391	40	91	17	2	16	45	40	82	1	1	.219	.238	.188	.132
Gonzales	Tor.	R	.195	.246	.289	71	118	16	23	3	0	1	6	12	22	0	0	.212	.188	.097	.200
Grebeck	ChiA	R	.281	.460	.386	107	224	37	63	16	3	6	31	38	40	1	3	.304	.257	.276	.161
Gruber	Tor.	R	.252	.443	.308	113	429	58	108	18	2	20	65	31	70	12	7	.277	.243	.238	.158
Hulett	Bal.	R	.204	.350	.255	79	206	29	42	9	0	7	18	13	49	0	1	.139	.239	.137	.115
Humphreys	NY-A	R	.200	.200	.347	25	40	9	8	0	0	0	3	9	7	2	0	.250	.150	.231	.222
Jacoby	Oak.	R	.224	.308	.274	122	419	28	94	21	1	4	44	27	54	2	1	.250	.215	.250	.283
P. Kelly	NY-A	R	.242	.339	.288	96	298	35	72	12	4	3	23	15	52	12	1	.263	.231	.188	.229
Lansford	Oak.	R	.063	.063	.063	5	16	0	1	0	0	0	0	0	2	0	0	.000	.143	.000	.000
Law	Oak.	R	.209	.276	.303	74	134	11	28	7	1	0	9	18	27	0	0	.259	.175	.297	.263
Leius	Min.	R	.286	.417	.378	109	199	35	57	7	2	5	20	30	35	5	5	.305	.254	.271	.250
Leyritz	NY-A	R	.182	.221	.300	32	77	8	14	3	0	0	4	13	15	0	1	.243	.125	.250	.143
Livingstone	Det.	L	.291	.378	.341	44	127	19	37	5	0	2	11	10	25	2	1	.417	.278	.233	.118

American League Third Basemen

Name	Team	B	BA	SLG	OBP	G	AB	R	H	2B	3B	HR	RBI	BB	SO	SB	CS	LHP	RHP	SP	SP2
Lovullo	NY-A	B	.176	.216	.250	22	51	0	9	2	0	0	2	5	7	0	0	.167	.178	.091	.000
Lyons	Bos.	L	.241	.354	.277	87	212	15	51	10	1	4	17	11	35	10	3	.167	.245	.200	.182
E. Martinez	Sea.	R	.307	.452	.405	150	544	98	167	35	1	14	52	84	72	0	3	.359	.286	.219	.160
Mulliniks	Tor.	L	.250	.333	.364	97	240	27	60	12	1	2	24	44	44	0	0	.083	.259	.400	.316
Newman	Min.	B	.191	.211	.260	118	246	25	47	5	0	0	19	23	21	4	5	.242	.172	.189	.132
Pagliarulo	Min.	L	.279	.384	.322	121	365	38	102	20	0	6	36	21	55	1	2	.188	.284	.195	.189
Palmer	Tex.	R	.187	.403	.281	81	268	38	50	9	2	15	37	32	98	0	2	.247	.160	.250	.333
Pecota	K.C.	R	.286	.399	.356	125	398	53	114	23	2	6	45	41	45	16	7	.336	.263	.320	.279
Petralli	Tex.	L	.271	.352	.339	87	199	21	54	8	1	2	20	21	25	2	1	.111	.279	.265	.269
Phillips	Det.	B	.284	.438	.371	146	564	87	160	28	4	17	72	79	95	10	5	.357	.256	.317	.296
Riles	Oak.	L	.214	.324	.290	108	281	30	60	8	4	5	32	31	42	3	2	.143	.219	.278	.333
Rose	Cal.	R	.277	.431	.304	22	65	5	18	5	1	1	8	3	13	0	0	.359	.154	.333	.286
Sax	NY-A	R	.304	.414	.345	158	652	85	198	38	2	10	56	41	38	31	11	.344	.284	.318	.246
Schaefer	Sea.	R	.250	.323	.272	84	164	19	41	7	1	1	11	5	25	3	1	.263	.232	.171	.143
Seitzer	K.C.	R	.265	.350	.350	85	234	28	62	11	3	1	25	29	21	4	1	.333	.238	.242	.229
Sheffield	Mil.	R	.194	.320	.277	50	175	25	34	12	2	2	22	19	15	5	5	.140	.212	.178	.250
Snyder	Tor.	R	.175	.265	.216	71	166	14	29	4	1	3	17	9	60	0	0	.164	.200	.163	.091
Sprague	Tor.	R	.275	.394	.361	61	160	17	44	7	0	4	20	19	43	0	3	.267	.286	.289	.278
Stanley	Tex.	R	.249	.381	.372	95	181	25	45	13	1	3	25	34	44	0	0	.277	.218	.250	.276
Surhoff	Mil.	L	.289	.372	.319	143	505	57	146	19	4	5	68	26	33	5	8	.255	.298	.313	.291
Sveum	Mil.	B	.241	.365	.320	90	266	33	64	19	1	4	43	32	78	2	4	.246	.236	.299	.368
Thome	Cle.	L	.255	.367	.298	27	98	7	25	4	2	1	9	5	16	1	1	.050	.308	.222	.300
Velarde	NY-A	R	.245	.332	.322	80	184	19	45	11	1	1	15	18	43	3	1	.253	.239	.196	.259
Ventura	ChiA	L	.284	.442	.367	157	606	92	172	25	1	23	100	80	67	2	4	.260	.295	.331	.271

American League Shortstops

Name	Team	B	BA	SLG	OBP	G	AB	R	H	2B	3B	HR	RBI	BB	SO	SB	CS	LHP	RHP	SP	SP2
Amaral	Sea.	R	.063	.063	.167	14	16	2	1	0	0	0	0	1	5	0	0	.143	.000	.000	.000
Bell	Bal.	R	.172	.249	.201	100	209	26	36	9	2	1	15	8	51	0	0	.104	.193	.106	.154
Beltre	ChiA	R	.167	.167	.286	8	6	0	1	0	0	0	0	1	1	1	0	.000	.200	–	–
Bordick	Oak.	R	.238	.268	.289	90	235	21	56	5	1	0	21	14	37	3	4	.224	.243	.340	.375
Brumley	Bos.	B	.212	.254	.273	63	118	16	25	5	0	0	5	10	22	2	0	.308	.165	.172	.167
Cora	ChiA	B	.241	.276	.313	100	228	37	55	2	3	0	18	20	21	11	6	.298	.222	.196	.154
Diaz	Tex.	R	.264	.319	.318	96	182	24	48	7	0	1	22	15	18	0	1	.268	.260	.292	.370
Disarcina	Cal.	R	.211	.246	.274	18	57	5	12	2	0	0	3	3	4	0	0	.222	.205	.250	.000
Espinoza	NY-A	R	.256	.344	.282	148	480	51	123	23	2	5	33	16	57	4	1	.261	.254	.250	.170
Fermin	Cle.	R	.262	.302	.307	129	424	30	111	13	2	0	31	26	27	5	4	.281	.254	.278	.250
Fryman	Det.	R	.259	.447	.309	149	557	65	144	36	3	21	91	40	149	12	5	.296	.244	.290	.260
Gagne	Min.	R	.265	.395	.310	139	408	52	108	23	3	8	42	26	72	11	9	.280	.259	.252	.286
Gallego	Oak.	R	.247	.369	.343	159	482	67	119	15	4	12	49	67	84	6	9	.311	.225	.250	.196
Gonzales	Tor.	R	.195	.246	.289	71	118	16	23	3	0	1	6	12	22	0	0	.212	.188	.097	.200
Grebeck	ChiA	R	.281	.460	.386	107	224	37	63	16	3	6	31	38	40	1	3	.304	.257	.276	.161
Guillen	ChiA	L	.273	.340	.284	154	524	52	143	20	3	3	49	11	38	21	15	.211	.300	.248	.197
Hernandez	Tex.	R	.184	.224	.208	45	98	8	18	2	1	0	4	3	31	0	1	.241	.159	.200	.182
Hill	Cal.	B	.239	.301	.335	77	209	36	50	8	1	1	20	30	21	1	0	.257	.236	.327	.105
Howard	K.C.	B	.216	.258	.267	94	236	20	51	7	0	1	17	16	45	3	2	.225	.212	.242	.243
Huson	Tex.	L	.213	.287	.312	119	268	36	57	8	3	2	26	39	32	8	3	.074	.228	.262	.148
Lee	Tor.	B	.234	.288	.274	138	445	41	104	18	3	0	29	24	107	7	2	.285	.209	.219	.264
Leius	Min.	R	.286	.417	.378	109	199	35	57	7	2	5	20	30	35	5	5	.305	.254	.271	.250
Lewis	Cle.	R	.264	.318	.293	84	314	29	83	15	1	0	30	15	45	2	2	.276	.260	.324	.317
Naehring	Bos.	R	.109	.127	.197	20	55	1	6	1	0	0	3	6	15	0	0	.125	.103	.125	.133
Newman	Min.	B	.191	.211	.260	118	246	25	47	5	0	0	19	23	21	4	5	.242	.172	.189	.132
Pecota	K.C.	R	.286	.399	.356	125	398	53	114	23	2	6	45	41	45	16	7	.336	.263	.320	.279
Perezchica	Cle.	R	.364	.455	.440	17	22	4	8	2	0	0	3	5	5	0	0	.300	.417	.250	.000
Phillips	Det.	B	.284	.438	.371	146	564	87	160	28	4	17	72	79	95	10	5	.357	.256	.317	.296
Riles	Oak.	L	.214	.324	.290	108	281	30	60	8	4	5	32	31	42	3	2	.143	.219	.278	.333
C. Ripken	Bal.	R	.323	.566	.374	162	650	99	210	46	5	34	114	53	46	6	1	.348	.315	.315	.291
Rivera	Bos.	R	.258	.384	.318	129	414	64	107	22	3	8	40	35	86	4	4	.315	.239	.202	.226
Schaefer	Sea.	R	.250	.323	.272	84	164	19	41	7	1	1	11	5	25	3	1	.263	.232	.171	.143
Schofield	Cal.	R	.225	.260	.310	134	427	44	96	9	3	0	31	50	69	8	4	.183	.240	.255	.283
Spiers	Mil.	L	.283	.401	.337	133	414	71	117	13	6	8	54	34	55	14	8	.222	.306	.320	.224
Stillwell	K.C.	B	.265	.361	.322	122	385	44	102	17	1	6	51	33	56	3	4	.266	.264	.297	.304
Sveum	Mil.	B	.241	.365	.320	90	266	33	64	19	1	4	43	32	78	2	4	.246	.236	.299	.368
Trammell	Det.	R	.248	.373	.320	101	375	57	93	20	0	9	55	37	39	11	2	.212	.263	.268	.255
Velarde	NY-A	R	.245	.332	.322	80	184	19	45	11	1	1	15	18	43	3	1	.253	.239	.196	.259
Vizquel	Sea.	B	.230	.293	.302	142	426	42	98	16	4	1	41	45	37	7	2	.230	.230	.312	.311
Weiss	Oak.	B	.226	.286	.286	40	133	15	30	6	1	0	13	12	14	6	0	.194	.235	.206	.190
Zosky	Tor.	R	.148	.259	.148	18	27	2	4	1	1	0	2	0	8	0	0	.167	.143	.143	.167

American League Left Fielders

Name	Team	B	BA	SLG	OBP	G	AB	R	H	2B	3B	HR	RBI	BB	SO	SB	CS	LHP	RHP	SP	SP2
Aldrete	Cle.	L	.262	.322	.380	85	183	22	48	6	1	1	19	36	37	1	2	.182	.267	.341	.273
Amaro	Cal.	B	.217	.261	.308	10	23	0	5	1	0	0	2	3	3	0	0	.000	.263	.375	.600
Anderson	Bal.	L	.230	.324	.338	113	256	40	59	12	3	2	27	38	44	12	5	.139	.245	.280	.318
Barnes	Det.	R	.289	.491	.325	75	159	28	46	13	2	5	17	9	24	10	7	.282	.297	.281	.313
Bell	Tor.	R	.143	.143	.314	18	28	5	4	0	0	0	1	6	5	3	2	.150	.125	.167	.000
Belle	Cle.	R	.282	.540	.323	123	461	60	130	31	2	28	95	25	99	3	1	.288	.280	.310	.283
Blankenship	Oak.	R	.249	.341	.336	90	185	33	46	8	0	3	21	23	42	12	3	.222	.262	.241	.233
Briley	Sea.	L	.260	.336	.307	139	381	39	99	17	3	2	26	27	51	23	11	.231	.263	.243	.219
Brosius	Oak.	R	.235	.397	.268	36	68	9	16	5	0	2	4	3	11	3	1	.208	.250	.143	.143
Browne	Cle.	B	.228	.269	.292	107	290	28	66	5	2	1	29	27	29	2	4	.231	.226	.270	.289
Bush	Min.	L	.303	.485	.401	93	165	21	50	10	1	6	23	24	25	0	2	.000	.307	.262	.261
Carter	Tor.	R	.273	.503	.330	162	638	89	174	42	3	33	108	49	112	20	9	.335	.247	.266	.308
Cochrane	Sea.	B	.247	.354	.286	65	178	16	44	13	0	2	22	9	38	0	1	.245	.248	.438	.438
Cole	Cle.	L	.295	.354	.386	122	387	58	114	17	3	0	21	58	47	27	17	.387	.277	.258	.231
Cotto	Sea.	R	.305	.463	.347	66	177	35	54	6	2	6	23	10	27	16	3	.323	.284	.308	.471
Daugherty	Tex.	B	.194	.264	.270	58	144	8	28	3	2	1	11	16	23	1	0	.233	.184	.128	.158
Ducey	Tor.	L	.235	.368	.297	39	68	8	16	2	2	1	4	6	26	2	0	.333	.214	.143	.100
Eisenreich	K.C.	L	.301	.392	.333	135	375	47	113	22	3	2	47	20	35	5	3	.322	.295	.324	.255
Fariss	Tex.	R	.258	.387	.395	19	31	6	8	1	0	1	6	7	11	0	0	.261	.250	.286	.400
Gallagher	Cal.	R	.293	.367	.355	90	270	32	79	17	0	1	30	24	43	2	4	.300	.288	.328	.444
Gibson	K.C.	R	.236	.403	.341	132	462	81	109	17	6	16	55	69	103	18	4	.197	.252	.229	.163
Gladden	Min.	R	.247	.356	.306	132	461	65	114	14	9	6	52	36	60	15	9	.254	.245	.222	.179
Gonzalez	Cle.	R	.159	.261	.284	33	69	10	11	2	1	1	4	11	27	8	0	.094	.216	.133	.125
Gonzalez	Tex.	R	.264	.479	.321	142	545	78	144	34	1	27	102	42	118	4	4	.299	.251	.266	.232
Greenwell	Bos.	L	.300	.419	.350	147	544	76	163	26	6	9	83	43	35	15	5	.327	.287	.307	.247
Griffey Sr.	Sea.	L	.282	.400	.380	30	85	10	24	7	0	1	9	13	13	0	0	.333	.280	.280	.286
Hall	NY-A	L	.285	.455	.321	141	492	67	140	23	2	19	80	26	40	0	1	.309	.273	.250	.211
Hamilton	Mil.	L	.311	.385	.361	122	405	64	126	15	6	1	57	33	38	16	6	.276	.321	.368	.367
D. Henderson	Oak.	R	.276	.465	.346	150	572	86	158	33	0	25	85	58	113	6	6	.354	.250	.279	.215
R. Henderson	Oak.	R	.268	.423	.400	134	470	105	126	17	1	18	57	98	73	58	18	.289	.261	.231	.208
Hill	Cle.	R	.258	.421	.324	72	221	29	57	8	2	8	25	23	54	6	4	.281	.240	.273	.238
Howitt	Oak.	L	.167	.262	.182	21	42	5	7	1	0	1	3	1	12	0	0	.000	.175	.000	.000
Huff	ChiA	R	.251	.346	.361	102	243	42	61	10	2	3	25	37	48	14	4	.231	.270	.293	.294
Humphreys	NY-A	R	.200	.200	.347	25	40	9	8	0	0	0	3	9	7	2	0	.250	.150	.231	.222
Incaviglia	Det.	R	.214	.353	.290	97	337	38	72	12	1	11	38	36	92	1	3	.206	.217	.169	.045
James	Cle.	R	.238	.318	.273	115	437	31	104	16	2	5	41	18	61	3	4	.198	.255	.237	.300
T. Jones	Sea.	R	.251	.360	.321	79	175	30	44	8	1	3	24	18	22	2	0	.203	.351	.250	.211
R. Kelly	NY-A	R	.267	.444	.333	126	486	68	130	22	2	20	69	45	77	32	9	.296	.254	.299	.254
Komminsk	Oak.	R	.120	.160	.185	24	25	1	3	1	0	0	2	2	9	1	0	.143	.091	.333	.333
Lyons	Bos.	L	.241	.354	.277	87	212	15	51	10	1	4	17	11	35	10	3	.167	.245	.200	.182
Mack	Min.	R	.310	.529	.363	143	442	79	137	27	8	18	74	34	79	13	9	.350	.292	.265	.194
Maldonado	Tor.	R	.250	.427	.342	86	288	37	72	15	0	12	48	36	76	4	0	.276	.241	.250	.275
McKnight	Bal.	R	.171	.195	.209	16	41	2	7	1	0	0	2	2	7	1	0	.150	.190	.125	.125
Mercedes	Bal.	R	.204	.241	.259	19	54	10	11	2	0	0	2	4	9	0	0	.212	.190	.111	.167
Meulens	NY-A	R	.222	.319	.276	96	288	37	64	8	1	6	29	18	97	3	0	.236	.200	.239	.250
Milligan	Bal.	R	.263	.406	.373	141	483	57	127	17	2	16	70	84	108	0	5	.229	.277	.305	.323
Moore	K.C.	R	.357	.429	.400	18	14	3	5	1	0	0	0	1	2	3	2	.455	.000	–	–
Moseby	Det.	L	.262	.396	.321	74	260	37	68	15	1	6	35	21	43	8	1	.239	.266	.316	.348
Munoz	Min.	R	.283	.500	.327	51	138	15	39	7	1	7	26	9	31	3	0	.295	.277	.231	.133
Newson	ChiA	L	.295	.424	.419	71	132	20	39	5	0	4	25	28	34	2	2	.143	.304	.356	.435
O'Brien	Sea.	L	.248	.402	.300	152	560	58	139	29	3	17	88	44	61	0	1	.235	.255	.287	.273
Orsulak	Bal.	L	.278	.358	.321	143	486	57	135	22	1	5	43	28	45	6	2	.234	.284	.239	.191
Palmer	Tex.	R	.187	.403	.281	81	268	38	50	9	2	15	37	32	98	0	2	.247	.160	.250	.333
Pasqua	ChiA	L	.259	.465	.358	134	417	71	108	22	5	18	66	62	86	0	2	.265	.258	.243	.298
Phillips	Det.	B	.284	.438	.371	146	564	87	160	28	4	17	72	79	95	10	5	.357	.256	.317	.296
Plantier	Bos.	L	.331	.615	.420	53	148	27	49	7	1	11	35	23	38	1	0	.320	.333	.356	.267
Polonia	Cal.	L	.296	.379	.352	150	604	92	179	28	8	2	50	52	74	48	23	.238	.319	.333	.359
Powell	Sea.	R	.216	.369	.288	57	111	16	24	6	1	3	12	11	24	0	2	.250	.163	.130	.111
Pulliam	K.C.	R	.273	.576	.333	18	33	4	9	1	0	3	4	3	9	0	0	.267	.333	.250	–
Raines	ChiA	B	.268	.345	.359	155	609	102	163	20	6	5	50	83	68	51	15	.279	.262	.286	.217
Reimer	Tex.	R	.269	.477	.332	136	394	46	106	22	0	20	69	33	93	0	3	.222	.274	.287	.276
Rose	Cal.	R	.277	.431	.304	22	65	5	18	5	1	1	8	3	13	0	0	.359	.154	.333	.286
Jo. Russell	Tex.	R	.111	.111	.138	22	27	3	3	0	0	0	1	1	7	0	0	.133	.083	.000	.000
Segui	Bal.	B	.278	.340	.316	86	212	15	59	7	0	2	22	12	19	1	1	.337	.228	.281	.226
Snyder	Tor.	R	.175	.265	.216	71	166	14	29	4	1	3	17	9	60	0	0	.164	.200	.163	.091
Stubbs	Mil.	L	.213	.359	.282	103	362	48	77	16	2	11	38	35	71	13	4	.218	.211	.150	.160
Thurman	K.C.	R	.277	.359	.320	80	184	24	51	9	0	2	13	11	42	15	5	.267	.297	.326	.200
Vaughn	Mil.	L	.244	.456	.319	145	542	81	132	24	5	27	98	62	125	2	2	.227	.250	.277	.263
Venable	Cal.	L	.246	.358	.292	82	187	24	46	8	2	3	21	11	30	2	1	.211	.250	.244	.143
Wilson	Tor.	B	.241	.349	.277	86	241	26	58	12	4	2	28	8	35	11	3	.209	.247	.294	.188
Wilson	Oak.	B	.238	.313	.290	113	294	38	70	14	4	0	28	18	43	20	5	.253	.231	.288	.407

American League Center Fielders

Name	Team	B	BA	SLG	OBP	G	AB	R	H	2B	3B	HR	RBI	BB	SO	SB	CS	LHP	RHP	SP	SP2
Abner	Cal.	R	.228	.366	.257	41	101	12	23	6	1	2	9	4	18	1	2	.204	.250	.261	.182
Anderson	Bal.	L	.230	.324	.338	113	256	40	59	12	3	2	27	38	44	12	5	.139	.245	.280	.318
Barnes	Det.	R	.289	.491	.325	75	159	28	46	13	2	5	17	9	24	10	7	.282	.297	.281	.313
Bell	Tor.	R	.143	.143	.314	18	28	5	4	0	0	0	1	6	5	3	2	.150	.125	.167	.000
Bichette	Mil.	R	.238	.393	.272	134	445	53	106	18	3	15	59	22	107	14	8	.253	.230	.216	.262
Briley	Sea.	L	.260	.336	.307	139	381	39	99	17	3	2	26	27	51	23	11	.231	.263	.243	.219
Brown	Min.	R	.216	.216	.256	38	37	10	8	0	0	0	0	2	8	7	1	.000	.286	.000	.000
Brumley	Bos.	B	.212	.254	.273	63	118	16	25	5	0	0	5	10	22	2	0	.308	.165	.172	.167
Burks	Bos.	R	.251	.422	.314	130	474	56	119	33	3	14	56	39	81	6	11	.259	.248	.226	.315
Cole	Cle.	L	.295	.354	.386	122	387	58	114	17	3	0	21	58	47	27	17	.387	.277	.258	.231
Cotto	Sea.	R	.305	.463	.347	66	177	35	54	6	2	6	23	10	27	16	3	.323	.284	.308	.471
Cuyler	Det.	R	.257	.337	.335	154	475	77	122	15	7	3	33	52	92	41	10	.270	.252	.186	.111
Devereaux	Bal.	R	.260	.431	.313	149	608	82	158	27	10	19	59	47	115	16	9	.293	.247	.257	.235
Eisenreich	K.C.	L	.301	.392	.333	135	375	47	113	22	3	2	47	20	35	5	3	.322	.295	.324	.255
Felix	Cal.	B	.283	.370	.321	66	230	32	65	10	2	2	26	11	55	7	5	.291	.280	.259	.250
Gallagher	Cal.	R	.293	.367	.355	90	270	32	79	17	0	1	30	24	43	2	4	.300	.288	.328	.444
Gonzalez	Cle.	R	.159	.261	.284	33	69	10	11	2	1	1	4	11	27	8	0	.094	.216	.133	.125
Gonzalez	Tex.	R	.264	.479	.321	142	545	78	144	34	1	27	102	42	118	4	4	.299	.251	.266	.232
Griffey Jr.	Sea.	L	.327	.527	.399	154	548	76	179	42	1	22	100	71	82	18	6	.314	.332	.331	.333
Hamilton	Mil.	R	.311	.385	.361	122	405	64	126	15	6	1	57	33	38	16	6	.276	.321	.368	.367
Harris	Tex.	R	.375	.750	.444	18	8	4	3	0	0	1	2	1	3	1	0	.333	.400	.000	.000
D. Henderson	Oak.	R	.276	.465	.346	150	572	86	158	33	0	25	85	58	113	6	6	.354	.250	.279	.215
Hill	Cle.	R	.258	.421	.324	72	221	29	57	8	2	8	25	23	54	6	4	.281	.240	.273	.238
Housie	Bos.	B	.250	.375	.333	11	8	2	2	1	0	0	0	1	3	1	0	.500	.167	1.000	–
Howitt	Oak.	L	.167	.262	.182	21	42	5	7	1	0	1	3	1	12	0	0	.000	.175	.000	.000
Huff	ChiA	R	.251	.346	.361	102	243	42	61	10	2	3	25	37	48	14	4	.231	.270	.293	.294
Johnson	ChiA	L	.274	.342	.304	159	588	72	161	14	13	0	49	26	58	26	11	.244	.285	.246	.247
R. Kelly	NY-A	R	.267	.444	.333	126	486	68	130	22	2	20	69	45	77	32	9	.296	.254	.299	.254
Komminsk	Oak.	R	.120	.160	.185	24	25	1	3	1	0	0	2	2	9	1	0	.143	.091	.333	.333
Lyons	Bos.	L	.241	.354	.277	87	212	15	51	10	1	4	17	11	35	10	3	.167	.245	.200	.182
Mack	Min.	R	.310	.529	.363	143	442	79	137	27	8	18	74	34	79	13	9	.350	.292	.265	.194
McRae	K.C.	B	.261	.372	.288	152	629	86	164	28	9	8	64	24	99	20	11	.294	.245	.254	.197
Moore	K.C.	R	.357	.429	.400	18	14	3	5	1	0	0	0	1	2	3	2	.455	.000	–	–
Pettis	Tex.	B	.216	.277	.341	137	282	37	61	7	5	0	19	54	91	29	13	.195	.224	.225	.268
Phillips	Det.	B	.284	.438	.371	146	564	87	160	28	4	17	72	79	95	10	5	.357	.256	.317	.296
Powell	Sea.	R	.216	.369	.288	57	111	16	24	6	1	3	12	11	24	0	2	.250	.163	.130	.111
Puckett	Min.	R	.319	.460	.352	152	611	92	195	29	6	15	89	31	78	11	5	.406	.289	.301	.266
Sheridan	NY-A	L	.204	.336	.286	62	113	13	23	3	0	4	7	13	30	1	1	.200	.204	.136	.111
Sierra	Tex.	B	.307	.502	.357	161	661	110	203	44	5	25	116	56	91	16	4	.335	.296	.342	.255
Sosa	ChiA	R	.203	.335	.240	116	316	39	64	10	1	10	33	14	98	13	6	.227	.186	.238	.216
Thurman	K.C.	B	.277	.359	.320	80	184	24	51	9	0	2	13	11	42	15	5	.267	.297	.326	.200
Venable	Cal.	L	.246	.358	.292	82	187	24	46	8	2	3	21	11	30	2	1	.211	.250	.244	.143
T. Ward	Tor.	B	.239	.301	.306	48	113	12	27	7	0	0	7	11	18	0	0	.250	.235	.226	.235
White	Tor.	B	.282	.455	.342	156	642	110	181	40	10	17	60	55	135	33	10	.302	.273	.172	.141
Whiten	Cle.	R	.243	.388	.297	116	407	46	99	18	7	9	45	30	85	4	3	.257	.238	.232	.130
Williams	NY-A	B	.238	.350	.336	85	320	43	76	19	4	3	34	48	57	10	5	.202	.255	.343	.237
Wilson	Tor.	B	.241	.349	.277	86	241	26	58	12	4	2	28	8	35	11	3	.209	.247	.294	.188
Wilson	Oak.	B	.238	.313	.290	113	294	38	70	14	4	0	28	18	43	20	5	.253	.231	.288	.407
Yount	Mil.	R	.260	.376	.332	130	503	66	131	20	4	10	77	54	79	6	4	.256	.262	.297	.288
Zupcic	Bos.	R	.160	.280	.192	18	25	3	4	0	0	1	3	1	6	0	0	.182	.143	.143	.000

American League Right Fielders

Name	Team	B	BA	SLG	OBP	G	AB	R	H	2B	3B	HR	RBI	BB	SO	SB	CS	LHP	RHP	SP	SP2
Anderson	Bal.	L	.230	.324	.338	113	256	40	59	12	3	2	27	38	44	12	5	.139	.245	.280	.318
Baines	Oak.	L	.295	.473	.383	141	488	76	144	25	1	20	90	72	67	0	1	.301	.294	.278	.306
Barfield	NY-A	R	.225	.447	.312	84	284	37	64	12	0	17	48	36	80	1	0	.315	.170	.253	.361
Barnes	Det.	R	.289	.491	.325	75	159	28	46	13	2	5	17	9	24	10	7	.282	.297	.281	.313
Bichette	Mil.	R	.238	.393	.272	134	445	53	106	18	3	15	59	22	107	14	8	.253	.230	.216	.262
Blankenship	Oak.	R	.249	.341	.336	90	185	33	46	8	0	3	21	23	42	12	3	.222	.262	.241	.233
Briley	Sea.	L	.260	.336	.307	139	381	39	99	17	3	2	26	27	51	23	11	.231	.263	.243	.219
Brosius	Oak.	R	.235	.397	.268	36	68	9	16	5	0	2	4	3	11	3	1	.208	.250	.143	.143
Brown	Min.	R	.216	.216	.256	38	37	10	8	0	0	0	0	2	8	7	1	.000	.286	.000	.000
Brunansky	Bos.	R	.229	.390	.303	142	459	54	105	24	1	16	70	49	72	1	2	.254	.218	.232	.176
Buhner	Sea.	R	.244	.498	.337	137	406	64	99	14	4	27	77	53	117	0	1	.240	.246	.215	.242
Bush	Min.	L	.303	.485	.401	93	165	21	50	10	1	6	23	24	25	0	2	.000	.307	.262	.261
Canseco	Oak.	R	.266	.556	.359	154	572	115	152	32	1	44	122	78	152	26	6	.250	.271	.266	.347
Carter	Tor.	R	.273	.503	.330	162	638	89	174	42	3	33	108	49	112	20	9	.335	.247	.266	.308
Cochrane	Sea.	B	.247	.354	.286	65	178	16	44	13	0	2	22	9	38	0	1	.245	.248	.438	.438
Cotto	Sea.	R	.305	.463	.347	66	177	35	54	6	2	6	23	10	27	16	3	.323	.284	.308	.471

American League Right Fielders

Name	Team	B	BA	SLG	OBP	G	AB	R	H	2B	3B	HR	RBI	BB	SO	SB	CS	LHP	RHP	SP	SP2
Deer	Det.	R	.179	.386	.314	134	448	64	80	14	2	25	64	89	175	1	3	.196	.171	.168	.130
Ducey	Tor.	L	.235	.368	.297	39	68	8	16	2	2	1	4	6	26	2	0	.333	.214	.143	.100
Eisenreich	K.C.	L	.301	.392	.333	135	375	47	113	22	3	2	47	20	35	5	3	.322	.295	.324	.255
Evans	Bal.	R	.270	.378	.393	101	270	35	73	9	1	6	38	54	55	4	2	.308	.245	.254	.316
Felix	Cal.	B	.283	.370	.321	66	230	32	65	10	2	2	26	11	55	7	5	.291	.280	.259	.250
Gallagher	Cal.	R	.293	.367	.355	90	270	32	79	17	0	1	30	24	43	2	4	.300	.288	.328	.444
Gibson	K.C.	L	.236	.403	.341	132	462	81	109	17	6	16	55	69	103	18	4	.197	.252	.229	.163
Gonzalez	Cle.	R	.159	.261	.284	33	69	10	11	2	1	1	4	11	27	8	0	.094	.216	.133	.125
Gonzalez	Tex.	R	.264	.479	.321	142	545	78	144	34	1	27	102	42	118	4	4	.299	.251	.266	.232
Hall	NY-A	L	.285	.455	.321	141	492	67	140	23	2	19	80	26	40	0	1	.309	.273	.250	.211
Hamilton	Mil.	L	.311	.385	.361	122	405	64	126	15	6	1	57	33	38	16	6	.276	.321	.368	.367
Hare	Det.	L	.053	.105	.143	9	19	0	1	1	0	0	0	2	1	0	0	–	.053	.000	.000
Hill	Cle.	R	.258	.421	.324	72	221	29	57	8	2	8	25	23	54	6	4	.281	.240	.273	.238
Howitt	Oak.	L	.167	.262	.182	21	42	5	7	1	0	1	3	1	12	0	0	.000	.175	.000	.000
Huff	ChiA	L	.251	.346	.361	102	243	42	61	10	2	3	25	37	48	14	4	.231	.270	.293	.294
Incaviglia	Det.	R	.214	.353	.290	97	337	38	72	12	1	11	38	36	92	1	3	.206	.217	.169	.045
James	Cle.	R	.238	.318	.273	115	437	31	104	16	2	5	41	18	61	3	4	.198	.255	.237	.300
Kirby	Cle.	L	.209	.256	.239	21	43	4	9	2	0	0	5	2	6	1	2	.000	.250	.273	.200
Komminsk	Oak.	R	.120	.160	.185	24	25	1	3	1	0	0	2	2	9	1	0	.143	.091	.333	.333
Larkin	Min.	B	.286	.373	.361	98	255	34	73	14	1	2	19	30	21	2	3	.273	.293	.190	.154
Lyons	Bos.	L	.241	.354	.277	87	212	15	51	10	1	4	17	11	35	10	3	.167	.245	.200	.182
Mack	Min.	R	.310	.529	.363	143	442	79	137	27	8	18	74	34	79	13	9	.350	.292	.265	.194
Maldonado	Tor.	R	.250	.427	.342	86	288	37	72	15	0	12	48	36	76	4	0	.276	.241	.250	.275
Martinez	Bal.	L	.269	.514	.303	67	216	32	58	12	1	13	33	11	51	1	1	.207	.278	.288	.278
Mercedes	Bal.	R	.204	.241	.259	19	54	10	11	2	0	0	2	4	9	0	0	.212	.190	.111	.167
Meulens	NY-A	R	.222	.319	.276	96	288	37	64	8	1	6	29	18	97	3	0	.236	.200	.239	.250
Munoz	Min.	R	.283	.500	.327	51	138	15	39	7	1	7	26	9	31	3	0	.295	.277	.231	.133
Newson	ChiA	L	.295	.424	.419	71	132	20	39	5	0	4	25	28	34	2	2	.143	.304	.356	.435
Orsulak	Bal.	L	.278	.358	.321	143	486	57	135	22	1	5	43	28	45	6	2	.234	.284	.239	.191
Pasqua	ChiA	L	.259	.465	.358	134	417	71	108	22	5	18	66	62	86	0	2	.265	.258	.243	.298
Phillips	Det.	B	.284	.438	.371	146	564	87	160	28	4	17	72	79	95	10	5	.357	.256	.317	.296
Plantier	Bos.	L	.331	.615	.420	53	148	27	49	7	1	11	35	23	38	1	0	.320	.333	.356	.267
Powell	Sea.	R	.216	.369	.288	57	111	16	24	6	1	3	12	11	24	0	2	.250	.163	.130	.111
Puckett	Min.	R	.319	.460	.352	152	611	92	195	29	6	15	89	31	78	11	5	.406	.289	.301	.266
Pulliam	K.C.	R	.273	.576	.333	18	33	4	9	1	0	3	4	3	9	0	0	.267	.333	.250	–
Quintana	Bos.	R	.295	.412	.375	149	478	69	141	21	1	11	71	61	66	1	0	.340	.274	.277	.308
Segui	Bal.	B	.278	.340	.316	86	212	15	59	7	0	2	22	12	19	1	1	.337	.228	.281	.226
Sheridan	NY-A	L	.204	.336	.286	62	113	13	23	3	0	4	7	13	30	1	1	.200	.204	.136	.111
Sierra	Tex.	B	.307	.502	.357	161	661	110	203	44	5	25	116	56	91	16	4	.335	.296	.342	.273
Snyder	Tor.	R	.175	.265	.216	71	166	14	29	4	1	3	17	9	60	0	0	.164	.200	.163	.091
Sosa	ChiA	R	.203	.335	.240	116	316	39	64	10	1	10	33	14	98	13	6	.227	.186	.238	.216
Stevens	Cal.	L	.293	.414	.354	18	58	8	17	7	0	0	9	6	12	1	2	.294	.293	.214	.250
Tartabull	K.C.	R	.316	.593	.397	132	484	78	153	35	3	31	100	65	121	6	3	.296	.325	.371	.345
Thurman	K.C.	R	.277	.359	.320	80	184	24	51	9	0	2	13	11	42	15	5	.267	.297	.326	.200
Venable	Cal.	L	.246	.358	.292	82	187	24	46	8	2	3	21	11	30	2	1	.211	.250	.244	.143
T. Ward	Tor.	B	.239	.301	.306	48	113	12	27	7	0	0	7	11	18	0	0	.250	.235	.226	.235
Whiten	Cle.	B	.243	.388	.297	116	407	46	99	18	7	9	45	30	85	4	3	.257	.238	.232	.130
Wilson	Oak.	R	.238	.313	.290	113	294	38	70	14	4	0	28	18	43	20	5	.253	.231	.288	.407
Winfield	Cal.	R	.262	.472	.326	150	568	75	149	27	4	28	86	56	109	7	2	.300	.248	.273	.278
Zupcic	Bos.	R	.160	.280	.192	18	25	3	4	0	0	1	3	1	6	0	0	.182	.143	.143	.000

American League Designated Hitters | Overall Batting

Name	Team	B	GS	AB	R	H	2B	3B	HR	RBI	BA	BA	SLG	OBP	G	AB	R	H	2B	3B	HR	RBI
Aldrete	Cle.	L	6	22	2	8	1	0	1	1	.364	.262	.322	.380	85	183	22	48	6	1	1	19
Alomar	Cle.	R	4	18	1	3	0	0	0	0	.167	.217	.266	.264	51	184	10	40	9	0	0	7
Baines	Oak.	L	122	447	69	133	22	1	18	81	.298	.295	.473	.383	141	488	76	144	25	1	20	90
Barnes	Det.	R	1	5	1	1	0	0	0	0	.200	.289	.491	.325	75	159	28	46	13	2	5	17
Belle	Cle.	R	31	129	18	37	12	1	5	24	.287	.282	.540	.323	123	461	60	130	31	2	28	95
Benzinger	K.C.	B	1	5	0	2	0	0	0	0	.400	.294	.386	.338	78	293	29	86	15	3	2	40
Bergman	Det.	L	9	31	4	7	2	0	1	5	.226	.237	.407	.351	86	194	23	46	10	1	7	29
Blankenship	Oak.	R	1	4	1	0	0	0	0	0	.000	.249	.341	.336	90	185	33	46	8	0	3	21
Brett	K.C.	L	118	463	73	121	40	2	10	60	.261	.255	.402	.327	131	505	77	129	40	2	10	61
Brosius	Oak.	R	1	2	0	0	0	0	0	0	.000	.235	.397	.268	36	68	9	16	5	0	2	4
Browne	Cle.	B	4	23	4	7	2	0	0	3	.304	.228	.269	.292	107	290	28	66	5	2	1	29
Burks	Bos.	R	1	4	1	2	1	0	0	1	.500	.251	.422	.314	130	474	56	119	33	3	14	56
Bush	Min.	L	6	26	5	9	1	1	1	4	.346	.303	.485	.401	93	165	21	50	10	1	6	23
Canseco	Oak.	R	23	87	21	24	6	0	7	26	.276	.266	.556	.359	154	572	115	152	32	1	44	122
Carter	Tor.	R	11	46	6	13	4	1	1	3	.283	.273	.503	.330	162	638	89	174	42	3	33	108
Clark	Bos.	R	134	476	75	120	18	1	28	87	.252	.249	.466	.374	140	481	75	120	18	1	28	87

American League Designated Hitters | Overall Batting

Name	Team	B	GS	AB	R	H	2B	3B	HR	RBI	BA	BA	SLG	OBP	G	AB	R	H	2B	3B	HR	RBI
Cochrane	Sea.	B	1	4	0	1	0	0	0	0	.250	.247	.354	.286	65	178	16	44	13	0	2	22
Cole	Cle.	L	4	14	6	5	2	0	0	1	.357	.295	.354	.386	122	387	58	114	17	3	0	21
Cotto	Sea.	R	1	7	2	1	0	0	0	0	.143	.305	.463	.347	66	177	35	54	6	2	6	23
Davis	Sea.	L	114	413	34	90	14	1	10	61	.218	.221	.335	.299	145	462	39	102	15	1	12	69
Davis	Min.	B	149	531	84	147	33	1	29	93	.277	.277	.507	.385	153	534	84	148	34	1	29	93
Davis	Bal.	R	10	37	5	5	0	0	3	6	.135	.227	.460	.307	49	176	29	40	9	1	10	28
Downing	Tex.	R	98	393	75	107	16	2	17	45	.272	.278	.455	.377	123	407	76	113	17	2	17	49
Ducey	Tor.	L	1	4	0	0	0	0	0	0	.000	.235	.368	.297	39	68	8	16	2	2	1	4
Eisenreich	K.C.	L	1	4	0	1	0	0	0	0	.250	.301	.392	.353	135	375	47	113	22	3	2	47
Evans	Bal.	R	9	39	5	11	2	0	1	6	.282	.270	.378	.393	101	270	35	73	9	1	6	38
Fariss	Tex.	R	1	4	0	1	1	0	0	3	.250	.258	.387	.395	19	31	6	8	1	0	1	6
Fielder	Det.	R	42	169	21	43	9	0	12	33	.254	.261	.513	.347	162	624	102	163	25	0	44	133
Fisk	ChiA	R	12	44	2	8	2	0	1	7	.182	.241	.413	.299	134	460	42	111	25	0	18	74
Gibson	K.C.	L	29	107	16	21	0	1	7	14	.196	.236	.403	.341	132	462	81	109	17	6	16	55
Gomez	Bal.	R	6	24	1	5	1	0	0	0	.208	.233	.409	.302	118	391	40	91	17	2	16	45
Gonzalez	Tex.	R	4	19	1	5	1	1	0	3	.263	.264	.479	.321	142	545	78	144	34	1	27	102
Greenwell	Bos.	L	1	4	0	0	0	0	0	0	.000	.300	.419	.350	147	544	76	163	26	6	9	83
Griffey Jr.	Sea.	L	1	4	0	0	0	0	0	0	.000	.327	.527	.399	154	548	76	179	42	1	22	100
Gruber	Tor.	R	2	7	1	2	1	0	0	0	.286	.252	.443	.308	113	429	58	108	18	2	20	65
Hall	NY-A	L	10	38	4	7	1	0	1	6	.184	.285	.455	.321	141	492	67	140	23	2	19	80
Hare	Det.	L	1	4	0	0	0	0	0	0	.000	.053	.105	.143	9	19	0	1	1	0	0	0
Harper	Min.	R	1	5	2	3	1	0	0	1	.600	.311	.447	.336	123	441	54	137	28	1	10	69
D. Henderson	Oak.	R	4	19	1	4	0	0	0	0	.211	.276	.465	.346	150	572	86	158	33	0	25	85
R. Henderson	Oak.	R	8	35	5	5	0	0	2	3	.143	.268	.423	.400	134	470	105	126	17	1	18	57
Hill	Cle.	R	17	61	8	14	1	1	2	5	.230	.258	.421	.324	72	221	29	57	8	2	8	25
Hoiles	Bal.	R	10	36	4	9	1	0	2	6	.250	.243	.384	.304	107	341	36	83	15	0	11	31
Horn	Bal.	L	92	302	42	70	15	0	21	58	.232	.233	.502	.326	121	317	45	74	16	0	23	61
Hulett	Bal.	R	8	37	4	7	2	0	0	4	.189	.204	.350	.255	79	206	29	42	9	0	7	18
Humphreys	NY-A	R	2	8	5	3	0	0	0	0	.375	.200	.200	.347	25	40	9	8	0	0	0	3
Incaviglia	Det.	R	40	145	23	36	5	1	6	14	.248	.214	.353	.290	97	337	38	72	12	1	11	38
Jackson	ChiA	R	21	69	7	15	4	0	2	12	.217	.225	.408	.333	23	71	8	16	4	0	3	14
James	Cle.	R	58	233	13	53	5	1	2	16	.227	.238	.318	.273	115	437	31	104	16	2	5	41
T. Jones	Sea.	R	19	80	10	17	2	0	1	11	.213	.251	.360	.321	79	175	30	44	8	1	3	24
Lansford	Oak.	R	1	4	0	0	0	0	0	0	.000	.063	.063	.063	5	16	0	1	0	0	0	1
Larkin	Min.	B	2	9	2	3	1	0	0	0	.333	.286	.373	.361	98	255	34	73	14	1	2	19
Lennon	Sea.	R	2	6	1	1	1	0	0	0	.167	.125	.250	.364	9	8	2	1	1	0	0	1
Leyritz	NY-A	R	1	3	0	1	1	0	0	0	.333	.182	.250	.364	32	77	8	14	3	0	0	4
Lopez	Cle.	R	5	18	1	3	1	0	0	1	.167	.220	.293	.261	35	82	7	18	4	1	0	7
Maas	NY-A	L	103	370	52	78	12	1	17	43	.211	.220	.390	.333	148	500	69	110	14	1	23	63
Macfarlane	K.C.	R	4	14	2	5	2	0	0	1	.357	.277	.506	.330	84	267	34	74	18	2	13	41
Maldonado	Tor.	R	7	26	3	5	1	0	2	6	.192	.250	.427	.342	86	288	37	72	15	0	12	48
Martinez	Cle.	R	41	156	11	44	8	0	3	16	.282	.284	.397	.310	72	257	22	73	14	0	5	30
T. Martinez	Sea.	L	3	12	1	5	1	0	0	1	.417	.205	.330	.272	36	112	11	23	2	0	4	9
E. Martinez	Sea.	R	2	8	0	3	2	0	0	1	.375	.307	.452	.405	150	544	98	167	35	1	14	52
Martinez	Bal.	L	4	15	7	7	1	0	4	9	.467	.269	.514	.303	67	216	32	58	12	1	13	33
Mattingly	NY-A	L	22	86	9	21	3	0	1	7	.244	.288	.394	.339	152	587	64	169	35	0	9	68
Maurer	Tex.	L	2	7	0	0	0	0	0	0	.000	.063	.125	.211	13	16	0	1	1	0	0	2
McIntosh	Mil.	R	2	9	2	4	1	0	1	1	.444	.364	.727	.364	7	11	2	4	1	0	1	1
McKnight	Bal.	B	2	9	1	2	1	0	0	2	.222	.171	.195	.209	16	41	2	7	1	0	0	2
Melvin	Bal.	R	1	8	0	2	0	0	0	1	.250	.250	.307	.279	79	228	11	57	10	0	1	23
Merullo	ChiA	L	3	14	2	2	0	0	1	3	.143	.229	.343	.268	80	140	8	32	1	0	5	21
Meulens	NY-A	R	13	42	7	9	2	0	0	4	.214	.222	.319	.276	96	288	37	64	8	1	6	29
Milligan	Bal.	R	20	83	12	24	3	0	3	11	.289	.263	.406	.373	141	483	57	127	17	2	16	70
Molitor	Mil.	R	112	476	88	153	23	10	10	45	.321	.325	.489	.399	158	665	133	216	32	13	17	75
Moseby	Det.	L	4	19	5	7	3	0	0	1	.368	.262	.396	.321	74	260	37	68	15	1	6	35
Mulliniks	Tor.	L	70	217	25	56	12	1	2	20	.258	.250	.333	.364	97	240	27	60	12	1	2	24
Munoz	Min.	R	1	5	0	2	0	0	0	2	.400	.283	.500	.327	51	138	15	39	7	1	7	26
Nokes	NY-A	L	3	11	0	2	0	0	0	0	.182	.268	.469	.308	135	456	52	122	20	0	24	77
O'Brien	Sea.	L	17	61	9	16	4	1	3	14	.262	.248	.402	.300	152	560	58	139	29	3	17	88
Palmeiro	Tex.	L	2	7	2	2	1	0	1	1	.286	.322	.532	.389	159	631	115	203	49	3	26	88
Palmer	Tex.	R	4	17	1	3	0	0	1	1	.176	.187	.403	.281	81	268	38	50	9	2	15	37
Parker	Tor.	L	129	500	47	118	26	2	11	58	.236	.239	.365	.288	132	502	47	120	26	2	11	59
Parrish	Cal.	R	5	21	2	3	0	0	1	1	.143	.216	.388	.285	119	402	38	87	12	0	19	51
Pasqua	ChiA	L	6	20	2	4	1	0	0	3	.200	.259	.465	.358	134	417	71	108	22	5	18	66
Petralli	Tex.	L	2	11	0	5	1	0	0	1	.455	.271	.352	.339	87	199	21	54	8	1	2	20
Phillips	Det.	B	17	62	13	17	3	3	2	15	.274	.284	.438	.371	146	564	87	160	28	4	17	72
Plantier	Bos.	L	4	13	0	3	0	0	0	3	.231	.331	.615	.420	53	148	27	49	7	1	11	35
Polonia	Cal.	L	4	16	3	5	0	0	0	1	.313	.296	.379	.352	150	604	92	179	28	8	2	50
Powell	Sea.	R	1	3	3	1	1	0	0	1	.333	.216	.369	.288	57	111	16	24	6	1	3	12
Raines	ChiA	B	19	80	13	27	3	2	2	7	.338	.268	.345	.359	155	609	102	163	20	6	5	50

American League Designated Hitters — Overall Batting

Name	Team	B	GS	AB	R	H	2B	3B	HR	RBI	BA	BA	SLG	OBP	G	AB	R	H	2B	3B	HR	RBI
Ramos	NY-A	R	3	9	2	2	0	0	0	1	.222	.308	.346	.310	10	26	4	8	1	0	0	3
Randolph	Mil.	R	2	9	1	2	0	0	0	1	.222	.327	.374	.424	124	431	60	141	14	3	0	54
Reimer	Tex.	L	48	178	23	46	10	0	9	27	.258	.269	.477	.332	136	394	46	106	22	0	20	69
Reynolds	Sea.	B	1	4	0	0	0	0	0	0	.000	.254	.341	.332	161	631	95	160	34	6	3	57
Rowland	Det.	R	1	2	0	1	0	0	0	0	.500	.250	.250	.333	4	4	0	1	0	0	0	1
Salas	Det.	L	8	27	1	3	1	0	0	2	.111	.088	.158	.117	33	57	2	5	1	0	1	7
Sax	NY-A	R	4	19	3	7	2	0	0	2	.368	.304	.414	.345	158	652	85	198	38	2	10	56
Sheffield	Mil.	R	5	17	4	4	0	1	1	6	.235	.194	.320	.277	50	175	25	34	12	2	2	22
Sheridan	NY-A	L	1	4	0	1	0	0	0	0	.250	.204	.336	.286	62	113	13	23	3	0	4	7
Sorrento	Min.	L	2	8	1	1	0	0	1	1	.125	.255	.553	.314	26	47	6	12	2	0	4	13
Sprague	Tor.	R	2	6	2	2	0	0	0	1	.333	.275	.394	.361	61	160	17	44	7	0	4	20
Stanley	Tex.	R	1	7	0	2	0	0	0	2	.286	.249	.381	.372	95	181	25	45	13	1	3	25
Steinbach	Oak.	R	1	5	0	1	0	0	0	0	.200	.274	.386	.312	129	456	50	125	31	1	6	67
Stubbs	Mil.	L	3	14	2	4	1	0	2	4	.286	.213	.359	.282	103	362	48	77	16	2	11	38
Surhoff	Mil.	L	5	21	1	7	2	0	1	3	.333	.289	.372	.319	143	505	57	146	19	4	5	68
Sveum	Mil.	B	3	10	0	3	0	0	0	2	.300	.241	.365	.320	90	266	33	64	19	1	4	43
Tabler	Tor.	R	29	116	13	29	5	0	0	12	.250	.216	.270	.318	82	185	20	40	5	1	1	21
Tartabull	K.C.	R	6	25	1	4	0	0	0	0	.160	.316	.593	.397	132	484	78	153	35	3	31	100
Tettleton	Det.	B	23	83	11	23	4	0	7	17	.277	.263	.491	.387	154	501	85	132	17	2	31	89
Thomas	ChiA	R	101	363	71	118	21	1	22	68	.325	.318	.553	.453	158	559	104	178	31	2	32	109
Trammell	Det.	R	5	20	3	5	1	0	0	1	.250	.248	.373	.320	101	375	57	93	20	0	9	55
Vaughn	Mil.	R	10	30	7	6	2	0	2	8	.200	.244	.456	.319	145	542	81	132	24	5	27	98
Vaughn	Bos.	L	16	63	4	19	6	0	1	9	.302	.260	.370	.339	74	219	21	57	12	0	4	32
Whitaker	Det.	L	3	9	4	3	1	0	1	2	.333	.279	.489	.391	138	470	94	131	26	2	23	78
Whiten	Cle.	B	3	13	1	1	0	0	0	1	.077	.243	.388	.297	116	407	46	99	18	7	9	45
Wilson	Tor.	B	21	94	13	22	5	3	0	13	.234	.241	.349	.277	86	241	26	58	12	4	2	28
Wilson	Oak.	B	1	10	5	5	1	0	0	0	.500	.238	.313	.290	113	294	38	70	14	4	0	28
Winfield	Cal.	R	34	125	14	32	5	0	5	16	.256	.262	.472	.326	150	568	75	149	27	4	28	86
Yount	Mil.	R	13	52	4	11	0	2	0	10	.212	.260	.376	.332	130	503	66	131	20	4	10	77

National League Pitchers

Name	Team	T	W	L	PCT	ERA	G	GS	CG	SHO	SV	INN	HR	BB	SO	WP	SB	CS	GAR	BA	SLG	OBP
Agosto	St.L	L	5	3	.625	4.81	72	0	0	0	2	86	4	39	34	6	7	5	2.57	.291	.408	.380
Andersen	S.D.	R	3	4	.429	2.30	38	0	0	0	13	47	0	13	40	1	6	2	1.55	.232	.262	.284
Armstrong	Cin.	R	7	13	.350	5.48	27	24	1	0	0	139.2	25	54	93	2	12	8	0.76	.293	.491	.354
Ashby	Phi.	R	1	5	.167	6.00	8	8	0	0	0	42	5	19	26	6	0	1	1.06	.256	.431	.341
Assenmacher	ChiN	L	7	8	.467	3.24	75	0	0	0	15	102.2	10	31	117	4	8	5	0.83	.223	.357	.284
Avery	Atl.	L	18	8	.692	3.38	35	35	3	1	0	210.1	21	65	137	4	21	11	1.28	.240	.372	.299
Barnes	Mon.	L	5	8	.385	4.22	28	27	1	0	0	160	16	84	117	5	20	8	1.06	.233	.371	.333
Beatty	NY-N	L	0	0	_	2.79	5	0	0	0	0	9.2	0	4	7	1	1	1	1.00	.250	.333	.317
Beck	S.F.	R	1	1	.500	3.78	31	0	0	0	1	52.1	4	13	38	0	2	3	0.82	.273	.412	.319
Belcher	L.A.	R	10	9	.526	2.62	33	33	2	1	0	209.1	10	75	156	7	17	10	1.13	.240	.318	.306
Belinda	Pit.	R	7	5	.583	3.45	60	0	0	0	16	78.1	10	35	71	2	13	3	0.60	.184	.327	.283
Benes	S.D.	R	15	11	.577	3.03	33	33	4	1	0	223	23	59	167	3	10	11	0.72	.232	.358	.285
Berenguer	Atl.	R	0	3	.000	2.24	49	0	0	0	17	64.1	5	20	53	0	3	1	0.62	.189	.303	.261
Bielecki	Atl.	R	13	11	.542	4.46	41	25	0	0	0	173.2	18	56	75	6	19	9	1.43	.262	.420	.319
Black	S.F.	L	12	16	.429	3.99	34	34	3	3	0	214.1	25	71	104	6	14	11	1.06	.251	.396	.313
Boever	Phi.	R	3	5	.375	3.84	68	0	0	0	0	98.1	10	54	89	6	12	2	0.72	.245	.383	.336
Bones	S.D.	R	4	6	.400	4.83	11	11	0	0	0	54	3	18	31	4	3	1	1.36	.269	.354	.321
Boskie	ChiN	R	4	9	.308	5.23	28	20	0	0	0	129	14	52	62	1	4	2	1.01	.294	.456	.361
Bowen	Hou.	R	6	4	.600	5.15	14	13	0	0	0	71.2	4	36	49	8	12	1	1.20	.268	.360	.353
Brantley	Phi.	R	2	2	.500	3.41	6	5	0	0	0	31.2	0	19	25	2	6	2	1.23	.228	.281	.341
Brantley	S.F.	R	5	2	.714	2.45	67	0	0	0	15	95.1	8	52	81	6	17	2	0.72	.225	.338	.332
Bross	NY-N	R	0	0	_	1.80	8	0	0	0	0	10	1	3	5	0	0	0	1.08	.200	.314	.263
Browning	Cin.	L	14	14	.500	4.18	36	36	1	0	0	230.1	32	56	115	3	21	6	0.72	.266	.427	.309
Burke	NY-N	R	6	7	.462	3.36	72	0	0	0	6	101.2	8	26	59	3	8	1	1.58	.249	.369	.301
Burkett	S.F.	R	12	11	.522	4.18	36	34	3	1	0	206.2	19	60	131	5	17	16	1.12	.277	.392	.332
Candelaria	L.A.	L	1	1	.500	3.74	59	0	0	0	2	33.2	3	11	38	1	1	3	1.46	.252	.415	.307
Carpenter	St.L	R	10	4	.714	4.23	59	0	0	0	0	66	6	20	47	1	3	4	0.83	.220	.365	.278
Castillo	NY-N	L	2	1	.667	3.34	17	3	0	0	0	32.1	4	11	18	0	3	1	1.00	.299	.425	.349
Castillo	ChiN	R	6	7	.462	4.35	18	18	4	0	0	111.2	25	33	73	5	7	4	1.19	.252	.351	.304
Charlton	Cin.	L	3	5	.375	2.91	39	11	0	0	0	108.1	6	34	77	11	10	7	1.23	.236	.336	.306
Christopher	L.A.	R	0	0	_	0.00	3	0	0	0	0	4	0	3	2	0	0	1	1.50	.167	.250	.333
Clancy	Atl.	R	3	5	.375	3.91	54	0	0	0	8	89.2	8	34	50	10	5	1	1.20	.223	.373	.295
Clark	St.L	R	1	1	.500	4.03	7	2	0	0	0	22.1	3	11	13	2	5	1	0.58	.215	.354	.301
Clements	S.D.	L	1	0	1.000	3.77	12	0	0	0	0	14.1	0	9	8	0	0	1	1.77	.255	.314	.349
Combs	Phi.	L	2	6	.250	4.90	14	13	1	0	0	64.1	7	43	41	7	12	2	1.29	.254	.389	.365
Cone	NY-N	R	14	14	.500	3.29	34	34	5	2	0	232.2	13	73	241	17	27	13	0.91	.235	.329	.296
Cook	L.A.	L	1	0	1.000	0.51	20	1	0	0	0	17.2	0	7	8	0	1	1	1.00	.203	.254	.279

Name	Team	T	W	L	PCT	ERA	G	GS	CG	SHO	SV	INN	HR	BB	G	AB	R	H	2B	3B	HR	RBI
Cormier	St.L	L	4	5	.444	4.12	11	10	2	0	0	67.2	5	8	38	2	1	3	0.94	.277	.401	.300
Corsi	Hou.	R	0	5	.000	3.71	47	0	0	0	0	77.2	6	23	53	1	8	3	2.25	.259	.357	.310
Costello	S.D.	R	1	0	1.000	3.09	27	0	0	0	0	35	2	17	24	2	4	0	1.05	.276	.366	.353
Cox	Phi.	R	4	6	.400	4.57	23	17	0	0	0	102.1	14	39	46	7	11	7	1.20	.258	.426	.323
Crews	L.A.	R	2	3	.400	3.43	60	0	0	0	6	76	7	19	53	3	10	2	1.22	.256	.392	.299
Dascenzo	ChiN	L	0	0		0.00	3	0	0	0	0	4	0	2	2	0	0	0	1.00	.154	.154	.267
DeJesus	Phi.	R	10	9	.526	3.42	31	29	3	0	1	181.27	128	118	10	19	11	1.04	.224	.318	.353
DeLeon	St.L	R	5	9	.357	2.71	28	28	1	0	0	162.215	61	118	1	12	12	0.81	.239	.378	.313
Deshaies	Hou.	L	5	12	.294	4.98	28	28	1	0	0	161	19	72	98	0	21	14	0.59	.259	.430	.336
Dibble	Cin.	R	3	5	.375	3.17	67	0	0	0	31	82.1	5	25	124	5	16	5	1.09	.223	.322	.280
Downs	S.F.	R	10	4	.714	4.19	45	11	0	0	0	111.2	12	53	62	4	15	4	1.09	.239	.373	.326
Drabek	Pit.	R	15	14	.517	3.07	35	35	5	2	0	234.216	62	142	5	29	15	1.26	.274	.385	.321
Fassero	Mon.	L	2	5	.286	2.44	51	0	0	0	8	55.1	1	17	42	4	3	1	1.78	.196	.266	.263
Fernandez	NY-N	L	1	3	.250	2.86	8	8	0	0	0	44	4	9	31	0	3	1	0.52	.222	.327	.262
Foster	Cin.	R	0	0		1.93	11	0	0	0	0	14	1	4	11	0	0	0	1.13	.143	.224	.208
Franco	NY-N	L	5	9	.357	2.93	52	0	0	0	30	55.1	2	18	45	6	4	2	2.66	.271	.360	.328
Fraser	St.L	R	3	3	.500	4.93	35	0	0	0	0	49.1	9	21	25	4	6	4	0.92	.242	.434	.325
Freeman	Atl.	R	1	0	1.000	3.00	34	0	0	0	1	48	2	13	34	4	2	2	2.24	.214	.283	.275
Frey	Mon.	L	0	1	.000	4.99	31	0	0	0	1	39.2	3	23	21	3	3	2	0.92	.281	.373	.374
Gardner	Hou.	R	1	2	.333	4.01	5	4	0	0	0	24.2	5	14	12	0	0	1	1.14	.218	.414	.327
Gardner	Mon.	R	9	11	.450	3.85	27	27	0	0	0	168.117	75	107	2	13	17	0.77	.230	.356	.318
Garrelts	S.F.	R	1	1	.500	6.41	8	3	0	0	0	19.2	5	9	8	0	4	2	0.92	.313	.563	.378
Glavine	Atl.	L	20	11	.645	2.55	34	34	9	1	0	246.217	69	192	10	18	10	1.35	.222	.330	.277
Gooden	NY-N	R	13	7	.650	3.60	27	27	3	1	0	190	12	56	150	5	33	16	1.73	.257	.369	.311
Gott	L.A.	R	4	3	.571	2.96	55	0	0	0	2	76	5	32	73	6	8	0	1.56	.223	.312	.304
Greene	Phi.	R	13	7	.650	3.38	36	27	3	2	0	207.219	66	154	9	18	7	0.80	.230	.361	.290
Grimsley	Phi.	R	1	7	.125	4.87	12	12	0	0	0	61	4	41	42	14	14	1	1.98	.242	.368	.364
Gross	L.A.	R	10	11	.476	3.58	46	10	0	0	3	115.210	50	95	3	15	6	1.45	.275	.380	.348
Gross	Cin.	R	6	4	.600	3.47	29	9	1	0	0	85.2	8	40	40	5	8	3	1.52	.279	.393	.355
Gunderson	S.F.	L	0	0		5.40	2	0	0	0	1	3.1	0	1	2	0	0	0	2.00	.353	.471	.389
Hammaker	S.D.	L	0	1	.000	5.79	1	1	0	0	0	4.2	0	3	1	1	1	0	2.20	.364	.409	.440
Hammond	Cin.	L	7	7	.500	4.06	20	18	0	0	0	99.2	4	48	50	3	8	3	1.62	.250	.340	.339
Haney	Mon.	L	3	7	.300	4.04	16	16	0	0	0	84.2	6	43	51	9	8	6	1.28	.280	.405	.362
Harkey	ChiN	R	0	2	.000	5.30	4	4	0	0	0	18.2	3	6	15	1	2	0	0.95	.273	.442	.321
Harnisch	Hou.	R	12	9	.571	2.70	33	33	4	2	0	216.214	83	172	5	27	6	0.75	.212	.313	.288
Harris	S.D.	R	9	5	.643	2.23	20	20	3	2	0	133	16	27	95	2	13	8	1.13	.233	.363	.273
Hartley	Phi.	R	4	1	.800	4.21	58	0	0	0	2	83.1	11	47	63	10	13	1	0.82	.237	.388	.347
Heaton	Pit.	L	3	3	.500	4.33	42	1	0	0	0	68.2	6	21	34	0	9	2	0.93	.275	.401	.334
Henry	Hou.	R	3	2	.600	3.19	52	0	0	0	2	67.2	7	39	51	5	7	3	0.60	.219	.361	.333
Heredia	S.F.	R	0	2	.000	3.82	7	4	0	0	0	33	4	7	13	1	2	2	1.96	.233	.379	.274
Hernandez	Hou.	R	2	7	.222	4.71	32	6	0	0	3	63	6	32	55	0	7	2	1.43	.263	.382	.345
Hernandez	S.D.	R	0	0		0.00	9	0	0	0	2	14.1	0	5	9	2	0	0	1.92	.157	.196	.232
Hershiser	L.A.	R	7	8	.778	3.46	21	21	0	0	2	112	3	32	73	2	11	2	1.62	.259	.330	.316
Hickerson	S.F.	L	2	2	.500	3.60	17	6	0	0	0	50	3	17	43	2	6	4	0.88	.275	.378	.333
Hill	St.L	R	11	10	.524	3.57	30	30	0	0	0	181.115	67	121	7	19	11	1.03	.224	.346	.299
Hill	Cin.	R	1	1	.500	3.78	22	0	0	0	0	33.1	1	8	20	1	4	4	0.93	.295	.402	.331
Howell	L.A.	R	6	5	.545	3.18	44	0	0	0	16	51	3	11	40	0	3	1	0.72	.213	.328	.259
Hurst	S.D.	L	15	8	.652	3.29	31	31	4	0	0	221.217	59	141	5	11	6	1.25	.241	.340	.292
Innis	NY-N	R	0	2	.000	2.66	69	0	0	0	0	84.2	2	23	47	4	6	5	3.04	.219	.291	.270
Jackson	ChiN	L	1	5	.167	6.75	17	14	0	0	0	70.2	8	48	31	1	8	2	1.68	.309	.451	.407
Jackson	S.D.	R	0	0		9.00	1	0	0	0	0	2	0	2	0	0	0	0	0.25	.375	.625	.500
Jones	Mon.	R	4	9	.308	3.35	77	0	0	0	13	88.2	8	33	46	1	8	6	1.65	.246	.369	.318
Jones	Hou.	R	6	8	.429	4.39	26	22	1	1	0	135.19	51	88	4	18	6	1.91	.270	.374	.336
Juden	Hou.	R	0	2	.000	6.00	4	3	0	0	0	18	3	7	11	0	3	1	1.56	.275	.449	.329
Kile	Hou.	R	7	11	.389	3.69	37	22	0	0	0	153.216	84	100	5	12	3	1.09	.246	.393	.344
Kipper	Pit.	L	2	2	.500	4.65	52	0	0	0	4	60	7	22	38	0	7	4	0.65	.276	.431	.335
Lancaster	ChiN	R	9	7	.563	3.52	64	11	1	0	0	156	13	49	102	2	14	14	1.01	.256	.376	.315
Landrum	Pit.	R	4	4	.500	3.18	61	0	0	0	17	76.1	4	19	45	3	9	1	0.91	.252	.329	.296
Lefferts	S.D.	L	1	6	.143	3.91	54	0	0	0	23	69	5	14	48	3	6	4	0.91	.285	.408	.318
Leibrandt	Atl.	L	15	13	.536	3.49	36	36	1	1	0	229.218	56	128	5	35	11	1.22	.245	.363	.292
Lewis	S.D.	R	0	0		4.15	12	0	0	0	0	13	2	11	10	1	1	0	1.82	.275	.490	.403
Lilliquist	S.D.	L	0	2	.000	8.79	6	2	0	0	0	14.1	3	4	7	0	0	1	1.13	.379	.606	.414
Litton	S.F.	R	0	0		9.00	1	0	0	0	0	1	0	3	0	0	0	0	0.50	.250	.750	.571
Maddux	ChiN	R	15	11	.577	3.35	37	37	7	2	0	263	18	66	198	6	25	7	1.88	.237	.345	.288
Maddux	S.D.	R	7	2	.778	2.46	64	1	0	0	5	98.2	4	27	57	5	5	7	2.22	.221	.300	.277
Mallicoat	Hou.	L	0	2	.000	3.86	24	0	0	0	1	23	2	13	18	1	1	1	1.55	.259	.388	.363
De. Martinez	Mon.	R	14	11	.560	2.39	31	31	9	5	0	222	9	62	123	3	22	4	1.38	.226	.311	.282
Martinez	L.A.	R	17	13	.567	3.27	33	33	6	4	0	220.118	69	150	6	16	9	0.76	.229	.337	.293
Mason	Pit.	R	3	2	.600	3.03	24	0	0	0	3	29.2	2	6	21	2	0	2	1.44	.200	.305	.248
McClellan	S.F.	R	3	6	.333	4.56	13	12	1	0	0	71	12	25	44	5	12	5	1.00	.252	.437	.316

National League Pitchers

Name	Team	T	W	L	PCT	ERA	G	GS	CG	SHO	SV	INN	HR	BB	G	AB	R	H	2B	3B	HR	RBI
McClure	St.L	L	1	1	.500	3.13	32	0	0	0	0	23	1	8	15	0	0	2	0.79	.282	.376	.340
McDowell	L.A.	R	9	9	.500	2.93	71	0	0	0	10	101.1	4	48	50	2	12	4	2.45	.262	.357	.346
McElroy	ChiN	L	6	2	.750	1.95	71	0	0	0	3	101.1	7	57	92	1	12	10	1.23	.210	.305	.317
Melendez	S.D.	R	8	5	.615	3.27	31	9	0	0	3	93.2	11	24	60	3	1	6	0.60	.221	.368	.269
Mercker	Atl.	L	5	3	.625	2.58	50	4	0	0	6	73.1	5	35	62	4	10	0	1.15	.211	.316	.303
Minutelli	Cin.	L	0	2	.000	6.04	16	3	0	0	0	25.1	5	18	21	3	2	0	0.49	.288	.519	.387
Morgan	L.A.	R	14	10	.583	2.78	34	33	5	1	1	236.1	12	61	140	6	24	7	2.17	.226	.307	.278
Mulholland	Phi.	L	16	13	.552	3.61	34	34	8	3	0	232	15	49	142	3	6	5	1.10	.260	.374	.299
Myers	Cin.	L	6	13	.316	3.55	58	12	1	0	6	132	8	80	108	2	4	7	1.01	.242	.342	.347
Nabholz	Mon.	L	8	7	.533	3.63	24	24	1	0	0	153.2	5	57	99	3	15	11	0.96	.237	.336	.307
Ojeda	L.A.	L	12	9	.571	3.18	31	31	2	1	0	189.1	15	70	120	4	23	15	1.49	.257	.376	.323
Olivares	St.L	R	11	7	.611	3.71	28	24	0	0	1	167.1	13	61	91	3	10	11	1.34	.243	.356	.316
Oliveras	S.F.	R	6	6	.500	3.86	55	1	0	0	3	79.1	12	22	48	2	5	9	0.78	.242	.400	.296
Oquendo	St.L	R	0	0	—	27.00	1	0	0	0	0	1	0	2	1	0	0	0	1.00	.400	.600	.571
Osuna	Hou.	L	7	6	.538	3.42	71	0	0	0	12	81.2	5	46	68	3	2	0	0.86	.201	.304	.311
Palacios	Pit.	R	6	3	.667	3.75	36	7	1	1	3	81.2	12	38	64	6	3	4	0.61	.228	.386	.315
Patterson	Pit.	L	4	3	.571	4.11	54	1	0	0	2	65.2	7	15	57	0	1	5	1.13	.267	.406	.306
Pena	Atl.	R	8	1	.889	2.40	59	0	0	0	15	82.1	6	22	62	1	8	4	0.72	.245	.341	.293
Perez	ChiN	L	1	0	1.000	2.08	3	0	0	0	0	4.1	0	2	3	2	0	1	0.50	.167	.333	.250
Piatt	Mon.	R	0	0	—	2.60	21	0	0	0	0	34.2	3	17	29	1	3	1	1.24	.230	.357	.322
Portugal	Hou.	R	10	12	.455	4.49	32	27	1	0	1	168.1	19	59	120	4	12	7	1.18	.256	.400	.318
Power	Cin.	R	5	3	.625	3.62	68	0	0	0	3	87	6	31	51	6	12	4	0.87	.265	.387	.329
Rasmussen	S.D.	R	6	13	.316	3.74	24	24	1	1	0	146.2	12	49	75	1	21	6	1.02	.271	.385	.328
Remlinger	S.F.	L	2	1	.667	4.37	8	6	1	1	0	35	5	20	19	2	1	1	0.95	.271	.451	.364
Reynoso	Atl.	R	2	1	.667	6.17	6	5	0	0	0	23.1	4	10	10	2	1	1	2.29	.299	.552	.390
Righetti	S.F.	L	2	7	.222	3.39	61	0	0	0	24	71.2	4	28	51	1	8	4	1.14	.240	.330	.317
Rijo	Cin.	R	15	6	.714	2.51	30	30	3	1	0	204.1	8	55	172	2	16	3	1.06	.219	.305	.272
Ritchie	Phi.	L	1	2	.333	2.50	39	0	0	0	0	50.1	4	17	26	1	10	0	0.87	.234	.346	.299
Robinson	S.F.	R	5	9	.357	4.38	34	16	0	0	1	121.1	12	50	78	1	10	5	0.99	.265	.417	.334
Rodriguez	S.D.	L	3	1	.750	3.26	64	1	0	0	0	80	8	44	40	4	6	4	1.37	.234	.365	.335
Rodriguez	Pit.	L	1	1	.500	4.11	18	0	0	0	0	15.1	1	8	10	2	0	1	1.19	.246	.333	.348
Rojas	Mon.	R	3	3	.500	3.75	37	0	0	0	6	48	4	13	37	3	5	1	0.83	.228	.375	.280
Ruffin	Phi.	L	4	7	.364	3.78	31	15	1	1	0	119	6	38	85	4	7	4	1.13	.272	.386	.327
Ruskin	Mon.	L	4	4	.500	4.24	64	0	0	0	6	63.2	4	30	46	5	7	3	1.00	.241	.371	.333
Sampen	Mon.	R	9	5	.643	4.00	43	8	0	0	0	92.1	13	46	52	3	16	8	1.05	.273	.452	.358
Sanford	Cin.	R	1	2	.333	3.86	5	5	0	0	0	28	3	15	31	4	4	0	0.56	.186	.294	.297
Scanlan	ChiN	R	7	8	.467	3.89	40	13	0	0	1	111	5	40	44	5	5	7	1.85	.269	.373	.332
Schilling	Hou.	R	3	5	.375	3.81	56	0	0	0	8	75.2	2	39	71	4	3	4	1.10	.271	.364	.356
Schourek	NY-N	L	5	4	.556	4.27	35	8	1	1	2	86.1	7	43	67	1	12	0	0.52	.248	.390	.334
Scott	Hou.	R	0	2	.000	12.86	2	2	0	0	0	7	2	4	3	0	2	1	0.78	.367	.667	.457
Scudder	Cin.	R	6	9	.400	4.35	27	14	0	0	0	101.1	16	56	51	7	12	6	1.02	.246	.362	.352
Searcy	Phi.	L	2	1	.667	4.15	18	0	0	0	0	30.1	2	14	21	1	5	0	1.84	.252	.400	.328
Segura	S.F.	R	0	1	.000	4.41	11	0	0	0	0	16.1	1	5	10	2	3	2	5.67	.303	.379	.352
Simons	NY-N	R	2	3	.400	5.19	42	1	0	0	1	60.2	5	19	38	3	5	4	1.30	.246	.379	.305
Sisk	Atl.	R	2	1	.667	5.02	14	0	0	0	0	14.1	1	8	5	0	2	0	2.15	.333	.476	.403
Slocumb	ChiN	R	2	1	.667	3.45	52	0	0	0	1	62.2	3	30	34	9	12	1	1.54	.231	.323	.321
Smiley	Pit.	L	20	8	.714	3.08	33	32	2	1	0	207.2	17	44	129	3	18	13	1.06	.251	.381	.292
B. Smith	St.L	L	12	9	.571	3.85	31	31	3	0	0	198.2	16	45	94	3	19	8	1.08	.251	.381	.297
Da. Smith	ChiN	R	0	6	.000	6.00	35	0	0	0	17	33	6	19	16	1	3	0	1.13	.302	.535	.396
L. Smith	St.L	R	6	3	.667	2.34	67	0	0	0	47	73	5	13	67	1	10	2	0.70	.249	.352	.281
P. Smith	Atl.	R	1	3	.250	5.06	14	10	0	0	0	48	5	22	29	1	13	1	1.07	.262	.437	.335
Smith	Pit.	L	16	10	.615	3.20	35	35	6	3	0	228	15	29	120	1	26	8	2.51	.268	.370	.292
Smoltz	Atl.	R	14	13	.519	3.80	36	36	5	0	0	229.2	16	77	148	20	14	13	1.06	.243	.360	.305
Stanton	Atl.	L	5	5	.500	2.88	74	0	0	0	7	78	6	21	54	0	9	1	1.22	.217	.325	.273
St. Claire	Atl.	R	0	0	—	4.08	19	0	0	0	0	28.2	4	9	30	4	1	3	1.57	.282	.445	.333
Sutcliffe	ChiN	R	6	5	.545	4.10	19	18	0	0	0	96.2	4	45	52	2	21	2	1.34	.264	.379	.338
Terry	St.L	R	4	4	.500	2.80	65	0	0	0	1	80.1	1	32	52	0	7	3	1.43	.249	.308	.320
Tewksbury	St.L	R	11	12	.478	3.25	30	30	3	0	0	191	13	38	75	0	10	10	1.17	.281	.413	.317
Tomlin	Pit.	L	8	7	.533	2.98	31	27	4	2	0	175	9	54	104	2	17	12	1.37	.254	.354	.315
Viola	NY-N	L	13	15	.464	3.97	35	35	3	0	0	231.1	25	54	132	6	16	11	1.14	.286	.423	.325
Walk	Pit.	R	9	2	.818	3.60	25	20	0	0	0	115	10	35	67	11	7	4	1.19	.240	.363	.302
Wetteland	L.A.	R	1	0	1.000	0.00	6	0	0	0	0	9	0	3	9	1	0	0	0.58	.161	.194	.250
Whitehurst	NY-N	R	7	12	.368	4.19	36	20	0	0	1	133.1	12	25	87	3	9	8	2.37	.274	.409	.311
Whitson	S.D.	R	4	6	.400	5.03	13	12	2	0	0	78.2	13	17	40	1	8	2	1.40	.299	.479	.332
Williams	Hou.	R	0	1	.000	3.75	2	2	0	0	0	12	2	4	4	0	1	2	2.10	.250	.386	.327
Williams	Phi.	L	12	5	.706	2.34	69	0	0	0	30	88.1	4	62	84	4	12	2	0.60	.182	.266	.330
Wilson	L.A.	L	0	0	—	2.61	19	0	0	0	2	20.2	1	9	14	0	1	0	0.81	.197	.282	.284
Wilson	S.F.	L	13	11	.542	3.56	44	29	2	1	0	202	13	77	139	5	8	12	1.72	.234	.343	.308
Wohlers	Atl.	R	3	1	.750	3.20	17	0	0	0	2	19.2	1	13	13	0	5	0	1.61	.239	.380	.368
Young	NY-N	R	2	5	.286	3.10	10	8	0	0	0	49.1	4	12	20	1	3	1	2.13	.257	.374	.303

National League Catchers

Name	Team	B	BA	SLG	OBP	G	AB	R	H	2B	3B	HR	RBI	BB	SO	SB	CS	LHP	RHP	SP	SP2
Berryhill	Atl.	B	.188	.325	.243	63	160	13	30	7	0	5	14	11	42	1	2	.051	.231	.158	.208
Biggio	Hou.	R	.295	.374	.358	149	546	79	161	23	4	4	46	53	71	19	6	.274	.306	.280	.264
Bilardello	S.D.	R	.269	.423	.345	15	26	4	7	2	1	0	5	3	4	0	0	.167	.300	.571	.667
Cabrera	Atl.	R	.242	.432	.284	44	95	7	23	6	0	4	23	6	20	1	1	.222	.268	.333	.294
Carter	L.A.	R	.246	.375	.323	101	248	22	61	14	0	6	26	22	26	2	2	.252	.237	.261	.231
Cerone	NY-N	R	.273	.357	.360	90	227	18	62	13	0	2	16	30	24	1	1	.315	.233	.204	.208
Daulton	Phi.	L	.196	.365	.297	89	285	36	56	12	0	12	42	41	66	5	0	.146	.222	.290	.240
Decker	S.F.	R	.206	.309	.262	79	233	11	48	7	1	5	24	16	44	0	1	.221	.197	.138	.139
Eusebio	Hou.	R	.105	.158	.320	10	19	4	2	1	0	0	0	6	8	0	0	.111	.100	.000	.000
Fitzgerald	Mon.	R	.202	.308	.278	71	198	17	40	5	2	4	28	22	35	4	2	.233	.179	.241	.286
Fletcher	Phi.	L	.228	.309	.255	46	136	5	31	8	0	1	12	5	15	0	1	.273	.219	.176	.200
Gedman	St.L	L	.106	.213	.140	46	94	7	10	1	0	3	8	4	15	0	1	.000	.119	.000	.000
Girardi	ChiN	R	.191	.234	.283	21	47	3	9	2	0	0	6	6	6	0	0	.229	.083	.273	.500
Hassey	Mon.	L	.227	.319	.301	52	119	5	27	8	0	1	14	13	16	1	1	.333	.224	.243	.278
Heath	Atl.	R	.209	.266	.250	49	139	4	29	3	1	1	12	7	26	0	0	.167	.235	.189	.111
Hernandez	L.A.	R	.214	.286	.250	15	14	1	3	1	0	0	1	0	5	1	0	.333	.125	.000	–
Hundley	NY-N	B	.133	.217	.221	21	60	5	8	0	1	1	7	6	14	0	0	.105	.146	.250	.231
Kennedy	S.F.	R	.234	.351	.283	69	171	12	40	7	1	3	13	11	31	0	0	.300	.230	.231	.158
Lake	Phi.	R	.228	.285	.238	58	158	12	36	4	1	1	11	2	26	0	0	.245	.188	.263	.263
Lampkin	S.D.	L	.190	.276	.230	38	58	4	11	3	1	0	3	3	9	0	0	.190	.200	.286	–
LaValliere	Pit.	L	.289	.360	.351	108	336	25	97	11	2	3	41	33	27	2	1	.222	.301	.263	.229
Manwaring	S.F.	R	.225	.275	.271	67	178	16	40	9	0	0	19	9	22	1	1	.308	.177	.262	.167
O'Brien	NY-N	R	.185	.256	.272	69	168	16	31	6	0	2	14	17	25	0	2	.167	.200	.111	.059
Oliver	Cin.	R	.216	.379	.265	94	269	21	58	11	0	11	41	18	53	0	0	.229	.203	.258	.259
Olson	Atl.	R	.241	.345	.316	133	411	46	99	25	0	6	44	44	48	1	1	.290	.225	.293	.373
Pagnozzi	St.L	R	.264	.351	.319	140	459	38	121	24	5	2	57	36	63	9	13	.254	.271	.261	.200
Prince	Pit.	R	.265	.441	.405	26	34	4	9	3	0	1	2	7	3	0	0	.375	.167	.125	.000
Reed	Cin.	L	.267	.370	.321	91	270	20	72	15	2	3	31	23	38	0	1	.192	.275	.203	.182
Reyes	Mon.	R	.217	.261	.285	83	207	11	45	9	0	0	13	19	51	2	4	.186	.245	.250	.148
Santiago	S.D.	R	.267	.403	.296	152	580	60	155	22	3	17	87	23	114	8	10	.284	.258	.276	.253
Santovenia	Mon.	R	.250	.365	.255	41	96	7	24	5	0	2	14	2	18	0	0	.265	.234	.296	.364
Sasser	NY-N	L	.272	.417	.298	96	228	18	62	14	2	5	35	9	19	0	2	.172	.286	.367	.276
Scioscia	L.A.	L	.264	.391	.353	119	345	39	91	16	2	8	40	47	32	4	3	.189	.297	.276	.200
Scott	Cin.	B	.158	.158	.158	10	19	0	3	0	0	0	0	0	2	0	0	.154	.167	–	–
Servais	Hou.	R	.162	.243	.244	16	37	0	6	3	0	0	6	4	8	0	0	.143	.167	.400	.500
Slaught	Pit.	R	.295	.395	.363	77	220	19	65	17	1	1	29	21	32	1	0	.262	.340	.284	.250
Stephens	St.L	R	.286	.286	.375	6	7	0	2	0	0	0	0	1	3	0	0	.167	1.000	.000	–
Villanueva	ChiN	R	.276	.542	.346	71	192	23	53	10	1	13	32	21	30	0	0	.280	.272	.233	.160
Wilkins	ChiN	L	.222	.355	.307	86	203	21	45	9	0	6	22	19	56	3	3	.237	.218	.233	.250

National League First Basemen

Name	Team	B	BA	SLG	OBP	G	AB	R	H	2B	3B	HR	RBI	BB	SO	SB	CS	LHP	RHP	SP	SP2
Anderson	S.F.	R	.248	.314	.286	100	226	24	56	5	2	2	13	12	35	2	4	.148	.303	.173	.172
Bagwell	Hou.	R	.294	.437	.387	156	554	79	163	26	4	15	82	75	116	7	4	.320	.279	.299	.271
Bell	Atl.	L	.133	.233	.188	17	30	4	4	0	0	1	1	2	7	1	0	.000	.154	.000	.000
Bonilla	Pit.	B	.302	.492	.391	157	577	102	174	44	6	18	100	90	67	2	4	.284	.313	.308	.276
Bream	Atl.	L	.253	.423	.313	91	265	32	67	12	0	11	45	25	31	0	3	.150	.271	.256	.200
Brewer	St.L	L	.077	.077	.077	19	13	0	1	0	0	0	0	1	5	0	0	.200	.000	.333	.333
Cabrera	Atl.	R	.242	.432	.284	44	95	7	23	6	0	4	23	6	20	1	1	.222	.268	.333	.294
Calderon	Mon.	R	.300	.481	.368	134	470	69	141	22	3	19	75	53	64	31	16	.354	.272	.303	.173
Carter	L.A.	R	.246	.375	.323	101	248	22	61	14	0	6	26	22	26	2	2	.252	.237	.261	.231
Clark	S.D.	R	.228	.352	.295	118	369	26	84	16	0	10	47	31	90	2	1	.175	.255	.236	.280
Clark	S.F.	L	.301	.536	.359	148	565	84	170	32	7	29	116	51	91	4	2	.239	.334	.338	.283
Donnels	NY-N	L	.225	.247	.330	37	89	7	20	2	0	0	5	14	19	1	1	.294	.182	.179	.273
Doran	Cin.	B	.280	.374	.359	111	361	51	101	12	2	6	35	46	39	5	4	.263	.285	.268	.195
Fitzgerald	Mon.	R	.202	.308	.278	71	198	17	40	5	2	4	28	22	35	4	2	.233	.179	.241	.286
Foley	Mon.	L	.208	.286	.269	86	168	12	35	11	1	0	15	14	30	2	0	.150	.216	.250	.368
Galarraga	Mon.	R	.219	.336	.268	107	375	34	82	13	2	9	33	23	86	5	6	.180	.239	.173	.109
Grace	ChiN	L	.273	.373	.346	160	619	87	169	28	5	8	58	70	53	3	4	.270	.275	.229	.169
Gregg	Atl.	R	.187	.308	.275	72	107	13	20	8	1	1	4	12	24	2	2	.000	.196	.111	.176
Guerrero	St.L	R	.272	.361	.326	115	427	41	116	12	1	8	70	37	46	4	2	.256	.281	.352	.262
Hollins	Phi.	B	.298	.510	.378	56	151	18	45	10	2	6	21	17	26	1	1	.444	.236	.250	.273
Hudler	St.L	R	.227	.309	.260	101	207	21	47	10	2	1	15	10	29	12	8	.252	.154	.298	.125
Hunter	Atl.	R	.251	.450	.296	97	271	32	68	16	1	12	50	17	48	0	2	.273	.233	.319	.214
Javier	L.A.	B	.205	.284	.268	121	176	21	36	5	3	1	11	16	36	7	1	.247	.152	.167	.143
Jordan	Phi.	R	.272	.452	.304	101	301	38	82	21	3	9	49	14	49	0	2	.310	.246	.303	.214
Karros	L.A.	R	.071	.143	.133	14	14	0	1	1	0	0	1	1	6	0	0	.000	.250	.250	.000
Kingery	S.F.	L	.182	.236	.280	91	110	13	20	2	2	0	8	15	21	1	0	.077	.196	.250	.056
Kruk	Phi.	L	.294	.483	.367	152	538	84	158	27	6	21	92	67	100	7	0	.297	.292	.275	.302

National League First Basemen

Name	Team	B	BA	SLG	OBP	G	AB	R	H	2B	3B	HR	RBI	BB	SO	SB	CS	LHP	RHP	SP	SP2
Litton	S.F.	R	.181	.276	.250	59	127	13	23	7	1	1	15	11	25	0	2	.159	.193	.171	.150
Magadan	NY-N	L	.258	.342	.378	124	418	58	108	23	0	4	51	83	50	1	1	.245	.266	.291	.380
Martinez	Cin.	R	.234	.383	.301	64	154	13	36	5	0	6	19	16	39	0	0	.225	.243	.194	.188
McClendon	Pit.	R	.288	.460	.366	85	163	24	47	7	0	7	24	18	23	2	1	.350	.130	.250	.250
McGriff	S.D.	L	.278	.494	.396	153	528	84	147	19	1	31	106	105	135	4	1	.272	.283	.273	.182
Merced	Pit.	B	.275	.399	.373	120	411	83	113	17	2	10	50	64	81	8	4	.208	.285	.326	.345
Morris	Cin.	L	.318	.479	.374	136	478	72	152	33	1	14	59	46	61	10	4	.252	.336	.284	.322
Murray	L.A.	B	.260	.403	.321	153	576	69	150	23	1	19	96	55	74	10	3	.217	.295	.258	.276
Perry	St.L	R	.240	.380	.300	109	242	29	58	8	4	6	36	22	34	15	8	.240	.239	.319	.172
Redus	Pit.	R	.246	.393	.324	98	252	45	62	12	2	7	24	28	39	17	3	.249	.241	.143	.200
Salazar	ChiN	R	.258	.432	.292	103	333	34	86	14	1	14	38	15	45	0	3	.271	.246	.192	.212
Santovenia	Mon.	R	.250	.365	.255	41	96	7	24	5	0	2	14	2	18	0	0	.265	.234	.296	.364
Sasser	NY-N	L	.272	.417	.298	96	228	18	62	14	2	5	35	9	19	0	2	.172	.286	.367	.276
Sharperson	L.A.	R	.278	.375	.355	105	216	24	60	11	2	2	20	25	24	1	3	.323	.155	.207	.207
Templeton	NY-N	B	.221	.304	.246	112	276	25	61	10	2	3	26	10	38	3	2	.344	.156	.205	.167
Teufel	S.D.	R	.217	.370	.319	117	341	41	74	16	0	12	44	51	77	9	3	.273	.182	.213	.192
Tolentino	Hou.	L	.259	.389	.305	44	54	6	14	4	0	1	6	4	9	0	0	.500	.229	.353	.250
Villanueva	ChiN	R	.276	.542	.346	71	192	23	53	10	1	13	32	21	30	0	0	.280	.272	.233	.160
Walker	Mon.	L	.290	.458	.349	137	487	59	141	30	2	16	64	42	102	14	9	.288	.291	.269	.217

National League Second Basemen

Name	Team	B	BA	SLG	OBP	G	AB	R	H	2B	3B	HR	RBI	BB	SO	SB	CS	LHP	RHP	SP	SP2
Alicea	St.L	B	.191	.235	.276	56	68	5	13	3	0	0	0	8	19	0	1	.250	.173	.111	.000
Anderson	S.F.	R	.248	.314	.286	100	226	24	56	5	2	2	13	12	35	2	4	.148	.303	.173	.172
Backman	Phi.	B	.243	.308	.344	94	185	20	45	12	0	0	15	30	30	3	2	.083	.267	.243	.304
Barberie	Mon.	B	.353	.515	.435	57	136	16	48	12	2	2	18	20	22	0	0	.270	.384	.296	.250
Benavides	Cin.	R	.286	.302	.303	24	63	11	18	1	0	0	3	1	15	1	0	.278	.289	.125	.000
Biggio	Hou.	R	.295	.374	.358	149	546	79	161	23	4	4	46	53	71	19	6	.274	.306	.280	.264
Blauser	Atl.	R	.259	.409	.358	129	352	49	91	14	3	11	54	54	59	5	6	.305	.232	.320	.327
Candaele	Hou.	B	.262	.362	.319	151	461	44	121	20	7	4	50	40	49	9	3	.285	.251	.304	.290
DeShields	Mon.	L	.238	.332	.347	151	563	83	134	15	4	10	51	95	151	56	23	.217	.249	.250	.155
Doran	Cin.	B	.280	.374	.359	111	361	51	101	12	2	6	35	46	39	5	4	.263	.285	.268	.195
Duncan	Cin.	R	.258	.411	.288	100	333	46	86	7	4	12	40	12	57	5	4	.314	.218	.342	.286
Faries	S.D.	R	.177	.215	.262	57	130	13	23	3	1	0	7	14	21	3	1	.239	.143	.214	.188
Foley	Mon.	L	.208	.286	.269	86	168	12	35	11	1	0	15	14	30	2	0	.150	.216	.250	.368
Gardner	NY-N	L	.162	.162	.238	13	37	3	6	0	0	0	1	4	6	0	0	.000	.207	.250	.000
Harris	L.A.	L	.287	.350	.349	145	429	59	123	16	1	3	38	37	32	12	3	.241	.298	.280	.189
Herr	S.F.	R	.209	.270	.344	102	215	23	45	8	1	1	21	45	28	9	2	.217	.205	.224	.231
Jefferies	NY-N	B	.272	.374	.336	136	486	59	132	19	2	9	62	47	38	26	5	.293	.260	.306	.241
Lemke	Atl.	B	.234	.312	.305	136	269	36	63	11	2	2	23	29	27	1	2	.254	.219	.230	.250
Lind	Pit.	R	.265	.339	.306	150	502	53	133	16	6	3	54	30	56	7	4	.269	.263	.280	.295
Litton	S.F.	R	.181	.276	.250	59	127	13	23	7	1	1	15	11	25	0	2	.159	.193	.171	.150
Miller	NY-N	R	.280	.411	.345	98	275	41	77	22	1	4	23	23	44	14	4	.247	.318	.345	.429
Morandini	Phi.	L	.249	.317	.313	98	325	38	81	11	4	1	20	29	45	13	2	.185	.265	.266	.286
Mota	Hou.	R	.189	.244	.198	27	90	4	17	2	0	1	6	1	17	2	0	.114	.236	.125	.167
Noboa	Mon.	R	.242	.305	.250	67	95	5	23	3	0	1	2	1	8	2	3	.253	.188	.158	.111
Oquendo	St.L	B	.240	.301	.357	127	366	37	88	11	4	1	26	67	48	1	2	.240	.241	.250	.186
Pena	St.L	B	.243	.400	.322	104	185	38	45	8	3	5	17	18	45	15	5	.301	.185	.212	.174
Quinones	Cin.	B	.222	.325	.297	97	212	15	47	4	3	4	20	21	31	1	2	.172	.243	.209	.154
Ramirez	Hou.	R	.236	.292	.274	101	233	17	55	10	0	1	20	13	40	3	3	.245	.228	.213	.080
Ready	Phi.	R	.249	.322	.385	76	205	32	51	10	1	1	20	47	25	2	1	.265	.207	.250	.200
Roberts	S.D.	B	.281	.347	.342	117	424	66	119	13	3	3	32	37	71	26	11	.254	.291	.316	.327
Samuel	L.A.	R	.271	.389	.328	153	594	74	161	22	6	12	58	49	133	23	8	.252	.285	.248	.266
Sandberg	ChiN	R	.291	.485	.379	158	585	104	170	32	2	26	100	87	89	22	8	.359	.253	.341	.246
Sharperson	L.A.	R	.278	.375	.355	105	216	24	60	11	2	2	20	25	24	1	3	.323	.155	.207	.207
Shipley	S.D.	R	.275	.341	.298	37	91	6	25	3	0	1	6	2	14	0	1	.318	.234	.333	.333
Teufel	S.D.	R	.217	.370	.319	117	341	41	74	16	0	12	44	51	77	9	3	.273	.182	.213	.192
Thompson	S.F.	R	.262	.447	.352	144	492	74	129	24	5	19	48	63	95	14	7	.281	.255	.229	.250
Treadway	Atl.	L	.320	.418	.368	106	306	41	98	17	2	3	32	23	19	2	2	.250	.325	.333	.280
Vizcaino	ChiN	B	.262	.297	.283	93	145	7	38	5	0	0	10	5	18	2	1	.216	.278	.233	.412
Walker	ChiN	B	.257	.337	.315	124	374	51	96	10	1	6	34	33	57	13	5	.210	.278	.286	.130
Wilkerson	Pit.	B	.188	.277	.243	85	191	20	36	9	1	2	18	15	40	2	1	.224	.176	.155	.167

National League Third Basemen

Name	Team	B	BA	SLG	OBP	G	AB	R	H	2B	3B	HR	RBI	BB	SO	SB	CS	LHP	RHP	SP	SP2
Anderson	S.F.	R	.248	.314	.286	100	226	24	56	5	2	2	13	12	35	2	4	.148	.303	.173	.172
Backman	Phi.	B	.243	.308	.344	94	185	20	45	12	0	0	15	30	30	3	2	.083	.267	.243	.304
Barberie	Mon.	B	.353	.515	.435	57	136	16	48	12	2	2	18	20	22	0	0	.270	.384	.296	.250
Blauser	Atl.	R	.259	.409	.358	129	352	49	91	14	3	11	54	54	59	5	6	.305	.232	.320	.327
Bonilla	Pit.	B	.302	.492	.391	157	577	102	174	44	6	18	100	90	67	2	4	.284	.313	.308	.276
Buechele	Pit.	R	.246	.412	.315	31	114	16	28	5	1	4	19	10	28	0	1	.324	.213	.244	.294
Caminiti	Hou.	B	.253	.383	.312	152	574	65	145	30	3	13	80	46	85	4	5	.310	.213	.288	.292
Candaele	Hou.	B	.262	.362	.319	151	461	44	121	20	7	4	50	40	49	9	3	.285	.251	.304	.290
Cooper	Hou.	B	.250	.313	.368	9	16	1	4	1	0	0	2	3	6	0	0	.000	.308	.667	.500
Donnels	NY-N	L	.225	.247	.330	37	89	7	20	2	0	0	5	14	19	1	1	.294	.182	.179	.273
Faries	S.D.	R	.177	.215	.262	57	130	13	23	3	1	0	7	14	21	3	1	.239	.143	.214	.188
Foley	Mon.	L	.208	.286	.269	86	168	12	35	11	1	0	15	14	30	2	0	.150	.216	.250	.368
Garcia	Pit.	B	.250	.417	.280	12	24	2	6	0	2	0	1	1	8	0	0	.400	.211	.000	.000
Hamilton	L.A.	R	.223	.298	.255	41	94	4	21	4	0	1	14	4	21	0	0	.192	.375	.333	.353
Hansen	L.A.	L	.268	.393	.293	53	56	3	15	4	0	1	5	2	12	1	0	.167	.280	.182	.200
Harris	L.A.	L	.287	.350	.349	145	429	59	123	16	1	3	38	37	32	12	3	.241	.298	.280	.189
C. Hayes	Phi.	R	.230	.363	.257	142	460	34	106	23	1	12	53	16	75	3	3	.258	.211	.239	.300
Hollins	Phi.	B	.298	.510	.378	56	151	18	45	10	2	6	21	17	26	1	1	.444	.236	.250	.273
Howell	S.D.	L	.206	.350	.287	58	160	24	33	3	1	6	16	18	33	0	0	.125	.215	.308	.308
Jefferies	NY-N	B	.272	.374	.336	136	486	59	132	19	2	9	62	47	38	26	5	.293	.260	.306	.241
Johnson	NY-N	B	.259	.535	.342	156	564	108	146	34	4	38	117	78	120	30	16	.253	.262	.276	.239
King	Pit.	R	.239	.376	.328	33	109	16	26	1	1	4	18	14	15	3	1	.323	.205	.286	.400
Lemke	Atl.	B	.234	.312	.305	136	269	36	63	11	2	2	23	29	27	1	2	.254	.219	.230	.250
Litton	S.F.	R	.181	.276	.250	59	127	13	23	7	1	1	15	11	25	0	2	.159	.193	.171	.150
Pendleton	Atl.	B	.319	.517	.363	153	586	94	187	34	8	22	86	43	70	10	2	.299	.328	.320	.281
Quinones	Cin.	B	.222	.325	.297	97	212	15	47	4	3	4	20	21	31	1	2	.172	.243	.209	.154
Royer	St.L	R	.286	.333	.318	9	21	1	6	1	0	0	1	1	2	0	0	.250	.308	.143	.250
Sabo	Cin.	R	.301	.505	.354	153	582	91	175	35	3	26	88	44	79	19	6	.358	.272	.306	.267
Salazar	ChiN	R	.258	.432	.292	103	333	34	86	14	1	14	38	15	45	0	3	.271	.246	.192	.212
Sharperson	L.A.	R	.278	.375	.355	105	216	24	60	11	2	2	20	25	24	1	3	.323	.155	.207	.207
Strange	ChiN	B	.444	.556	.455	3	9	0	4	1	0	0	1	0	1	1	0	.400	.500	.000	.000
Templeton	NY-N	B	.221	.304	.246	112	276	25	61	10	2	3	26	10	38	3	2	.344	.156	.205	.167
Teufel	S.D.	R	.217	.370	.319	117	341	41	74	16	0	12	44	51	77	9	3	.273	.182	.213	.192
Vizcaino	ChiN	B	.262	.297	.283	93	145	7	38	5	0	0	10	5	18	2	1	.216	.278	.233	.412
Walker	ChiN	B	.257	.337	.315	124	374	51	96	10	1	6	34	33	57	13	5	.210	.278	.286	.130
Wallach	Mon.	R	.225	.334	.292	151	577	60	130	22	1	13	73	50	100	2	4	.222	.227	.238	.202
Wehner	Pit.	R	.340	.406	.381	37	106	15	36	7	0	0	7	7	17	3	0	.346	.333	.333	.154
Wilkerson	Pit.	B	.188	.277	.243	85	191	20	36	9	1	2	18	15	40	2	1	.224	.176	.155	.167
Williams	S.F.	R	.268	.499	.310	157	589	72	158	24	5	34	98	33	128	5	5	.279	.264	.243	.299
Wilson	St.L	R	.171	.195	.222	60	82	5	14	2	0	0	13	6	10	0	0	.231	.067	.231	.250
Zeile	St.L	R	.280	.412	.353	155	565	76	158	36	3	11	81	62	94	17	11	.304	.262	.304	.250

National League Shortstops

Name	Team	B	BA	SLG	OBP	G	AB	R	H	2B	3B	HR	RBI	BB	SO	SB	CS	LHP	RHP	SP	SP2
Anderson	S.F.	R	.248	.314	.286	100	226	24	56	5	2	2	13	12	35	2	4	.148	.303	.173	.172
Barberie	Mon.	B	.353	.515	.435	57	136	16	48	12	2	2	18	20	22	0	0	.270	.384	.296	.250
Batiste	Phi.	R	.222	.222	.250	10	27	2	6	0	0	0	1	1	8	0	1	.333	.133	.000	.000
Bell	Pit.	R	.270	.428	.330	157	608	96	164	32	8	16	67	52	99	10	6	.289	.261	.286	.192
Belliard	Atl.	R	.249	.286	.296	149	353	36	88	9	2	0	27	22	63	3	1	.242	.252	.269	.292
Benavides	Cin.	R	.286	.302	.303	24	63	11	18	1	0	0	3	1	15	1	0	.278	.289	.125	.100
Benjamin	S.F.	R	.123	.208	.188	54	106	12	13	3	0	2	8	7	26	3	0	.167	.105	.050	.000
Blauser	Atl.	R	.259	.409	.358	129	352	49	91	14	3	11	54	54	59	5	6	.305	.232	.320	.327
Castilla	Atl.	R	.200	.200	.200	12	5	1	1	0	0	0	0	0	2	0	0	-	.200	-	-
Cedeno	Hou.	B	.243	.418	.270	67	251	27	61	13	2	9	36	9	74	4	3	.213	.257	.254	.229
Clayton	S.F.	R	.115	.154	.148	9	26	0	3	1	0	0	2	1	6	0	0	.200	.095	.200	.000
Duncan	Cin.	R	.258	.411	.288	100	333	46	86	7	4	12	40	12	57	5	4	.314	.218	.342	.286
Dunston	ChiN	R	.260	.407	.292	142	492	59	128	22	7	12	50	23	64	21	6	.232	.279	.271	.224
Elster	NY-N	R	.241	.351	.318	115	348	33	84	16	2	6	36	40	53	2	3	.296	.196	.271	.220
Faries	S.D.	R	.177	.215	.262	57	130	13	23	3	1	0	7	14	21	3	1	.239	.143	.214	.188
Fernandez	S.D.	B	.272	.360	.337	145	558	81	152	27	5	4	38	55	74	23	9	.261	.278	.308	.279
Foley	Mon.	L	.208	.286	.269	86	168	12	35	11	1	0	15	14	30	2	0	.150	.216	.250	.368
Garcia	Pit.	B	.250	.417	.280	12	24	2	6	0	2	0	1	1	8	0	0	.400	.211	.000	.000
Gardner	NY-N	L	.162	.162	.238	13	37	3	6	0	0	0	1	4	6	0	0		.207	.250	.000
Griffin	L.A.	B	.243	.271	.286	109	350	27	85	6	2	0	27	22	49	5	4	.270	.223	.263	.225
Harris	L.A.	L	.287	.350	.349	145	429	59	123	16	1	3	38	37	32	12	3	.241	.298	.280	.189
Johnson	NY-N	B	.259	.535	.342	156	564	108	146	34	4	38	117	78	120	30	16	.253	.262	.276	.239
Jones	St.L	R	.167	.250	.222	16	24	1	4	2	0	0	2	2	6	0	1	1.000	.190	.143	.250
Larkin	Cin.	R	.302	.506	.378	123	464	88	140	27	4	20	69	55	64	24	6	.326	.292	.288	.265
Litton	S.F.	R	.181	.276	.250	59	127	13	23	7	1	1	15	11	25	0	2	.159	.193	.171	.150

National League Shortstops

Name	Team	B	BA	SLG	OBP	G	AB	R	H	2B	3B	HR	RBI	BB	SO	SB	CS	LHP	RHP	SP	SP2
Offerman	L.A.	B	.195	.212	.345	52	113	10	22	2	0	0	3	25	32	3	2	.300	.111	.158	.000
Oquendo	St.L	B	.240	.301	.357	127	366	37	88	11	4	1	26	67	48	1	2	.240	.241	.250	.186
Owen	Mon.	B	.255	.366	.321	139	424	39	108	22	8	3	26	42	61	2	6	.305	.210	.215	.100
Quinones	Cin.	B	.222	.325	.297	97	212	15	47	4	3	4	20	21	31	1	2	.172	.243	.209	.154
Ramirez	Hou.	R	.236	.292	.274	101	233	17	55	10	0	1	20	13	40	3	3	.245	.228	.213	.080
Sanchez	ChiN	R	.261	.261	.370	13	23	1	6	0	0	0	2	4	3	0	0	.000	.333	.250	.500
Sharperson	L.A.	B	.278	.375	.355	105	216	24	60	11	2	2	20	25	24	1	3	.323	.155	.207	.207
Shipley	S.D.	R	.275	.341	.298	37	91	6	25	3	0	1	6	2	14	0	1	.318	.234	.333	.333
O. Smith	St.L	B	.285	.367	.380	150	550	96	157	30	3	3	50	83	36	35	9	.262	.305	.273	.190
Templeton	NY-N	B	.221	.304	.246	112	276	25	61	10	2	3	26	10	38	3	2	.344	.156	.205	.167
Thon	Phi.	R	.252	.351	.283	146	539	44	136	18	4	9	44	25	84	11	5	.259	.249	.220	.228
Uribe	S.F.	B	.221	.303	.283	90	231	23	51	8	4	1	12	20	33	3	4	.250	.211	.250	.273
Vizcaino	ChiN	B	.262	.297	.283	93	145	7	38	5	0	0	10	5	18	2	1	.216	.278	.233	.412
Wilkerson	Pit.	B	.188	.277	.243	85	191	20	36	9	1	2	18	15	40	2	1	.224	.176	.155	.167

National League Left Fielders

Name	Team	B	BA	SLG	OBP	G	AB	R	H	2B	3B	HR	RBI	BB	SO	SB	CS	LHP	RHP	SP	SP2
Azocar	S.D.	L	.246	.281	.267	38	57	5	14	2	0	0	9	1	9	2	0	.000	.255	.385	.500
Bass	S.F.	L	.233	.366	.307	124	361	43	84	10	4	10	40	36	56	7	4	.239	.230	.198	.186
Bell	ChiN	R	.285	.468	.323	149	558	63	159	27	0	25	86	32	62	2	6	.288	.283	.235	.213
Bonds	Pit.	L	.292	.514	.410	153	510	95	149	28	5	25	116	107	73	43	13	.284	.298	.345	.312
Boston	NY-N	L	.275	.416	.350	137	255	40	70	16	4	4	21	30	42	15	8	.194	.286	.288	.167
Braggs	Cin.	R	.260	.432	.323	85	250	36	65	10	0	11	39	23	46	11	3	.282	.238	.302	.281
Bullock	Mon.	L	.222	.319	.305	73	72	6	16	4	0	1	6	9	13	6	1	.500	.214	.111	.200
Calderon	Mon.	R	.300	.481	.368	134	470	69	141	22	3	19	75	53	64	31	16	.354	.272	.303	.173
Candaele	Hou.	B	.262	.362	.319	151	461	44	121	20	7	4	50	40	49	9	3	.285	.251	.304	.290
Carreon	NY-N	R	.260	.331	.297	106	254	18	66	6	0	4	21	12	26	2	1	.242	.292	.225	.263
Chamberlain	Phi.	R	.240	.399	.300	101	383	51	92	16	3	13	50	31	73	9	4	.271	.222	.247	.207
Clark	S.D.	R	.228	.352	.295	118	369	26	84	16	0	10	47	31	90	2	1	.175	.255	.236	.280
Daniels	L.A.	L	.249	.397	.337	137	461	54	115	15	1	17	73	63	116	6	1	.252	.247	.291	.339
Dascenzo	ChiN	B	.255	.314	.327	118	239	40	61	11	0	1	18	24	26	14	7	.299	.230	.167	.167
Davidson	Hou.	R	.190	.275	.263	85	142	10	27	6	0	2	15	12	28	0	0	.186	.200	.190	.190
Davis	Cin.	R	.235	.386	.353	89	285	39	67	10	0	11	33	48	92	14	2	.229	.239	.217	.290
Doran	Cin.	B	.280	.374	.359	111	361	51	101	12	2	6	35	46	39	5	4	.263	.285	.268	.195
Duncan	Cin.	R	.258	.411	.288	100	333	46	86	7	4	12	40	12	57	5	4	.314	.218	.342	.286
Felder	S.F.	B	.264	.328	.325	132	348	51	92	10	6	0	18	30	31	21	6	.271	.261	.279	.241
Gilkey	St.L	R	.216	.313	.316	81	268	28	58	7	2	5	20	39	33	14	8	.190	.244	.210	.172
Gonzalez	Hou.	L	.254	.433	.320	137	473	51	120	28	9	13	69	40	101	10	7	.172	.282	.272	.200
Gregg	Atl.	L	.187	.308	.275	72	107	13	20	8	1	1	4	12	24	2	2	.000	.196	.111	.176
Gwynn	L.A.	L	.252	.410	.301	94	139	18	35	5	1	5	22	10	23	1	0	.182	.258	.300	.444
Hatcher	Cin.	R	.262	.360	.312	138	442	45	116	25	3	4	41	26	55	11	9	.277	.256	.340	.351
V. Hayes	Phi.	L	.225	.285	.303	77	284	43	64	15	1	0	21	31	42	9	2	.267	.206	.179	.111
Howard	S.D.	B	.249	.356	.309	106	281	30	70	12	3	4	22	24	57	10	7	.286	.245	.286	.316
Hudler	St.L	R	.227	.309	.260	101	207	21	47	10	2	1	15	10	29	12	8	.252	.154	.298	.125
Hunter	Atl.	R	.251	.450	.296	97	271	32	68	16	1	12	50	17	48	0	2	.273	.233	.319	.214
Jackson	S.D.	R	.262	.476	.315	122	359	51	94	12	1	21	49	27	66	5	3	.264	.260	.266	.270
Javier	L.A.	R	.205	.284	.268	121	176	21	36	5	3	1	11	16	36	7	1	.247	.152	.167	.143
S. Jefferson	Cin.	B	.053	.053	.100	13	19	2	1	0	0	0	0	0	3	2	0	.000	.071	.000	–
Jones	Cin.	R	.292	.416	.304	52	89	14	26	1	2	2	6	2	31	2	1	.283	.302	.143	.286
Kingery	S.F.	L	.182	.236	.280	91	110	13	20	2	2	0	8	15	21	1	0	.077	.196	.250	.056
Kruk	Phi.	L	.294	.483	.367	152	538	84	158	27	6	21	92	67	100	7	0	.297	.292	.275	.302
Landrum	ChiN	L	.233	.279	.313	56	86	28	20	2	1	0	6	10	18	27	5	.385	.205	.375	.375
Leonard	S.F.	L	.240	.357	.306	63	129	14	31	7	1	2	14	12	25	0	1	.100	.252	.238	.130
Lindeman	Phi.	R	.337	.389	.413	65	95	13	32	5	0	0	12	13	14	0	1	.426	.176	.360	.429
Martinez	Cin.	R	.234	.383	.301	64	154	13	36	5	0	6	19	16	39	0	0	.225	.243	.194	.188
Da. Martinez	Mon.	L	.295	.419	.332	124	396	47	117	18	5	7	42	20	54	16	7	.237	.314	.302	.313
D. May	ChiN	L	.227	.455	.280	15	22	4	5	2	0	1	3	2	1	0	0	.000	.238	.250	1.000
McClendon	Pit.	R	.288	.460	.366	85	163	24	47	7	0	7	24	18	23	2	1	.350	.130	.250	.250
McDaniel	NY-N	B	.207	.241	.233	23	29	3	6	1	0	0	2	1	11	2	0	.267	.143	.222	.167
McReynolds	NY-N	R	.259	.416	.322	147	522	65	135	32	1	16	74	49	46	6	6	.259	.258	.308	.280
Miller	NY-N	R	.280	.411	.345	98	275	41	77	22	1	4	23	23	44	14	4	.247	.318	.345	.429
Mitchell	Atl.	R	.318	.409	.392	48	66	11	21	0	0	2	5	8	12	3	1	.345	.297	.273	.286
Mitchell	S.F.	R	.256	.515	.338	113	371	52	95	13	1	27	69	43	57	2	3	.272	.249	.242	.188
Morris	Phi.	B	.220	.276	.293	85	127	15	28	2	1	1	6	12	25	2	0	.333	.209	.217	.143
Nixon	Atl.	B	.297	.327	.371	124	401	81	119	10	1	0	26	47	40	72	21	.305	.294	.312	.375
Ortiz	Hou.	R	.277	.386	.381	47	83	7	23	4	1	1	5	14	14	0	0	.250	.314	.150	.200
Pena	St.L	B	.243	.400	.322	104	185	38	45	8	3	5	17	18	45	15	5	.301	.185	.212	.174
Perry	St.L	B	.240	.380	.300	109	242	29	58	8	4	6	36	22	34	15	8	.240	.239	.319	.172
Redus	Pit.	R	.246	.393	.324	98	252	45	62	12	2	7	24	28	39	17	3	.249	.241	.143	.200
Roberts	S.D.	B	.281	.347	.342	117	424	66	119	13	3	3	32	37	71	26	11	.254	.291	.316	.327

National League Left Fielders

Name	Team	B	BA	SLG	OBP	G	AB	R	H	2B	3B	HR	RBI	BB	SO	SB	CS	LHP	RHP	SP	SP2
Sanders	Atl.	L	.191	.345	.270	54	110	16	21	1	2	4	13	12	23	11	3	.125	.202	.346	.200
Sasser	NY-N	L	.272	.417	.298	96	228	18	62	14	2	5	35	9	19	0	2	.172	.286	.367	.276
Dw. Smith	ChiN	L	.228	.347	.279	90	167	16	38	7	2	3	21	11	32	2	3	.000	.235	.350	.350
L. Smith	Atl.	R	.275	.394	.377	122	353	58	97	19	1	7	44	50	64	9	5	.339	.244	.292	.385
Thompson	St.L	L	.307	.442	.368	115	326	55	100	16	5	6	34	32	53	16	9	.216	.333	.221	.235
Vanderwal	Mon.	L	.213	.361	.222	21	61	4	13	4	1	1	8	1	18	0	0	.063	.267	.208	.182
Varsho	Pit.	L	.273	.417	.344	99	187	23	51	11	2	4	23	19	34	9	2	.200	.275	.239	.286
Walker	ChiN	B	.257	.337	.315	124	374	51	96	10	1	6	34	33	57	13	5	.210	.278	.286	.130
Ward	S.D.	R	.243	.402	.308	44	107	13	26	7	2	2	8	9	27	1	4	.294	.154	.176	.200
Webster	L.A.	B	.222	.363	.296	94	171	21	38	8	5	2	19	18	52	0	1	.250	.195	.259	.222
Williams	Mon.	R	.271	.400	.311	34	70	11	19	5	2	0	1	3	22	2	1	.288	.222	.077	.000
Wilson	St.L	R	.171	.195	.222	60	82	5	14	2	0	0	13	6	10	0	0	.231	.067	.231	.250
Winningham	Cin.	L	.225	.290	.272	98	169	17	38	6	1	1	4	11	40	4	4	.154	.231	.185	.182
Young	Hou.	B	.218	.275	.327	108	142	26	31	3	1	1	11	24	17	16	5	.244	.188	.250	.188

National League Center Fielders

Name	Team	B	BA	SLG	OBP	G	AB	R	H	2B	3B	HR	RBI	BB	SO	SB	CS	LHP	RHP	SP	SP2
Boston	NY-N	L	.275	.416	.350	137	255	40	70	16	4	4	21	30	42	15	8	.194	.286	.288	.167
Butler	L.A.	L	.296	.343	.401	161	615	112	182	13	5	2	38	108	79	38	28	.281	.306	.309	.277
Candaele	Hou.	B	.262	.362	.319	151	461	44	121	20	7	4	50	40	49	9	3	.285	.251	.304	.290
Carr	NY-N	B	.182	.182	.182	12	11	1	2	0	0	0	1	0	2	1	0	.400	.000	.500	.500
Carreon	NY-N	R	.260	.331	.297	106	254	18	66	6	0	4	21	12	26	2	1	.242	.292	.225	.263
Castillo	Phi.	R	.173	.231	.189	28	52	3	9	3	0	0	2	1	15	1	1	.167	.179	.182	.333
Coleman	NY-N	B	.255	.327	.347	72	278	45	71	7	5	1	17	39	47	37	14	.248	.260	.281	.269
Dascenzo	ChiN	B	.255	.314	.327	118	239	40	61	11	0	1	18	24	26	14	7	.299	.230	.167	.167
Davis	Cin.	R	.235	.386	.353	89	285	39	67	10	0	11	33	48	92	14	2	.229	.239	.217	.290
Dykstra	Phi.	L	.297	.427	.391	63	246	48	73	13	5	3	12	37	20	24	4	.309	.289	.250	.211
Espy	Pit.	B	.244	.329	.281	43	82	7	20	4	0	1	11	5	17	4	0	.188	.258	.261	.385
Felder	S.F.	B	.264	.328	.325	132	348	51	92	10	6	0	18	30	31	21	6	.271	.261	.279	.241
Finley	Hou.	L	.285	.406	.331	159	596	84	170	28	10	8	54	42	65	34	18	.250	.301	.311	.328
Gant	Atl.	R	.251	.496	.338	154	561	101	141	35	3	32	105	71	104	34	15	.287	.237	.262	.195
Goodwin	L.A.	L	.143	.143	.143	16	7	3	1	0	0	0	0	0	0	1	1	.000	.200	.000	.000
Grissom	Mon.	B	.267	.373	.310	148	558	73	149	23	9	6	39	34	89	76	17	.284	.256	.288	.351
Hatcher	Cin.	R	.262	.360	.312	138	442	45	116	25	3	4	41	26	55	11	9	.277	.256	.340	.351
V. Hayes	Phi.	L	.225	.285	.303	77	284	43	64	15	1	0	21	31	42	9	2	.267	.206	.179	.111
Howard	S.D.	B	.249	.356	.309	106	281	30	70	12	3	4	22	24	57	10	7	.286	.245	.286	.316
Hudler	St.L	R	.227	.309	.260	101	207	21	47	10	2	1	15	10	29	12	8	.252	.154	.298	.125
Jackson	S.D.	R	.262	.476	.315	122	359	51	94	12	1	21	49	27	66	5	3	.264	.260	.266	.270
Javier	L.A.	B	.205	.284	.268	121	176	21	36	5	3	1	11	16	36	7	1	.247	.152	.167	.143
Kruk	Phi.	L	.294	.483	.367	152	538	84	158	27	6	21	92	67	100	7	0	.297	.292	.275	.302
Landrum	ChiN	L	.233	.279	.313	56	86	11	20	2	1	0	6	10	18	27	5	.385	.205	.375	.375
Lankford	St.L	L	.251	.392	.301	151	566	83	142	23	15	9	69	41	114	44	20	.236	.260	.286	.291
Lewis	S.F.	R	.248	.311	.358	72	222	41	55	5	3	1	15	36	30	13	7	.280	.231	.229	.240
Lindeman	Phi.	R	.337	.389	.413	65	95	13	32	5	0	0	12	13	14	0	1	.426	.176	.360	.429
Lofton	Hou.	L	.203	.216	.253	20	74	9	15	1	0	0	0	5	19	2	1	.250	.185	.000	.000
Da. Martinez	Mon.	L	.295	.419	.332	124	396	47	117	18	5	7	42	20	54	16	7	.237	.314	.302	.313
McDaniel	NY-N	B	.207	.241	.233	23	29	3	6	1	0	0	2	1	11	2	0	.267	.143	.222	.167
McGee	S.F.	R	.312	.408	.357	131	497	67	155	30	3	4	43	34	74	17	9	.338	.300	.343	.347
McReynolds	NY-N	R	.259	.416	.322	143	522	65	135	32	1	16	74	49	46	6	6	.259	.258	.308	.280
Morris	Phi.	R	.220	.276	.293	85	127	15	28	2	1	1	6	12	25	2	0	.333	.209	.217	.143
Nixon	Atl.	B	.297	.327	.371	124	401	81	119	10	1	0	26	47	40	72	21	.305	.294	.312	.375
Redus	Pit.	R	.246	.393	.324	98	252	45	62	12	2	7	24	28	39	17	3	.249	.241	.143	.200
Roberts	S.D.	B	.281	.347	.342	117	424	66	119	13	3	3	32	37	71	26	11	.254	.291	.316	.327
Sanders	Atl.	L	.191	.345	.270	54	110	16	21	1	2	4	13	12	23	11	3	.125	.202	.346	.200
Sanders	Cin.	R	.200	.275	.200	9	40	6	8	0	0	1	3	0	9	1	1	.125	.250	.400	.500
Dw. Smith	ChiN	L	.228	.347	.279	90	167	16	38	7	2	3	21	11	32	2	3	.000	.235	.350	.350
Thompson	St.L	L	.307	.442	.368	115	326	55	100	16	5	6	34	32	53	16	9	.216	.333	.221	.235
Van Slyke	Pit.	L	.265	.446	.355	138	491	87	130	24	7	17	83	71	85	10	3	.195	.307	.280	.231
Varsho	Pit.	L	.273	.417	.344	99	187	23	51	11	2	4	23	19	34	9	2	.200	.275	.239	.286
Walker	ChiN	B	.257	.337	.315	124	374	51	96	10	1	6	34	33	57	13	5	.210	.278	.286	.130
Walker	Mon.	L	.290	.458	.349	137	487	59	141	30	2	16	64	42	102	14	9	.288	.291	.269	.217
Walton	ChiN	R	.219	.330	.275	123	270	42	59	13	1	5	17	19	55	7	3	.195	.239	.173	.115
Webster	L.A.	B	.222	.363	.296	94	171	21	38	8	5	2	19	18	52	0	1	.250	.195	.259	.222
Williams	Mon.	R	.271	.400	.311	34	70	11	19	5	2	0	1	3	22	2	1	.288	.222	.077	.000
Winningham	Cin.	L	.225	.290	.272	98	169	17	38	6	1	1	4	11	40	4	4	.154	.231	.185	.182
Young	Hou.	B	.218	.275	.327	108	142	26	31	3	1	1	11	24	17	16	5	.244	.188	.250	.188

National League Right Fielders

Name	Team	B	BA	SLG	OBP	G	AB	R	H	2B	3B	HR	RBI	BB	SO	SB	CS	LHP	RHP	SP	SP2
Bass	S.F.	B	.233	.366	.307	124	361	43	84	10	4	10	40	36	56	7	4	.239	.230	.198	.186
Bonilla	Pit.	B	.302	.492	.391	157	577	102	174	44	6	18	100	90	67	2	4	.284	.313	.308	.276
Boston	NY-N	B	.275	.416	.350	137	255	40	70	16	4	4	21	30	42	15	8	.194	.286	.288	.167
Braggs	Cin.	R	.260	.432	.323	85	250	36	65	10	0	11	39	23	46	11	3	.282	.238	.302	.281
Brooks	NY-N	R	.238	.409	.324	103	357	48	85	11	1	16	50	44	62	3	1	.248	.233	.212	.174
Bullock	Mon.	L	.222	.319	.305	73	72	6	16	4	0	1	6	9	13	6	1	.500	.214	.111	.200
Candaele	Hou.	B	.262	.362	.319	151	461	44	121	20	7	4	50	40	49	9	3	.285	.251	.304	.290
Carreon	NY-N	R	.260	.331	.297	106	254	18	66	6	0	4	21	12	26	2	1	.242	.292	.225	.263
Clark	S.D.	R	.228	.352	.295	118	369	26	84	16	0	10	47	31	90	2	1	.175	.255	.236	.280
Dascenzo	ChiN	B	.255	.314	.327	118	239	40	61	11	0	1	18	24	26	14	7	.299	.230	.167	.167
Davidson	Hou.	R	.190	.275	.263	85	142	10	27	6	0	2	15	12	28	0	0	.186	.200	.190	.190
Dawson	ChiN	R	.272	.488	.302	149	563	69	153	21	4	31	104	22	80	4	5	.296	.256	.297	.301
Espy	Pit.	B	.244	.329	.281	43	82	7	20	4	0	1	11	5	17	4	0	.188	.258	.261	.385
Felder	S.F.	B	.264	.328	.325	132	348	51	92	10	6	0	18	30	31	21	6	.271	.261	.279	.241
Finley	Hou.	L	.285	.406	.331	159	596	84	170	28	10	8	54	42	65	34	18	.250	.301	.311	.328
Fitzgerald	Mon.	R	.202	.308	.278	71	198	17	40	5	2	4	28	22	35	4	2	.233	.179	.241	.286
Gregg	Atl.	L	.187	.308	.275	72	107	13	20	8	1	1	4	12	24	2	2	.000	.196	.111	.176
Grissom	Mon.	R	.267	.373	.310	148	558	73	149	23	9	6	39	34	89	76	17	.284	.256	.288	.351
Gwynn	S.D.	L	.317	.432	.355	134	530	69	168	27	11	4	62	34	19	8	8	.294	.332	.380	.370
Gwynn	L.A.	L	.252	.410	.301	94	139	18	35	5	1	5	22	10	23	1	0	.182	.258	.300	.444
V. Hayes	Phi.	L	.225	.285	.303	77	284	43	64	15	1	0	21	31	42	9	2	.267	.206	.179	.111
Howard	S.D.	B	.249	.356	.309	106	281	30	70	12	3	4	22	24	57	10	7	.286	.245	.286	.316
Hudler	St.L	R	.227	.309	.260	101	207	21	47	10	2	1	15	10	29	12	8	.252	.154	.298	.125
Javier	L.A.	B	.205	.284	.268	121	176	21	36	5	3	1	11	16	36	7	1	.247	.152	.167	.143
Johnson	NY-N	B	.259	.535	.342	156	564	108	146	34	4	38	117	78	120	30	16	.253	.262	.276	.239
Jones	Cin.	R	.292	.416	.304	52	89	14	26	1	2	2	6	2	31	2	1	.283	.302	.143	.286
Jose	St.L	B	.305	.438	.360	154	568	69	173	40	6	8	77	50	113	20	12	.298	.310	.343	.282
Justice	Atl.	L	.275	.503	.377	109	396	67	109	25	1	21	87	65	81	8	8	.277	.274	.347	.200
Kingery	S.F.	L	.182	.236	.280	91	110	13	20	2	2	0	8	15	21	1	0	.077	.196	.250	.056
Kruk	Phi.	L	.294	.483	.367	152	538	84	158	27	6	21	92	67	100	7	0	.297	.292	.275	.302
Leonard	S.F.	L	.240	.357	.306	63	129	14	31	7	1	2	14	12	25	0	1	.100	.252	.238	.130
Lindeman	Phi.	R	.337	.389	.413	65	95	13	32	5	0	0	12	13	14	0	1	.426	.176	.360	.429
Da. Martinez	Mon.	L	.295	.419	.332	124	396	47	117	18	5	7	42	20	54	16	7	.237	.314	.302	.313
McClendon	Pit.	R	.288	.460	.366	85	163	24	47	7	0	7	24	18	23	2	1	.350	.130	.250	.250
McGee	S.F.	B	.312	.408	.357	131	497	67	155	30	3	4	43	34	74	17	9	.338	.300	.343	.347
McReynolds	NY-N	R	.259	.416	.322	143	522	65	135	32	1	16	74	49	46	6	6	.259	.258	.308	.280
Miller	NY-N	B	.280	.411	.345	98	275	41	77	22	1	4	23	23	44	14	4	.247	.318	.345	.429
Mitchell	Atl.	R	.318	.409	.392	48	66	11	21	0	0	2	5	8	12	3	1	.345	.297	.273	.286
Morris	Phi.	L	.220	.276	.293	85	127	15	28	2	1	1	6	12	25	2	0	.333	.209	.217	.143
Murphy	Phi.	R	.252	.415	.309	153	544	66	137	33	1	18	81	48	93	1	0	.297	.227	.239	.264
Nixon	Atl.	B	.297	.327	.371	124	401	81	119	10	1	0	26	47	40	72	21	.305	.294	.312	.375
Noboa	Mon.	R	.242	.305	.250	67	95	5	23	3	0	1	2	1	8	2	3	.253	.188	.158	.111
O'Neill	Cin.	L	.256	.481	.346	152	532	71	136	36	0	28	91	73	107	12	7	.201	.281	.262	.276
Ortiz	Hou.	R	.277	.386	.381	47	83	7	23	4	1	1	5	14	14	0	0	.250	.314	.150	.200
Redus	Pit.	R	.246	.393	.324	98	252	45	62	12	2	7	24	28	39	17	3	.249	.241	.143	.200
Sasser	NY-N	L	.272	.417	.298	96	228	18	62	14	2	5	35	9	19	0	2	.172	.286	.367	.276
Simms	Hou.	R	.203	.317	.301	49	123	18	25	5	0	3	16	18	38	1	0	.212	.197	.212	.188
Dw. Smith	ChiN	L	.228	.347	.279	90	167	16	38	7	2	3	21	11	32	2	3	.000	.235	.350	.350
Strawberry	L.A.	L	.265	.491	.361	139	505	86	134	22	4	28	99	75	125	10	8	.276	.256	.285	.197
Thompson	St.L	R	.307	.442	.368	115	326	55	100	16	5	6	34	32	53	16	9	.216	.333	.221	.235
Varsho	Pit.	L	.273	.417	.344	99	187	23	51	11	2	4	23	19	34	9	2	.200	.275	.239	.286
Vatcher	S.D.	R	.200	.200	.333	17	20	3	4	0	0	0	2	4	6	1	0	.273	.111	.400	.250
Walker	ChiN	L	.257	.337	.315	124	374	51	96	10	1	6	34	33	57	13	5	.210	.278	.286	.130
Walker	Mon.	L	.290	.458	.349	137	487	59	141	30	2	16	64	42	102	14	9	.288	.291	.269	.217
Webster	L.A.	B	.222	.363	.296	94	171	21	38	8	5	2	19	18	52	0	1	.250	.195	.259	.222
Williams	Mon.	R	.271	.400	.311	34	70	11	19	5	2	0	1	3	22	2	1	.288	.222	.077	.000
Wood	S.F.	L	.120	.120	.185	10	25	0	3	0	0	0	1	2	11	0	0	.333	.091	.200	.000

M inor League Report

USA SNAPSHOTS®

A look at statistics that shape the sports world

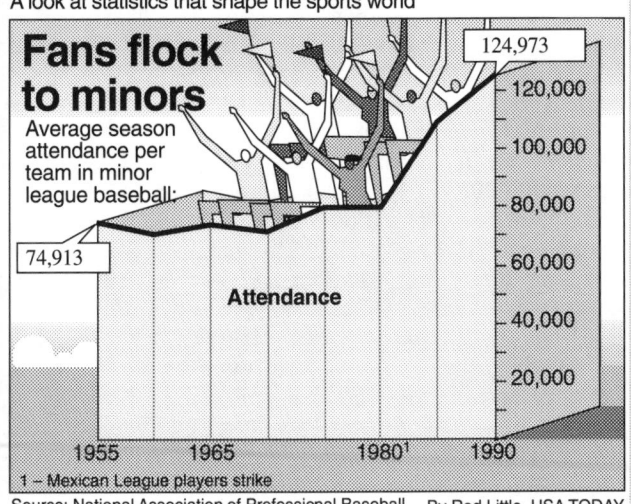

Fans flock to minors

Average season attendance per team in minor league baseball:

74,913

124,973

120,000

100,000

80,000

60,000

40,000

20,000

Attendance

1955   1965   1980¹   1990

1 – Mexican League players strike

Source: National Association of Professional Baseball   By Rod Little, USA TODAY

Minor leagues 1991: New rules, new clubs, new attendance marks

By Bill Koenig

The 1991 minor–league season began on a sour note, but ended with the sweet sound of turnstiles clicking. Many minor-league executives were upset about losing a lot of autonomy to the Major League commissioner's office under a new Professional Baseball Agreement signed in December 1990.

New guidelines were established for working agreements, TV money, player salaries, travel expenses, ballpark standards and the like. Without that agreement, minor league baseball as we know it could have disappeared, or so the major league owners threatened. They said they would handle their player development at their spring training sites and leave the owners of minor league clubs out to fend for themselves.

Unofficially, the face of the minor leagues is changing anyway. More and more of the best prospects are getting their fine-tuning at Class A . Class AAA, the last stop before the majors, still has prospects, but many of those rosters are now populated with more experienced players who can be emergency fill-ins when the major league team needs quick, short-term help.

Despite the initial acri-mony, the minors went on to draw 26,590,096 fans in 1991—the sixth-best figure of all time and a 5% increase over 1990.

No less than 12 leagues set attendance records. The American Association drew 4,093,525 fans, the most ever for any league in the USA. That broke the Pacific Coast League's mark of 4,008,432 set in 1947. The Mexican League holds the all-time mark of 4,591,286 in 1979.

Last season marked the first time that every full-season league drew at least 1 million fans. A total of 48 teams set individual club records. The Buffalo Bisons set a minor-league attendance record, drawing 1,188,972 to Pilot Field. Meanwhile, Salt Lake City became the first short-season team in history to draw 200,000.

On the field, the Los Angeles Dodgers farm system had the best cumulative record (424-323). That's a .566 winning percentage.

The Atlanta Braves were next at 429–333 (a .563 percentage). Rounding out the top five: Milwaukee .555, Montreal .552 and San Francisco .552.

The St. Louis Cardinals were last at .417. The only repeat minor-league champions were the Class AA Shreveport Captains, who won the Texas League title for the second consecutive year.

Other minor-league highlights:

▶Minor League Commissioner Sal Artiaga stepped down in January when his three-year term expired. Artiaga, 45, joined the National Association in 1982 and became its head in 1988 upon the death of John Johnson. A native of Albuquerque, N.M., he visited 115 of the 152 minor-league clubs during his tenure. He also oversaw the implementation of the new PBA.

"I was proud to play a small role in the renaissance of minor-league baseball," he said. "The appeal reached an all-time high. I was proud of the way the clubs presented baseball in their communities."

▶A young couple from Lyme Center, N.H.—Bill Craib, 27, and Sue Easler, 23—made news when they traveled to all 178 major- and minor-league ballparks. They are believed to be the first people to live out a fantasy dreamed by many.

Craib and Easler put 53,970 miles on their mini-van during their odyssey, which began in Oakland, April 9, and ended at Yankee Stadium, Oct. 6. To put the icing on the cake, they saw the playoffs and World Series as well.

They became folk

heroes in some cities, throwing out the first ball and signing autographs. They also filmed weekly highlights for ESPN's Baseball Magazine.

"I feel like we accomplished something," Craib said. "We didn't solve any of the world's problems, but we did what we set out to do."

They listed Pilot Field in Buffalo, Derks Field in Salt Lake City and Engel Stadium in Chattanooga among their favorite parks.

▶The 1991 season marked the end of the line for McCormick Field in Asheville, N.C. The stadium, which opened in 1924, was regarded as the oldest park in the minor leagues.

The wooden ballpark, currently the home of the Houston Astros' Class A South Atlantic League farm club, was replaced this season by a $2.5 million, 4,000-seat stadium

on the same site.

Another old park, Bowman Field in Williamsport, Pa., will be quiet in 1992. The New York Mets moved their Class AA club to Binghamton, N.Y., at the end of last season. The team will play in a newly constructed, 6,000-seat stadium.

▶Last season was the last year for the Triple-A Alliance, the four-year experiment that brought the International League and American Association together for an interlocking schedule and postseason playoff.

The American Association voted 8-0 to maintain the setup, but the International League voted 5-3 against it. Several IL clubs said they wanted more games against traditional rivals, especially the two New York farm teams (Columbus and Tidewater).

"I'm flabbergasted that

they walked away from such a successful arrangement," said Dale Owens, general manager of the American Association Louisville Redbirds.

▶There were two big All-Star Games in 1991. The National League beat the American League 6-5 in the Triple-A game before 20,725 in Louisville. Tucson's Gary Cooper provided the margin of victory with a two-run double in the eighth inning. The AL beat the NL 8-2 in the first Double-A game before 4,022 at Huntsville, Ala. Midland's Mark Howie homered and drove in four runs.

McCormick Field was the oldest park in the minor leagues.

Class AAA WRAP UPS

American Association

The Denver Zephyrs staged a furious comeback from a 10-game deficit on June 21 to win the Western Division title, then overcame a two-game deficit with three straight wins that brought them the league title. After that, it took just five games to take the best-of-seven Triple-A Classic from Columbus.

Denver outfielder Jim Olander hit .325 to win the league batting title and Most Valuable Player award. Oklahoma City's Dean Palmer (22), Steve Balboni (20) and Rob Maurer (20) ranked 1-2-3 in home runs, even though Palmer spent just 60 games in the minors. Denver first baseman Tim McIntosh won the RBI title with 91.

Buffalo right-hander Rick Reed was Most Valuable Pitcher. He led the league in victories (14-4) and ERA (2.15). Denver's Cal Eldred led with 168 strikeouts, while Iowa's Laddie Renfroe had 18 saves.

Denver's Tony Muser was Manager of the Year.

Final AAA Player Stats

American Association

Buffalo Bisons (Pirates)

BATTING	Avg.	AB	R	H	2B	3B	HR	RBI	SB
Jeff Banister, c	.244	234	23	57	7	1	2	21	1
Brian Dorsett, 1b	.272	103	17	28	6	0	2	18	0
Tommy Dunbar, of	.174	69	6	12	1	0	1	4	0
Cecil Espy, of	.312	398	69	124	27	10	2	43	22
Carlos Garcia, ss	.266	463	62	123	21	6	7	60	30
Scott Little, of	.242	165	22	40	5	3	0	18	3
Joey Meyer, 1b	.250	292	27	73	13	2	6	35	0
Keith Miller, of	.261	441	63	115	27	7	9	68	9
Armando Moreno, 2b	.226	221	39	50	11	2	5	30	2
Tom Prince, c	.208	221	29	46	8	3	6	32	3
Joe Redfield, 3b	.275	356	60	98	20	6	7	50	21
Jeff Richardson, 2b	.258	186	21	48	16	2	1	24	5
Jeff Schulz, of	.300	437	55	131	20	4	2	54	7
Greg Sparks, 1b	.180	128	13	23	7	0	3	16	1
Greg Tubbs, of	.273	373	71	102	18	11	3	34	34
John Wehner, 3b	.304	112	18	34	9	2	1	15	6
Eddie Zambrano, of	.340	144	19	49	8	5	3	35	1

PITCHING	W	L	ERA	G	SV	IP	H	BB	SO
Joe Ausanio	2	2	3.86	22	3	30.1	33	19	26
Kevin Blankenship	8	9	4.30	27	0	126.2	127	61	77
Marty Clary	5	8	4.31	40	1	100.1	108	36	42
Victor Cole	2	3	3.89	25	0	37	32	29	35
Steve Fireovid	9	8	2.90	34	3	130.1	127	43	72
Carl Hamilton	4	3	4.92	18	1	68.2	77	24	30
Roger Mason	9	5	3.08	34	0	123.2	115	44	80
Tim Meeks	4	8	3.89	36	1	143.1	146	31	66
Paul Miller	5	2	1.48	10	0	67	41	29	30
Blas Minor	2	2	5.75	17	0	36	46	15	25
Jeff Neely	2	5	4.63	42	7	58.1	67	27	45
Rick Reed	14	4	2.15	25	0	168.2	151	26	102
Rosario Rodriguez	4	3	3.00	48	8	51	38	31	43
Mike Roesler	5	4	3.56	33	8	48	46	21	33
Jim Tracy	2	2	5.17	11	0	47	61	10	20
Mike York	5	1	2.91	7	0	43.1	36	23	22

Denver Zephyrs (Brewers)

BATTING	Avg.	AB	R	H	2B	3B	HR	RBI	SB
Esteban Beltre, ss	.179	78	11	14	1	3	0	9	3
Mickey Brantley, of	.301	478	78	144	18	5	15	78	10
George Canale, 1b	.234	274	36	64	10	2	10	47	6
John Cangelosi, of	.294	303	69	89	8	3	3	25	26
Matias Carrillo, of	.276	421	56	116	18	5	8	56	11
Carmen Castillo, dh	.302	334	41	101	19	4	14	72	2
Sandy Guerrero, 3b	.282	216	29	61	11	4	4	32	2
Joe Kmak, c	.238	294	34	70	17	2	1	33	7
Dave Liddell, c	.270	89	15	24	4	1	1	13	0
Pat Listach, 2b	.252	286	51	72	10	4	1	31	23
Tim McIntosh, 1b	.292	462	69	135	19	9	18	91	2
Charlie Montoyo, ss	.239	394	68	94	13	1	12	45	15
Dave Nilsson, c	.232	95	10	22	8	0	1	14	1
Jim Olander, of	.325	498	89	162	32	10	9	78	14
Gus Polidor, ss	.272	103	8	28	2	1	0	5	0
Rolando Roomes, of	.164	61	9	10	0	3	0	2	0
D.L. Smith, 3b	.213	291	34	62	7	3	1	22	0
William Suero, 2b	.386	70	20	27	3	2	0	15	3

Denver Zephyrs (Brewers)

PITCHING	W	L	ERA	G	SV	IP	H	BB	SO
Jim Austin	6	3	2.45	20	3	44	35	24	37
Kevin Brown	4	3	4.67	12	0	62.2	71	34	31
Jim Davins	1	2	8.06	25	5	22.1	21	10	20
Cal Eldred	13	9	3.75	29	0	185	161	84	168
Narciso Elvira	04	5	96	18	0	80	100	40	52
Brian Fisher	10	6	4.78	44	2	98	98	39	66
Tim Fortugno	0	1	3.57	26	2	35.1	30	20	39
Chris George	4	5	2.33	43	4	85	74	26	65
Doug Henry	3	2	2.18	32	14	58.2	47	20	47
Manny Hernandez	1	1	.54	5	1	17.2	14	4	8
Jim Hunter	7	4	3.30	14	0	87.1	94	27	43
Mike Ignasiak	9	5	4.25	24	1	138.2	119	57	103
Jeff Kaiser	0	1	3.86	8	0	19.2	16	13	12
Mark Kiefer	9	5	4.62	17	0	101.1	104	41	68
Mark Knudson	4	4	5.40	13	1	52.2	73	13	28
Greg Mathews	6	3	3.86	13	0	61.2	62	27	25
Andy McGaffigan	0	2	3.58	33	7	65.1	72	26	45
Angel Miranda	0	1	6.17	11	2	12.2	10	17	14
Ed Puig	0	2	5.14	11	0	14	13	3	5

Indianapolis Indians (Expos)

BATTING	Avg.	AB	R	H	2B	3B	HR	RBI	SB
Bret Barberie, 3b	.312	218	45	68	10	4	10	48	10
Wil Cordero, ss	.261	360	48	94	16	4	11	52	8
Mike Davis, dh	.236	178	27	42	11	2	3	20	0
Alex Diaz, of	.243	370	48	90	14	4	1	21	16
Jerry Goff, c	.251	191	32	48	10	2	9	37	2
Todd Haney, 2b	.312	510	68	159	32	3	2	39	11
Steve Hecht, of	.243	210	34	51	8	2	4	26	9
Jimmy Kremers, c	.241	290	34	70	14	0	11	42	2
Quinn Mack, of	.272	416	35	113	19	8	5	49	4
Marlin McPhail, 3b	.273	319	40	87	23	2	7	38	1
Omer Munoz, ss	.283	92	7	26	2	0	0	12	0
Rich Renteria, 3b	.236	72	6	17	5	0	1	5	0
Nelson Santovenia, c	.263	194	23	51	7	1	6	26	0
Razor Shines, 1b	.251	471	61	118	28	0	7	60	2
David Stockstill, of	.240	50	9	12	3	1	3	11	0
John Vanderwal, of	.293	478	84	140	36	8	15	71	8

PITCHING	W	L	ERA	G	SV	IP	H	BB	SO
Brian Barnes	2	0	1.64	2	0	11	6	8	10
Kevin Bearse	0	2	3.15	12	0	34.1	33	10	17
Chris Bennett	1	0	7.94	6	0	11.1	12	1	5
Kent Bottenfield	8	15	4.06	29	0	166.1	155	61	108
Bret Davis	1	0	4.97	7	0	13.2	16	3	8
Eddie Dixon	6	7	2.91	53	5	118.2	120	30	63
Howard Farmer	6	4	3.86	20	0	105	93	37	67
Jeff Fassero	3	0	1.47	18	4	18.1	11	7	12
Steve Frey	3	1	1.51	30	3	36.2	25	15	45
Mark Gardner	2	0	3.48	6	0	31	26	16	38
Chris Haney	1	1	4.35	2	0	10.1	14	6	8
Bill Long	1	4	5.13	10	1	33.1	32	14	17
Chris Marchok	2	2	4.13	11	0	28.1	24	13	10
Dave Masters	4	6	6.04	27	1	70	82	63	64
Matt Maysey	3	6	5.14	12	0	63	60	33	45
Chris Myers	0	1	3.29	2	0	14.2	15	5	9
Chris Nabholz	2	2	1.86	4	0	19.1	13	5	16
Doug Piatt	6	4	3.45	44	13	47	40	27	61
Dana Ridenour	5	3	3.12	57	6	81.2	69	50	93
Mel Rojas	4	2	4.10	14	1	53.2	50	14	55
Bill Sampen	4	0	2.04	7	0	40.2	33	19	41
Scott Service	6	7	2.97	14	0	121.1	83	39	91
David Wainhouse	2	0	4.08	14	1	29.2	28	15	13
Darrin Winston	1	0	1.45	27	0	31	26	21	23

Class AAA WRAP UPS

International League

The Columbus Clippers won their seventh division title in 12 years, then completed a surprising three-game sweep against Pawtucket to win their fifth Governors' Cup. The Clippers lost to Denver in the Triple-A Classic.

The Clippers won despite sending a raft of quality players, including reliever Steve Howe, infielder Pat Kelly and outfielder Bernie Williams, to the parent New York Yankees.

Pawtucket enjoyed an amazing 18-game improvement over 1990 under Butch Hobson, who was named Manager of the Year and rewarded with a promotion to Fenway Park. Veteran Rick Lancellotti won the league title with 21 HRs.

Syracuse outfielder Derek Bell was named Most Valuable Player. He led the league in average (.346) and RBI (93), and had 13 homers.

Armando Reynoso of Richmond (10-6, 2.61) won the ERA title, while Pat Hentgen of Syracuse led the IL with 155 strikeouts. Mike Mussina of Rochester (10-4, 2.87) was Most Valuable Pitcher.

Class AAA WRAP UPS

Pacific Coast League

The Tucson Toros were 45-25 in the Southern Division the first half of the split season, but only 34-36 the second half. However, they got hot again in September, and beat Colorado Springs three games to one, and Calgary three games to two in the playoffs to win the PCL title.

Calgary first baseman Tino Martinez (.326-18-86) was named Most Valuable Player. Calgary shortstop Rich Amaral hit .346 to win the batting crown, with teammate Pat Lennon second at .329. Portland's Bernardo Brito and Colorado Springs's Luis Medina shared the home run crown with 27 each. Phoenix's Ted Wood (109) and Albuquerque's Eric Karros (101) ranked 1-2 in RBI.

Right-hander Gil Heredia of Phoenix was just 9-11, but won the ERA title at 2.82. Jeff Hartsock of Albuquerque nosed out Kyle Abbott of Edmonton 123-120 to win the strikeout title.

Tucson's Bob Skinner was Manager of the Year.

Iowa Cubs (Cubs)

BATTING	Avg.	AB	R	H	2B	3B	HR	RBI	SB
Jeff Baldwin, of	.210	62	5	13	2	0	1	8	0
Damon Berryhill, c	.330	97	20	32	4	1	8	24	0
Brad Bierley, of	.228	382	48	87	21	4	12	60	5
Dick Canan, of	.266	64	14	17	6	0	0	6	2
Steve Carter, of	.287	519	79	149	31	11	8	67	11
Brian Guinn, of	.236	343	46	81	11	2	4	32	10
Cedric Landrum, of	.336	131	14	44	8	2	1	11	13
Derrick May, of	.297	310	47	92	18	4	3	49	7
Russ McGinnis, 1b	.281	374	70	105	18	2	15	70	3
Erik Pappas, c	.275	284	41	78	19	1	7	48	5
Rey Sanchez, ss	.290	417	60	121	16	5	2	46	13
Gary Scott, 3b	.208	231	21	48	10	2	3	34	0
Craig Smajstrla, 2b	.278	385	55	107	17	5	3	38	7
Jeff Small, 2b	.295	122	11	36	8	1	0	11	2
Doug Strange, 3b	.293	509	76	149	35	5	8	56	10
Glenn Sullivan, 1b	.247	247	35	61	17	1	4	30	1
Rick Wilkins, c	.271	107	12	29	3	1	5	14	1

PITCHING	W	L	ERA	G	V	IP	H	BB	SO
Steve Adkins	4	4	5.14	13	0	63	57	32	48
Shawn Boskie	2	2	3.57	7	0	45.1	43	11	29
Jim Bullinger	3	4	5.40	8	0	47.2	47	23	30
Frank Castillo	3	1	2.52	4	0	25	20	7	20
Lance Dickson	4	4	3.11	18	0	101.1	85	57	101
Tom Filer	8	3	4.37	18	0	113.1	126	29	47
Joe Kraemer	8	7	4.60	20	0	119.1	127	48	77
Dave Lapoint	3	2	6.47	33	1	65.1	85	25	42
Scott May	4	4	2.97	57	10	94	75	54	93
Chuck Mount	1	2	5.40	10	0	23.1	29	18	15
Jose Nunez	12	9	4.58	28	0	165	157	87	118
Dave Pavlas	5	6	3.98	61	7	97.1	92	43	54
Laddie Renfroe	8	5	4.21	63	18	98.1	101	32	52
Dave Rosario	3	1	2.18	33	1	33	21	11	31
Bob Scanlan	2	0	2.95	4	0	18.1	14	10	15
Heathcliff Slocumb	1	0	4.05	12	1	13.1	10	6	9
Mike Sodders	2	4	6.69	16	0	38.2	48	18	33
Julio Strauss	1	0	.87	6	0	10.1	9	2	8
Rick Sutcliffe	1	2	9.69	3	0	13	23	6	8
Steve Wilson	3	8	3.87	25	0	114	102	45	83

Louisville Redbirds (Cardinals)

BATTING	Avg.	AB	R	H	2B	3B	HR	RBI	SB
Luis Alicea, 2b	.393	112	26	44	6	3	4	16	5
Rod Brewer, 1b	.225	382	39	86	21	1	8	52	4
Greg Carmona, ss	.175	143	16	25	2	1	2	10	7
Nick Castaneda, 1b	.271	140	24	38	11	1	3	18	0
Todd Crosby, 2b	.211	227	26	48	5	2	0	15	1
Joey Fernandez, 1b	.237	316	40	75	15	2	11	31	3
Bien Figueroa, ss	.204	269	18	55	8	2	0	14	1
Ed Fulton, c	.197	132	10	26	8	0	0	15	0
Tim Jones, ss	.256	305	34	78	9	1	5	29	19
Brian Jordan, of	.264	212	35	56	11	4	4	24	10
Lonnie Maclin, of	.287	327	35	94	12	2	4	37	19
Willie Magallanes, of	.224	116	10	26	4	1	1	6	0
Julian Martinez, of	.226	402	52	91	21	2	10	40	8
Jesus Mendez, of	.268	213	15	57	8	2	1	18	1
Scott Nichols, c	.222	54	9	12	1	1	3	8	1
Tom Nieto, c	.263	57	5	15	3	0	1	4	0
Don Prybylinski, c	.254	67	6	17	4	0	0	4	0
Mike Ross, of	.211	251	21	53	8	1	4	20	1
Stan Royer, 3b	.254	523	48	133	29	6	14	74	1
Ray Stephens, c	.279	165	16	46	7	0	7	28	0

PITCHING	W	L	ERA	G	SV	IP	H	BB	SO
Mark Clark	3	2	2.98	7	0	45.1	43	5	29
Stan Clarke	5	7	4.60	20	0	121.1	130	52	74
Fidel Compres	0	2	3.07	10	0	15.2	22	8	7
Rheal Cormier	7	9	4.23	21	0	128.2	140	31	74
John Corona	0	1	5.40	12	0	17.2	18	11	19
Bob Davidson	3	5	4.29	51	0	107	134	34	61
Mark Grater	3	5	2.02	58	12	80.1	68	33	53
Mike Hinkle	1	2	4.65	6	0	31	42	10	15
Mike Loynd	3	6	5.09	9	0	46	43	15	36
Mike Milchin	5	9	5.07	18	0	94	132	40	48
Jamie Moyer	5	10	3.80	20	0	126.2	125	43	69
Al Nipper	0	3	5.72	5	0	28.1	36	9	10
Omar Olivares	1	2	3.47	6	0	36.1	39	16	27
Dave Osteen	1	5	6.41	29	0	59	74	31	25
Mike Perez	3	5	6.13	37	4	47	54	25	38
Len Picota	3	6	5.83	28	0	88	112	51	42
Dave Richardson	1	0	7.15	13	1	23.2	29	16	8
Tim Sherrill	5	5	3.13	42	10	60.1	56	26	38

Nashville Sounds (Reds)

BATTING	Avg.	AB	R	H	2B	3B	HR	RBI	SB
Billy Bates, 2b	.242	165	22	40	3	3	3	15	1
Freddie Benavides, ss	.242	331	24	80	8	0	0	21	7
Jeff Branson, ss	.241	145	10	35	4	1	0	11	5
Adam Casillas, of	.275	422	44	116	17	3	5	52	3
Tony Defrancesco, c	.156	141	9	22	1	0	2	12	0
Leo Garcia, of	.244	450	49	110	12	5	9	37	17
Angel Gonzalez, 2b	.243	309	31	75	10	7	4	42	3
Denny Gonzalez, 3b	.289	242	41	70	17	1	9	38	3
Reggie Jefferson, 1b	.320	103	15	33	3	1	3	20	3
Stanley Jefferson, of	.244	78	10	19	4	3	2	5	2
Chris Jones, of	.243	267	29	65	5	4	9	33	10
Manny Jose, of	.224	67	5	15	1	0	0	2	5
Terry Lee, 1b	.304	437	70	133	21	4	15	67	12
Keith Lockhart, 3b	.260	411	53	107	25	3	8	36	3
Kevin Pearson, 3b	.240	229	23	55	13	1	0	19	3
Scott Pose, of	.192	52	7	10	0	0	0	3	3
Donnie Scott, c	.178	225	19	40	8	0	3	18	0
Glenn Sutko, c	.209	134	9	28	2	1	3	15	1
Todd Trafton, of	.285	263	37	75	16	1	9	41	1
PITCHING	W	L	ERA	G	SV	IP	H	BB	SO
Jose Alvarez	2	2	2.03	16	1	31	19	16	28
Jack Armstrong	2	0	2.65	6	0	37.1	31	5	28
Keith Brown	2	5	3.48	47	16	62	64	32	53
Steve Foster	2	3	2.14	41	12	55.2	46	29	52
Victor Garcia	2	0	2.63	15	0	24	15	14	12
Kip Gross	5	3	2.08	14	0	48.2	39	16	28
Milton Hill	3	3	2.94	37	3	67.1	59	15	62
Rodney Imes	3	7	6.30	25	0	86.2	103	49	49
Tim Layana	3	1	3.23	26	1	47.1	41	28	43
Rob Lopez	1	1	4.50	3	0	16	11	4	11
Gino Minutelli	4	7	1.90	13	0	80.1	57	35	64
Charlie Mitchell	6	9	4.17	35	0	108	110	33	61
Ross Powell	8	8	4.37	24	0	130.2	125	63	82
Tim Pugh	7	11	3.81	23	0	149.2	130	56	89
Bill Risley	3	5	4.91	8	0	44	45	26	32
Mo Sanford	3	0	1.60	5	0	34.2	19	22	38
Joe Turek	3	6	4.99	14	0	79.1	88	29	49
Luis Vasquez	1	2	5.12	8	0	39.2	40	29	15
Joey Vierra	5	4	4.33	62	2	96.2	81	43	84

Class AA WRAP UPS

Texas League

Shreveport capped an 86-50 regular season with its second consecutive playoff championship. The Captains were the first repeat winners since Jackson in 1984-85.

Midland third baseman Mark Howie won the batting title with a .364 average. El Paso catcher Dave Nilsson hit .418 before a subsequent promotion and injury, but didn't have enough plate appearances to qualify.

El Paso first baseman John Jaha had a fantastic year, hitting .344 with 30 home runs and 134 RBI. He was named Most Valuable Player. San Antonio second baseman Eric Young stole 71 bases.

Shreveport's Paul McClellan (11-1, 2.82) was Pitcher of the Year. Teammate Carter (9-8) won the ERA title at 2.95. Wichita's Frank Seminara (15-10) led the league in victories, while San Antonio knuckleballer Dennis Springer had a league-high 138 strikeouts.

Don Long of Midland was Manager of the Year.

Arkansas led in attendance with 265,268 fans, despite a last-place team.

Class AA WRAP UPS

Southern League

Like their parent club in Minnesota, the Orlando SunRays went from worst to first. They were last in the Eastern Division the first half, but won the second half with a 44-31 record. Then they knocked off Greenville in three straight games and Birmingham in four. It was their first title since 1981.

Greenville first baseman Ryan Klesko (.291-14-67) was named Most Valuable Player. Jacksonville first baseman Jim Bowie (.310) won the batting title and was the league's only .300 hitter. Charlotte first baseman Elvin Paulino led the league with 24 home runs and 81 RBI.

Orlando pitcher Pat Mahomes (8-5) had a league-leading 1.78 ERA, a shade better than Birmingham's Wilson Alvarez (10-6, 1.83). Greenville's Nap Robinson (16-6) led in victories, while Orlando's Mike Trombley was strikeout king with 175. Greenville reliever Mark Wohlers (21 saves) was named Outstanding Pitcher.

Charlotte drew 313,791 fans and landed a Triple-A expansion team for 1993. Birmingham was turned down in favor of Ottawa, Ontario, Canada.

Oklahoma City 89ers (Rangers)

BATTING	Avg.	AB	R	H	2B	3B	HR	RBI	SB
Steve Balboni, dh	.269	301	44	81	15	1	20	63	0
Kevin Belcher, of	.210	205	23	43	6	2	2	15	6
Mike Berger, of	.315	213	27	67	15	3	3	31	2
Nick Capra, of	.272	485	74	132	33	4	5	38	27
Jack Daugherty, of	.143	77	4	11	2	0	0	4	1
Monty Fariss, 2b	.271	494	84	134	31	9	13	73	4
Gary Green, ss	.218	308	36	67	4	2	2	30	1
Bill Haselman, c	.256	442	57	113	22	2	9	59	10
Chad Kreuter, c	.271	70	14	19	6	0	1	12	2
Rob Maurer, 1b	.301	459	76	138	41	3	20	77	2
Gar Millay, of	.233	257	38	60	12	1	6	27	1
Billy Moore, of	.220	123	16	27	11	0	5	16	0
Dean Palmer, 3b	.299	234	45	70	11	2	22	59	4
Dan Peltier, of	.229	345	38	79	16	4	3	31	6
Paul Postier, 3b	.242	219	22	53	4	0	1	20	1
Jim Presley, 3b	.271	207	30	56	10	2	6	29	1
Tony Scruggs, of	.203	182	19	37	4	0	3	21	4
PITCHING	W	L	ERA	G	SV	IP	H	BB	SO
Gerald Alexander	1	1	4.22	2	0	11.2	10	4	10
Brad Arnsberg	1	0	1.69	9	1	11.2	3	3	10
Jose Bautista	0	3	5.29	11	0	32.1	38	6	22
Joe Bitker	0	5	4.05	23	7	27.2	30	9	33
Brian Bohanon	0	4	2.91	7	0	46.1	49	15	37
Dan Boone	5	7	4.28	24	0	116.2	131	36	67
Jeff Bronkey	1	0	10.80	7	0	10	16	4	7
Jose Guzman	1	1	3.92	3	0	21.2	18	4	18
Drew Hall	1	3	6.75	23	0	32	34	27	17
Ray Hayward	3	3	4.88	19	1	48	59	21	27
Bill Laskey	3	5	4.40	31	2	47	50	30	33
Terry Mathews	5	5	3.49	18	1	95.1	98	34	63
Tony Menendez	5	5	5.20	21	0	116	107	62	82
Gary Mielke	2	1	9.74	10	0	20.1	34	6	14
Eric Nolte	1	3	5.91	25	1	56.1	74	31	41
Roger Pavlik	0	5	5.19	8	0	26	19	26	43
Steve Peters	3	3	5.57	24	0	32.1	43	19	28
Mark Petkovsek	9	8	4.93	25	0	150.2	162	38	67
Jim Poole	0	0	.00	10	3	12.1	4	1	14
Wayne Rosenthal	3	2	4.01	32	5	52.2	52	22	59
Calvin Schiraldi	1	2	5.64	18	0	30.1	32	23	24
Dave Schmidt	0	3	2.92	24	1	37	39	17	19
Dan Smith	4	17	5.52	28	0	152.2	195	75	85
Rich Thompson	0	2	6.51	16	0	28.2	47	11	16
Terry Wells	1	3	7.15	12	0	34	40	33	29

Omaha Royals (Royals)

BATTING	Avg.	AB	R	H	2B	3B	HR	RBI	SB
Sean Berry, 3b	.264	368	62	97	21	9	11	54	8
Jacob Brumfield, of	.267	397	62	106	14	7	3	43	36
Kevin Burrell, c	.227	211	22	48	10	1	4	17	1
Dave Clark, of	.301	359	45	108	24	3	13	64	6
Stu Cole, ss	.261	441	64	115	13	7	3	39	11
Jeff Conine, 1b	.257	171	23	44	9	1	3	15	0
Jeff Garber, 3b	.277	94	12	26	3	3	1	13	0
Bob Hamelin, dh	.189	127	13	24	3	1	4	19	0
Kevin Koslofski, of	.298	94	13	28	3	2	2	19	4
Jeffrey Leonard, dh	.244	258	28	63	9	1	10	50	1
Nelson Liriano, 2b	.274	292	50	80	16	9	2	36	6
Bobby Moore, of	.243	494	65	120	13	3	0	34	35
Russ Morman, 1b	.263	316	46	83	15	3	7	50	10
Jorge Pedre, c	.216	116	12	25	4	0	1	4	2
Harvey Pulliam, of	.257	346	35	89	18	2	6	39	2
Tim Spehr, c	.274	215	27	59	14	2	6	26	3
Andres Thomas, ss	.288	66	6	19	5	0	2	7	0
Paul Zuvella, ss	.269	219	28	59	14	1	1	20	3

PITCHING	W	L	ERA	G	SV	IP	H	BB	SO
Bob Buchanan	11	7	3.26	32	0	157.1	147	66	79
Don Carman	3	3	3.96	14	0	25	29	13	14
Scott Centala	6	9	3.58	18	0	101.2	109	37	64
Dera Clark	6	9	4.51	25	0	130.2	126	74	108
Mark Davis	4	1	2.02	6	0	36.2	27	9	36
Luis Encarnacion	3	3	3.76	50	4	93.1	77	41	65
Greg Everson	0	0	4.88	16	1	31.1	33	19	19
Wes Gardner	3	1	4.91	9	1	18.1	27	5	12
Mark Gubicza	2	1	3.31	3	0	16.1	20	4	12
Mark Huismann	6	5	3.16	45	17	68.1	70	18	50
Joel Johnston	4	7	5.21	47	8	74.1	60	42	63
Jim Lemasters	2	7	5.42	21	0	75.2	88	37	45
Mike Magnante	6	1	3.02	10	0	66.2	53	23	50
Carlos Maldonado	1	1	4.28	41	9	61	67	42	46
Dennis Moeller	7	3	3.22	14	0	78.1	70	40	51
Daryl Smith	4	5	3.39	23	0	93	82	33	94
Hector Wagner	5	6	3.44	17	0	86.1	88	38	36

International League

Columbus Clippers (Yankees)

BATTING	Avg.	AB	R	H	2B	3B	HR	RBI	SB
Keith Hughes, of	.271	424	64	115	18	8	8	66	6
Mike Humphreys, of	.283	413	71	117	23	5	9	53	34
Pat Kelly, 2b	.336	116	27	39	9	2	3	19	8
Jay Knoblauh, of	.309	94	16	29	4	1	3	19	2
Jim Leyritz, c	.267	270	50	72	24	1	11	48	1
Torey Lovullo, 3b	.271	395	74	107	24	5	10	75	4
Scott Lusader, of	.282	284	48	80	13	6	7	32	7
Jason Maas, dh	.352	71	16	25	6	1	1	6	6
John Ramos, c	.308	377	52	116	18	3	10	63	1
Carlos Rodriguez, ss	.255	212	32	54	9	3	0	21	1
Dave Sax, 1b	.285	270	45	77	19	2	8	54	1
Pat Sheridan, of	.271	70	15	19	3	2	2	12	2
Van Snider, 1b	.267	247	28	66	17	1	9	44	4
Don Sparks, 1b	.257	152	11	39	6	2	0	25	0
Andy Stankiewicz, 2b	.272	372	47	101	12	4	1	41	29
Jim Walewander, ss	.225	408	81	92	11	3	3	38	54
Bernie Williams, of	.294	306	52	90	14	6	8	37	9
Gerald Williams, of	.258	198	20	51	8	3	2	27	9
PITCHING	W	L	ERA	G	SV	IP	H	BB	SO
Steve Adkins	4	5	5.60	14	0	80.1	75	57	52
Daven Bond	4	8	5.70	32	1	85.1	103	41	52
Chuck Cary	5	3	5.72	8	0	46.2	44	26	28
Darrin Chapin	10	3	1.95	55	12	78.1	54	40	69
Royal Clayton	11	7	3.84	32	0	150	152	53	100
Andy Cook	5	5	3.52	13	0	79.1	63	38	40
Mike Draper	1	3	3.77	4	0	29.2	36	5	13
Dave Eiland	6	1	2.40	9	0	60	54	7	18
Victor Garcia	0	1	3.86	5	0	28	20	20	11
Steve Howe	2	1	.00	12	5	18	11	8	13
Jeff Johnson	4	0	2.61	10	0	62	58	25	40
Scott Kamieniecki	6	3	2.36	11	0	76.1	61	20	58
Alan Mills	7	5	4.43	38	8	114.2	109	75	77
Kevin Mmahat	3	3	3.58	12	0	65.1	54	34	59
Rich Monteleone	1	3	2.12	32	17	47.2	36	7	51
Hipolito Pena	1	0	8.38	6	0	10.2	11	9	7
Dave Rosario	4	0	2.11	29	2	47	30	20	34
Jerry Rub	3	2	3.44	44	1	52.1	42	30	51
Jeff Sellers	0	1	4.84	6	0	22.1	17	17	11
Don Stanford	3	3	4.01	15	0	34.2	30	15	14
Wade Taylor	4	1	3.54	9	0	61	59	22	36

Class AA WRAP UPS

Eastern League

The Harrisburg Senators took off in midseason, winning 26 of 32 games to win the regular-season crown with an 87-53 record. But it was the third-place Albany-Colonie Yankees who caught fire in the playoffs, sweeping Hagerstown and Harrisburg in three games each.

Matt Stairs, Harrisburg's Canadian-born second baseman, won the batting title with a .333 average and was named Most Valuable Player. Williamsport outfielder Jeromy Burnitz hit a league-leading 31 home runs and tied Albany's Vince Phillips for the RBI lead with 85.

Hagerstown left-hander Arthur Rhodes (7-4, 2.70, 115 strikeouts) was Pitcher of the Year. Jeff Mutis of Canton-Akron was 11-5 with a league-leading 1.80 ERA. Martel (13-6) led the EL with 141 strikeouts and tied Williamsport's Dave Telgheder (13-11) in victories.

Mike Quade from Harrisburg was Manager of the Year.

The New York Mets moved their Class AA franchise from Williamsport, Pa., to Binghamton, N.Y., after the season.

Class A WRAP UPS

California League

The High Desert Mavericks went 42-26 to win the second-half title in the Southern Division. Then they polished off Bakersfield in three straight games and Stockton in five to win the playoffs. Stockton had advanced to the finals by shocking San Jose in the Northern Division semis. San Jose had the best record in baseball at 92-44; Stockton was just 71-65 in the regular season.

High Desert swept most of the top offensive awards. Outfielder Matt Mieske won the batting title with a .341 average, drove in 119 runs and was named league Most Valuable Player. First baseman Jay Gainer led the league with 32 home runs and 120 RBI. Outfielder J.D. Noland stole 81 bases.

San Jose had the top pitching staff (2.67), led by Pitcher of the Year Rick Huisman. He led the league in victories (16-4), ERA (1.83) and strikeouts (216). Teammate Gary Sharko set a league record with 31 saves.

Ron Wotus of San Jose was Manager of the Year.

Pawtucket Red Sox (Red Sox)

BATTING	Avg.	AB	R	H	2B	3B	HR	RBI	SB
Luis Aguayo, 2b	.284	204	31	58	14	1	9	37	0
Tom Barrett, 2b	.269	331	42	89	15	1	0	27	8
Mike Brumley, 2b	.269	108	25	29	2	2	4	16	8
Scott Cooper, 3b	.277	483	55	134	21	2	15	72	3
Michael Dekneef, 2b	.188	16	3	3	0	0	0	0	0
John Flaherty, c	.186	156	18	29	7	0	3	13	0
Wayne Housie, of	.329	79	14	26	9	0	2	8	2
Rick Lancellotti, of	.209	330	43	69	15	1	21	64	1
Dave Milstien, 2b	.203	59	2	12	0	0	0	4	0
Jim Pankovits, 2b	.265	215	29	57	14	0	5	30	1
Mickey Pina, of	.208	298	40	62	11	1	8	33	2
Phil Plantier, of	.305	298	69	91	19	4	16	61	6
Todd Pratt, c	.292	219	27	64	16	0	11	41	0
Jeff Stone, of	.281	352	63	99	14	9	8	44	18
Mike Twardoski, 1b	.253	367	52	93	20	2	4	26	0
John Valentin, ss	.264	329	52	87	22	4	9	49	0
Mo Vaughn, 1b	.274	234	35	64	10	0	14	50	2
Eric Wedge, c	.233	163	24	38	14	1	5	18	1
Bob Zupcic, of	.240	429	70	103	27	1	18	70	10

PITCHING	W	L	ERA	G	SV	IP	H	BB	SO
Brian Conroy	6	4	4.58	17	0	98.1	95	51	66
Gar Finnvold	1	2	6.60	3	0	15	19	7	12
Tom Fischer	0	2	9.58	2	0	10.1	14	2	8
Mike Gardiner	7	1	2.34	8	0	58.2	39	11	42
Eric Hetzel	9	5	3.57	19	0	116	110	58	83
Peter Hoy	1	2	2.38	15	5	23.2	18	10	12
Daryl Irvine	1	1	3.00	27	17	33	27	13	19
Dana Kiecker	2	3	3.79	8	0	38	42	19	23
Derek Livernois	1	2	10.53	5	0	20.2	27	17	14
Josias Manzanillo	5	5	5.61	20	0	103.2	109	53	65
Kevin Morton	7	3	3.49	16	0	98	91	30	80
Dan O'Neill	5	7	5.30	55	1	70.2	76	44	54
Jeff Plympton	2	6	3.12	41	7	69.1	65	29	58
Paul Quantrill	10	7	4.45	25	0	156.2	169	30	75
Ken Ryan	1	0	4.91	9	1	18.1	15	11	14
Larry Shikles	8	4	3.88	41	3	128.2	130	34	74
Scott Taylor	3	3	3.46	7	0	39	32	17	35
Gene Walter	4	3	4.81	22	3	58	61	29	34
Dave Walters	5	3	3.07	48	12	85	83	30	48

Richmond Braves (Braves)

BATTING	Avg.	AB	R	H	2B	3B	HR	RBI	SB
John Alva, 2b	.287	129	16	37	3	0	3	17	2
Mike Bell, 1b	.249	341	37	85	12	2	5	29	2
Francisco Cabrera, 1b	.261	119	22	31	7	1	7	24	0
Rich Casarotti, 2b	.200	85	10	17	2	1	0	8	2
Vinny Castilla, ss	.225	240	25	54	7	4	7	36	1
Bruce Crabbe, of	.264	178	21	47	10	0	0	20	1
Bruce Fields, of	.225	111	9	25	5	0	0	8	0
Brian Hunter, of	.260	181	28	47	7	0	10	30	3
Mike Loggins, of	.165	91	7	15	0	0	0	6	3
Kelly Mann, c	.184	196	24	36	7	0	3	14	1
Al Martin, of	.278	151	20	42	11	1	5	18	11
Keith Mitchell, of	.326	95	16	31	6	1	2	17	0
Jerome Nelson, of	.288	215	34	62	6	6	0	18	10
Boi Rodriguez, 3b	.281	392	50	110	25	1	8	49	1
Rico Rossy, 2b	.257	482	58	124	25	1	2	48	4
Deion Sanders, of	.262	130	20	34	6	3	5	16	12
Joe Szekely, c	.260	227	24	59	10	1	3	30	1
Andy Tomberlin, of	.234	329	47	77	13	2	2	24	10
Jerry Willard, c	.300	277	42	83	24	0	8	39	1
Glenn Wilson, of	.270	100	13	27	4	0	2	15	1
Tracy Woodson, 3b	.277	441	43	122	20	3	6	56	1

PITCHING	W	L	ERA	G	SV	IP	H	BB	SO
Tony Castillo	5	6	2.90	23	0	118	89	32	78
Pat Gomez	2	9	4.39	16	0	82	99	41	41
Randy Kramer	3	3	2.80	11	0	64.1	60	24	26
Paul Marak	10	13	5.85	29	0	172.1	220	80	57
Tom McCarthy	4	6	4.24	21	0	85	80	34	51
Jeff Parrett	2	7	4.52	19	0	80.2	72	46	88
Yorkis Perez	12	3	3.79	36	1	107	99	53	102
Jeff Peterek	0	1	4.38	6	0	12.1	10	4	9
Dale Polley	2	3	3.26	50	4	66.1	70	30	38
Armando Reynoso	10	6	2.61	22	0	131	117	39	97
Rusty Richards	1	2	7.47	6	0	16.2	25	7	8
Mark Ross	3	6	3.50	39	9	82.1	84	13	50
Doug Sisk	0	0	1.59	9	0	11.1	14	4	2
Pete Smith	3	3	7.24	10	0	51	66	24	41
Randy St. Claire	6	2	1.19	29	2	68	39	11	60
Matt Turner	1	3	4.75	23	5	36	33	20	33
Randy Veres	0	2	5.04	9	0	25	32	10	12
Turk Wendell	0	2	3.43	3	0	21	20	16	18
Mark Wohlers	1	0	1.03	23	11	26.1	23	12	22

Rochester Red Wings (Orioles)

BATTING	Avg.	AB	R	H	2B	3B	HR	RBI	SB
Tony Chance, of	.251	355	61	89	14	3	14	55	4
Benny Distefano, 1b	.267	427	52	114	23	2	18	83	5
Tommy Dunbar, dh	.300	60	13	18	3	0	3	8	0
Mike Eberle, c	.178	90	8	16	2	0	0	5	0
Leo Gomez, 3b	.257	101	13	26	6	0	6	19	0
Ricky Gutierrez, ss	.306	157	23	48	5	3	0	15	4
Tyrone Kingwood, of	.312	138	20	43	8	2	1	18	12
Chito Martinez, of	.322	211	42	68	8	1	20	50	2
Oddibe McDowell, of	.231	264	31	61	13	2	4	22	12
Jeff McKnight, ss	.383	81	19	31	7	2	1	18	1
Mark McLemore, 2b	.281	228	32	64	11	4	1	28	12
Scott Meadows, of	.329	249	45	82	16	1	5	42	3
Luis Mercedes, of	.334	374	68	125	14	5	2	36	23
David Segui, 1b	.271	96	9	26	2	0	1	10	1
Tommy Shields, 3b	.289	412	69	119	18	3	6	52	16
Jeff Tackett, c	.236	433	64	102	18	2	6	50	3
Shane Turner, 2b	.282	404	49	114	13	2	1	57	6
Jack Voigt, of	.270	267	46	72	11	4	6	35	9
Jeffrey Wetherby, dh	.143	70	2	10	2	0	1	5	1
Craig Worthington, 3b	.298	57	10	17	4	0	2	9	0

PITCHING	W	L	ERA	G	SV	IP	H	BB	SO
Jeff Ballard	3	3	4.41	7	0	51	63	10	19
Jose Bautista	1	0	.59	6	1	15.1	8	3	7
Francisco Delarosa	4	1	2.67	38	3	84.1	71	33	61
Todd Frohwirth	1	3	3.65	20	8	25.2	17	5	15
Dave Johnson	0	1	4.15	2	0	13	18	5	8
Stacy Jones	4	4	3.38	33	8	51.2	53	20	47
Paul Kilgus	2	2	5.76	9	0	45.1	58	10	29
Richie Lewis	1	0	2.81	2	0	16	13	7	18
Mike Linskey	1	5	7.24	10	0	41	67	17	25
David Martinez	0	5	5.48	37	1	87	98	43	73
Jose Mesa	3	3	3.86	8	0	51.1	37	30	48
Mike Mussina	10	4	2.87	19	0	122.1	108	31	107
Chris Myers	8	7	4.49	23	0	118.1	141	44	57
Oswaldo Peraza	3	4	5.20	8	0	45	45	21	40
Jim Poole	3	2	2.79	27	9	29	29	9	25
Jeff Robinson	1	2	6.43	8	1	21	23	15	13
Israel Sanchez	6	2	3.42	24	2	95.2	94	33	74
Roy Smith	6	2	3.50	11	0	75.2	65	17	40
Anthony Telford	12	9	3.95	27	0	157.1	166	48	115
Rob Woodward	7	7	4.11	47	1	72.1	80	39	60

Class A WRAP UPS

Carolina League

The Cleveland Indians are off to a good start in rebuilding their farm system. Kinston went 89-49, won both halves in the Southern Division, then swept Lynchburg three straight to win the playoffs.

Indians' outfielder Tracy Sanders led the league with 18 home runs, while outfielder Brian Giles hit a solid .310. Right-hander Curtis Leskanic (15-8) led the league with 163 strikeouts and tied for the lead in victories. Sidearm reliever Mike Soper tied the minor-league record of 41 saves, set by Mike Perez in 1987.

Lynchburg outfielder Jeff McNeely hit .322 to win the batting title by four points over Salem's Paul List. Winston-Salem third baseman Pete Castellano drove in a league-high 88 runs and was named Most Valuable Player.

Prince William's Sam Militello (12-2, 1.22) was Pitcher of the Year. Lynchburg's Tim Smith (2.16) nosed out Durham's Scott Taylor (2.18) for the ERA title, while Winston-Salem's Ryan Hawblitzel had a great all-around year (15-2, 2.28, 103 strikeouts).

Brian Graham of Kinston was Manager of the Year.

Class A WRAP UPS

Midwest League

The Clinton Giants rode pitching—and plenty of it—to the Midwest League championship. They posted a sparkling 2.75 team ERA en route to an 81-58 record and a pair of playoffs sweeps against Burlington and Madison.

Most Valuable Player Salomon Torres led the way with a 16-5 record, league-leading 1.41 ERA and league-high 214 strikeouts. He won two more games in the play-offs. Teammate Dan Carlson was 16-7, while Rod Huffman had 35 saves.

Two Kenosha players shared the Triple Crown. Outfielder Midre Cummings won the batting title with a .322 average, while third baseman Paul Russo had a league-high 20 home runs and 100 RBI. Spring-field second baseman Mateo Ozuna led the league with 78 stolen bases.

The Kane County Cougars, based in Geneva, Ill., entered the league and won the Northern Division sec-ond-half title. After the season, the Angels changed their name to the River Bandits.

Gary Jones of Madison was Manager of the Year.

Scranton/WB Red Barons (Phillies)

BATTING	Avg.	AB	R	H	2B	3B	HR	RBI	SB
Gary Alexander, 1b	.239	209	31	50	9	0	17	48	1
Kim Batiste, ss	.292	462	54	135	25	6	1	41	18
Sil Campusano, of	.262	305	44	80	12	1	8	47	9
Braulio Castillo, of	.350	60	14	21	9	1	0	15	2
Wes Chamberlain, of	.257	144	12	37	7	2	2	20	7
Darrin Fletcher, c	.284	306	39	87	13	1	8	50	1
Jeff Grotewold, 1b	.257	276	33	71	13	5	5	38	0
Dave Hollins, 3b	.266	229	37	61	11	6	8	35	4
Chris Knabenshue, of	.200	35	3	7	2	0	0	8	1
Greg Legg, 3b	.290	352	58	102	15	4	3	41	4
Tony Longmire, of	.261	111	11	29	3	2	0	9	4
Louie Meadows, of	.210	186	23	39	9	3	4	16	2
Mickey Morandini, 2b	.261	46	7	12	4	0	1	9	2
Julio Peguero, of	.273	506	71	138	20	9	2	39	21
Steve Scarsone, 2b	.274	405	52	111	20	6	6	38	10
Rick Schu, 1b	.321	355	69	114	30	5	14	57	7
Gary Tremblay, c	.245	147	18	36	7	0	3	16	1
Scott Wade, of	.262	309	48	81	14	7	9	43	4
PITCHING	W	L	ERA	G	SV	IP	H	BB	SO
Darrel Akerfelds	3	3	6.32	11	0	53.2	52	39	36
Andy Ashby	11	11	3.46	26	0	161.1	144	60	113
Bob Ayrault	8	5	4.83	68	3	99.2	91	47	103
Jay Baller	4	4	4.98	61	17	72.1	84	33	79
Kevin Bearse	1	1	5.79	6	0	23.1	30	12	14
Cliff Brantley	2	4	3.80	8	0	47.1	44	25	28
John Burgos	1	3	2.95	24	0	64	54	29	32
Amalio Carreno	4	8	5.33	33	0	81	88	26	52
Pat Combs	2	2	6.67	6	0	27	39	16	14
Rocky Elli	1	0	4.26	18	0	19	23	20	13
Jason Grimsley	2	3	4.35	9	0	52.2	48	37	43
Ken Howell	2	0	5.11	6	0	25.2	30	16	20
Chuck Malone	0	3	17.31	5	0	13	16	32	9
Tim Mauser	6	11	3.72	26	1	128.1	119	55	75
Steve Ontiveros	2	1	2.90	7	0	31	29	10	21
Pat Perry	2	4	3.98	36	4	54.1	60	21	36
Wally Ritchie	1	0	2.42	7	2	26	17	7	25
Bruce Ruffin	4	5	4.66	13	0	75.1	82	41	50
Mark Sims	4	3	2.91	45	2	65	61	33	38
Gary Wilson	3	7	4.92	40	0	104.1	121	45	46

Syracuse Chiefs (Blue Jays)

BATTING	Avg.	AB	R	H	2B	3B	HR	RBI	SB
Derek Bell, of	.346	457	89	158	22	12	13	93	27
Rob Ducey, of	.293	266	53	78	10	3	8	40	5
Bruce Fields, dh	.251	259	28	65	10	0	2	21	1
Steve Jeltz, ss	.188	224	26	42	6	3	1	26	5
Shawn Jeter, of	.264	242	36	64	15	1	3	26	5
Randy Knorr, c	.260	342	29	89	20	0	5	44	1
Mike Maksudian, c	.330	97	13	32	6	3	1	13	0
Domingo Martinez, 1b	.313	467	61	146	16	2	17	83	6
Julius McDougal, dh	.253	182	26	46	9	3	1	11	1
Stu Pederson, of	.263	373	49	98	20	2	8	54	3
Marty Pevey, c	.280	193	24	54	8	2	3	23	1
Tom Quinlan, 3b	.240	466	56	112	24	6	10	49	9
Jerry Schunk, 2b	.248	327	34	81	9	0	5	29	0
Cory Snyder, of	.269	67	11	18	3	0	6	17	0
Ed Sprague, c	.364	88	24	32	8	0	5	25	2
William Suero, 2b	.198	393	49	78	18	1	1	28	17
Turner Ward, of	.330	218	40	72	11	3	7	32	9
Eddie Zosky, ss	.264	511	69	135	18	4	6	39	9

PITCHING	W	L	ERA	G	SV	IP	H	BB	SO
Doug Bair	0	1	2.50	13	0	18	21	7	21
Pete Blohm	2	5	4.71	37	2	99.1	96	43	45
Denis Boucher	2	1	3.18	8	0	57.2	57	19	28
Ken Dayley	0	1	9.64	10	1	14	26	11	13
Willie Fraser	0	1	3.68	7	1	15.2	12	6	12
Don Gordon	2	2	1.69	26	1	48	48	9	29
Juan Guzman	4	5	4.03	12	0	67	46	42	67
Pat Hentgen	8	9	4.47	31	0	171	146	90	155
Guillermo Hernandez	1	1	4.22	8	0	11.2	10	4	9
Doug Linton	10	12	5.01	30	0	162.2	181	56	93
Ravelo Manzanillo	3	0	3.42	12	1	24.2	26	14	20
Alex Sanchez	1	4	10.29	14	1	28	33	35	12
John Shea	12	10	4.55	35	2	172	198	78	76
Efrain Valdez	3	2	5.36	21	0	44.2	50	25	30
Steve Wapnick	6	3	2.76	53	20	72.2	68	25	58
Mickey Weston	12	6	3.74	27	0	166	193	36	60
Woody Williams	3	4	4.12	31	6	55.2	52	27	37
Frank Wills	3	5	4.84	22	1	61.1	71	21	38

Tidewater Tides (Mets)

BATTING	Avg.	AB	R	H	2B	3B	HR	RBI	SB
Kevin Baez, ss	.171	210	18	36	8	0	0	13	0
Tim Bogar, ss	.257	218	23	56	11	0	1	23	1
Chuck Carr, of	.195	246	34	48	6	1	1	11	27
Chris Donnels, 3b	.303	287	45	87	18	2	8	56	1
D.J. Dozier, of	.269	171	19	46	7	5	1	22	8
Jeff Gardner, 2b	.292	504	73	147	23	4	1	56	6
Terrel Hansen, of	.272	368	54	100	19	2	12	62	0
Todd Hundley, c	.273	454	62	124	24	4	14	66	1
Al Jimenez, 1b	.208	331	36	69	9	1	4	32	0
Tim Leiper, 3b	.252	282	33	71	11	1	2	30	0
Lee May, of	.257	113	16	29	6	5	0	8	5
Terry McDaniel, of	.248	399	63	99	23	6	9	42	17
Orlando Mercado, c	.270	159	13	43	12	0	4	26	0
Al Pedrique, 3b	.269	182	24	49	6	0	0	12	2
Jaime Roseboro, of	.294	279	34	82	12	0	2	29	0
Kelvin Torve, 1b	.274	336	57	92	20	2	9	49	4
PITCHING	W	L	ERA	G	SV	IP	H	BB	SO
Blaine Beatty	12	9	4.11	28	0	175.1	192	43	74
Terry Bross	2	0	4.36	27	2	33	31	32	23
Doug Cinnella	2	2	2.51	12	0	29.2	26	15	15
Mark Dewey	12	3	3.34	48	9	65.2	61	36	38
Sid Fernandez	1	0	1.15	3	0	16.2	9	6	22
Manny Hernandez	1	2	8.03	3	0	12.1	17	8	4
Eric Hillman	5	12	4.01	27	0	162.2	184	58	91
Brad Moore	8	5	3.33	50	13	78.1	73	45	53
Dale Plummer	4	3	3.99	46	3	97	95	32	33
Rich Sauveur	2	2	2.38	42	6	45.1	31	23	49
Dan Schatzeder	0	0	7.36	9	0	15.2	22	13	10
Pete Schourek	1	1	2.52	4	0	25	18	10	17
Ray Soff	8	7	3.52	28	0	138	118	48	84
Dave Trautwein	0	0	6.35	12	1	17	22	13	5
Julio Valera	10	10	3.83	26	0	176.1	152	70	117
Anthony Young	7	9	3.73	25	0	164	172	67	93

Toledo Mud Hens (Tigers)

BATTING	Avg.	AB	R	H	2B	3B	HR	RBI	SB
Karl Allaire, ss	.262	385	57	101	20	4	3	34	4
Skeeter Barnes, of	.330	233	48	77	14	0	9	40	27
Arnie Beyeler, ss	.174	69	14	12	2	0	0	2	0
Rico Brogna, 1b	.220	132	13	29	5	1	2	13	2
Phil Clark, of	.254	362	47	92	13	4	4	45	6
Dean Decillis, dh	.308	143	20	44	7	0	2	18	3
Luis Delossantos, 1b	.284	141	12	40	8	0	2	22	0
Curt Ford, of	.268	366	52	98	24	4	3	38	8
Shawn Hare, of	.310	252	44	78	18	2	9	42	1
Randy Kutcher, of	.232	237	26	55	11	1	3	28	0
Scott Livingstone, 3b	.302	331	48	100	13	3	3	62	2
Mitch Lyden, dh	.224	340	34	76	11	2	18	55	0

Class A WRAP UPS

New York–Penn League

The Montreal Expos' farm system had a great year with three playoff champions and another regular-season first-place finish. Nobody had an easier time of it than the Jamestown Expos. They won the NY-Penn League Stedler Division by 14 games, then polished off Erie and Pittsfield in the playoffs. Reliever Heath Haynes (10-1, 11 saves) figured in all three post-season games with a victory and two saves.

There was a tie for the league batting title between Erie second baseman Rick Juday and St. Catharine's outfielder Rob Butler. Each hit .338. Butler won the Kinsella Award as the league's Rookie of the Year.

Elmira's Felix Colon and Geneva's Ozzie Timmons shared the home-run crown with 12 each. Jamestown's Mike Daniel won the RBI title outright with 62. Auburn's James Mouton stole 60 bases.

The top pitchers were Jamestown's Brian Looney (7-1, 1.16) and Utica's Mike Call (6-1, 1.26). Erie's Mike Lynch led with 102 strikeouts.

Ed Creech of Jamestown was Manager of the Year.

Class A WRAP UPS

Northwest League

Good pitching once again stopped good hitting as Boise beat Yakima in two straight games to win the Northwest League championship. Boise had the top pitching staff (3.21) in the league, while Yakima was the top hitting team (.271).

The Hawks' Julian Heredia was the league's premier pitcher with an 8-1 record, 1.05 ERA and 99 strikeouts in 77 innings. He picked up a save in the playoffs.

Southern Oregon outfielder Mike Neill hit .350 and won the batting title by three points over Everett's Matt Brewer. Bend designated hitter Leon Glenn led the league with 15 home runs, while Yakima first baseman Murph Proctor had a league-high 61 RBI.

Eugene third baseman Joe Randa was named Most Valuable Player. He was third in average (.338), second in homers (11) and second in RBI (59). Yakima's Vern Spearman stole 56 bases.

Eugene's Tom Poquette was Manager of the Year.

Toledo (continued)

BATTING	Avg.	AB	R	H	2B	3B	HR	RBI	SB
Eric Mangham, of	.241	378	60	91	12	1	4	35	29
Johnny Paredes, 2b	.284	514	82	146	25	6	1	53	36
Steve Pegues, of	.225	222	21	50	13	3	4	23	8
Victor Rosario, ss	.300	423	59	127	21	12	1	48	12
Rich Rowland, c	.272	383	56	104	25	0	13	68	4

PITCHING	W	L	ERA	G	SV	IP	H	BB	SO
Scott Aldred	8	8	3.92	22	1	135.1	127	72	95
Steve Cummings	5	5	4.68	30	5	75	72	29	41
Mike Dalton	3	3	4.13	39	4	65.1	72	24	28
John Desilva	5	4	4.60	11	0	59.2	62	21	56
Dan Gakeler	2	3	3.50	23	4	44.2	44	13	32
Greg Gohr	10	8	4.61	26	0	148.1	125	66	96
Buddy Groom	2	5	4.32	24	1	75	73	25	49
David Haas	8	10	5.23	28	0	158.1	187	77	133
Jeff Kaiser	3	0	2.08	16	1	35.2	35	11	28
John Kiely	4	2	2.13	42	6	72	57	35	60
Kurt Knudsen	1	2	1.47	12	0	18.1	13	10	28
Rusty Meacham	9	7	3.09	26	2	125.1	117	40	70
Mike Munoz	2	3	3.83	38	8	54	44	35	38
Ron Rightnowar	1	1	3.94	23	3	30.2	30	15	5
Kevin Ritz	8	7	3.28	20	0	126.1	116	60	105
Don Vesling	1	0	5.48	12	0	23	28	19	20

Pacific Coast League

Albuquerque Dukes (Dodgers)

BATTING	Avg.	AB	R	H	2B	3B	HR	RBI	SB
Billy Bean, of	.297	259	35	77	22	6	2	35	7
Rafael Bournigal, ss	.293	215	34	63	5	5	0	29	4
Jerry Brooks, of	.294	429	64	126	20	7	13	82	4
Butch Davis, of	.313	284	55	89	19	10	7	44	12
Tom Goodwin, of	.273	509	84	139	19	4	1	45	48
Dave Hansen, 3b	.303	254	42	77	11	1	5	40	4
Bert Heffernan, c	.242	161	17	39	10	1	0	13	1
Carlos Hernandez, c	.345	345	60	119	24	2	8	44	5
Eric Karros, 1b	.316	488	88	154	33	8	22	101	3
Luis Martinez, 3b	.282	170	20	48	11	1	0	13	1
Jose Munoz, 2b	.326	389	49	127	18	4	0	65	15
Jose Offerman, ss	.298	289	58	86	8	4	0	29	32
Henry Rodriguez, of	.271	446	61	121	22	5	10	67	4
Greg Smith, 2b	.217	161	25	35	3	2	0	17	11

PITCHING	W	L	ERA	G	SV	IP	H	BB	SO
Mike Christopher	7	2	2.44	63	16	77.1	73	30	67
Dennis Cook	7	3	3.63	14	0	92.2	73	32	84
Jeff Hartsock	12	6	3.80	29	0	154	153	78	123
Brian Holton	7	7	3.87	29	0	107	121	19	77
Mike James	1	3	6.60	13	0	45	51	30	39
Chris Jones	4	1	4.97	29	0	54.1	68	23	23
David Lynch	1	3	6.63	33	0	37.2	51	26	29
Pedro Martinez	3	3	3.66	6	0	39.1	28	16	35
Jamie McAndrew	12	10	5.04	28	1	155.1	167	76	91
Jim Neidlinger	7	7	4.75	23	0	131.2	165	39	80
Dan Opperman	5	4	5.95	11	0	59	74	34	32
Zak Shinall	2	0	3.07	29	1	41	48	10	22
Dave Veres	7	6	4.47	57	5	101.2	89	52	81
Terry Wells	1	0	4.78	29	0	32	29	25	29
John Wetteland	4	3	2.79	41	20	61.1	48	26	55

Calgary Cannons (Mariners)

BATTING	Avg.	AB	R	H	2B	3B	HR	RBI	SB
Rich Amaral, ss	.346	347	79	120	26	2	3	36	30
Mike Blowers, 3b	.289	329	56	95	20	2	9	59	3
Jim Bowie, 1b	.340	50	9	17	3	0	1	7	0
Dave Brundage, of	.310	365	75	113	23	3	3	32	7
Dave Cochrane, c	.321	190	25	61	11	0	3	37	2
Alan Cockrell, of	.290	435	77	126	27	2	11	81	7
Dennis Hood, of	.178	314	52	56	9	2	11	42	18
Chris Howard, c	.246	293	32	72	12	1	8	36	1
Chuck Jackson, 2b	.285	488	80	139	28	5	15	85	2
Pat Lennon, of	.329	416	75	137	29	5	15	74	12
Tino Martinez, 1b	.326	442	94	144	34	5	18	86	3
Alonzo Powell, of	.375	192	45	72	18	7	7	43	2
Matt Sinatro, c	.260	131	13	34	8	0	3	19	1
Jack Smith, ss	.272	202	26	55	14	1	9	41	2
Steve Springer, 2b	.257	412	62	106	25	2	17	70	8

PITCHING	W	L	ERA	G	SV	IP	H	BB	SO
Rick Balabon	6	6	6.41	17	0	87	109	43	42
Shawn Barton	2	0	2.61	17	1	31	25	8	22
Dave Burba	6	4	3.53	23	4	71.1	82	27	42
Keith Comstock	3	1	3.28	15	2	36.2	25	16	38
Mike Cook	2	4	9.68	10	0	31.2	45	24	18
Gary Eave	3	6	5.52	21	0	93	120	50	39
Dave Fleming	2	0	1.13	3	0	16	11	3	16
Brian Givens	1	0	4.91	3	0	15.2	16	6	8
Gene Harris	4	0	3.34	25	4	35	37	11	23
Keith Helton	4	7	6.46	30	0	110	148	51	55
Calvin Jones	1	1	3.91	20	7	23	19	19	25
Randy Kramer	4	4	5.86	16	0	66	87	25	24
Vance Lovelace	0	2	7.58	13	0	19	21	22	6
Brian Meyer	2	3	4.01	18	1	34.2	39	10	10
Jeff Nelson	3	4	3.90	28	7	32.1	39	15	26
Dennis Powell	9	8	4.15	27	0	174.2	200	59	96
Pat Rice	13	4	5.03	21	0	122.2	138	37	59
Dave Richards	0	2	7.63	10	0	15.1	27	13	13
Ricky Rojas	0	0	9.10	16	0	30.2	54	14	19
Roger Salkeld	2	1	5.12	4	0	19.1	18	13	21
Ed Vandeberg	5	3	4.26	47	0	70.2	71	24	37
Ed Vosberg	0	3	6.87	28	2	38	57	17	29

Colo. Springs Sky Sox (Indians)

BATTING	Avg.	AB	R	H	2B	3B	HR	RBI	SB
Mike Aldrete, of	.289	76	4	22	5	0	0	8	0
Beau Allred, of	.250	148	39	37	12	3	6	21	1
Albert Belle, of	.328	61	9	20	3	2	2	16	1
Geronimo Berroa, of	.322	478	81	154	31	7	18	91	2
Marty Brown, 3b	.301	396	65	119	24	2	15	69	3
Kevin Burdick, 2b	.235	132	24	31	6	0	2	17	3
Carlos Diaz, c	.237	93	7	22	4	0	0	7	0
Jose Escobar, ss	.204	93	12	19	5	1	0	11	0
Reggie Jefferson, 1b	.309	136	29	42	11	0	3	21	0
Stan Jefferson, of	.284	74	11	21	2	1	2	9	3
Brian Johnson, c	.340	53	13	18	4	0	2	3	0
Wayne Kirby, of	.294	385	66	113	14	4	1	39	29
Mark Lewis, ss	.279	179	29	50	10	3	2	31	2
Luis Lopez, 1b	.347	176	29	61	11	4	1	31	0
Ever Magallanes, 2b	.285	305	37	87	13	1	1	33	1
Jeff Manto, 3b	.320	153	36	49	16	0	6	36	1
Luis Medina, dh	.324	450	81	146	28	6	27	98	0
John Moses, of	.295	298	58	88	18	3	3	31	11
Keith Smith, ss	.317	205	28	65	10	0	4	31	1

Class A WRAP UPS

South Atlantic League

Columbia pitcher Jose Martinez became the second 20-game winner in league history, posting a 20-4 record with a 1.49 ERA and 158 strikeouts. He added another win in the playoffs as the Mets swept Macon and Charleston (W.Va.) for the league crown.

Columbia third baseman Butch Huskey led the league with 26 home runs and 99 RBI, while teammate Kyle Washington won the batting title with a .343 average. Greensboro catcher Kiki Hernandez (.332-15-78) was named Most Valuable Player.

Three players stole 60 or more bases: Savannah's Terry Bradshaw (64), Macon's Lee Heath (61) and Charleston (S.C.) star Ray McDavid (60).

Wheelers' pitcher John Roper led the league with 189 strikeouts. Savannah's John Kelly had a league-leading 30 saves. Other top pitching years were turned in by Macon's Joe Roa (13-3, 2.11) and Greensboro's Rafael Quirico (12-8, 2.26).

Asheville's McCormick Field, the oldest ballpark in the minors, is being replaced in 1992 by a new $2.5 million stadium bearing the same name.

Dave Miley of Charleston (W.Va.) was Manager of the Year.

Class A WRAP UPS

Florida State League

The West Palm Beach Expos finished the job they started in 1990. Two years ago, they had the best record in baseball, but were upset in the league playoffs.

Last year, the Expos snuck into the playoffs as a wild card, then beat Vero Beach, Lakeland and Clearwater to win their first championship since 1974. They won despite a .218 team batting average.

Dunedin outfielder Robert Perez hit .302 and nipped teammate Nigel Wilson by one point to win the batting crown. Sarasota's Scott Cepicky was the league Most Valuable Player and won the RBI title with 76.

Port Charlotte's Jose Oliva and Fort Lauderdale's Rey Noriega shared the home-run lead with 14 apiece. Kerwin Moore of Baseball City stole 61 bases.

Bill Wengert of Vero Beach was 7-6 but had the top ERA of 2.06. Tom Michno of the Miami Miracle led with 190 strikeouts.

The independent Miracle again played its home games in Pompano Beach, Fla.

St. Petersburg drew 155,946 fans for the attendance crown.

Colo. Springs (continued)

BATTING	Avg.	AB	R	H	2B	3B	HR	RBI	SB
Eddie Taubensee, c	.310	287	53	89	23	3	13	39	0
Jim Thome, 3b	.285	151	20	43	7	3	2	28	0
Turner Ward, of	.196	51	5	10	1	1	1	3	2
Roberto Zambrano, of	.297	91	12	27	2	2	3	14	0
PITCHING	W	L	ERA	G	SV	IP	H	BB	SO
Eric Bell	2	1	2.13	4	0	25.1	23	11	16
Jeff Bittiger	9	12	3.90	27	0	148.2	158	83	93
Willie Blair	9	6	4.99	26	4	114.2	130	30	57
Denis Boucher	1	0	5.02	3	0	14.1	14	2	9
Jim Bruske	4	0	2.45	7	2	26.2	19	8	13
Steve Cummings	0	4	6.08	5	0	27.2	36	6	15
Mike Curtis	2	4	3.83	20	1	45.2	43	23	32
Bruce Egloff	1	2	3.38	15	2	29.1	31	13	17
Mauro Gozzo	10	6	5.25	25	1	130.1	143	68	81
Drew Hall	1	0	1.86	5	0	10.2	6	6	8
Grady Hall	1	5	5.57	22	1	73.2	97	45	37
Ricky Horton	3	2	6.67	22	1	27	37	7	18
Doug Jones	2	2	3.28	17	7	36.2	30	5	29
Eric King	1	0	9.53	3	0	11.1	18	5	3
Tom Kramer	1	0	.79	10	4	11.1	5	5	18
Steve Olin	3	2	4.47	22	6	44.1	45	10	36
Dave Otto	5	6	4.75	17	0	95.2	110	43	62
Greg Roscoe	2	1	5.74	3	0	16.2	20	9	6
Rudy Seanez	0	0	7.27	16	0	17.1	17	22	19
Jeff Shaw	6	3	4.64	12	0	76.2	77	25	55
Efrain Valdez	3	1	3.82	14	1	31.2	26	13	25
Sergio Valdez	4	12	4.11	26	0	131.1	139	27	71
Colby Ward	2	1	4.50	28	2	48	56	28	33
Kevin Wickander	1	0	2.31	12	2	12.2	9	5	10
Mike York	0	1	5.88	5	0	26	40	16	13

Edmonton Trappers (Angels)

BATTING	Avg.	AB	R	H	2B	3B	HR	RBI	SB
Ruben Amaro, of	.326	472	95	154	42	6	3	42	36
Kent Anderson, 2b	.210	271	30	57	9	2	2	26	6
Chris Cron, 1b	.293	461	74	135	21	1	22	91	6
Chad Curtis, 3b	.316	431	81	136	28	7	9	61	46
Doug Davis, c	.274	113	12	31	4	0	3	18	1
Kevin Davis, 2b	.237	118	14	28	7	2	2	20	2
Mark Davis, of	.278	424	86	118	20	6	13	58	32
Gary Disarcina, ss	.310	390	61	121	21	4	4	58	16
Dan Grunhard, of	.267	326	62	87	19	2	9	45	12
Barry Lyons, c	.309	165	15	51	13	0	2	23	0
John Orton, c	.224	245	39	55	14	1	5	32	5
Reed Peters, of	.266	207	32	55	13	1	1	19	10
Bobby Rose, 3b	.298	242	35	72	14	5	6	55	3
Lee Stevens, of	.314	481	75	151	29	3	19	96	3
Ron Tingley, c	.291	55	11	16	5	0	3	15	1
PITCHING	W	L	ERA	G	SV	IP	H	BB	SO
Kyle Abbott	14	10	3.99	27	0	180.1	173	46	120
Chris Beasley	3	5	5.26	23	1	89	99	26	51
Hector Berrios	3	1	3.86	17	1	16.1	15	8	12
Gary Buckels	5	3	4.18	51	7	56	66	20	34
Tim Burcham	7	7	4.98	31	5	137.1	161	57	70
Sherm Corbett	4	3	3.92	41	6	62	58	33	34
Mike Erb	1	0	3.76	31	5	41.2	40	23	26
Mike Fetters	2	7	4.87	11	0	61	65	26	43
Joe Grahe	9	3	4.01	14	0	94.1	121	30	55
Dave Leiper	1	0	7.64	13	1	18.2	30	5	8
Scott Lewis	3	9	4.50	17	0	110	132	26	87
Rafael Montalvo	1	0	6.84	25	2	26.1	39	12	15

PITCHING	W	L	ERA	G	SV	IP	H	BB	SO
John Pawlowski	0	0	3.97	10	1	1.1	16	3	10
Fred Toliver	7	4	4.15	18	0	95.1	89	49	68
Fernando Valenzuela	3	3	7.12	7	0	37.2	48	17	36
Cliff Young	4	8	4.90	34	5	72.2	88	25	39
Mark Zappelli	2	1	4.44	17	0	24.1	24	19	16

Las Vegas Stars (Padres)

BATTING	Avg.	AB	R	H	2B	3B	HR	RBI	SB
Oscar Azocar, of	.296	361	51	107	23	3	7	50	4
Dann Bilardello, c	.314	140	17	44	13	1	4	29	2
Scott Coolbaugh, 3b	.287	209	29	60	9	2	7	29	2
Edgar Diaz, ss	.232	56	6	13	0	1	0	4	1
Brian Dorsett, c	.307	215	36	66	13	1	13	38	0
Paul Faries, ss	.307	75	16	23	2	1	1	12	7
Kevin Higgins, 1b	.288	403	53	116	12	4	3	45	3
Thomas Howard, of	.309	94	22	29	3	1	2	16	11
Chris Jelic, ph	.275	91	23	25	5	1	3	23	1
Dean Kelley, 2b	.253	221	33	56	13	3	1	24	6
Tom Lampkin, c	.317	164	25	52	11	1	2	29	2
Jose Mota, 2b	.289	377	56	109	10	2	1	37	15
Ed Romero, ss	.284	74	16	21	4	0	1	14	1
Craig Shipley, ss	.300	230	27	69	9	5	5	34	2
Dave Staton, 1b	.267	375	61	100	19	1	22	74	1
Will Taylor, of	.259	468	82	121	11	5	4	33	62
Jim Vatcher, of	.266	395	67	105	28	6	17	67	4
Dan Walters, c	.317	293	39	93	22	0	4	44	0
Kevin Ward, of	.322	276	51	89	17	6	6	43	10

PITCHING	W	L	ERA	G	SV	IP	H	BB	SO
Ricky Bones	8	6	4.22	23	0	136.1	155	43	95
Pat Clements	0	0	8.25	11	0	12	15	5	4
John Costello	1	2	2.15	17	3	29.1	31	7	24
Terry Gilmore	2	7	6.90	26	0	73	128	17	52
Atlee Hammaker	0	0	6.46	3	0	15.1	21	3	9
Greg Harris	1	2	7.40	4	0	21.2	24	8	16
Jeremy Hernandez	4	8	4.74	56	13	68.1	76	25	67
Reese Lambert	1	0	3.86	11	0	28	24	12	21
Jim Lewis	6	3	3.38	48	3	85.1	93	34	76
Derek Lilliquist	4	6	5.38	33	2	105.1	142	33	89
Randy McCament	2	1	6.85	30	0	47.1	61	19	15
Jose Melendez	7	0	3.99	9	0	59.2	54	11	45
Adam Peterson	2	2	4.50	8	0	42	41	20	37
Joe Price	2	1	2.19	26	1	25.2	16	15	24
Dennis Rasmussen	1	3	5.47	5	0	26.1	23	15	12
Steve Rosenberg	2	4	7.54	36	0	68	95	26	61
A.J. Sager	7	5	4.71	18	0	109	127	20	61
Tim Scott	8	8	5.19	41	0	111	133	39	74
Roger Smithberg	3	7	6.61	17	0	79	112	33	34
Rafael Valdez	0	2	5.94	5	0	17.2	22	16	9
Brian Wood	3	8	5.48	47	2	69	73	39	68

Phoenix Firebirds (Giants)

BATTING	Avg.	AB	R	H	2B	3B	HR	RBI	SB
Rich Aldrete, 1b	.302	215	29	65	10	0	0	18	0
Mark Bailey, c	.301	186	33	56	16	1	6	36	1
Mike Benjamin, ss	.204	226	34	46	13	2	6	31	3
Jeff Carter, 2b	.272	246	47	67	5	2	2	24	11
Craig Colbert, c	.246	142	9	35	6	2	2	13	0
Darnell Coles, 3b	.290	328	43	95	23	2	6	65	0
Steve Decker, c	.252	111	20	28	5	1	6	14	0
Mark Leonard, of	.253	146	27	37	7	0	8	25	1
Darren Lewis, of	.340	315	63	107	12	10	2	52	32
Kirt Manwaring, c	.222	81	8	18	0	0	4	14	0

Rookie League WRAP UPS

Appalachian League

The Braves' 1991 success didn't stop in Atlanta. The organization's farm system posted the second-best winning percentage in baseball— .563 to the Los Angeles Dodgers' .566. That winning feeling stretched all the way down to short-season Pulaski, which swept Burlington 6-0 and 3-2 to win the Appalachian League championship.

Pulaski led the league in victories (45), shutouts (8) and strikeouts (628). Right-hander Kevin Lomon was 6-0 with a 0.61 ERA, but didn't have enough innings to qualify for league leaders.

Burlington outfielder Manny Ramirez, a first-round draft pick by Cleveland, was Most Valuable Player. He hit .326 and led the league with 19 home runs and 63 RBI. Kingsport's Ricky Otero (.345) and Quilvio Veras (.336) finished 1-2 in the batting race.

Martinsville's Joel Gilmore (1.53) won the ERA title over Johnson City's Steve Jones (1.61) and Kingsport's Jason Jacome (1.63). Elizabethton's Eddie Guardado (8-4, 1.86) led the league with 106 strikeouts while walking just 31.

Elizabethton's Ray Smith was Manager of the Year.

Rookie League WRAP UPS

Arizona League

The Arizona Rookie League was a hitter's league (no team's ERA was under 4.25), but when the smoke cleared, the Athletics were on top by five games. They earned the championship as there are no playoffs in the league.

The Athletics' top hitters were Juan Cabrera (.340) and Luinis Aracena (.335). Pitcher Keith Millay was 6-1 with a 3.43 ERA.

The Brewers' Michael Stefanski hit .369 to win the batting title. The Cardinals' Steve Cerio just missed the Triple Crown. He was second to Stefanski with a .360 average and first with nine home runs and 47 RBI. Brewers' outfielder Howard House (.332-6-45) was named Most Valuable Player.

The top pitcher was the Mariners' George Glinatsis (10-2, 2.19, 80 strikeouts). He led the league in wins, ERA and strikeouts. Cardinal Troy Koneman had a league-high 16 strikeouts.

Dick Scott of the Athletics was Manager of the Year.

Phoenix (continued)

BATTING	Avg.	AB	R	H	2B	3B	HR	RBI	SB
Jim McNamara, c	.170	53	3	9	1	0	0	2	0
Rick Parker, of	.300	297	41	89	10	9	6	41	16
Dave Patterson, 3b	.314	169	23	53	8	2	2	22	5
Tony Perezchica, 3b	.293	191	41	56	10	4	8	34	1
Gregg Ritchie, of	.287	157	23	45	8	0	0	16	13
Andres Santana, 2b	.316	456	84	144	7	5	1	35	45
Jim Wilson, 1b	.300	433	62	130	30	0	21	78	5
Ted Wood, of	.311	512	90	159	38	6	11	109	12

PITCHING	W	L	ERA	G	SV	IP	H	BB	SO
Johnny Ard	3	5	5.78	10	0	62.1	76	33	30
Rod Beck	4	3	2.02	23	6	71.1	56	13	35
Mark Dewey	1	2	3.97	10	4	11.1	16	7	4
Eric Gunderson	7	6	6.14	40	3	107	153	44	53
Gil Heredia	9	11	2.82	33	1	140.1	155	28	75
Bryan Hickerson	1	1	3.80	12	2	21.1	29	5	21
Dave Masters	1	2	6.46	8	0	31.2	34	17	28
Paul McClellan	2	2	2.82	5	0	38.1	27	21	18
Craig McMurtry	10	6	4.38	27	0	113	117	44	67
Rafael Novoa	6	6	5.96	17	0	94.2	135	37	46
Francisco Oliveras	2	0	2.45	3	0	18.1	18	7	12
Dan Rambo	0	1	4.61	3	0	14.2	18	6	10
Steve Reed	2	3	4.31	41	6	56.1	62	12	46
Mike Remlinger	5	5	6.38	19	0	109.2	134	59	68
Jose Segura	5	5	3.43	32	4	39.1	46	17	21
Stuart Tate	0	0	4.50	8	0	18	20	11	6
Mark Thurmond	0	3	3.42	26	2	24.2	29	12	15
Randy Veres	3	0	3.56	19	1	43	42	14	41
Jimmy Williams	7	9	5.96	30	0	160	192	93	69

Portland Beavers (Twins)

BATTING	Avg.	AB	R	H	2B	3B	HR	RBI	SB
Bernardo Brito, dh	.259	428	65	111	17	2	27	83	1
Jarvis Brown, of	.289	436	62	126	5	8	3	37	26
J.T. Bruett, of	.284	345	51	98	6	3	0	35	21
Chip Hale, 2b	.241	352	45	85	16	3	1	37	3
Barry Jones, of	.264	296	42	78	17	4	5	40	9
Terry Jorgensen, 3b	.298	456	74	136	29	0	11	59	1
Pedro Munoz, of	.316	212	33	67	19	2	5	28	9
Ed Naveda, of	.269	245	42	66	10	2	7	32	6
Jeff Reboulet, ss	.248	391	50	97	27	3	3	46	5
Victor Rodriguez, 2b	.304	270	36	82	17	0	6	32	0
Rolando Roomes, of	.235	136	21	32	4	3	4	25	5
Danny Sheaffer, c	.303	330	46	100	14	2	1	43	2
Paul Sorrento, 1b	.308	409	59	126	30	2	13	79	1
Lenny Webster, c	.252	325	43	82	18	0	7	34	1

PITCHING	W	L	ERA	G	SV	IP	H	BB	SO
Paul Abbott	2	3	3.89	8	0	44.	36	28	40
Allan Anderson	4	1	3.06	5	0	32.1	33	7	16
Willie Banks	9	8	4.55	25	0	146.1	156	76	63
Larry Casian	3	2	3.46	34	2	52	51	16	24
Tim Drummond	5	8	4.65	56	7	79.1	87	32	45
Tom Edens	10	7	3.01	25	0	161.1	145	62	100
Richard Garces	0	1	4.85	10	3	13	10	8	13
Pat Mahomes	3	5	3.44	9	0	55	50	36	41
Denny Neagle	9	4	3.27	19	0	105.2	101	32	94
Jack Savage	2	4	6.56	38	1	60.1	77	38	45
Charles Scott	3	6	3.83	18	1	80	75	30	59
George Tsamis	10	8	3.27	29	0	168.2	183	66	71
Rob Wassenaar	4	4	3.26	40	5	77.1	75	25	62
Gary Wayne	4	5	2.79	51	8	68.2	63	31	66
David West	1	1	6.32	4	0	16.2	12	12	15

PITCHING	W	L	ERA	G	SV	IP	H	BB	SO
Carl Willis	1	1	1.64	3	0	11	5	0	0

Tacoma Tigers (Athletics)

BATTING	Avg.	AB	R	H	2B	3B	HR	RBI	SB
Troy Afenir, c	.244	262	35	64	12	3	10	38	0
Lance Blankenship, ss	.294	109	19	32	7	0	1	11	9
Mike Bordick, ss	.272	81	15	22	4	1	2	14	0
Jorge Brito, c	.233	73	6	17	2	0	1	3	0
Scott Brosius, 3b	.286	245	28	70	16	3	8	31	4
Pete Coachman, 2b	.271	306	64	83	16	1	2	36	16
Ron Correia, 3b	.250	56	9	14	0	0	1	7	0
Eric Fox, of	.270	522	85	141	24	8	4	52	17
Webster Garrison, ss	.215	237	28	51	11	2	2	28	4
Scott Hemond, 2b	.272	327	50	89	19	5	3	31	11
Dann Howitt, of	.267	449	58	120	28	6	14	73	5
Doug Jennings, of	.268	332	43	89	17	2	3	44	5
Brad Komminsk, of	.293	270	38	79	15	4	5	43	11
Vance Law, 3b	.200	65	7	13	1	0	0	6	0
Troy Neel, of	.237	59	7	14	3	1	0	7	0
Gus Polidor, ss	.297	182	22	54	8	4	0	14	0
Nelson Simmons, dh	.272	427	48	116	18	2	8	67	0
Wil Tejada, c	.186	59	7	11	1	2	0	6	0
Ron Witmeyer, 1b	.262	431	64	113	18	4	15	80	2
PITCHING	W	L	ERA	G	SV	IP	H	BB	SO
Dana Allison	3	1	4.37	18	0	23.2	25	11	13
John Briscoe	3	5	3.66	22	1	76.1	73	44	66
Todd Burns	0	2	5.33	13	2	25.1	30	7	24
Kevin Campbell	9	2	1.80	35	2	75	53	35	56
Kirk Dressendorfer	1	3	10.88	8	0	24	31	20	19
Dan Eskew	0	3	9.91	7	0	26.1	46	19	23
Apolinar Garcia	0	4	10.92	7	0	30.2	49	20	12
Johnny Guzman	2	5	6.78	17	0	80.2	113	51	40
Reggie Harris	5	4	4.99	16	0	83	83	58	72
Gary Mielke	1	0	5.93	10	0	14.2	14	9	6
Jeff Musselman	5	9	5.79	25	0	138.1	176	69	81
Clay Parker	7	6	3.67	25	0	132.1	123	44	78
Jeff Pico	4	8	3.00	45	4	75	82	29	50
Will Schock	6	7	5.74	16	0	89.1	102	30	41
Eric Show	3	2	2.68	8	0	40.1	36	9	27
Joe Slusarski	4	2	2.72	7	0	46.1	42	10	25
Bruce Walton	1	1	1.35	38	20	47.2	39	5	49
Weston Weber	2	0	1.99	15	1	32.2	28	7	15
Pat Wernig	7	8	4.91	39	2	99	99	51	48

Tucson Toros (Astros)

BATTING	Avg.	AB	R	H	2B	3B	HR	RBI	SB
Eric Anthony, of	.336	318	57	107	22	2	9	63	11
Doug Baker, 3b	.183	164	17	30	1	2	1	15	0
Andujar Cedeno, ss	.303	347	49	105	19	6	7	55	5
Carlo Colombino, 3b	.273	198	38	54	12	1	1	25	0
Gary Cooper, 3b	.305	406	86	124	25	6	14	75	7
Kenny Lofton, of	.308	545	93	168	19	17	2	50	40
John Massarelli, c	.268	127	19	34	7	1	0	16	10
Terry McGriff, c	.288	146	18	42	15	1	0	24	0
Andy Mota, 2b	.299	462	65	138	19	4	2	46	14
Rob Nelson, 1b	.249	361	40	90	17	2	16	62	1
Carl Nichols, c	.215	121	13	26	4	1	3	17	0
Javier Ortiz, of	.323	127	20	41	13	0	3	22	0
Karl Rhodes, of	.260	308	45	80	17	1	1	46	5

Rookie League WRAP UPS

Pioneer League

What a year they had in Salt Lake City! Not only did the Trappers post a 49-21 record and beat Great Falls in the play-offs to win the champi-onship, they also drew 200,599 fans—a record for any short-season league.

Even though they could have had a working agreement under the new Professional Baseball Agreement, the Trappers elected to remain inde-pendent for the seventh consecutive year.

Outfielder Rick Hirten-steiner hit .356 with a league-leading 11 home runs and 71 RBI. (His contract was purchased by Montreal after the playoffs.) Helena's Andy Fairman hit .373 to win the batting title by two points over Idaho Falls' Dario Paulino.

Salt Lake had the top two pitchers in John Gilligan (6-1, 1.71) and Mark Stephens (6-3, 2.43). Stephens won the strikeout crown with 89.

P.J. Carey of Billings was Manager of the Year.

Rookie League WRAP UPS

Gulf Coast League

The Expos had the toughest dogfight in the Gulf Coast League, but enjoyed the last laugh. They won the tight Central Division, where four teams were separated by a mere game and a half. Familiar with the pressure, they beat the Red Sox and then the Orioles in the playoffs to win the league championship. They joined West Palm Beach and Jamestown as championship teams in the rich Montreal farm system.

Dodgers' outfielder Angel Dotel hit .400 (48-for-120) to win the batting crown by a large margin over Luis Ortiz of the Red Sox (.333) and Jason Wuerch of the Yankees (.333).

Orioles outfielder Duane Thomas was the home run champion with 10, while Pirates first baseman Joe Calder led with 45 RBI. Yankees outfielder Abdiel Cumberbatch had great speed to go with a great name. He stole 44 bases.

The Dodgers' Young Chul Sohn was 7-0 with a 1.27 ERA, but he was beaten out for the ERA title by the Orioles' Ihosvany Marquez (1.12). The Royals' Michael Bovee led the league with 76 strikeouts.

The Orioles' Ed Napoleon was Manager of the Year.

1992 BASEBALL WEEKLY ALMANAC

Tucson (continued)

BATTING	Avg.	AB	R	H	2B	3B	HR	RBI	SB
Dave Rohde, ss	.372	253	36	94	10	4	1	40	15
Scott Servais, c	.324	219	34	71	12	0	2	27	0
Mike Simms, of	.246	297	53	73	20	2	15	59	2
Jose Tolentino, 1b	.290	303	44	88	24	5	6	51	2
Gerald Young, of	.304	79	14	24	2	3	0	17	3

PITCHING	W	L	ERA	G	SV	IP	H	BB	SO
Harold Allen	0	2	19.50	5	0	12	25	22	6
Ryan Bowen	5	5	4.38	18	0	99.2	114	56	78
Mike Capel	4	2	2.40	30	3	56.1	49	17	44
Rocky Childress	0	1	6.92	7	0	13	21	2	6
Terry Clark	14	7	4.66	26	0	164	200	37	97
Dean Freeland	1	3	6.42	22	0	41.2	63	25	30
Dean Hartgraves	3	0	3.09	16	0	44.2	47	20	18
Randy Hennis	4	0	3.36	11	0	62.2	69	31	41
Butch Henry	10	11	4.80	27	0	154.2	192	42	97
Xavier Hernandez	2	1	2.75	16	4	36	35	9	34
Blaise Ilsley	8	6	4.27	46	0	86.1	105	27	52
Jeff Juden	3	2	3.18	10	0	57.2	56	25	51
Rob Mallicoat	4	4	5.48	19	1	48.2	43	38	32
Curt Schilling	0	1	3.42	13	3	24.2	16	12	21
Calvin Schiraldi	3	2	4.47	15	0	54.1	62	21	49
Bob Sebra	4	2	3.75	30	4	60	64	32	52
Lee Tunnell	5	3	3.84	20	0	73.2	78	27	41
Matt Turner	1	1	4.15	13	1	26	27	14	25
Dean Wilkins	8	7	4.20	65	20	84.2	84	43	65
Brian Williams	0	1	4.93	7	0	38.1	39	22	29

Vancouver Canadians (White Sox)

BATTING	Avg.	AB	R	H	2B	3B	HR	RBI	SB
Esteban Beltre, ss	.271	347	48	94	11	3	0	30	8
Cesar Bernhardt, 2b	.260	323	40	84	10	5	1	30	12
Kurt Brown, c	.248	274	22	68	12	2	4	27	2
John Cangelosi, of	.245	102	15	25	1	0	0	10	9
Joe Hall, 3b	.248	427	41	106	16	1	4	39	11
Danny Heep, of	.243	70	2	17	6	0	0	10	1
Dan Henley, ss	.195	190	30	37	5	1	1	13	0
Orsino Hill, of	.288	347	39	100	14	1	4	45	4
Shawn Jeter, of	.299	144	24	43	5	1	1	13	4
Ron Kittle, 1b	.310	71	9	22	4	1	4	21	1
Derek Lee, of	.295	319	54	94	28	5	6	44	4
Allen Liebert, c	.235	51	3	12	3	0	1	7	0
Norberto Martin, 2b	.278	338	39	94	9	0	0	20	11
Rod McCray, of	.230	222	37	51	9	5	0	13	14
Warren Newson, of	.369	111	19	41	12	1	2	19	5
Sammy Sosa, of	.267	116	19	31	7	2	3	19	9
Matt Stark, 1b	.284	394	47	112	21	1	10	68	0
Aubrey Waggoner, of	.205	156	23	32	4	4	1	10	5
Don Wakamatsu, c	.198	172	20	34	8	0	4	19	0

PITCHING	W	L	ERA	G	SV	IP	H	BB	SO
Mario Brito	0	10	7.12	19	0	78.1	106	25	41
Jeff Carter	3	7	3.05	41	4	80.2	78	35	40
Brian Drahman	2	3	4.44	22	12	24.1	21	13	17
Tom Drees	8	8	3.52	22	0	143	130	62	89
Mike Dunne	2	2	5.40	17	2	55	66	19	21
Wayne Edwards	3	9	6.26	14	0	65.2	73	37	35
Ramon Garcia	2	2	4.05	4	0	27.2	24	7	17
Curt Hasler	0	2	7.81	11	0	28.2	44	16	17
Roberto Hernandez	4	1	3.22	7	0	45.2	41	23	40

PITCHING	W	L	ERA	G	SV	IP	H	BB	SO
Bo Kennedy	3	4	7.85	17	0	37.2	56	29	25
Jerry Kutzler	5	10	5.06	29	0	158.1	199	62	64
Greg Perschke	7	12	4.65	27	0	176	170	62	98
Rich Scheid	6	7	6.08	47	3	67.2	65	33	57
Ron Stephens	3	4	3.42	53	4	105.1	103	58	58

Final AA Player Stats

Eastern League

Albany-Colonie Yankees (Yankees)

BATTING	Avg.	AB	R	H	2B	3B	HR	RBI	SB
Brad Ausmus, c	.266	229	36	61	9	2	1	29	14
Richard Barnwell, of	.263	19	4	5	0	0	0	0	2
Juan Blackwell, 2b	.195	41	6	8	2	0	0	1	0
Russ Davis, 3b	.218	473	57	103	23	3	8	58	3
Bobby Dejardin, 2b	.295	482	74	142	21	0	2	53	18
Brian Johnson, c	.000	8	0	0	0	0	0	0	0
Jay Knoblauh, of	.284	335	52	95	16	2	11	50	16
Jeff Livesey, c	.230	61	5	14	1	0	2	6	0
Billy Masse, of	.295	356	67	105	17	2	11	61	10
Vince Phillips, of	.274	482	71	132	26	1	8	85	12
John Quintell, c	.107	28	0	3	0	0	0	0	0
Dave Silvestri, ss	.262	512	97	134	31	8	19	83	20
Andy Skeels, c	.254	197	25	50	9	0	2	26	0
J.T. Snow, 1b	.279	477	78	133	33	3	13	76	5
John Toale, c	.000	2	0	0	0	0	0	1	0
Hector Vargas, dh	.278	345	49	96	16	3	1	39	23
John Viera, of	.266	308	52	82	11	4	5	40	12
Joey Wardlow, 2b	.133	15	1	2	1	0	0	1	0
Gerald Williams, of	.286	175	28	50	15	0	5	32	18
PITCHING	W	L	ERA	G	SV	IP	H	BB	SO
Jim Blueberg	3	2	3.18	8	0	45.1	43	21	37
Andy Cook	6	3	3.95	14	0	82	94	27	46
Mike Draper	10	6	3.29	36	2	131.1	125	47	71
Victor Garcia	5	5	3.85	18	0	110	94	61	80
Mike Gardella	4	5	3.82	53	11	78.2	70	55	76
Cullen Hartzog	6	6	5.80	18	0	90	100	55	64
Scott Holcomb	4	1	1.41	26	1	32	20	22	28
Ramon Manon	0	2	7.56	3	0	17.2	17	9	16
Mark Marris	2	2	4.35	8	1	31	35	9	17
Ed Martel	13	6	2.81	25	0	163.1	129	55	141
Sam Militello	2	2	2.35	7	0	46	40	19	55
Tom Newell	1	0	4.73	8	1	13.1	14	12	13
Jerry Nielsen	0	1	5.63	6	0	8	9	8	5
Pascual Perez	0	0	1.69	2	0	5.1	5	1	6
Tom Popplewell	4	10	4.40	52	3	86	81	83	63
Jerry Rub	1	0	2.45	10	0	11	7	7	17
Willie Smith	7	7	4.15	21	0	108.1	99	72	104
Russ Springer	1	0	1.80	2	0	15	9	6	16
Don Stanford	5	3	4.50	40	0	68	68	31	42
Larry Stanford	2	3	1.89	52	24	62	41	36	61
Mike Witt	0	0	9.00	1	0	2	2	2	2

Class AAA Directory

American Association

Buffalo Bisons (Pirates)
Pilot Field (capacity 19,500)

Denver Zephyrs (Brewers)
Mile High Stadium (76,000)

Indianapolis Indians (Expos)
Bush Stadium (12,500)

Iowa Cubs (Cubs)
Sec Taylor Stadium (7,600)

Louisville Redbirds (Cardinals)
Cardinal Stadium (33,500)

Nashville Sounds (Reds)
Herschel Greer Stadium (18,000)

Oklahoma City 89ers (Rangers)
All-Sports Stadium (12,000)

Omaha Royals (Royals)
Rosenblatt Stadium (15,000)

Class AAA Directory

International League

Columbus Clippers (Yankees)
Harold Cooper Stadium (15,000)
Pawtucket Red Sox (Red Sox)
McCoy Stadium (6,010)
Richmond Braves (Braves)
The Diamond (12,000)
Rochester Red Wings (Orioles)
Silver Stadium (12,503)
Scranton/Wilkes-Barre Red Barons (Phillies)
Lackawanna County Stadium (10,004)
Syracuse Chiefs (Blue Jays)
MacArthur Stadium (10,500)
Tidewater Tides (Mets)
Metropolitan Park (6,162)
Toledo Mud Hens (Tigers)
Ned Skeldon Stadium (10,025)

Canton-Akron Indians (Indians)

BATTING	Avg.	AB	R	H	2B	3B	HR	RBI	SB
Jeff Barns, 2b	.260	123	12	32	6	0	1	10	3
Ramon Bautista, 2b	.216	278	40	60	9	5	2	29	7
Joaquin Contreras, of	.225	240	27	54	13	3	1	19	1
Tim Costo, 1b	.271	192	28	52	10	3	1	24	2
Daren Epley, 1b	.253	451	58	114	24	0	9	52	9
Jose Escobar, ss	.059	34	0	2	1	0	0	1	0
Sam Ferretti, ss	.214	299	26	64	12	3	0	23	8
Reggie Jefferson, 1b	.280	25	2	7	1	0	0	4	0
Nolan Lane, of	.245	237	20	58	8	1	2	22	8
Jesse Levis, c	.264	382	31	101	17	3	6	45	2
Carlos Martinez, dh	.329	295	48	97	22	2	11	73	11
Rouglas Odor, ss	.199	236	24	47	5	2	1	29	8
Ken Ramos, of	.241	257	41	62	6	3	2	13	8
Gary Resetar, c	.227	154	14	35	3	0	1	13	3
Miguel Sabino, of	.219	392	52	86	11	2	5	26	23
Mike Sarbaugh, 2b	.067	15	1	1	0	0	0	1	1
Bernie Tatis, 2b	.333	30	5	10	3	0	0	3	3
Andres Thomas, ss	.290	169	15	49	14	1	0	20	2
Jim Thome, 3b	.337	294	47	99	20	2	5	45	8
Lee Tinsley, of	.295	139	26	41	7	2	3	8	18
Ken Whitfield, of	.240	200	24	48	9	2	3	24	5
Roberto Zambrano, of	.338	77	15	26	6	0	2	10	1

PITCHING	W	L	ERA	G	SV	IP	H	BB	SO
Jeff Barns	0	0	7.36	3	0	4.2	7	2	0
Eric Bell	9	5	2.89	18	0	93.1	82	37	84
Mike Birkbeck	2	3	3.89	21	5	39.1	39	18	40
Jim Bruske	5	2	3.47	17	1	80.1	73	27	35
Craig Chamberlain	0	0	7.50	2	1	6	8	3	4
Mike Curtis	2	0	1.83	10	1	20.2	20	10	20
Gerard Dipoto	6	11	3.81	28	0	156	143	74	97
Logan Easley	0	2	3.60	6	1	15	11	1	14
Apolonar Garcia	2	1	1.96	4	0	18.1	22	7	10
Grady Hall	2	3	3.26	8	0	47	39	11	24
Ricky Horton	1	2	3.67	25	1	27	25	5	23
Garland Kiser	2	3	2.03	17	0	44.1	35	11	34
Ty Kovach	2	6	6.02	11	0	58.1	72	28	30
Tom Kramer	7	3	2.38	35	6	79.1	61	34	61
Brian Meyer	1	0	1.50	14	3	24	18	4	9
Oscar Munoz	3	8	5.72	15	0	85	88	51	71
Jeff Mutis	11	5	1.80	25	0	170.2	138	51	89
Greg Roscoe	6	2	1.83	13	0	88.1	70	28	66
Rudy Seanez	4	2	2.58	25	7	38.1	17	30	73
Mike Walker	9	4	2.79	45	11	77.1	68	45	42
Colby Ward	0	1	.90	4	1	10	6	5	7
Kevin Wickander	1	2	3.91	20	0	25.1	24	13	21

Hagerstown Suns (Orioles)

BATTING	Avg.	AB	R	H	2B	3B	HR	RBI	SB
Manny Alexander, ss	.333	9	3	3	1	0	0	2	0
Dan Berthel, of	.161	31	0	5	1	0	0	2	0
Paul Carey, of	.252	373	63	94	29	1	12	65	5
Glenn Davis, 1b	.250	24	4	6	1	0	1	3	0
Bobby Dickerson, ss	.238	302	34	72	12	4	1	36	2
Roy Gilbert, of	.225	204	22	46	5	5	0	19	14
Ricky Gutierrez, ss	.236	292	47	69	6	4	0	30	11
Victor Hithe, of	.277	260	46	72	11	5	0	26	20
Tim Holland, 3b	.248	501	58	124	21	2	8	73	6
Tyrone Kingwood, of	.279	319	39	89	15	2	2	36	26
Mike Lehman, c	.281	331	42	93	24	1	3	46	2

BATTING	Avg.	AB	R	H	2B	3B	HR	RBI	SB
Rodney Lofton, 2b	.284	437	78	124	8	4	1	33	56
Scott Meadows, of	.300	120	18	36	7	1	1	11	1
Tim Raley, dh	.244	234	40	57	9	3	3	31	2
Billy Ripken, 2b	.600	5	1	3	0	0	0	0	1
Doug Robbins, c	.304	286	45	87	12	1	0	28	4
Greg Roth, of	.345	119	21	41	4	1	5	24	1
Ken Shamburg, 1b	.275	426	59	117	36	2	10	82	3
Jack Voigt, dh	.244	90	15	22	3	0	0	6	6
Melvin Wearing, dh	.299	107	18	32	6	0	3	24	1
Ed Yacopino, of	.343	268	51	92	16	4	2	47	4

PITCHING	W	L	ERA	G	SV	IP	H	BB	SO
Jeff Bumgarner	3	6	4.54	17	0	73.1	84	35	45
Stacey Burdick	11	4	2.99	26	0	136.2	99	100	102
Chris Codiroli	3	0	4.50	5	0	12	11	5	10
Andres Constant	0	1	18.00	1	0	2	7	1	1
Steve Culkar	0	0	.00	3	0	5	1	1	2
Kevin Hickey	0	1	1.83	15	3	20.2	15	6	20
Dave Johnson	3	0	1.00	3	0	18	13	3	9
Stacy Jones	0	1	1.78	12	1	30.1	24	15	26
Pat Leinen	10	6	3.03	23	0	149.2	143	33	63
Mike Linskey	6	5	4.46	16	0	107	128	37	71
Joel McKeon	3	2	4.19	33	0	62.1	72	27	34
Bob Milacki	3	0	1.06	3	0	17	14	3	18
Dave Miller	2	0	1.17	14	1	31.2	16	13	15
Daryl Moore	5	3	3.38	34	3	32	21	19	47
Mike Oquist	10	9	4.06	27	0	166.1	168	62	136
Oswaldo Peraza	6	7	3.98	19	0	106.1	97	60	97
Arthur Rhodes	7	4	2.70	19	0	107.2	73	47	115
Erik Schullstrom	1	0	2.77	2	0	13	11	3	9
Todd Stephan	5	5	2.12	53	14	89	68	41	67
Jeff Williams	3	5	2.60	39	17	55.1	52	32	42

Harrisburg Senators (Expos)

BATTING	Avg.	AB	R	H	2B	3B	HR	RBI	SB
Chris Cassels, of	.222	297	35	66	15	0	13	48	1
Archi Cianfrocco, 1b	.316	456	71	144	21	10	9	77	11
Jim Faulk, of	.251	267	32	67	10	3	5	47	22
Greg Fulton, 3b	.293	157	18	46	7	1	0	18	4
Cesar Hernandez, of	.254	418	58	106	16	2	13	52	34
Chris Hirsch, c	.235	17	6	4	1	0	1	4	1
Rob Katzaroff, of	.290	558	94	162	21	2	3	50	33
Bryn Kosco, 3b	.241	381	50	92	23	5	10	58	4
Ken Lake, of	.091	11	1	1	0	0	0	1	0
Tim Laker, c	.286	35	4	10	1	0	1	5	0
Chris Martin, ss	.224	294	30	66	10	0	6	36	1
Todd Mayo, of	.257	35	6	9	0	0	0	1	2
Omer Munoz, ss	.308	214	27	66	7	1	1	21	1
Bob Natal, c	.256	336	47	86	16	3	13	53	1
F.P. Santangelo, 2b	.245	462	78	113	12	7	5	42	21
Joe Siddall, c	.230	235	28	54	6	1	1	23	8
Matt Stairs, 2b	.333	505	87	168	30	10	13	78	23

PITCHING	W	L	ERA	G	SV	IP	H	BB	SO
Chris Bennett	5	6	3.16	28	1	74	82	22	35
William Brennan	3	2	3.12	21	1	35.2	35	30	33
Chris Bushing	1	0	1.04	3	0	9.2	3	8	8
Reid Cornelius	2	1	2.89	3	0	19.2	15	7	12
Dan Freed	11	8	4.32	26	0	162.1	176	41	83
Matt Grott	2	1	4.70	10	1	15.1	14	8	16
Chris Haney	5	3	2.16	12	0	83.1	65	31	68
Phil Harrison	7	1	2.20	23	2	57.1	42	28	41
Rich Holsman	0	0	2.84	4	0	6.1	8	6	7
Jonathan Hurst	5	0	.86	6	0	42	26	12	34
Chris Johnson	3	2	3.34	10	0	57.1	59	28	42
Carl Keliipuleole	0	1	2.84	6	0	6.1	6	3	5

Class AAA Directory

Pacific Coast League

Albuquerque Dukes (Dodgers)
Albuquerque Sports Stadium (10,510)

Calgary Cannons (Mariners)
Foothills Stadium (7,500)

Colorado Springs Sky Sox (Indians)
Sky Sox Stadium (6,130)

Edmonton Trappers (Angels)
John Ducey Park (5,000)

Las Vegas Stars (Padres)
Cashman Field (9,370)

Phoenix Firebirds (Giants)
Municipal Stadium (7,983)

Portland Beavers (Twins)
Civic Stadium (26,500)

Tacoma Tigers (A's)
Cheney Stadium (8,002)

Tucson Toros (Astros)
Hi Corbett Field (9,500)

Vancouver Canadiens (White Sox)
Nat Bailey Stadium (6,500)

Class AA Directory

Eastern League

Albany-Colonie Yankees (Yankees)
Heritage Park (5,700)
Binghamton Mets (Mets)
Municipal Stadium (6,000)
Canton-Akron Indians (Indians)
Thurman Munson Memorial Stadium (5,600)
Hagerstown Suns (Orioles)
Municipal Stadium (6,000)
Harrisburg Senators (Expos)
Riverside Stadium (5,600)

London Tigers (Tigers)
Labatt Park (5,400)
New Britain Red Sox (Red Sox)
Beehive Field (4,000)
Reading Phillies (Phillies)
Municipal Stadium (6,500)

Harrisburg (continued)

PITCHING	W	L	ERA	G	SV	IP	H	BB	SO
Rusty Kilgo	1	0	3.51	14	1	26.2	24	4	20
Richie Lewis	6	5	3.74	34	5	75.2	67	40	82
Chris Marchok	4	2	2.10	41	9	64.1	51	14	56
Matt Maysey	6	5	1.89	15	0	105.2	90	28	86
Chris Pollack	11	8	2.75	26	0	157	147	68	83
Stanley Spencer	6	1	4.40	17	0	92	90	30	66
John Thoden	0	0	2.59	5	0	31.1	30	3	19
David Wainhouse	2	2	2.60	33	11	52	49	17	46
Pete Young	7	5	2.60	54	13	90	82	24	74

London Tigers (Tigers)

BATTING	Avg.	AB	R	H	2B	3B	HR	RBI	SB
Doyle Balthazar, c	.258	264	28	68	8	1	1	22	4
Arnie Beyeler, 2b	.235	213	21	50	8	2	1	13	3
Rico Brogna, 1b	.273	293	40	80	13	1	13	51	0
Basilio Cabrera, of	.127	71	10	9	0	1	1	3	3
Ivan Cruz, 1b	.248	443	45	110	21	0	9	47	3
Dean Decillis, ss	.267	225	25	60	8	1	1	32	2
Lou Frazier, of	.239	439	69	105	9	4	3	40	42
Luis Galindo, 3b	.253	269	27	68	5	1	0	20	5
Mike Gillette, c	.187	241	25	45	10	1	5	21	2
Shawn Hare, of	.272	125	20	34	12	0	4	28	2
Jody Hurst, of	.278	187	33	52	8	0	8	24	8
Riccardo Ingram, of	.271	421	57	114	14	1	18	64	6
Keith Kimberlin, ss	.233	331	27	77	16	5	2	34	4
Dave Leonhardt, 2b	.200	15	5	3	0	0	0	0	0
Ron Marigny, 3b	.271	85	14	23	3	1	0	6	2
Domingo Michel, dh	.269	145	18	39	4	1	2	14	1
Steve Pegues, of	.301	216	24	65	3	2	6	26	4
Rob Reimink, 3b	.258	279	37	72	9	1	2	18	2
Pat Woodruff, of	.212	179	14	38	8	0	1	22	3

PITCHING	W	L	ERA	G	SV	IP	H	BB	SO
Ron Cook	0	1	10.13	3	0	5.1	11	8	2
John Desilva	5	4	2.81	11	0	74.2	51	24	80
John Doherty	3	3	2.22	53	15	65	62	21	42
Luis Galindo	0	0	7.36	3	0	4.2	5	2	4
Greg Gohr	0	0	.00	2	0	11	9	2	10
Buddy Groom	7	1	3.48	11	0	52.2	51	12	39
Mike Hansen	4	5	3.32	21	1	84	70	33	61
Darren Hursey	2	2	5.16	35	2	68	81	30	35
Charley Kerfeld	1	1	3.12	11	2	17.1	9	11	18
Kurt Knudsen	2	3	3.48	34	6	52.2	42	30	56
Todd Krumm	4	8	7.10	18	0	77.1	103	42	61
Vance Lovelace	1	0	5.52	9	0	15.2	18	9	12
Randy Marshall	8	10	4.47	27	0	159	186	27	105
Jose Ramos	2	5	3.80	34	0	64	67	25	44
Ron Rightnowar	2	1	3.91	15	3	25.1	28	8	18
Lino Rivera	2	2	3.71	17	0	27.2	25	11	19
Eric Stone	1	5	5.74	6	0	27.2	26	25	10
Don Vesling	7	8	4.49	18	0	112.1	127	47	53
Marty Willis	5	12	3.64	31	0	156.2	154	69	98
Steve Wolf	5	7	4.80	17	0	101.1	109	63	67

New Britain Red Sox (Red Sox)

BATTING	Avg.	AB	R	H	2B	3B	HR	RBI	SB
Mike Beams, of	.203	251	21	51	14	2	4	25	1
Greg Blosser, of	.217	452	48	98	21	3	8	46	9
Jim Byrd, ss	.240	292	28	70	9	1	0	15	14
Vinnie Degifico, dh	.231	199	12	46	4	0	4	19	0
Colin Dixon, 3b	.270	274	29	74	16	1	4	20	1

BATTING	Avg.	AB	R	H	2B	3B	HR	RBI	SB
Lou Dorante, c	.265	181	20	48	12	0	1	22	2
Ray Fagnant, c	.130	46	3	6	2	0	0	1	0
John Flaherty, c	.289	225	27	65	9	0	3	18	0
Blane Fox, of	.213	141	17	30	3	0	0	13	4
Steve Hendricks, 1b	.211	336	20	71	10	2	0	33	8
Wayne Housie, of	.277	444	58	123	24	2	6	26	43
Tom Magrann, c	.105	76	5	8	1	0	1	3	0
Dave Milstien, 2b	.278	309	36	86	6	1	4	31	3
Juan Paris, of	.243	419	32	102	17	3	3	41	4
Scott Powers, 3b	.208	250	21	52	9	2	0	16	3
Randy Randle, 3b	.193	347	33	67	12	2	2	31	7
Ruben Rodriguez, c	.270	100	11	27	5	0	3	9	1
John Valentin, ss	.198	81	8	16	3	0	0	5	1
Les Wallin, 1b	.202	89	13	18	8	2	0	9	0
Eric Wedge, c	.250	8	0	2	0	0	0	2	0
PITCHING	W	L	ERA	G	SV	IP	H	BB	SO
Tracy Allen	0	1	10.13	8	0	8	13	9	7
Paul Brown	1	1	3.60	12	2	20	22	6	13
Brian Conroy	1	5	3.02	10	0	66.2	51	26	34
Freddie Davis	2	3	5.45	45	2	78.2	102	29	42
Pete Estrada	2	12	6.05	25	0	97.2	113	58	53
Gar Finnvold	5	8	3.82	16	0	101.1	97	36	80
Tom Fischer	8	11	4.09	22	0	134.1	135	63	85
Don Florence	3	8	5.55	55	2	84.1	85	43	73
Peter Hoy	4	4	1.46	47	15	68	47	22	39
Tom Kane	4	8	4.55	41	1	115.2	121	42	75
Derek Livernois	3	2	3.25	5	0	28.2	28	10	31
Josias Manzanillo	2	2	2.90	7	0	50.2	37	28	35
Dan O'Neill	0	2	4.50	2	0	10	12	3	5
Gary Painter	3	7	4.84	15	0	87.1	89	35	51
Paul Quantrill	2	1	2.06	5	0	35	32	8	18
Ken Ryan	1	2	1.73	14	1	26	23	12	26
Al Sanders	4	15	4.95	26	0	158.1	160	77	80
Scott Taylor	2	0	.62	4	0	29	20	9	38
Gene Walter	0	1	3.60	3	0	5	5	0	3

Reading Phillies (Phillies)

BATTING	Avg.	AB	R	H	2B	3B	HR	RBI	SB
Sal Agostinelli, c	.200	35	4	7	1	0	0	3	0
Pat Austin, 2b	.289	329	57	95	21	1	4	39	21
Dana Brown, of	.244	271	39	66	5	2	2	25	24
Darren Daulton, c	.250	4	0	1	0	0	0	0	0
Bruce Dostal, of	.313	364	68	114	11	5	5	34	38
Doug Lindsey, c	.259	313	26	81	13	0	1	34	1
Tony Longmire, of	.288	323	43	93	23	1	9	56	10
Tom Marsh, of	.263	236	27	62	12	5	7	35	8
Joe Millette, ss	.246	353	52	87	9	4	3	28	6
Nikco Riesgo, of	.258	356	61	92	18	2	14	66	8
Rod Robertson, 2b	.245	416	52	102	19	0	9	51	20
Ed Rosado, c	.200	125	17	25	5	0	0	10	5
Sean Ryan, 1b	.241	439	54	106	22	0	8	70	0
Steve Scarsone, 2b	.306	49	6	15	0	0	3	3	2
Tony Trevino, ph	.253	83	10	21	6	1	0	12	1
Casey Waller, 3b	.261	402	64	105	25	1	12	52	2
Cary Williams, of	.278	421	55	117	21	3	6	62	12
PITCHING	W	L	ERA	G	SV	IP	H	BB	SO
Jason Backs	3	5	7.36	19	0	70.2	101	40	36
Toby Borland	8	3	2.70	59	24	77.2	68	56	72
Cliff Brantley	4	3	1.94	11	0	70.2	50	25	51
Brad Brink	2	2	3.71	5	0	34	32	6	27
John Burgos	2	0	4.70	15	0	23	27	13	10
Andy Carter	11	5	4.84	20	0	102.1	86	57	64
Frank Dimichele	0	2	6.61	22	2	31.1	39	9	21
Rick Dunnum	6	5	4.58	55	0	108	112	64	63

Class AA Directory

Southern League

Birmingham Barons (White Sox)
Hoover Metropolitan Stadium (10,000)

Carolina Mudcats (Pirates)
Five County Stadium (6,000)

Charlotte Knights (Cubs)
Knights Castle (10,917)

Chattanooga Lookouts (Reds)
Engel Stadium (8,000)

Greenville Braves (Braves)
Municipal Stadium (7,023)

Huntsville Stars (A's)
Bill Meyer Stadium (6,412)

Jacksonville Suns (Mariners)
Wolfson Park (8,200)

Knoxville Blue Jays (Blue Jays)
Bill Meyer Stadium (6,412)

Memphis Chicks (Royals)
Tim McCarver Stadium (10,000)

Orlando Sunrays (Twins)
Tinker Field (6,000)

Class AA Directory

Texas League

Arkansas Travelers (Cardinals)
Ray Winder Field (5,975)
El Paso Diablos (Brewers)
Cohen Stadium (10,000)
Jackson Generals (Astros)
Smith-Wills Stadium (5,200)
Midland Angels (Angels)
Angels Stadium (3,800)
San Antonio Missions (Dodgers)
V.J. Keefe Memorial Stadium (3,500)
Shreveport Captains (Giants)
Fairgrounds Field (6,200)
Tulsa Drillers (Rangers)
Drillers Stadium (8,234)
Wichita Wranglers (Padres)
Lawrence-Dumont Stadium (7,488)

342

Reading (continued)

PITCHING	W	L	ERA	G	SV	IP	H	BB	SO
Rocky Elli	5	7	3.15	16	0	74.1	65	33	48
Paul Fletcher	7	9	3.51	21	0	121.2	111	56	90
Bob Gaddy	1	1	4.71	10	0	21	20	15	16
Elliott Gray	0	2	5.16	7	0	30.2	35	26	18
David Holdridge	0	2	5.47	7	0	26.1	26	34	19
Chris Limbach	0	2	5.68	18	3	19	20	6	17
Darrell Lindsey	3	1	6.68	17	1	32.1	41	15	23
Tom Marsh	0	0	.00	1	0	2	0	1	0
Mark Sims	1	2	2.52	14	0	25	23	5	20
Matt Stevens	5	1	3.57	25	2	40.1	35	11	31
Jeff Tabaka	4	8	5.07	21	0	108.1	117	78	68
Bob Wells	1	0	3.60	1	0	5	4	1	3
Scott Wiegandt	2	3	2.67	48	1	81	66	40	50
Mike Williams	7	5	3.69	16	0	102.1	93	36	51

Williamsport Bills (Mets)

BATTING	Avg.	AB	R	H	2B	3B	HR	RBI	SB
Tom Allison, 2b	.225	89	13	20	4	1	0	9	2
Tim Bogar, 3b	.251	243	33	61	12	2	2	25	13
Jeromy Burnitz, of	.225	457	80	103	16	10	31	85	31
Hernan Cortes, 1b	.214	42	2	9	0	0	0	2	0
Steve Davis, of	.138	87	11	12	4	0	0	6	3
Joe Dellicarri, 3b	.242	215	30	52	10	2	5	23	7
D.J. Dozier, of	.278	259	49	72	11	6	8	30	25
Javier Gonzalez, c	.153	150	7	23	7	0	4	14	1
Rudy Hernandez, 2b	.217	346	38	75	9	0	0	22	25
Tim Howard, 3b	.257	245	23	63	7	6	1	16	7
Pat Howell, of	.281	274	43	77	5	1	1	26	27
Lee May, of	.203	296	29	60	9	5	1	19	19
Loy McBride, of	.216	283	23	61	13	0	4	30	7
Tito Navarro, ss	.288	482	69	139	9	4	2	42	42
Paul Williams, 1b	.259	463	62	120	29	1	8	72	0
Alan Zinter, c	.220	422	44	93	13	6	9	54	3
PITCHING	**W**	**L**	**ERA**	**G**	**SV**	**IP**	**H**	**BB**	**SO**
Terry Bross	2	0	2.49	20	5	25.1	13	11	28
Doug Cinnella	3	5	3.71	28	2	78.2	92	38	45
Todd Douma	2	4	4.33	10	0	60.1	78	17	42
Sid Fernandez	0	0	.00	1	0	6	3	1	5
Chris Hill	3	3	4.69	27	1	88.1	115	40	42
John Johnstone	7	9	3.97	27	0	165.1	159	79	99
Doug Kline	2	5	2.47	50	3	91	77	37	76
Toby Nivens	10	11	4.19	28	0	144	156	63	72
Dave Proctor	0	2	2.59	9	0	42.2	38	28	24
Bryan Rogers	6	8	4.72	41	15	61	73	18	33
Al Sieradzki	0	1	9.00	1	0	7	8	5	2
David Sommer	4	7	4.37	22	0	111.1	114	72	83
Greg Talamantez	3	2	4.76	32	0	59.2	65	38	47
Dave Telgheder	13	11	3.60	28	0	168.2	185	33	90
David Trautwein	3	9	6.79	42	3	58.1	75	23	21
Jose Vargas	2	1	3.80	16	2	21.1	19	13	10
Aguedo Vasquez	0	1	3.97	11	1	11.1	10	7	5

Southern League

Birmingham Barons (White Sox)

BATTING	Avg.	AB	R	H	2B	3B	HR	RBI	SB
Cesar Bernhardt, 2b	.272	103	15	28	2	0	3	16	3
Wayne Busby, ss	.162	198	18	32	3	2	1	14	2
Darrin Campbell, c	.221	289	39	64	7	3	7	32	0
Kevin Castleberry, ph	.000	1	0	0	0	0	0	0	0
Mark Chasey, 1b	.238	332	42	79	17	3	5	36	1
Ron Coomer, 3b	.255	505	81	129	27	5	13	76	0
Lindsay Foster, ss	.212	372	40	79	8	4	1	34	23
Kevin Garner, 1b	.249	430	54	107	19	3	14	74	0
Jeff Gay, c	.193	83	5	16	4	0	0	6	1
Bo Jackson, dh	.308	13	2	4	0	0	0	0	1
Scott Jaster, of	.265	362	40	96	14	4	7	44	1
Greg Kobza, c	.000	4	0	0	0	0	0	0	0
Derek Lee, of	.325	154	36	50	10	2	5	16	9
Allen Liebert, c	.183	109	7	20	3	0	1	7	0
Matt Merullo, c	.214	28	5	6	0	0	2	3	0
Javier Ocasio, 2b	.224	398	39	89	7	4	0	30	16
Kinnis Pledger, of	.218	363	53	79	16	8	9	51	15
Greg Roth, 2b	.190	126	15	24	8	1	1	12	0
Carl Sullivan, of	.234	128	11	30	6	1	3	12	2
Dean Tatarian, ss	.333	15	5	5	2	0	0	0	0
Scott Tedder, of	.294	337	34	99	14	3	0	32	5
Aubrey Waggoner, of	.230	248	39	57	11	4	3	21	20
Brandon Wilson, ss	.400	10	3	4	1	0	0	2	0
PITCHING	**W**	**L**	**ERA**	**G**	**SV**	**IP**	**H**	**BB**	**SO**
Wilson Alvarez	10	6	1.83	23	0	152.1	109	74	165
Rodney Bolton	8	4	1.62	12	0	89	73	21	57
Mario Brito	2	4	3.30	10	0	71	53	16	37
Travis Chambers	0	0	3.71	10	0	17	18	4	13
Conde Cortes	8	8	3.31	22	0	133.1	126	61	71
Mike Davino	1	4	3.45	25	4	47	41	16	27
Ramon Garcia	4	0	.93	6	0	39.2	27	11	38
Roberto Hernandez	2	1	1.99	4	0	23.2	11	6	25
Chris Howard	6	1	2.04	38	9	53	43	16	52
John Hudek	5	10	3.84	51	13	66 .2	58	28	49
Bo Kennedy	10	3	2.32	15	0	93	88	48	52
Brian Keyser	0	1	5.00	3	0	18	19	9	9
Frank Merigliano	3	2	3.89	36	4	69.1	58	31	51
Scott Middaugh	2	2	3.41	12	1	34.1	27	14	27
Dave Reynolds	2	0	1.97	19	1	46.2	36	20	38
Larry Thomas	0	0	3.00	2	0	6	6	4	2
Jose Ventura	8	10	4.06	25	0	149.2	129	64	91
Robert Wickman	6	10	3.56	20	0	131.1	127	50	81

Carolina Mudcats (Pirates)

BATTING	Avg.	AB	R	H	2B	3B	HR	RBI	SB
Felix Antigua, c	.091	11	1	1	0	0	0	0	0
Terry Crowley, 2b	.264	469	60	124	15	5	7	45	5
Greg Edge, ss	.220	350	43	77	10	2	1	22	13
Chris Estep, of	.243	300	34	73	17	2	4	34	4
Tom Green, of	.198	197	15	39	10	0	2	16	0
Tim Hines, c	.204	98	8	20	2	0	1	7	0
Mike Huyler, ss	.210	229	22	48	4	4	0	28	4
Paul List, of	.150	20	1	3	0	1	0	2	0
Tom Magrann, c	.222	18	1	4	0	0	0	2	0
Keith Osik, c	.302	43	9	13	3	1	0	5	0
Darwin Pennye, of	.257	455	53	117	20	7	5	43	19

Class A Directory

California League

Bakersfield Dodgers (Dodgers)
Sam Lynn Ballpark (3,000)

Modesto A's (A's)
Thurman Field (2,500)

Palm Springs Angels (Angels)
Angels Stadium (5,185)

Reno Silver Sox (Independent)
Moana Stadium (4,500)

High Desert Mavericks (Padres)
Maverick Stadium (3,500)

Salinas Spurs (Independent)
Municipal Stadium (3,000)

San Bernardino Spirit (Mariners)
Fiscalini Field (3,000)

San Jose Giants (Giants)
Municipal Stadium (5,200)

Stockton Ports (Brewers)
Billy Herbert Field (3,500)

Visalia Oaks (Twins)
Recreation Park (2,000)

Class A Directory

Carolina League

**Durham Bulls
(Braves)**
Durham Athletic Park
(5,000)
**Frederick Keys
(Orioles)**
Harry Grove Stadium
(4,500)
**Kinston Indians
(Indians)**
Grainger Stadium
(4,100)
**Lynchburg Red Sox
(Red Sox)**
City Stadium (4,200)
**Peninsula Pilots
(Mariners)**
War Memorial Stadium
(4,330)
**Prince William
Cannons (Yankees)**
County Stadium (6,000)
**Salem Buccaneers
(Pirates)**
Municipal Field (5,000)
**Winston-Salem Spirits
(Cubs)**
Ernie Shore Stadium
(4,280)

Carolina (continued)

BATTING	Avg.	AB	R	H	2B	3B	HR	RBI	SB
William Pennyfeather, of	.275	149	13	41	5	0	0	9	3
Daryl Ratliff, of	.215	93	10	20	3	0	0	9	8
Mandy Romero, c	.217	323	29	70	12	0	3	31	1
Bruce Schreiber, 2b	.243	325	25	79	11	1	1	22	4
Ben Shelton, 1b	.231	169	19	39	8	3	1	19	2
Greg Sparks, 1b	.273	220	19	60	10	0	5	35	0
Jessie Torres, c	.067	30	3	2	0	0	0	1	0
John Wehner, 3b	.265	234	30	62	5	1	3	21	17
Ed Yacopino, of	.224	147	19	33	2	1	0	14	3
Kevin Young, 3b	.342	263	36	90	19	6	3	33	9
Eddie Zambrano, of	.253	269	28	68	17	3	3	39	4
PITCHING	W	L	ERA	G	SV	IP	H	BB	SO
Steve Adams	2	2	3.92	8	3	21.2	25	6	10
Joe Ausanio	0	0	.00	3	2	3	0	0	2
Steve Buckholz	7	10	4.66	21	0	133.1	135	53	85
Victor Cole	0	2	1.91	20	12	28.1	13	19	32
Stephen Cooke	3	3	2.26	9	0	56.2	39	19	46
Hector Fajardo	3	4	4.13	10	0	61	55	24	53
Stan Fansler	6	6	3.50	19	0	90	77	28	78
Carl Hamilton	3	4	3.47	10	0	62.1	58	21	46
Lee Hancock	4	7	3.77	37	4	98	93	42	66
Paul Miller	7	2	2.42	15	0	89.1	69	35	69
Blas Minor	0	0	2.84	3	0	13.1	9	7	18
Pete Murphy	6	9	3.41	32	0	98.2	96	35	49
Jeff Neely	0	0	6.75	5	0	4	5	4	5
Mike Roesler	2	4	4.91	20	6	26.2	20	15	31
Dennis Tafoya	1	3	1.99	40	6	63.1	51	22	35
David Tellers	0	2	4.73	11	1	13.1	18	6	9
Jim Tracy	6	3	2.45	16	1	88.1	80	21	72
Tim Wakefield	15	8	2.90	26	0	183	155	51	120
Bob Walk	0	1	1.80	1	0	5	5	2	3
Ben Webb	1	6	3.15	37	3	69.2	61	30	38

Charlotte Knights (Cubs)

BATTING	Avg.	AB	R	H	2B	3B	HR	RBI	SB
Alex Arias, ss	.275	488	69	134	26	0	4	47	22
Jeff Baldwin, of	.246	207	24	51	8	0	1	27	4
Joe Biasucci, 2b	.220	50	4	11	2	0	0	2	2
Paul Blair, 2b	.179	67	13	12	3	0	0	3	2
Dick Canan, 3b	.214	84	10	18	2	1	1	10	3
Pedro Castellano, 3b	.421	19	2	8	0	0	0	2	0
Rusty Crockett, of	.214	280	36	60	7	1	1	23	14
Mike Grace, 3b	.207	261	22	54	8	0	6	32	3
Ty Griffin, of	.164	116	16	19	4	0	0	12	4
Mike Knapp, c	.256	266	19	68	12	0	1	33	4
Elvin Paulino, 1b	.257	460	67	118	27	1	24	81	9
Fernando Ramsey, of	.276	547	78	151	18	6	6	49	37
Kevin Roberson, of	.256	507	77	130	24	2	19	67	17
Dan Simonds, c	.247	97	17	24	6	1	0	6	0
Bill St. Peter, 3b	.192	146	14	28	2	0	3	9	4
Scott Taylor, c	.234	107	11	25	3	0	0	4	0
Doug Welch, of	.241	444	45	107	17	0	13	65	7
Billy White, 2b	.268	396	52	106	16	3	3	50	13
PITCHING	W	L	ERA	G	SV	IP	H	BB	SO
Jim Bullinger	9	9	3.53	20	0	143.2	132	61	128
Rusty Crockett	0	0	.00	2	0	3	1	1	1
Steve Dibartolomeo	4	3	3.79	45	1	76	80	34	46
John Gardner	7	8	3.51	29	0	154	122	97	116
Henry Gomez	5	8	4.88	34	1	122.2	114	47	82
Ryan Hawblitzel	1	2	3.21	5	0	34.2	31	12	25
Eric Jaques	3	1	4.19	20	0	19.1	20	9	15
Shannon Jones	1	1	6.52	4	0	10.2	5	11	12

PITCHING	W	L	ERA	G	SV	IP	H	BB	SO
Chuck Mount	4	5	3.78	17	0	105.2	97	27	55
Steve Muh	1	1	4.74	28	0	49.1	48	31	35
Tim Parker	11	9	3.73	24	0	145.2	131	73	74
John Salles	10	7	3.00	22	0	150	141	37	74
Candy Sierra	4	1	3.78	18	0	48.2	45	22	24
Mike Sodders	0	2	7.58	9	0	19	21	11	14
Julio Strauss	6	7	2.69	49	9	74.2	63	27	57
Derek Stroud	0	0	12.71	4	0	6.2	11	3	4
Dave Swartzbaugh	0	1	10.13	1	0	5.1	6	3	5
Tim Watkins	8	6	3.11	52	13	107	109	32	97

Chattanooga Lookouts (Reds)

BATTING	Avg.	AB	R	H	2B	3B	HR	RBI	SB
Rick Allen, 3b	.251	382	52	96	15	1	4	26	5
Pete Beeler, c	.201	204	26	41	7	1	6	16	2
Jeff Branson, ss	.263	304	35	80	13	3	2	28	3
Scott Bryant, of	.304	306	42	93	14	6	8	43	2
Benny Colvard, of	.281	463	62	130	23	8	17	68	11
Tim Costo, 1b	.280	293	31	82	19	3	5	29	11
Darren Cox, c	.184	38	2	7	1	0	0	3	0
K.C. Gillum, of	.161	31	3	5	3	0	0	0	1
Manny Jose, of	.302	169	22	51	8	6	2	17	13
Frank Kremblas, of	.241	320	35	77	17	0	3	41	3
Greg Lonigro, 2b	.261	460	47	120	24	3	5	54	12
Scott Pose, of	.274	402	61	110	8	5	1	31	17
Eddie Rush, ss	.165	91	11	15	0	0	0	3	0
Reggie Sanders, of	.315	302	50	95	15	8	8	49	15
Scott Sellner, 2b	.200	130	11	26	3	0	0	11	4
Glenn Sutko, c	.286	63	12	18	3	0	3	11	0
Todd Trafton, 1b	.260	231	30	60	18	0	6	34	2
Dan Wilson, c	.257	292	32	75	19	2	2	38	2
PITCHING	W	L	ERA	G	SV	IP	H	BB	SO
Mike Anderson	10	9	4.40	28	0	155.1	142	93	115
Bobby Ayala	3	1	4.67	39	4	91.2	79	58	92
Bill Dodd	3	4	4.32	35	7	75	68	40	64
Steve Foster	0	2	1.15	17	10	16.2	10	4	18
Victor Garcia	5	3	1.98	40	5	50	41	20	51
Trevor Hoffman	1	0	1.93	14	8	14	10	7	23
Rodney Imes	4	2	5.13	8	0	47.1	48	17	25
Frank Kremblas	0	0	.00	3	0	3.1	1	2	1
Reggie Leslie	0	1	18.69	1	0	4.1	8	3	4
Dave McAuliffe	4	6	6.47	33	3	40.1	37	24	26
Steve McCarthy	0	0	6.75	12	0	9.1	17	9	9
Tim Pugh	3	1	1.64	5	0	38.1	20	11	24
Bill Risley	5	7	3.16	19	0	108.1	81	60	77
Mo Sanford	7	4	2.74	16	0	95.1	69	55	124
Jason Satre	1	7	5.11	8	0	44	37	26	44
Will Schock	6	3	4.06	12	0	69.2	77	14	38
Jerry Spradlin	7	3	3.09	48	4	96	95	32	73
Kevin Tatar	3	8	5.19	12	0	68.2	75	31	37
Joe Turek	4	5	3.38	10	0	59.2	57	18	48
Luis Vasquez	7	5	3.12	17	0	121.1	104	43	64

Greenville Braves (Braves)

BATTING	Avg.	AB	R	H	2B	3B	HR	RBI	SB
Ed Alicea, of	.333	42	6	14	3	0	1	5	1
John Alva, ss	.207	256	27	53	12	1	2	24	0
Chris Burton, of	.208	144	18	30	3	2	1	9	8
Rich Casarotti, 2b	.258	264	38	68	9	2	0	15	2
Vinny Castilla, ss	.270	259	34	70	17	3	7	44	0
Brian Champion, dh	.226	332	45	75	17	1	7	35	1
Popeye Cole, of	.243	420	51	102	14	4	2	36	16

Class A Directory

Midwest League

Appleton Foxes (Royals)
Goodland Field (4,300)
Beloit Brewers (Brewers)
Pholman Field (3,800)
Burlington Astros (Astros)
Community Field (3,500)
Cedar Rapids Reds (Reds)
Veterans Memorial Ballpark (6,000)
Clinton Giants (Giants)
Riverview Stadium (3,600)
Kane County Cougars (Orioles)
Events Center Stadium (3,600)
Kenosha Twins (Twins)
Simmons Field (3,500)
Madison Muskies (A's)
Warner Park (3,923)
Peoria Chiefs (Cubs)
Meinen Field (5,000)
Quad City (Angels)
John O'Donnell Stadium (5,000)
Rockford Expos (Expos)
Marinelli Field (4,200)
South Bend White Sox (White Sox)
Stanley Coveleski Stadium (5,000)
Springfield Cardinals (Cardinals)
Lanphier Park (5,000)
Waterloo Diamonds (Padres)
Municipal Stadium (5,500)

MINOR LEAGUE STATISTICS

345

Class A Directory

Florida State League

Baseball City Royals (Royals)
Baseball City (7,000)
Charlotte Rangers (Rangers)
Charlotte County Stadium (6,026)
Clearwater Phillies (Phillies)
Jack Russell Stadium (7,385)
Dunedin Blue Jays (Blue Jays)
Grant Field (6,218)
Fort Lauderdale Yankees (Yankees)
Yankee Stadium (7,211)
Lakeland Tigers (Tigers)
Joker Marchant Stadium (7,500)
Miami Miracle (Independent)
Municipal Stadium (5,000)
Osceola Astros (Astros)
Osceola County Stadium (5,100)
Port St. Lucie Mets (Mets)
Port St. Lucie Sports Complex (7,347)
St. Petersburg Cardinals (Cardinals)
Al Lang Stadium (7,004)
Sarasota White Sox (White Sox)
Ed Smith Stadium (7,500)
Vero Beach Dodgers (Dodgers)
Holman Stadium (6,500)
West Palm Beach Expos (Expos)
Municipal Stadium (4,392)
Winter Haven Red Sox (Red Sox)
Chain O'Lakes Park (5,000)

Greenville (continued)

BATTING	Avg.	AB	R	H	2B	3B	HR	RBI	SB
Johnny Cuevas, c	.190	205	22	39	11	0	3	21	1
Brian Deak, c	.201	204	31	41	9	0	10	41	0
Pat Kelly, 3b	.300	90	14	27	6	2	0	5	5
Ryan Klesko, 1b	.291	419	64	122	22	3	14	67	14
Brian Kowitz, of	.232	112	15	26	5	0	3	17	1
Fred Lopez, c	.264	53	5	14	3	0	1	6	0
Rich Maloney, 2b	.261	111	12	29	6	1	0	13	0
Al Martin, of	.243	301	38	73	13	3	7	38	19
Keith Mitchell, of	.327	214	46	70	15	3	10	47	12
Rick Morris, 3b	.240	338	50	81	16	1	5	43	2
Jose Olmeda, 2b	.202	173	18	35	10	1	3	16	9
Eduardo Perez, 1b	.250	4	0	1	0	0	0	0	0
Boi Rodriguez, 3b	.283	92	14	26	10	1	1	14	0
Sean Ross, of	.282	429	52	121	28	3	8	40	20
Randy Simmons, of	.000	1	0	0	0	0	0	0	0
PITCHING	W	L	ERA	G	SV	IP	H	BB	SO
Brian Bark	2	1	3.57	9	1	18.2	19	8	15
Pedro Borbon	0	1	2.79	4	0	29	23	10	22
Brian Champion	0	0	.00	2	0	2	1	1	0
Pat Gomez	5	2	1.81	13	0	80.2	58	31	71
Judd Johnson	10	7	3.56	47	6	99.2	108	15	66
David Nied	7	3	2.41	15	0	90.2	79	20	101
Ben Rivera	11	8	3.57	26	0	159.2	155	75	116
Napoleon Robinson	16	6	2.27	29	0	175.2	172	48	107
Earl Sanders	4	7	3.65	48	0	79	82	51	85
Don Strange	1	0	13.50	4	1	5.2	9	2	8
Bill Taylor	6	2	1.51	59	22	77.1	49	15	65
Scott Taylor	3	4	4.19	8	0	43	49	16	26
Lee Upshaw	7	6	3.36	19	0	115.1	117	43	87
Preston Watson	5	6	4.24	49	1	81.2	74	44	53
Turk Wendell	11	3	2.56	25	0	148.2	130	51	122
Mark Wohlers	0	0	.57	28	21	31.1	9	13	44
Mike Young	0	0	14.90	10	0	10.2	10	19	9

Huntsville Stars (Athletics)

BATTING	Avg.	AB	R	H	2B	3B	HR	RBI	SB
Kurt Abbott, ss	.253	182	18	46	6	1	0	11	6
Marcos Armas, 1b	.226	305	40	69	16	1	8	53	2
Bob Bafia, 3b	.255	51	4	13	4	0	0	8	0
Eric Booker, of	.257	113	12	29	6	0	0	17	0
Dean Borrelli, c	.190	184	9	35	4	1	0	7	1
Jorge Brito, c	.202	203	26	41	11	0	1	23	0
James Buccheri, of	.212	340	48	72	15	0	0	22	35
Tom Carcione, c	.122	49	4	6	0	1	0	4	0
Joel Chimelis, 2b	.214	238	26	51	10	2	1	16	4
Mike Conte, of	.228	359	36	82	10	0	5	30	8
Fred Cooley, dh	.125	40	3	5	1	0	0	6	0
Rod Correia, 2b	.221	290	25	64	10	1	1	22	2
Kevin Dattola, of	.235	285	38	67	13	2	0	18	15
Webster Garrison, 2b	.264	110	18	29	9	0	2	10	5
Dwayne Hosey, of	.245	102	16	25	6	0	1	7	5
Francisco Matos, ss	.194	191	18	37	1	2	0	19	12
Troy Neel, dh	.277	364	64	101	21	0	23	68	1
Craig Paquette, 3b	.262	378	50	99	18	1	8	60	1
Scott Shockey, 1b	.240	229	26	55	9	1	4	31	1
Wil Tejada, c	.200	20	2	4	0	0	0	3	1
Lee Tinsley, of	.224	303	47	68	7	6	2	24	36
Darryl Vice, 2b	.244	287	46	70	11	1	0	28	3
PITCHING	W	L	ERA	G	SV	IP	H	BB	SO
John Briscoe	2	0	.00	2	0	4.1	1	2	6
Russ Cormier	3	4	5.64	17	0	67	75	31	29

Huntsville (continued)

PITCHING	W	L	ERA	G	SV	IP	H	BB	SO
Scott Erwin	1	4	3.63	19	2	22.1	15	17	30
Dan Eskew	1	3	3.92	6	0	39	37	17	29
Apolinar Garcia	6	3	3.18	13	0	79.1	76	22	40
Matt Grott	2	9	5.15	42	3	58.2	65	37	65
Johnny Guzman	2	1	3.48	7	0	44	46	25	23
Chad Kuhn	1	1	5.96	43	0	51.1	50	40	49
Dave Latter	6	4	4.06	58	1	89.2	69	51	81
Gary Mielke	0	0	1.93	4	0	5.2	4	3	4
Mike Mohler	4	2	3.57	8	0	53	55	20	27
Gavin Osteen	13	9	3.54	28	0	173	176	65	105
Tim Peek	2	4	3.26	56	26	66.1	65	15	52
Don Peters	4	11	5.00	33	0	126	131	70	59
Steve Phoenix	0	0	6.00	2	0	3	7	1	3
Todd Revenig	1	2	.98	12	0	18.1	11	4	10
Todd Van Poppel	6	13	3.47	24	0	132.1	118	90	115
Darryl Vice	0	0	9.00	2	0	2	4	2	2
Weston Weber	2	3	2.17	34	3	54	57	18	26
David Zancanaro	5	10	3.38	29	0	165	151	92	104

Jacksonville Suns (Mariners)

BATTING	Avg.	AB	R	H	2B	3B	HR	RBI	SB
Fernando Arguelles, c	.196	138	8	27	1	0	0	10	1
Frank Bolick, 3b	.254	468	69	119	19	0	16	73	5
Bret Boone, 2b	.255	475	64	121	18	1	19	75	9
Jim Bowie, 1b	.310	448	51	139	25	0	10	67	3
Jim Campanis, c	.248	387	36	96	10	0	15	49	0
Ruben Gonzalez, dh	.237	308	27	73	14	0	4	41	0
Bobby Holley, of	.282	103	20	29	6	2	2	17	0
Bryan King, ss	.080	25	2	2	0	0	0	0	1
Tony Manahan, ss	.254	410	67	104	23	2	7	45	11
Tow Maynard, of	.259	216	32	56	5	3	0	13	30
Mike McDonald, of	.232	112	16	26	9	0	0	11	2
Mark Merchant, of	.282	156	22	44	10	0	5	17	3
Marc Newfield, of	.231	26	4	6	3	0	0	2	0
Ken Pennington, of	.244	320	32	78	14	2	6	29	3
Ron Pezzoni, of	.318	22	3	7	0	0	0	2	0
Ruben Santana, 2b	.200	15	2	3	0	0	1	3	0
Jack Smith, ss	.212	104	17	22	2	1	3	11	1
Tim Stargell, of	.185	200	22	37	6	1	3	13	8
Brian Turang, of	.215	130	14	28	6	2	0	7	5
Jeff Wetherby, of	.288	264	39	76	15	2	7	36	6
Ted Williams, of	.219	269	47	59	10	3	4	16	34
PITCHING	W	L	ERA	G	SV	IP	H	BB	SO
Rick Balabon	5	1	3.09	10	0	64	60	26	42
Shawn Barton	3	3	3.12	14	0	35.2	36	8	24
Jim Blueberg	3	5	2.72	14	0	89.1	75	23	67
Jim Bowie	0	0	.00	1	0	2	3	0	2
Mark Czarkowski	4	9	5.31	20	0	85.2	107	26	46
Gary Eave	2	1	1.69	5	0	27.2	15	10	18
Dave Evans	5	9	5.21	21	0	116.2	118	49	76
Fernando Figueroa	6	3	2.53	41	5	64	57	24	55
Dave Fleming	10	6	2.64	21	0	140	129	25	109
Marcos Garcia	3	2	4.35	6	0	41.1	40	16	42
Jeff Nelson	4	0	1.27	21	12	28.1	23	9	34
Jim Newlin	6	5	2.25	47	12	64	58	29	48
Mike Pitz	1	5	3.98	36	1	86	87	22	67
Dave Richards	3	0	1.57	10	0	23	12	9	22
Ricky Rojas	1	3	5.87	15	1	23	29	4	15
Roger Salkeld	8	8	3.05	23	0	154.2	131	55	159
Mike Schooler	1	1	5.56	11	0	11.1	13	3	12
Johnny Wiggs	1	0	4.05	6	0	13.1	14	2	14

Class A Directory

South Atlantic League

Asheville Tourists (Astros)
McCormick Field (4,000)
Augusta Pirates (Pirates)
Heaton Stadium (4,000)
Charleston (S.C.) Rainbows (Padres)
College Park (4,300)
Charleston (W.Va.) Wheelers (Reds)
Watt Powell Park (6,500)
Columbia Mets (Mets)
Capital City Stadium (6,100)
Columbus Indians (Indians)
Golden Park (6,000)
Fayetteville Generals (Tigers)
J.P. Riddle Stadium (3,000)
Gastonia Rangers (Rangers)
Sims Legion Field (3,200)
Greensboro Hornets (Yankees)
War Memorial Stadium (7,500)
Macon Braves (Braves)
Luther Williams Field (3,000)
Myrtle Beach Hurricanes (Blue Jays)
Coastal Carolina College (3,500)
Savannah Cardinals (Cardinals)
Grayson Stadium (7,500)
Spartanburg Phillies (Phillies)
Duncan Park Stadium (3,900)

Leaders by position across all leagues

CATCHER

	Club (Level-Organization)	Avg.
Nilsson	Denver (AAA-Brewers).	.366
Hernandez	Albuquerque (AAA-L.A.)	.345
Hernandez	Prince William(A-Yankees)	.328
Ramos	Columbus (AAA-Yankees)	.308
Robbins	Hagerstown (A-Orioles)	.304
Sheaffer	Portland (AAA-Twins)	.303
Pirkl	S.Bernardino (A-Mariners)	.289
Ausmus	Albany (AA-Yankees)	.285
Delgado	Syracuse (AAA-Blue Jays)	.284
Massarelli	Tucson (AAA-Astros)	.284
Beasley	Springfield (A-Cardinals)	.284

FIRST BASE

Howie	Midland (AA-Angels)	.364
Jaha	El Paso (AA-Brewers)	.344
Eppard	Salinas (A-Co-op)	.339
Martinez	Calgary (AAA-Mariners)	.326
Barbara	Midland (AA-Angels)	.324
Schu	Scranton/WB (AAA-Phillies)	.321
Karros	Albuquerque (AAA-L.A.)	.316
Cianfrocco	Harrisburg (AA-Expos)	.316
Jim Bowie	Calgary (AAA-Mariners)	.313
Martinez	Syracuse (AAA-Blue Jays)	.313
Sorrento	Portland (AAA-Twins)	.308

SECOND BASE

Stairs	Harrisburg (AA-Expos)	.333
Munoz	Albuquerque (AAA-L.A.)	.324
Santana	Phoenix (AAA-Giants)	.316
Haney	Indianapolis (AAA-Expos)	.312
Carlsen	Madison (A-Athletics)	.311
Sondrini	Augusta (A-Pirates)	.306
Meares	Visalia (A-Twins)	.303
Frye	Tulsa (AA-Rangers)	.302
Mifune	Salinas (A-Co-op)	.300
Mota	Tucson (AAA-Astros)	.299
Santana	Jacksonville (AA-Mariners)	.298

Jacksonville (continued)

PITCHING	W	L	ERA	G	SV	IP	H	BB	SO
Kerry Woodson	4	6	3.06	13	0	79.1	73	39	50
Fernando Zarranz	2	0	2.09	24	4	43	29	11	42
Clint Zavaras	2	2	4.60	6	0	31.1	36	10	21

Knoxville Blue Jays (Blue Jays)

BATTING	Avg.	AB	R	H	2B	3B	HR	RBI	SB
Domingo Cedeno, ss	.223	336	39	75	7	6	1	26	11
Juan Delarosa, of	.215	382	37	82	11	1	4	33	17
Bobby Deloach, of	.266	364	42	97	16	4	5	37	12
Ray Giannelli, 3b	.276	362	53	100	14	3	7	37	8
Alexis Infante, 3b	.227	22	3	5	1	0	0	1	0
Jeff Kent, 2b	.256	445	68	114	34	1	12	61	25
Randy Knorr, c	.176	74	7	13	4	0	0	4	2
Mike Maksudian, c	.255	231	32	59	12	3	5	35	2
Rob Montalvo, ss	.161	31	3	5	1	0	0	0	0
Jose Monzon, c	.267	116	12	31	5	0	0	11	1
Bernie Nunez, of	.197	234	16	46	11	1	4	24	4
Greg O'Halloran, c	.254	350	37	89	13	3	8	53	11
Paul Rodgers, of	.193	114	15	22	3	2	0	4	11
Mike Taylor, ss	.165	139	16	23	3	1	0	10	9
Ryan Thompson, of	.241	403	48	97	14	3	8	40	17
Jason Townley, dh	.197	213	12	42	8	0	0	13	0
Julian Yan, 1b	.280	350	45	98	16	3	16	61	2
Mark Young, of	.233	317	43	74	10	3	1	21	24
PITCHING	W	L	ERA	G	SV	IP	H	BB	SO
Pete Blohm	0	1	1.69	3	0	11.2	7	4	6
Daren Brown	0	1	10.80	3	0	3.1	6	1	2
Nate Cromwell	2	9	4.95	16	0	80	73	53	61
Jesse Cross	10	9	2.83	31	1	172	141	71	128
Darren Hall	5	3	2.60	42	2	69.1	56	27	78
Vince Horsman	4	1	2.34	42	3	81.2	79	19	80
Chris Jones	2	2	2.22	12	0	28.1	20	22	20
Daren Kizziah	4	2	.89	11	1	30.1	26	11	19
Mike Ogliaruso	2	1	3.69	7	0	39	31	18	24
Jimmy Rogers	7	11	3.31	28	0	168.1	140	90	122
Alex Sanchez	4	2	3.07	14	0	59.2	43	36	38
Mike Taylor	0	0	.00	2	0	2	2	0	1
Rich Thompson	0	3	3.55	10	3	13.2	13	2	11
Rick Trlicek	2	5	2.45	41	16	51.1	36	22	55
Anthony Ward	6	10	3.73	31	0	128	122	53	110
Dave Weathers	10	7	2.45	24	0	139.1	121	49	114
Woody Williams	3	2	3.59	18	3	43.2	42	14	37
Rob Wishnevski	6	8	2.94	31	3	101	78	53	58

Memphis Chicks (Royals)

BATTING	Avg.	AB	R	H	2B	3B	HR	RBI	SB
Pete Alborano, of	.257	183	11	47	7	1	0	16	2
Jim Baxter, c	.219	187	25	41	11	0	3	22	1
Tony Bridges, ss	.224	371	34	83	11	0	3	30	18
Doug Davis, c	.169	89	9	15	3	0	0	4	0
Jeff Garber, 2b	.250	200	24	50	4	1	0	19	7
David Gonzalez, ss	.129	70	9	9	1	0	0	6	1
Phil Hiatt, 3b	.228	206	29	47	7	1	6	33	6
Kevin Koslofski, of	.324	287	41	93	15	3	7	39	10
Deric Ladnier, dh	.241	166	17	40	5	0	2	17	1
Frank Laureano, 2b	.298	359	58	107	17	2	3	34	12
Kevin Long, of	.275	407	60	112	18	2	3	35	27
Jorge Pedre, c	.253	363	43	92	28	1	9	59	1
Kyle Reese, c	.208	24	3	5	1	0	0	1	0
Darryl Robinson, 3b	.285	351	42	100	16	3	2	35	0
Colin Ryan, c	.125	16	0	2	0	0	0	4	0

BATTING	Avg.	AB	R	H	2B	3B	HR	RBI	SB
John Toale, 1b	.281	253	41	71	14	0	8	42	3
Rich Tunison, 1b	.250	208	23	52	11	0	1	19	6
Joe Vitiello, of	.219	128	15	28	4	1	0	18	0
Bernie Walker, of	.232	185	38	43	4	4	2	18	13
Hugh Walker, of	.231	407	40	94	16	6	4	43	13
Daren Watkins, of	.153	177	21	27	2	1	1	8	9
George Wright, of	.212	52	8	11	2	0	1	6	0
PITCHING	W	L	ERA	G	SV	IP	H	BB	SO
Archie Corbin	8	8	4.66	28	0	156.1	139	90	166
Andres Cruz	1	7	6.85	11	0	47.1	56	13	18
Chip Duncan	6	3	4.79	28	1	88.1	99	32	67
Brad Hopper	1	1	4.05	20	4	47.2	52	20	24
Jim Lemasters	2	2	3.79	12	0	57	52	26	34
Dennis Moeller	4	5	2.55	10	0	53	52	21	54
Randy O'Neal	1	4	4.33	12	0	54	48	22	29
Mark Parnell	4	5	3.04	58	17	74	60	37	67
Dario Perez	0	1	8.53	3	0	13.2	15	5	12
Doug Peters	5	8	5.34	19	0	98.2	113	36	64
Hipolito Pichardo	3	11	4.27	34	0	99	116	38	75
Ed Pierce	5	11	3.84	31	0	136	136	61	90
Mike Poehl	5	5	4.13	33	0	94.2	100	39	53
Peter Roberts	4	2	2.67	25	2	34.2	31	14	29
Darryl Robinson	0	0	.00	2	0	2	2	0	0
Steve Shifflett	11	5	2.15	59	9	113	105	22	78
Jim Smith	0	1	7.04	16	0	23	24	18	20
Lou Talbert	0	2	7.62	3	0	13	21	10	3
Terry Taylor	1	2	5.55	6	0	36.2	51	16	17

Orlando Sunrays (Twins)

BATTING	Avg.	AB	R	H	2B	3B	HR	RBI	SB
Carlos Capellan, 2b	.241	365	41	88	10	1	0	29	12
Rafael Delima, of	.249	394	45	98	14	4	4	46	13
Cheo Garcia, 3b	.282	496	57	140	24	4	9	75	13
Shawn Gilbert, of	.257	529	69	136	12	5	3	38	43
Pedro Grifol, c	.150	20	0	3	0	0	0	2	0
Jay Kvasnicka, of	.271	292	48	79	12	2	4	27	23
Todd Logan, c	.184	38	5	7	2	0	0	3	0
Jose Marzan, 1b	.262	229	29	60	13	2	2	22	2
Dan Masteller, 1b	.246	370	44	91	14	5	5	35	6
Dave McCarty, of	.261	88	18	23	4	0	3	11	0
Bob McCreary, ss	.206	345	25	71	9	1	2	22	3
Kenny Morgan, of	.239	184	24	44	7	2	3	17	2
Reed Olmstead, 1b	.196	107	12	21	6	0	2	11	0
Ray Ortiz, of	.247	470	58	116	19	3	9	71	3
Derek Parks, c	.215	256	30	55	14	0	6	31	0
Joe Siwa, c	.191	157	11	30	2	0	1	14	0
Frank Valdez, dh	.247	182	13	45	10	0	2	14	1
PITCHING	W	L	ERA	G	SV	IP	H	BB	SO
Pat Bangtson	12	11	3.44	26	0	162	161	42	110
Carlos Capellan	0	0	9.00	2	0	2	4	0	3
Pete Delkus	5	5	4.73	45	1	91.1	103	24	53
Rich Garces	2	1	3.31	10	0	16.1	12	14	17
Greg Johnson	3	3	2.40	53	25	56.1	40	28	61
Orlando Lind	9	8	2.67	52	3	108	96	39	110
Pat Mahomes	8	5	1.78	18	0	116	77	57	136
Alan Newman	5	4	2.69	11	0	67	53	30	53
Rusty Richards	6	7	3.45	19	0	112.1	111	37	61
Jack Savage	2	1	1.88	6	0	14.1	9	5	14
Mike Schwabe	3	2	1.77	6	0	36.2	24	7	34
Steve Stowell	2	1	2.70	50	1	50	41	24	38
Mike Trombley	12	7	2.54	27	0	191	153	57	175
George Tsamis	0	0	.00	1	0	7	3	4	5
Rob Wassenaar	2	2	1.44	15	1	25	18	7	21
Phil Wiese	6	9	4.42	21	0	112	136	48	47

Leaders by position across all leagues

THIRD BASE

Guerrero	Shreveport (AA-Giants)	.334
Patterson	Phoenix (AAA-Giants)	.332
Young	Buffalo (AAA-Pirates)	.328
Thome	Colo. Springs (AAA-Indians)	.319
Curtis	Edmonton (AAA-Angels)	.316
Castellano	Charlotte (AA-Cubs)	.308
Cooper	Tucson (AAA-Astros)	.305
Livingstone	Toledo (AAA-Tigers)	.302
Brown	Colo. Springs (AAA-Indians)	.301
Jorgensen	Portland (AAA-Twins)	.298
Lowery	Gastonia (A-Rangers)	.294

SHORTSTOP

Amaral	Calgary (AAA-Mariners)	.346
Colon	Tulsa (AA-Rangers)	.336
Jones	Macon (A-Braves)	.326
Tatum	El Paso (AA-Brewers)	.320
Wilson	Birmingham (AA-White Sox)	.315
Disarcina	Edmonton (AAA-Angels)	.310
Cedeno	Tucson (AAA-Astros)	.303
Rosario	Toledo (AAA-Tigers)	.300
Barker	San Antonio (AA-Dodgers)	.292
Batiste	Scranton/WB (AAA-Phillies)	.292
Hardtke	Columbia (A-Mets)	.290

OUTFIELD

Bell	Syracuse (AAA-Blue Jays)	.346
Washington	Kinston (A-Indians)	.342
Mieske	High Desert (A-Padres)	.341
Lewis	Phoenix (AAA-Giants)	.340
Mercedes	Rochester (AAA-Orioles)	.334
Lennon	Calgary (AAA-Mariners)	.329
Amaro	Edmonton (AAA-Angels)	.326
Olander	Denver (AAA-Brewers)	.325
Berroa	Colo. Springs (AAA-Indians)	.322
McNeely	Lynchburg (A-Red Sox)	.322
Cummings	Kenosha (A-Twins)	.322

Leaders across all minor leagues

BATTING AVERAGE

	Club	League	
Nilsson, Dave	Den	Amer	.366
Howie, Mark	Mdl	Tex	.364
Amaral, Rich	Cgy	Pcl	.346
Bell, Derek	Syr	Int	.346
Hernandez, C.	Abq	Pcl	.345

HOME RUNS

Gainer, Jay	Hds	Cal	32
Burnitz, J.	Wpt	East	31
Jaha, John	Elp	Tex	30
Piazza, Mike	Bak	Cal	29

RBI

Jaha, John	Elp	Tex	134
Tatum, Jim	Elp	Tex	128
Howie, Mark	Mdl	Tex	123
Gainer, Jay	Hds	Cal	120
Mieske, Matt	Hds	Cal	119

STOLEN BASES

Maynard, Tow	Jax	Sou	88
Noland, J.D.	Hds	Cal	81
Ozuna, Mateo	Spr	Mid	78
Young, Eric	Abq	Pcl	71
Tavarez, Jesus	Sbr	Cal	69

Texas League

Arkansas Travelers (Cardinals)

BATTING	Avg.	AB	R	H	2B	3B	HR	RBI	SB
Frank Abreu, 3b	.238	256	24	61	12	1	1	20	5
Cliff Brannon, of	.281	399	46	112	26	1	4	44	11
Greg Carmona, ss	.182	33	1	6	0	0	0	1	0
Ric Christian, of	.238	282	29	67	12	3	0	21	10
Tripp Cromer, ss	.229	227	28	52	12	1	1	18	0
Steve Fanning, 2b	.241	162	19	39	7	0	1	15	3
Joe Federico, 1b	.209	110	12	23	7	1	1	13	0
Joey Fernandez, 1b	.217	46	9	10	3	0	2	8	0
Jose Fernandez, c	.228	281	46	64	14	1	12	27	0
Mike Fiore, of	.263	453	60	119	31	4	8	50	7
Luis Martinez, of	.271	280	28	76	17	2	2	32	6
Scott Melvin, ph	.288	52	3	15	0	0	1	7	0
Don Prybylinski, c	.185	119	13	22	9	0	0	13	0
Tim Redman, c	.341	44	3	15	2	0	0	1	0
Mike Ross, 3b	.247	255	31	63	18	0	7	28	2
John Sellick, 1b	.245	387	57	95	18	2	18	63	3
Jeff Shireman, 2b	.242	368	49	89	12	1	1	28	2
Charlie White, of	.237	329	33	78	15	3	2	30	11
PITCHING	**W**	**L**	**ERA**	**G**	**SV**	**IP**	**H**	**BB**	**SO**
Cliff Brannon	1	0	6.75	2	0	3.2	3	4	3
David Cassidy	2	2	7.62	6	0	28.1	44	15	15
Mark Clark	5	5	4.00	15	0	92.1	99	30	76
Fidel Compres	4	2	3.94	27	9	32	37	12	18
John Corona	0	2	4.45	27	0	30.1	27	21	23
John Ericks	5	14	4.77	25	0	140.2	138	84	103
Luis Faccio	7	8	3.76	20	1	105.1	102	39	74
Todd Gonzales	0	1	3.86	3	0	9.1	6	10	5
Dale Kisten	1	5	6.57	36	1	49.1	66	40	41
John Lepley	1	2	4.41	16	0	16.1	17	14	7
Steffen Majer	4	6	4.44	34	0	97.1	91	57	72
Mike Milchin	3	2	3.06	6	0	35.1	27	8	38
Donovan Osbourne	8	12	3.63	26	0	166	177	43	130
Gab Ozuna	0	2	6.08	17	2	24.2	26	15	25
Lee Plemel	1	3	3.30	53	3	85.2	87	25	57
Dave Richardson	1	2	2.51	12	2	14.1	14	3	12
Troy Salvior	0	2	6.27	13	4	19.2	24	10	13
Brian Stone	0	1	7.11	2	0	6.1	9	6	6
Dean Weese	0	1	9.61	14	0	20.2	27	14	15
Dennis Wiseman	6	15	4.16	26	0	149.1	167	35	72

El Paso Diablos (Brewers)

BATTING	Avg.	AB	R	H	2B	3B	HR	RBI	SB
Shon Ashley, of	.308	493	86	152	28	5	24	100	2
John Byington, 3b	.273	501	60	137	27	1	9	89	3
Craig Cooper, 1b	.299	147	25	44	8	1	7	33	0
Ruben Escalera, of	.316	443	101	140	26	7	6	67	9
Craig Faulkner, c	.307	267	39	82	18	0	10	46	1
John Finn, 2b	.300	230	48	69	12	2	2	24	8
Mike Guerrero, 2b	.205	117	23	24	2	0	0	13	2
Mitch Hannahs, 2b	.244	86	23	21	5	1	1	9	1
Dave Jacas, of	.264	511	103	135	26	9	6	53	27
Kenny Jackson, of	.302	427	77	129	25	9	17	66	9
John Jaha, 1b	.344	486	121	167	38	3	30	134	12
Dave Liddell, c	.205	39	5	8	1	0	1	6	0
Pat Listach, ss	.253	186	40	47	5	2	0	13	14
Dave Nilsson, c	.418	249	52	104	24	3	5	57	4
Randy Snyder, c	.208	24	7	5	1	0	0	1	1
Jim Tatum, ss	.320	493	99	158	27	8	18	128	5
Tim Wallace, ss	.269	167	20	45	2	0	1	16	7

PITCHING	W	L	ERA	G	SV	IP	H	BB	SO
Gibson Alba	1	1	11.57	3	0	2.1	5	4	2
Mark Ambrose	10	6	4.26	19	0	112	120	58	81
Larry Carter	0	0	9.00	1	0	3	5	1	1
Mark Chapman	4	3	3.72	45	5	92	90	37	63
Jim Czajkowski	5	2	4.94	43	11	78.1	100	29	69
Mike Davino	1	1	5.61	12	2	26.2	36	14	13
Greg Everson	0	0	7.36	7	0	11	18	5	3
Tim Fortugno	5	1	1.99	20	1	54.1	40	25	73
Dean Freeland	3	2	4.76	8	1	40.2	46	17	25
Don Gordon	0	0	7.98	7	0	15.2	20	2	7
Otis Green	3	3	3.18	9	0	51	35	25	49
Chris Johnson	4	4	6.48	13	0	67.2	85	40	43
Mark Kiefer	7	1	3.33	12	0	76.2	62	43	72
Steve Lienhard	9	9	4.83	26	0	121	157	43	69
Greg Mathews	0	0	6.30	2	0	10	11	6	8
Tom McGraw	1	1	5.80	9	1	36.2	43	21	28
Angel Miranda	4	2	2.54	38	11	74.1	55	41	86
Steve Monson	3	4	5.91	17	0	64	84	28	38
Jeff Schwarz	11	8	4.89	27	0	142.2	139	97	134
Mike Smith	3	3	5.22	11	0	50	52	29	44
Steve Sparks	1	2	9.53	4	0	17	30	9	10
Brandy Vann	2	3	9.85	19	0	25.2	41	26	24
Tim Wallace	0	0	1.50	4	0	6	2	2	3
Rob Wishnevski	4	0	3.94	7	0	16	17	6	9

Jackson Generals (Astros)

BATTING	Avg.	AB	R	H	2B	3B	HR	RBI	SB
Willie Ansley, of	.232	233	43	54	15	5	1	20	9
Jeff Baldwin, 1b	.206	34	7	7	0	0	0	4	0
Ed Beuerlein, c	.263	19	4	5	1	0	1	4	0
Kevin Dean, of	.237	278	34	66	11	4	2	33	9
Tony Eusebio, c	.261	222	27	58	8	3	2	31	3
Tom Forrester, ph	.231	39	4	9	3	0	0	5	0
David Hajek, 3b	.191	94	10	18	6	0	0	9	2
Rusty Harris, ss	.240	150	21	36	9	0	0	18	4
Trent Hubbard, 2b	.297	455	78	135	21	3	2	41	39
Bert Hunter, of	.256	379	58	97	17	7	1	43	32
Bernie Jenkins, of	.260	335	42	87	14	4	5	36	21
Frank Kellner, ss	.270	311	47	84	7	4	2	25	6
Lance Madsen, 3b	.221	407	54	90	20	5	7	50	8
Scott Makarewicz, c	.231	229	23	53	9	0	2	30	1
John Massarelli, c	.211	38	3	8	2	0	0	0	4
Mark McLemore, 2b	.227	22	6	5	3	0	1	4	1
Joe Mikulik, of	.293	492	76	144	17	4	15	94	20
Orlando Miller, ss	.186	70	5	13	6	0	1	5	0
Howard Prager, 1b	.305	357	57	109	26	2	11	65	9
Ed Renteria, 2b	.288	59	11	17	3	0	1	6	1

PITCHING	W	L	ERA	G	SV	IP	H	BB	SO
Harold Allen	4	7	4.50	26	0	92	90	74	61
Sam August	1	2	5.24	7	0	34.1	27	19	25
Pete Bauer	3	7	3.81	46	2	78	50	33	80
Kevin Coffman	8	7	5.03	30	1	106.2	79	101	105
Chris Gardner	13	5	3.15	22	0	131.1	116	75	72
Carl Grovom	1	1	3.63	10	0	17.1	18	8	17
Dean Hartgraves	6	5	2.68	19	0	74	60	25	44
Bert Hunter	0	0	.00	3	0	2	3	0	2
Todd Jones	4	3	4.88	10	0	55.1	51	39	37
Jeff Juden	6	3	3.10	16	0	96.2	84	44	75
Keith Kaiser	1	4	11.54	14	0	39	40	71	41
Steve Larose	1	3	4.05	26	6	33.1	34	22	30
Rob Mallicoat	4	1	3.77	18	1	31	20	11	34

Leaders across all minor leagues

HITS

Howie, Mark	Mdl	Tex	188
Lofton, Kenny	Tcn	Pcl	168
Stairs, Matt	Hrb	East	168
Mieske, Matt	Hds	Cal	168
Jaha, John	Elp	Tex	167

DOUBLES

Amaro, Ruben	Edm	Pcl	42
Maurer, Rob	Okc	Amer	41
Guerrero, Juan	Shr	Tex	40
Lee, Derek	Van	Pcl	38
Becker, Rich	Ken	Mid	38
Jaha, John	Elp	Tex	38
Wood, Ted	Phx	Pcl	38

TRIPLES

Lofton, Kenny	Tcn	Pcl	17
Flora, Kevin	Mdl	Tex	15
Murray, Glen	Rkf	Mid	14

EXTRA BASE HITS

Jaha, John	Elp	Tex	71
Maurer, Rob	Okc	Amer	64
Karros, Eric	Abq	Pcl	63
Medina, Luis	Csp	Pcl	61
Guerrero, Juan	Shr	Tex	61

Leaders across all minor leagues

SLUGGING PCT.

Jaha, John	Elp	Tex	.619
Medina, Luis	Csp	Pcl	.593
Plantier, Phil	Paw	Int	.557
Schu, Rick	Swb	Int	.552
Karros, Eric	Abq	Pcl	.551
Martinez, Tino	Cgy	Pcl	.548

ON-BASE PCT.

Mieske, Matt	Hds	Cal	.456
Eppard, Jim	Sln	Cal	.453
Patterson, Dave	Phx	Pcl	.447
Robbins, Doug	Hag	East	.444
Meadows, Scott	Roc	Int	.441

TPA/SO RATIO

Sherman, Darrell	Wch	Tex	21.18
Vina, Fernando	Clb	Sal	21.07
Hale, Chip	Por	Pcl	18.64
Sanchez, Rey	Iwa	Amer	17.56
Casillas, Adam	Nvl	Amer	17.11

SWITCH-HITTERS

Colon, Cris	Tul	Tex	.336
Amaro, Ruben	Edm	Pcl	.326
Jones, Chipper	Mac	Sal	.326
Munoz, Jose	Abq	Pcl	.324
Cummings, Midre	Ken	Mid	.322
Santana, Andres	Phx	Pcl	.316

Jackson (continued)

PITCHING	W	L	ERA	G	SV	IP	H	BB	SO
Bob Resnikoff	1	1	3.00	26	1	42	40	13	34
Shane Reynolds	8	9	4.47	27	0	151	165	62	116
Dave Richards	1	1	2.66	29	1	44	30	22	55
Bob Sebra	0	0	.00	1	0	2.1	1	0	2
Rich Simon	4	2	2.18	56	20	70.1	55	30	54
Wally Trice	1	3	4.18	20	1	24.2	26	5	27
Brian Williams	2	1	4.20	3	0	15	17	7	15
Rodney Windes	1	0	1.29	13	0	21	23	14	19

Midland Angels (Angels)

BATTING	Avg.	AB	R	H	2B	3B	HR	RBI	SB
Ed Alfonzo, 3b	.277	83	13	23	1	1	4	13	0
Don Barbara, 1b	.362	224	43	81	13	0	10	40	0
Jeff Barns, 3b	.219	32	5	7	0	0	0	3	0
Mick Billmeyer, c	.305	128	15	39	7	2	1	25	0
Frank Dominguez, c	.222	18	2	4	1	0	0	1	0
Damion Easley, ss	.254	452	73	115	24	4	6	57	22
Kevin Flora, 2b	.285	484	97	138	14	15	12	67	40
Larry Gonzales, c	.319	257	27	82	13	0	4	56	2
Mark Howie, 1b	.364	516	101	188	32	2	18	123	7
Bobby Jones, of	.221	285	35	63	12	0	1	35	4
Marcus Lawton, of	.287	435	76	125	25	8	5	53	29
Walt McConnell, dh	.284	264	41	75	14	1	7	65	1
Ken Rivers, c	.257	109	11	28	6	0	2	15	1
Tim Salmon, of	.245	465	100	114	26	4	23	94	12
Ramon Sambo, of	.286	161	29	46	5	2	0	10	14
Daryl Sconiers, dh	.275	102	15	28	8	0	4	14	2
Terry Taylor, 3b	.196	102	15	20	6	1	0	8	0
Alex Trevino, c	.227	44	8	10	3	0	2	10	0
Reggie Williams, of	.310	319	77	99	12	3	1	30	21
PITCHING	W	L	ERA	G	SV	IP	H	BB	SO
Clemente Acosta	0	6	7.39	37	0	71.2	109	27	59
Jeff Barns	0	0	.00	1	0	2	0	0	2
Hector Berrios	2	1	2.81	18	2	16	13	3	17
Randy Bockus	3	0	7.27	12	0	17.1	28	6	10
Mike Butcher	9	6	5.22	41	3	88	93	46	70
Glenn Carter	1	6	8.26	8	0	40.1	69	26	13
Marvin Cobb	2	2	4.04	42	3	78	73	45	72
Sherman Corbett	0	1	3.33	13	1	24.1	24	9	17
Mark Holzemer	0	0	1.42	2	0	6.1	3	5	7
Todd James	12	10	4.81	27	0	161	186	73	94
Steve King	0	3	12.39	5	0	20.1	40	16	12
Phillip Leftwich	1	0	3.00	1	0	6	5	5	3
Fili Martinez	4	5	6.37	15	0	82	104	50	42
Rafael Montalvo	5	1	5.62	22	0	58.2	89	15	30
John Pawlowski	1	3	2.49	15	0	47	42	16	36
Doug Robertson	2	2	4.82	36	9	52.1	65	23	40
Dave Shotkoski	5	11	4.28	23	0	130.1	161	40	85
Alan Sontag	2	3	6.33	15	0	70.2	90	37	26
Fernando Valenzuela	3	1	1.96	4	0	23	18	6	17
Don Vidmar	13	5	3.16	22	0	145.1	168	47	64
Mark Zappelli	2	2	2.48	32	11	33.2	26	13	31

San Antonio Missions (Dodgers)

BATTING	Avg.	AB	R	H	2B	3B	HR	RBI	SB
Jorge Alvarez, 2b	.298	225	33	67	14	2	3	23	9
Bryan Baar, c	.224	348	33	78	19	0	10	51	3
Tim Barker, ss	.292	401	70	117	20	4	2	46	32
Tony Barron, of	.235	200	35	47	2	2	9	31	8
Rafael Bournigal, 3b	.323	65	6	21	2	0	0	9	2
Adam Brown, ph	.270	37	3	10	1	0	1	4	0
Braulio Castillo, of	.300	297	49	89	19	3	8	48	22
Dino Ebel, ss	.275	40	3	11	3	0	0	2	1
Steve Finken, 3b	.288	386	53	111	19	4	5	48	8
Freddy Gonzalez, of	.167	24	1	4	0	0	1	5	0
Garey Ingram, of	.000	1	0	0	0	0	0	1	0
Alan Lewis, 3b	.109	46	3	5	1	0	1	5	0
Brett Magnusson, of	.265	358	69	95	22	2	11	66	5
Scott Marabell, of	.217	83	11	18	4	0	1	7	1
Raul Mondesi, of	.272	213	32	58	10	5	5	26	7
Chris Morrow, of	.360	89	13	32	6	0	2	8	1
Jose Munoz, of	.317	123	25	39	6	2	0	13	4
Rex Peters, 1b	.204	108	19	22	2	0	1	7	0
Lance Rice, c	.200	215	23	43	8	0	3	28	2
Brian Traxler, 1b	.256	379	50	97	24	0	7	61	1
Mike White, of	.290	255	25	74	13	4	1	37	5
Eric Young, 2b	.280	461	82	129	17	4	3	35	71

PITCHING	W	L	ERA	G	SV	IP	H	BB	SO
Steve Allen	1	0	4.43	12	1	20.1	22	10	25
Pedro Astacio	4	11	4.78	19	0	113	142	39	62
Cameron Biberdorf	0	3	8.84	14	1	18.1	23	12	18
Jason Brosnan	0	1	17.61	2	0	8.2	15	11	8
Albert Bustillos	5	5	4.65	16	0	93	113	23	47
Ray Calhoun	0	3	6.37	21	1	30.2	34	18	11
Dale Coleman	1	2	3.42	32	1	50	56	24	36
Dennis Cook	1	3	2.49	7	0	51.2	43	10	45
Orel Hershiser	0	1	2.57	1	0	7	11	1	5
Mike James	9	5	4.53	15	0	89.1	88	51	74
Dave Lynch	0	1	6.75	11	1	13.1	17	6	10
Isidrio Marquez	4	1	2.09	34	3	47.1	42	19	36
Pedro Martinez	7	5	1.76	12	0	77.2	57	31	74
Zak Shinall	2	4	2.80	25	9	55.2	53	21	29
Dennis Springer	10	10	4.43	30	0	165.2	153	91	138
Jose Tapia	0	0	9.00	2	1	2	4	0	3
Ramon Taveras	0	1	12.81	8	0	20.2	31	15	15
Jimmy Terrill	2	6	3.25	27	0	72	69	33	36
Jody Treadwell	3	3	4.72	10	0	61	73	22	43
Mike Wilkins	6	6	4.30	22	1	111	130	38	87
James Wray	6	4	3.48	43	1	67.1	58	25	56

Leaders across all minor leagues

PITCHING ERA

Torres, Salomon	Cln	Mid	1.41
Martinez, Jose	Clb	Sal	1.49
Militello, Sam	Alb	East	1.57
Wegmann, Tom	Slu	Fsl	1.65
Bolton, Rodney	Bir	Sou	1.78
Mutis, Jeff	Can	East	1.80

WINS

Martinez, Jose	Clb	Sal	20
Martinez, Pedro	Abq	Pcl	18
Vidmar, Don	Mdl	Tex	17

COMPLETE GAMES

Michno, Tom	Mia	Fsl	13
Martinez, Jose	Clb	Sal	9
8 tied			8

SHUTOUTS

Bolton, Rodney	Bir	Sou	4
Mutis, Jeff	Can	East	4
Painter, Lance	Wlo	Mid	4
Huisman, Richard	Sjo	Cal	4

MINOR LEAGUE STATISTICS

353

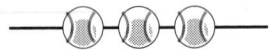

Leaders across all minor leagues

SAVES

Soper, Michael	Kin	Caro	41
Huffman, Rod	Cln	Mid	35
Wohlers, Mark	Rmd	Int	32
Keller, Clyde	Spr	Mid	32
Sharko, Gary	Sjo	Cal	31
Kelly, John	Sav	Sal	30

GAMES

Bailey, Roy	Sav	Sal	73
Eversgerd, Bryan	Sav	Sal	72
Ayrault, Bob	Swb	Int	68
Wilkins, Dean	Tcn	Pcl	65
A., Francisco	Rno	Cal	64

INNINGS PITCHED

Michno, Tom	Mia	Fsl	216.0
Torres, Salomon	Cln	Mid	210.2
Painter, Lance	Wlo	Mid	200.0
Sparks, Steve	Stk	Cal	196.2
Williams, Mike	Rea	East	195.2
Martinez, Jose	Clb	Sal	193.1

STRIKEOUTS

Huisman, Richard	Sjo	Cal	216
Torres, Salomon	Cln	Mid	214
Painter, Lance	Wlo	Mid	201
Martinez, Pedro	Abq	Pcl	192
Michno, Tom	Mia	Fsl	190

Shreveport Captains (Giants)

BATTING	Avg.	AB	R	H	2B	3B	HR	RBI	SB
Frank Carey, ph	.000	5	0	0	0	0	0	0	0
Royce Clayton, ss	.280	485	84	136	22	8	5	68	36
Jamie Cooper, of	.230	374	57	86	9	2	2	25	25
Adell Davenport, 1b	.230	165	19	38	3	0	7	24	0
Tom Ealy, of	.201	199	29	40	5	4	3	21	1
Dan Fernandez, c	.250	12	3	3	0	0	0	1	0
Juan Guerrero, 3b	.334	479	78	160	40	2	19	94	14
Steve Hosey, of	.293	409	79	120	21	5	17	74	24
Erik Johnson, 3b	.219	146	27	32	7	0	2	20	6
Kevin Kasper, 2b	.250	72	13	18	2	0	1	9	2
Dan Lewis, 1b	.291	422	66	123	30	1	13	90	6
James McNamara, c	.275	109	13	30	8	2	2	20	2
Dave Patterson, 1b	.350	177	35	62	15	0	2	29	3
John Patterson, 2b	.295	464	81	137	31	13	4	56	40
Reuben Smiley, of	.230	318	57	73	8	4	5	31	37
Scooter Tucker, c	.284	352	49	100	29	1	4	49	3
Pete Weber, of	.250	116	21	29	8	0	0	7	6

PITCHING	W	L	ERA	G	SV	IP	H	BB	SO
Johnny Ard	9	3	2.74	13	0	89.2	77	36	58
Larry Carter	9	8	2.95	24	0	149.1	124	51	133
Bryan Hickerson	3	4	3.00	23	2	39	36	14	41
Tom Hostetler	4	1	3.55	9	0	46.2	39	20	33
Paul McClellan	11	1	2.82	14	0	96.2	75	30	63
Kevin Meier	9	6	5.04	33	0	136.2	157	38	79
Jim Myers	6	4	2.48	62	24	76.1	71	30	51
Kurt Peltzer	0	1	8.53	5	0	6.1	13	7	1
Jim Pena	7	4	4.77	45	2	83	84	41	51
Vlad Perez	1	1	3.35	27	1	43	40	19	22
Dan Rambo	12	6	3.67	26	0	147	146	43	103
Pat Rapp	6	2	2.69	10	0	60.1	52	22	46
Steve Reed	2	0	.83	15	7	22.2	17	3	26
Kevin Rogers	4	6	3.36	22	0	118	124	54	108
Rob Taylor	3	3	4.14	39	2	67.1	62	30	68

Tulsa Drillers (Rangers)

BATTING	Avg.	AB	R	H	2B	3B	HR	RBI	SB
Kevin Belcher, of	.250	84	16	21	5	1	3	17	2
Mike Berger, c	.185	27	2	5	1	0	0	2	1
Paco Burgos, 3b	.222	216	15	48	5	1	1	16	0
Mike Burton, 1b	.241	361	43	87	18	2	7	49	0
Cris Colon, ss	.392	102	20	40	6	2	3	28	0
Jeff Frye, 2b	.302	503	92	152	32	11	4	41	15
Pat Garman, dh	.224	98	9	22	6	0	2	16	0
Dave Green, dh	.285	200	22	57	16	0	4	32	2
Rusty Greer, of	.297	64	12	19	3	2	3	12	2
Donald Harris, of	.227	450	47	102	17	8	11	53	9
Jose Hernandez, ss	.239	301	36	72	17	4	1	20	4
Greg Iavarone, c	.148	27	2	4	0	0	0	1	0
Chad Kreuter, c	.234	128	23	30	6	1	2	10	1
Peter Kuld, c	.211	218	20	46	6	0	6	19	2
Trey McCoy, dh	.241	137	21	33	7	0	10	32	0
Rod Morris, of	.269	383	44	103	17	8	0	35	9
Ivan Rodriguez, c	.274	175	16	48	7	2	3	28	1
Dan Rohrmeier, of	.292	418	67	122	20	2	5	62	3
Luke Sable, 3b	.289	339	32	98	12	7	0	33	9
Fred Samson, 3b	.208	207	31	43	12	1	2	15	2
Rick Wrona, c	.159	82	4	13	0	1	3	7	0

PITCHING	W	L	ERA	G	SV	IP	H	BB	SO
Brian Bohanon	0	1	2.31	2	0	12.2	9	11	6
Jeff Bronkey	0	0	9.39	4	0	8.2	11	5	5
Rob Brown	7	6	3.29	43	4	118.2	130	39	86
Mike Campbell	5	7	5.23	23	1	108.1	104	51	90
Nick Felix	0	0	6.65	11	0	22.2	22	10	16
Christopher Gies	2	2	4.82	8	0	37.1	51	13	25
Bryan Gore	7	8	4.28	27	2	107.1	122	33	60
Ray Hayward	0	3	4.45	8	0	28.1	33	13	21
Jon Hurst	2	1	2.16	5	1	25	18	6	17
Barry Manuel	2	7	3.29	56	25	68.1	63	34	45
Eric McCray	4	3	4.65	21	0	41.2	32	32	31
Tony Menendez	3	0	1.29	3	0	14	9	4	14
Robb Nen	0	2	5.79	6	0	28	24	20	23
David Perez	5	14	4.22	25	0	147	130	69	97
Bobby Reed	4	4	2.55	12	1	67	62	22	33
Brian Romero	6	5	4.98	23	1	94	92	52	79
Steve Rowley	2	4	6.02	10	0	43.1	48	27	24
Luke Sable	0	0	36.00	2	0	2	5	4	0
Cedric Shaw	9	8	4.06	26	0	142	142	66	111
Chris Shiflett	0	0	5.59	4	0	10.2	7	5	12

Wichita Wranglers (Padres)

BATTING	Avg.	AB	R	H	2B	3B	HR	RBI	SB
Mike Basso, c	.242	165	17	40	10	0	3	26	0
Brian Cisarik, of	.284	384	68	109	24	3	5	52	27
Greg Conley, c	.308	65	7	20	3	0	1	10	0
Greg David, c	.255	306	42	78	11	0	6	46	5
Vince Harris, of	.286	381	78	109	12	1	0	39	48
Charles Hillemann, of	.268	291	45	78	19	1	7	44	10
Luis Lopez, 2b	.268	452	43	121	17	1	1	41	6
Tim McWilliam, of	.296	307	40	91	20	1	7	56	1
Tom Redington, 3b	.284	394	54	112	23	0	5	57	2
Darrell Sherman, of	.295	502	93	148	17	3	3	48	43
Phil Stephenson, dh	.471	34	4	16	5	0	0	8	0
Jose Valentin, ss	.251	447	73	112	22	5	17	68	8
G. Velasquez, 1b	.295	501	72	148	26	3	21	100	4

PITCHING	W	L	ERA	G	SV	IP	H	BB	SO
Doug Brocail	10	7	3.87	34	6	146.1	147	43	108
Renay Bryand	3	2	3.09	37	1	55.1	53	14	34
Rafael Chavez	3	0	5.20	38	3	71	80	41	49
Everett Cunningham	0	5	7.43	37	0	67.2	77	41	48
Rick Davis	5	6	3.98	50	13	72.1	82	19	57
Luis Galindez	2	8	6.41	17	0	86.2	116	43	43
Terry Gilmore	1	2	6.04	9	0	25.1	28	7	18
Atlee Hammaker	0	1	3.52	5	0	8.2	10	0	9
Chris Haslock	0	0	6.62	10	0	18.2	21	13	9
Howard Hilton	3	1	4.78	26	3	38.2	37	17	31
Kerry Knox	4	4	4.91	28	0	114.2	133	36	51
Jim Lewis	0	0	.00	2	1	3.2	4	4	3
Pedro Martinez	11	10	5.23	26	0	157.2	169	57	95
Darrin Reichle	4	3	5.02	14	0	57.1	63	27	32
A.J. Sager	4	3	4.13	10	0	65.1	69	16	31
Frank Seminara	15	10	3.38	27	0	176	173	68	107
Roger Smithberg	2	3	4.79	7	0	41.1	49	16	23
Tito Stewart	0	0	3.38	7	0	8	10	1	1
Brian Wood	4	2	2.30	11	2	16.2	12	7	20

Leaders across all minor leagues

SO/9 IP (starters)

Sanford, Mo	Nvl	Amer	11.30
Green, Otis	Elp	Tex	11.07
Huisman, Richard	Sjo	Cal	10.66
Mlicki, Dave	Clm	Sal	10.58
Elliott, Donnie	Clw	Fsl	10.48

AVG. vs. (starters)

Green, Otis	Elp	Tex	.172
Quirico, Rafael	Gbo	Sal	.187
Hutton, Mark	Col	Int	.187
Wall, Donnie	Osc	Fsl	.192
Rhodes, Arthur	Hag	East	.194

SO/9 IP (relievers)

Seanez, Rudy	Csp	Pcl	14.87
Scott, Darryl	Qcy	Mid	14.69
Hoffman, Trevor	Cng	Sou	14.16
Pennington, B.	Fre	Caro	13.64
Fletcher, Dennis	Spr	Mid	12.21

AVG. vs. (relievers)

Scott, Darryl	Qcy	Mid	.137
Keller, Clyde	Spr	Mid	.146
Vasquez, Julian	Slu	Fsl	.163
Ponte, Edward	Osc	Fsl	.166
Wohlers, Mark	Rmd	Int	.167

355

F.Y.I.

Farm teams chewed out

By Rod Beaton

Chew on this, minor leaguers. Commissioner Fay Vincent ordered smokeless tobacco to be outlawed (starting in 1991) at ballparks in Class A Appalachian and Northwest leagues, and in rookie Pioneer and Gulf Coast leagues. That means all on-field personnel.

"I'm not sure baseball has the right to dictate a person's personal habits," said Eddie Watt, a coach for Bradenton (Fla.), Atlanta's Gulf Coast team. Watt has chewed tobacco for 30 years.

"I could give it up, but it would be a difficult thing," he said. "I gave up drinking and haven't had a drink in three years. I smoked for 25 years, and I no longer smoke. But I gave up those things because it was my decision. I had a choice."

Major leaguers can still dip and chew, but some, such as Padre Tony Gwynn, are trying to do without: "To be honest, I think [the ban] is good. I'm a guy who has dipped a long time and I'm trying to quit . . . I know the risks."

AAA expansion teams: Charlotte, Ottawa

By Bill Koenig

Charlotte, N.C., and Ottawa, Ont., won the expansion derby and are to begin play in 1993 in conjunction with National League expansion. They won out over semi-finalists Birmingham (Ala.), Bowie (Md.) and Tulsa (Okla.) in a pool of 18 possible applicants.

Minor League Commissioner Sal Artiaga and Major League Commissioner Fay Vincent had the final say in approving the two teams. Charlotte is home to the Chicago Cubs' Double-A farm team, and Ottawa hasn't hosted a team since 1954. The new Ottawa franchise is owned by cable TV magnate Howard Darwin, who also owns the Ottawa 67s Junior A hockey team.

Interleague play is out

By Bill Koenig

Triple-A fans in International League and American Association cities will be seeing fewer major-league prospects in 1992.

The IL voted July 9 to end interleague play, which the two 8-team leagues had used the last four seasons.

IL teams voting to end interleague play: Columbus, Pawtucket, Scranton/Wilkes-Barre, Syracuse and Toledo. Three voted to keep it: Richmond, Rochester and Tidewater.

The American Association, which favored the current system, is made up of Buffalo, Denver, Indianapolis, Iowa, Louisville, Nashville, Oklahoma City and Omaha. The end of interleague play means:

▶Rochester and Buffalo, little more than an hour apart, no longer will play each other.

▶New York Mets fans in Tidewater won't see prospects from NL East rivals Pittsburgh (Buffalo), Montreal (Indianapolis), St. Louis (Louisville) or Chicago (Iowa).

▶Fans in Nashville—considered to be Atlanta Braves territory—no longer will get to see Braves prospects with Richmond.

▶Geographic rivalries such as Indianapolis-Toledo and Louisville-Columbus will be dropped.

▶The American Association officials asked the IL to reconsider its vote and report back at the annual Triple-A fall meetings in September in Palm Springs, Calif.

With the elimination of interleague play, IL teams will play a 144-game schedule next season: 24 against each team in the same division and 18 against teams in the other division. The American Association will play a 142-game season: 26 against teams within the division and 16 against clubs from the other division.

Youth Leagues

USA SNAPSHOTS®

A look at statistics that shape the sports world

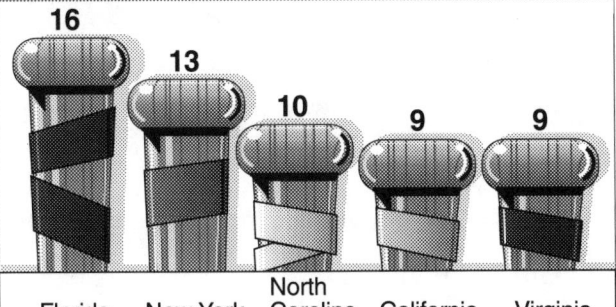

States with the most minor league baseball teams

Florida	New York	North Carolina	California	Virginia
16	13	10	9	9

Source: National Association of Professional Baseball Leagues

By Suzy Parker, USA TODAY

Little League: Diamonds in the rough

Little League facts

Here's a nutshell look at Little League:

‣**Founded:** 1939
‣**Ages:** 11-18
‣**Divisions:** Little League (11-12); Junior League (age 13); Senior League (13-15); Big League (16-18)
‣**Total active players:** 2.5 million
‣**Countries:** USA; 45 foreign

In the beginning, there was Little League. This is where it all begins—real uniforms, organized teams, umpires, proud moms and dads, and dreams of one day smacking a home run out of a major league ballpark.

Perhaps the greatest thrill of Little League—aside from the delight of the players themselves—is watching the talents of these youngsters develop under the guidance of devoted coaches. Brien Taylor, 1991's top overall free-agent draft pick, was once a wild Little League pitcher who walked more batters than he struck out. Today he is the New York Yankees' promise of the future—and it all started in Little League.

But youth baseball is much more than an incubator for future big-league stars. It teaches youngsters how to be part of a team, how to accept the losses along with the victories and, most of all, how to have a lot of fun every step of the way.

The best-known of all youth baseball associations, Little League was founded in 1939 in Williamsport, Pa., the site of its annual World Series for 11- and 12-year-olds. Now encompassing 46 countries and 2.5 million youngsters, competitions are held in four age groups in baseball, as well as three age groups for girls playing softball.

The Tai Chung Little League from Taiwan won the 45th annual Little League World Series (1991), the fifth time in the last six seasons a Taiwanese team has won the series. Teams from Taiwan also took two other age groups: a Taiwanese all-star team in Big League (16- to 18-year-olds) and Ping Tung in Senior League (ages 13-15). The only USA winner: Spring, Texas in Junior League (for 13-year-olds).

How to find a team

Little League Baseball's national headquarters is located at the site of its annual World Series—in Williamsport, Pa. To find your local offices, contact the regional headquarters for your state, listed below:

‣**National Headquarters**, P.O. Box 3485, Williamsport, PA 17701; (717) 326-1921
‣**Western Region Headquarters**, 6707 Little League Drive, San Bernardino, CA 92407; (714) 887-6444
‣**Central Region Headquarters**, 4360 N. Mitthoeffer Rd., Indianapolis, IN 46236; (317) 897-6127
‣**Southern Region Headquarters**, P.O. Box 13366, St. Petersburg, FL 33733; (813) 344-2661
‣**Eastern Region Headquarters**, P.O. Box 3485, Williamsport, PA 17701; (717) 326-1921
‣**Texas State Headquarters**, 1612 University-Parks Dr., Waco, TX 76706; (817) 756-1816

Little League World Series

By Pete Williams

The Little League World Series is the world's largest tournament—and the only postseason event that can stake a literal claim to being a world series.

Players from 7,000 teams worldwide played for the chance to become one of only eight teams to earn the trip to Williamsport, Pa., Aug. 20-24, to compete for the title, arguably the most elusive of baseball championships.

Memories of the tournament might eventually fade for the players, ages 11 to 13. But some are continually reminded, even after going on to bigger leagues.

"People ask me about it all the time," said Pirate McClendon, who hit five home runs in five at-bats in 1971 for runner-up Gary, Ind. "Nobody forgets and it's been 20 years. It's kind of frightening to say that.

"I don't remember that vividly, but I know it was exciting. It was almost like a fairy tale and a dream. Everything I hit was going out. It helped put Gary, Indiana, on the map. I've had moments in professional ball, but as far as one accomplishment, nothing that compares with it."

Oakland A's third baseman Carney Lansford was on the Santa Clara, Calif., team that lost 5-0 to Taipei, Taiwan, in 1969. Former Cubs pitcher Billy Connors is the only big leaguer to have played on a champion team from the USA, although former utility infielder Hector Torres was a member of the 1958 champ from Monterrey, Mexico.

YOUTH LEAGUES

359

Taiwan wins again

By Pete Williams

Taiwan tightened its stranglehold on the Little League World Series in 1991. San Ramon Valley Little League of Danville, Calif., offered only token resistance to the Far East's 23-year dynasty in an 11-0 loss in the title game.

For Hsi Nan Little League of Tai Chung, the victory gave Taiwan its 15th championship since 1968. Since 1976, a Far East team has made the final game every year except 1983. Taiwan's dynasty is all the more impressive considering that the eight-team world series tournament is heavily stacked in favor of the USA.

The USA has four of the eight teams in the tournament and its own bracket, thereby being assured of a berth in the final. But Taiwan must first win the Far East championship against talented teams from Japan and Korea just to get to the world series, where it must defeat the Latin American champion, then the winner of Canada vs. Europe, just to get to the final.

PONY League: Filling the gap

How to find a team

PONY League's national headquarters are located in Washington, Pa., where the league was founded. There are separate headquarters for each of the 50 states, many of which change from year to year. To find your state's current headquarters, contact the national headquarters, listed below:

▶ **National Headquarters**
P.O.Box 225,
Washington,PA
15301-0225;

PONY facts

Here's a nutshell look at PONY League Baseball and Softball.

▶ **Founded:** 1951
▶ **Age range:** 5-18
▶ **Total active players:** 360,000+
▶ **Total players since 1951:** 5,000,000+
▶ **Total teams:** 24,000+
▶ **Total countries:** USA, 12 foreign
▶ **Total leagues:** 6 besides PONY
▶ **Girls:** Softball and baseball

Q: Where do budding ballplayers go when they are too old for Little League, but not quite ready to compete with 17- and 18-year-olds?

A: PONY League. Founded in 1951 in Washington, Pa., PONY stands for "Protect Our Nation's Youth." It was started primarily to fill the gap between Little League and high school ballplayers, both in age and rules. PONY league baselines are set at 80 feet, longer than Little League's 60 feet, but shy of the 90 feet for high schoolers and up.

Today, PONY baseball is played by 360,000 youths in the USA and 12 foreign countries.

San Juan, Puerto Rico, won the 13-14 age group at the 1991 Pony World Series held in Washington, Pa. Winners in the other age groups: Seoul, South Korea in the Bronco series (11-12 year olds); Tustin, Calif. in the Colt series (15-16 year olds); and Weirton, W.V., in the Palomino series (17-18 year olds).

PONY League keeps youths on diamond

In 1951, Lew Hays, then sports editor of the *Washington (Pa.) Observer*, realized that kids still wanted to play baseball when their Little League careers were over at age 12.

The only place to play, though, was American Legion ball. Although anyone under 18 was eligible, it was highly unusual for a 12-year-old to be good enough to compete with a 17- or 18-year-old.

"There was no youth ball that took care of kids after you were 12 years old," Hays said. So in 1951 Hays founded Protect Our Nation's Youth (PONY), a league designed to give 13- and 14-year-olds the opportunity to continue their baseball careers.

PONY League baseball presented a transition for players from the Little League diamond to the regulation baseball field, with bases set at 80 feet and a pitching distance of 64 feet. But Hays said his reason for creating PONY wasn't only to help kids better their skills.

"The primary purpose was to keep kids occupied during the summer time," he said.

PONY baseball took off and now, in its 41st year, there are over 360,000 players on 24,000 teams in the USA and 12 foreign countries, including the Soviet Union. It has been estimated that more than 5 million young people have played in PONY baseball since 1951.

"I am interested in young people," said Hays, who retired as PONY chief in 1981, "and you have to provide them an opportunity of involvement. It's a team experience."

American Legion: The original

Though it is not as well known as some of the baseball programs for young players, American Legion is the oldest of all the youth leagues. Founded in 1925 for players 17 years old and under, American Legion now includes players up to age 19, and has been a springboard for many talented young ballplayers. Major league scouts are a common sight at the American Legion national playoffs, which have been staged since 1926. Headquartered in Indianapolis, the league has more than 760,000 registered players.

American Legion notes

▶**New Jersey team captures Legion crown:** Brooklawn, N.J., won the 1991 American Legion World Series with a 5-3 victory over Newark, Ohio. Scott Lavender pitched seven innings in relief, yielding one run and two hits and was named to the first All-Star Legion series team. Newark shortstop Ryan Beeney was spectacular in the field and at bat, displaying the talent that made him a high draft pick of the Boston Red Sox. He was named the series Player of the Year and won a scholarship to Kent State University.

▶**All-Star team selections:**
C—Michael Cormier, East Hartford, Conn.; 1B—Brian Cummings, Newark, Ohio; 2B—David Gautreau, Gonzales, La.; SS—Beeney; 3B—Mike Harris, Brooklawn, N.J.; CF—Chris O'Dell, Newark, Ohio; RF—John Mader, Brooklawn, N.J.; P—Lavender.

▶**Triple honors:**
Bob Failthorpe of Union City, Calif., won the Rawlings Big Stick Award for 36 total bases in regional and World Series play, the Louisville Slugger Award for highest batting average (.585), and the Bob Feller Award for 36 strikeouts as a pitcher during the tournament. —*Carl Lundquist*

How to find a team

American Legion Baseball's national headquarters are located in Indianapolis. There are separate headquarters for each of the 50 states, many of which change from year to year. To find your state's current headquarters, contact the national headquarters, listed below:

▶**National Headquarters**
700 N. Pennsylvania, Indianapolis, IN 46204; (317) 635-8411

Road to the title

Results of the 1991 American Legion World Series:

▶**Championship Round**
Brooklawn (N.J.) 5, Newark (Ohio) 3

▶**Consolation Round**
Newark 10, Gonzales (La.) 3

▶**Fourth Round**
Gonzales 12, Brooklawn 7
Newark 7, E. Hartford (Conn.) 6

▶**Third Round**
Brooklawn 12, E. Hartford 10
Gonzales 8, Escondido (Calif.) 5
Newark 11, Union City (Calif.) 9

▶**Second Round**
Brooklawn 3, Escondido 2
E. Hartford 14, Union City 2
Newark 4, Sarasota (Fla.) 3
Gonzales 9, Kansas City (Kan.) 4

▶**First Round**
Brooklawn 3, Newark 1
Union City 1, Gonzales 0
Escondido 6, Sarasota 1
E. Hartford 5, Kansas City 3

Here's a nutshell look at Babe Ruth Baseball:

▶**International Headquarters:** 1770 Brunswick Ave., P.O. Box 5000, Trenton. N.J. 08638; (609) 695-1434
▶**Founded:** 1951
▶**Ages:** 7-18
▶**Divisions:** age 16-18; age 13-15; Prep (age 13); Bambino (8-12); Rookie (7-9)
▶**Total active players:** 600,000+

Something for everybody

No matter what your age—or level of skill—there is a baseball league made for you. Listed below are some of the more established leagues with national organizations:

▶**Babe Ruth Baseball.** Begun in 1951 for players from 13 to 15, it was started in Hamilton Township, N.J., a suburb of Trenton. An older division (ages 16-18) was started in 1968, with a separate division for 13-year-olds formed in 1974. More than 600,000 youngsters played Babe Ruth in 1991.

Marietta, Ga., won the 13-15 Babe Ruth World Series in Lebanon, Mo., while Cincinnati won the 16-18 series in Falmouth, Mass. LaCrescenta, Calif., won the Prep series (13-year-olds); Oakland won the Bambino World Series (8-12). Bambino incorporates Rookie League, started by Major League Baseball for 7- to 9-year-old players. It uses pitching machines, softer balls and 12 players on the field.

▶**Junior Olympic Super Series**. A national championship for junior-age teams, the super series matches the winners (from the USA) of amateur organizations in the 15-16 age group. Suffolk County, N.Y., won the Police Athletic League national championship. Winners in the AABC, NABF, PONY leagues and the Dixie Baseball Association (an amateur organization based in the South with four age groups) also participated in the '91 series.

▶**National Amateur Baseball Federation.** Founded in 1914, the NABF is the oldest amateur baseball organization in the USA. Started to organize sandlot baseball across the USA, the first participants were high school age and older. The NABF holds national competitions in six different age groups and in the only national baseball organization with an all-volunteer staff.

Host Louisville was the winner in the NABF Major (unlimited ages) series, held for the 77th time in 1991. Kansas City, Mo., won the College NABF title (ages 19-20), while No. Atlanta won the Senior NABF crown in Youngstown, Ohio. Other winners: Orlando took the High School division (17-18), while Cincinnati won the Junior division (15-16) and Miamisburg, Ohio, won the Sophomore class (13-14).

▶**American Amateur Baseball Congress.** Another organization primarily started as a competition among senior teams across the country. The first AABC world series, called the Stan Musial World Series (ages 19 and up) was held in 1935 in Battle Creek, Mich. A division for younger players (18 and under) was started in 1954, and since 1968, has since become a six-division association. The Dallas A's won the last Stan Musial series.

H

igh School &
College Baseball

USA SNAPSHOTS®

A look at statistics that shape the sports world

Signing up

The all-time largest signing bonuses offered for baseball players[1]:

Bonus

Player, Team	Bonus
Brien Taylor, N.Y. Yankees	$1.6 million
Shawn Green, Toronto	$700,000
Mike Kelly, Atlanta	$575,000
John Olerud, Toronto	$575,000
Tony Clark, Detroit	$500,000
Todd Van Poppel, Oakland	$500,000

X

1—All players signed 1991 except Olerud (1989), Van Poppel and Clark (1990)

Source: *Baseball America*

By Keith Carter, USA TODAY

USA TODAY Super 25 Final High School Rankings

▶1. **Fairfield, Ohio (32–3)** Won second Division I state title as Tracy Moore posted 10–0 record with 2.12 ERA. Spence Gunnell batted .464 with 44 RBI, 9–2 pitching record and Terry Mitchum batted .422 with 46 RBI, 11 HR.

▶2. **Cherry Hill, N.J. West (25–2)** Won first Group III state title after winning previous two Group IV titles. Junior Dan Farling batted .573 with 14 doubles, 29 RBI and Chad Crovetti batted .400. Junior Bo Gray was 12–0 with 1.74 ERA.

▶3. **South Holland, Ill. Thornwood (35–3)** Won first Class AA state title as All-USA first baseman Cliff Floyd (6–4, 215 pounds) set school records with .556 batting average, 69 RBI. Jon Dunlop batted .480 with 34 RBI and Sam Antkiewicz batted .371.

▶4. **Jacksonville, Fla. Parker (26–6)** Won first Class 4A state title behind hitting of Aaron Sedgwick (.455, 27 RBI) and Mark Lassiat (.389, 30 RBI, 23–23 stolen bases). Scott Garren was 9–3 with 1.31 ERA.

▶5. **Lancaster, S.C. (29–5)** Won second Class 4A state title. John Barnes was 12–2 with 0.81 ERA and Pep Harris was 9–3 with 1.02 ERA. O'Brien Cunningham batted .385 with seven HRs, 36 RBI.

▶6. **LaMesa, Calif. Grossmont (29–1)** Won second consecutive San Diego Section Class 2A title and last 18 games. Todd Cady set San Diego Section career records with 150 hits, 27 HRs, 149 RBI. Mike Spears was 10–0 with four saves, 1.61 ERA and sophomore John Heinrich batted .340 with 18 stolen bases.

▶7. **Jacksonville, Fla. Bolles (26–3)** Won last 15 games, third Class 2A state title with 244–108 scoring advantage, .348 batting average. Steve Carver batted .456 with 36 RBI. Junior Danny Wheeler batted .436 with 12–1 pitching record.

▶8. **Munford, Tenn. (29–1)** Won last 27 games, first Class AAA state title with .364 team batting average, 0.77 ERA. Aaron Fultz batted .433 with 24 RBI, was 10–0 with 0.32 ERA, 133 strikeouts in 65 innings. John Griffin batted .510 with 35 RBI.

▶9. **Long Beach, Calif. Millikan (24–6)** Won fourth Southern Section Class 5A title as Dante Powell batted .440 with a school-record 48 runs and 46 stolen bases. Junior Greg Gregory was 13–0 with 1.12 ERA and Pat Thacker batted .404.

▶10. **Ontario, Calif. (26–0)** Won first Southern Section Class 3A title behind hitting of Cesar Barrera (.526, 37 RBI) and Mike Sweeney (.470, 32 RBI). Mike Hernandez was 10–0 with 0.65 ERA.

▶11. **Edwardsville, Ill. (39–1)** Ran state-record winning streak to 64 games before placing second in Class AA tournament. Junior Dean Suhre set school records with 64 runs, 42 walks, 65 stolen bases, .710 on-base percentage. Dave Slemmer set records with 63 hits, 54 RBI and Joe Blasingim set records with 14 wins (24–0 in career), 1.55 ERA. Team batted .387, averaging 8.5 runs.

▶12. **Gilbert, Ariz. (22–6)** Won first Class 5A, seventh overall state title. Marcos Chaira batted .445 with 31 RBI, Jeff Holland batted .440 with 38 RBI and junior Widd Workman was 7–2 with 2.90 ERA.

▶13. **Pasadena, Md. Northeast (24–0)** Set state record for most wins while claiming third Class 2A state title. Charlie Buckheit was 11–0 with 10 walks in 73 innings, 2.10 ERA. Don Shump batted .473 with state-record 45 RBI; Russ Curry batted .462 with 39 RBI.

▶14. **Logansport, Ind. (31–3)** Won last 13 games, fourth state title, 9–5, against Marion. Willy Hilton (11–0) won twice and had a save in final game. Greg Korreckt was 6-for-12 with five

RBI, John Curl 4-for-8 with four RBI and Greg Diekman tied state record with 4-for-4 in title game.

▶**15. Springfield, Va. West Springfield (25–3)** Won first Class 3A state title as Chad Olms posted 9–1 record with 1.21 ERA, 113 strikeouts in 74 innings. Jamie Warren batted .312 with 33 RBI and Jim Francis batted .366.

▶**16. San Mateo, Calif. Serra (26–5)** Won second Central Coast Section Class 4A title as pitching staff struck out 304 batters in 31 games. Mike Wolger was 10–1 with 0.98 ERA, 120 strikeouts in 78 innings. Junior Dan Serafini was 9–1 with 1.07 ERA, 122 strikeouts in 71 innings. Matt Bazzani had 12 HRs, 47 RBI, school-record .528 batting average.

▶**17. Anaheim, Calif. Esperanza (26–3)** Won Upper Deck Classic and reached semifinals of Southern Section Class 5A playoffs. Jon Pitts batted .452 and threw out 14 of 20 on steal attempts. Keith McDonald batted .415 with 29 RBI. Jeff Bowman was 3–0 with 1.77 ERA, Southern Section-record 12 saves.

▶**18. League City, Texas Clear Creek (28–6)** Won first Class 5A state title behind hitting of Eric Silvas (.387, 20 RBI), Shawn Buhner (.375, 28 RBI), Thomas Uptegrove (.343, 26 RBI). Brendan Daly was 12–1 with 1.77 ERA.

▶**19. Pine Bluff, Ark. Watson Chapel (21–4)** Won second Class AAA state title as Abb Hayden was 11–1 with 2.14 ERA. Junior Richie Workman batted .481 with 28 RBI and John Roberts batted .455 with 22 RBI, 30 stolen bases.

▶**20. Boyertown, Pa. (25–2)** Became first Pennsylvania team to win two Class AAA state titles. Matt Spade was 11–1 with 0.47 ERA and junior Jed Johnson was 10–0 with 2.61 ERA. Jason Benyo batted .462 with 32 RBI and junior Steve Mest batted .430 with 18 RBI, 34 stolen bases.

▶**21. Hope Mills, N.C. South View (26–3)** Won first Class 4A state title as Brian Ford posted 14–0 record with 0.45 ERA, 213 strikeouts in 108 innings. Pat Barber batted .422 with eight HRs, 39 RBI and junior Stewart Ezzell batted .404 with seven HRs.

▶**22. Orlando, Fla. Dr. Phillips (28–4)** Gatorade National Player of the Year Brian Barber set school records with 11–0 record, 0.82 ERA, 82 strikeouts in 68 1/3 innings. Juniors Johnny Damon and Kevin Chabot batted .372 and .360, respectively, and combined for 56 RBI.

▶**23. San Diego, Calif. Mira Mesa (28–4–1)** Won second consecutive San Diego Section Class 3A title as pitchers yielded eight hits in four playoff wins. Mike Bovee was 11–2 with 1.19 ERA, 142 strikeouts in 87 2/3 innings and batted .390. Marc Nielsen was 6–1 with 0.76 ERA and batted .320. Junior Brendan Hause was 7–1 with 0.68 ERA and batted .340.

▶**24. Vallejo, Calif. (30–2)** Set school records with .378 team batting average, 32 home runs, 165 stolen bases in 174 attempts while winning Sac-Joaquin Section Class 3A title. Chris Kirk was 13–0 with 1.30 ERA, and Ivory Jones was 9–1 with 2.00 ERA and batted .500. Each had an 18-strikeout game.

▶**25. Petal, Miss. (29–5)** Won second consecutive Class 4A state title as Bryan Strahan batted .394 with 40 runs, 35–36 stolen bases. Brian Clark batted .376 with seven HRs, 43 RBI and was 13–2 with 2.09 ERA. Todd Carpenter batted .352 with seven HRs, 43 RBI.

OTHERS CONSIDERED: Birmingham (Ala.) Vestavia Hills (25–4); Broken Arrow (Okla.) (30–16); Burtonsville (Md.) Paint Branch (19–1); Edison (N.J.) (25–4); Gambrills (Md.) Arundel (20–4); Independence (Mo.) Fort Osage (20–2); Newnan (Ga.) (29–10); Pensacola (Fla.) Escambia (25–8); Redmond (Wash.) (21–5); Shenandoah Junction (W.Va.) Jefferson (35–3).

Ranked for USA TODAY by consulting high school editor Dave Krider

USA TODAY
1991 All-USA High School Team

1991 Player of the year
▶**BRIEN TAYLOR, P,** Beaufort, N.C.
East Carteret
> Ht: 6-3 Wt: 205
> Class: Senior
> Bats: L
> Throws: L
> W-L: 9-2. ERA: 0.47
> Innings: 88
> Strikeouts: 213
> Walks: 28

Signed with New York Yankees; No. 1 overall pick in free-agent draft.

**KENNY HENDERSON,
P,** Ringgold,(Ga.)
> Ht: 6-7. Wt: 185
> Class: Senior
> Bats: R
> Throws: R
> W-L: 11-1. ERA: 0.41
> Innings: 69
> Strikeouts: 154
> Walks: 14

No. 5 free-agent draft pick by Milwaukee Brewers.

EDDIE WILLIAMS, C,
Miami (Fla.) Edison
> Ht: 6-2. Wt: 220
> Class: Senior
> Bats: R-L
> Throws: R
> BA:.469 Runs: 14
> HR: 3. RBI: 22

Drafted No. 39 by St. Louis Cardinals.

CLIFF FLOYD, 1B,
South Holland (Ill.) Thornwood
> Ht: 6-4. Wt: 215
> Class: Senior
> Bats: L
> Throws: R
> BA: .556 Runs: 52
> HR: 9 RBI: 69

Drafted No. 14 by Montreal Expos.

DMITRI YOUNG, SS
Oxnard (Calif.) Rio Mesa
> Ht: 6-2. Wt: 215
> Class: Senior
> Bats: L-R
> Throws: R
> BA: .425 Runs: 38
> HR: 11 RBI: 31

Drafted by St. Louis Cardinals first round and signed.

BENJI GIL, SS, Chula Vista (Calif.) Castle Park
> Ht: 6-2 Wt: 180
> Class: Senior
> Bats: R
> Throws: R
> BA: .443 Runs: 36

> HR: 7 RBI: 25

Drafted No. 19 by Texas Rangers.

SHAWN LIVSEY, SS,
Chicago (Ill.) Simeon
> Ht: 6-0 Wt: 169
> Class: Senior
> Bats: L-R
> Throws: R
> BA: .520 Runs: 48
> HR: 11 RBI: 68

Drafted No. 29 by Houston Astros.

**MANNY RAMIREZ,
OF,** New York (N.Y.)
George Washington
> Ht: 6-0. Wt: 195
> Class: Senior
> Bats: R
> Throws: R
> BA: .650 Runs: 40
> HR: 14 RBI: 40

Signed with Cleveland Indians (No. 13 draft pick).

AL SHIRLEY, OF,
Danville (Ga.) George Washington
> Ht: 6-1 Wt: 210
> Class: Senior
> Bats: R
> Throws: R
> BA: .429 Runs: 23
> HR: 8 RBI: 22

No. 18 draft pick by New York Mets.

SHAWN GREEN, OF,
Tustin (Calif.)
> Ht: 6-4 Wt: 180
> Class: Senior
> Bats: L
> Throws: L
> BA: .479 Runs: 37
> HR: 2 RBI: 25

No. 16 draft pick by Toronto; enrolled at Stanford.

Brien Taylor: A stone's throw from the majors

By Dave Krider

He started by throwing rocks at age 3 and took on birds at 10. Today, Beaufort (N.C.) East Carteret High graduate Brien Taylor stands to make a fortune by throwing fastballs past professional baseball players.

He's already signed a million-dollar deal with the New York Yankees after being chosen No. 1 overall in the free-agent draft.

Scouts say he looks like a young Dwight Gooden, firing fastballs past mystified batters. As a senior, the 6-3, 205-pounder threw back-to-back no-hitters with pitches clocked as high as 99 mph. During that 9-2 season (88 innings, 0.47 ERA) he struck out 213 batters, allowing only six earned runs. In his four-year career, Taylor was 29-6 (half of the losses were to state champions) with a 1.25 ERA. He struck out 476, walked 158 and allowed 85 hits in 239 1/3 innings.

His eventual high school coach, Gary Chadwick, got an eyeful of Taylor while umpiring Little League games.

"He was just a wild kid," Chadwick said. "He walked as many as he struck out."

But at the end of his sophomore year, Taylor attended a camp at the University of Virginia and learned "how to bend my knee to hold my weight. They showed me the balance points." His improvement has been remarkable.

"His control—along with his mechanics—has gotten better every year," Chadwick said.

In addition to his searing fastball, Taylor throws a curve, changeup and slider. He is a superb athlete, hitting .490 as a junior, and Chadwick said "he goes from first to third as fast as anybody in the world "

Brien Taylor held out for "Van Poppel-type money."

Famous prep school closes

By Mike Hlas

The Norway Tigers—Iowa's most fabled prep baseball power—are now history. Winning 19 state baseball championships wasn't enough to keep the small rural high school's doors open.

Norway High captured nine of its 19 crowns since 1981, but the town of 585 residents and its school had a great baseball reputation long before the first state title in 1965. Hal Trosky, who hit 228 major league home runs in the 1930s and '40s, was born and raised here.

Veteran major league pitcher Mike Boddicker notched 1,122 strikeouts for Norway in the 1970s. San Diego Padres' coach Bruce Kimm—Mark Fidrych's favorite Detroit Tiger catcher in 1976—was a Norway star.

There will still be baseball in Norway, though. The town team—one of 10 in the Iowa Valley League—will continue to play in the ballpark with clover in the outfield and cornfields in plain sight.

Mike Hlas writes for the Cedar Rapids (Iowa) Gazette.

College baseball 1992:
A look at the top teams

By Rick Lawes

The 1992 college baseball season will be a year for the traditional powers to try to regain some stature—but it won't be easy. If anything, the 1991 season showed that the distance from top to bottom is short.

Although Louisiana State won the national championship (their fifth trip to the College World Series in the last six years) the 1991 series was notable for the unknown—but not undeserving—field.

Hometown Creighton, host of the series since 1950, made its first-ever appearance. Florida State and Long Beach State made just their second appearances, and Fresno State made its third. Absent: traditional powers Miami (Fla.), Texas and Oklahoma State.

But the powerhouse programs should again dominate the top schools in 1992. A look at the top teams:

▶**Wichita State** (66-13 in 1991): The Shockers lost to LSU in the national championship 6-3, two seasons after winning their first national title. Coach Gene Stephenson has built a power in Wichita, with 10 NCAA postseason appearances since 1980—including four trips to Omaha and the CWS. The Shockers return two 1991 All-Americans, both members of the USA national team that won the bronze medal in the Pan American Games: Kennie Steenstra and Chris Wimmer. Steenstra, a junior right-handed pitcher, set an NCAA mark with his 17-0 record, then followed with a 2-1, 3.16 record with Team USA. Wimmer, a junior shortstop, hit .399 with 54 steals last year. Wichita loses pitcher Tyler Green, the No. 10 pick in the June draft and four everyday starters.

▶**Florida** (51-21): The Gators face a major rebuilding job on the offensive side, but their strength lies in their starting pitching—including an unexpected bonus in John Burke. Burke, a junior right-hander, was the No. 6 pick of the draft, but returned to Gainesville when he and the Houston Astros could not come to terms. Two other key hurlers return: Marc Valdes (13-4, 2.63) and Ron Scott (10-2, 4.13) who are only sophomores. But the Gators lose nearly their entire starting lineup, including C Mario Linares (.350, 14 HR, 55 RBI) and 3B Herbert Perry (.346, 15 HR) with 1B Brent Killen (.306, 9 HR) the only everyday player coming back.

▶**Louisiana State** (55-18): The defending national champions face a rebuilding year, but don't count out experience. Five of the Tiger starters were seniors, and Lyle Mouton (.354, 13 HR, 62 RBI) and series MVP Gary Hymel (.310, 25 HR, 79 RBI) went to the pros. But in the CWS, C Adrian Antonini, LHP Ronnie Rantz, IF Keyaan Cook, IF Mike Neal and OF Harry Berrios all saw valuable playing time. The Tigers also face a void on the mound, where starters Paul Byrd (8-3) and Chad Ogea (14-5) were signed. Coach Skip Bertman is another of the new breed of college coaches who has built a winning program at Baton Rouge.

▶**Miami** (46-17): Led by junior catcher Charles Johnson and freshman pitcher Kenny Henderson, the Hurricanes are in line to return to Omaha after a two-year absence—their biggest gap since 1975-77. Johnson was the USA's starting catcher this summer, after a .329-13-48 regular season last year. Henderson, the No. 5 pick in the nation by the Brewers out of Ringgold (Ga.) H.S., opted for Miami after a signing dispute. The 'Canes also have a key returnee in senior CF Johnathen Smith, who hit .320 in the Cape Cod League this summer after a .329, 13 HR regular season last year. Another factor is coach Ron Fraser, who will also coach the USA Olympic team in Barcelona. Fraser may be coaching his last season at Miami, to take a job with the expansion Florida Marlins.

▶**Oklahoma State** (47-20): The Cowboys are expecting another strong season after a year when they were upset in the NCAA regional final by Long Beach State. Coach Gary Ward has not been able to bring a national title to Stillwater, despite eight trips to Omaha since 1980. The 'Boys lose Big 8 Player of the Year Mike Daniel (.350, 27 HR, 107 RBI), but OF Danny Perez and three of the infield (2B Lou Lucca, SS Fred Ocasio and 3B Manny Gagliano) all return. Also coming back is junior pitcher Billy Kanwisher.

▶**Texas** (48-18): The Longhorns were upset in the regional on their home field for the second straight season. Returning is all-everything freshman Brooks Kieschnick, who led the 'Horns in nearly every offensive category while posting a 7-1 record on the hill. 3B Clay King and Calvin Murray, who both played in Alaska during the summer, return as does sophomore hurler Jay Vaught, who was undefeated in his freshman campaign. Texas is the all-time leader with 25 CWS trips, including 15 under coach Cliff Gustafson—but have been to Omaha only once since 1987.

▶**Florida State** (57-14): The Seminoles, the No. 1-ranked team most of the year, were rudely bounced from the CWS in two games—including an elimination-game loss to arch-rival Florida. But coach Mike Martin will have some key players return, including pitcher/outfielder Chris Roberts. Roberts, who played for Team USA in the Pan Am Games, saw action mostly in the outfield, but pro scouts like his arm on the mound. He'll join Roger Bailey (11-3, 3.78) and Bryan Harris (7-2, 2.83) as the keys to the 'Noles rotation. FSU was hard hit by the draft, losing 1B Eduardo Perez, C Pedro Grifol and LHP Tim Davis.

▶**Clemson** (60-10): The winningest team in the country received an early exit from the CWS, but should have enough to learn from the experience in a return trip this year. Sophomore Billy McMillon (.386, 10 HR, 48 RBI, 12 SB) received an invitation to Team USA, and will be joined by pitchers Jason Angel (14-2), Scott Miller (8-3) and Paxton Briley (7-3). The offense will be hard to match though: the Tigers averaged 10 runs per game.

▶**Fresno State** (42-23): The Bulldogs return some key starters from their CWS team, including catcher Todd Johnson, a member of Team USA last summer. But the loss of pitchers Bobby Jones (16-1) and Robbie Saitz (9-5) leaves a large hole in the Fresno mound staff.

▶**Arizona State** (35-27): After suffering through an injury-plagued off year, the Sun Devils have to cope this year without All-American Mike Kelly—the second player chosen overall in the draft. But coach Jim Brock has a stable of youngsters that gained valuable experience last year. If the pitching comes together, they could return to Omaha.

USA SNAPSHOTS®

A look at statistics that shape the sports world

Striking out in the Series

Team	Times in CWS
Florida State	11
Northern Colorado	10
Maine	7
Clemson	6
St. John's	6
Western Michigan	6

Colleges that have played most in the College World Series without winning it:

Source: NCAA   By Marcia Staimer, USA TODAY

College Round–up

LSU Tigers take the Series

The unsung and unheralded Louisiana State Tigers came to the College World Series for the fifth time in the last six years — a record unequaled in college baseball —and left with their first national championship. They defeated Wichita State 6-3 on June 8, after exploding for 42 runs in their first three games.

LSU succeeded on both sides of the plate: They tied a College World Series record with nine home runs and set a record with 12 runs per game. They also set a CWS record for fielding percentage (.993) committing just one error.

"I think this victory belongs to Ben McDonald, Wes Grisham and some of the great players that helped us get here in the past," said LSU head coach Skip Bertman. "You've got to come here and lose first to win."

LSU arrived in Omaha as the No. 4 seed. They defeated rival Florida twice and Fresno State once, outscoring their opponents 42-12. In Wichita State, they faced the nation's top-ranked team, though the Shockers were the tourney's No. 3 seed.

— *Rick Lawes*

World Series Game Scores

Game 1, May 31:
Fresno St. 6, Florida St. 3
Game 2, May 31:
LSU 8, Florida 1
Game 3, June 1:
Creighton 8, Clemson 4
Game 4, June 1:
Wichita St. 8, Long Bch. St. 5
Game 5, June 2:
Florida 5, Florida St. 0
Game 6, June 2:
LSU 15, Fresno St. 3
Game 7, June 3:
Long Bch St. 12, Clemson 11
Game 8, June 3:
Wichita St. 3, Creighton 2
Game 9, June 4:
Florida 2, Fresno St. 1
Game 10, June 4:
Creighton 13, Long Bch St. 4
Game 11, June 5:
LSU 19, Florida 8
Game 12, June 6
Wichita St. 11, Creighton 3
Game 13, June 8:
LSU 6, Wichita St. 3

College Players go for gold

The 1992 USA Olympic team will be comprised entirely of the best college players, hoping to bring the first baseball gold medal back to the USA. Coach Ron Fraser has an added bonus: the 20 Olympic players will be protected, meaning they can negotiate contracts with pro teams while playing for Team USA. Players to watch:

▶**Kennie Steenstra, Wichita St.**: Junior right-hander; undefeated in 1991 (17–0, 2.17 ERA), tying Jim Gideon's 1975 record.

▶**Charles Johnson, Miami**: Junior catcher; 34th pick by the Angels; considered by some scouts to be ready for the majors.

▶**Chris Roberts, Florida St.**: Dual threat, pitches and plays outfield; led Team USA (.331, 11 HR, 40 RBI); scouts feel he will pitch in the pros.

▶**John Burke, Florida**: Right-hander; No. 6 pick in the nation (9-5, 2.25 ERA); passed up a $400,000 offer from the Astros to return to school.

▶**Jeffery Hammonds, Stanford**: Outfielder (.327, 14 HR, 57 RBI); has tremendous speed (69 stolen bases in two seasons).

▶**Steve Rodriguez, Pepperdine**: All-American at second base; hit .419 for the Waves with 32 stolen bases.

▶**Greg Thomas, Vanderbilt**: Batted .401 (16 HR, 71 RBI) for the Commodores as a freshman.

▶**Jose Prado, Miami**: Pitcher (9-4, 3.66 ERA); second-round pick of the San Francisco Giants out of high school in 1990, but chose to attend Miami.

▶**Calvin Murray, Texas**: Center fielder; has great speed (92 stolen bases in two seasons).

▶**Brooks Kieschnick, Texas**: Another two-way threat; led the 'Horns in batting, home runs and RBI while also leading the pitching staff in ERA; freshman of the year.

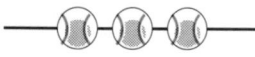

Fantasy Report

USA SNAPSHOTS®

A look at statistics that shape the sports world

The game's the thing

Despite growing popularity of baseball fantasy leagues, USA TODAY Sports Team members aren't ready to give up the real thing. What members preferred:

Watching baseball games **73%**

Playing in fantasy leagues **8%**

They're about the same **19%**

Source: Call-in survey of 448 USA TODAY Sports Team members. All are sports fans.

By Julie Stacey, USA TODAY

Sailing the trade winds to more wins

By John Benson

The well-informed trader always negotiates from strength. Point out the benefits of a trade and educate your trading partners, while strengthening your own roster. Here are a few tips to get the most out of your deals:

▶**Focus on the other team's needs, not just your own surpluses.** If you are leading your league in SB while Greg Briley and Lance Johnson have been dragging down your batting average, don't just pick up the phone and start offering Briley and Johnson. Pick up your league rosters first, and see who needs stolen bases.

▶**Focus on other teams' surpluses, not just your own needs.** If you want help in batting average, don't just call up the guy who owns Wade Boggs and start throwing offers around. Start by looking for the roster with the highest team average, and you will find some good, high-BA names that ought to be available cheap.

▶**Look for prejudices.** Owners are not always rational. People who love Red Sox or Dodgers (or any home town team) can be spotted quickly in any league. Mets' fans will gladly give you more than Dwight Gooden is worth, and most Phillies' fans will jump at Von Hayes. Some people love certain stat categories, usually home runs.

▶**Be aware of love-hate relationships among your competitors.** When the Yankees once wanted a young Cleveland outfielder named Roger Maris, they knew better than to make a direct bid for him. Yankee GM George Weiss simply helped Kansas City understand the value of Maris. The Athletics traded for Maris in 1958 and then gave him to the Yankees in 1959 for a package including 37-year-old Hank Bauer and Marv Throneberry.

▶**If you want a player from your archrival's roster, consider using an intermediary.** And if you want to keep a player away from your toughest competitor, don't trade him to your rival's best friend.

▶**Anticipate moves.** In fantasy leagues, the future-moves frontier is the free agent pool. You can get a feeling for the probabilities by looking at other teams' rosters. You can also gauge future availability by looking at players in the pool today. Watching other teams' disabled lists will give you more clues about imminent changes in the available pool. When you see a wave of pitchers coming off the DL, you can expect a richer supply of talent to be available soon.

1991 AL PITCHING

ERA IN HOME GAMES

BEST		WORST	
Moore, Oak.	2.14	Milacki, Bal.	5.16
Swindell, Cle.	2.52	Gullickson, Det.	4.95
J. Abbott, Cal.	2.57	Terrell, Det.	4.84
Clemens, Bos.	2.59	Wells, Tor.	4.81
Wegman, Mil.	2.62	Delucia, Sea.	4.72
Holman, Sea.	2.65	Sanderson, NY-A	4.66
Saberhagen, K.C.	2.76	Fernandez, ChiA	4.48
Tapani, Min.	2.79	Hanson, Sea.	4.25
Appier, K.C.	2.79	Stewart, Oak.	4.21
Finley, Cal.	3.03	Brown, Tex.	4.14

ERA IN ROAD GAMES

BEST		WORST	
Candiotti, Tor.	2.25	Stewart, Oak.	6.18
Key, Tor.	2.64	Welch, Oak.	5.87
Langston, Cal.	2.64	Delucia, Sea.	5.46
Guzman, Tex.	2.64	Swindell, Cle.	5.21
Clemens, Bos.	2.66	Hibbard, ChiA	5.10
Bosio, Mil.	2.74	Hough, ChiA	4.76
McDowell, ChiA	2.82	Finley, Cal.	4.73
Erickson, Min.	2.86	Brown, Tex.	4.70
Wells, Tor.	2.88	Nagy, Cle.	4.59
Gullickson, Det.	3.01	Fernandez, ChiA	4.53

1991 NL PITCHING

ERA IN HOME GAMES

BEST		WORST	
De. Martinez, Mon.	2.16	Bielecki, Atl.	4.74
Drabek, Pit.	2.40	Leibrandt, Atl.	4.35
Harnisch, Hou.	2.41	Viola, NY-N	4.26
DeLeon, St.L	2.42	Barnes, Mon.	4.24
Boyd, Mon.	2.47	Smoltz, Atl.	4.10
Belcher, L.A.	2.67	Cone, NY-N	3.91
Wilson, S.F.	2.71	Avery, Atl.	3.75
Glavine, Atl.	2.71	Benes, S.D.	3.73
Smith, Pit.	2.78	Gooden, NY-N	3.55
Black, S.F.	2.81	Burkett, S.F.	3.54

ERA IN ROAD GAMES

BEST		WORST	
Rijo, Cin.	2.06	Deshaies, Hou.	5.83
Morgan, L.A.	2.23	Portugal, Hou.	5.76
Benes, S.D.	2.33	Black, S.F.	5.28
Glavine, Atl.	2.44	Browning, Cin.	4.94
Belcher, L.A.	2.56	Burkett, S.F.	4.90
De. Martinez, Mon.	2.57	Wilson, S.F.	4.81
Cone, NY-N	2.68	Gardner, Mon.	4.69
Leibrandt, Atl.	2.81	Mulholland, Phi.	4.44
Avery, Atl.	3.01	B. Smith, St.L	4.24
Harnisch, Hou.	3.05	Hill, St.L	3.94

▶**Don't confine your friendly chats to a small group of owners.** Get to know everybody. To win a fantasy league, you will have to pass a quiz including questions like where your opponents went to school and their favorite teams and players. The more you know, the better you do.

How to evaluate run production

By Steve Mann

Common baseball sense and years of rigorous research have fully established that team runs are linked directly to wins. You would think that somewhere in the vast pile of baseball numbers you could find a stat or two that goes directly to the matter of individual run production. Sorry, Joe, it just ain't so.

What you get instead are a slew of clues in the form of hits, walks, steals and home runs. There are a few red herrings—batting average, runs scored and runs batted in—that seem to deal with the matter, but they lead only to blind alleys.

A number of stats have emerged over the years that have proved to be excellent measures of offensive run productivity. But they, too, have hang-ups: The formulas for computing them are as long as your arm and they need careful post-season tenderizing to hammer out the differences between the two major leagues and the unique effects of the 26 ballparks.

Now for the good news: There is a straightforward way to add up a player's offensive contribution. It has three major benefits: (1.) It's easy to compute a hitter's true value from individual runs produced to run production average per plate appearance. (2.) It's an accurate way to track hitting performance during the season. (3.) It can be the basis for a fantasy baseball league. Here's how it works:

▶**Score 1 point for each time on base.** Just hits and walks. Don't use other stats such as hit-by-pitch.

▶**Add 1 point for each total base.** 1 for a single, 2 for a double, 3 for a triple, and 4 for a home run.

▶**Add 1 point for each stolen base, and subtract 2 points for each time caught stealing.** This factors in the run-producing effects of base stealing.

The result of this calculation represents a player's overall offensive value, expressed in points. It's a direct reflection of run production and a highly reliable way to rank hitters.

1991 AL BATTING

HOME GAMES

BEST		WORST	
Thomas, ChiA	.371	Valle, Sea.	.162
Griffey Jr., Sea.	.365	Huson, Tex.	.177
Franco, Tex.	.344	Maas, NY-A	.178
Palmeiro, Tex.	.339	McGwire, Oak.	.185
Randolph, Mil.	.336	Deer, Det.	.193
Knoblauch, Min.	.328	Incaviglia, Det.	.205
Puckett, Min.	.326	Schofield, Cal.	.209
Sierra, Tex.	.320	Pettis, Tex.	.212
E. Martinez, Sea.	.320	Buhner, Sea.	.212
		Parker, Tor.	.214

ROAD GAMES

BEST		WORST	
C. Ripken, Bal.	.358	Deer, Det.	.165
Molitor, Mil.	.354	James, Cle.	.185
Franco, Tex.	.339	Browne, Cle.	.200
Polonia, Cal.	.332	Brunansky, Bos.	.200
Joyner, Cal.	.325	Parrish, Cal.	.204
Baines, Oak.	.322	Stubbs, Mil.	.207
Tartabull, K.C.	.318	Reynolds, Sea.	.208
Randolph, Mil.	.318	Vizquel, Sea.	.209
Sax, NY-A	.317	Williams, NY-A	.211
Puckett, Min.	.311	Davis, Sea.	.212

1991 NL BATTING

HOME GAMES

BEST		WORST	
Biggio, Hou.	.343	Griffin, L.A.	.203
Pendleton, Atl.	.340	Bass, S.F.	.210
Sabo, Cin.	.339	Clark, S.D.	.210
Larkin, Cin.	.326	Daulton, Phi.	.211
O. Smith, St.L	.323	Owen, Mon.	.211
Morris, Cin.	.319	Wallach, Mon.	.213
Butler, L.A.	.312	Gilkey, St.L	.215
Sandberg, ChiN	.309	Galarraga, Mon.	.224
Bonilla, Pit.	.309	Pagnozzi, St.L	.226
Calderon, Mon.	.308	Van Slyke, Pit.	.226

ROAD GAMES

BEST		WORST	
McGee, S.F.	.345	C. Hayes, Phi.	.193
Gwynn, S.D.	.325	Olson, Atl.	.196
Clark, S.F.	.319	Duncan, Cin.	.205
Morris, Cin.	.317	Teufel, S.D.	.207
Bonds, Pit.	.313	Chamberlain, Phi.	.209
Jose, St.L	.313	Walton, ChiN	.213
Van Slyke, Pit.	.310	Galarraga, Mon.	.215
Bell, ChiN	.304	Elster, NY-N	.216
Kruk, Phi.	.302	DeShields, Mon.	.218
Walker, Mon.	.300	Oquendo, St.L	.220

Twelve steps for the rotisserie-impaired

1991 AL BATTING

WITH RUNNERS ON BASE

BEST		WORST	
Randolph, Mil.	.375	Valle, Sea.	.165
Hamilton, Mil.	.370	Maas, NY-A	.181
Tartabull, K.C.	.355	Deer, Det.	.196
Harper, Min.	.352	Cuyler, Det.	.204
Franco, Tex.	.344	Stubbs, Mil.	.208
Griffey Jr., Sea.	.343	Shumpert, K.C.	.210
Molitor, Mil.	.333	Myers, Tor.	.210
Sierra, Tex.	.331	Barfield, NY-A	.214
Boggs, Bos.	.324	James, Cle.	.214
Surhoff, Mil.	.323	Pena, Bos.	.215

w/RUNNERS IN SCORING POSITION

BEST		WORST	
Randolph, Mil.	.373	Stubbs, Mil.	.150
Tartabull, K.C.	.371	Valle, Sea.	.163
Thomas, ChiA	.347	Deer, Det.	.168
Sierra, Tex.	.342	Incaviglia, Det.	.169
Polonia, Cal.	.333	White, Tor.	.172
Griffey Jr., Sea.	.331	Maas, NY-A	.180
Ventura, ChiA	.331	Cuyler, Det.	.186
Joyner, Cal.	.329	Gomez, Bal.	.188
Molitor, Mil.	.326	Newman, Min.	.189
Buechele, Tex.	.324	Pagliarulo, Min.	.195

1991 NL BATTING

WITH RUNNERS ON BASE

BEST		WORST	
Gwynn, S.D.	.368	Gilkey, St.L	.196
McGee, S.F.	.339	Galarraga, Mon.	.199
Sandberg, ChiN	.339	Brooks, NY-N	.210
Clark, S.F.	.332	Bass, S.F.	.212
Biggio, Hou.	.332	Thon, Phi.	.215
Bonds, Pit.	.327	Teufel, S.D.	.218
Calderon, Mon.	.323	Lemke, Atl.	.221
Jose, St.L	.322	Wallach, Mon.	.223
Bonilla, Pit.	.321	C. Hayes, Phi.	.225
Pendleton, Atl.	.318	Thompson, S.F.	.227

IN LATE/PRESSURE SITUATIONS

BEST		WORST	
Bagwell, Hou.	.407	Jackson, S.D.	.140
Jose, St.L	.384	Blauser, Atl.	.143
Dunston, ChiN	.378	Mitchell, S.F.	.145
Calderon, Mon.	.367	Elster, NY-N	.146
Butler, L.A.	.341	Galarraga, Mon.	.162
McGee, S.F.	.333	Magadan, NY-N	.175
Gwynn, S.D.	.329	Da. Martinez, Mon.	.179
Caminiti, Hou.	.326	Clark, S.D.	.182
Walker, ChiN	.326	Grissom, Mon.	.183
Thompson, S.F.	.324	Walton, ChiN	.184

Batting average in 7th inning or later with score tied or batter's team trailing by 1, 2 or 3 runs–or 4 if there are 2 or more runners on base.

▶**Step 1: Admit that you are addicted to fantasy baseball**. If you know who David Rohde and Matt Sinatro are, you qualify.

▶**Step 2: Hang up the phone.** You do not need to talk to your competitors every day to discuss the previous night's games, especially since the conversation is so littered with strategic bluffs that nothing is ever communicated anyway.

▶**Step 3: Remember that you already have a job.** It's very cute when you call yourself "Mr. McIlvaine," but it won't pay the rent.

▶**Step 4: Preserve that job**. When you boss asks how you're doing, do not say, "Cerutti's ratio is killing me, but it looks like I'm going to have a great week for stolen bases."

▶**Step 5: Never pester the front office of an injured player's team.** The club's representative, whether a minimum-wage receptionist or the GM himself, will severely mock you.

▶**Step 6: Stay away from TBS**. The glowing praise lavished on all Atlanta Braves will sucker you into waving rubber tomahawks in the air and joining the Lemke for President campaign.

▶**Step 7: Don't root for injuries.** In 1990, while I was praying for John Franco's arm to fall off and wither in the dust, the voodoo backfired and my $32 production-god Nick Esasky suddenly developed inexplicable dizzy spells and double vision.

▶**Step 8: Use your resources wisely.** If you're going to sit in your parked car secretly listening to that distant broadcast of the game that your staff's ace is scheduled to pitch, remember to turn off the ignition.

▶**Step 9: Repeat the following sentence to yourself every morning**. "No one cares about my team but me."

▶**Step 10: Keep your perspective.** If a trade is taking more than three weeks to hammer out, take a moment to recall how little time you spent with your mother last year.

▶**Step 11: Remember: You can wait for the morning paper to see the box scores.** Nothing is more pathetic than a Rotisserie owner who insists that he just happened to be awake at 2:30 Tuesday morning and figured he might as well check ESPN.

▶**Step 12: Forgive yourself.** If you're so addicted to the Rotisserie high of knowing everything first and discussing it all day long that you couldn't possibly abide by any of these rules without the aid of a straitjacket, let yourself off the hook.

— Eric Zicklin is a fantasy baseball player and freelance writer in New York City.

Raw numbers don't indicate impact

Impact Player Ratings, a system devised by Rob Feinstein, does not give equal weight to each statistical category. It takes note of the difference between "whole number" and "averages" categories.

"The whole-number categories—home runs, victories, saves, for example—accumulate in building blocks," he says. "Every one helps. Averages—batting averages and earned run averages—are different. The solid foundation built by a few players can cave in under the weight of mediocre performers on your roster."

Impact Player Ratings also focus on the ability of individual players to dominate. Categories such as home runs and victories require input from many players for a fantasy team to do well. Others such as stolen bases can practically be won by one player.

So, Feinstein's system ranks each player on his ability to contribute to winning categories for your team. His Impact Rating is a single number that identifies the player's impact on winning teams' scores in a typical fantasy league. Here are some examples:

Johnny Impact last year scored 100 runs and stole 50 bases. The league-leading teams in those categories had 500 runs and 200 stolen bases. Johnny's runs were 20% of the team's total, his stolen bases 25%. So, his impact rating was .20 for runs, .25 for stolen bases.

Johnny's batting average was .320 on 160 hits in 500 at-bats. The league-leading team's average was .300 on 1,050 hits in 3,500 at-bats. This would seem to make him a good player for your team, but look again. Adding his batting stats to the winning team would increase the team average to .3025, an impact of just .0083.

Feinstein has eight-stat and 10-stat ratings. The eight stats are batting average, home runs, RBI and stolen bases for hitters; victories, saves, ERA and hits plus walks per inning for pitchers. The 10-stat ratings add runs for hitters and strikeouts for pitchers. Three tips from Feinstein:

▶**Help determine the value of a player by noting the drop-off in his area.** That is, the difference is wide between the top echelon of hitters and other hitters. Among pitchers, the drop-off isn't nearly as drastic.

▶**Don't neglect position needs while you religiously follow the ratings**.

*More information on **The Impact Player Ratings Report** is available from **Impact Player**, 9903 Santa Monica Blvd., Suite 313, Beverly Hills, Calif. 90212.*

Fantasy owner goes on offensive

Is fantasy baseball gambling? For Randy Bramos, a part-time baseball fantasy became a full-time, real-life nightmare. Bramos, 37, a former North Lauderdale, Fla., firefighter and fantasy baseball commissioner, lost his job after being charged with gambling. The charge was dismissed Aug. 20.

The nightmare started Sept. 11, when Bramos was suspended without pay for 60 days after his Rotisserie League statbook was confiscated and given to the Broward County state attorney's office. He was fired Nov. 27, and charged with gambling, a second-degree misdemeanor that carried a potential 60-day prison sentence and $500 fine.

Bramos' first attorney urged him to plead no contest. But Fort Lauderdale attorneys—and fantasy baseball players—John George and Gary Lazarus offered to defend him free of charge. They argued that Bramos' notebook was illegally seized from his duffel bag, a violation of his fourth amendment rights. Broward County Judge Leonard Feiner agreed, and the case was dropped before the gambling issue was addressed.

Future cases might turn on the issue of whether fantasy baseball is a game of chance or skill. But until lawmakers enact legislation protecting fantasy baseball, similar cases are sure to arise.

—Pete Williams

Come in low on your pitchers

By John Baragona

The key to winning baseball is good pitching. And anyone who plays fantasy baseball seriously knows that the secret is not identifying the superstars, but identifying the average players who give you superior seasons—or finding the low-rung player that gives you average production. Some rules of thumb:

▸**Never pay an extravagant amount for one pitcher.** This quickly deletes your money supply and prevents you from filling out a solid and complete staff. The idea is to get five good starters at mid-range prices, three good relievers, and a cheap middle reliever.

▸**Bid on all closers.** You certainly won't get them all, but you'll find yourself landing two or three good ones at reasonable prices. You almost never have too many closers. And if you do, they're great trade bait.

▸**Prior to the draft, establish a price distribution chart to help you during the draft.** My chart looks something like this:

SP-17 (SP: Starting Pitcher)
SP-14
SP-11
SP-10
SP-8
MRP-3 (MRP: Middle Relief Pitcher)
RP-7 (RP: Relief pitcher/closer)
RP-10
RP-20

As you buy pitchers, mark them down at the appropriate salary. If they don't meet one of the numbers exactly, place them as close as possible and adjust the other numbers.

▸**Look for pitchers who don't walk people.** Look back through a pitcher's major and minor league career and see how his control has been. Pitchers who walk a lot of batters may give up a lot of runs.

▸**Ignore wins.** Pitchers have very little control over their win-loss records. If your pitcher pitches well and doesn't walk people, he'll have just as good a chance to earn wins as anyone.

▸**Never draft a pitcher who is wild.** One bad pitcher can destroy a pitching staff on his own.

▸**Look for pitchers coming off injuries, especially injuries unrelated to their arms.** They will generally go for less money than they are worth and can often be the key to your staff.

1991 AL PITCHING

RECORD IN HOME GAMES

WINS		LOSSES	
Morris, Min.	13	McCaskill, Cal.	10
Moore, Oak.	11	Swindell, Cle.	9
Erickson, Min.	10	Ballard, Bal.	8
Gullickson, Det.	10	Boddicker, K.C.	8
McDowell, ChiA	10	Gordon, K.C.	8
Ryan, Tex.	10	Key, Tor.	8
Tapani, Min.	10	Mesa, Bal.	8
6 tied	9	7 tied	7

RECORD IN ROAD GAMES

WINS		LOSSES	
J. Abbott, Cal.	10	Nagy, Cle.	10
Clemens, Bos.	10	Delucia, Sea.	9
Erickson, Min.	10	McCaskill, Cal.	9
Gullickson, Det.	10	Morris, Min.	9
Langston, Cal.	10	Navarro, Mil.	9
Bosio, Mil.	9	Stewart, Oak.	8
Finley, Cal.	9	7 tied	7
Key, Tor.	9		
Sanderson, NY-A	9		
Wells, Tor.	9		

1991 NL PITCHING

RECORD IN HOME GAMES

WINS		LOSSES	
Mulholland, Phi.	11	Armstrong, Cin.	8
Smith, Pit.	11	Drabek, Pit.	8
Browning, Cin.	10	Leibrandt, Atl.	8
Glavine, Atl.	10	Viola, NY-N	8
Smiley, Pit.	10	Bielecki, Atl.	7
7 tied	9	Black, S.F.	7
		Cone, NY-N	7
		Smoltz, Atl.	7
		Whitehurst, NY-N	7

RECORD IN ROAD GAMES

WINS		LOSSES	
Glavine, Atl.	10	Mulholland, Phi.	11
Smiley, Pit.	10	Browning, Cin.	10
Avery, Atl.	9	Black, S.F.	9
Benes, S.D.	9	Deshaies, Hou.	9
Leibrandt, Atl.	9	Martinez, L.A.	9
Cone, NY-N	8	Tewksbury, St.L	9
Hurst, S.D.	8	Gross, L.A.	8
Maddux, ChiN	8	Myers, Cin.	8
Martinez, L.A.	8	Rasmussen, S.D.	8
Morgan, L.A.	8	10 tied	7

Collectibles

USA SNAPSHOTS®

A look at statistics that shape the sports world

Fans foot bill

Teams with the highest average cost for a family of four
to attend a major league baseball game[1]:

Toronto Blue Jays	$93.29
New York Mets	$87.40
Boston Red Sox	$86.02
Oakland Athletics	$83.00
Chicago Cubs	$83.00

1 – Cost includes
tickets, hot dogs,
drinks, souvenir
caps, programs
and parking.

Source: Team Marketing Report Fan Cost Index   By Rod Little, USA TODAY

Game–worn jerseys rare (continued)

one year or for one game only (turn-back-the-clock nights, etc.), bring novelty value.

▸**Home or away:** Home jerseys are generally more sought after.

▸**The quantity.** A team or player has the option of ordering extra jerseys, and many teams do for charity auctions. The quantity of some uniforms, therefore, is never exactly known.

Regardless of the jersey, collectors should demand letters of authenticity.

Minor league cards collect value

Security tips for investors

Like any investment on display, baseball cards are a lure for thieves. The best security depends on the size of your collection and the nature of the your business.

Advice from the experts:

▸**Split up your collection to guard against a total loss.** Put valuable cards that you don't often look at in a safe deposit box and the rest in a home safe.

▸**For smaller collections, a fine arts waiver within a standard homeowner's policy usually will offer sufficient coverage.** Collectors with large holdings or businesses should consider separate policies, such as those offered by Cornell & Finkelmeir, Inc., of Ohio.

▸**Shop owners should never underestimate the value of their wares.** A security system with a motion detector and silent alarm is a must. Barred windows and in-store safes have become standard equipment.

By Bill Koenig

If you happened to be in San Bernardino, Calif., three years ago and bought a set of Spirit baseball cards for $6, don't throw them out. Thanks to outfielder Ken Griffey, Jr., that set is now worth $28.

A set of 1982 Oneonta (N.Y.) Yankees cards is worth $175. Why? It includes the only baseball card ever made of Denver Broncos quarterback John Elway.

A set of 1979 Ogden (Utah) A's cards—which includes Rickey Henderson's only minor-league card—is worth more than $200.

Then there are the 1980 Reading (Pa.) Phillies with Ryne Sandberg, George Bell, Mark Davis, Bob Dernier and Ozzie Virgil, Jr. The set sold for $3 at Municipal Stadium that summer.

"It's worth $550 now," said Julian McCracken, a former Reading general manager who is now GM for ProCards in nearby Pottstown, Pa. (He ought to know. He recently had two sets stolen from his personal possessions.)

"Minor league cards probably will be the next hot market," predicted Don White, marketing director for Best Cards, a subsidiary of Classic Games in Atlanta. "I think minor-league cards will outsell Hoops (NBA) cards in three or four years."

This season, ProCards is producing sets for 148 of the 152 communities which have minor-league baseball—everyone except Class A Bakersfield (Calif.), Reno (Nev.) Greensboro (N.C.) and Columbus (Ga.). Best Cards is putting together sets for 114 teams, as well as random foil packs of 12 cards from various teams. Impel Marketing in Durham, N.C., is producing "Line Drive Pre Rookie" cards for all 52 Triple-A and Double-A clubs.

Minor-league cards have been around for about 100 years, according to Bob Lemke, publisher of *Sports Collector's Digest*.

"The first issue of Old Judge baseball cards in 1887 included minor-league cards," he said.

The "modern era" of minor-league cards began in 1974 when two partners named Tom Collier and Mike Aronstein began doing cards for a handful of teams. Things picked up in the early 1980s when independent producers such as Larry Fritsch of Stevens Point, Wisc., got into the act. Fritsch worked the Midwest League, where his sets included the 1983 Madison Muskies —the first card issued of Jose Canseco.

Some teams had what is called "police sets." The local police department would issue the cards, often with safety tips on the back. One of the most valuable police cards today is the set of 1980 Charlotte Orioles, featuring Cal Ripken, Jr. It is listed at $1,200 now, primarily because the edition is limited.

One word of caution: Buy a whole set rather than an individual player's card.

"You want to protect yourself from counterfeiters," Lemke explained. "There is some speculation, for instance, that Rickey Henderson's Ogden card has been counterfeited extensively."

USA SNAPSHOTS®

A look at statistics that shape the sports world

The road to Cooperstown

Baseball players with the shortest, longest times between end of career and election to the Hall of Fame:

Player	Team	Length of time
Roberto Clemente[1]	Pittsburgh Pirates	5 months (1972-73)
Mickey Welch	New York Giants	81 years (1892-1973)

1 — Died while still an active player

Source: Baseball Hall of Fame   By Sam Ward, USA TODAY

How to avoid pitfalls

Houston card dealer Ted Stokes offers the following tips for young dealers:

▶ **Keep your cards in top condition,** including the commons (cards that aren't stars or rookies). A player could become great. For example, Kevin Mitchell became a star, and everyone went back to their commons.

▶ **Stay away from error cards,** which have the wrong position or the wrong statistics of a player. The demand has gone down. An overabundance of these cards has lessened the value.

▶ **Always inspect the card or set when you make a purchase.**

▶ **If you like a certain rookie, don't buy just one, buy several.** Later, if you ever want to sell it, you'll still have one or two left.

▶ **Do not get rookie cards autographed.** You'll reduce the market. Use second- to fourth-year cards for autographs.

▶ **Don't take advantage of people.** Sooner or later that person will find out you took advantage of him, and he'll tell his friends, who could be potential trading partners. Then no one will want to trade with you.

Taking Care of Business

Right signature checks fraud

One quick test of the authenticity of a baseball autograph is to check out which league president's signature appears on the ball. An autograph simply can't be authentic if the player died before the president's tenure.

Be wary of baseballs signed right after a president takes office: Balls stamped with a new league president's name usually come out three to five months after he takes office.

NL presidents

John A. Heydler	Dec. 19, 1918–Dec. 11, 1934
Ford C. Frick	Dec. 12, 1934–Oct. 8, 1951
Warren Giles	Oct. 9, 1951–Dec. 31, 1969
Charles S. Feeney	Jan. 1, 1970–Dec. 11, 1986
A. Bartlett Giamatti	Dec. 12, 1986–March 31, 1989
William D. White	April 1, 1989–present

AL presidents

William Harridge	May 27, 1931–Jan. 31, 1959
Joseph E. Cronin	Feb. 1, 1959–Dec. 31, 1973
Leland S. MacPhail, Jr.	Jan. 1, 1974–Dec. 31, 1983
Robert W. (Bobby) Brown	Jan. 1, 1984–present

Source: John L. Raybin's Baseball Autograph News

Cover your collection

Protecting one's investment in baseball cards and memorabilia is as necessary as protecting one's car or health, especially as values increase. Peter van Aartrijk of the Insurance Information Institute said there are a number of things card owners should do to insure their investments.

▸**Contact your insurance agent.** Even if you have just one high-value card and keep it at home, you should check with your agent to see if the full value of the card is covered. If you have limited coverage, or if the card is especially valuable, you should get a "floater" which will cover the full value of the card.

▸**Make a full inventory.** Catalog every card and collectible in your collection, no matter how big, and append it to your property list.

▸**Have the memorabilia appraised.** Since baseball card prices change so often and there is not a set value for any one piece of memorabilia, you should find a reputable dealer to evaluate your collection's worth and append it to the inventory.

▸**Photograph or videotape the item.** Especially if there are no receipts, a photo or video of you with the card will help speed the claim process if the item is stolen or destroyed.

Subscribe now and Save 20%
PLUS get a *free* baseball cap!

Order the most complete guide to baseball for just $35 a year. You'll get 44 exciting issues packed full of stats, scores and standings delivered for just $35 a year — *it's like getting 9 issues free!* And, for a limited time, with this offer only, you'll get a free Baseball Weekly baseball cap. Mail the coupon below or call toll-free: **1-800-USA-1415.** Please ask for operator 181.

YES, Start my year-long subscription to **USA TODAY Baseball Weekly** at just $35 for 44 stat-packed issues — that's only 80¢ an issue.

Name _____
(please print)

Address _____

City _____ State _____ Zip _____

Phone (_____) _____

_____ Check enclosed *(payable to Baseball Weekly)*

Charge my: _____ VISA _____ MC _____ AMEX

Credit Card # _____ Exp. _____

Signature _____
(if paying by credit card)

CALL TOLL FREE:
1-800-USA-1415
operator 181
Visa, MasterCard and American Express accepted.

BB Delivery by mail only. Rates may vary outside the continental USA. Savings based on newsstand rates. Offer expires December 31, 1993. BQB

For subscription rates and information outside the continental USA call: 1-301-622-7430